Learn more about marketing by visiting our World Wide Web site at

http://www.worthpublishers.com/marketing

About the cover

Just as the long shadows of people reach across the entire cover, the voices of people—customers, employees, suppliers, dealers, stockholders, and the community—must penetrate every marketing decision. Listening and responding to people leads to long-term mutually beneficial exchange relationships. Those *relationships* are established and maintained by constantly providing products and services that meet and exceed expectations (quality) at a fair price (value). The bright colors represent the excitement and opportunity that world-class marketing generates.

MARKETING

Relationships, Quality, Value

MARKETING

Relationships, Quality, Value

William G. Nickels

University of Maryland

Marian Burk Wood

Strategic Marketing Group

Worth Publishers

MARKETING

Relationships, Quality, Value

Copyright © 1997 by Worth Publishers, Inc.
All rights reserved
Printed in the United States of America
Library of Congress Catalog Card Number: 96-60599
ISBN: 1-57259-144-7
Printing: 5 4 3 2 1
Year: 00 99 98 97

Executive Editor: **Paul Shensa**
Design: **Malcolm Grear Designers**
Art Director: **George Touloumes**
Project Editor: **Timothy Prairie**
Production Supervisor: **Patricia Lawson**
Line Art: **Demetrios Zangos**
Layout: **Fernando Quiñones**
Composition and Separations: **TSI Graphics**
Printing and Binding: **R.R. Donnelley & Sons**
Cover: **Malcolm Grear Designers**

Illustration credits begin on page IC-1 and
constitute an extension of the copyright page.

Worth Publishers
33 Irving Place
New York, NY 10003

About the Authors

William G. Nickels
University of Maryland

Dr. William G. Nickels is Associate Professor of Marketing at The University of Maryland, College Park. He has taught marketing at the University of Maryland for over 26 years. In addition to receiving many teaching awards within the College of Business, Dr. Nickels won the Outstanding Teacher on Campus Award in 1981 and again in 1995. He holds an M.B.A. degree from Case Western Reserve University and a Ph.D. from The Ohio State University. He also has extensive sales and entrepreneurial experience.

A prolific author, Dr. Nickels' *Understanding Business* text is the market leader among introduction to business texts. His *Marketing Communication and Promotion* text was the first to stress integrated marketing communication. Dr. Nickels has also written numerous articles in academic journals. He has long been active in the area of macromarketing, and has helped define the field. Dr. Nickels is now deeply involved in relationship marketing, a major theme of this text.

Marian Burk Wood
Strategic Marketing Group

Marian Burk Wood is President of Strategic Marketing Group, a consulting firm in Connecticut that helps organizations develop strategy for marketing and communication. Her executive experience covers vice-presidential level positions at several corporate and nonprofit organizations, including Citicorp/Citibank, Chase Manhattan Bank, and the National Retail Federation. Her business background also includes retail management positions at Tandy, Sam Goody, and Bloomingdale's.

Wood holds an M.B.A. in marketing from Long Island University. She has co-authored a number of textbooks on business subjects, including *Advertising Excellence*. In her consulting work, she develops a variety of marketing, advertising, and training strategies and materials for internal and external business audiences.

This unique partnership of an experienced faculty member with a seasoned business professional brings a highly practical dimension to the text. As a team, they have the knowledge and background to show students how concepts are applied to the problems and opportunities that marketers face every working day. They also provide instructors with the tools they need to be effective in the classroom and to bring the material to life for their students.

Contents in Brief

Contents

What does it take to compete successfully in a dynamic global economy? What are the new rules and strategies for relationship building? Part 1 addresses the challenges and opportunities today's marketers face.

Is green marketing here to stay? Part 2 explores this and other issues related to ethics, social responsibility, and international and cross-cultural marketing.

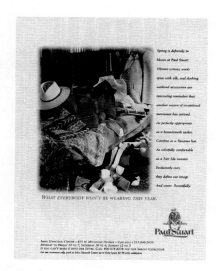

How important is image and product quality to the customer? The marketer? Part 3 examines the topics of marketing research, consumer and business buying behavior, as well as market segmentation, targeting, and positioning.

Would you like to choose your next date through a vending machine? You could if you lived in Japan. The development and management of goods and services are covered in Part 4.

How does Sprint do it? How should their competitors respond? Part 5 introduces the concepts of establishing and managing prices to provide customer value and profits.

What is the value chain and why is it increasingly important to marketers? You'll discover the answer to this question and explore channel management, wholesaling, retailing, and logistics in Part 6.

PART **7**

Management of Integrated Marketing Communication 499

CHAPTER **17** Integrated Marketing Communication 500

Who is or should be selling on the Internet? What is IMC? Is technology rapidly transforming the way goods and services are sold? These questions are considered in Part 7.

Marketing on the Net and VideoCases

Marketing on the Net

VideoCases

Preface

This is one of the most exciting and demanding times in the history of marketing. Never before have changes in the business environment occurred so quickly and relentlessly. In recognition of those changes, this text is designed to equip students, regardless of major or specialization, with the knowledge and skills they will need to take advantage of the opportunities that continuous change can present. Here are just a few of the dynamic concepts and trends *Marketing: Relationships, Quality, Value* covers:

Benchmarking
Boundarylessness
Continuous improvement
Core competencies
Cross-cultural marketing
Cross-functional teams
Customer focus
Customer loyalty
Database marketing
Efficient consumer response (ECR)
Electronic data interchange (EDI)
Empowerment
Everyday low pricing (EDLP)
Green marketing
Integrated marketing communication (IMC)
Interactive marketing
Internal customers
Internal marketing
Internal products
ISO 9000 quality standards
ISO 14000 environmental standards
Lifetime value of customers

Marketing on the Internet
Mass customization
New ethical challenges
Niche marketing
One-to-one marketing
Outsourcing
Quality function deployment
Quick response
Relationship marketing
Sales partnering
Service encounters
Service recovery plans
Stakeholder relationships
Strategic alliances
Total quality management (TQM)
Value-chain management

These concepts and trends are revolutionizing the way organizations approach marketing. World-class marketers are now aiming to "delight the customer," a phrase that comes from the literature on total quality management. To delight the customer, organizations have to adopt the latest marketing and management techniques—techniques that are integrated throughout this text.

The Need for World-Class Marketing

It is increasingly evident that, in the coming years, the most successful marketers will be those that have adopted world-class marketing techniques, whether or not they compete in global markets. Such organizations are continuously benchmarking their processes against the world's best and are making continuous improvements that strengthen relationships with customers and partners throughout the value chain. Throughout the development of this text, instructors asked for a book that would introduce students to these and other tools and then motivate them to apply the tools as they actively engage in the learning process.

Marketing: Relationships, Quality, Value will help students understand the roles of total quality management, core competencies, value-chain management, and other elements in the practice of world-class marketing. Students will also learn how marketers are competing more effectively through cooperative arrangements such as outsourcing, strategic alliances, and joint ventures that contribute efficiencies, increase profits, and build relationships among marketing organizations.

In this new era of intense competition, marketing departments no longer bear the sole responsibility for building relationships. Every employee—in every profit-seeking, nonprofit, and government organization—now shares in that responsibility. Therefore, every student in business needs an understanding of the principles, processes, and challenges involved in successful world-class marketing.

Marketing's New Era

The new era in marketing is one based on relationship building, and *relationship marketing* is a major theme of this text—along with quality and value. Marketing has always been concerned with building relationships with customers. Today, however, marketing has broadened its focus to include relationship building with employees (internal marketing), suppliers and dealers (value-chain management), stockholders (profit seeking), and other stakeholders of the firm, including the community (social responsibility). More attention is being focused on long-term customer satisfaction; thus transactional marketing (creating one-time exchanges) is being replaced by relationship marketing (establishing and maintaining long-term exchange relationships). As a result, relationship marketing has become one of the most active special interest groups (SIGs) in the American Marketing Association.

Shaping this new era of marketing are technological advances, global competition, total quality management, consumer activism, ethical considerations, and countless other influences. In short, the fundamental focus of marketing has changed forever, making marketing more complex, more demanding, and more exciting than at any time in its long history.

Discussing the new era of marketing, Christian Gronroos (professor of marketing at the Swedish School of Economics) has noted that

The mass marketing and transactional orientation, as well as the adversarial approach to customers and the functionalistic organizational solution inherent in the marketing mix approach, do not allow the firm to adjust its market performance to the demands of more and more customers today, i.e., enhanced value around the core product, reliable service to accompany the product, a trustworthy relationship with customers, suppliers, distributors, etc.[1]

In a similar vein, a recent *Marketing News* article by A. H. Walle of the University of Nebraska stressed that "in the future, marketing must aggressively broaden its scope beyond the traditional marketing management paradigm, which has dominated for the last 30 years."[2]

We agree. The four Ps of marketing management—product, price, place, and promotion—are still foundational. However, marketers today must succeed as relationship builders, creating and sustaining enduring linkages both inside and outside the organization, because that is what the best marketers in the world are now doing. The four Ps are an incomplete model for guiding marketing efforts in this new marketing era: the relationship-building approach extends far beyond traditional marketing. Indeed, everyone who has to build relationships—on the job, in the classroom, and in the community—should understand and learn to apply these techniques.

How This Text Differs from Traditional Texts

For the last 30 years or so, most marketing texts have stressed a *managerial* approach. They assumed that marketing decisions were handed down from top management and that managers were expected to plan, implement, and control the marketing process. This marketing management view resulted in an inside-out approach whereby managers decided how to control the four Ps of marketing. The idea was to get the right product to the right place at the right price and then promote it to potential buyers.

Customer Focus

This text emphasizes a *customer-focused* approach. Thus, before a good or service is developed or produced, we advocate inclusion of the customer's voice. Using this research, the organization then designs or refines its products (goods or services) to meet customer needs, tests them, and throughout maintains a dialogue with customers. Rather than a top-down approach, this text takes a bottom-up approach.

More than ever before, frontline employees are empowered to respond to customer wants and needs, and managers have become coaches, trainers, and supporters. The goal is an outside-in approach, emphasizing the needs of the customer, rather than inside-out, focusing on the marketer's ideas. One process for accomplishing this is quality function deployment, and quality is another one of the major themes of the text, a theme reinforced by numerous illustrations.

Exchange Relationships

Traditional texts focus on creating marketing *exchanges* with customers. This text focuses on building long-term *exchange relationships*—not only with customers, but with suppliers, dealers, employees, and other stakeholders of the organization.

Commitment to all organizational stakeholders is an emerging theme throughout the business literature. For example, Stephen Covey, author of *Seven Habits of Highly Effective People,* recently wrote:

> What represents the next paradigm shift leading to higher levels of performance capability? It is the principle-based foundation of 360 degree total stakeholder commitment: understanding, anticipating, prioritizing, balancing, organizing and executing to meet and exceed the needs of **all** your stakeholders [emphasis in original]. This means more than customer satisfaction. It means striving to cultivate the total commitment of your organization to customers and other essential stakeholders. It means developing stakeholder relationships built on total trust.[3]

Quality Service

Typically, customer service is not given a central role in traditional texts, but here it is fundamental. In the past, some organizations were able to succeed without giving outstanding service. In contrast, customer-oriented companies such as Home Depot, Nordstrom, and FedEx (and many smaller firms) are now capturing market share from traditional companies by offering superior service.

Diverse Examples

Traditional texts frequently read like encyclopedias of facts and principles. They also tend to have an overwhelming focus on larger, U.S. companies. This text introduces students to a wider variety of marketing organizations. There are many more small business examples, and many examples feature marketers based in other countries. However, world-class large businesses are also included. Students thus gain insight into the inner workings of a more diverse group of marketers.

The title, *Marketing: Relationships, Quality, Value,* offers additional clues as to other ways this text is set apart from traditional texts. For example, there is a much greater integration of total quality concepts. Most texts do mention total quality, but the concepts tend to be added on rather than integrated into marketing strategy. The same is true of value concepts. Traditional texts discuss channels of distribution; this text looks at the entire value chain. Traditional texts look at pricing; this text looks at price as just one element in the total value package. In other words (as our reviewers consistently confirmed), relationships, quality, and value permeate this text like no other.

Updating the Marketing Definition

We believe that the changes in marketing over the last decade—and the changes coming in the twenty-first century—demand an updated definition of marketing. Our reviewers agreed. The American Marketing Association's definition of marketing, quoted in most marketing texts, is: "The process of planning and executing the conception, pricing, promotion, and distribution of ideas, goods, and services to create exchanges that satisfy individual and organizational objectives."

The American Marketing Association's definition has three limitations: (1) it defines marketing as a managerial activity (planning, etc.) rather than as a process of creating exchange relationships, (2) it emphasizes the creation of mutually beneficial exchanges with customers only, and (3) it leaves out the important role of internal marketing in organizations. The definition is too limited because world-class marketing involves maintaining exchanges that result in longer-term relationships with many stakeholders, not just customers.

This text defines marketing as the process of establishing and maintaining mutually beneficial exchange relationships with customers and other stakeholders. This is our own definition, one that is solidly built on current marketing literature. The American Marketing Association's official definition of marketing has, of course, been changed several times to reflect marketing's evolutionary nature. We believe, and trust that you'll agree, that it is again time for a change.

Updating the Marketing Concept and the Four Ps of Marketing

The marketing concept is one of the foundations upon which modern marketing is built. However, the concept is now over 40 years old and we believe it requires updating to reflect the emergence of practices such as total quality management and internal marketing. We have taken the components of the marketing concept and integrated them into a new framework called the "ABCs of Marketing," as detailed in Chapter 1. Basically, we have kept the three parts of the marketing concept—a consumer orientation, a profit orientation, and coordination of functions—and added quality concepts such as benchmarking, continuous improvement, empowerment, and value creation.

Although the four Ps of marketing are the foundation of most introductory marketing textbooks, they provide an incomplete framework for the practice of marketing today. The four Ps fail to cover critical marketing processes such as environmental scanning and analysis; marketing research; segmentation, targeting, and positioning; and relationship building.

It is easy for students to memorize the four Ps, but it misleads them into thinking that these four areas are all that marketing requires. How can marketers understand and reach out to customers without marketing research, segmentation, targeting, and positioning? How can marketers understand their markets and their competitors without environmental scanning and analysis? How can they be successful today and tomorrow without forging strong relationships with customers and other stakeholders?

Today, marketers of all sizes and all product orientations are broadening their activities beyond the four Ps. As a result, tomorrow's business and marketing graduates need to understand all eight marketing processes: the four Ps plus the four critical processes discussed above. We demonstrate how these eight processes are combined into a unified strategy in Chapter 2.

Comprehensive Coverage Meets the Needs of Tomorrow's Marketers

The content of *Marketing: Relationships, Quality, Value* has been carefully developed to meet the needs of today's students, who are tomorrow's marketers. Blending fundamental principles, cutting-edge concepts, and compelling examples, this text offers comprehensive coverage of the ideas and applications necessary for marketing success.

A Text That Responds to Customer Input

You—faculty members and students—are *our* customers. William Nickels teaches introductory marketing to classes of 500 at the University of Maryland. His students made many suggestions that were incorporated into this text. The most frequent suggestion was: "Make it more interesting to read and use more up-to-date examples." Focus groups with students and professors from other schools provided further helpful input.

Given the new customer-driven orientation of marketing, it certainly made sense for the authors to conduct extensive research with faculty and students before writing the text and to maintain a dialogue with them as the text evolved. Three different panels of experienced marketing faculty reviewed every chapter (a total of 42 reviewers). We composed three full drafts in response to their suggestions, then sent individual chapters to reviewers and asked how these compared with the best texts now available (yes, we benchmarked). Consequently, we're confident that no other marketing principles text has ever benefited from such broad and comprehensive input from students and instructors.

Faculty members consistently urged us to "Put more focus on the customer." In responding to this advice, we have given the text the strongest customer focus of any on the market. We weave relationship marketing strategies into every chapter and involve students in decision making that guides their thinking into a relationship-building mode. Just as important, we teach students how to provide the kind of customer service that will delight customers.

Responding to faculty comments, we offer custom-produced videocases describing world-class service providers such as Zane's Cycles and Union Square Cafe to drive home the concepts. We also include in the text 14 innovative "Marketing on the Net" cases to help prepare students for the fast-paced challenges and opportunities they will face with online marketing.

The Importance of Internal Marketing

Our reviewers told us that marketing texts must pay more attention to the importance of an organization's internal customers (employees). Businesses that want to be customer oriented must hire, train, motivate, compensate, and empower their employees to delight customers. Doing this requires an emphasis on internal marketing.

By marketing to their employees, organizations create environments of friendly, helpful service that result in customer satisfaction and greater profits. The text describes in detail how internal marketing is done in organizations around the world. A videocase on Von Maur department stores shows how internal marketing can lead to such strong customer service that the company is able to compete with Nordstrom and other legendary service providers.

Small Business Emphasis

As giant corporations continue to downsize and reengineer, the majority of tomorrow's graduates will build their careers in smaller firms. Therefore, any modern text needs to show students how to apply the latest marketing tools to small businesses of all kinds. Our reviewers confirmed that we have more small business examples than any other text. These include:

- Zane's Cycles, a small bicycle retailer in New Haven, Connecticut. Chris Zane will do almost anything to attract and keep customers: give lifetime service, guarantee the lowest price, and serve customers cappuccino while he repairs their bikes. This is all part of his philosophy of relationship marketing.

- Nantucket Nectars, founded by two college buddies who mixed up a fruit-flavored soft drink to compete with Snapple. Using personalized service and unusual flavor combinations, the pair have built Nantucket Nectars into a market leader in some Eastern states.

- Collegiate Health Care, a small business that operates medical care facilities on college campuses. Careful attention to the needs of both students and college decision makers has helped this service business expand.

- Capitol Concierge, a service business growing on the strength of its owner's dedication to delighting customers. Customers can hire Capitol Concierge to do almost anything, from buying theater tickets to picking up laundry—with the personal touch.

- Brock Control, a high-tech marketer that offers software to help businesses sell to other businesses. Brock emphasizes partnering with its business customers to build mutually beneficial relationships that endure.

By weaving these small business examples (including many from other countries) throughout the text, we teach students how to become world-class marketers regardless of the marketer's size, location, or product.

Meeting and Beating International Competition

We carefully and deliberately searched the global marketplace to find world-class organizations that would show students the best marketing the *world* has to offer. Global competition is now so stiff that every marketer needs to be aware of international marketing trends to stay competitive. Chapter after chapter presents examples of international and cross-cultural marketing in both consumer and organizational markets. Examples include:

- Samsung Electronics, based in South Korea, which has mapped an aggressive, quality-based strategy for global market leadership.

- Amil Assistencia Medica International, a fast-growing Brazilian medical company that successfully mixes excellent customer service and profitability.

- Grupo Casa Autrey, a Mexican wholesaler that uses warehouse automation to offer its small business customers same-day delivery.

- Nestlé, based in Switzerland, which uses one-on-one marketing research to learn about the needs of baby-food customers in France.

- The Vien Dong International Supermarket, a San Diego grocery retailer that actively targets customers from a variety of cultures.

Showcasing market-leading businesses from around the world helps students see that competition has become global and that the best practices and strategies may be found anywhere. It also offers insights into the kind of challenges they may face as they work for organizations that market in other countries and cultures—or compete with international marketers.

Learning How to Build Relationships

Marketing to employees and marketing to customers are just two parts of a total relationship marketing approach. Relationship marketing calls for establishing and maintaining mutually beneficial exchange relationships with a variety of stakeholders. Here are a few examples from the text:

- Spector Photo in Belgium uses relationship marketing to forge closer ties with independent photography shops that act as distributors for Spector's film-processing service.

- Florida Division of Tourism has a program for building relationships with travel writers, travel agents, and vacationers.

- Dell Computer uses relationship marketing to cement its connection with Roadway Logistics Systems, a company that handles Dell's inbound and outbound transportation.

- Volvo, based in Sweden, uses a sophisticated computer network to maintain close communications with suppliers and dealers in order to better satisfy car buyers' needs.

These are only some of the dozens of examples included in the text to show how marketers around the world use relationship marketing to maintain relationships with other businesses and with ultimate consumers.

The Impact of Technology

It would be difficult to overstate the impact that technology continues to have on both global and domestic competition. Today's technology allows marketers to gather and analyze a mass of details about customer needs, preferences, and buying behaviors. With comprehensive, interactive databases, marketers have the capability to develop strategies custom-tailored to each individual. The result is mass customization and one-to-one marketing, two trends that are picking up speed as technology advances.

Assisting marketers in building one-to-one relationships are the Internet, lap-top computers, modems, fax machines, CD-ROM catalogs, pagers, and more. A salesperson's car can now serve as an executive office on wheels where he or she can keep in constant contact with customers, suppliers, and others in the value chain. Every chapter in Marketing: Relationships, Quality, Value integrates coverage of technology, showing how such resources are applied to create or maintain relationships.

Some examples include:

- Levi Strauss's use of a computerized logistics-management program to let retailers know when and where products are being shipped.

- General Electric Plastics' relationship-building strategy with international businesses that features access to product specifications and details via the Internet.

- Nickelodeon's use of online focus group research to probe children's reactions to its programming and promotions.

There is no aspect of marketing that hasn't been greatly affected by new technological breakthroughs. We introduce these state-of-the-art ideas throughout the text, from research surveys on the Internet to EDI and efficient consumer response in logistics.

Marketing on the Internet

Few changes in marketing are occurring more rapidly than the growth of marketing on the Internet. Businesses, nonprofit groups, and government agencies are rushing to establish World Wide Web sites so they can offer goods and services of all kinds in the boundaryless online environment. Tomorrow's graduates must be as familiar with such online marketing as they are with marketing in today's shopping malls.

We have integrated Internet marketing throughout the text and, in addition, have developed 14 interactive "Marketing on the Net" cases, two at the end of each part. Some of the 14 organizations profiled are small businesses, such as Hot Hot Hot and Relax the Back; some are global, such as Unilever and Weekend in Florence; some are service marketers, such as WebConnect and Security First Network Bank; and some are nonprofit, such as the state of Ohio. Here are three examples:

- Yahoo works up a pricing schedule for advertising banners on its Web site. Along the way, students are asked to visit Yahoo, Lycos, and Excite, three search engines that accept banner ads. They are also asked to click on an ad banner and follow the link to compare the banner advertising with the Web site and offerings of the marketer.

- Ohio uses its Web site to target businesses, tourists, and residents. Students are asked to visit the Ohio Web site and the Rock and Roll Hall of Fame Web site. They also use a search engine to locate and visit two other state Web sites.

- Amazon.com is a book retailer that operates only on the World Wide Web. Students are asked to visit the Web sites of Amazon.com and its competitor, Borders, as they contrast Internet retailing with traditional retailing operations.

All the "Marketing on the Net" cases have been designed to actively involve students in creating, analyzing, and improving marketing efforts on the Internet and the World Wide Web. In this way, students gain hands-on experience with online marketing. In addition, Appendix A discusses how to use the Internet for a job search and for career development. It also includes a sampling of World Wide Web sites where students can find job openings and upload their resumés for review by potential employers.

Emphasis on Service and Quality

Among the most important challenges a business must successfully meet in order to delight customers is providing excellent service and quality. This text leads the way in helping students understand how to plan, implement, and evaluate outstanding customer service and quality. The emphasis on quality begins in Chapter 1 with a discussion of total quality, then continues chapter by chapter as students see how marketers around the world build quality into their products and processes.

Chapter 11 is dedicated to more thoroughly exploring services marketing in profit-making and nonprofit organizations alike, stressing the crucial link to customer satisfaction and relationship building. Service examples permeate other chapters as well, including:

- Montgomery County, Ohio, applying service excellence to improve local government service.
- Jacob Smith, of the Bank of America in Los Angeles, delivering outstanding service to internal customers.
- Sunkyong, a Korean producer of petroleum products, benchmarking on the world's best to achieve world-class quality.

Reviewers consistently indicated that this textbook has the best and most comprehensive coverage of services marketing of any on the market.

Marketing Ethics and Social Responsibility

Marketing: Relationships, Quality, Value thoroughly explores the concepts and applications of ethics and social responsibility. These key concepts are introduced in Chapter 1 and examined in detail in Chapter 3. In addition, extended examples throughout the text show how marketers deal with ethical issues and responsibilities to society. Here are a few examples:

- Tierra Pacifica, a small construction company in Irvine, California, donates a construction project to every community in which it operates.
- Au Bon Pain, a national restaurant chain, grapples with the ethics of using mystery shoppers to test service quality.
- Siemens Nixdorf, based in Germany, designs its computers with environmentally friendly components that can be recycled or safely discarded.

Every effort is made to keep ethical considerations at the forefront of student thinking. For example, in Chapter 5, the research chapter, when discussing the choice of alternative courses of action, it is the best *ethical* alternative that is recommended. We also introduce global ethical principles as they apply to *all* stakeholders, as shown in Chapter 3.

Organization and Coverage

Part 1. Chapter 1 begins with the updated definition of marketing discussed earlier. Students are introduced to the contemporary concepts that successful marketers need to establish and maintain relationships with all organizational stakeholders. Chapter 2 presents a strategic model that integrates the eight marketing processes and teaches students how to manage both internal marketing and external marketing. The result is an overview of how and why firms are using relationship marketing to gain and sustain a competitive advantage.

Part 2. This part explores the use of environmental scanning and analysis to examine the rapidly changing marketing environment. Chapters 3 and 4 explore strategies for monitoring and keeping up with a wide spectrum of environmental changes. Constant change is shown as a dynamic market force, and seven of the most dramatic changes are presented. Special emphasis is given to marketing ethics and social responsibility. Chapter 4 discusses effective strategies for global marketing and for marketing to culturally diverse target markets.

Part 3. This part covers the process of marketing research and analysis. Chapter 5 looks at the role of marketing information and research, including the gathering of information on the Internet. In Chapters 6 and 7, students study both traditional and emerging concepts of consumer and organizational buying behavior. Chapter 8 discusses principles and applications of market segmentation, targeting, and positioning, including emerging concepts such as mass customization and one-to-one marketing.

Part 4. Part 4 focuses on developing and managing goods and services. Chapter 9 looks at products, value, and differentiation, while Chapter 10 takes up product development and management. The latest advances in product development strategies, such as quality function deployment, are presented. Chapter 11 examines services marketing, explores customer perceptions of service quality, and discusses the importance of service recovery plans in achieving customer satisfaction.

Part 5. This part investigates the related concepts of value and pricing. Chapters 12 and 13 cover the traditional pricing concepts, adding a new dimension by looking at customer value and the creation of such value. All of the concepts are related within the framework of establishing and maintaining relationships, not just making a single sale.

Part 6. Part 6 explores the new relationships that are developing among organizations in the value chain (the more contemporary term for channels of distribution). In Chapter 14, students are introduced to traditional channel concepts and value-chain management. Wholesaling and retailing are the focus of Chapter 15; reviewers strongly approved of this combination after reading the chapter. In Chapter 16, students learn about the pivotal role of logistics management in the value chain. The latest concepts such as electronic data interchange and efficient consumer response are discussed in a framework of providing seamless customer service throughout the value chain.

Part 7. Part 7 is the most complete presentation of integrated marketing communication (IMC) ever offered in an introductory marketing textbook. Chapter 17 provides a comprehensive overview of IMC. Chapter 18 discusses advertising and direct marketing, covering the latest developments such as marketing on the Internet, product placement, and database marketing. Sales promotion and public relations are examined in Chapter 19. Sales promotion is one of the fastest-growing parts of marketing, and strategies are discussed in detail. Personal selling, including relationship selling and sales management, are explored in Chapter 20. One of the key ingredients of a relationship marketing effort is the dialogue that takes place between salespeople and customers. Students learn about such current concepts as team selling, system selling, and consultative selling in detail.

Integrative Capstone Case. The text ends with a case from the travel/tourism industry, one of the world's largest and fastest-growing industries. This up-to-date case incorporates key marketing concepts and demonstrates their application in a lively real-world example. Students are shown the value of establishing a marketing plan. Then they follow along as Biltmore Estate, a well-known travel destination, develops and implements its marketing plan with the help of an IMC agency. Reviewers recommended the use of such a case because of increased interest in travel and tourism and because it offers an opportunity for students to apply their skills to a challenging marketing situation.

Appendixes. Appendix A discusses careers in marketing and how students can get *the* job they want. Appendix B explores the quantitative techniques that marketers are using today. For example, given the text's emphasis on relationship building, it is important to understand and calculate the lifetime value of a customer. Appendix C is a detailed outline of how to prepare a marketing plan. Once students have learned all the terms and concepts of marketing, they are ready to tackle such a challenge.

Skill-Building Pedagogy and Applications

The pedagogy used throughout the text has been developed specifically to enhance student competency in accordance with AACSB guidelines and the U.S. Secretary of Labor's SCANS program. SCANS, the Secretary's Commission on Achieving Necessary Skills, has identified skills that people should have in order to succeed in the workplace. The purpose is to help students translate classroom learning into skills that apply to the world of work.

The pedagogical tools in this text and its supplements package are fully integrated and designed to facilitate SCANS competencies and meet AACSB guidelines. Here is an overview of the major pedagogical tools used in the text.

Applying the Concepts. Unique to this text and enthusiastically endorsed by reviewers, each chapter contains a short case that encourages students to practice making marketing decisions. These cases are intentionally brief and are meant to involve students in applying concepts while they are reading and engaged in the chapter. Each case is embedded within the chapter, rather than appearing at the end, in order to avoid a lag between studying a concept and applying it. Answers to case questions are included in the Instructor's Resource Manual. These real-world cases are designed to assist students in achieving SCANS competencies.

VideoCases. As the SCANS report notes, students benefit from video and multimedia materials that create the realistic contexts in which course competencies are developed. The 15 custom-made videocases for this text range in length from 8 to 15 minutes and are suitable for use in the classroom, home, or lab. These engaging videos feature companies, processes, practices, and managers that highlight and bring to life the principles and themes examined in the text. The written videocases, which appear at the end of chapters, can stand alone as the basis for in-class discussion and assignments for individual or team work. Detailed notes on case content, running time, suggested applications, and questions are provided in the VideoCase Instructor's Manual.

Skill-Building Applications. Six skill-building exercises at the end of each chapter stimulate creativity, concept application, and critical thinking. They also involve students in writing reports and making presentations. Challenging questions help students apply what they have learned to their own lives, to small businesses, to businesses selling to other businesses, to nonprofit organizations, to service organizations, and to international marketing.

Getting Involved in Marketing. These end-of-chapter exercises, questions, and problems encourage students to work alone, in partnerships, and in larger teams to research and analyze marketing issues and develop marketing applications and programs. In completing these exercises, students will learn to use the library, do off-campus research, use online database services and other electronic resources, write reports, make presentations, and work effectively in teams. All of these exercises are designed to increase SCANS competencies.

Cross-Reference System. This system, unique in a marketing text, refers students back to the primary coverage of selected key concepts. A *specific page reference* is given when a key concept appears in a chapter subsequent to its original discussion and development. This allows students, when necessary, to quickly review that

concept in context and thus enhance their comprehension of the material. Inclusion of such references precludes the need to reintroduce concepts, and through elimination of this redundancy overall text length is reduced. Our student focus groups ranked this learning/ study tool first in utility among more than 20 different learning aids.

Chapter Opening Profiles. Each chapter begins with a profile of an organization that has successfully applied important concepts covered in that chapter. These examples show marketing in action in large and small, domestic and global businesses. Some feature entrepreneurs and others focus on key executives. These attention-getting profiles provide a lively transition between chapters and a thought-provoking introduction to the text material.

Before You Go On . . . . Each chapter has several groupings of review questions under this title, carefully positioned at the end of each major topic. Students can use these questions to test their understanding and recall of material they have just read. If they are unable to answer these periodic questions, they will know that they need to review a section before proceeding.

Issues for Critical Thinking. These periodic inserts, two in each chapter, ask students to pause and consider the implications of specific marketing concepts or situations. This tool is an excellent medium for linking the text material to a student's experiences or conclusions, which enhances retention.

Extended Examples. Each chapter includes three extended examples showing how chapter concepts apply to particular themes, including ethics and social responsibility, global marketing, small business, and contemporary marketing issues. Although dozens of examples of such topics are integrated throughout the text, these extended examples add emphasis to key concepts.

Learning Goals. These appear at the beginning of each chapter and are tied directly to the summaries at the end of the chapter and to questions in the Test Bank. The learning goals will assist students in previewing what they should know after reading the chapter. In addition, the Study Guide is carefully keyed to the learning goals as part of a totally integrated teaching, learning, and testing system.

Key Terms. Key terms are developed and reinforced through a four-pronged system. They appear initially in boldface, are repeated and defined in the margin on the same two-page spread where they first appear, are listed at the end of the chapter along with page references, and are included in a comprehensive glossary at the end of the book.

Photos and Illustrations. We live in a visual age. In a typical principles of marketing text, photos and illustrations account for at least 25 percent of the space and content, yet few authors take the care to ensure that this important element is as pedagogically relevant as the narrative. Today's students notice. We believe our text overcomes this shortcoming. Each photo and ad was carefully researched and chosen for its ability to augment and reinforce key concepts. Additionally, over one-third of the photos were commissioned specifically for use in this text in order to maximize their pedagogical value. All photos and ads are accompanied by detailed captions, which extend and reinforce key concepts. Each concludes with one or more questions designed to promote critical thinking and concept application.

Interactive Summaries. Summaries at the end of each chapter are tied directly to the learning goals and are written in a question-and-answer format. The questions and concise answers help students retain chapter material and prepare for quizzes and exams. Focus groups have shown that students find this test-simulating format a more effective study tool than the typical content review.

Diverse Examples. Nothing brings a text to life more effectively than exciting examples showing principles in action. This text includes the very best examples of marketing practices from organizations throughout the world. The examples include small and large businesses, nonprofit and government organizations, consumer and business-to-business marketing. Our reviewers acknowledged that no other text has as many current examples or as diverse a selection.

Developing the Supplements Package

As mentioned earlier, this text is customer-oriented and the result of extensive research into the needs of both faculty and students. We have addressed their concerns not only in the text, but in the supplementary materials as well.

From the more than 40 instructors who critiqued the manuscript and answered our questions, we received consistent advice: the need for a great test bank, relevant transparencies and videocases, and more. We have worked closely with these reviewers to develop materials so that the supplements package provides the level of quality and utility needed to meet instructors' teaching requirements. This extensive research even shaped the title of the text.

The integrated package includes the following:

A Comprehensive Test Bank

We list this first for the simple reason that our research confirms that the Test Bank is the most widely used, and thus important, supplement in the course.

Our Test Bank was prepared by three experienced marketing professors: James Hazeltine of Northeastern Illinois University, James Kellaris of the University of Cincinnati, and John Weiss of Colorado State University, who also served as overall coordinator. All questions were reviewed by the text authors and Joseph Brown of Ball State University and James Gaubert of Clemson University. The final Test Bank was carefully revised and refined to reflect their detailed feedback.

Several aspects of the Test Bank are unique or exceptional and worth noting:

- Questions are tied directly to the text's learning goals. In this way, no concept in the book is left uncovered in the testing system.

- Questions are structured to test three levels of learning:

  1. Knowledge of key terms

  2. Understanding of concepts and premises

  3. Application of principles

- Each chapter includes a unique Test Table that categorizes each question according to both learning objectives and the three levels of learning. This table allows instructors to more quickly arrange a balanced and thorough exam.

- All questions include the correct answers with text page references and, where applicable, a rationale for the correct answer.

Computerized Test Bank

The printed Test Bank forms the database for test-generation software available for use on Windows, DOS, and Macintosh computer systems. Instructors can edit questions, add new questions, scramble questions, and create multiple versions of the same test.

Transparency Acetates

The package contains 200 full-color acetates. The subject matter of these acetates was carefully chosen to support and reinforce the text's themes and key concepts—for example, relationship marketing, cross-cultural and global marketing, marketing in small business, business-to-business and services marketing, and IMC.

Classroom Presentation Software Using Microsoft PowerPoint

Created by Kathleen Stuenkel of Northeastern State University, the software contains approximately 150 electronic transparencies that can be modified with PowerPoint. Lecture notes accompany these illustrations and are available for Windows and DOS word processors.

Instructor's Resource Manual

Co-authored by Gayle M. Ross and William Nickels, this manual fully reflects the feedback received from our reviewers and focus group participants. We believe its design and content will provide extraordinary utility for experienced and inexperienced instructors alike. The manual contains the following features for each chapter:

- Chapter Preview
- What's in This Chapter—a listing of each resource
- What Makes This Chapter Unique—notes describing significant organizational and substantive differences compared with other texts
- Brief Outline
- Learning Goals
- Key Terms (list)
- Available Resources—a listing of lecture material, supplemental cases, videocases, etc., in the supplements package
- Lecture Outline Resources and Teaching Notes—using a unique side-by-side format
- Answers to "Applying the Concepts" Cases
- Resource Materials—summaries of articles and lectures instructors can use as supplemental lecture material
- Resource Lectures—additional examples formatted as supplemental lectures
- Supplementary Cases—with discussion questions

VideoCases

Fifteen video cases ranging in length from 8 to 15 minutes are available to adopters. The print versions of these cases appear at the end of selected chapters. The cases feature organizations and individuals carefully selected to reinforce key themes of the text. For example, marketing in small businesses is highlighted by Zane's Cycles, Larry's Shoes, and *Option* magazine. Services marketing is featured in the Union Square Cafe and Von Maur cases. Cross-cultural issues are explored in the case of Ornelas & Associates, a Dallas, Texas, agency specializing in advertising to the Latino community. Business-to-business services marketing is highlighted through Upp Business Systems. Customer-focused retailing is the subject of the case on Von Maur department stores. Commercial use of the Internet is demonstrated through the Fly & Field case. Issues surrounding new product development are featured in McDonald's development and launch of the Arch Deluxe. The Biltmore Estate is the subject of the case used to explore the activities and concepts involved in implementing integrated marketing communication.

All organizations featured in these cases share a common trait—they are customer-focused. Each is also known for the quality and value of its products and services.

VideoCase Instructor's Manual

This resource provides a detailed description of each video, running times, suggested uses, and answers to the case questions.

Study Guide

Written by Rockney Walters of Indiana University, this guide builds upon the solid foundation of marketing basics in the textbook. It reinforces the major concepts of the book, supplements them with real and hypothetical examples, and tests retention and comprehension of key terms and concepts. Each chapter includes the following features:

- Major Concepts. The chapter's major concepts are reviewed through a summary, a variety of compelling examples, and illustrations of real-world applications.
- Chapter Summary. A fill-in-the-blank format enables students to quickly recall the chapter's material and recognize relationships between key concepts.

- Key Term Matching.
- True/False Scenario. A scenario with embedded chapter concepts promotes practical application of the chapter's main ideas.
- Fill-in-the-Blanks Scenario.
- Multiple-Choice Questions.
- Similarities and Differences. Short-answer essays use a compare/contrast approach to facilitate a deeper understanding of chapter material.
- Applied Exercise. Two case studies focus on fictitious businesses, allowing the student to further explore the impact of marketing ideas and strategies upon individual companies.
- Experiential Exercises. These learning extensions engage students through research via the Internet, personal interviews, observation of local and national companies, and hands-on interaction with the business community.

Integrating traditional review formats with the more innovative and expansionary approach of the applied and experiential exercises provides an in-depth exploration of text material. The Internet exercises in particular allow students to take full advantage of available resources to form real-world decisions based on the knowledge they acquire from the textbook.

Marketing Planning Software

A student version of Tim Berry's Marketing Plan Pro™ will be available to students to accompany the textbook. Students will be able to create and print a complete marketing plan with text, tables, and charts. The document writer prompts the student through every topic of the plan to make sure all the major points are covered. The software provides students with the tools to create the kind of sound, strategic plan that professional marketing managers do.

Marketing Web Page

Worth Publishers has established a World Wide Web site for users of this text. Please check it out at http://www.worthpublishers.com/marketing. The authors will reference current articles and commentary on these Web site pages. Internet links to case studies in the book and various organizations mentioned in the text will be posted, as well as additional Internet case studies and student projects. Many articles that represent important new research will be summarized and chapter-correlated.

The Web site is linked to *Inc.* magazine's Web site (http://www.inc.com) and articles and interviews from their extensive archives are available; visitors will also be able to interact with entrepreneurs and *Inc.* editors.

Lecture Presentation CD-ROM

The presentation CD-ROM software will make it easy for instructors to include multimedia in classroom lectures. The disk, available in Macintosh and Windows formats, includes electronic lecture outlines and digital images of figures and tables from the textbook. Lecture and teaching notes from the Instructor's Resource Manual will be included for instructors who can modify and edit them to suit individual preferences.

Self-Test Software

A diskette, in Windows format, provides students with a multiple-choice test for each chapter. The disk both encourages use of the computer and offers the opportunity for advance preparation and study for scheduled examinations.

Acknowledgments

As we have stressed, this project is customer-focused and market-driven. Throughout the process of composing three comprehensive drafts of the manuscript we enjoyed essential and enormously helpful advice from a wide array of instructors and students. Without their dedication and insights this project would not have been possible. In the end we believe this team approach has achieved an exceptionally modern and pedagogically refined text. We extend our sincere and profound thanks to the following reviewers for their countless contributions.

Stephanie Bibb, Chicago State University
Abe Biswas, Louisiana State University
Joseph Brown, Ball State University
William G. Browne, Oregon State University
William Carner, University of Texas
Gerri Chaplin, Joliet Junior College
Susan Cisco, Oakton Community College
Robert Collins, University of Nevada at Las Vegas
Kenneth Crocker, Bowling Green State University
Lowell E. Crow, Western Michigan University
Denver D'Rozario, Temple University

Tom DeLaughter, University of Florida
James Gaubert, Clemson University
Peggy Gilbert, Southwest Missouri State University
John Grant, Southern Illinois University
Matthew Gross, Moraine Valley Community College
Robert Gwinner, Arizona State University
Timothy Hartman, Ohio University
James Hazeltine, Northeastern University
James Kellaris, University of Cincinnati
Phil Kemp, DePaul University
Doug Kornemann, Milwaukee Area Technical College
Marylou Lockerby, College of DuPage
H. Lee Meadow, Northern Illinois University
Robert O'Keefe, DePaul University
Eric Panitz, Ferris State University
Marie Pietak, Bucks County Community College
Robert Roe, University of Wyoming
James Spiers, Arizona State University
Michael Swenson, Brigham Young University
Clint Tankersley, Syracuse University
Debbie Thorne, University of Tampa
Frank Titlow, St. Petersburg Junior College
Sue Umashankar, University of Arizona
Steve Walker, St. Cloud State University
Rockney Walters, Indiana University
David Wasson, Johnson County Community College
John Weiss, Colorado State University
Edward Wheatley, East Carolina University

Special thanks go to the following instructors who gave up an entire weekend in order to give us face-to-face counsel on every facet of this project: Bill Carner, Lowell Crow, John Grant, Robert Gwinner, Doug Kornemann, H. Lee Meadow, Robert O'Keefe, Rockney Walters, and John Weiss.

We have been blessed to work with a great team of publishing professionals in making this text and supplements package a reality. Paul Shensa, executive editor for Worth Publishers, served as a strong advocate and knowledgeable sounding board throughout the entire process. George Touloumes, Worth's creative director, supervised the reader-friendly innovative book design and cover (the theme is relationships among people). Thanks to Elisa Adams for her input on early drafts of the manuscript. We thank our production editors, Timothy Prairie and Margaret Comaskey, who guided the manuscript, features, and art into their final form. They ably juggled deadlines and changes to make this book a reality. We would also like to thank Patricia Lawson in production and Fernando Quiñones and Demetrios Zangos in design, who handled critical details and rendered final art to ensure the quality of the final product, and Malcolm Grear Designers for their beautiful design.

We want to thank John Britch for his enthusiastic planning and coordinating of the launch effort of our text. He has successfully shepherded the bond of commitment between our marketers and their stakeholders. We appreciate the service and commitment of the dedicated sales representatives from the Scientific American–St. Martin's Press College Publishing Group. They will provide an ongoing commitment to the needs of students and faculty alike.

Our thanks also go to the industry sources for their suggestions and advice on current technologies and real-world business concepts. Special thanks to Edward Tennent of IBM and Devar Burbage of GRC International for their ideas and help.

We could not have developed a new marketing text without the assistance of the faculty and graduate students at the University of Maryland. Expert faculty members in marketing and logistics read various chapters and made suggestions: Ruth Bolton (services marketing), Roxanne Lefkoff-Hagius (consumer behavior), Phil Evers (transportation and logistics), Dan Sheinin (integrated marketing communication), Janet Wagner (retailing), Sanjit Sengupta and Abdul Ali (overall marketing concepts), and Amy Smith (reviewed all chapters). Carol Emerson of Denver University helped conceptualize the text and reviewed all the chapters. Graduate assistants also read and commented on chapters. They include Marcy Friedman, Ryan Holmes, Tricia Raiken, and Ron Zussman.

Special thanks go to Susan and Jim McHugh, coauthors of *Understanding Business*, who helped shape and refine many of the features in the resource package for instructors. Finally, thanks to Ronald Michaels of the University of Central Florida and Erica Michaels who reviewed much of the first draft.

We dedicate this book to our families, friends, and colleagues who show us daily the value of relationship building, and to Heather Mazzenga, Andrea Mazzenga, Katie Beth Goodwin, Joel Nickels and all the other young people who will benefit from customer-driven marketing in the future.

William G. Nickels   Marian Burk Wood

November 1996

MARKETING

Relationships, Quality, Value

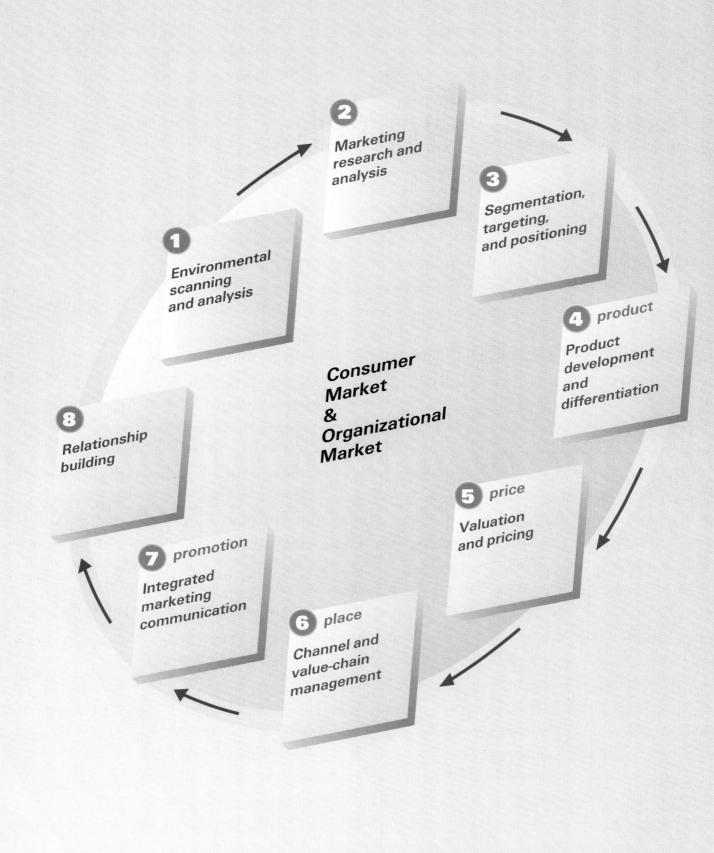

Foundations of Marketing and Relationship Building

Marketing is all about building relationships, as Part 1 explains. Chapter 1 presents a customer-driven vision of marketing, with an overview of relationship building with customers, employees, suppliers, retailers, government officials, media representatives, and other stakeholders. The chapter opening profiles of Mr. CB's, a small business, and Biltmore Estate, a major tourist attraction, highlight the use of marketing to build relationships that last. Chapter 1 also introduces the eight universal processes that are fundamental to marketing any good or service. Chapter 2 integrates these universal marketing processes into a strategic framework for guiding the development and implementation of internal and external marketing plans. The chapter opening profile shows how marketing strategy helped Samsung Electronics build relationships in global markets.

1

Introduction to the New Marketing Vision

Learning Goals

After you have read and studied this chapter, you should be able to:

1. Explain how and why the definition of marketing has changed over the years.
2. Differentiate between relationship marketing and transactional marketing.
3. Relate utility to customer needs and wants, and describe the six types of utility that marketing can provide.
4. Discuss how the practice of marketing has evolved from a production orientation to a sales orientation to a way of doing business based on the marketing concept.
5. List and explain the ABCs of marketing.
6. Define the marketing mix and explain the need for its expansion.
7. Identify the eight universal marketing processes.

PROFILE

Building relationships for the twenty-first century

Mr. CB's, a small boat-rental business, and Biltmore Estate, the grandest home in America, share something vitally important. They both have the marketing skill needed to build enduring relationships with customers, employees, and suppliers.

Aledia Hunt Tush, the owner of Mr. CB's in Siesta Key, Florida, bought the bait-and-tackle shop in 1976. In addition to boat and bicycle rentals, the store meets customer needs by offering seminars on fishing and maps to where the big ones are biting. Tush knows that her store competes with Wal-Mart and other large stores. To attract and keep customers, she provides what customers can't get at the chain stores: boat rentals, live bait, reel repairs, and plenty of personalized attention.

Tush realizes that her most important asset is her employees. The first thing she tells new hires is: "The customer is number one." The second thing is: "You have to work together as a group." She also works hard to establish friendly relationships with her suppliers, who reward her loyalty with good deals.

Biltmore Estate, a major tourist destination in Asheville, North Carolina, also uses marketing—on a larger scale—to build relationships with visitors. The Estate annually attracts more than 800,000 visitors to its magnificent mansion, gardens, winery, and restaurants. One of its key marketing tools is a database of details about visitors, which helps Estate marketers gear offers to the interests of specific customer groups.

Passholders, who buy one-year admission passes, are mailed newsletters and special offers to reinforce loyalty. General visitors, who buy one-day admissions, are mailed seasonal brochures to encourage return visits. The Estate also keeps a close eye on quality and service, both of which influence long-term customer relationships. You'll read more about Biltmore Estate's marketing in the Integrative Capstone Case at the end of the book.[1]

Marketing is an exciting and ever-changing activity that touches all of our lives. This chapter introduces the world of marketing, starting with old and new views of marketing, how marketing exchanges are formed, and why stakeholders are important. The chapter ends with a preview of eight universal marketing processes that form the foundation of marketing for the twenty-first century.

Emergence of the New Marketing Vision

*T*he attitude changed from "the customer is inconveniencing you and preventing you from doing your job" to "the customer is your job."

Chris Zane
of Zane's Cycles, describing his customer-oriented approach

For Mr. CB's and for Biltmore Estate, as well as for many other organizations heading into the twenty-first century, building relationships that survive the test of time is the top priority. Electrolux, based in Sweden, wants an ongoing relationship with the customers who buy its appliances throughout the world, just as U.S.-based Pizza Hut wants an ongoing relationship with people everywhere who buy its pizzas. From appliance manufacturers to fast-food restaurants, from colleges to museums, organizations of all kinds are using marketing to discover what customers want and are doing whatever it takes to keep customers coming back again and again.

This vision of marketing isn't entirely new. Early in this century, Henry Ford worked hard to build relationships with car buyers, as did L.L. Bean, founder of the mail-order sports and apparel business that bears his name. Then, as today, whenever and wherever money or something else of value changes hands, marketing plays a leading role.

What exactly is marketing? If you had asked that question forty years ago, you would have received one answer. Just ten years ago, you would have received another. But all past efforts fall short of conveying the dynamics of marketing today.

Old and New Views of Marketing

As early as 1948, the American Marketing Association (AMA) defined marketing as "the performance of business activities directed toward, and incident to, the flow of goods and services from producer to consumer or user."[2] According to that definition, which the association modified slightly in 1960, marketing was a highway along which goods and services traveled from producers to customers and users.

An updated version, prepared by the AMA in 1985, defined marketing as a management activity: "the process of planning and executing the conception, pricing, promotion, and distribution of ideas, goods, and services to create exchanges that satisfy individual and organizational objectives." This definition, however, does not recognize the value of building long-term relationships with customers and with other groups and individuals who are involved with the organization. These relationships are now easier to develop because of technology such as databases containing information about customers.

Since relationship building has become an integral part of marketing, the authors of this text believe that the evolving definition needs to be updated once again. Today marketing in most organizations has a new meaning, one that takes into account the relationship between participants:

> **Marketing** is the process of establishing and maintaining mutually beneficial exchange relationships with customers and other stakeholders.

In this definition, several key concepts stand out—"mutually beneficial exchange relationships," "customers," and "stakeholders"—and each is extremely important. The sections that follow take a closer look at these key concepts.

marketing
the process of establishing and maintaining mutually beneficial exchange relationships with customers and other stakeholders

product

a good, a service, or an idea that the customer acquires to satisfy a need or want through the exchange of money or something else of value

Mutually Beneficial Marketing Exchange

Marketing doesn't occur unless there is an *exchange*, the action of trading or selling something of value, as seen, for example, in Figure 1.1. When you buy a chair at the local store, you are exchanging money for seating. Similarly, when you respond to a Red Cross blood drive, you are exchanging your blood for the satisfaction of helping others. A marketing exchange occurs only when three elements are in place:

1. Each of two or more people or organizations has something of value to trade.

2. Both parties are willing and able to trade what they have for something else they value.

3. The parties are able to communicate with each other about the exchange.

In a marketing exchange, both the marketer (provider) and the customer must benefit. Think again about going shopping and about donating blood. Each party in the exchange—you as the customer and the store or Red Cross organization as the provider—receives something of value as a result of these exchanges. This makes the exchange *mutually beneficial*.

During a marketing exchange, the marketer receives money or something else of value, and the customer receives a product. A **product** is a good, a service, or an idea that the customer acquires to satisfy a need or want through the exchange of money or something else of value. *Goods* are products such as pens and potatoes, bananas and buildings, that are tangible—that is, physically able to be touched. *Services* are products such as medical care, education, and haircuts that are intangible but offer health, information, cosmetic, or other valuable benefits. *Ideas* are thoughts or images such as "Wear your seat belts" or "Safety First" that businesses and nonprofit organizations promote to customers, employees, and others to increase their knowledge or contribute to their well-being.

F I G U R E **1.1** **Examples of Marketing Exchanges**

Marketing creates mutually beneficial exchanges. Those exchanges may be between a local store and the customers it serves (goods exchanged for money) or between a restaurant and the organization to which it gives food (donations for the satisfaction of helping others). Another way in which businesses participate in marketing exchanges is by trading money or products for goods and services offered by other businesses.

transactional marketing

marketers focus on individual, isolated exchanges that satisfy a customer's needs at a particular time and place

relationship marketing

the process of establishing and maintaining mutually beneficial long-term relationships among organizations and their customers, employees, and other stakeholders

Transactional Marketing

For years, most organizations approached marketing as a set of unconnected transactions between marketer and customer. In **transactional marketing** marketers focus on individual, isolated exchanges that satisfy a customer's needs at a particular time and place. Marketers tended to concentrate more on attracting *new* customers for future exchanges than on encouraging additional exchanges by developing closer relationships with current customers.

Because of the emphasis on new exchanges, marketers and their customers developed little trust or commitment to the relationship. Customers soon learned to search for the best deal, and they chose among products largely on the basis of price. This led many marketers to stress lower prices, which in turn led to cost-cutting, layoffs, and lower profits. With profitability a key issue and international competition growing, marketers today are increasingly interested in fostering customer loyalty and commitment.

Relationship Marketing

Relationship marketing is the process of establishing and maintaining mutually beneficial long-term relationships among organizations and their customers, employees, and other stakeholders.[3] The key words in this definition are "maintaining" and "long-term." The relationship approach is used by Mr. CB's, Biltmore Estate, and a growing number of organizations around the world. It expands the concept of the marketing exchange from a single transaction to an ongoing series of transactions, as shown in Table 1.1. Each transaction is just one link in the chain of the relationship between the marketer and the customer or other stakeholders. Over time, each transaction has the potential to strengthen the bond of commitment and trust between marketers and their stakeholders.

Businesses have practiced relationship marketing for years in their dealings with other businesses (business-to-business marketing). For example, Volkswagen and other automobile companies have established and maintained long-term mutually beneficial relationships with many of their suppliers and dealers. Supermarkets such as Finast are also establishing such relationships with their suppliers to compete with Wal-Mart, one of the better practitioners of the process.

TABLE **1.1**   **Transactional Marketing Versus Relationship Marketing**

Transactional Marketing	Relationship Marketing
1. Emphasis on getting new customers	1. Emphasis on keeping customers as well as getting new ones
2. Short-term orientation	2. Long-term orientation
3. Interest in making a single sale	3. Interest in multiple sales and enduring relationships
4. Limited commitment to customers	4. High level of ongoing commitment to customers
5. Research on customer needs used to complete one transaction	5. Continuing research on customer needs used to enhance relationship
6. Success means making a sale	6. Success means customer loyalty, repeat purchases, customer recommendations, and low customer turnover
7. Quality is a production concern	7. Quality is every employee's concern
8. Limited service commitment	8. High degree of service commitment

Relationship marketing is now coming into its own in the consumer market. Consider how two retailers—a discount chain and an upscale chain known for high fashion—use relationship marketing with consumers. Zellers is a 272-store retail chain in Canada. The store uses a combination of guaranteed lowest prices and shopper rewards to build a strong relationship

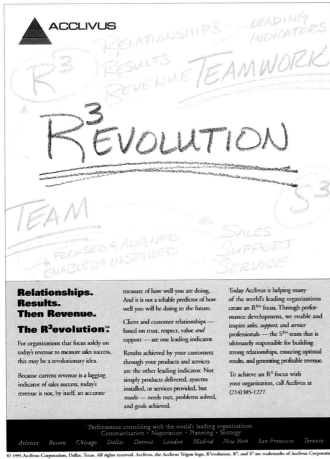

**Relationships.
Results.
Then Revenue.**

The R³evolution™

For organizations that focus solely on today's revenue to measure sales success, this may be a revolutionary idea.

Because current revenue is a lagging indicator of sales success, today's revenue is not, by itself, an accurate

measure of how well you are doing. And it is not a reliable predictor of how well you will be doing in the future.

Client and customer relationships — based on trust, respect, value *and* rapport — are one leading indicator.

Results achieved by your customers through your products and services are the other leading indicator. Not simply products delivered, systems installed, or services provided, but *results* — needs met, problems solved, and goals achieved.

Today Acclivus is helping many of the world's leading organizations create an R³ℳ focus. Through performance development, we enable and inspire *sales, support, and service* professionals — the S³ℳ team that is ultimately responsible for building strong relationships, ensuring optimal results, and generating profitable revenue.

To achieve an R³ focus with your organization, call Acclivus at (214)385-1277.

Performance consulting with the world's leading organizations.
Communication · Negotiation · Planning · Strategy

Atlanta   Boston   Chicago   Dallas   Detroit   London   Madrid   New York   San Francisco   Toronto

Relationship marketing is a relatively new concept for many organizations. Acclivus Corporation is a performance-development company based in Dallas that helps organizations build strong relationships, ensure optimal results for their products and services, and generate profitable revenue. Acclivus teaches the skills and strategies that allow individuals and companies to build trust, respect, value, and rapport with customers. What other organizational stakeholders should be approached with a relationship-building strategy?

customer

an individual or organization that buys or exchanges something of value for a marketer's products

with its customers. Through Club Z, customers earn points for every dollar they spend at Zellers. Since these points are redeemable for gifts, the system gives customers an incentive to remain loyal to Zellers.

Neiman-Marcus, a Dallas-based retailer known for quality and service, also uses relationship marketing to create closer connections with customers. Searching for ways to make its top-spending customers feel appreciated and thus more loyal, the store established two programs, InCircle and NM Plus. Both programs reward customers with glamorous merchandise when their spending reaches preset levels, starting at $1,000 per year. Neiman's customers are clearly pleased with the recognition: Participation has been six times greater than expected.[4]

Many customers and marketers actively seek long-term relationships. For example, people want ongoing relationships with their physicians, dentists, hair stylists, and other marketers that provide personal services. For their part, these service providers, who prosper only when customers return again and again, want to encourage long-term relationships. Now makers of supermarket foods and other everyday products are adopting this approach.[5] In the future, even more marketers will be moving toward strengthening relationships with customers and other stakeholders. Some marketers and customers are not interested in establishing long-term relationships. For them, transactional marketing may be sufficient.

Customers and Other Stakeholders

The marketer is one of the main parties in any marketing transaction. Another key player is the **customer**, an individual or organization that buys or exchanges something of value for a marketer's products. All marketers—businesses, nonprofit organizations, government agencies, and individuals—have customers, although they may be called something else (such as patients or citizens). The exact term isn't important as long as each marketer is customer-oriented, attuned to satisfying every customer in every marketing exchange.

For their part, customers are becoming more active participants in the exchange process. A growing number of businesses, for example, are working closely with suppliers to develop products that more closely meet the businesses' needs. Consider Nintendo, which markets video games and equipment around the world. As a customer, it has formed long-term relationships with 20 hardware manufacturers and 150 software developers that make products for Nintendo's customers.[6]

In addition, some government agencies are trying to strengthen relationships with their customers. For example, the Madison, Wisconsin, police chief recently asked a team of employees to research what local citizens—customers—want from the department. Was enforcement of traffic regula-

stakeholders

individuals and organizations, including employees, suppliers, stockholders, and the community, that influence or are influenced by what the organization does

tions a top priority? Noise control? Control over street violence? Once the employees had identified the city's most important needs, they were able to set specific goals for satisfying those needs—and to measure results to see how well customer needs were being met.[7]

The satisfaction of other stakeholders is also a consideration in any marketing exchange. **Stakeholders** are individuals and organizations, including employees, suppliers, stockholders, and the community, that influence or are influenced by what the organization does, as illustrated in Figure 1.2. Employees, in particular, are a vitally important stakeholder group because they're often the people who take care of customers. Just as satisfied employees are likely to feel more motivated to satisfy their customers, dissatisfied employees are likely to feel less motivated to satisfy their customers.

Organizations have learned that one way to satisfy employees is to treat them as internal customers. An *internal customer* is an employee who receives help and cooperation from other employees in completing the organization's work. Everyone in the organization is thus an internal customer, and everyone in the organization serves certain internal customers.

FIGURE **1.2**   **Building Relationships with Organizational Stakeholders**

Marketers need to establish and maintain good relationships with the many stakeholders that can influence (or are influenced by) the organization's activities. The marketer benefits by earning profits from sales to customers and from the money and support it receives from the other stakeholders. In turn, the marketer provides goods, services, support, and information for its stakeholders.

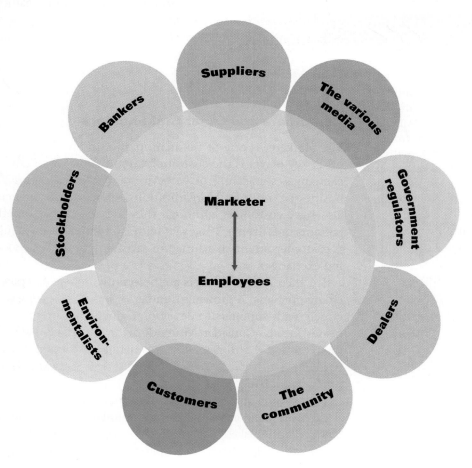

internal marketing

the process of satisfying internal customers (employees) as a prerequisite to satisfying external customers

Think about your local Burger King restaurant. The employees who ring up customer purchases are the internal customers of kitchen employees, who are expected to cook the food properly and on time. The goal is to make every internal function operate as if its output is going to a customer, whether the customer is inside or outside the organization. Inside the organization, this is known as **internal marketing**, the process of satisfying internal customers (employees) as a prerequisite to satisfying external customers.[8]

Other stakeholders, such as suppliers, bankers, dealers, environmentalists, the local community, the media, and stockholders, also play a key role in the exchange process. Therefore, it is important to establish good relationships with all these stakeholders. Without good suppliers, for example, General Motors will not get the right supplies and parts to make high-quality cars. Without good dealers, GM will not be able to get its cars to customers. Without the backing of stockholders and bankers, GM may not have the resources to buy necessary supplies or factory equipment. Without cooperation from the community, GM may not find a good location for its dealerships serving that area. Environmentalists may have an important say in how GM acquires or builds on property. Similarly, because stories in the media can support or hurt GM's image, media relations are another priority.

Publicly held corporations like General Motors are especially concerned with maintaining relations with stockholders, who are interested in profitability. Although marketers have to focus on satisfying customers, they cannot let that focus result in unsatisfactory returns to stockholders. That's why a substantial portion of GM's marketing effort goes toward establishing and maintaining good relationships with stockholders and with all its stakeholders.

Issues for critical thinking

Why would a petroleum marketer such as Royal Dutch/Shell want to establish friendly relations with environmental activists? Government regulators? Stockholders? What other stakeholders would be important to this company's success?

Customer Needs and Wants

To benefit the customer, a marketing exchange must satisfy a need or a want. A *need* is the feeling of deprivation over the absence of food, clothing, shelter, or some other necessity for basic survival. While every human being can feel the need for such necessities, how a need is satisfied varies a great deal from person to person. A *want* is a desire to satisfy a need in a specific way, a way that is influenced by the individual's background and culture, as well as by other forces, including marketing.

To understand the distinction between a need and a want, imagine that you *need* clothing as protection against cold weather. Among the items of clothing you might buy to satisfy this need are a ski parka, a wool coat, or a down vest. Which garment you choose to satisfy your need depends on your *wants*: your desire for warmer, more fashionable, or more functional clothing. Any of these three items of clothing will satisfy your need. You'll choose one that fulfills a want *and* is sold at a price you're willing to pay (the one with the best value).

utility

the value a product provides for the customer

Although marketers have no control over people's needs, they can influence people's wants. Eddie Bauer and Eastern Mountain Sports are two marketers that want you to buy their ski parkas, for example. In effect, a customer with an unsatisfied need is a customer with a problem—and it's the marketer's job to create and market a product to solve that problem.[9] How well a product satisfies customer needs and wants is a function of its utility.

Utility and Value

Utility describes the value a product provides for the customer. Marketers may satisfy customer needs and wants through six types of utility: form, time, place, possession, information, and service. *Form utility* is the value provided by changing (forming) raw materials into a finished product. Sony creates form utility when it produces a cassette player from plastic, metal, and electronic components.

Time utility is the value of making a product available *when* the customer needs it. Store 24 in Boston, for example, creates time utility by allowing hungry customers to buy Smartfood popcorn at any hour of the day or night. *Place utility* is the value of making a product available *where* the customer needs it. Instead of having to go all the way to the factory in Spring Hill, Tennessee, customers can buy Saturn cars at local dealers, a more convenient place for such a transaction.

Possession utility is the value provided by enabling customers to obtain and use the product over time. Marketing activities included in possession utility are credit (allowing customers without cash to buy immediately), delivery, installation, and guarantees. When you buy a washing machine from a nearby store, for example, you may benefit from all these activities.

Information utility is the value of communicating to the customer information about the product, such as its price and instructions for use. Retailers like Hudson's Bay in Canada create information utility by offering product details in catalogs, advertisements, and store signs, as well as through sales help and instruction booklets.

Service utility is the value added to products through services such as friendly employees, return privileges, quick repairs, customer support, and

Store 24 provides time utility to consumers by staying open 24 hours a day. It works toward a true customer focus by stressing elements such as friendliness, cleanliness, value, and quality. It has introduced a "ban boredom" theme to create some excitement in all its stores. What kinds of things could a convenience store do to make shopping more fun for customers?

value package

the combination of tangible and intangible elements that potential customers evaluate when deciding whether to buy a particular product

updating of information about product uses to increase the item's value over time. Service utility is becoming critical because it creates a competitive advantage that is not easily matched.[10]

Beyond Customer Satisfaction

From the customers' perspective, a product is a package of tangible and intangible elements that in combination offer value to satisfy their wants and needs.[11] When people shop for a car, for example, they take for granted that every model will have four wheels, a chassis, and other standard features. But the car must have much more than these basic elements. People also look at color, styling, service, financing, price, company reputation, and other elements that have nothing to do with satisfying the need for reliable transportation. In effect, everything about that car and its manufacturer plays a role in creating customer satisfaction and loyalty.

Thus, a **value package** is the combination of tangible and intangible elements that potential customers evaluate when deciding whether to buy a particular product. When the value package goes beyond meeting ordinary needs and expectations, it has the potential of delighting the customer.* Consider Saturn cars. The value package created by an attractive car design, good performance, no-haggle pricing, and attentive dealer service doesn't merely satisfy customers, it delights them. The proof? When Saturn put on a three-day festival for customers, more than 20,000 people came to tour the factory, meet with Saturn employees, and listen to country music. Clearly, Saturn's value package delights these customers.[12]

As Saturn's experience shows, offering a superior value package does more than satisfy customers. It also encourages customer loyalty, which leads to stronger, longer lasting relationships and, ultimately, higher profitability. As a result, both marketer and customer benefit when value packages are designed to elicit delight, not to merely meet customer needs.[13]

Integrated Marketing and You

At one time, the marketing department was the only place in the organization that handled marketing—and its managers were the only people who made marketing decisions. For a growing number of organizations, however, the idea of isolating marketing activities in a single department has been replaced by the concept of marketing as an organization-wide activity. In the words of marketing consultant Regis McKenna, "Marketing today is not a function; it is a way of doing business. . . . Marketing has to be all-pervasive, part of everyone's job description, from the receptionists to the board of directors."[14]

These days, marketing is part of every job in the organization. Even if you're not planning a marketing career, you can expect to be involved in marketing wherever you work. The decisions you make and the actions you take in dealing with customers and other stakeholders will certainly affect your organization's marketing performance. For a closer look at two employees who satisfy internal and external customers, follow along as Paula Doricchi and Jacob Smith apply marketing concepts.

---

*Delighting customers is a concept that emerged from total quality management (TQM).

MARKETING IDEAS

Learning marketing on your own

You can learn a lot about marketing by finding people who are good at it and watching how they do it. One good marketer to watch is Paula Doricchi, a waitress at the Ruby Tuesday restaurant in Greenville, South Carolina. Doricchi knows every dish on the menu and how each one is prepared. She remembers her customers' names and the kind of food they prefer, and she recommends specific dishes customers might like.

All in all, Doricchi thoroughly enjoys serving her customers, and it shows. That's why people stand in line for up to an hour to be seated at one of her tables. She has turned regulars into friends by developing a close, personal relationship with them. Doricchi's commitment has a positive effect on her co-workers, her managers, and her customers.

Another good marketer to watch is Jacob Smith of the Bank of America in Los Angeles. He approves or rejects loan applications that are forwarded by employees in the bank's California branches. Although branch employees are paid a commission for each loan they make, evaluators are cautious about approvals, because some customers may not be able to repay their loans.

This inherent conflict caused tension until the bank taught all evaluators to do what Smith does: Treat branch employees as internal customers. Smith looks for ways to approve loans. But when a loan can't be made, he calls the branch and carefully explains why. Neither Smith nor Doricchi is in the marketing department, yet as individuals they do everything they can to strengthen marketing relationships.[15]

Whom do you know who exemplifies successful marketing?

Integrated marketing unites the activities of many firms to satisfy the needs of consumers and industrial buyers. To bring the customer a beautiful dining room ensemble, a furniture retailer has to establish a good relationship with a furniture factory. The factory, in turn, has to establish a successful relationship with a lumber supplier, which has to establish a good relationship with a tree-harvesting firm. The smooth flow of materials among all these organizations should result in profit for each and satisfaction for consumers, who can purchase fine furniture at reasonable prices. From this example, can you see how important the marketing process is to the economic system?

integrated marketing

the unification and coordination of the marketer's internal activities with its partners' activities to complete marketing exchanges that delight customers

Marketing success also depends on the actions of employees in other organizations. First, organizations need the cooperation of suppliers that provide raw materials, services, and other resources that go into producing goods and services for customers. Second, organizations need the cooperation of dealers and others that make goods and services available to customers. All these organizations have to work together in a seamless marketing system that results in satisfying customer needs.

Integrated marketing is the unification and coordination of the marketer's internal activities with its partners' activities to complete marketing exchanges that delight customers. Much as a conductor coordinates the playing of each musician in the orchestra, the marketer coordinates the role of its employees and its partners' employees in satisfying customers. Integrated marketing keeps everyone, in every department and organization, focused on the objectives and activities that lead to long-term relationships by satisfying customers' needs and wants.[16]

The best way to remember important concepts and terms from a text is to periodically review what you have read to see whether you are retaining the material. The following exercise, called "Before you go on . . . ," is one of two found in every chapter. By answering these questions, you will reinforce what you have read and increase your retention rate dramatically.

Before you go on . . .

A. How does transactional marketing differ from relationship marketing?

B. What are stakeholders and why is it important for marketers to satisfy them?

C. What six utilities do marketers add?

D. What is a value package?

Marketing Yesterday, Today, and Tomorrow

To understand where marketing is going, it helps to understand how it evolved over time. In the eighteenth and nineteenth centuries, companies in Europe and the United States developed the capacity to turn out products in large quantities at low prices. Many of these marketers stressed production as the foundation of the marketing exchange. At a time when families had to make nearly everything they needed, the mere availability of a finished product at a reasonable price was often enough to stimulate demand. Choices were few, so customers bought whatever products were available. This *production orientation* is still the approach of some organizations, especially in developing countries where demand often outstrips supply.[17]

By the 1920s, most U.S. manufacturers had learned how to use marketing research, advertising, distribution, and other marketing methods to get closer to customers. Since, however, supply exceeded demand in many cases, there was increased competition among manufacturers who made similar products. Faced with the problem of getting rid of their output, most producers

The computer industry changed dramatically after Intel invented the computer chip in 1971. Instead of producing and selling gigantic computers for a few very large organizations, Intel applied the marketing concept to make and sell chips for smaller computers that enable companies and individuals to be more productive. How do you think Intel might investigate future uses of personal computers so it can plan the next generations of computer chips?

increasingly stressed selling as the foundation of the marketing exchange. This stronger *sales orientation* helped producers to find customers for what they made, and many contemporary companies approach marketing in the same way—those who still practice traditional marketing.[18]

As important as selling is to many organizations, it's not the same as marketing. Harvard marketing professor Theodore Levitt notes that marketing puts the focus squarely on satisfying the needs of the customer. Instead of thinking only in terms of sales activities, marketing is based on the idea "of satisfying the needs of the customer by means of the product and the whole cluster of things associated with creating, delivering, and finally consuming it."[19]

The Marketing Concept

By the 1950s, General Electric, Pillsbury, and other forward-thinking U.S. businesses were looking beyond a sales orientation to better adapt to the needs of customers. Producers wanted to avoid making—and trying to sell—what customers didn't want or need. Instead, they decided to put their resources into making what their research showed customers wanted and needed.[20]

This orientation became known as the **marketing concept,** the idea that organizations can satisfy their own long-term objectives, such as profitability, by coordinating and focusing all their activities on identifying and satisfying customer needs and wants. The marketing concept is based on three principles:

1. A customer orientation
2. The coordination and integration of all marketing activities
3. A profit orientation

Procter & Gamble, Michelin, and many other large corporations have built worldwide profits by applying the marketing concept. The French tire manufacturer, for example, has worked hard to respond to the needs of makers and buyers of automotive vehicles. Michelin's cross-functional work teams cooperate to develop innovative products that customers want. One example is the environment-friendly "green" tire, 20 years in the making, that reduces fuel consumption. Such products help the company keep its 19 percent share of the world tire market.[21]

Smaller businesses have also adopted the marketing concept, as have nonprofit organizations such as charities and government agencies.[22] Although nonprofits are not in business to make a profit, they do need to understand who their customers are and how to satisfy their needs and wants in a financially responsible way. For example, Joanne Lawson, senior director of direct marketing for the American Society for the Prevention of Cruelty to Animals (ASPCA), thinks carefully about the needs and wants of potential donors before starting a campaign to raise funds. By applying the marketing concept, Lawson helps the ASPCA raise nearly $9 million annually.[23]

World-Class Marketing

As you saw earlier, marketers today are very much aware that the marketing exchange doesn't end when a transaction is completed. If anything, the relationship between marketer and customer can become more intense after the first exchange.[24] Car buyers need service, equipment buyers need training and replacement parts, and so on. Even a seemingly simple transaction, such as the sale of a package of chewing gum, isn't quite so simple when you think about the many packages your customers might buy if they like your gum, and the many sales you'll lose if they don't. In effect, you can think of every marketing transaction as the prelude to the next one and the one after that, a series of transactions in an ongoing relationship.

Remember that customers can choose among suppliers from many countries, just as suppliers can reach out to customers across geographic borders. With so much at stake and so many choices, the best way to build strong and enduring relationships is to be the best. *World-class marketing* is marketing that is as good as marketing done by the best organizations in the world. This means pleasing customers with quality products, fair prices, and outstanding service. It also means on-time delivery and informative communication.

One way to work toward world-class marketing is by benchmarking. **Benchmarking** is rating your practices, processes, and products against the world's best to see how they got that way so you can do the same. For instance, L.L. Bean is known for filling customer orders without a hitch. It recently mailed 500,000 packages and correctly filled every order. Manchester

marketing concept

the idea that organizations can satisfy their own long-term objectives, such as profitability, by coordinating and focusing all their activities on identifying and satisfying customer needs and wants

benchmarking

rating your practices, processes, and products against the world's best to see how they got that way so you can do the same

Stamping Corporation is trying to match that record. Not long ago, it shipped some 540,000 parts to Honda of America, with only seven bad ones. Manchester's goal, like L.L. Bean's goal, is 100% satisfaction. Marketers can benchmark Wal-Mart to learn how to handle distribution, Motorola to learn product development, and Xerox for effective supplier management.[25]

The process of handling customer orders is so fast and efficient at L.L. Bean that businesses come from all over the world to benchmark on its processes. Slower service is unacceptable to customers. Do you know of other businesses that are models of fast and efficient service that slower companies could benchmark?

World-class marketing is also *boundaryless* marketing, in which everyone in the organization, regardless of location, is working toward satisfying the needs and wants of customers, wherever they may be. Here's how General Electric describes this approach: "Boundaryless behavior combines 12 huge global businesses—each number one or number two in its markets—into a vast laboratory whose principal product is new ideas, coupled with a common commitment to spread them throughout the [company]."[26] In short, every customer in every market benefits from the ideas of every employee in every GE business.

The ABCs of Marketing

Like all world-class marketers, you can use the basics of marketing to give your customers the best value in goods and services, and you can work hard to deserve their loyalty. In return, customers will keep coming back, giving you the profits (or donations or votes) you need. The seemingly simple formula for world-class marketing, which updates the marketing concept, is known as the *ABCs of marketing:*

- *Always be customer-driven.* The point of marketing is to establish and maintain a mutually beneficial exchange relationship with customers. Although other stakeholders are important, customers are the key to marketing success. The whole organization needs to be united in serving the customer.

- *Benchmark against the best in the world.* Your goal is to match the best. Ideally, you can go further, creating more value for the customer and generating higher profits at the same time.

- *Continuously improve your product and performance.* Your customers' needs—and your competitors' responses—are constantly changing. Therefore, you have to keep looking for ways of making your product, your service, and your employees better and better. Continuous improvement is just one part of *total quality management (TQM)*, which is discussed in more detail in Chapter 2.

- *Develop the best value package.* Use research to find out what the customer values and then provide more of it than your competitors. Your value package should bundle the best array of goods and services at the best price to satisfy your customers' needs.

- *Empower your employees.* **Empowerment** allows employees at all levels of the organization to use their power and discretion to make decisions and take steps to satisfy customers. Thus employees must receive thorough and continuous training to enable them to understand organizational objectives and customer requirements. To be effective, employees need the tools and the authority to respond appropriately—and enthusiastically—to customer needs.

- *Focus on relationships.* Aim to attract new customers as well as to reinforce your relationships with current customers. Every transaction is an opportunity to remind customers of why they should remain loyal to you rather than switching to a rival. Strengthen, too, your relationships with suppliers, retailers, and other stakeholders.

- *Generate profit and meet other organizational objectives.* The ABCs of marketing provide a means to help organizations achieve their primary objectives. For most businesses, this means generating profits. For nonprofits and for government agencies, it means meeting the needs of the organization and its constituents alike. Therefore, you should keep organizational objectives (such as profit) in mind throughout the marketing process.

Issues for critical thinking

To keep the ABCs simple, only seven letters are used, covering the critical marketing tasks. However, the concept can be carried through the rest of the alphabet. For example, H could stand for "**Hire** the best people." How would you extend the list through the end of the alphabet?

Note that the ABCs of marketing is an update of the marketing concept. The marketing concept is merged into the ABCs as follows: **A** (Always be customer-driven) replaces the marketing concept's *customer orientation*, **F** (Focus on relationships) replaces the marketing concept's *coordinate and integrate marketing functions*, and **G** (Generate profits) replaces the marketing concept's *profit orientation*.

In the following case, you can see how the ABCs of marketing have made a difference at snack marketer Frito-Lay. After you've finished reading the case, you can practice making marketing decisions by answering the case questions as if you were handling Frito-Lay's marketing program.

empowerment

allows employees at all levels of the organization to use their power and discretion to make decisions and take steps to satisfy customers

Applying the Concepts

Marketing is everybody's job at Frito-Lay

Less than a decade ago, Frito-Lay's sales force sold about $700 million in snack foods yearly to supermarkets, grocery stores, delicatessens, and other commercial customers. These days, annual sales are over $8 billion. What made the difference? Frito-Lay began to look at marketing in an entirely new way. Now everyone's job is to market the company's products. Where salespeople were once expected to merely carry out orders, now they are empowered to build relationships by putting the customer first. In turn, they're treated as valued internal customers who need help to satisfy their external customers' needs.

In all, Frito-Lay salespeople call on over 100,000 stores a day, selling Doritos, Ruffles, and other snacks. To help salespeople satisfy these customers, Frito-Lay reoriented its entire organization toward supporting the needs of salespeople. Every department, from product development and distribution to human resources and production, is ready to provide information and anything else the salespeople need to be effective.

One way Frito-Lay made the salesperson's job easier was to give each a handheld computer to track and place orders. The computers calculate sales (including any tax and discounts), print out receipts (using printers in the sales truck), and send data back to the company for analysis. Salespeople can also receive data from the company about the status of a customer's order. When a customer has a question or problem, the salesperson can use this technology to respond immediately.

Because they get quick answers—and action—from other Frito-Lay employees, the salespeople are able to ensure that snacks on store shelves are never more than two days old. That's why Ruffles, Lay's, Cheetos, and other Frito-Lay foods taste fresh and crisp. Fresh snacks please everyone, stores and consumers alike. For Frito-Lay, this cycle of continually improving internal and external customer satisfaction is the best fuel for higher sales and profits.[27]

Make marketing decisions

1. How could the meat and fish departments in supermarkets and delicatessens apply these concepts?

2. What barriers do organizations face when trying to implement customer-oriented programs such as the one at Frito-Lay?

3. What other services might Frito-Lay offer to make its value package even more attractive to commercial customers?

4. Apart from customers and employees, what other stakeholders should Frito-Lay target for marketing activities? Why?

Social Responsibility and Ethics

Managing relations with customers and other stakeholders involves issues of social responsibility and ethics. *Social responsibility* is the idea that organizations should look beyond their own interests and make a contribution to society. Accordingly, every organization should act in ways that benefit

A key organizational objective of Chicago's South Shore Bank is making a profit for its stockholders. But another important goal is community development. About 75 percent of the 34,000 housing units in the area are apartments, many of them deteriorating, and the area was in general economic decline. The bank's management, shown here, decided to act aggressively to turn things around by financing the rehabilitation of 6,000 rental units. They also helped finance a local shopping center. As a result, the bank and the community have both profited, and the local economy has improved. Should all organizations have such community-minded objectives?

society, such as improving the community, safeguarding the environment, and protecting consumer rights.

The *societal marketing concept* emerged from the marketing concept. It is the idea that marketing owes more to society than simply giving customers what they want. It means that social obligations are seen not as an imposition, but as an integral part of marketing.[28] Marketers that adopt this view give more and more attention to stakeholders such as the community.

Marrying social responsibility and marketing can have a definite influence on stakeholders. For example, Ben & Jerry's Homemade, which makes premium ice cream and frozen yogurt, is a successful and socially conscious business that benefits many stakeholders. The company supports its Vermont community by buying dairy ingredients only from local farmers. The brownies for its Chocolate Fudge Brownie ice cream are baked by homeless people in a New York bakery. The nuts in its Rainforest Crunch ice cream come from the Amazon rain forest. The labels of its Peace Pops ice cream bars explain company support for a nonprofit group that promotes humanitarian efforts. In addition, Ben & Jerry's donates 7.5 percent of its profits to worthy causes. However, the company has had profit problems, and some groups complain that it now puts profits ahead of social causes.[29]

Another complex area involving the rights of stakeholders is *marketing ethics:* the values and moral standards that govern marketing actions and decisions. As a marketer, you'll sometimes face decisions about actions open to you that are legal but may not measure up to society's values and standards. Social responsibility and ethics are part of the overall marketing environment, and marketers can incorporate both into successful marketing strategies. You'll explore these concepts in more detail in Chapter 3.

Before you go on . . .

A. What happens when producers stress production in the marketing exchange? When they stress sales?

B. What is the marketing concept? The societal marketing concept?

C. What are the ABCs of marketing? How do they incorporate the three parts of the marketing concept?

The New Role of Marketing Management

marketing management

the system-wide process of planning and implementing marketing programs, measuring results, and making adjustments to ensure the establishment and maintenance of mutually beneficial exchange relationships with customers and other stakeholders

The new marketing vision of enduring, mutually beneficial relationships between marketers and customers has brought about changes in the way organizations manage their marketing activities. **Marketing management** is the system-wide process of planning and implementing marketing programs, measuring results, and making adjustments to ensure the establishment and maintenance of mutually beneficial exchange relationships with customers and other stakeholders. As you can see from this definition, marketing management is responsible for focusing the attention of everyone inside and outside the organization on profitably satisfying customers and stakeholders.

To do this, the marketer works with all its suppliers and dealers to make sure that the entire system is both efficient (accomplishes its goals while spending the least amount of money) and effective (accomplishes what it sets out to do better than others). It also works with every internal department to maintain a marketing focus. Finally, marketing management, like all other management functions, involves planning, coordinating, and evaluating internal processes to achieve the organization's objectives.

One of the newest and most dramatic marketing tools available today are online services such as America Online and the World Wide Web. What you see here is the America Online site for Tower Records. As the uses of this technology are refined, it is expected that the Internet will be used to market all kinds of goods and services. What are some of the challenges faced by marketers trying to sell over the Internet?

The Marketing Mix Expanded

In the past, marketing management was centered on the marketing mix. The **marketing mix** is the combination of product, price, distribution, and marketing communication that most effectively satisfies customer needs. The marketing mix is also known as the **four Ps** because the elements can be remembered by their initials: product, price, place, and promotion. These four elements are under the control of the marketing manager, who varies them to create the right combination (mix) of elements for the needs of the market.[30]

The simple formula of the marketing mix was developed when mass marketers were selling standardized products and changes in the marketplace were relatively slow. Today, rapid change is the norm. The world of marketing is being transformed by new technology, new customer needs, new markets, new competitors, new media, and other changes. Applications of advanced technology such as the Internet have given customers more information and more choices. Competitors not only can copy most products but also can customize them for specific customers.[31]

These changes are moving marketers in the direction of a more comprehensive method of marketing management that builds on the four Ps model. Marketers need to monitor the environment more carefully, research the market continuously, choose customers and suppliers more carefully, and establish longer term relationships. In the next section, you'll see how to extend marketing management beyond the traditional four Ps.

The Eight Universal Marketing Processes

Marketers at organizations like Biltmore Estate and Mr. CB's have added four more processes to the original four Ps to construct a new approach to marketing management, one that is universal because it applies to any marketer of any product. The eight universal marketing processes are (1) environmental scanning and analysis, (2) marketing research and analysis, (3) segmentation, targeting, and positioning, (4) product development and differentiation, (5) valuation and pricing, (6) channel and value-chain management, (7) integrated marketing communication, and (8) relationship building.

marketing mix

the combination of product, price, distribution, and marketing communication that most effectively satisfies customer needs

four Ps

the elements product, price, place, and promotion

F I G U R E   **1.3**   **The Universal Marketing Processes**

The eight universal processes of marketing, which incorporate the four Ps of marketing, are coordinated by marketing strat-egy and management. These eight processes apply to both consumer and organizational marketing.

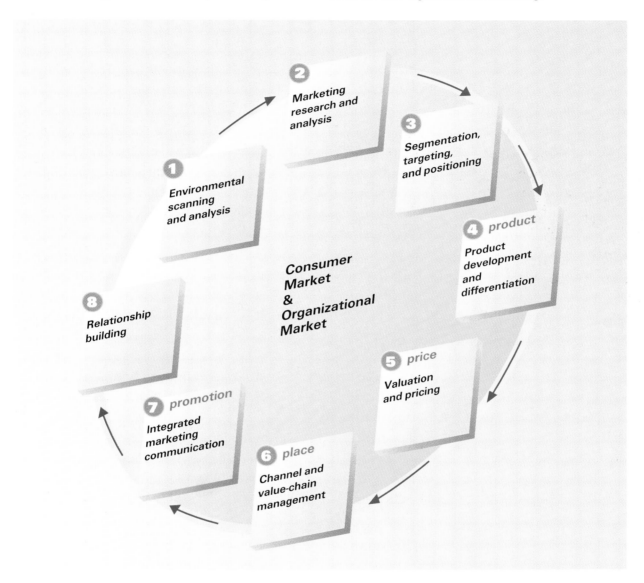

These eight processes are the foundation for the rest of this text; they are shown in Figure 1.3. How you put these eight processes together to guide your marketing efforts is *marketing strategy*, the subject of Chapter 2. Note that the four Ps of marketing are incorporated in the eight processes: *product* in the product development process, *place* in the channel and value-chain management process, *price* in the valuation and pricing process, and *promotion* in the integrated marketing communication process. In the following sections you will get a brief overview of each of the eight processes. Details about each process are found in the later chapters.

Environmental Scanning and Analysis

No matter what you're marketing, success depends on a wide variety of internal and external factors that, combined, make up the *marketing environment*. To better understand these factors and prepare for an appropriate response, you need to continually gather information about the environment and carefully examine it, including the identification of all important stakeholders. *Environmental scanning* is the process of identifying internal and external factors that can affect marketing success. *Environmental analysis* is the evaluation, interpretation, and distribution of information about environmental factors to all organizational employees.

In the processes of environmental scanning and analysis, you look at the effects on marketing of social, political, technological, economic, and competitive factors, which are all outside the organization. An environmental analysis should also examine the influence of employees and factors inside the organization as well as at the effects of the global environment. Chapters 2, 3, and 4 discuss the marketing environment in detail.

Marketing Research and Analysis

Marketers use *marketing research and analysis* to identify potential markets, understand the forces that shape those markets, and uncover ways of marketing effectively to the most profitable or most attractive markets. Marketers also do research to uncover customer needs and wants, attitudes, and behavior. No marketing analysis would be complete without an evaluation of past marketing programs.

By studying the actions that you (and other marketers) have taken, you can gain an understanding of what has been successful in the past and, just as important, what has been unsuccessful. You can use this information to craft new marketing programs, adjust existing programs, or eliminate unproductive ones. Chapters 5, 6, and 7 explain how to conduct marketing research and analysis.

It's important to remember that markets don't stay the same forever; rapid change can and does occur in every product area. MCI executives are keenly aware of how quickly and profoundly telecommunication markets can change. "A month here is like a decade in a lot of other industries," observes Angela Dunlap, MCI's president of marketing.[32] As Dunlap knows, unless companies use market analysis to stay on top of what's happening in their markets, any successful marketing program can come undone in the face of rapid change.

Segmentation, Targeting, and Positioning

Market segmentation is grouping people or organizations within a market according to similar needs, characteristics, or behaviors. Your objective is to identify groups of customers (and potential customers) so you can establish marketing relationships with appropriate groups both efficiently and effectively. You start by determining which characteristics to use in selecting certain groups and in eliminating any groups you cannot effectively serve. Next, you evaluate the groups, called segments, and decide which are most desirable. Finally, you select the segments you want to market to (*targeting*) and set out to create an image of your product in these markets (*positioning*).

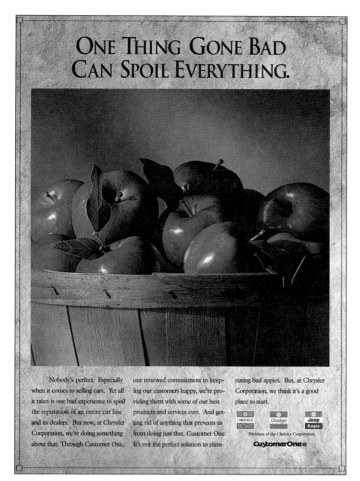

ONE THING GONE BAD CAN SPOIL EVERYTHING.

Nobody's perfect. Especially when it comes to selling cars. Yet all it takes is one bad experience to spoil the reputation of an entire car line and its dealers. But now, at Chrysler Corporation, we're doing something about that. Through Customer One, our renewed commitment to keeping our customers happy, we're providing them with some of our best products and services ever. And getting rid of anything that prevents us from doing just that. Customer One. It's not the perfect solution to eliminating bad apples. But, at Chrysler Corporation, we think it's a good place to start.

Divisions of the Chrysler Corporation.

CustomerOne

Product quality entails much more than simply designing a good product. It also means providing after-sale service that will please and keep customers. Just as Ford's slogan "Quality Is Job One" is intended to promote an image of reliability, Chrysler's Customer One program suggests continuous improvement and the idea that its automobiles and service are the best. A poor product or bad experience for customers can damage a firm's reputation, so excellence in quality and service are a never-ending quest. What could automobile dealers do to please customers who may have received less-than-delightful service from them in the past?

In some cases, you build a market for your product one person or organization at a time.

For example, Minnesota-based Marvin Windows has used market segmentation to narrow the overall market for windows into smaller, more manageable segments. Among the many segments the company identified are home and office builders, architects, building owners, remodelers, and building supply dealers. Marvin Windows' marketing experts segmented the market using a variety of factors, and then targeted marketing programs to appeal to the segments with the most profit potential. This segmentation process helped the company increase sales so dramatically that it jumped from eighth to third place among U.S. window suppliers.[33] More details on segmentation, targeting, and positioning are presented in Chapter 8.

Product Development and Differentiation

Product development is the creation or improvement of a product to meet the needs and wants of customers. In product development, the objective is to find out what customers need and want, then create a new product— or improve an existing one—to satisfy those needs and wants. Because a product is a bundle of values that satisfy customers, everything about the product has to be specifically geared toward customer satisfaction and, increasingly, customer delight.

Product differentiation means setting your value package apart from the competition in a way that is meaningful to the customers. When customers perceive that your product is not only different from but better than those of your rivals, you can gain a competitive edge. Quality has become one of the key differentiating elements that brings customers back again and again. However, quality isn't restricted to production or service operations. If internal and external customers alike are to be satisfied, a commitment to quality must pervade the organization. At the same time, marketers should be careful to define quality from the customer's perspective.

Compaq Computer got into trouble in the early 1990s because it had a product orientation instead of a customer orientation. It kept improving its high-quality computers until customers could not afford to pay for the improvements. As James Garrity, the director of marketing communications for North America, notes, Compaq's prices were much higher than those of competitors. The other companies were "delivering what customers were looking for—adequate quality at a respectable price," says Garrity. "Not the ultimate in quality at a high price." When Compaq introduced new products featuring good quality at much lower prices, sales and profits soared.[34] Product development and services marketing are discussed in Chapters 9, 10, and 11.

Product differentiation is just as important for small marketers as it is for large marketers such as Compaq, as you can see from the experience of General Stair.

SMALL BUSINESS WATCH

General Stair steps up differentiation

Competition was heating up when Saby Behar went looking for a way to differentiate his company's prefabricated staircases. His small business, General Stair, held a solid market share in southern Florida. But he knew that home builders, his customers, thought all staircases were "pretty much the same; they go up, and they go down." Behar wanted to set his products apart from those of competitors and, in the process, focus the entire organization on activities that lead to customer satisfaction.

Behar's research showed that customers particularly valued on-time delivery and installation. So he set out to guarantee that his staircases would be installed exactly when needed—or the customer would get a $50 credit for each day that General Stair was late. To keep this promise without incurring unacceptably high outlays of credit, General Stair had to boost its on-time delivery above the current 95 percent level.

Employee teams set to work studying internal processes and installation systems. They figured out how to firm up delivery dates, track jobs more accurately, and improve internal and external communications. They also suggested a bonus system to reward employees for on-time performance. Within nine months, productivity was up, costs were down, and profits were holding at a healthy level. Just as important, only five vouchers had been issued. Now Behar wants to put more emphasis on the guarantee. "It shows people that we are serious about this," he says.[35]

How might he make prospective customers aware of the guarantee?

Valuation and Pricing

Valuation is the process that buyers and sellers use to determine whether a marketing exchange will be beneficial. Remember, the goal is a mutually beneficial exchange relationship, so both parties must see value in the exchange. *Price*, the amount of money a seller asks in exchange for a product, is only one dimension of valuation. You, as a marketer, have a variety of ways of valuing your products to make them attractive to customers.

For example, many cosmetics companies offer a small gift with every purchase over a certain dollar amount, such as $35. This gift makes the merchandise seem more valuable to customers. You might also give extra service for the same price, or include more features with no or minimal increase in price. Chevrolet, for example, recently added air bags and many extras to its new models, folded in the cost of shipping (which many competitors tack on later), and kept price increases below 3 percent.[36] Pricing is discussed in greater detail in Chapters 12 and 13.

Channel and Value-Chain Management

As a marketer, you can succeed only when your customers are able to obtain your products in a convenient way. So, to complete the marketing exchange, you need a way of bringing your product to your customer. This is the function of the *marketing channel*, the organizations involved in moving goods from producers to consumers. But the marketing channel is only part of the process needed to complete an exchange. You also have to manage the entire *value chain*, the linkage of activities that must be performed by suppliers and channel partners—as well as by producers—to create and deliver a value package that satisfies customers.

Whether you're interested in consumer or organizational markets, you'll need to think carefully about how your customers want to complete their transactions. Where do they want the exchange to take place? How will they pay? How and when will they take possession of what they buy, or use the service they have contracted for? These are some of the issues you'll face in channel management.

Sometimes your customers will want to be in direct contact with you. Dell Computer, for example, broke new ground in the personal computer business when it started selling by telephone and delivering to the customer's door. Instead of ordering through a salesperson or visiting a store, customers simply call Dell, discuss the features they want, and give their credit card numbers. A few days later, the computers arrive. If problems develop, customers can talk to Dell experts on a toll-free hotline. What could be more convenient?

At other times customers will want the convenience of buying through channel partners, businesses such as wholesalers and retailers that are set up to handle specific marketing activities such as transportation, storage, and sales. If you want to make it easy for customers all over the United States to buy cat food, laundry detergent, or tennis balls, for instance, you might get your products onto the shelves of Wal-Mart, Kmart, and other stores. You will learn more about channel and value-chain management in Chapters 14, 15, and 16. For now, read how Jeff Klindt used channel management to market skateboards in Europe.

GLOBAL ISSUES

Skating into foreign markets

Jeff Klindt was surprised when he started getting calls from eastern Europe. The young owner of Deluxe Productions in San Francisco had been concentrating on the U.S. market for jazzy-looking skateboards. Then some U.S. skateboarding magazines made their way across the Atlantic, and Deluxe's ads wound up in the hands of street skaters in Prague and Budapest. As the calls kept coming, Klindt woke up to the potential profits he could make by getting his products to foreign markets.

To gauge interest—and drum up business—the entrepreneur traveled to Europe with a group of skilled San Francisco skateboarders. The enthusiasts who attended Deluxe's skateboarding demonstrations liked what they saw, and they began placing orders. Now Klindt had to get his skateboards overseas.

Jeff Klindt didn't know the legal ins and outs of sending goods to Europe, but he couldn't afford to set up an office abroad. Nor was he able to pay European dealers to handle his products. Since, however,

Jeff Klindt's company sells skateboards in many different countries. Exports now make up more than 25 percent of Deluxe's revenues, which exceed $6 million. Initially, Klindt didn't have the funds necessary to aggressively promote his products in international markets, so he organized demonstration tours featuring some of the best California skateboarders. What other products could Klindt now add to his line of products to appeal to his skateboarding customers?

he didn't want to turn down orders, he decided to ship skateboards directly from California, using transportation firms experienced in sending goods to Europe.

These days, Deluxe is selling more skateboards in foreign markets than ever. More than one-quarter of its $6 million in annual sales is made abroad, and the orders continue to come in. [37]

Do you think Klindt would sell more skateboards if he arranged for European stores to carry his products?

Integrated Marketing Communication

Integrated marketing communication (IMC) establishes and strengthens profitable relationships with customers and other stakeholders by controlling or influencing all marketing messages and maintaining a continuing dialogue.[38] Unlike integrated marketing, which seeks to coordinate all the internal and external activities that lead to a marketing exchange, IMC is concerned only with communication activities. These activities include advertising, sales promotion, direct marketing, public relations, and personal selling.

As you can see in the definition, IMC calls for cutting across functional lines to involve the entire organization. The definition also recognizes that the purpose of IMC is to maintain an ongoing dialogue with stakeholders. In the past, marketers tended to think of marketing communication as flowing only one way, from the marketer to the stakeholder. Most of this one-way communication was *promotion*, marketing communication designed to inform and influence customers and potential customers. One form of promotion, advertising, was traditionally intended to persuade people that the advertised products would fulfill their needs and wants. However, advertising generally did not provide a way for customers to respond with questions, comments, or orders.

What marketers need is a running dialogue that allows customers to influence organizational decisions about products and other aspects of marketing.[39] Such an interactive, two-way communication process strengthens marketing relationships by providing a mechanism for listening to stakeholders and responding appropriately. Of course, when you use a variety of IMC techniques and messages, it's important to control the look and content of the messages so stakeholders won't be confused by conflicting messages. Chapters 17, 18, 19, and 20 explain how to use integrated marketing communication. Then, in a capstone case, you'll see how one marketer used IMC as part of a highly successful marketing strategy.

Relationship Building

Relationship building is the process of attracting and keeping customers over time by maintaining contact and providing service before, during, and after the sale. It is part of relationship marketing. As you saw earlier, savvy marketers prefer relationship marketing to transactional marketing. These marketers understand the *lifetime value* of a customer, the total amount a customer is likely to spend with one marketer throughout the marketing relationship. General Motors, for example, estimates that over time, a loyal customer spends as much as $400,000 on GM cars, service, and auto loan financing.[40]

Of course, the lifetime value of a customer varies from marketer to marketer and from industry to industry, but the principle of relationship building is the same: get a customer and keep that customer through communication and service. In this way, you can profitably support the relationship for the long term. How can you find out what the customer wants from your relationship? Many times, all you have to do is ask.

For example, Shoebox Greetings, a Hallmark division, placed a short questionnaire in Hallmark Card shops. A customer who filled in his or her name, address, phone number, and birth date, and answered three questions, received a free card with the purchase of two others. The questions concerned the number of greeting cards purchased in recent months, the number of cards purchased at a card store, and the occasions for sending cards. Armed with these answers, Shoebox could estimate how much individuals tend to spend on cards, how much they spent in card stores (an important marketing channel), and when people are likely to buy.[41] This enabled the company to identify its customers and plan IMC messages geared to their needs and habits.

Like Shoebox, more and more marketers are gathering information about customers and potential customers, storing the details in computer files, and then analyzing the files to find out how to best support ongoing relationships. This is known as *database marketing*. You'll see numerous examples of relationship building and database marketing throughout this text.

Before you go on . . .

A. What is marketing management?

B. What are the four Ps, and how are they incorporated into the eight universal marketing processes?

C. What is relationship building, and why is it important?

Summary

1. **Explain how and why the definition of marketing has changed over the years.**

   Before 1960, marketing was defined as a system for bringing goods and services from producers to customers and users. By 1985, this definition had assumed a managerial orientation but did not reflect recognition of the value of building long-term relationships with customers and stakeholders. Today, marketing is defined as the process of establishing and maintaining mutually beneficial exchange relationships with customers and other stakeholders.

2. **Differentiate between relationship marketing and transactional marketing.**

   In transactional marketing, marketers focus on individual, isolated exchanges that satisfy a customer's needs at a particular time and place. In contrast, relationship marketing is the process of establishing and maintaining mutually beneficial *long-term* relationships between organizations and their customers and other stakeholders.

3. **Relate utility to customer needs and wants, and describe the six types of utility that marketing can provide.**

   Utility is the value a product provides for the customer by satisfying needs and wants. Marketers may satisfy customer needs and wants through six types of utility: form, time, place, possession, information, and service.

4. **Discuss how the practice of marketing has evolved from a production orientation to a sales orientation to a way of doing business based on the marketing concept.**

   Starting in the eighteenth century, producers who could turn out items in large quantities at low prices stressed production as the foundation of marketing because demand outstripped supply. By the 1920s, supply had outstripped demand, so producers eager to move their products put increasing emphasis on selling as the foundation of marketing. In the mid-1950s, producers were faced with growing competition. To avoid making and selling what customers didn't want or need, they used the marketing concept to make what customers wanted and needed.

5. **List and explain the ABCs of marketing.**

   Always be customer-driven, **B**enchmark against the best in the world, **C**ontinuously improve your product and performance, **D**evelop the best value package, **E**mpower your employees, **F**ocus on relationships, and **G**enerate profits. The ABCs of marketing are an extension and a replacement of the marketing concept. By putting the customer first and developing the best value package, marketers can optimize profits through long-term customer and stakeholder relationships.

6. **Define the marketing mix and explain the need for its expansion.**

   The marketing mix is the combination of product, price, place, and promotion that most effectively satisfies customer needs. The marketing mix was appropriate when mass marketers were selling standardized products, and changes in the marketplace were relatively slow. However, today's rapidly changing business environment calls for a more comprehensive method of marketing management. Marketers need to monitor the environment more carefully, research the market continuously, choose customers and suppliers more carefully, and establish relationships over the longer term.

7. **Identify the eight universal marketing processes.**

   The eight universal marketing processes are (1) environmental scanning and analysis, (2) marketing research and analysis, (3) segmentation, targeting, and positioning, (4) product development and differentiation, (5) channel and value-chain management, (6) valuation and pricing, (7) integrated marketing communication, and (8) relationship building. The eight universal functions expand on and replace the marketing mix (the four Ps). (Review Figure 1.3, which provides a visual outline for the entire text.)

KEY TERMS

benchmarking **15**

customer **7**

empowerment **17**

four Ps **20**

integrated marketing **13**

internal marketing **9**

marketing **4**

marketing concept **15**

marketing management **19**

marketing mix **20**

product **5**

relationship marketing **6**

stakeholders **8**

transactional marketing **6**

utility **10**

value package **11**

Skill-Building Applications

1. You have been hired as the manager of a local 7-Eleven convenience store. What would you do to develop a closer relationship with regular customers? With new customers?

2. You're a merchandise buyer for local Sears stores in Mexico. How can you find out what types of toy your customers will buy?

3. Who are the stakeholders of your school? Is the school doing a good job of marketing to all of them? Identify one stakeholder group's needs and wants. What is the school doing to address these needs?

4. How does a local H&R Block tax preparation service provide form, time, place, possession, information, and service utility?

5. As a manufacturer of telephone equipment, what partners would you seek out to help market to businesses across your state?

6. You're starting your own advertising agency. What value package would you offer?

Getting Involved in Marketing

1. *On Your Own* Think of two long-time marketing relationships you have had, such as habitually buying the same toothpaste or always seeing the same hair stylist. What keeps you coming back? Contrast these relationships with an exchange you view as transactional marketing because it was an isolated incident. How could the marketer have induced you to become a long-time customer?

2. *On Your Own* As a customer, what utility do you get from your college? How do you benefit from this utility? What value package do you think your college offers to prospective students? Are you a delighted customer of your college? Why or why not?

3. *Find Out More* Go to the library or browse the Internet and find a recent magazine or newspaper article about a successful product. How do you think this product satisfies customer needs and wants? What type of market is this product geared toward? How do you know?

4. *In a Partnership* With a classmate, look up a recent news report of representatives of a city or state who convinced a manufacturer to locate its plant in their area. Is this marketing? What is the product? Who is the customer, who is the marketer, and what is being exchanged? Present your findings to the class in a two-minute talk.

5. *In a Team* With other students, interview the owner of a small business—a dentist, perhaps, or a baker or a building contractor. Does the person consider himself or herself to be a marketer? Why or why not? Which of the eight universal marketing processes does this person handle for the business? Write a brief (one or two page) report answering these questions.

6. *In a Team* Team up with at least two classmates and visit a local mall. Observe how salespeople in two clothing stores work with customers who are making purchases. Do the customers seem satisfied? List at least three ways each store might use marketing to delight its customers. Compare your group's list with those created by other groups. What similarities and differences do you see?

VideoCase   Zane's Cycles Is Customer Driven

Independent bicycle shops are under siege, being driven out of business by Wal-Mart or other retail giants. But not Zane's Cycles of Branford, Connecticut. Drawing customers from New Haven and beyond, this independent is thriving in a competitive environment so fierce that three local bike shops went out of business in a single year. How does owner Chris Zane do it?

Zane has maintained his success by following the first of the ABCs of marketing: Always Be Customer Driven. He will do almost anything to attract and keep customers: provide free lifetime repairs, give away a free cellular phone with each bike purchased, even serve cappuccino while he fixes a customer's bike.

Zane knows that customers who are delighted with his service will tell other customers, and word of mouth will help him grow his business. That's why he doesn't charge customers for parts that cost less than $1, why he guarantees free service

forever, and why he built an in-store play area for children. In addition, he publishes a glossy catalog featuring biking tips and product specifications. This serves to educate customers and give them the details they need to make informed buying decisions. All of this is part of Zane's philosophy of relationship marketing.

Competitive pricing is also important. Zane has a 90-day price guarantee to reassure customers that they are paying the lowest price in the state. Because Zane keeps a sharp eye on pricing, he has had to rebate less than $1,000 in two years.

Zane wants to make the buying experience as enjoyable as possible for his customers. As a result, he looks specifically for employees who are genuinely interested in helping people. "I can teach anyone about a bike," he comments, "but I can't teach them to be helpful or courteous."

To generate even more positive word of mouth, Zane practices relationship marketing with the community as well. His Zane Foundation funds college scholarships for local high school seniors. He also talks to school children about bike safety and began selling children's helmets at cost when Connecticut passed a law mandating their use. Such community service wins him positive publicity and customer loyalty.

Zane works hard to offer the best value package in the area, benchmark against the best practices, and continuously improve his operation. This hard work is paying off, bringing in more customers and generating higher profits. Zane's Cycles has become the best-known bicycle shop in the area, and its reputation is spreading throughout New England.

Early in his career, Zane was told, "If you give good service, you'll stay in business. If you don't, you won't." That advice is serving him well as the giant chains come to town. "You have to work to be as strong as they are and kill them where they're weak," he notes. "And customer service is where they're weakest." Clearly, customer-driven relationship marketing is going to keep Zane's Cycles in high gear.[42]

Strategies and applications

1. How does Zane's Cycles provide service utility? Information utility? Why would customers value these utilities?

2. What world-class marketing concepts could Zane benchmark against to improve his ability to satisfy customers?

3. What kind of market research and analysis should Zane do to assure that he maintains his strong relationship with customers and the community?

4. How can Zane compute the lifetime value of a customer of his bike shop?

5. What inexpensive techniques could Zane apply as part of an integrated marketing communication program to reach college-age bicycle buyers?

6. How could a small ski shop apply the concepts from this case to compete with Sports Authority and other giant sporting-goods chains?

Team project

With other students, consider what Zane's Cycles might do to strengthen relations with customers and attract new ones once a Wal-Mart opens nearby. In addition to the techniques discussed in this case, what else might customers expect from a bicycle retailer? How do you think Zane's Cycles should meet those expectations? Outline your team's ideas in a letter to Chris Zane.

2

Strategic Planning for Relationship Marketing

Learning Goals

After you have read and studied this chapter, you should be able to:

1. Define strategy and explain how it is used to build and strengthen customer relationships.
2. Show how marketing strategy links the eight universal marketing processes.
3. Analyze the organization's strategic alternatives using the growth–share matrix, the business strength–market attractiveness matrix, and the industry–competition model.
4. Identify the components of internal marketing strategy and explain their importance to relationship building.
5. Discuss the components of external marketing strategy and explain how value chains are created.
6. Explain the principles marketers can use to build relationships with customers and other stakeholders.
7. Describe the components of the marketing plan, and outline the marketing control process.

PROFILE

Samsung Electronics maps strategy for high-tech success

What do you do when you're a global success with one of the world's hottest products? If you're South Korea's Samsung Electronics, a leading computer chip manufacturer, you map a strategy for your next success. That's what chief executive officer Kim Kwang-Ho did. Eyeing the emerging market for reasonably priced high-tech products, Kim decided to move boldly beyond chips. He focused the energies of employees, suppliers, and partners by setting a deadline of the year 2000 for making Samsung one of the world's top five electronics marketers.

Tackling the task, company analysts examined a number of possible business directions, starting with research into customers' needs, competitive pressures, and other environmental factors. This information helped Kim decide that Samsung should concentrate on meeting growing customer needs for multimedia computer gear, digital television, telecommunications equipment, and other electronics. This top-level decision set the direction for plans at lower levels of the organization. In the marketing area, individual strategies guided activities in product development, pricing, channel management, and integrated marketing communication, carefully coordinated to support Kim's long-term goal of industry leadership.

Because the company lacked the know-how to design and produce all the products envisioned, Kim forged alliances with several companies, including General Instrument (for digital television) and Fujitsu (for computer displays). He also made quality improvement an organization-wide priority. Earmarking billions of dollars for research and operation upgrades, Kim then applied strategy internally to "change our internal process, cut delivery time, reduce overhead costs, and innovate all processes." Samsung's strategies are keeping the company on target for global marketing success in the twenty-first century.[1]

In this chapter, you'll learn how to develop a strategy for establishing and maintaining relationships that lead to long-term marketing success. First you'll learn about putting the customer at the center of your strategic focus. Then you'll see how to unite the eight marketing processes into a coherent marketing strategy. After you have examined the components of internal and external marketing strategies and looked at the use of marketing plans, you'll learn the use of marketing controls.

To satisfy the customer, it means that everybody in the company has to understand that the total existence of a company depends upon the customer, so if the customer is not satisfied, he is not going to be a customer tomorrow, and if he is not a customer tomorrow, we don't have a business tomorrow.

Harvey Lamm
of Subaru of America[2]

Ruth Owades, the founder of Calyx & Corolla, has used marketing strategy to build her business into a world-class organization. She set out to establish strong, long-term relationships with flower growers, a distribution firm, and her customers. Those relationships are maintained through an effective communication system. The results are profits for her firm and happy customers who have fresh flowers that last longer. Could you find equal success bringing consumers fresh meats or vegetables? What kind of relationships would you have to establish?

Strategy Development and a Customer Focus

Kim Kwang-Ho knows that decision making is part of every marketer's life. He had to decide which markets to enter, which customers to serve, which products to make, and how to make those products. Whether you work for a business, a nonprofit organization, or a government agency, you'll be making marketing decisions almost every day. But how do you know which actions you should take—and which you should *not* take?

The marketing choices you make depend on your organization's overall strategy. A **strategy** is a broad plan used to guide the decisions and actions of everyone in the organization. In essence, strategy is a summary of where you are, where you want to go, and how you'll get there. Marketers use strategy to help everyone from the chief executive officer to the receptionist understand where the organization wants to go and how it will get there. Given today's pressured, competitive marketing environment, a customer-oriented strategy is essential for shaping organizational decisions and actions.[3]

There are three levels of strategy. *Corporate-level strategy* establishes the overall direction for the entire organization (e.g., the kinds of businesses or markets it will enter). *Business-level strategy* sets the direction for how a particular business or division within the organization will be run. *Functional-level strategies*, the narrowest in scope, guide activities in marketing, finance, and other functions.

Small and large organizations around the world use marketing strategy to profitably satisfy customers. Just as Samsung is applying marketing strategy to electronics, Calyx & Corolla is applying it to fresh flowers. Founder Ruth Owades started her small business with a simple idea: Flowers shipped directly from grower to customer will arrive fresher and last longer, giving customers more value for their money. She also wanted to make buying more convenient by inviting customers to select from bouquets in a colorful catalog and then order by phone. In addition, she could differentiate her product with a money-back guarantee of customer satisfaction. But to succeed, she needed a strategy for forging solid relationships with her suppliers and her shipper as well as with the upscale customers she was targeting.

The strategy Owades developed laid out a plan for ensuring quality, reliability, and responsive service by working one-on-one with small growers to meet customer needs. She asked several small growers for advice, and she got help with protective packaging for flower orders. Once she had commitments from growers who would supply flowers, she signed with Federal Express for guaranteed overnight delivery. Then Owades installed a computer system to link her company with the growers and with FedEx, allowing instantaneous communication among all parties.

Now when customers call in orders, the details are immediately transmitted to growers along with a prepared FedEx label. The growers wrap the flowers, and

FedEx picks up for next-day delivery. The price: $30 and up for a just-picked bouquet that lasts and lasts. Customers are delighted with the value package and the personal attention, and they buy again and again. This strategy for building customer, supplier, and shipper relationships has helped Calyx & Corolla blossom into a $15 million business.[4]

Customer-Oriented Strategy for Integrated Marketing

Both Kim Kwang-Ho of Samsung and Ruth Owades of Calyx & Corolla focused their strategies on the customer. Without a customer orientation, marketers risk marketing myopia. **Marketing myopia** is Theodore Levitt's phrase for the tendency to view the organization as a means of producing goods or services rather than as a means for creating and satisfying customers.[5] Thus a company may define its markets too narrowly and miss out on profit opportunities. For example, railroads failed to define their product (transportation) from the customer's perspective and were left behind in the wake of the airline revolution. So, no matter what you're marketing, you need a thorough understanding of customer needs, wants, and expectations. Over time, this approach will attract new customers and enhance relationships with existing customers.[6]

To build these ongoing relationships effectively, your strategy must support integrated marketing ◄———┘ **(p. 13)**. By creating a strategy that crosses departmental and organizational boundaries, you can unify and coordinate internal activities with those of partners outside the organization. Samsung's integrated marketing strategy guides employees in marketing, research, finance, and other internal departments, and also provides direction for suppliers, channel partners, and retailers. In this way, Samsung has created a solid foundation for strengthening internal and external relationships.

Marketing Strategy Builds Profits

In planning a strategy for relationship marketing ◄———┘ **(p. 6)**, you have to look beyond single transactions. An effective relationship marketing strategy should be designed to help you (1) attract new customers and (2) get more business from current customers, thus maximizing their lifetime value. In many product categories, the investment needed to *retain* a customer is as little as 25 percent of the investment needed to win over a new one. As a result, getting more business from the customers you have leads to higher profits.[7]

For example, MBNA Corporation, a Maryland-based credit card marketer, spends about $100, on average, to attract each new customer. The longer the duration of the relationship, the higher MBNA's yearly profits per customer. A 5-year customer represents about $100 in yearly profits, while a 10-year customer represents about $300 in yearly profits. For MBNA, as for every marketer, strategies for maintaining good customer relationships pay off in bottom-line profits.[8]

However, rapid changes in customers, technologies, and other areas of the marketing environment can quickly date even the most successful marketing strategy. Therefore, to help the organization prosper over the long run, strategy must be *dynamic*, looking beyond today to the customers and markets of the future.[9]

strategy

a broad plan used to guide the decisions and actions of everyone in the organization

marketing myopia

the tendency to view the organization as a means of producing goods or services rather than as a means for creating and satisfying customers

Japan's NEC, for example, used this dynamic approach to transform itself from a regional telecommunications marketer to a global marketer of computers and communications devices. Twenty years ago, the company foresaw how businesses and individuals would benefit from digital technologies for the processing and transmission of information. With this foresight, the company crafted a strategy to profitably apply the new technologies to meet emerging customer needs. This strategy helped NEC quadruple sales in the years that followed.[10]

Marketers also use strategy to meet the needs of noncustomer stakeholders. Here's how two marketers do it.

ETHICS & SOCIAL RESPONSIBILITY

Strategies for balancing stakeholder interests

If strategy begins with the customer, what about the rights and interests of other stakeholders, such as employees and community residents? Marketers like Manor Care and State Farm Insurance Companies realize that their business interests are interwoven with the interests of their stakeholders. Although customers are important—as are profits—these marketers are experienced in using socially responsible strategies to satisfy other stakeholders as well.

"We want to strike a balance between all the key stakeholders in the organization," explains Stuart Bainum Jr., chairman of Manor Care, a Maryland-based operator of hotels, hospitals, nursing homes, and pharmacies. Bainum's strategies are designed to satisfy employees, customers, and other stakeholders. In particular, he emphasizes how his 23,000 employees can achieve personal growth and gain self-esteem from accomplishing meaningful work tasks.

State Farm Fire & Casualty has a vested interest in satisfying community stakeholders. The company's slogan, "Like a good neighbor, State Farm is there," sums up its strategy. "State Farm is particularly interested [in social investment] because we insure people, houses, and vehicles in these communities," says chairman Roger Joslin. "The neighborhoods impact all of us in terms of our social fabric, so it's important for all of us to be supportive." That's why employees get time off to volunteer with the Special Olympics, teach about fire safety, and work with local schools.[11]

What else can marketers do to incorporate employee and community stakeholders into their strategies?

Strategy Unites All Eight Marketing Processes

Marketing strategy provides the structure and purpose that unites all eight marketing processes (pp. 20–21). As you can see in Figure 2.1, each process has a place in the organization's overall marketing strategy. Marketing strategy built on the eight marketing processes has to begin with a focus on customer needs and wants. Remember, "Always be customer-driven" is the first of the ABCs of marketing (pp. 16–17).

F I G U R E **2.1** The Framework of Marketing Strategy

Marketing strategy starts with the customer. Internal and external marketing are linked by the goal of creating long-term exchange relationships. Marketing control provides feedback indicating whether customers are satisfied—or delighted—with the marketer's goods and services.

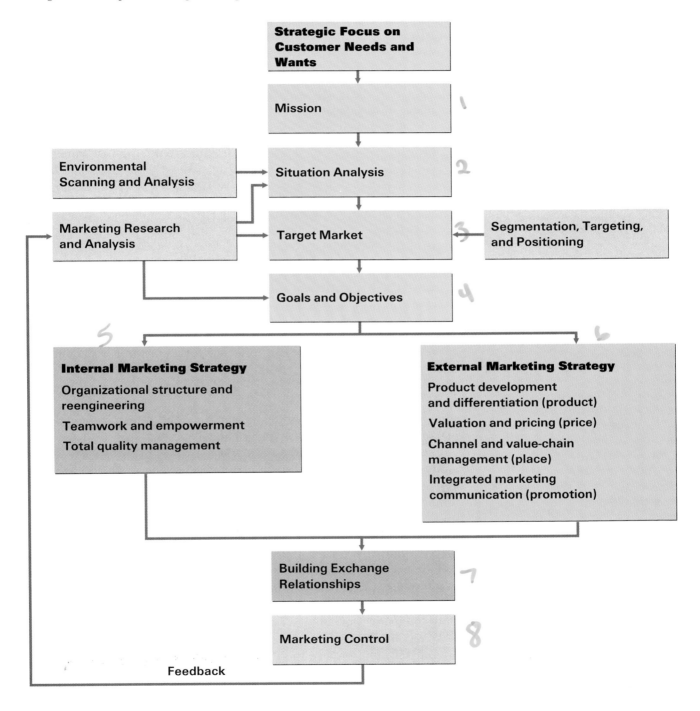

1. Group Mission Statement

The Unipart Group of Companies aims to be an enduring upper-quartile-performing company, in which stakeholders are keen to participate, performing principally in the automotive-related market by:

Pursuing our values

Ensuring the continuing relevance and synergy of the divisions' missions

Creating an environment within which the divisions can and do pursue their mission

2. Group Philosophy

To understand the real and perceived needs of our customers better than anyone else, and to serve them better than anyone else.

3. Group Corporate Goal

To make the Unipart logo the mark of Outstanding Personal Customer Service.

4. Lifetime Customer Relationships

We will strive to build lifetime relationships with our customers, and we realize that to do so, we will need to harness the intellectual energies and creativity of all our stakeholders, based on long-term, shared-destiny relationships.

5. The Supplier Partnership

We see our suppliers as stakeholders, and are increasingly working in partnership with them, continuously striving to make our total enterprise activities, from raw material to the end-user, as lean and efficient as possible through a process of continuous mutual learning and up-skilling, underpinned with the confidence of a long-term relationship.

6. The People Commitment

We will strive to create a community of employee stakeholders who are committed to the company, the customer, quality, and continuous improvement.

7. Interdependence with the Community

We realize that the vitality of the communities in which we trade and from which we recruit is crucial to our prosperity, and we will lead or participate in our community, sometimes in partnership with others, for our mutual long-term benefit.

8. Unipart U's Vision

To build the world's best lean enterprise.

9. Unipart U's Mission

To train and inspire people to achieve world-class performance with Unipart and amongst its stakeholders.

Unipart Group of Companies' mission statement.

mission

the fundamental purpose of the organization, which forms the foundation of all organizational activities

mission statement

a declaration of an organization's purpose and direction

SWOT analysis

an assessment of the organization's strengths (S) and weaknesses (W) as well as its opportunities (O) and threats (T)

Top management sets the parameters for customer-driven marketing strategy, goals, and objectives by spelling out the firm's mission. The **mission** is the fundamental purpose of the organization, which forms the foundation of all organizational activities. By looking ahead to where the organization wants to be 5, 10, or 15 years out, top managers can shape the organization's mission to make that future a reality.[12]

So that the mission can be communicated inside and outside the organization, managers work with employees to prepare a **mission statement**, a declaration of purpose and direction. One good model for mission statements reads as follows: "We exceed CUSTOMER requirements by creating a working environment that empowers EMPLOYEES to do everything right the first time. This in turn will make Chicago Pipe & Boiler Covering Company the most prestigious, largest and successful company in our industry." [13] See the Unipart Group of Companies' mission statement at the left.

Analyze Your Situation

Once an organization has developed its mission statement, it's time to analyze the current situation. A *situation analysis* is a review of the organization's present state and an evaluation of the external and internal factors that can influence future prospects. Marketers conduct a situation analysis using the first universal marketing process, *environmental scanning and analysis* ◄——┘ **(p. 20)**. This process helps marketers look at a variety of factors that influence the ability to build relationships with customers and other stakeholders. You'll learn more about the marketing environment in Chapters 3 and 4.

One part of an overall situation analysis is a SWOT analysis. A **SWOT analysis** is an assessment of the organization's strengths (S) and weaknesses (W) as well as its opportunities (O) and threats (T). A *strength* is an organizational capability that enables it to meet customer needs more effectively than competitors. In contrast, a *weakness* is an internal factor that can keep you from exceeding competitors in customer satisfaction. At Motown Record Company, for example, one strength is the vast catalog of music, ranging from the Supremes to Boyz II Men, and other artists from the 1960s to the 1990s. A weakness is Motown's lack of up-and-coming streetwise acts, which puts the label at a disadvantage to rivals such as Interscope, which represent many popular newcomers.[14]

An *opportunity* is an external situation that offers the potential to improve the organization's ability to satisfy customers. A nostalgia craze for 1960s rhythm and blues, for instance, would allow Motown to make the most of its extensive catalog from that era.

A *threat* is some external problem that has the potential to impair your ability to provide customer satisfaction. Threats can come from competitors, government actions, or other factors outside the organization. One threat that might hurt Motown is a shift in popular interest away from the label's music. In the example that follows, you'll see how a small marketer makes the most of its strengths to compete more effectively.

SMALL BUSINESS WATCH

Building on strengths to battle big rivals

How can a neighborhood bookstore compete with two giant bookstore chains? That was the threat facing Elaine Petrocelli, owner of the Book Passage in Corte Madera, California. Her rivals "have unlimited amounts of money and ways of advertising that we will never have," and they offer discounts she can't afford. But Petrocelli used her store's strengths to fight back.

One strength was Book Passage's 18 years of building strong relationships with Marin County stakeholders, a record the newcomers couldn't match. A second was its writers' workshops, which drew students and faculty from around the world. A third was its regular schedule of writers' autograph parties, readings, and lectures. A fourth strength was its coffee bar, which attracted both customers and authors.

Petrocelli's marketing strategy enhances relationships with customers, employees, and the community. She sends out customer newsletters filled with information about books and special events. She'll go out of her way to track down obscure books that customers request. Her community activities include fund-raising for a local hospice and a counseling service for abused women.

Petrocelli can't slash prices, because her costs are higher than those of the big stores, but she did cut 10 percent from the price of many books. By playing on its strengths, Book Passage has continued ringing up nearly $3 million yearly. Petrocelli can write the book on how to compete with the big chains.[15]

If you were competing against Petrocelli, what strengths would you stress to take advantage of her weaknesses?

Build on Core Competencies

A SWOT analysis helps reveal core competencies. **Core competencies** are an organization's competitively superior knowledge and use of particular technologies, processes, and specialists' skills. Core competencies, also known as *distinctive competencies*, enable marketers to do better than competitors at satisfying customer needs. This means that a core competence must be something that benefits customers. For example, one core competence of Ericsson, a Sweden-based telecommunications marketer, is its ability to develop reliable mobile telephone systems that help businesses and individuals communicate where and when they want.[16]

Du Pont, Toshiba, Nike, and many others among the world's most successful marketers recognize that they don't have all the competencies needed to serve their customers.[17] They prefer to concentrate on what they do best and gain access to the needed capabilities through strategic alliances or outsourcing.

Strategic alliances are long-term relationships with other organizations in which the partners pool their resources to develop or share competencies. The partners learn from each other and minimize both risks and costs, which is especially important in industries characterized by costly technology or rapid change.[18] Toshiba, for example, has forged strategic alliances to gain competencies that enable it to make, with its partners, computers, medical equipment, and other products.[19]

core competencies

an organization's competitively superior knowledge and use of particular technologies, processes, and specialists' skills

strategic alliances

long-term relationships with other organizations in which the partners pool their resources to develop or share competencies

Effective outsourcing has always been a necessity for Bill Thomas of Bills Khakis. Thomas' pants are sold entirely by mail order or wholesale. Therefore, the marketing relationships Thomas has with his subcontractors are critical because he needs top quality goods to stay competitive in this niche market. What other functions (e.g., accounting, distribution, marketing, design, personnel) might Thomas outsource to other companies to stay competitive? What core competencies, if any, should he keep rather than outsource?

Marketers can also gain access to a needed competence through **outsourcing**, hiring other companies to perform certain functions that the selected firms can handle more efficiently or more effectively. About one-third of the largest U.S. corporations handle a good portion of their manufacturing through outsourcing. But even small businesses can use outsourcing. When Bill Thomas, founder of Bills Khakis, wanted to make and sell khaki trousers, he had no manufacturing plant. So he decided to outsource the cutting and sewing functions of his operation by hiring a plant with a reputation for making high-quality pants. Thomas knows that his customers expect quality, and outsourcing allows him to have his products made by a factory that can meet exacting standards.[20]

Analyze Your Strategic Alternatives

Strategy has the potential to take the organization in any number of directions. But how does a marketer choose among these strategic alternatives? Marketers use a variety of tools to evaluate their options, including the growth–share matrix, the business strength–market attractiveness matrix, and the industry competition model.

The **growth–share matrix**, developed by the Boston Consulting Group, is an analytical tool for comparing the market growth and market share of various products or divisions (called strategic business units—SBUs). High or low market growth is measured by the growth of the market in which the business operates. **Market share** measures the marketer's portion of total units or dollar sales of a given product, relative to competitors.

The two-by-two grid shown in Figure 2.2 slots businesses or products into four categories: stars, question marks, cash cows, and dogs. In this growth–share matrix, the idea is to sustain the cash-generating cows, divest or harvest the dogs, take cash from the cows, selectively invest in question marks to make them stars, and invest to increase the profits of stars. Not all companies have multiple units or products like this, however, and there is a danger of focusing too much on market share and not enough on customer wants and needs.[21]

The **business strength–market attractiveness matrix**, pioneered by General Electric, compares strategic alternatives according to business strength and market attractiveness. This matrix, shown in Figure 2.3, is more comprehensive than the growth–share matrix. It takes into account a wider range of factors that affect success in a particular market or business, including market share, profitability, and technical capabilities. Like the growth–share matrix, however, it lacks a strong focus on customers and future market potential.

outsourcing

hiring other companies to perform certain functions that the selected firms can handle more efficiently or more effectively

growth-share matrix

an analytical tool for comparing the market growth and market share of various divisions or products

market share

measures the marketer's portion of total units or dollar sales of a given product, relative to competitors

business strength–market attractiveness matrix

compares strategic alternatives according to business strength and market attractiveness

FIGURE **2.2** **The Growth–Share Matrix**

Using this matrix, marketers can compare divisions or products on the basis of market growth and market share. Some, the dogs, may need to be dropped; others, stars and question marks, may need an inflow of cash. However, the matrix isn't keyed to customer wants and needs, so its usefulness is limited.

Relative Market Share

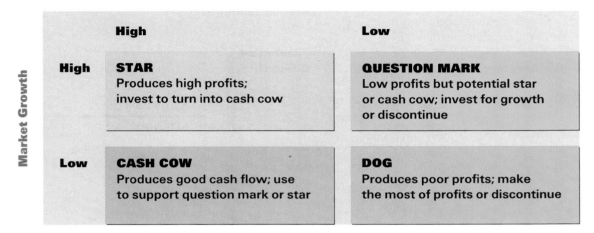

FIGURE **2.3** **Business Strength–Market Attractiveness Matrix**

This matrix, developed by General Electric, helps marketers analyze their strategic choices according to the attractiveness of the market and the strength of the business. Businesses and markets that rank high are good candidates for growth. Like the growth–share matrix, this matrix is of limited value because it isn't geared toward customer needs and wants.

Market Attractiveness

Market Attractiveness Criteria	Business Strength Criteria
Size	Size
Market growth, pricing	Growth
Market diversity	Share
Competitive structure	Position
Industry profitability	Profitability
Technical role	Margins
Social	Technological position
Environmental	Strengths/ weaknesses
Legal	Image
Human	Pollution
	People

Business Strength

	High	Medium	Low
High	Grow	Grow	Hold
Medium	Grow	Hold	Harvest
Low	Hold	Harvest	Harvest

FIGURE **2.4**   Industry–Competition Model

To understand their competitive position in the industry—and examine the impact on profits— marketing managers can use Michael Porter's industry-competition model. Note that existing competitors are only one component. Marketers also have to explore potential competitors and the bargaining power of the organization's partners in the value chain. Such information is invaluable when making marketing plans for the future.

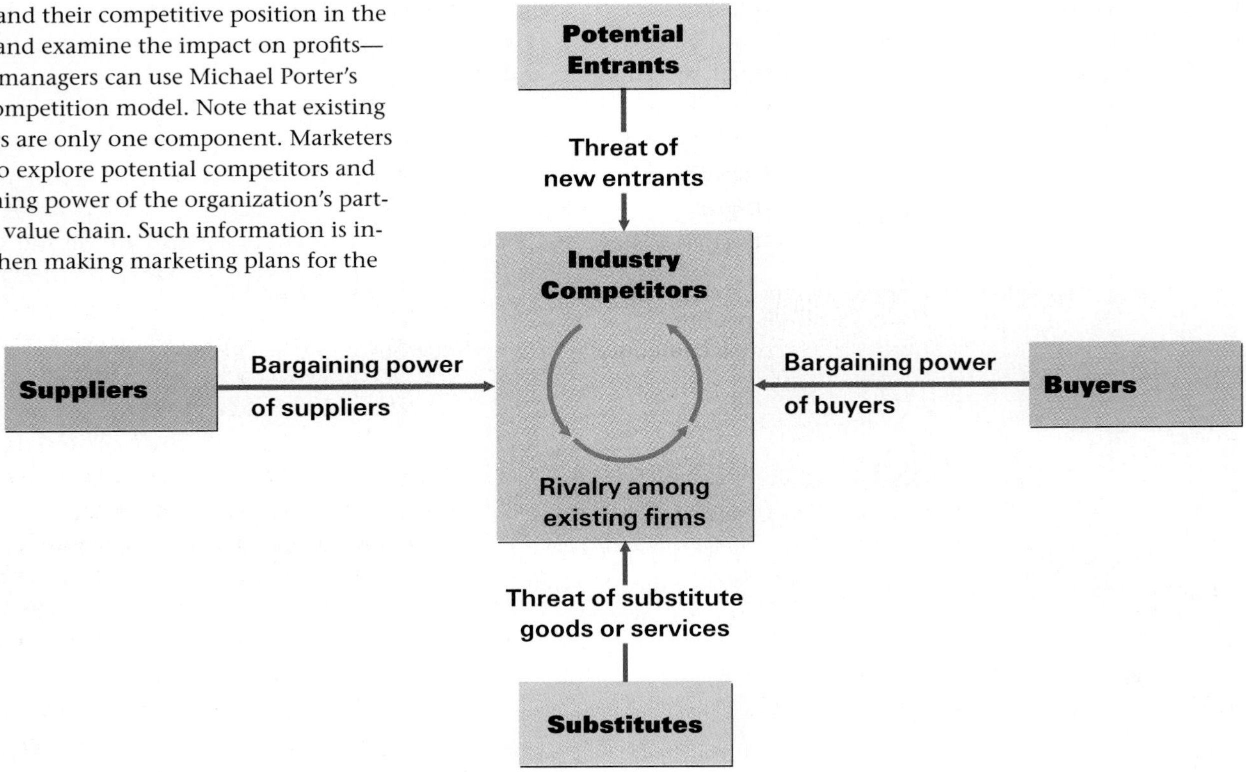

The **industry–competition model**, developed by Michael Porter of the Harvard Business School and shown in Figure 2.4, provides a structure for analyzing the effect of *competition* on profitability within an industry. This model shows the role of five competitive forces that influence industry profitability: (1) the threat of potential entrants coming into the industry, (2) the bargaining power of suppliers, (3) the bargaining power of buyers, (4) the threat of available goods and services to substitute for the industry's products, and (5) rivalry among current competitors.[22]

The industry–competition model is a useful strategic tool because it focuses on relationships among customers, suppliers, and competitors, and their effects on profits. The model points up the importance of collaboration among competitors, which can strengthen individual companies as well as the entire industry.[23] On the other hand, the model offers no guidance about incorporating existing or emerging customer needs into strategy. Moreover, it doesn't lead to ideas for specific strategies to build relationships within an industry.

Each of the foregoing tools for analyzing strategic alternatives has benefits and limitations. Thus when you are planning strategy and selecting a target market, it is necessary to study the competition, the profitability of various units, and all other environmental elements. The models outlined above provide helpful direction. You will learn about them in more detail if you take an advanced course in marketing management.

industry–competition model

provides a structure for analyzing the effect of competition on profitability within an industry

Select and Segment the Target Market

One of the key questions a marketing strategy answers is, "Whom do we want as customers?" Finding the answer involves two universal marketing processes. With the process of *marketing research and analysis*, marketers investigate specific market and customer needs. They also gather data to determine how various decisions and actions are likely to affect marketing results. Then, using the process of *segmentation, targeting, and positioning*, they select the most appropriate customer groups to target as well as the way to position products to those groups. Since this process is discussed in detail in Chapter 8, the following is only a brief description and example.

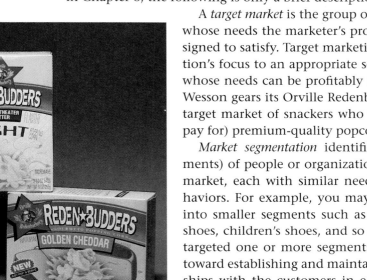

A *target market* is the group of people or organizations whose needs the marketer's products are specifically designed to satisfy. Target marketing narrows the organization's focus to an appropriate set of potential customers whose needs can be profitably met. For example, Hunt-Wesson gears its Orville Redenbacher products toward a target market of snackers who want (and are willing to pay for) premium-quality popcorn snacks.

Market segmentation identifies separate groups (segments) of people or organizations within a broad target market, each with similar needs, characteristics, or behaviors. For example, you may divide the shoe market into smaller segments such as athletic shoes, women's shoes, children's shoes, and so on. Once a marketer has targeted one or more segments, it can gear its strategy toward establishing and maintaining long-term relationships with the customers in each. For example, David Rohdy, Orville Redenbacher's marketing director, has segmented the popcorn market into a series of distinct groupings including younger consumers interested in highly flavored snacks and consumers interested in con-

Orville Redenbacher popcorn can be formulated to appeal to a number of different market segments. The Reden⋆ Budders line includes a light version for dieters; a jalapeño popcorn for those who like it hot, hot, hot; and a buttered popcorn for traditionalists. How many niche markets should Reden⋆Budders aim for and how would you go about making this decision?

venience. Each segment receives separate relationship-marketing treatment. Such Reden⋆Budders products as jalapeño popcorn add zing for the younger flavor seekers, while Popcorn Cakes make popcorn an on-the-go treat for convenience seekers.[24]

To help customers in each segment relate the product to their needs, wants, and expectations, marketers use positioning. *Positioning* means creating a specific image of the product in the minds of people in your target market. This image sets the product apart from competing products. At Orville Redenbacher, the Reden⋆Budders products are positioned as a flavorful indulgence for young adults. Vibrant television commercials and colorful packaging reinforce this view of the products.

Issues for critical thinking

Are marketers acting ethically when they select children as their target market? Do the ethics depend on the marketing strategy being used? Can you think of any ethical marketing programs that target children?

goals

specific long-term results a marketer wants to achieve

objectives

specific, measurable interim targets that must be met to reach the organization's goals

Set Marketing Goals and Objectives

Once you have determined who you're targeting, you have to establish clear goals and objectives. **Goals** are the specific long-term results a marketer wants to achieve. Top managers generally set the organization's overall goals. **Objectives** are specific, measurable interim targets that must be met to reach the organization's goals. Short-term objectives may be set for weekly, monthly, and yearly results. Top-level goals are incorporated into these objectives and into the strategies that lower level managers and employees set for each organizational unit, function, and team. When other organizations are involved, clear objectives help all participants follow a single unified strategy.

For goals and objectives to be meaningful in guiding a marketer's decisions and actions, they have to:

1. *Support the organization's mission.* The mission is the ultimate destination, so goals and objectives should help the organization move in that direction.
2. *Be challenging but attainable.* Goals and objectives should be aggressive enough to stretch the organization's capability without discouraging employees and partners.
3. *Be measurable.* Clear, precise goals and objectives that are also measurable will allow the organization to trace its progress over time.
4. *Include a deadline or schedule.* All employees need to know when they're expected to achieve results.

Marketers can set a variety of goals for relationship-building strategies, some of which are shown in Table 2.1. It is important not to focus narrowly on a profit goal, a sales goal, or any other goal that doesn't help build or sustain customer relationships. Of course, profits and sales definitely influence how the organization moves toward its future and must be incorporated into any strategy. However, the real purpose of any organization is to create and keep customers. If it does this successfully, profits will follow.[25]

T A B L E   **2.1**   Sample Marketing Goals

Goal	Examples
Customer satisfaction	Achieve 100% scores on U.S. customer satisfaction surveys about delivery, quality, and service, within one year.
Market share	Achieve a 10% share of the South African market in one product category by December 31.
Sales	Sell 1,000 units in the first year in New Zealand. Sell $10,000 worth of products in the first quarter in Cleveland. Sell 30% more units next month in the Southern Region, compared with last month.
Product development	Develop and launch three new products during the next 12 months. Reduce the time needed to develop new products from 10 months to 6 months.
Market development	Sell 30,000 products in two new markets next year.
Market penetration	Sell 30,000 additional products in current markets next year.
New customer relationships	Attract 35 new local customers from January to March. Increase the European customer base by 20% within 6 months.
Customer development	Increase sales to current South American customers by 15% during the next 12 months.
Customer loyalty	Have 25% of current U.S. customers make two or more purchases during the coming month.
Profit margin	Make a 25% profit in domestic markets next year. Increase next year's overseas profits 20% over the preceding year.

TABLE **2.2** Forecasting Tools for Strategy Planning

Tool	Definition	Advantages and Disadvantages
Jury of executive opinion	Managers give educated guesses about future sales.	Inexpensive and fast. However, may miss the mark if managers aren't knowledgeable or objective.
Sales force composite	Combine the estimates of salespeople who know the market and the customers.	Inexpensive and fast. However, salespeople may not be objective about some products or markets. This forecast is best used with other estimates.
Survey of buyer intentions	Ask customers about their future buying intentions.	Works well with small market, but not with a large number of customers.
Delphi technique	Ask a panel of outside experts to work independently to submit forecasts (often by mail); compile results and return to panel for revised forecasts until a consensus is achieved.	Effective with knowledgeable experts, but can be time-consuming.
Test marketing	Estimate sales by evaluating customer response to a new product during a limited period in a given market.	Expensive, but can show what customers think of the product.
Simulated test marketing	A version of test marketing by computer (to estimate test-market results) or by bringing customers to a special site (to gauge their reaction to a product).	Less expensive than test marketing; able to test many more elements.
Trend analysis	Look at sales history and project future sales based on a similar pattern.	Can be computerized for easy calculation and interpretation. However, beware of assumption that trends of the past will continue unchanged in the future.
Regression analysis	Statistical method of analyzing the cause-and-effect relationship of factors that affect sales.	Complex calculation; larger samples improve accuracy.

Nonprofit organizations don't focus on profit goals, but they do set goals that relate to their mission. For example, the mission of the American Heart Association is to prevent premature death and disability from cardiovascular disease and stroke. Its goals are to convince a certain number of people to stop smoking or not to start in the first place, to convince a certain number of people to change their dietary habits, and to raise money to fund research into heart disease. These goals benefit people who have heart problems as well as people who want to stay healthy.[26]

Marketers often have to estimate future sales as they prepare marketing goals. *Market potential* estimates industry-wide sales of a certain product during a future period. *Sales forecasts* estimate how much a company expects to sell in a future period. There are a variety of planning tools for preparing such estimates, as shown in Table 2.2. With computer-based forecasting, marketers can speed up the forecasting process and quickly analyze the effects of market, competitive, or other changes. However, sophisticated planning tools can't substitute for a marketer's informed judgment.

Before you go on . . .

A. What are the three levels of strategy?

B. How is a SWOT analysis used in developing strategy for relationship marketing?

C. Why do marketers use outsourcing and strategic alliances?

D. What are target markets and why do marketers segment them?

Develop Internal Marketing Strategy

Building good relationships with customers and other stakeholders outside the organization requires a high degree of teamwork and cooperation within the organization. So, before developing a relationship marketing strategy for external stakeholders, marketers need a strategy that can serve to build internal relationships.

Internal marketing strategy guides activities inside the organization. Just as external marketing strategy helps marketers reach customers outside the organization, internal marketing strategy is aimed at reaching internal customers by smoothing the way for closer cooperation among individuals, departments, and units.[27] Three critical elements of internal marketing strategy are (1) organizational structure and reengineering, (2) teamwork and employee empowerment, and (3) total quality management.

Organizational Structure and Reengineering

For years, many organizations have maintained separate departments for marketing, finance, production, and other functions. The director of marketing supervises product or brand managers, each with responsibility for a particular brand or group of products. At General Motors, for example, brand managers concentrate on understanding and meeting the needs of customers in the target market for their assigned brands.[28] Such structures are still in use, but a growing number of marketers are making their organizations looser and flatter (with few layers of management).

These organizations want to react more quickly to customer shifts, environmental changes, and competitive challenges. The hierarchy of managers giving orders to the people below them is therefore on its way out, the result of a revolution in the way organizations are put together to serve their customers.

The most advanced organizations have actually turned the traditional organizational structure upside down, as shown in Figure 2.5. These *inverted organizations* put people who deal with customers at the top of the organization—and the chief executive officer at the bottom. There are few layers of managers, and their job is to assist and support frontline employees in giving customers what they need. In essence, these organizations use structure to show employees that customer relationships are the top priority and everything (and everybody) else is secondary.

A good example of an inverted organization is NovaCare, a provider of rehabilitation care. At the top of the organization are some 3,500 physical, occupational, and speech therapists. The rest of the organization is structured to serve those therapists, who work directly with patients. Managers support the therapists by arranging contacts with nursing homes, handling accounting and credit activities, and providing professional training.

Many organizations use reengineering to examine internal operations and to rebuild from scratch processes and activities for more productivity, better quality, and improved customer satisfaction. **Reengineering** is the fundamental rethinking and radical redesign of organizational processes to achieve dramatic improvements; it completely changes the flow of work as well as the jobs and groupings needed to get work done faster and better.[29]

reengineering

the fundamental rethinking and radical redesign of organizational processes to achieve dramatic improvements

FIGURE **2.5** Inverted Versus Traditional Organization Structures

Many marketers are moving from a traditional, top-down organization structure, where employees follow orders given by their managers, to an inverted structure, where employees are empowered to make decisions—and managers support their efforts.

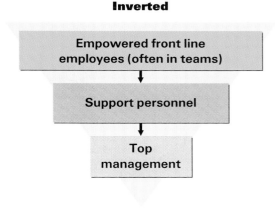

For example, IBM Credit recently analyzed its procedure for evaluating customer applications for financing computer purchases. In the traditional organizational structure, a customer waited six days while the application bounced from department to department. When IBM Credit reengineered the process, it replaced the departments with a team that did everything necessary to evaluate applications in only four hours.[30]

Teamwork and Employee Empowerment

As traditional organizational structures change, more marketers are breaking down internal boundaries by forming **cross-functional teams**—groups of employees from various functions or departments, such as design, engineering, and marketing, who work together to satisfy customers. Aerojet, which manufactures propulsion systems and chemical products, won the 1995 Enterprise Award for motivating and retraining employees. Empowered employees ◄┘ **(p. 17)** on some 144 cross-functional teams are a way of life at Aerojet. Its team-oriented culture has led to greater productivity and profits.[31]

**Issues for critical thinking**

How much power should "empowered" employees have? Should they be able to respond to any customer need or request without checking with management? Should they have guidelines to direct their activities? What do employees need to know to satisfy customers most effectively?

cross-functional teams

groups of employees from various functions or departments who work together to satisfy customers

organizational culture

the pattern of shared values and beliefs that influences employee attitudes and behavior

total quality management (TQM)

puts quality at the heart of every organizational operation, because quality is defined as satisfying the needs of both internal and external customers

An atmosphere of empowerment can be created at the top and carried through to all levels by the **organizational culture**, the pattern of shared values and beliefs that influences employee attitudes and behavior. Organizational culture, also known as *corporate culture*, shows employees what is important and how things are done in the organization. Here's how one Hong Kong company used organizational culture to build its global business through employee empowerment.

GLOBAL ISSUES

Empowerment and teamwork fuel double-digit growth

When Patrick Wang Shui Chung's father founded Johnson Electric Holdings in Hong Kong, all significant decisions—about marketing and every other organizational activity—were made at the top. Using this top-down style, the founder built Johnson into a successful toy-motor manufacturer. Then the younger Wang set a goal of shooting past $250 million in global sales by marketing small motors to makers of hair dryers and other equipment. To support his marketing strategy, Wang needed the ideas, creativity, and total involvement of every employee.

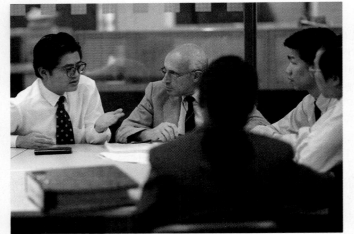

Diverse cross-functional teams work well at Johnson Electric Holdings in Hong Kong. The company also works closely with its customers by linking design centers in the United States and Europe with engineers and factories in Asia. To create the appropriate corporate culture to support teamwork and international cooperation, the company sponsors a U.S.-run Outward Bound camp in Hong Kong where team members from China can bond with similar teams in Hong Kong.

That's why top-down management is out and employee empowerment is in at Johnson. By instilling a culture of empowerment, Wang cleared the way for every employee to participate fully. "My job is basically to create the culture so that professionals can do their job," he says. Technology plays a central role here. Employees share information via comprehensive databases, allowing them to respond quickly to market trends and customer requirements without many layers of managers.

Another element of Wang's internal marketing strategy is the switch from big functional departments to an organizational structure featuring more than 30 smaller, cross-functional teams. These teams are responsible for making and marketing specialized products to particular customer segments, such as manufacturers of automobiles and power tools. Between the small, agile teams and the culture of empowerment, Wang has laid a solid foundation for Johnson's ambitious growth strategy.[32]

How can Wang use internal marketing to reinforce the empowerment mandate?

Total Quality Management

Quality is an essential component of every marketing strategy. **Total quality management (TQM)** puts quality at the heart of every organizational operation, because quality is defined as satisfying the needs of both internal and external customers. With TQM, employees (as well as suppliers and channel partners) never lose sight of customer requirements.

Benchmarking ◀──┘ **(p. 15)** is a TQM process that helps marketers match the quality of the world's best practices, processes, and products. With *continuous improvement*, another TQM process, marketers endlessly search for ways to improve quality. That means that everyone is constantly thinking of better ways to do their jobs and serve their internal and external customers. These and other TQM methods, such as statistical process control for improving production quality, help employees deliver quality that satisfies—or delights—their customers. Table 2.3 shows the criteria for winning the National Quality Award, given in honor of Malcolm Baldrige by the National Bureau of Standards and Technology. (The NBST is part of the U.S. Department of Commerce, where Baldrige served as secretary between 1981 and 1987.) Note the focus on the customer.

T A B L E **2.3** **Points Given for Various Criteria Used in the Baldrige Award**

Examination Category	Maximum Points Awarded
Customer satisfaction	300
Quality results	180
Quality assurance of products/services	140
Human resource utilization	150
Strategic quality planning	60
Information and analysis	75
Leadership	95
Total points	1,000

Note that customer satisfaction gets the highest weighting. Since the customer determines quality, all the other criteria build upon customer satisfaction.

Incorporating quality into a marketer's strategy is critical for profitability as well. Quality was part of a comprehensive study by the *Profit Impact of Market Strategy (PIMS) project*, started by General Electric and continued by the Strategic Planning Institute. The PIMS findings, covering 450 companies, suggest that the single most important factor influencing profitable returns is product quality relative to that of competitors.[33]

Procter & Gamble, the giant U.S. marketer of soaps, toothpastes, and other household products, has crafted a powerful internal marketing strategy around TQM. Recognizing that quality is essential to building long-term relationships with consumers and retailers, the company first adopted TQM in the early 1980s. Now TQM has been extended throughout the organization and to its suppliers as well. The results: better quality raw materials from suppliers, fewer product defects, improved teamwork, higher customer satisfaction—and higher profits.[34]

Before you go on . . .

A. What are the critical elements of an internal marketing strategy?

B. What is total quality management, and why is it important?

Develop External Marketing Strategy

Your internal marketing strategy ensures that everyone in the organization (and in supplier and dealer organizations) is working on the same goals and objectives. Once you have set the organizational structure, created a culture of empowerment, and implemented TQM, you are ready to develop an external marketing strategy. *External marketing strategy* guides activities conducted outside the organization to satisfy external customers.

As shown in Figure 2.1, external marketing strategy covers four of the eight universal marketing processes: *product development and differentiation* (product), *valuation and pricing* (price), *channel and value-chain management* (place), and *integrated marketing communication* (promotion). These four processes correspond to the original four Ps of marketing, which form the marketing mix ◄——┛ **(p. 20)**.

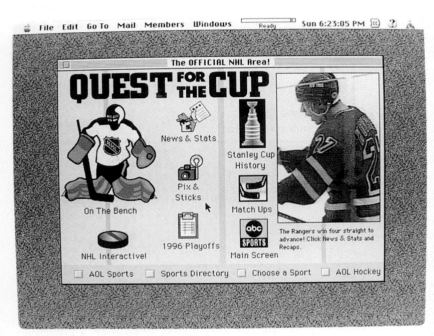

The National Hockey League maintains sites on both America Online (shown here) and the World Wide Web. These online sites enable and encourage stakeholders to keep in touch any time of the day or night. Interested fans can now ask questions and provide input without leaving their homes. What future uses can you see for online sites developed by the various sports leagues and their teams?

Applying the Marketing Mix

Individual strategies for each of the four parts of the marketing mix help marketers start and sustain relationships with customers in their target markets. Although these processes will be examined in detail in later chapters, a quick overview shows how each fits into the external marketing strategy.

- *Product development and differentiation.* The product is the basic building block of marketing. Product strategy guides the development of new products, the refining of existing products, and the determination of actions for setting all products apart from those of competitors. In developing a product, the key is to understand its value from the customer's viewpoint.

- *Valuation and pricing.* Pricing strategy is the set of decisions and actions used to create product value and set an appropriate price that will lead to a mutually beneficial marketing exchange. When customers weigh a product's value, they look beyond price to consider the cost (in money and time) of buying, installing, and using the product. And, although prices must give customers value for their money, they also have to return sufficient profit to the marketer.

- *Channel and value-chain management.* A strategy for channel and value-chain management lays out a course of action for managing relationships with other organizations in the value chain. The **value chain** is the sequence of linked activities that must be performed by suppliers, channel partners, and the marketer to create and deliver a value package that satisfies customers.

value chain

the sequence of linked activities that must be performed by suppliers, channel partners, and the marketer to create and deliver a value package that satisfies customers

- *Integrated marketing communication.* Integrated marketing communication strategy supports relationship building by coordinating all marketing messages and opening a dialogue with customers and other stakeholders. The National Hockey League, for example, uses two-way communication to stay in touch with fans, corporate sponsors, owners, players, employees, and other stakeholders. The NHL's IMC techniques include television and magazine advertising, personal selling, and online messages posted on a World Wide Web site.[35]

Creating the Value Chain

Value-chain development creates alliances among marketers, suppliers, and dealers that gives them, as a whole, more competitive power than would be available if they acted alone, as illustrated in Figure 2.6. To create a value chain, the marketer researches customer needs and identifies the internal departments or outside organizations that will handle activities connected with

- obtaining raw materials and supplies,
- transforming these materials into useful goods and services,
- bringing products to customers through the marketing channel,
- communicating with customers, and
- adding services to form the value package for the exchange.[36]

Because the value chain starts with raw materials and ends with the customer, any one company usually tackles just a few of the activities, relying on suppliers and partners to handle the others. Therefore, a complete value chain is really a connection of many value chains. Suppliers have their own suppliers, for example. The printer that produces textbooks for a publisher has to get paper—its raw material—from a mill. The printer is part of the publisher's value chain, and the mill is part of the printer's value chain. As a result, competition is often between two or more *value-chain systems*, all the organizations in each marketer's value chain, instead of between one value chain and another. The following case will help you apply strategic thinking to managing suppliers in the value chain.

FIGURE **2.6** Links in the Value Chain

Customer needs trigger a whole web (or chain) of interlinked functions that result in a value package to satisfy customers.

Often value chains are linked with other value chains in a total system to create value for customers throughout the system.

Applying the Concepts

Ford steers into a simpler value chain

How many suppliers does it take to provide a car lightbulb? If you had asked the Ford Motor Company five years ago, you would have gotten a surprisingly large number. Today, however, the number is much lower—and moving lower still. From lightbulbs to interior trim to floor carpet, Ford is simplifying its value chain to reduce the number of suppliers and slash overall costs. These changes are helping the carmaker gain faster access to the latest technology, keep quality high, and boost profits.

Just a few years ago, Ford bought auto parts from more than a thousand suppliers in the United States as well as hundreds of vendors abroad. But tracking orders, parts, and invoices was an expensive nightmare. Worse, using so many suppliers complicated the manufacturing process and threatened consistent quality.

Then Ford decided to use the same kind of part in more than one car, to buy from fewer suppliers, and to work closely with its suppliers on quality standards. It also started requiring suppliers to use electronic data interchange (EDI), a computerized system of documenting orders. To speed delivery, suppliers were asked to locate near Ford factories. Ford also requested that suppliers lower their prices. In return, the automaker agreed to buy more from the remaining suppliers (although it wouldn't agree to longer term contracts).

Ford's goal is to have fewer than 300 suppliers around the world. Ultimately, the revamping of supplier relationships—coupled with improvements in manufacturing productivity—will allow Ford to quickly and easily fine-tune car designs to meet the requirements of different customer segments. In the meantime, Ford is keeping a watchful eye on its value chain to stay competitive in the worldwide automotive market.[37]

Make marketing decisions

1. If you were a Ford supplier, would you agree to locate your facility near a Ford plant and lower prices without a long-term contract? Why or why not?
2. How does the interchangeability of parts help Ford tailor its car designs to the needs of customers in Canada and England?
3. What standards would you use to measure Ford's progress in meeting its goal of reducing the number of suppliers?
4. Do you think Ford's value-chain system is a strength or a weakness? Explain your answer.

Before you go on . . .

A. What four marketing processes are covered by external marketing strategy?

B. Why does a marketer create a value chain?

Relationship Building and the Marketing Plan

Both internal and external marketing strategies support *relationship building,* the eighth universal marketing process, which focuses on establishing and maintaining mutually beneficial exchange relationships with employees, customers, and other stakeholders ◀──┘ **(p. 8)**. Although you can benchmark on many marketers that are expert in creating long-term relationships with customers, you'll find far fewer that are adept at simultaneously strengthening ties with other stakeholders. But you can learn relationship-building strategies from other disciplines and incorporate those ideas into your marketing plans, as the following sections show.[38]

Planning for Relationship Building

You can plan for long-lasting relationships with customers and other stakeholders by applying the same principles that strengthen relationships among individuals. Relationship marketing will be discussed throughout the text. Here are some basics to get you started.

1. *Relationships are based on open communication.* To build relationships, you must be a good listener, interested in what the other person has to say. Marketers must therefore pay careful attention to customers, employees, suppliers, and others with whom they want to have a relationship; they also must ask questions and act on the answers. Facilities Management, a small Maryland-based government contractor, is so concerned about open communication that it trains its employees to ask probing questions and listen harder. The training helped the company win a $3.5 million contract.[39]

2. *Relationships are built on reliability.* Help customers learn to trust you by doing what you say you'll do. A marketer that delivers as promised, time after time, demonstrates that it is worthy of customers' trust and commitment. Allen Breed, the inventor of the air bag car safety device, built his $400 million business on reliability. Competing with TRW and other giants, he finally won huge contracts from Ford and other automakers by proving over and over that he could supply quality products on time—and at a reasonable cost.[40]

3. *Relationships are strengthened when the parties stay in contact.* Good marketers talk with customers before developing new goods or services. They maintain contact as the product is developed, ask customers what they think, and check after the product has been purchased to make sure that buyers are satisfied. The more you stay in contact with customers, the better you are able to identify their wants and needs and respond accordingly.[41] The same holds true for contacts with employees, suppliers, stockholders, bankers, and other stakeholders.

4. *Relationships depend on trust, honesty, and ethical behavior.* Stakeholders want to be able to trust marketers. Any hint that a marketer is not being fully honest and ethical with employees, customers, or other stakeholders will greatly weaken the relationship. Chapter 3 discusses ethics in more detail.

5. *Partners in a relationship show they care.* Marketers can show customers and other stakeholders that they care in a variety of ways, from follow-

marketing plan
a detailed document that describes (1) the target market, (2) the goals, objectives, and strategies for reaching that market, (3) the marketing tactics, budget, and timing needed to reach those goals, and (4) the expected return to the organization

ing up after the purchase to offering incentives to reward continued loyalty. The best marketers use research to develop such a deep understanding of their stakeholders that they can actually anticipate future requirements and then move ahead to satisfy those requirements. For example, WelcomGroup in India doesn't just offer a business center and hotel rooms designed for business travelers. It goes further, offering free plane tickets for travelers' spouses to spend the weekend at the hotel.[42]

However, even though a marketer may be eager to establish long-term relationships, customers may be reluctant to commit. In today's global economy, customers have many choices. What keeps customers in a long-term marketing relationship is consistent satisfaction with the marketer's value package. To ensure customer satisfaction time after time, a marketer needs a well-developed and thoughtfully implemented marketing plan.

Developing and Implementing the Marketing Plan

The entire strategic marketing process is outlined in the organization's marketing plan. A **marketing plan** is a detailed document that describes (1) the target market, (2) the goals, objectives, and strategies for reaching that market, (3) the marketing tactics, budget, and timing needed to reach those goals, and (4) the expected return to the organization; the contents of a typical marketing plan are shown in Figure 2.7. A marketing plan starts with the organization's overall mission and goals and situation analysis. Then it lays out the organization's plan for using marketing to reach its goals and to make progress toward its mission. Details about creating a marketing plan can be found in Appendix C at the back of this text.

F I G U R E   **2.7**   **Table of Contents of a Marketing Plan**

All eight marketing processes are involved in the creation of a marketing plan. You need to do environmental scanning and marketing research to write a situation analysis. Segmentation and positioning are both part of clearly stating who your target market will be. Clear marketing goals and objectives help you focus on the proper internal and external strategies to follow. Those strategies become marketing programs, complete with budgets, and are then implemented according to a planned schedule.

Contents

I. **Situation Analysis**

II. **Target Market**

III. **Marketing Goals and Objectives**

IV. **Marketing Strategies**

V. **Marketing Programs**

VI. **Program Budgets**

VII. **Program Schedules**

Preparing the Marketing Plan

Although the marketing plan is generally guided by the marketing department, its preparation is a joint effort representing many functions, departments, and employees. For instance, when Johnson & Johnson marketers are considering new products, they work with many departments in the course of developing their marketing plans. First, J&J marketers research customers' health care needs and collaborate with specialists in research and development (R&D) to create quality products. Then they meet with financial experts to review profit forecasts and with production experts to examine operational requirements. For J&J, as for all marketers, the final marketing plan should represent the ideas and commitment of everyone who will carry it out.[43]

What makes the marketing plan so important is its role in keeping every employee focused on the specific goals, objectives, activities, and results that make a difference to the organization's future. The details in the plan also provide a budget and schedule for planning and implementing marketing tactics. *Marketing tactics* are the daily actions a marketer will take to implement internal and external marketing strategies and achieve marketing goals and objectives.

Marketing plans are absolutely essential in large businesses such as Delta Air Lines and Panasonic, whose employees need a single blueprint laying out the organization's present situation, its future aims, and the steps to take toward the future. But marketing plans are no less valuable to small marketers, who use them to bring focus and discipline to decisions made by owners and employees.

That's what Harlan Accola and his brother Conrad found out with American Images, their small aerial photography business in Marshfield, Wisconsin. Started as a sideline to the brothers' flying hobby, the business initially grew rapidly and without clear direction. In many cases, the photographers simply shot photos and then tried to sell them to farmers, business owners, and homeowners. Then, after financial disaster nearly grounded them, the Accola brothers started to plan for marketing.

The planning process helps the company pinpoint which segments to pursue and lays out steps for communicating with the target market through mailings, telephone calls, and personal selling. Goals and objectives are set by the Accolas and their department heads, with the participation of every employee. These objectives are then translated into individual objectives for each employee. In this way, all employees understand how their contributions affect customer relationships and—equally important—the bottom line. Thanks to careful attention to planning, American Images has grown to $4.7 million in sales.[44]

Implementing the Marketing Plan

With the marketing plan in place, you are ready to implement the marketing tactics that carry out the strategies. Implementation is the reality check for everything in the plan. This is the point at which the ideas and decisions are translated into actions that move the organization in the right direction. "Strategy is a piece of paper," observes Andrea Jung, president of product marketing at Avon. "It doesn't mean a thing unless you can implement it."[45] Unfortunately, strategies can fall apart during implementation.

For example, when Sony implemented a strategy to introduce Betamax videocassette technology, it had a two-year lead over Matsushita's VHS technology. However, Sony was slow to allow other manufacturers to use its technology. In contrast, Matsushita quickly signed up RCA and others, in addition to using VHS in its own Panasonic, Quasar, and JVC VCRs. Soon

marketing control

the four-step process of setting standards for performance, measuring progress toward marketing goals, comparing results with the standards, and making changes or reinforcing good results to stay on track

the U.S. market was filled with VHS-compatible equipment, which offered longer playing time and lower prices than Betamax. Ultimately, Sony abandoned its Betamax strategy and switched to VHS.[46]

Still, failure can lay the groundwork for successful future marketing. Sony continues to innovate, finding new product ideas for emerging customer needs. As many as 200 of the 1,000 new or improved products Sony introduces every year are aimed at creating new markets. That's why Sony doesn't judge overall success by customer acceptance of a single product. Instead, it applies the lessons learned to the situation analysis, strategy, and implementation of later marketing plans.[47]

Exercising Marketing Control

No marketing plan for building relationships is complete without plans for marketing control. **Marketing control** is the four-step process of setting standards for performance, measuring progress toward marketing goals, comparing results with the standards, and making changes or reinforcing good results to stay on track, illustrated in Figure 2.8. Without marketing control, you won't know whether you're going in the right direction; you may even be unaware that you have arrived at your destination when you get there. With good marketing control, you can follow your progress and adjust your decisions and actions if you find you're not achieving the expected results.

FIGURE **2.8**   **The Marketing Control Process**

Marketing control starts with clear, specific performance standards. Such standards make it easier to measure progress and results.

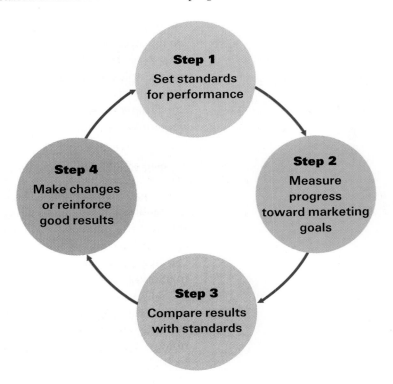

Marketing control starts during the planning stage, when marketers translate goals into measures to be used in evaluating performance. If there are goals for customer satisfaction, for instance, the marketer must be able to measure progress toward those goals. Marriott measures its success in achieving customer satisfaction goals by asking each departing hotel guest to fill out a "Guest Services Index" survey. The results help Marriott to evaluate its marketing performance and also reveal relationship-damaging problems that need immediate attention.[48]

Using the Marketing Audit

A key element in marketing control is the **marketing audit**, a comprehensive review of an organization's marketing strategies, tactics, and performance. By showing where the marketing is up to standard and where it falls short, this information can help to catch small problems before they cause big headaches and to uncover ideas that will help the organization do better in the future. Ideally, a marketing audit should be conducted yearly so the results can be used to control current marketing activities and plan future activities. Some marketers conduct the marketing audit less often, however, because of its wide scope.

Although the exact questions asked during a marketing audit may vary, any marketing audit should include

- an assessment of previous goals, objectives, and results,
- an assessment of the environmental elements that influenced the organization's performance during the past year,
- an assessment of stakeholder satisfaction, including customers, employees, and other groups, and
- an assessment of the current external and internal marketing strategies and implementation.[49]

Some marketers supplement the marketing audit with a quality audit similar to the one performed by judges for the National Quality Award, which honors businesses with exceptionally effective quality and customer satisfaction management processes. Motorola and Cadillac are two of the leading companies that have been recognized for their high standards of quality and customer satisfaction.

Planning Marketing Control Actions

The information gathered during the marketing audit is used to compare actual performance with the standards set in the goals and objectives. If an organization is meeting or exceeding the standards and making timely progress toward the goals, it should acknowledge the achievement of its employees. Not only is this good internal marketing practice, it also lets people know that they're doing well and encourages them to keep up the good work.

On the other hand, if marketing performance doesn't measure up, marketers face two steps. The first is to reexamine the standards to be sure they're reasonable. If they are, marketers move to step two, namely, to make corrections to the marketing strategy and implementation to get back on track. By quickly adjusting activities, you have a better chance of bringing results back in line with expectations.

marketing audit

a comprehensive review of an organization's marketing strategies, tactics, and performance

For example, AT&T's "i" marketing campaign for long-distance telephone services didn't encourage many new customer relationships. While it ran, archrivals MCI and Sprint were gaining market share. When AT&T saw what was happening, it changed its approach within three months. The next marketing campaigns, titled True Voice and True Choice, introduced simpler discount calling plans and rewards for customer loyalty. These campaigns sparked many new customer relationships and reinforced relationships with existing customers. The result: AT&T enjoyed the most significant market share gain since 1984, when its long-time monopoly on long-distance calling was ended.[50] But AT&T must now continually adjust to new competition or lose its lead.

Marketers use marketing research and analysis to monitor the results of their marketing strategies and plans over time. The information obtained from such research helps marketers select new target markets and establish new goals and objectives. Marketing research is thus a critical part of the overall marketing process, allowing individuals or organizations to monitor results and adjust practices to assure long-term success in building relationships.

Before you go on . . .

A. What basic principles can marketers follow to build relationships with customers and other stakeholders?

B. What is the purpose of a marketing plan?

C. How does a marketing audit support marketing control?

Summary

1. **Define strategy and explain how it is used to build and strengthen customer relationships.**

   A strategy is a broad plan used to guide the decisions and actions of everyone in the organization. Over time, customer-oriented strategies for integrated marketing will attract new customers and enhance relationships with existing customers.

2. **Show how marketing strategy links the eight universal marketing processes.**

   Environmental scanning helps marketers conduct a situation analysis. Marketing research and segmentation, targeting, and positioning help define the target market. Four of the universal processes (product development, pricing, value-chain management, and integrated marketing communication) are part of external marketing strategy. Both internal and external marketing strategies support relationship building.

3. **Analyze the organization's strategic alternatives using the growth–share matrix, the business strength–market attractiveness matrix, and the industry–competition model.**

   The growth–share matrix is an analytical tool for comparing the market growth and market share of various products or strategic business units. The business strength–market attractiveness matrix compares strategic alternatives according to business strength and market attractiveness. The industry–competition model provides a structure for analyzing the effect of competition on profitability within an industry. These analytical tools are used to help marketers decide among various strategic alternatives for relationship building.

4. **Identify the components of internal marketing strategy and explain their importance to relationship building.**

   Internal marketing strategy guides activities inside the organization to help reach internal customers. Three components of internal marketing strategy are (1) organizational structure and reengineering, (2) teamwork and employee empowerment, and (3) total quality management. This strategy smooths the way for closer cooperation among individuals, departments, and units in building relationships with external stakeholders.

5. **Discuss the components of external marketing strategy and explain how value chains are created.**

   The external marketing strategy consists of product development and differentiation (product), valuation and pricing (price), channel and value-chain management (place), and integrated marketing communication (promotion). Value chains are developed by linking together suppliers, dealers, and other organizations into a unified system that is designed to respond to customer wants and needs.

6. **Explain the principles marketers can use to build relationships with customers and other stakeholders.**

   Marketers can build relationships with stakeholders based on the principles of (1) open communication, (2) reliability, (3) continuous contact, (4) trust, honesty, and ethical behavior, and (5) caring.

7. **Describe the components of the marketing plan, and outline the marketing control process.**

   The components of a marketing plan are situation analysis, target market, marketing goals and objectives, marketing strategy, and marketing programs, budgets, and schedules. Marketing control is the four-step process of setting standards for performance, measuring progress toward marketing goals, comparing results with the standards, and making changes or reinforcing good results to stay on track.

KEY TERMS

business strength–market attractiveness matrix **40**

core competencies **39**

cross–functional teams **47**

goals **44**

growth–share matrix **40**

industry–competition model **42**

market share **40**

marketing audit **57**

marketing control **56**

marketing myopia **35**

marketing plan **54**

mission **38**

mission statement **38**

objectives **44**

organizational culture **48**

outsourcing **40**

reengineering **46**

strategic alliances **39**

strategy **34**

SWOT analysis **38**

total quality management (TQM) **48**

value chain **50**

Skill-Building Applications

1. As the marketing director for Orville Redenbacher, how would you use total quality management to improve your popcorn products?

2. Consider a job search as a marketing challenge. Which of your core competencies would you stress when applying for a job as (a) a bank teller, (b) a veterinary assistant, and (c) a house painter? Explain your reasoning.

3. You've just taken over a local Dairy Queen business. Draft a marketing plan to meet a goal of doubling the number of customers served within five years.

4. Assume you're the new marketing director for Intel, which markets computer chips to PC manufactur-

ers. How can you use external marketing strategy to encourage your business customers to buy more from you?

5. As the marketing director of Wrangler, you're developing a strategy to market jeans to South American customers. How will you select a target market, set goals and objectives, and evaluate your marketing results?

6. How would you use a marketing audit to help the Boy Scouts of America evaluate a campaign to attract more scoutmasters?

Getting Involved in Marketing

1. *On Your Own* Select a small local business, such as a building contractor, gas station, or accounting firm. What mission statement would you write for the marketing plan if you were the owner? Why?

2. *On Your Own* If you were the marketing manager of a local PIP printing franchise, what kind of marketing goals would you set? What standards would you establish for measuring performance of your strategy? How would you measure your performance?

3. *Find Out More* Find a recent magazine or newspaper article that discusses how a company used a strategic alliance to gain access to the core competencies of a company based in another country. How did the strategic alliance help both partners?

4. *In a Team* Working with three or four classmates, identify the core competencies of your college or university. What additional capabilities do you

think should be acquired through a strategic alliance or through outsourcing?

5. *In a Partnership* With another student, list the strengths, weaknesses, opportunities, and threats you see for a McDonald's or another franchise restaurant near your campus. Based on this analysis, one student should write a paragraph explaining what can be done to capitalize on the opportunities, while the other student writes about what can be done to avoid the threats.

6. *In a Team* With other students visit the college bookstore (or another store) and talk with employees about the store's internal marketing. Ask how goals and strategies are communicated to employees and how quality fits into the strategy. Work together on a two-minute presentation offering suggestions for improving internal marketing in the store you visited.

Practice Case Home Depot Tools Up to Satisfy Internal and External Customers

Two decades ago, the first Home Depot store opened in Atlanta, Georgia—and the home improvement industry has never been the same.

Home Depot stores are a combination of cavernous hardware store, warehouse-style home improvement center, and well-stocked lumberyard. Thanks to the business's internal and ex-

ternal marketing strategies, Home Depot's sales have soared past $12 billion.

Home Depot begins its marketing plan with the goal of serving internal and external customers with exceptional care. For external customers, Home Depot has developed a successful external marketing strategy using the four Ps. It offers quality products, at competitive prices, in good locations, with an effective marketing communication program covering advertising, how-to seminars, and many other tactics.

The cornerstone of this external strategy is strengthening customer relationships through outstanding service. "Customer service is our top priority," announces the company's World Wide Web home page. This statement is translated into action at every one of the company's 375 stores in North America.

Home Depot's staff of trained employees can answer virtually any question about home maintenance and remodeling. On any given day, customers can attend in-store seminars about installing faucets, wiring three-way switches, or laying patio blocks. Then they can browse among 50,000 products—with expert help at hand, ready to offer advice and guidance.

The company's internal marketing strategy is equally comprehensive. Home Depot treats its 70,000 employees like internal customers. The information system department maintains a help desk to answer questions from any employee. Support calls come from all kinds of workers: salespeople working with external customers, shippers on the loading dock, and managers on the service desk. This system gets fast, accurate information to Home Depot's empowered employees, who can then satisfy internal and external customers.

Working toward its longer-term goals of expanding to 500 stores and expanding beyond North America, Home Depot is using market segmentation to target attractive customer groups. One priority is building relationships with women customers, who make up half the customer base. Research indicates that women often initiate home improvement projects and that they are deeply involved in buying decisions. Also, many women handle all kinds of home improvement projects on their own. Responding to research about this segment's needs and expectations, Home Depot has made its stores a little quieter, widened the aisles, and begun displaying some products fully assembled.

Despite its success, Home Depot is not standing still. Its strategies are dynamic to meet the changing conditions in the marketplace and the evolving needs of new and existing customer segments. As a result, look for changes ahead as this do-it-yourself pioneer gets ready for the twenty-first century.[51]

Strategies and applications

1. What other marketing tactics would you recommend that Home Depot use to build relationships with women customers?

2. In addition to suppliers, employees, and customers, what other stakeholders should Home Depot target for establishing mutually beneficial long-term relationships? Why?

3. What do you think are Home Depot's core competencies? What functions do you think they should outsource or handle through strategic alliances? Why?

4. Some of Home Depot's products include components such as nickel cadmium batteries that must be recycled to protect the environment. What actions do you think the company should take to show community stakeholders its commitment to environmental protection?

5. What kinds of threats should Home Depot watch out for as it conducts a SWOT analysis? What kinds of opportunities?

6. Where in the value chain does a store such as Home Depot stand? Explain your answer.

Team project

With other students, analyze Home Depot's situation using the industry-competition model. Gather data for your analysis through the Internet or through library research. What threats do you see from potential entrants to the industry or from substitutes for the company's products? What do you estimate is the bargaining power of suppliers and customers? What can you learn about rivalry among Home Depot's competitors? Write a two-page report summarizing your findings, and include your team's recommendations for how Home Depot can meet competitive threats in the coming years.

http://www.hothothot.com

Marketing on the Net   Hot Sauces Sizzle on the Web

Fiery tastes are fueling sales at Hot Hot Hot, the California-based small business founded by entrepreneurs Monica and Perry Lopez. The original strategy was to open a modest store in Pasadena and stock hot sauces from around the world, targeting people who crave fiery foods.

Then, following a customer's suggestion, the Lopezes decided they could cost-effectively reach more customers by expanding onto the World Wide Web. The first day the Web site was active, the couple announced the grand opening by sending e-mail messages to an Internet news group for chili enthusiasts and to other related news groups. Just 30 minutes later, Hot Hot Hot had made its first cyberspace sale—to a customer on the East Coast. No longer was the company confined to serving store customers. By thinking big, Hot Hot Hot had expanded its business opportunities virtually overnight.

As part of Hot Hot Hot's external strategy, the company maintains an electronic catalog featuring hundreds of special sauces. What differentiates Hot Hot Hot from its competitors is the exceptionally large number of choices it offers in this single product category. The diversity of offerings is reflected in colorful brand names such as Hot Lava, Rica Red Habanero, and Ring of Fire.

Customers can find just the right sauce for their taste buds by conducting a search according to brand name, heat level, where the sauce comes from, and sauce ingredients. For customer convenience, orders can be placed through a simple electronic order form or by toll-free telephone.

The Lopezes stay in close contact with customers to track their needs, preferences, and complaints. They encourage a dialogue by inviting customers to submit comments and product reviews online. They also have a Frequent Fire Club to reward customer loyalty and continued purchasing. The purpose is to move beyond single transactions and bring customers back again and again, creating a series of mutually beneficial marketing exchanges that satisfy both marketers and customers.

The internal strategy is to build a relatively small team of knowledgeable employees who believe in quality and are dedicated to relationship building. The internal teamwork is geared toward satisfying customers both on and off the Web. With the help of a few staff members, the Lopezes are able to carefully read and respond to all e-mail messages received at the Hot Hot Hot Web site. At Christmas, they add temporary workers to their team so they can keep up with the orders that pour in from customers in New Zealand, Brazil, and other far-flung locations. Year-round "Gift of Fire" orders from customers keep the team busy, too.

The site has won awards for its user-friendly graphics and fun-loving attitude. As it has become better known, it has attracted a larger number of visitors. More than 1,500 people visit the Hot Hot Hot Web site every day. Instead of spending $50,000 to mail printed catalogs, the Lopezes spend about $100 in monthly Internet usage fees to interact with customers worldwide. "Our 300-square-foot store is now a global company," notes Monica Lopez. [1]

Strategies and applications

1. Visit the Hot Hot Hot Web site. How can the company make it easier for first-time visitors to learn about the products offered in the electronic catalog?

2. What do you think are Hot Hot Hot's core competencies? What should they consider outsourcing? Explain your answers.

3. Think about the suppliers who provide the hot sauces that Hot Hot Hot features in its catalog. How can the Lopezes use the Internet and the World Wide Web to strengthen relationships with these suppliers?

4. Sending relevant messages to members of Internet newsgroups is an inexpensive way to reach highly targeted market segments. What specific newsgroups would you suggest that Hot Hot Hot target for ongoing communication and participation? Why?

5. With what other Web sites would you recommend that the Lopezes create links in order to make the Hot Hot Hot Web site even more valuable and interesting for visitors? Why?

6. How can Hot Hot Hot apply total quality management to continuously improve its Web site and its customer service?

Team project

With other students, carefully review the Hot Hot Hot Web site and think about the company's current situation. What do you think are its strengths and weaknesses? What opportunities and threats does it face? Summarize your team's ideas in a brief written report or a presentation to your class.

http://www.sprintbiz.com

Marketing on the Net Sprint Is Calling All Business Callers

For a look at a truly world-class Web site, point your Web browser toward Sprint Business's home page. The new marketing vision is embodied in this Web site, an integral part of Sprint's marketing strategy to build long-term relationships with businesses, government agencies, and healthcare organizations that buy long-distance telephone services. Following the ABCs of marketing, Sprint seeks to delight its customers and help them delight *their* customers.

To do this, Sprint has set up its Web site as a convenient clearinghouse for information that helps organizations work smarter. In addition to posting business news, the site offers links to other useful Web sites. Need to know the current exchange rate for buying or selling Japanese yen? Want to make travel reservations? Interested in exploring career opportunities? It's all just a mouse-click away. And, of course, visitors are invited to read all about the benefits of Sprint telecommunication products.

Sue Sentell, vice president of marketing communications for Sprint Business, knows that when organizations go looking for information, they want something very specific—and they want it in a hurry. That's why Sprint's Web site has been designed to be straightforward as well as graphically inviting. "Everything on the site is focused around a very friendly-looking file cabinet," says Sentell. "The theme is targeted to the business community, and it downloads super quickly so people aren't wasting time waiting for complicated graphics."

In planning its Web site, Sprint wanted to allow as many visitors as possible to access all the information. So, despite the emphasis on attractive graphics, Sprint also offers a text-only version of the Web site, available at the click of a mouse. This avoids disappointing potential customers who aren't equipped with Netscape or another Web browser capable of handling graphics.

The look of the Web site has been carefully coordinated with Sprint's conventional IMC materials. Using marketing research and analysis, Sprint tracks the number of visits and the number of new customers brought in by the site. It also compares the cost of reaching people electronically with the cost of reaching the same number of people through advertising in brochures, newspapers, and magazines.

In this way, Sprint can determine how effectively its Web site is creating new customer relationships and keeping its brand name in front of prospective and current customers. It can also evaluate the cost of using the Web site for relationship building in the context of the cost-effectiveness of typical advertising media.

From the beginning, Sprint viewed the World Wide Web as more than an opportunity to build its brand name. The challenge was to develop the web as a valuable sales channel to reach Sprint's targeted customer segments. To date, the site has exceeded the marketer's expectations, opening the door to many new customer relationships and adding value to existing customer relationships. Now that's world-class marketing.[2]

Strategies and applications

1. Visit the Sprint Business site. How do the graphic elements reflect the organizational market that Sprint is targeting? What suggestions can you offer for enhancing the graphics to appeal to the target market?

2. What types of utility are being provided through Sprint's Web site? What do you think is the value of each utility to organizational customers?

3. How should Sprint invite specific comments about the usefulness of its Web site? Browse Sprint's site and evaluate its feedback form. What can you suggest to improve it?

4. Since many businesses have to deal with a local telephone service provider as well as a long-distance service provider, should Sprint's Web site contain links to local telephone companies? Why or why not?

5. Should Sprint's Web site include a head-to-head comparison of its services with competing services? What are the legal and ethical issues involved in such a comparison?

6. How does the Web site help Sprint communicate with the various segments it is targeting within the organizational market? Be specific.

Team project

With another student, visit the Web sites of Sprint's two major competitors, AT&T (http://www.att.com) and MCI (http://www.mci.com). How do these competitors reach out to organizational customers using their Web sites? Knowing how competitors use their Web sites, what can Sprint do to its Web site to compete more effectively?

internetempowerment

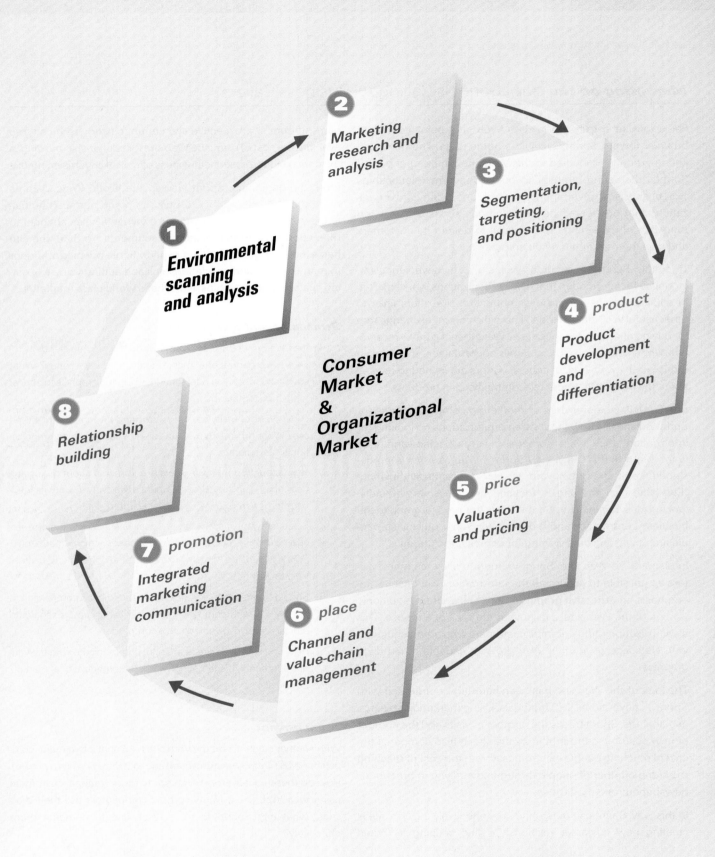

Environmental Scanning and Analysis

Part 2 explains the use of environmental scanning and analysis to understand the rapidly changing marketing environment inside and outside the organization. As discussed in Chapter 3, ethics and social responsibility are critical components of the marketing environment. The chapter opens with a profile of McDonald's, which constantly scans and analyzes its environment so that it can keep up with changes that affect marketing relationships. Chapter 4 examines the challenges and opportunities of building relationships by marketing across national boundaries and across cultures. The chapter opening profile follows Blockbuster's marketing plans for building relationships in global markets.

3

Environmental Analysis, Ethics, and Social Responsibility

Learning Goals

After you have read and studied this chapter, you should be able to:

1. Explain the uses of environmental scanning and environmental analysis, and distinguish between the internal and external environments.

2. Identify the factors in the internal environment that can influence marketing.

3. Analyze how demographic changes and cultural influences in the social environment affect marketing.

4. Explain why marketers need to analyze the political and technological environments.

5. Discuss how the economic environment affects marketing and identify the three forms of product competition.

6. Define marketing ethics and apply three questions to help resolve ethical issues in marketing.

7. Describe how marketers can apply social responsibility, and discuss the role of a social audit.

PROFILE

McDonald's appetite for environmental change

Hamburgers are still hot, and McDonald's isn't letting them cool off. The world's biggest fast-food chain has seen the future, and it extends beyond large sit-down restaurants on major intersections. Nowadays, up to 500 smaller McDonald's units are popping up inside gas stations, stores, and airports every year.

Why scale down and scatter fast-food outlets? The answer comes from changes in the marketing environment. The company's research showed that 75 percent of busy shoppers decide to visit a McDonald's just 5 minutes before they walk in. To be able to offer instant access when and where shoppers want to eat meant looking beyond traditional sites. Competitors such as Checkers Drive-In Restaurants were putting drive-throughs in prime but tiny locations where larger McDonald's outlets couldn't fit.

Understanding these trends helped McDonald's cook up a plan to follow customers through their busy days by opening small outlets inside Wal-Marts and Home Depots, and in other such locations. But opening smaller outlets isn't McDonald's only response to its environment. Seeing a slow-moving economy and value-conscious customers who need to stretch their budgets, the chain added a series of specially priced hamburger meals. It has also developed a special sandwich to appeal to adults and has made its hamburger patties larger.

As a good corporate citizen, McDonald's has teamed up with Conservation International to protect Central American rain forests. The chain also demands that its food suppliers follow strict guidelines for humane treatment of animals. The company isn't legally required to take these steps, just as it isn't required to open smaller restaurants. Nonetheless, McDonald's believes that ethics and social responsibility should be part of its profitable recipe for building relationships with customers, employees, and other stakeholders.[1]

In this chapter, you'll see how scanning, analyzing, and managing the marketing environment can help you make better marketing decisions. You'll also explore the many facets of the marketing environment, including internal, social, political, technological, economic, and competitive factors. Then you'll learn about marketing ethics and social responsibility, which are growing in importance for marketers all over the world.

Constant Change in the Marketing Environment

The movement for social responsibility [is] about balance. We are saying that short-term profits can no longer be the only motive in making business decisions, but must be balanced with the interests of our employees, our customers, our community and our natural environment.

Judy Wicks
owner of the White Dog Cafe

Never before in history has change been so fast and so dramatic. The only way marketers can stay ahead of such swift, profound change is to use environmental scanning and analysis, the first universal marketing process. As the marketing environment shifts, marketers can use this process to constantly monitor and decipher the changes.

Imagine what it's like to be a marketer in this situation:

Rapid, relentless, and uncertain change is the most unsettling marketplace reality that companies and people must cope with today. New products, even whole markets, appear, mutate, and disappear within shorter and shorter periods of time. The pace of innovation continues to quicken, and the direction of innovation is often unpredictable. Product variety has proliferated to a bewildering degree (Seiko markets 3,000 different watches; Philips sells more than 800 color TV models), and imitative competition is swift and profit destroying.[2]

Ignoring or misinterpreting the marketing environment can have serious consequences, even for the most sophisticated marketers. Walt Disney, for example, didn't pay close enough attention to its marketing environment when it announced plans for a Disney America history theme park in Virginia. Disney moved ahead quickly and forcefully without consulting local community organizations and history preservation societies, important stakeholder groups who opposed the plan. After months of bad publicity and opposition, Disney was forced to abandon the site.[3]

Major Change Factors Affecting Marketing's Future

Market leaders such as McDonald's have succeeded because they're customer-driven, technology-based, relationship-oriented organizations built on a foundation of quality, service, and value. But such companies may not remain leaders unless they stay attuned to the marketing environment. Here are seven of the major environmental challenges marketing managers now face:

1. *Change is constant and rapid.* Customers, rivals, and markets are moving targets. Everything is subject to change, and the pace of change is increasing. As a result, marketers need to respond quickly to both opportunities and challenges. Time itself has become a major competitive element.

2. *Competition is global.* Just as customers can cross geographic borders to deal with marketers, marketers can cross borders to meet their customers. Competing in such a boundaryless environment requires world-class marketing.

3. *Technology is dramatically changing marketing exchanges.* Integrated marketing communication, product development, and virtually every aspect of marketing have been touched by advances in information technology, telecommunication, and so on. The challenge is to study these new technologies and use them to serve customers better and faster.

Technological change continues to have a dramatic impact on companies and competition throughout the world. This woman, who works for a knitting company in Philadelphia, Pennsylvania, is using computer-aided design (CAD) software to design a sweater. Computers and software now make it possible to turn out customized goods quickly and efficiently and thus to be more responsive to the wants and needs of individual customers. Which recent technological changes have had the greatest effect on you and your friends as you have interacted with marketers?

4. *Collaboration is as important as competition.* Marketers need to move beyond the question of whom to beat. They also need to figure out whom to join. Alliances with competitors, suppliers, governments, unions, even customers, can help marketers compete more effectively and strengthen stakeholder relationships.

5. *Quality isn't optional, it's standard.* International quality standards such as ISO 9000 require marketers to meet uniformly high levels of quality before they can enter certain markets. That's why more marketers are adopting total quality management ◄──┘ **(p. 48)**.

6. *The focus is on the individual.* Mass production, mass media, and mass marketing efforts are often being replaced. Products, media, and marketing can be and are being tailored to the needs of individual customers, a process made easier by technology.[4]

7. *An ethical and socially responsible approach to marketing is critical.* Relationship building is based on trust and reliability. Unethical or irresponsible marketers will soon lose market share. New global environmental standards will soon be widely adopted.

These factors give you a flavor of what's in store for marketing managers in the twenty-first century. It will be necessary to monitor world markets as well as local conditions, adapting to the constant shifts. To do this means understanding both the internal and external factors in the marketing environment.

Internal and External Factors in the Marketing Environment

marketing environment

all the internal and external factors that directly or indirectly influence a marketer's success

The **marketing environment** consists of all the internal and external factors that directly or indirectly influence a marketer's success. Although marketers can influence some of the factors in the marketing environment, others are largely beyond their control. For instance, marketers have little direct influence over their competitors. What's more, the marketing environment is constantly changing, creating uncertainty, opportunities, and threats. Therefore, conducting a SWOT analysis ◄──┘ **(p. 36)** is critical to understanding how environmental changes may affect the marketer's ability to satisfy its stakeholders.

internal environment

the set of factors inside the marketer's value chain that can influence marketing success

external environment

the set of factors outside the marketer's value chain that can influence marketing success

Marketers must monitor both the internal and external marketing environment. The **internal environment** consists of the set of factors inside the marketer's value chain that can influence marketing success. Members of the internal environment include employees, stockholders, and partners, as shown in Figure 3.1. For example, PepsiCo markets soft drinks and snacks, and operates fast-food restaurants, including Kentucky Fried Chicken. Adapting to Pepsi's internal environment involves training 400,000 *employees*, providing returns to 147,000 *stockholders*, and working closely with franchise owners, who are *partners*.[5]

F I G U R E **3.1** **The Internal and External Environment for Marketing**

No marketing decision or action occurs in a vacuum. Factors in the internal and external marketing environments affect what marketers can do. To monitor changes in these factors, marketers use environmental scanning and analysis. In addition, every marketing manager needs to apply marketing ethics and social responsibility when making marketing decisions.

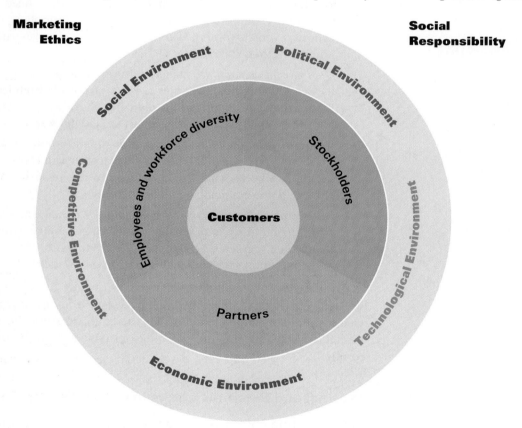

The **external environment** is the set of factors outside the marketer's value chain that can influence marketing success. Some of the factors in the external environment that can affect Pepsi are societal pressures for healthier products (*social factors*), government food regulations (*political factors*), new artificial sweeteners (*technological factors*), customer spending (*economic factors*), and actions taken by Coca-Cola (*competitive factors*).

TABLE **3.1** Sources for an Environmental Scan

Internal Sources	External Sources
Employees (through meetings, suggestions, surveys, memos)	Government agencies (through publications and direct contact)
Organizational records (of sales and other activities)	Scholarly, professional, business, and general publications
Organizational newsletters and other communications	Computerized online databases
Board of directors (through meetings and other communications)	Trade associations
	Trade shows and conferences
	Unions
	Industry consultants
	Customers (through suggestions, complaints, compliments)
	Better Business Bureau and other regulatory bodies
	Stockholders (through meetings and communications)
	Chamber of Commerce groups

Scanning and Analyzing the Environment

To better understand marketing trends and prepare for an appropriate response, you need to continually gather information about the environment and examine its effect on stakeholders. *Environmental scanning* is the process of identifying internal and external factors that can affect marketing success. *Environmental analysis* is the process of interpreting, evaluating, and sharing information about the environment with all employees.

Information for an environmental scan comes from a variety of sources, some inside and some outside the organization, as shown in Table 3.1. Of course, the sheer volume of data gathered in an environmental scan can be overwhelming, preventing marketers from incorporating everything into their strategies. That's why analysts identify the specific changes that are likely to affect marketing success now or in the future.

An environmental analysis examines the meaning of information uncovered in an environmental scan. Then, having analyzed the data, marketers can apply what they've learned, enabling them to guard against threats and take advantage of opportunities to build stakeholder relationships.

Managing Change to Build Stakeholder Relationships

There are two approaches to managing changes in the marketing environment. The first approach is to be *reactive*, taking steps to adapt to environmental factors that can't be controlled or influenced. For example, Vitro, a $3 billion Mexican manufacturer, saw that rising local incomes were fueling demand for consumer products. The expanded market, in turn, was attracting more competitors. In response, Vitro found partners to provide innovative technologies for upgrading operations and making new products. It also reduced its dependence on sales in Mexico by branching out into other markets, buying a U.S. competitor, and forming alliances with Whirlpool and other global marketers.[6]

In the second, or *proactive* approach to change, you seek ways to influence your environment when you think you can modify or shape certain factors. For example, computer software giant Microsoft is proactive in creating new technology. One of its top priorities is to shape the information superhighway, which is dramatically changing the way people work and live.[7] The choice to be proactive or reactive depends on the marketer's situation and the environmental forces that it confronts. Here's how a group of high school students parlayed proactive marketing into a successful business based in a difficult environment.

SMALL BUSINESS WATCH

Proactive marketing in the inner city

Every kind of organization can practice proactive marketing. A case in point is Food from the 'Hood, an organization formed by students at Crenshaw High School in Los Angeles. As a school project, the teens renovated a garden behind the inner-city school. Then they started a company to manage the garden as part of an effort to rebuild the riot-torn city and to provide money for college. They planned to give one-quarter of the produce to needy families and use the profits from selling the remainder to award themselves scholarships. However, the first year's profits came to $600, which funded only three scholarships.

Marketers can have a positive affect on the cities and town where they are located. For example, Food From the 'Hood' feeds needy people and uses some of its revenue to send children to college. Individuals with marketing expertise can improve their communities by consulting with start-up companies and helping them grow, providing more jobs. Are there any new companies in your area that could benefit from your assistance? What other proactive steps could other marketers take to improve your community?

At that point, the teens became more proactive. They realized that they could raise more scholarship money with a branded product that was widely marketed. With a state grant, they hired a marketing expert who came up with the idea of marketing a bottled salad dressing. Publicity about the project attracted Norris Bernstein, a successful salad-dressing entrepreneur, who volunteered his services. Bernstein helped the teens sort through issues such as relationships with retailers, and he introduced them to influential people in the food and supermarket industries.

These relationships helped the students get their first product, a creamy Italian dressing, into local grocery chains. Now Lucky Stores, Vons, and nearly every other southern California supermarket carries the product. But the students aren't keeping their energies bottled up. They're looking ahead to rebuilding more of their neighborhood. Using some of their profits, they plan to renovate a greenhouse behind the school and use it to raise basil for their dressing. That's another sign of proactive marketing in the inner city.[8]

Make marketing decisions

1. Does Food from the 'Hood salad dressing face competition from other bottled salad dressings? What would you do to investigate these competitive products?

2. If you were running Food from the 'Hood, would you let customers know how the profits would be used? Why or why not?

3. What are Food from the 'Hood's strengths and weaknesses?

4. Given the company's core competence in food products, what do you think its second product should be? Why?

The Changing Internal Marketing Environment

One of the most important influences on any marketer's success is the internal environment. After all, your organization can't delight customers if your employees aren't enthusiastic about what they do and how they do it. At the most basic level, this means using internal marketing ◄——▐ **(p. 9)** to meet the needs of employees so they can meet the needs of customers. "We discovered a long time ago that customer satisfaction really begins with employee satisfaction," notes Frederick Smith, the founder and CEO of Federal Express. "That belief is incorporated in our corporate philosophy statement: People—Service—Profit."[9]

You'll want to be proactive in handling three areas within the internal environment: (1) employees and workforce diversity, (2) relationships with stockholders, and (3) relationships with suppliers and other partners.

Building Relationships with Employees and the Workforce

The more you know about what motivates your employees, the better you can design proactive internal marketing programs that fulfill their needs. Then they can concentrate on fulfilling customers' needs. Regular surveys and other research techniques can help you learn what *your* employees want and expect.[10]

How do organizations show employees that their work is important? When *Family Circle* presented its Car of the Year Award to Nissan, the automaker didn't advertise the honor to the general public. Instead, it used the award as part of an internal marketing program designed to boost morale throughout the company.[11] Nissan managers realized that employees who know that their product is appreciated will feel good about themselves.

Organizations have to go beyond award programs and understand *who* their employees are. The U.S. workforce is undergoing major changes as more women and minorities enter the labor pool. Government projections show that white males, who accounted for 51 percent of the U.S. workforce in 1980, will account for just 44 percent by 2005, as shown in Figure 3.2 .[12] In fact, many human resources managers say that workforce diversity gives their companies a competitive advantage.[13]

F I G U R E **3.2** **Workforce Diversity in the United States**

The U.S. workforce is becoming increasingly diverse. As a result, management of diversity has become an important priority for marketers.

Share of Total U.S. Labor Force (16 years and older)

	White males	White females	Blacks	Hispanics	Asians and others
1980	51	36	10	6	NA
1993	47	38	11	8	NA
2005 (projected)	44	39	12	11	4

■ 1980 ■ 1993 ■ 2005 (projected)

Data totals more than 100% because Hispanics are counted in other segments of the population

For example, Hallmark (the number one greeting card company) recently doubled the number of greeting cards geared toward African American customers, thanks to ideas from its diverse workforce. To account for such nuances as the preference for "Mama" and "Daddy" instead of "Mother" and "Father," Hallmark turned to its African American designers and staffers. It also solicited opinions from African American employees in other departments.[14]

Building Relationships with Stockholders

A publicly held company—one whose stock is traded on a stock exchange—has a strong incentive to build long-term relationships with its *stockholders*, the people or institutions that own shares of its stock. If stockholders are satisfied with a company's profitability, policies, and social responsiveness, they'll buy and hold shares of its stock. If not, they will sell them—depriving the company of needed funding. Another pair of reasons for strengthening this relationship is as follows: to relieve stockholder pressure for short-term profits and to gain support for strategies that build profits over the long term.

Large institutions such as the California Public Employees' Retirement System hold a sizable block of shares in many companies. They can make their voices heard even when companies don't like the message. In fact, pressure from *institutional investors* disappointed with company results helped to unseat top executives at IBM and American Express and led to marketing changes at both companies. By building strong relationships with institutional investors, marketers can retain the confidence and investments of these important stakeholders.[15]

Issues for critical thinking

If you held stock in Walt Disney, would you favor a long-term or a short-term perspective on marketing? If the company had to sacrifice profits for two years to invest in new theme parks—depressing the stock price and lowering dividends—would you hold or sell your shares of the stock? How could Disney influence your decision?

Building Relationships with Partners

Suppliers, dealers, and banks are key partners whose cooperation can give you a *collaborative advantage*, an edge you gain because of strong relationships with partners. Carmakers, for example, have to consider the needs of the dealers that sell their products as well as the suppliers that provide the parts. So Honda teaches its suppliers how to boost productivity because "ultimately, that makes us a better company," explains Honda executive Richard Mayo.[16] Here's how Levi Strauss builds partnerships with overseas suppliers.

GLOBAL ISSUES

Levi's sews up supplier and community relationships

Stitching together a loyal, capable group of suppliers takes time, patience, and internal marketing. But Levi Strauss, maker of Levi's jeans, Dockers clothing, and Britannia pants, takes the long view to maintaining supplier relationships. With brand competition from Lee, Wrangler, and Rustler heating up, Levi's simply can't afford to take its partners for granted.

One sticky issue Levi's had to resolve was its stance with respect to international suppliers' labor practices. A supplier in Dhaka, Bangladesh, employed children as young as 11 to sew Dockers pants. Levi's objected, pointing to International Labor Organization standards that set the minimum employment age at 14. The supplier countered that many of the child workers were their family's only wage earners and their salaries were important.

To resolve the issue, Levi's agreed to pay for the children to return to school if the supplier would continue paying wages, then rehire the children when they reached 14. This satisfied the parents of the children, the supplier, and Levi's—and cost just a few thousand dollars. It also allowed the company to maintain its good public image. For Levi's, and for every other global marketer, having good supplier relations translates into better sales, more satisfied customers, and better community relations.[17]

Can you think of another way this conflict could have been resolved?

Banks can also help organizations grow. Jennifer Norrid's relationship with First National Bank in Albuquerque helped her company, PC Support, grow to $1.2 million in sales. Although Norrid could save $1,200 by changing banks, she won't. "I concluded that the relationship I had was worth a lot more to me than $1,200," she says.[18]

Before you go on . . .

A. What are seven major environmental changes marketing managers are now facing?

B. How does the external environment affect marketing?

C. Why do marketers need to establish strong relationships with employees, stockholders, and partners?

The Social Environment for Marketing

social environment

the set of characteristics, cultural elements, and attitudes that affect customers' perceptions of and reactions to marketers

The **social environment** is the set of characteristics, cultural elements, and attitudes that affect customers' perceptions of and reactions to marketers. Among the most important factors in the social environment are demographic changes and cultural influences.

demography

the study and measurement of a population as described by such factors as age, gender, birthrate, education, family size, income, nationality, race, and occupation

Adapting to Demographic Changes

You can get a sense of who your customers are and what their lives are like by doing a demographic analysis. **Demography** is the study and measurement of a population as described by such factors as age, gender, birthrate, education, family size, income, nationality, race, and occupation. Keeping up on demographic changes helps reveal the possible future demand for certain types of products. For example, a survey conducted by the Bureau of Labor Statistics found that households headed by 35- to 44-year-olds spend more on clothing than do other households. Translating this demographic data into marketing action, Liz Claiborne, Giorgio Armani, and other apparel marketers are well advised to put extra marketing emphasis on people in this age group.

Demographics are constantly changing as people are born, grow up, go to work, get married, move, and start families. This makes the customer a moving target, which you and every other marketer must continually watch and analyze. In the United States, major demographic trends include changes in the population and shifts among various states, cities, and regions.

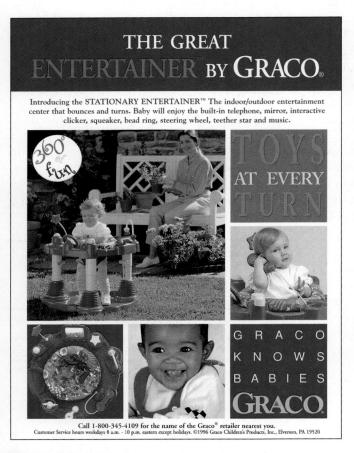

Demographic changes in the population greatly affect companies like Graco. Its entertainment centers are geared toward young toddlers. If birthrates decline, what can Graco do to maintain its growth in sales? How important is environmental scanning and marketing research to companies that cater to toddlers?

Reacting to Population Changes

Population growth in the United States continues in the 1990s. One-third of the growth is coming from increased immigration and two-thirds from a healthy birthrate. Nearly one million legal immigrants (and many illegal immigrants) enter the United States every year. However, this number may drop as a result of a backlash against immigration. Since, in addition, the birthrate is expected to decline slightly through the year 2000, *American Demographics* projects that the population will grow only modestly from the 1995 figure of 262 million.[19]

By 2000, more than half the U.S. population will be over 35, a big change from 1970, when the median age was 28. As the population ages, its needs change and so does its income. Americans over age 50 control half the nation's discretionary income (money left after necessities are paid for). By 2030, all baby boomers (people born between 1946 and 1964) will be senior citizens—one in five Americans, compared with one in eight today.[20]

Population trends are important because they determine the size of the market for products geared toward specific age groups or particular ethnic or racial segments. For example, the large number of youngsters in the U.S. population presented a profitable opportunity for entrepreneur Richard Caudle. Meeting the needs of this expanding group helped Caudle build a successful educational audiocassette business called Rock 'n' Learn.[21]

Recognizing Population Centers and Shifts

Where are your customers today—and where will they be tomorrow? The answer can be found in population movements, which you can analyze to determine where customer groups tend to live and where they move. Overall, the most populous state in the nation is California, followed by Texas, New York, and Florida. African American population centers include areas in and around New York City, Chicago, Washington, D.C., and Los Angeles. Los Angeles, New York City, and Miami are Hispanic American population centers. The Asian American population is highest in Los Angeles, New York City, and Honolulu. And the Northeast is growing more slowly as people move west and south, according to Figure 3.3.[22]

F I G U R E   **3.3**   **Population Shifts in the United States**

People are constantly on the move, not only within the United States but among countries. By following such patterns, marketers can anticipate the growth of some markets and the decline of others and make needed adjustments in marketing strategy. Here you see that a state's population can increase due to births and immigration, even when the state experiences a net out-migration (more people move out than move in). Note that two states—Connecticut and Rhode Island—had an overall loss in population, 1994 to 1995.

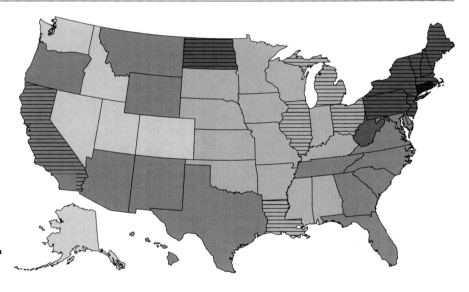

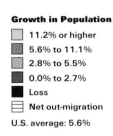

Growth in Population
- 11.2% or higher
- 5.6% to 11.1%
- 2.8% to 5.5%
- 0.0% to 2.7%
- Loss
- Net out-migration

U.S. average: 5.6%

These shifts create opportunities for marketers that operate or target groups in specific geographic areas. Where areas are gaining new residents, marketers can put up homes and commercial buildings, offer home furnishings, sell more clothing, and so on. At the same time, the shifts create financial challenges for the areas that are losing taxpayers to the new population centers, such as Washington, D.C. Think of the implications for marketers that are either losing or gaining potential employees and customers.

Adapting to Cultural Influences

Culture is the set of values and beliefs shared by a group of people and passed down from one generation to the next. A *subculture* is a separate group within a dominant culture that preserves its own unique values and lifestyle. Your customers' culture (or subculture) influences the way they buy and use products, which is why you need to consider cultural influences when you plan marketing activities.

culture

the set of values and beliefs shared by a group of people and passed down from one generation to the next

TABLE **3.2**   **Cultural Diversity in the United States**

Cultural Group	Population (in millions)	Percentage of Total
White, non-Hispanic	193	73.7
Black, non-Hispanic	31	11.8
Asian, non-Hispanic	9	3.4
Hispanic	26	9.9
Native American, Eskimo, and Aleut, non-Hispanic	2	0.8
Total U.S. population	262	100

Note: Hispanics may be of any race. Numbers in columns do not add to totals due to rounding.

Making the Most of Cultural Diversity

The United States, like many countries, is a culturally diverse marketplace within which numerous subcultures flourish, as shown in Table 3.2. Heavy immigration and high population growth in certain subcultures mean that ethnic minorities will soon make up half the population in some age categories. Far from being the traditional "melting pot" where people of various backgrounds blend together, today the country is home to many subcultures that treasure their original values, heritages, and languages. As a result, marketers must make their activities relevant to a subculture's tradition if they want to communicate with that group.[23]

Welcoming cultural diversity has helped Your DeKalb Farmers Market in DeKalb, Illinois, grow to sales of more than $50 million. Market employees come from some 36 countries and wear name tags such as "Patel, I speak Gujarati and Hindi," which encourages a diverse group of customers to mingle and shop.[24]

Issues for critical thinking

Some U.S. cities have newspapers, radio stations, and television stations that present news and entertainment in Spanish and other languages. In some cities, government forms are printed in two or more languages. Can you think of other ways in which language affects marketing and marketing affects language?

Social changes reflect the more subjective (yet measurable) behaviors, beliefs, lifestyles, attitudes, and character of society at large. Major social changes that are affecting marketing in the United States include redefined households, women in the workplace, and two-income families.

Finding Opportunity in Redefined Households

A *household* is a family, or two or more non–family members, living together. In 1960 more than half of all U.S. family households included three or more members. By 1990, however, the traditional family of two parents and two children represented only 7 percent of all U.S. households. Today, most family households have two or fewer members, and well over half of all new households are set up by single individuals. Smaller households mean more individual units and the opportunity to market more basic household items and furniture.[25]

Responding to Women in the Workplace

As recently as 1969, only 49 percent of the women between the ages of 25 to 54 worked outside the home. The percentage is expected to rise to 81 percent by the year 2000. Many women actively pursue careers for the same reasons as their male counterparts (self-fulfillment, financial security, and so on). Also, because of changing social attitudes toward both marriage and divorce, many women are returning to work to support their children. In addition, the number of female-owned companies is growing.[26] Working women create marketing opportunities for goods and services that save precious time and solve problems such as the need for affordable day care and home-delivered meals.

Responding to the Needs of Two-Income Families

The inability of many households to live on just one income has led to a dramatic growth in two-income families. One result of this trend—the absence of both parents from the home during the work week—has led to changes in attitudes and beliefs. For example, some working parents feel concern about being away from their families and want their children to learn independence. Marketers have reacted to these changes by providing after-school programs and activities. Retailers at local malls notice higher spending by young teens as some parents try to provide their sons and daughters with material goods. These shifts present opportunities for many marketers.

The Political Environment for Marketing

No matter what or where you market, you're subject to the rapidly changing **political environment**, the governmental rules, policies, and legal rulings that influence marketing. Local, state, and federal laws and regulations, and court rulings, are designed to protect consumers, promote fair competition, and improve the natural environment. A positive public image is based, in part, on how closely you follow these rules. The reputation of Food Lion, a supermarket chain, was tarnished after a television program criticized the company's food-handling techniques, which are under government regulation. The company quickly started a wide-ranging quality control program, but its reputation had been damaged. Food Lion's growth slowed, and its profits and stock price suffered.[27]

Today, organizations need to monitor hundreds—sometimes thousands—of laws and rules governing product safety, product labeling and packaging, transportation, communication with customers, and other marketing concerns. As a marketer, you should scan your environment for legislation, regulation, court rulings, and political influences that can affect your actions.

Legislation and Marketing

Early in U.S. history marketers had few legal or regulatory guidelines to follow. Then, late in the nineteenth century, laws such as the Interstate Commerce Act and the Sherman Antitrust Act were passed to promote fair competition.[28] This new regulatory climate widened consumer choice and encouraged businesses to compete vigorously yet fairly, priorities that remain part of the marketing environment today. Software marketer Microsoft is one of several big companies that have been scrutinized under antitrust

political environment

governmental rules, policies, and legal rulings that influence marketing

TABLE **3.3**   Major Federal Laws Affecting Marketing

Legislation	Effects on Marketers
Sherman Antitrust Act (1890)	Outlaws some anticompetitive practices
Pure Food and Drug Act (1906)	Sets purity and labeling requirements for food and drug products
Clayton Antitrust Act (1914)	Prohibits additional anticompetitive practices; more specific than the Sherman Act
Federal Trade Commission Act (1914)	Outlaws unfair and deceptive practices
Robinson–Patman Act (1936)	Prohibits price discrimination
Food, Drug, and Cosmetics Act (1938)	Regulates food, drug, and cosmetics companies
Lanham Act (1946)	Protects trademarks and brand names
Truth in Lending Act (1968)	Protects consumers by regulating credit granting
Consumer Product Safety Act (1972)	Establishes formal regulation of product safety
Alcohol Labeling (1988)	Requires health warning labels on alcoholic beverages
Nutrition Labeling Education Act (1990)	Requires uniform and truthful food labeling

laws in recent years. The company was forced to change the way computer makers pay for preloaded Microsoft programs.[29] In addition to antitrust legislation, federal laws such as those listed in Table 3.3 protect consumers and businesses and affect marketing activities.

- *Consumer protection.* Marketers must comply with laws that protect consumers from price discrimination, unhealthy or unsafe products, and unfair business practices. The first push for consumer protection came with the passage of the Pure Food and Drug Act in 1906, setting purity and labeling standards for food and drug products. A second push came in the 1950s and 1960s with the rise of **consumerism**, a movement to promote the rights and powers of buyers in relation to marketers as listed in Table 3.4. Recent federal laws have improved food labeling and required businesses and government agencies to accommodate people with disabilities.

- *Business protection.* Brand names and logos can be registered and protected from improper use by the Lanham Act. Patented products are protected by laws that bar unauthorized copying or use for 17 years. Written, musical, and artistic works can be copyrighted to protect against illegal copying or use.

TABLE **3.4**   The Consumer Movement

President John F. Kennedy declared that consumers are entitled to four basic consumer rights:

1. The *right to safety* mandates that products not be hazardous.
2. The *right to be informed* holds that consumers should be given information about products and their proper usage.
3. The *right to choose* assures consumers that they have the freedom to decide among many products in the marketplace.
4. The *right to be heard* allows consumers to express their needs, expectations, and displeasure.

consumerism

a movement to promote the rights and powers of buyers in relation to marketers

- *Pricing regulation.* Unfair pricing can destroy competition and boost prices. The Robinson–Patman Act prohibits price discrimination that hurts competition or leads to a monopoly. The Miller–Tydings Act, later modified by the Consumer Goods Pricing Act, aims for fair price competition between large and small marketers.[30]

- *Marketing communication regulation.* Laws such as the Truth-in-Lending Act and the Truth-in-Savings Act require financial service marketers to communicate the full costs and returns of credit and savings products. The American Automobile Labeling Act requires carmakers to tell U.S. consumers where components come from and where the vehicles are assembled.[31] Other laws govern telephone sales, ban tobacco ads on television and radio, and require health warnings on tobacco and alcohol packages.

Regulations Affecting Marketing

Federal lawmakers have created a variety of regulatory agencies, some of which are listed in Table 3.5, to protect consumers and businesses from deceptive or unfair actions. Some agencies watch over particular industries. For example, the National Highway Traffic Safety Administration (NHTSA) oversees motor vehicles and the Food and Drug Administration (FDA) oversees food and drug products.

TABLE **3.5** Major Federal Agencies That Regulate Marketing

Agency	Function
Consumer Products Safety Commission (CPSC)	Enforces laws that protect consumers from harmful products
Environmental Protection Agency (EPA)	Regulates business practices to prevent pollution
Federal Communications Commission (FCC)	Regulates communication by wire, radio, telephone, and television
Federal Trade Commission (FTC)	Enforces laws that prevent unfair and deceptive practices
Food and Drug Administration (FDA)	Enforces laws that maintain purity and safety in food and drug products

Other agencies regulate activities that cross industry boundaries. The Federal Trade Commission (FTC) is charged with watching for misleading or unfair marketing actions in any industry. It can force marketers to change or stop deceptive advertising or to run ads correcting false impressions made by earlier ads. That's why Steve Bronstein, who photographs Domino's Pizza ads, can't show more than 27 pepperoni slices on a large pie. Showing more might be construed as an attempt to mislead consumers if evidence were offered that the pizzas have fewer slices.

For the past 30 years, the U.S. government has moved toward *deregulation*, changing or loosening regulations to encourage freer competition within an industry. Deregulation of the telecommunications industry broke up AT&T and did away with fixed, regulated pricing, which spurred long-distance telephone competition from MCI and Sprint, among others. The Telecommunications Act of 1996 broke down the barriers between local and long-distance calling, cable TV, broadcasting, and wireless services. Competition is now wide open.[32] Similar changes during deregulation of the airline industry brought dozens of new companies into the field, increasing competition. However, some of the newer competitors—such as People's Express and New York Air—didn't survive the competition. Some pioneers, like Eastern Airlines, also went under, unable to cut costs enough to keep their prices competitive in a deregulated environment.

A major influence on consumers, who feel that its information is unbiased and accurate, is *Consumer Reports*. This box, which appears in every issue of the magazine, shows why *Consumer Reports* is such a trusted source. What other sources do you, as a consumer, turn to for information before buying major goods and services?

Court Rulings

A third layer in the political, regulatory, and legal environment is the effect of court rulings, which can be time-consuming, costly, and damaging to a marketer's image. After a jury decided against McDonald's in a lawsuit brought by a customer who was scalded by the chain's hot coffee, Dunkin' Donuts and other marketers reviewed their procedures to see whether changes in coffee temperature were advisable.[33] Transporting raw materials that can harm the environment is another area receiving closer attention after a jury assessed $5 billion in punitive damages for the 1989 oil spill from the oil tanker *Exxon Valdez*.[34]

Even small marketing details, like the look and color of a product package, have important legal implications. Chesebrough-Ponds, maker of Vaseline Intensive Care moisturizers, recently sued Venture Stores over packaging of the chain's private-brand moisturizer. The Venture package was so much like that of Vaseline Intensive Care that Chesebrough-Ponds charged the store with infringing its copyright. A lower court ruled for Chesebrough, but a federal court reversed that ruling; then the reversal was appealed.[35] The moral of the story: Watch court rulings carefully to see how your marketing may be affected.

The facts you need before you choose

Consumer Reports is published by Consumers Union, an independent, nonprofit testing and information organization serving only consumers. We are a comprehensive source for unbiased advice about products and services, personal finance, health and nutrition, and other consumer concerns. Since 1936, our mission has been to test products, inform the public, and protect consumers. Our income is derived solely from the sale of CONSUMER REPORTS and our other services, and from nonrestrictive, noncommercial contributions, grants, and fees.

We buy all the products we test on the open market. Our shoppers go into the stores and buy the products off the shelf, just as you do; we receive no special treatment. We accept no free samples; if a manufacturer sends us a free product, we send it right back.

We test products in 50 state-of-the art labs at our National Research and Testing Center in Yonkers, N.Y. Our Ratings are based on lab tests, controlled-use tests, and expert judgments by our technical and research staff. If a product is high in overall quality and relatively low in price, we deem it a **CR Best Buy**. A Rating refers only to the brand and model listed.

We survey our millions of readers to bring you information on the reliability of hundreds of auto models and of major products like appliances and electronic gear. Reader-survey data also help us rate insurance and other consumer services.

We report on current issues of concern to consumers. Our staff of researchers and editors brings you in-depth information on matters that affect your health, your money, and your well-being as a consumer.

We accept no ads from companies. We do advertise our own services, which provide impartial information and advice to consumers. We don't let any company use our reports or Ratings for commercial purposes. If that happens, we insist that the company stop, and take whatever additional steps are open to us.

Illustrations by Mike Quon Design Office

Other Influences

Other influences on marketing come from elected officials, consumers, businesses, unions, and other individuals or groups. *Special interest groups* are organizations of people who work together to take action on particular issues. Nearly every cause has spawned special interest groups, from environmental issues and nuclear power to gay rights and gun control. Since some of these special interest groups can influence your stakeholders, their views are important to your success.

Millions of readers depend on the Consumers Union magazine *Consumer Reports*, for example, as a source of straight talk and advice about goods and services. As a result, the magazine—like the media outlets of other special interest groups—can influence the actions of marketers whose products are reviewed.

In some cases, the industry itself exerts pressure on businesses to conform to acceptable marketing practices.

Self-regulation can take the form of voluntary guidelines for advertising and other activities. The National Advertising Review Board is one of several industry groups helping to maintain high standards of truth and accuracy in advertising.[36]

In addition, each country can influence marketing through trade agreements, regulations, and pressures that foster or hinder product movement across national borders. Pressure to buy local products, such as the "Buy American" movement, can also affect global marketing success.

Marketers can influence the political, regulatory, and legal environment in two ways. The first is by *lobbying*, the process of persuading public officials to enact, defeat, or change particular laws. Lobbyists meet with legislators and their staff members to provide facts, figures, and background about relevant political issues. The second is through *political action committees (PACs)*, groups that contribute to the campaigns of candidates running for public office. PACs support politicians who will listen to their views and represent their interests in government.[37]

Before you go on . . .

A. Define demographics and explain its effect on marketing.

B. Give an example of a cultural or subcultural influence on marketing.

C. What is deregulation and how can it influence marketing?

D. What are special interest groups and how do they affect marketers?

The Technological Environment for Marketing

Everywhere you look, you can see evidence of the **technological environment**, innovations and new ideas from scientific or engineering research that help marketers satisfy customers in a new or better way. Apple's first personal computer and Sony's first Walkman cassette player were developed to satisfy customer needs not being met by other products. Apple, Sony, and many other companies maintain research and development departments that continually work on new processes, tools, and materials. Moreover, research by government laboratories and nonprofit organizations benefits customers through new products, higher quality, better service, and improved productivity.

Thanks to new technology, marketers are now able quickly to give customers what they want—customized for each customer's unique requirements. For example, Cannondale will make a bicycle that fits a customer's exact size and weight. Cannondale's computerized manufacturing system turns out a custom bike in hours rather than weeks or months.[38] Technology also helps marketers communicate using new media such as interactive television and CD-ROM catalogs that bring information to customers when and where they want it.

technological environment

innovations and new ideas from scientific or engineering research that help marketers satisfy customers in a new or better way

Technological Innovation

Innovation can help marketers compete more effectively by offering customers a better solution to their problems. It also allows marketers to overcome competitive barriers to entering new industries. What's more, technological innovation has changed the way companies design, produce, and market goods and services. For example, Elektrobit, a small business in Finland, recently applied leading-edge technology to develop the world's first cellular pay telephone.[39]

In addition, marketers of all sizes are using the latest in technology to communicate with their customers. The owner of Allawos Mikana Manufacturing, a small tool-and-die shop in California, uses a laptop computer to transmit orders and verify parts availability right from the customer's office. Pizza Hut uses information technology to capture customer phone orders, track what its 9 million customers request, and then mail offers that appeal to those specific tastes.[40]

Technological Standards

In many industries, the technological environment also includes specific product or industry standards that you must meet if you want to compete. For example, a videotape must be VHS-compatible to play in nearly every videocassette machine sold in the United States, regardless of its brand. In addition, industry standards for high-definition television and other emerging technologies are shaping the product development activities of many marketers. Also, global quality standards such as ISO 9000 greatly affect technological products marketed in other countries, as you'll see in Chapter 4.

The Economic Environment for Marketing

The **economic environment** is the set of economic factors that influence customer buying and organizational marketing efforts. These economic factors include business cycles, levels of income and employment, and availability of resources. Even though you as a marketer can't control such factors, you need to think about how the changing economy influences demand for your products and how it changes access to resources such as supplies.

The Business Cycle, Employment, and Income

The **business cycle** is the pattern of economic activity created by successive stages of prosperity, recession, and recovery. This up-and-down cycle influences how businesses operate, the number of people hired or fired, and consumers' buying decisions. During periods of prosperity, the *gross domestic product (GDP)*—the total value of all goods and services produced in the country—grows at a healthy level. Businesses invest in new facilities and products, creating new jobs. Consumers spend more, fueling demand and spurring more business expansion.

During a recession, production slows and less money is available for investment. Businesses cut back their spending, stop hiring, and start laying people off as fewer orders come in. Consumers pass up expensive products and buy basic goods and services that offer maximum value for the money.

economic environment
the set of economic factors that influence customer buying and organizational marketing efforts

business cycle
the pattern of economic activity created by successive stages of prosperity, recession, and recovery

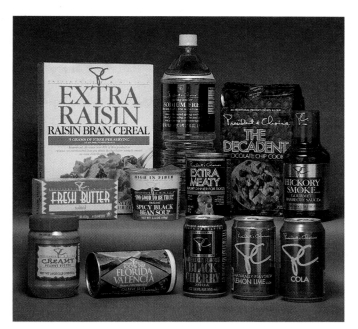

When the economic outlook is unfavorable, some consumers turn to private brands in order to get more value for their dollar. Why don't consumers typically seek such value when they have more disposable income? What value does buying brand names add to goods and services? What could retailers of private brands do, if anything, to increase your value perception of private brands?

During recessions, more customers seek out *private brand products*—items that bear the store's brand rather than a manufacturer's brand and usually are priced lower than manufacturer brands. Private brand products, which account for about half of J.C. Penney's sales, generated enough profits to help the department store weather the 1990–1991 recession.[41] When the economy shifts into recovery, on an upswing from a recession to prosperity, the cycle begins again.

Every marketer who targets a group of customers has to consider what those people can afford to buy. One measure of what consumers can afford is their *disposable income*, the amount that remains after paying taxes. Part of anyone's disposable income goes for food, housing, clothing, and other necessities. What's left is *discretionary income*, money that can be saved or used to buy nonessential items. Marketers such as Kraft, General Foods, and Midas Muffler compete for the part of disposable income that is earmarked for buying essentials and nonessentials. Banks and financial services marketers like NationsBank and Fidelity Investments compete for the part of discretionary income that consumers and businesses earmark for savings and investment.

Resource Availability and Inflation

Another important element of the economic environment is the amount of resources—human, physical, financial, and informational—available to both organizations and consumers. Rarely is any resource available in unlimited quantities. To cope with shortages, marketers use **demarketing**, a type of marketing that discourages demand for goods and services in short supply.

When demand heats up, prices move higher as people offer more money for the limited stock available. Higher demand and higher prices can fuel *inflation*, a decline in the purchasing power of money due to rising average prices. For the marketer, inflation means paying more for supplies and other resources, then trying to pass these added costs along to customers in the form of higher prices. For the customer, inflation means stretching money further to buy things that had cost less just months before—and a greater sensitivity to price increases.

The Global Economy

In an age when faxes and phone lines can instantaneously carry orders and information halfway around the world to a waiting supplier or customer, when FedEx can move a package across the continent in a day, every marketer is influenced by the global economic environment. As a marketer, you may work with suppliers and customers in markets that are located hundreds or thousands of miles away, competing with both local and international marketers. For example, customers in Vietnam, where the economy is growing more than 8 percent every year, can buy Pepsi soft drinks and Sony televisions and use Bank of America Visa credit cards.[42] See Chapter 4 for more about the global economy.

demarketing

a type of marketing that discourages demand for goods and services in short supply

The Competitive Environment for Marketing

competitive environment

includes all organizations offering product alternatives to your target markets

competition

every alternative that a customer might consider in place of your product

The **competitive environment** includes all organizations offering product alternatives to your target markets. Every alternative that a customer might consider in place of your product is **competition** for you. It works the other way around as well: your product provides competition for others who want to build relationships with the same customers.

Types of Competition

Your product can face three types of competition: (1) competition from other brands, (2) competition from substitute products, and (3) competition for the customer's attention and money. In the first type, your product competes with similar products being marketed under other brands, as illustrated in Figure 3.4. A good example of brand competition is found in the antibacterial soap market, where Dial Soap competes with Lever 2000.

FIGURE **3.4** Three Types of Competition for Carnival Cruise Lines

Many companies are building bigger and fancier ships, creating new and challenging competition for Carnival Cruise Lines. Potential customers may choose other vacation alternatives, or they may choose to spend money on something entirely different, such as clothing or furniture. Carnival Cruise Lines has to consider all three types of competition when developing its marketing strategy.

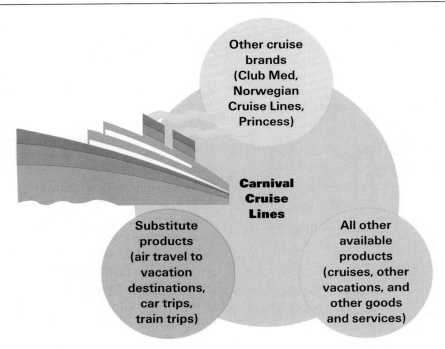

In the second type, your product faces competition from other goods or services that customers may choose as a substitute. What customers choose isn't exactly like your product, but it solves the same problem or offers the same benefits. For example, a customer who wants to color her hair may decide to substitute an application of L'Oréal hair coloring at home for a trip to the hairdresser.

In the third type, your product faces competition from anything else that a customer can buy or use. This is a more general type of competition because in place of your product customers may choose virtually any other option that's available, including saving the money in a bank. Consumers and businesses have a limited amount of money to spend, so they must make choices. People can spend their leisure time watching a rented videotape, dancing, or in some other activity. Thus, the video rental store competes with all other leisure activities. In a broader sense, however, the store also competes with restaurants, clothing, and everything else a customer can spend money on to buy or use.

MARKETING IDEAS

Flexing your competitive muscles

Marketers can compete in many ways, not just on price. Here's a sampling of how marketers are competing to build meaningful relationships with customers.

- *Time.* Time-based competition means hurrying to make or deliver something to customers faster than rivals can do it. Bringing out new products faster than competitors falls into this category. Also in this category is Jiffy-Lube's while-you-wait oil change.

- *Innovation.* When you compete on the basis of innovation, you appeal to customers who want to be first with new products or need new solutions to old problems. Intel does this, continually introducing new, more powerful computer chips to speed up calculations and run more complex, demanding programs.

- *Values.* By competing on the basis of values, you attract customers who agree with your philosophy. By making purchases from Body Shop, for example, many customers are expressing agreement with the company's stand against animal testing of cosmetics and in favor of other values.

- *Service.* When you compete on service, you offer your customers special attention. Mercedes-Benz buyers get special services such as 24-hour roadside assistance if they have car troubles.

- *Relationships.* Competing on the basis of relationships means meeting more of your customers' needs to build a multipronged relationship. Customers of People's Bank in Connecticut save on bank fees and earn more interest by keeping checking and savings accounts in one bank. This relationship orientation works well for the bank and the customer.[43]

Can you identify additional examples of companies that use these competitive methods?

Competitive Barriers and Competitive Advantage

Competitive barriers are problems, such as the high cost of constructing or operating a facility, that restrict competition in some way. In cookies, for example, one competitive barrier is the high cost of advertising. Nabisco spends $13 million annually advertising its Oreo brand.[44] Marketers that can't come close to such expenditures may have difficulty competing with Nabisco.

The point of analyzing the competitive environment is to find ways of building *competitive advantage*, gaining an edge over rivals by giving customers more reasons to choose your product. Use marketing research to understand how customers compare you to your competition. Watch, too, for competition from suppliers or customers who can develop the skills to do what you do. Also watch for businesses that get around competitive barriers by concentrating on small segments of a larger market. For example, Checkmate Electronics has a narrow focus on helping banks and retailers detect counterfeits by using equipment that determines a check's authenticity. This niche in the overall market for payment processing is worth $25 million a year to Checkmate.[45]

Marketing Ethics

An increasingly important influence on the marketing environment is the role of **marketing ethics**, the moral standards and values that are applied to marketing issues. Marketers can address ethical issues at five levels: personal, organizational, industrial, societal, and international. This means that ethics are shaped by your own values, by the values of your employer and your managers, by what your industry considers to be ethical, by the standards and laws of your society, and by the values and laws of other countries. You'll sometimes face standards as well as actions that are legal but don't seem ethical. That's why you won't always find a clear-cut answer when you ask, "What is the right thing to do?" A code of business ethics can be found on pages 90 and 91; these principles are global in scope and cover all stakeholders.[46]

Ethical Issues in Marketing

Nearly every marketing decision opens the door to a potential ethical question. Here are two of the many ethical issues in marketing today:

- *Should a marketer sell something when another product would be better for the customer?* Wetherill Associates in Royersford, Pennsylvania, faced this dilemma when a customer wanted to buy a rebuilt electrical component. Finding only new components in stock, the salesperson could have sold one of those. Instead, he suggested that the customer save money by buying a rebuilt part from a competitor. Although the company lost a sale, it strengthened its long-term relationship with that customer.[47]

- *Should a marketer advertise a product very widely believed to be unhealthy?* This is a dilemma for cigarette marketers. As long as they observe government rules such as the ban on television advertising, tobacco marketers are allowed to advertise, because their products are legal. However, critics charge that tobacco ads encourage nonsmokers—and children—to start smoking. If the Food and Drug Administration declares nicotine a drug, the industry will likely face new restrictions on advertising.[48]

marketing ethics
the moral standards and values that are applied to marketing issues

Both ISO 9000 standards (quality management systems) and ISO 14000 standards (environmental management systems) are often managed by the same people. That is true at Eastman Kodak and Lucent Technologies, for example. Both standards call for systems thinking, design, development, and auditing. Often companies turn to quality professionals for help in designing those systems. The goal in becoming certified under such standards is to satisfy customers and other stakeholders in an ethical and socially responsible way.

In some cases, you'll be faced with a decision involving an action that may not be illegal but doesn't measure up to your personal ethical standards or those of your organization, the industry, or society. For example, it is unethical for marketing researchers to reveal the names of people who answer a survey if the respondents have been promised that names will be held confidential. Other examples of unethical marketing behavior include conspiring with competitors to fix prices, manipulating the amount of products offered through various dealers, using packaging techniques that cause customers to believe they are getting more of a product than the container in fact carries, and overpromising what a product can deliver. All these actions are unethical, and some are illegal.[49]

Ethical questions become more complex when you have marketing operations in other countries. Businesspeople say that requests for payments to government officials who decide what can be exported or imported are not unusual in Venezuela, Egypt, and many other countries. But U.S. businesses have to abide by the Foreign Corrupt Practices Act, legislation that lays out what actions marketers can and cannot take when they operate abroad.[50] Chapter 4 has more details on this issue.

Principles for Business

These principles are rooted in two basic ethical ideals: kyosei and human dignity.

The Japanese concept of kyosei means living and working together for the common good—enabling cooperation and mutual prosperity to coexist with healthy and fair competition. "Human dignity" refers to the sacredness or value of each person as an end, not simply as a means to the fulfillment of other's purposes or even majority prescription.

The General Principles in Section 2 seek to clarify the spirit of kyosei and "human dignity," while the specific Stakeholder Principles in Section 3 are concerned with their practical application.

SECTION 1. PREAMBLE

The mobility of employment, capital, products, and technology is making business increasingly global in its transactions and its effects.

Laws and market forces are necessary but insufficient guides for conduct.

Responsibility for the policies and actions of business and respect for the dignity and interests of its stakeholders are fundamental.

Shared values, including a commitment to shared prosperity, are as important for a global community as for communities of smaller scale.

For these reasons, and because business can be a powerful agent of positive social change, we offer the following principles as a foundation for dialogue and action by business leaders in search of business responsibility. In so doing, we affirm the necessity for moral values in business decision making. Without them, stable business relationships and a sustainable world community are impossible.

SECTION 2. GENERAL PRINCIPLES

PRINCIPLE 1. *The Responsibilities of Businesses: Beyond Shareholders Toward Stakeholders*

The value of a business to society is the wealth and employment it creates and the marketable products and services it provides to consumers at a reasonable price commensurate with quality. To create such value, a business must maintain its own economic health and viability, but survival is not a sufficient goal.

Businesses have a role to play in improving the lives of all their customers, employees, and shareholders by sharing with them the wealth they have created. Suppliers and competitors as well should expect businesses to honor their obligations in a spirit of honesty and fairness. As responsible citizens of the local, national, regional, and global communities in which they operate, businesses share a part in shaping the future of those communities.

PRINCIPLE 2. *The Economic and Social Impact of Business: Toward Innovation, Justice, and World Community*

Businesses established in foreign countries to develop, produce, or sell should also contribute to the social advancement of those countries by creating productive employment and helping to raise the purchasing power of their citizens. Businesses also should contribute to human rights, education, welfare, and vitalization of the countries in which they operate.

Businesses should contribute to economic and social development not only in the countries in which they operate, but also in the world community at large, through effective and prudent use of resources, free and fair competition, and emphasis upon innovation in technology, production methods, marketing, and communications.

PRINCIPLE 3. *Business Behavior: Beyond the Letter of Law Toward a Spirit of Trust*

While accepting the legitimacy of trade secrets, businesses should recognize that sincerity, candor, truthfulness, the keeping of promises, and transparency contribute not only to their own credibility and stability but also to the smoothness and efficiency of business transactions, particularly on the international level.

PRINCIPLE 4. *Respect for Rules*

To avoid trade frictions and to promote freer trade, equal conditions for competition, and fair and equitable treatment for all participants, businesses should respect international and domestic rules. In addition, they should recognize that some behavior, although legal, may still have adverse consequences.

PRINCIPLE 5. *Support for Multilateral Trade*

Businesses should support the multilateral trade systems of the GATT/World Trade Organization and similar international agreements. They should cooperate in efforts to promote the progressive and judicious liberalization of trade, and to relax those domestic measures that unreasonably hinder global commerce, while giving due respect to national policy objectives.

PRINCIPLE 6. *Respect for the Environment*

A business should protect and, where possible, improve the environment, promote sustainable development, and prevent the wasteful use of natural resources.

PRINCIPLE 7. *Avoidance of Illicit Operations*

A business should not participate in or condone bribery, money laundering, or other corrupt practices: indeed, it should seek cooperation with others to eliminate them. It should not trade in arms or other materials used for terrorist activities, drug traffic, or other organized crime.

SECTION 3. STAKEHOLDER PRINCIPLES

Customers

We believe in treating all customers with dignity, irrespective of whether they purchase our products and services directly from us or otherwise acquire them in the market. We therefore have a responsibility to:

❖ provide our customers with the highest quality products and services consistent with their requirements;
❖ treat our customers fairly in all aspects of our business transactions, including a high level of service and remedies for their dissatisfaction;
❖ make every effort to ensure that the health and safety of our customers, as well as the quality of their environment, will be sustained or enhanced by our products and services;
❖ assure respect for human dignity in products offered, marketing, and advertising; and
❖ respect the integrity of the culture of our customers.

Employees

We believe in the dignity of every employee and in taking employee interests seriously. We therefore have a responsibility to:

❖ provide jobs and compensation that improve workers' living conditions;
❖ provide working conditions that respect each employee's health and dignity;
❖ be honest in communications with employees and open in sharing information, limited only by legal and competitive restraints;
❖ listen to and, where possible, act on employee suggestions, ideas, requests, and complaints;
❖ engage in good faith negotiations when conflict arises;
❖ avoid discriminatory practices and guarantee equal treatment and opportunity in areas such as gender, age, race, and religion;
❖ promote in the business itself the employment of differently abled people in places of work where they can be genuinely useful;
❖ protect employees from avoidable injury and illness in the workplace;
❖ encourage and assist employees in developing relevant and transferable skills and knowledge; and
❖ be sensitive to serious unemployment problems frequently associated with business decisions, and work with governments, employee groups, other agencies and each other in addressing these dislocations.

Owners/Investors

We believe in honoring the trust our investors place in us. We therefore have a responsibility to:

❖ apply professional and diligent management in order to secure a fair and competitive return on our owners' investment;
❖ disclose relevant information to owners/investors subject only to legal requirements and competitive constraints;
❖ conserve, protect, and increase the owners/investors' assets; and
❖ respect owners/investors' requests, suggestions, complaints, and formal resolutions.

Suppliers

Our relationship with suppliers and subcontractors must be based on mutual respect. We therefore have a responsibility to:

❖ seek fairness and truthfulness in all of our activities, including pricing, licensing, and rights to sell;
❖ ensure that our business activities are free from coercion and unnecessary litigation;
❖ foster long-term stability in the supplier relationship in return for value, quality, competitiveness, and reliability;
❖ share information with suppliers and integrate them into our planning processes;
❖ pay suppliers on time and in accordance with agreed terms of trade;
❖ seek, encourage, and prefer suppliers and subcontractors whose employment practices respect human dignity.

Competitors

We believe that fair economic competition is one of the basic requirements for increasing the wealth of nations and, ultimately, for making possible the just distribution of goods and services. We therefore have a responsibility to:

❖ foster open markets for trade and investment;
❖ promote competitive behavior that is socially and environmentally beneficial and demonstrates mutual respect among competitors;
❖ refrain from either seeking or participating in questionable payments or favors to secure competitive advantages;
❖ respect both tangible and intellectual property rights; and
❖ refuse to acquire commercial information by dishonest or unethical means, such as industrial espionage.

Communities

We believe that as global corporate citizens, we can contribute to such forces of reform and human rights as are at work in the communities in which we operate. We therefore have a responsibility in those communities to:

❖ respect human rights and democratic institutions, and promote them wherever practicable;
❖ recognize government's legitimate obligation to the society at large and support public policies and practices that promote human development through harmonious relations between business and other segments of society;
❖ collaborate with those forces in the community dedicated to raising standards of health, education, workplace safety, and economic well-being;
❖ promote and stimulate sustainable development and play a leading role in preserving and enhancing the physical environment and conserving the earth's resources;
❖ support peace, security, diversity, and social integration;
❖ respect the integrity of local cultures; and
❖ be a good corporate citizen through charitable donations, educational and cultural contributions, and employee participation in community and civic affairs.

code of ethics

a written guide to help employees understand what is considered ethical and what is unethical

Ethical Marketing Standards

What can be done to encourage ethical behavior? Ethical behavior begins at the personal level. If marketers are committed to acting ethically, they contribute to the overall ethical climate and set an example for others. Ethics leadership starts at the top. When government officials, business executives, or university deans act unethically or fail to punish unethical behavior, they influence everyone around them. Leaders who live up to world-class moral standards and values set a tone for everyone to duplicate. Robert Haas, CEO of Levi Strauss, is a business leader with a dedication to high moral values. This ethical standard is carried through in a written code that helps employees resolve ethical questions they may face.[51]

Like Levi's, more organizations are adopting and unconditionally supporting an explicit **code of ethics**, a written guide to help employees understand what is considered ethical and what is unethical. About 95 percent of the *Fortune* 500—the largest U.S. corporations—have ethics codes. To spread ethical behavior and thinking throughout the organization, management must make clear that everyone is expected to follow the ethics code—and that anyone who does not will suffer. Many organizations offer special training to teach employees to consider the ethical implications of their decisions and actions. Some organizations have appointed ethics officers and set up ethics hotlines, encouraging employees to report suspected ethical lapses and permitting them to discuss ethical questions in confidence.[52]

How can you resolve ethical issues you encounter in marketing? Ask yourself these questions:[53]

- *Is it legal?* Am I violating laws or company policies? If an action doesn't seem to be legal, chances are it won't be ethical, either.

- *Is it balanced?* Am I acting fairly? Would I want to be treated this way? Should my stakeholders be treated this way? Will I win at the expense of someone else? Every situation can't be completely balanced, but you should aim for a win–win outcome.

- *How will I feel about myself, and how will others feel about me?* Would I feel proud if my family, supervisor, company president, or customers learned of my decision? Decisions that go against your personal sense of right and wrong can make you feel bad and corrode your self-esteem. Think not only of how you feel but of how your actions would make others feel.

LEVI STRAUSS & CO.

CODE OF ETHICS

Levi Strauss & Co. has a long and distinguished history of ethical conduct and community involvement. Essentially, these are a reflection of the mutually shared values of the founding families and of our employees.

Our ethical values are based on the following elements:
- A commitment to commercial success in terms broader than merely financial measures.
- A respect for our employees, suppliers, customers, consumers and stockholders.
- A commitment to conduct which is not only legal but fair and morally correct in a fundamental sense.
- Avoidance of not only real, but the appearance of conflict of interest.

From time to time the Company will publish specific guidelines, policies and procedures. However, the best test whether something is ethically correct is whether you would be prepared to present it to our senior management and board of directors as being consistent with our ethical traditions. If you have any uneasiness about an action you are about to take or which you see, you should discuss the action with your supervisor or management.

Note Levi's commitment to multiple stakeholders, including suppliers and stockholders. Note also its commitment beyond legal conduct to being fair and morally correct. Is it important, given the competitive nature of today's society, for companies to be "morally correct"? What does that mean to you, and which companies would have the most positive impact on society if they were to adopt such a position?

Marketing and Social Responsibility

Closely related to marketing ethics is the concept of **social responsibility**, the belief that organizations should look beyond their own interests and profits to make a real contribution to society. Social responsibility is influ-

social responsibility

the belief that organizations should look beyond their own interests and profits to make a real contribution to society

enced by marketing, just as marketing is influenced by social responsibility. *Macromarketing* is the study of marketing's effect on society and the effects of societal changes on marketing.[54]

Like marketing ethics, social responsibility is an important part of the marketing environment that influences how marketers build and strengthen relationships with stakeholders. "Two out of three consumers say that they are concerned about a company's social performance when they shop," observes J.D. Choate, chairman of Allstate Insurance. "What they are really doing is broadening the definition of quality."[55] In this context, the quality of a marketer's actions is defined not just by your customers but by society at large.

Social responsibility makes marketers accountable for what their organizations take from and give back to society. This means balancing sometimes conflicting pressures from different stakeholder groups. If a company spends money to clean up the river behind its plant, it may be short-changing stockholders whose share of earnings will be smaller. If it sends an employee to a community career fair, is it forcing other employees to work harder as they cover the absent co-worker's duties? If it donates money to one charity, should it donate to five or ten?

Questions such as these have no easy answers. Still, many companies believe that they can successfully balance stakeholder pressures and improve society. "For the first time in American history, we all need to accept the fact that there is no longer a difference between what's good for society and what's good for business," says Darryl Hartley-Leonard, chairman of Hyatt Hotels.[56]

Socially responsible behavior is more than simply avoiding what is unethical or illegal. It also means getting involved in society to help improve conditions or solve problems. Half the people who responded to a recent U.S. poll said they were involved in charitable or social service activities such as helping poor, sick, or elderly people. This indicates that people are not just talking about social responsibility, they are also behaving in socially responsible ways. Marketers, too, are taking action on many fronts, including the natural environment, community service, health and welfare, and philanthropy. One marketer's experience in this area is instructive.

Applying the Concepts

Walking the walk of social responsibility

Debbie Aguirre started Tierra Pacifica, a construction company in Irvine, California, because she wanted to combine personal values and business goals. One of her values was community service, and her business goal was to learn about corporate real estate. Her company therefore contributes an extra project to each city in which it does business. For example, the company has built a shelter for battered women and constructed a library reading area for senior citizens. "It's good business," explains Aguirre. "It makes me feel good, it empowers our employees and it helps the community. The people hiring us know we're doing something bigger and broader than just constructing a building."

Aguirre isn't alone in her commitment to social responsibility. More than 900 people are members of Business for Social Responsibility, an organization that educates businesses about their societal roles. The organization's cofounder, Helen Mills, wants companies to make a difference. "We have more resources, more creativity and more energy than even the government," she says. "We have the ability to touch many, many lives, and to create new, more ingenious ways of solving society's problems." Author Joel Makower (*Beyond the Bottom Line: Putting Social Responsibility to Work for Your Business and the World*) sees more movement toward social responsibility.

> "As the number of companies embracing socially responsible visions and values continues to grow, and the links between their social performance, their impact on stakeholders, and [their] financial performance become more firmly established, the overriding question will not be whether companies should adopt these policies and practices but rather when, and how quickly, they should do so.[57]

Make marketing decisions

1. Name a company that you believe is socially responsible. How did it get this reputation? How can it enhance this good name so it can continue to grow and prosper?

2. Would you hire Debbie Aguirre's construction company? What, if anything, do you like or dislike about her approach? What are the implications for marketing the company's services?

3. Name a company that you believe is not socially responsible. Does its reputation have any effect on the company's success? If so, what can the company do to change this reputation?

4. How can Debbie Aguirre use environmental scanning and analysis to find potential customers for her construction company?

Protecting the Natural Environment

One of the most critical issues facing everyone on the planet is protecting, restoring, and sustaining the natural environment. Twenty years ago, many marketers were reluctant to embrace this expensive and time-consuming proposition, but today marketers have become active problem solvers.[58] A common method is through **green marketing**, marketing products that are safe or beneficial to the environment. Green marketing signals that a marketer's actions won't disturb the ecological balance—and, if possible, will have a positive effect. This approach builds relationships with customers concerned about the natural environment. For example, Lee uses

Protecting the natural environment should be a concern for all marketers. That is why "green marketing" has become so popular. It means marketing environmentally safe or beneficial products. Lee's Ecolojeans are made from recycled denim. Many companies are making products from recycled bottles, cans, paper, and plastics. Can you cite examples where marketers are damaging the environment? What changes would you like to see them make?

green marketing to offer Ecolojean dungarees for preteens, made from a textile combining denim with recycled plastics.

Many companies that are implementing ISO 9000 quality standards are also seeking certification in ISO 14000 standards. **ISO 14000** is a collection of the best practices for managing an organization's environmental impacts. ISO 14001 is an environmental management system (EMS). Certification in ISO 9000 and ISO 14000 would show that an organization has a world-class management system in both quality and environmental standards.[59]

Relationship Building Through Community Service

From aiding local schools to helping out during natural disasters, marketers are deeply involved in community service projects. Kragie/Newell, a small Des Moines advertising agency, helped local schools start a guidance program. Oracle, a California software company, worked closely with San Mateo schools to foster computer literacy. Pizza Hut offers free pizza to students who hit their reading goals and Texas Instruments employees teach mathematics to Dallas school students.[60] Such community involvement programs help organizations to establish and maintain relationships with the community. Close relations with customers are fostered, in turn.

Relationship Building with Health and Welfare Projects

Many marketers focus efforts on the health and welfare of customers and people in the community. McDonald's operates Ronald McDonald Houses to provide housing for families of seriously ill children being treated in nearby hospitals. Half a million people stay every year in 157 houses in North America, Great Britain, Germany, Australia, and other countries. Avon, the global cosmetics marketer, puts special emphasis on women's health issues. Its representatives in the United States, Canada, and the United Kingdom raise money for breast cancer research; representatives in Thailand raise awareness of AIDS.[61] Such attention to the needs of the community cannot help but create better long-term relationships.

Philanthropy and Cause-Related Marketing

Marketers can channel money to socially responsible causes in two ways. Corporate **philanthropy** is the direct donation of money, goods, and services to nonprofit organizations of all sorts. Dayton Hudson is just one of many companies that has a special foundation to coordinate philanthropic donations. Philanthropy isn't merely corporate giving—it's relationship building, reaching out to stakeholders in the community.[62]

A second way to see that money goes to a worthy cause is through **cause-related marketing**, a marketing program that links donations to sales of a particular product. Cause-related marketing has become a popular way for companies to connect certain products with specific causes and, at the same time, help customers feel good about buying from a socially responsible and responsive company. Going a step beyond, Working Assets Long Distance and others use cause-related marketing to donate a percentage of every sale to causes that customers help choose.[63]

green marketing

marketing products that are safe or beneficial to the environment

ISO 14000

a collection of the best practices for managing an organization's environmental impacts

philanthropy

the direct donation of money, goods, and services to nonprofit organizations of all sorts

cause-related marketing

a marketing program that links donations to sales of a particular product

social audit

evaluates an organization's progress toward
implementing programs that are socially
responsible and responsive

Measuring Social Programs with a Social Audit

It is one thing to talk about becoming more socially responsible. It is another to implement such programs and measure the results. A **social audit**
evaluates an organization's progress toward implementing programs that are
socially responsible and responsive. One of the more difficult problems is
defining "socially responsible and responsive" to each stakeholder's satisfaction. Is a company socially responsible if it postpones putting in the latest
technology (for example, robots and computers) to save jobs, even if the
delay makes the firm less competitive or less profitable? Such questions
make the design of social audits particularly challenging.

Social audits help companies plan and evaluate a coordinated program of
socially responsible activities. First, consider what organizational stakeholders expect of your company. Next, identify specific social causes that are
worthy of your support *and* have some connection to your company's mission, then prioritize them. After your plan has been put into action, you assess the results to see whether you've accomplished what you set out to do.
Social responsibility revealed through a thorough social audit is fast becoming a measure of success that is recognized by a business's stakeholders.

Before you go on . . .

A. Why are technological standards important?

B. How does disposable income differ from discretionary income?

C. What is marketing ethics and why is it important?

D. Why does social responsibility mean balancing sometimes conflicting stakeholder interests?

Summary

1. **Explain the uses of environmental scanning and environmental analysis, and distinguish between the internal and external environments.**

    Environmental scanning helps marketers to identify internal and exter-
    nal factors that can affect marketing success. Environmental analysis
    helps marketers evaluate, interpret, and distribute information about
    the marketing environment to employees and managers. The internal
    environment is the set of factors inside the marketer's value chain that
    can influence marketing success. The external environment covers fac-
    tors outside the value chain that can influence marketing success.

2. **Identify the factors in the internal environment that ca ence marketing.**

The factors in the internal environment that can influen are employees and workforce diversity, relationships with stockholders, and relationships with suppliers and other partners.

3. **Analyze how demographic changes and cultural influences in the social environment affect marketing.**

Demographics is the study and measurement of a population as described by such factors as age, gender, birthrate, education, family size, income, nationality, race, and occupation. Culture is the set of values, beliefs, and attitudes shared by a group and passed down from one generation to the next. Both are part of the social environment, the set of characteristics, cultural elements, and attitudes that affect customers' perceptions of and reactions to marketers.

4. **Explain why marketers need to analyze the political and technological environments.**

The political environment, including laws, governmental rules, and other regulations, can influence virtually every aspect of marketing because it covers consumer protection, fair competition, and protection of the natural environment. The technological environment, which consists of innovations and new ideas from scientific or engineering research, can help marketers satisfy customers in a new or better way.

5. **Discuss how the economic environment affects marketing and identify the three forms of product competition.**

The economic environment is the set of economic factors that influence both customer buying and organizational marketing efforts, affecting product demand and access to resources. A product can face three types of competition: (1) competition from other brands, (2) competition from substitute products, and (3) competition for the customer's attention and money.

6. **Define marketing ethics and apply three questions to help resolve ethical issues in marketing.**

Marketing ethics refers to the moral standards and values that are applied to marketing issues. Three questions to resolve ethical issues are (1) Is it legal? (2) Is it balanced? (3) How will I feel about myself, and how will others feel about me?

7. **Describe how marketers can apply social responsibility, and discuss the role of a social audit.**

Social responsibility is a reflection of the belief that organizations should look beyond their own interests and profits to make a real contribution to society. Marketers apply social responsibility to the natural environment, community service, health and welfare, and philanthropy. A social audit is a systematic evaluation of an organization's progress toward implementing programs that are socially responsible and responsive.

KEY TERMS

business cycle 84	demarketing 85	marketing environment 69
cause-related marketing 95	demography 76	marketing ethics 88
code of ethics 92	economic environment 84	philanthropy 95
competition 86	external environment 70	political environment 79
competitive environment 86	green marketing 94	social audit 96
consumerism 80	internal environment 70	social environment 75
culture 77	ISO 14000 95	social responsibility 92
		technological environment 83

Skill-Building Applications

1. What are some of the social, political, and techno-logical changes that will affect your career in the future? What can you do to monitor and take advantage of those changes?

2. What are some actions U.S. marketers like Good-year can take to build relationships with companies like Honda that buy from U.S. suppliers as well as from suppliers in other countries?

3. What are some of the environmental changes that may affect donations to the Sierra Club and other nonprofit environmental groups? What can such groups do to anticipate and respond to these changes?

4. How are small businesses in your area using green marketing to strengthen relationships with customers? What examples can you find, and how do these examples illustrate relationship building?

5. Wal-Mart has faced opposition from local communities and government officials who don't want the stores in their towns. Why would communities oppose Wal-Mart? What might Wal-Mart do to better manage this part of its marketing environment?

6. If an international marketer like Exxon completed a global social audit today, what are some of the actions that would be classified as beneficial to society? Harmful to society?

Getting Involved In Marketing

1. *On Your Own* Think about how the technological environment will soon affect textbook marketing. Will texts be offered in different forms, such as on CD-ROM? Will they be advertised in new media? Write a paragraph summarizing your thoughts.

2. *On Your Own* Imagine you're hiring college students to help in your new business—renting in-line skates at public parks in your area. Prepare a two-minute talk to your class on how you would use organizational culture to make your business a success.

3. *Find Out More* Research how a marketer has been socially responsible by helping the community or taking other actions. What is this marketer gaining from its actions? What are its stakeholders gaining?

4. *In a Partnership* With a classmate, list at least three ethical issues involved in liquor marketing.

Explain the ethical questions and discuss your viewpoint about each in a brief (one to two page) report.

5. *In a Team* Work with two other students to analyze the competitive environment of the U.S. Postal Service. Name at least four companies that compete with U.S.P.S. What type of competition does each company represent? How might the U.S.P.S. respond to each?

6. *In a Team* With other students, interview three people who were laid off in the past year or so. Have their food-buying habits changed? Do they eat out as much or at the same places as they did when they were working? If you and your classmate were running a restaurant, how would you use your interview data to craft a marketing strategy that would attract such diners?

VideoCase Making Ethical Marketing Decisions

Deciding what is right and what is wrong in a marketing situation isn't always easy. A decision may seem legal but still not meet the ethical standards and values of the individual, the organization, the industry, society, or another culture. This videocase examines five ethical issues in marketing.

The first ethical issue is how to sell products that will soon be obsolete. In the "Dumping Inventory" video segment, the store's sales manager receives inside information about an improved product that will replace the existing Lasertron. By aggressively selling before competitors learn about the improved product, the store will avoid being stuck with outdated inventory—and will receive more manufacturer rebates, boosting profits. However, a top salesperson is concerned about violating the trust of customers. Should the store act on inside information? Should the store put short-term profits ahead of long-term customer relationships? What is the store's responsibility to customers in this situation?

The second ethical issue, explored in the "Sexist Campaign" segment, is how to handle advertising that seems sexist. The client is paying the bill—and specifically wants a controversial campaign. What is the agency's ethical responsibility to consumers, especially women, who are the target market? Should the advertising agency move ahead even if the account executive and copywriter agree that the commercial is in questionable taste?

The third ethical issue, explored in the "Sales Hype" segment, is how to sell without damaging customer relationships. The department store wants to sell furniture. Should its salespeople stretch the truth? Do customers expect to be treated that way? Should management be informed when a salesperson uses questionable practices that boost sales?

The fourth ethical issue is the interplay between personal values and professional responsibilities. In the "Furrier" segment, the salesperson sells advertising space. Because she is against fur coats, she is reluctant to take advertising from a local furrier. Still, her family budget depends on the commissions she earns from sales. What decision can she make that will meet both personal and professional ethical standards?

The fifth ethical issue, illustrated in the "Priced to Go" segment, is how to price a product that can relieve human suffering and, at the same time, preserve profits. The new drug will help Alzheimer's patients, but a company task force is under pressure to set a high price to recoup costs more quickly and make profits before competitors catch up. The assistant product manager, however, wants to set a lower price on the product. Although this will result in a longer payback period, it will also make the drug more affordable for more patients. What is one individual's ethical responsibility as part of a team that is working together on an assignment? How do the competitive pressures and the drug's high acquisition costs affect the ethical issues?

Strategies and applications

1. Can you resolve any or all of the ethical issues in each scenario by referring to legal and regulatory guidelines? Explain your answer.

2. What stakeholders are involved in each scenario? Are some stakeholders more important than others? Explain your answer.

3. What would be the most balanced decision to make in each scenario? How does this decision affect the stakeholders involved?

4. What would *you* do in each scenario? Why? How would you feel about yourself?

5. In what ways can companies encourage open discussion of ethical issues, thus avoiding ambiguity about what is right and wrong in situations like these?

6. Assuming the role of a company manager in one scenario, draft a code of ethics. How would this code help resolve the issues in the scenario?

Team project

With another classmate, prepare to debate the ethical issues in one video segment. First agree on the specific ethical issues that your chosen segment raises. Then, working separately, prepare to defend your argument by researching what other companies or individuals have done in similar situations. Hold the debate in front of your class, then poll the class to find out which side was more persuasive—and why.

4

International and Cross-Cultural Marketing

Learning Goals

After you have read and studied this chapter, you should be able to:

1. Discuss why more marketers are entering international marketing.
2. Describe how NAFTA and the EU affect relationship building through international marketing.
3. Explain the impact of trade protectionism on domestic and international marketers.
4. Distinguish among straight extension, product adaptation, and product invention as product strategies for international markets.
5. Identify four ways of entering the international marketplace.
6. Contrast global and customized international marketing strategies.
7. Compare international marketing and cross-cultural marketing.

PROFILE

Blockbuster bursts into global markets

Blockbuster Entertainment had only 19 video rental stores in 1986, all in the United States. Eventually it became the largest and fastest-growing video rental chain in the world, with more than 4,500 video stores in 22 countries. Why transform this U.S. giant into an international marketer? The answer, in a word, is growth. The U.S. market for video rentals has been growing slowly, and Blockbuster wants to expand at a more rapid pace.

To do so, the chain's marketers looked for new opportunities in other countries, where demand for video-taped movies was high but largely untapped. The United States accounts for only about half of the $25 billion spent annually on home video rentals and sales around the world. The remainder of this large and lucrative market is in other countries. Applying the company's marketing expertise to global markets, Blockbuster opened its first video store outside the United States in London in 1989. When it bought the 800-store Ritz video chain in 1992, Blockbuster gained a 20% share of the U.K. market and an opening into the broader European market.

Because regulations and requirements vary from country to country, the company works with local businesses in joint ventures and franchises to enter some markets. In this way, Blockbuster can benefit from its partners' knowledge of local needs. The franchise holder in Tel Aviv, for example, has succeeded by offering a wider selection of videos for rent and more convenient service than competitors. Blockbuster plans future growth in South America, Asia, Canada, and Europe.

What's next? Music superstores and state-of-the-art entertainment complexes are being tested in the United States. If successful, these will be expanded to other countries. Blockbuster marketers all over the world are working hard to continue expanding the company's entertainment empire, aiming for 50 percent of the company's growth from non-U.S. markets.[1]

This chapter examines how marketers build relationships with customers in other countries and in other cultures. After looking at the growth and the components of the international environment, you'll explore various ways of marketing across national boundaries and cultural boundaries.

Building Relationships Across National Borders

Much of what constitutes the phrase *"globalization" begins with redefining one's thinking. The first order of business of decision-makers—in both the public and private sectors—is to think beyond national borders and to embrace a mind-set that says all world markets constitute one economy.*

Fred Smith
FedEx CEO

TABLE **4.1**

U.S. Companies with Large International Sales

Company	Percentage of Revenue from International Sales
Exxon	77.4
Manpower	68.8
Colgate-Palmolive	68.4
Coca-Cola	68.3
Gillette	68.0
Avon	64.0
IBM	62.3
Citicorp	62.3
Digital Equipment Corporation	61.5

domestic marketing

marketing exchanges with customers in the marketer's country

international marketing

exchange relationships between marketers and customers located in two or more countries

For Blockbuster, as for many other marketers, crossing national borders is the key to rapid growth. Look around and you'll see how many marketers have entered the U.S. market to build relationships with customers. Saab (based in Sweden), Panasonic (based in Japan), and Philips (based in the Netherlands) are just three of the many foreign companies that market in the United States. Their products have become so familiar to U.S. customers that it's difficult to remember that their roots are in other nations.

In the past, it was quite possible for an organization to survive and grow without going beyond the borders of its own country. As recently as the 1980s, some 90 percent of U.S. companies concentrated on **domestic marketing**, marketing exchanges with customers in the marketer's country. Since then, many more have started marketing in Canada, Mexico, and elsewhere, building relationships with some of the 5 billion potential customers who live and work outside the United States.

By reaching out to customers in other countries, these marketers are engaging in **international marketing**, exchange relationships between marketers and customers located in two or more countries. Some international marketers have sought out customers in only one or two countries; others have fanned out to many countries. In fact, one-fifth of the U.S. companies that market internationally are active in more than five foreign markets.[2] The number of U.S. marketers that draw over half of their revenues from international marketing has been increasing as more join such veterans as Hewlett-Packard (computers) and Caltex (oil products) in courting overseas customers.[3] Table 4.1 lists some major players.

Even though marketing in other countries can help build sales and profits, most businesses in the United States have not yet adopted an international orientation. Many are unaware of the opportunities that are available. And even marketers who understand the potential of international markets sometimes shy away from doing business abroad. The reasons they give include the expense of traveling to other countries, fluctuating exchange rates that can wipe out profits overnight, too much red tape, too many bureaucratic obstacles, unstable foreign economies, high transportation costs, cultural differences that complicate marketing activities, and a lack of knowledge about how to start.

A common feeling is that international marketing is nothing like domestic marketing. In many cases it is indeed different, but often the differences can be overcome if you focus on your customers and if you study—but avoid getting bogged down in—the unfamiliar political systems, laws, monetary systems, languages, cultures, and customs. International marketing also brings more intense competition, so you'll have to stress quality and use world-class marketing to build and maintain a loyal customer base.

Can U.S. marketers find success in countries where local marketers have long-standing customer relationships? Consider Italy, a country known for the quality and fit of locally made shoes. Despite the success of the domestic shoe industry, the Allen-Edmonds Shoe Corporation of Wisconsin is able to market its line of high-quality shoes to Italian customers. Goods and services, parts, and completed products alike are all increasingly crossing national borders.

The Move to International Marketing

When you **export**, you're marketing products to customers in other countries. On the other hand, when you **import**, you're bringing another country's products into your own. Both exports and imports are part of international marketing. Thanks to advances in communication and technology, marketers can both look for supplies and market their products far from home.[4] High-speed communication and technology allow marketers to buy materials, find funding, make products, and market products all over the world. Using faxes, phones, computer links, and other technology, marketers can manage production plants thousands of miles away. Using air delivery and other methods, they can send products from Argentina to Zimbabwe more safely and easily than ever before.

In such an environment, national boundaries mean little. What does matter is finding the most efficient place to make and market goods and services that satisfy customers' needs. In the words of Jack Welch, CEO of General Electric, "If you can't sell a top-quality product at the world's lowest price, you're going to be out of the game."[5]

This is why Honda builds Accords in Ohio and ships them to Japan, and why Ford designs Aspires in Michigan and, through its Japanese partner Mazda, assembles them in South Korea.[6] Are these U.S. cars, Japanese cars, or South Korean cars? In today's global marketplace, such distinctions aren't very important. In fact, the line between domestic and international marketing is being blurred by a *transnational* system of product development, design, production, and marketing.[7]

Today's marketers see the entire world as their marketplace. Using television and other communications, they can bring information about goods, services, and ideas to far-flung areas. They operate wherever they can develop relationships with customers, obtain resources, and make profits. A company with operations and activities in more than one country has traditionally been called a **multinational corporation (MNC)**. An organization that has gone worldwide is called a **global corporation**. Global corporations constantly check opportunities for buying or expanding all over the globe, and they aggressively market wherever they can build solid customer relationships.

Comparative Advantage and Competitive Advantage

Going international can be easier when your country is known for producing a particular good or service. But why are Italy and the Netherlands considered to be leaders in leather shoes and fresh flowers, respectively? In the past, the guiding principle behind international marketing was the theory of *comparative advantage*, which states that a country's companies should make and export the goods and services they can produce more efficiently than their trading partners.

export

marketing products to customers in other countries

import

bringing products from other countries into your own

multinational corporation (MNC)

company with operations and activities in more than one country

global corporation

an organization that has markets worldwide

National competitive advantage may be more important than comparative advantage when it comes to being competitive in the global marketplace. This plant in the Finnish village of Oulu, for example, benefits from an educated workforce, technological expertise in surrounding countries, and related industries. What other countries have fewer natural resources but nonetheless have a competitive advantage technologically?

According to this theory, factors such as naturally occurring raw materials or the talents of the local labor pool give a country a relative advantage over other countries in the production of certain products. Each country should therefore export the products in which it has a relative advantage and that provide a more profitable return. In addition, it should import products in which it has a relative disadvantage, because other countries can produce those more efficiently.

However, this theory doesn't explain why Italy excels at shoes or the Netherlands at flowers. The reason isn't simply better Italian leather or better Dutch seeds. Michael Porter of the Harvard Business School argues that the reason is *national competitive advantage*, the theory that a country's ability to compete depends on four elements:[8]

1. *Factor conditions*. Factors such as a country's educated labor pool, a developed infrastructure (the availability of communications, transportation, and other basic services), and technological expertise help companies to market more effectively than rivals in other countries.

2. *Demand conditions*. A sizable, sophisticated, competitive domestic market teaches companies how to compete on quality and price, better preparing them for global competition.

3. *Related and supporting industries*. Having access to world-class value-chain partners (especially suppliers) in their own country contributes to marketers' ability to compete elsewhere.

4. *Company strategy, structure, and rivalry*. The way companies manage their strategies, organization structures, and approach to domestic competition strengthens their ability to compete against marketers in other countries.[9]

Porter argues that the presence of raw materials and similar resources is less important than the four factors just listed. By constantly innovating and improving technology and productivity, a country's companies can harness these factors to compete more effectively with each other and, ultimately, with foreign rivals. Thus, Italian shoe designers are always preparing innovative new fashion designs, working closely with local leather producers, and adjusting strategies to compete both domestically and globally. In the United States, world-class companies have worked with domestic suppliers and skilled researchers to make the country a center of basic science, biotechnology, and environmental technologies.[10]

Opportunities for International Marketing

Many major U.S. marketers are already taking advantage of marketing opportunities throughout the world. From Nike to Pizza Hut, Citicorp to FedEx, their familiar names and logos circle the globe. At the same time, some of the best-known brands in the United States belong to marketers based in other countries. These include Benetton (based in Italy), Perrier (owned by Swiss-based Nestlé), and Shell Oil (owned by Royal Dutch/Shell in the Netherlands). Being big isn't a prerequisite for international marketing, however; opportunities are available for any sharp entrepreneur.

Just ask Pamela Coker, a San Diego businesswoman who put a new face on an old product—COBOL computer language—and brought her company from $200,000 to $12 million in sales in just 6 years. Her company, Acucobol, gives COBOL users a new and easier way to work with the early computer language on today's equipment. Coker realized that COBOL was in widespread use in Brazil, Germany, India, Italy, and other countries. Like Blockbuster's management, she started out by hooking up with partners abroad who could navigate through the local environment; Acucobol now draws about half its revenue from international marketing.[11]

Marketers of services, like marketers of tangible goods, can also find appropriate marketing opportunities in other nations. Services of all types can be marketed in other countries, from translation and accounting to catering and rail transport. Some services, such as communication and transportation, can be offered across national boundaries. For example, European Passenger Service, based in the United Kingdom, has joined with French and Belgian railroads to jointly market and operate Eurostar, a high-speed train service through the tunnel under the English Channel. Eurostar is successfully challenging airlines that connect London, Paris, and Brussels.[12]

In particular, manufacturers and service marketers alike see opportunity in satisfying the needs of nations for *infrastructure* improvements, upgrades to basic communication, energy, and transportation facilities. Developing nations such as China, Russia, and Thailand are moving quickly to add new energy plants, telecommunications systems, environmental cleaning procedures, highways, and airports. Marketers around the world are vying for these lucrative contracts, paving the way for importing and exporting additional goods and services.[13]

The following case shows how a U.S. sport is scoring marketing points in other countries.

Applying the Concepts
Shooting hoops around the world

Layups and slamdunks have gone global, thanks to the worldwide visibility of the Olympic Dream Team and the marketing savvy of David Stern. As commissioner of the National Basketball Association, Stern has presided over a period of expansion during which basketball fever has spread from the United States into Canada, Mexico, even Japan. Now he's seeking growth on six continents through television rights, merchandise sales, and special sporting events.

International marketing is helping Stern move the action beyond the United States, where interest in basketball is high but growing only slowly. The regular NBA schedule now includes games in Canada with the Toronto Raptors and the Vancouver Grizzlies, two expansion teams. An expansion team in Mexico City is also planned. The USA Basketball Women's National Team, assembled for the 1996 Olympics in Atlanta, whipped up excitement by playing collegiate and international teams in the months leading up to the Olympics.

There are attractive profits to be made selling sports-related clothing and equipment. However, not all of this merchandise has been officially licensed by the various professional leagues. Some items are unauthorized copies produced by companies trying to profit from someone else's image. By promoting their official label, the NBA hopes to fend off such competitors. Why would some consumers want to buy unlicensed merchandise? How could the leagues respond to these desires?

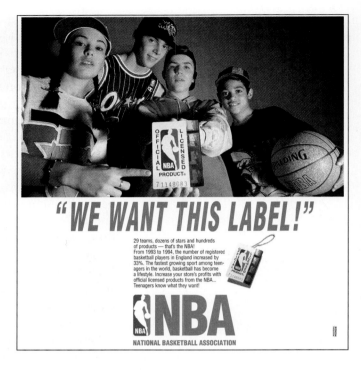

Basketball has become a worldwide sport, with fans in more than 160 countries tuning in to televised NBA games. McDonald's, Coca-Cola, IBM, and Nike are NBA global marketing partners, advertising during televised NBA events and supporting local marketing events as well. Stern is targeting the hottest growth markets, including Australia, Israel, and Japan, for special marketing attention. In addition, merchandise sales are fueling growth in global revenues: sales of shirts and other NBA-branded merchandise tops $3 billion every year. And as the NBA adds fans in other countries, Stern is planning the right marketing plays for growing global revenues more than 20 percent per year.[14]

Make marketing decisions

1. How would you use personal appearances by NBA stars to boost basketball's popularity in other countries?

2. If you handled McDonald's marketing, what would you consider before advertising during televised NBA games in 160 countries?

3. Does the United States have national competitive advantage where basketball is concerned? Why or why not?

4. If you were David Stern, who would you consider to be your customers? Explain your answer.

Before you go on . . .

A. How do multinational corporations differ from global corporations?

B. How does national competitive advantage explain a country's world leadership in a particular product?

home country

the nation where your organization has its headquarters

host country

any nation where you market or set up operations

Not everyone is thrilled by the prospect of free trade agreements among countries. Ross Perot and his followers, for example, protested vigorously against NAFTA at this Michigan rally. Many believe that as a result of trade agreements, U.S. workers are losing their jobs to workers in other countries who receive less pay. On the other hand, U.S. consumers will be able to buy some products for less. What role does politics play in world trade? In general, do you perceive this role as positive or negative?

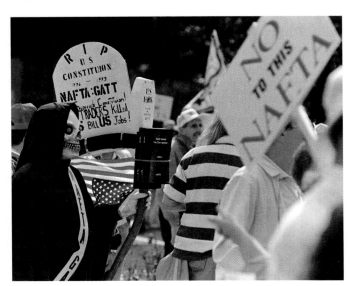

Understanding the International Marketing Environment

Before any company enters the international marketplace, its marketers must understand how political, economic, social, and cultural influences can affect marketing relationships. Conducting research into these issues is the role of the first universal marketing function, environmental scanning and analysis. As you read the following sections, think about the impact these influences can have on your relationships with customers across the continent or across the ocean.

Political and Economic Influences

The political environment of your **home country**, the nation where your organization has its headquarters, can have a major effect on your ability to market in other countries. One example: The United States, like many countries, regulates what marketers can and cannot sell to customers in other countries—and what can and cannot be purchased by domestic customers. For instance, the government doesn't allow materials or equipment related to nuclear technology to be shipped to certain countries because of concern about nuclear nonproliferation.[15] It also is essential to understand the political environment of your **host country**, any nation where you market or set up operations. Both opportunities and challenges are presented by the trade relationship between your home and host countries.

Trade Agreements and Economic Integration

Many promising opportunities can arise when your home country is party to a *free-trade pact*, an agreement that encourages trade by lowering or eliminating restrictions on marketing exchanges among the countries that have signed on. Such pacts build bridges between countries that want to enhance trade ties through closer economic integration. The United States participates in a free-trade pact known as the *North American Free Trade Agreement (NAFTA)*, which reduces barriers to marketing goods and services across the borders of Canada, the United States, and Mexico.

Thanks to NAFTA, Canada's Bank of Montreal can invite customers in all three countries to invest in its mutual funds with a minimum of paperwork; Ford can market many more U.S.-made cars in Mexico—and many more Mexican-made cars in the United States. Despite concerns about the movement of U.S. jobs to Mexico, where wages are lower, NAFTA has helped U.S., Canadian, and Mexican marketers reach customers throughout the area.[16]

Another opportunity comes from operating inside a *common market*, a group of nations that agree to a single set of regulations governing trade within and outside the unified market. Again, the purpose is to stimulate marketing exchanges inside the market. The *European Union (EU)* is a common market composed of Austria,

Belgium, Denmark, Finland, France, Germany, Great Britain, Greece, Ireland, Italy, Luxembourg, the Netherlands, Portugal, Spain, and Sweden. The total market includes about 400 million people. Other nations are expected to join the EU in the future.[17]

Marketing within the EU is easier for companies that are based in the member countries and conform with ISO 9000 quality standards ◄───┘ **(p. 95)** and other marketing considerations. However, the EU also sets uniform requirements governing marketing exchanges with companies outside the common market. As a result, EU marketers can compete more effectively within the market than outsiders trying to break in. For this reason, outsiders often buy local companies to enter the EU. United Parcel Service (UPS), which is based in the United States, gobbled up 16 European businesses over 7 years in its quest to compete in the EU goods-transport business. Such growth wasn't painless—UPS spent about $1 billion getting set up—but the company is now established as Europe's largest delivery service.[18]

Barriers to international trade are being reduced by the *General Agreement on Tariffs and Trade (GATT)*, a series of trade pacts initiated in 1948. The 1994 agreement, known as the Uruguay round, lowered or eliminated charges levied on goods and services entering 124 countries. It also set guidelines for protecting copyrights and patents and established the World Trade Organization (WTO) to resolve trade disputes. This agreement should help marketers operate more cost effectively across national borders, with fewer restrictions than before.[19]

Issues for critical thinking

Opponents of NAFTA and GATT worry that foreign marketers will have a price advantage over domestic marketers because many use low-wage employees to produce their goods and services. What are some other disadvantages of free trade? Do you think the advantages outweigh the disadvantages?

Trade Protectionism

Trade protectionism is the use of government regulations to set limits on the marketing of goods and services by foreign producers. Countries use trade protectionism to protect domestic industries against foreign competition and to help domestic marketers survive and grow. The U.S. government, for example, has practiced trade protectionism to shield domestic automakers and steel producers from foreign rivals.

But trade protectionism can have the opposite effect if it also protects domestic marketers from having to face the realities of world competition. If local marketers don't feel pressure to achieve world-class status, their products may not be as good as those of foreign marketers—and they may lose sales and jobs in the long run. Consider what happened when fuel-efficient compact cars from Japan came on the U.S. market nearly 30 years ago. As customers snapped up the peppy imports, U.S. automakers sought protection against the foreign competition. Even with voluntary restraints capping Japanese imports, General Motors and other U.S. automakers suffered market-share and profitability losses, and layoffs followed. Only in recent years have U.S. automakers regained ground by researching and meeting customer needs and upgrading quality to better compete with foreign rivals.[20]

trade protectionism

the use of government regulations to set limits on the marketing of goods and services by foreign producers

tariffs

taxes levied on specific products going into the country

quotas

limits on the number of products in certain categories that can be imported or exported

embargo

a ban on importing or exporting certain products

exchange rate

value of one currency relative to the currencies of other countries

FIGURE **4.1**

The United States carefully monitors its balance of trade with top trading partners. When there is an imbalance, such as the gap between imports from and exports to Japan, U. S. officials look for ways to stimulate additional trade to improve the balance.

Nearly every country protects its domestic industries through the use of **tariffs**, taxes levied on specific products going into the country. Tariffs raise the price of foreign products, which makes domestic products seem less costly and more attractive by comparison. Even though the Uruguay round of GATT reduced tariffs by an average of one-third, these fees are still part of global trade. Still, lower tariffs should save U.S. customers more than $9 billion a year.[21] As an international marketer, you need to consider how much tariffs will raise the price your customers have to pay for your products—and then you must look for ways of lowering costs while raising quality or finding nonprice ways to compete with locally made products.

In the name of trade protectionism, many governments also set **quotas**, limits on the number of products in certain categories that can be imported or exported. In the past, the United States set import quotas on many products, including peanuts and sugar. Import quotas were outlawed by the Uruguay round of GATT, although countries can substitute tariffs for quotas.[22]

Another technique used to protect local producers—and to retaliate against other countries—is the **embargo**, a ban on importing or exporting certain products. During the Persian Gulf War, for example, Canada banned exports of domestic grains to Iraq. This move stopped Canadian farmers from selling 800,000 tons of wheat and 282,000 tons of barley to Iraq, and idled many Canadian ship operators as well.[23]

Balance of Trade and Balance of Payments

When a country looks at its position in the international marketplace, one figure it considers is its *balance of trade*, the relationship of the value of its merchandise exports to the value of its imports. A second figure it checks is the *balance of payments*, the difference between the value of the products and money entering the country and the value of the products and money leaving the country. These figures show whether a country imports more than it exports and whether it receives money from or owes money to other countries. Values for the United States for 1995 are shown in Figure 4.1. As a result, a country may revise quotas and tariffs to better balance trade and payments.

Foreign Exchange

Both customers and marketers are interested in the **exchange rate**, the value of one currency relative to the currencies of other countries. Take the value of the Brazilian real, for example. When this monetary unit has a high value relative to other currencies, one real buys more foreign goods (or can be traded for more foreign currency) than is possible when the real has a low relative value. In such a situation, Brazilian customers often find foreign products a better bargain than local goods.

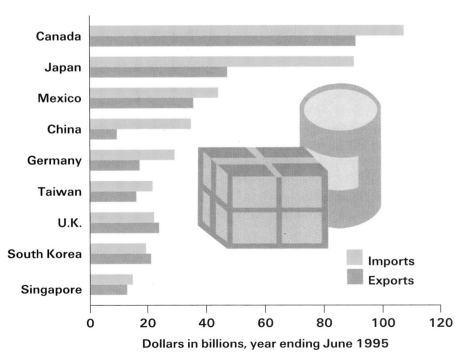

Canada
Japan
Mexico
China
Germany
Taiwan
U.K.
South Korea
Singapore

☐ Imports
☐ Exports

0   20   40   60   80   100   120

Dollars in billions, year ending June 1995

To compete when the real is high, Brazilian marketers may have to change prices or enhance the value package. Industria de Calcados Wirth, a shoe manufacturer based in Dois Irmaos, Brazil, faced this situation not long ago. As low-price shoes imported from China flooded the market, Industria de Calcados Wirth held its prices but slashed its response time from 60 days to 21 days for product orders. This strengthened the company's competitive stance, allowing it to grow nearly 50 percent in five years.[24] Of course, when the real's value is low compared with other currencies, foreign goods are more expensive for local customers because it takes more reals to buy them. However, the low real makes Brazilian goods cheaper for foreign customers.

Foreign exchange rates fluctuate from minute to minute as currency traders in financial institutions around the world buy and sell currencies. These fluctuations mean that the value of what you pay a foreign supplier (or the price you are paid by the foreign customer) can change at any time. As a result, you may pay more (or less) for supplies and receive more (or less) for your products. For example, Friedrich Grohe, a German maker of plumbing fixtures, knows that changing prices due to shifts in foreign exchange can affect sales to other countries. "The translation of just the peseta, lira, pound sterling and dollar into [German] marks will cost us about 20 million marks less sales," says Klauss Weisshaar, Grohe's chairman.[25]

Barter and Countertrade

Before money existed, people met their needs by trading goods and services with one another. In some areas of the world, marketing still relies on **barter**, exchanging products without the use of money (or money substitutes). For example, barter tourism is alive and well along the China–Russia border. Tourists from Heihe, China, can cross into Blagoveshchensk, Russia, while the same number of tourists from Heihe cross into Blagoveshchensk. Tourists in both cities receive the same services, so no money has to be exchanged.[26] Thus, barter allows companies and individuals to acquire what they need by trading their products for those of other producers.

At times, customers in another country will not be able to pay cash for products. One reason may be government concern over balance of trade and balance of payments; another may be laws forbidding people to take money out of the country. In such situations, many international marketers turn to **countertrade**—marketing exchanges in which customers pay for their purchases with local products instead of money.

When you use countertrade, whatever you accept in payment is then sold for cash to customers elsewhere. Be prepared for some creative trades when you take products instead of cash from a customer in another country. For example, Chrysler has traded its vehicles in Jamaica for bauxite, and Telelex Media has traded television shows for advertising time in several countries. These countertrade examples show that lack of cash to pay for products needn't halt a deal that satisfies both marketer and customer.

Social and Cultural Influences

No two nations or cultures are exactly alike, and marketers may succeed or fail because of social and cultural differences. Even when operating in countries that are linked by economic integration, marketers must be sensitive to the differences that distinguish each nation. The European Union countries

barter

exchanging products without the use of money (or money substitutes)

countertrade

marketing exchanges in which customers pay for their purchases with local products instead of money

share a common market, but they're as different from one another as sauer-braten and spaghetti. Similarly, Canada, Mexico, and the United States share a continent and a free-trade pact, but cultures and business customs differ widely.

Language

Whether you're naming a product, preparing a package, or scripting a television commercial for another country, communicating in another language can be challenging. For example, brand names or words that make sense in your home country's language may sound wrong or carry negative connotations in translation. Kellogg's Bran Buds cereal had to be renamed for the Swedish market after a translator revealed that the local meaning was something like "burned farmer."[27] And GM's Nova was hard to sell where the name translates in Spanish to "No go."

As Kellogg and other international marketers well know, you can't just translate your marketing communications word for word. You'll do best if you work with translators who have long experience in the language and in the host country. In fact, this specialty opens new marketing opportunities: Yuri and Anna Radzievsky, owners of YAR Communications, built their business helping U.S. corporations market in more than 100 countries using accurate language and cultural references. For extra insurance, use *back-translation*: have another person put the translation back into your language to be checked for problems.[28] Such a check would have helped the dry cleaner in Bangkok who advertised in English, "Drop your trousers here for best results."

This store in Quebec Province, Canada, has signs in both English and French. In many parts of the United States, stores have signs in both English and Spanish. Such trends mean that cultural and language differences must be taken into consideration not only when selling in international markets but also when selling in domestic markets. In a multicultural society, marketers must meet the needs of diverse groups or miss out on opportunities. A customer-oriented marketer might maintain contacts with all such groups and design products and promotions customized for each. What are the advantages and disadvantages to such adaptation?

Around the globe are nearly 200 countries and territories that use as many as 3,000 different languages and dialects. Two, three, or more languages may be spoken in a single country. Apart from the official national language (or languages), people in certain regions of each country tend to use their own dialects, slang, gestures, even other languages. People in Belgium speak French or Flemish or both; in Canada people speak English, French, and several Native North American languages.[29] The complexities of marketing to people in diverse cultures within a country are discussed later in the chapter.

Culture

Just as people in other countries use differing languages, they also belong to differing cultures, marked by unique values, beliefs, attitudes, and traditions. Cultural differences can present both opportunities and challenges. In India, for example, where 80 percent of the population is Hindu, these religious beliefs are powerful influences on marketing and shopping patterns. Because Hindus believe that cows are sacred, McDonald's can't offer beef hamburgers in India. But a local competitor, Nirula's, took this cultural value as an opportunity: its menu offers burgers made only from lamb or vegetables.[30]

ethnocentrism

the assumption that your culture is superior to others

geocentrism

the assumption that successful international marketing requires respecting both home- and host-country cultures

Although a host country's attitudes toward food, colors, time, or family relationships may differ from those of your home country, one set isn't necessarily better than the other. As an international marketer, you have to avoid **ethnocentrism**, the assumption that your culture is superior to others. Ethnocentric marketers stress the home country's cultural values when marketing abroad, even when such values are inappropriate. Because ethnocentric marketing doesn't take local differences into account, a better approach is **geocentrism**, the assumption that successful international marketing requires respecting both home- and host-country cultures.

PepsiCo used geocentric marketing when it began making Cheetos in China. Rather than assuming that the cheesy flavor of the U.S. version would travel well, PepsiCo marketers asked Chinese customers what they liked and disliked. Upon learning that cheese would not be popular, PepsiCo developed two flavors, Zesty Japanese Steak and Savory American Cream, for local tastes. The name Cheetos was translated into Chinese as "new surprise," and television commercials showed Chester Cheetah singing in Cantonese or Mandarin, depending on the region.[31]

Business Customs

To be effective in another country, you should be familiar with local business customs. Many books, seminars, and newsletters can give you hints about how to behave when doing business in other countries. Be prepared to encounter differences in greetings, in forms of physical contact such as handshakes, and in conventions relating to punctuality, distances between people, gift giving, and entertaining.

International marketers also grapple with overseas business customs that reflect ethical values at odds with those of their home countries. One area of conflict is the question of bribes, which foreign officials sometimes expect in exchange for awarding contracts or expediting transactions. These payments aren't considered unethical in many countries; rather, they're looked at as a cost of doing business. However, large payoffs are illegal under the Foreign Corrupt Practices Act, passed in 1977, which sets guidelines for U.S. marketers doing business in other countries. Under this law, U.S. companies can't bribe foreign officials, but they can give small tips for completing routine transactions.[32]

Choices involving ethical issues and questions of social responsibility are rarely clear-cut, whether you're operating domestically or internationally. What is considered appropriate in your home country may be less acceptable in your host country; the reverse is also true. For a starting point, check the laws of both countries, talk to marketers who have experience in other countries, and think carefully about your stakeholders' interests. Remember, too, that your objective is to build relationships that stand the test of time.

Before you go on . . .

A. What are quotas and tariffs?

B. Why is foreign exchange important to international marketers?

C. How does ethnocentrism differ from geocentrism?

Entering the International Marketplace

Once you've completed your analysis of the international environment, you'll need to decide how to enter those markets. You can choose among four basic methods: (1) exporting and importing, (2) licensing and franchising, (3) joint ventures, and (4) direct investment. Exporting, importing, and licensing and franchising require less commitment and carry less risk. Joint ventures and direct investment involve more commitment and more risk but also allow more control, as shown in Figure 4.2. These methods can be combined to reach different customers and markets.

F I G U R E **4.2** Entering International Markets

Importing and exporting are the easiest ways for marketers to enter international markets, because little risk and commitment are involved. At the other end of the spectrum, direct investment allows marketers more control over their international activities, but it also carries more risk and commitment.

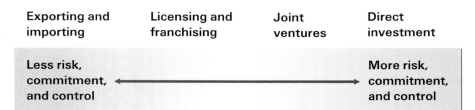

Exporting and importing	Licensing and franchising	Joint ventures	Direct investment
Less risk, commitment, and control ←———————————————→			**More risk, commitment, and control**

Exporting and Importing

Both exporting and importing bring goods and services across national boundaries. Because these arrangements do not call for high initial investments, they are the least risky way of entering the international marketplace. With *indirect exporting*, a marketer works through a channel partner that deals with customers in other countries. This setup is especially helpful when a marketer is unfamiliar with a country's customs or when it has a partner that is well established in the host country. For example, Narayan Bhat, chairman of Namaste Exports in India, uses indirect exporting to market his leather coats through Liz Claiborne, which has fashion contacts all over the United States.[33]

Another method of indirect exporting entails *export trading companies*, channel partners that match marketers and customers from different countries, buy products for resale in another country, and arrange for shipping and other services. *Export management companies* offer similar services, although instead of buying your products, they may simply arrange for others to be buyers or dealers.[34]

In contrast, *direct exporting* lets marketers deal directly with customers. Many exporters choose this method, making arrangements to send their products overseas to waiting customers. Paul MacLardy, president of Arise, uses direct exporting to send Bart Simpson dolls and other U.S. merchandise to its company-owned stores in Japan. MacLardy also uses *direct importing*, dealing directly with suppliers to buy products for sale in the home country. He buys clothing in Japan and imports it for sale in the United States.[35]

Products also can be brought into a country through *indirect importing*, either buying imports from channel partners who deal with foreign suppliers or buying imported parts for domestic products. This approach is growing in importance as more marketers cross national boundaries in search of the

Auburn Farms is a small U.S. importer. Producers throughout the world are making sweets such as these that few people in the United States have ever seen. By carefully selecting the best of these products, an importer can generate profit for the firm and provide an attractive choice to those consumers who enjoy variety. What kinds of products do you use that are made in other countries? What do you think are the keys to prospering in international trade?

licensing

an agreement in which one company pays for the right to make or sell another company's product

franchising

a form of licensing in which a company pays a fee for the right to use another company's brand name, products, and operational methods in a particular area

joint venture

a partnership in which two or more companies share the work, costs, and rewards of a major project

best materials and technology. After you have incorporated the parts or technology into your products, you can market them in your home country—or export them.

Licensing and Franchising

Marketers can avoid both direct involvement and direct investment by entering the international marketplace through the arrangement called **licensing**, whereby one company pays for the right to make or sell another company's product. The company providing the license may help set up the production or the marketing channel in the host country and may also provide marketing advice. Sometimes marketers license only the brand name. For example, Saban International holds the license to the Mighty Morphin Power Rangers brand outside Pacific Rim countries. It pays the brand's Japanese owners a licensing fee and, in turn, licenses the brand to 300 other marketers, bringing in fees of $80 million.[36]

Franchising is a form of licensing in which a company pays a fee for the right to use another company's brand name, products, and operational methods in a particular area. Franchising is popular both domestically and in international markets. Firms such as Ramada Inn, Avis, and Dunkin' Donuts have many international units operated by *franchisees*, local businesses that own franchises. Like all marketers, franchisees adapt to the needs of their local customers. For example, Pizza Hut accommodates local tastes by serving spinach and sauerkraut pizza in Germany; corned beef, corn, and pea pizza in Hong Kong; and sardine, tuna, and mackerel pizza in Russia.[37]

Licensing can build revenues without the cost and management headaches of manufacturing or marketing in other countries. The foreign company bears the costs and the problems of actually marketing the product. However, if your product sells well in other countries, you won't earn as much money as if you had marketed the product yourself. Also, if the foreign company learns your processes, it may break the agreement and start to operate on its own. Finally, your brand name is linked to the quality and customer service offered by the foreign company. If it doesn't meet high standards, your reputation will suffer, too.

Joint Ventures

A **joint venture** is a partnership in which two or more companies share the work, costs, and rewards of a major project. Such arrangements are particularly useful when a marketer has little or no experience in the host country and is able to team up with an experienced marketer. For example, Honda, the Japanese automaker, has formed a joint venture with Siel, an Indian manufacturer, to produce small cars for the Indian market. Even service marketers can benefit from joint ventures: A Washington, D.C. law firm that specializes in transportation law has a joint-venture law practice with a Belgian firm.[38]

direct investment

owning manufacturing or marketing facilities in another country

An international joint venture helps you learn from your partner and compete in markets where foreign goods are not allowed unless produced by local companies. Joint ventures require more investment and risk than importing, exporting, licensing, or franchising, but they also allow more control. On the other hand, a partner may turn around and use your technology and practices to compete with you later.

Disagreements with your partner constitute another potential problem. For example, WIN Laboratories, a small computer maker in Virginia, decided to withdraw from a joint venture in Chile, blaming its local partner for poor sales.[39] To make joint ventures work, therefore, you must pay close attention to the needs and priorities of your partners as well as those of your customers.

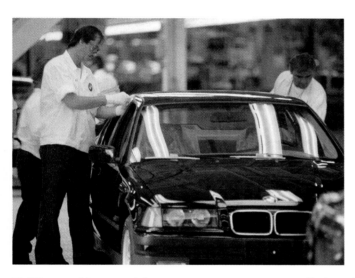

BMW, one of Germany's largest auto makers, now builds cars in Spartanburg, South Carolina. By locating plants close to the markets they serve, BMW and other manufacturers can save on transportation costs and in many cases take advantage of skilled labor pools. Direct investment in other countries can be an expensive way to enter those markets, but often, as in the United States, there are offsetting savings, such as tax breaks from local communities seeking the jobs provided by manufacturing facilities. How could BMW use the fact that these autos are made in the United States to increase their appeal to U.S. consumers?

Direct Investment

You maintain the most control over your international marketing activities if you use **direct investment**, owning manufacturing or marketing facilities in another country. Because of the costs of buying or building—and the potential risks—this is a less popular method of moving into the international marketplace. Still, cross-border investments can be a good way to enter countries that restrict access to outsiders. For example, Commercial Union Group, a large U.K. insurance marketer, bought Groupe Victoire, the sixth-largest insurer in France, to gain access to the French market.[40]

One reason for direct investment is to move closer to your customers or to locate near sources of supply for materials or skilled labor. Read-Rite, a California-based company that makes computer disk-drive components, has invested $100 million to build a huge production facility in Thailand. More than 90 percent of Read-Rite's components are marketed to computer makers located in Southeast Asia, which is one reason for the choice of location. Another is the availability of skilled but inexpensive personnel to assemble the products.[41]

First Steps in International Marketing

No matter how you decide to enter international markets, getting started is easier if you benchmark on the experiences of others to learn how the best competitors in the world operate. It's also easier if you take the time to acquire information about the mechanics of working with foreign suppliers and customers as well as about each market's needs, government regulations, and other environmental details.

Benchmarking on the Experiences of Others

Businesses of any size can benchmark on the experiences of successful international marketers. A good example is the experience of Jeffrey Ake, vice president of sales and marketing at Electronic Liquid Fillers, a U.S. manufacturer of equipment used in liquid packaging. In 3 years, Ake traveled to 42 countries to build relationships with customers who use his products. This helped him increase international sales from $150,000 to $6 million, nearly half the company's total sales.

One secret of Ake's success: not being afraid to look for help. "There are dozens of experts—bankers, freight forwarders, shipping agents, customs brokers, trade reps and consultants—who are dying to get your business and to teach you exactly what you need to know to fill those first orders," he says.[42]

Large companies can be quite helpful, as Cornnuts, Inc., learned when it rode into Spain on the coattails of McDonnell Douglas. Details follow.

SMALL BUSINESS WATCH

International matchmakers for small marketers

If you're a small marketer looking into the international market, you may get free advice from a giant corporation in your own backyard. Why should big marketers help small marketers? Because some countries insist that their suppliers help establish other trade links . . . or lose their contracts. When U.S.-based McDonnell Douglas wanted to sell jets to Spain, Spanish officials insisted that the aerospace giant promote trade and technological advancement in Spain—or risk losing the $1.5 billion order.

To fulfill this obligation, McDonnell Douglas decided to guide a small Ohio food producer, Cornnuts, Inc., into the Spanish market. The big company arranged meetings between the small company and several Spanish food executives. In addition, McDonnell Douglas helped Cornnuts locate local marketing research experts and prepare a marketing presentation in Spanish. In all, Cornnuts received thousands of dollars' worth of international marketing advice and services from McDonnell Douglas—free.

McDonnell Douglas is not the only large U.S. company playing matchmaker in international markets. What are the benefits of international matchmaking? In this case, Spain acquired a new hybrid corn technology and more jobs from Cornnut's local operations; Cornnuts entered a new market more quickly and more efficiently than would have been possible without an experienced guide; and McDonnell Douglas persuaded a customer to place a large order for aircraft.[43]

How might McDonnell Douglas help its U.S. suppliers enter other markets?

Finding Sources of Information

Before you invest a nickel (or a shekel) in international marketing activities, look for sources of information on the subject. Some local libraries can help you gain access to the Internet and electronic database services and to CD-ROM databases such as Business Periodicals On-Disc. These sources can help you find out more about a particular country, such as the current business climate, the local culture and customs, and the most popular imports and exports. Check books, magazines, and other library materials for additional background.

Another source of information is your own government, which helps marketers compete with foreign rivals at home and internationally. Some

TABLE **4.2**   Selected U.S. Government Sources of Information on International Marketing

U.S. Agency for International Development helps marketers go international through its Center for Trade and Investment Services.

U.S. & Foreign Commercial Service helps marketers determine whether products are ready for export; assists in developing a marketing plan and making contact with overseas customers and value-chain partners.

U.S. Department of Commerce collects trade statistics and customs information from other countries and publishes guides to international marketing; its National Trade Data Bank summarizes trade information from 15 federal agencies.

U.S. Department of State offers information on travel requirements, foreign currency, and health precautions to help marketers prepare for trips to other countries.

U.S. Government Printing Office offers a wide variety of publications about exporting and importing.

U.S. International Trade Commission offers information about exporting to other countries, including trade agreements and legal rulings that affect international trade.

U.S. government sources are listed in Table 4.2. Both state and federal agencies can help. For example, the U.S. Department of Commerce offers a wide range of free or low-cost services to support international marketing. The U.S. & Foreign Commercial Service (US&FCS) can help you determine whether your product is ready for exporting. The National Trade Data Bank (NTDB), accessed through Department of Commerce offices, holds information about trade regulations, exchange rates, marketing research, and much more.[44]

Government agencies can also help marketers locate financing for international marketing ventures. For example, Russell Mazakas, owner of RAMCO Finishing Systems in Ontario, California, wanted to export his paint finishing systems to China, but he needed additional financing to take this step. The California Export Finance Office in Los Angeles gave Mazakas a loan guarantee that helped him get funding at an attractive interest rate. He was so successful that he was recently named exporter of the year by the World Trade Association International.[45]

Before you go on . . .

A. In what four ways can marketers enter the global marketplace?

B. Why would someone new to international marketing choose a joint venture over direct investment?

Developing Strategies for International Marketing

Once you've completed your research and determined the level of investment and control to use in entering the international marketplace, you face decisions about marketing strategy. With a **global marketing strategy**, you standardize your product, pricing, channel management, and communication activities, wherever possible, for use in all countries. As described by marketing expert Theodore Levitt, this strategy focuses on the similarities rather than the differences among customers in various countries. Individuals and businesses around the world have many similar wants, needs, and

global marketing strategy

standardization of product, pricing, channel management, and communication activities, wherever possible, for use in all countries

concerns, says Levitt, especially for high quality and reasonable pricing. Marketers who concentrate on these similarities can standardize their products for global markets, achieving economies of scale and ultimately competing more effectively through lower prices.[46]

The best-known user of global marketing strategy is Coca-Cola, which markets its soft drinks in more than 160 countries. The company standardizes its marketing activities for widespread appeal but also allows for minor local variations. The same Coca-Cola formula is used from Australia to Zambia. The distinctive red and white can is in every market, with the brand name and label copy translated for local customers. The advertising carries the same theme of enjoyment everywhere, with the words and images interpreted for local markets.[47]

Issues for critical thinking

Coca-Cola has a drink, an advertising theme, and an image that have been successful all over the world. What kinds of products do you think can be successfully introduced in other countries using a global marketing strategy? What adjustments, if any, would you need to market these products internationally?

At the other end of the spectrum from global marketing strategy is **customized marketing strategy**, which means tailoring marketing activities to each local market. With such *localization*, marketers focus on the differences between countries and adapt products, channel management, pricing, and communication to the unique characteristics of each local market. Of course, localization is more costly than globalization because it is necessary to fit marketing activities to every market, rather than using one overall strategy with minor adjustments for local differences. But the result is a coordinated set of marketing activities that is carefully matched to the needs of each country's customers.

Many international marketers use a combination of global and customized marketing strategies. They think globally, replicating appropriate product, channel management, pricing, and communication activities as required. They also act locally, adjusting to differences in each country. This is how Matsushita, based in Japan, markets home appliances and electronic gear around the world. With its state-of-the-art product design and manufacturing technology as a global base, the company customizes products for local needs. "Germans like their potatoes overcooked, but the British like them almost crunchy, so you have to design the cooking controls differently," says Tsuneo Takahashi, a marketing specialist for microwave ovens. "It's hard for product engineers sitting in Japan to understand all that."[48]

Whether you use a global, customized, or combination marketing strategy for entering international markets, you'll need to think about how your product, channel management, pricing, and communication fit local customer needs and market conditions. Your marketing decisions and actions will, of course, depend on your own situation and the countries you target. For that reason, you should consider the following sections as a starting point to spark ideas for marketing in other countries.

customized marketing strategy
tailoring marketing activities to each local market

Product Strategies

Product strategies for international markets include (1) marketing an existing product, known as *straight extension*, (2) modifying an existing product, known as *product adaptation*, and (3) developing a new product, known as *product invention*. These strategies are shown in Figure 4.3. The choice depends on the marketer's experience in international marketing, local customer needs, local competition, and the product's application of technology. Makers of technologically advanced products such as scientific instruments usually can market their products without change, because such equipment is used the same way all over the world.[49]

FIGURE **4.3** Product Strategies for International Marketing

When planning products for other countries, marketers can choose from three strategies. Using straight extension, they can export an existing product. Using product adaptation, they can change an existing product to fit new markets. Using product invention, they can create a new product for new markets.

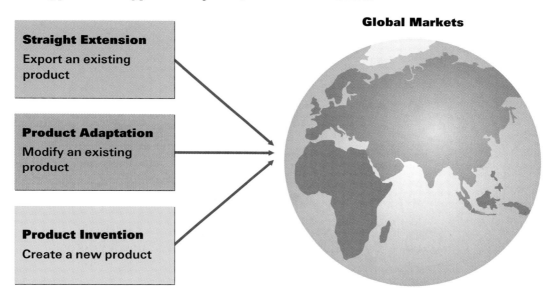

Straight Extension
Export an existing product

Product Adaptation
Modify an existing product

Product Invention
Create a new product

Global Markets

For other marketers, product adaptation and product invention are the keys to establishing and strengthening relationships with foreign customers. Unilever, the giant Anglo-Dutch household products marketer, has adapted its laundry detergents for use in a variety of markets. Its Omo detergent is now the leading international detergent brand in China.[50] German automaker Mercedes-Benz has used product invention to satisfy car buyers in the United States. Using marketing research, the company investigated the preferences of U.S. buyers of sport-utility vehicles. Then it designed its All Activity Vehicle specifically for that target market.[51]

As these examples show, planning products for international markets means using environmental scanning and market analysis to understand local conditions and customer needs. Check requirements for electrical voltage (which varies around the world), measurement systems (such as metric standards), quality standards (such as ISO 9000), even size and packaging (to fit local customers' incomes and lifestyles).

Channel Strategies

When entering other markets, examine the available marketing channels (wholesalers, retailers, dealers, and others) to determine which ones make sense for your goods or services. If you find that domestic marketers have locked up the best channel partners, you can look for alternative ways into the market. At the same time, you can keep building relationships to improve channel management in the future. Also, because total quality is a global, not a domestic, issue, see whether dealers and retailers can provide the kind of after-sale service necessary to keep your customers happy.

In addition, you'll need appropriate locations for your facilities. Some marketers can operate anywhere, thanks to electronic communications. Shell/Mullaney, a New York ad agency, can create advertising for marketers in 29 countries because it sends its ads and messages via the Internet using America Online and other online services.[52] But manufacturers have to worry about getting their products from factories to customers, a process that is complicated by border crossings. Interceramic, a Mexican tile manufacturer, built a factory in Dallas to be closer to U.S. customers. Still, trucking between its two plants is a problem because of delays at the border. Victor Almeida, Interceramic's CEO, hopes that a proposed expansion to the highways linking the two countries will reduce the delays.[53]

When pricing a luxury car like the Mercedes, marketers have to evaluate many factors, including the state of the economy and competitive pressures. They also, of course, have to consider the cost of making the automobile. Do you see any strategic advantages or disadvantages for Mercedes in bringing out a lower-priced model?

Pricing Strategies

Pricing is an important but tricky part of international marketing, complicated by local economic influences such as the business cycle and customers' incomes. For example, Germany's Mercedes-Benz had to cut U.S. prices to attract price-conscious car buyers when the American economy was recovering from a recession a few years ago. Dropping its price more than $4,000 helped Mercedes increase U.S. sales by 22 percent over the previous year; during the same period, rival Toyota raised the price on its Lexus models—and its U.S. sales plummeted.[54]

As you set and manage prices, think about your costs and profits, local demand for your products, competition from local and foreign marketers, and government regulation. Moreover, in many countries, price is seen as an indicator of quality and of product image, two key considerations. Also think about what local customers can afford to pay and what they can substitute for your product. For example, U.S.-based Procter & Gamble figured out what customers in Brazil could afford to pay for disposable diapers, then developed a low-priced version of Pampers for that market.[55] International pricing can trip up even experienced marketers, as you'll see next.

Global Issues

Learning from international marketing missteps

A good way to prepare for the challenges and opportunities of international marketing is to learn from the mistakes of others. Even big marketers can stumble, as this brief overview demonstrates. How would *you* have solved these marketing problems?

- *Setting inappropriate pricing.* Walt Disney initially set high admission, hotel, and food prices for Disneyland Paris, its theme park in France. Because the park was unique and Disney characters were so popular, Disney believed that premium prices would be acceptable. However, European visitors balked. They stayed just a day or two, not four days as was common at Florida's Disney World, and many brought their own food. Disney soon cut hotel and restaurant prices and pruned off-season ticket prices, which lured more visitors and eventually led the way to profits.

- *Underestimating local competitors.* Adidas, a German maker of athletic footwear, was the worldwide industry leader when it entered the U.S. market. However, the company didn't pay close enough attention when Oregon-based Nike developed new shoe technology and an imaginative marketing strategy. As the U.S. market for running and sports shoes grew, Nike took the lead, leaving Adidas behind. In fact, Adidas soon had to defend its turf in Europe against both Nike and Reebok.

- *Designing inappropriate packaging.* When Johnson & Johnson first introduced baby powder in a shaker canister in Japan, sales were modest. Puzzled, J&J marketers investigated and found that mothers were reluctant to use the shaker because they didn't want powder flying around their homes. In response to this research, J&J changed to a flat box with a powder puff, and sales soared.[56]

Communication Strategies

More often than not, you'll have to adapt your promotional communications to the local market. Beyond the obvious differences in language, you need to consider how local customers get and use the information in integrated marketing communication. Where customers are accustomed to having many product choices, you may need to communicate only brand and benefit details. In China and other developing countries, where customers have traditionally had few product choices, you'll have to explain what your product is, what it does, and other basics.

Customers who are unfamiliar with foreign brands may make the first purchase out of curiosity. You might try pumping up interest in a new product before it's even available. Procter & Gamble introduced Ariel laundry detergent in China using this approach. For a month before Ariel appeared in stores, P&G used television advertising to promote the new product, making consumers curious and creating such pent-up demand that Ariel grabbed nearly 5 percent of the market within a month of its introduction.[57]

cross-cultural marketing

marketing to people who belong to various cultures

Sears is just one of many U.S. retailers located in areas where many Hispanic and Latino customers reside. Although most of these customers can speak English, ads in their native language have a different, and often more effective, appeal. It is important, however, to recognize the differences among the various groups in this general population. Just as people from New York differ in culture and tastes from people in New Orleans, people from Cuba differ from those in Mexico or Chile. How do you think you differ in the way you dress, act, and shop from people in other parts of the country?

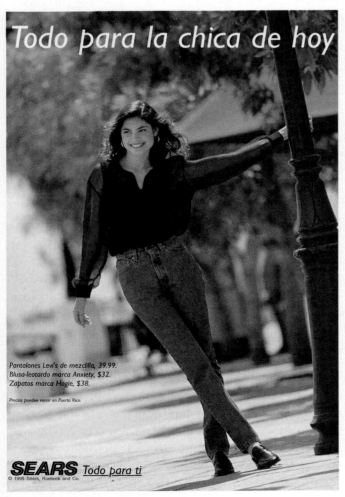

Todo para la chica de hoy

Pantalones Levi's de mezclilla, 39.99.
Blusa-leotardo marca Anxiety, $32.
Zapatos marca Hogie, $38.

Precios pueden variar en Puerto Rico.

SEARS *Todo para ti*
© 1995 Sears, Roebuck and Co.

When placing advertising, investigate local media options, which vary from country to country. Be aware of local literacy rates, television ownership patterns, and local attitudes toward advertising when you plan advertising. For example, nearly every household in Beijing, Shanghai, and Guangzhou, three major Chinese cities, owns a television receiver. You can reach China and other Asian markets through programming beamed by Star TV and the Gang of Five television companies.[58] Almost anywhere you market, you can reach viewers through MTV and CNN. And with interactive options such as CompuServe and the Internet, you can maintain a dialogue with customers who need technical assistance or want to order goods and services.

Marketing Across Cultures

No matter which country you market in, you're likely to find customers in a wide range of cultural groups. The United States, for example, is a culturally diverse country made up of people from a variety of religious, ethnic, and racial groups. Marketing to people who belong to various cultures is known as **cross-cultural marketing**. Cross-cultural marketing, also known as *multicultural marketing*, presents both challenges and opportunities. Like international marketing, it requires sensitivity to the differences that set subcultures apart.

Understanding U.S. Diversity

The cultural makeup of the United States is rapidly changing. Although members of U.S. subcultures are proud Americans, they also have unique characteristics, values, family roles, and lifestyles that affect their buying behavior. Here is a brief profile of three major groups that contribute to cultural diversity in the United States **(p. 77)**.[59]

- *African Americans.* Nearly 32 million African Americans live in the United States, with a combined yearly buying power estimated to be as high as $300 billion. According to the U.S. Census, the average yearly household income for African Americans is $14,051; 10 percent of all African American households have an annual income of $50,000 or more.

- *Hispanic and Latino Americans.* The 24 million Hispanic and Latino Americans in the United States have a total annual purchasing power of more than $200 billion and an average household income (in 1990) of $16,271. This diverse group includes people with roots in Cuba, Puerto Rico, Mexico, and the Caribbean.

• *Asian Americans.* More than 6.5 million Asian Americans live in the United States, and the value of their yearly purchases is about $35 billion. The average yearly household income in 1990 was $23,671, higher than that of African Americans or Hispanic and Latino Americans. Asian American subcultures include those of China, Japan, Korea, the Philippines, Vietnam, and the Pacific islands.

Many other groups contribute to the country's cultural diversity, including Native Americans, religious groups, and descendants of immigrants who settled in the United States decades ago. No matter which culture you're targeting, you have to look carefully at individuals' needs and research their values, interests, and sensitivities to develop an appropriate cross-cultural marketing program. It is also essential to remain sensitive to the pitfalls of stereotyping.

ETHICS & SOCIAL RESPONSIBILITY

Stereotyping and cross-cultural marketing

One danger in cross-cultural marketing is the possibility of *stereotyping*, or assuming that people have certain traits or behave in certain ways because they are members of a particular culture. Too often a stereotype is inaccurate or overly simplistic, perpetuating an unrealistic view of people who share a given culture. This point was driven home by a New York City study of national advertising, which found that only 3 percent of the people portrayed were African American—and these were athletes, entertainers, laborers, or children. City official Mark Green, whose department conducted the study, was outraged. "This racial neglect is both economically dumb and morally offensive," he said. "What we see affects what we think."

Even humor can backfire, as snack marketer Frito-Lay found out when it created a Mexican character, the Frito Bandito, for its advertising. Company research showed that Mexican Americans liked the bandit character in these tongue-in-cheek ads, but the Mexican American Anti-Defamation Committee objected. Frito-Lay withdrew the Bandito campaign soon afterward.

How can you reach out to various cultures without stereotyping? Marketing experts advise incorporating appropriate language, fashion, and other *realistic* details and situations to which members of a culture can relate. [60]

Can you think of other ads geared toward one cultural group that successfully avoid stereotyping?

Planning Cross-Cultural Marketing

As much as they have in common with other groups, people of various cultures also have unique differences and interests, which pose both challenges and opportunities for marketers. Language is one obvious difference. Marketers targeting U.S. subcultures must be prepared to speak many languages. Nearly 14 percent of the population (32 million people) speaks a language other than English at home. The most prevalent non-English languages are Spanish, French, German, Italian, and Chinese. Recent immigration has put Asian and Eastern European languages among the fastest growing in the United States.

Choosing which language to use in your marketing can be tricky. For example, fewer than half of all Hispanic/Latino Americans consider themselves to be fluent in English, and more than 80 percent speak Spanish at home. At the same time, many younger people in this cultural group prefer to speak English, although many older people continue to use Spanish.[61] Your decision depends on the exact customers *you* want to reach.

If you decide to market in Spanish, you can choose among a wide variety of media, including Spanish-language television, radio stations, newspapers, and magazines. Similarly, you can reach Asian Americans through media that are geared to people who speak specific Asian languages. Marketers in San Francisco can use the Asian Yellow Pages, published in Chinese, Japanese, and Vietnamese.[62] But don't just translate your materials into other languages. As with international marketing, your communications also have to reflect the attitudes, images, and contexts appropriate for each group.

Reaching non–English speakers inside the United States can be rewarding for marketers who find the right words and methods. When AT&T advertised its long-distance services to Asian American customers, it shot three separate commercials showing grandparents in Korea, China, and Japan, hearing their U.S.-born grandchildren coo and cry via telephone. Each commercial used songs and baby talk from the group it was targeting, a touch that made the commercials more realistic.[63]

Understanding the values and interests that are unique to each subculture can help you market more effectively. For example, the owner of the Vien Dong International Supermarket in San Diego is of Vietnamese descent, and he understands what people from his culture like. His store plays Vietnamese songs and offers Vietnamese food specialties. He also stocks perfectly fresh vegetables and fish, an important consideration for Asian American customers but one that traditional supermarkets sometimes overlook. However, the supermarket doesn't restrict itself to one subculture. It also draws white, Hispanic American, and African American shoppers by offering standard foods such as tomatoes and onions as well as exotic foods such as mussels from New Zealand and shrimp from Ecuador.[64] By successfully building relationships with a diverse group of customers, Vien Dong's owner has proven his savvy as a cross-cultural marketer.

Before you go on . . .

A. Why would an international marketer combine global and customized marketing strategies?

B. What are three possible product strategies for international marketers?

C. What is cross-cultural marketing?

Summary

1. **Discuss why more marketers are entering international marketing.**

   Advances in communications and technology have made it possible for marketers to get supplies, operate facilities, and market products anywhere in the world. Pushing to grow sales and profits, more marketers are crossing national boundaries in search of the most efficient place and way to make and market their products to customers.

2. **Describe how NAFTA and the EU affect relationship building through international marketing.**

   NAFTA, a trade pact, encourages commerce among Mexico, Canada, and the United States by allowing marketers to build relationships with customers in all three countries with few restrictions. The European Union (EU) is a common market in which a single set of regulations governs trade among all member countries and trade with countries outside the market. The purpose is to stimulate more marketing exchanges inside the market.

3. **Explain the impact of trade protectionism on domestic and international marketers.**

   Trade protectionism is the use of government regulations to set limits on the marketing of goods and services by foreign producers. Trade protectionism aims at shielding domestic marketers from foreign competition by using tariffs (taxes) to raise the prices of imported products or quotas to limit the amount of foreign products allowed into the country.

4. **Distinguish among straight extension, product adaptation, and product invention as product strategies for international markets.**

   Product strategies for international markets include marketing an existing product (straight extension), modifying an existing product (product adaptation), and developing a new product (product invention).

5. **Identify four ways of entering the international marketplace.**

   Marketers can enter the international marketplace by exporting and importing, licensing and franchising, joint ventures, and direct investment.

6. **Contrast global and customized international marketing strategies.**

   In a global marketing strategy, whenever possible, marketers standardize product, pricing, channel management, and communication activities for use in all countries. In contrast, a customized international marketing strategy calls for the tailoring of marketing activities to each local market.

7. **Compare international marketing and cross-cultural marketing.**

   In international marketing, marketers cross national borders to market to people in other countries. Cross-cultural marketing targets people who belong to one or more subcultures within a single nation or globally.

KEY TERMS

barter 110
countertrade 110
cross-cultural marketing 122
customized marketing strategy 118
direct investment 115
domestic marketing 102
embargo 109
ethnocentrism 112

exchange rate 109
export 103
franchising 114
geocentrism 112
global corporation 103
global marketing strategy 117
home country 107
host country 107

import 103
international marketing 102
joint venture 114
licensing 114
multinational corporation (MNC) 103
quotas 109
tariffs 109
trade protectionism 108

Skill-Building Applications

1. Given what you know about various countries throughout the world, which countries seem most attractive as places you would like to work to get global marketing experience? Why?

2. Government officials from the United States and Japan often disagree on trade practices. If you marketed 3M's industrial adhesives, how could you build relationships with Japanese manufacturers without government assistance?

3. The International Red Cross provides emergency relief throughout the world. To raise funds for this organization, would you use a universal marketing appeal to all countries or customized appeals? Why?

4. What would be the advantages of buying an existing Mister Donut franchise in Europe, as opposed to starting your own small business? What are some of the problems a small, independent business might encounter in Europe?

5. The United States leads the world in services exporting. How would you use marketing research to investigate global marketing prospects for Liberty Travel, a large travel agency?

6. With the world's major nations forming trade agreements, what will happen to countries that don't join a free-trade pact? What dangers do you see in excluding countries from such pacts?

Getting Involved In Marketing

1. *On Your Own* Visit a clothing store and an electronics store. Look at labels and boxes to see who markets the products and where they are made. Write a brief report summarizing what you learned about international marketing in these stores.

2. *On Your Own* Keep a record of the foreign exchange value of the British pound sterling compared with the U.S. dollar over a two-week period. What movement did you note? How might this movement affect General Electric's exports to England? Give a two-minute talk to your class summarizing your findings.

3. *Find Out More* Check the annual report of Compaq Computer or IBM. Does the company use a global, customized, or combination marketing strategy? Why? How does the company adjust its marketing to local customers and conditions?

4. *In a Team* With three other students, debate this issue: "Resolved: The United States should reduce

trade protectionism to encourage international marketing and foreign investment." Have two students prepare the "pro" argument and two prepare the "con" argument. Which side is more persuasive? Why?

5. *In a Team* With two other students, watch an hour of network television, paying close attention to the commercials. What words, actions, or images do the commercials include that might be misunderstood by someone from another country or culture? How would you correct these potential problems?

6. *In a Partnership* With another student, select a specific culture within the United States, such as Mexican American people, and a specific product, such as long-distance telephone services. List at least five questions you would need to have answered as background for marketing to this group. How can you find the answers?

VideoCase Reaching Latino Customers

Marketing to an increasingly diverse population can challenge even the most accomplished marketers. To be successful, a marketer must research and understand the unique needs, characteristics, values, family roles, and lifestyles that affect each group's buying behavior. In addition, marketers have to be careful to avoid basic language or cultural problems that can hurt their marketing programs and damage their credibility.

Many savvy marketers choose not to tackle cross-cultural marketing on their own. Instead, they hire advertising and marketing agencies that specialize in reaching specific audiences. Mobil Oil, Anheuser-Busch, Inc., GTE and Bank One are just four of the many marketers that have hired Ornelas & Associates to prepare marketing programs targeting Hispanic and Latino customers.

Ornelas & Associates is a Latino-owned advertising and marketing communications agency based in Dallas. Since Victor Ornelas founded the agency in 1988, it has grown to more than three dozen employees and has annual billings over $25 million. Ninety percent of the agency is both bilingual and bicultural, which allows employees to effectively communicate with English- and Spanish-speaking clients and customer segments.

Spanish-language marketing materials account for about 90 percent of the agency's work. The agency uses research about Hispanic and Latino attitudes to help clients formulate marketing plans and prepare integrated marketing communication materials. Based on this research, the agency is able to suggest creative ways of presenting a good or service to the targeted segment. It can also recommend the appropriate advertising media for presenting the marketer's message.

The "Pepsi Man" character, played by comedian Paul Rodriguez, was created by Ornelas for Pepsi-Cola. This character has figured in a number of successful Pepsi-Cola promotions. Other campaigns, such as those for Bank One and GTE, have been crafted around the traditional family values of Hispanic and Latino people.

Ornelas worked for Levi Strauss, Anheuser-Busch, and Seven-Up before founding his agency. He works with two partners—one of whom is his wife Marjorie, who serves as director of human resources. Ornelas was recently named National Hispanic Business Entrepreneur of the Year by *Hispanic Business*

magazine in recognition of his accomplishments. Looking ahead, he sees even more need for his agency's services as an increasing number of marketers seek to tap the profit potential of meeting the needs of Hispanic and Latino customers all over the United States.[65]

Strategies and applications

1. Imagine that, as a marketer of canned vegetables, you want Victor Ornelas to help you reach Hispanic and Latino customer segments. In addition to language preferences, what other issues might you ask Ornelas to research as background for your marketing plan?

2. What sources could you use to research the size and composition of the Hispanic and Latino segments in the United States? If you were conducting online research through electronic databases, what key words would you use? Be specific.

3. Find two ads that have appeared in the United States for the same product, one in English and one in another language. Apart from language, how do the ads differ? How are they the same? What cultural elements are emphasized in each? Why?

4. Look again at the ads collected for question 3. How do these ads avoid stereotyping the target segments?

5. Open a discussion with your classmates who are from other countries or who have visited other countries recently. What are some of the marketing differences they have observed in different parts of the world?

6. If you were targeting the Hispanic and Latino segments, would you adapt your product, pricing, and channel management in addition to your marketing communication? Explain your answer.

Team project

Your team is working with Victor Ornelas on a new advertising campaign for GTE or Bank One, targeting Hispanic and Latino college students in your area. What media would you use to reach these segments? How would you research the message to use in this campaign? Prepare a brief presentation to your class summarizing your recommendations.

http://www.unilever.com

Marketing on the Net   Welcoming Web Visitors in Their Own Language

English-only Web sites are fine for English-speaking countries. But a growing number of marketers entering global markets want to welcome Web visitors in the local language. As interest in the Internet expands around the world and more computer users log on to access sites on the Web, the language issue is becoming even more urgent for marketers.

Why not stick with English? "You wouldn't market a car in Japan using an English ad campaign," says William Hunt, an entrepreneur who helps companies with Web sites for Japanese net surfers. He develops Japanese-language Web sites that meet the needs of net surfers in Japan. He also helps companies get listed with Web search engines that cover Japanese sites. This allows browsers to easily find such sites.

Getting listed with search engines is important, because surfers use these to locate sites in specific languages. One such search engine is Ecila, which lists all Web sites created in France. In addition, more translation programs are coming on-line to break the English-only barrier and allow visitors to view Web pages and e-mail in Japanese, German, French, Spanish, and other languages.

Some global marketers have broken through the English-only barrier by inviting electronic visitors to choose the language they wish to use when viewing the marketer's Web pages. Although this drives up the marketer's costs (because of the expense of translation and designing multiple Web pages), it broadens the base of potential visitors. As a result, the marketer is able to reach more people and start more customer relationships.

Unilever, for example, is an Anglo-Dutch company that markets packaged foods and household products around the world. Its Web site can be accessed in either English or Dutch. Visitors can look at product information, corporate financial data, and more.

Although Unilever does not offer electronic ordering—it markets through supermarkets, drug stores, and other channel partners—it does provide an extensive listing of brands by product category. Of course, some brands will initially be unfamiliar to visitors, because they are not available locally. However, that will change as Unilever brings more brands across national borders.

Unilever welcomes comments from visitors by offering a variety of communication options. In addition to e-mail, visitors can choose to write, fax, or telephone their questions, ideas,

and suggestions. By offering so many communication options—in both languages—Unilever reinforces its positioning as a customer-driven transnational marketer. [1]

Strategies and applications

1. Visit the Unilever Web site. Go to the English Index page and click on "Where Am I?" to see a chart of the site. As a first-time visitor, do you find this chart valuable? How could it be enhanced?

2. You're Unilever's Webmaster. How would you design a Web page for a new laundry detergent to be introduced across Western Europe? What information would you include on the page? To which other pages or sites would you link this page? Why?

3. Imagine you work for Procter & Gamble, which competes with Unilever in many markets around the world. What information on the Unilever Web site can give you clues about competing more effectively against this company?

4. You're the Webmaster for Carrefour, a France-based retailer that has stores in many countries. Review the Carrefour Web site (http://www.carrefour.fr). Suggest three ways that Carrefour can enhance its site to encourage customers outside France to browse the site and, ultimately, visit Carrefour stores.

5. Choose a U.S.-based company and visit its Web site. You can find URLs (universal resource locators, which are Web addresses) for major companies using Hoover's Online (http://www.hoovers.com). Suggest three ways that this company can use its Web site to strengthen relationships with non-U.S. customers and suppliers.

6. Choose a specific product and conduct Internet research into opportunities for exporting to global markets, using search engines such as Altavista. Are you able to find up-to-date information about attractive markets? Are you able to find good information about customer needs? What else might you research using the Internet before starting to export?

Team project

With other students, assume the role of co-owners of a small business that wants to reach Japanese customers in Japan and elsewhere. In planning your Web site, how would your business handle inquiries and orders? Write a brief report summarizing the issues you would have to address if you entered the Japanese market via a Web site.

http://www.greenmarket.com

Marketing on the Net Green Marketing Goes High-Tech

Where in cyberspace can the socially responsible marketer offer environmentally correct products? The answer is Green Market, an online mall that features only green products. Green Market is more than an online shopping center. In addition to browsing pages of green products, visitors—consumers and businesspeople—can find information about energy, pollution, and more.

Green marketers that want to differentiate their products can benefit from connecting with malls such as Green Market. Being listed on a green mall site can reinforce a product's green positioning and draw the attention of people who care about the environment. Once visitors find Green Market and explore its offerings, they are likely to return again and again, looking for updates on the issues and for green products that meet their needs. In this way, Green Market serves as an additional channel for marketers to use in reaching this particular market segment.

Identifying and reaching customers who are interested in environmentally correct products is not an easy task for marketers. Green Market makes it easier by providing an electronic meeting site where customers and marketers can find each other and complete mutually beneficial exchanges.

What's more, listing with a mall such as Green Market can help a marketer strengthen customer relationships by encouraging an ongoing electronic dialogue. With this dialogue, marketers can find out more about what customers want and what they think of products already on the market. This is also a good way to gather information for a marketing database.

Larger businesses such as Ben & Jerry's Homemade can afford a separate Web site to showcase their products and explain their stand on environmental issues. But for smaller marketers, a listing on a green cyberspace mall page can be more cost-effective. Marketers can have their products listed on green mall Web sites for as little as $500. Adding links to related sites can drive up costs, but it's another way to reach Internet surfers who may be interested in green products.

Jay Watts, vice president of marketing for the green marketer AFM, is enthusiastic about Green Market, where his company promotes Safecoat paints. "It's another way for us to communicate with people and to get our message out there," he says.

"It lets our competitors know we're first and helps us to promote an image of cutting edge." That edge can help AFM reach the right customer and pave the way for an ongoing relationship with customers while keeping rivals at bay. In the end, using a green cyberspace mall to promote green products can help a marketer make more "green."[2]

Strategies and applications

1. Visit the Green Market Web site. Does the Webmaster make it easy for customers to find specific products? What suggestions can you offer for improvements?

2. How can a visitor be sure that products listed on Green Market are actually green? What, specifically, does Green Market do to help customers feel comfortable about the environmental correctness of the products it features?

3. Why is it important for Green Market to offer general information and links to compatible Web sites as well as company offerings? How does this add value for customers? For marketers that list their products on the Green Market pages?

4. How can Jay Watts use non-Web advertising to let people know about his company's listing on the Green Market site?

5. What external factors in the marketing environment should Jay Watts be watching for signs of change that indicate increasing public apathy toward environmentally correct products? Would such signs be considered threats or opportunities? How might Watts adapt his marketing to such changes?

6. Customers are just one stakeholder group to which a green marketer such as AFM should be paying attention. How can an affiliation with Green Market help Jay Watts build relationships with noncustomer stakeholders? Identify specific stakeholder groups and explain how the affiliation is important to these groups.

Team project

With another student, visit and explore the Web site of Eco Expo (http://www.ecoexpo.com), a green mall that competes with Green Market. If you were a green marketer, on which site would you prefer to be listed? Why? Draft a letter to the Webmaster of the site you *don't* choose, presenting at least three ideas for improving the site so that it can be more responsive to the needs of marketers and visitors.

internetempowerment

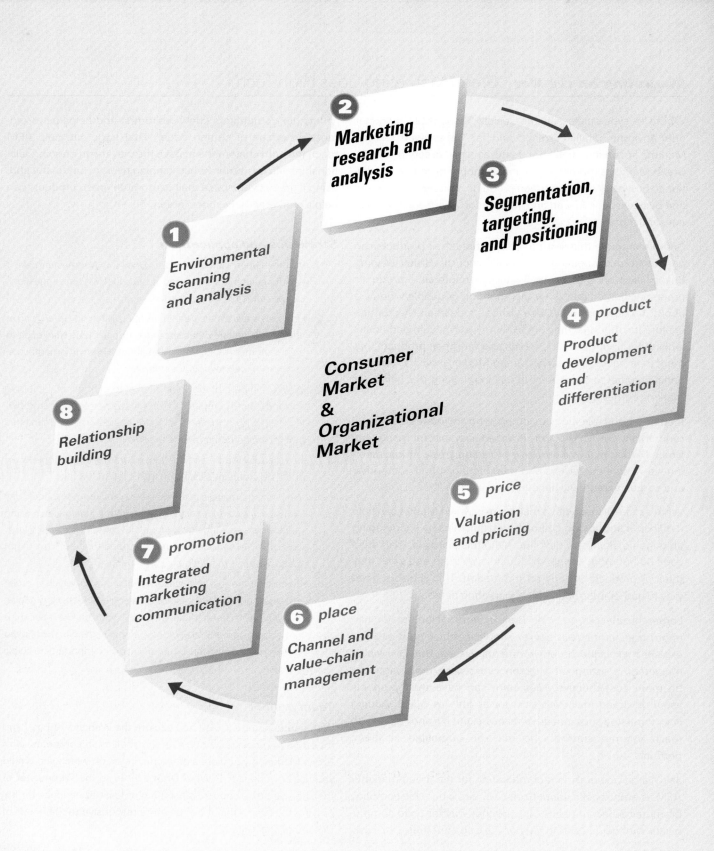

3

Marketing Research, Buyer Behavior, and Market Segmentation

Part 3 explores the use of marketing information, knowledge of buyer behavior, and segmentation for relationship building. Chapter 5 looks at how customer-focused marketers gather, analyze, and apply information about customers and markets. The profile discusses Nestlés ongoing research into customer needs and satisfaction. How consumers make buying decisions is the focus of Chapter 6, which explores internal and external influences on consumer buying. The chapter opens with a profile of Saturn, which has profited by taking the hassle out of buying cars. Chapter 7 shows how manufacturers, retailers, government agencies, and nonprofit institutions make buying decisions. The Brock Control profile describes the company's partnership approach to forging closer relationships with business buyers. Chapter 8 explores the use of market segmentation, targeting, and positioning. The profile of Luxottica shows these processes in action in a global marketing situation.

5

Marketing Information, Research, and Analysis

Learning Goals

After you have read and studied this chapter, you should be able to:

1. Identify four uses of marketing research.
2. Distinguish among marketing information systems, databases, and marketing decision support systems.
3. Describe the six steps in the formal marketing research process.
4. Differentiate between secondary data and primary data.
5. Explain the use of probability and nonprobability samples.
6. Analyze the three methods of collecting primary data and show how follow-up and tracking research are used.
7. Examine three ethical questions related to data collection.

PROFILE

Nestlé blends bits, bytes, and baby food

How can a marketer of baby food identify new parents and find out more about their concerns? That was the challenge facing Nestlé Baby Foods in France, a division of Switzerland-based Nestlé, the world's largest food marketer. Marketing director Fabienne Petit met the challenge by setting out to determine how Nestlé could make life easier for new parents. Her approach was so successful that it catapulted Nestlé into the number two slot behind Blendina, the top-selling baby food brand in France.

One of Petit's ideas was to get closer to parents by easing the strain of traveling with babies during summer vacations. A family driving tour is a tradition in France. However, long car trips can be difficult for parents of infants and toddlers. To help out—and to establish a dialogue with Nestlé's customers—Petit set up eight "Le Relais Bébé" rest stops along main highways. These roadside oases welcome 120,000 babies every summer, giving away 600,000 free samples of baby food and, with a diaper marketer, offering free disposable diapers and changing areas.

For the 20 minutes or so that the babies are being fed and changed, Nestlé hostesses talk with the parents about their likes and dislikes. This research helps Nestlé sharpen its marketing. Petit also accesses hospital maternity records to build a computerized database listing the names and addresses of new mothers. In the first mailing to mothers, the company asks for additional details such as the baby's name. If mothers respond, Nestlé sends six more mailings over two years, with samples and tips on baby care keyed to specific stages in child development.

To continue the dialogue with customers, every Nestlé advertisement, mailing, and product label invites customers to call for free nutritional advice from Nestlé's licensed dieticians. The nutrition hotline demonstrates the company's dedication to helping new parents. It also allows the company to learn firsthand about customers' concerns, providing ideas for creating new products and improving existing products, as well as developing communications that reinforce customer relationships.[1]

This chapter looks at the role of marketing research in providing marketing information. After learning about the four uses of marketing research and exploring applications of marketing information to marketing decisions, you'll examine the six steps in the formal marketing research process. The chapter closes with a look at ethical issues in marketing research.

The Role of Marketing Information and Research in Relationship Building

Fabienne Petit boosted Nestlé's baby food sales by getting good firsthand information about customers and their needs. As Petit's experience shows, such information is the lifeblood of any organization seeking to create and sustain customer relationships. It supports both environmental analysis and market analysis, the two universal marketing processes that enable organizations to (1) determine how the environment can affect marketing and (2) analyze customers and markets.

Marketing information is vital to organizations as they make dozens of big and small decisions. Among the big decisions are: To whom should we market? What product should we offer? What price should we set? How should we communicate with customers?

To make sound decisions that lead toward profitably satisfying customer needs, marketers need a steady flow of information about the world around them. Guesswork just isn't good enough. Only with accurate, timely information can organizations choose among the many paths they might take to reach out to customers.

Organizations obtain the facts and figures they need to support marketing decisions (and other organizational decisions) through marketing research. The American Marketing Association defines **marketing research** as "the function that links the consumer, customer, and public to the marketer through [the gathering of] marketing information."[2] This definition reflects the fundamental role of information in the relationship among customers, stakeholders, society, and the marketer. Without information, managers and employees can't make decisions that are appropriate for the organization and for exchange relationships with others.

In fact, marketing research plays far too vital a role in relationship building to be locked away in the marketing department. Employees in every department need access to the full range of marketing information so they can do their part to support exchange relationships. For that reason, some are saying that the term "marketing research" should be changed to "business information," showing that the information gathered is for everyone in the organization.[3]

Just as access to information is important, so is timing. When Nabisco marketers were reviewing trends in the marketing environment, they found that the number of older Americans was increasing. They also learned that people were more concerned about healthful eating. In response to these trends, the company developed a cross-functional team to create the Snack-Well's line of low-fat cookies and foods. Nabisco's timing was excellent: Customers flocked to buy the products, which now generate $400 million in yearly sales. Competitors didn't spot the trends in time, and they had to scramble to catch up.[4]

marketing research

the function that links the consumer, customer, and public to the marketer through the gathering of marketing information

Uses of Marketing Research

Neither the Nabisco situation nor the Nestlé example is unique. Throughout the business world—and in government and nonprofit organizations as well—people are putting marketing research to work as they strive to satisfy customers or constituents. There are four primary uses of marketing research:

- to analyze customers, their needs, and their level of satisfaction,
- to analyze markets and opportunities,
- to analyze the effectiveness of a marketer's strategy and tactics, and
- to analyze whether the marketing process is meeting the goals of both customers and the organization.

To Analyze Customers, Needs, and Satisfaction

Marketing research is a support function within marketing. The first use of marketing research is to analyze customers as well as their needs and their level of satisfaction. The results of this effort help firms to become more customer oriented and to determine which people or organizations to target; to learn what customers need, want, and expect; and to find out whether customers are satisfied with what marketers (and their competitors) are offering. For example, Fox Valley Technical College in Appleton, Wisconsin, sees local businesses as well as students as its customers. It regularly surveys businesses to ask about their interest in training courses and economic development services. Also, to determine satisfaction with college courses, it checks with graduates to find out how many are able to get jobs. With this feedback, the college can refine its course offerings to give both customer groups what they need and want.[5]

In the days of standard products and mass production, marketers took aim at mass audiences. As a result, they were interested in what *large groups* of people had to say about various products. Today, however, marketing is becoming much more focused. Marketers now have the sophisticated technology necessary to research the needs and preferences of *individual customers*. They can use such data to maintain ongoing customer relationships by developing quality products tailored to each customer's needs.[6]

To Analyze Markets and Opportunities

The second use of marketing research is to analyze both markets and opportunities. **Market** refers to the group of customers or prospects who need or want a product and have both the resources and willingness to exchange something of value to get it. With marketing research, organizations can answer question such as: Where should we market? How big is the market for certain products? What in the marketing environment can help or hurt our marketing efforts?

Premier Bank in Baton Rouge uses marketing research to locate promising markets for banking services. Market data is analyzed in PRIZM, a demographic segmentation system showing lifestyle information about U.S. households arranged into 62 ZIP code groups. Using the data from PRIZM (which stands for Potential Rating Index by ZIP Market), the bank locates neighborhoods of households with traits that are similar to those of its best customers. Then it puts together marketing campaigns to pitch the appropriate bank products to people in those new markets.[7]

market

the group of customers or prospects who need or want a product and have both the resources and willingness to exchange something of value to get it

Custom PRIZM Target Groups

Creation of target groups is a key element of many marketing applications using PRIZM. The process typically begins with a profile that organizes a consumer file about product usage, survey responses, or other data according to PRIZM Clusters. The clusters within a target group show similarities in behavior and in fundamental lifestyle characteristics that represent a significant percentage of the overall market. The PRIZM Profile shown right illustrates the starting point for creating target groups. The index rates consumers' propensity to purchase; average equals 100. The chart shows that all of the S1 Clusters index considerably higher than average for purchasing a particular midsize import sedan. However, only three of the U1 clusters ("Money & Brains," "Young Literati," and "American Dreams") would be good candidates for this car. Claritas provides classroom training to teach PRIZM users how to develop accurate and reliable target groups.

PRIZM Profile for Midsize Import Sedans

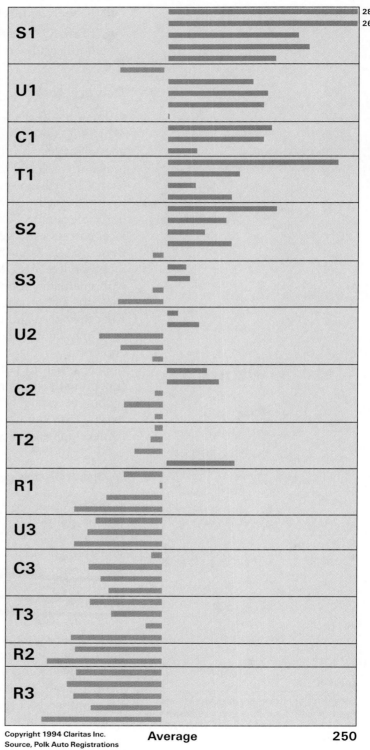

Copyright 1994 Claritas Inc.
Source, Polk Auto Registrations

Average   **250**

To Analyze The Effectiveness of Marketing Strategy and Tactics

The third use of marketing research is to analyze marketing effectiveness. Such evaluations help organizations measure their ongoing marketing performance and identify areas ripe for improvement. Marketing research can answer questions such as: Does our advertising communicate effectively with people interested in buying our product? Is our product reaching customers through the right channels? Are people buying our product more than once? Answers to these and similar questions can help organizations evaluate their marketing success and determine which changes in their marketing plans will yield the results they want.

Using marketing research to check marketing effectiveness is a high priority for Pharmacia Biotech, a Swedish marketer of chemicals and instruments to biotechnological researchers. Pharmacia sets aside up to 10 percent of its marketing dollars for marketing research. The company's research shows whether its integrated marketing communication are reaching the target market of business customers, whether customer attitudes are affected, and how the firm's Swedish origins affect foreign customers.[8]

To Analyze Whether the Marketing Process Is Meeting the Goals of Both Customers and the Organization

The fourth use of marketing research is to analyze the overall marketing process. Did we achieve our marketing goal? What can we do better? What is likely to happen if we make certain changes in our marketing process? You can become a better marketer by using marketing information to evaluate the steps you take in the process and then fix or improve the appropriate functions. Remember: "Always be customer-driven" ◄——⏐ **(p. 7)** when using research data.

For example, M&M/Mars recently teamed up with a large supermarket to study the effectiveness of its candy marketing efforts. Comparing the supermarket's sales of M&M candy brands and all candy brands against results in other stores, the executives discovered plenty of room for improvement. As a result of this research, M&M evaluated a wide variety of options before deciding on new pricing strategies and a new mix of products and sizes for the store.[9]

Marketing Information and Marketing Decisions

In the course of conducting marketing research, organizations will generally gather a varied collection of facts and figures. Depending on the decisions they are facing at the time, they may use some of the data right away and put the rest aside for later use. Because the marketing environment is so changeable, however, marketers never know when they'll need that marketing information to solve a sudden problem. Three tools can help manage marketing information and use it to make sound decisions: marketing information systems, marketing databases, and marketing decision support systems.

Marketing Information Systems

A **marketing information system (MIS)** is a structured system for managing the ongoing collection, analysis, storage, and reporting of marketing data. From sales figures to product prices to customer-satisfaction ratings, a good marketing MIS can gather and store a mass of details needed for marketing decisions. Although being short of marketing data is the reason for conducting marketing research, marketers often face the opposite problem as well. Some organizations have so much data that they don't know how to make sense of everything in their files. An MIS is a good way to collect and organize facts and figures for availability in a timely fashion. The MIS can be computerized or, for smaller organizations, paper-based.

A world-class marketing information system has at least four components:

1. *A mechanism for gathering data from inside and outside the organization.* A continual process is essential, rather than a sporadic series of events or a one-time poll. Otherwise, you'll have gaps in the information, and you may miss important changes.

2. *A mechanism for processing and storing the data.* Facts and figures have to be put into usable form and held until needed. The mechanism can be as simple as grouping data into appropriate categories and holding them in files, ready for access.

3. *A mechanism for making the information available to everyone in the organization.* With computerized systems, employees at all levels and in all locations can tap into the MIS files by means of personal computers. With paper-based systems, employees can visit a central location to check the files for data.

4. *A mechanism for allowing employees to request additional information from the system.* If what is needed isn't readily available, the MIS should include a method for searching other files or even other systems to find key information.

The trick is to make everyone in the organization aware of the kind of information needed for making marketing decisions that will build long-term relationships and encourage people to contribute to as well as request data from the system. To meet this goal, Xerox has a formal program featuring a technique known as *reverse engineering*. When a competitor introduces a product, Xerox engineers buy it and take it apart to see how it functions and to estimate the cost of design and production. Employees, who receive this information through online communications and company newsletters, can then compare Xerox products to those of rivals and get ideas from what competitors have done.[10]

Marketing Databases

marketing information system (MIS)

a structured system for managing the ongoing collection, analysis, storage, and reporting of marketing data

database

a computerized file of data that can be searched for particular details

The second tool for managing marketing information is a **database**, a computerized file of data that can be searched for particular details. Databases are used to store facts and figures gathered by the MIS. *Internal databases*, which are built and maintained by one organization, can hold a variety of details about customers, markets, and products. Marketers such as Radio Shack typically concentrate everything they know about their customers into a single internal database. Radio Shack's customer database, for example, holds the names and addresses of millions of customers along with their recent purchases. Using this database, the store chain can identify past buyers of radios and telephones and mail them separate offers for similar products.[11] This helps them maintain a relationship with their customers.

Details about prospective customers, new markets, industry sales, competitors, legal and regulatory rulings, and virtually anything else marketers might want to research can be obtained by checking *external databases*—that is, databases maintained by other organizations. Using external databases, organizations can access information needed for specific marketing decisions. They can also identify potential markets and customers for their products. And, most importantly, they can better meet the wants and needs of specific customers by obtaining more information about them.

North American Life Assurance of Toronto, one of Canada's largest insurance marketers, taps external databases to find potential customers. It buys names and addresses from several outside databases, then adds telephone numbers from a database held by a telephone company division. The resulting information is loaded into North American's computers as an internal database for mailings and telephone marketing programs.[12] However, privacy advocates are alarmed by the amount of data held in marketing databases.

ETHICS & SOCIAL RESPONSIBILITY

Does marketing research invade customers' privacy?

If you live in a small town outside Chicago, your buying habits may have been studied by Foote Cone & Belding, a Chicago advertising agency. The agency isn't saying which town has been under its marketing research microscope since 1989, when researchers began gathering data on small-town life. Is this an invasion of privacy or an appropriate way of helping marketers gain insight into customer wants and needs?

Advertising agencies are among the many marketing organizations that collect and analyze data on interests, lifestyles, and other aspects of people's personal lives. Marketers argue that they need accurate, timely information to satisfy customer needs. On the other hand, critics are concerned about the volume and accuracy of personal information that is available in marketing databases. They also worry that the U.S. government isn't adequately safeguarding personal privacy. "Existing laws regulating privacy simply aren't effective," says Robert S. Bulmash of Private Citizen, a public advocacy group.

To keep customers' trust, marketers should put in place a four-pronged customer privacy policy. First, advise customers that you would like to share their data with other marketers—and let them say no. Second, be sure customers understand that their data may be used to send them more offers. Third, prevent sensitive data such as credit card numbers from leaving the files. And fourth, consider whether a particular use of database information *seems* unethical; if it does, don't do it.[13]

Can you think of a situation in which a marketer should *not* reveal data to others?

marketing decision support system (MDSS)

a computerized system that links internal databases and allows marketers to analyze data for marketing decisions

Marketing Decision Support Systems

A **marketing decision support system (MDSS)** is a computerized system that links internal databases and allows marketers to analyze data for marketing decisions. The key words in this definition are "analyze data." An MDSS serves only for data analysis; thus it is less comprehensive than an MIS.

Using sophisticated formulas, the MDSS pulls appropriate data from databases and winnows the mass of details to uncover trends and patterns. This information is then presented in an easy-to-read format for marketers who are preparing to make decisions. Marketers can also simulate the future by asking the MDSS to show how profits would change based on higher sales, fewer customers, and other possible scenarios.[14]

One important application of MDSSs is to analyze the results of marketing efforts. In the past, marketers spent weeks after a program ended gathering details about sales. Then they faced the tedious task of analyzing the data to interpret the meaning. Today, MDSSs help Kraft and other marketers study a program's profitability right after completion. Just as important, the MDSS can use the results of past programs to project the profitability of marketing programs under consideration.[15]

Informal and Formal Marketing Research

Organizations can gather information about customers, markets, and the marketing environment informally as well as formally. *Informal marketing research* means gathering marketing data whenever the opportunity arises. For example, almost every employee in an organization hears comments from customers and potential customers about the organization, its goods or services, and its competitors. The accumulation of such information is informal marketing research because organization members simply collect data when possible, without waiting for a deliberately planned study.

Building a database to support a marketing decision system calls for creativity. Each time a company does a demonstration like this one, it can ask for the names and addresses of participants who sample products. It can also record customer reactions and suggestions. This data can then be analyzed and added to the decision support system. What other information do marketing decision makers need on a regular basis?

Pizza Hut uses informal marketing research to gather data about customer complaints. The chain invites customers to call a toll-free telephone hotline when they have a problem with food or service. Employees of an outside service that specializes in handling complaints listen to callers and find out what store was involved, and what product. They then send the details via computer to the store that experienced the problem. Within 48 hours, that Pizza Hut's manager calls the customer to resolve the problem—and to demonstrate commitment to strengthening customer relationships.[16]

In almost any company, from time to time, employees hear something that competitors do better. This informal benchmarking can be used to gradually improve the way the organization operates. Such informal marketing research is one of the reasons for the success of Wal-Mart, the largest U.S. retail chain. Founder Sam Walton visited Wal-Mart's competitors almost daily. He made comparisons, took notes, and then ordered small changes in his own operations. Using data gathered in this way, Walton kept improving Wal-Mart, a practice the company continues today.[17]

Informal marketing research is only one part of the equation, however. Even organizations with a systematic way of collecting data through informal marketing research may not have enough information to solve certain problems or answer particular marketing questions. To fill in the gaps, marketers turn to *formal marketing research*, the use of planned research studies to gather specific marketing information. Together, informal and formal marketing research provide the details needed to make an informed decision. The next section explains the process of planning, conducting, and evaluating formal marketing research.

Before you go on . . .

A. **What is marketing research, and how is it used?**

B. **Why are marketing information systems (MIS) important?**

C. **What are marketing databases, and how are they used?**

D. **How does informal marketing research differ from formal marketing research?**

The Marketing Research Process

Formal marketing research consists of six steps: (1) define the problem and determine the present situation, (2) design the research, including hypotheses, and identify data sources, (3) collect primary data, (4) analyze and interpret research data, (5) select and implement the best ethical alternative, and (6) evaluate the results. Step 5 is often performed by top management with or without the consultation of researchers. The process is circular, not linear. What you learn at each step helps you continuously improve your research, as illustrated in Figure 5.1. As you progress, you gain more insight into the situation and the best way to approach it. By the sixth step, your evaluation of the results will show whether you need to retrace earlier steps and refine the process for a better solution.

As you might imagine, marketing research can be complex. Even companies that have professional marketing researchers on staff often hire outside research suppliers to handle some or all of

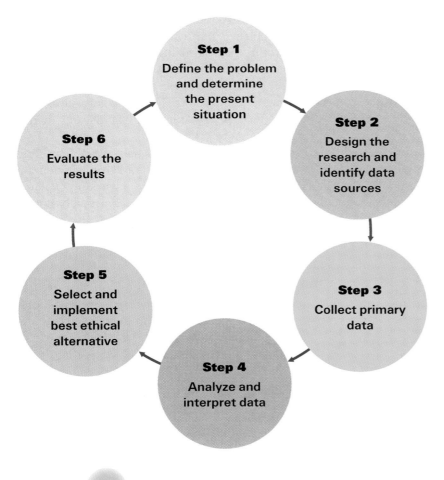

FIGURE **5.1** **The Marketing Research Process**

When planning formal marketing research, marketers move in six steps from defining a problem that affects marketing performance to selecting the best ethical alternative and evaluating results.

the steps just listed. For example, you might have a supplier collect the data or analyze the data you have collected. Grocery and drug marketers frequently hire suppliers to test customer reaction to proposed advertising programs or new product ideas.[18] Although the supplier can recommend a particular alternative to solve your problem or to improve your research process, the final decision is, of course, up to you as the marketer.

Step 1: Define the Problem and Determine the Present Situation

The marketing research process starts when you need facts and figures to make an informed decision that will solve a marketing problem. When things are not as you want or expect them to be, something needs to be solved, or opportunities are being missed, you have a marketing *problem*. Not long ago, MicroScan, a maker of medical analysis equipment used by hospitals and physicians, identified what appeared to be a symptom of a critical marketing problem. The symptom: The company wasn't sustaining as many customer relationships as it wanted.[19]

MicroScan recognized that a problem existed, but that was only the start. Next the company had to determine the kind of data needed to make a decision that would eliminate the problem. That requires defining the problem in very specific terms. People do this by looking beyond the general "symptoms" of the problem to get a more specific idea of why the problem is occurring. What was behind MicroScan's loss of customers? "MicroScan insisted it lost customers only when they [the customers] went out of business or got acquired," says Scott Garrett, president of MicroScan's owner, Baxter Diagnostics. "We were a little skeptical."

Garrett suspected that a rival firm was taking customers away. This kind of tentative explanation of the relationship between marketing elements is called a **hypothesis**. The hypothesis points you toward a working explanation for what is happening. Not every research problem requires a hypothesis, but such proposed explanations are helpful when trying to discover why a problem exists. Garrett's hypothesis—that MicroScan was losing customers because it couldn't match what competitors were doing—could be tested by marketing research.

Because marketing problems don't occur in a vacuum, you also need to consider the context of the present situation. How do employees, stockholders, and the public perceive your company and its products? What is the competitive environment? What products are profitable? Where are the market opportunities and threats? These are the kinds of questions that define your situation and help you limit your research to areas that will give you data for a meaningful decision. In the MicroScan case, the president's hypothesis pointed the company toward investigating the competitive situation.

hypothesis

tentative explanation of the relationship between marketing elements

Issues for critical thinking

Sometimes the people closest to a marketing problem can't see it objectively enough to define it or form a hypothesis. What role do you think other employees, suppliers, and customers can play in this process? Should this step be an individual or a team effort?

exploratory research

a type of preliminary research designed to disclose more fully the nature of the problem and of the present situation, and to point the way toward further research

descriptive research

gives a rather precise picture of the nature of a marketing problem and the frequency with which it occurs

Many government and civic organizations survey their members with questionnaires such as this one that ask respondents to rate various aspects of the service and its facilities. Typical responses are "yes," "no," "strongly agree," "strongly disagree," and so on, but the questionnaires provide very little space for written comments. How would you go about designing such a questionnaire? Would you begin with a focus group? Why? Would you leave more room for comments? Why?

Step 2: Design the Research, Including Hypotheses, and Identify Data Sources

Once a marketer has defined its problem and characterized its present situation, it is ready to design the marketing research study and determine where to get needed data. The research design serves as a plan of action for studying the marketing problem.

Marketing Research Designs

Depending on the problem definition and the hypotheses to be explored, you can conduct any of three types of research: exploratory, descriptive, or causal. When you have only a vague idea of what the problem entails, you'll sometimes start with exploratory research. Then, as you acquire a better sense of the problem, the cause, and the probable alternative solutions you might choose, you may conduct either descriptive or causal research. The results of those two types of research will give you data to help decide which ethical course of action to take.[20]

Exploratory Research **Exploratory research** is a type of preliminary research designed to disclose more fully the nature of the problem and of the present situation, and to point the way toward further research. By exploring first, marketers gain a deeper understanding of the opportunities and challenges they face; they also come to realize what additional information they need to resolve their problems. Exploratory research can include talking to experts in the target area and checking available marketing databases or outside sources for information on similar problems.

For example, when Scott Garrett suspected that MicroScan's customers were going to competitors, he began exploratory research to see whether he was on the right track. Using an outside research supplier, Garrett surveyed former customers to learn why they had stopped doing business with MicroScan. It developed that many customers left because MicroScan couldn't match an attractive mid-priced product offered by a competitor.

Descriptive Research Descriptive research gives a rather precise picture of the nature of a marketing problem and the frequency with which it occurs. This type of research helps describe in detail what is happening in a specific market or how members of a certain group of customers are using the marketer's products. An organization that has studied these detailed descriptions can answer many questions about the marketing problems it is facing.

What do citizens—the customers of a local government—think of municipal government and services? This is the kind of descriptive research that Dallas, Texas, St. Petersburg, Florida, and many other U.S. cities undertake every year. By finding out what citizens like and dislike, government officials and employees can get a detailed picture of what they should continue doing and what they should consider changing.[21]

Causal Research   Causal research is designed to help identify cause-and-effect relationships among certain elements in marketing problems. What will be the effect of changing specific parts of the product, the pricing, the integrated marketing communication, or the marketing channel? These are the kinds of questions causal research is designed to investigate. When you understand how one element affects another—for instance, how customers react to a new product—you have more information to consider when deciding among possible solutions to the problem.

Although causal research can give you clues to the way one marketing element affects another, it isn't infallible. Suppose you want to test whether supermarket sales will rise if your product gains additional shelf space. Thus if sales do in fact go up when your product is displayed on two shelves instead of one, you have to think about other possible explanations for this result. Did competitors raise prices or stop advertising? Did the supermarket put competing products in less visible shelf positions? Because controlling every element in such a test is nearly impossible, you should use care when interpreting the results of causal research and making decisions that will affect marketing relationships.

Sources of Data

Imagine that you are a marketing manager. As you think about your research design, you also need to consider the sources of data to be used in studying the marketing problem. You can collect two types of data: secondary data and primary data. In fact, marketers generally use both in marketing research projects.

Secondary Data   Secondary data are facts and figures that have already been collected for another purpose. Such available materials make a good place to start when you're searching for a description of a new market or customer segment, or when you need additional information to form a hypothesis. Even though secondary data were gathered for another purpose (such as a previous research project), the information can be valuable when you want a quick and inexpensive study of a current marketing problem. Secondary data can also yield valuable ideas about the nature or extent of your problem, areas for further research, and possible solutions.

However, secondary data have limitations. Information from secondary sources may not be sufficiently detailed. It may also be entirely irrelevant to the current study. In addition, secondary data from published sources may be out of date and therefore unusable in some situations. Old data cause headaches for Thomas Buchert, director of Japanese operations for General DataComm, a Connecticut-based maker of computer networking equipment. Buchert is always looking for information about overseas customers and markets, but most of what he finds in secondary sources isn't timely enough to be useful.[22]

Secondary data can come from both internal and external sources. Try internal sources first because they are easily accessible and inexpensive. You can often find valuable facts and figures in your own organization's records. Internal secondary data sources include accounting and sales records, cost figures, customer records, inventory protocols, and management and employee experience. A constant stream of information flows into internal records, including compliments and complaints from customers, supplier

causal research

designed to help identify cause-and-effect relationships among certain elements in marketing problems

secondary data

facts and figures that have already been collected for another purpose

	DOLLAR SALES	DOLLAR SALES	CTGRY DOLLAR SHARE	CTGRY DOLLAR SHARE	VOLUME SALES	VOLUME SALES	AVG_$ PER VOLUME	AVG_$ PER VOLUME	EST_AV ACV_WT DIST	EST_AV ACV_WT DIST	%VOL ANY MERCH	%VOL ANY MERCH
	52-WEEK ENDING 12/31/95	52-WEEK ENDING 12/31/95 VS. 52 WKS AGO	52-WEEK ENDING 12/31/95	52-WEEK ENDING 12/31/95 VS. 52 WKS AGO	52-WEEK ENDING 12/31/95	52-WEEK ENDING 12/31/95 VS. 52 WKS AGO	52-WEEK ENDING 12/31/95	52-WEEK ENDING 12/31/95 VS. 52 WKS AGO	52-WEEK ENDING 12/31/95	52-WEEK ENDING 12/31/95 VS. 52 WKS AGO	52-WEEK ENDING 12/31/95	52-WEEK ENDING 12/31/95 VS. 52 WKS AGO
CATEGORY - COCOA MIXES	302,228M	1.05	100.00	0.00	119,833M	-3.58	2.52	4.80	100.0	-0.01	32.0	-3.68
TYPE - CHOCOLATE MLK FLAVRNG/COC M	302,228M	1.05	100.00	0.00	119,833M	-3.58	2.52	4.80	100.0	-0.01	32.0	-3.68
PARENT - CHOCOLATERA DE JALSC S A	2,030M	-2.20	0.67	-0.02	1,164M	3.25	1.74	-5.29	11.8	1.31	44.0	-8.83
VENDOR - CHOCOLATERA DE JLSC S A	2,030M	-2.20	0.67	-0.02	1,164M	3.25	1.74	-5.29	11.8	1.31	44.0	-8.83
IBARRA	2,030M	-2.20	0.67	-0.02	1,164M	3.25	1.74	-5.29	11.8	1.31	44.0	-8.83
PARENT - CONAGRA INC	82,782M	4.48	27.39	0.89	26,135M	1.65	3.16	2.77	97.5	0.60	34.8	-3.30
VENDOR - HUNT-WESSON	82,782M	4.48	27.39	0.89	26,135M	1.65	3.16	2.77	97.5	0.60	34.8	-3.30
SWISS MISS	68,117M	-2.40	22.53	-0.80	21,412M	-5.69	3.18	3.48	96.5	0.22	36.7	-2.80
SWISS MISS CHOCOLATE SENSATION	1,790M	*	0.59	0.59	600,951	*	2.97	*	34.1	34.12	31.6	31.68
SWISS MISS MARSHMALLOW LOVERS	8,311M	30.98	2.74	0.62	2,827M	30.84	2.93	0.11	64.9	10.85	27.2	-1.62
SWISS MISS PREMIERE COCOAS	4,564M	48.28	1.50	0.48	1,295M	54.51	3.52	-4.03	52.4	28.87	19.9	-1.71
PARENT - HEINZ USA	1,154M	-56.65	0.38	-0.50	109,387	-58.70	10.55	4.98	20.5	-18.23	1.9	-1.39
VENDOR - WEIGHT WATCHERS COMPANY	844,779	-60.49	0.27	-0.43	91,213	-60.63	9.26	0.37	20.5	-18.23	2.1	-1.22
WEIGHT WATCHERS	844,779	-60.49	0.27	-0.43	91,213	-60.63	9.26	0.37	20.5	-18.23	2.1	-1.22
- HERSHEY FOODS CORP	18,691M	41.23	6.18	1.75	7,588M	24.10	2.46	13.80	87.6	4.82	27.8	0.22
CHOCOLATE USA		41.23	6.18			24.10		13.80	87	.82	27.8	

MARKET: TOTAL U.S.
CATEGORY: COCOA MIXES
VOLUME: EXPRESSED IN 16OZEQ

infoScan®
SUPERMARKET REVIEW

OUTLET: FOOD
PAGE 000051
TIME PERIODS: 01/03/94 - 12/31/95
IRI WEEKS: 749 - 852

Information Resources Incorporated (IRI) provides detailed secondary data that can be used by marketers to compare their product's sales with sales of competitive brands. In this sample, the product category is cocoa mixes. Overall category sales are up from year to year, but sales of certain brands tend to fluctuate. Using this information, a marketer can determine its relative share and track results of retail promotions.

letters, and other information picked up by executives, employees, and friends. Also, data and results from earlier company studies may be of value.

External secondary data sources include published industry studies, library sources, syndicated research suppliers, and government records. Industry studies are published by trade associations and other groups, which collect data about company activities, products, and so on. Sometimes industry studies are free and sometimes they carry a price tag. Although these studies may not supply all the details you require, they can provide good background.

Often public, university, and company libraries offer convenient gateways to an abundance of information (in published form or through the Internet and other online database services). For example, you can search through Business Periodicals Online, a computerized database, to find articles from business magazines and journals. If you're researching legal issues, check the LEXIS database of legal cases and the PATSEARCH database of U.S. patents. For background on new markets, you might check Rezide, an encyclopedia that profiles residents in all 42,496 U.S. ZIP codes.[23]

You can search for external sources of secondary data on the Internet using a variety of tools. One is a *gopher*, which helps you search external databases stored in other systems. Another tool is a *browser* such as Netscape, which allows you to access information on World Wide Web sites. A third tool is a *search engine* such as Infoseek, which points the way to Internet sites that have information related to the subject you're researching.

Syndicated research data comprise marketing information collected by private research firms to be resold to companies that require facts and figures about markets, customers, and so on. Syndicated research firms such as Nielsen Marketing Research, Information Resources Inc., and Arbitron can give you details about product usage, shopping patterns, customer demographics, media usage, and other information needed for marketing decisions.

Some syndicated research suppliers can provide *single-source data*, details about customers, product sales, media usage, and communications that are available from one research source. Instead of having to pull together details from many sources, the marketer can get everything from one source, in a form already suitable for analysis. With the data, marketers can examine buying patterns and relate individuals' purchases to specific marketing activities such as couponing. Much of the sales information is drawn from the *scanner data* collected by store checkout scanning devices that record brand purchases, payment methods, and coupon usage for storage in store and supplier databases.[24]

Marketers looking for secondary data on markets, customers, dealers, and competitors can check U.S. government sources. At the federal level, the Bureau of the Census provides a vast array of statistics about area population, household sizes, and residents' occupations and levels of education, as well as data on housing, transportation, wholesaling, retailing, and other elements essential to effective marketing. At the state and local level, other government agencies can provide details about economic conditions, car and house ownership, and so on. For international markets, contact foreign embassies as well as the sources shown in Chapter 4.[25]

Primary Data   Often marketing decisions are too important to base them solely on secondary data or the data needed to make a marketing decision aren't available from secondary sources. That's when you need **primary data**: facts, figures, or details gathered for a specific marketing research study. Gathering this information can be costly and time-consuming. However, primary data are valuable because they fit your needs exactly and are as current as possible.

Primary data are essential for the marketing decisions made by Thomas Buchert for General DataComm. As you saw earlier, Buchert found that secondary data about other countries are frequently out of date. That's why many company managers gather primary data themselves. "Twice a year we have to go on a world tour and get our questions answered first-hand," he says. Talking with potential customers helps the company determine the best way to approach each new market and customer relationship.[26]

Primary data can help you determine *how* to best satisfy your customers. Think back to MicroScan, which wanted to find out why it wasn't retaining customer relationships. The only way to uncover the reason was to gather primary data—specifically, to poll former customers about why they'd left. MicroScan went further, questioning the 3,000 buyers of its own and competitors' products about equipment, service, and other issues. The answers to these questions helped the company better understand its customers' needs and paved the way for making decisions that would improve customer satisfaction and enhance customer relationships.[27]

Step 3: Collect Primary Data

At this point in the marketing research process, the organization has defined the problem, determined the present situation, reviewed data sources, and designed the research needed to collect primary data. Now it's time for the third step, collecting primary data for analysis and interpretation. In this step, the marketer thinks about exactly who (or what) should be included in the study. Then the organization collects data, using the observation, survey, or experimental method.

primary data

facts, figures, or details gathered for a specific marketing research study

population

the total group that might be included in a particular research study

census

a study incorporating every person, place, or thing in the defined population

sample

a segment of the total population selected to represent the whole

sampling error

a measure of the difference between the results obtained from studying a sample and the results that would have been obtained from studying the entire population

probability sample

one in which every person, place, or thing in the population has a known chance of being selected for the research

Sample Design

To yield information for marketing decisions, research has to focus on the right group of people, places, or things. The **population** or universe is the total group that might be included in a particular research study. In a study of customer satisfaction, the population would consist of all customers. In a study of a new perfume for teenagers, the population would consist of all the 13- to-19-year-old females in a given market.

In some cases, marketers take a **census**, a study incorporating every person, place, or thing in the defined population. This broad approach is appropriate if the population is small enough and the marketer knows how to reach it. For example, Solectron, a maker of components for powerful computers, contacts every one of its nearly 70 customers when it studies customer satisfaction.[28]

Often marketers don't have the time, money, or ability to study the entire population. That's when they use a **sample**, a segment of the total population selected to represent the whole. How the sample is chosen greatly affects the results. Larger sample sizes provide more complete information for marketing decisions, but they cost more.[29]

Bear in mind that when you use a sample, your results won't be the same as you would have obtained if you had surveyed the entire population. **Sampling error** is a measure of the difference between the results obtained from studying a sample and the results that would have been obtained from studying the entire population. The level of sampling error varies from one type of sample to another, something to consider when designing a sample for your research.

Sample designs can be described as either probability or nonprobability as shown in Figure 5.2. A **probability sample** is one in which every person, place, or thing in the population has a known chance of being selected for the research. You can calculate the chance, or probability, that a particular member of the population will be included in your probability sample. In contrast, a **nonprobability sample** is one in which you can't accurately calculate the chance that any one member of the population will be selected.

F I G U R E **5.2** **Alternative Sample Designs**

When you use probability samples, you can calculate the sampling error to see how the results differ from what you would find if you surveyed the entire population. You can't calculate the sampling error of nonprobability samples, however.

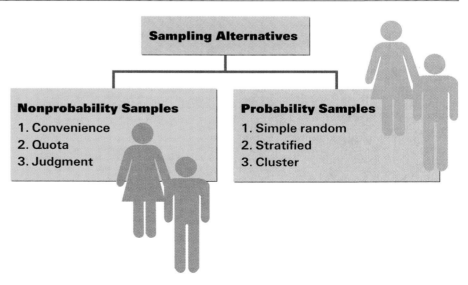

This is because nonprobability samples are chosen to suit the researcher's convenience or judgment, or according to a quota. As a result, the sampling error of such samples can't be statistically measured—and you can't be sure that the sample accurately represents the population you want to study.

Probability Samples   The most basic of the probability samples is the simple random sample, in which all the members of a population have an equal chance of being included. To design a *stratified sample*, you divide the population into distinct subgroups and then select a simple random sample of each group. To design a *cluster sample*, you divide the population into certain areas (or clusters) and then randomly select which will be surveyed.

No matter which probability sample you design, you can calculate the sampling error and see how closely the results would match results from the entire population. But because you need a list of every member of the population to work with simple random samples and stratified samples—and a list of all the members of the areas randomly selected in a cluster sample—these designs can be costly and take time. On the other hand, probability samples allow you to statistically test the results, an important consideration for analysis and interpretation.

Nonprobability Samples   You can guess from the name what a *convenience sample* is: a sample gathered from members of the population that can be reached easily by the researcher. When you go to a shopping center and ask shoppers about their preferences for political candidates, you're using a convenience sample. Such samples are easy to design, but the results are often of questionable validity because of potential sampling error.

Philips, the global electronics marketer based in the Netherlands, recently used convenience samples to uncover ideas for a new online interactive product for children. Researchers fanned out to communities across Italy, France, and the Netherlands, inviting adults and children to talk about online products. This dialogue helped Philips develop a product that would interest children and be acceptable to their parents.[30]

A *quota sample* is one in which respondents are selected according to predetermined characteristics that reflect the population as a whole. A quota sample might consist of an equal number of women and men or a certain percentage of people who use each of three competing products. For example, Delta Air Lines recently had to decide whether to extend a ban on smoking to all its international flights. Using a quota sample, the carrier's marketers surveyed 4,200 passengers flying to Pacific destinations during two months. The results showed overwhelming support for the ban, and Delta became the first U.S. carrier to outlaw smoking on all flights around the world.[31]

In a *judgment sample*, members of the population are selected on the basis of what the researcher believes will be a good sample. When Colgate-Palmolive conducted research leading to a relaunch of Irish Spring soap, its researchers talked to people in Marion, Indiana, and Visalia, California. The researchers believed that statements from people in these cities were representative of the reactions of U.S. consumers generally to new advertising and promotion.[32]

Of course, with nonprobability samples, you can't measure how the results are likely to differ from those of research that covers the entire population. Still, such sample designs are often used in exploratory research to

nonprobability sample
one in which you can't accurately calculate the chance that any one member of the population will be selected

refine the problem definition, formulate hypotheses, and point the way for additional research.

Observation

Once you've prepared the sample design and selected members of the population to study, you can begin collecting data. One of the three methods used to collect data is **observation**, watching and recording the actions of the people, objects, or events being studied. A.C. Nielsen uses special equipment to record which television programs are watched by a sample of U.S. households. This information helps marketers make decisions about airing commercials designated for various target markets.

Nearly all marketers use informal observation to get clues to customer buying behavior, competitive actions, and other data needed for marketing decisions. For example, Donald Cassel came up with the idea of loose-fitting shirts and shorts for skateboarders after he observed freestylers struggling in restrictive clothing. His California company, Grind King, makes clothing as well as skateboard accessories.[33]

Informal observation can help in narrowing a marketing problem or in arriving at a suitable hypothesis. However, it can lead to sampling errors and other mistakes. That's why marketers also use formal observation and other techniques when gathering primary data. For example, Jon Steel of the advertising agency Goodby, Silverstein & Partners used formal observation, watching and reporting teenagers' at-home behavior, for its client Sega.[34]

Surveys

When you want to find out why people act the way they do, you can use a **survey** to collect data by asking the target population a series of questions. Survey questions are arranged in a document known as a *questionnaire*. You can get answers from the **respondents**, the people being studied, in four ways: by mail or fax, by Internet, by telephone, or in person, as shown in Table 5.1.

TABLE   **5.1**   **How the Four Survey Methods Compare**

Basis of Comparison	Mail/Fax	Internet	Telephone	In Person
Flexibility	Little	Moderate	Moderate	High
Speed of completion	Moderate	Fast	Fast	Slow
Control of sample	Relatively good	Fair	Good	Good
Quantity of data that can be collected	Large amount	Large amount	Moderate amount	Large amount

observation

watching and recording the actions of the people, objects, or events being studied

survey

collecting data by asking the target population a series of questions

respondents

the people being studied

Mail and Fax Surveys and Panels   If your respondents are spread over a wide geographic area, you can mail out questionnaires or send them by fax. This is an economical way to survey large groups. To get people to answer, however, you'll have to keep the questionnaires fairly short.

Mail surveys help USAA research customer needs and satisfaction. The Texas-based company markets insurance and financial services to military officers and their families all over the country. It mails questionnaires to 500,000 customers annually, asking about satisfaction with company products, future needs, and new product ideas. Some 60 percent of the respondents return the questionnaires (10–20 percent response is average for direct mail surveys). By designing products based on this research, such as new mutual funds, USAA has strengthened its relationship with customers.[35]

In some cases, marketers want to question the same respondents again and again. They can do this using a *panel*, a group of people who participate in a series of surveys, usually by mail, over time. Many marketers contact panels through outside suppliers. The NPD Group, a New York research supplier, mails monthly surveys to a panel of 300,000 U.S. households to find out about product purchases and attitudes.[36]

Surveys on the Internet   A growing number of companies are using the Internet to conduct surveys. Respondents send their answers to an e-mail address, thereby providing quick feedback. The Internet also allows marketers to establish a dialogue with respondents and to delve deeper into their views and suggestions.

Telephone Surveys   Many marketers use telephone surveys when they want immediate answers to their questions. Computerized telephone questioning systems and lower telephone rates are bringing the price of telephone surveys down. What's more, limited contact with the respondents reduces the possibility that the researcher will influence the answers. *Bias*, which is undesirable, may result when a researcher reveals emotional reactions, approval, or disapproval, leading some respondents to modify their answers acccordingly.

Issues for critical thinking   Is it ethical for researchers to influence respondents by words or actions that show their bias? How can researchers guard against bias in conducting marketing research?

Still, you generally can't ask people to answer a lengthy questionnaire over the telephone. And no matter where you conduct your research, you're open to sample error because not everyone has a telephone or a listed telephone number. Telephone surveys are completely impractical in China and other developing countries, where few households have telephones.

Personal Surveys   When you need in-depth answers to your questions, you can use personal surveys, meeting respondents face to face. You can often combine observation with personal surveys by watching and recording what respondents do as they answer. From checking people's reactions to advertising materials to finding out about product usage, the list of topics you can research using personal surveys is nearly endless. Focus group interviews and individual interviews are two types of personal surveys.

In a **focus group interview**, a researcher meets with a group of 8 to 12 people to discuss a particular product or topic. Marketers generally watch focus groups from behind a one-way mirror (so researchers see the group but

focus group interview
meeting of a researcher with a small group of people to discuss a particular product or topic

Using mall intercepts such as the one shown here, some cities and towns conduct descriptive research to determine exactly what the concerns of citizens are. Using that research, officials can design programs to better meet the needs of the community. If such research were conducted in your home town, what kinds of problems might emerge? What kinds of questions would you ask to reveal the most important needs and concerns of citizens?

mall intercepts

individual interviews conducted in shopping centers

respondents are not constantly reminded that they are being observed). The interviews may be videotaped or audiotaped, or videoconferencing may be used to transmit the group discussion to researchers in other locations.[37] The video material allows researchers to study body language and other nonverbal clues that reveal personal attitudes.

Because of the potential for sampling error, focus groups are best used as exploratory research studies or in combination with other methods. Focus groups can help fine-tune a questionnaire and provide insight into how people think and feel. GM recently used this technique to learn how Cadillac owners relate to their cars. Then the automaker's advertising agency incorporated the respondents' emotions and thoughts into television commercials that stressed feelings rather than facts.[38]

Researchers who want to talk with respondents individually can go to each respondent's home or office, or to a mall. Individuals may also come to the researcher's office to be interviewed in person or may respond by means of a computer-administered survey. Individual interviews conducted in shopping centers are known as **mall intercepts** because individuals are stopped (intercepted) as they shop. Mall intercepts use convenience samples, so they're susceptible to sampling error.

Sometimes you want to talk with people in more private surroundings or get a better sense of how they act in their homes or offices. In such cases the in-home or in-office interview is appropriate. This is a costly research method, but it can provide data you wouldn't be able to collect any other way. The case that follows shows how Nickelodeon conducts research online.

Applying the Concepts

Nickelodeon tunes into online focus groups

Wednesday night is Nickelodeon night. No, not on cable television, but on CompuServe, the online computer service. On Wednesdays, 150 children from around the United States gather electronically to discuss Nickelodeon, the children's cable channel. This cyberspace focus group of 8- to 12-year-olds helps Nickelodeon probe reaction to its programming and its marketing.

Electronic focus groups yield results faster and are cheaper to implement than traditional face-to-face marketing research methods, and Nickelodeon's marketers get immediate feedback on programs and proposals. About one-third of the time, the children discuss recent episodes of *The Ren and Stimpy Show* and other programs. Other discussions touch on current events and new ideas.

When Nickelodeon marketers asked the group about a proposed "winter blues" promotion, for example, the children talked about playing in the snow, taking winter holidays, and enjoying school vacation. "The idea of winter blues and not liking winter was not something that kids related to," says Karen Flischel, Nickelodeon's senior vice president of research and development worldwide. "That thinking got scrapped right away."

Nickelodeon marketers recognize that online research has limitations. Because the participants aren't physically together, "the thing that you miss is that you don't see them laugh or smile, or that confused look on their face," notes Flischel. "You can't replace something like that. But you also can't have a focus group for every issue that this organization faces."

Nickelodeon doesn't rely solely on online surveys. It continues to conduct other marketing research studies, and it uses the on-line sessions as a supplement. Now MTV (like Nickelodeon, owned by Viacom) is considering electronic surveys. Stay tuned for more high-tech marketing research.[39]

Make marketing decisions

1. What kinds of issues might Nickelodeon researchers explore when talking to respondents?

2. What hypothesis do you think Nickelodeon's marketers were testing when they asked about the "winter blues" promotion?

3. Should Nickelodeon be using a nonprobability sample in its online survey? Why?

4. How would you define the population from which Nickelodeon should select participants for its marketing research?

Marketing research is such an important function that many firms would be wise to outsource it to professionals. Maritz, for example, not only measures customer satisfaction, it also helps firms to become more customer-driven. It can assist in training employees and will even design a reward system for them. Maritz uses an integrated approach to marketing research that matches the integrated marketing approach presented in this text. What are the advantages and disadvantages you can see to outsourcing marketing research?

Questionnaires No matter which survey method you use, you need to design your questionnaire carefully. Three types of questions are often used: dichotomous, multiple choice, and open ended. *Dichotomous* means that the question offers just two answers, often yes or no: "Have you ever bought an umbrella at the campus bookstore?" Another approach would be to have respondents pick which of two products (or two ads) they prefer.

Multiple-choice questions require respondents to choose answers from a list. If you wanted to know where students shop for umbrellas, you might offer four choices: the campus bookstore, the local department store, the local discount store, and "other." Dichotomous and multiple-choice questions have the advantage of simplicity: You can easily count up the answers you collect. However, you won't get any details about *why* people answered as they did. Furthermore, respondents may feel they have to choose one of the available answers, even when none of the options accurately reflect their true reaction.

When you want to collect data about people's thoughts, attitudes, and behavior, you can ask *open-ended questions*, which respondents answer in their own words. To learn where students buy umbrellas, for example, you might ask, "Where have you bought umbrellas in the past?" Such data can be harder to summarize and analyze, which increases the cost of the survey.

Although conducting research in other countries and cultures can be especially complicated, planning helps, as the next section shows.

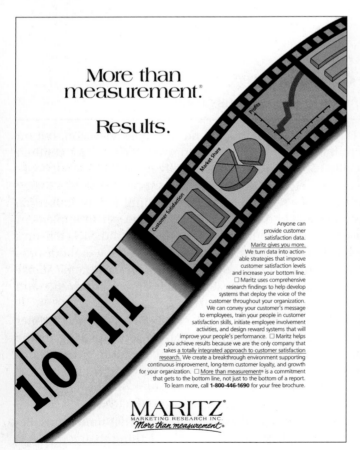

experiment

a scientific way of comparing and measuring data under controlled conditions—that is, one or more elements are changed while others remain the same

test marketing

research to measure reaction to a new product offered in a specific geographic area

GLOBAL ISSUES

Researching other countries and cultures

[handwritten: the assumption that a specific culture is specific to others.]

If you plan carefully—and avoid ethnocentrism ◄———┘ **(p. 112)**—designing a marketing research project to collect primary data in another country or culture needn't give you a world-class headache. The key is to adjust your methods to local cultural and legal differences. For example, door-to-door personal surveys are illegal in Saudi Arabia. The best approach there is to ask local businesspeople for introductions to their relatives and friends. That's only one of many nuances you need to consider when you gather primary data around the world.

When using focus group interviews, think about the mix of people in each group. In some countries or cultures, young people will defer to older people, and women will defer to men. Because such behavior influences the dynamics in a group, consider the age, gender, and other characteristics of each group's participants. Also be alert to cultural tendencies that can squelch disagreement or free expression of opinions. Sometimes participants say what they think the researcher wants to hear, instead of offering their true opinions. This isn't the case in Norway, however, where respondents tend to answer forthrightly.

Telephone surveys are becoming more common in Europe, where as much as 35 percent of all research is conducted by telephone (compared with 65 percent in the United States). However, this method won't work in countries where few people have home telephones. In Russia and China, for example, face-to-face interviews remain the best way to gather firsthand marketing data.[40]

What other circumstances might influence your ability to gather accurate data in another country or culture?

Test marketing can be done in the laboratory or in the field. After doing taste tests in the lab, a company might make a sample batch and try selling it in a test market, such as Columbus, Ohio. Simulated test marketing is often a less expensive way to explore new promotions and new product concepts. What are the advantages of doing test marketing in the field rather than in a lab or in a simulated setting?

Experiments

A marketer can also conduct marketing research through an **experiment**, a scientific way of comparing and measuring data under controlled conditions—that is, one or more elements are changed while others remain the same. An experiment is a form of causal research. The purpose is to identify cause-and-effect relationships between the *variables*, marketing elements that are being studied. The *independent variable* is the element being manipulated to study the influence on a second element, the *dependent variable*.

Experiments can be conducted in a laboratory setting or in the field (meaning the real world). A widely used form of field experiment is **test marketing**, in which marketers measure reaction to a new product offered in a specific geographic area. During test marketing, marketers change the advertising and other variables to see the effect on sales and product usage. Competitors can see what is being done, however—and they may introduce a similar product before the test is over or distort the results by running special sales or trying other tricks.[41]

To avoid such problems, some companies now turn to the laboratory equivalent of test marketing. *Simulated test marketing (STM)* uses computer modeling to predict a product's success or future based on consumer behavior in a laboratory setting, on details of the competitive environment, and on the product's planned marketing approach. Respondents are exposed to ads for the new product as well as for competitors. Then they're allowed to shop in a storelike setting. Weeks later, respondents are surveyed about their reactions to the products and their future buying plans.

All these data are fed into a computer, which *simulates* what would happen to a new product's sales as a result of various marketing decisions. Many marketers use STM to screen out poor products before they're actually tested or launched.[42] However, lab results may not be the same as real-world results. Ore-Ida found this out when it used STM to forecast future sales of a new food product. The computer model assumed that the food would be available continuously in stores. But when the food was actually introduced, grocers weren't willing to carry it year-round, so actual sales didn't match the predictions of the lab experiment.[43] In the following section, you'll see how marketers use other technological tools to collect research data.

MARKETING IDEAS

High-tech data collection

Marketing research has gone high tech, thanks to advanced communication and computerized systems. For example, Spiegel and other marketers use computer-assisted telephone surveys to maintain a research dialogue with customers. A computer with a pleasant, human-sounding voice asks questions, and respondents answer by touching numbers on their telephone keypads. The computer can recognize a few spoken words, but longer verbal answers are taped for later transcription and analysis.

Marketers who want to study customer buying decisions can use computer software that makes research participants sitting in a lab feel as though they're browsing in a store. Watching a personal computer screen that displays store shelves, participants can zoom in for a closer look at items, turn products to read the labels, and put items into their shopping carts. Researchers can change the order of products on the shelves and vary other elements to see the effect on customers who take this virtual shopping trip.

Technology is also helping marketers analyze reaction to products that are too new or unusual to be easily understood. One example is interactive television, a service that most people have never seen. U.S. West, a telecommunications provider, gets around that problem by putting respondents into high-tech kiosks that imitate the way interactive television services work. This technology lets U.S. West observe people exploring the services to find out what works and what doesn't.[44]

What other new products might be researched using such high-tech methods?

Step 4: Analyze and Interpret Research Data

Once you've collected data, you (or your research supplier) need to analyze and interpret them. First *tabulate* the responses by counting, categorizing, and summarizing the facts and figures. Next, analyze the data, by breaking them down, sorting, comparing, and searching for patterns that reveal meaning. You may have to do this several times before useful patterns emerge.[45]

Often, you can apply statistical tests that help you describe the sample, uncover relationships among variables, and form judgments about the overall population based on the sample results. Statistical tests, usually computerized, also help you calculate the possibility of errors in your research and the degree to which the results are representative of what you'd find if you researched the entire population.

Depending on who has to make the marketing decision, the analysis may be presented to other people in the organization. At this point, you interpret your findings, making inferences about the meaning and implications of the research. Guard against trying to make the data fit a preconceived hypothesis. Instead, keep an open mind as you interpret the results.

For example, Lubrizol, an Ohio chemical company, analyzed and interpreted its marketing research data to uncover what customers wanted and how Lubrizol compared with competitors. An outside supplier collected data about the level of satisfaction expressed by various people in the businesses that used the company's products. Analysis showed that purchasing agents were less pleased than technicians, and competitors were quicker at filling customer orders. Lubrizol's interpretation: It needed to make changes to boost customer satisfaction.[46]

Step 5: Select and Implement the Best Ethical Alternative

Now the organization has the data it needs to evaluate its options and implement the one that best solves its marketing problems. Marketing researchers can then turn the research results over to others. Bringing in people from other parts of the organization can provide fresh ideas and insights. Together they might list the pros and cons of each alternative and select the one with the most advantages. It is important at this point to consider the ethics of any proposed behavior. Such an analysis helps your organization maintain good relationships with all stakeholders.

You might use numerical values to weight the pros and cons of each ethical choice and then make your selection based on the total scores. The process you use depends on the time and data available for evaluation and selection, as well as the importance and risk of the marketing problem you face.[47]

In Lubrizol's case, analysis and interpretation indicated that competitors were doing a better job of building customer relationships in several service areas. Rivals were more willing to rush customer orders or respond to changing customer needs, and they processed orders more quickly and accurately. Lubrizol chose to solve its problem and boost customer satisfaction by revamping operations for both speed and flexibility. It slashed delivery times, responded more quickly to customers, and accelerated new product introductions.[48]

Step 6: Evaluate the Results

After the best ethical alternative has been selected and implemented, it is time for researchers to evaluate the results. In this final step of the marketing research process, you look at (1) what happens after the chosen solution has been implemented and (2) the process you used to research that solution. This helps you determine whether you have chosen the right solution—and shows how you can do better in the future.

One method of evaluation is to conduct *follow-up research*, studying what happens after a particular solution has been implemented. This closes the loop on marketing research, allowing you to go back to earlier steps in the process and make any necessary adjustments. Imagine that your marketing problem was low product sales in supermarkets and your solution, based on research, was to change the product package. You would use follow-up research to determine how the new package affected product sales. As another example, follow-up research helped Lubrizol determine whether changes made in response to the first customer surveys had any effect on satisfaction ratings.

When you want to monitor long-term results, you can use *tracking research*, surveys involving various samples that help you detect (track) trends over time. Tracking research can show how people in the target market react to new advertising and how these reactions change during a period of time. Another use is to see how people's attitudes toward your product or brand

Marketing research may help you identify a market, but you still have the task of reaching it efficiently and measuring the results. Mediamark Research helps marketers understand the media consumption patterns of targeted segments and select the most appropriate media for marketing communication messages. What other marketing research questions would a marketer want to outsource to research specialists?

change over time. Data collected during such studies help you refine your solution and the marketing process overall, leading to a better solution and improved results in the long run. Follow-up research is especially important to measure online marketing efforts because they are so new and different. [49]

Before you go on . . .

A. **Why is the marketing research process considered to be circular?**

B. **Why do researchers review secondary data before collecting primary data?**

C. **In what ways can researchers collect primary data?**

D. **How are follow-up research and tracking research used?**

Ethical Issues in Marketing Research

In seeking to create and strengthen stakeholder relationships **(p. 8)**, marketing research can ultimately lead to changes in every aspect of marketing and every part of the organization. This potential power carries with it ethical responsibilities for those who conduct or apply marketing research. That is why step 5 calls for selecting the best *ethical* alternative. In fact, the whole marketing research process raises ethical issues: how the information is obtained and the uses made of it.

Over time, unethical practices such as making sales calls or soliciting charitable contributions under the guise of marketing research have caused respondents to be wary or to decline to participate. Marketing research also gets a bad reputation when unethical researchers change respondents' data or deliberately misinterpret results to support a particular conclusion.

Sometimes you'll face gray areas, where the line between right and wrong isn't immediately clear. In particular, observation, surveys, and experiments bring up sticky ethical questions about deception, confidentiality, and privacy. Here are three ethical questions you may face as you collect data.

It is important to maintain ethical standards when conducting marketing research. It is proper to tape a focus group or a sales presentation only if the participants are made fully aware that taping will take place. To minimize disruptions, however, the taping can be done as discreetly as possible, such as by taping through two-way mirrors. What would happen if customers began to distrust marketing researchers?

1. *Should respondents be misled about the nature or purpose of the research?* One argument for deception is the possibility of distorting respondents' reactions if they know too much about the research. Some researchers prefer to explain things to respondents after the data have been collected. On the other hand, respondents have the right to be informed fully enough to have an accurate idea of what they're undertaking. This is particularly important when the research involves possible harm or stress.[50] When to explain and how much to say are additional considerations relating to this ethical question.

2. *Should respondents be allowed to answer anonymously?* Often, people will not agree to participate unless the researcher promises that names will not be revealed. If you promise anonymity, is it ethical to mark the questionnaires in a way that will let you identify the respondents later? What if the names are known to the researchers but not to anyone else? And what if some respondents agree to have their names and data used, but change their minds later? These questions complicate the issue of anonymity.

3. *Should respondents' behavior be secretly observed or recorded?* Observing or recording what people say or do in private—without disclosing that the activities are being studied—invades the respondents' privacy. However, when people are in stores or other public places, anyone can see or record their behavior. Getting consent, even from people in a public setting, raises another problem: If people know that someone is watching, they may change their behavior. Should respondents always be asked before researchers observe or record their actions?

The preceding list is only a sampling of the ethical questions that can crop up in any company, government agency, or nonprofit organization that uses marketing research. As you think through these questions and confront others during your marketing career, remember the guidelines for resolving ethical issues. You can also consult the codes of ethics ◄———▏ **(p. 92)** adopted by the American Marketing Association, the Marketing Research Association, and other groups. These documents have been carefully designed to clarify the standards of right and wrong and to point the way toward ethical marketing research around the world. After all, the whole purpose of marketing research is to build better relationships with customers and other stakeholders by creating more trust, more involvement, and more responsiveness.

Before you go on . . .

A. What ethical issues are involved in secretly observing or recording people's behavior?

B. How do codes of ethics help marketers resolve ethical issues in marketing research?

Summary

1. **Identify four uses of marketing research.**

   Four uses of marketing research are (1) to analyze customers, needs, and satisfaction, (2) to analyze markets and opportunities, (3) to analyze marketing effectiveness, and (4) to analyze the marketing process.

2. **Distinguish among marketing information systems, databases, and marketing decision support systems.**

   A marketing information system (MIS) is a structured system for managing the ongoing collection, analysis, storage, and reporting of marketing data. A database is a computerized file of data that can be searched for particular details. A marketing decision support system (MDSS) is a computerized system linking the MIS and internal databases, allowing marketers to analyze data for marketing decisions.

3. **Describe the six steps in the formal marketing research process.**

The six steps in the marketing research process are (1) define the problem and determine the present situation, (2) design the research and identify data sources, (3) collect primary data, (4) analyze and interpret research data, (5) select and implement the best ethical alternative, (6) evaluate the results. Step 5 is often done by top management, not the researcher.

4. **Differentiate between secondary data and primary data.**

Secondary data are available facts and figures that have been collected for another purpose. Primary data are facts, figures, or details gathered for a specific marketing research study.

5. **Explain the use of probability and nonprobability samples.**

A probability sample is one in which every member of the population has a known chance of being selected for the research, which means that you can statistically test your results. A nonprobability sample is one in which you can't accurately calculate the chance that any one member of the population will be selected. Nonprobability samples are often used in exploratory research.

6. **Analyze the three methods of collecting primary data and show how follow-up and tracking research are used.**

The three methods of collecting primary data are observation, surveys, and experimentation. Follow-up research is used to evaluate the results of decisions based on marketing research by studying what happens after a particular solution has been implemented. Tracking research evaluates the results of implementing a solution by surveying various samples to help detect trends over a longer period.

7. **Examine three ethical questions related to data collection.**

Three ethical issues related to data collection are: (1) Should respondents be misled about the nature or purpose of the research? (2) Should respondents be allowed to answer anonymously? (3) Should respondents' behavior be secretly observed or recorded?

KEY TERMS

causal research **144**
census **147**
database **138**
descriptive research **143**
experiment **153**
exploratory research **143**
focus group interview **150**
hypothesis **142**
mall intercepts **151**

market **135**
marketing decision support system (MDSS) **140**
marketing information system (MIS) **138**
marketing research **134**
nonprobability sample **147**
observation **149**
population **147**

primary data **146**
probability sample **147**
respondents **149**
sample **147**
sampling error **147**
secondary data **144**
survey **149**
test marketing **153**

Skill-Building Applications

1. How would you use the six steps in the marketing research process to find a good job with a company that has a corporate culture that best meets your needs?

2. Some businesses try to obtain information about rivals by hiring employees away from competitors and asking about competitive secrets. Is this practice ethical? What might businesses do to keep competitors from gaining access to sensitive information in this way?

3. What kind of research should the United Way conduct before deciding which causes to support and which individuals to target for donations?

4. Minh Nguyen started Automated Office Products, a company that recycles laser printer cartridges. Nguyen donates money to an environmental group or charity when companies agree to send their used cartridges to him. What kind of research should this marketer conduct to gain more customers?

5. Evan Kemp Associates, Inc. is a service firm that offers communication, marketing, and public affairs consulting to companies that sell to disabled people. What kind of marketing research should Kemp Associates do to keep current with its customer base?

6. One of the biggest controversies about marketing research today is the use of telephone surveys, especially those conducted at the dinner hour. Can you think of a better way for Bank of America to research customers' banking needs and habits?

Getting Involved in Marketing

1. *On Your Own* Imagine that you're preparing to market a new kind of toothbrush for toddlers just learning to brush. Which survey method(s) would you use to collect primary data about this group's needs?

2. *On Your Own* As you prepare to conduct the research in exercise 1, which sampling technique(s) would you use? Why? What population would be appropriate for this study?

3. *Find Out More* Identify and contact a marketing research company that conducts mall intercepts or telephone surveys. Ask what kinds of product they've recently researched and how they design their survey samples. What kinds of questions do they use? Why?

4. *In a Partnership* With a classmate, discuss with the manager or owner of a new store what formal and informal marketing research was conducted before the opening. What kind of ongoing marketing research is being conducted? Write a report about how this retailer can obtain the information it needs to be successful.

5. *In a Team* With two other students, research the sources of secondary data you would check for information about introducing a new in-line skate to compete with Rollerblades. What do you need to know? Where might you find this information? Summarize your findings for the class in a two-minute presentation.

6. *In a Team* With three other students, draft at least eight questions that could be used to uncover students' reactions to marketing research as an invasion of privacy. What type of question would you ask? Would you conduct this survey in person, by mail, or by telephone? Why?

VideoCase Larry's Steps Up Marketing Research

What business owner would feel dissatisfied about growing annual sales from $500,000 to $21 million in 25 years? Yet Elliot Goodwin, president of Larry's Shoes, a Texas-based chain of men's shoe stores, knew his business had more potential. Using marketing research, Goodwin set out to tap that potential.

Goodwin's father, Larry, started the business in 1949. Emphasizing large sizes, the store, through its selection, quality, and service, attracted members of the Dallas Cowboys and other athletes as regular customers.

When Elliot Goodwin succeeded his father as president, he continued the focus on large sizes and expanded the chain. Soon, growth and profits began to plateau, and Goodwin became concerned. Rather than simply wait for things to get better, he used marketing research to learn how to forge better relationships with customers.

Although Goodwin had reservations, he hired a marketing research firm to conduct formal marketing research into men's shoe-buying habits. The firm conducted focus groups with a sample of Larry's customers and people who had never visited Larry's stores. The findings: some men thought that Larry's was no different from other shoe stores; others thought it offered no special services or that it was high-priced; and some actually thought it was a women's shoe store. Another finding stood out: these men truly hated shopping for shoes.

Initially, Goodwin didn't believe that the findings applied to his target market, and he postponed taking any action. But as flat sales continued, he reconsidered. "We had to know what customers really thought of us to get the company moving again," remembers Goodwin. So he asked the research firm to get more information as a basis to make decisions about advertising, store design, pricing, and inventory.

The researchers designed a questionnaire to conduct 20-minute telephone surveys with 650 men—450 from a random sample of men living near the Larry's stores and 200 from Larry's customer database. The results showed that men wanted an abundance of sizes and widths; quality, brand-name shoes at reasonable prices; a large selection; a customer-friendly return policy; and helpful, knowledgeable salespeople. Goodwin realized that his stores already offered most of these elements. The problem was that he wasn't effectively communicating his store's strengths to potential customers.

Acting on the research results, Goodwin began an integrated marketing communication plan focused on relationship marketing. He used direct mail to reach current customers and cable television commercials to reach potential customers. To differentiate his chain, he also began offering in his stores foot massages, free espresso and fruit juices, and coloring books for kids. He set up big-screen televisions so customers could watch sporting events. And he founded a shoe museum featuring celebrity footwear from Clark Gable, Cher, Marilyn Monroe, and other famous names.

Acting on the research has paid off. Larry's has become the highest-volume independent men's shoe store in the United States and was voted independent Retailer of the Year in 1995. But Elliot Goodwin isn't resting on his laurels. He's constantly scanning the environment for new challenges and opportunities, and he's staying close to his customers.[51]

Strategies and applications

1. Do you think Goodwin could find data about men's shoe-buying habits in secondary research sources? Explain your answer.

2. What could Goodwin learn about men's shoe-buying habits through observation? Is this technique appropriate in this situation? Why?

3. What can Goodwin do to evaluate the results of the actions he takes based on research?

4. To get even more information about customer needs and preferences, do you recommend that Goodwin conduct a census of his customers? Why?

5. If you were designing a questionnaire to learn more about customer attitudes toward competitors of Larry's Shoes, would you use dichotomous, multiple-choice, or open-ended questions? Explain your answer.

6. What informal marketing research might Goodwin conduct to stay abreast of changes in customer needs and expectations?

Team project

With other classmates, make a list of all the types of information that Larry's Shoes should have in its internal customer database. How would the store obtain this information? What would it do with it? Draft a memo to Elliot Goodwin to explain your team's ideas.

CHAPTER

6

Consumer Buying Behavior

Learning Goals

After you have read and studied this chapter, you should be able to:

1. Define consumer behavior and discuss why marketers have to continually study it.
2. List the five stages in the consumer purchase-decision process.
3. Explain how the consumer's level of involvement affects the purchase-decision process.
4. Identify five internal influences on consumer behavior.
5. Discuss the three ways in which the family can influence consumer behavior.
6. Explain the role of opinion leaders, word-of-mouth communication, and reference groups in consumer buying decisions.
7. Describe the five situational influences on consumer purchasing decisions.

PROFILE

Saturn accelerates consumer-driven marketing

For many people, car shopping means a tiresome round of dealer negotiations, price comparisons, and worries over quality and service. That's the bad news. The good news is that someone is listening—and responding—to car buyers' complaints. Haggling is out and customer appreciation is in at Saturn, a General Motors division that has introduced U.S. consumers to a new way of buying cars. Saturn wants to give consumers what they want, when they want it—before, during, and after the sale.

Saturn was started literally from the ground up, with a state-of-the-art factory in Spring Hill, Tennessee, that has been praised for its efficiency and product quality. Because sales are made—or lost—at the dealership, Saturn emphasized sales and service training. Dealer employees, including salespeople, were taught to work as a team to satisfy customers. Saturn "sales consultants" were trained to listen to tire kickers, give out price sheets, and encourage comparison shopping. After-sale service, another consumer headache at most dealerships, was also redesigned to produce customer satisfaction.

Delighted customers told friends, relatives, and colleagues about their experiences with Saturn. Many learned about Saturn on the Internet. As the word spread, more people bought Saturn cars. For a brief time, demand outstripped supply. Independent studies of customer satisfaction gave Saturn high marks. Excitement ran so high that Saturn hosted a three-day "homecoming celebration" in Spring Hill, opening the factory for customer tours and offering country music in a festival atmosphere. More than 40,000 happy customers attended. "We're being treated like royalty," observed one. "You can't beat it."[1]

This is the first of two chapters that examine *buyer behavior*—how consumer and organizational buyers make their purchase decisions. In this chapter, you'll learn how and why marketers use their knowledge of consumer behavior to build lasting customer relationships. The first part of the chapter explores consumer behavior and the need to respond to behavioral changes. Then, you'll learn about the purchase-decision process and examine the role of consumer involvement. The last part of the chapter discusses key internal and external influences on consumer behavior.

Marketing, Relationships, and Consumer Behavior

When two marketers are competing for the same customer's business, all other things being equal, the marketer with the greatest scope of information about that particular customer—the marketer with the most extensive and intimate relationship with that customer—will be the more efficient competitor.[2]

Don Peppers and Martha Rogers
in The One-to-One Future

The insights GM's Saturn division used to build a successful car-marketing strategy came from studying consumer behavior. **Consumer behavior** comprises all the consumer decisions and activities connected with choosing, buying, using, and disposing of goods and services. As you can see from this definition, marketers have to pay attention to consumer behavior that occurs before the purchase and goes on well after the product has been used, extending all the way to the disposal of the product after usage.[3] Saturn marketers didn't just consider how consumers buy cars. They also studied the way people search for price and option information *before* the purchase and their concerns about dealer service *afterward*.

Why do people buy? What influences their buying decisions? How do they decide between competing products? What makes them buy one brand repeatedly or switch from brand to brand? What relationship do consumers want with the brands they buy? How do marketing activities affect consumer attitudes and behavior? These are only a few of the questions that marketers try to answer by analyzing what, when, where, how, and why consumers buy.

Studying consumer behavior is one of the steps in marketing research and analysis, the universal marketing process of collecting and analyzing data about consumers and organizations, buyer behavior, and markets **(p. 134)**. By conducting research, marketers can uncover clues about how and why people in the target market plan, make, use, and evaluate purchases. Such clues provide the raw material for responding to consumer needs through a suitable marketing strategy and value package. Although understanding the basic principles that guide overall consumer behavior is a good start, marketers also need to study the decisions and actions of real people in their target markets.

Real People, Real Individuals

Until recently, the study of consumer behavior was relatively abstract, focusing on generalized consumer decisions and actions. The approach provided helpful insights, but it didn't address the behavior of *individual consumers*. As a result, organizations were making marketing decisions without knowing specific details about *their* customers.

These days, thanks to information technology, marketers can collect and analyze a great deal of data about consumer behavior, one person at a time. As you saw in Chapter 5, external databases **(p. 138)** that hold supermarket scanner and single-source data can give a detailed picture of specific people's purchases, as well as their product usage, media usage, and so on. Thus armed, marketers can reach out to consumers, using an approach geared to the individual needs that have been uncovered. This is the relationship approach to marketing **(p. 6)**.

New technology allows marketers to track the specific purchase and usage behavior of their customers. Once information has been gathered and stored in an internal database, marketers can explore what each customer wants and tailor the marketing processes to meet those needs. No guesswork here:

consumer behavior

comprises all the consumer decisions and activities connected with choosing, buying, using, and disposing of goods and services

Some marketers know exactly what their customers want—and they try to give their customers exactly that.[4]

For example, when customers call Pizza Hut outlets to place their orders, the local restaurants capture names, addresses, and purchase information for the chain's database. Marketers have programmed the system to search the database and periodically mail customers discount coupons for their favorite foods. "It's really as simple as keeping up with our customers and making it easier for them to get what they want," explains Bob Perkins, Pizza Hut's senior vice president of marketing.[5]

Some marketers have been able to go a step further. August Max Woman, Petite Sophisticate, and some other retail chains, have built a comprehensive internal database on consumer behavior that is used to drive their integrated marketing communication programs. August Max salespeople enter the customer's merchandise purchases and telephone numbers into the electronic cash register system. The system automatically searches external databases to find the customer's name and address and other demographic details.

The computer keeps tabs on customers, recording how much they spend during subsequent transactions, how often they shop, and the merchandise, sizes, and colors they prefer. August Max uses these details to tailor its communications to individual customers' needs, such as sending information on pantyhose products to women right after they have purchased suits. The company also sends thank-you notes after a customer's first purchase, mails sale notices to people who like to buy during sales, and so on. In addition, the database can single out people who *haven't* shopped in some time for special marketing treatment, such as a letter and a money-saving coupon.[6]

Consumers as Moving Targets

The marketers at August Max have a good reason for continually examining consumer behavior. Consumer behavior changes over time as people and situations change. (This is also true of organizational behavior, the subject of the next chapter.) As a result, marketers can't assume that a person who buys a certain product or brand today will make the same purchase decision tomorrow. To maintain their relationships with customers, marketers have to be alert to changes and adjust their marketing activities accordingly.

Of course, every marketer has to allow for *individual* variations in consumer behavior—and be ready to customize marketing tactics as needed. But marketers can't afford to miss the signals of broad-based changes in consumer behavior either. For example, a shift toward dressing down (instead of dressing up) for work and other activities is spreading across the country and around the world. In response, apparel manufacturers and retailers are adjusting their marketing strategies to meet increased demand for casual clothing and to find new ways of marketing more formal attire.

The most nimble marketers try to fan the flames of change so they can profit by being the first or best at giving customers what they want. Casual shoe manufacturer Hush Puppies has helped shape the movement toward more casual office attire by producing a video guide for human resource personnel who need help planning corporate dress-down policies. The result? A blazing 37 percent increase in the company's shoe sales during a single year.[7]

The study of consumer behavior doesn't end when a product hits the market. Marketers have to go on to analyze consumer response. Are consumers buying and using the product? Are they satisfied with the value package? **(p. 11)** Are they coming back for more? Depending on how consumers respond, a marketer may need to adjust its marketing strategy and tactics to build more profitable relationships with customers. Nonprofit organizations also study consumer behavior, as the following section shows.

MARKETING IDEAS

Nonprofits profit from consumer behavior

The American Heart Association knows. Stanford University knows. The Dallas Parks and Recreation Department knows. Many nonprofit organizations, in fact, know the value of studying and responding to consumer behavior. And the value isn't always measured in dollars and cents.

In Dallas, the Parks and Recreation Department looked at the lifestyle of local residents and realized that many worked odd hours. People who wanted to use the city's recreational facilities couldn't because of their work schedules. In response to this information about consumer behavior, the department began operating a full-service recreational center around the clock. Now residents can play volleyball or softball and attend concerts and art shows day and night. By the way, the entire city benefits: crime is down.

Consumer behavior means dollars and cents to the American Heart Association. CEO Dudley Hafner has found that asking contributors for a specific amount prompts people to give more because it appeals to their self-image of generosity. "People who find the appeal sets its sights a little bit too high are not offended; they're usually flattered," observes Hafner. But the association doesn't just single people out at random for suggested donations. It separates donors into 41 discrete groups and designs a special marketing approach for each, based on the behavior of individuals in that group.

Stanford University's fund-raising programs are based on the premise that alumni respond differently to different appeals. By varying the timing, content, and method of communication, university fund-raisers found out through trial and error how and when people respond. This helped the university design a structured and cost-effective fund-raising program. Now those who donate up to $75 receive three to four letters a year, while those who donate more than $75 also receive a phone call.[8]

If you were leading a major university's fund-raising effort, what else would you want to know about alumni behavior?

How Consumers Buy

To provide what customers want before, during, and after the marketing exchange, you (and all marketers) have to understand how consumers buy. This knowledge will enable you to develop an appropriate marketing strategy to satisfy customer needs and build lasting customer relationships. The consumer purchase-decision process consists of five stages, which are outlined in Figure 6.1: (1) need recognition, (2) information seeking, (3) alternative evaluation, (4) purchase, and (5) postpurchase evaluation.

Since the actual purchase is just one part of the process, marketers need to provide what consumers require at every stage. Consumer purchasing is affected by the way marketers apply the eight marketing processes as well as by involvement, external, situational, and internal influences, which are discussed later in the chapter.

F I G U R E   **6.1**   **Consumer Purchase-Decision Process**

Consumers move through five steps as they decide on a purchase to satisfy a recognized need. This process is affected by (1) their level of involvement with the product, (2) marketing processes, (3) external influences, (4) situational influences, and (5) internal influences.

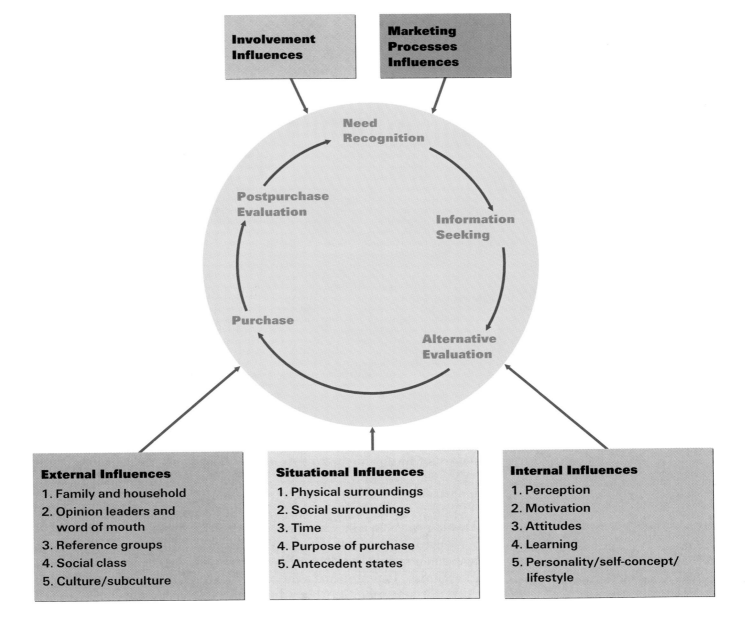

The Need-Recognition Stage

The first stage, need recognition, occurs when a consumer realizes that his or her actual state is not what he or she would like it to be.[9] This recognition is triggered by some stimulus, such as running out of a product, seeing an ad for a product, or being dissatisfied with the product currently in use. If the difference between the desired state (what the consumer would like) and the actual state (what the consumer perceives as already existing) is large or important enough, the consumer will start the decision-making process that leads to a purchase.

Although the process doesn't start until the consumer has recognized a need, marketing can play a role in this stage. Imagine a woman who is considering joining the in-line skating crowd. Her decision to make a purchase might be triggered by need recognition awakened when she sees how much others enjoy the activity. Advertising by Rollerblade and other manufacturers of in-line skates can help nurture her interest by reminding her of the fun and health benefits of in-line skating. Product labeling and product demonstrations can also increase need recognition.

Issues for critical thinking

Look at the advertising on local area billboards or campus bulletin boards. Do many of these sales pitches try to spark recognition of a need? Do the ads suggest how consumers, by visiting a store, for example, or by calling a toll-free number, can move from need recognition to the information-seeking stage? Why do you think this is important?

The Information-Seeking Stage

During the second stage of the purchase-decision process, the consumer looks for information about ways of satisfying the recognized need. Initially, the consumer will use an *internal search* (reviewing past purchases) to recall experiences with products that might satisfy the need. If this need occurs regularly, the internal search may be all that's necessary to come up with an acceptable way of satisfying the need. Thus a person who has run out of milk probably can arrange to remedy the situation without an elaborate search for information.

If, however, more information is needed, the consumer can begin an *external search*, looking to other sources for ways of satisfying the need. The consumer who needs in-line skates might talk to friends or relatives, check magazines such as *Consumer Reports*, read ads, or ask a salesperson. If the consumer is especially interested in the product or determined to make the optimal choice, the search may take some time.[10]

Consumers may be prompted to search for even more information because of **perceived risk**, the chance that the wrong choice of product to satisfy a need might result in negative consequences. Perceived risks can be financial, functional, safety, social, and psychological.[11] In the in-line skating example, the prospective buyer might worry about (1) spending too much (financial risk), (2) choosing uncomfortable skates (functional risk),

perceived risk
the chance that the wrong choice of product might result in negative consequences

(3) choosing an unsafe product (safety risk), (4) choosing an unfashionable style (social risk), or (5) choosing such an expensive model that a guilty feeling results (psychological risk).

Because consumers perceive risk in making the wrong choice in skates, Rollerblade and other marketers of skates provide a good deal of information about brands, features, usage, prices, delivery, and so on.

The Evaluation Stage

Consumers who have done their homework and uncovered a number of ways of satisfying their needs then come to the third stage of the decision-purchase process: evaluating the alternatives. In this stage, consumers consider the perceived risks and benefits of each option. To do this, they establish *evaluative criteria*, specific dimensions used to compare alternatives. Criteria for comparing in-line skates might include brand reputation, product guarantee, and price.

Not every criterion receives the same weight during a consumer's evaluation. Some consumers weigh price more heavily, while others are more concerned with style or quality. For consumers in many cultures, brand names are seen as an important index of quality to be used in evaluating products.[12]

By applying these criteria, the consumer comes up with a **consideration set** of alternatives, the options that he or she considers before deciding on a purchase. Rollerblade uses advertising to get its name into the consideration set for consumers considering the purchase of in-line skates. An informative brochure or a hands-on trial can help consumers evaluate alternatives as well.

This ad for Rollerblade emphasizes the skate's customizable fit. Other ads promote different features and benefits. From your perspective, what kind of information is most important to you in order to remove the perceived risk of buying a particular brand of skate? Are you more comfortable with a well-known name like Rollerblade? Why?

The Purchase Stage

Next the consumer chooses among the alternatives in the consideration set and decides where and when to make the purchase. As deliberate as this sounds, you know from personal experience that not all purchases are carefully planned before the shopping trip. For example, an estimated two-thirds of the purchases made in supermarkets are decided in the store, not in advance. Retail marketers therefore use a variety of in-store marketing techniques such as product displays and demonstrations, signs, and announcements to focus shopper attention on specific products and brands.[13]

One way the makers of in-line skates reach their market is by selling skates to stores that rent skates. By trying various brands, consumers are able to choose the style that best meets their needs. Therefore, selling to rental stores is a great way to influence consumers.

The Postpurchase Evaluation Stage

The final stage of the consumer purchase-decision process is postpurchase evaluation. During this stage, the consumer decides whether the product and purchase experience meet or exceed expectations (creating customer satisfaction) or fall short of expectations (creating dissatisfaction). Evaluating the purchase may also cause a consumer to rethink the need that

consideration set

options considered before deciding on a purchase

Postpurchase dissonance can be especially important when using services because the quality can vary so greatly. But Promus Hotel Corporation and its Embassy Suites, Homewood Suites, and Hampton Inns guarantee your satisfaction or you don't pay. This is about as strong a commitment as a consumer can expect from a service organization. Do you think consumers are more tempted to stay at such places because of the 100% satisfaction guarantee?

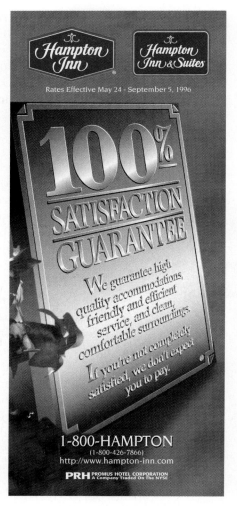

sparked the purchase, starting the cycle again.

Consumers may also ask themselves, "Did I make the right decision?" This common question reflects **postpurchase dissonance**, feelings of anxiety or doubt about the wisdom of the purchase decision. As a marketer, you want to do everything in your power to satisfy or delight customers as a way of encouraging repeat purchases, loyalty to your brand, and a long-term relationship that defies competitive pressure. You also want to reassure customers that they've made the right decision.

Many marketers try to minimize postpurchase dissonance by guaranteeing satisfaction, which eases consumer worry over making the wrong decision. Hampton Inns has found that some travelers choose the hotel chain because of its money-back guarantee. The guarantee earns $8 in revenues for every dollar refunded to settle a customer complaint.[14] Some marketers follow up by calling or writing customers to ask them about any postpurchase problems. For example, Fox Valley Technical College in Appleton, Wisconsin, surveys graduates up to five years later to find out whether they're satisfied with their education.[15]

What could Rollerblade and other marketers of in-line skates do to assure consumer satisfaction over time? Would a trade-in policy help people move up to better skates on second and later purchases? Ski manufacturers often use such a strategy.

Involvement and the Purchase-Decision Process

Does every consumer purchase decision follow the full five-stage process? To find the answer, consider the last time you bought a soft drink. Did you take more than a moment or two to decide which to buy? Probably not, because the decision didn't seem very important or risky. Now think about your decision to buy a new stereo system or an expensive piece of jewelry. Did you take more time to consider this purchase? If you approached the second decision in a reasoned, logical way, you probably researched your alternatives. You may even have worried later about whether you had made the right choice—or wished afterward that you had bought something else.

The purchase decisions above differed because your involvement was different in each case. **Involvement** is the level of importance or interest that a consumer attaches to a certain product or purchase situation. Consumer in-

postpurchase dissonance

feelings of anxiety or doubt about the wisdom of a purchase decision

involvement

the level of importance or interest that a consumer attaches to a certain product or purchase situation

volvement tends to be high when (1) a buying decision carries significant perceived risks (such as the financial risk of buying the wrong stereo system or inappropriate jewelry), (2) the product or decision has considerable personal or emotional meaning (such as the feeling you get or want to convey when you buy jewelry as a gift), or (3) the product enhances a long-standing interest (such as your long-time enthusiasm for state-of-the-art sound equipment).[16] One way to explore consumer involvement with products is to follow people through the purchase process. The following case illustrates that process and allows you to make marketing decisions on your own.

Applying the Concepts
Now showing: A real-life shopping trip

What really happens when consumers get involved with a product or a purchase? That's what Bugle Boy, a manufacturer of casual clothing for young men, wanted to know. To understand how young men in its target market buy, wear, and evaluate clothing, Bugle Boy and its advertising agency, DDB Needham Los Angeles, needed to go beyond the mere facts and figures of consumer behavior. So they went to the source, asking a group of teens to videotape their actions before, during, and after a purchase.

The young men were given video cameras to take along when they shopped for clothing, with instructions to tape what they liked and disliked about clothing stores. They also taped a journey through their closets as they put together an outfit. Much of what emerged confirmed what Bugle Boy and DDB Needham already suspected, such as the importance of comfort. But some of the footage held surprises. For one thing, buying on sale was a significant factor in these consumers' clothing purchases. For another, closets represented more than storage. "Your closet is where old clothes go to die," observed one young man.

Overall, the videotapes revealed nuances of behavior that Bugle Boy and its agency couldn't have uncovered by simply asking questions. By analyzing the videotapes, Bugle Boy gained a better understanding of what the young men wanted in clothing, how they felt about clothing stores, and how they assembled an outfit. This information helped the agency develop ads that reflected the values and lifestyles of the young men in its target market. As Bugle Boy has found, basing marketing on real-life consumer behavior is especially crucial for high-involvement products and purchases such as clothing.[17]

Make marketing decisions

1. If you were marketing Bugle Boy clothing, what might you do to trigger recognition of a need?

2. How would you get the Bugle Boy brand into the consumer's consideration set?

3. What criteria might young men use when evaluating Bugle Boy and other clothing alternatives? How can Bugle Boy marketing play a role in this stage of the purchase-decision process?

4. Do you think postpurchase dissonance affects young men buying casual clothing? If so, how would you use marketing to handle it?

F I G U R E   **6.2**

Involvement and the Purchase-Decision Process

Consumers generally use extended problem solving for high-involvement products such as cars or costly vacations. In contrast, they use routine problem solving for low-involvement products such as milk or taxi services.

As you might imagine, the level of consumer involvement determines the complexity of the purchase-decision process, as shown in Figure 6.2. When consumers are quite involved with a product or purchase, they will move more deliberately through every stage of the purchase-decision process. This is **extended problem solving**, an approach to decision making in which the consumer consciously searches for information, carefully evaluates the alternatives, and analyzes the result.

Consumers who perceive significant differences between brands are likely to use extended problem solving as a way of gathering information about alternatives and evaluating the options using specific criteria. A consumer shopping for a fancy camera or a computer would use extended problem solving to carefully research available products, come up with criteria against which to assess the products under consideration, and evaluate the purchase.

High Involvement ←		→ Low Involvement
Extended Problem Solving	**Limited Problem Solving**	**Routine Problem Solving**
Products: cars, expensive vacations	Products: shoes, appliance repair	Products: milk, taxi service
Need recognition	Need recognition	Need recognition
Information seeking (internal and external)	Information seeking (internal and limited external)	Information seeking (limited internal)
Evaluation (many alternatives, many criteria, complex decision rules)	Evaluation (few alternatives, few criteria, simple decision rules)	
Purchase	Purchase	Purchase
Postpurchase Evaluation (dissonance, complex evaluation)	Postpurchase Evaluation (no dissonance, limited evaluation)	Postpurchase Evaluation (no dissonance, very limited evaluation)

When consumers are less involved in the product or process, they may use **limited problem solving**, in which a consumer chooses among a number of unfamiliar alternatives in a familiar purchase situation. In such situations, the consumer may already have a few criteria for evaluation, but will not yet have applied them to the new alternatives. Searching out alternatives and making a decision takes less time with limited problem solving than with extended problem solving. Consumers deciding between restaurants in a strange city would use limited problem solving.

When involvement is even lower, you have **routine problem solving**, in which the consumer makes a quick choice, taking little time to consider the alternatives or the outcome of the decision. This mode of purchase occurs when people habitually buy the same product or brand with little conscious thought. When buying candy bars or paper cups, for example, consumers often leave out some of the stages in the purchase-decision process. In building customer relationships, a marketer tries to move customers from limited to routine problem solving. In this way, the purchase of the marketer's product becomes a habit.

In addition to involvement, external and internal influences affect consumer behavior. These influences help determine whether a consumer plans carefully and rationally for a purchase, following the purchase-decision process, or acts more impulsively.[18] How marketers research, anticipate, and react to the external and internal influences depends on their products, their target markets, and their analysis of the marketing environment.

extended problem solving

an approach to decision making in which the consumer consciously searches for information, carefully evaluates the alternatives, and analyzes the result

limited problem solving

a consumer chooses among a number of unfamiliar alternatives in a familiar purchase situation

routine problem solving

the consumer makes a quick choice, taking little time to consider the alternatives or the outcome of the decision

Before you go on . . .

A. How does advanced technology help marketers analyze consumer behavior on an individual level?

B. What is perceived risk and why is it important to marketers?

C. Why do marketers want to be sure their products are in the consumer's consideration set?

D. How does postpurchase dissonance affect consumers?

External Influences on Consumer Behavior

Consumer decisions and actions don't come about in a vacuum. External forces play an important role. The next sections examine the key external influences on the purchase-decision process, including family and household, opinion leaders and word of mouth, reference groups, social class, and culture and subculture. In addition, situational influences can affect how, what, when, and where consumers buy.

Family and Household Influences

The family influences consumer behavior in three ways. The first is through *consumer socialization*, the process by which children learn the skills, knowledge, and attitudes they use when they function as consumers making purchase decisions. What children learn from parents about investigating, evaluating, selecting, and using products will carry over into their adult lives. Recognizing this, many marketers seek relationships with parents in the hope that their influence on children's buying habits will lead to brand loyalty as the children mature.

Family also influences consumer behavior through the *family life cycle*, the sequence of stages from young, single person to young married couple, followed by couple with children, couple whose children have left home, and retirement. At each stage, the family has needs that drive purchasing decisions and, of course, present opportunities for marketers. However, today's family life cycle doesn't necessarily follow the traditional path just outlined.[19] Divorce and remarriage are redefining the 70 percent of all U.S. households that are *family households*, residential units with a married couple or a parent and children. Some families are headed by a single parent, while others include members of the extended family, such as a grandparent.

Children learn consumer behavior skills from their family and friends through consumer socialization. By working closely with families and maintaining information in a database regarding their product preferences and buying habits, marketers can develop very strong relationships with adults and their children. As the children mature, marketers can adapt their products and promotions to fit their changing needs. How could a clothing store, for example, adapt its promotions over time to meet a family's changing needs as the children grow older?

More grown children are living at home for longer periods. At the same time, more people are staying single but sharing living quarters—and purchase decisions—with others.[20] This trend has led to an increase in *nonfamily households*, households of unrelated people who live together, which now represent 30 percent of U.S. households.[21] Marketers are therefore responding to ever-changing needs and demands for furniture, cookware, banking services, and other products used by family and nonfamily households.

Finally, the family influences consumer behavior through *family decision making* (or, in nonfamily households, household decision making). Individual family members, even young children, may play a role in any or all stages of the purchase-decision process. By themselves, children under 12 in the United States spend about $7.5 billion a year. Their influence on family purchase decisions is even larger, estimated at about $130 billion of the parents' annual spending. Teens also have influence. Parents listen more carefully to teens' opinions when they believe the young people are knowledgeable about a particular product. Teens are especially motivated to influence family purchase decisions for products they use.[22]

Little wonder, then, that marketers try to get more than one family member on their side when a purchase is in order. To this end, Ralston Foods, which makes Chex cereals, used product packaging, advertising, and promotions to reach both parents and children. Ralston redesigned its cereal packages with a banner announcing that "8 out of 10 kids like Chex," a message to parents who doubt that their children will enjoy the Ralston cereals. The message was repeated in television and print advertising. At the same time, a promotional tie-in with the video release of Walt Disney's *The Lion King* was designed to appeal to children.[23]

Issues for critical thinking

Watch an hour or two of Saturday morning television, paying close attention to the commercials. How do marketers of foods, toys, and other products try to influence parental purchasing by advertising to children? Do you think such promotion is ethical? Explain your answer.

Opinion Leaders and Word of Mouth

Before consumers decide what to buy, they often seek advice or guidance from people who are knowledgeable about or involved with the products under consideration. These product experts are **opinion leaders**, people who can influence the attitudes or behaviors of others. Opinion leaders are frequently among the first on the block to try new goods or services, which is why people ask them about product features, advantages, and disadvantages before buying. In addition, opinion leaders are seen as objective and as specialists in a certain product or category. For all these reasons, the recommendations of opinion leaders are important to consumers who are planning a purchase.

opinion leaders

people who can influence the attitudes or behaviors of others

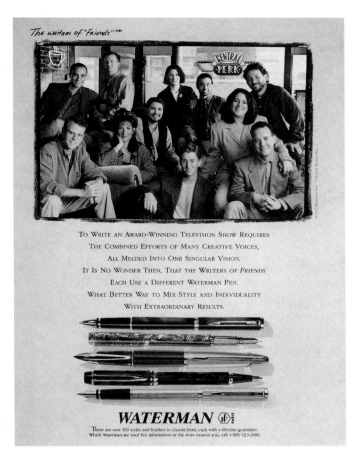

To Write an Award-Winning Television Show Requires
The Combined Efforts of Many Creative Voices,
All Melded Into One Singular Vision.
It Is No Wonder Then, That the Writers of FRIENDS
Each Use a Different Waterman Pen.
What Better Way to Mix Style and Individuality
With Extraordinary Results.

WATERMAN ⓦ

There are over 100 styles and finishes to choose from, each with a lifetime guarantee.
Which Waterman are you? For information or the store nearest you, call 1-800-523-2486.

Few television shows were as popular as "Friends" when this ad was produced. As a result, many potential customers were attracted by this ad and learned about Waterman pens. Ads of this type revolve around word-of-mouth communication whereby opinion leaders such as the writers of "Friends" influence what people buy. Would it be a wise promotional strategy for Waterman to give away pens to others who can influence consumer purchasing?

word-of-mouth communication

transmission of information informally from person to person

reference groups

groups that influence the behavior of members, people wanting to be members, and people who do not want to be members

Because opinion leaders are in a position to recommend products, as well as to disparage them, some marketers develop marketing programs especially for this group. Reebok, for example, signed on as an official sponsor of the U.S. gymnastics team for the 1996 Olympic Games, arranging for the gymnasts to wear Reebok clothing. The gymnastics team toured 20 cities in 1995 as a prelude to the 1996 Olympics, and they participated in fashion shows in local malls—a perfect opportunity for fans to see them wearing Reebok active fashions.[24]

Opinion leadership operates through **word-of-mouth communication**, the transmission of information informally from person to person. Word-of-mouth is believable because it comes from opinion leaders, family members, friends, and other sources not officially connected with marketers. Seen as trustworthy and unbiased, word-of-mouth communication can deal a marketer a powerful blow when negative, even as positive word-of-mouth can give a strong boost. Jim Easton has seen what positive word-of-mouth can do for his Jas. D. Easton sports equipment company. The firm placed little advertising. However, it did pay four National Hockey League players to use its sticks. These players praised the equipment so highly that soon 36 NHL players were using Easton's sticks.[25]

Reference Groups

Reference groups are groups that influence the behavior of members, people wanting to be members, and people who do not want to be members. Consumers can be influenced by reference groups in three ways: in their search for information before a purchase, in their attitudes toward a product or purchase, and in the way they buy or use a product.[26] For example, teenagers are a reference group for preteens. The youngsters aspire to be just like teenagers, especially older siblings, so they're influenced to wear teen fashions. The Gap, like many other apparel marketers, taps into the power of teen reference groups by offering child-sized versions of its teen clothing at its Gap Kids retail chain.

Similarly, teens have their own reference groups. J.C. Penney builds on connections to the reference group of fashion models by holding an annual cover-girl contest for young teenage women. The chance to become a model—and to hobnob with Jamie Walters, Matthew Fox, and other heartthrobs who walk the runway with the winning teens—draws thousands to enter the contest every year.[27] It's important to remember that the influence of reference groups works in reverse, as well. Some marketers, especially nonprofit groups, try to influence behavior by using images of reference groups (such as drug dealers or criminals) to which consumers *don't* want to belong.

Social Class

In every society, consumer behavior is subtly influenced by **social class**, groupings of people who share similar lifestyles, values, interests, behaviors, and status. In the United States, social class is determined partly by factors such as education, occupation, income, possessions, and attitudes. People in the United States tend to fall into one of seven social classes: upper-upper, lower-upper, upper-middle, middle, working, lower, and lower-lower. Of course, the distinctions between classes are not firm. Through hard work, education, and other means, people can and do move up to a higher class in their own eyes or in the eyes of others.[28] They can also slip down, however, through long-term loss of income brought on by layoffs or through other problems.

Social class is important to marketers because it has much to do with the way people buy and use products. From clothing to real estate, sporting goods to banking services, the preferences and buying habits of one social class often differ from those of others. Upper-class parents, for instance, want baby clothing and furniture that reflects their social status. "It's 'Look at my child and see who this family is,'" explains James McNeal, a Texas A&M marketing professor. They are the market for Ralph Lauren's infant and toddlers' clothing, including $350 cashmere receiving blankets and $22 cotton shirts.[29]

Social classes vary in description in different countries. Given those differences, however, rising incomes and aspirations of middle-class consumers around the world are fueling sales of a variety of products. Cadbury Schweppes, the British-based maker of desserts and beverages, is taking advantage of this phenomenon in Russia by building a chocolate plant near St. Petersburg. Russian consumers with extra rubles to spend are buying from television home shopping channels and traveling to Western countries to buy fashion apparel. These consumer buying trends present opportunities for marketers of a wide variety of products.[30]

This Ralph Lauren ad in San Francisco portrays the lifestyle of people in one social class. The idea is to inspire others to copy that lifestyle and purchasing behavior by buying Polo Boys products. Do you think this ad would work well in countries with a small but growing middle class? Why?

Culture, Subculture, and Core Values

Culture is the set of values, beliefs, and attitudes that is shared by a group and passed down from one generation to the next **(p. 77)**. Youngsters learn the basic underpinnings of their nation's culture from family, school, and other institutions. As adults, they transmit the culture to their children. In each generation, some cultural attitudes or beliefs change in importance. But over time the *core values*—basic, enduring values that pervade the culture—change only slowly. For example, the core values of individualism and freedom have formed the foundation of U.S. culture since the nation's birth. Other emerging values, including concern for the natural environment, have become a significant part of the cultural fabric only in recent decades.

A subculture is a group of people that preserves its unique values and lifestyle within a dominant culture. As you saw in Chapter 4, the United States (like most other countries) is home to a diverse group of thriving subcultures. Among the most important for companies targeting the U.S. market are ethnic and religious subcultures, cohort subcultures, and regional subcultures.

social class

groupings of people who share similar lifestyles, values, interests, behaviors, and status

Some like it hot! Typically, each subculture has its own preferences for food and other products. This ad features the familiar brand of Tabasco pepper sauce and is directed at Hispanic people who prefer their food hot. Would this ad also appeal to other subcultures who like spicy food?

cohort subculture

people of similar ages who have undergone similar experiences

Ethnic and Religious Subcultures

A wide variety of ethnic and religious subcultures exist within the U.S. culture, set apart from the mainstream by their unique traditions and beliefs. The list of ethnic subcultures in the United States reads like a world atlas, including groups descended from homelands on every continent. As discussed in Chapter 4, the three major U.S. subcultures are those of African Americans, Hispanic Americans, and Asian Americans. Major religious subcultures in the United States include Catholics, Protestants, Jews, and Muslims. Given the growing numbers and buying power of the people in these subcultures, you can understand why more and more marketers are studying and responding to their groups' buying behavior, which can affect how they eat, what they wear, and many other aspects of daily life.

Kraft Foods, for example, hired Burrell Advertising to research African American attitudes toward Stove Top Stuffing and develop advertisements geared specifically to that subculture's attitudes and interests. After conducting a series of focus group interviews, Burrell designed a campaign that likened Stove Top's cornbread stuffing to cornbread dressing, a favorite side dish. The theme was "The box says stuffing. The taste says dressing." Posttesting found that the ads were both likable and realistic.[31]

Of course, you can't automatically assume that all members of a subculture will display identical buying behaviors. Each consumer is different from every other, and the role of subcultural influences may vary from individual to individual. Remember, too, that the power of these influences may change over time as subculture members adapt to the broader environment. In Hispanic cultures, for example, husbands traditionally have had much influence over major family purchases such as automobiles, whereas wives have made decisions about home-related products, such as appliances. Research shows that this buying behavior often changes as Hispanic families in the United States adopt the joint decision-making behavior more frequently found in the mainstream U.S. culture.[32]

Cohort Subcultures

Every consumer is part of a **cohort subculture**, people of similar ages who have undergone similar experiences.[33] The values, attitudes, and beliefs of cohort subcultures are shaped by common memories about historical events, cultural heroes, and so on. In turn, these shared cultural bonds shape the way people in each age cohort buy and use products such as recorded music and clothing. "Baby boom" (men and women born between 1946 and 1964) and "Generation X" (men and women now in their twenties) are the names given to two cohort subcultures with unique values, needs, and interests shaped by the popular culture and products of their times. And one way marketers appeal to these cohorts is through nostalgia, especially music of the era, that links a product to vivid memories of the past.

For example, the California Raisin Advisory Board used the 1960s Motown hit "I Heard It Through the Grapevine" in an advertising campaign aimed at baby boomers. The campaign brought new life to the slow-growing raisin industry. Similarly, a small but steadily growing number of radio stations such as WWLG in Baltimore play nostalgic music from the big-band era, aiming at the cohort of people aged 50 and over. "If you're advertising to the 50-plus crowd, you really don't have a lot of options," says Jim Ward, WWLG station manager.[34] His station provides that option.

Regional Subcultures

Regional subculture—the culture of a particular region within a country—can also affect consumer behavior. One obvious aspect of regional subculture is climate, which influences outdoor sports, driving styles, and other aspects of product usage. Beyond climate, regional subcultures can be defined by differences in food preferences and other buying or usage patterns.

For example, people in Philadelphia have a weakness for cheese–steak sandwiches, and people in Buffalo are fond of spicy chicken wings. Many northerners have a taste for blueberries, which are mostly grown in New Jersey, Michigan, and other northern states. And when people from the north move south, they take their food preferences with them. "Before so many Northerners moved to Florida, it wasn't a particularly big market for New Jersey highbush blueberries," observes Dennis Doyle, general manager of the Tru-Blu Cooperative Association, an organization of blueberry growers. But as more people have retired to the sunny south, says Doyle, "Our Florida blueberry business has increased about 60 percent over the past decade."[35]

Situational Influences

The purchase-decision process is also subject to **situational influences**, elements of time and place that can affect consumer behavior. In particular, five situational influences can make a difference in how, when, or where consumers buy. These influences are physical surroundings, social surroundings, time, purpose of the purchase, and antecedent states.[36]

- *Physical surroundings.* Where the purchase is being made—and the physical conditions under which the transaction occurs—can affect consumer behavior. Weather, geographical location, store decor, product displays, even music, can help or hinder consumers as they gather information, weigh their alternatives, or make purchases. For example, Campbell's Soup uses weather forecasts to schedule radio commercials during cold or foul weather, when consumers are most likely to be interested in soup.

- *Social surroundings.* Other people present during the purchase-decision process can influence what, when, and how consumers buy. Consumers are frequently influenced by the comments and perceptions of companions on a shopping trip or by people in the room when a television commercial comes on. Mullen Advertising, an agency in Wenham, Massachusetts, carefully considers social surroundings when helping clients communicate with Generation X consumers. "They're making dates with their friends to get together to watch 'Melrose Place'," says Kevin Kolbe, senior account planner. Understanding this behavior helps the agency to place its clients' commercials during the appropriate programs to take advantage of the influence of social surroundings.[37]

- *Time.* Consumer behavior is also influenced by the amount of time available for gathering information, making the decision, and buying and using the product. Saving time has become a priority for many people, offering an opportunity for marketers who show consumers how to avoid wasting time in buying or using products. The need to cater to people who are pressed for time has transformed the restaurant industry, for example. Fast food now accounts for 45 percent of all

situational influences

elements of time and place that can affect consumer behavior

Many consumers feel they don't have enough time to accomplish everything they want to accomplish. This situational influence of time pressure creates an opportunity for Bennigan's, a national chain of restaurants. The chain is offering a special "Time Crunch Lunch," guaranteeing to get customers in and out of its restaurants quickly. In addition to restaurants, what other marketers might be successful with such an approach?

restaurant business, and 99 percent of all restaurants offer food for take-out.[38]

- *Purpose of purchase.* The reason for the purchase will have a significant impact on consumer behavior. People often approach gift purchases differently from purchases made for personal or household use. They also think about who will receive a particular gift. When Levi Strauss marketers spotted the lifestyle shift toward dress-down days at work, they realized that consumers needed clothing that could be worn for both work and play. So the company positioned its Dockers clothing as appropriate for leisure activities yet professional enough to wear to work.[39]

- *Antecedent states.* Both momentary conditions and moods before and during the purchase can affect consumer behavior. Momentary conditions such as being short on cash or feeling tired can influence the way consumers act. People may search for information, analyze the alternatives, and make decisions differently when they are in a good mood and when they feel sad or bored. For example, Northwest Airlines counted on the good mood of Super Bowl XXIX viewers when it aired a commercial asking for donations to help victims of the earthquake in Kobe, Japan. The reasoning was that consumers enjoying the game would be in a generous frame of mind and would be more likely to contribute to the cause.[40]

Before you go on . . .

A. What is word-of-mouth communication and why does it influence consumer behavior?

B. How do opinion leaders influence consumer behavior?

C. What are cohort subcultures?

D. How do situational influences affect consumer buying?

Internal Influences on Consumer Behavior

How people think, act, and buy is also determined, in part, by a number of internal forces. Among these forces are perception, motivation, attitudes, learning, and the interaction of personality, self-concept, and lifestyle. Because the effects of these influences on behavior can vary from person to person, the marketer's goal of understanding—and molding or changing—consumer behavior is both complex and exciting. Researchers often refer to the mind as a "black box" because it is so difficult to determine what goes on inside. The following discussion considers some of the insights that researchers have had into the internal influences on consumer behavior.

Perception

Consumers make sense of the outside world through their perception of what surrounds them. **Perception** is the process of determining meaning by selecting, organizing, and interpreting stimuli in the environment. Its four stages are exposure, attention, interpretation, and memory.

In the first stage, the consumer is exposed to a stimulus such as a product, package, or advertising message, through the senses. In the second stage, the consumer actively attends to a selected stimulus, such as by consciously watching or listening to a particular commercial. The third stage is interpreting what the senses have detected, such as by understanding the meaning of words in an ad. And the fourth stage is storing the meaning in memory to facilitate the use of the information during the purchase-decision process.

Because the environment is filled with stimuli—more advertisements and products than any one person can notice or try to understand—consumers choose to focus on only a few. *Selective exposure* means that consumers will not expose themselves to products they believe they won't enjoy. For example, some people avoid television shows that they expect will be violent. *Selective perception* is a phenomenon in which people often see what they expect to see. That is, if you expect a television show to be violent, you may perceive it to be more violent then others without this preconception might. Finally, *selective retention* means that you forget messages that have little relevance to your life.

Such *selective processes* present communication challenges for marketers in all four stages of the perception process. This is where marketing research comes into play. Through research, for example, you can find out how many people were exposed to your ad, paid attention to it, remembered the message, and accurately interpreted it. You can also show your ad message to people before using it; this tactic, called *pretesting*, helps you to determine whether consumers in your target market are likely to properly interpret the ad's meaning.

Once you've done your homework, you can apply marketing techniques that help your product or marketing communication stand out amid the clutter. Retailers, for example, have studied the way consumers perceive products in the store, then designed aisles and shelves to encourage exposure to more products, especially higher profit items. They also use eye-catching displays, special lighting, and other techniques to draw consumer attention. Brand names are another way to help consumers focus on—and remember—individual products. For example, the Compaq Computer brand, developed by a name specialist, combines "com" (to convey computer and communications) and "paq" (to convey small); the unconventional spelling attracts attention.[41]

Motivation

perception

the process of determining meaning by selecting, organizing, and interpreting stimuli in the environment

motives

the internal factors that propel individuals to take actions that satisfy their needs

As the discussion of perception demonstrates, much of what influences decisions and actions occurs inside the individual. To identify what drives someone to fulfill a need, you must look below the surface. A *need* is the feeling of deprivation over the absence of food, clothing, shelter, or some other necessity for basic survival. When people feel a need, they are driven to act by their **motives**, the internal factors that propel individuals to take actions that satisfy their needs.

TABLE **6.1**   **Maslow's Hierarchy and Marketing Communications**

Need	Product Examples	Marketing Communication Examples
Physiological	Foods, medicines	Quaker Oat Bran: "It's the right thing to do"
Safety	Alarm systems, retirement investments	Radio Shack: "If security is the question, we've got the answer"
Social	Grooming products, clothing	Pond's: "For younger looking skin"
Esteem	Cars, credit cards	Lexus: "The relentless pursuit of perfection"
Self-actualization	Education, travel, hobbies	Canada: "The world next door"

Psychologist Abraham Maslow identified a hierarchy of human needs, listed in Table 6.1: physiological, safety, social, esteem, and self-actualization. When he developed this classification, Maslow believed that people are initially motivated to satisfy their basic needs for survival, such as physiological and safety needs. Then they are able to concentrate on satisfying higher level needs such as esteem and self-actualization.

The five classifications in Maslow's hierarchy of needs describe in simple terms how needs and motives operate, but the model doesn't completely explain consumer behavior. It doesn't fully explain why people choose to satisfy a higher level need (such as education) before accommodating a lower level need (such as food or sleep). It also doesn't recognize that one behavior may satisfy more than one need. Entrepreneur Joe Marino understands the power of satisfying two needs at once. At his Area Code Cafe in New York City, each customer can make a free three-minute call anywhere in the United States with a food purchase of $5 or more, satisfying both physiological and social needs at once.[42]

Attitudes

Attitudes are enduring positive or negative responses to people, products, or information. A consumer's attitudes toward any brand or type of product are formed over time through experience and information gathering as well as through interaction with other people. Clearly, consumers' attitudes toward your product or brand can affect their actions. People whose attitudes are positive are more likely to buy what you're marketing than those whose attitudes are negative or neutral. This is why marketers spend so much time and money investigating and influencing consumer attitudes.

Attitudes are complex, consisting of three components, any of which can be molded or changed through marketing strategy. The *cognitive component* is the set of beliefs or knowledge a consumer has of the product. Marketers can play an active role in helping consumers formulate or change their beliefs by providing appropriate information during the purchase-decision process. For example, the Pork Producers Council's "other white meat" ad campaign explained that pork is not high in fat. By changing consumer beliefs about pork, the campaign reversed a sales decline and brought U.S. pork consumption to new levels.[43]

attitudes

enduring positive or negative responses to people, products, or information

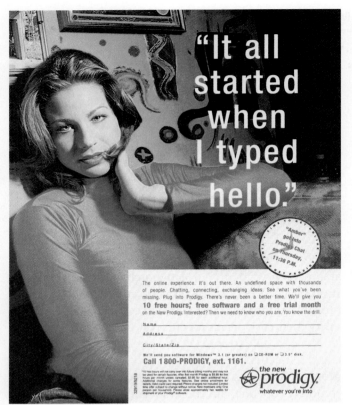

"It all started when I typed hello."

"Amber" got into Prodigy Chat on Thursday, 11:38 P.M.

The online experience. It's out there. An undefined space with thousands of people. Chatting, connecting, exchanging ideas. See what you've been missing. Plug into Prodigy. There's never been a better time. We'll give you **10 free hours, free software and a free trial month** on the New Prodigy. Interested? Then we need to know who you are. You know the drill.

Name

Address

City/State/Zip

We'll send you software for Windows™ 3.1 (or greater) on ☐ CD-ROM or ☐ 3.5" disk.
Call 1 800-PRODIGY, ext. 1161.

the new **prodigy**
whatever you're into

Consumers have greater uncertainty when buying services because they have more difficulty actually trying the product. For that reason, service marketers are wise to make it as easy as possible for consumers to experience what they have to offer. In this ad, for example, Prodigy offers 10 free hours and free software. What else could Prodigy do to influence consumer attitudes toward its product?

The *affective component* represents the consumer's feelings about or emotional reaction to the product. Extremely powerful emotions such as fear and love can be generated by a company's ads. Thus an Allstate Insurance television commercial appeals to feelings of fear by showing the remains of a house gutted by fire. On the other hand, the Hallmark Cards theme, "When you care enough to send the very best," used for its greeting cards and stationery products, appeals to feelings of love.[44]

Marketers can reinforce the positive feelings that consumers have about their products and, at the same time, influence the feelings that prospects have. For example, Chrysler's print and television ads have featured letters from customers discussing how happy they were with the overall car-buying experience, encouraging similar attitudes in customers and prospects alike.[45]

The *behavioral component* is the consumer's tendency to act in a certain way. Marketers can use coupons, free samples, and other incentives to persuade people to take actions such as buying and trying products. Once consumers have used a product and experienced its benefits, they may behave the same way in the future—buying the product again and again. Jolly Rancher used an appeal geared to the behavioral component when it introduced its MegaFruit Gummis candy. The company used a "try me" coupon to invite candy lovers to buy one, get one free, on the premise that buyers who enjoy the new product will go on to buy more.[46]

ETHICS & SOCIAL RESPONSIBILITY

True colors of green

When is green really green? More than ever, consumers are interested in socially responsible activities and products that help the environment. But what attitudes and behaviors can marketers expect from such consumers? A wide range, as a recent study by Roper Starch Worldwide reveals.

Environmentally conscious consumers come in five shades of green. "True-blue greens," about 14 percent of all U.S. adults, are deeply committed to environmental causes. They want to protect the environment through their buying decisions, as well as other forms of personal behavior. "Greenback greens," about 6 percent of the adult population, are less willing to make significant changes in purchasing behavior. "Sprouts," 35 percent of the population, sometimes purchase environment-friendly products.

By contrast, the 13 percent of the population who are "grousers" respond grudgingly to environmental issues, and the 32 percent in the "basic browns" category are apathetic. The ranks of "basic browns" have grown slightly in recent years, in part because of confusion about marketers' environmental claims. At the same time, more people are moving up to become "true-blue greens" and "sprouts."

The survey has two lessons for green marketers. First, aim your marketing efforts at consumers who are committed to the environment, and explain your product's environmental benefits, backing up claims with facts so consumers can make an informed decision. Second, don't exaggerate environmental claims.[47]

If you were a green marketer, how would you uncover your customers' attitudes and reactions to green marketing?

Learning

Learning, the process of applying experience or knowledge to consumer behavior, is another influence that marketers must consider. Over time, learning can affect the way people recognize needs, collect and assess product information, make buying decisions, and evaluate the results. In a recent study, 82 percent of the respondents cited past experience with a brand as an important factor in their purchase decisions.[48] Changes in consumer behavior can come about because of behavioral learning and cognitive learning.

Behavioral Learning

The first type of learning, *behavioral learning*, occurs when a person behaves in a certain way in response to the experience of an external stimulus. Behavioral learning can happen both automatically and consciously. Suppose you feel hungry and go to a Burger King to eat. Over time, you may automatically feel hungry when exposed to the Burger King brand (an external stimulus) because you associate the brand with food. This response can also be consciously learned through *reinforcement*. If you're rewarded every time you react to the Burger King brand—the reward being a trip to the restaurant for a hamburger—you're more likely to knowingly repeat the behavior.

Marketers can apply behavioral learning concepts by using stimulus generalization and stimulus discrimination. *Stimulus generalization* means that people who have learned to respond to one stimulus learn to respond in the same way to another, similar stimulus. Once people have grown accustomed to buying a particular product, they may continue the response—buying—when presented with a similar product. That's the thinking behind copycat store products packaged in the same size, shape, and color container as brand-name competitive products.[49] It's also the reason marketers cite for putting established brands on new products, building on consumers' positive associations with the brand. For example, Dole has put its brand, best known for canned fruits and vegetables, on fresh produce.

Stimulus discrimination occurs when people detect differences between similar stimuli and learn not to respond in the same way to all such stimuli. Campbell's Soup applies stimulus discrimination in an ad for Healthy Request Hearty Vegetable soup, which urges consumers to "Taste the Difference! Taste Preferred Over Progresso Healthy Classics Vegetable Soup." By calling attention to the taste difference between the two products, the marketer hopes to convince consumers that all healthful soups are not alike.

Cognitive Learning

learning

the process of applying experience or knowledge to consumer behavior

The second type of learning, *cognitive learning*, occurs when people change their behavior as a result of thinking about their situations. By putting ideas together in their minds, or by watching other people, consumers can learn

No caffeine. No alcohol. No sushi. When you're a pregnant or nursing mother there are lots of nos. But there is one big yes. Milk. And there's practically nothing your body needs more right now than all that calcium. Except sleep, but let's be realistic.

MILK
What a surprise!

Drinking milk in the past often was not considered as "cool" as drinking other beverages. But ads like this one have created new interest in milk. The ads feature famous people from the entertainment and sports industries. This one features Christie Brinkley and her children. When famous personalities are shown drinking milk, consumers may be led to copy such behavior or at least consider milk as an "in" beverage. How much are you and your friends influenced by ads featuring celebrities?

brand loyalty

a favorable attitude toward a brand that prompts consistent purchasing over time

behavior that will satisfy their needs. One way marketers can build on cognitive learning is by helping consumers remember the connection between the brand and what the brand represents. That's why the labels "Low Fat Crackers" or "Reduced Fat Crackers" appears prominently on Today's Choice cracker packages. It's also why the packages carry a reminder that the product is "from the makers of Wheat Thins," a related product that consumers may have enjoyed.

A second way marketers build on cognitive learning is through the use of *modeling*, encouraging people to learn new behaviors by imitating what others do. For example, a recent ad campaign from the Milk Industry Foundation featured photographs of Christie Brinkley, Lauren Bacall, and other celebrities sporting a milk mustache. The campaign encouraged consumers to imitate the behavior of these famous people, who were drinking milk for better health.[50]

Brand Loyalty and Relationship Marketing

Both behavioral and cognitive learning can lead to buying by habit, which is what happens during routine problem solving. When consumers learn that a particular brand meets their needs, they tend to purchase it more consistently, skipping steps in the purchase-decision process. Soon these consumers develop **brand loyalty**, a favorable attitude toward a brand that prompts consistent purchasing over time. Brand loyalty is what drives Rhona Daniels, a young British woman, to buy only Armani jeans. "Nothing suits me as well as these do," she says. Would she wear another brand? "Not in a million years."[51]

To build up purchasing habits that lead to brand loyalty and long-term profitable customer relationships, many marketers have created programs that reward consumers for sticking with certain brands. By giving consumers tangible reasons to remain loyal to one brand, such as free gifts or free travel, marketers reinforce their customers' purchasing behavior. General Mills, maker of Betty Crocker baking products and other food products, has been rewarding brand loyalty since 1931. Buyers cut coupons from General Mills packages and redeem them for household items featured in the Betty Crocker Catalog. Some marketers, such as the Spanish retail chain Caprobo, automatically track customer purchases and send monthly statements showing how many points customers have earned toward prizes.[52]

Such relationship marketing programs strengthen long-term connections with customers and discourage brand switching. Because consumer behavior can change from purchase to purchase, however, marketers need to continually measure and reinforce brand loyalty. Also, studies show that consumers are usually loyal to brands only in certain product categories. Nonetheless, marketers in other categories may plan strategies to reinforce repeat purchasing. What's more, when consumers don't perceive a difference in quality among brands, lower prices can break the bond of brand loyalty.[53] As a result, marketers should use caution when setting prices as part of a strategy to build long-term loyalty in a profitable marketing relationship. Here's how two restaurateurs are building brand loyalty among customers.

personality

the unique set of behavior patterns an individual exhibits in response to recurring situations

self-concept

the way a person feels and thinks about himself or herself

Consumers in every country respond to symbolism in ads. The symbolism in this ad for the sporty MGF Roadster convertible appeals to the lifestyle and self-concept of people in the target market. How does the car maker's decision not to show any people in the ad allow consumers to make the connection between their own lifestyles and the lifestyle suggested by the MGF Roadster? How does this decision allow both men and women to relate to the product?

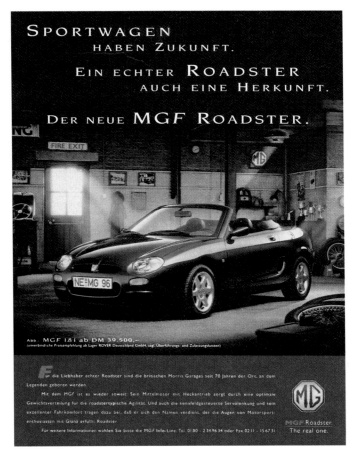

SMALL BUSINESS WATCH

Feeding restaurant brand loyalty

Entrepreneurs Michael Franks and Robert Bell have made brand loyalty a key ingredient in their recipe for restaurant success. Franks and Bell wanted to encourage repeat business at their four California restaurants, Depot, Chez Melange, Fino, and Misto Caffe & Bakery. Borrowing a marketing technique from the airlines, who used frequent-flier programs to build brand loyalty, the two decided to create a frequent-diner club.

Club members earn points every time they eat at one of the four restaurants. On occasion, the restaurants offer double points on certain menu items they want to push as well as on gift certificates. The 4,000 club members track their own points, which can be redeemed for restaurant meals, gourmet picnic lunches, even the chance to be guest chef for a day. The top prize? For 12,000 points, says Franks, "Robert and I will come to your home and personally cook a meal for 10 people."

Even though their frequent-diner club sounds costly, it isn't. The total of prizes awarded every year, worth more than $100,000, is only about one percent of the business's total expenses. Compared with the cost of advertising, Franks says, the club is fairly inexpensive. Best of all, says Franks, the club is a way of showing gratitude to the customers who dine at his restaurants most often.[54]

Can you identify other types of small business that might prosper by rewarding brand loyalty?

Personality, Self-Concept, and Lifestyle

Personality is the unique set of behavior patterns an individual exhibits in response to recurring situations. Some marketers group consumers according to certain personality *traits*—characteristics such as impulsiveness—and develop positioning and marketing approaches to fit each group. For example, if an automaker's research reveals that convertible owners are more active, vigorous, and impulsive than other car owners, the marketer would then advertise its convertibles using images of active, carefree people.[55]

A few personality traits, such as innovativeness (the desire for new experiences), seem to predict who will purchase certain products.[56] People who crave variety or new experiences are more likely to switch brands. This tendency creates opportunities for marketers who position their products accordingly. Despite years of study, however, researchers have found little evidence that personality can be consistently linked to buying behavior.

On the other hand, research shows that consumer behavior is clearly influenced by **self-concept**, the way a person feels and thinks about himself or herself. Of course, the way people see themselves is not necessarily the way they really are, how others see them, or the way they would like to be. Self-concept is a powerful driver of

lifestyle

an individual pattern of living as exhibited in a person's activities, interests, and opinions

consumer behavior. People buy and use products that shape, support, or express their inner selves. This fact has not been lost on the marketers at Sara Lee Knit Products, maker of Hanes underwear. "Underwear is becoming more of a fashion statement for men," says Jeanie Snow, director of marketing for men's underwear. "It's not just underwear anymore. Men are starting to see it as an expression of themselves, whether it's funny boxer shorts or briefs in wilder colors."[57]

Another reflection of self-concept is **lifestyle**, an individual pattern of living as exhibited in a person's activities, interests, and opinions. When marketers analyze consumer lifestyles, they look at a wide range of characteristics (known as *psychographic variables*), including people's work, hobbies, sports, community interests, and convictions. Lifestyle shifts can open vast marketing opportunities—and pose threats, as well. In the car industry, the movement toward more active lifestyles has boosted sales of sport-utility vehicles such as the Jeep Cherokee and the Toyota 4Runner. At the same time, the lifestyle shift has chilled sales of big luxury cars.[58]

Before you go on . . .

A. What is perception and why is selective perception important to marketers?

B. List the five categories of needs in Maslow's hierarchy.

C. How does behavioral learning differ from cognitive learning?

D. How does self-concept affect consumer behavior?

Summary

1. **Define consumer behavior and discuss why marketers have to continually study it.**

   Consumer behavior consists of all the consumer's decisions and actions connected with choosing, purchasing, using, and disposing of goods and services. Marketers have to continually study this area of behavior because it changes over time as people and situations change.

2. **List the five stages in the consumer purchase-decision process.**

   The five stages in the consumer-purchase-decision process are need recognition, information seeking, alternative evaluation, purchase, and postpurchase evaluation.

3. **Explain how the consumer's level of involvement affects the purchase-decision process.**

   Involvement is the level of importance or interest that a consumer attaches to a certain product or purchase situation. The level of consumer involvement determines the complexity of the purchase-decision process. When consumers are highly involved, they use extended problem solving, consciously searching for information, carefully evaluating the alternatives, and analyzing the result. When consumers are less involved, they use limited problem solving, choosing among a number of unfamiliar alternatives in a familiar purchase situation. Even less involvement leads to routine problem solving, as shown in the making of a choice quickly, without taking much time to consider the alternatives or the outcome of the decision.

4. **Identify five internal influences on consumer behavior.**

   Five internal influences on consumer behavior are perception, motivation, attitudes, learning, and the interaction of personality, self-concept, and lifestyle.

5. **Discuss the three ways in which the family can influence consumer behavior.**

   The family can influence consumer behavior through (1) consumer socialization (the process by which children learn the skills, knowledge, and attitudes they need to function as consumers, making purchase decisions), (2) family life cycle (the sequence of steps that take a family from formation to retirement), and (3) family decision making (or, in nonfamily households, household decision making).

6. **Explain the role of opinion leaders, word-of-mouth communication, and reference groups in consumer buying decisions.**

   Opinion leaders are people who exert influence on the attitudes or behaviors of others because they are knowledgeable about or involved with the products under consideration. Opinion leadership operates through word-of-mouth communication, the transmission of information informally from person to person. Reference groups are groups that influence behavior on the basis of consumers' being members, wanting to be members, or not wanting to be members.

7. **Describe the five situational influences on consumer purchasing decisions.**

   The five situational influences on consumer purchasing decisions are (1) physical surroundings, including where the purchase is made and under what conditions; (2) social surroundings, including who is present during the process; (3) time, including the time available for gathering information, making the decision, and buying and using the product; (4) purpose of the purchase; and (5) antecedent states, which are moods and momentary conditions in effect before and during the purchase.

KEY TERMS

attitudes 181	lifestyle 186	reference groups 175
brand loyalty 184	limited problem solving 172	routine problem solving 172
cohort subculture 177	motives 180	self-concept 185
consideration set 169	opinion leaders 174	situational influences 178
consumer behavior 164	perceived risk 168	social class 176
extended problem solving 172	perception 180	word-of-mouth communication 175
involvement 170	personality 185	
learning 183	postpurchase dissonance 170	

Skill-Building Applications

1. Retail stores and other marketers that cater to consumers work hard to establish a mutually beneficial exchange relationship with you and other customers. What could you do to assist in creating such a relationship, and what benefits might you receive from doing so?

2. Show how the concepts of brand loyalty, cohort subculture, involvement, learning, reference groups, and word-of-mouth communication apply to the marketing of Birkenstock sandals.

3. What are the major influences on a student looking for a barber or a dentist in a new college town?

4. Heartland Value Fund is a mutual fund that invests in small undervalued companies. Describe how the company could lead people to buy shares in its mutual fund by assisting them at each stage of the consumer decision-making process.

5. City Year Inc., a Boston nonprofit group, developed a "franchisable" model for privately funded youth service corps that create value for sponsors and the community. What consumer behavior concepts might the organization use to get more volunteers?

6. Pick a country with which you are not familiar. Do research to determine which situational influences are likely to have the greatest effect on consumer buying there. How would these influences affect buyers of a global product such as Coca-Cola?

Getting Involved in Marketing

1. *On Your Own* Think of the last time you made what was, for you, a major purchase. Chart the decision-making process you followed in buying that product. Did you use extended, limited, or routine problem solving? How could the maker of that product use information about your decision-making process to market more effectively? Write a letter to the marketer, offering advice and explaining the concepts underlying your ideas.

2. *On Your Own* Think again about the major purchase in exercise one. Identify the external influences that played a role in your decision. Did you include a particular product or brand in your consideration set—or eliminate it—because of these influences? Write a one-page report explaining how you would use your knowledge of external influences to market the product you purchased.

3. *Find Out More* Find a published article about a marketer introducing a new product. What level of involvement might consumers have with this product? What perceived risks might be associated with it? How does the marketer seem to be countering the perceived risks?

4. *In a Partnership* Collaborate with another student on this exercise. Separately, select one reference group to which you would like to belong, and write a paragraph explaining how this reference group influences your personal buying behavior. Exchange answers and write a brief report describing how you would use the other student's answer to market a particular product to him or her.

5. *In a Team* With two other students, find ads from three competitors that market similar consumer products such as fast-food or banking services. Discuss which aspects of consumer buying behavior seem to be addressed in each ad. Summarize your findings in a two-minute talk to your class. Do your classmates agree with your team's assessment?

6. *In a Team* Team up with other students for this exercise. Talk about what caused a feeling of postpurchase dissonance in a buying situation each of you made recently. Would you feel postpurchase dissonance if you had been in your teammates' buying situation? Write a one-page report explaining how you would minimize postpurchase dissonance if you were marketing what one of your teammates purchased.

VideoCase Fly & Field Reels In Customers by Mail and by Modem

Database marketing and fly-fishing—this unique combination has helped Marcos Vergara build a successful store, catalog operation, and Web site to serve customers around the world. Vergara's business, Fly & Field, specializes in goods and services for fly-fishing enthusiasts. By collecting data on the needs and behaviors of customers and prospects in an internal database, Vergara has been able to more precisely target his consumer marketing efforts.

Vergara's store is located in Glen Ellyn, Illinois. To supplement the retail operation, he spent $50,000 building a database of 65,000 prospects and customers that he could reach by mail. He selected 25,000 people from this database to receive his first catalog, and received a 24 percent response, which is very high. These days, to maintain relationships with customers, Vergara sends customers a continuous stream of mailings, including catalogs, newsletters, promotional pieces, and announcements of fly-fishing trips and seminars.

As surfing the Internet became more popular, Vergara began fishing there for more customers. He established a World Wide Web site for Fly & Field (http://www.flyfield.com). The site is extremely interactive, allowing visitors to chat with others who are interested in the sport of fly-fishing, talk with experts about the best fishing areas, and read about the most exciting adventures. Of course, visitors can browse through pages and pages of fly-fishing merchandise in the online catalog, which features a special section for sale items.

The Fly & Field Web site guides customers through the buying process. Consumers can recognize their needs as they look at the latest equipment and accessories and move through the articles about expert fly-fishers. The information-seeking stage is covered by a whole series of Web site pages devoted to subjects such as fly-tying and fly-fishing locations.

In the process of querying online experts, customers can evaluate their alternatives. Before and after they make purchases, visitors can trade fly-fishing stories on a special swap page. In this way, Vergara incorporates word of mouth into his Web site, allowing opinion leaders to influence what other fly-fishers pur-

chase. Then, when they're ready to buy, customers can order in any of four ways: they can request a catalog, print out an order form to be mailed, print out a separate order form for art prints and videos, or call toll-free to talk with a staff member.

The catalog and Web site share an upbeat tone and mirror the enthusiasm that customers have for fly-fishing. By understanding the buying behavior of fly-fishers, Vergara has hooked thousands of customers around the world.[59]

Strategies and applications

1. Many fishing equipment retailers try to hook customers on the World Wide Web. How might Vergara encourage customers to develop brand loyalty and consistently buy from Fly & Field rather than from competitors?

2. How would you measure the level of involvement that people interested in fly-fishing have in their product purchases? Do you think the level of involvement would be high or low? Why? How could Vergara use this information in his marketing efforts?

3. Which would be likely to have the greatest effect on customers who buy after visiting the Web site: opinion leaders, word of mouth, reference groups, or some combination? How could Fly & Field increase such influences?

4. How do you think the contents of the Fly & Field Web site might affect a customer's antecedent states? Would the Web site be likely to have any effect on the social surroundings? On the physical surroundings? Explain your answers.

5. If you were building Vergara's customer database, what information about each customer and purchase would you want to capture and store? How would you use this information to strengthen long-term customer relationships?

6. Would a study of the way shoppers perceive the Field & Fly store help Vergara enhance his Web site? What might Vergara want to know about the perceptions of Web visitors? About perceptions of store shoppers?

Team project

With other students, visit the Fly & Field Web site and compare it to shopping in a store. What are the differences? The similarities? If you were a customer, which experience would more motivate you to buy? Why? Can your team suggest ways of enhancing the site to make it even more inviting to fly-fishing enthusiasts? As a team, prepare a brief report to present your ideas.

7

Organizational Buying Behavior

Learning Goals

After you have read and studied this chapter, you should be able to:

1. Demonstrate how organizational buying behavior differs from consumer buying behavior.
2. Differentiate among the four types of organizational markets.
3. Describe how derived demand operates and explain its importance in organizational marketing.
4. List the six stages in the organizational buying process.
5. Identify the six roles in the organizational buying center.
6. Explain the use and importance of reverse marketing in the value chain.
7. Discuss four approaches to building strong value-chain relationships.

PROFILE

Brock Control sees customers as partners

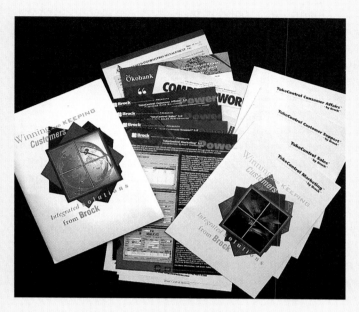

Mercedes-Benz is a Brock partner, Bank of Montreal is a Brock partner, and hundreds of other businesses around the world are Brock partners. In fact, Brock Control Systems, an Atlanta-based technology company that specializes in sales software and consulting, considers all its business customers to be partners. As founder Richard Brock says, "If somebody doesn't want to be a partner, we don't want to sell them software." In just 10 years, this partnership approach has propelled the company from a tiny start-up to a global marketer with $31 million in annual sales.

Richard Brock sees customers as partners because he knows they aren't buying software; they're buying solutions to their problems. What customers want is to manage their sales and service contacts more efficiently and, at the same time, build long-term relationships with their own customers. Goals this important can't be reached by buying a disk and popping it into the computer. Instead, customers need expert help in assessing their problems, determining what to do, and implementing the solutions. That takes a partnership relationship.

For every customer, Brock sets up a partnership team. The first member of the team is the new-account representative, who makes the initial contact and follows through on the first sale. The second member is the customer-development representative, who stays in touch with the customer after the sale to track ongoing needs and customer satisfaction. The third is the service technician, who assists with the installation. The fourth is the customer, whose active participation is vital to properly diagnosing and solving the problem.

Brock personnel work with the people who actually use the software, offering training and guidance at every step. In this way, the company becomes a partner in its customers' success. Does the partnership approach work? Brock's rapid growth shows that the answer is definitely *yes*.[1]

Brock Control Systems is one of many marketers that focus on building customer relationships with organizations rather than individual consumers. In this chapter, you'll go inside the organizational market, examining organizations as customers, comparing consumer and organizational markets, and learning about the links between consumer and organizational demand. You'll also analyze the organizational buying process and explore why and how smart marketers build stronger relationships in the value chain.

Marketing and Organizational Buying Behavior

The first essential task in business marketing is to develop a profile of your customers—find out who they are, and which are the most valuable; define their wants and needs; understand why they buy from your company, and why from competitors; and develop a system for gathering information from them on a regular basis.

Michael P. Collins
in *The Manufacturer's Guide to Business Marketing*[2]

Brock Control Systems specializes in marketing to businesses, which form part of the lucrative organizational market. In contrast to the *consumer market*, which consists of individuals who buy products for personal use or for use in the household, the *organizational market* consists of businesses, government agencies, and institutions that buy products to be used in their operations, as components of the products they make, or for resale to other customers. The organizational market in the United States is responsible for more than $5 trillion worth of purchases every year.[3] Organizations around the world buy many billions of dollars worth of goods and services, which illustrates the immense purchasing power that this market controls.

Given the market's attractiveness, it is not surprising that some marketers, like Brock, focus only on organizational customers. For example, Ballard Medical Products in Utah sells disposable patient-care products to hospitals. Creative Marketing Corporation in Wisconsin creates advertising for business clients such as Deere (producer of farm equipment) and Mack Trucks. But just because a marketer reaches out to the organizational market doesn't mean it has to ignore ultimate consumers. By using marketing strategies that are keyed to the needs of each customer group, a marketer can serve *both* markets. United Parcel Service, Johnson & Johnson, and IBM are three of the many marketers that successfully target both organizational customers and ultimate consumers. **Organizational marketing**, also known as *business-to-business marketing*, is the process of marketing to customers in the organizational market. Customers in this market think of marketers as *suppliers* or *vendors*. Typically, organizational marketing means reaching out to fewer but larger customers. Brock, for example, deals with 1,000 customers, a smaller number than if the company marketed to individual consumers. Its customers also buy more—and spend more—than consumers, because they need multiple copies of the company's software for different departments and locations. In all, Brock's 1,000 customers have bought software for 27,000 employees.

Even though, like consumers, they're looking to solve problems, not buy products, organizational customers often have needs that are more complex. In the case of Brock Control Systems, solving those problems requires more than a single, standard piece of software. The company meets this challenge by offering a series of programs that can be tailored to each customer's unique needs. It also provides consulting and training services to help customers plan, implement, and optimize the use of their purchases. When you consider that Brock's sales grew 240 percent in just one year, you can see that the founder's commitment to solving the problems of his organizational customers is paying off.

Organizations Are Customers Too

Building profitable long-term relationships with organizations demands the same dedication to customer satisfaction as building relationships with consumers. Whether you're marketing to manufacturers, stores, government agencies, or institutions, you'll start by using the universal marketing processes of environmental and market analysis. Using marketing research, you can find out what, how, when, and why people in these organizations buy. Given that information, you're ready to develop a marketing strategy

organizational marketing

also known as business-to-business marketing, it is the process of marketing to customers in the organizational market

and value package  **(p. 11)** that will satisfy—and ideally delight—your organizational customers.

As in consumer marketing, the goal is not to complete one or two transactions, but to nurture a lasting *relationship* that benefits both the marketer and its organizational customers. Trust and commitment are pivotal in such profitable relationships. Research shows that the longer a customer remains with a marketer, the higher the potential for profits. The increased profits come from frequent, larger reorders, lower selling costs, and new customers drawn by word of mouth from loyal customers. On the other hand, getting a new customer costs up to five times as much as keeping a current customer. Therefore, marketers will be less profitable if they aggressively go after new accounts and neglect relationships with existing customers.[5]

Organizational and Consumer Buying Behavior Compared

To reach the organizational market successfully, marketers need an understanding of both consumer behavior and organizational buying behavior. Remember, when an organization places an order, one or more *employees* are actually doing the buying. As a result, many of the same influences that affect consumer behavior **(p. 164)** come into play with organizational purchases.[6]

The organizational buying team's personal involvement **(p. 170)** with the product or purchase, for example, determines how much research and planning go into the buying decision. In addition, organizational buyers can be affected by internal influences such as perception, motivation, attitudes, and learning, as well as by external influences such as opinion leaders, word of mouth, reference groups, culture, subculture, and situational factors.[7]

Eco Specialties of Baltimore bases its marketing strategy partly on the attitudes of the individuals who make buying decisions in nonprofit organizations. Knowing that many buyers are conscious of environmental concerns, this marketer offers products that are reusable and made from recycled materials. One product is paper made from kenaf (a quick-growing southern plant). Because kenaf doesn't depend on the destruction of forests or the use of chemical pesticides or artificial brightening agents, it appeals to buyers who want to help their organizations take an active role in protecting the environment.[8]

As in consumer marketing, when you reach out to organizational buyers in other countries, you need to pay special attention to cultural differences **(p. 77)**. Customs, attitudes, and preferences, as well as local policies and regulations, all affect relationships between marketers and organizational customers. For example, buyers in China prefer to build a personal relationship with marketers by getting together for meals or in other nonwork situations. Buyers in Russia act more formally in negotiations with marketers.[9]

No matter where you market, you also need an understanding of how organizational buying behavior differs from consumer buying behavior. The main points of difference are the size of the purchases and the structure of the two types of markets, the product needs, and the buying procedures, as listed in Table 7.1. As you'll see next, each of these differences poses unique challenges and opportunities for organizational marketers.

Much of the search for products by organizational buyers takes place at trade shows like this one for electronics. Buyers can see and touch products and, often, watch videos of the products in action. They can also ask questions of knowledgeable company representatives who work in the booths. This interaction generates leads that are usually followed up by one of the producer's salespersons. Moreover, buyers get to talk with other buyers to learn about their experiences. All in all, trade shows can be a great help to business-to-business marketers. Have you ever visited such a show? What did you learn?

TABLE **7.1**   Comparing Organizational and Consumer Buying Behavior

	Organizational Market	Consumer Market
Market structure	Relatively few potential customers	Many potential customers
	Larger purchases	Smaller purchases
	Geographically concentrated	Geographically dispersed
Products	Require technical, complex products	Require less technical products
	Frequently require customization	Sometimes require customization
	Frequently require technical advice, delivery, and after-sale service	Sometimes require technical advice, delivery, and after-sale service
Buying procedures	Buyers are trained	No special training
	Negotiate details of most purchases	Accept standard terms for most purchases
	Follow objective standards	Use personal judgment
	Formal process involving specific employees	Informal process involving household members
	Closer relationships between marketers and buyers	Impersonal relationships between marketers and consumers
	Often buy from multiple sources	Rarely buy from multiple sources

Organizational Customers Make Larger Purchases

Compared with consumer markets, organizational markets have fewer potential customers who make larger purchases. Imagine if you could count Ericsson as one of your customers: the telecommunications giant, based in Sweden, buys goods and services worth billions every year. Ericsson buys in quantity so it can serve its own large customer base. Similarly, PepsiCo buys sugar and other ingredients by the ton so it can turn out flavored concentrate for its soft drinks. Of course, not every organization buys as much as Ericsson and PepsiCo, but the idea of fewer customers, larger purchases holds for the organizational market overall.

Consider the markets for two transportation products: jet airplanes and bicycles. The worldwide organizational market for jets consists of approximately 200 airlines. Each jet costs millions of dollars, and most customers buy several at a time. In contrast, the U.S. consumer market for adult bicycles consists of about 90 million people. Each bike costs as little as $100 or as much as $7,000, and most customers buy one at a time.[10]

Another difference between consumer and organizational markets is the *location* of potential customers. Organizational customers tend to be concentrated in certain locations because of the need to be near raw materials, labor, other resources, or customers. Most U.S. manufacturing plants are in the Midwest because planners saw the advantages of being near steel, tire, and parts manufacturers as well as skilled labor. In contrast, consumers are more difficult to reach because they're spread over a much wider area.

You can see this difference at work in the jet and bicycle markets. Airlines are clustered near airports in capital cities around the world, but consumers who buy bicycles are scattered all over every country. That's why it is easier for Boeing and other manufacturers of jet air craft to contact customers than for bicycle makers, who must try to identify individual buyers, research their needs, and reach out with marketing programs.

Organizational Products Are More Complex

As Richard Brock's experience shows, organizational customers often require complex, technical products designed to play a particular role in helping the company, institution, or agency achieve its goals (making profits, educating students, and so on). In many cases, organizations expect products to be tailored to exacting technical standards—and increasingly, they're willing to be actively involved in product development.

For example, employees of Ross Controls in Michigan regularly visit their customers to see how the company's pneumatic valves are used. They learn firsthand about customer problems, then collaborate with customers in designing new products to meet specific needs. Using computer-aided design and production techniques, Ross specialists quickly turn out samples for customers to test. Feedback from these tests helps the company fine-tune each new product, with the result that customers get exactly what they want. One big customer, General Motors, is so pleased that it won't buy pneumatic valves from anybody but Ross—and it won't let its suppliers buy elsewhere either.[11]

Service components of the total value package are especially important to organizational customers. Speedier delivery is, of course, vital to the growing number of organizations that are racing the clock to serve their own customers. In addition, most organizational customers need technical advice about buying and using technical goods and services. They also want to be able to call with questions after a purchase. In one recent survey, organizational buyers said they place the highest value on a supplier's reliability, responsiveness to customer demands, willingness to help customers, and prompt service support.[12]

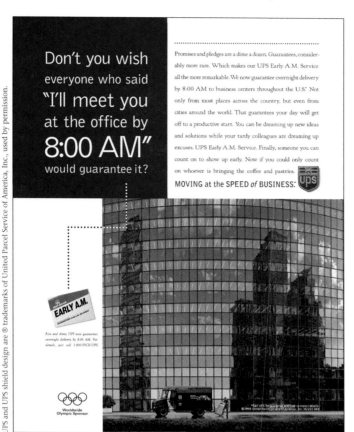

Don't you wish everyone who said "I'll meet you at the office by 8:00 AM" would guarantee it?

Promises and pledges are a dime a dozen. Guarantees, considerably more rare. Which makes our UPS Early A.M. Service all the more remarkable. We now guarantee overnight delivery by 8:00 AM to business centers throughout the U.S. Not only from most places across the country, but even from cities around the world. That guarantees your day will get off to a productive start. You can be dreaming up new ideas and solutions while your tardy colleagues are dreaming up excuses. UPS Early A.M. Service. Finally, someone you can count on to show up early. Now if you could only count on whoever is bringing the coffee and pastries.

MOVING at the SPEED *of* BUSINESS.™ **ups**

EARLY A.M.

Worldwide Olympic Sponsor

Because speed and reliability are frequently critical in business-to-business transactions, many businesses turn to UPS to assure their customers of early morning delivery. The service component of the total value package is often more important in organizational markets than it is to consumers. By outsourcing what they can't do on a world-class basis—like delivery—businesses free themselves to do a world-class job in the functions they do perform. What other service components would be important to customers of UPS?

Organizational Buying Procedures Are More Complicated

As you might expect, buying expensive, technical products takes more time and effort than shopping for consumer products. Marketers working with overseas customers sometimes confront an even slower, more complicated buying process. Westinghouse found out how slowly the wheels of foreign government purchasing can grind when it finally delivered its first steam turbine to China, seven years after going into partnership with the government on the project.[13]

Because of the complexities of buying technical products, most organizations use professional buyers (purchasing agents) who are trained (and sometimes certified by an industry association) to make purchases. Associations also establish objective standards to guide buyers in evaluating products being considered for purchase. For example, marketers who want to supply some of the 300,000 tons of paper used by the U.S. government have to comply with the purchasing rule that paper have at least 20 percent recycled content.[14]

Unlike ultimate consumers, organizational buyers are expected to follow a set of formal procedures when they place orders. Thus less emotion may go into the buying decision. Because buyers purchase large quantities and often order customized products, they negotiate with suppliers over price, service, and other details. In contrast, ultimate consumers in the United States rarely negotiate purchases except for cars and homes and other expensive products. As you'll see later in the chapter, buyers often need official approval from other organization members before they can complete certain purchases, whereas consumers typically discuss purchases informally with family members.

Since organizational markets have fewer customers than consumer markets, marketers are able, over time, to foster closer relationships with organizational buyers than they normally develop with consumers. Instead of using advertising and other impersonal communication methods, organizational marketers rely primarily on salespeople who call on buyers and other influencers. This helps the marketer learn firsthand about the organization's buying process as well as the influences on the individual buyer.

When you think of the business-to-business market, the tendency is to think of big businesses. The organizational market, however, is made up of firms of all sizes. Ernestina Galindo runs a small tortilla factory in Austin, Texas, but like all organizational buyers, she needs and seeks good, reliable suppliers who also provide outstanding service. The better her suppliers, the better she is able to compete by providing her customers with a superior product.

Unlike consumers, purchasing agents who place huge orders or order on short notice worry about their suppliers' ability to comply with these requests. Some organizations rely on *single sourcing*, in which the buyer purchases from just one supplier. The organization can often negotiate a lower price by concentrating its purchases in this way. It can also command a good deal of loyalty and commitment from that single supplier. On the other hand, many buyers prefer working with several suppliers, or *multiple sourcing*. When a purchasing agent can turn to several qualified suppliers, all around the world, the organization is much less likely to be caught short if one supplier has problems filling an order.

Working with too many sources can be confusing and costly, however, which is why the trend today, among large buyers in particular, is toward reducing the number of suppliers. Whereas Xerox once bought from 5,000 suppliers, it now buys from 500. Motorola cut the number of suppliers from 6,000 to 1,000. Marketers who continue to supply such customers get larger orders—but they're also asked to make a bigger commitment to meeting customer needs at lower costs. Many buyers are forming global alliances with suppliers to assure world-class standards. That's what relationship marketing is all about.

One example of relationship marketing occurred at AlliedSignal. This company, which makes auto and aerospace parts, brought in the Dutch-owned supplier Van Leeuwan to replace 400 suppliers of valves and pipes. In exchange for yearly purchases worth $10 million, Van Leeuwan agreed to charge lower prices. It also set up an electronic ordering system to minimize purchasing paperwork and speed delivery.[15] The result is a mutually beneficial exchange relationship.

Inside the Organizational Market

Although the organizational market covers all nonconsumers, that description doesn't begin to convey this market's size, range, and diversity. The total market includes individual lawyers and multinational law firms; giant retail chains and tiny stores; governmental offices for countries, cities, and hamlets; state universities; hospitals; and one-room schoolhouses. When you think of the organizational market, you have to think small as well as large, because well over 90 percent of all U.S. businesses employ fewer than 500 people.[16] In all, millions of organizations make up this varied market.

Rather than approach the organizational market as a single market, therefore, think instead of a variety of organizational markets, each with distinct needs and characteristics. There are four types of organizational markets: the industrial market, the reseller market, the government market, and the institutional market. These are listed in Table 7.2.

TABLE **7.2** Four Types of Organizational Markets

Industrial Market	Reseller/Commercial Market	Government Market	Institutional Market
Goods	Wholesalers	Federal government	Hospitals
• Manufacturing	Retailers	State governments	Schools
• Construction	• Department stores	Local governments	Charities
• Agriculture, forestry, fishing	• Specialty stores	Foreign governments	Museums
• Mining	• Discount stores		Prisons
Services	• Other retailers		Associations
• Transportation			Libraries
• Utilities			Other nonprofit organizations
• Communication			
• Finance, insurance, real estate			
• Other services			

Some marketers target more narrowly, using the U.S. government's *standard industrial classification (SIC) codes*, a coding system that groups organizations according to their main products. A similar system, *international standard industrial classification codes*, applies to the worldwide organizational market. Segmenting according to SIC can be helpful for studying industry-specific needs and estimating the number of possible customers, total employees, and sales by industry. You'll read more about SIC segmentation in Chapter 8.

The Industrial Market

The **industrial market** consists of businesses that buy goods and services to use directly or indirectly in producing other goods and services. Among the millions of businesses in this category are manufacturers, mining and construction firms, farms, service companies, banks, insurers, utilities, and transportation companies. *Original equipment manufacturers (OEMs)* buy materials from suppliers to use in the course of creating the products they sell to others. For example, motorcycle manufacturers, such as Japan's Suzuki and Yamaha, are OEMs that buy machinery, steel, and parts to be incorporated into motorcycles. In addition, organizations in the industrial market buy desks, banking services, and other goods and services that are used in business activities that indirectly support their production operations.

industrial market

businesses that buy goods and services to use directly or indirectly in producing other goods and services

The Reseller Market

The **reseller market** or *commercial market* is made up of wholesalers and retailers that buy products for resale to others. As you'll see in Chapters 14 and 15, resellers are a vital link in the chain between producers and customers. Wholesalers buy from producers and then sell to retailers and other channel partners such as other wholesalers and various producers. Retailers (such as department stores, automobile dealers, and catalog merchants) buy from manufacturers or wholesalers and then resell to consumers.

Often, resellers transport and repackage items before offering them to their customers. For example, supermarket chains, such as Vons in California, buy fruits and vegetables by the carton and then truck the produce to local stores where consumers can buy by the item.

The Government Market

The **government market** is composed of federal, state, local, and foreign government agencies that buy goods and services. This is a sizable segment of the organizational market. From airplanes to submarines, from telephone services to cleaning services, government agencies buy a wide variety of products, mostly to serve their customers (citizens). The U.S. Army buys so many vehicles that it is considered to be the largest fleet operator in the world. Every nation buys on behalf of its central government. In addition, many nations have state or provincial government offices plus many town and local government offices. In the United States alone, nearly 87,000 governmental units buy a total of more than $1.2 trillion worth of products.[17] Here's how small marketers can more effectively reach U.S. government customers.

SMALL BUSINESS WATCH

Getting a piece of a $200 billion pie

What small business marketer wouldn't want even a tiny wedge of a $200 billion pie? That huge pie represents the federal government's total spending on goods and services every year. Until recently, however, Uncle Sam's slow and cumbersome purchasing processes frustrated—and sometimes defeated—smaller marketers. Now, thanks to the Federal Acquisition Streamlining Act of 1994, small businesses have a better chance of getting their share.

Most government purchases are made by competitive bidding for contracts. The new legislation sets aside all government purchase contracts between $2,500 and $100,000 for small businesses, which will compete for the orders through a new, simpler bidding process. In addition, the government is going online with a computerized system that will eliminate paperwork every step of the way. By the end of the decade, a small business with a computer and a modem (a device that allows a computer to communicate with other computers) will be able to troll the government database looking for marketing opportunities. The small-business marketers will also submit bids, receive responses, and get paid electronically.

reseller market

also called commercial market; wholesalers and retailers that buy products for resale to others

government market

federal, state, local, and foreign government agencies that buy goods and services

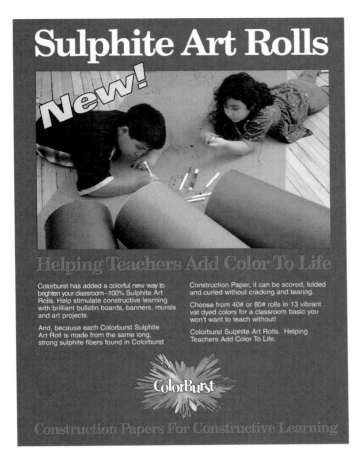

Sulphite Art Rolls

New!

Helping Teachers Add Color To Life

Colorburst has added a colorful new way to brighten your classroom–100% Sulphite Art Rolls. Help stimulate constructive learning with brilliant bulletin boards, banners, murals and art projects.

And, because each Colorburst Sulphite Art Roll is made from the same long, strong sulphite fibers found in Colorburst

Construction Paper, it can be scored, folded and curled without cracking and tearing.

Choose from 40# or 80# rolls in 13 vibrant vat dyed colors for a classroom basic you won't want to teach without!

Colorburst Sulphite Art Rolls. Helping Teachers Add Color To Life.

ColorBurst

Construction Papers For Constructive Learning

This colorful ad is directed at the institutional market, specifically schools and teachers. Certainly teachers are eager to supply their students with the best materials available, but often budgets are tight. What could Colorburst do to attract teachers with small budgets? What kind of public relations programs might increase the visibility of Colorburst among educators?

Already, small businesses such as E. Maka, Inc., a Washington, D.C., marketer of pharmaceutical supplies, are experimenting with online contracts and communication with government agencies. By browsing the government's online system, owner Barbara Koné can spot new selling opportunities. "If it weren't for [the online system]," she says, "right now I'm not sure I'd be in business."[18]

What other benefits do you think small marketers will gain from this computerized system?

The Institutional Market

The **institutional market** consists of hospitals, charities, civic groups, religious institutions, schools, prisons, museums, libraries, and other profit-making and not-for-profit organizations that, as a class, are called "institutions." Most of the products purchased relate to services these institutions provide for their customers (patients, clients, students, and so on). For example, Yale–New Haven Hospital in Connecticut buys bed sheets, surgical equipment, electricity, and other products to be used in the care of patients. Like other institutions, the hospital also buys fire insurance, lightbulbs, and other products that aren't directly related to medical care but are needed to run the hospital.

Demand Links Organizational and Consumer Markets

When a company develops a strategy for reaching organizational markets, it needs to be able to estimate the demand for its products. This is tricky because demand for organizational products is often linked to (or derived from) the demand for consumer products; hence the term **derived demand**. Demand for most consumer products can change quickly and unpredictably, affecting demand for related organizational products. By building closer relationships with its organizational customers—and continuously researching trends in consumer buying—a marketer can stay alert to changes in demand that are likely to affect demand for its own products.

Here's how the link between consumer and organizational demand works. General Electric buys aluminum, rubber, steel, motors, and other materials and components that go into the manufacture of its dishwashers. When consumers buy more dishwashers, GE has to buy more materials and parts to keep up with consumer demand, which is good news for GE's 10,000 suppliers. On the other hand, when fewer consumers buy dishwashers, GE needs smaller amounts of materials and fewer components, which is bad news for suppliers.[19] In this case, aluminum suppliers have to look ahead to the influence that changes in consumer demand for GE's products will have on the demand for aluminum.

institutional market

hospitals, charities, civic groups, religious institutions, schools, prisons, museums, libraries, and other profit-making and not-for-profit organizations

derived demand

demand for organizational products is often linked to (or derived from) the demand for consumer products

Issues for critical thinking

How would you go about estimating the demand for a basic industrial product such as steel? How would you determine which consumer products to research? How could you enlist the aid of your organizational customers in this process?

The wait for new technology is getting shorter.

In some places, there's no wait at all.

Bravo MS-T, 130 MHz Intel Pentium Pro processor

Pronto. Right now. Yesterday even. AST and the latest Intel Pentium® Pro chip are ready to accelerate through your workload in a new AST desktop. The Bravo MS-T is one feature-packed machine designed to run all your most powerful 32-bit software. (Even the stuff some techno-wizard will think up next year.) Windows NT®? It could be on your desk by, let's say, Tuesday. Instead of waiting for a faster computer, you'd be using one. Call 800-876-4AST. Or on the net: http://www.ast.com. Today, running a little fast is a good thing.

AST COMPUTER

International marketers have to keep an eye on consumer demand in all the countries where their organizational customers operate. Global trade barriers are falling **(p. 107)**, allowing marketers to cross borders and reach consumers all over the world. General Electric, for example, is a major player in Europe and North America, and it's aggressively entering fast-growing consumer markets across Asia. GE's success in global expansion is translating into stronger demand for parts and materials from its suppliers.

In some cases, suppliers create marketing programs to stimulate consumer demand for products made by their organizational customers. Aluminum producers, for example, have gotten together to fund television and magazine advertising to remind consumers that aluminum beverage containers are convenient and recyclable. The purpose is to persuade consumers to buy soft drinks in cans rather than in plastic bottles. A lot is at stake for the aluminum producers. Every year, almost 5 billion pounds of aluminum goes into making the cans used by Coca-Cola and other beverage marketers.[20]

Demand for Intel Pentium Pro chips is derived from the demand for personal computers made by AST and other manufacturers. Thus, Intel needs to track the current and anticipated sales volume of personal computers in order to plan the manufacture of Pentium Pro chips. Intel also pays part of the cost when AST and other manufacturers feature the "Intel Inside" logo in their ads, as shown here. How does such advertising help Intel in its brand-building efforts among consumers and organizational buyers?

Before you go on . . .

A. Why should marketers aim for long-term relationships with organizational customers?

B. Why do organizational marketers need to understand consumer behavior as well as organizational buying behavior?

C. How does organizational buying behavior differ from consumer buying behavior?

D. How does demand in the consumer market affect demand in the organizational market?

How Organizations Buy

To build long-lasting business relationships, organizational marketers have to understand how other organizations buy. In addition to studying the stages in the organizational buying process, such marketers should take into consideration the type of buying decision each organizational customer is making and the roles of the people in each organization's buying center. Then they will be better prepared to develop an appropriate marketing strategy to satisfy their customers' needs.

The Organizational Buying Process

Like the consumer buying process, the organizational buying process is a form of problem solving that covers a series of stages, as shown in Figure 7.1. The stages are problem recognition, specification, supplier identification, evaluation, purchase, and postpurchase evaluation. Typically, buyers move through these six stages in a few weeks or months, although the experience of Westinghouse in China, mentioned earlier, shows that the process can take much longer, even years on occasion.

F I G U R E **7.1** **The Organizational Buying Process**

The organizational buying process begins when someone in the organization recognizes a problem that can be solved by a purchase. As in the consumer purchase-decision process, the final step leads back to the first step so that organizational buyers can determine how well their purchases have solved the problem.

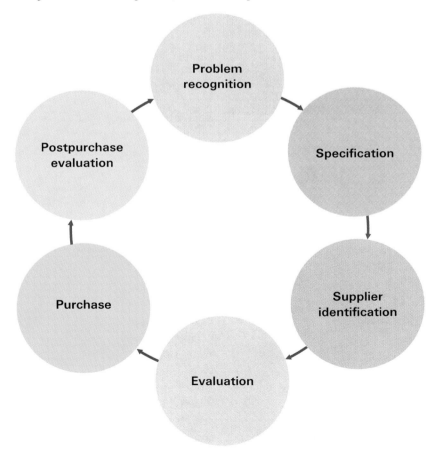

make-or-buy decision

decision to produce what is needed to solve the problem or to buy (or lease) from an outside supplier

value analysis

examination of the balance between a product's cost and its design, quality, and performance

Just as Sir Speedy is trying to win over business customers for its printing services, Savin is trying to convince companies like Sir Speedy to purchase its copiers and fax machines. Ads like this are intended to help open the door for Savin's salespeople to call on Sir Speedy and other organizations by demonstrating Savin's commitment to satisfying customer needs. How could Savin help its prospects recognize a problem that can be solved by buying Savin's products?

The Problem-Recognition Stage

The organizational buying process begins when someone in the firm perceives a gap between the actual state—the current situation—and the desired state—the situation the organization would prefer. Just as marketing can play a role in helping consumers recognize needs and problems, it can spark the same recognition among organizational buyers, turning a customer's problem into a selling opportunity. When an individual realizes that a purchase can solve the problem, bringing the organization closer to its desired state, he or she sets the buying process in motion.

For example, at Sir Speedy, a California-based national franchise chain of quick printers, president Don Lowe looked at the kinds of problems faced by customers and at the buying process those customers used. Through marketing research, Lowe discovered that most customers were small businesses, such as law firms, resellers, and medical firms, which wanted to develop and distribute brochures and other materials. Sir Speedy could lead such customers to recognize the need for help in designing, printing, and mailing their materials.[21]

The Specification Stage

In the second stage of the buying process, the organization faces a **make-or-buy decision**: should it produce what it needs to solve the problem or should it buy (or lease) from an outside supplier? At times, an organization may believe it can better control costs, quality, or other factors by manufacturing needed parts or by handling its own printing, delivery, or other services. In a growing number of cases, however, firms decide on outsourcing **(p. 40)** certain services or operations.

Whether the decision is to produce internally or to outsource, the organization has to determine the *specifications*—the exact requirements—for the purchased product (quality and quantity, technical features, and so on). With these specifications in hand, the organization can conduct a **value analysis** to examine the balance it wants between a product's cost and its design, quality, and performance. Sometimes a change in design can dramatically lower costs. At the same time, an increase in quality or performance may add only a little to the cost. Expert marketers who are alert to the opportunity can often help organizations complete a thorough value analysis.

Sir Speedy's Don Lowe found that price and service were important to small business customers—and so were trust and dependability. Lowe also discovered that these customers weren't getting help from vendors when preparing specifications or value analyses. "Research told us that for every business customer we saw, scores of others never came through the door," explains Lowe. "They didn't have the time or staff to get out of the office. We had to go to them." As a result, Sir Speedy franchisees visit each prospect, to learn about the organization and its goals, as well as about what the organization prints and who makes the buying decisions.

The Supplier Identification Stage

In the third stage of the buying process, the organization looks for suppliers that can provide the goods or services needed to solve the problem. Marketers bring their products to the attention of buyers through personal selling, direct mail materials, advertising, trade shows, and other marketing communication techniques. A growing number of buyers narrow the list of potential suppliers by insisting on *supplier certification*—that is, they consider only suppliers that meet stringent standards for quality, response time, and other requirements. Buyers at Dell Computer go even further, considering only suppliers that meet their requirements *and* impose the same requirements on their own suppliers.[22]

Once buyers have developed a list of qualified suppliers, they typically send out a **request for proposal (RFP)**, also known as a request for quotation, which asks vendors to compete for an order by showing how they will meet the product specifications, the delivery dates, and other requirements. Each interested marketer then submits a **bid** indicating the price the company will charge, the goods and services it will provide, and other details about how the marketer will meet the buyer's requirements. The RFP system is used extensively in government and institutional buying to spark competition.

Don Lowe of Sir Speedy realized that franchisees wouldn't get orders until organizational buyers understood how the company's capabilities matched their needs. When he analyzed customer buying behavior, he found that the company "landed 80 percent of our accounts after the sixth contact." Therefore, he advised franchisees to take some time to get to know buyers and their needs. "It's arrogant to ask for business during the first sales contact," he explains. "Customers want a relationship. That's why it can take six contacts before getting a shot." In addition, Lowe began a new advertising campaign to showcase Sir Speedy's capabilities as a business printer.[23]

The Evaluation Stage

At this point in the organizational buying process, the buyer (and sometimes others involved in the purchase) should be ready to evaluate alternatives. Organizations care about price but they also evaluate each supplier's value package ◄────┘ **(p. 11)** on the basis of quality, performance, capacity, technical services, warranties, delivery schedule, and other such factors. In addition, organizational buyers take into account what their own customers (organizations or ultimate consumers) want and need. Buyers evaluating purchases for department stores, for example, have to consider what shoppers have requested.[24]

As in consumer purchases, organizational buyers face the uncertainty of perceived risk. Even when buyers don't actually use the product, they are responsible for making a purchase that will meet the organization's needs. No buyer wants to make a costly mistake, which is why this perceived risk is one of the most important influences on organizational buying. In markets for high-tech products such as computer workstations, the perceived risk is

request for proposal (RFP)

asks marketers to compete for an order by showing how they will meet the product specifications, the delivery dates, and other requirements

bid

indicates the price the company will charge, the goods and services it will provide, and other details about how the marketer will meet the buyer's requirements

Organizational buyers of expensive products such as this CD-ROM Credit Reference Service face the uncertainty of perceived risk, because they can't easily evaluate the product until after completing the purchase. To counter this perceived risk, American Business Information offers a 30-day free trial, allowing customers to decide whether the product meets their needs. What else might the marketer do to calm prospects' fears before they buy?

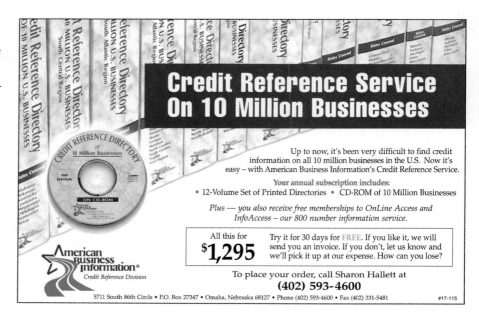

complicated by uncertainty over evolving standards and rapid changes in features and prices.[25]

Sir Speedy franchisee Ken Mathes works hard to minimize any perceived risk on the part of organizational buyers using his printing services for the first time. "We ask customers to test us with a single piece," he says. "If they don't like it, there's no charge. But once they see our capabilities, they're usually pleased." Using this technique, Mathes courted and won the printing business of a large restaurant chain based in Long Beach, California. He convinced the buyer to let Sir Speedy design, produce, and distribute a promotional mailing. Because the promotion looked good and brought a favorable response from restaurant patrons, the buyer has made Sir Speedy its primary printer.[26]

The Purchase Stage

After the buyer has evaluated all the alternatives—a process that can take weeks when there are complicated bids to be examined—it's time to make a purchase. The purchasing agent contacts the selected vendor and negotiates a firm agreement for quantity, delivery, payment, and other details. At that point, the organization signs a contract with the seller that spells out the purchase and payment agreement. If technical products are being purchased, the buyer may arrange to postpone paying the bill until the goods have been inspected or tested to be sure that specifications have been met.

Even though Sir Speedy's products aren't technically complex, its organizational customers don't pay until they have inspected and approved the printed materials. This lowers any perceived risk. Ken Mathes, like many of the franchisees, delivers orders directly to the buyer, demonstrating the personal service he's used to build profitable long-term relationships with customers. He also takes a moment to ask customers for referrals to other organizations that might need Sir Speedy's printing services. In attempting to influence organizational purchasing, however, marketers may find themselves at risk of crossing ethical lines, as you'll see in the following section.

ETHICS & SOCIAL RESPONSIBILITY

A friendly cup of coffee or a bribe?

Imagine you're selling to a buyer for a chain of retail stores. She does business with dozens of suppliers, ordering millions of dollars worth of merchandise every year. Grateful suppliers offer to buy her lunch or dinner, provide tickets for sporting events, and so on. Where is the ethical line between offering a gift to strengthen the personal relationship, and offering a bribe in exchange for future business?

Many times, organizational guidelines indicate what buyers can accept. Buyers for Wal-Mart Stores can't accept even a cup of coffee from suppliers. This avoids conflicts that could prevent buyers from getting the best deals for the store. Buyers for J.C. Penney can say yes to meals or golf dates paid for by suppliers, as long as each buyer can return the favor. People who work for the city of Chicago can accept gifts worth $50 or less on occasion, while state employees in Indiana need written permission to accept gifts worth more than $25. (As you saw in Chapter 4, the rules differ in countries where small gifts and payments are part of daily life.)

The exact guidelines vary from organization to organization, but the intent is the same: to keep buyers out of ethically questionable situations that could influence buying decisions. Of course, offering cash payments in exchange for an order is unethical as well as illegal in the United States. Ethics experts advise marketers to avoid offering valuable gifts, to wait to offer small gifts until after a customer relationship has been established, and to set a limit on the value of gifts that are offered. [27]

From the marketer's viewpoint, when is a meal really a bribe and not a way of conducting business?

The Postpurchase Evaluation Stage

During the postpurchase evaluation stage of the buying process, the buyer determines whether the product and the supplier met or exceeded the organization's needs and expectations (resulting in customer satisfaction) or fell short (resulting in dissatisfaction). This analysis serves as feedback to refining the buying process in the future. Some organizations conduct a formal **vendor analysis**, rating each supplier's performance on factors such as price and service. Buyers drop suppliers that don't score well on these analyses. However, suppliers that do well are eligible to receive future orders and strengthen the relationship.

Sir Speedy franchisee Ken Mathes knows that high marks during the postpurchase evaluation stage can lead to higher future sales. First, satisfied customers are encouraged to buy again. Second, only customers who are satisfied will be willing to divulge the names of other buyers who may need Sir Speedy's services. Referrals from satisfied customers can have a strong impact on other buyers. On the other hand, word-of-mouth communication can work against Sir Speedy—or any marketer—when dissatisfied buyers tell other buyers about bad experiences. All the more reason for Sir Speedy franchisees to work hard to build lasting relationships with their customers.

vendor analysis

rating each supplier's performance on factors such as price and service

Types of Buying Situations

Just as consumers face different buying situations according to whether a purchase represents extended, limited, or routine problem solving ←⌐ **(p. 172)**, organizational buyers face three *buyclasses*, buying situations, that affect the way they move through the buying process, as shown in Table 7.3.[28] By understanding how buyers react to these situations, marketers can be prepared to provide the right amount of information and other assistance when needed.

T A B L E   **7.3**   **Organizational Buying Situations**

Buyclass	Type of Problem Solving	Characteristics of Purchase	Example of Purchase
New-task buy	Extended	Problem has not come up before; need much information about the problem, suppliers; occurs infrequently	Buying a central air-conditioning system for a new office
Modified rebuy	Limited	Evolves from a new-task buy or straight rebuy; alternatives are known but have changed; need more information before buying	Switching to new, more efficient filters for air-conditioning system
Straight rebuy	Routine	Occurs regularly because of recurring requirements; only regular suppliers are considered; little prepurchase information needed	Reordering filters for the air-conditioning system

At one extreme is the **new-task buy**, a situation in which the buyer has no experience making a particular type of purchase. A buyer who has never made the kind of purchase in question uses extended problem solving, taking more time and care in the buying process as a way of minimizing the perceived risk. Marketers can help by recognizing the buyer's specific needs and supplying both product information and technical advice.[29]

As the name implies, **modified rebuy** is a purchase situation in which a buyer who has made a particular kind of purchase before now faces some changed circumstances such as additional alternatives. Because the purchase is not routine, the buyer uses limited problem solving, gathering needed information as he or she moves through the buying process. Marketers can strengthen their relationships with buyers in this situation by analyzing the changes and presenting appropriate alternatives that will solve the organization's problem.

In a **straight rebuy**, the buyer is making a routine repeat purchase. Because the buyer has made this purchase time and again, routine problem-solving techniques, such as automatic reordering, can be used to move through the reordering process fairly quickly. To encourage loyalty and repeat orders, marketers should continually look for ways to meet and exceed their customers' expectations. A marketer that wants to break into the ranks of suppliers that routinely receive reorders has to show how the buyer would benefit by switching. The following section shows how New Zealand's 3M Pharmaceuticals used marketing to encourage its customers to use straight rebuys.

new-task buy

situation in which the buyer has no experience making a particular type of purchase

modified rebuy

a purchase situation in which a buyer who has made a particular kind of purchase before now faces some changed circumstances such as additional alternatives

straight rebuy

a situation in which the buyer is making a routine repeat purchase

GLOBAL ISSUES

The rewards of rewarding loyalty

The marketers at 3M Pharmaceuticals in New Zealand realize that buyers in the organizational market, like their consumer counterparts, can develop brand loyalty over time. In marketing to pharmacists, 3M personnel faced two major challenges. First, knowing that pharmacists stock

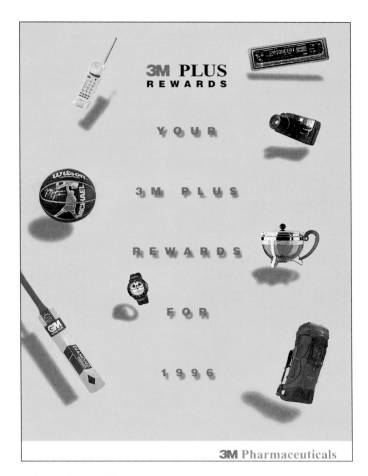

Relationship marketing programs may be aimed at wholesalers and retailers as well as consumers. In fact, many buyers in businesses such as retail pharmacies react to special incentives in the same way consumers do. That's why 3M Pharmaceuticals in New Zealand developed a frequent-buyer program offering pharmacists the opportunity to earn valuable gifts when they continue to buy 3M products. Do you think pharmacies should start similar programs to reward consumers for repeat purchasing and store loyalty?

both branded and generic (nonbranded) drugs, they wanted to encourage loyalty to 3M brands. Second, the company wanted to get 3M products into more of the country's 1,100 pharmacies without slashing prices. The answer to these challenges was 3M Plus, a relationship marketing program.

Like a frequent-flyer program, 3M Plus rewards pharmacists for buying again and again from 3M. With every purchase, the pharmacist earns points toward valuable rewards ranging from electric carving knives, electric kettles, and electric fans to refrigerators, personal computers, and overseas travel. Participating pharmacists receive a monthly order form and a recap of points earned. They also earn bonus points for ordering monthly specials such as new products.

Heather Whinesay, 3M's business manager in New Zealand, says the program is flexible enough to make small customers feel as important as big customers. For example, regardless of size, all 3M Plus participants receive a monthly newsletter packed with business tips. They're also invited to attend product seminars and ask for expert help with advertising materials. The 3M Plus program has been extremely successful. Now, about 75 percent of the country's pharmacists participate, and 3M's market share is growing.[30]

If you were in Heather Whinesay's position, how would you encourage nonparticipants to enroll in 3M Plus?

Who's Who in the Buying Center

One of the most important influences on organizational buying behavior is the **buying center**, the group of people within an organization who participate in the buying process. The buying center is not a department, but a group of loosely aligned people with an interest in the product being purchased. Each participant has his or her own goals and responsibilities, all of which affect the buying process, as shown in Table 7.4. Within the buying center, individual employees can play one (or more) of six roles:

- *Initiators* are the people who first suggest a need for the product.
- *Users* will actually use the goods or services being purchased.
- *Influencers* provide information for evaluating alternatives or establishing specifications for the purchase.
- *Gatekeepers* manage the flow of information to buying center members.
- *Deciders* actually make the buying decision.
- *Buyers* are responsible for placing the purchase order.

The buying situation, the perceived risk, and the individual and collective actions of all buying center participants can affect a supplier's chances of being considered during the buying process and of receiving an order once the purchase decision has been made.[31] Furthermore, the size of the buying

buying center

the group of people within an organization who participate in the buying process

TABLE **7.4** Buying Center Roles

Role	Influence on Buying Process	Examples of Organizational Members Playing the Role
Initiators	Are the first to point out the need for a product	Could be anyone in the organization; need often triggered by an ad or a salesperson
Users	People who actually will use the product; may write the specifications for technical products	Production-line workers, various staff people
Influencers	Provide information for evaluating alternatives; establish specifications	Quality assurance personnel, financial analysts
Gatekeepers	Affect the search for information by distributing or screening information such as marketing materials, bids	Secretaries, receptionists, purchasing agents
Deciders	Decide among alternatives; may also approve product and supplier	Presidents, vice presidents, plant managers
Buyers	Place the order to buy a particular product from the chosen supplier; may also select the supplier	Purchasing agents, buyers

Grainger goes right to the heart of the industrial buying process by acknowledging the fact that such purchases can be costly. They also note that these purchases are often made by teams of buyers. By offering fast, error-free delivery and acting as a single source for many items, Grainger has developed a powerful business-to-business advertisement. If you were to develop a follow-up ad for the company, what appeal might you use?

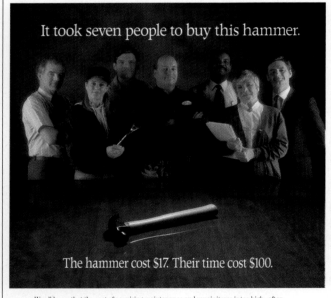

It took seven people to buy this hammer.

The hammer cost $17. Their time cost $100.

We all know that the cost of acquiring maintenance and repair items is too high—often higher than the cost of the item itself.

Grainger can help you cut that cost dramatically. As a matter of fact, we're already doing it for two thirds of the Fortune 100. How? Here are some examples:

We supply thousands of products—broad selections, many lines—enabling you to eliminate hundreds of suppliers and leverage your purchases with just one. Grainger.

With our sophisticated systems and error-free ordering processes, we can help you dramatically reduce your inventory cost.

Through Grainger Consulting Services, we can even help you re-engineer your entire materials management process to make it more cost-effective. And your people more productive.

Maybe you should take advantage of our experience and capabilities to achieve your cost reduction goals. Call 1-800-905-3338 Ext. 1388.

GRAINGER
Industrial and Commercial
Equipment and Supplies

http://www.grainger.com
©1996 W. W. Grainger, Inc.

center varies from organization to organization and from country to country. In Italy, an average of three people play a role in the buying decision, while in France, an average of 20 people play a role.[32]

With all these variables, marketers often have difficulty determining who is playing which buying role within the organization. Also, an individual's role can change in different buying situations. That's why marketers need to research the identity and roles of the individuals who influence a particular purchase.

Many organizations are searching for ways to slice time and costs from the sometimes cumbersome buying process used by buying centers. Marketers that present good ideas will likely gain an edge in building and sustaining customer relationships.

An increasing number of organizations are preparing for major purchases by assembling *buying teams* composed of people from purchasing, manufacturing or operations, quality assurance, sales, design, maintenance, and other groups that have a stake in the purchase. The team approach allows a company to gather information and evaluate alternatives more quickly than would be possible if it had to wait for all departments to approve the purchase one by one. Teams also build commitment among the various departments involved in the process.

Warren Consolidated Industries in Ohio, for example, used the team buying approach to ensure that all the departments affected by the purchase of steel-making equipment had a say in the buying process. In all, about 100 employees participated in the $100 million purchase, which was completed in record time. The outcome was a good buying decision and successful installation process.[33]

Having a buying team of their own helps marketers sell to customers with similar buying teams. For example, Cincinnati Milacron, an Ohio maker of high-tech production equipment, calls its buying teams "wolf packs," explains John Effmann, vice president of marketing services. "We form multidisciplinary teams with eight or nine members from all over the company. We'll have a purchasing person and a marketing person, plus a design engineer, the hydraulics expert, etc." Because of his company's knowledge of team buying, Effmann knows how to put together a sales team to work effectively with its customers' buying teams.[34]

Building relationships among value-chain members is just as important to many marketers as building relationships with ultimate consumers and employees. In this ad, American Express points out the many advantages it offers the restaurant industry, an important client. American Express even has a newsletter that goes to restaurants. What other industries might American Express target in its effort to build business-to-business relationships?

Before you go on . . .

A. What is a make-or-buy decision?

B. How and when is a vendor analysis used?

C. What three types of buying situations do organizations face?

D. What roles do individuals play in the buying center?

Relationship Marketing in the Value Chain

Through relationships with both suppliers and customers, every organizational marketer is part of a value chain (p. 50). Suppliers are the source for materials brought through the value chain to create the value package consumers buy. Depending on the exact features in each value package, the value chain may be short or long, simple or complex.

Marketing relationships connect every one of the links in the value chain. Savvy marketers realize that their relationships with organizational customers also affect other parts of the value chain. Chevron, for instance, supplies natural gas to a company that resells it to a chemical company for use in producing a leaching agent necessary for gold mining. Exploring the needs of the chemical company's customers, including the gold mine at the end of the value chain, Chevron learned about problems that could be solved through cooperation among all the organizations. By helping to solve problems throughout the value chain, Chevron has strengthened its place in the system and demonstrated its commitment to strong relationships with its customers and *their* customers.[35]

Using Reciprocity and Reverse Marketing in the Value Chain

Some organizational marketers build value-chain relationships through **reciprocity**, the practice of buying from suppliers that are also customers. For example, General Motors buys auto engines from Borg Warner, a supplier that buys many of the cars and trucks it needs from GM. Reciprocity is legal in the United States as long as it's not enforced through coercion or does not harm competition. Suppliers may voluntarily buy from customers to show commitment to the relationship, but attempting to force suppliers to buy is unethical.[36]

With **reverse marketing**, customers use marketing to build stronger relationships with suppliers. In essence, organizational customers are consciously applying relationship marketing techniques to enhance their links with suppliers. This is important because customers want loyal suppliers that will not only satisfy very specific needs but also anticipate and react to changed needs. World-class suppliers capable of such far-reaching commitment are in great demand. By using reverse marketing, customers can develop and maintain enduring relationships with suppliers, a practice that benefits both parties.[37]

Reverse marketing helped entrepreneur Joanna T. Lau save a Massachusetts electronic systems manufacturer that had lost money under its previous owner. Renaming the company Lau Technologies, the new owner shuttled between suppliers, sharing her plans for rebuilding the company—and reassuring suppliers that she would pay bills on time. Suppliers rallied to help turn the company around. With suppliers' support and a total quality management program implemented by dedicated employees who worked nearly around the clock, Lau's company notched $2.7 million in profits just 4 years later.[38]

Fiat, Italy's largest company, uses reverse marketing to strengthen ties with its suppliers, which helps it compete with automakers based elsewhere in Europe and in Asia. Fiat encourages such close relationships that major suppliers have miniplants inside the Melfi factory where the Punto model is made. Continuous, open communication is the key to the company's reverse marketing. The company takes every opportunity to share ideas and procedures, and it even codesigns parts with important suppliers. Responding to Fiat's efforts, suppliers such as Sila Group have worked even harder to enhance their value packages, adding new features and lowering costs.[39]

Issues for critical thinking

Why do you think a supplier might be reluctant to take on a particular customer? Is it ethical for a supplier to refuse to work with a particular customer? How would you resolve this issue if the same type of product were available from many suppliers? If the supplier were the only source for a product?

reciprocity
the practice of buying from suppliers that are also customers

reverse marketing
customers use marketing to build stronger relationships with suppliers

Using Information Technology in the Value Chain

Throughout the value chain, organizational marketing depends on information technology for faster, more accurate transactions. One key technology is

electronic data interchange (EDI)

the computer-to-computer exchange of information between marketer and customer

electronic data interchange (EDI), the computer-to-computer exchange of information between marketer and customer. Some marketers are using the Internet; others dial into their customers' computers for EDI. No matter which system is used, EDI cuts paperwork and speeds up any exchange. For example, the U.S. Department of Defense uses EDI to manage a complex purchasing system covering 100,000 suppliers and a \$4 billion budget for food, clothing, and medical supplies used by defense personnel. Through this system, suppliers can check on the agency's product usage, bid on purchases, receive orders, send shipment notices, and receive electronic payments.[40]

Another important application of information technology is the tracking of customer needs and purchasing patterns. Tracking allows marketers to gain a clearer picture of how derived demand will affect products by using external computer databases ◄—┘ **(p. 138)** to check sales of related consumer products (based on supermarket scanner data and other sources discussed in Chapter 6). In addition, the use of information technology enables marketers to spot the peaks and valleys of consumer buying and to examine how individual brands and products are selling. With these clues, it is possible to better estimate future demand for goods or services and gear up to meet customer needs.

An internal database is an effective organizational marketing tool because it allows marketers to track the purchase and product usage behavior of the customers that buy their products. By analyzing what and when organizational prospects and customers buy, marketers can tailor their activities to better meet customer needs and strengthen customer relationships.

Germany's Commerz Bank, for example, uses its internal database to monitor its business customers' use of credit and to track the need for additional funds. Correlating the data with details gleaned from external databases, such as the number of businesses that open and close in an area, the bank can better determine loan demand and help customers with funding and advice that will improve their chances for success.[41]

Internal databases are important to Dun & Bradstreet Information Services (D&B). This company provides business marketers with mailing lists as well as financial information about businesses. Over a 10-year period, D&B has built a comprehensive internal database that helps its marketers determine which prospects are likely to become customers and which marketing tactics will be most effective for new and existing customers. In the process, D&B saved as much as \$5 million in marketing costs while increasing its sales.[42]

Gerald Reisberg, the company's vice president of marketing, says that the biggest challenge for business-to-business marketers is to "know your customers and prospects better than your competitors know theirs—and to build your strategies based on that knowledge." In the following case, you can learn more about D&B and begin applying the concepts you have learned.

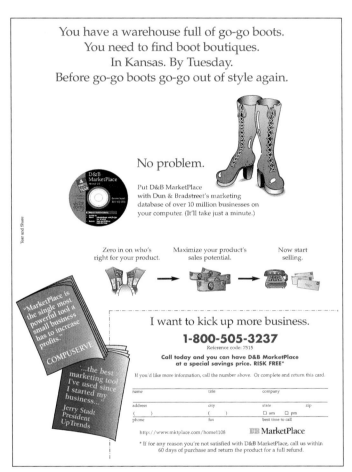

One of the most important products in the organizational market today is information. Getting the right information at the right time is critical. That's where Dun & Bradstreet shines. This information provider has a database of over 10 million businesses and can help other businesses find the right customers quickly. Note the use of endorsements in the lower left hand corner of the ad. Do you think that such endorsements add credibility to the message in the ad?

Applying the Concepts

Dun & Bradstreet digs into its database

Suppose you had spent a marketing budget of $5.6 million to acquire new customers and later found that these customers' purchases totaled only $5 million? What if you then discovered that 75 percent of your new customers were leaving after a year? Few businesses would survive for long with marketing results like these. Yet that was exactly the situation facing Dun & Bradstreet during the 1980s.

Dun & Bradstreet is a global leader in providing business and financial information to organizational marketers. D&B maintains the world's largest private database, with details about businesses in every industry in the United States and abroad. The challenge confronting D&B was to use the information in its internal database to become a more effective marketer itself.

The first step was an analysis of past marketing efforts and results. That analysis revealed the imbalance between marketing spending and customer purchases as well as the rapid turnover in customers. It also showed that each new customer was buying less than $2,000 annually in services from D&B, although some long-time customers were buying more than $10,000. Next, D&B specialists took a closer look at both big and little spenders to better understand their individual needs.

Finally, the company used its knowledge of customer purchasing patterns to develop a computer model for predicting which noncustomers were likely to respond to various D&B marketing programs. Originally, the computer model took into account fewer than a dozen factors that affect product needs, including type of business, size, and location. Over time, D&B's experts added other factors related to product needs and purchasing requirements. The company now uses over 50 factors to analyze customers and prospects. The payoff: annual sales increases of up to 6 percent—and more profitable marketing programs.[43]

Make marketing decisions

1. If you were a D&B marketer, how would you estimate demand for your products?

2. How would you determine whether big spenders are satisfied with D&B's services?

3. What would you do to determine the reason for the turnover in new customers?

4. Would you use the same marketing strategy to reach $2,000 customers as you would to reach $10,000 customers? Why or why not?

Building Relationships Within the Value Chain

How can you, as an organizational marketer, build a strong value chain to satisfy your customers and, at the same time, obtain needed materials? The following sections provide some answers.

Collaborating with Customers

By joining with your customers to tackle issues that are important to both parties, you can strengthen relationships and create bonds of trust that extend to future marketing transactions. For example, electronics marketer Motorola worked closely with an Illinois customer to help speed up deliveries throughout its value chain. Thanks to this collaboration, Tellabs—a telecommunications equipment manufacturer—cut its delivery time from 50 days to under 24 hours. Now Tellabs is beating its competitors, and Motorola has nearly tripled sales to this satisfied customer.[44]

Linking with Other Organizations

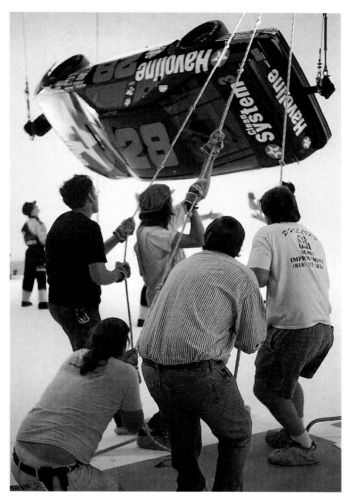

Instead of going it alone, you can get together with another marketer—or more than one—to supply what organizational customers need. Two or more marketers may be more effective than a single marketer working alone in meeting customer needs. The tiny firm Cowart and Company in Lexington, Kentucky, learned this when it landed a lucrative contract to supply cabinets for a housing development. Because his 20 employees couldn't produce everything within the 95-day deadline, owner Andy Cowart divided the design, production, and assembly chores among three of his competitors. That successful linkage spawned the Kentucky Wood Manufacturers Network, a nonprofit group of 17 small businesses that share ideas and resources to compete against larger businesses.[45]

Other value-chain linkages include strategic alliances  **(p. 39)** and joint ventures ◀—┘ **(p. 114)**. Often, such partnerships are not permanent but are forged on a customer-by-customer, project-by-project basis. For example, when the Hollywood company Cinnabar gets an order from a film maker needing props or special effects, cofounder Jonathan Katz quickly puts together a temporary group of organizations to fit that customer's needs. "We decide to do a film on Friday and have a team on Monday," explains Katz. In any linkage, temporary or permanent, all parties have to be committed to collaborating for the benefit of the customer.[46]

Cinnabar California is an example of a firm that prefers to create short-term value-chain linkages with other companies as needed to satisfy customer needs. In this way, Cinnabar retains the flexibility to quickly assemble the right team of companies to tackle each customer project. Here the company is helping Texaco promote the use of its Havoline motor oil in racing cars. Can you think of other companies that would be better able to satisfy their customers if they forged links with other organizations only on a short-term basis?

Crossing Functional and National Borders

Another way to build strong value-chain relationships is to cross functional borders within companies or geographic boundaries between countries. Some firms can do both. For example, Cisco Systems, in California, makes electronic routing devices for computer networks. Originally, the company supplied only the U.S. market, but multinational customers soon convinced Cisco to expand. A cross-functional team from research and development, manufacturing, customer support, marketing and sales, and other functions examined the needs of customers in many countries. Then the team developed products to fit electricity and computer systems around the world and satisfy local government regulations. This effort helped Cisco ring up international sales topping $500 million a year.[47]

Benchmarking World-Class Standards

No matter which of the organizational markets you're targeting, you can serve your customers better—and get better performance from your own suppliers—by benchmarking  **(p. 15)** world-class standards. You can benchmark purchasing costs, delivery time, product quality, and any other measures that are meaningful to you and your customers. Here are some samples:

- *Delivery time.* Look inside and outside your industry at those who make just-in-time deliveries. Marketers can benchmark or try to beat Wal-Mart, which requires its suppliers to deliver goods to stores within three days after receiving an order. That time will soon be cut to two days.[48]

- *Order fulfillment.* Customers want to receive exactly what they order. Many marketers benchmark L.L. Bean, which fills customer orders correctly 99.9 percent of the time, even during the chaotic holiday shopping season.[49]

- *Quality.* Work to meet or exceed product quality standards set by ISO 9000, an official standard that applies globally, as well as standards set by award programs such as the Baldrige Award in the United States and Japan's Deming Award, both of which recognize the achievements of quality leaders.

- *Purchasing costs.* See how you measure up to the results of a recent study of world-class purchasing. The top companies need, on average, about 2.2 purchasing agents to handle $100 million worth of purchases, while the typical company needs 5.4 agents. Top companies spend less than 1 percent of their budgets on the purchasing process, while the typical company spends 3.3 percent.[50]

You can benchmark competitors, suppliers, customers, big corporations, small businesses, or any other organizations that demonstrate superior performance. Don't just go by the numbers—analyze how the other organizations *achieved* their results and determine how you can adapt their ideas. After all, standards are useful only when they make sense in the value chain that links you, your suppliers, and your customers.

Best Domestic Long-Flight & Best Domestic Short-Flight

According to J. D. Power and Associates, frequent travelers ranked only one airline the best in customer satisfaction. Delta Air Lines. They awarded us honors for both "best domestic short-flight airline" and "best domestic long-flight airline." And now we'd like to say thanks. To the millions of frequent travelers who fly with us. And to the 60,000 Delta Air Lines people around the world who give you nothing less than their best.

▲Delta Air Lines
You'll love the way we fly

Frequent Flyer/J.D. Power and Associates 1995 Domestic Airline Frequent Flyer Satisfaction Study.℠ Study conducted among frequent airline travelers who completed 7,694 individual flight evaluations. Long flight is defined as 500 air miles or more. Short flight is defined as less than 500 air miles. ©1995 Delta Air Lines, Inc.

This ad for Delta Air Lines establishes Delta as the company to benchmark in satisfying the demanding needs of frequent flyers, as demonstrated by Delta's number-one ranking in annual surveys conducted by J.P. Power and Associates. Delta knows that business travelers care about the quality of an airline's service and may be more inclined to fly with an airline that is known for taking care of its passengers. What else might Delta do to communicate its world-class quality to business customers?

Before you go on . . .

A. **What is electronic data interchange (EDI) and why is it used?**

B. **What is reverse marketing, and how does it enhance value-chain relationships?**

Summary

1. **Demonstrate how organizational buying behavior differs from consumer buying behavior.**

   Organizational buying behavior differs from consumer buying behavior in three main ways: (1) organizations make larger purchases, and these markets are more concentrated than consumer markets; (2) organizational customers often require more complex, technical products than consumers; and (3) organizational buying procedures are more complicated than those of consumers.

2. **Differentiate among the four types of organizational markets.**

   The four types of organizational market are (1) the industrial market (businesses that buy goods and services to directly or indirectly use in producing other products), (2) the reseller or commercial market (wholesalers and retailers that buy products for resale to others), (3) the government market (federal, state, local, and foreign government agencies that buy goods and services), and (4) the institutional market (public and private nonprofit and for profit organizations that buy goods and services in the course of serving their customers).

3. **Describe how derived demand operates and explain its importance in organizational marketing.**

   Demand for most organizational products is linked to and therefore influenced by the demand for consumer products, which can change quickly and unpredictably. As a result of such derived demand, organizational marketers have to be aware of how consumer demand affects their organizational customers' demand for products.

4. **List the six stages in the organizational buying process.**

   The six stages in the organizational buying process are problem recognition, specification, supplier identification, evaluation, purchase, and postpurchase evaluation.

5. **Identify the six roles in the organizational buying center.**

   The buying center comprises the people within an organization who participate in the buying process. Initiators are those who first suggest the need for a new product. Users are employees who actually use the purchased products. Influencers provide information for evaluating alternatives or establishing specifications for the purchase. Gatekeepers control the flow of information to buying center members. Deciders make the final buying decision. Buyers place purchase orders.

6. **Explain the use and importance of reverse marketing in the value chain.**

   Reverse marketing attempts to build strong relationships with suppliers so a marketer can better serve its customers. Since world-class suppliers are in demand, organizational customers use reverse marketing to develop long-term relationships that benefit customer *and* supplier.

7. **Discuss four approaches to building strong value-chain relationships.**

   Four approaches to building strong value-chain relationships are collaborating with customers, linking with other organizations, crossing functional and national borders, and benchmarking world-class standards.

KEY TERMS

bid 203
buying center 207
derived demand 199
electronic data interchange (EDI) 211
government market 198
industrial market 197

institutional market 199
make-or-buy decision 202
modified rebuy 206
new-task buy 206
organizational marketing 192
reciprocity 210

request for proposal (RFP) 203
reseller market 198
reverse marketing 210
straight rebuy 206
value analysis 202
vendor analysis 205

Skill-Building Applications

1. What role do you as a consumer play in creating derived demand for tires, windshields, air bags, and other equipment? Do any manufacturers of such equipment reach out to consumers to influence purchases?

2. Wal-Mart has relationships with its suppliers just as it has relationships with its customers. How do those relationships differ? Which are easier to establish and maintain? Why?

3. What differences, if any, do you see between marketing cleaning supplies and office supplies to a large manufacturer like GE and a large government organization like the Internal Revenue Service?

4. How might a small retailer use reverse marketing to get better and faster service from larger suppliers?

5. Why might it be harder to sell a service like auto and truck repair to a city (say, Los Angeles) than to a trucking firm like Hertz?

6. Russia is having trouble creating a global market for its oil. It needs expertise in finding, pumping, and marketing oil. What benefits would Russia get from forming a joint venture with oil companies from the United States? What benefits would a U.S. oil company get by working with the Russians?

Getting Involved in Marketing

1. *On Your Own* Find out how your college purchases classroom furniture. Compare this process to the organizational buying process presented in this chapter. If your college uses a buying center, identify the participants and trace their influence on the buying process. How is the need for furniture affected by enrollment trends?

2. *On Your Own* Imagine you're a manufacturer eager to sell classroom furniture to your college. What information would help you market more effectively to this potential customer? How would you research the college's buying process? Once you had gained the college as a customer, what would you do to strengthen the relationship?

3. *Find Out More* Research the value chain for a basic consumer product such as milk or bread. Where does the manufacturer get the raw materials for this product? How do the producers who supply the raw materials market to the manufacturers? How do the manufacturers market to the resellers who have contact with consumers? Summarize your findings in a brief talk to your class.

4. *In a Partnership* Team up with another student. One of you will play the role of an office manager for an advertising agency, and the other will pretend to be a telephone equipment marketer. Prepare to role-play a meeting in which the office manager is researching the new-task buy of a new telephone system. What are the goals of each participant? What does each need to know to discuss the buying process and decision with the other? Conduct the role-playing exercise in front of the class and discuss the results. How close did each participant come to achieving his or her goals?

5. *In a Team* With two classmates, select an organization and identify which of the four organizational markets it represents. Next, list 10 products the organization is likely to buy. Assume that your group is marketing one of those products, and the organization is one of your customers. What details would you want to capture in your customer database? How would you use these details to strengthen your relationship with this customer?

6. ***In a Team*** With other students, list at least five ways that Brock Controls, featured in this chapter's opening profile, might use reverse marketing to build relationships with suppliers of its computers and floppy disks. Next to each, list the benefit(s) to Brock and the benefit(s) to the supplier. Of the five, which would you recommend that Brock implement first? Why?

VideoCase Upp Business Systems Helps Businesses Shape Up

No organizational marketer can succeed unless it understands and satisfies its customers' needs, wants, and expectations. For that reason, the motto of Upp Business Systems is, "Our business is knowing yours." Upp provides consulting services to the commercial market, to government agencies, and to institutions across the United States. The company's expertise is in information systems tecnologies such as customized business applications, databases, and warehouse management systems. The goal is to help clients leverage technology to improve their business practices so that they can better serve *their* clients.

Each time Upp begins to build a new relationship, it first studies the client's business objectives, technological environment, skill-level requirements, and overall corporate culture, while offering complete confidentiality. Upp is then able to work closely with the client's employees to identify and select the optimum consultants to plan, develop, and implement the specific solution that will address the client's unique requirements. Over the years, this solution-oriented approach has helped Upp build long-term relationships with its business customers.

For example, Upp has worked with a large cereal company for more than a decade. It was Upp's first client and is today, in fact, Upp's largest customer. At first, Upp provided consultants to help the company develop mainframe-based business applications. Later, Upp worked with the company's employees to plan a comprehensive outsourced information technology training program. Soon afterward, Upp became its sole information systems education facilitator, helping its employees prepare for the transition from mainframe to client/server systems. All the services Upp provides ultimately contribute to this Fortune 500 company's level of service in maintaining relationships with value-chain partners.

Each of the services Upp offers is based on the needs of its clients. Helping business, government, and institutional clients succeed takes a variety of core competencies, and Upp has continually expanded its skills and offerings. For example, the company added Integrated Warehouse Solutions to its roster of services a few years ago, in response to a growing need among companies to improve the inventory accuracy and flow in their high-volume distribution centers.

Identifying early clues that might indicate a client's future needs is all in a day's work at Upp. Technology is changing so rapidly that Upp is continually reevaluating how to best serve its clients today—while thinking ahead to the needs of tomorrow. Small wonder that nearly 90 percent of Upp's clients buy its services again and again.[51]

Strategies and applications

1. Go through the organizational buying process (problem recognition, specification, etc.) and describe how Upp could help clients with information and ideas in each stage, leading up to a decision to purchase Upp's services.

2. A client's first contract with Upp is a new-task buy situation. But working with a client over time results in a modified rebuy. How would Upp's approach differ in each selling situation?

3. How does Upp's relationship-building challenge in the organizational market differ from that in the consumer market? Describe two specific differences and show how Upp might act in each case to establish relationships with new organizational clients or strengthen relationships with current ones.

4. How would you describe the value package that Upp sells? Imagine that you are a marketer working for Upp. Write a letter to a hot new prospect of your choice, describing the Upp value package and linking it to benefits that would be valued by that prospect. (Make up any details you need.) Exchange letters with another student, and critique each other's work.

5. Which functional areas at Kellogg do you think might benefit from contracting with Upp consultants for a custom-built internal database? List the specific functional areas and show the position that each might assume in the buying center. How could Upp market to each member of the buying center?

6. Contracts for information systems consulting services are relatively costly and can span months or years. What could Upp do throughout the contract's duration to satisfy clients and provide them with the tools to evaluate the entire contract at the end? How would this help Upp in a modified rebuy situation?

Team project

Several students should assume the various roles in the buying center of a major manufacturing firm. Other students should assume the roles of salesperson, consultant, and support personnel from Upp. Role-play the process of meeting each other, talking about how the relationship might develop and the procedures for evaluating the results of a purchase. Discuss the process afterward and compare it to a marketing exchange in the consumer area.

8

Market Segmentation, Targeting, and Positioning

Learning Goals

After you have read and studied this chapter, you should be able to:

1. Discuss the four major benefits of market segmentation and explain when markets can be segmented.
2. Describe the four steps in the market segmentation process.
3. Identify the five types of segmentation for consumer markets.
4. List the three types of segmentation for organizational markets.
5. Explain how market segments can be evaluated.
6. Show how the four target marketing strategies are used.
7. Differentiate between positioning and repositioning.

PROFILE

Luxottica frames a fashion positioning

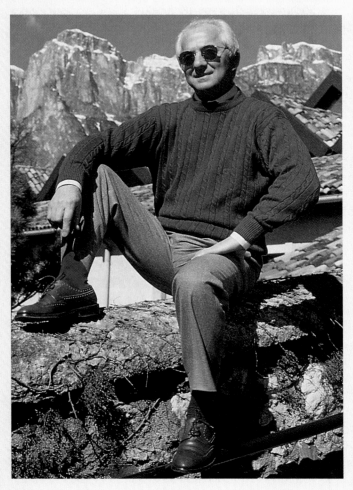

For 700 years, eyeglasses were anything but a fashion accessory. Then Leonardo Del Vecchio, the chairman of Luxottica Group, based in the Italian Alps, saw his way clear to making stylish eyeglass frames under designer names. The result was a high-fashion image that sent global frame sales soaring.

Del Vecchio started in 1961 with a small factory that made parts for eyeglass frames. During the 1970s, he began making the entire frame. By continually upgrading and expanding manufacturing capacity, Del Vecchio improved product quality and lowered costs for his Luxottica brand frames.

In 1989, after nearly two decades of turning out basic frame styles, Del Vecchio tried something new. He produced his first line of designer frames branded with the Giorgio Armani name, which he licensed from the designer. By encouraging customers to think of eyeglasses as fashion accessories rather than merely sight-corrective devices, he launched a movement toward designer eyeglasses. Although designer eyeglasses were but a small segment of the overall eyeglass market, Del Vecchio saw great potential for building profitable relationships with customers eager to make a fashion statement.

Riding this trend, Del Vecchio acquired licenses for a number of eyeglass frame brands from top European designers such as Yves St. Laurent and Byblos. These mid- and high-priced frames became extremely popular, transforming Luxottica from a niche marketer into the world's largest eyeglass frame maker, with sales exceeding $500 million. Del Vecchio recently bought Lenscrafters, a U.S. chain that promises finished eyeglasses in "about an hour," to fuel further expansion in North America. That's just one of the avenues Luxottica is using to build relationships in world markets and compete more effectively with global rivals.[1]

This chapter will show you how and why marketers have moved from mass to target marketing. First you'll learn why market segmentation makes sense, when to segment markets, and how to focus on desirable segments. Then you'll examine the four steps in the market segmentation process and see how target marketing and positioning are used.

From Mass Marketing to Target Marketing

By reducing our product line and clarifying our distribution policy, we became more important to our customers, and I learned that there is more growth potential in focusing yourself than in answering every call.

Les Burch
of Sashco Sealants Inc.

Most marketers today can't be all things to all people. Focusing on a certain group of people—those interested in fashion accessories—helped Leonardo Del Vecchio grow Luxottica into a world leader. His experience illustrates the shift from mass marketing to target marketing. **Mass marketing** is the process of using one standardized strategy to market standardized, mass-produced products to everyone in the market.[2] This "one size fits all" marketing approach was used in the past by Ford, Procter & Gamble, Campbell's Soup, and others to sell the large quantities of products they manufactured.[3]

Over time, mass marketing has largely given way to **target marketing**, the process of selecting customer groups within a larger market (p. 134) and developing products and marketing programs geared to their specific wants and needs. In contrast to mass marketing, which assumes that all people in the market have similar wants (to be filled by the same product), target marketing recognizes that all customers do *not* have the same wants. In fact, markets can be quite diverse, consisting of people or organizations with differing needs or uses for a product type. Del Vecchio reasoned that some people wanted fashion as well as function from their eyeglass frames. Fashion taste is highly individual, so it calls for careful target marketing.

Competing more effectively in today's global economy requires marketers to focus on an appropriate target market. A **target market** is the group of people or organizations whose needs a product is specifically designed to satisfy.

Not everyone can be a customer. Markets consist of **prospects**, people or organizations that are potential customers, and **nonprospects**, people or organizations that are not potential customers. How do marketers find the right target market—the market with the most prospects? The answer is **market segmentation**, the process of grouping people or organizations within a market according to similar needs, characteristics, or behaviors. Leonardo Del Vecchio used market segmentation to analyze the overall market for eyeglasses and identify a smaller target market of people interested in high-fashion frames.

A **niche market** is a very small segment identified through market segmentation. At first, Del Vecchio's fashion segment was a niche, but his marketing efforts and the overwhelming response from customers turned a niche into a much bigger segment. Niche markets are not the only application of market segmentation. With advanced information technology and marketing research, marketers can find large groups or small groups of potential customers, all the way down to target markets of one customer, as shown in Figure 8.1. One-to-one marketing is discussed later in the chapter.

mass marketing

the process of using one standardized strategy to market standardized, mass-produced products to everyone in the market

target marketing

the process of selecting customer groups within a larger market and developing products and marketing programs geared to their specific wants and needs

target market

the group of people or organizations whose needs a product is specifically designed to satisfy

prospects

people or organizations that are potential customers

nonprospects

people or organizations that are not potential customers

market segmentation

the process of grouping people or organizations within a market according to similar needs, characteristics, or behaviors

niche market

a very small market segment

The "Sneakerization" of Markets

Sneakers were once general-purpose, inexpensive, mass-marketed commodities with moderate profits. Adidas, Nike, Reebok, and other sneaker marketers learned that by segmenting the market to meet specialized customer needs, they could attract more loyal customers, command higher prices, and achieve higher profits. This is not a new concept, but the approach has become more widespread. For example, sneakers today have been replaced by "sport shoes"—special-purpose, expensive, and directed at niche markets.

F I G U R E **8.1** **Market Segmentation and Niche Markets**

A marketer can target one or many segments. This figure shows that of the six available segments, the marketer decided to target only one, market segment #2. Within that segment are two smaller niche markets that can also be targeted.

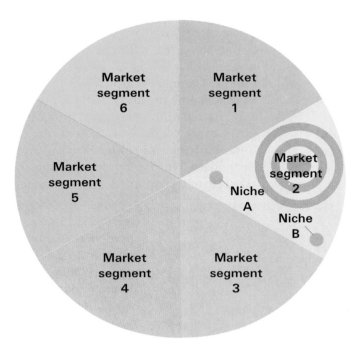

Customers can now buy shoes specialized for tennis, basketball, track, field, walking, hiking, jogging, running, aerobics, bicycling, and cross-training. Smaller niches have been created within these categories. For example, bicycle shoes are aimed at road, criterium, track, and off-road racers.[4]

The opportunity to profitably serve small market segments has led to the "sneakerization" of other markets. Like sneakers, sunglasses were once a low-priced commodity item that you could buy at any drug store. Ray-Ban, a subsidiary of Bausch & Lomb, brought out fashion sunglasses and created whole new market segments. Revco, another Bausch & Lomb company, offers 80 different frame styles and four different lenses, with a top price of $200. There are now sunglasses specifically designed for skiing, hiking, flying, shooting, volley ball, and water sports.[5] Thus market segmentation, targeting, and positioning have come to comprise one of the more important of the eight universal marketing processes. With the diversity of markets and customer needs, marketers have difficulty in besting competitors at being all things to all people. That's why the ideal approach is to group people or organizations according to common characteristics or behaviors that can be addressed by specific marketing plans.

Why Market Segmentation Makes Sense

When you focus only on specific customer groups, you can more carefully analyze their wants and needs and then develop products and marketing programs geared to those wants and needs—and establish closer long-term relationships. Over time, you can become even better at satisfying the needs of your selected customers, which gives you a competitive edge. This holds true whether you are working in a business, a government agency, or a nonprofit organization. Used properly, market segmentation offers four benefits:

1. *Opportunities for building and strengthening long-term relationships with key customers.* By devoting your resources to doing a better job than any rivals in satisfying the needs of customers in a desirable market segment, you're able to develop an enduring bond with those customers. The more narrowly you focus, the stronger the bond is likely to be. Imagine the loyal relationships you can build by tailoring goods and services to the needs and interests of *each customer*. At Dell Computer, every computer is built to the exact specifications of the customer placing the order. Service and technical support are also customized, which reinforces the idea that Dell is ready and willing to take care of its customers over the long term.[6]

Rap Snacks, founded by James Lindsay, is targeted to a very specific group of inner-city teens who buy snacks in convenience stores. Using segmentation allowed James Lindsay to be efficient in focusing on establishing good relationships with consumers and convenience stores in the targeted segment without investing too much money. Do you think Rap Snacks should partner with a drink manufacturer to prepare joint ads for this target? Why or why not?

2. *Improved marketing efficiency and effectiveness.* You won't waste time and money on unprofitable or inappropriate market segments. Because you have a better understanding of whom you want to reach and what they need, you can better allocate your limited resources to satisfy (even delight) your customers. That's why entrepreneur James Lindsay used market segmentation to break into the competitive snack-food market in Philadelphia with just $40,000. His product, Rap Snacks, was targeted toward inner-city youths who buy snacks in convenience stores. By aiming just at that group, he has built sales to $1.5 million a year.[7]

3. *Better understanding of the competitive marketing environment.* You can more easily detect emerging trends, potential problems, and marketing opportunities by looking at segments rather than the entire market. In addition, you can see competitive moves clearly, watch how customers react to rival products, and determine how your product and marketing compare to those of other industry players.[8] Natural Nectar Products, a California maker of healthy foods, used market segmentation to identify small segments where competition is less intense. "We can't compete head-on with the big companies, so we find a little niche that works," says Rick Persley, vice president of marketing and new-product development. This approach led the company to avoid chocolate and peanut granola bars in favor of fruit and nut granola bars.[9]

4. *Faster response to the changing needs of customers.* Customers are a moving target. Their needs, wants, and expectations can change from month to month, even from day to day. Market segmentation helps you stay on top of changes in your target market. Instead of marketing to a vague mass market, you're marketing to a well-defined group whose needs you can track and use to drive everything you do. SAS, the Scandinavian airline, uses information technology to separate its frequent flyers into three segments. By analyzing the travel patterns of each segment, SAS can stay abreast of changes and key its marketing activities to each segment's unique requirements and priorities.[10]

When to Segment Markets

As powerful as market segmentation can be, it's not appropriate in every situation. In some cases, you won't be able to identify distinct differences between customer groups. In others, the differences you find won't help you market more effectively. So when should you segment your market? Use market segmentation when you can answer "yes" to these questions:[11]

1. *Can you find an objective, reliable way to define groups of people that have similar needs but differ from other groups?* You need a sound basis, such as analysis of demographic or geographic data, for grouping people or organizations that have something in common. You also need to be sure that no two segments are alike. Otherwise, you won't be able to design unique marketing programs for each segment.

2. *Can you measure the sales and profit potential of the segments?* Segmenting your market and then developing marketing programs for each segment you target takes time and money. Since, however, some segments are too small or unprofitable to warrant separate marketing attention, you won't want to use market segmentation if you can't gauge the payback in dollars (or pesos) or some other measure.

3. *Can these segments be profitably reached using marketing?* Identifying a segment is one thing, reaching it is another. How would you design a marketing program to reach people who prefer large, not small, paper clips? Where would you advertise? What would you say? Market segmentation isn't meaningful if the segment identified can't be reached through marketing or if reaching it is not profitable.[12]

4. *Can you expect a different response from the unique marketing plans you offer each segment?* The point of identifying segments is to allow you to meet differing needs more effectively. If every segment responds the same way to every product or marketing program you try, you need not segment. In such a situation, one size may very well fit all.

How to Focus on Market Segments

If market segmentation is appropriate for your situation, you'll study the overall market, look for logical ways to assemble customer groups that have something in common, evaluate the segments, and then pick out desirable ones to target. The steps in this process are detailed in the next section. As you might imagine, you need sharp research and analysis skills to understand and categorize customer characteristics and behaviors during the segmentation process. Your planning skills come into play as you decide how to focus on the targeted segments.

First, you'll develop a target marketing strategy to guide your efforts. Your strategy determines whether you'll treat all segments alike, use a

It is one thing to identify a market segment, yet quite another to develop a strategy to reach it. Reebok, for example, has developed a line of sneakers with a Navajo theme. These attractive shoes appeal to a group of consumers who are interested in Native American culture. What kind of positioning strategy would be effective in promoting such shoes?

positioning

the use of marketing to encourage people in your target market to form a particular mental image of your product relative to competing products

product differentiation

creating a value package that is better than the competition in a way that is meaningful to your target market

different approach for every segment, market to only one or two narrow segments, or treat every customer in every chosen segment as a separate target market. Only then can you design the product or products you'll offer and plan the specifics of the marketing programs you'll implement.

Next, you'll want to shape the way customers think of your product or brand. **Positioning** is the use of marketing to encourage people in your target market to form a particular mental image of your product relative to competing products. The image might be one of greater product value or superior performance. By encouraging the right positioning for the right target market, you can more effectively start relationships with new customers and maintain relationships with existing customers.

For example, Contac is positioned (through advertising, packaging, and other elements of marketing) as an all-day cold relief tablet. This position contrasts with products that offer relief for a few hours. Nyquil is positioned, through marketing, as all-night cold relief, which contrasts with products used in the daytime. Both Contac and Nyquil have built strong customer relationships using positioning to create a consistent image of their products in the minds of people in their target markets.

Note that positioning isn't something you do to a product. Rather, it's the image that your marketing forms among customers and prospects as they compare your product's advantages with those of competing products. As discussed later in the chapter, positioning is a way to give your product an edge in today's competitive, dynamic marketing environment, especially when customers have little time to mull over buying decisions.[13]

Product differentiation is creating a value package ⟵⎯⎯⏉ **(p. 11)** that is better than the competition in a way that is meaningful to your target market. By gearing the differentiation to the needs of the target market, you can attract new customers and retain those you already have. A product can be differentiated on the basis of quality, technology, value, channel availability, service, and many other dimensions.[14] However, a product that is competitively superior on any or all these dimensions may still be perceived as merely comparable by the target market. Changing such perceptions is the job of positioning.

Consider how Apple Computer originally used positioning along with product differentiation. The company differentiated its first computer from those of IBM and other competitors by offering a compact processing unit, user-friendly operation, and a lot of power at a reasonable price. At the time, Apple wasn't big or well known, so its claims of superiority were less believable. That's why the company positioned its computer as a "personal computer." In the minds of people in the target market, a personal computer was something new and different, not at all like anything on the market. This positioning launched a new computer category and gave Apple a strong start. Years later, Microsoft Windows software brought user-friendly operation to IBM-compatible PCs, which made Apple's user-friendly differentiation less distinctive.[15]

Before you go on . . .

A. **How does mass marketing differ from target marketing?**

B. **What is the relationship between product differentiation and positioning?**

The Market Segmentation Process

The market segmentation process consists of four steps: (1) define the markets to be segmented, (2) identify and apply the segmentation variables, (3) evaluate the segments, and (4) select segments you want to pursue. Then come target marketing and positioning, setting the stage for decisions about your product, pricing, channel management, and integrated marketing communication, as shown in Figure 8.2.

Bear in mind that market segmentation is a journey that never ends. Markets are dynamic, which means that they're subject to change at any time. The entire market can change; segments can grow, shrink, or evolve; and the needs of people and organizations within segments can change.[16] So even when you've followed all four steps in the market segmentation process, chosen a target marketing strategy, and developed a positioning strategy, you have to be ready to respond to environmental changes that may influence the results.

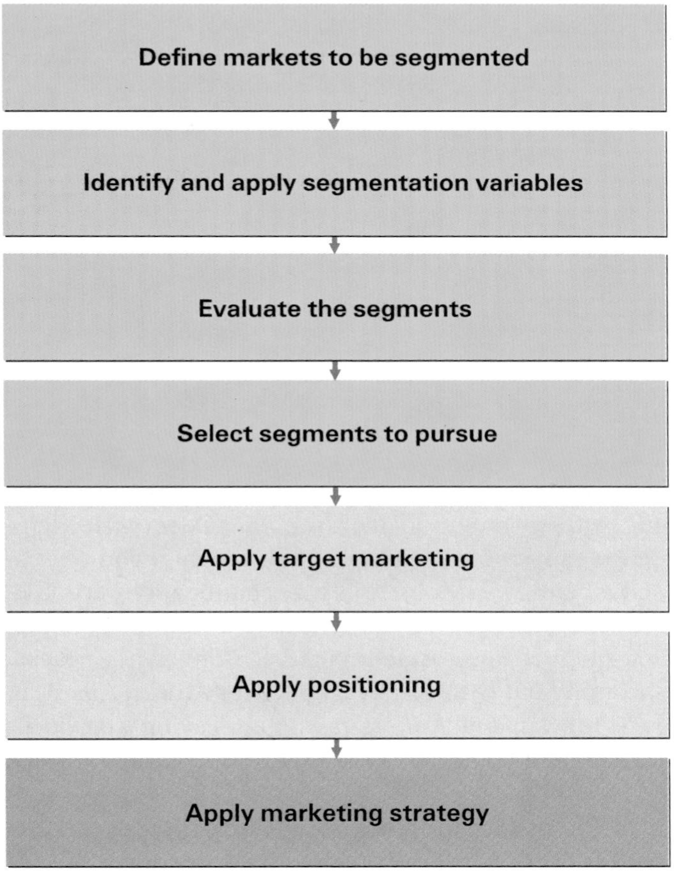

Step 1: Define the Market to Be Segmented

Before you can start segmenting, you have to define, in general terms, your overall market. This helps you narrow down the market (from "everybody" to "possible customers") by eliminating inappropriate or unwanted groups. In broad terms, you should decide whether you're interested in the consumer or the organizational market, whether you're going to market internationally, nationally, or within a smaller region, and so on. Then you can screen out groups that would not use your product, no matter how good it is. A politician running for office would exclude citizens too young to vote, while a steel mill would exclude businesses that don't buy or use steel.

Jim Baum, the president of Baum's, a small women's apparel store in Morris, Illinois, defined his overall market as older women who wear larger dress sizes. Because he could describe his market specifically, Baum was no longer dealing with a huge, undefined market. His targeted market excluded men (inappropriate for the product) and women who wear small sizes. That left a more manageable market.[17]

Step 2: Identify and Apply Segmentation Variables

The next step is to identify and apply one or more variables to segment your market. You want the people or organizations in each segment to be similar to each other and, at the same time, different from those in other segments. One variable may be enough, although marketers often use two or more, in sequence, to define segments as precisely as possible. Marketing research comes into play during this step, because without research you generally can't tell which variables are best for your product and market.[18]

Define markets to be segmented

↓

Identify and apply segmentation variables

↓

Evaluate the segments

↓

Select segments to pursue

↓

Apply target marketing

↓

Apply positioning

↓

Apply marketing strategy

FIGURE **8.2**

Market Segmentation, Targeting, and Positioning
After completing the four-step process of market segmentation, you move on to apply target marketing and positioning. Then you're ready to apply your marketing strategy using the four Ps.

Consumer Market Segmentation

As you saw in Chapter 6, the overall consumer market is both complex and diverse. Even after you've eliminated the unwanted and inappropriate groups, you're usually left with a large market to be segmented. You can group people within the consumer market on the basis of demographic segmentation, geographic segmentation, geodemographic segmentation, psychographic segmentation, and behavioral segmentation, as listed in Table 8.1. The following sections discuss each variable in detail.

TABLE **8.1**   **Variables for Consumer Market Segmentation**

Demographic Segmentation	Geographic Segmentation	Geodemographic Segmentation
Age	Country	Geographic and demographic data as shown at left
Gender	Region	**Psychographic Segmentation**
Marital status	State	Attitudes
Family/household size	County	Interests
Income	City or metropolitan area	Opinions
Occupation	Neighborhood or block	Lifestyles
Education	Climate	**Behavioral Segmentation**
Religion	Transportation	Product usage
Race	Government	Product loyalty
Nationality	Mobility	Benefits sought
Property ownership		

These Black Radiance products are targeted toward African-American women and women with darker skin tones. This is a large target and a profitable market segment to pursue. If Pavion wanted to further segment the market by age, how could it promote Black Radiance cosmetics to teens in the target market?

Demographic Segmentation   **Demographic segmentation** is a way of creating smaller groups within a larger market using variables, such as age and income, that describe the population. Among the variables you can use are gender, marital status, family or household size, nationality, race, religion, occupation, education, and property ownership. For example, cosmetics maker Pavion has segmented the cosmetics market along gender, racial, and nationality lines, coming out with Black Radiance for African American women and Solo Para Ti for Hispanic American women. Pavion's products, marketing communication, and brand names are specifically geared to each segment.[19]

Using age to segment the market for hotel stays, Choice Hotels has created a type of room with features specifically designed for senior citizens. At the other end of the age spectrum, Capcom sees great potential in the children's market for video game software. Its games, such as Disney's Aladdin for Super Nintendo, are geared to 7- to 12-year-olds.[20]

Many marketers combine demographic variables to identify suitable segments. The Maid Brigade, a franchised cleaning service based in Atlanta, uses a combination of variables to find appropriate markets for new franchises. Demand for the company's services is highest in areas with at least 12,000 households having incomes of $50,000–$200,000 and headed by young or middle-aged people. Art Guyton, director of franchise development, uses a software program to search and analyze U.S. Census data. When a franchisee wanted to open a Maid Brigade in Augusta, Georgia, Guyton found that Aiken, South Carolina—just across the Savannah River from Augusta—was a better market.[21]

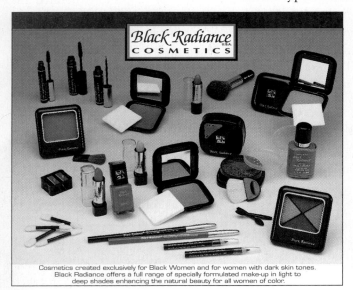

Cosmetics created exclusively for Black Women and for women with dark skin tones. Black Radiance offers a full range of specially formulated make-up in light to deep shades enhancing the natural beauty for all women of color.

Research about the demographics of U.S. and major international markets is available from the federal government and from private sources. However, demographic information about people in some countries, particularly developing countries, may be sketchy or outdated. Thus it is important, when data are available, to avoid faulty assumptions that can derail your segmentation. In the United States, for example, the traditional pattern of children leaving home when they become adults affects the number, size, and composition of U.S. households. In China, however, the number of households changes little over time because children often remain with their parents after they marry. Counting the number of households in China would give you an incomplete demographic picture, since three or four generations may live under one roof.[22]

You can segment any market according to household makeup and family life cycle, then use appropriate marketing efforts to satisfy the unique needs and requirements of each segment. More than ever before, children play a direct role in family purchases. The list goes beyond toys to computers, food, cars, even vacations, a fact not lost on marketers such as Holiday Inn and Delta Air Lines. These and other companies market directly to children in an attempt to influence family buying.[23]

Geographic Segmentation **Geographic segmentation** is a way of grouping people within a market using geographic variables such as countries or regions. Other geographic variables include state, county, city or metropolitan area, neighborhood or block, climate, and amount of mobility (movement into or out of an area). Think about how these variables can influence your marketing efforts. Would you market snow boots in balmy Corpus Christi, Texas? Probably not. Would you market them in snowy Montreal, Canada? Yes, if you used geographic segmentation to identify appropriate segments within your market.

Multinational companies such as Toyota use geographic segmentation to focus on how consumer needs differ by country. This helps Toyota plan its car designs, advertising, and other marketing tactics for each country. However, one danger in segmenting by country is the possibility of missing important consumer differences *within* countries. Another is the potential for overlooking similarities in consumer needs or tastes that transcend national boundaries. By viewing each country as a separate market, you may lose the chance to broaden production or advertising and lower your overall costs.[24] Colgate-Palmolive saves money, for example, by using larger geographic segments. Many of its household products, such as Fabuloso floor cleaner, are marketed across an entire continent rather than in just one country.[25]

Many national marketers are paying closer attention to regional segments within countries, because tastes and preferences tend to differ from area to area. The Olive Garden chain of Italian restaurants segments the United States by region, and then prepares menus and dishes specifically for each one. The chain even varies its marinara sauce to meet regional needs. "In some parts of the country, it has a little more garlic," explains spokesperson Cathie Weinberg. "In the Southern part of the U.S., they like it a little chunkier, more resembling a salsa, while in the Northeast, they would think that wasn't cooked enough."[26]

You can apply geographic segmentation to urban areas using standard definitions developed by the U.S. government. These definitions recognize that traditional city and state boundaries don't necessarily reflect the eco-

demographic segmentation

a way of creating smaller groups within a larger market using variables, such as age and income, that describe the population

geographic segmentation

a way of grouping people within a market using geographic variables such as countries or regions

geodemographic segmentation

combines geographic and demographic data to define market segments

geographic information system (GIS)

a computerized method of merging and analyzing details about an area and displaying the results in map form

psychographic segmentation

groups people or organizations in a market according to similarities in lifestyles, interests, activities, and opinions

GIS technology integrates traditional business information management tools, such as spreadsheets, with maps to facilitate market research analysis, customer information analysis, analysis of sales statistics, and analysis of other related information. Combining maps with traditional tools greatly eases development of better business strategies. Here, GIS technology is used to determine the best location for a new grocery store based on customer profiles, ease of access, and competitor penetration. Can you see the value of having this type of information when selecting a store location?

nomic or social reality of urban communities. People can work in or near one urban area, live in another, and shop in yet another. To reflect the close connection between such areas, the government has grouped them according to population size instead of geography.

A *metropolitan statistical area (MSA)* is an urban area covering either one or more cities having a population of at least 50,000 or an urbanized area with a population of 50,000 or more as well as a total area population of at least 100,000 (75,000 in New England). Larger still is a *primary metropolitan statistical area (PMSA)*, an urban area covering a population of at least 1 million and often a part of a *consolidated metropolitan statistical area (CMSA)*, which is an area covering two or more PMSAs.[27]

Geodemographic Segmentation Combining geographic and demographic data into one segmentation method, known as **geodemographic segmentation**, creates another powerful way of segmenting a market. By adding relevant demographic details to geographic data, you can locate groups of potential customers with appropriate income levels, household sizes, or other desirable characteristics. This type of segmentation is based on the "birds of a feather flock together" premise—that people who live in the same neighborhood generally have many similarities.[28]

Outside research suppliers such as Claritas combine geographic and demographic data to classify U.S. neighborhoods into "clusters" or groupings based on specific demographic attributes. The Claritas clustering system, called PRIZM (for Potential Rating Index by ZIP Markets), reveals 62 distinct clusters in the United States, each containing households with similar demographic characteristics. Of the 1.7 million households in the smaller cities included in the "Upward Bound" cluster, for example, many consist of college-educated couples who have professional jobs and, frequently, children.[29]

Because geodemographic segmentation generalizes about a community on the basis of overall demographic statistics, you can't assume that it will be accurate for individual households. Despite this limitation, the approach is often useful.

For example, Cellular One of Washington–Baltimore applies geodemographic segmentation to help its dealers find potential customers for cellular phone systems. James Carter, director of marketing operations, uses average household income and other demographic indicators to segment the market and create neighborhood clusters judged to be good, better, and best for marketing Cellular One's systems. Similarly, DePauw University in Greencastle, Indiana, uses PRIZM's geodemographic segmentation system to locate neighborhoods in which the college can feasibly market itself to high school seniors.[30]

Computerized mapping systems can help you literally visualize geodemographic segmentation data. A **geographic information system (GIS)** is a computerized method of merging

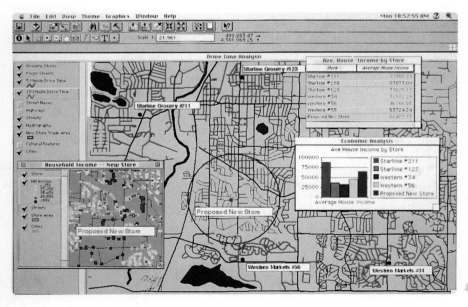

The Irish Card is a MasterCard, bearing the colors of the Irish flag, which is targeted toward Irish Americans. Many credit card issuers segment their markets using psychographic variables. This is what segmentation is all about: finding new niches where your product has a special advantage. Do you belong to a group that might be a good target market for a credit card?

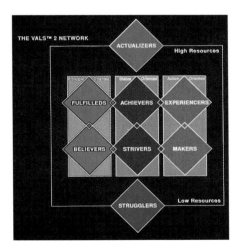

VALS 2, which stands for Values and Lifestyles Systems, segments the United States into eight broad psychographic groupings. The purpose is to explain consumer behavior and help marketers pinpoint appropriate segments to target. How might a credit card issuer apply VALS 2 to find prospective card holders?

and analyzing details about an area and displaying the results in map form. When Connecticut General Life Insurance explored the market for managed health care prior to launching CIGNA Healthcare, it used a GIS to produce maps matching the locations of its network of physicians with the locations of potential clients' employees. "Mapping reassured people that if they were to go to managed care, they would have access to the providers and specialists they desired," says CIGNA's Marina Pye.[31]

Psychographic Segmentation When you use **psychographic segmentation**, you group people or organizations in your market according to similarities in consumer lifestyles, interests, activities, and opinions. By establishing such groupings, you will achieve a better understanding of why people buy as they do, and thus you'll be better prepared to respond to their needs and buying patterns. Because you can't easily infer from demographic, geographic, or geodemographic segmentation how people think or feel, psychographic segmentation is designed to provide additional clues to what goes on in consumers' minds and hearts.

Psychographic segmentation is being applied throughout the credit card industry, where card issuers battle furiously for a place in the consumer's wallet. For example, First Consumers National Bank in Oregon issues the Irish Card, a MasterCard with the colors of the Irish flag. Potential cardholders are 10 million Irish Americans who "tend to be fairly well-educated, affluent, and to travel to Ireland," explains David Alexander, the bank's marketing manager. "We consider this card a form of self-expression," says Alexander. "And it's a whole lot easier to carry in your wallet than the Irish flag."[32]

Jodee Stevens is an entrepreneur who uses psychographic segmentation variables to identify groups whose needs aren't being met by mainstream marketers. Jodee Stevens's greeting card company, Cardthartic, segments on the basis of lifestyle, targeting gay and lesbian customers. "People have asked me, 'Why do gay people need their own cards?' But when you're trying to connect with people's situations, it's important to be true to their real lives," she explains. Now Cardthartic is branching out. "We think of ourselves as a lifestyle company," says Stevens. "Even as we expand into cards for what we call 'thinking people' and for true romantics, we think what we're doing is still out of the ordinary."[33]

You can go to a number of outside suppliers for help with psychographic segmentation. A well-known psychographic consumer segmentation system is SRI Consulting's VALS™ 2 (Values and Lifestyles) system, which categorizes U.S. adults by similar psychological attributes and focuses explicitly on explaining consumer purchase behavior. Companies and advertising agencies use VALS 2 to:

- identify appropriate consumer targets for their products/services
- design advertising and other communication devices using words and images that will grab the attention of the target
- test their ads with focus groups made up of their target
- place advertising in media that the target prefers
- design new products and services

National product and media data are available through VALS 2 linkages with the Simmons' annual *Survey of the American Household*, SRI's retail fi-

behavioral segmentation

groups people within a market on the basis of product usage, benefits sought, or brand loyalty

nancial services survey, MacroMonitor, and other databases. VALS 2 both identifies and explains *why* consumers choose the products and services they buy, the media they use, and the activities they engage in.

Another source is the Yankelovich Monitor, which categorizes U.S. consumers based on an annual survey of social trends and values.[34] Recognizing that cultural differences influence lifestyles, some psychographic systems have been developed for other countries as well. For example, the ad agency McCann-Erickson London classifies British men and women according to separate lifestyle categories.[35]

Despite the many uses for psychographic segmentation, the necessary data on consumer attitudes and lifestyles can be difficult to collect. Furthermore, some experts believe that psychographic segmentation is of limited value because the groupings don't always respond differently to different marketing techniques. You can't tell from psychographics alone how any segment is likely to react to a particular kind of product, let alone *your* product.[36] Finally, when you use psychographic segmentation in international markets, remember that segments sometimes cross national and cultural lines.

Behavioral Segmentation **Behavioral segmentation** is a way of grouping people within a market on the basis of product usage, benefits sought, or brand loyalty. Segmenting by product usage allows you to distinguish between users and nonusers as well as between heavy, medium, and light users. It also helps you identify specific usage occasions that offer opportunities for marketing activities.

Careful research and analysis of buyer habits and preferences in each country you serve can lead to profitable relationships. For example, these Whirlpool refrigerators in Bangkok, Thailand, come in bright colors because buyers often put them in their living rooms as a status symbol. In Japan, appliances often need to perform multiple tasks because there is insufficient storage space available in most homes. Have you observed products being used in unusual ways that the manufacturer could use as a promotional tool?

Issues for critical thinking

Are heavy users—those who use your type of product the most—necessarily the best segment for you to go after? Do you think heavy users are the most likely to switch from their regular brand to another? What might cause them to switch? How can you as a marketer take advantage of such switching opportunities?

Segmentation by benefits sought helps marketers create one or more products and marketing programs that deliver exactly the benefits each group seeks.[37] Using this approach, the marketer concentrates its marketing programs on the benefits that each segment wants.

Behavioral segmentation can be effective in any market, as long as you understand how the behavior influences consumer buying behavior. For example, Whirlpool marketers looked at consumer behavior in each country where the company sells its home appliances. In Thailand, they found that one of the benefits sought by refrigerator buyers was status. Buyers often stand new refrigerators in the living room to impress guests. Whirlpool responded by making its refrigerators in red, blue, and green, to give the appliances the fashionable look buyers wanted.[38]

Product usage is another key variable. Kodak, for example, found that single-use, preloaded disposable cameras were being placed on tables for guests to use during weddings and other special occasions. Responding to this usage, the company brought out a five-pack set of single-use cameras, enclosed in festive wrappings, for special-occasion photography. This segment is only one of several that have responded to Kodak's marketing and led the company to a share of more than 70 percent in the category of single-use cameras.[39] The following case shows how one wise entrepreneur used behavioral segmentation.

Applying the Concepts

Wholesome & Hearty targets vegetarians

Where's the beef? At Paul Wenner's company, it isn't in the hamburgers. His Portland, Oregon, company, Wholesome & Hearty, makes the Garden-burger, a low-fat, low-cal mixture of vegetables, grains, and spices shaped into a patty as a vegetarian substitute for the traditional beef burger.

Wenner is using behavior to target the vegetarian segment of the U.S. market. He's reaching out to the 12 million people who never eat meat and the more than three-quarters of the population who eat two or more meatless meals a week. As a vegetarian, he has firsthand knowledge of this behavioral segment.

With more Americans seeking the benefit of lower dietary fat by becoming part-time vegetarians, the organizational market for Gardenburgers is likely to grow. Even now, Wenner sells his burgers through nearly 3,000 supermarkets and more than 20,000 food outlets, including the Hard Rock Cafes and Astroburger in Hollywood. Next, Wenner wants to convince major fast-food chains to add Gardenburgers to their burger menus. By selling through more supermarkets and food outlets, Wenner is working hard to keep sales growing beyond $20 million a year.

Competition is also heating up. One major competitor is Archer Daniels Midland, a global food processing corporation with deep pockets and a long-term commitment to its vegetarian Harvest Burger. Worthington Foods, an Ohio health-food marketer, offers low-fat soy and vegetable burgers. Linda McCartney (of the rock band Wings) is marketing meatless entrées under her brand, Linda McCartney's Home Style Cooking. Nestlé and other mainstream food marketers have begun marketing pasta meals, bean dishes, and other nonmeat entrées. Intense competition—plus the changing behavior and tastes of consumers—will put Wenner's marketing and cooking skills to the test for some time.[40]

Make marketing decisions

1. What kind of marketing research should Paul Wenner conduct to estimate the size of the market for vegetarian burgers?

2. What smaller segments might Wenner look for within the vegetarian segment?

3. Should Wenner eliminate any part of the overall consumer market as inappropriate? Explain your answer.

4. What kinds of environmental change could influence Wenner's niche marketing strategy in the future?

Marketers can also use brand loyalty in behavioral segmentation. The ultimate objective is to build and strengthen customer relationships that lead to long-term brand loyalty. For example, the airlines' frequent-flyer programs reward travelers with free airline travel or other gifts in exchange for their loyalty. The most loyal customers, those who fly farther and more frequently than the average customer, receive special recognition and rewards because they're a more valuable segment. Both American Airlines and Northwest Airlines, like most other carriers, offer additional premiums to this group.[41]

Organizational Market Segmentation

Like the consumer market, the organizational market is multifaceted. Within the overall market, as you saw in Chapter 7, are four distinct markets (industrial businesses, resellers, government agencies, and institutions), each of which can be further divided into segments. You can analyze the organizational market using demographic segmentation, geographic segmentation, and behavioral segmentation, as listed in Table 8.2.

TABLE **8.2**   Variables for Organizational Market Segmentation

Demographic Segmentation	Geographic Segmentation	Behavioral Segmentation
Industry	Country	Product usage
Number of offices/branches/plants	Region	Benefits sought
Number of employees	State	Brand loyalty
Number of years in business	County	Purchasing and payment policies
Sales revenues	City or metropolitan area	
Products offered	Neighborhood or block	
Organizational ownership	Climate	
Property/equipment ownership	Transportation	
	Government	
	Mobility	

Demographic Segmentation   Among the demographic variables you can use to segment the organizational market are type of industry; number of offices, branches, or plants; number of employees; number of years in business; sales revenues; products offered; organizational ownership; and property and equipment ownership. To segment on the basis of industry type, you can use **standard industrial classification (SIC) codes,** a U.S. government system for categorizing organizations according to the products they sell. Every major industry group has a two-digit SIC code and can be further divided into more specific categories—there's a three-digit code for each industry group and a four-digit code for specific industry segments, as in the sample shown in Figure 8.3. Paint maker Sherwin-Williams segments its market by SIC code, sending its magazine *Professional Painting Contractor* to customers in three SIC codes that identify painting and contracting businesses.[42]

Although SIC codes are widely accepted and fairly simple to use, the system doesn't meet every marketer's needs. Because the government revises SIC codes only once a decade—sometimes less often—up-to-date developments such as cutting-edge technological products and newly emerging service businesses aren't well represented.[43] Because of the limitations, a new system called NAICS (National Industry Classification System) will soon be available. It will cover the United States, Canada, and Mexico.

standard industrial classification (SIC) codes

U.S. government system for categorizing organizations according to the products they sell

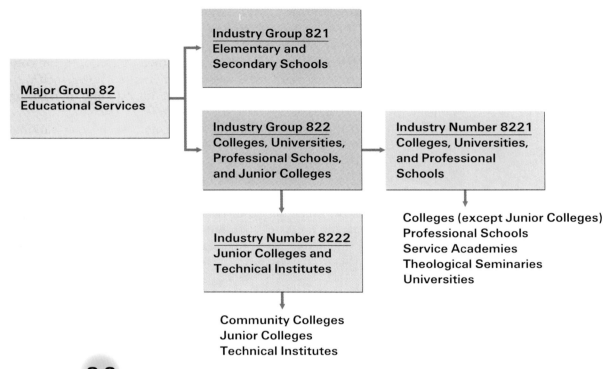

FIGURE **8.3**

SIC Codes for Educational Services
Using standard industrial classification (SIC) codes, marketers can segment the organizational market according to the products being sold. This figure shows how all U.S. organizations offering educational services can be subdivided into industry groupings. What kinds of products do you think marketers would want to sell to the market segment of colleges?

Statistics about the size of an organization and its operations are important for many marketers. For example, Ameritech, a midwestern telephone operating company, segments its market according to the number of phone lines it assigns to each business.[44] Because many of the needs of smaller organizations are unlike those of larger ones, size (as measured by annual sales, number of employees, or other measures) can be a useful way of dividing a market into meaningful segments.[45]

Banks often use size to segment the market for business banking services. Standard Chartered Bank, based in London, segments each country's market for trade banking services (such as financing for import and export transactions) according to company sales. The bank works with U.S. companies having annual sales of $10 to $200 million that are becoming more involved in global trade.[46]

Geographic Segmentation   A second way to approach organizational markets is through geographic segmentation. Like the consumer market, the organizational market can be divided by country and then into smaller geographic segments. You'll want to think in terms of where potential customers have located their headquarters, plants, or branches. Look, too, at whether potential customers are concentrated in certain areas or are spread out, because their locations can affect your ability to build and maintain a strong relationship with your customers.

Consider how WellCare Management Group, a health maintenance organization (HMO) in Kingston, New York, used geographic segmentation to expand into new market segments. WellCare's customers are employers, such as IBM and the Archdiocese of New York, that contract for employee medical services. Eyeing the large number of employers with offices in Westchester County and New York City, WellCare decided to move first into those areas. The next move may be to Long Island, which is promising because of the concentration of employers there.[47]

Behavioral Segmentation   A third way to approach organizational markets is through behavioral segmentation. Using behavioral segmentation along with demographic or geographic segmentation (or both, on occasion) will help you isolate smaller segments for marketing attention. In the context of the organizational market, behavioral segmentation covers such variables as product usage, benefits sought, brand loyalty, and purchasing policies.

Segmenting on the basis of product usage is common in organizational markets, where buyers may use products in their business operations, as components for the products they make, or to be resold. For example, Hotel Fort Des Moines, in Iowa, distinguishes between organizations whose employees rent hotel rooms when traveling on business and organizations whose employees plan meetings and special events held in banquet facilities. Both segments use hotel facilities, but in different ways. Responding to those differences, the hotel's marketing activities are geared to the needs of each segment.[48]

Hotels are using behavioral segmentation to target women business travelers who are interested in the benefits of more personalized service. This ad appeared in *Executive Woman* magazine, a publication that addresses the specific needs of businesswomen. What are some of the special benefits a woman traveling on business might seek in a hotel?

Step 3: Evaluate Segments

In steps 1 and 2, you defined your overall market and applied appropriate segmentation variables. Now you're ready to evaluate the segments you've identified. Depending on the market and the product, you can use one or more of the following criteria to evaluate the segments.[49]

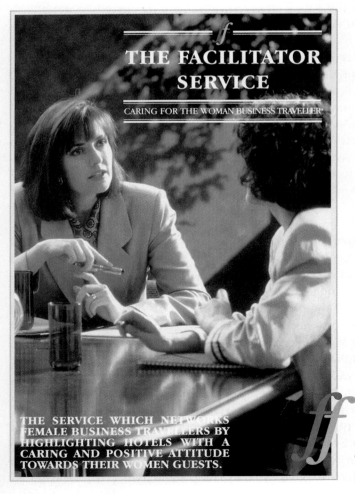

- *Potential sales and profits.* A segment that is likely to buy or use more of your products is more valuable than one with less potential for sales and profits.
- *Potential for growth.* A segment that is poised for future growth—leading to higher sales and profits—may be more valuable in the long run than a segment that is shrinking or stable.
- *Potential for retention.* Segments in which you can build strong relationships and retain customers for an extended period are the most desirable. The ideal is to target customers who will collaborate with you to forge an enduring relationship.[50]
- *Potential marketing cost.* Estimate what you might have to spend to market to each segment. Some segments may be too costly (or difficult) to reach or to service.
- *Potential risks.* Weigh any competitive, environmental, political, technological, or legal and regulatory risks you might face in these segments. Think, too, about how you might convert a risk—such as an environmental one—into a customer benefit by using recycled materials or another technique.

Consider how Southwest Airlines, based in Texas, evaluated the market for short-route air travel within Texas. Southwest's marketers segmented the market and forecast both good sales and profits for flights between

Dallas, Houston, and San Antonio. It could reach price-sensitive flyers in those three cities at a reasonable cost, using billboards and newspapers. The airline kept costs low, which translated into lower air fares and helped draw and retain a loyal customer base. Because expenses and ticket prices were so low, Southwest faced little risk of competition from higher cost rivals, which couldn't afford to match the fares. Later, the airline identified and evaluated additional segments to support expansion beyond Texas.[51]

Step 4: Select Segments

Once you've evaluated the various segments, you can screen out those that contain nonprospects and select those you want to pursue. Since you may not have the resources or time to market to every attractive segment, you'll want to put the segments in priority order. One way to do this is to rate each segment on each of the evaluation criteria, then add up the scores. Market first to the segment(s) with the best overall scores, then work your way down the list.

Another way to select segments is to use a *market segmentation matrix*, a grid that graphically portrays the segments created by applying two or three segmentation variables. Look at the potential market segments evaluated by Louis Brown, Jr., founder of Micros Systems, which makes electronic cash registers. He segmented the organizational market according to industry, size, and benefits sought, as shown in Figure 8.4.

FIGURE **8.4**

**Micros Systems'
Segmentation Approach**
Given the strengths of the company and the needs of each segment, Micros Systems decided to first target medium-sized firms in the restaurant industry. Once the company has successfully established relationships in these segments, it can branch out into other segments.

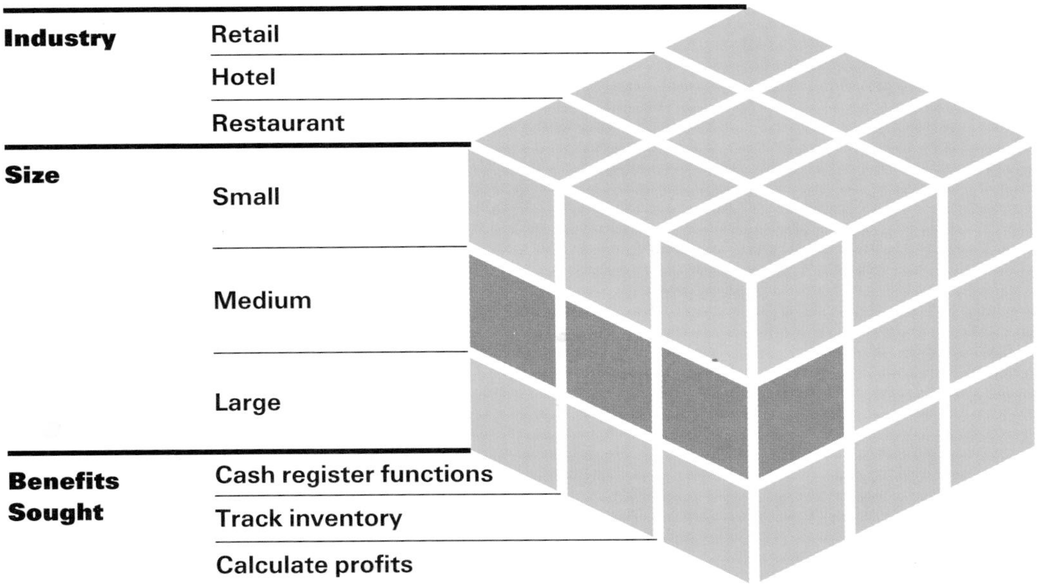

Of the three industries evaluated, Brown decided to avoid the retail and hotel segments because of strong competition from IBM and others. He saw little competition in the restaurant segment, a real plus. Size, too, was a factor. The smallest restaurants might not be able to afford Micros's systems, but the largest chains would be unlikely to try an unproven product from an unknown supplier. Brown looked at the benefits sought, including basic cash register functions and more extensive functions that linked purchases to inventory and profit calculation. Midsized and larger restaurants wanted more functionality—and were willing to pay for these benefits, not available from many other suppliers. Brown gave the segment of midsized restaurants requiring extensive functionality first priority. Later, he expanded to restaurant chains and hotel computer systems.[52]

Before you go on . . .

A. What are the four steps in the market segmentation process?

B. How is demographic segmentation used in the consumer market? In the organizational market?

C. How is behavioral segmentation used in the consumer market? In the organizational market?

D. What are geodemographic segmentation and psychographic segmentation?

Target Marketing and Positioning to Build Relationships

The market segmentation process is complete once you've selected and prioritized the segments you want to address. But your marketing work continues, as you move on to make decisions about target marketing and positioning. These decisions are important because they point the way toward the specific marketing actions used to build relationships with individuals or organizations within each segment you've selected.

Target Marketing Decisions

Target marketing decisions determine the number of segments to target and your plans for product, price, channel management, and integrated marketing communication to reach these segments. You can choose among four target marketing strategies: undifferentiated marketing, differentiated marketing, concentrated marketing, and customized marketing, all shown in Figure 8.5.

Undifferentiated Marketing

In **undifferentiated marketing**, a single marketing strategy is used to reach the entire market. The extreme is mass marketing, in which you market to the world rather than to individual segments, using the same product, price, channel partners, and integrated marketing communication. Few marketers today use undifferentiated marketing. Even Coca-Cola, once a devoted practitioner, has long since moved away from this strategy.

As recently as 1981, Coca-Cola offered only one type of cola under that brand name. But competitive pressure from Pepsi-Cola and a slow drop in market share led the company to launch New Coke, with a new formula, in

undifferentiated marketing
a single marketing strategy is used to reach the entire market

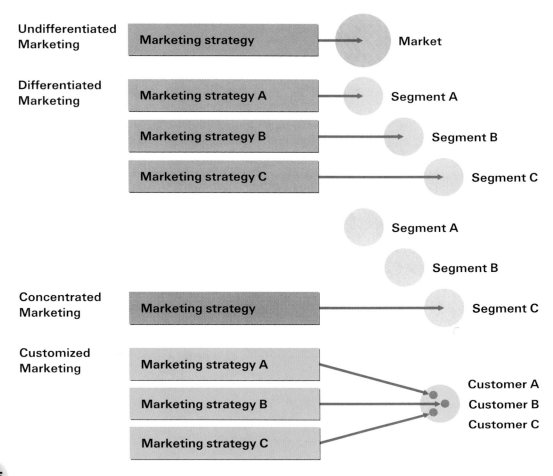

FIGURE **8.5**

Target Marketing Strategies
Once you've segmented your market, you can use any of four target marketing strategies to reach your chosen market or segments. At one extreme is undifferentiated marketing, which uses a single marketing strategy to reach an entire market. At the other extreme is customized marketing, which uses a separate strategy for each customer in the market.

differentiated marketing

separate and distinct marketing strategies are devised for each of the segments to be reached

1985. The new product sparked anger and controversy among those loyal to the original product, which was quickly reintroduced as Coca-Cola Classic. By 1986, the company had put undifferentiated marketing (and New Coke) behind it and was marketing seven soft drinks under the Coca-Cola umbrella.[53]

Differentiated Marketing

In **differentiated marketing**, separate and distinct marketing strategies are devised for each of the segments you want to reach. Differentiated marketing means varying the product, pricing, channel partners, and integrated marketing communication as needed for each segment. In this way, you can use marketing to support the unique positioning you want to create for each market.

When you use differentiated marketing, you look carefully at the needs of each segment with a view to designing an appropriate marketing program. Banco del Pais in Honduras, for example, targets small business owners as well as individual consumers who need banking services. The bank studied the small business market and saw a need for streamlining the financial transactions between Honduras exporters and their U.S. customers. In response, the bank began offering checking accounts that can accept U.S. dollars as well as lempiras, the Honduran currency. For this segment, the bank's marketing communication relies primarily on direct mail sent to local business organizations.[54]

Concentrated Marketing

In **concentrated marketing**, one marketing program is directed toward a single market segment. Because you're concentrating on one segment only, you can become extremely familiar with that market's needs, wants, and expectations and be better prepared to respond. Of course, the segment you choose must have sufficient potential to make your efforts worthwhile. In particular, start-ups and small businesses prefer concentrated marketing. For example, Polyconversions, a small Illinois company owned by brothers Dennis, Robert, William, and Ronald Smith, aims at the hospital market with only one product, disposable hospital gowns.[55]

Even niche markets too tiny for larger rivals can be the right size for a smaller marketer. Terri's Consignment World is a chain of five furniture consignment shops in Arizona. Although the business is growing, the segment is small and therefore isn't drawing the attention of big furniture chains.[56] When big marketers notice your niche, however, competition can really heat up. The frenzy that Snapple and other small marketers caused with ready-to-drink tea beverages quickly caught the attention of PepsiCo, Coca-Cola, and other giants. The niche is only a drop in the bucket of the soft-drink industry as a whole, but its potential has ignited an expensive marketing struggle.[57]

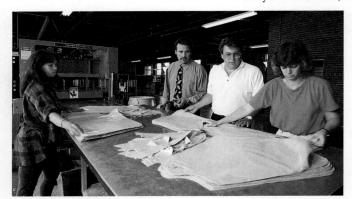

Concentrated marketing can be an effective strategy if the company is successful in getting close enough to potential customers to understand their wants and needs better than their competitors. As shown, Polyconversions has developed a process to efficiently produce disposable hospital gowns—the company's only product. How might the company prioritize the large number of potential customers in the overall market for its product?

Customized Marketing

At the other extreme from undifferentiated marketing is **customized marketing**, in which marketing programs are tailored for each individual consumer or organization in the market. In customized marketing, also known as *individualized* or *one-to-one marketing*, each customer or prospect is a market segment. You adjust your product (and sometimes your pricing, channel management, and integrated marketing communication) for each person you target.

Issues for critical thinking

Once a customized marketer, always a customized marketer? Digital Equipment Corporation marketed personal computers by mail and telephone, building each to the customer's specifications. Then the company found marketing through dealers to be more efficient. What would a switch like this mean for Digital's customers? For competitors?

Not long ago, mass marketers lacked the manufacturing equipment or know-how to mass-customize what they made. That's changed now, as high-tech, flexible manufacturing methods allow nearly endless variations to satisfy individual customers.[58] For instance, the National Bicycle Industrial Company in Japan uses computer-aided design and manufacturing to make bicycles that exactly fit the customer's height, weight, riding style, and skill level. The company can offer more than 10 million customized bicycles with this system.[59] The next section explains how a large service marketer and a small manufacturer use customized marketing to satisfy customers.

concentrated marketing

one marketing program is directed toward a single market segment

customized marketing

marketing programs are tailored for each individual consumer or organization in the market

MARKETING IDEAS

Customizing for a segment of one

What do giant American Express and tiny Software Sportswear have in common? Both use customized marketing to reach out to individuals. The key is information technology that allows the two businesses to build customer relationships one at a time.

American Express markets its charge cards to a variety of segments, including personal cardholders, small business cardholders, and corporate cardholders. The company further segments each group into markets of one, using computer power to analyze the spending details in customer charge transactions. These details show Amex how to shape its marketing communication to each customer's needs and preferences.

One example: The company produces 1,349 variations of its newsletter for corporate card customers. Although this sounds unwieldy, it's actually quite manageable, because the company has a large online library of articles and graphics. Printing newsletters is simply a matter of matching each customer's buying patterns with appropriate articles and graphics. Customers' enjoyment derived from reading material selected specifically for them gives them more incentive to stay with American Express.

Meg Felton, president of Software Sportswear, uses information technology to design and custom-manufacture women's swimsuits. She uses a computerized video system to take measurements and show women how they'd look in swimsuits of various styles and fabrics. Once a customer has made a decision, the system creates a pattern for the swimsuit, which fits perfectly because it's made for the wearer. More than a thousand customers used Felton's system in the first 30 months.[60]

Can you think of other products suitable for customized marketing?

Positioning Strategies

After you've decided on a target marketing strategy, you have to decide how to position your product or brand. This step is important because the marketing decisions you make will affect the opinion or image of your product held by people in your target market. Think of Volvo, a car brand that's positioned as safe, or Heinz, a ketchup brand that's positioned as thick.

Customers and prospects use these positions as a kind of shorthand to catalog certain categories of products. In a buying situation, these positions come to mind and help people in the target market choose among the various brands and products. Remember that a position should be seen from the customer's perspective, based on what customers want.[61] Volvo's position as a safe car is meaningful because customers want safety, and the same holds true for Heinz's position as a thick ketchup.

By creatively applying the eight marketing processes, you create and reinforce the chosen position in the minds of customers and prospects, a position unlike those of competing products in the same category. Positioning also keeps every employee focused on the total value package you are providing to customers. To effectively maintain a unique and preferred position, your entire organization must deliver on the promise made by the position you choose.

perceptual map

a graph of how customers perceive the competing products in a category along two or more important dimensions

No matter how wonderful an image your marketing creates in the minds of customers, the real test occurs when customers come into contact with employees. "The only thing we offer is service, and service is our people," says Gary Mahn, president of Fisher's Office Products in Boise, Idaho. As Mahn knows, empowering **(p. 17)** employees to satisfy customers goes a long way to reinforcing a competitive position and building relationships that stand the test of time.[62]

Consider the positioning of Roto-Rooter Plumbing Service, which promises one-hour emergency service night and day, for peace of mind that sends plumbing troubles "down the drain." Advertising supports the marketer's positioning, but what really makes the difference is the employees. When a customer calls, the dispatcher sends the next available service person, then calls the customer back to confirm. When Roto-Rooter personnel arrive, they diagnose the problem, fix it, and clean up the mess. Roto-Rooter staffers make a final call after the service to check on customer satisfaction. Clearly, everyone in the Roto-Rooter organization is working to support the company's positioning.[63]

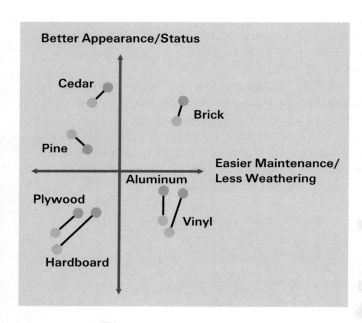

FIGURE **8.6**   Perceptual Map

This perceptual map shows how users and nonusers perceived a variety of home siding products. Users' perceptions are represented by green dots, while nonusers' perceptions are represented by blue dots. After looking at this perceptual map, a marketer of vinyl siding might create a strategy for positioning its product as both better in appearance/status and better in maintenance/weathering.

Positioning and the Customer

The only way you can know what is important to customers is through marketing research. Once you have learned what customers like and dislike, you can see the relative standings of every product in the category, including yours. After all, no product is marketed in isolation. The position a product holds is related to those of competing products being considered by customers.

To visualize how your product stands, you can draw up a **perceptual map**, a graph of how customers perceive the competing products in a category along two or more important dimensions. A perceptual map, like the one in Figure 8.6, also known as a *product positioning map*, shows the positions of your product and its rivals as well as other position opportunities in its market. Using this map, you may decide to move your product from one position to another.

Understanding how customers and prospects view the product forms the foundation of marketing activities for positioning a product. The following section shows how Lea & Perrins, which markets a 150-year-old product, revitalized customer relationships and attracted new customers by positioning its product for targeted segments.

GLOBAL ISSUES

Segmentation and positioning for saucy marketing

Does one taste fit all? Not these days, as Lea & Perrins found out. A U.K. company now owned by the French food giant BSN, Lea & Perrins markets Worcestershire sauce in 130 countries. After a century and a half of success, Lea & Perrins was experiencing intense competition from marketers of hot pepper sauces, soy sauces, and other liquid flavor enhancers. A mass-market approach was leaving the company vulnerable to these competitors. To fight back, the company used marketing to spice up its position in the minds of customers and prospects.

First, the company researched consumer cooking habits and attitudes toward food throughout Europe, where the brand already enjoyed high recognition. Then, it identified segments of cooks and consumers who wanted easy-to-use spice flavorings that could be applied during cooking or at the table. Responding to the needs of customers in these segments—and mindful of cultural differences in cooking and taste—the company formulated 14 new variations of liquid spices.

Next, Lea & Perrins used marketing to associate its brand with "added piquancy." This positioning made the brand distinct from competitive products that entirely change the flavor of a dish. The company's promotional programs stressed the differences and suggested recipes and uses for the products. In this way, Lea & Perrins has updated its marketing to compete more effectively across Europe.[64]

How might Lea & Perrins research market segments and possible positionings for the U.S. market?

Positioning and Repositioning

Repositioning is the use of marketing to change a product's relative position in the minds of the target market. If you want to move to a more favorable position on the perceptual map, you can use your marketing mix ◄⎯⎯⎦ **(p. 20)** to reposition your own product—or even a competitor's product. In some markets, the pace of change is so rapid that you have to be ready for *dynamic positioning*, frequent adjustments to your positioning approach as a response to shifts in the marketing environment.[65] But rapid changes can be confusing to customers. Some organizations have lost their image because of such changes. However, here's how one business owner used dynamic positioning to stay on top of her target market.

SMALL BUSINESS WATCH

Fast and flexible repositioning

Maria Elena Toraño is a positioning chameleon. Her Miami-based company, Maria Elena Toraño Associates (META), has been positioned as an expert government supplier in a variety of activities. This dynamic positioning allows Toraño to adapt to changing needs and opportunities in the marketplace.

The Cuban-born entrepreneur is a former airline marketer and a one-time associate director of the U.S. Community Services Administration. After leaving her government post, Toraño went into business for herself. She positioned her firm as a public relations agency with Washington savvy and connections, and she soon attracted both government and corporate clients.

One of her clients was the U.S. Small Business Administration, which offers business development assistance to minority-owned companies.

repositioning

the use of marketing to change a product's relative position in the minds of the target market

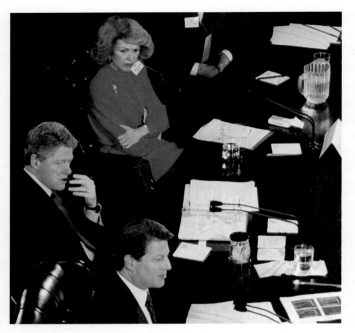

Positioning is a concept that can be applied not only to individual products but to entire businesses as well. No organization illustrates this better than Maria Elena Toraño Associates. The company has positioned itself as a public relations agency, as an MIS (management information systems) supplier to the government, and as a preparer of environmental impact statements. Here, Maria Elena Toraño is shown attending an economic conference with President Clinton and Vice President Gore. What are some possible disadvantages of positioning a small business to serve several markets?

Toraño used the SBA program as an entrée to management information systems work with the Defense Contract Audit Agency. Eventually META was positioned as a government MIS supplier. When defense contract work slowed, Toraño saw growth in the environmental field. She went after—and was awarded—contracts to prepare environmental impact statements for the Department of Energy.

META next expanded into management consulting to satisfy another need in the target market. Because of continuing changes in customers' needs, Toraño is ready to reposition for additional opportunities such as health care management and administration. "To me, being alert to new opportunities means knowing what people want, what they need, and where the country is going," she observes.[66]

Do you know of other positioning chameleons? Why have these marketers repositioned their products or brands?

Whether you're positioning or repositioning your product, you have a variety of options. One approach is to position your product *against* your leading competitor. When MCI first began battling for a piece of the long-distance telephone market, the upstart positioned itself as cheaper than AT&T, which held the lion's share of the market.[67]

A second approach is to position your product according to who uses it. This is the approach Lever Brothers took when it positioned Lever 2000 as the soap that can be used by the whole family. Surprisingly, no other marketer had sought this position, and it helped Lever grab the lead in the bath soap market.[68]

A related approach is to position your product according to when or where it's used. Campbell's Soup has done this by repositioning its condensed soups as time-saving ingredients to be used in cooking main-meal recipes. "With an 80 percent share of the condensed soup business, our game is to make Red and White Soups [condensed soups] relevant and contemporary versus other food options," says Gary T. Fassak, business director for Red and White Soups. "We want people to pull out those six cans they already have in the pantry, and start cooking with them."[69]

You can also position your product or brand according to the values of the people in your target market. For example, the Body Shop has positioned itself by making sure consumers know that the organization uses natural ingredients in its personal care products, opposes animal testing, and acts to protect the environment.[70] Another strategy is to position your product according to its benefits. Japanese cosmetics maker Shiseido did this with its Perfect Rouge line of long-lasting, no-smear lipsticks.[71]

Finally, you can use the differences between your product and its competitors to develop an effective position. Dennis M. Hedlund, founder of Kulture International Films, did this when he positioned his mail-order videotape rental business as different from all the others. Few marketers carry the kind of classical music or ballet videos that Hedlund rents, so stressing the difference has helped build Kulture into a $5 million business.[72]

Before you go on . . .

A. When are undifferentiated marketing, differentiated marketing, and concentrated marketing appropriate?

B. What is a perceptual map and how is it used?

C. In what ways can marketers use marketing to position their products?

Summary

1. **Discuss the four major benefits of market segmentation and explain when markets can be segmented.**

   The four major benefits of market segmentation are opportunities for building and strengthening long-term relationships with key customers, improved marketing efficiency and effectiveness, better understanding of the marketing environment, and faster response to the changing needs of customers.

2. **Describe the four steps in the market segmentation process.**

   The four steps in the market segmentation process are: define the markets to be segmented, identify segmentation variables, evaluate segments, and select segments.

3. **Identify the five types of segmentation for consumer markets.**

   Five types of segmentation for consumer markets are demographic, geographic, geodemographic, psychographic, and behavioral segmentation.

4. **List the three types of segmentation for organizational markets.**

   Three types of segmentation for organizational markets are demographic, geographic, and behavioral segmentation.

5. **Explain how market segments can be evaluated.**

   Market segments can be evaluated on the basis of potential sales and profits, potential growth, potential for retention, potential marketing costs, and potential risks.

6. **Show how the four target marketing strategies are used.**

   Undifferentiated marketing is a strategy in which a single marketing mix is used to reach the entire market. Differentiated marketing uses separate and distinct marketing mixes for each segment. Concentrated marketing uses one marketing mix directed toward a single market segment. And customized marketing uses a marketing mix tailored for each individual consumer or organization.

7. **Differentiate between positioning and repositioning.**

   Positioning is using marketing to encourage people in the target market to form a particular mental image of the product. Repositioning is changing a product's relative position in the minds of the target market.

KEY TERMS

behavioral segmentation 230
concentrated marketing 238
customized marketing 238
demographic segmentation 226
differentiated marketing 237
geodemographic segmentation 228
geographic information system (GIS) 228
geographic segmentation 227

market segmentation 220
mass marketing 220
niche market 220
nonprospects 220
perceptual map 240
positioning 224
product differentiation 224
prospects 220

psychographic segmentation 229
repositioning 241
standard industrial classification (SIC) codes 232
target market 220
target marketing 220
undifferentiated marketing 236

Skill-Building Applications

1. How would you use segmentation, targeting, and positioning to find *the* job in *the* organization that you want?

2. What are the dangers of niche marketing in the organizational market, such as making driveshafts only for Ford?

3. Should a nonprofit organization like United Way use an undifferentiated marketing appeal to generate contributions or should it use a segmentation strategy? Why?

4. How could a small barbershop like Kids Cuts position itself against the larger chains? Are there potential niche markets in the children's market?

5. How effectively has MCI positioned itself relative to AT&T and Sprint? It is time for a repositioning? Explain your answer.

6. Should Ben & Jerry's use the same segmentation, targeting, and positioning strategy in Japan as in the United States? Why?

Getting Involved in Marketing

1. *On Your Own* Imagine that you're marketing an inexpensive children's archery set with a bow and six arrows. How might you use segmentation to analyze the consumer market for this product? Be specific.

2. *On Your Own* You've opened an auditing service that checks commercial property tax bills and helps small businesses recover overpayments. How might you use segmentation to analyze the organizational market for this product? Be specific.

3. *Find Out More* Go to the library or use an online database service to look up the U.S. Census statistics for a nearby Metropolitan Statistical Area. What area(s) does this MSA cover? What is the MSA population? How much population data is available and how old is the material? What is the source of the data? Write a one-page summary of your findings.

4. *In a Partnership* With another student, select a magazine ad for a particular product, such as a car. Work separately to analyze the ad and write a brief

statement of the position you believe this product is seeking in the minds of the target market. Then compare your statements and prepare a joint two-minute presentation to the class about your conclusions.

5. *In a Team* With other students, identify three goods or services you agree would benefit from market segmentation. If you could choose only one segmentation method for each, which would it be? Explain your choices in a few paragraphs.

6. *In a Team* With three other students, you are handling the marketing for a new business, Clean Sweep, which cleans student dormitory rooms in colleges in your state. Each student should select one of the target marketing strategies and offer at least three reasons why it is appropriate for this product and market. Once your group has voted on the strategy that seems best, compare the decision with that of other groups in your class.

VideoCase Targeting the Alternative Market

No mass markets for Scott Becker. Instead, the Santa Monica, California, magazine publisher is targeting two specific segments: people interested in alternative music and people interested in alternative fashion. By focusing on these market segments through differentiated marketing, Becker has built a profitable, cutting-edge magazine business.

Becker started *Option*, his bi-monthly magazine on alternative music, in 1985. Each issue contains news, features, and at least 200 brief reviews of groups and performers such as Ambient Time Travelers, Beastie Boys, Children of Dub, Loop Guru, and Toast.

Now *Option* has more than 75,000 readers, and Becker has researched those customers extensively. In terms of demographics, most subscribers are college-educated males, with an average age of 31. In terms of behavior, subscribers are frequent purchasers of prerecorded music, often buying by mail. In terms of psychographics, subscribers tend to be avid music fans and many are musicians, retailers, or otherwise directly involved in the music industry. To meet the eclectic tastes of this targeted segment, *Option* covers many types of music, including rock, jazz, and country.

By staying close to his customers and continuing to research the market, Becker identified another market segment, one that wasn't being addressed by existing magazines. He saw an opportunity to fill the need for a magazine geared toward alternative fashion and culture. Becker started *U.H.F.* in 1995 as an alternative to *Vogue* or *GQ* in the fashion industry, just as *Option* is an alternative to *Rolling Stone* in the music industry. The acronym U.H.F. stands for "ultra high frequency," and the clothes in *U.H.F.* certainly fit that description.

Geared toward both sexes, *U.H.F.* showcases styles that are heavily influenced by music culture. It also features fashions related to active sports such as snowboarding, skateboarding, motocross racing, and surfing. *U.H.F.* has become a valuable resource for readers seeking new designers and new fashion ideas.

To get his magazines out to more potential readers, Becker is building relationships with other organizations. He has arranged for customers to be able to buy single copies of *Option* and *U.H.F.* at newsstands, record and book stores, and boutiques. In addition, Becker has hired an advertising director to market the magazines as good advertising vehicles for makers of apparel, recorded music, consumer electronics, and other products. These are advertisers that want to reach the same segments as Becker. With his magazine publishing business growing so quickly, Becker is determined to keep his focus squarely on specific segments—and away from the mainstream mass market.[73]

Strategies and applications

1. Thinking about the demographic, psychographic, and behavioral characteristics of *Option* readers, what other kinds of advertisers should Becker's advertising director approach?

2. Do you think Becker should segment his two market segments into smaller, even more specific customer groupings? If so, how do you suggest he segment the market?

3. What effect, if any, has the alternative music and clothing trend had on people you know? Does the market for such items seem to be growing in your area? Why? How could Becker use such informal marketing research to better target his magazines?

4. How should Becker position *Option* to appeal to his target market? Should he position the magazine against competing magazines? Explain your answers.

5. How could Becker use customized marketing to tailor his magazines for individual readers? What should he consider before starting such an effort?

6. *Option* isn't the only alternative music magazine on the market. As competition heats up, how could Becker use repositioning to change the way his target market thinks about *Option*?

Team project

With other students, visit a newsstand or music store and look through *Option* and several other alternative music magazines. Analyze the articles as well as the advertisements. Can you identify the specific segment that each of *Option*'s competitors is targeting? Working as a team, develop a detailed description of each magazine's targeted segment. What differences and similarities can you find?

http://www.spiegel.com

Marketing on the Net   Mail Order Moves Online

Once a mail-order only catalog, Illinois-based Spiegel has jumped into cyberspace with a Web site that offers merchandise and more. By understanding the buying behavior of catalog shoppers and adding services that fit customers' lifestyles, Spiegel has boosted sales—and strengthened long-term relationships with loyal customers.

The Spiegel Web site is first and foremost an online store. Many of the clothing and home furnishing items found in the company's printed catalog can be found on the Web site. Browsers can click to order a CD-ROM version of the latest catalog. And there's even a CyberSale section for bargain-hunters.

Spiegel offers many ways to buy. Customers are invited to call toll-free, to fax toll-free, to download and mail in an order form, or to use a toll-free TDD telephone line (for hearing- and speech-impaired customers). If they prefer, customers can order and arrange payment online. "You don't have sales without the ability to order online," notes Randy Heiple, Spiegel's director of advertising. The company found this out the hard way. The first four months its site was open, no online ordering was available—and customers complained. "People told us it's their business to decide which way they want to order, while it's our business to provide that ability to choose," Heiple says.

Now, about 90 percent of the site's sales come through online orders. However, some shoppers are reluctant to input credit-card numbers because they fear security leaks. In response, the company has set up elaborate security procedures, which are outlined on the Web site. If customers are still wary of inputting card numbers, they can simply check a box to have Spiegel personnel call them back and take the information over the phone.

But the Web site goes well beyond shopping. It also addresses customers' lifestyle needs and concerns, offering advice, information, and resources to help them live the way they want. For example, a visit to the Web site in June turned up pages of tips for planning weddings, and a wedding consultant is always available to answer online questions. Customers can also e-mail experts with questions about gardening, travel, and home decoration.

To keep browsers coming back, the Web site contains an online magazine featuring articles by knowledgeable writers who cover fashion, travel, and other topics. Other unique elements also draw people back. For example, there has been a soap opera, complete with daily updates, to add a little spice to the Spiegel site. With so much to see and buy, why would customers ever leave?[1]

Strategies and applications

1. Visit Spiegel's Web site and analyze its on-screen order process. What suggestions can you offer for making online buying easier and more convenient for shoppers?

2. Imagine that Spiegel wants to put particular emphasis on the segment of customers who are newly married. How can the company research their needs and concerns? What type of merchandise do you think this segment might need? How would you use Spiegel's home page to alert browsers from this segment that they will find useful items and information at the site?

3. If Spiegel wanted to conduct marketing research to uncover customer interest in a new line of children's merchandise, what questions would you include in an online questionnaire? How would you lead visitors to the survey from Spiegel's home page?

4. Can Spiegel use its Web site to strengthen relationships with suppliers? Would you recommend that the company set up a special area for suppliers to leave questions and comments? Are there other ways of using the site to maintain a dialogue with suppliers?

5. Looking at Spiegel's Web site, how do you think it is positioning itself to customers? Write one sentence to describe Spiegel's positioning. Suggest a specific idea for enhancing the Web site that would help Spiegel reinforce this positioning.

6. With what other Web sites do you think Spiegel should be linked? Browse the Web and find two other sites that would be good links to help Spiegel attract new customers. What kinds of customers do you think visit these sites? How do you know? Why are they good links for Spiegel?

Team project

With other students, think about any special help that online shoppers might want during peak gift-giving periods such as Christmas, Mother's Day, and graduation time. Choose one such period and develop two ideas that Spiegel could incorporate into its Web site. Explain how each idea addresses the buying behavior and concerns of online catalog shoppers.

http://www.worldata.com

Marketing on the Net   WebConnect Helps Businesses Connect Online

If you build it, they will come. Or will they? Roy Schwedelson knows that there's more to a successful Web site than a spiffy home page. As CEO of Worldata, based in Boca Raton, Florida, Schwedelson originally specialized in helping software and hardware marketers handle direct marketing. He helped clients locate mailing lists, build marketing databases, and analyze customer response for companies that sell by mail.

Then commerce on the Internet became big business, and Schwedelson saw an opportunity to show clients how to profit from the Web. So Schwedelson set up a division called WebConnect to help businesses draw traffic to their Web sites. To do this, he needed to understand the segments each business is targeting, learn how its potential customers use the Web, and then analyze the response to fine-tune the techniques.

For Schwedelson, the leap from direct mail to Web marketing wasn't too hard, since both media are interactive—that is, they encourage two-way communication between the marketer and the customer. However, instead of the marketer controlling the communication, now it's the customer who controls it. "Because the Internet is interactive, consumers are now telling the marketers what they want, rather than simply viewing what the marketers want them to see," says Schwedelson. This customer control presents a special challenge to marketers who want to build relationships with new customers.

That's why clients such as First Union Bank, Publishers' Clearing House, and Omaha Steaks have come to WebConnect for help in attracting Net surfers to their Web sites. WebConnect arranges banners to bring its clients' sites to the attention of someone browsing in another, related area of cyberspace. Banners are like miniature billboards that appear on someone else's Web site, paid advertisements for a particular brand or company. Click on the banner, and the advertiser's home page comes up.

WebConnect starts by selecting Web sites that attract a client's targeted segment. Once the banner is up and running, WebConnect analyzes the number of visitors that land on the site where a client's banner appears and the number of clicks on the banner, then compares these figures with the number of visitors to the client's Web site. The goal is to continuously improve the banner to increase traffic at the Web site.

"If a banner is not doing well, the [client] can change it so it will draw a higher response," Schwedelson notes. "In other words, if you have 2,000 people visiting your site and you're only getting five clicks on your banner, something is wrong with the banner, not the site." More clicks means more opportunities to start an exchange relationship—and keep it going.[2]

Strategies and applications

1. Visit Worldata's Web site. How does the company provide information to help various members of the organizational buying center make a decision?

2. Visit the Web site of NetCreations, a Web design and promotion agency (http://www.netcreations.com). Examine The PostMaster, a service to help clients announce their sites to the media and get listed on popular Web sites. Why would businesses choose this service in addition to WebConnect's banner placement services?

3. How might the choice of sites for banners reflect the way a customer perceives the client and its products? What role can banners play in positioning a Web marketer?

4. What kind of marketing research do you think WebConnect should conduct before launching a new division to design and manage Web sites for small businesses? Explain what the research needs to uncover and how WebConnect might conduct this research.

5. What ethical issues are involved in researching not only how many hits a site receives but also which pages within the site are being visited and for how long? How can WebConnect avoid acting unethically when it measures site visits?

6. If you were designing a banner for WebConnect and could include six words plus the brand name, what would you say? How does your suggested message relate to the target market?

Team project

Team up with other students to explore the Web and identify three additional sites where Worldata might buy a banner to advertise WebConnect. Prepare a report or a class presentation explaining the kinds of visitors that would be attracted to each site and how those visitors fit with WebConnect's target market.

internetempowerment

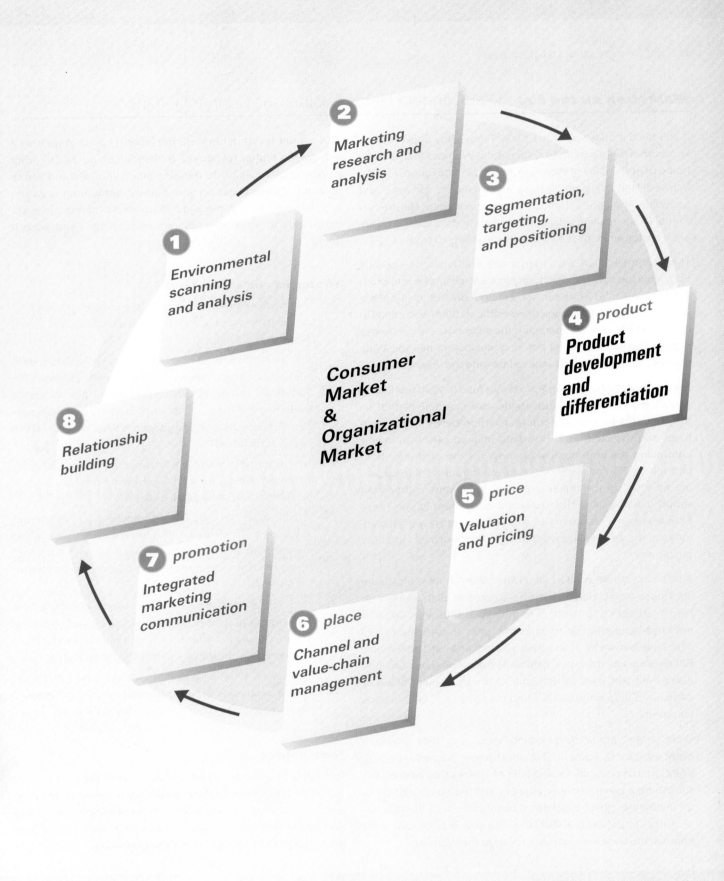

2 Marketing research and analysis

3 Segmentation, targeting, and positioning

1 Environmental scanning and analysis

4 product
Product development and differentiation

Consumer Market & Organizational Market

8 Relationship building

5 price
Valuation and pricing

7 promotion
Integrated marketing communication

6 place
Channel and value-chain management

4

Product Development and Services Marketing

Part 4 focuses on the development, management, and differentiation of goods and services. Chapter 9 looks at the many elements that make up the unique value package of a good or service. The chapter opening profile shows how the founders of Nantucket Nectars put together a service-oriented value package to compete with Snapple beverages. Chapter 10 examines how marketers develop and manage their product mixes. Learn how Individual Inc., the subject of this chapter's profile, became successful by developing customized information services for business customers. Chapter 11 presents a detailed look at services marketing, covering service quality, customer satisfaction, and the marketing of nonprofit services. The profile of Collegiate Health Care describes how the business was built around the concept of delivering quality health care to college students.

9 Products, Value, and Product Differentiation

Learning Goals

After you have read and studied this chapter, you should be able to:

1. Analyze the types of consumer and organizational products that marketers use to build customer relationships.

2. Show how basic, expected, augmented, and potential products relate to customer needs and satisfaction.

3. Demonstrate how the seven elements in the product value package contribute to stronger customer relationships.

4. Explain how the customer's view of quality affects the product value package.

5. Apply the strategies of brand extension, line extension, family brands, individual brands, and brand licensing.

6. Show the importance of brand loyalty and brand equity.

7. Explain how marketers link product differentiation with positioning to compete more effectively.

PROFILE

Quenching Nantucket Nectars' thirst for success

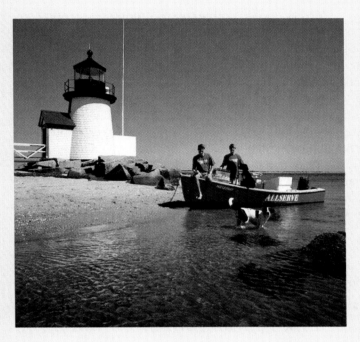

Tom First and Tom Scott wouldn't listen when friends and family warned them against competing with Snapple, Apple & Eve, and other large marketers of fruit beverages. The two started Nantucket Nectars with little more than a splash of entrepreneurial spirit and a recipe for a tangy peach drink. In just four years, they parlayed that first product into a $10-million-a-year business spanning 16 states.

The young entrepreneurs met at Brown University. After graduation, they opened a small supermarket on Nantucket as they searched for a new business idea. Opportunity knocked the night friends tasted First's version of a peach-flavored drink from Spain. Listening to the raves, the two men decided to form Nantucket Nectars.

Initially, they tested their product on a small scale. They bought bottles and caps, created a label, and mixed a batch of juice that they sold in local stores. After the first batch quickly sold out, First and Scott hired a bottling plant to produce another 1,700 cases, which again sold out.

First and Scott knew they needed more than a tasty recipe and quality ingredients to compete with big rivals. They redesigned their labels and bottles, concocted additional recipes, and began visiting stores, promising fast, convenient delivery. "The stores liked our approach, appreciating the fact that we not only delivered a good product but guaranteed personal service," says First.

Thanks to superior customer service and continually upgraded products, Nantucket Nectars has been able to expand north to Maine, south to North Carolina, and west to selected markets. First and Scott hope to overtake Snapple someday.[1]

The founders of Nantucket Nectars succeeded because they realized that a product is more than the sum of its ingredients. This chapter is the first of three about product development and differentiation, one of the universal marketing processes. You'll see how products provide value that builds customer relationships. Then you'll explore how marketers manage the product value package and how they compete through product differentiation. With this foundation, you'll learn in Chapter 10 how products are developed and managed, and you'll examine services as products in Chapter 11.

Building Relationships Through Product Value

Nothing is more basic to the marketing exchange than a product. But what exactly is a product? A *product* is a good, a service, or an idea that a customer acquires through a marketing exchange to satisfy a need or want.

In the case of Nantucket Nectars, the product is a fruit-flavored drink to satisfy a customer's thirst. Similarly, Jiffy-Lube's product is a quick oil change, a service that satisfies the customer's need for speedy auto maintenance. Boston Consulting Group's product consists of recommendations for improving organizations, ideas that satisfy a business customer's need for better organizational performance. These are just three examples of the products that marketers offer for exchange with consumer and organizational customers; the variety is endless.

Of course, customers of Nantucket Nectars, Jiffy-Lube, and Boston Consulting Group are buying more than a bottle of juice, an oil change, or a report about the organization. What they're really buying is a value package ◄──┛ **(p. 11)** of tangible and intangible elements that in combination offer benefits to satisfy their wants and needs. For example, Nantucket Nectars' customers buy a value package of juice, bottle, label, quality, competitive price, brand, and service.

Savvy marketers emphasize the *benefits* of their value packages, not the *features*. **Benefits** are the satisfaction or need-fulfillment gains that customers receive from products. In contrast, **features** are characteristics or attributes of products. Green laundry detergent crystals are features; clean clothes are the benefit. What customers buy is clean clothes, not green detergent. Distinguishing between benefits and features helps marketers see their products from the customers' perspective. No matter how many fancy features a marketer may put into a product, its actual benefits are determined by the customers whose needs it satisfies.

Of course, the benefits that customers value today may not be what they will want or need tomorrow. Because wants can change at any moment, marketers can't remain competitive and build long-term customer relationships if they think only one marketing transaction ahead. Good marketers use marketing research ◄──┛ **(p. 134)** on an ongoing basis to keep up with customer needs, identify benefits to be delivered by new or improved products, and assess customer satisfaction with products. With the right value package, marketers can provide need-satisfaction benefits to start profitable new customer relationships and profitably strengthen relationships with current customers.

benefits

the satisfaction or need-fulfillment gains that customers receive from products

features

characteristics or attributes of products

goods

tangible products which can physically be touched

services

products that are intangible and offer financial, health, cosmetic, or other benefits that satisfy customer needs

Goods, Services, and Ideas as Products

Depending on customer needs, marketers may offer products in the form of goods, services, or ideas. **Goods** are tangible products, such as fax machines and soft drinks, which can physically be touched. *Durable goods* are products such as trucks, which are used over an extended period. In contrast, *nondurable goods* are products, such as pencils, that are used over a shorter period.

This distinction is important because customers approach the purchase of durable and nondurable goods (as well as services and ideas) in different ways, which affects marketing planning. Faced with the purchase of a

Even an engineer has trouble understanding how his Maytag washer keeps running.

Mr. Thomas Fisher of Newport News, Virginia is oaffled. As a professional engineer, he's studied lots of machines before. In fact, he's got a pretty good sense how everything from a car to a computer operates. But he can't quite figure out how his Maytag washer keeps working. His family of five has had their machine for ten years now. In all those years of constant use, it's only needed a couple of minor repairs. And that's only half the story, because originally the Fishers got their washer from neighbors. And their family of five had used it for years before the Fishers even did a load. We can't promise every Maytag washer will last this long, but we build them all to last longer than any other brand. So take it from an expert like Mr. Fisher. He'll be the first to tell you a Maytag washer will keep running for years and years. Just don't ask him to explain it.

© 1994 Maytag Co.

MAYTAG
THE DEPENDABILITY PEOPLE™

When buying a durable good like a washing machine, customers often spend a good deal of time evaluating the benefits of the purchase. Two of the more important benefits are durability and reliability, and as this ad illustrates, few appliance manufacturers have had Maytag's success in building a reputation around these two attributes. What other appeals or features might Maytag use to attract more buyers?

durable product such as a computer or a furnace, consumers and organizations normally move more slowly and deliberately through the buying process. They spend time gathering information and evaluating their alternatives, and they may also feel postpurchase dissonance ◄──┘ **(p. 170)**. Knowing this, most marketers provide a great deal of information about a durable product's long-term benefits, design the product to overcome usage problems that may arise, and offer service before and after the purchase.

For example, IBM positioned its AS/400 minicomputers for businesses as easy to use and powerful. The computer was shipped ready to be plugged in and used, eliminating problems of installing software and getting printers to work, which customers had suffered through (and hated) with earlier models. Also, IBM salespeople were trained to help buyers determine their data-processing needs so they could select the appropriate AS/400 configuration. To head off postpurchase doubts, IBM contacted every customer 90 days later, thanking each one, checking on any problems, and asking for ideas about improving the product. As a result, IBM sold 25,000 AS/400 units within 4 months, the most successful new computer launch in the company's history.[3]

In contrast, customers who buy inexpensive, nondurable products such as Nantucket Nectars juice don't worry as much about the consequences of the purchase. After all, if they don't like the juice, they haven't lost much time or money. They can easily try another flavor or switch to a different brand, which poses a challenge to marketers seeking to build customer loyalty.

Services are products such as car repairs and tax preparation that are intangible and offer financial, health, cosmetic, or other benefits that satisfy customer needs. Also intangible are *ideas*, such as "stay in school" or "practice random acts of kindness," which provide intellectual, emotional, or spiritual benefits. Success in marketing intangible products depends on the ability to prove to customers that the service or idea offers real benefits. You will learn more about marketing services in Chapter 11.

Some products fall between pure goods and pure services. For example, businesses such as The Olive Garden restaurants and Jiffy-Lube represent combinations. They offer tangible items (food, oil) along with intangible services (table service; oil change and lubrication services). Selling such products means marketing the benefits of the goods as well as the benefits of the services.

Issues for critical thinking

Which products do you think are harder to market: goods or services? Why? What are some ways that marketers can show customers the benefits of services before purchase or use?

Products to Satisfy Consumer Needs

The distinction between goods, services, and ideas is only one of several to be considered when marketing a product. As you saw in Chapters 6 and 7, consumers and organizations make their purchasing decisions in different ways, and the resulting distinctions affect the way consumer and organizational products are marketed. Products that satisfy consumer needs, which can be classified into the four categories shown in Table 9.1, reflect differences in the way customers approach the purchase of convenience products, shopping products, specialty products, and unsought products.

T A B L E **9.1** **Classifying Consumer Products**

	Convenience Products	Shopping Products	Specialty Products	Unsought Products
Consumer Behavior				
Time and effort invested in buying	Very little	Considerable	A great deal	Varies; often relatively little
Purchase frequency	Frequent	Less frequent	Least frequent	Less frequent
Perceived risk	Low	Higher	Highest	Varies; more than convenience products
Marketing Process Considerations				
Price	Low	Fairly high	Varies; value to customer is the key	Varies; more costly than convenience products
Channel management	Widely available in many outlets	Few outlets	Few outlets, often one in a market	Sometimes limited number of outlets
Integrated marketing communication	Widely advertised; price and brand often stressed	Personal selling important; store name important	Personal selling important; both store and brand important	Point-of-purchase advertising important; advertise to build awareness

convenience products

fairly inexpensive goods and services that consumers buy frequently, quickly, and with a minimum amount of effort

shopping products

goods and services that are relatively costly and bought infrequently, and consumers usually take time and effort to compare alternatives

specialty products

goods and services that consumers value and see as unique, so they are willing to expend considerable time and effort when purchasing them

Convenience products are fairly inexpensive goods and services such as eggs and dry cleaning that consumers buy frequently, quickly, and with a minimum amount of effort. Consumers usually don't perceive much risk in purchasing convenience products, which is why they don't spend much time seeking out and evaluating alternatives. Marketers of convenience products therefore arrange marketing channels that will put their products in front of as many potential customers as possible.

On the other hand, **shopping products** such as videocassette recorders and language training are more costly and bought less frequently, so consumers usually take more time and effort to compare alternatives. Consumers perceive more risk in buying these products, so they gather as much information as possible about price, quality, and performance before making a decision. Marketers of shopping goods often use advertising to stress product benefits and value.

Specialty products are goods such as parachutes and services such as child care that consumers value and see as unique, so they are willing to ex-

Bentley.
You don't park it, you position it.

Beneath the stunning lines of the Bentley Azure is the sophisticated technology of a 150 mph supercar. Its turbocharged, intercooled 6.75 liter V-8 engine can launch it from standstill to 60 mph in 6.3 seconds.

Inside, this Bentley is as sensuous as it is sporting. A sumptuous leather cockpit, enhanced by hand-polished burr walnut veneer, will accommodate four occupants in traditional Bentley style.

For lease or purchase information and nearest dealer, call (800) 237-6557.

The Reward of a Lifetime.

©Rolls-Royce Motor Cars Inc., 1995. The name "Bentley" and the badge and radiator grille are registered trademarks.

A Bentley is a specialty product; interested consumers will spend considerable time making their purchase decision and will pay a high price for the status and quality the car represents. Ads such as this contribute to the car's exclusive image. Note the adjectives used in the ad: sophisticated, hand-polished, sumptuous, sensuous. How do such words reinforce the car's image?

unsought products

goods and services that consumers are unaware of, haven't necessarily thought of buying, or find that they need to solve an unexpected problem

raw materials

basic, natural materials and agricultural goods that become part of manufactured products

components

parts supplied by other marketers that are incorporated into finished products

pend considerable time and effort when purchasing them. Because of their uniqueness, specialty products aren't easily compared with other alternatives, which complicates buying and increases the risk that customers perceive to be associated with the process. Marketers of specialty products often use branding and seek word-of-mouth endorsements to emphasize product value and uniqueness.

Unsought products are goods and services that consumers are unaware of, haven't necessarily thought of buying, or find that they need to solve an unexpected problem. Examples of unsought products are emergency car-towing services, burial services, and the services provided by charitable organizations that solicit donations. Products such as food processors and smoke detectors were unsought when they were new on the market; once consumers became aware of their benefits, however, sales took off. That's why many marketers use point-of-purchase displays and demonstrators to bring unsought products to the attention of consumers.[4]

Individual consumer differences can come into play with any of these product categories. What is a specialty product to one consumer may be a shopping product to a second consumer or an unsought product to a third. Thus car-towing service, an unsought product to many consumers, is a shopping product to members of the American Automobile Association and other auto clubs.

Products to Satisfy Organizational Needs

Just as consumer products can be classified according to customer need satisfaction, buying behavior, and perceptions, organizational products can be similarly classified. Organizational products fall into six classifications, shown in Table 9.2: raw materials, components, installations, accessory equipment, supplies, and business services.

Raw materials are basic, natural materials such as iron ore and agricultural goods such as wheat that become part of manufactured products. For example, lumber is the raw material that James River, a large U.S. papermaker, uses for its Brawny paper towels and Dixie drinking cups.[5] Organizations often buy raw materials in massive quantities. Think of the amount of lumber James River uses to make miles of paper toweling and millions of drinking cups.

In addition, many organizations buy **components**, parts supplied by other marketers that are incorporated into finished products. Compaq buys computer chips, display screens, and other components to be installed in its personal computers. Chrysler buys rearview mirrors, tires, and other components to be installed in its cars, trucks, and minivans. Organizational buyers look carefully at price, delivery, quantity, reliability, and quality when buying raw materials and components.

TABLE **9.2**   **Classifying Organizational Products**

	Raw Materials	Components	Installations	Accessory Equipment	Supplies	Business Services
Organizational Behavior						
Quantities purchased	Large	Large	Very small	Small	Small	Small
Purchase frequency	Infrequent; but frequent delivery	Infrequent; but frequent delivery	Very infrequent	Medium frequency	Frequent	Varies
Brand preference	Not very important	Somewhat important	Very important	Very important	Relatively unimportant	Somewhat important
Marketing Process Considerations						
Price	Low to high unit prices	Relatively high	Highest	Varies	Relatively low	Varies
Channel management	Direct to buyers	Direct to volume buyers, but through dealers or wholesalers to small buyers	Direct to buyers	Dealers used in most cases	Dealers used often	Dealers used in some cases
Integrated marketing communication	Little promotion; often stress price, delivery	Some promotion; often stress price, quality	Personal selling most important; often stress customization	Personal selling and promotion; often stress price, quality	Some promotion, some personal selling; often stress quality, price	Some promotion, some personal selling; often stress technical expertise, price

installations

large, expensive, long-lasting capital purchases such as buildings

accessory equipment

relatively small and inexpensive items, shorter-lived than components

supplies

items that are used up in the course of business but don't become part of the finished product

business services

specialized, intangible products that keep operations running smoothly

To shape raw materials and components into finished products, manufacturers need **installations**, large, expensive, long-lasting capital purchases such as buildings. Personal selling is an important part of the marketing process for selling installations. Buyers generally gather detailed information about alternatives, request competitive bids, and carefully weigh their options before buying. Smaller, less expensive, and shorter-lived pieces of equipment, such as portable tools, are known as **accessory equipment**. Buyers often obtain such products from industrial suppliers or wholesalers.

Every organization needs **supplies**, also known as *maintenance, repair, and operating items (MRO items)*, which are used up in the course of business but don't become part of the finished product. Supplies are relatively inexpensive items such as pens, copier supplies, and cleaning products. Once the organizational buyer has identified a reliable product and source of supply, reordering items usually becomes a matter of routine. Thus, only by offering a superior value package can other suppliers start a relationship with such users.

In addition, organizations use many **business services**, specialized, intangible products such as accounting, legal, and financial services that keep their operations running smoothly. Buyers check prices, but they also pay close attention to the service quality and technical expertise of sellers. For example, Cable & Wireless in Virginia provides long-distance telephone services to small U.S. businesses. Company salespeople call on businesses, research their telecommunications requirements, and put together a value package to exactly fit each customer's needs. As a result, the company is growing at a rate of 20 percent every year.[6]

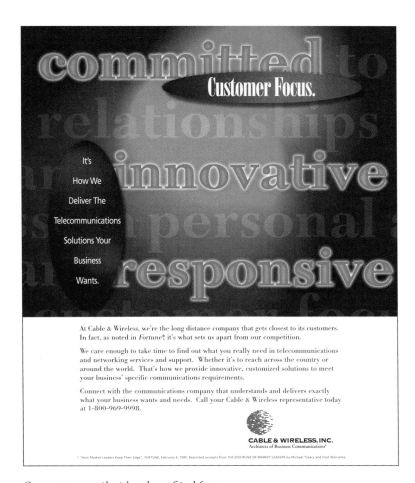

At Cable & Wireless, we're the long distance company that gets closest to its customers. In fact, as noted in *Fortune*, it's what sets us apart from our competition.

We care enough to take time to find out what you really need in telecommunications and networking services and support. Whether it's to reach across the country or around the world. That's how we provide innovative, customized solutions to meet your business' specific communications requirements.

Connect with the communications company that understands and delivers exactly what your business wants and needs. Call your Cable & Wireless representative today at 1-800-969-9998.

CABLE & WIRELESS, INC.
Architects of Business Communications®

One company that has benefited from a consistent customer orientation is Cable & Wireless. It has a reputation for listening carefully to its small-business customers and then customizing communication systems to meet specific customer needs. Thus, Cable & Wireless applies mass customization to differentiate its services. Note how "customer focus" stands out in this ad. Would Cable & Wireless be able to compete with larger rivals without catering to its customers? Why?

internal products

reports and advice delivered to internal customers (employees) in organizations

Not included in the traditional classification of organizational products are **internal products**, such as reports and advice, that are delivered to internal customers (employees) in organizations. This is a separate category of product because it isn't purchased by an external customer, although it does have to be marketed to internal customers. As you saw in Chapter 1, the needs of internal customers **(p. 13)** must be satisfied if these individuals are to meet the needs of external customers. For example, Telecommunications Europe, which does telephone installations, found that focusing on internal products helped the company translate external customer requirements into internal priorities that employees could act on. Improving internal products, such as customer and market information, boosted employees' ability to satisfy the company's external customers.[7]

Product Profitability and Customer Satisfaction

Although every successful marketer wants to create a product that satisfies customers, this isn't the only goal. In striving for the best value package, with top quality and service that pleases customers, marketers can't lose sight of another fundamental goal of business—to make a profit. The point of marketing products is to provide *mutually beneficial* exchange relationships. Stakeholders such as stockholders, employees, and managers expect to benefit (profit) from the exchange, as do customers and all the partners in the value chain. Therefore, marketers have to weigh the financial investment in products against the profits to be gained from selling them.[8]

For example, when Du Pont was developing its StainMaster carpet fiber, it had a cross-functional team from marketing, research and development, and finance investigate how the product would benefit everyone in the value chain. The team consulted with retailers as well as carpet mill operators before launching the product, a stain-resistant fiber that revived carpet sales industry-wide and earned Du Pont $2 billion in revenues. Everybody benefited from the StainMaster product: Du Pont, its value-chain partners, stockholders, ultimate consumers, and organizational customers.[9]

Other marketers can emulate Du Pont's approach by creating a value package that benefits their organizations as well as their customers, value-chain partners, and other stakeholders. Nonetheless, it's important to remember that the value package to which customers respond best may be the least profitable, because complete customer satisfaction is a costly proposition.[10] That's why balancing the offer of a customer-satisfying value package with an appropriate level of profitability can be tricky but it is essential to a marketer's financial health.

Before you go on . . .

A. How do features differ from benefits?

B. How are consumer and organizational goods classified?

C. Why do marketers have to consider profitability as well as customer satisfaction when developing a value package?

Managing the Product Value Package

Research into customer wants and needs is just the start of product development. Next comes the process of managing the value package to profitably satisfy customer needs. At the heart of any value package is the *basic product* (also called the generic product), the fundamental element that makes the product what it is, shown in Figure 9.1. The basic product of a steel mill is steel. The basic product of a real-estate broker is land or homes for sale. Without the fundamental element, the marketer has nothing to sell.[11]

In reality, however, customers usually demand more than basic products. *Expected products* are value packages that meet *minimum* expectations. The expected product of a steel mill is delivery of a certain grade of steel at a specific price with specific payment terms. The expected product that a marketer offers will help it compete more effectively and start or reinforce customer relationships.

Beyond the expected product is the *augmented product*, a value package that *exceeds* customer expectations. The augmented product provides additional benefits that research shows customers value, such as installation and training. For a steel mill, the augmented product might include longer payment terms or steel having a higher strength grade. When marketers start matching rivals' augmented products, however, customers come to expect the enhancements. In 1984, driver and passenger air bags for cars were part of the augmented product. By 1993, so many cars had them—and so many customers responded—that dual air bags became part of the expected product. "It's become the price of entry," says Thomas G. Elliott, Honda's executive vice president of U.S. sales.[12]

The *potential product* represents *all* the possible enhancements a marketer can add to its value package to satisfy targeted customer segments. The potential product of a steel mill might include continuously improved quality at no increase in price, or specialized steel products tailored to individual customer requirements.

Building a long-term relationship with customers means moving beyond offering basic and expected products to creating distinctive value packages that exceed customer expectations. Key elements of value packages include quality, features, branding, packaging and labeling, safety, customer service, and warranties and guarantees, as shown in Figure 9.2. Combined with a fair price, product information, and availability through convenient marketing channels, the right value package can delight customers while returning increased profits to the marketer.

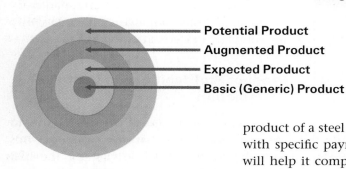

Potential Product
Augmented Product
Expected Product
Basic (Generic) Product

F I G U R E **9.1**

Expanding Beyond the Basic Product

At the heart of every value package is the basic product, the fundamental element that makes a product what it is. The expected product meets customer expectations, while the augmented product exceeds customer expectations. In the course of developing the value package, marketers look at the potential product, all the elements that can be used to enhance the product in the course of building and maintaining customer relationships.

quality

the degree to which the product meets customer needs, wants, and expectations

FIGURE **9.2** Elements in a Product Value Package

By varying the basic building blocks of the value package, marketers can deliver benefits that customers want and need. In combination with appropriate pricing, product information, and availability through marketing channels, this product value package forms the cornerstone of a profitable customer relationship.

Total Quality Enhances Product Value

From the customer's perspective, one of the most important elements in any value package is **quality**, the degree to which the product meets customer needs, wants, and expectations. Through marketing research and customer feedback, marketers can determine how customers view quality, then use that information to enhance the value of their products. Remember, every time customers buy or use a product, they're judging the value package on one or more of the dimensions of quality shown in Table 9.3.

Good quality will satisfy consumers and organizational customers; superior quality will delight them. Poor quality, which will drive buyers to competitive products, also hurts profitability by driving up costs associated with reworking defective products and handling complaints. Consider the experience of Samsung Electronics, the South Korean manufacturer of appliances and other durable goods. Rushing to export to growing markets, Samsung had concentrated on boosting production, and quality suffered. As a result, 6,000 employees were needed to fix 20,000 defective products every year. Now Samsung has changed, stressing quality to reduce costs and strengthen relationships with customers, employees, suppliers, and retailers.[13]

TABLE **9.3** Eight Dimensions of Product Quality

Dimension	Description	Example
Performance	The product's primary operating characteristics	Ability of contact lenses to correct vision comfortably
Features	Supplements to the basic operating characteristics	Side air bags in vehicles to supplement driver and passenger air bags
Reliability	Probability that the product will not break down for a specified period	Car manufacturer's five-year/60,000-mile warranty
Conformance	The degree to which a product's design and operation meet established standards	Test results showing that a biodegradable product breaks down within the specified period
Durability	Measure of length of a product's life	Number of hours a candle will burn
Serviceability	Speed and ease of repair and servicing	Ability to quickly and conveniently replace an empty toner cartridge in a laser printer
Aesthetics	The look, feel, taste, and smell of a product	The taste, color, and texture of a tortilla chip
Perceived quality	How the customer views the quality of a product	Assessment of service quality at local bank based on accuracy and speed of transactions, employee responsiveness, other factors

To be sure that quality is built into all parts of the value package, many marketers have adopted *total quality management (TQM)* ◀—┛ **(p. 48)**, a management approach that puts quality at the heart of every organizational operation, delivering quality to both internal and external customers. By integrating quality into the organization's operations, marketers can help the firm design, manufacture, market, and deliver products correctly the first time. Through benchmarking ◀—┛ **(p. 15)**, continuous improvement, and other TQM methods, employees can improve organizational processes, with the goal of having products measure up to customers' quality standards.

Building a reputation for product quality is critical for marketers that want to sustain long-term customer relationships. According to Jim Alleborn, who has researched product quality, customer perceptions of quality translate directly into sales and profits. "We learned [from a recent research survey] that consumers' perception of quality is all-important in the brands they choose," he says. "Brands that recognize that and communicate that quality image to consumers will do well in the marketplace."[14]

Alleborn's advice holds for organizational products as well. Business buyers are particularly concerned about the quality of the product, service and support, and delivery. To gain public recognition for quality, some marketers apply for quality awards such as the Deming Prize, awarded by Japan, or the U.S. National Quality Award, the Malcolm Baldrige Award. Even if they don't win an award, these marketers are able to boost customer satisfaction, secure added market share, enhance financial performance, and improve employee relations by striving for higher quality.[15]

Building a reputation for product quality is very important for firms hoping to become world-class competitors. The Malcolm Baldrige Award, which recognizes superior quality, can greatly enhance a company's reputation. Wainwright Industries, which recently received the award, can capitalize on the distinction the award conveys. Here, company CEO A. Don Wainwright and President W. Nelson Wainwright II are honored by Vice President Al Gore and late Secretary of Commerce Ron Brown for their quality achievements.

To compete in the global marketplace, a marketer must meet or exceed quality levels established on the international level by ISO 9000 and ISO 14000 ◀—┛ **(p. 95)** and comply with quality standards set by individual countries. Many organizational buyers won't even consider products that don't meet such quality standards. However, constantly improving products can be costly and counterproductive. Marketers have to keep profitability in mind when applying the ideals of total quality to the pursuit of customer satisfaction. That's why Nations-Bank, for example, calculates how much additional revenue a quality improvement could be expected to bring in before moving ahead.[16]

Features Deliver Customer Benefits

A value package has to include features that deliver the benefits that customers want and need, as determined by marketing research. In services, features define what the service provider will do to give the customer desired benefits. For example, a photo finisher promoting its use of Kodak paper and its one-hour developing service is citing features linked to the benefits of quality prints and speedy results. Similarly, marketers of goods need to show

New high-tech products are being introduced at an unprecedented pace and they're not always easy to master. Consequently, marketers must find ways to make it easier for the customer to enjoy the benefits the product is supposed to provide. These Resource Kits from Microsoft are just one example of how marketers seek to be problem solvers for consumers, while enhancing the value of their products at the same time. What else can Microsoft do to help customers master new software?

customers how features provide the desired benefits. So when Vaseline Intensive Care products tout the use of alpha-hydroxy acids and nongreasy formulas, they link those features to the benefits of younger-looking skin and nonstaining creams.

In planning product features, marketers look at five areas:

- *Utility*. Do the features function as they should? Are they safe and easy to use?

- *Appearance*. Is the product pleasing and practical in its physical form and in its features?

- *Maintenance*. Can the product and its features be easily maintained and repaired?

- *Cost*. Does the product include only the features that satisfy real customer wants? Are the materials and components appropriate to the features and utility? Can the product's features and form be achieved in a cost-effective manufacturing process?

- *Communication*. Do the product's features and form visually communicate the marketer's approach and position in the target market? Do they help to differentiate the product from competing products?[17]

For high-tech products, research and development efforts are the key to offering new features that deliver benefits customers can't get elsewhere or don't yet know they want. Consider the marketing battle between Microsoft and Netscape, two software marketers that want to gain market share by developing the most user-friendly technological advances in Internet communication and browsing. As the two rivals vie to produce better Internet software and grab more market share, customers will gain the benefit of being able to use the Internet more efficiently and effectively than ever before.[18] Another example is the German company Rational, which makes computer-controlled ovens that can effectively cook a wide variety of foods. The inspiration for this product came from discussions company owner Siegfried Meister had with restaurateurs and chefs who wanted a single cooking unit for baking, steaming, and roasting. After more than 10 years of development, Meister produced an oven that uses steam as well as forced hot air to cook meats, vegetables, and desserts. These unique features made Rational's ovens a hit all over the world.[19]

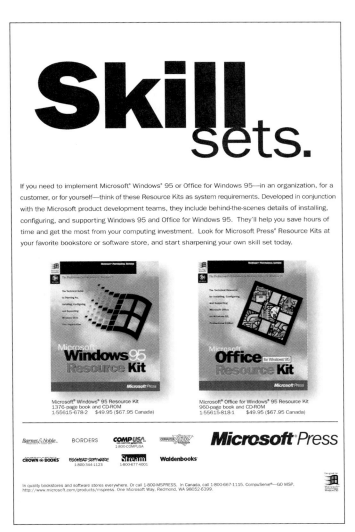

Branding Reinforces Marketing Relationships

As a marketer, how can you reinforce marketing relationships by identifying your value package as separate and distinct from competing products? The answer is to use a **brand**, a name, phrase, design, symbol, or a combination that identifies your products and differentiates them from rival products.

To customers, brands are a kind of shorthand representing the unique combination of features and benefits offered by each branded product. Customers nowadays make so many purchases on the Internet and through telephone and mail orders that branding is essential as a way of distinguishing a marketer's products. Both products and companies can be branded for identification and differentiation, as shown in Table 9.4.

TABLE 9.4 Branding Products and Companies

Element of Branding	Description	Example
Brand name	Verbal part of a brand, including words, letters, or numbers	Barbie, Lexus, WD-40
Brand mark	Graphical part of a brand	The "swoosh" symbol on Nike products; the red roof graphic above the Pizza Hut brand name
Trademark	Any brand or part of a brand legally registered by a marketer for its exclusive use	Lexan, registered by General Electric for its superstrong resin product
Service mark	A service brand legally registered by a marketer for its exclusive use	CompaqCare, registered by Compaq for its service and support programs
Trade name	Business name that a marketer legally registers with the government	Nordstrom, Mattel

Brand Types

Both manufacturers and channel partners can use brands to distinguish their value packages from those of competitors and to strengthen customer relationships. A **manufacturer brand**, which is owned by the product's maker, is also known as a *national brand* because it is frequently advertised throughout the country. For example, Hewlett-Packard puts the HP LaserJet brand on certain laser printers, and ConAgra puts the Healthy Choice brand on certain frozen and prepared foods.

When two or more marketers collaborate on a product, they may apply *cobranding*, using more than one manufacturer's brand to identify a jointly developed product. This convention alerts customers to the added value they're getting from a product with two trusted brand names. For example, United Airlines and Visa offer a cobranded credit card that rewards loyalty by giving users one frequent-flier mile for every dollar charged. These mileage awards allow customers to accumulate points that will enable them to travel free.[20]

A **private brand** is one that is owned by a wholesaler or retailer. Also called a *private-label* or *store brand*, this type of identification is used to strengthen relationships with customers. From the customer's perspective, private brands are a lower-priced alternative to manufacturer brands, which accounts for their popularity. Private-brand products are usually made by companies other than the retailer or wholesaler.

Supermarkets, for example, pay manufacturers to make private-brand food and household products. A&P, which introduced private-brand groceries to the industry, offers products under a basic private brand, America's Choice, as well a premium private brand, Master's Choice. Private-brand groceries account for $30 billion in annual sales in the United States, challenging sales of manufacturer brands, as you can see in Figure 9.3.[21]

manufacturer brand
a national brand frequently advertised throughout the country

private brand
one that is owned by a wholesaler or retailer

generic brand
identifies a product by the category alone

What products, if any, have you purchased with no brand name on them? What was your experience with those products? Do some generic goods seem just as good as their brand-name counterparts? How are generic brands typically marketed to consumers? Is this marketing effective? Why or why not?

F I G U R E **9.3** Growth in Private-Brand Food Sales

Channel partners such as wholesalers and retailers are increasingly offering private-brand food products to build relationships with their customers. Such private-brand products compete with manufacturer-brand food products.

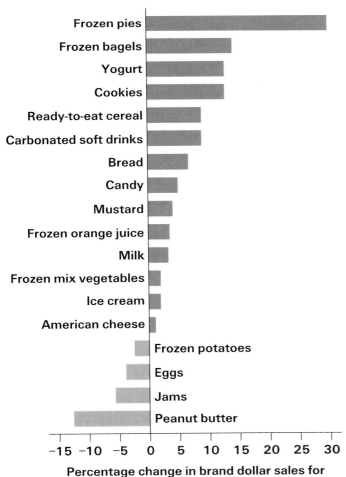

Percentage change in brand dollar sales for selected private-brand foods, 1992–1993

A **generic brand** carries no brand name. It is identified by the product category alone. Generic brands usually receive no promotional support from marketers or retailers, so they are cheaper than other brands. Drugs marketed in this way, for example, are available as lower-priced substitutes for many pharmaceutical products. For obvious reasons, the practice of generic branding appeals to price-conscious shoppers.

Effective Branding

To help customers keep a product in mind and tell it apart from others, a brand should be simple, memorable, and distinctive. Brand names such as Ivory and Xerox are easy to say and easy to remember. An effective brand name should also remind customers of the product's key features and benefits. For example, think of Ruffles, the brand name for Frito-Lay's potato chips that have ridges to hold snack dip, or Diet Coke, the brand name for Coca-Cola's low-calorie soft drink. If a brand will be available in other areas or cultures, be sure it is appropriate and translates well. Check also for any legal or regulatory restrictions that might prevent the brand from being used.

Julie Lobdell, cofounder of a California chain of cinnamon roll shops, tells how she and her partner planned the brand name. "We knew 'Bodacious Buns' would be well received in Southern California, but we wanted to make sure it would not be too provocative or misunderstood in other parts of the country," she says. The partners hired a lawyer to review use of the brand in other states. They also legally registered the trademark.[22]

What many marketers fear is having their brand names become generic. A *generic name* identifies an entire product category. Did you know that *aspirin, linoleum, nylon, escalator,* and *zipper* were once brand names? When the brands became identified with all versions of the products, they lost their distinctiveness and became generic. The trademark owners could no longer enforce their exclusivity. The manufacturers then had to come up with new brand names. The original Aspirin, for example, became Bayer aspirin. It's easy to see why Rollerblade's lawyers want people to say "in-line skating" rather than using the brand name as the generic term for this activity.[23] Protecting brands in other countries can be problematic, as the following section shows.

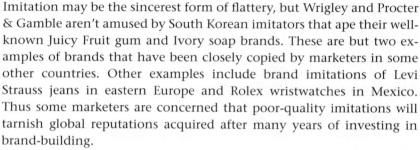

GLOBAL ISSUES

Battling international brand copycats

Imitation may be the sincerest form of flattery, but Wrigley and Procter & Gamble aren't amused by South Korean imitators that ape their well-known Juicy Fruit gum and Ivory soap brands. These are but two examples of brands that have been closely copied by marketers in some other countries. Other examples include brand imitations of Levi Strauss jeans in eastern Europe and Rolex wristwatches in Mexico. Thus some marketers are concerned that poor-quality imitations will tarnish global reputations acquired after many years of investing in brand-building.

Marketers of nearly every type of product can tell stories of international brand rip-offs. Despite country-by-country laws that call for registration and protection of *intellectual property* such as brands and trademarks, product designs, and product ideas, marketers charge that some developing nations are lax in enforcing these legal rights. As a result, brand copycats can exploit the cachet of globally known brands by unfairly imitating their brands, logos, and packaging.

Fortunately, relief is on the way. More than 120 countries signed the 1994 update of the General Agreement on Tariffs and Trade, calling for more vigorous protection of intellectual property rights. Now marketers that legally register brands in other countries can expect more consistent enforcement. Some marketers are also moving on their own to root out copycatters. Levi Strauss and Ralph Lauren have hired investigators to find imitators so they can be prosecuted. Other marketers are offering rewards to people who find brand copies.[24]

What factors do you think influence a customer to buy an imitation product rather than the real brand? What are the implications for brand marketers?

A major issue in global trade during the 1990s has been the protection of intellectual property, including brand names, copyrights, and trademarks. The items in this photo are all fake copies of brand-name goods. Members of the international trade community are now working hard to protect the rights of copyright holders and producers. What more could producers do to discourage competitors in other countries from illegally or unfairly appropriating their brand names?

brand extension

applying an existing brand to a new product in another category

Brand Strategies

Marketers use a variety of brand strategies to compete more effectively with rivals. If a brand is well established, a marketer may leverage it through **brand extension**, applying an existing brand to a new product in another category. For example, the brand name Virgin, created by U.K. entrepreneur Richard Branson, has been extended from Virgin Atlantic Airways (airline) to Virgin Megastores (retailing) and Virgin Cola (soft drink).[25]

Brand extensions can give new products a head start. Marketing consultant Allen McCusker advises, "If you can put the right brand name with the right new category, it's a tremendously less expensive way to introduce a new product than starting from scratch with a new brand name." Because customers already know the brand, brand extensions can capture market share without sky-high advertising costs. However, customers may be confused by seeing the brand on different products—and they may shun the brand altogether if the new product doesn't live up to expectations.[26]

Brand extensions such as these products are one way to get instant recognition for a new product offering. Many consumers use Arm & Hammer's Baking Soda for deodorizing their refrigerators and sinks. The company is well-positioned, therefore, to introduce a cat litter deodorizer. Given that some brand extensions seem obvious to consumers once they're available, such as Reese's Peanut Butter, does it surprise you that they enter the market many years after the original brand is established?

Another brand strategy is *line extension*, which puts an existing brand on a related product in the same category. Appropriate brand extensions can reinforce customer perceptions of the brand, building the value of the brand.[27] For example, Procter & Gamble used line extension to stretch the Tide brand from powdered detergent to liquid detergent. The brand name Liquid Tide sets the newer product apart from the original and promises the quality and performance customers expect from Tide. Although line extensions allow marketers to address the needs of individual customer segments, they can also clutter store shelves and bewilder customers with many choices, each one only slightly different from the others, under a single brand umbrella.[28]

A *family brand* is one that is used on a variety of related products (a family). Hanes Hosiery has used a family brand strategy to put its Hanes brand on a wide range of products in related categories: legwear such as pantyhose and socks; legwear care products such as hosiery wash mixture; and leg care, such as foot and leg moisturizers. This puts the halo of a proven brand over a series of related products and lets the marketer build awareness for all by promoting a single brand. If one of the products falls down on quality or another part of the value package, however, the brand name may suffer, hurting sales.

In contrast, an *individual brand* is used on only one product in a family. This strategy makes sense for a new product geared to a separate customer segment or for an entirely new, unproven product. The idea is to give the product an opportunity to develop its own identity. For example, the Swiss watch marketer Asuag-SSIH aims individual brands at specific customer segments around the world. Rado, Longines, and Omega are targeted toward high-end watch buyers. Tissot, Hamilton, and Certina are targeted to medium-price buyers, and Swatch is targeted toward popular-price buyers.[29] Because of the high rate of new product failure, individual branding is also a way to protect the rest of the family if a product doesn't succeed.

You may decide that some other marketer's brand would be more appropriate for a product you're planning, or another marketer may ask for permission to put your brand on its products. Such strategies call for *brand licensing*, paying a fee to use another marketer's brand. For example, Time Warner's DC Comics owns the Batman trademark in more than 140 countries, and it licenses the brand to marketers of trading cards, cereal, and other products offered around the world.[30] Brand licensing can bring revenues to both parties, and it can help launch a brand in new markets. How-

Children, especially younger ones, are easily attracted to brand images promoted by some of their favorite movie, television, and sports stars. For example, this bicycle is more attractive because it carries the Batman image on its front. Time Warner, owner of the Batman character, allows other businesses to license the popular likeness or name for a fee. What are the risks of licensing a brand that already appears on a large number of products?

brand equity
the long-term value of a marketer's brand in the marketplace

ever, it can also bring headaches if the licensees make inferior products or misuse the brand, producing a negative effect on the way customers see a marketer's branded products.

Issues for critical thinking

Are marketers who license brands from others misleading customers? To avoid inconsistencies in quality or service, and to forestall other problems that customers might encounter with products from licensees, should brands be used only by their owners? Why or why not?

Brand Loyalty and Brand Equity

Once customers have come to recognize and appreciate certain benefits and satisfaction from a branded product, they often develop *brand loyalty*, a favorable attitude toward a brand that prompts consistent purchasing **(p. 184)**. Brand loyalty strengthens the relationship between marketer and customer. As customers come to know and trust a brand, they are less likely to risk trying unfamiliar brands. Over time, brand loyalty can contribute to brand equity.[31]

Brand equity is the long-term value of a marketer's brand in the marketplace. This is the value a brand develops as a business asset when customers see it as more than the sum of the elements in the package. With brand equity, customers (both ultimate consumers and businesses) come to associate a brand with specific benefits as well as a certain level of quality and need satisfaction. Customers' buying decisions are influenced by their perceptions of the brand as well as by the product itself. "What really matters is that people are buying a product because of your brand, not just because of the underlying product," explains marketing specialist Sharon Slade.[32]

The power to build customer loyalty as well as sales and profitability is what makes brand equity so valuable. Marketers estimate the business value of some major global brands at $1 billion or more. Because of perceived added value, customers are apt to react more positively to integrated marketing communication, brand extensions, and family branding. As a result, brand marketers can get more mileage out of new products and marketing communications. Wholesalers and retailers are also interested in handling top brands that customers want, which strengthens relationships throughout the value chain.[33]

Brand equity can be particularly critical in organizational marketing, where buyers compare brands during the supplier identification and evaluation stages of the purchasing process. The power of a brand not only can help a product be considered, it can also allow the marketer to charge a premium. For example, businesses surveyed about buying personal computers for the workplace said they would pay $260 more for Hewlett-Packard PCs and $230 more for Dell Computer PCs than for nonbranded PCs. Knowing the importance of brand equity in organizational marketing, Hewlett-Packard and other PC manufacturers are stressing brand building more than ever. They're increasing advertising to communicate brand value, quality, and service, and they're forging alliances with other strong brands for more competitive leverage.[34]

Packaging and Labeling Add Value

Packaging and labeling help marketers communicate with customers and provide protection, storage, and convenience as products move through the value chain. As a result, packaging and labeling add value that helps marketers differentiate their products and build brand equity among ultimate consumers and organizational buyers.[35] In addition, marketers now are keeping environmental concerns in mind when they design both packaging and labeling.

Packaging as Communication

As you learned in Chapter 6, roughly two-thirds of the purchases made in supermarkets are decided on when the shopper is in the store. That's why savvy marketers use packaging and labeling to attract shopper attention and communicate product benefits directly from the store shelf. Rice-A-Roni, for example, beat back competitive threats by redesigning its package and label to focus more on product quality and appetite appeal. When the repackaged product landed on supermarket shelves, brand sales jumped 20 percent over the previous year.[36]

Of course, labels on all products have to provide basic details such as weight, ingredients, and instructions. They also must carry any needed warnings about product safety and usage.[37] In many cases, the information on product labels must conform with government regulations. So international marketers like Sony (electronics) and Crabtree & Evelyn (foods) often print packages and labels in several languages. This gives their brands an international veneer while satisfying local regulations and providing shoppers with needed product facts.

Packaging can also help a marketer target new customer segments. For example, Kimberly-Clark packaged its Kleenex for Kids tissues in fun cartons dressed up in colorful animal themes such as dinosaurs to reach the under-12 set. Kimberly-Clark's unique package for an established product is designed to stand out when parents (and children) stand in front of the tissue shelf trying to decide among manufacturer, private, and generic brands. New lower-cost technology for package printing will soon allow marketers to reach out to even smaller customer groups without spending a fortune.[38]

However, retailers are increasingly resistant to more and more product variations. Such retailers use another tactic to limit the number of different products offered: *category management*, the selection of a group of products in each category that can be profitably carried. Manufacturers, therefore, are now working more closely with retailers before introducing new versions of already available products.

In some cases, packaging and labeling are integral parts of the value package that become synonymous with the brand. Think of the hourglass Coca-Cola bottle or the red and white Campbell's Soup label. Instant brand recognition is important because customers view 20 products per second during a typical scan. So when Campbell's recently updated its soup label—which has remained much the same for nearly 100 years—it didn't do anything radical. The marketer simply shrank the red band a bit to expand the white area, where a mouth-watering photo of the soup beckons hungry shoppers.[39] Coca-Cola is now introducing an hourglass can to take advantage of its established appeal.

Packaging for Protection, Storage, and Convenience

On a purely functional level, packaging keeps a product safe until the customer buys it and brings it home or to the office. Then the package stores the product until all or part of it has been used at the customer's convenience. This function isn't as glamorous as the communication function, but it's critical to marketing success. Fisher Scientific found this out when its international business customers complained that their laboratory tubes were arriving broken. With the help of its shipper, UPS, Fisher determined that a stronger package was needed to prevent damage during shipment.[40]

Packaging helps marketers give customers as much or as little of a product as they need and want. From beverages to pizza to laundry detergents, customers can choose single-serve packages, jumbo packages, and everything in between. Look at the success of Arizona, which made a big splash when it introduced a 24-ounce can of tea. Or consider Procter & Gamble's Ultra Tide, a highly concentrated detergent sold in a smaller than usual package.[41] Customers may even reuse the package long after the product is gone, an extra benefit. Aware of the attractiveness of recyclability, the marketers at Sucrets conducted marketing research before changing the packaging of its throat lozenges from a tin to a plastic box that is "every bit as reusable as the old, with the added advantage that it doesn't rust," says Frank Dzvonik, associate brand manager.[42]

Packaging often plays a significant role in making products attractive to consumers. Arizona brand drinks, for example, come in large, 24-ounce cans. Anyone with a big thirst would appreciate the larger serving. In fact, Arizona has captured a profitable share of the soft drink market with its attractive packaging and creative distribution. Besides size, what other aspects of Arizona's packaging make it attractive to consumers?

Marketers are increasingly looking to packaging to differentiate products and provide new uses or extra convenience for selected customer segments. Packaging was the innovative power behind such product successes as toothpaste pumps and microwavable popcorn packages. In each case, the package changed the product in the minds of consumers and opened additional market segments. Packaging adds value for resellers too. For example, packaging materials made by Cryovac keep fruit and vegetable products bought by retailers from becoming prematurely ripe during shipment and storage. And nearly every consumer product is labeled with the familiar bars of the Universal Product Code (UPC), which helps wholesalers and retailers track inventory and sales more efficiently.[43] The following case shows how a small business effectively uses packaging and labeling.

Applying the Concepts

Packaging Annie's Homegrown as homespun

Ann Withey is back in the kitchen cooking up new products. Her first product, Smartfood, ignited a national craze for popcorn coated with white Cheddar cheese. After Frito-Lay bought Smartfood, Withey branched out to develop all-natural pasta and cheese products. Her new company's name is Annie's Homegrown and the family brand is Annie's, chosen to "personalize the product," says Withey, who cofounded the company with one of her Smartfood partners.

Knowing that macaroni and cheese is a mainstay of many children's diets, Withey positioned her products as healthy alternatives because they use no preservatives and come in both whole-wheat and white pasta versions. The products are packaged in cardboard boxes with folksy graphics and a friendly bunny. The labeling includes a letter from Withey, who introduces herself as a "real person" living on a farm with her pet rabbit Bernie. The letter also tells customers that Annie's products aren't like those put out by her gigantic competitor. Her recipes, she points out, don't include chemicals or artificial coloring like that other marketer's macaroni and cheese products.

"The letter is an effort to make us seem homespun and small," explains Withey. "And we are, compared to our competition." She sells more than $3 million of Annie's products a year, but her sales are tiny compared with those of Kraft, her largest competitor. When Kraft launched a white Cheddar version of its macaroni and cheese, Annie's felt the competition. Still, Withey is counting on unique packaging and labeling to help Annie's Homegrown products leap off supermarket shelves and into shopping carts across the country.[44]

Make marketing decisions

1. How would you design Annie's packaging to convey the products' benefits?

2. Do you agree that the letter on Annie's packages should allude to the competitor's use of artificial coloring and chemicals? Should the letter name the competitor?

3. How would you design packaging for Annie's to appeal to young couples and older, retired people?

4. How might Kraft use packaging and labeling to help customers distinguish its white Cheddar macaroni and cheese from its yellow Cheddar version?

Packaging and Environmental Concerns

Many marketers have been looking for ways to minimize the environmental impact of their packaging. In part, they're responding to mandates for reduced packaging by government agencies such as the Environmental Protection Agency. Similar pressures are being felt by marketers throughout Europe.[45]

As part of its green marketing effort, Nike encourages stores to collect old athletic shoes. Nike then grinds these old shoes up and gives the rubber to Atlas Track & Tennis for use in producing running tracks. This recycling program has a positive impact on the environment and on Nike customers. What other green marketing initiatives might Nike undertake to help the environment?

Marketers are also rethinking packaging in response to consumer activism. For example, public pressure persuaded McDonald's to switch from foam hamburger containers to paper wrappers. This change reduced by 70 percent the landfill waste generated by the chain's hamburger packaging.[46] Pasqua Coffee Bars in San Francisco responded differently to its community's environmental concerns. Reluctant to sacrifice the heat-retention qualities of disposable foam coffee cups, the company retained this packaging but began a recycling program.[47]

As an offshoot of green marketing ⟵⟶ **(p. 95)**, more marketers are labeling their products to indicate the environmental impact of the product or package. Most packages show whether the product or package is biodegradable, recyclable, or made from recycled materials. To ensure that customers won't be misled by inaccurate or deceptive claims, the Federal Trade Commission regulates environmental labeling in the United States. Many other nations do the same. The ISO 14000 environmental standards may soon be commonplace.

Product Safety Protects Customers

One of the more basic requirements of a value package is safety. Both the product and its packaging should keep buyers and users from hazards associated with the product's usage or product tampering. At a minimum, marketers must comply with a variety of government regulations that dictate product safety standards and the content of warning labels, such as those developed by the U.S. Consumer Product Safety Commission. Toy makers, for example, are required to label toys and games to alert parents to parts that could pose a choking hazard to young children.[48]

Other government agencies watch over a range of consumer and business products. Many have the power to order marketers to recall products that may cause harm. For example, the National Highway Traffic Safety Administration can order carmakers to recall vehicles to repair defects involving safety or pollution controls, and the Food and Drug Administration can order food, drug, and cosmetics marketers to recall unsafe products. In addition, special interest groups such as Consumers Union test and report on product safety, giving customers more information on which to base purchase decisions. Many marketers go above and beyond government standards, voluntarily looking for ways to make their products safer. However, as you'll see next, a product deemed unfit for one country may be sold in another, raising serious ethical issues.

ETHICS & SOCIAL RESPONSIBILITY

Unsafe in U.S. but safe abroad?

Should U.S. marketers offer products in other countries that are banned for sale in the United States because of safety concerns? This ethical question is being raised because U.S.-based firms go to developing nations around the world to market chemicals, pharmaceuticals, and other products that cannot legally be sold domestically. Dow-Elanco, for example, can't sell its Galant weed killer in the United States because of concerns about cancer-causing ingredients. Is Dow-Elanco acting ethically by exporting Galant to Costa Rica?

Before you answer, consider that banned-in-U.S. products are sold in markets that either don't forbid their sale or don't enforce such regulations. If Costa Rica doesn't ban Galant, why should DowElanco hesitate to market there? By exporting, DowElanco and other marketers are not breaking any U.S. laws. Although President Carter signed an executive order in 1981 to stop marketers from exporting such products, President Reagan revoked the order when he took office a few weeks later. President Bush's administration took the position that the United States has no standing to rule on what should or should not be allowed outside its borders.

Critics charge that Bangladesh and other developing nations are dumping grounds for banned products. Some marketers, such as Upjohn, are offering in other countries new products they have been refused permission to market in the United States. Product development is costly, and marketers are understandably eager to recoup their investments. Moreover, if U.S. marketers don't provide weed killers and other products desired by consumers, foreign competitors will.[49]

Do you think U.S. marketers should be allowed to export what have been called unsafe products in the United States? What about products that may offer important benefits to developing nations?

Despite all the efforts made to make products safe, the specter of product liability looms large. *Product liability* means that marketers can be held responsible for damages or injuries caused by their products. Even when marketers carefully design products, test them, and provide safety warnings, they're not immune from product liability lawsuits that can, in worst-case situations, result in multimillion-dollar judgments. In response, businesses routinely buy liability insurance, which carries a high price tag—when it's available at all—and raises the ultimate price that customers pay for products. Businesses are hoping to stem the rising tide of liability lawsuits through proposed changes in product liability legislation.[50]

Customer Service Builds Satisfaction

Customer service is assistance that marketers provide to customers when they buy or use a product. A vital but intangible element of the value package, customer service covers a wide range of activities, including delivery, installation, repair, training, and credit, that marketers use to build relationships with customers and, at the same time, differentiate their products from competitive offerings.

Customer services often come *bundled* as part of the value package; that is, they are included in the price of the product, regardless of whether the customer needs or wants them. Bundling can be a competitive advantage if most customers find the bundle desirable—especially if rivals can't offer the same bundle. However, customer services can also come *unbundled*, allowing customers to buy just the services they need. This strategy can be effective as long as competitors don't offer the full bundle at a better price.[51] Sears

customer service

assistance that marketers provide to customers when they buy or use a product

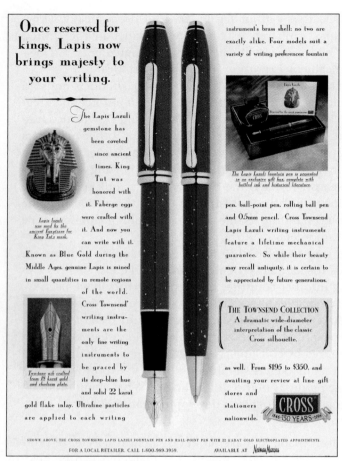

Once reserved for kings. Lapis now brings majesty to your writing.

The Lapis Lazuli gemstone has been coveted since ancient times. King Tut was honored with it. Faberge eggs were crafted with it. And now you can write with it.

Lapis lazuli was used by the ancient Egyptians for King Tut's mask.

Known as Blue Gold during the Middle Ages, genuine Lapis is mined in small quantities in remote regions of the world. Cross Townsend® writing instruments are the only fine writing instruments to be graced by its deep-blue hue and solid 22 karat gold flake inlay. Ultrafine particles are applied to each writing

Two-tone nib crafted from 18 karat gold and rhodium plate.

SHOWN ABOVE, THE CROSS TOWNSEND LAPIS LAZULI FOUNTAIN PEN AND BALL-POINT PEN WITH 22 KARAT GOLD ELECTROPLATED APPOINTMENTS

FOR A LOCAL RETAILER, CALL 1-800-989-3959.   AVAILABLE AT *Neiman Marcus*

instrument's brass shell: no two are exactly alike. Four models suit a variety of writing preferences: fountain

The Lapis Lazuli fountain pen is presented in an exclusive gift box, complete with bottled ink and historical literature.

pen, ball-point pen, rolling ball pen and 0.5mm pencil. Cross Townsend Lapis Lazuli writing instruments feature a lifetime mechanical guarantee. So while their beauty may recall antiquity, it is certain to be appreciated by future generations.

THE TOWNSEND COLLECTION
A dramatic wide-diameter interpretation of the classic Cross silhouette.

as well. From $195 to $350, and awaiting your review at fine gift stores and stationers nationwide.

CROSS
1846·150 YEARS·1996

Cross Townsend Lapis Lazuli writing instruments offer a lifetime mechanical guarantee. Do you think customers would pay more for a pen that offers such a promise? What other aspects of the value package would be important to customers who are considering purchasing this product?

bundles some services (such as credit, which is free if charges are repaid promptly) and unbundles others (such as appliance service contracts, which are available for an extra fee). This way, Sears customers can pick and choose, paying for only the services they want.

In many cases, customer service can make or break customer satisfaction. But until customer service is actually delivered—that is, until a marketer's employees have answered questions, installed products, repaired equipment, or trained product users—customers can't fairly judge service benefits. Customers can only rely on information they get from product packages, integrated marketing communication, and word-of-mouth recommendations from other purchasers. That's why marketers need to carefully explain customer services and associated benefits in their marketing materials, and then deliver as promised.

Warranties and Guarantees Add Value

Customers usually see more value in a product that carries a warranty or a guarantee. A *warranty* is a marketer's statement of its procedure for compensating customers if products are defective or fail to perform properly. Warranties reassure customers about product quality and performance. They can also help differentiate a product from competing items. For example, A.T. Cross will fix free, forever, any of its pens or pencils that malfunction, a warranty that demonstrates the company's extraordinary commitment to quality and customer satisfaction.

A *guarantee* is a promise that the product is as represented and that it will provide the expected performance. In offering a guarantee, many marketers pledge to refund the purchase price or replace a product if the customer isn't satisfied. In West Virginia, for example, some high schools offer employers a guarantee of graduates' basic job skills. The high schools promise to work without charge to bring graduates' skills (the product) up to the proper level if needed.[52]

Before you go on . . .

A. What are brand names, brand marks, trademarks, and service marks?

B. What is the difference between brand loyalty and brand equity?

C. How do packaging and labeling add value to products?

D. Why are marketers concerned about product liability?

Competing Through Product Differentiation

Every marketer's value package is a little different from those offered by rivals. The challenge is to make the most of these differences to battle competitors and build long-term customer relationships. To give a product a sense of uniqueness and to emphasize product value, marketers need to choose points of differentiation that customers care about. For example, Caterpillar differentiates its tractors on the basis of durability, parts availability, and reliable, responsive dealer service. These points of differentiation are important to tractor buyers, and they set Caterpillar apart from its competitors.[53]

Positioning ◀——┛ **(p. 224)** helps marketers create an image of a product that differentiates it from competitive products. The linkage between differentiation and positioning allows marketers to convey the unique value and benefits of every complete value package. When customers get the message that the differentiation makes the product more unique and attractive than competing products, they tend to form a more positive impression of the product.[54]

Chrysler, for example, used product differentiation and positioning to market a new version of its Dodge Ram truck. Chrysler redesigned the truck using the input of a cross-functional team that carefully studied customer needs and competing products. The team put together a value package with desirable styling, safety, and comfort features that differentiated the product from Ford and General Motors trucks. The advertising theme "The rules have changed" set the tone for positioning the Dodge Ram as the source of features and benefits not ordinarily found in trucks. When the target market became aware that the trucks had changed, they came to look—and to buy, sending sales soaring.[55]

Marketers can use all the elements of external marketing strategy—product, channel management, pricing, and integrated marketing communication—to create a differentiation strategy. The sections that follow present just some of the differentiation strategies marketers can use to build enduring customer relationships.

Differentiation Through Superior Quality

One effective differentiation strategy is to stress superior quality. Of course, "superior" is a relative term. What seems superior one day—creating an augmented product—can be merely ordinary the next, as competitors catch up and make better quality part of the expected product.

At Sunkyong, a Korean producer of petroleum products, employees worked toward superior quality by benchmarking against the world's best. They also set and achieved a goal of getting every part of the manufacturing process right the first time. "If we merely try to be excellent, our gap with the world's top companies will remain because they keep improving," says chairman Chey Jong-Hyon. "Only by seeking super-excellence can we reach their level or overtake them." By differentiating its products on the basis of superior quality, Sunkyong can compete with global rivals.[56] Here's how Harley-Davidson and other marketers differentiate products on the basis of zero defects.

MARKETING IDEAS

The quest for zero defects

One of today's product quality concepts is *zero defects*, the idea that no product defects are acceptable. With zero defects, customers get defect-free quality and marketers don't waste time and money fixing problems. Given the competitive global economy, anything less than perfect isn't good enough. That's why more marketers are differentiating their products on the basis of zero defects. "An 'acceptable' imperfection a few years ago . . . won't be tolerated today by our customers. Nor by us," states a recent Harley-Davidson annual report.

Motorcycle marketer Harley-Davidson is far from alone in its quest for perfection. Why are zero defects important? Consider what 99.9 percent quality would bring in daily life:

- 1 hour of unsafe drinking water every month
- 2 unsafe plane landings per day at O'Hare International Airport in Chicago
- 16,000 pieces of mail lost every hour by the U.S. Postal Service
- 20,000 incorrect drug prescriptions per year
- 500 incorrect surgical operations each week
- 50 newborn babies dropped at birth by doctors every day
- 22,000 checks deducted from the wrong bank accounts each hour

Does the zero-defects approach seems sensible? Can you think of any situations in which customers would accept products with less than 100 percent defect-free quality?[57]

Differentiation Through Speedy Response

With a differentiation strategy of speedy response, marketers move products more quickly downstream through the value chain to the customer. They also move information about customer wants, sales, and orders more quickly upstream (through technological applications such as electronic data interchange), to permit planning for future demand by marketers and their value-chain partners.

For example, speedy response has helped Fourgen Software become the fastest growing marketer in the accounting software industry. The key is getting new products to small and midsize business customers faster than competitors. Software makers normally provide enhanced versions of their accounting programs every 18 months. In contrast, Fourgen differentiates itself by providing improved software every 3 months.[58]

Differentiation Through Mass Customization

mass customization

offering individually tailored, quality goods and services to a large number of customers at a relatively low cost

Technology is helping marketers shape products to the needs of specific customers. With **mass customization**, marketers have the ability to offer individually tailored, quality goods and services to a large number of customers at a relatively low cost. Because such products more closely fit customer needs, they are easily differentiated from off-the-shelf products.[59]

Motorola, for example, can manufacture pagers to fit each customer's requirements. Similarly, Levi Strauss can produce women's jeans to fit each customer's measurements. In both cases, the marketers have differentiated their products by offering customization that customers can't find elsewhere.[60]

Differentiation Through Superior Customer Service

Some firms market as though no level of service is too high for their customers. These marketers differentiate their products by offering superior service that can't easily be matched. In turn, they're rewarded by loyal customers.

Department store shoppers, for example, keep coming back to Nordstrom because they are routinely delighted by the legendary service. Toyota's Lexus is another example. Lexus car dealers pamper their customers with many free services. Superior service sets Lexus apart from other luxury brands, as shown by the brand's scores on surveys of customer satisfaction.[61]

Differentiation Through Channel Management and Value

Marketers can differentiate their products by using unique or emerging channels that offer particular speed, price, or convenience advantages for customers. Marketing channels unchoked by rival products are especially attractive as marketers seek unique points of differentiation.

T-Shirts Online, a small business in Maine, uses speedy electronic channels to differentiate itself from competitors that rely on traditional retail channels. Customers with PCs can tap into the marketer's automated ordering system and electronically transmit the graphics they want on their shirts. T-Shirts Online renders the design and puts it on a customized T-shirt that's shipped within a few days. This way, customers get T-shirts decorated exactly as they want without setting foot in a store.[62]

Of course, some organizations effectively differentiate their products through offering superior value. The "value menu" at certain fast-food restaurants is an example.

One of the fastest-growing marketing channels is the Internet, or the World Wide Web. It is a relatively inexpensive way to reach consumers, who find it fast and convenient. Customers of 1-800-MUSIC NOW can listen before they buy. Can you think of other products that are particularly suited to being marketed online?

Differentiation Through Information

Another effective differentiation strategy is to provide important information with the product. Comprehensive usage and safety instructions are helpful, as are newsletters, recipes, and decorating tips. For maximum impact, however, marketers need to give customers vital information they can't get anywhere else. This approach helps build enduring customer relationships that leave competitors out in the cold.

For example, tractor manufacturer Massey-Ferguson developed a system that provides farmers with detailed information to analyze and improve harvest yields. Each

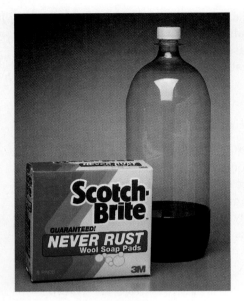

The marketing of "green," or environmentally sound, products is a major trend. These soap pads, for example, are manufactured from recycled plastic bottles. What other products are successfully differentiated by being socially responsible?

Massey-Ferguson tractor holds a computer that collects details about the farmer's acreage and yield. The tractor's computer sends this information to the farmer's personal computer in the form of maps that compare actual and expected yields for each field. Such information helps the farmer identify fields that need special attention. Given such service, why would a Massey-Ferguson customer switch?[63]

Differentiation Through Social Responsibility

Demonstrating social responsibility ◁———| **(p. 93)** makes customers feel good about the brands they buy and the marketers they support. However, whether a marketer wants to save the rain forest, clean up the environment, or contribute to medical research, the socially responsible cause a product supports must be meaningful to customers.

Consider how 3M developed a "green" product that was environmentally friendly, worked well, and satisfied consumers. The Never Rust Wool Soap Pad is made of recycled plastic bottles and uses a nonpolluting soap. Information about the product and its benefits appears on the package. The 3M product, positioned as an environmentally correct scrubbing pad, is drawing customer interest, judging by the product's rising sales.[64]

Before you go on . . .

A. **How do marketers marry product differentiation and positioning strategies to compete more effectively?**

B. **Why do marketers need a product differentiation strategy?**

Summary

1. **Analyze the types of consumer and organizational products that marketers use to build customer relationships.**

   Products that marketers use to build relationships with consumers include convenience products, shopping products, specialty products, and unsought products. Products that marketers use to build relationships with organizational customers include raw materials, components, installations, accessory equipment, supplies, and business services.

2. **Show how basic, expected, augmented, and potential products relate to customer needs and satisfaction.**

   The basic product is the fundamental element that makes the product what it is. The expected product is the value package that satisfies customers' minimum expectations. The augmented product exceeds customers' expectations for satisfaction. The potential product represents all the possible enhancements that can be added to a value package to satisfy customers.

3. **Demonstrate how the seven elements in the product value package contribute to stronger customer relationships.**

   Quality (the degree to which a product meets customer needs, wants, and expectations) enhances product value. Features (characteristics or attributes of products) deliver benefits that customers want and need. With branding (a name, phrase, design, symbol, or combination of these), marketers can identify and differentiate products. Packaging and labeling serve several functions: communication and protection, storage, and convenience. Product safety protects customers from harm. Customer service is assistance that marketers provide when customers buy or use a product. Warranties and guarantees reassure customers about a product's quality and promise that the product will perform.

4. **Explain how the customer's view of quality affects the product value package.**

   Quality is the degree to which a product meets customer needs, wants, and expectations. To satisfy customers and build strong relationships, marketers need to develop product value packages that meet their customers' perceptions of quality.

5. **Apply the strategies of brand extension, line extension, family brands, individual brands, and brand licensing.**

   Brand extension is the application of an existing brand to a new product in another category. Line extension puts an existing brand on a related product in the same category. A family brand is one that is used on a variety of related products. An individual brand is used on only one product in a family. Brand licensing is the practice of paying a fee to use another marketer's brand.

6. **Show the importance of brand loyalty and brand equity.**

   Customers who recognize and appreciate the benefits and satisfaction they get from a branded product often develop a favorable attitude toward that brand, prompting consistent purchasing and strengthening the relationship between marketer and customer. Over time, such brand loyalty contributes to brand equity, the long-term value of a marketer's brand in the marketplace that builds sales and profits.

7. **Explain how marketers link product differentiation with positioning to compete more effectively.**

   Product differentiation helps marketers set a product apart from competitors in a way that is meaningful to the target market. Marketers then use positioning to create an image of the product based on the points of differentiation.

KEY TERMS

Skill-Building Applications

1. Consider yourself as a product to be marketed to potential employers. Identify the expected, augmented, and potential products that you represent.

2. What are the differences between Windows 95 (the PC operating system) as a consumer product and as an organizational product? What is the potential product in a business setting?

3. How could your local elementary school use the concept of mass customization to develop an educational program for each of its students? Would computers help in the process?

4. Dina Magazines is a store in New York City that sells a wide selection of magazines. Owned by Ezzat Reda and his brother Hussein, who are from Lebanon, the store employs immigrants from several countries. How can the brothers enhance the product value package and use differentiation to attract more customers?

5. H&R Block is the most recognized service for preparing income tax returns in America. TaxHelp Express is a Los Angeles preparer. How can TaxHelp use product differentiation to capture local customers from its larger competitor?

6. In-line skating is increasingly popular among people who are, for example, playing street hockey. What steps can Rollerblade take to protect its brand name from becoming generic?

Getting Involved in Marketing

1. *On Your Own* What is the basic product of a college? What is the expected product? The augmented product? What might the potential product look like? Write a two-page report about how your college could deliver the potential product.

2. *On Your Own* Visit an electronics store and compare the warranties and guarantees offered by makers of, for example, CD players. What similarities and differences can you find? How does each marketer communicate the benefits of its warranty or guarantee? Draft a letter to one marketer with advice on how to gain more competitive leverage from the warranty or guarantee.

3. *Find Out More* Find information in a magazine, newspaper, book, or online database about how one marketer won a quality award. How did the marketer improve its product? How was quality measured? Report your findings in a five-minute classroom talk.

4. *In a Partnership* With another student, select a consumer marketer and an organizational marketer to research. Identify the types of products each offers and the kinds of customer needs the products satisfy. How does branding convey these products' features, quality, and benefits? Report your findings to the class.

5. *In a Team* With other classmates, visit a supermarket to analyze one product category such as toothpaste. Note how many manufacturer brands, private brands, and generic brands are available, and compare packaging, labeling, and pricing. Suggest how one manufacturer's brand might enhance its value package to compete more effectively against rival brands.

6. *In a Team* With other students, find an ad about a product bundled with customer service and an ad about a product with unbundled customer service options. How do the ads convey the benefits of the bundle and the options? How might customers choose between the bundle and the options? Write a two-page report summarizing your team's findings.

VideoCase Dakin Farm Differentiates Products Through Quality

Sam Cutting, Jr., encourages customers to bring home the bacon . . . and the cheese, the maple syrup, and many other Vermont products. Customers from anywhere in the United States can quickly and easily order any of these mouth-watering foods by mail from Cutting's Dakin Farm catalog. What sets these products apart from competitive products is an emphasis on top quality.

For Dakin Farm, the basic product is fresh-from-the-farm food. The expected product includes the intangible services of accurate order fulfillment and prompt delivery. The augmented product—which is where Dakin Farm really shines—is the quality service that enables customers to order a gift at the very last minute and have it delivered in only two days.

Dakin Farm, started by Cutting's father in 1960, originally consisted of a working farm and a small, roadside farm stand. At that time, the target market was tourists who wanted to buy the farm's Vermont maple syrup, although clothing and other products were added over the years. When Cutting became active in the business in 1980, he reevaluated the product offerings and decided to drop clothing so he could concentrate on selling specialty food products by mail. The target market became those consumers who wanted a convenient way to send Vermont-style food gifts to friends, relatives, and business associates. Because the company relied heavily on repeat business, winning the customer's loyalty and maintaining a good relationship was critical to Cutting's success.

Rather than continue making all his own products, Cutting arranged to buy raw materials in bulk from local suppliers and then complete the processing, packaging, and labeling to suit Dakin Farm's quality standards. For example, Dakin Farm buys maple syrup from several local sources and then creates a blend with the distinctive taste that its customers desire. The same is true for hams and cheeses, which are processed in a smokehouse operation that the company carefully controls to maintain consistent flavor standards. This way, Cutting can ensure the quality of every product he sells, enhancing the brand equity of Dakin Farm.

Next, Cutting set out to improve the total value package. He installed a new computer system to speed customer ordering.

However, the computer didn't completely solve the problem of on-time order fulfillment during the year-end holiday season, when about 90 percent of the company's orders were received. Because picking, packing, and shipping orders took a long time, customers who ordered at the last minute couldn't be guaranteed delivery by Christmas. By benchmarking on other mail-order firms, Cutting learned what to do. He put in conveyor belts and other new equipment and revamped the packing system—part of the company's internal product—to help employees process orders more efficiently.

As the business continued to grow, the next step was to upgrade the computer system to process a higher volume of orders and capture database information about customers. The new system worked fine until it crashed on one of the busiest days of the holiday season. The supplier fixed the problem within three days, but Cutting quickly established a backup system in case such a failure should occur again. Now customers can call or fax orders at any time and feel confident that Dakin Farm's quality extends to its delivery as well as its foods.

Strategies and applications

1. Is the quality of the internal products (such as the packing system) as important to the success of Dakin Farm as the quality of its consumer products? Explain your answer.

2. Within the value package, do you think the quality of the food or the quality of the service is more important to customers? Why?

3. What are some of the packaging and environmental issues that Dakin Farm faces in marketing its food products?

4. What are some features and benefits of the potential product for Dakin Farm?

5. What kind of guarantee do you think Dakin Farm could offer to reassure customers of its ability to deliver on time?

6. What else can Cutting do to build brand loyalty and brand equity?

Team project

How can Cutting apply technology to differentiate Dakin Farm from competitors? Would a differentiation strategy based on channel management be a good idea if Cutting put his products in a CD-ROM catalog? Would a differentiation strategy based on information be a good idea if Cutting created a Web site for Dakin Farm? With other students, consider these ideas and prepare a two-page report summarizing your team's suggestions.

10 Product Development and Management

Learning Goals

After you have read and studied this chapter, you should be able to:

1. Differentiate among the types of new product.
2. Analyze why some new products succeed and others fail.
3. Identify the sequence of activities in the new product development process.
4. Describe the four product development strategies.
5. Define product line and product mix, and contrast product mix width with product line length.
6. List and discuss the four stages in the product life cycle.
7. Show how the product adoption process drives product diffusion.

PROFILE

Individual Inc. sells information for a fee

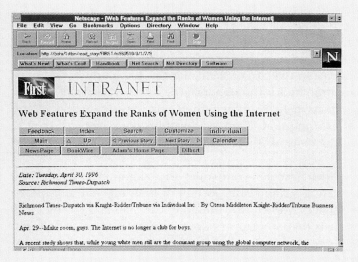

In the organizational market, no product is more valuable than information. The problem today is that there is often too much information available. It is time-consuming and very expensive to monitor all the newspapers, magazines, television shows, and the like. That's where Individual Inc. comes in. Founded in 1989 in Burlington, Massachusetts, this company customizes news information for thousands of customers, based on each customer's unique needs and wants. The company feels that less information is more—as long as it is the right information.

Each day Individual Inc. receives some 20,000 news stories from approximately 600 suppliers. The stories are then indexed and stored in a computerized database. Story content is matched to its customers' reading interests based on key words stored in another database. The company screens thousands of stories to identify those of interest to particular customers and then prioritizes them according to each customer's specific requirements.

The market for information is segmented by industry. Thus there are stories targeted toward the following industries: computers, energy, electronics, finance, and government, among others. As customers receive news stories, they grade them by level of interest and provide that feedback to the company. In this way, Individual Inc. can continuously improve its selection of stories to better meet the needs of individual users.

Users can receive stories by fax, e-mail, and through the World Wide Web or Lotus Notes. The company has developed various products to meet the needs of diverse business customers. Heads-Up, for example, provides only summaries of stories. After glancing through Heads-Up, customers can choose to order the full text. Individual's major product is called "First." It provides the full text of articles on an on-line browser. "iNews" is a news-flash service.[1]

Now that it has information from many sources, Individual Inc. can custom-design new information-based products for a variety of customer groups. Every marketer needs new products to fuel growth and keep customers satisfied. This chapter discusses why and how marketers develop and manage new products. First you'll look at the types of new products, at new product success and failure rates, and at trends in product development, all of which influence marketing relationships. Next, you'll go inside the new product development process to see how it operates and how to manage it. Then you'll explore product planning and management in more detail.

New Products, New Opportunities for Marketing Relationships

There are really only two important functions in business: marketing and innovations.

Peter F. Drucker

The inventor of the mountain bike, Michael Sinyard, has a favorite slogan for his employees at Specialized Inc.: "Innovate or die!"[2] Seem extreme? Not to successful marketers, who know that tomorrow's profits depend on today's new products. To see why this is so, think about the dynamic marketing environment.

Every marketer faces continual shifts in competitive pressures, customer needs, social and cultural influences, and international forces, among other environmental elements. In the face of such changes, the products you now offer may not be appropriate for the opportunities or threats you'll face in the future. New products help you strengthen relationships with current customers and, just as important, start relationships with new customers. This is true for both the consumer and industrial markets, as the Profile on Industrial Inc. showed.

In many cases, market leaders—companies that dominate their industries—set goals for earning a significant portion of their revenue from sales of newer goods or services. At 3M, for example, the standard set by CEO L. D. "Desi" DeSimone is that 30 percent of company sales must come from products launched in the past four years. This goal is even more ambitious than the earlier one, which specified that 25 percent of company sales should come from products introduced during the past five years.[3]

Types of New Product

Thousands and thousands of products are introduced every year. But is every one of these products *really* new? As simple as the question may seem, its answer depends on the viewpoint you take. As you can see from Table 10.1, the newness of a product depends on whether you're looking at it from the perspective of the customer or the marketer.

Few products are truly *new to the world*. Still, products that create new categories, such as the first cellular phone or the first overnight delivery service, can be a marketer's entrée to relationships with new customers and new markets. Studies show that despite the higher risk in launching them, these breakthrough products, which are only 10 percent of all new products, can return higher profits than other types of new products.[4]

When you introduce a product that's not new to the world but is new for your organization, you again face some risks. The product may not meet

TABLE **10.1**   **Defining New Products**

Type of New Product	Definition	Example
New-to-the-world	A product innovation that creates an entirely new product category	FedEx overnight delivery
New-to-the-marketer	A product that's new to the marketer but already offered by other marketers	Lysol Drain Opener
Line extension	A product that applies the marketer's brand to products added to the marketer's existing line in a particular category	Dance Moves Barbie
Repositioned	A product marketed in a new way to change its position in the minds of the target market	Kodak Royal Gold (formerly Ektar film)
Improved	An improved version of an existing product	Microsoft Word 7.0 software

line extensions

products bearing the marketer's brand that are added to the marketer's existing line of products in a particular category

customer expectations. Costs may be higher than anticipated. Customers may prefer competing products. Because the category is already in existence, however, you can learn from other marketers' mistakes, which helps reduce the risk compared with entirely new products. Your goal is to make a *creative imitation* so that you don't merely copy someone else's product, you perfect and position it for your target market.[5]

Issues for critical thinking

Why would a marketer bring out a new product that's virtually identical to a competing product (a "me-too" product)? Which do you think is less risky: creative imitation or me-too products? Which has the potential to build a more loyal customer base?

McDonald's Arch Deluxe is the "burger with the grown-up taste." It features a quarter pound of beef, optional hickory-smoked bacon, American cheese, lettuce, tomato, onions, and sauce. McDonald's, like all companies, must constantly monitor competition and develop new products to expand its market share. In recent moves, McDonald's decided to drop both the McLean Deluxe and its cookie selection, added the Arch Deluxe to appeal to adults, and signed an exclusive movie tie-in agreement with Disney in order to strengthen its appeal to kids. How else might McDonald's broaden its appeal to adults?

The majority of new products are actually **line extensions**, products bearing the marketer's brand that are added to the marketer's existing line of products in a particular category. Look at the food category. According to *New Product News*, most of the 15,000-plus food products introduced in one recent year were actually new flavors (line extensions) of existing brands. For example, new products such as Frito-Lay's Doritos Flamin' Hot Tortilla Chips put the Doritos brand on a new flavor of tortilla chips, a snack category in which Frito-Lay is already active.[6]

Repositioned products **(p. 242)** (including those aimed at new segments or markets) are less risky than line extensions because the marketer already has some experience with the product. An example is Johnson & Johnson's baby powder repositioned for adults. However, there's some chance that the new positioning won't fit customer needs or won't help the product compete effectively with rival products. Least risky and least innovative are improved versions of existing products, which help maintain strong bonds with current customers. At the same time, such products don't attract many new customers, so they don't have as high a profit potential as breakthroughs.[7]

Another way to classify new products is according to their effect on consumer behavior, as outlined in Table 10.2. A product incorporating *continuous innovation* builds on existing consumer behaviors and consumption patterns. It's *continuous* because consumers can maintain current behaviors and patterns using the new

TABLE **10.2** How New Product Innovation Affects Consumer Behavior

Degree of Innovation	Product Example	Effect on Consumers
Continuous innovation	Dial soap's improved fragrance Mountain Fresh soap	Consumers continue behaviors and patterns as before, with no change required
Dynamically continuous innovation	Motorola's cellular phone	Consumers need to adapt previous behaviors and patterns to learn to use new product
Discontinuous innovation	Citibank's Direct Access PC-based banking	Consumers need to develop new behaviors and patterns to learn to use new product

product. A product with *dynamically continuous innovation* requires only a few changes in consumer behavior. In contrast, a product with *discontinuous innovation* is so different from other products that it requires consumers to form new behaviors and patterns. Marketing activities should be geared toward helping consumers adapt to the degree of innovation in new products.

Why New Products Succeed

Every marketer hopes its new products will succeed, despite the risks. After all, competition is fierce, and customers are unforgiving. If a product doesn't meet their needs, customers will quickly move on to one that does. So what drives new product success? Researchers point to a number of factors:[8]

If you think you can take your time going to market, think again.

In today's volatile business environment, yesterday is ancient history. Succeeding in the modern marketplace takes speed. It takes agility. It takes GE Information Services.

GE Information Services can help you integrate your suppliers, manufacturers, distributors and customers so that you can respond to your market in minutes instead of days or weeks. In supply chain management, cash management, marketing and sales, we show you how to increase productivity and save time—the time you need to keep a step ahead of your competition.

At GE Information Services, our business productivity solutions enhance the fitness and survival skills of some of the world's best-known companies. In a rapidly evolving marketplace, we give you the edge you need to prevail.

Productivity. It's All We Do.

GE Information Services

For more information, call 1-800-560-GEIS, or write GE Information Services, MC07F1, 401 N. Washington St., Rockville, MD 20850. Find us on the Internet at http://www.ge.com/geis.

One key to new-product success is the ability to produce and deliver products or services in a timely fashion. GE Information Services help companies integrate suppliers, manufacturers, distributors, and customers into a smooth-flowing system. Such coordination is important because time of development has become a major factor in determining whether a product succeeds. Why has timing become such an important factor for new products?

- *Product superiority.* To be successful, a new product needs a competitively superior value package with unique benefits, better quality, and/or better performance at a reasonable price. This set of requirements is particularly critical for success in organizational markets.

- *Customer orientation.* To be successful, a product must spring from and satisfy customer wants. At times, it may solve a problem that customers have yet to recognize.

- *Market attractiveness.* To support new product success, the target market has to be sizable and, ideally, growing.

- *Early entrance.* Products that come to market early can select the most desirable marketing channels, locking out competitors and gaining access to attractive markets.

- *Careful timing.* Success depends on speedy development and introduction and on launching the right product at the right time. Also essential is the patience to test and support a product for a time, gauging the market's response.

- *Excellent teamwork and execution.* To translate a good idea into a great product, the entire organization must be focused on getting the details right and on working closely with suppliers, retailers, and other partners in the value chain. Studies show that new products need such cooperative efforts to succeed.

All these factors came into play when Compaq developed the SystemPro, a new product designed to hook personal computers into a communication network. Compaq believed that groups of PCs would take over data processing chores traditionally handled by mainframe computers, and customers would need a convenient way to link PCs together. Confident that the product, known as a server, would fill a real need—and that enough customers would need it in the future—the computer maker forged ahead with SystemPro.

Compaq employees crisscrossed the country demonstrating to customers how the new product allowed PCs to do what mainframes did, only at a lower cost. Slowly but steadily, SystemPro sales grew. Within a few years, Compaq's server sales were nearly $2 billion. SystemPro now leads the worldwide server market and accounts for one-sixth of Compaq's total sales.[9]

Product managers learn valuable lessons by visiting the New Products Showcase and Learning Center in Ithaca, New York. The center has some 75,000 household items that were deemed marketing failures. They include everything from food to detergents. The museum owner says that people won't buy products with names they can't pronounce or that are too out of the ordinary (like microwave ice-cream sundaes). In fact, about 90 percent of the 16,000 new products that are introduced in supermarkets each year fail. As a product manager, what would you want to learn from the marketing failures of others?

Why New Products Fail

Considering the many things that have to go right to make a product successful, it's hardly surprising that an estimated 80 to 90 percent of all new products fail. Of course, if a product can succeed for the reasons outlined in the preceding section, it can fail for the opposite reasons. Researchers have pinpointed other reasons for failure, some of which relate to the product and some to marketing planning and execution:[10]

- *Improper targeting and positioning.* A new product can't succeed if it's not targeted to the right market, if its positioning isn't meaningful to the market, or if the market is too small.

- *Problems in product and marketing planning.* Any of a number of problems with marketing research, product testing, timing, competitive strategy, and other aspects of product and marketing planning can contribute to product failure.

- *Overpromising satisfaction.* Don't expect success if a product fails to live up to its overstated promise of satisfying customer needs.

- *No competitive differentiation.* If a product doesn't meet customer needs better than rival products, customers are not likely to buy.

- *Not good value.* Customers want to feel that they're getting a good value for the money they pay. A product is doomed if customers think it isn't worth the price.

- *Inadequate marketing communication.* Customers can't buy a product they don't know about. Even when they're aware of a new product, they won't buy if they don't know how the product's benefits will satisfy their needs.

- *Poor channel management.* Products can fail when customers don't have convenient access to them.

- *Inadequate profits.* A product can't succeed without the eventual promise of an acceptable level of profitability.

Some of these factors contributed to the downfall of Procter & Gamble's Citrus Hill orange juice. P&G marketers positioned the product as a better-tasting orange juice, despite research indicating that consumers don't see much difference between brands. In this case, the positioning of better taste wasn't meaningful to the target market. After a brief market test, the marketers got so excited about early indications of success that they pushed to get the product into more stores. Meanwhile, the test continued, and later results showed that only half the consumers who tried the new product bought it again.

As P&G geared up to market Citrus Hill throughout the United States, a winter freeze damaged the orange crop, forcing the company to change the blend of juices it used. As a result, the juice that appeared on store shelves wasn't the same blend that had been tested. Then competitors doubled their advertising and promotional spending, slowing Citrus Hill's momentum. Even reformulating the juice and offering more flavors attracted few customers.

After spending more than a decade and losing $200 million on Citrus Hill, P&G gave up. Edwin Artzt, who was P&G's CEO at the time, commented, "You can't make money in a business if your primary entry is a number-three brand, and you can't have a market leader if you don't have a competitive advantage. We just didn't have it and couldn't get it."[11]

New Product Development Trends

Given today's dynamic marketing environment, the constant stream of technological advances, and changes in competitive pressures, marketers are moving toward streamlining new product development. Among the most important trends are concurrent product development, reduced cycle time, value-chain teamwork, and continuous improvement.

Concurrent development puts specialists from every part of the organization to work simultaneously on a new product so they can share their expertise and make key decisions together throughout the development process, as shown in Figure 10.1. All departments work at the same time, not sequentially. They share ideas and results, which speeds up the process and eliminates costly surprises at the end. Using concurrent development, the Govan Shipyard in Scotland, owned by the Kvaerner Company of Norway, has all departments working simultaneously on developing new ships. Employees in every department are empowered ◄──┘ **(p. 17)** to take actions that will move new products forward.[12]

Reduced cycle time slashes the time needed to develop and bring new products to market, allowing marketers to take advantage of opportunities on a timely basis and stay ahead of competitors. Xerox, for example, worked to slice nearly half the time from its product development cycle after years of losing ground to Japan-based Canon, which captured market share by launching new photocopiers much more quickly. However, reducing cycle time can be costly and is not appropriate in every situation.[13]

Involving both customers and suppliers in new product development is another global trend gaining acceptance. Such cooperation among members of the value chain ◄──┘ **(p. 50)** requires a high level of trust because everyone involved has access to sensitive data such as costs. When the teamwork clicks, the result can be reduced cycle time, improved productivity, and a market-driven product. For example, cooperation among Boeing's suppliers, customers, and employees helped get the company's 777 jetliner off the ground. Thanks to effective teamwork, the thousands of parts for the first 777 fit together almost perfectly. And because customers were involved early in the process, the final product had features airlines really wanted.[14] Here's how Hewlett-Packard involved customers in the development of new printers for personal computer users.

FIGURE **10.1**   Sequential Versus Concurrent Product Development

Traditionally, employees in each department worked on new products according to a standard sequence, with marketing becoming involved at the end of the process. In concurrent product development, all departments participate from the beginning of the process. This speeds up product development and allows employees to share their knowledge and ideas throughout the process.

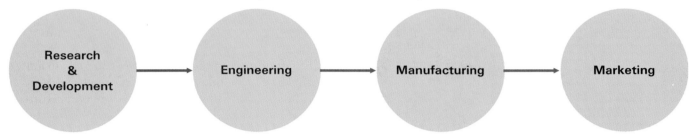

Sequential Product Development

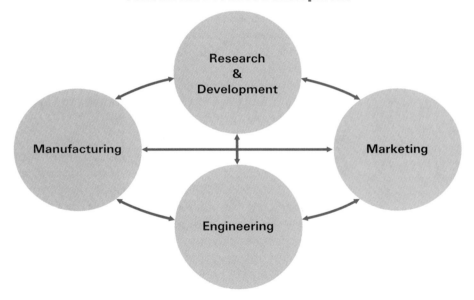

Concurrent Product Development

MARKETING IDEAS

Anatomy of a long-term success

High quality at a low price sounds like a contradictory notion to some marketers, but not to Hewlett-Packard. The computer products marketer was determined to bring out a convenient, technologically superior printer for personal computers at an affordable price. The company also wanted the new product to serve as the basis of a new line of printers for the coming decade. How HP employees rose to this challenge is a textbook study in new product success.

The members of a cross-functional team at Hewlett-Packard are shown here on the DeskJet printer they developed. One of the reasons cited for the team's success was a strategy of maintaining a dialogue with potential customers and having them test working prototypes. Consumer suggestions were then incorporated into the final product. This is just one more example of how marketers are successfully working on teams with colleagues from other departments and with consumers to develop and market products that consumers want. How can Hewlett-Packard use a similar approach to develop a new generation of printers that can also scan documents?

First, a cross-functional team of experts from research and development, manufacturing, and marketing defined their new product goal: to quickly create and market a laser-quality printer that would sell for much less than laser printers. Next, the team identified the target market and the features required to meet customer needs. For example, the printhead had to be convenient to replace, yet inexpensive, to keep overall product price down. To reduce cycle time, several subteams worked concurrently on the printer's parts and technology.

After months of development, the HP team brought working models to shopping malls for testing by potential customers, who were encouraged to offer comments. Nearly all the changes suggested by prospects in the target market were incorporated in the final product. Indeed, without these changes, such as faster drying ink, the new product would have been far less successful. The DeskJet printer, launched in just 22 months, was an instant success. Over the next 10 years, HP continually upgraded quality and slashed prices. It also added related products such as color and portable printers, designed with input from suppliers and, of course, customers.[15]

Should marketers act on all customer and supplier suggestions for improving new products? Why or why not?

Finally, more marketers are adopting **continuous improvement**, a total quality management process that leads to constant, incremental improvements in products (as well as in all organizational processes). This approach moves marketers toward ever-better quality by constantly reinventing the value package. It also helps marketers stay on top of market changes, such as shifting customer buying patterns, to ensure that products remain relevant.[16] Many marketers, including Renault, the French automaker, benchmark **(p. 15)** on world-class marketers to determine the next level of improvements to be made. Renault is benchmarking on Japanese car manufacturing plants as it sets standards for quality and efficiency.[17] With a steady stream of "new, improved" products, marketers can go beyond satisfaction to delighting customers, an ideal result that strengthens relationships over the long haul.

Before you go on . . .

A. Why do marketers develop new products?

B. How do new-to-the-world products differ from line extensions and repositioned products?

C. What factors lead to product success? Product failure?

continuous improvement

a total quality management process that leads to constant, incremental improvements in products (as well as in all organizational processes)

Inside the New Product Development Process

Part inspiration and part perspiration, the **new product development process** is the sequence of activities a marketer uses to transform product ideas into marketable goods and services. In the course of developing a new product, marketers scan the environment and generate ideas, screen them, develop and test product concepts, analyze the business potential, design and develop the product, test it in the market, and then commercialize the product by bringing it to market, as illustrated in Figure 10.2.[18] In effect, the process works like a funnel. Many ideas go in at the start. Then the marketer systematically tests, changes, and eliminates ideas until only those that satisfy both customer and organizational expectations emerge as new products.

FIGURE **10.2** The New Product Development Process

The process of creating new products to satisfy customer needs involves seven distinct activities. At the start, the marketer has a large number of product ideas. By the end, the marketer has systematically tested, modified, and eliminated ideas until only those that satisfy both customer and organizational expectations emerge as new products.

Activity	Purpose
Environmental scan and idea generation	Uncover new product ideas
Screening out inappropriate ideas	Weed out unsuitable and impractical ideas
Concept development and testing	Determine how potential customers respond to the new product concept
Business analysis	Examine projected sales and profits and relate to organizational goals
Product design and development	Transform the concept into an actual product
Product and market testing	Find out whether any changes are needed before the product is launched
Commercialization	Bring the new product to market

Scan the Environment and Generate Ideas

New product ideas are all around. Start with an environmental scan, looking closely at markets, customer segments, opportunities, challenges, competition, technology, and so on. Study marketing research and examine consumer and organizational buying behavior for clues to problems that new products might solve. Then generate ideas for these products by looking both outside and inside your organization.

You can get ideas for new products from letters, phone calls, complaints, and suggestions from customers and prospects as well as from retailers, suppliers, and others outside the organization. Also analyze competitive products, both successes and failures, looking for insights. Inside the organization, new

new product development process

the sequence of activities a marketer uses to transform product ideas into marketable goods and services

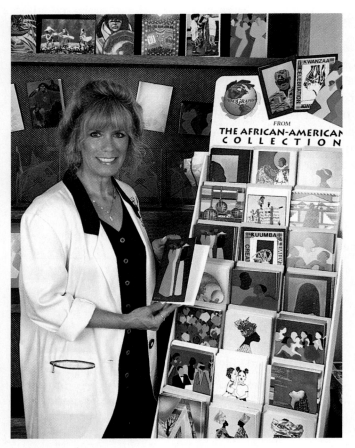

The founder of EthnoGraphics in Santa Barbara, California, introduced a new product idea into a line of greeting cards targeted toward African Americans. By targeting a defined market segment, the company has been able to research and respond to customers' needs. Can you suggest other narrowly defined market segments that might be appropriate for greeting card products?

ideas can come from employees at any level in any department.

In many organizations, specialists in research and development search for new technologies and processes that can be turned into new products. Intel, which makes the Pentium Pro computer chip, invests more than $1 billion yearly on R&D. This investment helps Intel stay ahead of competitors and customers by coming up with ideas for new, more powerful chips well before sales of its most popular chips peak.[19]

Ideas for new products can come from virtually anywhere, as the example of the Sky Dancer doll shows. One day, toy inventor John Gentile stood by as his young daughters played with wing-shaped maple seedlings by throwing them into the air and watching them spiral to the ground. Suddenly Gentile realized that although he'd seen many flying toys for boys, he'd never seen a girls' flying toy like this. He and his twin, Anthony, brought the idea to their partner, Marty Abrams, to put into the new product development pipeline. They hoped to sell the idea to one of the major toy manufacturers.[20]

Screen Out Inappropriate Ideas

Once you have a number of new product ideas, filter out those that don't make sense for your customers, your target market, or your organization, based on a SWOT analysis **(p. 38)**. Savvy marketers recognize that trying to develop too many products at one time can stretch employees and finances to the limit—and distract the company from concentrating on those ideas with the most potential.[21] Rubbermaid, for example, comes up with as many as 4,000 new product ideas every year. It can't possibly develop them all, so its product development teams quickly narrow the field by intuitively screening out inappropriate or impractical ideas. Ultimately, Rubbermaid retains enough ideas to introduce more than 400 new products a year (more than one a day!).[22]

One way to screen ideas is to rate each against a checklist of criteria such as ease of production and number of competitive points of differentiation. Another way is to use a weighted scoring system to assign points based on the relative importance of each of the screening criteria. After you tote up the ratings on the checklist or the points from the weighted scoring system, you can eliminate the low-scoring ideas and rank the others for development.

In the case of Sky Dancer, the Gentile brothers continued to nurse the idea of a flying doll. Based on their years of experience in the toy industry, the Gentiles and partner Abrams felt that this idea was worth taking to the next stage. So they moved ahead to develop the idea more fully, planning to test it by showing it to toy manufacturers that might buy it for further development. The Sky Dancer was initially intended for the U.S. market, but screening ideas for other countries poses a special challenge, as you'll see in the following section.

concept testing

marketing research to determine what potential customers think of an idea for a new product

70% WATER 30% LAND 100% CNN

CNN
THE WORLD'S NEWS LEADER

When designing products, there are times when it is not always beneficial to ask customers what they want. In some instances, customers don't have a clear idea of what they want or what benefits they would receive from a new product. CNN is a good example. At the time of CNN's inception, few people felt they needed a 24-hour-a-day news source. CNN's management persisted, however, and it is now one of the most respected and successful global news sources. How might marketers test products that customers have never experienced or envisioned?

GLOBAL ISSUES

Screening product ideas for developing countries

Many marketers want to tap the growing buying power of developing nations. But which new products are suitable for which markets? This is a complex question, since markets in developing countries are not like those in countries that have been industrialized for generations. When screening new product ideas, marketers need to take into account differences in culture, income, employment, health, and education. These differences influence customer needs and buying behavior as well as governmental policies in developing countries. The World Bank suggests asking these questions:

1. *Is the product appropriate to the country's development goals?* The government might want new products to create new jobs, stabilize the balance of payments, or improve health standards.

2. *Will the product's intended users find the product useful, acceptable, and affordable?* Functionality and acceptability are key, but affordability is also a major issue in many nations.

3. *For locally made products, is the production process appropriate for the country's technological and economic development?* Countries may want to encourage (or discourage) the development of certain technologies or the use of locally produced raw materials and components.

4. *Are the production processes, products, and marketing channels appropriate for the local culture and environment?* The new product must fit with the cultural values, lifestyle, environmental initiatives, and energy use patterns of the target nation.

A high-protein Quaker food product failed in Venezuela because raw materials weren't locally available. A Ford tractor for Latin American markets failed because local banks wouldn't loan farmers money to buy it. Learn from these new product failures, and screen product ideas carefully before entering developing nations.[23]

What other questions would you ask when screening new product ideas for developing countries?

Develop and Test Product Concepts

Up to this point, all you have is an idea. Now you have to shape the idea into a concept of the value package ◄──┘ **(p. 11)** and see how potential customers (and channel partners in many cases) react. First flesh out the idea into a full-blown concept, describing the proposed product in as much detail as possible. In addition to a written description, you might provide a drawing of the product and its package and label, or even a prototype to show what the new item would be like.

Once you've developed the idea more fully, you can use **concept testing**, a type of marketing research to determine what potential customers think of an idea for a new product. If customers are pleased, you might continue with development. If customers are critical, it is advisable to modify the concept to answer their objections. If customers are too critical, however, you might want to drop the concept and work on other ideas. Customer feed-

Blockbuster Entertainment Group, in an effort to increase its share of the entertainment market, is testing a new concept: amusement centers for adults featuring theme restaurants and interactive and virtual-reality games. What kind of questions would you ask adults in order to test this concept for your area? Which questions would be the most important indicators of whether the center would be a success?

back early in the new product development process helps you make an informed decision about whether to cancel a product before moving into the more costly stages of design, development, and full production.[24]

Concept testing isn't infallible. In fact, a product people dislike at first can turn into a big hit. The initial concepts for CNN, fax machines, and cellular phones were greeted skeptically because prospective users couldn't see the benefits of these forward-thinking products. The marketers moved ahead anyway, confident that their products would satisfy real customer needs and that the benefits could be easily communicated. Concept testing can be problematic because, says Mil Ovan, a Motorola marketer, "Our biggest competitor . . . isn't IBM or Sony. It's the way in which people currently do things."[25]

Going back to Sky Dancer, the Gentiles and Marty Abrams developed the concept by preparing samples and choosing a name. Abrams showed the concept to several companies, and Lewis Galoob Toys bought it. Galoob's staff then put the doll through concept testing. Of the 50 children who saw the concept, 45 said that Sky Dancer would be either their first or second choice over competing dolls. The results persuaded Galoob to do a business analysis.[26]

Analyze the Business Potential of Products

Products that survive the concept test are put through a rigorous business analysis to compare potential costs with potential results. In this part of the process, you estimate how much you can expect to spend to develop, produce, and market the value package, as well as how much you can expect to make from sales. Of course, nonprofit organizations and government agencies don't expect profitability, but before proceeding with a new product they weigh costs against likely results such as client or citizen satisfaction and pollution reduction.

Look into the immediate future as well as toward the long term when you forecast costs, sales, and profits. Think, too, about how the product might be affected by competitive actions. Then, if the product concept meets your organization's goals for relationship building, sales, and profits, you can embark on the next step—product design and development. If the concept doesn't meet your goals, you can drop it before you invest another penny, and look at other concepts.

During a business analysis, you also investigate the possibility of **cannibalization**, the potentially undesirable result of a new product cutting into sales of the marketer's existing product line. If a new product can succeed only at the expense of your other products, you may want to think twice about introducing it. On the other hand, some marketers argue that if they don't cannibalize their own products, rivals will. "When you are at the top, you have to have the courage to say, 'I have to stop investing in this great product, and I'm going to use the money to generate a new product that will kill it,'" says Willem Roelandts of Hewlett-Packard. "If you're not doing that,

cannibalization

the potentially undesirable result of a new product cutting into sales of the marketer's existing product line

prototype

a sample of the actual product made to test production methods as well as product performance

let me tell you, there's going to be some competitor that's going to do it for you."[27]

Mark Goldman, CEO of Lewis Galoob Toys, anticipated a multi-million dollar investment in producing and marketing Sky Dancers. He expected to sell at least 1.5 million dolls in the first year. Thinking long term, Goldman decided to go ahead, estimating that the doll would cost about $3.30 to make. Resellers (stores such as Toys 'Я' Us and Target) would pay $7.49 and charge consumers $9.99 for Sky Dancer. "Granted, if we only sell a half-million of these, it's going to be very bad news," admitted a Galoob executive. "But this is what the toy industry is all about. If you have a multiyear success, you get past that narrow margin. You already have the molds. Suddenly, the toys are easy to make. The company's sliver of profit becomes a chunk."[28]

Design and Develop the Product

In this stage of the new product development process, you're ready to transform your detailed concept of the value package into an actual product. Often the first step is to build a **prototype**, a sample of the actual product made to test production methods as well as product performance. The prototype helps you check the new product's quality and determine how to incorporate all the features needed to satisfy customer requirements. Sony, for example, moves from concept to rough working prototype in a week. This amazingly short time is possible because Sony's marketers prefer to evaluate new products more fully when they're in prototype form rather than when they're in the description stage.[29]

During the development and design stage, designers at Lewis Galoob Toys made Sky Dancer look good and fly gracefully. After the company made a prototype that could successfully glide through the air, Galoob brought in freelance designers to create Sky Dancer's face, body, and hair. Only then did Galoob invest in molds to turn out Sky Dancer dolls by the thousands.[30]

Many marketers are turning to *computer-aided design (CAD)*, electronically integrated graphic and mathematic modeling techniques used to design and test new products on the computer screen. Some marketers now use virtual-reality software to try out prototypes before they build. Caterpillar, for example, tests computer designs of new earthmoving equipment in a virtual-reality environment that simulates actual field conditions. Thus engineers who can see how new products would operate are able to make important changes in design before investing in prototype construction. "We take CAD data that describe the vehicles, put them in the virtual environment, and instead of using iron, we manufacture our machines in electrons and light," explains Caterpillar engineer Kem D. Ahlers.[31]

When you design a product these days, you also must take into account its impact on the natural environment and ISO 14000 standards ◄──┘ **(p. 95)**. The German firm of Siemens Nixdorf is one of many durable-goods marketers that use *design for disassembly (DFD)* methods to develop a product with components that can be recycled or safely discarded. A new Siemens Nixdorf computer, from Germany, was designed to have two-thirds fewer parts than a six-year-old model, and those parts can be quickly and easily taken apart for recycling in toys and other products.[32]

One of the newer developments in product testing and development is virtual reality. This photograph shows an employee testing a Caterpillar tractor using a virtual-reality model. It is much easier to learn where to put controls, how much visibility is needed, and so forth when you can simulate real-life situations and practice use of new products in a virtual world. Virtual-reality models can also be used to train people in product usage. What other products can you think of that would benefit from this technology?

simulated test marketing (STM)

a form of computer modeling that predicts a new product's future based on consumer behavior in a laboratory setting, on details of the competitive environment, and on the planned marketing activities

Test Products in the Market

At this point, you need to determine how customers react to the product and to the marketing mix so you can make any necessary changes—or stop production—before the product makes its full-scale debut. You can use *product testing* to determine how a product holds up under actual customer use. Gerber, for example, assembles panels of 2,500 infants (with parental help) to try out the company's new food products. Similarly, Fruit of the Loom asked male musicians in the New Haven Symphony Orchestra, in Connecticut, to evaluate underwear with a new type of waistband.[33]

If you make high-tech products such as computers or software, you'll probably want to use *beta testing*, in which customers try a nearly complete version of a new product to uncover problems that show up under regular use. For example, Oracle, a software marketer, asked its business customer Westinghouse for feedback during a beta test of the Oracle 7 database. In exchange, Westinghouse employees received free training in ways to use the new product more effectively. Not every product beta tests well, of course. By some estimates, one-third of new products are dropped at this point.[34]

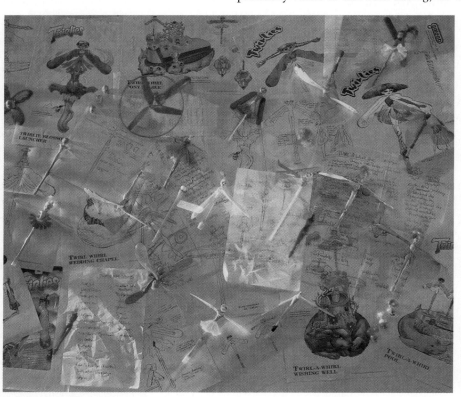

Sky Dancer has been one of the more successful new toys introduced recently. This photo illustrates the product development process, from studying the aerodynamics to designing the proper face. Today, creating and marketing a product are integrated functions. As you develop a product, you need to constantly obtain input from customers in the target market in order to design it in a manner that is attractive to them and best meets their needs. Would you use STM to test a product like Sky Dancer? Why?

Many marketers won't put out a product without first test marketing **(p. 153)** it to measure reaction to the item (and its marketing mix) in a specific geographic area. Before Johnson & Johnson's Vistakon unit brought out Acuvue, a disposable contact lens, the company test marketed it for less than a year—even as it built a factory in anticipation of a nationwide launch. This unorthodox approach gave Vistakon a six-month head start over rivals, and Acuvue quickly captured 25 percent of the U.S. market for contact lens products.[35]

Galoob Toys tested Sky Dancer in three cities. The San Francisco test market site was F.A.O. Schwarz, an upscale toy store. Store employees demonstrated the flying doll, and a case of Sky Dancers flew off the shelves in a week. A new shipment of 12 cases sold out in only three days, prompting an F.A.O. Schwarz toy buyer to comment, "I now expect to sell thousands before Christmas, ten times the number I'd planned for."[36]

Not all marketers choose to put a product out in the market to test customer reaction (where competitors can see what the company is doing). Some use **simulated test marketing (STM)**, a form of computer modeling that predicts a new product's future based on consumer behavior in a laboratory setting, on details of the competitive environment, and on the planned marketing activities. Ore-Ida and many other marketers use this testing approach. It's less costly than an actual field market test; it's con-

commercialization

putting the product into full-scale production and introducing it with full marketing support into the market

ducted in a private laboratory setting, out of range of rivals' eyes; and it's less time-consuming than putting a product in stores and waiting for a reaction to measure.[37]

Commercialize the Product

The final stage in the new product development process is **commercialization**: putting the product into full-scale production and introducing it with full marketing support into the market. As expensive as development and testing can be, commercialization typically costs even more, since the price tag includes all the investments in manufacturing, packaging, shipping, and promoting the new product to get it into the marketing channel and, from there, into the hands of customers.

Of course, you can't stop listening for customer feedback when your new product reaches the commercialization stage. In fact, smart marketers listen even harder at this point so they can move quickly to fix any problems and work on improvements or new product ideas that bubble up. For example, at Norton McNaughton, a women's apparel marketer, designers are constantly in touch with department store salespeople who report what sells and what shoppers say. "It's my direct link to the woman at the register buying my product," says Carrie Cline-Tunick, a Norton McNaughton designer. "If there is a problem, I can immediately react to it and correct it."[38]

The time and cost involved in developing and bringing a new product to market varies. As you look at Table 10.3, which compares the development of five products, remember that these data don't include marketing costs. Also note that some products will be on the market for only a few years, while others will be offered for decades.[39] Even when a product's life span is expected to be quite long, however, many marketers prefer to speed new products to market before the window of opportunity slams shut—or rivals have a chance to launch competing products.

The commercialization stage for Sky Dancer started months before the dolls showed up on toy store shelves. Galoob Toys hired a factory in Shajing, China, to manufacture the dolls. It then showed samples to toy store repre-

T A B L E   **10.3**   **Product Development Efforts Compared**

	Stanley Tools Jobmaster Screwdriver	Rollerblade Bravoblade In-Line Skates	Hewlett-Packard DeskJet 500 Printer	Chrysler Concorde Automobile	Boeing 777 Airplane
Annual production volume (units/year)	100,000	100,000	1.5 million	250,000	50
Sales lifetime (years)	40	3	3	6	30
Sales price	$3	$200	$365	$19,000	$130 million
Number of unique parts	3	35	200	10,000	130,000
Developmental time (years)	1	2	1.5	3.5	4.5
Internal development team (peak size)	3 people	5 people	100 people	850 people	6,800 people
External development team (peak size)	3 people	10 people	100 people	1,400 people	10,000 people
Development cost	$150,000	$750,000	$50 million	$1 billion	$3 billion
Production investment	$150,000	$1 million	$25 million	$600 million	$3 billion

sentatives at trade shows around the world. As the doll appeared on store shelves, it was supported by $4 million in television advertising to reach girls between the ages of 5 and 9. In all, Sky Dancer moved from idea generation to commercialization in 24 months, becoming one of the most popular toys of the 1995–1996 holiday season.[40]

Managing the New Product Development Process

Marketers can manage the new product development process in a variety of ways. In many cases, going outside the organization is a good way of getting help for bringing out a new product. Some marketers form strategic alliances **(p. 39)** with other companies to develop new products by sharing the work, the risks, the costs, and the profits. NYNEX, among others, finds strategic alliances particularly useful for entering international markets. Other marketers, including Lewis Galoob Toys and Apple Computer, use outsourcing **(p. 40)** for many development activities.[41]

As you saw earlier, an increasingly popular approach to managing new product development relies on cross-functional teams **(p. 47)**. More and more, suppliers (in addition to customers) are joining cross-functional teams to help marketers meet customers' wants and needs. Some marketers set up *venture teams* to work only on new product projects. When these teams are isolated from the remainder of the organization and allowed to operate outside normal company channels, they're known as *skunkworks*. Skunkworks are used to develop breakthrough products that might have been slowed, distorted, or derailed by ordinary management procedures. In the following case, you'll see how Rubbermaid manages product development.

Applying the Concepts
Rubbermaid stokes its new product engine

Imagine turning out new products at the rate of more than one a day without market testing. That's the breakneck pace set by Rubbermaid, the $2.2 billion new product juggernaut that makes ordinary, everyday plastic products extraordinarily well. From lunchboxes to mailboxes to window boxes, the Ohio-based company's 5,000 household and business products are designed and marketed uncommonly well. The company enjoys an incredible 90 percent new product success rate. How does Rubbermaid do it?

To start, the new product development process is a team effort. Cross-functional teams of five to seven people are assigned to specific product lines. Although Rubbermaid believes in marketing research and concept testing, it doesn't want its products prematurely exposed to competitor scrutiny. "We don't want to be copied," explains CEO Wolfgang Schmitt. "It's not that much riskier to just roll it out. Plus, it puts pressure on us to do it right the first time."

The teams have to meet high hurdles that Schmitt has set for new products. He expects Rubbermaid to move into a new product category every 12 to 18 months and to get one-third of its sales from products launched in the preceding five years. He's also aiming to double overall sales and get one-fourth of all sales from markets outside the United States by 2000. That's

why Schmitt puts 14 percent of profits into research and development.

Rubbermaid's teams are expert at spotting trends in the marketing environment. Many new products, including the Litterless Lunchbox line, were designed with an eye toward the natural environment. Other new products, such as an antimicrobial mop bucket, provide health-conscious consumers with a germ-fighting feature unmatched by competing products. Rubbermaid's new product success is one reason for the company's long-time status as one of America's most admired corporations.[42]

Make marketing decisions

1. Do you agree with Wolfgang Schmitt's policy of not putting new products into test marketing? Outline the pros and cons.

2. If you were Schmitt, would you invite suppliers or retailers (or both) to join your new product teams? Explain your answer.

3. Why do you think Schmitt set goals for the amount of sales that should come from products made in the past five years?

4. Where should a team look for new product ideas in kitchen accessories?

One of Rubbermaid's goals is to turn out a new product every day. However, it is one thing to make a product and quite another to make it a success. This Rubbermaid ad effectively highlights the benefits of one of its products and focuses on the company's responsiveness to customer wants and needs. Given the high cost of advertising, what else could Rubbermaid do to promote new products to potential consumers and business buyers?

quality function deployment (QFD)

a cross-functional effort to identify customer requirements and translate them into specifications to be used in defining, designing, producing, and marketing a quality product

Applying Quality Function Deployment

Today's attention to new product quality means building quality into every stage of the development process, from idea to commercialization. To do this, Campbell's Soup, Fidelity Trust, and many other world-class marketers are using **quality function deployment (QFD)**, a cross-functional effort to identify customer requirements and translate them into specifications to be used in defining, designing, producing, and marketing a quality product.[43] QFD helps marketers define quality from the customer's perspective, an important consideration when working toward building long-term customer relationships.

The *house of quality* is a graphical QFD technique that brings the voice of the customer into the new product development process. The first step is to research what customers need and the benefits they expect (called *customer attributes* in this context). The next step is to segment the market according to the needs and benefits you've identified, putting them into priority order for each segment.

After determining how well customers think their requirements are being met by competing products, you can plan product features (called *engineering characteristics*) and other elements of the value package to meet or exceed the level of quality customers say they require. Before you actually make a new product, you evaluate the cost and the difficulty of including each element in the value package and see which are most important to customers.

Then you're ready to move ahead to make and market the product, with customer-defined quality built in.[44]

Before you go on . . .

A. What is the purpose of screening new product ideas?

B. What is concept testing and why is it important?

C. What is cannibalization, and why do marketers conduct a business analysis?

D. Why are marketers using quality function deployment?

Product Planning and Management

Developing and marketing a new product is only one aspect of planning and managing your product mix. The product strategy you choose drives the actions you take to plan, launch, and manage new products. But you also have to think about how each new product fits among your existing products and among the products you plan to offer in the future. This exercise helps you make decisions about line and brand extensions as well as about adding, modifying, and eliminating individual products.

Developing Product Strategies

How you manage new and existing products depends in part on which of the four product development strategies shown in Figure 10.3 your organization is pursuing. If you're following a *market penetration strategy*, your goal is to boost sales of existing products in existing markets. Hershey did this by setting up eye-catching store displays for its candy bars, offering cents-off

F I G U R E **10.3** **Product Strategy Choices**

Marketers can pursue any of four product strategies. Two strategies help marketers build relationships in existing markets using new or existing products, and two strategies help marketers build relationships in new markets using new or existing products.

	Existing Product	**New Product**
Existing Market	Market penetration strategy	Product development strategy
New Market	Market development strategy	Product diversification strategy

product line

a group of closely related products offered by one marketer

product mix

the assortment of product lines and individual products offered by one marketer

coupons to encourage buying, and building excitement through sweepstakes promotions.[45] In a *market development strategy*, you want to introduce an existing product to *new* markets or segments. Blimpie International, a submarine sandwich chain that competes with Subway, used this strategy to expand beyond retail outlets into hospitals and airline food service.[46]

When you follow a *product development strategy*, you're launching a new product in a market where you're already active. Southland used this strategy to introduce the 7-Eleven Phone Card, a prepaid telephone card, in its national convenience store chain.[47] In a *product diversification strategy*, you develop a new product for a new market, which can be tricky because you have no experience with the product or the market. Following this strategy, Slim-Fast Foods brought out a new line of reduced-fat cookies to compete with Nabisco's SnackWell's cookies in the healthier snack market, where Slim-Fast hadn't been active.[48]

Working with Product Lines and Product Mixes

To implement your product strategy, you build both a product line and a product mix. A **product line** is a group of closely related products offered by

Adding to its line of consumer imaging products, Kodak has introduced the Advanced Photo System under the Kodak Advantix brand. These new products are designed to make it easier to load a camera and to produce pictures of various sizes. Does a large, successful firm like Kodak need to continuously add new offerings to its product mix? Does Kodak risk confusing consumers with too many types of cameras and film? Why?

one marketer. The relationship may exist because products are marketed to the same customer segments, satisfy similar customer needs, or move through the same channels. For example, among Eastman Kodak's multiple lines are consumer imaging products (films, cameras, and videotapes); motion picture and television imaging products (films and digital motion picture imaging systems); office imaging products (copiers, scanners, and microfilmers); and professional, printing, and publishing products (films, chemicals, and graphic reproduction products). By grouping products into lines defined according to customer segments, Kodak can better coordinate the marketing activities it uses to reach each segment. The Advanced Photo System (APS) is a newer product that Kodak is using to maintain its consumer market share.[49]

When you have more than one product line, you have to manage your **product mix**, the assortment of product lines and individual products offered by one marketer. Many marketers use tools such as the growth–share matrix **(p. 40)** to balance their investments among products in the mix. Kodak's product mix includes four lines of imaging products as well as product lines for health care markets. Every time Kodak introduces new products or changes the number or type of products in a line, it considers the effect on its overall product mix. For example, by selling off its Sterling Winthrop pharmaceuticals line to SmithKline Beecham, Kodak was able to redirect investment to its imaging product lines. The following section shows what happened when one small business changed its product mix.

SMALL BUSINESS WATCH

Nixing a me-too product mix

One new-to-the-world product changed the entire product mix of Sashco Sealants, a small business in Commerce City, Colorado. That new product, Lexel, was a clear sealant for doors, windows, and gutters that was differentiated from competing products by its unique ability to be painted. What Lexel taught Sashco president Les Burch is that his company needed a mix of innovative products to compete more effectively with rivals.

When Sashco launched Lexel, it invested heavily to buy special machinery and expand production space for the new product, which was packaged in a clear cartridge to emphasize its most outstanding feature. Three years after the launch, Sashco's sales had tripled, with Lexel accounting for 90 percent of sales.

The runaway success of Lexel started Burch thinking about new products. "When I compared [Lexel] with the rest of the product line, it was obvious that most of our other goods were 'me-too' items—made because the competition had them first, not because we had something better," he observes. So Burch pushed ahead with an innovative new adhesive. He also proposed eliminating the eight imitations, a radical step that some employees feared would drive retail customers away.

After three years of internal debate, Burch dropped the me-too products. With the focus on unique products alone, company's sales and profits soared. Burch also decided to sell only to specialty stores, where customers were more concerned about product functionality than low prices. These two decisions repositioned Sashco as a company with an uncommon product mix. Today the company has more than $7 million in annual sales.[50]

Do you think most companies should follow Sashco's example and discontinue me-too products?

Once a brand name has been successfully established in consumers' minds, that same brand name and image can be used to introduce new product lines. Anyone who loves Snickers candy bars may be tempted to try Snickers ice cream bars, and the same is true of those who love Butterfingers. How successful would the Snickers name be if it were used for other food products?

Managing your product mix means taking into account both the width of the mix and the length of your product lines. The number of product lines you offer is the *product mix width,* while the number of products in each line is the *product line length.* Of course, no product mix stays static for very long. Marketers are constantly reevaluating their product offerings in response to changes in customer needs, competitive pressures, or other forces in the marketing environment.

Extending Lines and Brands

In recent years, marketers have tended to shy away from the expense and risk of introducing new-to-the-world products and new product lines that widen the product mix. Instead, the trend is toward lengthening product lines by line extension or brand extension, banking on brand equity to draw customer interest and build sales.

For example, Mars and Nestlé are both extending their well-known candy brands into new ice cream product lines.[51]

Many marketers see line and brand extensions  **(p. 264)** as a relatively low-cost, low-risk way to satisfy customers in various market segments. After all, customers who trust the brand are likely to respond well to new products under the same umbrella, a tendency that increases your marketing efficiency. Extensions can boost sales by giving customers more choices such as new flavors, colors, and price, so they won't defect to competing products. This strategy worked for Hidden Valley, which retained existing customers and attracted new ones by introducing another salad dressing flavor. In addition, line and brand extensions can help the marketer fill store shelves to keep competitors out.[52]

However, experts warn that extensions can dilute brand equity **(p. 266)** if the products are only loosely related to those currently being marketed under a given brand. What's more, channel members may resent carrying multiple extensions, especially if they seem to be redundant or are not clearly differentiated from competing products. You also risk cannibalizing existing products and disrupting customer buying patterns without an offsetting increase in sales or profits to balance the added marketing investment. There are always exceptions, of course. For example, sales of all Frito-Lay corn chips increased after the company launched its Cool Ranch Doritos extension. So plan carefully if you want brand and line extensions to be profitable.[53]

Adding, Modifying, and Eliminating Products

You can change your product mix by adding, modifying, and eliminating products. These product decisions help you balance the level of investment, risk, and profits across the entire product mix. They also help you deal with changes in your marketing environment, such as sudden opportunities or threats, that affect one or more products in your mix.

You can add a new product (or product line) in several ways. One way is to develop the product (by yourself or with a partner). Another way is to buy it, complete, from another marketer. Smucker's used this approach to widen its product mix beyond jellies and jams by entering a new product category with its purchase of Mrs. Smith's frozen pies from Kellogg. A third way is to license a brand or a technology to boost a new product offering. Kellogg, for example, licensed ConAgra's established Healthy Choice brand for a new line of breakfast cereals.[54]

You can modify a product in any number of ways to carry out a market penetration or market development strategy. One way is through repositioning, which changes the way customers think of the product. A second way is to modify one or more elements in the product's value package. Coca-Cola, for example, modified the packaging of Coke Classic as a new weapon in the cola wars. By bringing back the original green contour bottle, Coke differentiates the product from Pepsi-Cola and other competitors and adds nostalgic appeal for thirsty baby boomers.[55]

Some marketers never stop modifying their products. At Dow, employees use continuous improvement to constantly upgrade the company's agricultural, chemical, and consumer products. Using a new catalyst technology, Dow improved the performance of polyolefin products bought by makers of appliances, sports equipment, and other products.[56] Similarly, Honda (among other automotive marketers) regularly adds safety and performance

Coca-Cola is constantly adapting its product line to meet the changing marketplace. When New Coke didn't prove a success, Coca-Cola quickly recovered by repositioning the original flavor as Coke Classic. Despite the fact that Coca-Cola is one of the world's most recognized brand names, the company realizes that global competition requires aggressive and continuous promotion of its existing products as well as the introduction of new ones. What are competitors currently doing to challenge Coke's leading position in the soft drink market? How should Coke respond?

All of these products have been or are being replaced by newer, more advanced products. For example, typewriters are being replaced by personal computers. The makers of these older products must anticipate such changes and move quickly to the next level of competition in order to remain successful. Given the increasing level of international competition and the rapid development of new products, failure to do so may result in a critical loss of market share. What products are gaining ground in the phone industry? The recorded music industry?

features to its cars to stay ahead of competitors and meet buyers' ever-higher expectations for quality.

No matter how successful a product has been, you may, at some point, decide to eliminate it from your product mix. This is an option if sales and profits are nearly gone, if technology has made your product obsolete, or if customers no longer need your product. Procter & Gamble, for example, eliminated its Clarion line of women's cosmetics because of poor sales. Then the company was able to shift its resources to two better selling cosmetics brands, Cover Girl and Max Factor.[57] Some 80 percent of your profit may come from 20 percent of your products, so it is often wise to trim some products from the mix in order to focus on the most profitable.

Retailers use the same reasoning when they eliminate products. However, without retail channels to reach consumers, manufacturers must find other ways to reach customers or, ultimately, they'll have to eliminate the products. Still, because eliminating a product is a drastic move, marketers don't take this step until they have considered the impact on their product lines, their product mixes, and their customers.

Understanding the Product Life Cycle

Just as people pass through various stages during their life cycle, so too do products pass through a series of stages during their time in the market. The **product life cycle** is the four-stage cycle of introduction, growth, maturity, and decline that characterizes a product's movement through the marketplace. The product life cycle, shown in Figure 10.4, applies only to a product category, not to an individual product or brand. A particular product may spend more time in one stage and less time in another. As with perennial sellers such as Crayola crayons, you may be able to use the marketing mix to extend the life cycle indefinitely. So even though you can't foresee the exact length or shape of your product's life cycle, you can consider your marketing actions in light of these four stages:[58]

- *Introduction.* During the first stage of the product life cycle, you develop and introduce a new product. Bringing a product from idea generation to commercialization to the first round of customer purchasing requires a hefty investment that may not pay back for months or years, if at all. During this stage, the aims are to set up a marketing channel and to build awareness of and demand for the new product.

- *Growth.* The new product enters the second stage when industry sales grow from a trickle to a torrent. Now you face competition from imitators that either copy or improve on your product. To continue building sales, you need to emphasize product differentiation, add channels, revise pricing to combat rivals, and promote your product's benefits and superiority.

- *Maturity.* Slower sales growth signals the start of the third stage. The market is saturated because most customers or prospects have already bought or at least tried the product. You and your competitors battle over fewer buyers by promoting brands, further segmenting the mar-

product life cycle

the four-stage cycle of introduction, growth, maturity, and decline that characterizes a product's movement through the marketplace

	Introduction	Growth	Maturity	Decline
Sales	Low but slowly rising	Rapidly growing	Peak	Falling off
Competition	None yet or few	Growing number	Many rivals	Fewer and fewer
Product stategy	Develop, launch product to meet customer needs	Improve product to keep current customers, attract new ones	Differentiate product to defend against rivals; segment market	Minimize investment and consider elimination or modify for new markets, new uses
Price strategy	Either high (to innovators) or low (to gain market share)	In line with competitors and lower costs	Lower price to retain share	Possible increase if rivals leave; or decreases to get rid of eliminated products
Channel strategy	Limited but growing number of channels, partners	More channels, partners	Widest number of channels, partners	Decreasing number of channels, partners
IMC strategy	Build awareness and trial	Stress brand, competitive superiority	Reinforce customer loyalty	Reduce investment, use tactics to get rid of eliminated products

Sales

Time

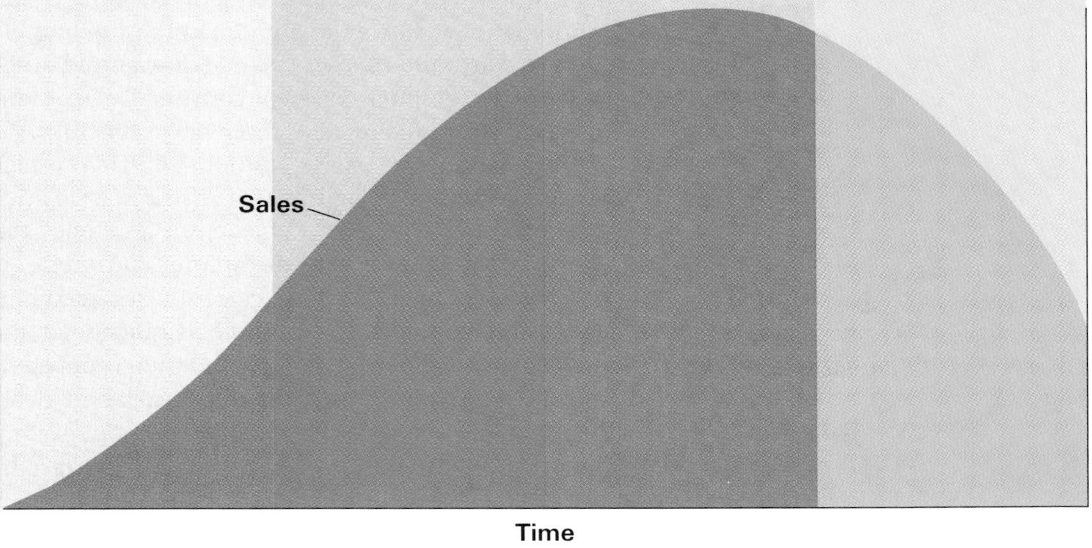

FIGURE **10.4**

Product Life Cycle
Each stage in the product life cycle is characterized by changes in sales and competition. By creating strategies for each of the four Ps of the marketing mix, marketers can establish and manage customer relationships in each of the four stages.

ket, trying to hold onto channels, and adding or modifying product lines to revive sales. To compete, you may have to drop your price, which could cut profits.

- *Decline.* In the last stage of the product life cycle, sales and profits taper off. You and your competitors are chasing fewer customers, and you're losing channel partners to newer products. If many rivals leave the market, you may be able to charge a higher price and boost profits. You may also be able to use marketing activities to defend your product. If the product isn't profitable enough, however, you may want to stop investing in it. Ultimately, you (or your channel partners) may eliminate the product from the product mix.

market modification

looking for new users or increased use among present users

product modification

changing product quality, features, or style to attract new users or more usage from present customers

Issues for critical thinking

Have you ever looked for a product only to find that it's no longer available? How long had the product been available? Why do you think the manufacturer or retailer dropped it? As a marketer, what questions would you ask before eliminating a product?

Some marketers have learned to extend the product life cycle through market modification and product modification. **Market modification** means looking for new users or increased use among present users. Backpacks, for example, were designed for the military. Students were a new, and highly profitable, user group. Arm & Hammer has greatly increased sales by finding new uses for its baking soda.

Product modification involves changing product quality, features, or style to attract new users or more usage from present customers. Makers of personal computers have been quite successful in introducing new features to keep sales growing.

No product life cycle is preordained. What happens in each life cycle stage is influenced by customer needs, competition, and every other element in the marketing environment. In some industries, the rapid pace of technological advance has shortened the product life cycle or allowed marketers to postpone its later stages. For example, Intel breathes new life into its existing computer chips by continually upgrading their performance—even as it's introducing new, more powerful chips.[59]

On the other hand, style, fashion, and fad products follow unique life cycles, as illustrated in Figure 10.5. A *style* is a distinctive form of expression carried through by product characteristics. Styles are popular for a time, recede as other styles come to the fore, and often enjoy a resurgence years later. A *fashion* is a style that's currently accepted or popular in a given market. Designer apparel, for example, is quickly adopted by a few customers, later copied for the mass market, and then dropped in favor of new fashions. A *fad* is a short-lived fashion that peaks and declines rapidly because it doesn't satisfy a long-term customer need. For example, the Teenage Mutant Ninja Turtles caught on quickly and faded fast, replaced by the fad of Mighty Morphin Power Rangers.

FIGURE **10.5**

Life Cycles of Style, Fashion, and Fad Products

Sales of fad products peak and fall off more quickly than sales of fashion products, which decrease less dramatically. In contrast, style products follow a pattern of increasing, decreasing, and increasing sales over time.

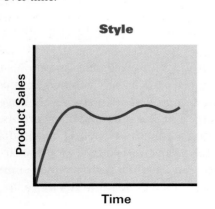

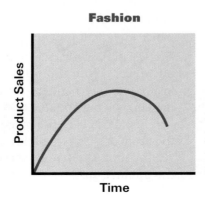

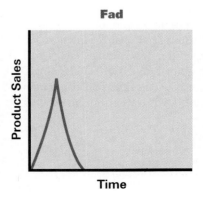

product adoption process

(or response model) the series of attitudinal and behavioral changes leading up to product purchase and adoption

product diffusion process

the process by which new products are adopted by various groups in the market

Planning for Product Adoption and Diffusion

Unfortunately, you can't predict the exact peaks, valleys, or schedule for your product's life cycle. By understanding what may happen in each stage, however, you're able to plan for the future by preparing appropriate marketing strategies. As you plan for marketing throughout the product life cycle, you also have to consider how and when customers adopt your product.

The shape and length of the product life cycle is based on sales to customers. But as you know from personal experience, people don't simply go out and buy a new product. The **product adoption process**, also known as the *response model*, is the series of attitudinal and behavioral changes leading up to product purchase and adoption. In the first stage, *awareness*, potential customers first learn about a new product. If they want to know more, they look for information during the *interest* stage. In the *evaluation* stage, they weigh information about the product's benefits and decide whether to try it. If they want to go ahead, they move into the *trial* stage, where they test the new product. In the *adoption or rejection* stage, people decide whether to continue buying the product or to reject it.

Traditionally, marketers viewed this progression from awareness to adoption of a product as a linear process. In the context of mass marketing, it was assumed that marketing activities would move customers in an orderly fashion from one stage to the next. However, within the context of target marketing and market segmentation, marketers now have the tools to identify individual customers, research individual needs and buying behavior, tailor marketing activities to individual needs, and track individual response. Because different customers move toward adoption at different times and in different ways, marketers are seeking to develop and maintain relationships with customers throughout the process.

The key is to work backward from adoption to arrive at an understanding of how customers in the segment actually use, buy, try, evaluate, develop interest, and become aware of a product. Using ongoing research and two-way communication with customers, marketers can then shape their marketing activities to give users what they need, regardless of the stage of the adoption process. Thus, strengthening relationships with customers throughout the process leads to adoptions that influence the product life cycle.[60]

The possibilities for using marketing to build and sustain relationships at any stage of the adoption process are endless, as you've seen throughout this book. You can combine product, price, channel management, and IMC **(p. 13)** in a variety of marketing mixes to fit your target market, your marketing environment, and your organization's goals. As many marketers do, you may choose to introduce your new product in a limited number of markets and gradually expand into other markets as you gain more adopters.

Not all customers adopt a new product at the same time, of course. Some consumer and organizational customers are quick to adopt something new, while others wait. The **product diffusion process**, graphed in Figure 10.6, is the process by which new products are adopted by various groups in the

FIGURE **10.6**

Product Diffusion
The product diffusion process shows how various customers adopt a new product. The innovators are the first, while the laggards are the last to buy a new product.

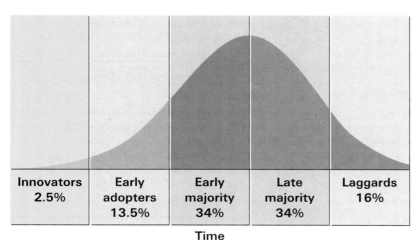

| Innovators 2.5% | Early adopters 13.5% | Early majority 34% | Late majority 34% | Laggards 16% |

Time

product managers

plan and implement marketing decisions for specific products or brands

product management

form of organization that groups employees according to the products they work on

market. First to try a new product are the *innovators*, followed by the *early adopters*, the *early majority*, and the *late majority*. The last to adopt a new product are the *laggards*.

Innovators and early adopters begin buying a new product early in the diffusion process, building the sales curve that brings the product from the introduction to the growth stage of the life cycle. Often, your first marketing efforts will be geared toward these early purchasers, because they influence later purchasers through opinion leadership and word of mouth. As early and late majority customers adopt the product, it moves from the growth stage into the maturity stage. Now you want to reinforce your customers' adoption decision and defend against competitors. By the time laggards start buying, the product is in maturity—and in fact may be in decline. At this point, you're using marketing to extend the product's life and encourage continued purchasing.

Managing Products and Categories

The way marketers organize to manage their products and categories has changed in recent years. For decades, many marketers assigned **product managers** (also known as brand managers) to plan and implement marketing decisions for specific products or brands. Procter & Gamble, for example, was a pioneer in assigning marketing responsibilities for one brand (such as Pampers disposable diapers) to one manager. This form of organization, known as **product management**, groups employees according to the products they work on.

However, as P&G and some other marketers geared up to turn out more and more new products, they needed a way to manage potential duplication and optimize profits. De-emphasizing product management, marketers are now moving toward *product category management*, an organizational approach in which one manager or group of managers is responsible for coordinating the marketing decisions for an entire product category. Product category management focuses on the category rather than on individual brands. Thus, decisions made for one brand (such as Pampers disposable diapers) are coordinated with those made for the company's brands in the category (such as Luvs disposable diapers).[61] This avoids potential conflicts among a marketer's brands and helps the marketer compete more effectively within the category.

Product and category management applies to consumer and organizational products, goods, and services alike. As you'll see in the next chapter, however, marketers face unique challenges when they manage service products.

Before you go on . . .

A. Identify the four new product development strategies.

B. How does a product line differ from a product mix?

C. What is the product life cycle and why is it important?

D. How does product adoption and product diffusion work?

Summary

1. **Differentiate among the types of new products.**

   The five types of new products are (1) new to the world, (2) new to the marketer, (3) line extensions, (4) repositioned, and (5) improved. In terms of how innovation affects consumer behavior, new products may use continuous innovation, dynamic innovation, or discontinuous innovation.

2. **Analyze why some new products succeed and others fail.**

   New products succeed because of product superiority, customer orientation, market attractiveness, early entrance to markets, careful timing, and excellent teamwork and execution. New products fail for the opposite reasons and because of improper targeting and positioning, problems with product and marketing planning, overpromised satisfaction, lack of competitive differentiation, inadequate value, poor marketing communication, faulty channel management, and inadequate profits.

3. **Identify the sequence of activities in the new product development process.**

   The activities in the new product development process are: scanning the environment and generating ideas, screening out inappropriate ideas, developing and testing product concepts, analyzing business potential, designing and developing the product, testing it in the market, and commercializing the product.

4. **Describe the four product development strategies.**

   A market penetration strategy aims for more sales in current markets from current products. A market development strategy brings current products to new markets. A product development strategy brings new products to current markets. A product diversification strategy brings new products to new markets.

5. **Define product line and product mix, and contrast product mix width with product line length.**

   A product line is a group of closely related products offered by one marketer. A product mix is the assortment of product lines and individual products offered by one marketer. Product mix width describes the number of product lines being offered. Product line length describes the number of products in each line.

6. **List and discuss the four stages in the product life cycle.**

   The four stages in the product life cycle are introduction, growth, maturity, and decline. The product is developed and launched in the introduction stage. Sales build during the growth stage. In the maturity stage, sales growth slows as the market is saturated. Sales taper off in the decline stage.

7. **Show how the product adoption process drives product diffusion.**

   The product adoption process consists of five stages: (1) awareness, when customers learn about a new product; (2) interest, when they look for information; (3) evaluation, when they consider trying it; (4) trial, when customers test the product; and (5) adoption or rejection, when they decide to buy or reject the product. Customers move through these stages at their own pace and in their own ways. That's why you need to shape your marketing activities to build relationships throughout the process. In the product diffusion process, the new product is adopted over time by various groups in this order: innovators, early adopters, early majority, late majority, and laggards.

KEY TERMS

cannibalization 292

commercialization 295

concept testing 291

continuous improvement 288

line extensions 283

market modification 304

new product development process 289

product adoption process 305

product diffusion process 305

product life cycle 302

product line 299

product management 306

product managers 306

product mix 299

product modification 304

prototype 293

quality function deployment (QFD) 297

simulated test marketing (STM) 294

Skill-Building Applications

1. How can you test the market for yourself as an employee or a business owner in the field of your choice?

2. What is the product mix of a nonprofit organization such as the American Cancer Society? Does this mix change over time? Why?

3. As the European marketing director for Adidas, how would you screen ideas for new types of athletic shoe?

4. Generate ideas for new products that Flexible Personnel, an employment service in Indiana, might offer corporate customers. How would these product ideas solve personnel problems faced by the company's customers?

5. What kind of business analysis should American Medical Response, a Boston-based ambulance service, use to evaluate proposed new services?

6. How can Toshiba use product design to make its newest laptop computer more functional and to differentiate it from competitors?

Getting Involved in Marketing

1. *On Your Own* Contrast the product life cycles of CB (citizens band) radio and cellular phones. In which life cycle stage is each? In which stage of the diffusion process is each? Do you think sales will grow or drop for each product next year? Summarize your conclusions in a brief report.

2. *On Your Own* If you were developing a new CD-ROM fantasy game, how would you use concept testing and market testing before commercialization? Write a memo to your marketing research firm, explaining what you want to learn from testing.

3. *Find Out More* Research how a marketer developed a recently introduced product. Did the company omit any steps in the new product development process? How did it manage the process? How quickly did it move from idea to commercialization? In a five-minute talk to your class, report your findings, including your assessment of whether the product is likely to succeed or fail.

4. *In a Partnership* With another classmate, collect magazine and newspaper ads for a new product. Analyze the ads to determine the target market and the customer needs the product is designed to satisfy. List the product's features and benefits, and do the same with a competing product already on the market. What competitive advantages do you see for each? What, if anything, about the new product helps it compete more effectively?

5. *In a Team* With other students, interview the head of a department on campus to find out how new courses—new products—are developed. Where do ideas come from? What business analysis is performed before a course is offered? What testing does the department or college do? Compare your findings with those of other students. What improvements can you suggest for your college's product development process?

6. *In a Team* With other students, select a product in the decline stage of its life cycle. In front of the class, conduct a debate in which one student ar- gues for modifying the product to extend its life while the other student argues for eliminating the item. What does the class think of each argument?

VideoCase McDonald's Cooks Up a Burger for Grown-Up Tastes

McDonald's has a long history of cooking up new food prod- ucts that sell . . . and sell . . . and sell. Since 1955, when founder Ray Kroc opened his first fast-food restaurant in Des Plaines, Illinois, hamburgers have been the main menu attraction. But over the years, as the company expanded to dot the globe with over 18,500 restaurants, it has introduced a steady stream of additional food items to bring customers back again and again.

Some, like the Big Mac and the Egg McMuffin, were invented by franchisees who own individual McDonald's units. Since the product's introduction in 1967, 18 billion Big Macs have been sold. For its part, the Egg McMuffin, introduced in 1973, has endured for more than two decades as the focus of the chain's breakfast promotions.

Other new products, like the Arch Deluxe, came from the ex- perts working in McDonald's test kitchens. Andrew Selvaggio, the executive chef at McDonald's, guided the development of the Arch Deluxe. His philosophy about food products: they must be fun. "Fun is a sandwich with a lot of action, a lot of layers," Selvaggio says. The Arch Deluxe has plenty of layers: a quarter- pound hamburger on a bed of ketchup, topped by American cheese, a tomato slice, lettuce leaves, slivered onions, and a mustard-mayonnaise sauce, on a soft, bakery-style roll.

As with any McDonald's food product, the amount, flavor, and assembly of the ingredients has been carefully planned to ap- peal to a specific market segment. In this case, adults are the targeted segment. Selvaggio sees a trend toward stronger fla- voring for adult tastes, and he has developed the Arch Deluxe in line with this trend. The pepper and mustard flavors are more distinct than in other McDonald's foods. In addition, cus- tomers who crave an "outdoorsy" taste can order the Arch Deluxe with optional hickory-smoked bacon (at a higher price).

The order in which ingredients are positioned in the bun, known in McDonald's test kitchens as the "sandwich build," makes a great deal of difference in the flavors that the cus- tomer perceives. Selvaggio tested a number of sandwich builds before deciding on the final order of the layers. For a time, the Arch Deluxe was test marketed in McDonald's units

in the Baton Rouge area, allowing the company to gauge cus- tomer reaction before launching the product across the United States and Canada in 1996.

To build sales momentum quickly, McDonald's put a $75 mil- lion advertising campaign behind the Arch Deluxe introduction. Commercials ran on broadcast network and cable television, in- cluding networks such as Telemundo, which reaches Hispanic and Latino viewers. Images of Ronald McDonald—in a business suit—heralded the appearance of a product specifically for adults. The company also arranged for "Arch Deluxe Day" at the Summer Olympic Games in Atlanta. Thanks to the strong pro- motion, sales of the Arch Deluxe were running above company expectations after only two months.[62]

Strategies and applications

1. How might McDonald's have test marketed the Arch Deluxe without allowing competitors to find out about the new product?

2. Where in the product life cycle would you place McDonald's Big Mac hamburger product? The Egg McMuffin? How can Mc- Donald's extend the life cycle of these products?

3. Would you have classified the new Arch Deluxe sandwich as entirely new to the world, a line extension, or a repositioned product? Why?

4. In its product development process, how would you suggest that McDonald's generate ideas for future sandwiches geared toward adults? Toward children? Be specific.

5. With the Arch Deluxe introduction, which of the four product development strategies do you think McDonald's was pursu- ing? Support your answer.

6. Was McDonald's using continuous innovation, dynamically continuous innovation, or discontinuous innovation when de- veloping the Arch Deluxe? Explain your answer.

Team project

With other students, assume the role of franchise owners operat- ing a McDonald's restaurant near your campus. Your franchise has been chosen to test market a new meatloaf-sandwich product, which has been specially developed to appeal to adults. How would you promote this product during the test to encourage adults to try the new sandwich? What goals would you set for evaluating the results? How long a test would you recommend— and why? Write a brief report outlining your team's ideas.

11

Services Marketing

Learning Goals

After you have read and studied this chapter, you will be able to:

1. Describe the goods–services continuum and show how the lines between goods and services are blurring.
2. Explain the four unique characteristics of services.
3. Discuss how services can be classified.
4. Demonstrate how customers use search qualities, experience qualities, and credence qualities to evaluate products.
5. Define service gaps, which customers use to judge service quality.
6. Show the steps marketers can take to manage service quality for customer satisfaction.
7. Identify the unique challenges of marketing nonprofit services.

PROFILE

Collegiate Health Care makes the grade in service

Only an entrepreneur like Brett Prager could turn a sprained ankle into a $2 million business . . . and he did it to improve service. When Prager was a graduate business student at Columbia University in New York City, he had to wait an hour at the student health center for treatment of this minor injury. Could an outside company, he wondered, provide health care services more efficiently?

Pursuing the idea as a school project, Prager questioned 200 colleges about their student health centers. Eighty colleges returned his survey, and 28 expressed interest in outsourcing such services. What started as a sprained ankle became a golden opportunity to tap a $2 billion market for student medical services at 2,500 U.S. campuses.

After graduation, Prager raised $1.2 million from Oxford Health Plan and two venture capital firms. As he marketed his service, he learned that college deans care more about service quality than about low costs. So he repositioned his business as an outsourcing alternative offering an intangible but important benefit: efficient health care for students at the same cost as in-house health centers. He included services such as a library of recorded telephone messages on medical topics and a 24-hour medical hotline staffed by nurses. Through his link with Oxford Health, he also offered discounted prescription drugs.

Within a year, Prager signed Sacred Heart University in Connecticut as his first customer. Today, Collegiate Health Care centers serve 16,500 students at six northeastern campuses. The entrepreneur is aiming for $100 million in annual revenues by the turn of the century—quite a handsome payback for the frustration of slow service at a college health care center.[1]

Brett Prager found that marketing a service isn't quite the same as marketing a physical product. In this chapter, you'll explore the special challenges of services marketing. First you'll look at the nature and classification of services as products. Then you'll see how service marketers manage service quality for customer satisfaction. The chapter closes with an overview of nonprofit services marketing.

Services Are Products Too

Services aren't always just a part of the product value package. They can also stand on their own as intangible products that offer educational, legal, financial, health, cosmetic, or other benefits to customers. Brett Prager's Collegiate Health Care center is a service product. Its value package **(p. 11)** provides organizational customers—colleges—with the benefit of improved health for the colleges' customers—their students. Bandages and pills may be involved, but the main component of this value package is expert medical services.

The list of service products is diverse and virtually endless. From air travel to advertising, banking to building maintenance, entertainment to education, services are an important part of the global economy. In fact, in the past few decades, services have come to the forefront as the fastest growing category of products in the world.

Services in the Global Economy

Perhaps you've heard about the *service economy*, also known as the *service sector*. Both phrases refer to the segment of a nation's economy represented by services of all kinds, as shown in Table 11.1. In the United States, the service sector has grown explosively. It now generates three-quarters of the country's gross domestic product and accounts for nearly four out of five of the country's jobs.[2] That means that there is an excellent chance that you will be working in the service sector when you graduate.

The health services industry is one of the largest in the service sector. Many service providers, including Collegiate Health Care, fall into this category. Like business services, this category will continue to expand in the coming years as baby boomers age and look for medical advice and treatment. Technology is also a major factor in this category's growth. Consider a business like Team Radiology in Durham, North Carolina. The company helps rural hospitals send medical scans over telephone lines for analysis by trained experts hundreds or even thousands of miles away.[3]

T A B L E **11.1**   **Selected Components of the Service Sector**

Type of Service	Example
Amusement and recreation services	Movie theaters
Automotive services	Auto rental firms
Business services	Collection agencies
Educational services	Schools
Financial services	Banks
Health services	Medical laboratories
Legal services	Law offices
Lodging services	Hotels
Repair services	Appliance repair stores
Social services	Job training institutions

Business-to-business marketers such as Upp Business Systems, based in Oakbrook Terrace, Illinois form a major part of the service sector. Upp, whose slogan is "Our Business Is Knowing Yours," provides information systems specialists to assist clients in meeting their business application development requirements on a project and fixed-fee basis. As with many highly successful service providers, founder and president Scott Upp, shown at right, believes his company's reputation depends entirely on relationship building. The wisdom of his approach is evident in results—launched in 1985, Upp now provides customized services for over 200 clients. Why would a strong relationship be as important to business customers as the technical expertise that Upp can provide?

Another large category of services is business services. These services—which include accounting, research, temporary office help, and legal, financial, and janitorial services—help organizations of all sizes keep their operations running smoothly. People who start their own businesses need such services, as do larger organizations that are seeking new ways to grow, downsizing or outsourcing to boost efficiency. As a result, this category of services will certainly grow.[4]

Services are also a major factor in the global economy. Indeed, world trade in services has been growing more quickly than trade in goods. Many U.S. service marketers are taking advantage of the boom. Telecommunications giant AT&T is just one example. The company has customers all over the world. In many places it joins with local companies to offer services such as data links.[5] At the same time, foreign service providers are entering U.S. markets. However, the value of U.S. services exported every year far outweighs the value of services imported, creating a yearly balance-of-trade *surplus* in services of nearly $60 billion. Compare this to the balance-of-trade *deficit* in goods, which hovers around $130 billion, and you can see how important services are to the United States and to the global economy.[6]

The Goods–Services Continuum

Rarely are services purely intangible. In many cases, the value package blends some tangible and intangible elements. To visualize the full range of goods and services products, look at the **goods–services continuum** in Figure 11.1 on the next page, a tool for classifying products according to their tangibility. At one extreme are goods such as milk and bicycles that can physically be examined, hence are predominantly tangible. At the other extreme are services, such as legal advice and nursing, that are predominantly intangible. In between are products from organizations such as restaurants that are a blend of goods (food) and services (cooking, table service).

goods–services continuum

a tool for classifying products according to their tangibility

FIGURE **11.1**   **The Goods–Services Continuum**

All products can be classified according to their tangibility. Products such as salt, which can be physically examined, are classified as goods on this continuum. In contrast, products such as teaching, which cannot be physically examined, are classified as services.

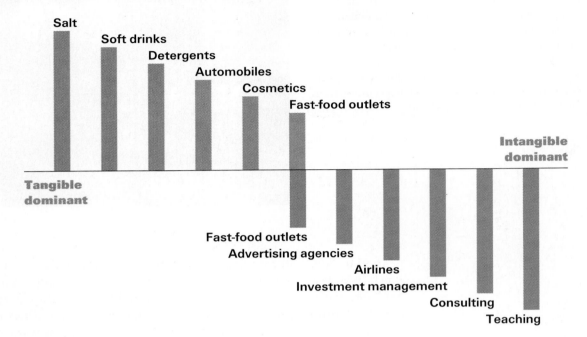

The majority of products combine tangible and intangible elements. For example, nearly every manufacturer offers services **(p. 253)** bundled or unbundled with its goods. When supermarkets buy milk products (goods), they also get delivery (services). When consumers buy cars (goods), they also have the option of obtaining loans (services) from the automakers. By offering services, manufacturers are able to satisfy more of their customers' needs and build relationships of longer standing. This is especially true for makers of complex or technical products whose customers often need training, along with repair and other services that can be as important—and as expensive—as the goods themselves.[7]

Similarly, service providers often offer something *tangible* with their services. For example, the main business of Bloomberg Financial Markets is providing details about stocks, bonds, and other financial instruments. To deliver this information, Bloomberg leases computer terminals to securities traders and other businesses. The company knows that the convenience and speed of the terminals have a lot to do with its customers' purchasing decisions and satisfaction with the Bloomberg relationship.[8]

Services have become so much a part of the business of traditional manufacturers like Bethlehem Steel, AT&T, and IBM that the result is a blurring of the distinction between goods and services. In fact, the line is so blurred that *Fortune* magazine recently combined its lists of the largest industrial companies and the largest service providers into a single Fortune 500 list.[9] *Forbes* magazine does the same. "The convergence of goods and services . . . is forcing a reconceptualization of what we mean by the terms 'production' and 'product,'" say professors Steven Goldman, Roger Nagel, and Kenneth Preiss of Lehigh University.[10]

Unique Characteristics of Services

Although the line between goods and services is blurring, it is certainly not disappearing. Services are set apart from goods by four unique characteristics: intangibility, inconsistency, inseparability, and inventory restrictions. Collectively, these are known as the *four I's of services*. Each affects the way service marketers build and sustain relationships with customers, as shown in Table 11.2.

TABLE 11.2 How Characteristics of Services Affect Relationship Building

Characteristic	Implications for Customers	Relationship Marketing Ideas
Intangibility	Service can't be physically examined	Make benefits more tangible
		Apply branding for unique identification and differentiation
		Offer samples to allow customers to experience the benefits
Inconsistency	Service may vary owing to reliance on employees	Emphasize employee training
		Emphasize automation to provide standardization (if applicable)
		Emphasize personalized nature of service (if applicable)
		Emphasize service standards
Inseparability	Production and consumption are simultaneous	Pay attention to atmospherics
		Emphasize quality of entire service delivery process
		Emphasize internal marketing for closer collaboration among employees
Inventory restrictions	Service can't be stored for later use	Use pricing and other marketing tactics to match supply and demand

Intangibility

First, services, unlike goods, have **intangibility**; that is, the services can be marketed, but they cannot be physically examined beforehand. Customers can see and drive a car (a good), but they can't see and use an airline trip (a service) before buying. If customers can't use their senses (touch, taste, etc.) to examine services, they can't easily try before they buy or judge value and quality in advance.

To overcome the problems of intangibility, some service marketers offer samples to allow customers to experience the benefits before committing to a long-term contract or an expensive purchase. Marketers can also work to make benefits as tangible as possible. For example, Andersen Consulting maintains a staff of some 22,000 experts who work on high-tech consulting projects for businesses in 47 countries. Clients can't examine the physical properties of a consulting project. They can, however, visit any of seven Andersen laboratories to get a personal sample of cutting-edge business technology. This is just one of the ways the company makes the benefits of its services more tangible to strengthen relationships with business customers.[11] In the next section, you'll learn how a doctor markets the tangible benefits of an intangible product.

intangibility

quality of services that cannot be physically examined before purchase

inconsistency

variability that occurs because delivery is highly dependent on the people providing the service or operating the equipment that provides the service

The reputation of service organizations, like those of all businesses, is based on quality, value, and service. Trust is also a crucial element in relationship marketing. Therefore, companies that sell to service organizations often stress consistency in the quality and value of the products they provide. They know, for example, that the reputation of a restaurant depends strongly on the consistent quality of the food served. Would you pay higher prices to suppliers of quality products knowing that your customers are price sensitive?

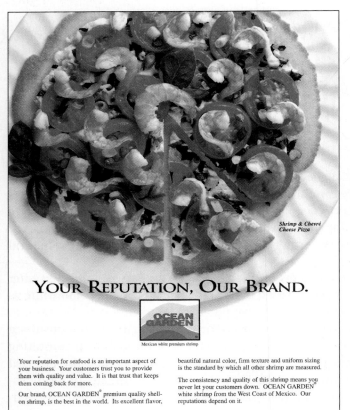

YOUR REPUTATION, OUR BRAND.

Shrimp & Chevré Cheese Pizza

OCEAN GARDEN

Mexican white premium shrimp

Your reputation for seafood is an important aspect of your business. Your customers trust you to provide them with quality and value. It is that trust that keeps them coming back for more.

Our brand, OCEAN GARDEN® premium quality shell-on shrimp, is the best in the world. Its excellent flavor,

beautiful natural color, firm texture and uniform sizing is the standard by which all other shrimp are measured.

The consistency and quality of this shrimp means you never let your customers down. OCEAN GARDEN® white shrimp from the West Coast of Mexico. Our reputations depend on it.

OCEAN GARDEN PRODUCTS, INC.
3585 Corporate Ct. San Diego, CA 92123
800-4-SHRIMP (474-7467)

FOR FURTHER INFORMATION CIRCLE 27 ON READER SERVICE CARD.   ©1995

GLOBAL ISSUES

Amil's RX for Brazilian medical plan

Edson de Godoy Bueno has the prescription for marketing the tangible benefits of medical plans. This physician's Brazilian company, Amil Assistencia Medica International—Amil for short—has grown 40-fold in just a decade and now tops $230 million in annual revenues. Dr. Bueno's secret? He dramatizes innovative service features through an aggressive television advertising campaign.

Amil's clients have access to many valuable services that are uncommon for Brazil. Those who need emergency treatment can call at any hour to talk to a doctor. If the condition warrants hospitalization, the caller is sent to a nearby hospital, where another doctor is waiting. For emergencies, clients can count on the Amil Health Rescue Plan, which provides airlift by helicopter to the nearest intensive care facility. It also provides mobile surgery and intensive care units staffed by specialists who treat the patient en route to the hospital.

Dr. Bueno makes the benefits of these services more tangible by means of television commercials that show them in action. For example, the commercial for the rescue plan features a reenactment of a rescue mission. At the end of the commercial, the company's telephone number appears on the screen with the slogan, "We take care of you." When the commercial first appeared, Amil was swamped by calls—and enrolled 100,000 people within weeks.[12]

Where on the goods–services continuum would you place Amil? Why?

Inconsistency

Second, services are subject to **inconsistency**, the variability that occurs because delivery is highly dependent on the people providing the service or operating the equipment that provides the service. This variability can be an advantage when a marketer wants to build a relationship with customers by responding to individual needs.[13] Thus a customer orientation is even more important in the service sector than it is in the manufacturing sector.

Although people expect consistently good service, doctors, chefs, teachers, and other service providers are only human, which means that their actions can vary. So the service at one restaurant chain won't be exactly the same as at the next, and the service at one outlet in a chain may differ from the service at another. Such inconsistency adds to the risk that customers perceive when buying a service—and points up the importance of internal marketing to give employees the support they need to maintain quality standards when serving external customers.

Taking the inconsistency out of services is what world-class marketers like McDonald's do best. Whether customers visit a McDonald's in Salt Lake City or Singapore, they can expect clean conditions, good food, and fast counter service. This consistency comes from training employees rigorously and setting standards that assure customers of quality service at every outlet. Through such consistency and adaptation to customer demands, McDonald's encourages repeat purchasing and customer loyalty.[14]

Inseparability

Third, services are subject to **inseparability**, which means that production can't be separated from consumption. Unlike goods marketers, who make products and pass them on to channel members such as retailers to deliver to customers for later consumption, service marketers produce nothing until customers buy and use the services. When you go for a haircut, the stylist cuts your hair then and there. When you get dental care, the dentist treats your problem on the spot. Customers start to gain benefits only when services are consumed; services can't be produced until customers are ready to consume them.

Because of this inseparability, customers usually judge services by every employee contact and every experience related to buying and receiving the service. As you read earlier, Brett Prager judged his college's medical services by the length of the wait he experienced as well as by the medical treatment he finally received. That's why it is important for service marketers to strengthen customer relationships before, during, and after a purchase. Sandra Wilkin, president of Bradford Construction in New York City, knows that the community judges her work by the quality of the finished building, including furnishings. Even though she isn't responsible for late delivery of furniture, which plagued a recent school reconstruction project, she supervises those details, too. "I just could not have looked those parents in the eye if the school was not finished," she explains.[15]

Inventory Restrictions

Fourth, services have **inventory restrictions**, meaning that they can't be stored in inventory. Goods such as lamp shades, which are physical, can be stored until customers are ready to buy them. However, you can't create and then store haircuts or airline flights for future use. Service happens in the moment.[16] If fewer customers come into your hair salon, or if your jet takes off with empty seats, you can't keep those haircuts or flights in inventory to be marketed at a later date. Of course, customers can't hold services aside for future use either.

Therefore, service marketing is significantly time oriented. You have to market services to encourage purchase and usage when your providers are available and the conditions are right. To avoid disrupting customer relationships, you may also have to use demarketing to *discourage* customers from demanding services when you have limited capacity to provide them. Many service marketers use pricing policies to manage demand. Movie theaters, for example, adjust their prices to charge more during periods of peak demand and less during periods of lower demand.

inseparability

service production can't be separated from service consumption

inventory restrictions

services can't be stored in inventory

TABLE **11.3**   Classifying Services

Classification	Examples
By Customer	
Consumer	Medical services, bus transportation
Organization	Commercial banking, industrial cleaning services
Internal customer	Legal advice, real estate management services
By Profit Goal	
For-profit	Hair stylist, auto repair service
Nonprofit	Environmental preservation, police protection
By Delivery	
People	College instruction, plumbing repair
Equipment	Telephone service, ATM banking services
By Skill Level	
Professional	Dental care, accounting services
Nonprofessional	Delivery service, shoe-shine service
By Contact Level	
High	Optical services, tennis instruction
Low	Trucking, appliance repair

Classification of Services for Relationship Building

All services are characterized by the four I's of intangibility, inconsistency, inseparability, and inventory restrictions. Since, however, all services are not alike, you have to match your relationship-building efforts to the type of service you're offering. You can classify services in five ways, according to customer, profit goal, delivery method, skill level, and contact level. Table 11.3 summarizes this classification system.

By Customer

Is the service marketed to ultimate consumers, organizations, or both? Is it aimed at internal or external customers? You can classify your service according to the customers you're targeting. This helps you determine the marketing strategies that make sense for building relationships with your customers.

For example, Lexis/Nexis provides computer-accessed online information services for law firms, advertising agencies, and other businesses. The company gears its pricing and other marketing tactics to the requirements of this market. In contrast, Discover markets its credit services only to ultimate consumers, using direct mail, television commercials, and other communications. Many marketers, including Westpac Bank in Australia, target both ultimate consumers and organizations. The bank's pricing, value package, and integrated marketing communication differ for each customer group. It uses advertising to reach consumers but adds personal selling to build relationships with organizations.[17]

By Profit Goal

Is the service provided for a profit? For-profit marketers such as Pip Printing are in business to return profits to owners and stockholders. As a result, when they make marketing decisions, they keep financial returns firmly in mind. In contrast, **nonprofit marketing** seeks to achieve a goal other than generating profits. Some nonprofit marketers exist to protect the natural environment, some to safeguard the health and welfare of citizens, and some to advance a social or political cause. To be officially designated as nonprofit organizations, nongovernment organizations apply for special tax status.

Of course, nonprofit service marketers such as Riverside Methodist Hospital in Columbus, Ohio, can't entirely ignore the financial consequences of their marketing actions. Even though they aren't operating to generate profits, they still try to produce revenue for construction, salaries, expansion, and repairs, and they face a marketing and competitive environment similar to the one that challenges for-profit marketers. Like many nonprofits, Riverside competes with other nonprofits as well as with profit-making organizations

nonprofit marketing

seeks to achieve a goal other than generating profits

that offer medical services. That's why the hospital has rebuilt facilities, upgraded its technology, and taken other steps to attract patients.[18]

Government agencies also compete with profit-making organizations for service tasks of all kinds: collecting garbage, building and managing prisons, delivering the mail (in some countries this service is provided by profit-making organizations), and more. In Phoenix, Arizona, for-profit businesses can bid against city garbage collectors for the right to collect trash. This competition pushed the city employees to upgrade operations and cut costs so they would win contracts.[19] Here's how a small nonprofit business uses marketing to serve its customers.

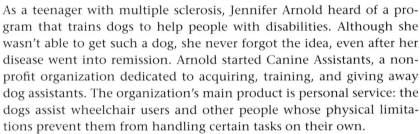

SMALL BUSINESS WATCH

Nonprofit service goes to the dogs

As a teenager with multiple sclerosis, Jennifer Arnold heard of a program that trains dogs to help people with disabilities. Although she wasn't able to get such a dog, she never forgot the idea, even after her disease went into remission. Arnold started Canine Assistants, a nonprofit organization dedicated to acquiring, training, and giving away dog assistants. The organization's main product is personal service: the dogs assist wheelchair users and other people whose physical limitations prevent them from handling certain tasks on their own.

Arnold doesn't charge recipients for the dogs, so she has to use smart marketing to raise the $10,000 needed to acquire and train each animal. To attract corporate, foundation, and individual donors, she gets her story out through the local and national news media. Another successful marketing tactic is to ask people to sponsor a dog. "They donate $10,000 to sponsor a canine assistant and [in return] get to know something about that dog and the person who eventually receives it," explains Arnold.

After three years in operation, Canine Assistants has an annual budget of $240,000 and a staff of four full-time and five part-time employees. Arnold is busier than ever responding to applications from people who want dogs and using her marketing skills to raise funds. But money is beside the point for this nonprofit entrepreneur, who says, "I would deliver pizzas to make enough money to support myself if I had to."[20]

What marketing ideas do you have for helping Arnold raise money?

Jennifer Arnold started the nonprofit service organization Canine Assistants to provide trained dogs to people with disabilities. These dogs have been trained to assist with everyday tasks that their masters can't handle on their own. What other nonprofit service organizations can you identify where marketing is geared toward helping people rather than making profits?

By Delivery

Is the service delivered by people, by equipment, or by both? Often, service marketers can more effectively control the consistency of services by using equipment rather than people. For example, MCI's fiber-optic network and computerized equipment can complete a large volume of telephone calls more quickly and less expensively than human operators. Of course, operators are available, but—barring equipment breakdowns—the vast majority of calls are routed without human intervention. This allows MCI to build relationships with millions of customers at one time.

As a means of both attracting new customers and maintaining relationships with existing subscribers, *Wired* magazine communicates information through its online sites as well as through the traditional print format. What do you see as the advantages and disadvantages of obtaining information by computer? If you were a publisher, would you move quickly to develop an online site on the Internet? Why?

However, many services—such as equipment repair and hair styling—must be delivered by people. When you market such services, your survival depends on strengthening the relationship between the person providing the service and individual customers. For example, CEO William A. Klein of the Cerplex Group in California builds customer relationships through personalized service. His technicians repair machinery for businesses in the United States and Europe. Although Klein's technicians use some diagnostic equipment, the CEO stresses the value of individually delivered, expert repair services.[21]

Service marketers also can build relationships by offering a choice of delivery methods to suit individual customer needs. *Wired* magazine, for example, offers information both in printed form and on *HotWired,* its site on the World Wide Web. Banks also offer choices to meet customer needs. Germany's Deutsche Bank uses state-of-the-art computer technology to electronically deliver updated information about customer investments that are being held for safekeeping. If they choose, customers can call or visit a branch to obtain the same information.[22] Channels for delivering services are discussed in more detail in Chapter 14.

By Skill Level

Are the people who provide the service professional or nonprofessional? Highly skilled professionals such as lawyers, teachers, accountants, and nurses can reassure customers about the quality of their services by pointing to their educational credentials and showing that they're licensed. These professionals also have to follow strict rules (set by industry associations or government agencies) about how to market their services. Of course, even skilled service providers can't ignore customer relations. To reinforce the importance of this critical area, the National Board of Medical Examiners in Philadelphia recently added questions on doctor–patient relations to its licensing exam.[23]

Some nonprofessionals, such as the repair technicians that work for Cerplex, can point to advanced training or certification. But the people who do janitorial work, deliver packages, and provide many other services often can't prove their qualifications by talking about education or licensing. If you're marketing such a service, you might offer testimonials from satisfied customers or guarantee that your results will live up to your promises. For instance, the point of the U.S. Postal Service's on-time guarantee for Express Mail is to let customers rest easy about the quality of the delivery service.

By Contact Level

Does the service require much or little contact with customers? When customers use airline and other *high-contact services,* they have extensive interaction with the service providers. Internal marketing ◄——┛ **(p. 9)** is as important as external marketing in such situations, because all employees have to collaborate to make customer contact pleasant and productive.[24]

Few competitive environments are more challenging than the restaurant business in New York. But Danny Meyer has managed to capture more than an average share of this market with outstanding food and service at fair prices. Mr. Meyer is shown here with his chef and partner, Michael Romano. His two restaurants, Gramercy Tavern and Union Square Cafe, are so successful that restaurateurs throughout the country now benchmark on them for quality and service. Why is success in the restaurant industry so difficult to achieve?

When you market high-contact services, you'll emphasize friendly relationships, comfortable surroundings, and other elements that make customers feel good about the contact. One key element is *atmospherics*, the design of the physical surroundings in which high-contact services are bought or delivered. Stores, restaurants, and hospitals can improve customer satisfaction by paying close attention to atmospherics.[25] For example, Danny Meyer, owner of the Union Square Cafe and the Gramercy Tavern in New York City, creates restaurant environments that make customers feel welcome and pampered. "Danny has an extraordinary way of making you feel like you're the most important person on earth," says one regular.[26]

On the other hand, when customers use *low-contact services* such as mail delivery and auto repair, they're not as directly involved with the service providers. Customers often pick up their mail from mailboxes and leave their cars to be repaired. In such situations, convenience, reliability, and security considerations may count for more than a strong personal relationship with the service provider. Safety-Kleen, an Illinois company, provides low-contact business services such as waste disposal and parts cleaning. Except for 24-hour emergency services, company reps visit customers only weekly or monthly, work quickly, then move on to the next assignment. Customers are happy to have Safety-Kleen handle these services, and they don't require a close relationship with the company's service providers.[27]

Before you go on . . .

A. **What role do services play in the U.S. economy?**

B. **What are the unique characteristics of services, and what challenges do they pose to marketers?**

C. **How can services be classified to facilitate marketers' application of appropriate relationship-building techniques?**

Service Quality and Customer Satisfaction

Given the unique characteristics of services, consumers and organizations approach such purchases slightly differently from the way they plan the purchase of goods. They also judge service quality in a different way, creating particular challenges and opportunities for service marketers that seek to establish and sustain enduring relationships with customers.

How Customers Buy Services

Products that can be physically examined are clearly easier for customers to evaluate and compare during the purchase-decision process. As shown in

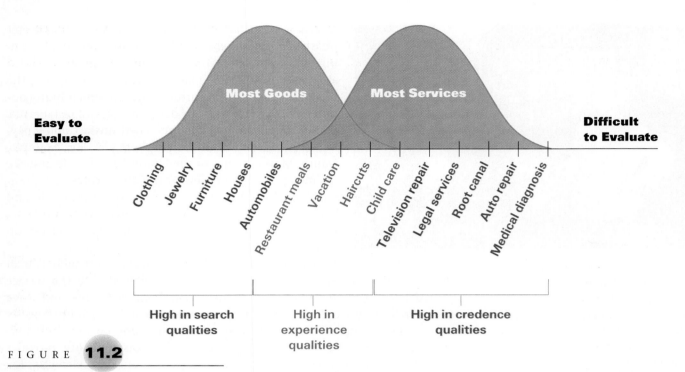

FIGURE **11.2**

Using Search, Experience, and Cre-dence Qualities to Evaluate Services
Tangible products such as clothing are high in search qualities, which means they can easily be examined and evaluated before a purchase. Less tangible products such as restaurant meals are high in experience qualities, which means they can be evaluated only after being purchased or consumed. However, medical services are much more intangible and therefore high in credence qualities. This means that they aren't easily evaluated even after purchase and use.

search qualities

qualities such as color and fit that customers can examine before they purchase

experience qualities

qualities such as taste that customers can evaluate only after purchase or consumption

credence qualities

qualities that customers can't easily evaluate even after purchase and consumption

Figure 11.2, tangible products are high in **search qualities**, qualities such as color and fit that customers can examine before they purchase. The unique characteristics of services prevent customers from evaluating a service before they buy. However, many services have elements that can be evaluated after a purchase.

Services such as restaurant meals are high in **experience qualities**, qualities such as taste that customers can evaluate only after purchase or consumption. Less tangible still are pure services such as legal advice and medical diagnosis, which are high in **credence qualities**, qualities that customers can't easily evaluate even after purchase and consumption. When customers have mysterious aches diagnosed, they have to trust their doctors and believe in the promise of a job well done. In the absence of tangible features to examine, service customers rely more on marketing cues, word of mouth, and other factors.[28]

To help customers evaluate their products, service marketers must offer appropriate information about benefits, quality, customization, price, and other aspects that customers weigh in the purchase decision. Although price is a key factor that is weighed during service purchases, quality is usually more important for expensive services that are high in credence qualities. Quality is especially critical when a customer perceives high risk in making a service purchase.[29]

How Customers Judge Service Quality

As you saw in Chapters 6 and 7, the last step in the purchase-decision process for consumers and organizations is postpurchase evaluation. The customer makes the purchase with an expectation of service quality that's formed by previous experiences, individual needs, and word-of-mouth recommendations, as well as by the marketer's communications. After buying and consuming the service, the customer compares the actual quality of the

service gap

discrepancy between the service provider's performance and the customer's expectations

service to the expected quality. At this point a discrepancy, or **service gap**, may be noticed between the service provider's performance and the customer's expectations. Service gaps may occur in these five areas of service delivery:[30]

1. *Misunderstanding of customer expectations.* Although the service marketer may have provided what it believed customers expected, customers perceived a gap because their actual expectations weren't met. That is why it is important for service marketers to carefully research consumer wants and needs.

2. *Inadequate standards for service delivery.* Customers saw a gap because the marketer's standards didn't support an adequate level of performance.

3. *Failure to deliver service according to the expected standards.* Here, customers identified a gap between their understanding of the expected service standards and the marketer's actual performance.

4. *Failure to communicate service benefits accurately and realistically.* Customers saw a gap between the actual service benefits and the expectations they had developed based on communications from the marketer.

5. *Overpromising of results in integrated marketing communications.* Because the delivery fell short of what the service marketer promised, customers noticed a gap between their expectations and the marketer's performance.

Remember, quality is determined by the customer, not by the marketer. A gap between the quality the customer expects and the quality you deliver can damage your relationship with customers. Avoiding service gaps in every transaction will help you win new customers and retain current patrons, because for most people and businesses, reliability is a top priority.

Service gaps aren't the only measure customers use to judge service quality. As shown in Table 11.4, other considerations include reliability, responsiveness, assurance, empathy, and tangibles. Especially in high-contact services, these measures of service quality are directly related to employee performance. Research indicates that customers are likely to change service providers when their current provider fails to measure up in any of these areas, a threat that makes employee performance even more critical to customer retention.[31]

TABLE **11.4** **Five Factors Customers Use to Judge Service Quality**

Factor	What Customers Are Judging
Reliability	Is the marketer dependable and accurate in providing service as promised, over time?
Responsiveness	Is the service provider willing and able to give prompt service?
Assurance	Are the service employees knowledgeable, competent, and trustworthy?
Empathy	Does the marketer provide caring, individualized service attention?
Tangibles	What is the appearance of the facilities, service personnel, equipment, materials, and so on?

On the other hand, by exceeding customers' expectations, a marketer can strengthen customer relationships and gain more customers from word-of-mouth referrals. The same goes for internal customers, who must have good service quality so they can give external customers the level of service quality they expect.

One airline that consistently meets or exceeds customer expectations of service quality is Southwest Airlines. Each of the thousand customer letters

Southwest Airlines is determined to meet or exceed the primary standards of service quality discussed in Table 11.4: reliability, responsiveness, assurance, empathy, and tangibles. Southwest's service quality, combined with its commitment to keeping prices low, leads to a high level of customer satisfaction. When measured against other airlines, Southwest consistently comes out a winner. How can Southwest demonstrate its empathy to customers who are evaluating the airline's service quality?

received every week is read (a good way to monitor service gaps), and each receives a personal response. Employees avoid nasty surprises by immediately announcing flight delays or other problems that can affect service quality. They also work to meet the service quality expectations of their internal customers. As CEO Herb Kelleher says, "If you don't treat your own people well, they won't treat other people well." No wonder Southwest is one of the most successful carriers in the United States today.[32]

How to Manage Service Quality for Customer Satisfaction

As a service marketer, you put your reputation, customer relationships, and profits on the line with every contact. Research shows that good service can bring you more customers and higher profits, in part because people are willing to pay more for being treated well. On the other hand, the cost of losing a loyal service customer is as much as eight times higher than the cost of retaining one, when you add in foregone future profits. And to retain a customer who's been dissatisfied with your service, you must prove yourself up to 12 more times to overcome the effects of one bad experience.[33]

Although good service can mean the difference between satisfied, loyal customers and dissatisfied defectors, too many service providers aren't measuring up to customer expectations. In one recent study, credit card telephone service representatives and rental car desk clerks were named the best service providers. Grocery store cashiers and airline check-in personnel got the lowest marks. To track national trends in service satisfaction, the U.S. government now conducts quarterly surveys. For several quarters, Americans have said that service at fast-food restaurants is improving—but service at retail stores, especially department stores, is deteriorating.[34]

The implications are clear: to build and strengthen mutually beneficial, long-term relationships with customers, you must pay close attention to what happens during every service encounter. A **service encounter** is a point of interaction between a customer and a service provider. A service encounter is also known as a *moment of truth* because it's the point at which a customer forms an impression of your service. Service marketers manage multiple service encounters every day, and each is an opportunity to prove service quality. Scandinavian Airline Systems (SAS), for example, manages 50,000 such encounters on any given day.[35]

Issues for critical thinking

As a customer, think of the service encounters you had during your most recent visit to a doctor or dentist. Which of these encounters were the most critical? Did the health care providers (and staff) seem aware of how important those moments are to you? How could they improve the quality of these encounters?

service encounter

point of interaction between a customer and a service provider

The stakes are high, and the pressure is on—so how do service marketers prepare for quality service? First, find out what customers expect. Second, prepare a service strategy to satisfy customer needs and expectations. Third, train, empower, and support employees so they can provide quality service. Fourth, communicate with customers to manage their service expectations. And, fifth, conduct research to find out whether service quality satisfies (or even delights) customers.

Examine Customer Expectations

To examine your customers' service expectations, start by mapping the sequence of service encounters that take place before, during, and after a purchase. Take the customer's perspective as you map every point of interaction. Even if a service encounter doesn't include direct interaction with employees, include it (because some employee, somewhere, is responsible for the quality of the encounter). Then you can determine how each encounter fits with every other encounter.

For example, the 16 service encounters shown in Figure 11.3 relate to a shopper's trip to the supermarket. Cashiers, customer service reps, store clerks, pharmacists, security guards, and baggers all have direct interaction with the customer. In addition, behind-the-scenes people are responsible for the quality of other service encounters. After all, someone polices the parking lot, puts merchandise on the shelf, and mops the floors. And if you include encounters beyond the shopping trip itself, such as store advertising, you add the work of even more employees who, along with the frontline employees, represent service quality to the customers.[36]

F I G U R E **11.3**   Service Encounters in a Shopping Trip

The first step in understanding a customer's service expectations is to map the sequence of service encounters that takes place before, during, and after a purchase. This model shows the service encounters in a typical trip to the supermarket. Each encounter is an opportunity to satisfy or even delight the customer in the course of building a mutually beneficial relationship.

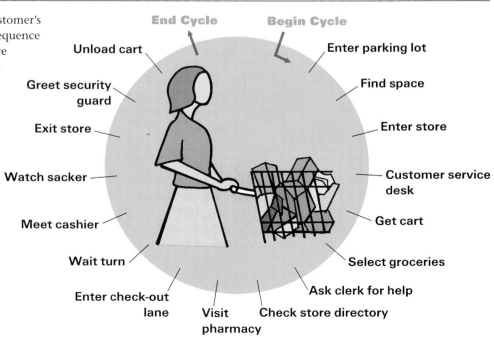

End Cycle · Begin Cycle · Unload cart · Enter parking lot · Greet security guard · Find space · Exit store · Enter store · Watch sacker · Customer service desk · Meet cashier · Get cart · Wait turn · Select groceries · Enter check-out lane · Ask clerk for help · Visit pharmacy · Check store directory

Next, find out, through marketing research, what your customers want, need, and expect from your services. You can use focus group interviews, surveys, personal interviews with customers (and prospects), customer advisory panels, postage-paid comment cards, and other methods to gather information about customer requirements. In addition, ask employees for their thoughts. Don't talk just with customer service representatives; survey all employees who are involved in service encounters. This is the raw material you need to develop a service strategy.

You may find, as Hyatt Hotels did, that you and your customers have different ideas of what makes quality service. For 20 years, Hyatt had added services and, as a result, raised costs. Then the company researched customer expectations. Many guests didn't care about having their beds turned down at night, so now guests who want the service can call for it. Customers did want coffee without having to phone for it, so Hyatt puts a coffee pot in each room. On request, Hyatt will also install a fax machine or a modem in a guest's room. These changes, which delighted customers, at the same time lowered Hyatt's costs while raising revenues and profits.[37]

Develop a Service Strategy

You can't expect employees to meet customers' needs unless you set the appropriate groundwork. Research shows that many service employees genuinely want to deliver quality services. However, they're often hampered by inadequate service plans and a lack of skills and tools.[38] So, once you know what customers want and need, you need to prepare a **service strategy**, a broad plan for delivering quality service. This plan sets standards for service quality based on customer expectations, and it indicates how to coordinate employee efforts to meet those standards.

For example, Roberts Express, a freight expediter in Cleveland, Ohio, has a smooth-running service strategy for delivering customer goods. Customer assistance teams handle each business customer's order from start to finish. Team members take delivery orders over the phone, arrange drivers and trucks, schedule pickups and deliveries, and dispatch trucks. Quality standards call for picking up freight within 90 minutes of the customer's call and delivering within 15 minutes of the promised time. Now 95 percent of all shipments arrive on time. If a shipment is two hours late, the customer gets a 25 percent discount. If it's four hours late, the customer gets a 50 percent discount. This strategy has helped Roberts Express grow to $125 million in annual sales.[39]

Service standards can work in health care too. Administrators at Mission Oaks Hospital in Los Gatos, California, understand that people don't like waiting for medical treatment. They established a standard for emergency room service and backed the standard with a guarantee: If a patient has to wait longer than five minutes to be seen in the emergency room, the bill is cut by 25 percent. Service is so good that the hospital owes discounts to only two patients in a thousand.[40]

The most successful service marketers are those whose leaders have a *service vision*, a view of the organization's future that becomes the driving force behind its service activities. Bruce Simpson, president of Roberts Express, puts quality service at the top of his priority list. He and his managers meet

service strategy

a broad plan for delivering quality service

service recovery plan

a set of actions designed as a response to service problems

every day to review the previous day's service problems and find ways of preventing such problems in the future.[41] Top management commitment inspires employees to do whatever it takes to turn the service vision into reality.

Include in this strategy a **service recovery plan**, a set of actions designed as a response to service problems. This is a critical part of a comprehensive service strategy, as Donald Porter of British Airways knows well: "'Recovery' was the term we coined to describe a very frequently repeated concern: If something goes wrong, as it often does, will anybody make a special effort to set it right?" he says.[42] Studies show that customers who experience problems want service providers to apologize, propose an appropriate solution, show consideration, offer reimbursement for the customer's trouble, and deliver on the promised recovery.[43]

For speed and consideration, consider the example set by Richard Branson, chairman of Virgin Atlantic Airways. When a transatlantic flight was delayed, Branson picked up the telephone and dictated a letter, with instructions to hand a copy to every passenger waiting to board in New Jersey. In the letter, the chairman apologized for the inconvenience and explained the reason for the delay. He also quoted a new departure time and offered to get messages to people in London who were expected to meet the delayed flight. This response made passengers feel that Virgin was working hard to solve the service problem.[44]

A small shop often has only one or two employees to assist customers. Consequently, since these employees are critical to the shop's success, the hiring, training, motivating, compensating, and empowering of these employees is a major responsibility of the owners/managers. What kind of training would you recommend that the owners of the Beadazzled Shop give their employees to ensure that they are responsive to customers' needs?

Train, Empower, and Support Employees

The next step is to train, empower, and support employees so they can deliver the service quality that customers want and expect. Start by hiring the right people. Says Scott Bruner of the Hard Rock Cafe Orlando, "We are very selective. We bring top-notch people on board. We look for people with the right attitude and a willingness to learn."[45]

Hiring is only the start. After studying service quality and customer satisfaction, marketing consultants Leonard A. Schlesinger and James L. Heskett observed: "The growing body of data we have collected thus far suggests that customer satisfaction is rooted in employee satisfaction and retention more than anything else."[46] To avoid turnover and morale problems that can sabotage quality service, use internal marketing, train your employees, and give them opportunities to learn on the job.

Large service marketers like Macy's as well as small service marketers like Beadazzled in Virginia work on the basics by giving courtesy training to all frontline employees. Some service marketers go beyond basic training. Ukrop's, a Virginia supermarket chain, set up a Center for Retail Food Studies. On company time, new employees attend five classes during their first 18 months to learn about company values, service, teamwork, safety, and industry conditions. Later, they can take additional classes in business writing and other subjects, in an effort to upgrade their knowledge and skills.[47]

Internal marketing plays a key role in giving employees the support they need to serve external customers. At Bank One Texas, members of the trust division meet every six months to coordinate work activities. They discuss the needs of internal customers and set service quality standards for meeting those needs. Employees sign a copy of the internal service pledge shown in Figure 11.4, which spells out these standards and expectations. Six months later, the bankers evaluate each other's performance and reaffirm or change the expectations for the coming six months.[48]

With training and internal support in place, you're ready to turn your employees loose to make decisions that will satisfy customers. Nordstrom empowers its employees to make decisions without checking with supervisors. The department store chain has only one rule: "Use your good judgment in all situations." Employees are trusted to do whatever it takes to provide quality service.[49] Other service marketers take a team approach to empowerment. Allina, a Minnesota company that operates nonprofit hospitals, organizes teams and gives them power to solve service problems. The teams have saved Allina millions of dollars and, in the process, have expanded employee pride in a job well done.[50]

Marketers can motivate employees to give quality service by rewarding their efforts. Rewards can include cash, recognition, gifts, and trips. For example, Ukrop's supermarkets recently rewarded top service employees with cruise vacations. No matter what rewards are offered, the point is to show employees that their efforts are noticed and appreciated.[51] Do you feel more motivated to do good work when you are rewarded for doing so?

Communicate with Customers

At this point, you've determined what customers expect, set a service strategy and service standards, and developed and empowered your employees to deliver that service quality. Now you have to communicate with customers through advertising or face to face, to impart a realistic idea of what to expect from your service. Customers become disillusioned when they perceive a gap between what was promised and what was delivered. By managing your customer's prepurchase expectations, you can close this gap.[52]

Customers feel more confident dealing with a service marketer when they know what will happen and when. Wheaton Van Lines, based in Indianapolis, manages customer expectations via personal contact. Sales representatives sit down with customers to fill out a form about the details of the move and any special re-

FIGURE **11.4**

Bank One Texas Trust Internal Service Pledges

Top-quality internal service provides the support that internal customers need to give top-quality service to external customers. The internal service pledges shown here set service quality standards that employees in the corporate trust and finance departments are expected to meet.

BANK ONE TEXAS TRUST INTERNAL SERVICE PLEDGE

CORPORATE TRUST pledges to FINANCE

1. By the 25th of each month, provide forecast for remainder of current month and for remainder of year.
2. Provide a copy of A/P transmittal and/or T & E Report with explanations of transactions to prepaid expenses or customer reimbursable expenses by the first business day of the following month.

FINANCE pledges to CORPORATE TRUST

1. Provide monthly, by the 10th business day, a printout of status on customer prepaid expenses and customer reimbursable expenses.
2. Provide monthly, by the 10th business day, general ledger reports on cost center.
3. Provide procedures or information on what is needed for forecast.

CORPORATE pledges to FINANCE

FINANCE pledges to CORPORATE TRUST

UNIVERSAL MUTUAL PLEDGES

1. Communicate with honesty and understanding: discuss problems with those involved.
2. We will treat each other, regardless of position, with courtesy and respect.
3. All service problems will be treated as "OUR" problem and we will work together on the immediate solution.
4. We will reconize that we are here to serve our ultimate client–the customer–and will focus our efforts on providing unsurpassed quality service.

Corporate Trust:

Department Members

Liz Galindo

Jeannene Gaston

Phillip D. Gatlin

Lynn McCullough

Donna McFarland

Finance Department:

Department Members

Karen Spuria

Fran Toliver

quirements. Once agents have quoted a price and customers have agreed, the company schedules pickup and delivery dates to set customer expectations. Customers can call a toll-free number to track goods in transit or to discuss changes. Wheaton's results reflect its quality service: 99 percent of Wheaton's shipments are picked up early or on time, 98 percent are delivered early or on time, and 99 percent don't involve a damage claim over $100.[53]

Sometimes customers simply don't know what to expect from your service. This is a special problem for a service high in credence qualities. In such a case, you'll want to educate your customers so they know when to seek your services, how to evaluate alternatives, how to communicate their needs and concerns, and what to expect. Many professional firms use newsletters, seminars, advertising, and public speaking opportunities to communicate with customers and prospects. The Baltimore accounting firm of Kamanitz, Uhlfeder, and Permison for example, offers seminars on tax, financial, and estate planning. Such communication gives customers a better picture of service capabilities.[54]

Bear in mind that by simply living up to your promised service standards, you're only offering an *expected* product. By *exceeding* customer expectations, you can offer a value package that customers see as an *augmented* product. Then, through environmental analysis, market analysis, and new product development, you can add enhancements that bring you closer to the *potential* product. This delights customers and helps protect a customer relationship from competitive pressure. Are there any service organizations in your area that give outstanding service? If so, you can benchmark on them to learn how they do it.

Research Service Performance

You can find out whether your service meets customers' expectations by conducting research to evaluate your service performance. Do this by using all the research tools you used to uncover customer needs, plus comment cards, toll-free telephone hotlines, complaint and suggestion boxes, and other methods. You can search out complaints you wouldn't ordinarily get by talking with customers who start to buy less, customers who stop buying, and frontline employees who are likely to hear complaints.[55]

Especially when competition is fierce, service marketers that want to retain their customers take special steps to investigate customer complaints—and, in some cases, prevent complaints. This is true of for-profit and nonprofit marketers alike. The Massachusetts Bay Transportation Authority and the Housing Authority of Louisville are just two of many government service marketers that use customer surveys to research service performance.[56]

The best service marketers never stop searching for feedback on service quality. Entergy Corporation, an electrical utility serving Arkansas, Louisiana, Mississippi, and Texas, surveys a sample of its customers every month. The utility also holds focus group interviews to explore customer perceptions of service quality. This research yields important information for changing the way the utility communicates with its customers about policies, repairs, and other elements of service quality.[57]

The ABCs of Services Marketing

In Chapter 1, you were introduced to the ABCs of marketing **(pp. 16–17)**. These simple but powerful rules apply to service organizations as well. Here are the ABCs of services marketing:

- *Always be customer driven.* Because production and consumption of services are inseparable, the way your treat your customers is an integral part of your product. To build enduring relationships, you have to make customers the focal point of everything you do—and give them what they want. At Nordstrom, president Jim Nordstrom says, "In this company, when a salesperson says the customers are asking for such and such, that carries more weight than the opinions of the buyers."[58]

- *Benchmark against the best in the world.* Nordstrom is only one of many service marketers you can use as a benchmark. In fact, this chapter is loaded with good examples. But don't confine yourself to benchmarking in your industry. You can learn from any top service marketer, anywhere in the world.

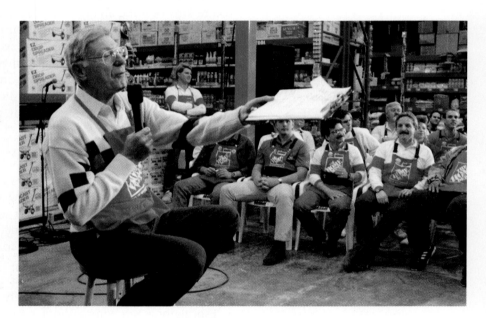

One of the primary ways Home Depot has been winning market share is by offering superior service. The store can assure outstanding service because it hires experienced people, trains them, and then creates a corporate culture built around service. What specific things can Home Depot and other huge stores do to build closer relationships with their customers?

- *Continuously improve your product and performance.* Karl Albrecht, who has studied service organizations around the world, says about the best: "They are constantly looking for ways to improve or refine their service product. They measure and evaluate their quality on an ongoing basis and look for areas that may need attention. However effective they may be, they are never willing to accept the status quo."[59] Of course, customers and competitors change, so keep looking for ways to improve.

- *Develop the best value package.* Satisfy customers by developing and delivering the best package of services you can. Here's what Southern Bell says of its services: "We deliver our service in a manner that causes our customers to perceive value added. . . . A promise to a customer by an employee commits all employees to help fulfill it."[60]

- *Empower your employees.* Hire good people, train them, and then give them authority for delivering quality service so they can attract new customers and retain existing ones. John Longstreet, general manager of the Harvey Hotel in Plano, Texas, tells employees: "You can do anything you want to do to exceed guest expectations as long as it is not illegal or immoral, and as long as you use your best judgment in making that decision."[61]

- *Focus on relationships.* With every service encounter, you have an opportunity to gain a new customer and please an existing one. And don't forget supplier and other stakeholder relationships. Rosenbluth Travel, for example, builds long-term relationships with customers and suppliers by sharing travel information and resources with them. Owner Hal Rosenbluth has found that stronger relationships benefit all participants.[62]

- *Generate profits.* Give customers quality service and they'll remain loyal, contributing to your sales and profits year after year. Customers today have so many choices that you can't survive—let alone thrive— unless you deliver quality service to profitably satisfy your customers, patients, or citizens.

Every service marketer can apply these ABCs to build strong relationships with customers. The following case shows the process in action in a government agency.

Applying the Concepts

Montgomery County becomes the place to benchmark

Montgomery County is an area of half a million people, 19 urban centers, 12 townships, and 16 school districts around Dayton, Ohio. Governing the county was a tough job even before industrial and military employers began moving away or shutting down. Instead of watching from the sidelines as businesses and residents packed up, county administrator Claude Malone hatched a five-year program named "Service Excellence" that ultimately became a case study for improving government service.

Under Malone's program, all county agencies started by determining who they were serving. Their customers included residents, patients, employers, and other government agencies. Next, many of the agencies began to survey customers about what they liked and disliked. With the results of this research in hand, Montgomery County was able to respond to customer needs.

For example, surveys showed that clients of the Department of Human Services, which is in charge of food stamps, financial assistance, counseling, and referral service, judged service to be slow and impersonal. The department responded by setting specific service standards. Employees now confirm the time for appointments, meet with clients within 15 minutes of the scheduled time, and greet clients amiably. Moreover, caseworkers are empowered to do what it takes to resolve service problems when people have become caught in a bureaucratic web.

Malone also proposed a high-tech industrial park that attracted Kodak, Mead, and 12 other businesses. In all, the customer-oriented "Service Excellence" approach improved the quality of life for residents and businesses alike. Government officials from all over the United States now come to Montgomery County to benchmark its service successes.[63]

Make marketing decisions

1. What would you ask clients to determine how they feel about services provided by the Department of Human Services?
2. How would you research the kind of service standards to set in that department?
3. Do you think the department's clients use search, experience, or credence qualities to evaluate its services?
4. Why should government agencies search for client complaints?

Before you go on . . .

A. How do customers evaluate products on the basis of search, experience, and credence qualities?

B. What five service gaps might customers notice in the quality of service delivery?

C. Why are service encounters also known as moments of truth?

D. What is a service recovery plan, and what should it cover?

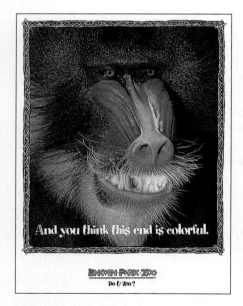

And you think this end is colorful.

LINCOLN·PARK·ZOO

Do U Zoo?

As you can see, advertising for nonprofit organizations can be colorful and provocative. This ad for the Lincoln Park Zoo of Chicago really catches your eye, doesn't it? Do you think reminder advertising of this type is effective in drawing people to the zoo?

Nonprofit Services Marketing

The world of nonprofit services marketing is large and diverse, including colleges and universities, museums, zoos, political organizations, religious institutions, health care facilities, and government agencies. Students Against Drunk Driving, the U.S. Department of Education, the League of Women Voters, the Salvation Army, the Republican National Committee, and the Smithsonian Institution are all nonprofit marketers because they don't exist to make profits. So, too, are National Public Radio, the Roman Catholic Church, and Jennifer Arnold's Canine Assistants.

For the most part, nonprofit marketers emphasize services. Of course, many offer tangible products such as books, food, gifts, and other goods to raise funds for their service activities. For example, the Rockland Family Shelter in New York State raises money to house victims of domestic violence by selling gifts through a catalog. The Girl Scouts of America raise money for troop activities by selling cookies.[64] Marketing these goods generates revenue, but profit is not the main focus of the organizations. The money raised by marketing goods goes toward funding services that satisfy customer needs.

Unique Challenges of Nonprofit Services Marketing

Nonprofit service marketers confront the same challenges faced by other service marketers in the course of building and sustaining mutually beneficial exchanges. In addition, however, nonprofit marketers face several unique challenges.

First, they often deliver services to one group of people but receive funding from another. The people who receive services may pay little or nothing, so nonprofits look for contributions of money, goods, or volunteer services to cover the full cost of services. For their part, contributors—including the 80 million U.S. adults who volunteer their time—find this to be a mutually beneficial exchange because they gain satisfaction from helping others.[65] Still, balancing the needs of these two stakeholder groups—contributors and customers—requires careful planning.

Second, the services that nonprofit marketers provide are sometimes controversial. Not everyone agrees with the objectives of nonprofit groups such as the American Civil Liberties Union, Planned Parenthood, or the National Rifle Association. Similarly, public schools sometimes come under fire for what they teach or how they teach it. Nonprofit service marketers that deal with controversial activities or ideas can use marketing to reach out to people who use their services as well as to enlist supporters and combat counterattacks from dissenters.

Issues for critical thinking

Think about a nonprofit service organization's stand on a controversial issue such as gun control. What marketing techniques has this organization used to communicate its position? What techniques have others used in opposition? Which marketing techniques do you find most effective? Why?

Third, setting goals and measuring success is less straightforward. For-profit marketers can easily evaluate their efforts against financial goals such as sales and profits. Since, however, nonprofit marketers aren't in business to make profits, they need to set goals and evaluate results using different measures, such as number of people served or degree of awareness of the cause.

The next two sections show how some nonprofit service marketers deliver quality service. Their goals, customers, and services may differ, but notice how each uses marketing concepts to develop and maintain long-term, mutually beneficial exchanges with its customers. To start, here's a look at how some hospitals help doctors gain a better understanding for the needs of patients—their customers.

Understanding customers by playing patient

Unless they've been seriously ill, few physicians really know what patients experience during a hospital stay. But that's changing. Responding to charges that many doctors can't understand or empathize with patients' worries and concerns, more hospitals are turning doctors into patients.

New resident physicians at Long Beach Memorial Medical Center, California, check in for an 18-hour stay as a patient. Each gets a phony name and diagnosis, and each is assigned a disability, complete with an eye patch or a leg cast to make the disability feel real. "Most new residents have never experienced the anxiety and helplessness of being in a hospital, and the dehumanizing aspects of hospital care," says Dr. Stephen Brunton, who started the program. Among the lessons that Dr. Deborah L. Pauer learned from the experience was how much intravenous procedures can hurt. "Now I try to wait until [such procedures are] really needed because I know how uncomfortable they can be," she says.

A similar program is in place at Hunterdon Medical Center in Flemington, New Jersey, where medical residents play the role of elderly patients. Wearing smeared, yellowed contact lenses that blur their vision, rubber gloves that dull their sense of touch, and ear plugs that reduce their hearing, they try to read medicine labels, open childproof drug containers, and interpret what's said to them by busy staff members. Afterward, they discuss how to apply their insights.

The Long Beach Memorial and Hunterdon experiences are just two of the programs that are helping doctors better understand and empathize with their customers' needs.[66] If you were the head of marketing at one of these hospitals, would you publicize the program? Why or why not?

Marketing Nonprofit Services

To nonprofit services marketers, students, patients, congregants, and clients are all customers with specific needs and expectations. As basic as this insight may seem, only in recent years have many nonprofits approached marketing as a customer-oriented process. For a long time, people were wary of applying marketing to certain nonprofit services, such as health care and religion. However, this attitude is starting to fade, in part because of increased competition from nonprofits and for-profit organizations and in part because of public acceptance of marketing techniques.

Understanding customer needs helps nonprofit health care providers do a better job of attracting and caring for patients. Planetree, a nonprofit organization based in San Francisco, helps hospitals in the United States, England, and Norway adopt a customer-oriented approach to medicine. Angelica Thieriot founded Planetree after feeling afraid and confused during a hospital stay. She knew that patients needed information to make informed choices. She also knew that proper atmospherics, good communication, and sensitivity to patients' needs could humanize hospital care.

Hospitals that link up with Planetree receive a library of medical materials so patients can read about their medical conditions and the available treatments. The hospitals also follow Planetree's suggestions for making facilities more customer-friendly. For example, Planetree affiliate Beth Israel Medical Center in New York City replaced its glaring fluorescent lights with softer, indirect lighting. Just as important, the Planetree approach makes patients partners in health care. They (and their families) participate in treatment planning meetings. Treating patients as customers is a powerful marketing idea that helps Planetree's affiliates deliver quality service.[67]

Colleges and universities are also earning their marketing stripes by adapting to the changing needs of students. One example is the televised instruction program at University of Maryland's University College. "Today's students are often working," explains Paul Hamlin, a dean at the University College. "Because of time constraints—children, jobs, commutes—they can't go to the typical campus." So the university allows students to earn a four-year degree via cable television. Through this and other programs, the University of Maryland delivers quality service that satisfies its student customers.[68]

Marketing Government Services

Federal, state, and local government agencies have become quality service converts. By viewing citizens as customers and applying marketing principles, government offices are moving toward delivering better service at a lower cost. Now more than 100 federal agencies, including the Social Security Administration, must meet quality service standards.[69]

The National Park Service, which is responsible for 367 sites around the country, uses marketing research to investigate customer needs. It found that 75 percent of the visitors to California's Death Valley are tourists from Europe. To keep these visitors safe as they drive through the two million acres of Death Valley, the National Park Service now provides instructions for emergency situations in French, German, and Italian. And, in response to seasonal demand, the agency is keeping visitor centers open longer.[70]

State governments are jumping on the quality service bandwagon, as well. Look at motor vehicle departments, once the scene of endless delays and paperwork. Changes made by Connecticut and other states are turning frowns into smiles as drivers receive faster, more convenient service. The Department of Motor Vehicles in Connecticut, like its counterparts in Oregon, Georgia, Maryland, and Massachusetts, has branches in shopping centers so drivers can transact business where they shop. In Illinois, drivers can order license plates from home, using an automated service operated via Touch-Tone telephone.[71]

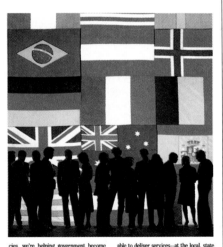

This ad for Unisys emphasizes the fact that all organizations, including government organizations, need to be customer focused. Unisys calls this "customerizing." Unisys partners with government agencies to create information systems to provide outstanding service to the agencies' customers. How does this ad communicate the company's emphasis on relationship building?

Local governments are also emphasizing quality service. In Sunnyvale, California, municipal officials set standards and measure performance for thousands of services, such as job training and road maintenance. Any manager who exceeds departmental service and productivity goals is eligible for a bonus. This system allows Sunnyvale to deliver more and better services at lower cost.[72]

Services on the Internet

Most service organizations, including nonprofit organizations, are now using the Internet to establish better relationships with customers and other stakeholders. The Nature Conservancy, for example, is experimenting with an Internet site to expand its conservation programs. It is also gathering the e-mail addresses of its 850,000 members to test response to e-mail solicitations. The Internet brought in up to 10 new members a day and led to the development of a Web site.

Various profit-making service organizations are also making greater use of the Internet, Web sites, and e-mail. Visitors to American Airlines' Web site can sign up to receive e-mail messages about special offers. There are now on-line virtual travel agencies, and people seeking rooms can check into TravelWeb.[73] L.L. Bean now offers an electronic catalog so customers can select items and place credit-card orders on the Internet. The Internet is fast becoming a major medium for all marketers.[74]

Before you go on . . .

A. What unique challenges do nonprofit service marketers face?

B. Why is it important for marketers of government services to stress quality and customer satisfaction?

Summary

1. **Describe the goods–services continuum and show how the lines between goods and services are blurring.**

   The goods-services continuum is a tool for classifying products according to their tangibility. Pure goods, which are tangible, are at one extreme, while pure services, which are intangible, are at the other. Since most products are a blend of goods and services, they fall between these extremes. The line separating goods and services is blurring because services have become so much a part of the business of goods manufacturers.

2. **Explain the four unique characteristics of services.**

   These are intangibility (the inability to physically examine the product), inconsistency (the variability that results from services being dependent on the human service providers), inseparability (the inability to separate service production and service consumption), and inventory restrictions (the inability to store services for later consumption).

3. **Discuss how services can be classified.**

   Services can be classified according to customer (including consumers and organizations or both and internal customers), profit goal (including for-profit or nonprofit services), delivery method (including people and equipment or both), skill level and contact level (including high- or low-contact services).

4. **Demonstrate how customers use search qualities, experience qualities, and credence qualities to evaluate products.**

   Customers evaluate tangible products according to search qualities, such as color and fit, which can be examined before the purchase. They evaluate services, which are intangible, according to experience qualities, such as taste, which can be examined only after purchase or consumption. The most difficult services to evaluate are high in credence qualities, which can't easily be evaluated even after purchase and consumption.

5. **Define service gaps, which customers use to judge service quality.**

   A service gap is a gap between the service provider's performance and the customer's expectations. Service gaps reflect misunderstandings of customer expectations, inadequate standards for service delivery, failure to deliver according to the expected standards, failure to communicate service benefits accurately and realistically, and overpromising of results in the marketer's communications.

6. **Show the steps marketers can take to manage service quality for customer satisfaction.**

   The five steps to managing service quality are: examine customers' expectations; develop a service strategy; train, empower, and support employees so they can deliver quality service; communicate with customers to manage their service expectations; and research service performance.

7. **Identify the unique challenges of marketing nonprofit services.**

   First, nonprofit services often deliver services to one group of people but receive funding from another, so they must market to both. Second, the services provided are sometimes controversial. Third, setting goals and measuring success is less straightforward compared with for-profit service marketers because the goals and measures of results are so diverse.

KEY TERMS

credence qualities 322
experience qualities 322
goods–services continuum 313
inconsistency 316
inseparability 317

intangibility 315
inventory restrictions 317
nonprofit marketing 318
search qualities 322
service encounter 324

service gap 323
service recovery plan 327
service strategy 326

Skill-Building Applications

1. To make money while in college, you decide to give minimassages to students and faculty. How would you examine customer expectations and measure customer satisfaction?

2. Apply the ABCs of service marketing to the marketing of AT&T's phone services to business clients.

3. How would you measure service quality at your local house of worship? How could the organization determine what members and potential members want and need in services?

4. Stephen Lovett began mowing lawns when he was 11 and expanded his services to washing cars. Now he runs Lovett Enterprises with four teenagers doing lawn work, auto detailing, and odd jobs.

   Which of the concepts from this chapter should Lovett use to keep his current customers and gain new ones?

5. Little Caesars Pizza wants to expand by building minirestaurants inside discount stores. What should management do to avoid service gaps that can damage customer relationships?

6. The National Rifle Association is often in the news because of its stands on gun ownership and assault weapons. Should the association focus only on its relationship with members or should it try to establish friendly relations with all its stakeholders, including proponents of gun control?

Getting Involved in Marketing

1. *On Your Own* Where do you think the following belong on the goods–services continuum? Write one or two sentences to justify your placement of each.
   a. A snack at Dunkin' Donuts
   b. Legal advice from Jacoby & Meyers legal services
   c. A Caribbean vacation on Carnival Cruise Lines
   d. A skin cancer screening from the American Cancer Society
   e. Information from the U.S. Department of Commerce about how to market in other countries

2. *On Your Own* Pick a specific service marketer, such as a restaurant, hospital, or cleaning service. Classify its services by customer, profit goal, delivery, skill level, and contact level. Next, indicate whether customers rely primarily on search qualities, experience qualities, or credence qualities when buying this service. How can this marketer make its benefits more tangible for customers? Write a two-page report on your ideas.

3. *Find Out More* Read the annual report of a high-tech manufacturer such as Hewlett-Packard or IBM, or access the company's site on the World Wide Web. What portion of the company's revenues and profits come from goods? From services? What services does the company provide? How do these services relate to the company's manufactured goods?

   Does the company market its services differently from its goods? Write a brief report summarizing your findings.

4. *In a Partnership* Working with a classmate, select one of the services shown in Exercise 1. Analyze how customers would be likely to buy this service and predict how they might judge service quality. What suggestions can you make for setting standards for service quality? What suggestions can you make for a service recovery strategy? Explain your ideas in a letter to the marketer.

5. *In a Team* With two classmates, map the service encounters a customer (student) would experience when registering for classes at your college. Identify one or more problems that could affect service quality at each contact. How can your college improve service quality at each encounter? What should your college put into a service recovery plan? Prepare a five-minute presentation to your class to explain your suggestions.

6. *In a Team* Working with two other students, research the services provided by a landscape service, carpet cleaner, or another local business. How can this business advertise realistic, desirable standards for service quality? Write a newspaper or television advertisement that would accomplish this. Exchange ads with another team. What suggestions can you make for improving the ads?

VideoCase   Meet the Maestro of Service

Few organizations provide a better benchmark for outstanding service than Danny Meyer's two New York City restaurants, Union Square Cafe and Gramercy Tavern. Meyer's goal is not just to set new standards for restaurant service, value, and food. It's also to participate actively in helping to feed the hungry.

Union Square Cafe, opened in 1985, was modeled on Meyer's personal vision of a good restaurant. "I don't like getting ripped off, I don't like to get dressed up too much, and I like to enjoy good wine and food with friends in a place you can return to a lot," he says. Transforming this vision into reality meant building a team of like-minded employees and empowering them to give the best possible service.

When Meyer opened Gramercy Tavern in 1994, just a few streets away, he wanted to target a more upscale crowd. He's now competing with top restaurants such as Le Cirque, Daniel, and The Four Seasons. To differentiate Gramercy Tavern, Meyer relies on sophisticated atmospherics, creative meals, and the same sense of warmth and hospitality that customers experience at Union Square Cafe. Prices are higher than your average restaurant, mainly because of the use of more expensive ingredients, but demand for tables at lunch and dinner shows that customers appreciate the value.

Both restaurants are prime examples of how Meyer applies the first of the ABCs of service marketing—Always Be Customer Driven. Meyer has traveled throughout Europe, searching for new ways to delight his customers. Planning the physical look of his restaurants took months, with special attention to details such as the image presented to customers in the entryway, the main dining room, even the bathrooms.

Building relationships with customers is a top priority. Meyer and his staff have analyzed every contact point and planned to meet customer expectations every step of the way. Employees receive days of intensive training so they know every menu item and understand the service concept. Meyer initiates a two-way dialogue with customers by asking for feedback on satisfaction and publishing a relationship-building Union Square Cafe newsletter, featuring news, recipes, and contests. Next is a World Wide Web home page which customers can visit between meals.

But Meyer is responsible for more than the runaway success of his two restaurants. He has also used his resources to fight against hunger. Working with organizations such as Share Our Strength, City Harvest, and the Food and Hunger Hotline, Meyer has taken a leadership role in donating excess food and money to feed people in need.

One winter night, for example, blizzard conditions prevented these organizations from picking up excess food from local restaurants for delivery to pantries and shelters that feed hungry families. Anticipating the problems that the blizzard would cause, Meyer donated 20 percent of that night's dinner revenue—from both restaurants—to pay for overtime and special deliveries so thousands of people would get fed. Community service fits well with Meyer's philosophy of superior guest service. "By providing food to those who need it most, well, that's true hospitality," he says.[76]

Strategies and applications

1. Are the Union Square Cafe and Gramercy Tavern high-contact or low-contact service businesses? Why? What are the implications for customer perceptions of service quality?

2. How can Meyer research customer expectations and satisfaction? What specific marketing research techniques would you suggest? Why?

3. What should Meyer include on his Web page to build relationships with visitors and encourage patronage of both restaurants?

4. Should Meyer enlist the help of his customers in the fight against hunger? Why? If so, what two specific suggestions can you offer?

5. How is Meyer's relationship with the community likely to affect the success of his restaurants?

6. Where have you experienced outstanding service from an organization? Describe what a restaurant owner such as Danny Meyer could learn from your experience.

Team project

You and several other classmates are planning the next Union Square Cafe newsletter. List at least six articles you want to include. How does each help build the restaurant's relationship with customers? Outline your ideas in a memo to Danny Meyer.

http://www.joeboxer.com

Marketing on the Net   Joe Boxer's Shorts Are Showing on the Net

Joe Boxer isn't your father's underwear. Entrepreneur Nicholas Graham knows his customers are looking for more than cloth and elastic when they buy Joe Boxer shorts—they're making a fashion statement. So Graham has crafted his value package around a hip brand name that differentiates the product from every other underwear product on the market.

The Joe Boxer Web site is an integral element in Graham's IMC strategy to build brand equity. Targeting a young audience (18 to 35 years old), Graham emphasizes fun as well as function. He explains, "We don't try to sell anything [on the Web]. We consider Job Boxer to be an entertainment company, and so the site is an amusement park and the underwear is the souvenir." The Web site is not a substitute for conventional advertising. In fact, it enhances the value package by providing "an experience that you can't get through the advertising or product," says Graham.

The Web site has been designed around tongue-in-cheek interactive games that draw visitors back again and again. One recent game invited visitors to "undress Nick" down to his Joe Boxers and send him via virtual delivery to any address on the Internet. For less-advanced visitors, the site offered an Internet primer and instructions on how to adjust Web browsing software to make the most of the music, sounds, and graphics available on the site. And in the spirit of traditional marketing, the site showed a map to help visitors find the nearest Joe Boxer retailer.

Graham is always looking for ways to stir up excitement around the Joe Boxer brand. For example, e-mail sent via the Joe Boxer Web site also appears on a giant electronic billboard in New York City's Times Square. Taking the billboard tie-in a step further, Graham arranged to appear with the mayor of New York at a wedding ceremony in Times Square—while the vows exchanged by the bride and groom flashed across the billboard.

Keeping the Joe Boxer brand in the public eye can be costly. Just getting the Web site up and running cost about $50,000. But Graham is pleased with the results, which show that the brand is gaining popularity around the world. As many as 90,000 visitors now land on the Web site every month, and nearly one in five e-mail messages comes from another country. Retailers report that the Web site has brought in shoppers, and media coverage of the Web site reinforces the cool brand image Graham wants to maintain.

Despite the Web site's success, Graham realizes that it isn't a marketing panacea. "I think [the Web] is a fantastic medium and it's changing the world, but I don't think anyone's Internet site should be all-encompassing." Still, if Graham has his way, he'll keep the Joe Boxer Web site on the list of "must see" stops for cyberspace surfers.[1]

Strategies and applications

1. Visit the Joe Boxer Web site and browse the games. How does game-playing reinforce the brand name and image?

2. Do you think a competitor could successfully mimic the Joe Boxer Web site to build a hip image for its brand? Why or why not?

3. Suggest two ideas for using the Joe Boxer Web site to strengthen relationships with retailers and other channel partners.

4. One of Joe Boxer's competitors in the underwear industry is Fruit of the Loom. Visit the Fruit of the Loom Web site (http://www.fruit.com) and compare that brand's image with the image presented by Joe Boxer. Do you think both are aiming for the same target market? Explain your answer.

5. Should Graham expand his product line by adding other apparel such as T-shirts and socks? How can he test such new product ideas before commercializing them?

6. Where in the product life cycle does Joe Boxer seem to be? Since Joe Boxer is a fashion product, how would you suggest that Graham extend its product life cycle for a longer period?

Team project

Work with other students to design an online treasure hunt that Graham can use on the Joe Boxer Web site. Would it be a good idea to ask players to visit a nearby Joe Boxer retailer? Should players be required to buy something to participate in the game? What ethical issues might be raised by an online treasure hunt? Present your game idea in a report to the class.

http://www.sfnb.com

Marketing on the Net   Pioneering Bank Cashes In on the Internet

The first bank to open for business on the Internet still has only one branch—in Pineville, Kentucky. Security First Network Bank (SFNB) is a full-service bank that invites cyberspace customers from all 50 states. Originally set up as a subsidiary of Cardinal Bancshares in Lexington, Kentucky, SFNB is growing even faster now as a separate publicly traded company. Banking online is a new type of product that appeals to computer-savvy early adopters looking for speedy, convenient, low-cost banking.

Customers don't have to stand in line waiting for a teller. Instead, they can simply tap their PC keyboards to open a checking or savings account, open a certificate of deposit, pay bills electronically, request a credit card, or use other banking services. Opening a new account takes just five minutes, and the bank even sets up an electronic check register that automatically records transactions and balances each customer's account. Customers can also examine electronic images of checks they have written to review payments. These product features have been specifically designed to deliver top-quality service despite the intangibility of banking services.

The Web site is open for banking transactions 24 hours a day, every day of the year, and customer service representatives are always available to help or answer questions. Of course, SFNB isn't entirely electronic. Customers can make deposits by mail, and they receive automated-teller-machine cards so they can withdraw money at local ATMs. They can also download records of their banking transactions to their own PCs using personal finance programs such as Quicken. And because SFNB doesn't maintain far-flung branches or hire local banking personnel, its costs and its prices are lower than at many neighborhood banks.

What about the security of banking data? SFNB had to address this issue before federal bank regulators would approve its online operations. The bank uses special security software similar to that used by U.S. intelligence agencies. After passing the government's security checks—and opening a single branch building, the minimum requirement for a bank—SFNB was approved for full-service banking so its deposits could be insured by the Federal Deposit Insurance Corporation.

Nearly 3,000 customers opened accounts during the bank's first year, and the number of customers keeps growing as SFNB adds new services such as brokerage and insurance. Now the online banking concept has become so popular that SFNB is the bank to benchmark—and other banks are licensing the software so they can do business on the Internet.[2]

Strategies and applications

1. Visit the SFNB Web site and move through the demonstration of the bank's operation. How does this demonstration help the bank address the problems customers have in evaluating services before they buy? What can you suggest to improve the demonstration?

2. Does SFNB offer high-contact or low-contact service? How would you characterize the service in terms of delivery? Explain your answers. What are the implications for online banking providers?

3. Play the role of SFNB's marketing director. Which service gaps are most likely to occur in online banking? What can you do to uncover customer expectations and avoid these gaps?

4. Examine the simulated bank lobby on SFNB's home page. Why would SFNB maintain the look of a traditional bank branch on its Web site? What other graphics does SFNB use that lend a more traditional banking look to its Web pages? Is this a good idea? Why or why not?

5. How does SFNB maintain a two-way dialogue with customers? Why is this especially important for an online service provider?

6. In the spirit of continuous improvement, what would you suggest that SFNB do to enhance its service offering? Show how your suggestions relate to the ABCs of services marketing.

Team project

Team up with several other students to investigate online banking services by visiting the Web sites of Salem Five Cents Savings Bank (http://www.salemfive.com), La Jolla Bank (http://www.ljbank.com), and 1st Source Bank (http://www.pawws.com/1stsource). How do the offerings of these banks compare with that of SFNB? Next, choose a single product, such as a one-year certificate of deposit, and compare rates at all four banks. How important do you think rates are to customers who are choosing among online banks? Write a report summarizing your team's findings. Include at least four measures of service quality you believe customers use in evaluating electronic banking services.

internetempowerment

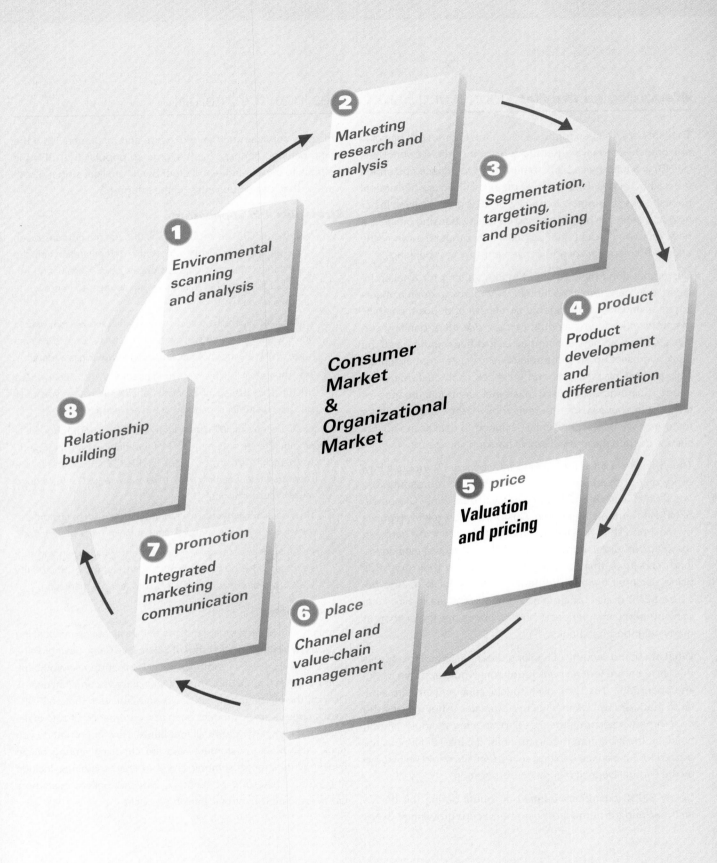

Product Valuation and Pricing

Part 5 explores the related concepts of product value and pricing. In Chapter 12, the customer's value equation is presented. The chapter also looks at pricing objectives and the role of pricing in marketing management. The profile shows how pricing at Direct Tire Sales supports a positioning strategy of top-quality service. Chapter 13 examines pricing strategies and management in the context of building and maintaining marketing relationships. The chapter opening profile of Southwest Airlines describes the use of a no-frills, low-price strategy to build market share and customer satisfaction.

12

PRICING AND VALUE

Learning Goals

After you have read and studied this
chapter, you should be able to:

1. Define price and state the value equation.
2. Characterize value marketing and value
   pricing from the customer's viewpoint.
3. List five long-term objectives marketers
   can set when planning pricing.
4. Distinguish between price competition
   and nonprice competition.
5. Describe the demand curve and show how
   price elasticity of demand operates.
6. Demonstrate how price leaders and price
   wars affect pricing.
7. Analyze how legal and regulatory
   influences affect pricing practices.

PROFILE

Value drives pricing at Direct Tire Sales

Barry Steinberg knows that people with cars don't like spinning their wheels over service. As the owner of Direct Tire Sales in Watertown, Massachusetts, Steinberg is out to build long-term relationships with customers who will pay a little more for better service. He sums up his philosophy this way: "I don't want a *consumer* who will drive all over town to save a few cents on a can of tuna fish. I want a *customer* we can keep for life."

Direct Tire sells tires and repairs cars. Turning up the heat on pricing are competitors like Sears, Firestone, and a number of discount tire outlets in the Boston area. Rather than get caught in a profit-crippling price war, Direct Tire stresses the value of its top-notch service, not the bottom-line price. "We let the public know that we *are* more expensive," Steinberg says. "I won't compete in the low price arena, and they [competitors] can't compete in the service arena."

Direct Tire's prices represent good value because they cover a variety of extras. Customers can borrow one of the company's 21 free loaner cars. The spotless customer waiting lounge is stocked with complimentary gourmet coffees, teas, and baked goods. Nimble teamwork between the front office employees and garage technicians gets customers back on the road as quickly as possible. And certain tire products come with lifetime warranties. With pricing linked to services that customers value, Direct Tire Sales has grown steadily and now rings up $7.2 million in annual sales.[1]

Direct Tire's customers, like all customers, expect good value in exchange for the price they pay. This chapter is the first of two that look at the pricing and valuation process, one of the eight universal marketing processes. First you'll examine the relationship between value and pricing and learn the five pricing objectives that marketers can set. Next, you'll consider the role of pricing in marketing management. Then, you'll analyze the market economics and environmental issues that influence pricing strategy. In the next chapter, you'll learn how to set and manage prices.

Pricing, Value, and Customer Relationships

The value decade is upon us. If you can't sell a top-quality product at the world's lowest price, you're going to be out of the game.

Jack Welch
CEO of General Electric

What makes a marketing exchange mutually beneficial? The answer lies in the universal process of valuation and pricing, which is concerned with whether an exchange benefits both the marketer and the customer. Both parties want something of value from the exchange. The customer gets the value package, with all its associated benefits. And the marketer gets the **price**, the amount of money or some other valuable that the marketer asks in exchange for a product. For marketers, the pricing process is critical because it directly affects both revenues and profitability.

What customers pay isn't always called price. Students pay *tuition* for college courses; passengers pay a *fare* for bus, train, or air transportation; members pay *dues* to clubs; and borrowers pay *interest* on loans. No matter what word is used, the price of a product is what a marketer expects to receive in exchange for a good, a service, or an idea.

In some cases, price isn't paid in money. **Barter** is the exchange of goods, services, and ideas without the use of money (or money substitutes like credit cards). When money didn't exist, people met their needs by bartering—trading pottery for chickens, for example. Barter is still common in some areas of the world. Still, whether an exchange involves money or barter, the effect is the same: the marketer receives something of value, as does the customer.

The Customer's Value Equation

Before they buy, customers weigh what they expect to get from a marketer against what they expect to give in exchange. By weighing the trade-off between these two, each customer arrives at a perceived value for the product. Thus, from the customer's perspective, **value** is the ratio of perceived benefits to perceived price. Here's the equation form of this definition:

$$\text{perceived value} = \frac{\text{perceived benefits}}{\text{perceived price}}$$

Marketers can increase perceived value by increasing the perceived benefits or by lowering the perceived price. **Perceived benefits** are anything and everything customers believe they receive from the overall value package. Remember that quality, services, and other product elements have value *only* when their presence results in the delivery of benefits that customers want and need. Consider the hotel business. Hotel owner Bill Kimpton says that "most customers in a hotel want only a bed and a room, but they are paying for the ballrooms and the discos. Out of a $150 room rate, they use maybe $90 worth." Knowing this, Kimpton designed his hotels, including the Prescott in San Francisco, to deliver only the benefits that customers value— at a reasonable price.[2]

Perceived price refers to whatever customers believe they have to give up in exchange for the benefits received. The perceived price includes the offering of money, products, or another form of payment. For example, Standard Equipment & Supply in Indiana, which markets tools, supplies, and manufacturing equipment, doesn't always pay cash. It has bartered its products for computers, copying machines, and fax machines.[3]

price

the amount of money or some other valuable that the marketer asks in exchange for a product

barter

the exchange of goods, services, and ideas without the use of money (or money substitutes)

value

the ratio of perceived benefits to perceived price

perceived benefits

anything and everything customers believe they receive from the overall value package

perceived price

whatever customers believe they have to give up in exchange for the benefits received

Often the perceived price covers more than the initial purchase price. It may include the time, inconvenience, and extra money a customer must invest to buy or benefit from a product. Organizations that buy personal computers, for instance, also pay for software, training, and other necessities. The price of the hardware—which has dropped steadily over the years even as performance has improved—is now only 10 percent of the total outlay. Shopping for PCs also takes time. So organizational customers are obliged to weigh the overall price against the benefits to determine the value of the PCs they buy.[4]

In essence, customer perceptions of value drive the marketer's pricing process. This is because marketers can sell only at a price customers are willing to pay for perceived value. However, the value equation is dynamic, changing as customer wants change, products and benefits change, and prices change. That's why you need to maintain a customer orientation and to research your customers and their views of the value equation, study the marketing environment, and watch competitive prices as you plan a pricing strategy aimed at starting new customer relationships and strengthening existing ties.[5]

In addition, think about what customers might substitute for your product. When customers apply the value equation to a product purchase, they frequently compare prices and benefits of other products that can satisfy the same needs and wants. Remember, customers seek to maximize the perceived benefits while minimizing the perceived price. Reacting to their customers' search for a better value equation, more marketers are using strategies such as value marketing and value pricing.

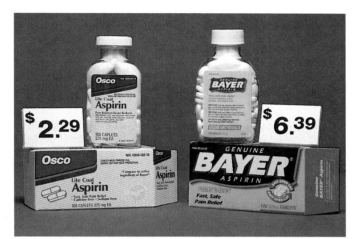

Nothing illustrates perceived value better than a side-by-side comparison of two similar products, one a well-known brand name and the other a private brand. Customers who believe that the brand-name product has superior quality are willing to pay a higher price for it. How can Bayer learn more about its customers' value perceptions?

The Rise of Value Marketing and Value Pricing

As marketers continue to improve the quality of their products, customers come to expect higher quality from all products in a category. Almost as soon as an augmented product appears, customers accept it as standard: an expected product. In Japan, this phenomenon is called *atarimae hinshitsu*, which means quality taken for granted. Customer emphasis not withstanding, however, quality is not always the deciding point in purchase decisions. One study showed that customers consider reasonable price even more important than a manufacturer's reputation for quality.[6]

These days, more marketers are adopting **value marketing**, the process of designing, developing, and marketing products to give customers extra benefits and higher quality at fair prices. Value marketing is one of *the* major marketing trends of the decade. It's growing in importance as more marketers emphasize a customer focus and long-term customer relationships. Customers want consistent value, and the company that provides it is more likely to win long-term customer loyalty. So many marketers are joining the value parade that the word "value" is popping up on products galore. In one recent year, as many as 200 trademark applications covered brands that contained the word "value."[7]

value marketing

the process of designing, developing, and marketing products to give customers extra benefits and higher quality at fair prices

The more benefits you add to your value package, the more value customers might perceive in it (if those benefits are communicated properly). Customers are generally willing to pay a higher price for added value, which can lead to higher profitability. Alternatively, by holding price steady as you improve quality, you can attract and keep more customers and expand your market share, which can lower your unit production costs and boost profits.[8] Either way, the exchange becomes more beneficial for you and your customers alike.

Value pricing is the process of holding prices steady or cutting them while improving product benefits. When you use value pricing, you look at the trade-off between benefits and price from your customer's viewpoint. Instead of setting prices according to internal concerns such as production costs and profitability objectives, you set them to reflect your customers' perceptions of value.

Although you can't ignore costs, you can't use them as the sole basis of pricing decisions, because they don't have a connection to the price that customers may accept. The key is to research customer needs, examine competitors' value packages **(p. 11)** and prices, and design and price your product accordingly. As management expert Peter Drucker says, "Customers do not see it as their job to ensure manufacturers a profit. The only sound way to price is to start out with what the market is willing to pay—and thus, it must be assumed, what the competition will charge—and design to that price specification."[9]

This photo of Taco Bell's automated ordering system illustrates its strategy of value pricing. Taco Bell's value menu offers selections that are priced especially low. Such aggressive pricing has forced other fast-food chains to adopt similar strategies. The trick is to ensure that the value price offered to customers includes an acceptable profit for the marketer. After all, the goal is a mutually beneficial exchange relationship. What do you think were Taco Bell's major goals in lowering prices?

For example, Taco Bell was among the first fast-food chains to adopt value pricing. The chain developed a special "value menu" of popular Mexican foods at lower prices, which lured customers away from competitors. But you don't have to develop a special product to use value pricing. Coca-Cola used value pricing when it reintroduced its soft drinks in India after a 16-year absence. The company reduced its prices by 10 percent while increasing the amount of Coke per bottle by 20 percent. Coke's integrated marketing communication stressed the beverage's affordability, availability, and suitability for many occasions. The result: local bottlers had to pump out 40 percent more product to meet customer demand.[10]

Issues for critical thinking

What is the difference between value pricing and discount pricing? Are you using value pricing when you lower your price to match a competitor's price? What examples of value pricing have you seen? Were they effective?

Value Pricing Applies in Consumer and Organizational Markets

Taco Bell, Procter & Gamble, Delta Air Lines, Coca-Cola, and thousands of other firms know how important value pricing has become in consumer

value pricing
the process of holding prices steady or cutting them while improving product benefits

markets. Consumer behavior has been shifting away from the freer spending of the 1980s toward a search for the right quality at the right price in the 1990s. At the same time, a growing number of marketers are vying for consumer relationships in nearly every product category. To prosper in this high-pressure environment, consumer marketers are using value pricing to give their products an edge.

Examples of effective value pricing are all around, from the success of no-frills Southwest Airlines in the service sector to the low-price, full-option car package of Chrysler's fast-selling Neon in the manufacturing sector. Another approach to value pricing is the mass customization  **(p. 274)** approach used by Motorola in its pager factory in Boynton Beach, Florida. Thanks to sophisticated technology, Motorola can help a customer design a pager for a specific use (combining parts in 29 million different ways) and start production within a few hours. This technology allows Motorola to enhance the value equation by customizing pagers at the price of a mass-produced product.[11]

Organizational customers are as concerned with value as ultimate consumers. They can't afford to overpay, and they want the best value for their money. Therefore, business-to-business marketers need to pay as much attention to value pricing as their consumer marketing counterparts. Manufacturers and service marketers alike are reexamining their value packages and balancing price tags with extra features that deliver important customer benefits. Consider how Boeing uses value pricing with its 777 jet, priced at about $100 million.

As you might expect, airlines get more than a stripped-down model for such a hefty price. Boeing asked its customers, including United Airlines, to help design the jet. At their request, the plane was designed to be quickly reconfigured to adapt to market changes. The flexibility to move the seats, the galleys, and the lavatories is a feature that yields benefits for customers throughout the jet's life. This customer-pleasing benefit is only one of many built into the jet's price.[12]

Kiwi Airlines offers low-cost fares to the cities listed on this billboard. However, low prices alone may not be enough to keep customers coming back. What are some other factors travelers consider when choosing an airline? What kinds of incentives or services might Kiwi provide to help establish long-term, friendly relationships with customers without substantially increasing operating costs?

Customer-Driven Pricing and Market Segmentation

Customer-driven pricing is very different from the "one price fits all" mode relied on by many marketers in the past. By using market segmentation  **(p. 220)** to identify discrete customer groups that will respond to products priced to meet their needs, you can improve both customer satisfaction and profitability. The key is to understand the value that each segment places on the product. For example, Sealed Air Corporation, a marketer of protective packaging, found that some business customers were shipping heavy items over long distances. Because such customers valued the superior cushioning of the air-bubble packaging material marketed by Sealed Air, they would pay more for the product. This type of segmentation for pricing helped Sealed Air boost sales and profits.[13]

When you target more than one segment, you'll want to adjust your prices accordingly. The Drake Swissotel, a New York City hotel, has two sets of room rates—a lower range (depending on room size) for airlines that need overnight accommodations for crew members and a higher range for business travelers and tourists. However, the higher rates are offset by remodeled rooms and access to banquet rooms and business services. "You still need to find a way to offer value," observes Janis Cannon, vice president of sales and marketing at Swissotel North America.[14]

Taking segmentation a step further, you can tailor a product to individual customer needs and set the price accordingly. To mention a familiar example, carmakers allow customers to specify leather seats and other nonstandard features but charge extra for these special options. At times, carmakers offer a specially priced value package that includes many desirable extras such as air conditioning and a sun roof. One result of this practice is that customers pay different prices based on the package they choose to meet their automotive desires.

How the Pricing Process Works

No matter what product you're marketing, the process of pricing starts with a thorough understanding of the wants and value perceptions of customers. Even when you're not customizing a product for an individual customer, your prices must reflect value to which customers will respond. That's the only way to build a customer relationship that will stand the test of time.

In planning a pricing strategy, think about the objectives you want to achieve. Also consider the interaction of pricing with other marketing processes. Once you've analyzed the effect of market economics and environmental influences, you're ready to set and manage prices, as you'll see in Chapter 13.

Before you go on . . .

A. Why do marketers need to understand the value equation?

B. What is value pricing and how do marketers use it?

Setting Pricing Objectives

Before you start pricing your products, stop to consider the role of pricing in your broader marketing and organizational strategies. Depending on what your organization wants to achieve and the specific objectives written into your marketing plan, you can set long-term pricing objectives corresponding to the five types shown in Figure 12.1: pricing for profit, pricing for sales growth, pricing for competitive advantage, pricing for positioning, and pricing for social goals.

To be effective in supporting relationships with customers, you must develop these objectives in the context of the value customers perceive in a product. However, pricing objectives aren't mutually exclusive. You can strive for two or even three different objectives during a given period. In addition, you may adopt short-term pricing goals to meet specific environmental threats or to take advantage of opportunities.

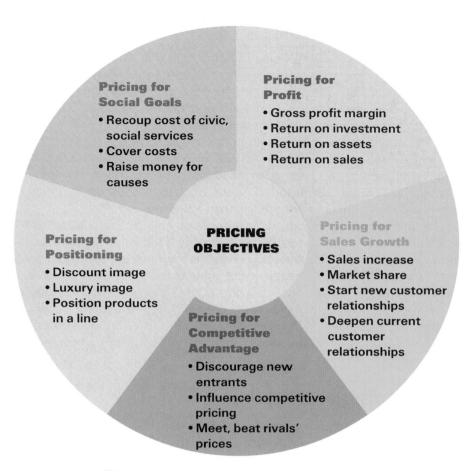

When an organization is strapped for cash, for example, the marketer may see survival as the main pricing goal until finances improve. During and after bankruptcy proceedings, both Continental Airlines and TWA set survival as their pricing goal. They undercut rivals' airfares to attract passengers and generate enough money to cover the cost of operations. Of course, pricing for survival will give a short-term boost, but it won't help a marketer grow or meet other long-term objectives.

Pricing for Profit

Most for-profit marketers use pricing to support their profit objectives, and they set specific targets to measure their profitability. *Profit* is what remains after paying for costs and expenses out of sales revenues. You can set pricing objectives to meet specific targets for profit returns, such as return on investment, return

FIGURE **12.1**

Pricing Objectives
Marketers can set five types of pricing objectives, as shown here. The specific objectives set will depend on the organization's overall objectives and the objectives established in the marketing plan.

on assets, and return on sales. (See Appendix B for details.) Rubbermaid, for example, sets its prices to achieve a target of a 13.5 percent return on the assets used in its business.[15]

You can also use pricing to achieve targets for *gross margin*, the amount that remains after deducting the cost of goods sold from sales revenues. Gross margin is usually expressed as a percentage of revenues. To increase your profit margin, you can raise prices, lower the cost of goods sold, or do both.

Pricing to achieve gross margin targets can be tricky. Until competition became too fierce, Apple Computer used pricing to support aggressive profit objectives. The company wanted to boost gross profit margin to 55 percent by maintaining relatively high prices as it pursued cost efficiencies. Because rivals were regularly shaving gross margins, this objective hampered Apple's ability to compete.[16]

Under pressure to achieve immediate returns, many marketers use pricing to *maximize current profits*, trying to make the highest profits right now. This approach is fostered, in part, by the need to satisfy investors and market analysts, who watch quarterly returns. By downplaying long-term customer satisfaction in favor of short-term profits, however, a marketer is exposed to competition from more patient marketers, willing to invest in long-term customer relationships. Toshiba, for example, didn't price its first digital video player to cover development costs. Instead, it spread the costs by reusing the technology to improve existing products. This long-term view helped Toshiba strengthen its relationships with a wider group of customers.[17]

Pricing for Sales Growth

Growth in sales is a second type of pricing objective. Growth in sales can mean starting more new customer relationships as well as deepening your relationships with current customers by encouraging them to buy more from you. You can set prices to sell a higher number or dollar amount of products, or to achieve a higher market share.

For example, Pacific Telesis Group wanted to accelerate sales growth of its integrated services digital network (ISDN) telephone lines, which send voice and digital information faster than standard telephone lines. After initially charging $24.50 per month for ISDN, the company sought broader market acceptance by cutting the price to less than $20 per month.[18]

Gaining market share can be an important objective, according to researchers in the Profit Impact of Market Strategy (PIMS) project at the Strategic Planning Institute. PIMS research suggests a strong link between market share and profitability. Although critics argue that the relationship has not been proven to be one of cause and effect, PIMS and other studies indicate that companies with high market share generally enjoy lower costs of goods, yielding higher profits. PIMS also concludes that companies can boost market share by offering quality that customers see as superior to competing products.[19]

Pricing for Competitive Advantage

Pricing for competitive advantage is one of the most common marketing objectives. Often you'll adjust your prices to match or beat competitors' prices, neutralizing their advantage and refocusing customers on your value message. That's how David Schwartz of Schwartz Bookshops in Milwaukee responded to competition from Barnes & Noble and other giant bookstores.

Schwartz discounted top-selling hardcover books by 40 percent, top paperbacks by 30 percent, a special group of 100 books by 20 percent, and a changing category of books by 10 percent. He also put a coffee bar in each store and hired a specialist to work with business customers around the world. "We have given away about 2.6 points of gross margin in discounting, but we increased the volume by about 35 percent," says Schwartz of the results.[20]

Pricing for Positioning

Price helps customers form a particular impression of a product or a marketer. Toys 'Я' Us uses low pricing to position itself as a discount retailer. Mitsubishi, on the other hand, used high price to support a positioning of exclusivity and luxury when introducing the Spyder convertible sports car. The company made a limited number of Spyders, priced at $65,000 each. Dick Recchia, vice president of marketing, says the Spyder is "a way to build our brand image. We'll use it to support the other cars in the line, plus we think we'll be setting the benchmark for luxury convertibles."[21]

Independent booksellers like David Schwartz (left) and Avin Domnitz (right), who own Schwartz Bookshops in Milwaukee, attract customers by pricing some products low and providing superior service. Borders Books, a national retailer, has captured market share using wide selection as its appeal. Crown Books, another large chain, uses price discounts as its primary competitive strategy. However, small bookstores often can't purchase in the same volume or offer the wide selection that these national stores do; such competition drives many of them out of business. What pricing strategy would you recommend to small bookstores trying to compete with giant chains?

In addition, you can position each product in your line by linking its price to a particular level of quality. Kodak does this with its Funtime, Gold, and Royal Gold films. Funtime, positioned as a brand-name alternative to store-brand films, is priced lower than other Kodak films. Royal Gold, positioned as a high-quality film for special occasions, is the highest priced of the three brands, and Gold is positioned as a good-quality film for everyday use, priced lower than Royal Gold.[22]

Pricing for Social Goals

Nonprofit marketers use pricing to achieve a variety of social goals. Government agencies use price to recoup some or all of their operating costs while delivering needed services, such as public transportation. Pricing can also help save taxpayers money. Within Minnesota's Department of Administration, for example, internal departments compete with outside suppliers for the right to supply state agencies with photocopying, management consulting, computer and telecommunications services, and other goods and services. The Department of Administration isn't in business to make a profit, but to provide government with quality products at reasonable prices. Thanks to the department's cost-cutting measures and competitive pricing, the state has saved its citizens millions of dollars.[23]

Charities, health care institutions, museums, and other nongovernment organizations that don't seek a profit use pricing to cover their costs where possible and to raise money for their activities. They also use pricing to reach out to new customers. At most times the Whitney Museum of American Art, in New York City, charges a $10 entry fee, but it periodically offers free admission. The free nights introduce the museum's art to the community and attract people who might not otherwise come.[24]

A number of companies, including Working Assets Long Distance, use pricing to raise money for selected social causes as well as to achieve profit objectives. Working Assets, a telecommunications marketer, prices its long-distance telephone services to include a percentage of profit to be donated to causes its customers help select.[25]

Before you go on . . .

A. What objectives can marketers set when they price for profit?

B. How can a marketer set pricing objectives to support its positioning?

The Role of Pricing in Marketing Management

Regardless of your specific pricing objectives, you must research customer needs and perceptions to be able to create a product customers value at a price they see as fair. By taking this route to satisfying customers and building enduring customer relationships, you are likely to improve profits.[26]

Of course, pricing doesn't exist in a vacuum. To be effective, pricing has to be carefully coordinated with other elements of external marketing strategy, including product management, value-chain management, and integrated marketing communications.

Pricing and Product Management

Pricing can vary throughout the stages of the product life cycle ⟵⎤ **(p. 302)**. How you set and adjust prices in each stage depends, in large part, on customer demand, competitive pressures, your production capabilities, and your pricing goals.[27] In many cases, you'll maintain your price in the growth stage but reduce it in the maturity stage as you defend against rivals entering the market. In the decline stage, you may slash your price to quickly clear stock if you decide to eliminate your product. On the other hand, you may be able to raise your price if many competitors have left the market and your product continues to satisfy the wants of enough customers.[28]

It is necessary to manage pricing across your entire product line to reflect the value of each product's unique benefits. Through marketing research, you can find out the highest and lowest prices customers will accept. Also, to help customers distinguish among your offerings, you'll want to maintain a price and benefit differential from each product to the next.[29]

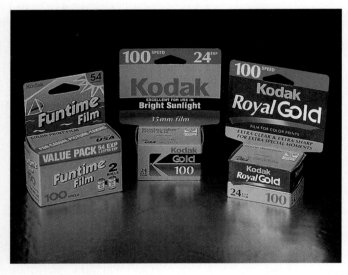

Kodak offers a variety of film product lines at various prices; the price reflects each line's quality, features, and benefits. A company with this kind of variety in its product line must establish a separate set of prices for each product in each line, then carefully monitor its competitors' prices. Which of these three lines of film do you think carries the highest price? Why?

Pricing and Value-Chain Management

Your product's price both influences and is influenced by your value-chain relationships. When you market through wholesalers and retailers, each organization reprices your product to reflect its own goals and the market's economics.[30] As a result, the price you set is incorporated into the price each intermediary charges its customers. Although you can't control the pricing decisions made by these channel members, you can choose to work with those that will keep the final price in line with customer expectations.

If you're marketing a luxury apparel product, for example, you can sell to a high-end retailer such as Saks Fifth Avenue, where shoppers expect to pay higher prices for higher quality. If you're marketing a basic household cleaner, you can sell to Wal-Mart or Kmart, whose shoppers look for good quality at low prices. These discount chains expect to buy in large quantities at low prices and resell to their customers at competitively low prices, as well.[31]

What you pay your suppliers is also a cost to factor into your pricing decisions. When the price of paper rose sharply in the mid-1990s, magazines and newspapers had to decide whether to absorb the increases or pass them along in the form of higher prices. The publisher of *TV Guide* decided to increase the magazine's price by 10 cents per issue. Taking a different approach, the *News-Times*, a daily newspaper in Danbury, Connecticut, cut pages from its Sunday magazine and bought more efficient printing equipment instead of raising its price.[32]

Pricing and Integrated Marketing Communication

Through integrated marketing communication, you can bring your pricing and value message to customers. Using advertising, sales promotion, and other tactics, you can show how your pricing reflects the value of your product's features and benefits. Your communication can also compare your value package and pricing with those of your competitors. And if you communicate via the Internet, you can give customers up-to-the-minute details about pricing and benefits.

Look at the battle between MCI and AT&T in long-distance telephone services. MCI originally positioned itself as the low-price alternative to AT&T's full-priced services. This approach helped MCI take customers from AT&T. For its part, AT&T initially responded by talking about superior quality, not price. Then the company shifted strategy. By offering a discount rate plan and advertising its service as a better value than MCI, AT&T was able to rebuild customer relationships and regain market share.[33]

Of course, products with higher price tags can trumpet themselves just as loudly as products with bargain prices. For example, Yonex advertises that its golf clubs are priced higher than competing brands. The company explains the higher prices by pointing to two benefits: better accuracy and longer drives.

Price and Nonprice Competition

Price competition is the practice of differentiating your product from competitive products primarily on the basis of price. Price competition can help you highlight your products' value in relation to rival products. Most often, you do this by cutting the price while holding benefits constant. Thanks to the flexibility of pricing tactics, you can lower prices in many ways, including putting a product on sale, offering a rebate, giving away discount coupons, and permanently discounting prices.

Although price competition can be an effective way to respond to an immediate competitive threat, it isn't necessarily good for the long term. "Anyone can imitate price—that's the problem with it," notes Chris Hoyt of Reach Marketing West, a California consulting firm. If you cut your price, your competition can quickly match or beat you, which neutralizes your advantage. This is common in retailing, where one store's discounting usually is matched quickly by other stores.[34]

However, customers who flock to you because of lower prices are just as likely to leave if rivals cut theirs even more. What's more, a very low price may lead some customers to question the quality and value of your products. In addition, a low price can influence a customer's perception of what is a "reasonable" price long after you (and your competitors) are ready to apply a new pricing approach. The low price becomes a reference point against which customers measure the value of your product and others when making future purchase decisions.[35]

You may have difficulty conveying the value of your benefits at a higher price as long as people remember the lower price. In short, although price competition can be a good short-term tactic, it's not usually an effective way to build enduring customer relationships. The following section shows how small businesses compete by adding value to the value equation.

price competition

the practice of differentiating a product from competitive products primarily on the basis of price

SMALL BUSINESS WATCH

Putting more value in the value equation

How can small businesses compete with mammoth discounters like Wal-Mart? Although they can't afford to compete on price, small businesses can still find plenty of ways to add value to the value equation. Here's a sampling of marketing tactics that have proven successful for small businesses:

- *Offer extra convenience.* Customers of the Locker Room in Montgomery, Alabama, don't have to visit the store to buy men's clothing. A mobile showroom brings a selection of items in the right size directly to the customer's door.
- *Offer extra help.* Customers who buy computers at CompuSystems in Washington, Missouri, can call the store's toll-free hotline and get free help. Owner Joe Wolf doesn't put a time limit on his help: customers can ask questions forever.
- *Offer unique products.* Breed & Company in Austin and San Marcus, Texas, specializes in hard-to-find and distinctive hardware products and housewares that discounters rarely stock. Each store carries more than 45,000 individual items and will order whatever customers need.
- *Highlight your value.* Fisher Office Products in Boise, Idaho, uses a one-page flyer to spell out the benefits customers get by shopping at Fisher's instead of at discount competitors.[36]

What other relationship-building ideas can you suggest for small businesses that can't compete on price?

There are many ways to create value for customers. One way is to make it easier for them to shop. The Locker Room, for example, brings traditional men's clothing to customers' homes or offices; this allows customers to shop when it's convenient for them. What other marketers would benefit from adapting Locker Room's strategy of bringing products to the customer?

As marketing expert Theodore Levitt warns, "The trick is to combine price competitiveness with competitiveness in all respects." So instead of simply cutting price when competition looms, many marketers are turning to **nonprice competition**, the practice of differentiating a product on the basis of elements other than price, including fast, friendly service and quality. Marketers can use nonprice competition to improve the benefits without increasing the price, or to improve the benefits faster than the price is increased.[37]

In the express delivery business, for example, FedEx and UPS are price conscious, but both carriers compete on more than price. Each offers a variety of delivery schedules and services, including computerized package tracking. Price and service convinced Phil Schaecher, senior vice president of cataloguer Lands' End, to choose UPS, because "there isn't an address that UPS won't go to, and they were better on price."[38]

nonprice competition

the practice of differentiating a product on the basis of elements other than price

demand curve

a graphic illustration of the way customer demand responds to a series of possible prices

Before you go on . . .

A. How do marketers vary price in the product life cycle?

B. Why would a marketer use nonprice competition instead of price competition?

FIGURE **12.2**

Analyzing Market Economics to Support Pricing Strategy

Demand Curves

The demand curve for a particular product graphically depicts how customer demand responds to a series of possible prices. In the downward sloping demand curve shown in (a), demand decreases as the price increases. In contrast, the luxury priced product demand curve shown in (b) indicates that demand for such products will actually increase at some higher prices.

As you plan your pricing strategy, think about how supply and demand affect your product. Market economics have a direct effect on the number of products you can sell at a particular price. How many bottles of iced tea can Snapple expect to sell at $0.99? How many at $1.29 or $1.99? To plan a price that makes sense in the context of its pricing and marketing objectives, Snapple, like all marketers, needs to understand the relationship between price and customer demand. Finding complete and accurate data about price and demand can be difficult, which is why many marketers use estimates.

Along the Demand Curve

The **demand curve** is a graphic illustration of the way customer demand responds to a series of possible prices. In most cases, the quantity demanded by customers goes up as price goes down. But demand doesn't always follow a straight line, nor does the demand curve remain constant, as Figure 12.2 shows. Sometimes demand will increase, not drop, at one or more higher price points, depending on customers' perceptions of the value of the product at that price. When the price goes up, therefore, the quantity demanded may go up as well. This may happen with luxury cars; for example, some people are more interested as the prestige increases because of the high price.

Of course, price isn't the only influence on customer demand, which complicates pricing along the demand curve. Competition also plays a role. If a comparable substitute is available at a lower price, customers may buy it, raising the quantity demanded for the substitute and lowering the quantity demanded for the other product.

In addition, customer affluence affects demand. For example, Procter & Gamble studies consumer income levels before it makes and prices products for international markets. By calculating what Brazilian shoppers could pay for disposable diapers, the company was able to develop and launch Pampers Uni, a lower priced version of Pampers geared to the economics of the South American market.[39]

Economists also recognize that individual needs, behaviors, and social interactions can influence demand. For example, many successful restaurants and sporting events experience continued heavy demand at high prices. Why? Because many consumers watch what other consumers buy or do. The popularity of a restaurant or event, not the price, can boost demand.[40] The case that follows shows how paper marketers have profited from understanding supply and demand.

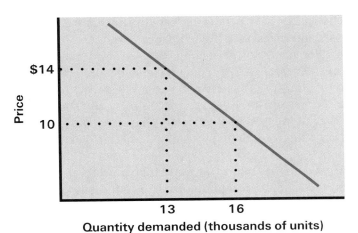

(a) Downward sloping demand curve

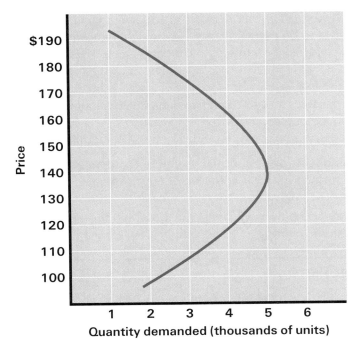

(b) Luxury priced product demand curve

Applying the Concepts

Paper profits from supply and demand

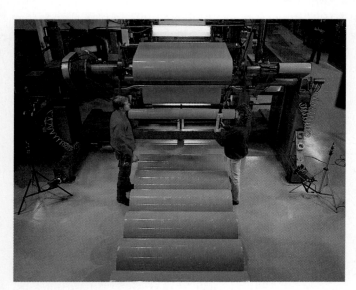

Few industries have had to adapt to pricing changes as often and as quickly as those that manufacture paper. For example, when retailers and other marketers reduce their newspaper and magazine advertising, publishers are forced to cut back, and this results in lower demand for paper. When the economy improves, demand increases. Big pushes for recycled paper also affect the paper industry at various times. What impact, if any, do you think the Internet will have on the demand for paper?

Weyerhaeuser, Champion International, and other paper marketers have to ride a pricing and demand roller-coaster. Not long ago, demand for paper was weak. A shaky economy had caused advertisers to cut back, which led publishers to slim down their newspapers and magazines. In addition, many papermakers had invested in more efficient production equipment, so they were churning out paper by the megaton. This combination of low demand and high supply sent paper prices tumbling. Not surprisingly, paper marketers posted poor—or no—profits through that period.

In recent years, however, paper's economics have changed. Advertisers came back in force, and newspapers and magazines needed paper. Marketers were looking for paper for packaging, catalogs, and many other uses. As sales soared, papermakers cranked up production, almost to capacity. They also hiked prices as much as 50 percent in a year to make up for the lean times. "We are still raising prices every chance we can get," says Dan King, president of Wausau, a paper-making company.

Paper recyclers started enjoying higher sales and higher prices as well. Recycled newsprint that sold for $20 a ton jumped to $150 a ton one year later. Despite the increase, recycled newsprint was quite affordable compared with new, priced at $744 a ton. Businesses and consumers still wanted recycled paper, so recyclers geared up to meet demand—at a price, of course.

Even though demand is expected to outstrip supply for a few years to come, paper marketers aren't out of the woods yet. If everybody moves full speed on bigger plants to turn out more paper, the market's economics will be changed again. Then, to keep the expensive new machines running when demand drops, marketers may be tempted to cut paper prices—yet again.[41]

Make marketing decisions

1. What pricing objectives do you think paper marketers should set when demand is high? When demand is low?

2. Why do you think many paper marketers use price competition?

3. If newspapers and magazines shift many subscribers to online delivery of news and information, what is the likely effect on paper demand? What price response might paper marketers make?

4. As a paper producer, how would you use value pricing to compete when demand starts to drop?

Price Elasticity of Demand

Along the demand curve, customer buying changes as pricing changes. This observable trend indicates that customers are sensitive to pricing. But how

price elasticity of demand

measures the degree to which customers are sensitive to changes in product pricing

much change in customer buying can you expect at each price along the curve? **Price elasticity of demand** measures the degree to which customers are sensitive to changes in product pricing. The formula is:

$$\text{price elasticity of demand} = \frac{\text{percentage change in quantity demanded}}{\text{percentage change in price}}$$

In a typical demand curve, the quantity demanded goes down as price goes up. For example, if demand drops by 10 percent when you raise your price by 4 percent, the price elasticity of demand is 10.0 divided by 4, or 2.5. However, if demand drops by 2 percent when you raise your price by 6 percent, the price elasticity of demand is 2 divided by 6, or 0.33.

When the price elasticity of demand is less than 1, demand is *inelastic*. Faced with inelastic demand, some marketers will increase revenues by raising prices, even though unit sales may decrease slightly. On the other hand, a small price cut will cause a smaller rise or no rise in demand and a potential loss of profit.

The demand for gasoline and other necessities is inelastic (at least in the short run) because customers can't drastically cut back on purchasing these products when prices go up. Thus a small increase in price may result in a large increase in revenue and profit. But demand for products of other kinds can also be inelastic. When Harley-Davidson was limiting production to keep quality high, affluent customers unable to obtain new models willingly paid more than the new-model price for slightly used Harleys.[42]

When the price elasticity of demand is larger than 1, demand is *elastic*. A small price cut will cause a larger increase in demand and revenue, potentially increasing profits. However, a small price increase will cause a larger decrease in demand. For example, if you were to lower the price of a movie ticket a little, you might attract a lot of people to your theater and thereby increase your profits (assuming your competitors don't do the same). On the other hand, if you raised prices with no perceived increase in benefits, even a small increase could drastically cut profits if competition remained the same.

Both demand and revenues change with price changes, as Table 12.1 shows. With inelastic demand, a small price increase will result in higher revenues, although a small price cut will result in lower revenues. The reverse is true for elastic demand, where a small price increase will result in lower revenues but a small price cut will result in higher revenues. A more sophisticated analysis is called the *arc* elasticity of demand. By understanding the relationship between price and demand, therefore, you can figure out whether to raise or lower your price to reach a certain level of sales revenue.

TABLE **12.1**
Price Elasticity of Demand and Revenues

Price Elasticity of Demand	Price Change	Effect on Sales Revenue
Inelastic	Small increase	Increase
Inelastic	Small cut	Decrease
Elastic	Small increase	Decrease
Elastic	Small cut	Increase

What Determines Price Sensitivity?

Since revenues depend on price and demand, you also need to anticipate how customers are likely to react to higher and lower prices. Why is the demand for one product elastic while the demand for another is inelastic? Customers are more sensitive to price when they know that they can choose among many products to satisfy their needs. Suellen Schussel, the founder of New York food manufacturer Steve's Mom, says this is why she can't pass higher costs along to customers. "I'd love to boost my prices," she explains. "But some customers will even buy something that doesn't taste very good just because the price is lower."[43]

When customers can't easily substitute another product, however, they're not as sensitive to the price of a needed product. They're also less sensitive when they can't easily compare the value of competing products that are differentiated by package size, formulation, and other elements. In addition, customers are less sensitive to the prices of products they see as necessities. They're less sensitive to the price of smaller purchases (such as paper towels) than they are to the price of larger purchases (such as cars). Finally, they're less sensitive to price when they anticipate better personal and general economic conditions.[44] Bank customers can be quite sensitive to price changes, as First National Bank of Chicago found out.

MARKETING IDEAS

Adjusting to fee, not free, banking

First National Bank of Chicago didn't expect the protests that greeted its announcement of new bank accounts and new fees. After 18 months of researching customers' banking needs, behavior, and preferences, the bank had developed new accounts and new pricing. When it called a news conference to launch the products, officials were stunned by public reaction.

What irked customers (as well as community activists, politicians, and news commentators) was the story that customers with balances under $2,500 would incur a $3 charge for seeing a teller instead of using an ATM. But First Chicago didn't back off. Instead, it immediately wrote its customers to clarify the fees and to stress the enhanced benefits of the new accounts. The bank emphasized that more than 80 percent of its customers wouldn't pay teller charges because they fell below the cutoff point of four teller transactions in a month.

Despite customer sensitivity to bank pricing, First Chicago is only one of a growing number of banks charging fees for services that used to be free. Fees on checking and savings accounts bring in more than $15 billion annually for U.S. banks. Even so, estimates show that half of all consumer accounts are unprofitable for the banks, which explains the need to put a price tag on formerly free services. But as First Chicago and other banks realize, judging price sensitivity is a tricky business.[45]

If you had been writing to First Chicago's customers, how would you have communicated the value equation for the new policy?

First Chicago's $3 fee charges on

Sister banks may have to pay; meanwhile, firm opposes extra costs for ATM users

By John Schmeltzer
TRIBUNE STAFF WRITER

The $3 fee that the First National Bank of Chicago charges some customers to see a teller is going companywide.

By the end of the year, customers of First Chicago's sister banks, NBD Bank, Michigan, and NBD Bank, Indiana, could also be paying the fee, officers of First Chicago NBD Corp. said Friday.

"The product menu will be the same," said Verne G. Istock, who was elected chairman and chief executive officer of the bank holding company. "I would expect that to be done this year from a consumer product standpoint."

But while First Chicago NBD will charge customers a fee for som[...] [...]nsactio[...] to see a teller for some transactions or maintaining a minimum balance in order to see a teller for free.

But First Chicago officials said Friday that the account has turned out to be more successful than they anticipated when it was rolled out last year.

"It was as misunderstood by the media as it was by some of the customers because of the media," said Istock. "When the media is saying one thing and the customers are choosing another, we don't have our communications hooked up."

Now, 71 percent of the bank's customers are choosing the account because they don't have to maintain a minimum balance, bank officials said.

More frequently than ever, customers are seeking services that [...]

Are customers a nuisance? Many customers of First National Bank of Chicago thought that was the bank's attitude when it announced that it would begin charging fees for frequent use of tellers. Any increases in fees are likely to be taken badly by the public. However, the negative publicity about First National's fee increase made the change particularly difficult. Nonetheless, the bank has not dropped this unpopular policy. In fact, the bank is trying hard to convince customers that such a change is actually to their benefit, pointing out that transactions at its ATM machines are free to customers while most banks charge for this service. What could First National have done to minimize the negative reaction and publicity prior to announcing this change?

Before you go on . . .

A. How does inelastic demand differ from elastic demand?

B. When are customers likely to be less sensitive to price?

Analyzing Environmental Influences to Support Pricing Strategy

Like every other process in marketing, pricing is subject to the forces in the marketing environment. Among the most important environmental influences on pricing are customer demand, competitive issues, value-chain relationships, cost factors, legal and regulatory changes, ethical standards, and international competition, as shown in Figure 12.3.

FIGURE **12.3**

Environmental Issues Affecting Pricing
Pricing isn't handled in a vacuum. In setting and managing prices to build relationships with customers, marketers have to consider these seven environmental issues.

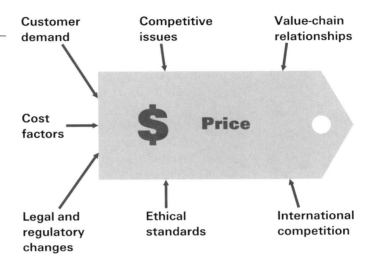

Customer Demand

As you saw earlier, customer demand and price sensitivity are two environmental elements that influence the price level of goods and services. If you don't know how customers are likely to react to your pricing, you may make misjudgments that can lead to serious problems. Walt Disney found this out when it opened its giant theme park in Paris. Management of Disneyland Paris reasoned that the park would enjoy inelastic demand because visitors couldn't easily substitute an experience comparable to the American-style atmosphere. Accordingly, the company set high profitability objectives and high prices.

However, Disney didn't count on customer reaction to the value equation. Visitors didn't stay as long or spend as much as Disney had anticipated because the price was perceived to be too high. Adult admission was $42.25 (higher than at Disney's U.S. parks), and the best hotel rooms cost more than $300 per night (about the same as a luxury hotel in Paris). Food and gift prices were also perceived to be high. So visitors tended to arrive early in the morning, spend one night at a Disney hotel, and leave on the second day. In contrast, many visitors to the highly profitable Disney World in Florida stay more than four days.

Once Disney officials in Paris had analyzed customer reaction to the value equation, they made changes. They offered admission discounts and cut prices on some hotel rooms, gifts, and restaurant food. They also adjusted menus to European tastes and made other changes to improve the perceived value of the package. The park is drawing more visitors these days, and officials see an even better long-term profit picture ahead.[46]

price leader

the first company to announce price changes that competitors quickly imitate

price war

a situation in which competitors continually undercut each other's prices in an effort to be perceived as offering the lowest price

Competitive Influences

In a market characterized by *pure competition*, where a great many marketers compete with nearly identical products, all marketers would theoretically price their products the same. One marketer could do little to control the prevailing price, and higher prices would cause customers to defect to competitors. At the other extreme, in a *monopoly*, one marketer operates without competition and doesn't have to worry about competitors when setting prices. However, a lone marketer might have to follow strict pricing guidelines set by government regulators.

These days, most marketers don't compete in either the pure competition or the monopoly framework. Instead, they may face competitive markets characterized by oligopoly or monopolistic competition. In an *oligopoly*, just a few marketers compete, so every marketer is highly sensitive to the marketing actions taken by its rivals, including pricing. The cereal industry is an example. In *monopolistic competition*, many marketers compete with products that are not identical, and they can differentiate their products in many ways, not by price alone. The computer industry is an example, as are shoe stores. Marketers faced with oligopoly and monopolistic competition find pricing an important element in their competitive strategies.

Watching what competitors do with price is essential, especially since prices can change quickly. In some industries, one marketer may assume the role of a price leader. A **price leader** is the first company to announce price changes that competitors quickly imitate. If the usual price leader isn't the first to signal a particular price change, other competitors may wait before responding. If the price leader doesn't change price, rivals usually follow this example (and the initiator of the change generally backs down).[47]

When competitors continually undercut each other's prices in an effort to be perceived as offering the lowest price, they're caught in a **price war**. Customers benefit from falling prices, but marketers suffer from falling profits.

There are many competing brands in the gasoline industry, establishing a situation of monopolistic competition where price is an important consideration. Each gasoline brand is positioned slightly differently, and each gasoline retailer puts together a different value package of gasoline, station service, food offerings, and other elements. How important is price when you are deciding where to buy gas?

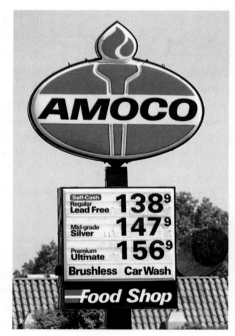

Consider air travel, for example, where American, USAir, and others regularly battle over price even though the steep cuts can wipe out profits and push weak airlines into bankruptcy. Travelers remember the super-low airfares long afterward, and regular fares seem much higher by comparison.[48] Thus, price wars upset the value equation and focus marketers on short-term gains rather than on long-term customer relationships.

Issues for critical thinking **Why do price wars hurt profitability? Do you think a marketer is likely to make enough revenues to keep profits up by matching or beating competitors during a price war? How do you think marketers should respond when rivals try to start a price war?**

Value-Chain Relationships

Value-chain partnerships play an important role in planning prices. You will need to line up suppliers that can help you keep quality and prices in line with your customers' perceptions of value. Ford, for example, has long-term agreements with most of its suppliers that call for lowering parts costs by 1 percent or more every year. This practice helps the automaker maintain competitive prices for its cars.[49]

Not every supplier relationship runs smoothly. Isao Nakauchi, head of Japan's largest retailer, has had difficulty with some suppliers. Observing that "People have changed their way of buying things," Nakauchi has used deep discounting to build his $50 billion Daiei chain. But discounting runs counter to the policies of Matsushita and other Japanese manufacturers. That's why Nakauchi buys from global suppliers and offers private-brand products. Daiei's private-brand colas and film products are marketed at less than half the price of brand-name items.[50]

It is important to plan prices that are appropriate for dealers, retailers, and other value-chain customers. Joseph Curley, director of marketing for Tseng Laboratories in Pennsylvania, is keenly aware of how his prices affect customers. Tseng makes graphics chips for personal computers, a market where prices go down and quality goes up day by day. "Since our customers are computer companies embroiled in their own price war, we have to empower them with products with a good price-to-performance ratio," says Curley. Tseng's well-priced products have earned it a high degree of customer loyalty as well as a 15 percent share of the global market for graphics chips.[51]

Cost Factors

Joseph Curley understands that cost is as important for Tseng as it is for the marketers who are the company's customers. No matter what you're marketing, you can't survive for long if you consistently price below cost. Nor can you succeed if you don't make enough money, after covering your costs, to reinvest in building customer relationships. (Chapter 13 investigates costs in more detail.)

Of course, when your suppliers raise their prices, you take these higher costs into consideration in your pricing planning. Sometimes you won't be able to raise your price because of customer sensitivity. But this isn't always the case. Recent price increases in aluminum, for example, pushed beverage marketer Arizona to rethink its pricing. Originally, Arizona's 24-ounce cans were priced the same as Snapple's 16-ounce bottles. But then the price of aluminum cans rose more than 60 percent in a year. Arizona managers believed that their customers would see the brand's value even at a higher price, so they raised prices to cover the increased costs.[52]

Some marketers keep costs under control by bartering for particular goods or services. This is how Barrie Pace, a catalog marketer of women's apparel, has managed costs associated with photographing on location in luxury resorts. In exchange for mentioning the resorts in the catalogs, Barrie Pace receives free or reduced-rate accommodations for its models and crew.[53]

Legal and Regulatory Considerations

As you plan your pricing strategy, be sure to comply with legal and regulatory guidelines that cover pricing practices. Chapter 3 provided an overview of some of the key actions taken by the U.S. government to protect consumers and businesses from unfair price competition and deceptive pricing practices. This section looks at four pricing practices that are restricted by legal and regulatory guidelines: price fixing, predatory pricing, price discrimination, and deceptive pricing. Table 12.2 summarizes these practices.

T A B L E   **12.2**   **Pricing Practices Restricted by Legal and Regulatory Guidelines**

Pricing Practice	Definition
Price fixing	Conspiring with competitors to set prices for products of particular types
Predatory pricing	Setting unreasonably low prices to force competitors out of business
Price discrimination	Unfairly pricing the same quality, grade, and quantity of goods differently for different customers
Deceptive pricing	Setting prices to mislead and deceive customers by hiding the true or final price for a product

Price Fixing

Price fixing is an illegal conspiracy among competitors to set prices for products of particular types. The Sherman Antitrust Act outlawed price fixing in 1890, seeking to protect customers against business agreements that reduced competition and raised prices. Subsequent U.S. Supreme Court decisions have ruled against anticompetitive agreements that fix maximum prices as well as against those that fix minimum prices.[54]

At one time, U.S. marketers were legally able to insist that dealers sell their products at specific prices, a practice known as *resale price maintenance*. The Consumer Goods Pricing Act banned the practice in 1975. These days, a product may carry a "manufacturer's suggested retail price," but marketers cannot force dealers to stick to that price. However, resale price maintenance still exists in Japan and other countries.[55]

price fixing

an illegal conspiracy among competitors to set prices for particular products

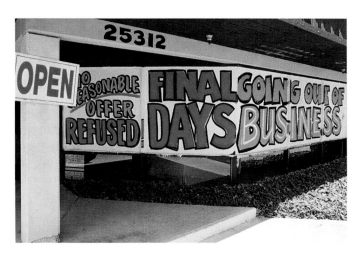

As this photograph demonstrates, there is no guarantee of success for businesses. Small retailers, for example, often fail when large competitors locate in their markets and offer discount prices. To maintain some order in the competitive marketplace and to protect consumers, government agencies act as watchdogs. Should governments regulate marketers to ensure fair price competition?

Predatory Pricing

Predatory pricing is the illegal practice of setting unreasonably low prices to force competitors out of business. With competitors out of the way, the marketer is then free to raise prices. Predatory pricing is covered by the Sherman Act and the Federal Trade Commission Act as well as by a variety of state laws.

Wal-Mart was ordered to pay a fine and stop selling products below cost in a predatory pricing case in Arkansas several years ago. Independent pharmacies had charged that Wal-Mart was pricing drug and health care products below cost to drive out the competition. In general, such cases are difficult to prosecute because the plaintiff has the burden of proving intent to eliminate competition.[56]

Price Discrimination

The Clayton Act and the Robinson–Patman amendment to it forbid **price discrimination**, the practice of unfairly pricing the same quality, grade, and quantity of goods differently for different customers. This is a complicated legal issue, because not all price discrimination is illegal. Essentially, price discrimination that is aimed at reducing competition is forbidden. It is illegal, for example, for a marketer to offer the same goods at different prices if the differences are not justified by cost differences or by variations in demand. It is also illegal to charge two or more customers the same price for the same goods if different costs are associated with serving each customer.[57]

Marketers that offer special pricing arrangements have to be sure they're not straying into the area of illegal price discrimination. One reason for the enactment of the Robinson–Patman Act was to prevent marketers from granting giant wholesalers and retailers volume discounts disproportionately higher than those available to smaller dealers. Marketers can, however, charge different customers different prices when the prices (1) are justified by cost differentials, (2) represent a good-faith effort to match competitors' prices rather than to reduce competition, or (3) reflect changing market conditions such as the need to clear obsolete seasonal goods.[58]

predatory pricing

the illegal practice of setting unreasonably low prices to force competitors out of business

price discrimination

the practice of unfairly pricing the same quality, grade, and quantity of goods differently for different customers

deceptive pricing

pricing that misleads and deceives customers by hiding the true or final price for a product

Deceptive Pricing

The Federal Trade Commission Act forbids **deceptive pricing**, defined as pricing that misleads and deceives customers by hiding the true or final price for a product. One form of deceptive pricing is advertising a price as lower than a fraudulent "regular" or "suggested" price. If the product hasn't sold at the regular price for any period, or if few products have been sold at the suggested price, such a comparison is misleading. Some marketers have pressured manufacturers to inflate suggested retail prices to make the stated price look like a bargain. "Retailers would ask us to set high suggested retail prices, so they could claim their retail prices were 50 percent off list," says the president of Serta, a bedding manufacturer. "Now we only set wholesale prices."[59]

In another form of deceptive pricing, one product is priced very low to lure customers to a store, where they're pressured to buy a more expensive product instead. Such pricing is deceptive because the store really intends to sell the higher priced item rather than the lower priced product. This illegal technique is known as *bait and switch*.

A third variation of deceptive pricing is the misleading promotion of a product at a bargain price when purchased with the same or another product. Price promotions that offer "2 for 1" or "Buy the second for a penny" are legal only when the first product is offered at a regular, not an inflated price. The FTC considers pricing to be deceptive when the first product's price is raised for the period of the offer or when lower quality products are substituted in such an offer.

Ethical Standards

In both consumer and business markets, pricing brings up a variety of ethical issues. First, is it ethical to set high prices for a product that people must have for medical or other reasons? This is a particular point of contention with respect to high-priced drugs. Pharmaceutical companies say they need to recoup the expense of developing drugs, but critics worry that people who can't afford the price won't have access to treatment they need. In some cases, the U.S. government has offered subsidies to make drugs more affordable for lower-income people. Furthermore, the price for some drugs is much lower in other countries.[60]

A second ethical issue in pricing is: How (and how much) should marketers tell customers when they advertise special prices? Banks, airlines, automakers, and other marketers have to follow local, state, and federal guidelines for revealing certain details of price promotions. However, they have some latitude in what they say and how they say it. Most often, marketers downplay restrictions such as making available only a limited number of products at the special price. Many observers say this approach makes it impossible for all but the most sophisticated customers to gauge the value equation, and it hinders shoppers who attempt to compare prices and benefits of competing products.[61] In the next section, you'll look at the ethical issue of setting prices that are subject to restrictions shown in fine print.

ETHICS & SOCIAL RESPONSIBILITY

Getting down to the fine print

Everybody loves a bargain. But not every advertised bargain is really a good buy once the customer gets down to the fine print at the bottom of the advertisement. Amtrak, for example, recently advertised prices for train travel from New York to five cities. Four of the five prices were promoted as one-way fares. The fifth carried an asterisk, which directed the prospective customer to a warning, in fine print, that the price was based on the purchase of a round-trip ticket and was subject to other restrictions. This is a typical (and legal) way marketers use to indicate restrictions on special pricing.

*Restrictions

Come and go as you please!

Los Angeles	$159	Miami	$89
Oakland	$159	Paris	$249
San Juan	$109	and More!

Tower/Air
MORE THAN JUST A GREAT FARE

★ When you fly Tower Air, we don't make you purchase your tickets in advance. We don't require a minimum stay and you can change your fully refundable tickets as often as you like with no charge. Just buy your tickets within 24 hours of making a reservation and you'll fly on one of our comfortable wide body 747s, non-stop. And you thought you were going to see a bunch of restrictions down here!

Note: Prices quoted are one way, vary by season and are subject to change. Taxes up to $9.00 additional.

Call 800-34-TOWER or 718-553-8500

New York   Los Angeles   Miami   Paris   Oakland   San Juan   Sao Paulo   Rio DeJaneiro   Tel Aviv

Tower Air knows that consumers don't like to be surprised by limitations to promotional prices that are mentioned only in the fine print. So this Tower ad boldly makes a simple promise of "No Restrictions" to customers. (Note, however, that the ad does state—as you might expect—that prices are subject to change and that taxes are additional.) Can you think of other companies or industries that might successfully adopt a similar pricing strategy?

The downsizing of products has become an ethical issue. Is it fair to give the consumer less while charging the same—without any notification? There are legitimate reasons for downsizing products, but how do you think consumers should be notified of such changes?

Is it ethical to promote a special price while burying information about restrictions or disclosing only some of the restrictions? When the Better Business Bureau of New York looked at 29 ads for rental cars and air travel, it found that 14 failed to completely explain restrictions, even in the fine print. "It's what I call marketing slipping and sliding," observes marketing expert Jack Trout. "Businesses want to attract people to buy their products, but they also want to find a way to not exactly give it to them at those prices."

Government agencies are looking into the possibility that some ads are misleading because they don't disclose all the details. Legalities aside, some marketers have chosen to quote prices without restrictions. Tower Air, a New York–based airline, printed the following in tiny type at the bottom of an ad not long ago: "Hello. You're reading the part of the ad where you usually see all the restrictions you have to meet to get the low fare. But this is Tower Air. There are no restrictions."[62]

How do you think Tower Air's approach affects customer relationships?

A third ethical issue is nonprice price increases. How can a marketer justify keeping the price the same when it reduces product quality or lowers quantity? Downsizing or downgrading a product without reducing its price effectively raises the price customers pay. When a marketer can't easily pass rising costs on to customers because of economic or competitive pressures, it may see downsizing (putting less into the same-size package) or downgrading (lowering the quality) as an acceptable alternative, because the unit the customer buys doesn't cost more. However, critics say that these practices are misleading.[63]

International Forces

When you market in other countries, you have an additional layer of pricing issues to consider. As you saw in Chapter 4, the value of the currency of any given country is constantly changing, causing the exchange rate for your product's price to move up or down. In some cases, you may want to hold prices steady to help maintain or increase market share—or profitability. But to maintain profits, you may choose to raise or lower your price in line with major foreign exchange fluctuations, depending on the elasticity of demand for your product and the competitive situation.

Currency fluctuations may make a product less attractive in a local market but more attractive in a foreign market, as Mexico-based Empresas La Moderna found out. This marketer of packaging and agricultural products recently saw the value of the Mexican peso drop

dumping

the practice of pricing products in host countries below cost or for less than their price in the marketer's home country

sharply against some other currencies. So the company stepped up exports to markets where the peso was weak and its products had a price advantage compared with local products. Now non-peso product sales account for more than 90 percent of the company's overall sales revenues.[64]

Setting extremely low prices for exported goods may trigger complaints about dumping. **Dumping** is the practice of pricing products in host countries below cost or for less than their price in the marketer's home country. Nearly every country outlaws dumping as unfair to local marketers, even though customers benefit from lower prices. When a government determines that a marketer is dumping, it can add a duty to raise the product's price. Dumping is a complex issue because some nations use antidumping regulations to shield local marketers from foreign competition.[65]

Finally, look at host country laws and regulations governing pricing, which vary from country to country. Germany bans advertisements comparing the prices of competing products, but it allows truthful comparisons of a marketer's original and new prices after a change. Denmark, Canada, and other countries outlaw deceptive pricing and other practices. So when planning prices for host countries, be sure to check local guidelines.[66]

Before you go on . . .

A. What is a price war?

B. What is predatory pricing and why is it illegal?

C. How does dumping affect pricing in international markets?

Summary

1. **Define price and state the value equation.**

   Price is the amount of money or other valuable that the marketer asks in exchange for a product. Value is the ratio of perceived benefits to perceived price. In equation form, perceived value equals perceived benefits divided by perceived price.

2. **Characterize value marketing and value pricing from the customer's viewpoint.**

   Value marketing is the process of developing and marketing products to give customers extra benefits and higher quality at reasonable prices, which builds and strengthens customer relationships. Value pricing is the process of improving product quality and offering additional benefits while holding prices steady or cutting them. In both cases, customers gain more benefits at the same or a lower price.

3. **List five long-term objectives marketers can set when planning pricing.**

Marketers can set five types of long-term pricing objective: pricing for profit, pricing for sales growth, pricing for competitive advantage, pricing for positioning, and pricing for social goals.

4. **Distinguish between price competition and nonprice competition.**

Price competition is the practice of differentiating a product from competitive products primarily on the basis of price. In contrast, nonprice competition is the practice of differentiating a product on the basis of elements other than price.

5. **Describe the demand curve and show how price elasticity of demand operates.**

The demand curve is a graphic illustration of the way customer demand responds to a series of possible prices. Price elasticity of demand measures the degree to which customers are sensitive to price changes. When demand is elastic, a small price cut causes a larger increase in demand, and a small price increase causes a larger decrease in demand. When demand is inelastic, a small price cut causes a smaller rise or no change in demand; a small price increase causes a smaller decrease or no decrease in demand.

6. **Demonstrate how price leaders and price wars affect pricing.**

When a marketer plays the role of price leader, it is the first to announce price changes, which competitors quickly imitate. In a price war, competitors continually undercut each other's prices in an effort to be perceived as offering the lowest price.

7. **Analyze how legal and regulatory influences affect pricing practices.**

Four pricing practices are restricted by legal and regulatory guidelines: price fixing (an illegal conspiracy among rivals to set prices for particular types of products), predatory pricing (an illegal practice in which a marketer sets unreasonably low prices to force competitors out of business), price discrimination (the practice of unfairly pricing the same quality, grade, and quantity of goods at different prices for different customers), and deceptive pricing (pricing that misleads or deceives customers by hiding the true or final price).

KEY TERMS

barter 346
deceptive pricing 365
demand curve 357
dumping 368
nonprice competition 356
perceived benefits 346

perceived price 346
predatory pricing 365
price 346
price competition 355
price discrimination 365
price elasticity of demand 359

price fixing 364
price leader 362
price war 362
value 346
value marketing 347
value pricing 348

Skill-Building Applications

1. You plan to start a dojo in your hometown. What factors should you consider when setting a price for karate lessons?

2. What factors affect the pricing decisions of GM when it sells cars to cities for police cars rather than to the general public?

3. Is it proper for the National Park Service to charge fees for use of public lands? Why? Research some of the fees charged for park admission and camping. Would you raise these prices? Why or why not?

4. City Center Supplies is a small office supply store that competes with Staples and other large office supply stores. What can City Center do with price and nonprice competition to keep current customers and attract new ones?

5. Sports fans often face price increases for tickets, parking, food, and other products sold at sports arenas. Is there a point at which consumers are likely to rebel against such high prices? What factors are likely to trigger such a revolt?

6. Walt Disney's Disneyland Paris park initially faced resistance to its pricing policies in France. What other U.S. service providers are likely to find price resistance as they expand to other countries? What can be done about such resistance?

Getting Involved in Marketing

1. *On Your Own* Visit a supermarket and compare prices on the same-size packaging of three brands of one type of product, such as shampoo or soup. What are the perceived benefits of each brand? How does each brand communicate the benefits and relate them to price? Which seems to offer the best perceived value? Why? How do you view the value equation for this type of product?

2. *On Your Own* Imagine you're marketing a good or a service such as cordless telephones or lawn care. Who are your competitors? How can you find out whether they compete on the basis of price? Prepare a brief presentation on how you would use price competition and how you would use nonprice competition.

3. *Find Out More* Find an article in a magazine, newspaper, or on an online database service that describes the supply and demand in a particular industry, such as paper, coffee, or aluminum. What is happening to demand, and what is the effect on prices? How are suppliers' prices affecting their customers? Summarize your findings in a report to the class.

4. *In a Team* Imagine that you and two classmates are marketing a new soft drink (or another product). Identify the target market, then determine the needs the product's benefits will satisfy. Decide which pricing objectives make sense for your product. Then calculate price elasticity of demand under the following conditions and explain the impact on revenues:

   a. Demand goes up 16 percent with a price cut of 4 percent

   b. Demand drops 2 percent with a price increase of 7 percent

5. *In a Team* With the same team and product used in Exercise 4, list the specific customer, competitive, value-chain, and cost influences to be considered before you set a price for your new product. How can you research these issues? List the sources or type of research you would use to investigate each.

6. *In a Partnership* With another student, research a recent price war in air travel, personal computers, or another product. Who started the price war? Why did it break out? What happened as a result? Play the role of marketing consultant for one of the companies involved in the price war. Would you suggest matching or beating rivals' prices? Would you recommend that the company take other measures? Write a brief report on the situation, including specific recommendations for your client.

VideoCase Customers Go Outback for Value

There are many ways to discover marketing opportunities. One way is to see whether all price ranges have been covered in an industry. In the restaurant business, fancy eateries satisfy upscale customers who can afford higher prices, while fast-food outlets and inexpensive local restaurants cater to those who want to spend much less. The founders of Outback Steakhouse saw an opportunity in the middle—and built it into a $700 million corporation.

Chris Sullivan, Robert Basham, and Timothy Gannon started the company back in the late 1980s. They realized that the market was relatively saturated with high-end steak houses like Morton's of Chicago and Ruth's Chris Steakhouse. They also noted that budget steak houses like Ponderosa and Golden Corral were well established. An opportunity seemed available, however, in the mid-priced range. So the partners set out to build a restaurant chain that created value through a stylish blend of quality and service—at moderate prices.

The original idea was to open four or five restaurants in the Tampa Bay area. When the first two restaurants became profitable before their second year of operation (a rare situation in this highly competitive business), the partners moved quickly to open more restaurants. Now there are over 300 Outback restaurants, with dozens more being opened every year.

Quality is always on the menu, beginning with the ingredients. One of the premier chefs in New Orleans recommended that the founders buy their beef from Bruss Company of Chicago, which carefully monitors the quality of the meat it receives from suppliers. Outback is equally demanding when buying chicken, pasta, shrimp, and fish. For example, it buys only chicken that has never been frozen. Quality of food is matched by quality of service. The servers are hired for their friendliness and then receive training in customer relations.

However, Outback's moderate prices don't mean moderate profits. Although the typical customer pays $16 for dinner, the company's return on investment (52 percent) is very high for the restaurant industry. Outback maintains its profit margins and its quality, service, and value by doing what it does well, given the chain's core competencies.

For example, the restaurants are open only for dinner. This allows Outback to locate restaurants in residential areas where real estate is less expensive than in central business districts.

Also, their dinner-only policy makes for fewer operating hours and allows the kitchen staff to focus on a single meal.

Other steak houses may beat Outback on price, but they can't beat Outback's nonprice competition. In addition to outstanding service and food quality, the chain is differentiated by its unique image, which is based on an Australia theme. The founders have carried through the theme in the decorations and in the menu offerings. For example, the walls are festooned with boomerangs, Aboriginal art prints, Foster's beer signs, and the like. The menu features items like Aussie-Tizers and Kookaburra Wings.

Outback managers are expected to establish good relationships not only with customers, but with the community and other stakeholders as well. For example, some restaurants offer a free dinner to local students who get top marks, and many Outback managers are active in local community events and charities. With the winning combination of quality, service, and value—and an attention to stakeholder satisfaction—you can see why the three Outback founders have been honored as Entrepreneurs of the Year by *Inc.* magazine.[67]

Strategies and applications

1. Do you think the price elasticity of demand at a local Outback is elastic or inelastic? Why?

2. What can top management at Outback do to keep costs down, especially the cost of meat and other food products, so moderate prices can be maintained?

3. Outback restaurants do not take reservations. As a result, there is often a long waiting line. How might this affect consumers' perception of the value of a meal?

4. Given Outback's target market of 25- to 45-year-olds, does an average meal price of $16 seem about right? How would you research price sensitivity in this market?

5. What pricing objectives would you say Outback's founders are pursuing? Explain your answer.

6. How are value-chain relationships likely to influence Outback's pricing policy? Be specific.

Team project

With other students, interview a local restaurant owner or do research to determine the cost influences that restaurants consider when setting prices for menu items. Rank these influences in order of importance, then compare your team's ranking with that of other teams. Which does the class agree is the most important? Why?

13

Pricing Management

Learning Goals

After you have read and studied this chapter, you should be able to:

1. Show how marketers can research customer reaction to pricing.
2. Distinguish among fixed, variable, total, and marginal costs, and demonstrate the use of breakeven analysis.
3. Identify the seven types of demand-based pricing.
4. Differentiate among markup pricing, cost-plus pricing, and experience curve pricing.
5. Explain how profit-based pricing operates and analyze two variations.
6. Apply four approaches to competition-based pricing.
7. Show how pricing adjustments affect prices paid by ultimate consumers, organizational customers, and value-chain partners.

PROFILE

Southwest Airlines's pricing keeps passengers flying high

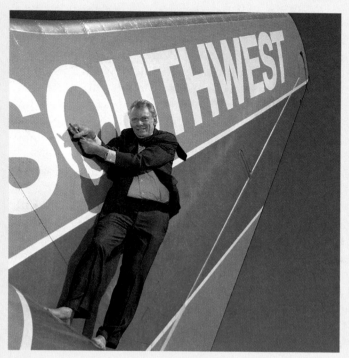

Pennies do add up. Just ask Southwest Airlines CEO Herb Kelleher. While operations cost full-service competitors like Northwest Airlines and Delta Air Lines about 9 cents per mile, Kelleher has stripped away the frills and capped Southwest's costs at 7 cents per mile. At a time when most airlines are struggling to stay aloft, the pennies that Kelleher pinches allow Southwest to offer prices well below competitors' fares. In the process, he's racked up an enviable reputation for customer satisfaction and profitability.

How does Kelleher do it? He focuses on low costs and high customer value, offering frequent flights at everyday low prices. The airline flies short-hop routes in a limited number of states; most flights last about an hour. The service is dependable but basic: no meals, no baggage transfers to other flights, no assigned seats, no special seating sections. Kelleher also reins in the budget, personally approving every expense over $1,000.

Southwest's pricing and value package has attracted a new customer segment, people who might otherwise take the bus or drive. In return for an everyday low fare that's well below competitors' fares for the same route, passengers get courteous, efficient, on-time service with a smile. Because Southwest emphasizes fun as well as teamwork and employee empowerment, its employees feel appreciated, and they make customers feel appreciated too. The entire value package is designed to build and strengthen relationships with passengers by offering good value for the money, flight after flight.[1]

Everyday low pricing based on low costs helps Southwest build enduring customer relationships by offering good value. In this second of two chapters about pricing and valuation, you'll learn about setting and managing prices. A look at setting prices with customers in mind is followed by a discussion of pricing in the context of costs, sales, and profitability. Then you'll examine four pricing strategies and their connection to building customer relationships. Finally, you'll learn how to manage and adjust pricing to build stronger customer relationships.

Customers and potential customers are the true drivers of price. No matter what your costs are, the ability to sell at a given price depends on customers' willingness to pay. Therefore, pricing decisions must start with the customer.[2]

Linda Gorchels
of the Management Institute at the School of Business, University of Wisconsin—Madison

Each customer has a different value equation based on individual wants and needs. CSX recognizes the existence of these differences and tries to maximize customer value by offering the best range of services at competitive prices. Naturally, the company has to consider profits when setting prices, but the final price is usually one that is mutually beneficial and satisfactory to both CSX and its customers.

Setting Prices with Customers in Mind

Because it is customer oriented, when Southwest Airlines sets prices, it considers how customers weigh the value of a flight against the cost of the ticket. Surprisingly, setting prices with customers in mind is a fairly new idea. Just four decades ago, most businesses treated pricing more as a financial decision than as an integral part of the marketing process. Customers often weren't part of the pricing formula at that time. Instead, firms stressed internal factors such as costs and production when setting prices.

Since then, pricing has slowly but steadily assumed more importance as one of the eight universal marketing processes. Today, pricing is seen as an important key to building customer relationships. Despite this shift, many marketers have not developed a customer-oriented pricing strategy based on in-depth studies of customers, competitors, and market economics. Only half the North American marketers who responded to one survey were researching customer reactions to pricing. In all, about 40 percent of all U.S. marketers have neither pricing strategies nor pricing research to support their pricing decisions.[3]

Given the growing emphasis on value marketing and value pricing **(p. 348)**, marketers today simply can't afford to ignore their customers' perceptions of price. Remember, the purpose of pricing is to facilitate a mutually beneficial exchange between marketers and customers. If customers don't buy, you have no exchange—and your pricing isn't doing its job or your value package doesn't beat the competition. By looking at price from your customers' perspective, you can more effectively set and manage prices that will enhance the value package and lead to long-term, profitable customer relationships.

CSX Corporation, for example, is a giant transportation company based in Virginia. Like many marketers, the company uses computer models to help in pricing specific shipping services. David E. Wise, vice president of pricing and yield management, scrutinizes value from the customer's perspective. "We look at what alternatives are available and the value we bring to a specific shipper," he says. In addition, CSX pricing takes into account each customer's price sensitivity, the type of freight, and supply and demand.[4]

As you saw in Chapter 12, price sensitivity is a key element in determining the price elasticity of demand. You can research your customers' reaction to pricing in several ways. The first way is to use *test marketing* to gauge customer reaction to various prices in representative markets. Dominick's Finer Foods, a supermarket chain in Chicago, used this approach to test several pricing strategies in selected stores. This kind of testing can be expensive, however, and it lets competitors see your pricing options.[5] Some marketers offer their products by mail to test customer reaction to various prices. This way, competitors can't see the prices being tested, and the marketers can measure results by counting the number of orders at each price.

Approach Software tested customer reaction when it planned a limited-time price promotion to introduce a database software product. To determine how much to charge, the company interviewed several dozen prospective customers and found that a price under $149 would be too low compared with competing products. When the company mailed offers to 50,000 prospects testing three prices ($99, $129, and $149), just as many people ordered at the $149 price as at the lower prices. Then the company tested $199, but that proved too high at the time. After the introductory promotional period was over, the company was able to charge an even higher price because word of mouth raised consumer perceptions of quality.[6]

A second alternative is to use *simulated test marketing* to test prices in a laboratory setting, without real-world experimentation. You might invite prospects from your target market to "shop" in a simulated store set up in a research facility. By observing how people compare competing products and prices, then asking questions about their decisions, you can learn more about the customers' view of the value equation. In addition, you can feed the results into a computer model to obtain predictions of sales and profits at various prices.[7]

A third alternative is to use *multiple trade-off analysis*. This marketing research tool helps you understand how customers respond to various value packages at various prices. For example, a financial services marketer tested reactions to pricing a service for buying and selling stocks and bonds through personal computers. The researchers asked 500 customers to react to a series of value packages, each with its own features, benefits, and monthly service charges. The results helped the researchers project how many customers might buy each potential value package, which led the marketer to an optimal product and price.[8]

Thanks to technological advances, more marketers are moving toward incorporating the results of pricing research into computerized pricing models like the one used by CSX. By constructing mathematical models that simulate actual customer response to pricing, marketers will be better able to analyze past results and forecast future sales and profits. Developing an effective model is a complicated undertaking, however, because of the interplay of the various unpredictable influences on pricing.[9] That's why modeling is not yet part of every marketer's pricing process.

Understanding Costs, Sales, and Profitability

Regardless of their pricing objectives, marketers—even nonprofit organizations—usually aim to set prices to at least cover costs. Costs are a basic fact of marketing life: Producers pay for raw materials, salaries, packaging, marketing, and other expenses related to developing and bringing a product to market. Before setting initial prices, marketers analyze costs and relate these to sales revenues and profits. Then they can use breakeven analysis to determine the price at which they begin to show a profit.

Cost Analysis

fixed costs

all the expenses that remain the same no matter how many goods or services are sold

variable costs

expenses that change according to the level of production and sales

In the course of developing, producing, and marketing products, marketers incur costs of two types. **Fixed costs** are all the expenses that remain the same no matter how many goods or services are sold. Among the expenses that make up fixed costs are the amount paid to rent a factory, warehouse, or office, and the amount paid for business insurance. In contrast, **variable costs** change according to the level of production and sales. Included in variable costs are the expenses for the materials used in making products and the bonuses paid to employees.

Total cost is the total amount spent to produce every unit—every haircut, every bicycle, every photocopier—and it is made up of both fixed and variable costs. Figure 13.1 shows the total costs for capuccino. The equation for total cost is:

$$total\ cost = fixed\ cost + variable\ cost$$

F I G U R E **13.1**   **How Costs Affect the Price of Cappuccino**

When you add up rent, overhead, labor, and product costs, the total cost of a mug of cappuccino is $1.72. If the cappuccino is priced at $2.00, the marketer makes a profit of $0.28.

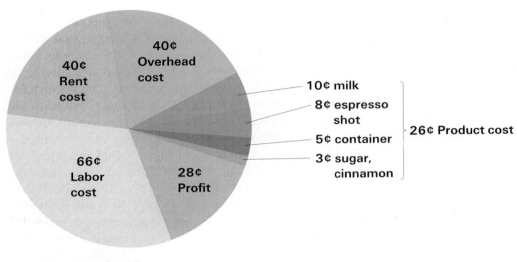

Price $2.00
Less total costs −1.72
_____
Profit $0.28

As you consider how many units to make, you also need to understand your **marginal cost**, the change in total expense of producing one more unit. Marginal cost differs for every additional unit you produce because your variable cost changes. In some industries, however, the change is extremely small. For example, marketers of long-distance telephone service use superefficient optic fibers that carry a huge number of calls simultaneously. Because they pay next to nothing to add another call, some marketers don't worry about marginal cost. Instead, they set one price for a three-minute call anywhere in the continental United States.[10]

Determining exact costs isn't always easy, however, in part because the cost of serving one customer or segment may not be the same as the cost of serving another. UPS found this out when it developed a sophisticated computer model to analyze costs at the customer level. Then UPS learned that serving residential customers was more costly than serving business customers because the former were more widely dispersed. This information led the shipper to set separate prices for serving the two customer segments.[11] Also, multinational marketers, such as Germany's Daimler-Benz Aerospace, face the task of managing costs incurred in more than one currency. The company has to deal with cost fluctuations caused by changes in foreign exchange rates.[12]

total cost
_____
total amount spent to produce every unit

marginal cost
_____
change in total expense of producing one more unit

More marketers are looking at how costs incorporated into product pricing affect the customer's perception of value ◄────┘ **(p. 346)**. *Target costing* is the process of working backward from what customers want—and will pay for—to develop and price a product with costs, quality, and functionality geared to targeted customer segments. Japan-based Olympus used target costing to start new customer relationships by creating lower-priced compact cameras for one segment based on lower product costs. Viewed in terms of the customer's value equation, the combination of quality at a lower price made these cameras more attractive.[13]

Marginal Analysis

When you know your marginal cost, you can calculate how many units you should produce to maximize your profitability. This calculation depends on marginal analysis. **Marginal analysis** is a tool for understanding the financial implications of producing one more unit and determining the point of maximum profitability. Marginal analysis shows how selling one more unit affects your revenue, cost, and profit.

Ordinarily, you calculate sales revenue by multiplying price times number of units sold. In marginal analysis, you look at **marginal revenue**, the change in sales revenue generated by selling one more unit. This change occurs because you must cut or raise your price to sell an additional unit, which either increases or decreases the amount of revenue you receive. To maximize your profits, look for the point at which your marginal cost is the same as your marginal revenue.

In Figure 13.2, you can see that marginal revenue drops as the number of units sold rises. This happens when you have a typical downward-sloping demand curve, where higher prices result in lower quantity demanded. At the same time, marginal cost initially drops and then rises with the quantity sold. Your profits are highest at the point at which marginal cost meets marginal revenue. You can confirm this by checking Table 13.1.

F I G U R E **13.2**

Marginal Analysis Relates Marginal Cost and Marginal Revenue
Using marginal analysis, you can determine how to maximize your profits by finding the point at which marginal cost is the same as marginal revenue. This analysis shows that pricing to stimulate demand beyond the point where marginal cost equals marginal revenue will hurt profits.

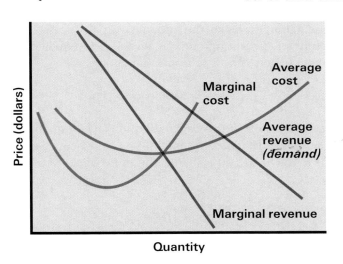

Quantity

T A B L E **13.1** Using Marginal Analysis to Maximize Profit

Price ($)	Quantity Sold	Total Revenue (price × quantity) ($)	Marginal Revenue ($)	Total Cost ($)	Marginal Cost ($)	Profit (total revenue – total cost) ($)
180	1	180	180	181	—	−1
175	2	350	170	326	145	24
170	3	510	160	467	141	43
165	4	660	150	604	137	56
160	**5**	**800**	**140**	**744**	**140**	**56** ←
155	6	930	130	889	145	41

Arrow indicates price where marginal cost = marginal revenue, maximizing profit.

---

marginal analysis

a tool for understanding the financial implications of producing one more unit and determining the point of maximum profitability

marginal revenue

the change in sales revenue generated by selling one more unit

breakeven analysis

a tool for analyzing revenues and costs to find the profit at various levels of quantity sold

breakeven point (BEP)

the point at which revenues equal costs and beyond which you begin to make a profit

As long as the marginal revenue from selling an additional unit is higher than that unit's marginal cost, you'll earn profits by expanding output. However, as you move beyond the point at which marginal cost equals marginal revenue, your marginal cost will rise while your marginal revenue will fall with each additional unit. As a result, your profit will be smaller and smaller beyond this point.

Breakeven Analysis

Once you know your costs, you can determine how many products you must sell at a given price to cover costs and make a profit. **Breakeven analysis** is a tool for analyzing revenues and costs to find the profit at various levels of quantity sold. The **breakeven point (BEP)** is the point at which revenues equal costs and beyond which you begin to make a profit. The formula for finding the breakeven point, expressed in units, is

$$\text{breakeven point (BEP)} = \frac{\text{fixed cost (FC)}}{\text{price of one unit} - \text{variable cost (VC) of one unit}}$$

To see how this operates, imagine that your publishing company has a fixed cost (FC) of $200,000 (for rent, equipment, and management salaries). You plan to price a book at $20. The variable cost (VC) per unit is $10 (for printing, packaging, and labor to make the product). In this case, the breakeven point (the point of generating enough revenues to equal your costs) would be 20,000 books. Here is how to reach that figure:

$$\text{BEP} = \frac{\$200,000}{\$20 - \$10} = \frac{\$200,000}{\$10} = 20,000 \text{ books}$$

Figure 13.3 shows how the results of this calculation look when graphed. Notice that when you sell fewer than 20,000 books, you don't cover your costs, which results in a loss. On the other hand, the more books you sell

FIGURE **13.3**

Breakeven Analysis
In breakeven analysis, the breakeven point is the point at which revenues equal costs. Beyond this point, marketers begin to make profits. This breakeven analysis shows that the publisher must sell 20,000 books at $20 each to reach the breakeven point of $400,000 in sales. At higher sales levels, the publisher enjoys higher profits.

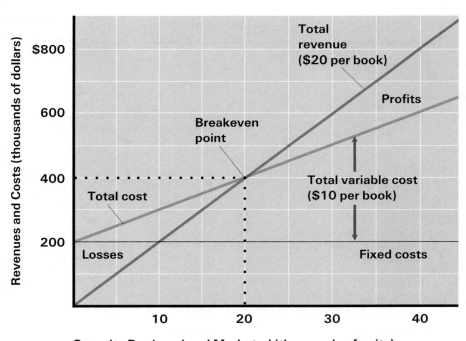

The breakeven point for stage productions in New York City is determined by a variety of factors, one of which is location of the theater. Theaters located within the Broadway district charge more. However, the Union Square Theater enables producers to have a much lower breakeven point and thus the opportunity for higher profit—given the same attendance. As you can see from the photo, customers still experience plush surroundings at this off-Broadway theater. How do you think a customer weighs the perceived value of a play on Broadway versus off-Broadway?

over 20,001, the higher your profits. To express the breakeven point in terms of dollars, multiply the number of units you need to sell to cover costs by the price per unit. In this example, the breakeven point comes when your company makes and markets 20,000 books at $20 each, for a total of $400,000 worth of books.

Breakeven analysis is as helpful for marketing theater tickets as it is for marketing tangible goods. After one of his plays lost over $600,000 on Broadway, playwright Neil Simon used breakeven analysis to compare potential profits on and off Broadway. The results convinced him to open his next show off Broadway at the Union Square Theatre. "At a place like the Union Square [Theatre]," Simon noted, "out of the 499 seats, literally if we only sold 200 seats, we'd break even every week."[14] Here's how one small business owner uses breakeven analysis.

SMALL BUSINESS WATCH

A dentist chews over breakeven analysis

Breakeven analysis can help small business owners make big pricing decisions. Katherine G. Collier had been operating her dental practice in Baltimore for seven years when she had an opportunity to open in an additional location. Concerned about the financial implications of the proposed expansion, Dr. Collier turned to her accountant, Louis G. Hutt, Jr., for help.

Hutt reviewed Collier's pricing, her customer base, and the estimated sales volume and revenues for the second location. Then he helped the dentist apply breakeven analysis to find the point at which the expansion would cover costs and begin to show profits. "We calculated the minimum volume of business that Katherine needed to break even," Hutt says. "In the end, she decided that it wouldn't be a wise financial move because the necessary volume of business wasn't there."

Collier admits that she didn't know much about the financial end of running a dental practice when she started. Now that her practice has grown to $1.3 million in annual revenues, she sees breakeven analysis as an objective way of supporting pricing decisions. Without breakeven analysis, she says, "I'd be so much less aware of how to run my business."[15]

Should Collier rely on breakeven analysis alone for her pricing decisions?

You can use breakeven analysis to see what happens to revenues, costs, and profits when you sell various quantities at a particular price. You can also use it to find the breakeven point of several prices under consideration and to see the potential profits and losses at each price. In turn, you'll be able to rule out prices that yield unacceptable levels of revenue, cost, or profit.

However, breakeven analysis has several limitations and should be used as only one tool, in conjunction with other data, to make pricing decisions. You can't use it as the sole basis for pricing because it looks only at profitability, leaving out other influences. Also, using breakeven analysis doesn't guarantee that you'll sell the quantities you need to earn the projected profit. In addition, since breakeven analysis is static and quite simplistic, it doesn't take into account changes such as increased fixed costs you may incur for the expanded plant or equipment needed to produce higher quantities.

Before you go on . . .

A. How can marketing research help marketers see pricing from their customers' perspective?

B. What is the purpose of marginal analysis?

C. What is breakeven analysis and what are its limitations?

Establishing a Pricing Strategy for Relationship Marketing

At this point, you're ready to establish a pricing strategy. You'll build on your knowledge of the marketing environment and customer needs as well as your pricing planning, your pricing research, and your analysis of costs, revenues, and profits. Four categories of pricing strategies that marketers commonly use are demand-based pricing, cost-based pricing, profit-based pricing, and competition-based pricing. These pricing strategies are outlined in Figure 13.4.

Of course, no single strategy works for everyone. Typically, you'll investigate more than one strategy before deciding how to price your product. And if you market several products, target several customer segments, or target several markets, you may apply a different pricing strategy for each as you work toward attracting customers and maintaining good customer relationships.

FIGURE **13.4**

Pricing Strategies
Marketers can use any of four categories of pricing strategies in building relationships with consumers and organizational customers.

Demand-Based Pricing	Cost-Based Pricing	Profit-Based Pricing	Competition-Based Pricing
Skimming pricing Penetration pricing Prestige pricing Price lining Odd–even pricing Bundle pricing Demand-backward pricing	Markup pricing Cost-plus pricing Experience curve pricing	Target-profit pricing Target-return pricing	Customary pricing Promotional pricing Everyday low pricing Competitive bidding and negotiated pricing

skimming pricing

a pricing strategy in which a new product is initially priced high to attract customers who are willing to pay for unique benefits and high quality

penetration pricing

a pricing strategy in which a new product is given a low initial price to attract many customers quickly while discouraging competitors

Demand-Based Pricing

When you use a pricing strategy based on demand, you place more emphasis on the influence of customer needs and interests than on the influence of costs, profits, or competitive forces. Among the demand-based strategies are skimming pricing, penetration pricing, prestige pricing, price lining, odd–even pricing, bundle pricing, and demand-backward pricing. Skimming pricing and penetration pricing are used for pricing new products at introduction.

Skimming Pricing

Skimming pricing is a pricing strategy in which a new product is initially priced high to attract customers who are willing to pay for unique benefits and high quality. You "skim the cream" from your target market when you use this strategy, appealing first to early adopters who are willing to pay more for an innovative product that has few, if any, substitutes. Over time, you can reduce your price to attract successive customer segments that are somewhat more price sensitive. From the start, you're able to generate high sales revenues to finance additional market expansion.

For example, Lotus used skimming pricing for the introduction of its Notes computer software. This program allows people at different workstations to share ideas and work on the same computer documents simultaneously. Many companies bought Notes at $495 per copy so their employees could collaborate on work projects. Two years after the launch, Lotus started lowering the price to appeal to more price-sensitive customer segments and to gain market share amid growing demand for similar products. Later, as more companies began sending documents via the Internet, Lotus slashed the price to $69 to compete with Internet software.[16]

Penetration Pricing

Penetration pricing is a pricing strategy in which a new product is given a low initial price to attract many customers quickly while discouraging competitors. This is the opposite of skimming, as shown in Table 13.2. Rather than pricing high initially, you price low to *penetrate* the market and move rapidly from the introduction to the growth stage of the product life cycle **(p. 302)**. This strategy builds sales momentum and reduces unit

TABLE **13.2** Comparison of Skimming Pricing and Penetration Pricing

Skimming Pricing	Penetration Pricing
Relatively inelastic demand	Relatively elastic demand
Product is unique, so few substitutes	Competitors are expected to enter the market quickly
Market can be segmented according to price sensitivity	Market can't be segmented according to price sensitivity
Used to generate revenues	Used to gain market share

Nintendo prices its video game consoles low, knowing that the greater profit comes from selling new games to console owners. However, as more and more people begin playing these and similar games on the Internet, pricing strategies for consoles may cease to be a key competitive issue. What impact will this shift have on Nintendo's pricing strategy for its video games? On retailers?

costs so you can gain market share and reach breakeven in short order. At the same time, you attract customers who might otherwise be sensitive to price, which is good for products with highly elastic demand ⟵┘ **(p. 359)**. In addition, the low prices and the prospect of low profits give your competitors second thoughts about entering the market.[17]

Nintendo has used penetration pricing to gain market acceptance for its video game consoles as quickly as possible. "There's no way to charge a premium on hardware," notes Hiroshi Yamauchi, Nintendo's president. Knowing this, Nintendo prices its consoles near or even below cost to get them into customers' hands. This effectively shuts out competitors and boosts demand for games that play on the consoles. By design, Nintendo reaps the bulk of its profits from games, not consoles.[18]

Prestige Pricing

The demand for some products grows stronger, not weaker, with higher prices. You can ride this demand curve ⟵┘ **(p. 354)** using **prestige pricing**, a strategy of setting a higher price than competitors to attract customers who are willing to pay more for a product that is higher in quality or status. This practice is different from skimming, which is used only in the introductory phase of the product life cycle. Prestige pricing is used at any stage. It's particularly effective when customers associate high quality with high price.

From Dior perfume to Christian Lacroix clothing, Paris-based LVMH Moet Hennessy Louis Vuitton markets luxury products at prestige prices to customers who are accustomed to buying the finest. "The appetite for luxury is as strong as ever," observes LVMH chairman Bernard Arnault. Even everyday products can carry prestige pricing. Thomas Kemper Soda Company prices its six-pack of soda at $5, more than twice the price of some competing brands, because Kemper's root beer is brewed, not produced as a syrup and then carbonated. The company's pricing reflects recognition that customers like to buy premium root beer as a treat.[19]

Thomas Kemper Root Beer is premium priced because it is brewed rather than produced from a syrup and then carbonated. Many customers are willing to pay twice as much for the unique taste. Note the attractive packaging. Do you ever buy premium-priced products? Beyond better quality, what value do you expect to get from such purchases?

Issues for critical thinking Does a prestige price necessarily indicate higher quality? What are the ethics of using prestige pricing to signal the promise of quality that a product can't fulfill? How are customers likely to react to such pricing?

Price Lining

When you offer a number of products, you may use **price lining**, a pricing strategy in which you set a separate, specific price for each product in your line. You want customers to link each product's value to its selling price and to recognize the relative differences among products in the line. In addition, the highest and lowest prices in your product line should reinforce the perceptions you want customers to have of your products and brand overall.[20]

Colgate-Palmolive uses price lining for its line of Colgate toothpaste products. At the high end is Platinum, a whitening toothpaste priced at $5.99 for 3 ounces, more than three times the price of regular Colgate toothpaste at the other end of the pricing scale. In between are the Colgate Baking Soda and Peroxide brand and other Colgate toothpastes, priced to reflect the value that customers will find in their specific features and benefits.[21]

Odd–Even Pricing

Retailers in particular attempt to influence customer perceptions by means of **odd–even pricing**, a strategy in which prices end in a certain digit. Many prices at Kmart, for example, are not round dollar amounts. Instead, they end in odd numbers—for example, you might see a $39.99 price tag on a window fan. The rationale behind this strategy is that people tend to compare prices by examining the numbers from left to right. Thus a unit priced at $39.99 seems a bargain compared with one costing $40.00. Research shows that putting grocery products on sale with prices ending in 9 can substantially boost volume.[22]

Because less expensive goods often carry prices ending in odd numbers, some marketers use round numbers, such as $50 or $250, to encourage a perception of quality and value. For example, Franklin Mint's Japanese subsidiary markets collectibles such as plates, coins, and jewelry through newspaper and magazine advertising. The company uses prices such as $2,000 to reinforce the perception of quality.[23]

Bundle Pricing

Bundle pricing is the strategy of setting one price for a package (bundle) of two, three, or more products. This pricing approach is used to market season tickets for sporting events, transportation and lodging vacation packages, computer systems complete with monitor and keyboard, and many other combinations of related units. The bundle you offer—and the price you set—will reflect the value customers perceive in a particular combination of products. Then, over time, as customer perceptions change and competitors enter and leave the market, you should be ready to respond by changing your bundle's products and pricing.[24]

prestige pricing

setting a higher price than competitors to attract customers who are willing to pay more for a product that is higher in quality or status

price lining

setting a separate, specific price for each product in a line

odd–even pricing

prices end in a certain digit rather than being rounded to whole dollars

bundle pricing

setting one price for a package (bundle) of two, three, or more products

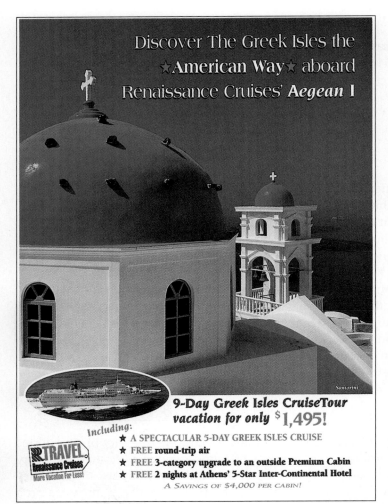

Discover The Greek Isles the
★American Way★ aboard
Renaissance Cruises' *Aegean I*

Santorini

9-Day Greek Isles CruiseTour
vacation for only $1,495!

Including:

★ A SPECTACULAR 5-DAY GREEK ISLES CRUISE
★ FREE **round-trip air**
★ FREE **3-category upgrade to an outside Premium Cabin**
★ FREE **2 nights at Athens' 5-Star Inter-Continental Hotel**

A SAVINGS OF $4,000 PER CABIN!

TRAVEL.
Renaissance Cruises
More Vacation For Less!

Renaissance Cruises offers bundled tour packages at attractive prices. This Greek Isles cruise tour includes a round-trip airline ticket, two free nights at a five-star hotel, and free upgrades. To what customer segment is this offer likely to appeal? Would such customers prefer to buy each of the components individually? Why?

demand-backward pricing

the price that will create a desired level of demand is determined first; the product is then developed and marketed to fit that price

If you offer a bundle rivals can't match at a price customers find attractive, you'll both increase demand and fend off competition. In most cases, you'll price your bundle below what customers would pay for the products individually. For example, the Swanson Chicken Salad Lunch Kit includes a small can of chicken, packets of mayonnaise and seasonings, and Pepperidge Farm crackers, for a convenient light meal at one low price.[25] However, if your bundle includes products customers don't need and don't want to pay for, you may lose business to competitors with more appropriate bundles or individually priced products.[26]

Demand-Backward Pricing

In **demand-backward pricing** the price that will create a desired level of demand is determined first; the product is then developed and marketed to fit that price. With this approach, all the activities connected with production, value-chain management, and marketing are tailored to fit the price that has been set. Thus you watch your costs, select your raw materials and components, examine the margins required by resellers, and do everything else necessary to keep the price at the point where it will generate the expected demand.

Chrysler did this with its Neon compact car. A cross-functional team ◄─┘ **(p. 47)** worked with suppliers to develop a low-cost, low-priced car with many standard features. The team had to keep costs for parts, materials, and production in line. It also had to allow adequate margins for dealers while creating a car priced to attract a large number of price-sensitive customers. The Neon was so successful that Toyota disassembled one to see how Chrysler controlled costs enough to charge the low base price.[27]

Cost-Based Pricing

The second category of pricing strategies (after demand-based) is cost-based pricing, which emphasizes the marketer's costs over other pricing considerations. Of course, before you can set a price, you need to understand what you're spending to buy parts or materials, handle production, and bring your product to market. But as you saw earlier, many marketers are at a disadvantage in setting prices because they don't know their exact costs. Moreover, since cost-based pricing doesn't consider market forces, it doesn't reflect what customers will pay or how customer relationships are affected by price. Still, the three types of cost-based pricing—markup pricing, cost-plus pricing, and experience curve pricing—are in common use, in part because they're relatively easy to apply.[28]

markup pricing

resellers in the marketing channel set prices by adding a standard, predetermined percentage to the cost of each product

Markup Pricing

Wholesalers and retailers generally don't find demand-based pricing practical. Because they carry many products and appeal to a number of customer segments, they can't easily determine the demand for each product and each segment. So most use **markup pricing**, a strategy in which resellers in the marketing channel set prices by adding a standard, predetermined percentage to the cost of each product. The percentage to be added, known as the *markup*, is intended to cover the wholesaler or retailer's costs and return a profit. Markup pricing can be calculated on either cost or selling price. You'll find details about such pricing in Appendix B.

During the journey through the value chain from producer to customer, a product may be marked up three times. First, the producer uses markup pricing to set the price the wholesaler will pay. Next, the wholesaler who buys from the producer uses markup pricing to determine how much to charge the retailer. Finally, the retailer who buys from the wholesaler uses markup pricing to set the price that the consumer will pay. As shown in Figure 13.5, all three markups are reflected in the final customer's price.

FIGURE **13.5** Markups in the Marketing Channel

The price paid by a store's customer has to cover as many as three markups in the marketing channel. The first markup is applied by the producer that markets the product to the wholesaler. The second markup is applied by the wholesaler that markets the product to the retailer. And the third markup is applied by the retailer that markets the product to the customer who shops in the store.

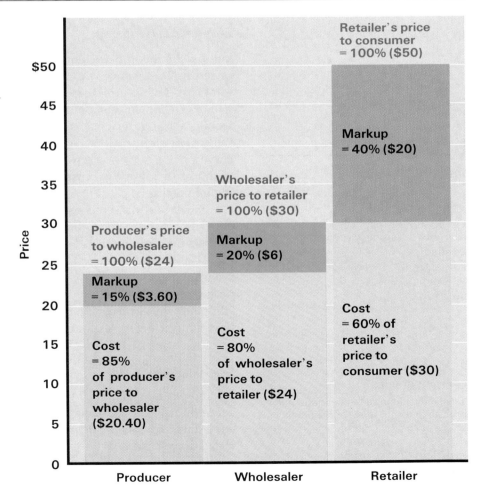

In many cases, the markup varies by product category. Products to which customers are more price sensitive, such as milk, often carry a smaller markup. On the other hand, nonnecessities like apparel and jewelry carry a considerably higher markup.

Cost-Plus Pricing

Cost-plus pricing is a strategy in which a marketer adds a certain amount or percentage to cost to arrive at the product's selling price. Many business-to-business marketers and professional firms select this pricing strategy, which is similar to markup pricing used by retailers and other channel partners. To implement cost-plus pricing, you add either a fixed dollar amount or a percentage to your total costs. In this way, your price both covers your costs and yields a profit.

Patty DeDominic, the CEO of PDQ Personnel Services in Los Angeles, used cost-plus pricing when she priced the services of the temporary employees who worked for her clients. To price each assignment, she added 30 to 80 percent on top of PDQ's costs; 30 percent brought her to the breakeven point, and higher percentages yielded profit. She varied the percentage to be added according to client, length of assignment, and other factors.[29]

Experience Curve Pricing

Manufacturers, in particular, may use **experience curve pricing**, a strategy of setting lower prices to increase the number of units sold, which drives total cost down as the marketer gains experience making the product. As a marketer learns more about making and marketing a product, gains more technological proficiency, and buys parts and materials in larger quantities, the cost of producing each unit goes down.[30] Marketers who use experience curve pricing set prices low enough to generate sufficient sales volume to significantly lower total cost. This strategy eventually yields higher profits at higher volumes.

A variety of marketers use experience curve pricing, including computer chip makers. Intel, the California maker of the Pentium Pro and other chips for personal computers, sets prices knowing that it will be able to turn out more—and better—chips at lower cost as time goes on. Like other cost-based pricing strategies, however, experience curve pricing ignores market economics and customer reaction. In addition, this strategy assumes that cost will go down as predicted, even though some costs may vary or fail to behave as anticipated. Use of experience curve pricing is therefore limited.[31]

Profit-Based Pricing

When you use *profit-based pricing*, you set prices to reach certain profit targets. You may express your profit targets in dollars or as a percentage of revenue. Like cost-based pricing, profit-based pricing stresses internal finances rather than market economics, so the result is a price that may bear no relation to what customers will pay or what will keep customers in a relationship with you. Despite this limitation, marketers who want an uncomplicated, easy-to-implement pricing strategy use profit-based pricing. Two types are target-profit pricing and target-return pricing.

cost-plus pricing
a marketer adds a certain amount or percentage to cost to arrive at the product's selling price

experience curve pricing
selecting a low price to maximize sales while keeping total costs down; made possible as a marketer gains technical proficiency in making the product

Target-Profit Pricing

In **target-profit pricing**, you establish the dollar amount of profit you want to achieve through pricing. You may express the profit target in terms of dollar profit per unit or total dollar profit for a period. For example, you may need to price a cordless telephone to hit a profit target of $20 per unit sold or an annual profit target of $200,000.

Calculating prices to meet the targets established is fairly straightforward. Like other profit-based pricing strategies, however, this approach ignores customer reaction and changes in demand. Therefore, your price may not result in a sales level that brings you to your profit target. What's more, because demand affects variable costs, you can't be sure that your pricing will bring you to your per-unit profit target, either.

Black & Decker has used target-return pricing to price some lines of tools. However, this kind of pricing ignores competitive challenges as well as changes in the economy and consumer demand. Would it be a good idea for Black & Decker to have a different pricing strategy for new, highly innovative products? Why?

target-profit pricing

establishing the dollar amount of profit you want to achieve through pricing

target-return pricing

setting prices to reach a specific measure of profit, such as return on sales, return on investment, or return on assets

Target-Return Pricing

In **target-return pricing**, you set prices to reach a specific measure of profit, such as return on sales, return on investment, or return on assets. As you saw in Chapter 12, many marketers set profit goals, which are achieved through pricing as well as through cost-containment policies and productivity gains. For example, Black & Decker uses pricing to achieve a 9 percent return on sales of tools and locks.[32]

Like target-profit pricing, target-return pricing relies on a series of calculations that neglect a consideration of how customers view prices. Yet despite its limitations, many marketers use this strategy to set prices, sometimes building computer models that allow them to factor in various levels of demand and cost changes that can affect pricing and profits. Aided by these models, marketers can project the effects specific prices may have on demand and on return targets.

Competition-Based Pricing

Competition is one influence that demand-based pricing, cost-based pricing, and profit-based pricing don't deal with. With competition-based pricing, you base your price on what others charge, setting a price that's equal to, higher than, or lower than that of your rivals. At times, you may set prices by bidding against competitors. Competition-based pricing covers a range of strategies, including customary pricing, promotional pricing, everyday low pricing, competitive bidding, and negotiated pricing.

Of course, competition-based pricing isn't appropriate if you're marketing an innovative new product or if your product is quite different from competing products. Nor does it allow for the possibility that competitors may have different cost structures, which would make their prices wrong for you. Finally, competition-based pricing ignores customer reaction. Despite these limitations, though, this form of pricing is a way of studying the market and analyzing the effect of rivals' prices. After all, you're not pricing in a vacuum. As soon as you price your product, your competitors will be able to respond.[33]

Customary Pricing

When you use **customary pricing**, you price your product according to a traditional or standardized price. You assume that customers won't accept any price other than the one they're accustomed to paying. In such a situation, all competitors offering the product will stay at the customary price, even if they have to adjust the product to do so. Although customary pricing isn't widely used today, it still applies for certain products, such as some candy bars and gum.[34]

Customary pricing prevails when the marketing situation discourages marketers from setting prices that vary from what is usually charged. For example, products marketed through vending machines are usually priced so that customers won't have to pay in pennies. Thus pricing a candy bar at 77 cents rather than 75 cents could hurt demand, especially if a competing product is available at 75 cents.

Promotional Pricing

Promotional pricing is a strategy of temporarily setting and communicating lower prices on selected products. Nearly every marketer uses promotional pricing at some point. It's helpful when you want to counter competitive pressures, draw new customers, enter new markets, break into a new customer segment, or open a new location. You might use promotional pricing to put all products on sale, to reduce prices on individual products or an entire product line, or to promote a particular brand of products. After the promotion, prices revert to the regular, higher level, which is why promotional pricing is sometimes called *high–low pricing*.

An extreme form of promotional pricing is **loss-leader pricing**, a strategy of pricing selected products well below what competitors ordinarily charge, to attract customers. As the name implies, loss-leader prices are set near or even below cost. The marketer hopes that when customers are drawn in by the extremely low prices on the so-called loss leaders, they will buy other, more profitable items. In the meantime, the marketer has gained a reputation for loss-leader pricing, which helps it sustain relationships with price-sensitive customers. The following case shows how a big marketer got hurt by a loss-leader promotion.

Applying the Concepts

Hoover loses on loss-leader promotion

Travel free when you buy Hoover appliances. Who could resist? Few did, which is why Hoover, Maytag's British subsidiary, wound up with amazingly high sales—and shockingly high losses. The promotional pricing strategy called for Hoover to give two round-trip tickets to European cities to British customers who bought more than £100 worth of Hoover products, and two round-trip tickets to New York or Florida to customers who bought more than £250-worth of products.

Sales skyrocketed as customers realized that the tickets were worth far more than the appliances. More than 200,000 customers responded—only 50,000 had been expected—and Hoover factories worked around the clock

customary pricing

pricing a product according to a traditional or standardized price

promotional pricing

temporarily setting and communicating lower prices on selected products

loss-leader pricing

pricing selected products well below what competitors ordinarily charge, to attract customers

Marketing Madness

An ingenious giveaway scheme by Hoover backfires by working too well

BUY A VACUUM CLEANER OR WASHING MACHINE from Maytag's British subsidiary, Hoover, and get air tickets to the U.S. or continental [...] Sound like a good [...]? You bet! S[...] Hoo[...]

This headline from *Time* magazine on April 12, 1993, highlighted the story of Hoover's free airline ticket promotion. The cost of the promotion went well beyond anticipated costs. A similar headline appeared on June 27, 1996, when Pepsi offered T-shirts and other merchandise with proof-of-purchase of Pepsi products. They too were overwhelmed by the response but cut back the offer before it got out of hand. How are customers likely to react to changes in offers that have been very popular?

to pump out enough vacuum cleaners, washers, and dryers to meet the demand. The response swamped the company, and thousands of people waited months for their tickets, were locked out of their travel dates, or simply never received their tickets. Hoover's special complaint hotline received 2,000 calls a day from angry customers.

In the end, the promotion hurt customer relationships and led to the firing of several Hoover executives. It also cost Hoover the equivalent of $50 million, making the promotion an extreme example of loss-leader pricing. What should Hoover have done? If its marketers had looked at the promotion from the customers' viewpoint, they would have seen that the value equation was too attractive to resist. To keep the promotion in bounds, the company could have set limits to restrict the response level and contain costs, raised the amount of merchandise to be purchased, or given away less valuable tickets.[35]

Make marketing decisions

1. If you were pricing Hoover products, would you limit promotional pricing to a certain period? Why or why not?

2. Would you limit each promotion to a certain number of people? If so, how would you decide how many requests to honor?

3. Why do you think Hoover marketers underestimated customer response to this pricing strategy?

4. In the future, should Maytag, the parent company, approve all Hoover promotional pricing strategies before implementation? Why or why not?

Everyday Low Pricing

Everyday low pricing (EDLP) is a strategy that calls for setting prices that are consistently low. When you use EDLP, you avoid the seesaw of raising and lowering prices that characterizes promotional pricing strategies. Instead, you price your products low at all times, which makes rivals' regular prices seem relatively high. This helps strengthen relationships with customers who want to feel they're paying a reasonable price every time they buy.

Both manufacturers and retailers can use EDLP, which was pioneered by Procter & Gamble to set lower prices on products it markets to supermarkets and other resellers. Although some retailers initially protested, P&G has persisted with EDLP, in part to stop the roller-coaster of periodic price adjustments and demand that used to raise costs and complicate production planning. Now Colgate-Palmolive and a growing number of manufacturers are joining P&G in switching to EDLP.[36]

Some supermarkets, discount chains, and department stores have also picked up on EDLP. Wal-Mart, for example, built its reputation on EDLP. The 7-Eleven convenience store chain has also converted some stores to EDLP. It

everyday low pricing (EDLP)

setting prices that are consistently low

Many consumers plan their purchases around special deals when shopping at the supermarket. However, when producers use everyday low pricing (EDLP), shoppers see steady, competitive pricing all the time instead of occasional price cutting by couponing or other methods. The Procter & Gamble products shown here are representative of the EDLP strategy. Do you think consumers prefer slightly lower prices all the time or slightly higher prices with an occasional substantial discount? Why?

found that EDLP increased store traffic and led to higher sales. Still, fewer than half of all U.S. retailers use EDLP. The nonbelievers see loss-leader pricing as a more effective way of bringing customers into their stores.[37] Of course, EDLP isn't right for everyone, as the following section shows.

MARKETING IDEAS

Pros and cons of EDLP

Is everyday low pricing (EDLP) a pricing panacea? Although EDLP has helped Toys "Я" Us and Wal-Mart compete, it has been much less successful for department stores, such as Dillard's and Sears, where customers are accustomed to high–low pricing. When considering EDLP, think about these advantages and disadvantages:

- *Advantage: Adds credibility to year-round pricing.* Customers can trust that prices will be consistently and reasonably low.

- *Advantage: Flattens sales peaks and valleys.* Customers don't have to wait for a sale to get a good price; they can buy at any time.

- *Advantage: Strengthens supplier partnerships.* Marketers and suppliers work collaboratively to reduce costs and lower prices.

- *Advantage: Reduces production and marketing costs.* Manufacturers can better anticipate and match demand; marketers spend less on advertising and changing prices.

- *Disadvantage: Possible erosion of customer relationships.* If customers believe that the everyday price is too high, they'll lose trust in the marketer—and take their business elsewhere.

- *Disadvantage: Limited ability to promote special pricing.* Having fewer sales means fewer opportunities to build excitement through temporary price reductions.

- *Disadvantage: Potential for lower profits.* Higher EDLP sales volume may not make up for lower profit margins.
- *Disadvantage: Depends on supplier relationships.* If suppliers won't co-operate, marketers may have difficulty cutting costs to set prices low enough to draw customer attention.

As long as some marketers are successful with EDLP, the debate will continue.[38] If you were running a convenience store near your campus, would you use EDLP? Why or why not?

Competitive Bidding and Negotiated Pricing

For consumers, one of the most frustrating aspects of buying a car is haggling over price. A consumer never knows whether the price is a good deal or not. In response, Oldsmobile and other companies are offering no-haggle pricing. They put the most popular options on the car and then price it attractively. What is your reaction to this ad? Does it clearly convey a customer-oriented message?

THE 1995 LAND·SHARK SEDAN
When it comes to Value...It Bites.

Standard Equipment

ALL FEATURES STANDARD (EXCLUDES TRANSMISSION, BRAKES, REAR DOORS, FRONT SEATS, GAS CAP AND ENGINE), AVAILABLE ONLY ON OPTION PACKAGES A, C, D, DD, AND ZZZ. WINDSHIELD, ANIMAL SAFETY SEAT. FULLY INDEPENDENT AND/OR DEPENDENT FRONT & TRANSVERSE REAR LEAF SPRING SUSPENSIONS OPTIONAL ONLY ON PACKAGE D, WHICH IS NOT OPTIONAL.*

GAS CHART THINGY

City MPG   Highway MPG
396   **567**

MILEAGE BASED ON ALL STANDARD EQUIPPED VEHICLES TRAVELING DOWNHILL AT 89 DEGREE GRADE. ACTUAL MILEAGE WILL VARY WITH OPTIONAL AND NON-OPTIONAL OPTIONS, DRIVING CONDITIONS, DRIVING HABITS, PERSONAL HYGIENE HABITS, AND VEHICLE CONDITION. GAS PUMP NOT INCLUDED.

Final Vehicle Price:
$**8,985.25**

MANUFACTURER'S SUGGESTED RETAIL PRICE. PRICE INCLUDES BASE VEHICLE WITH OPTION PACKAGE C, WHICH INCLUDES NO OPTIONS EXCEPT BRAKES, BUT DOES HAVE AN ASHTRAY. OPTION QQQ WITH NO BRAKES IS AVAILABLE, ALTHOUGH MANUFACTURER WOULD NOT SUGGEST IT. ADD BUMPER-TO-TRUNK WARRANTY, DEALER HAGGLING FEE, PLUS:

$$\text{MSRP} \times \sqrt{\text{MPG}} - \text{PDo}$$
- July rebate (if July) x .789%
$$\text{E=MSRP}^3 - \text{warp factor } 8 +$$
*@&#!! x π + 🌍
equals:

REALLY FINAL VEHICLE PRICE!!!
$**27,586.00****

We think we've figured out why people hate shopping for a car.

Oldsmobile Simplified Pricing

It's very simple, really. Shopping for a car has become too complicated. All those confusing option packages and rebates. Hours of haggling. Ugh. That's why we're making it simpler. By equipping every new Oldsmobile with the most popular options, standard. By taking out confusing rebates—but leaving in the savings. So our retailers can give you their best price right upfront. Without a lot of haggling. Funny, but people really seem to like our new way of doing business. Go figure. Demand Better. **Oldsmobile**

As you saw in Chapter 7, marketers who pursue organizational customers are often asked to submit bids indicating the price they will charge to provide specific products. This *competitive bidding* system is used by many government and business buyers to induce suppliers to try to outdo each other on price. To start a round of competitive bidding, the customer circulates a request for proposal (RFP), in which vendors are asked to compete for an order by showing how they will meet the product specifications, the delivery requirements, and other criteria. When the bids are in, the customer evaluates each marketer's value package and price and then accepts the bid that best suits its requirements and budget.

When Illinois-based Header Die & Tool is asked to bid on supplying parts to auto-fastener manufacturers, executive vice president Pat Derry uses two computerized models to estimate the costs he expects to incur. One model looks at the cost of producing the parts manually. The other looks at the cost of producing the parts using computer-aided manufacturing (CAM) equipment. Derry can quickly analyze a number of possible scenarios before coming up with a final bid, which he faxes to prospective customers within 24 hours.[39]

Some situations call for *negotiated pricing*, a system in which marketer and customer discuss and agree on price. When the customer's requirements or the marketer's value package is unique, negotiated pricing helps both sides settle on an acceptable price for a nonstandard product. Many organizational customers ask for negotiated pricing on construction contracts, major equipment purchases, and a variety of other purchases.

Negotiated pricing was once the only strategy used by auto dealers to price their cars. These days, however, *no-haggle pricing* has become more popular as a response to consumer frustration with the negotiation process. General Motor's Saturn division was one of the first major car companies to abandon negotiated pricing and label its cars with the lowest acceptable price. Studies reflect growing customer satisfaction with no-haggle pricing, which is why Oldsmobile and some other carmakers have followed suit.[40]

International Pricing

When you market in other countries, you may need special pricing strategies. If you're exporting, your pricing must cover expenses not incurred in domestic markets. Tariffs and taxes are two major costs that influence international pricing. Some marketers set standard world prices, a simple but somewhat inflexible strategy. Others set prices country by country, to be able to factor in local market economics, local competition, and other local influences.[41]

For example, Ray-O-Vac's Micro Power division makes and markets batteries for hearing aids and wristwatches. Marketers in the European and Asian countries where Micro Power operates are empowered to price according to local market conditions. This gives the company the flexibility to respond quickly to competitive forces, currency fluctuations, and other situations that affect pricing in local markets.[42]

Multinational companies often grapple with *transfer pricing*, pricing that relates to the movement of goods or services between a marketer's internal departments and divisions. In essence, the producing department (which may be based in one country) sells the product at a transfer price to the department that markets it (in another country). Thus transfer pricing helps you more accurately assign costs and measure profits in each department. You may, however, have difficulty settling on a price that makes sense for both departments.[43]

Government officials are concerned that transfer pricing raises the possibility for manipulating profits, tax liabilities, and tariff fees. An international marketer may try to reduce its overall tax burden by using transfer pricing to show higher profits in low-tax markets and lower profits in high-tax markets. It may also try to reduce tariff payments by understating product values, using lower transfer pricing in high-tariff markets. Small wonder that the Internal Revenue Service and its counterparts in many countries closely watch transfer pricing.[44] The following section examines pricing in the global gray market.

GLOBAL ISSUES

Marketers see red over gray market pricing

Makers of cameras, wristwatches, cars, and chewing gum are up in arms over the *gray market*, unauthorized marketing channels that bring products from other countries at lower prices than authorized channel members pay, leading to lower retail prices. Unauthorized channels are those that a product's marketer has not designated in a particular market. Warner-Lambert, for example, didn't plan for its chewing gum plant in Lebanon to market Chiclets in New York. The unauthorized sale of Chiclets and other items through the U.S. gray market adds up to as much as $10 billion every year, by some estimates.

Gray market activities flourish when currency fluctuations make unauthorized imports look more attractive. For example, Caterpillar builds and markets earthmoving equipment all over the world. When the dollar was strong against foreign currencies, gray market oppor-

list price

the official price you quote for your product

market price

the price that customers actually pay for your product

tunists bought Caterpillar products at low prices in Europe and Japan to sell in the United States at prices considerably lower than products offered by authorized U.S. dealers.

Gray market prices undercut those in legitimate marketing channels, but customers may not get the same value package. Many warranties, for example, are valid only in the country where the product was originally sold. For their part, more marketers are taking legal action against the importers. They're also publicizing the limitations of gray market goods to discourage customers from buying.[45]

Can manufacturers fight back by adjusting prices to authorized resellers?

Before you go on . . .

A. Identify seven demand-based pricing strategies. Which of these apply specifically to new products?

B. What are the limitations of cost-based pricing?

C. How does everyday low pricing differ from promotional pricing?

D. What is transfer pricing?

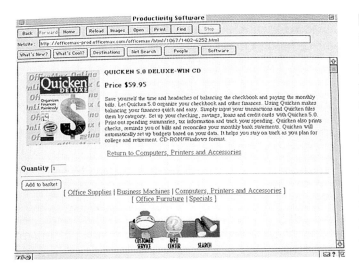

Products offered by OfficeMax on its World Wide Web site generally feature market prices, the price that customers actually pay. This Quicken software is being sold at the product's list price, the price set by the manufacturer. Do you think customers would prefer that OfficeMax show the list prices as well as the market prices on products sold through its Web site? Why?

Managing Pricing Adjustments for Relationship Marketing

Rarely do you set a price and leave it forever. Like every part of marketing strategy, pricing must be actively managed; only in this way can you build customer relationships and achieve your marketing and organizational objectives. All the influences on pricing, including customer requirements, competitive pressures, market economics, and value-chain relationships, can lead you to adjust your prices. There are four types of adjustment for managing your prices: monetary price adjustments, product adjustments, price discounts and allowances, and geographic price adjustments.

Some adjustments will affect the **list price**, the official price you quote for your product. You show list prices in your catalogs and other integrated marketing communication. By making adjustments that bring your list price up or down, you arrive at the **market price**, the price that customers actually pay for your product. The market price results from negotiating with various customers. For example, customers that buy in huge volume may get a discount.

Monetary Price Adjustments

Although promotional pricing is a temporary price change, raising or lowering the list price is not. Inflation, for example, can hike your costs and, in turn, prompt you to raise your list price. In countries where inflation runs particularly high and government controls don't forbid such actions, some marketers increase their prices quite often.

By the same token, you may decide to bring your price down for an extended period. When interest rates drop, for example, banks lower their mortgage and loan rates. But competitive pressures can also nudge marketers toward a long-term price cut. Not long ago, Post Cereal reduced the list prices on its ready-to-eat cereals by an average of 20 percent to boost sales. It also released new coupons that applied to all of its cereals, not just one.[46]

Product Adjustments

When you're reluctant to adjust your monetary price, you may adjust the product you offer at the same price. As part of a value pricing strategy, many marketers have increased the amount or the quality of product they offer, without increasing the price. Marketers can also choose to reduce the amount or the quality of the product offered for the same price. With this approach you may be able to avoid setting prices that run above customary pricing or are out of step with market economics.

For example, British candy maker Rowntree recently incurred higher costs for ingredients of its Kit Kat bar but couldn't easily raise the price because competitors were holding the line. The company therefore used less chocolate covering and kept the unit price constant. But competitor Jacob's Club Biscuits maintained its quality and price and drew customers away from Kit Kat. As Rowntree found out, adjusting the product instead of the price can be risky.[47]

Price Discounts and Allowances

A third way to adjust price is through discounts and allowances that reduce the final amount your customer pays. Properly applied, such adjustments can help you maintain relationships with organizational customers and ultimate consumers and, at the same time, strengthen your competitive position. Discounts and allowances that are too numerous or too deep, however, may confuse customers and reduce profits. That's why discounts and allowances are most effective when coordinated with an overall pricing strategy.

Discounts

When you offer a discount, you give customers (ultimate consumers as well as channel partners) a direct price break for taking a specific action such as buying when or how you want them to buy. This is often a good way to influence customer buying behavior. Discounts that marketers commonly offer include cash discounts, quantity discounts, seasonal discounts, and trade discounts.

- *Cash discounts* are price breaks used to reward customers for paying invoices within a certain period. In many industries, marketers quote prices such as "2/10 net 30" to indicate that the bill is due within 30 days, but the customer can deduct 2 percent if payment is made within 10 days. Imagine that you offer this discount to a customer who owes you $2,000. When the customer pays in 10 days or less, it can subtract $40 and send you $1,960. When the customer pays in 30 days, it must send the entire $2,000.

- *Quantity discounts*, or price breaks per unit, allowed on large-volume orders, give customers a reason to buy more from you. Quantity discounts can take one of two forms. *Noncumulative quantity discounts* are applied one order at a time. This means that a customer can't qualify for discounts by adding up the quantities bought over two, three, or more orders. As a result, customers are encouraged to buy more in each order. In contrast, *cumulative quantity discounts* give discounts for the quantity a customer buys over a period, generally a year. With this arrangement, customers who continue purchasing from you can qualify for larger discounts over time.

- *Seasonal discounts* reward customers for buying products out of season. Manufacturers can iron out the peaks and valleys in their production and marketing activities by providing discounts to customers who buy early. For example, Snapper might offer discounts to retailers and consumers in northern states for buying lawn mowers in January rather than waiting for May. Such price adjustments can also help service marketers build off-season demand. Caribbean cruise lines, for instance, often offer seasonal discounts to fill spring and fall cruises.

- *Trade discounts* are price breaks offered in exchange for specific services to wholesale and retail customers—those in the trade. These discounts are also known as functional discounts, because they reward resellers for handling functions such as answering customer questions and doing installations and repairs. Trade discounts allow your channel partners to set prices that cover the cost of the functions they must perform to bring the product to your customers.

For example, Schwartz Bookshops in Milwaukee typically receives a trade discount from publishers of 44 percent off the list prices of hardcover books. The retailer prices the top 35 best-sellers at 40 percent off list to maintain relationships with customers who might otherwise patronize the giant bookstore chains. But other books are priced at a lower discount—and some are sold at list price—to return needed profits and to recover costs, including employee wages and utilities.[48]

Allowances

Allowances are pricing adjustments that indirectly lower the price paid by customers in exchange for taking an action such as buying during a certain period or promoting your product. Trade-in allowances, rebates, and promotional allowances are among the most common types. Not every customer will earn an allowance, but those who do will pay a lower price. As a result, you don't need to reduce your list price. Like discounts, allowances can help you influence customer buying behavior.

Auto dealers frequently offer rebates to move stock late in the model year or during slow sales periods. Since these rebates are substantial, many customers take advantage of them. The problem for car dealers is that some customers refuse to pay the full price, preferring instead to wait for rebates. What could dealers do to persuade these customers not to wait?

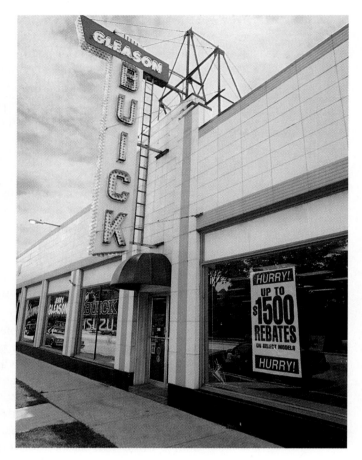

1. *Trade-in allowances* are reductions in price offered by marketers in exchange for a product from the customer. Car dealers offer trade-in allowances that give buyers a certain amount of credit toward a new car when they sign over a used car as part of the transaction. This allows the dealers to maintain their list prices and provide breaks only to customers who want to trade in their cars.

2. *Rebates* are refunds to customers who buy certain products during a specified period. Rebates don't affect list prices, but they do give customers a reason to buy when marketers want to sell. Carmakers use rebates to jump-start sales during slow periods. When minivan sales leveled off after a decade of growth, for example, Chrysler and Ford offered rebates to move specific models. Both marketers can afford the rebates: their average gross profit margins on minivans range from $4,500 to over $6,000.[49]

3. *Promotional allowances* are used to reward resellers for promoting products to customers through personal selling, advertising, displays, or other techniques. To encourage promotions, marketers can offer cash payments or give an extra allotment of products without charge. List prices and trade discounts remain the same, but dealers get a special incentive to promote these products.

Some marketers are concerned that dealers buy more than they need when promotional allowances are offered, then slow down or stop buying when promotional allowances aren't available. That's one reason Procter & Gamble de-emphasized promotional allowances and introduced everyday low prices. Do you agree with P&G's approach? Why or why not?

Geographic Price Adjustments

Geographic price adjustments allow you to include all, some, or none of the shipping costs in your price. Whether your customers are next door or around the world, you have to get products from your location to theirs. So your pricing should take into account, in addition to customer preferences and customer locations, how much your product weighs and how competitors handle geographic price adjustments. Two types of geographical price adjustment are FOB origin pricing and delivered pricing.

FOB Origin Pricing

When you exclude shipping charges from your price, you use *FOB (free on board) origin pricing*. This means that you'll load the products for transportation at the origin (your plant), but your customers pay shipping charges. Your responsibility ends once you've loaded your products for shipment.

With this approach, your price is lower than it would be if you included some or all of the shipping costs, which can be a competitive advantage when selling to customers close by. Also, some customers prefer to negotiate shipping on their own. On the other hand, customers that can't negotiate favorable shipping contracts or are located far from you may object, because they have to arrange for shipping and pay the charges as well.

Delivered Pricing

With delivered pricing, your price includes shipping charges to bring products to the customer's door. Customers don't have to make shipping arrangements, and they don't get a separate bill from the shipper. Also, they don't have responsibility for purchased goods until they're delivered. It's your responsibility to see that goods are delivered safe and sound.

Delivered pricing can take several forms. When you use *single-zone pricing*, you add an average shipping charge to your price so that all customers pay the same price, regardless of location. Often, this means that nearby customers pay a little more than they would with FOB origin, while distant customers pay a little less. The U.S. Postal Service (U.S.P.S.) uses single-zone pricing for first-class mail. No matter where in the 50 states a first-class letter is going, the cost is the same.

United Parcel Service uses multiple-zone pricing for packages sent by truck. With this pricing approach, the further a consumer or business ships a package—and the heavier the weight—the higher the shipping costs. How easy is it for customers to understand this pricing system? How would you explain this system to a customer who is using UPS Ground Service for the first time?

UPS Ground Service
1 to 70 pounds

- All rates are effective February 3, 199X
- Any fraction of a pound over the weight shown takes the next higher rate.
- See page 24 for additional charges, weight and size information, service restrictions, and general information.

Commercial Deliveries

WEIGHT IN POUNDS	ZONES						
	2	3	4	5	6	7	8
1	$2.52	$2.70	$2.94	$3.03	$3.10	$3.19	$3.24
2	2.57	2.76	3.20	3.32	3.51	3.62	3.83
3	2.65	2.91	3.40	3.55	3.82	3.96	4.28
4	2.76	3.04	3.56	3.74	4.05	4.23	4.63
5	2.90	3.19	3.65	3.86	4.22	4.44	4.87
6	3.03	3.28	3.72	3.94	4.35		
7	3.14	3.35	3.77				
8	3.26	3.42					

In contrast, when you use *multiple-zone pricing*, you divide your markets into geographic zones and vary your prices according to the shipping costs you incur to deliver to each zone. Customers in each zone pay the same price, but prices differ from zone to zone. This is the approach that both the U.S.P.S. and UPS take for delivering packages in the United States. The price a customer pays varies depending on the zone in which the package will be delivered.

With *freight absorption pricing*, you absorb (pay) the distribution cost by allowing your customers to deduct the shipping amount from your bills. Your price remains the same, but the customer winds up paying less. This approach can help you break into distant markets or meet competitive pricing pressures.

Under *basing-point pricing*, you establish one or more locations (basing points) from which you charge shipping costs as part of your price. Your plant is not a basing point. Instead, other locations serve as the starting point for pricing. Even if your products don't actually move through those locations, customers pay as if they had. Although this adjustment is less popular today, it has been used in the steel industry and others. For example, a New York manufacturer might use a location in California as a basing point to spare customers in California from paying high shipping costs, which would have made the firm noncompetitive in that market.

Before you go on . . .

A. Why do marketers use cash discounts, quantity discounts, seasonal discounts, and trade discounts?

B. How can marketers use discounts and allowances to build relationships with customers and value-chain partners?

C. What geographic pricing adjustments can marketers make?

Summary

1. **Show how marketers can research customer reaction to pricing.**

   Marketers can research customer reaction to prices in three ways. The first is to use test marketing to gauge customer response to various prices in representative markets or by mail. The second is to use simulated test marketing to test prices in a laboratory setting. The third is to use multiple trade-off analysis to understand how customers respond to various value packages at various prices.

2. **Distinguish among fixed, variable, total, and marginal costs, and demonstrate the use of breakeven analysis.**

   Fixed cost refers to the expenses that remain the same no matter how many goods or services are sold. Variable cost changes according to the level of production and sales. Total cost is the sum of fixed and variable costs. Marginal cost is the change in total expense of producing one more unit. Marketers use breakeven analysis to analyze revenues and costs and to find the profit at various levels of quantity sold. Breakeven analysis helps determine the breakeven point (BEP), the point at which revenues equal costs and beyond which profits begin.

3. **Identify the seven types of demand-based pricing.**

   With skimming pricing, marketers initially price a new product high to attract customers who are willing to pay for unique benefits and high quality. Penetration pricing means initially pricing a new product low to attract many customers quickly and discourage competitors. With prestige pricing, marketers set a price higher than that of the competition to attract customers who will pay more for a higher quality or higher status product. Price lining is setting a separate, specific price for each product in the line. Odd–even pricing is setting prices to end in a certain digit, to influence customer perceptions of the price. With bundle pricing, marketers set one price for two or more related products. With demand-backward pricing, marketers determine the price that will create a desired level of demand, then develop and market the product to fit that price.

4. **Differentiate among markup pricing, cost-plus pricing, and experience curve pricing.**

   All three are cost-based pricing strategies. With markup pricing, resellers in the marketing channel set prices by adding a standard, predetermined percentage to the cost of each product. With cost-plus pricing, marketers add a certain amount or percentage to the cost to arrive at the product's selling price. With experience curve pricing, the marketer prices low to increase the number of units sold. This drives total cost down while the organization gains experience in making the product.

5. **Explain how profit-based pricing operates and analyze two variations.**

   Profit-based pricing is a strategy for setting prices to reach a certain profit target. One variation is target-profit pricing, in which marketers set the dollar amount of profit to be achieved through pricing. A second variation is target-return pricing, in which prices are set to reach a specific measure of profit, such as return on sales, return on investment, or return on assets.

6. **Apply four approaches to competition-based pricing.**

   In customary pricing, you use a traditional or standardized price. In promotional pricing, you temporarily set and communicate lower prices on selected products. In everyday low pricing (EDLP), you set prices that are consistently low compared with the competition. Competitive bidding is pricing that is submitted at the request of a customer, who compares bids among suppliers before making a decision. Negotiated pricing is a system in which marketer and customer discuss and agree on a price.

7. **Show how pricing adjustments affect prices paid by ultimate consumers, organizational customers, and value-chain partners.**

   Monetary price adjustments are upward or downward changes to the list price. Product adjustments are changes to the amount or quality of product offered at the same price. Price discounts and allowances are direct and indirect price breaks to reward customers or value-chain partners for taking actions such as buying during a specific period. Geographic price adjustments may include none, some, or all the shipping costs in the price paid by customers or value-chain partners.

KEY TERMS

breakeven analysis 378
breakeven point (BEP) 378
bundle pricing 383
cost-plus pricing 386
customary pricing 388
demand-backward pricing 384
everyday low pricing (EDLP) 389
experience curve pricing 386
fixed costs 375

list price 393
loss-leader pricing 388
marginal analysis 377
marginal cost 376
marginal revenue 377
market price 393
markup pricing 385
odd–even pricing 383
penetration pricing 381

prestige pricing 382
price lining 383
promotional pricing 388
skimming pricing 381
target-profit pricing 387
target-return pricing 387
total cost 376
variable costs 375

Skill-Building Applications

1. If you were planning to sell your house or apartment, which pricing strategy would you use? Many homeowners expect to negotiate with customers to arrive at a final price. Is this always the best strategy? Why or why not?

2. Wal-Mart uses everyday low pricing (EDLP), while some competitors rely on high–low pricing. What are the advantages and disadvantages of each strategy? Identify a local retailer that competes with Wal-Mart. Should this store switch to EDLP? Why or why not?

3. When selling computers to businesses, companies such as IBM often compete on greater value rather than low price. What can these marketers offer customers to add value rather than adjusting price to compete with lower priced products?

4. The National Geographic Society is a nonprofit organization that makes millions of dollars from the sale of books, magazines, and videos. A rival charges that National Geographic's tax-exempt status allows the organization to price products lower than for-profit competitors. Is it ethical for nonprofit organizations to price in this way? Explain your answer.

5. What are some of the local situations that affect the prices companies like Dunkin' Donuts can set in other countries?

6. How would you go about pricing the plumbing services offered by Roto-Rooter? Would you use cost-based, demand-based, profit-based, or competition-based pricing? Are customary pricing or target-profit pricing good alternatives? Explain your answers.

Getting Involved in Marketing

1. *On Your Own* Calculate the breakeven point for these products:

   a. A bicycle priced at $250 with fixed costs of $400,000 and variable unit costs of $50; the same product with a desired profit of $40,000

   b. A Nike sneaker priced at $65 with fixed costs of $275,000 and variable unit costs of $25; the same product with a desired profit of $35,000

   c. A haircut priced at $30 with fixed costs of $8,000 and variable unit costs of $5; the same product with a desired profit of $1,500

2. *On Your Own* You're a buyer at Viking Office Products, a marketer that sells office supplies by mail to businesses. Would you prefer to buy from a wholesaler or from a manufacturer? How would each choice affect the percentage you add using markup pricing? How would each affect the price your customer pays?

3. *Find Out More* Interview a small business owner about costs, or select a company represented in an online database and develop answers to these questions: What are the fixed costs of the business? What variable costs does the business incur, and how do these costs vary with volume? How does the owner take these costs into account when pricing products? Summarize your findings in a two-page report.

4. *In a Partnership* Work with another student to consider pricing for a new product of your choice. Should you use penetration pricing or skimming pricing? During a classroom debate, let one student argue for penetration pricing and the other argue for skimming pricing. Which argument is more compelling? Why?

5. *In a Team* With two classmates, consider geographic pricing adjustments for a U.S. product being exported to South America.

   a. What geographic pricing would apply if customers want to arrange and pay for their own shipping?

   b. What geographic pricing would help you pass on shipping costs more fairly to customers across South America?

6. *In a Team* With at least two other students, scan newspaper, magazine, television, and World Wide Web advertising for examples of prestige pricing, loss-leader pricing, and everyday low pricing. In each case, how do the ads present the product's value to justify the price? What positioning does the price support in each case? Prepare a presentation to your class about your findings, and include the ads.

INTERNET

Marketing on the Net How Much Is an Advertising Banner Worth?

Once you get a World Wide Web site up and running, how do you attract visitors? For many Web marketers, the answer is to pay for banners, advertising links that appear on someone else's Web site. When a visitor clicks on the banner, the advertiser's home page comes up.

Every site controls the pricing for the banners that appear on its pages. Some set pricing objectives according to the profit they need to generate from advertising in order to support other activities. Others use pricing as a competitive tool to build long-term relationships with major marketers who might otherwise advertise on competing sites.

There are three broad pricing methods used for banners: flat fee, per-exposure, and per-contact. With a flat-fee pricing structure, the site sets a specific price for accepting a banner. The *Wall Street Journal*, for example, has set a flat fee of $20,000 for a month-long banner on some of its Interactive Edition screens. AT&T and Siemens are among the marketers that have bought banner space on selected *Wall Street Journal* screens.

With per-exposure pricing, advertisers pay for every 1,000 hits on the site where their banners are located. The price of the banner is the same whether or not visitors follow the link to the advertiser's site. The cost per thousand exposures ranges from approximately $10 to $80 at major Web sites. Yahoo, for example, is a popular search engine that charges advertisers a price of $20 for every 1,000 exposures. Lycos, another search engine, charges the same price, while a third search engine, Excite, charges $24 for every 1,000 exposures. However, specialized sites—such as those that attract businesspeople—generally require a higher price. On the other hand, the price is often discounted for higher volume, so the more exposures a banner garners, the lower the price paid per exposure.

In contrast, per-contact pricing means that advertisers pay according to the number of people who actually click on the banner to connect with the advertiser's Web site. Whereas per-exposure pricing covers everyone who visits the site where the banner is placed, per-contact pricing covers only those visitors who choose to use the link to the advertiser's Web site. Procter & Gamble negotiated with Yahoo for a so-called "click-through" rate, in which pricing is based on the number of times a banner is clicked divided by the number of exposures. The deal with Yahoo, for banners advertising five brands, gives P&G about the same price as it would have paid per exposure.

Most Web sites are reluctant to use per-contact pricing, and those that do want to set a higher price than would be paid for per-exposure pricing. Given the tremendous growth in Web commerce, pricing structures will probably evolve in new directions as advertisers and Webmasters alike continue to consider what a banner is worth.[1]

Strategies and applications

1. Visit the Yahoo Web site. Why is this an attractive site for an advertising banner? Which marketers do you think might benefit from buying a banner on the Yahoo site?

2. Click on one of the banners at the Yahoo site to follow the link to the marketer's home page. How well did the banner represent what the marketer is offering? Do you think the banner does a good job of encouraging people to click on it? How would you improve the banner?

3. As a marketer placing a banner, which of the three pricing methods would you prefer? As a Web site accepting banners? Indicate the advantages and disadvantages of each method for the company placing the banner and for the site accepting it.

4. How might an organizational marketer use banner pricing at its Web site to strengthen relationships with its suppliers and its business customers?

5. Why would a specialized Web site that draws business or technical visitors be able to charge a higher price for banners?

6. How could a Web marketer gauge the price sensitivity of companies that are seeking banner placements?

Team project

With another student, compare the size, shape, and placement of banners at the Yahoo site with those on both the Lycos site (http://www.lycos.com) and the Excite site (http://www.excite.com). As marketers, which would you prefer? Why? As visitors, on which would you and your partner be more likely to click? Why? Draft a memo to the Webmaster of one of these sites, critiquing the banners and offering suggestions for improvement.

one-to-one IM

http://www.creativecomputers.com

Marketing on the Net   Creative Computers Showcases Pricing on the Web

Fast-changing prices are no problem for Creative Computers. The California-based catalog marketer offers 12,000 hardware and software products in its MacMall catalog (for Macintosh PC users) and its PC Mall catalog (for IBM-compatible PC users). In this highly competitive market, technology is continually evolving even as prices drop, so customers are constantly adjusting their value equations. However, printed materials can't easily keep up when prices are so volatile, changing weekly or even daily in some cases. That's where Creative Computers' Web site comes in.

The company's home page sets the tone for price competition by using colorful graphics to highlight up-to-date prices on selected items. Then, as visitors browse the product listings in either the MacMall or PC Mall section, they can read about each item and see the current price. When they call the catalog center toll-free to order, customers repeat the priority code shown on each screen to ensure that they are charged the correct price.

Creative Computers knows that its shoppers are always interested in promotional pricing. In each online catalog, visitors can check the Bargain Basement for specially priced products offered in limited quantities. As in the Bargain Basement sections of the printed MacMall and PC Mall catalogs, these special prices are valid only as long as supplies last—which might be a day, a week, or a month. Online shoppers can't tell how many of each product is left, which adds a sense of urgency to the purchase decision.

Regulars at the Creative Computers Web site know to look for the Deal of the Day, which is valid until 5 p.m. Pacific Standard Time. Each day, the site features some computer product at a super-low price. This price promotion is one of the ways Creative Computers encourages return visits from shoppers and browsers alike.

Price competition isn't the only way Creative Computers differentiates itself from rivals. Creative Computers also maintains a comprehensive online listing of manufacturers' Web sites. At this section, visitors are just a mouse click away from hundreds of computer company home pages. That kind of special service enhances the value that customers perceive and gives them another reason, in addition to price, to visit the Creative Computers Web site again and again.[2]

Strategies and applications

1. Visit the Creative Computers Web site and go to the Bargain Basement section of the PC Mall or the MacMall. How does the company showcase the special prices on these items? Can you suggest another way to highlight these prices on the Web site? Would you add a Bargain Basement link to the company's home page? Explain your answer.

2. Where else on the Web would you suggest that Creative Computers buy banners to advertise its business? Would you mention specific Bargain Basement products and prices on any banners? Why or why not?

3. Why would Creative Computers limit its Deal of the Day pricing to orders placed before a certain time? What are the advantages and disadvantages of setting a deadline?

4. Why is it particularly important for marketers on the Web to be aware of the prices set by competitors for the same or similar goods or services? How would shoppers know about a lower price offered by a competitor? Should Creative Computers track price changes by every Web-based or catalog competitor? Why or why not?

5. Why does Creative Computers use odd-even pricing? Take into consideration the competitive environment and customer perceptions as you answer. Do you think Creative Computers should apply a different pricing strategy? If so, which do you think would be appropriate? Why?

6. Should Creative Computers allow negotiated pricing on higher-priced computer systems? List the advantages and disadvantages to the company. How do you think customers would react to being able to negotiate prices on some products but not on other products?

Team project

With other students, compare the Creative Computers Web site with the Web site of a competitor such as MicroWarehouse or MacWarehouse (both reached at http://www.warehouse.com). Does the competitor offer any special prices or bargains? How does it alert visitors to these special offers? Which Web site's presentation of special prices is more effective? Why? Summarize your team's findings in a report to the class.

internetempowerment

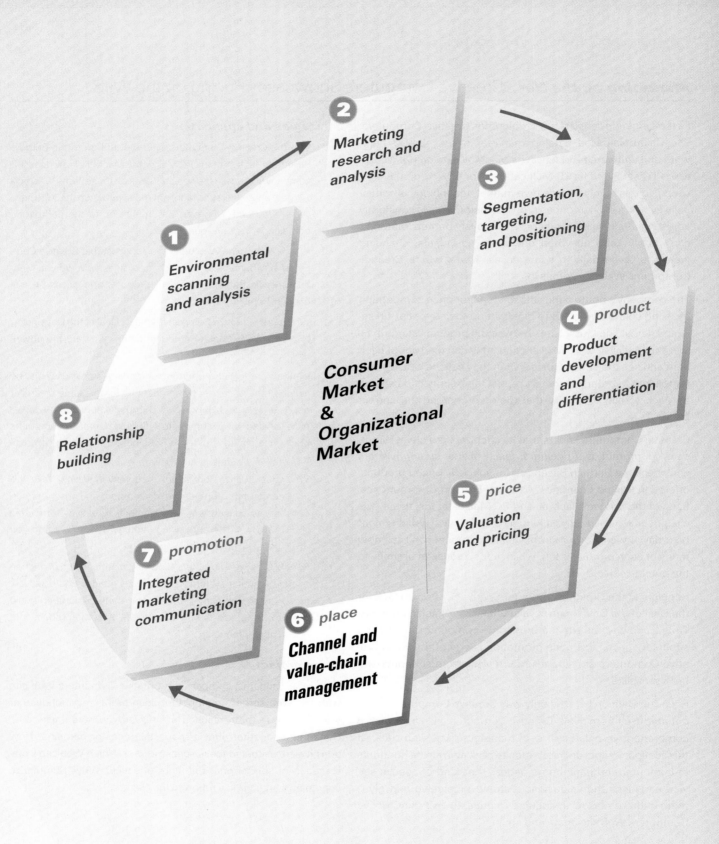

2 Marketing research and analysis

3 Segmentation, targeting, and positioning

1 Environmental scanning and analysis

4 product
Product development and differentiation

Consumer Market & Organizational Market

8 Relationship building

5 price
Valuation and pricing

7 promotion
Integrated marketing communication

6 place
Channel and value-chain management

PART **6**

Channels and Value-Chain Management

Part 6 focuses on the new relationships being forged among organizations in the value chain. Chapter 14 introduces channel concepts and the interdependencies among partners in the value chain. The chapter opening profile shows how the founders of American Connoisseur built a successful small business by linking with channel partners to reach targeted customers. Chapter 15 explores the role of wholesaling and retailing in the value chain. The profile shows how Yaohan is expanding to reach shoppers around the world. Chapter 16 examines the use of logistics management to support relationship building throughout the value chain. The profile describes how Dell Computer teamed up with Roadway Logistics Systems to cut delivery costs and boost efficiency.

14

Channel Concepts and Value-Chain Management

Learning Goals

After you have read and studied this chapter, you should be able to:

1. Define the marketing channel and explain its position in the value chain.
2. Show how channel partners add value to satisfy customers along the value chain.
3. Contrast direct and indirect channels.
4. Explain how marketers use multiple channels, strategic channel alliances, and reverse channels.
5. Demonstrate how intensive, selective, and exclusive forms of distribution allow for the proper market coverage.
6. Identify the issues marketers must analyze before making channel decisions.
7. Differentiate between horizontal and vertical channel conflict, and show how vertical marketing systems operate.

PROFILE

American Connoisseur meets customers in many channels

When David Zilko and Peter Gikas started their new business, American Connoisseur, they had four marinade recipes—and no way to get the finished products to customers. The two Michigan entrepreneurs had noticed that no one was marketing gourmet meat marinades targeted to home cooks. As cooking enthusiasts, they mixed oils, vinegars, and herbs until they came up with four tasty flavors. Then they set out to bring their products to home chefs across the United States. To do this, they had to sell to businesses that reach such customers.

Reasoning that upscale customers shop for gourmet cookware and specialty foods at department stores, they initially sent samples to 13 top stores. Within three weeks, they had an order from Hudson's. Within six months, they had orders from eight more big stores, including Macy's. The entrepreneurs also sold the marinades through several midwestern supermarkets.

Looking beyond traditional stores, Zilko convinced a buyer for the QVC television home-shopping channel to try the Dijon marinade. "She loved it and put it on the air in a 45-second spot that produced $16,000 of [customer] orders," he says. He also arranged for CompuServe, a commercial online service, to offer the marinades to its subscribers.

These days, American Connoisseur is an international marketer. Worldwide sales are close to $1 million a year as the company markets marinades in Europe and Japan. More expansion is on the way as Zilko and Gikas find additional channels to bring their products to cooks all over the globe.[1]

Hudson's, Macy's, QVC, and CompuServe are just a few of the partners that help bring American Connoisseur together with customers who want their products. In this first of three chapters about channel and value-chain management—one of the eight universal marketing processes—you'll examine how customers benefit when everyone in the marketing channel works together to serve their needs. You'll see what channel partners do, and you'll look at quality and customer satisfaction in marketing channels. After a discussion of both consumer and business-to-business channels, this chapter explores a variety of channel options. Given those options, you'll learn how to design marketing channels and manage relationships with channel partners.

Linking Customers and Marketers Through the Value Chain

To gain and sustain competitive advantage, a firm must not only understand its own value chain, but that of upstream and downstream suppliers and consumers.

Jennifer Patterson
Grainger Center for Distribution Management[2]

David Zilko and Peter Gikas learned that products sell better when customers can obtain them conveniently. If American Connoisseur marketed just by selling to home cooks who visited the company's Michigan offices, customers who live far away would have to make a long trip to buy a relatively inexpensive product—and few would bother. To serve customers who did make the trip, Zilko and Gikas would have had to complete dozens or even hundreds of individual marketing exchanges every day. The entrepreneurs would have needed to stock enough marinades to satisfy customer demand. They would also have had to accept cash, checks, or credit cards in payment and wrap the marinades for customers to take home.

Handling these and all the other functions connected with individual marketing exchanges can be time-consuming and costly. That's why American Connoisseur partnered with businesses that have contact with customers in other cities and countries. Those businesses assumed responsibility for completing the exchange process with customers and establishing close relationships. In the context of the four Ps ◄———⏌ **(p. 20)**, this process corresponds to *place*.

A **marketing channel** is the network of partners in the value chain that cooperate to bring products from producers to ultimate consumers. *Ultimate consumers* are people who buy products for their own use. For example, your family members are ultimate consumers when they buy food at the grocery store or services from Jiffy-Lube. To reach ultimate consumers, American Connoisseur partnered with department stores, supermarkets, television home-shopping channels, and commercial online information services. Figure 14.1 shows how channels make marketing exchanges more efficient.

In the past, marketers tried to establish relationships with partners in the marketing channel, but there was often conflict between them, and the flow of goods could be slow and inefficient. There was often no customer orientation among channel members. More recently, however, technology such as electronic

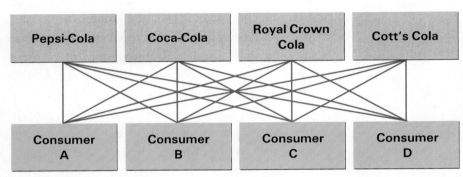

Number of exchanges without channel partners:
4 cola marketers × 4 consumers = 16 exchanges

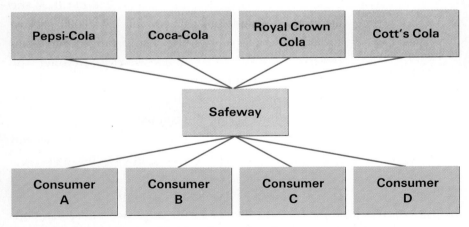

Number of exchanges with one channel partner:
4 cola marketers + 4 consumers = 8 exchanges

F I G U R E   **14.1**   **How Channels Make Marketing More Efficient**

Without marketing channels, four cola marketers would have to complete a total of 16 exchanges to get their products to four consumers. However, going through one channel partner, such as the Safeway supermarket chain, cuts in half the number of exchanges, from 16 to 8.

marketing channel

the network of partners in the value chain that cooperate to bring products from producers to ultimate consumers

logistics

the management of product and information flows throughout the value chain to increase efficiency and speed

data interchange ◄———┘ **(p. 210)** has made it possible for members of the value chain to become more closely linked, making the flow of goods much faster and more efficient. There is also a much stronger customer orientation that has led organizations in the value chain to respond better to their customers' wants and needs.

Marketing Channels and the Value Chain

The value chain ◄———┘ **(p. 50)** is the sequence of activities that must be performed to create, deliver, and service a value package that satisfies customers. The value chain spans all the functions concerned with researching customer needs, obtaining raw materials, turning them into useful products, transporting products to the marketplace, combining them with services to form the value package, and communicating with customers to complete the exchange. The new focus on a customer orientation has led all organizations to see each partner in the value chain as the customer for the partner in the preceding link and the supplier to the customer in the following link.

The value chain, then, consists of a series of exchange relationships that end with business customers or ultimate consumers. Figure 14.2 shows the value chain for American Connoisseur. Upstream partners (suppliers) in the value chain have adopted a customer orientation and are now seen as a valuable resource when their customers are designing and producing products (value packages). Through partners at the upstream end of its value chain, American Connoisseur obtains marinade ingredients such as oils and herbs, bottles and labels for packaging, and other supplies.

Suppliers
- Oils
- Herbs
- Vinegars
- Bottles
- Labels

Upstream

American Connoisseur

Channel Partners
- Department stores
- Specialty stores
- Television home-shopping channels
- Commercial online database services

Consumers

**Downstream
(marketing channel)**

F I G U R E **14.2**

Value Chain for American Connoisseur
In American Connoisseur's value chain, suppliers upstream provide the ingredients and materials needed to produce the company's flavored marinades. Downstream, the company brings its products to consumers through relationships with partners in the marketing channel.

For producers, another set of marketing exchanges takes place downstream as products flow to the ultimate consumer. Involved in such exchanges are marketers such as wholesalers and retailers, as discussed in detail in Chapter 15. American Connoisseur's owners must establish close relationships with a variety of channel partners to bring their products to consumers. Similarly appliance manufacturers such as General Electric work with channel partners that not only sell but also install and service GE products to complete the exchange and satisfy consumers.

Logistics is the management of product and information flows throughout the value chain to increase efficiency and speed and thus strengthen relationships among the participants.[3] The result is that customers can acquire products how, where, and when they want, and in the form that satisfies their needs. You'll learn more about logistics in Chapter 16.

Value-chain management (or *supply-chain management*) is the coordination of all the functions and partner relationships in the value chain. Using value-chain management, marketers look at the value added by each function and each partner at every step in the value chain, both inside and outside the organization. They also check for problems that slow the flow of products and information through the value chain, hurting efficiency and delaying response to customer needs. Then marketers can improve the system by making changes such as adding or changing channel partners, speeding delivery, and cutting costs.[4] Continuous improvement ⬅ **(p. 288)** of the value chain can be a powerful competitive advantage for any organization.

Channel Partners and the Value They Add

Channel partners include agents or brokers, wholesalers, retailers, and value-added resellers, as shown in Table 14.1. (At times, some channel partners are termed *distributors* or *dealers*.) Channel partners are sometimes referred to in a general way as *intermediaries* or *middlemen*. These vague terms, however, fail to describe the precise role of partners in channels. In addition, the terms are becoming outdated: they assume that channel partners stand between marketers and their customers, whereas in reality, channel partners form a web that enhances the exchange process by performing functions of three basic types that add value for customers. These are exchange functions, logistical functions, and facilitation functions.[5]

TABLE **14.1** **Roles of Partners in the Marketing Channel**

Channel Partner	Role in Marketing Channel
Agents, brokers	Channel partners that match marketers with wholesalers or, in organizational markets, with customers
Wholesalers	Channel partners that buy from marketers or through agents and resell products to retailers
Retailers	Channel partners that sell products to consumers
Value-added resellers	Channel partners that buy products from marketers, add value by modifying or otherwise enhancing them, and resell products to customers

Exchange functions are activities related to matching buyers and sellers. Instead of selling to customers on an individual basis, a marketer can arrange for a channel partner, such as a retailer, to match products with customers, which is an efficient way for producers to reach more customers in more markets. Customers benefit because they don't have to approach many different marketers to find what they need. For example, Goodyear sells tires to Sears, which in turn sells the tires to customers who shop at local stores. This helps Goodyear get tires to customers in markets that have Sears stores, and it helps customers find a selection of tires at a single location.

Logistical functions are activities related to transporting, storing, and sorting products. Channel members bring products to convenient locations and hold them until customers buy. They also separate products according to quality or other considerations, bring similar products together to supply customers' needs, and make smaller quantities available to suit customers' use patterns. For example, paper marketers sell in large, truckload quantities to Alco Standard, a North American wholesaler. Alco Standard then breaks these huge shipments down to the smaller quantities that its business customers want to buy.[6]

value-chain management

the coordination of all the functions and partner relationships in the value chain

Facilitation functions are activities related to completing the marketing exchange, such as financing purchases and gathering and disseminating information. For example, Sears offers a credit card that customers can use to charge their store purchases of products from Goodyear and other marketers. To help customers buy Goodyear tires, Sears offers information about tire sizes, warranties, and so forth. Sears mounts the tires and handles any follow-up services needed. The retailer also provides Goodyear with marketing information such as the number and type of tires sold in each market. This helps Goodyear plan production and new products.

Depending on the number of partners involved, a marketing channel may be long or short. In *long channels*, products pass through the hands of several partners to reach ultimate consumers. Many consumer products move through long channels because marketers need partners to reach the large and diverse consumer market. In *short channels*, fewer partners—sometimes no partners at all—are needed to help handle the products. Shorter channels are often used for organizational products, because the organizational or business-to-business market is smaller and less geographically dispersed than the consumer market.

There are marketing channels for both goods and services, although service channels are usually much shorter. Partners in a service channel provide many of the same functions as partners that work with tangible products (with the exception of physically handling and transporting products). For example, travel agents bring together buyers and sellers of travel services, helping customers make airplane, train, and hotel reservations. Similarly, brokerage firms such as Charles Schwab bring together buyers and sellers of stocks and other financial instruments. Customers can buy in person, by telephone, or by computer, any of the thousands of investments that are offered.[7]

Regardless of the type of product being marketed, the exchange, logistical, and facilitation functions are required in any exchange process. Depending on the arrangement with each marketer, channel partners may perform some or all of these functions. Here's how one small business prospered by becoming a specialist in the marketing channel for restaurants.

SMALL BUSINESS WATCH

Takeout Taxi takes off

Kevin Abt, the founder of Takeout Taxi, tells his value-chain partners to "leave the driving to us." Each Takeout Taxi franchise is a small business that provides the logistical and exchange functions to link participating restaurants with eat-at-home families. Takeout Taxi delivers restaurant meals to people who wish to save time by avoiding trips to restaurants—a convenience that adds place utility. The process starts when a consumer calls Takeout Taxi to order a take-out meal from a restaurant menu, setting the wheels in motion for an at-home marketing exchange.

Takeout Taxi's employees log each consumer's order and the delivery details, using a sophisticated computerized system. Then they alert the restaurant to prepare the food. A company driver picks up the meal from the restaurant and whisks it to the customer's door. For this service, Takeout Taxi collects the cost of the meal (to pay the restaurant) plus 15 percent from the customer, and charges restaurants an additional percentage.

Takeout Taxi's services add value for consumers and restaurants alike. "Busy people don't want to fit their lives around their dinner schedule," says Abt, explaining why take-out meals are booming. For their part, restaurants don't have to maintain a delivery staff, and they benefit from Takeout Taxi's marketing efforts as well. "Takeout Taxi drops 40,000 mailings advertising delivery from our restaurant every few months," says Stacy Kincaid of the restaurant Red Hot & Blue in Alexandria, Virginia. "Since we signed on with them in June, delivery more than doubled."[8]

What marketing information might Takeout Taxi offer restaurants to help them market even more effectively?

Marketing Channels, Quality, and Customer Satisfaction

In the past, marketing channels were regarded as merely convenient pipelines through which products traveled in the journey from producer to consumer. The relationships between channel members were often relatively weak. That type of marketing channel is disappearing. Marketers now recognize that channels offer real opportunities to create a competitive advantage by working jointly to satisfy customer needs more efficiently and more effectively than rivals. As Greg Podshadley, an executive with high-tech marketer Silicon Graphics in California, says about working with his channel partners: "You have to work as a team and do what has to be done, or you lose the market."[9]

This is especially true in today's global economy, where marketers and customers can easily buy and sell in other countries. The ability to use efficient marketing channels to please customers is now a key skill for success in world markets. No less important is the need to maintain quality throughout the value chain, ensuring that products are available when, where, and how consumers and organizational customers want them.

One marketer's survey of 18,000 business customers in 16 countries revealed that higher customer satisfaction—and higher sales—were linked to such quality-related activities in the marketing channel as on-time deliveries, quick response to orders, products delivered in good condition, and prompt attention to customer problems.[10] As you design and manage your channels for customer satisfaction, you'll want to pay particular attention to using cross-border channels to reach international customers, using technology in your channels, and adding extra value to channel relationships. These tasks are discussed next.

For many marketers, the world has become one huge market. This display of Kodak products is in Luxor, Egypt. However, it is not always easy to establish a network of wholesale and retail outlets to service consumers in other countries. To do that, marketers need to establish close global marketing networks that smooth the flow of goods among countries. What products from other countries have you noticed in large department stores?

Using Cross-Border Channels to Reach International Customers

Channel partners can perform two key roles for international marketers. First, they move products between countries. Trading companies and export management companies are two channel organizations that specialize in global trade. They can be particularly helpful when marketers are unfamiliar with certain markets and do not know how to develop the necessary relationships. Mitsubishi, the world's largest company, began as a trading company importing raw materials for Japanese manufacturers and exporting manufacturers' products to far-flung destinations. The company now serves 45,000 international customers, including many in its _keiretsu_, a group of companies with interlocking ownership that work cooperatively.[11]

Second, channel partners match imported products with customers within their countries. This helps marketers from other countries get their products to convenient locations where local customers can buy. Without this ability, marketers often can't start or continue relationships with customers in the targeted countries. For example, the Swedish wholesaler Ferro Engros handles 30,000 gardening and building products from manufacturers all over the world. Manufacturers that want to reach Swedish consumers can work through Ferro, which has established relationships with local retailers using CD-ROM catalogs and electronic online ordering systems.[12]

Working through the right marketing channels within a country can make the difference between market leadership and lagging market share. Just ask Eastman Kodak, which has been battling archrival Fuji Photo Film in Japan. For decades Kodak was unable to establish relationships with four channel partners that, together, make 70 percent of all the film sales to stores across the country. Kodak's problem was that the distributors had long-standing relationships with Fuji, the market leader. In an attempt to gain access to more marketing channels, Kodak finally filed a trade complaint with the U.S. government.[13]

Using Technology in Marketing Channels: ECR and EDI

Channel members in both consumer and organizational markets are using information technology to improve customer satisfaction throughout the value chain. The idea is to exchange details about customer purchases. With such details, each channel partner can apply its expertise in a cooperative effort to cost-efficiently bring products to customers when and where needed.

Marketers in the grocery industry now use efficient consumer response. **Efficient consumer response (ECR)** is an electronic system that creates an efficient, continual flow of grocery products through the value chain in response to store-by-store data on consumer purchases. With ECR, supermarkets electronically speed scanner data about consumer purchases to upstream members of the value chain. Manufacturers use the data to plan what and when to produce, and channel partners use the data to restock stores. Products move through the value chain at the right time and in the right amounts, cutting costs for all participants. This coordination strengthens value-chain relationships and improves consumer satisfaction because the stores always have what shoppers want.[14] In addition, such systems create a competitive advantage for participants because of improved response time and efficiency.

efficient consumer response (ECR)

an electronic system that creates an efficient, continual flow of grocery products through the value chain in response to store-by-store data on consumer purchases

Many other industries use electronic data interchange (EDI), the computer-to-computer exchange of purchasing documents and information between marketers and their organizational customers. Because information flows quickly through the value chain, channel members can process orders more effectively and less expensively than is possible with paper-based systems. As a result, customers at each link in the value chain know exactly when and where to expect their products, and this certainty helps cement long-term relationships.[15]

At the retail end of the value chain, Wal-Mart and other stores have gained a competitive edge by combining EDI with an automatic reordering system known as *quick response*. Quick response allows nonfood retailers to do what food retailers do with ECR: quickly replace what customers buy so that stores never run out. For example, Wal-Mart works with VF, the maker of Wrangler jeans, to keep store shelves full. Every night, VF's computers get store-by-store data from Wal-Mart's computers about Wrangler sales. Replacements reach stores quickly. Since Wal-Mart sells millions of pairs of Wrangler jeans every year, quick response helps keep its (and VF's) customers happy.[16]

Adding Extra Value to Channel Partnerships

An increasing number of channel partners are building closer customer relationships by taking on functions their customers once performed. This practice, which blurs the defining line between certain channel members, frees business customers to concentrate on what they do best. For example, Sales Systems Ltd. in Virginia, a $20 million distributor of industrial fasteners, now performs quality control tests formerly handled by its manufacturer customers. The distributor even assembles, packages, and labels parts kits, another task its customers used to do. These extra services have strengthened the company's channel partnerships—and boosted sales by $5 million annually.[17]

In addition, channel members can offer extra value and build relationships by simply providing more or better information. This is the approach used by Karen Caplan, president of Frieda's, a distributor of shallots and other specialty produce in Los Angeles. Caplan sends out tip sheets to help grocery stores display products and keep them fresh. The sheets also offer ideas for teaching shoppers to use the products when they cook.[18] Frieda's customers learn from these tip sheets and pass information on to customers, adding value all the way to the end of the value chain.

One secret to being a successful marketer is to add more value to products than is expected by others in the value chain or by consumers. Frieda Caplan, left, and her daughters, Jackie and Karen, apply that concept to their distributorship. They provide tips sheets for their dealers on how to use their exotic produce for creating healthy and delicious meals; retailers then pass this information along to consumers. Have you seen produce and other products in the grocery store that you didn't know how to use? Would you be willing to try them if someone showed you how they are used?

Before you go on . . .

A. What is a marketing channel and how does it fit in the value chain?

B. What functions do value-chain partners perform?

direct channels

marketing channels in which the marketer completes the marketing exchange directly with the customer

indirect channels

marketing channels that include one or more channel partners that help the marketer complete exchanges with customers

Analyzing Channel Options for Building Customer Relationships

Marketers can get their products to customers in a variety of ways. **Direct channels** are marketing channels in which the marketer completes the marketing exchange directly with the customer. In contrast, **indirect channels** include one or more channel partners that help the marketer complete the exchange with customers.

The channel option you choose depends on which of the functions of channel management your organization is willing to handle. Remember, all the exchange, logistical, and facilitation functions are needed to complete a marketing exchange with customers. In deciding whether to use direct or indirect channels—or both—think about which channel functions match your core competencies **(p. 39)**. Also determine how each channel option fits into your overall marketing strategy for achieving organizational goals and satisfying customer needs. The next sections analyze both direct and indirect channel options.

Reaching Consumers Through Marketing Channels

Marketers of consumer goods or services can reach customers in four ways, as shown in Figure 14.3. Some marketers use just one of these channels, while others use two, three, or all four. With a direct channel, the marketer brings products to customers without help from channel partners. For example, Discover offers its credit card services to consumers by mail and telephone.

Marketers can also reach consumers using three other types of channels, all of which are indirect. First, the marketer can reach consumers through retailers. This is often the choice for carmakers and food manufacturers, which produce expensive products and large quantities of goods, respec-

FIGURE **14.3**

Four Channels to Reach Consumers
Both direct and indirect marketing channels can help marketers reach consumers. In a direct channel, the marketer doesn't work with any channel partners, whereas in an indirect channel, the marketer works with one or more channel partners to reach consumers.

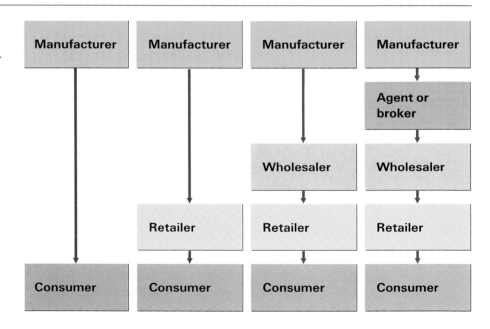

tively. For example, Spanish olive growers, the world's largest producers of olive oil, have tapped channel partners such as the Cortes Ingles department store in Spain to sell their product to cooks in Europe and around the world.[19] The following case shows how a small software company strengthened relationships with its partners in consumer marketing channels.

Applying the Concepts
Courting partners in consumer channels

Sally Narodick wants children to learn thinking skills from orangutan drummer Oranga Banga. Narodick is CEO of Edmark, a $23 million company that

markets award-winning educational software for young people from toddlers to teens. Not long ago, Edmark's sales had stalled because its products, offered through indirect marketing channels, weren't reaching enough consumers. Like many smaller businesses, Edmark faced the challenge of moving its products into more stores.

Narodick decided to apply value-chain management to get Edmark products into the giant retail chains, one of the first destinations for parents who buy educational software. Looking at chain-store buyers as customers in the next link of the value chain, her sales staff researched buyers' needs, demonstrated Edmark software, and shared the company's integrated marketing communication plans. Narodick also sent out teams to train store employees and demonstrate Edmark products across the country.

Courting the chain-store buyers took time and money, but the investment paid off: CompUSA and other big chains bought the product line. Within a year, Narodick doubled the number of stores in her marketing channel to 5,000. Edmark's sales and profits soared—and channel partners prospered by satisfying their customers too.[20]

Typically, products such as children's software are most easily sold through established retail stores. However, promoting a new product in these stores is difficult because they are already overloaded. Therefore, a marketer must create more value in the value chain than competitors in order to win shelf space. That's what Edmark has done with its educational software. How important do you think the shelf display shown here is to the total value package?

Make marketing decisions

1. Why would chain-store buyers care about Edmark's integrated marketing communication plans for reaching parents?

2. How can CompUSA help Edmark learn more about its target market?

3. How do you think CompUSA would react if Edmark began selling its most popular products exclusively through direct channels?

4. What should Narodick do if CompUSA wants to carry one of Edmark's popular products exclusively, so competing retailers can't sell it?

Second, marketers can go through wholesalers to get products to retailers for purchase by consumers. Wholesalers often make the process more efficient by breaking down shipments of products from manufacturers into the smaller lots needed by individual stores. This efficiency appeals to marketers that produce in limited quantities or that make specialized or low-price products. Alpine Lace Brands is one example. The company gets its specialty low-fat cheeses to supermarkets and other food retailers through food wholesalers.[21]

Smaller marketers or marketers that are not familiar with wholesale and retail channels may use agents. Serving as matchmakers for consumer marketers, agents help get the producer's products to the wholesalers and retailers that can bring them to the appropriate consumer segments and markets. Bear in mind, however, that working through agents lengthens the marketing channel and adds another layer of complexity—and costs.

Issues for critical thinking

Fruits and vegetables usually cost more at the supermarket than at the farm stand. What functions do channel partners perform when bringing fresh produce to local supermarkets? Do you think the value of these functions justifies the increase in price? Why or why not?

Reaching Organizational Customers Through Marketing Channels

To reach organizational customers, business-to-business marketers can use as many as four types of marketing channels, as illustrated in Figure 14.4. Since the organizational market covers fewer buyers and is more concentrated than the consumer market, marketers don't need as many channel partners to reach organizational customers as they do to reach consumers. That's why marketing channels to organizational customers are generally shorter than channels to consumers.

FIGURE **14.4**   **Four Channels to Reach Organizational Customers**

Marketing channels to reach organizational customers are usually shorter than those used to reach consumers, because the organizational market has fewer buyers and is more concentrated. As in the consumer market, channels to reach organizational customers may be direct (with no channel partners) or indirect (with one or more channel partners).

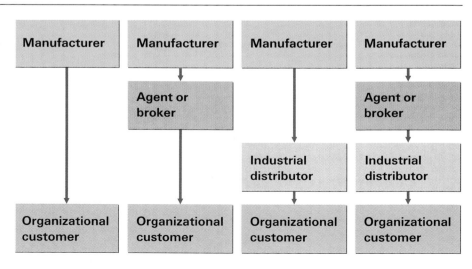

Like consumer marketers, organizational marketers can bring their products directly to their business, government, or nonprofit customers. A direct channel is appropriate when you're marketing expensive or complex products, and when you target large organizations that require considerable service before, during, or after the purchase. By going direct, you can be more responsive to customer needs. For example, L.M. Ericsson, a $10 billion telecommunications equipment marketer based in Sweden, uses a direct channel to reach corporations that buy its products, so it can provide design, installation, and testing services.[22]

The three other business-to-business marketing channels used to reach organizational customers are all indirect. For example, you may want to go through an agent, known as a *manufacturer's representative*, to reach organizational customers. Because agents focus on particular product categories or markets, they have contacts and information that can be useful in bringing buyers and sellers together. Another option is to work with one or more *industrial distributors*, marketing organizations that perform many of the functions that wholesalers perform in consumer marketing channels. Such distributors have ready access to certain markets. Black & Decker, for example, sells commercial tools and fasteners through manufacturer's reps as well as through industrial distributors and by approaching customers directly.[23]

In addition, you may want to market your products through agents who call on industrial distributors. Industrial distributors are responsible for reaching the organizational customers that buy and use your products. This is one of the longest channels you can use to reach organizational customers, but it is appropriate when you need to connect with industrial distributors that understand and service specialized markets.

Using Direct Channels

Some producers prefer to shorten their channels by reaching out directly to customers. It is easier to establish close relationships by going direct. Producers that use direct channels can contact customers in one of two ways: direct marketing or direct selling. *Direct marketing* is a two-way process of marketing communication through which marketers offer products and customers buy without contact with channel partners. For example, apparel marketer Lands' End mails catalogs directly to customers, inviting purchases by telephone, mail, fax, or via the Internet. This is a direct channel, because no partners are involved in the marketing exchange.

Direct selling refers to direct *sales* contacts between sales people and customers. When Mary Kay representatives visit customers' homes or workplaces to market cosmetics, they're using direct selling in a direct channel. Direct selling can also be used in indirect channels. For example, Edward D. Jones & Company is a stock brokerage firm that uses direct selling to market investments door to door to consumers in small communities. Financial services firms such as Goldman Sachs link with channel partners such as Edward D. Jones to sell investments to consumers.[24]

Direct marketing by catalog has become more and more popular as marketers have discovered how to target smaller and smaller market segments. These customized catalogs are popular not only in the United States, but in countries throughout the world. Do you think the majority of catalogs you receive are well targeted to your needs?

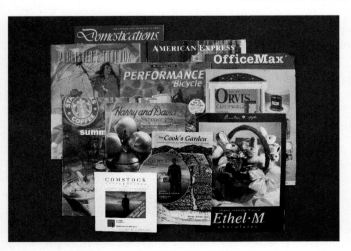

Marketers such as Mary Kay, Avon, and Amway combine a direct channel with a variation of direct selling called *multilevel marketing* or *network marketing*. In this arrangement, the marketer sells products to individuals who serve as independent distributors in their local areas. These distributors both sell to customers and recruit and sell to other independent distributors, a practice that expands the number of customers the marketer can reach. Multilevel marketing is growing as more marketers use direct channels to reach global markets. Using multilevel marketing, U.S.-based Amway annually sells $40 million worth of household products in Hungary.[25] Here's how Avon uses multilevel marketing around the world.

GLOBAL ISSUES

Avon meets worldwide customers one-on-one

Direct and personal: that's the best description for the multilevel marketing arrangement used by Avon. Nearly 2 million representatives ring doorbells around the world to market Avon's personal care and household products. This direct, door-to-door contact brings in $4.5 billion in annual sales, two-thirds from North and South America and one-third from Europe and Japan.

Representatives, who market to friends, neighbors, and work associates, are the backbone of Avon's direct channel. The company is also adapting to the buying behavior of local customers. In the United States and the United Kingdom, where an increasing number of women work outside the home, customers can call a toll-free number to receive a catalog and to place orders. Now Avon has arranged to mail Avon brochures to prospects by using names from the huge customer database of *Reader's Digest*.

Thanks to the direct channel, Avon representatives can meet one-on-one with customers, learn about individual needs, and then recommend and demonstrate appropriate products to satisfy those needs. Representatives show new catalogs every few weeks and respond to what, when, and where customers want to buy. This kind of personal contact helps Avon maintain profitable, long-standing relationships with customers in 125 countries.[26]

Do you think Avon should also offer its products in department stores? Why or why not?

Using Multiple Channels

Depending on the markets and customer segments you're targeting, one marketing channel may not be enough. After you've segmented your target market, you may find that you can establish relationships more effectively through different channels. Then you'll choose another approach: **dual distribution**, the use of more than one channel to bring the same product (or similar products under different brand names) to several customer segments.[27] Figure 14.5 shows how multiple channels operate to allow customers in each segment to obtain products how, when, and where they prefer.

dual distribution

the use of more than one channel to bring the same product (or similar products under different brand names) to several customer segments

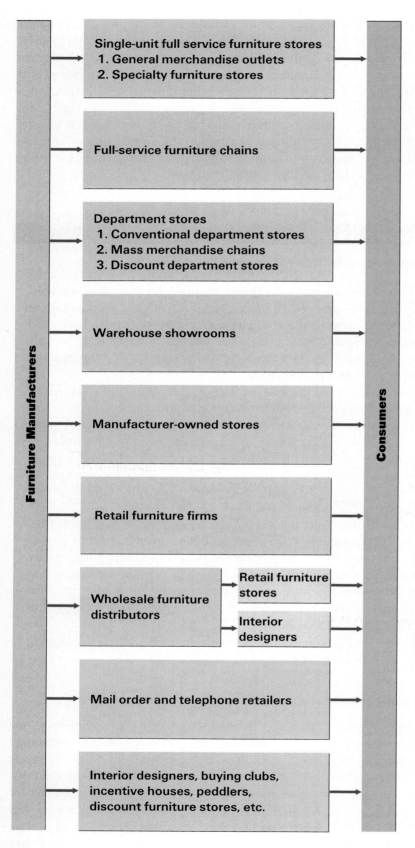

FIGURE **14.5** Multiple Channels for Furniture Marketing

Dual distribution is common in the furniture industry, where manufacturers work through a variety of channels to reach consumers. Think of the large number of consumers that a manufacturer can reach by establishing relationships with these channel partners.

For example, Cidco, based in California, markets caller-identification equipment through two channels. About 15 percent of its products are sold through stores. The rest are sold through local telephone companies, which offer caller-ID services that require the kind of equipment Cidco provides. This latter channel is convenient for customers, who can arrange to buy Cidco's device when they order services from the telephone company.[28]

Forging Strategic Channel Alliances

What if you want to bring your products to customers who are already being served by another marketer's channel? The solution lies in the forging of strategic channel alliances, a form of relationship marketing. A **strategic channel alliance** is an agreement in which a marketer uses another marketer's channel to reach customers. By linking with a noncompeting marketer, you can reach the same set of customers and create more value for the customer, who gains convenient access to two products through one channel.

For example, Blockbuster Entertainment arranged to place Coca-Cola soft drinks in its video stores, so customers can buy refreshments as they check out. In a similar arrangement, Calvin Klein Cosmetics placed displays of its CK One unisex fragrance in Tower Records stores. This strategic channel alliance helped catapult CK One to an estimated $65 million in sales.[29]

strategic channel alliance

an agreement in which a marketer uses another marketer's channel to reach customers

reverse channels

channels that bring products from customers to marketers

Arranging Reverse Channels

Traditional marketing channels are intended to bring products to customers. However, customers sometimes need channels to get products (or parts) back to marketers. In such cases, they use **reverse channels**, channels that bring products from customers to marketers. Such channels are particularly important for recycling plastics (such as bottles and printer cartridges) and other materials that would otherwise clog landfills. Many customers care about environmental issues, and reverse channels help them return products to marketers in a convenient way. BMW of North America, for example, has recycling centers to deal with old cars. Drivers receive $500 when they bring a car to BMW for recycling.[30]

Reverse channels can also serve when customers bring broken appliances to regional repair centers maintained by the manufacturers. In addition, marketers can use reverse channels to gather donations of money or goods. For example, the international clothing marketer Benetton set up a reverse channel when it gathered clothing donated by customers in its stores, then distributed the clothes to needy people worldwide.[31]

Planning Channels for Services

As noted earlier, when you're marketing a service, you'll usually use a shorter channel than you might use for a tangible good. After all, you don't have to store or transport services, so you don't need channel partners to handle those functions. But shorter channels also make sense from the customer's perspective. Because services are intangible, customers can't examine your services before they're performed. And because consumption is inseparable from production, customers don't benefit until your services are actually produced. So shorter channels make the purchase, production, and consumption of services faster and more convenient for customers.

Hairdressers, restaurants, financial services firms, and tax preparers are just a few of the service marketers that generally complete marketing exchanges directly with customers. Often relationships with customers are quite close. On the other hand, a number of service marketers use multiple channels, usually a mix of direct and indirect channels, to reach their customers. American Airlines, for example, markets through direct channels (by telephone, by mail, through the Internet, and at company-owned ticketing offices) as well as through indirect channels such as travel agents. This allows customers in various segments to choose the channels that best fit their needs.

Before you go on . . .

A. How do direct channels differ from indirect channels?

B. How are dual distribution, strategic channel alliances, and reverse channels used?

intensive distribution

a channel design in which you market your products through as many outlets as possible

selective distribution

a channel design in which products are marketed through a limited number of outlets

Intensive distribution requires getting your products into as many stores as possible. However, new products such as Milky Way Lite must first compete for shelf space. Due to the abundance of products, stores are reluctant to place new products on the shelves unless producers pay them a fee. On the other hand, new low-fat products appeal to many consumers, and stores may be willing to carry them as a test. Can you see the importance of building store relationships into any product design and development program?

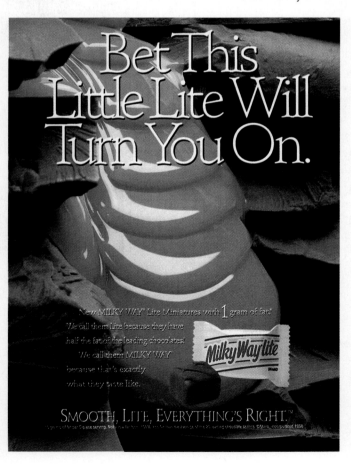

Designing and Managing Marketing Channels to Build Relationships

For marketers of goods and services alike, channel management is the key to profitably bring products to customers. Channel strategy starts with an assessment of your overall organizational and marketing objectives. A customer orientation is a critical part. Then you look at the role you expect channel management to play in building customer relationships. This analysis lays the groundwork for designing appropriate marketing channels.

In designing channels, consider the coverage you need to reach the markets and customer segments you're targeting. As you weigh your channel alternatives, you have to analyze issues that can affect channel decisions. Six basic types are presented later in this chapter. Once you've selected your channels, you must actively manage relationships with channel partners by understanding channel cooperation, conflict, leadership, and, in some cases, vertical marketing systems.

Designing Channels for Market Coverage

Some marketers need only one location to reach their markets and customer segments, while others need thousands of locations. When you do market analysis to determine the market coverage necessary to reach your customers, think about how and where customers in each segment buy products like yours. Also think about your product's stage in the product life cycle **(p. 302)**, which affects the number and type of channel locations you'll need. Then you can design channels that provide either intensive, selective, or exclusive distribution to cover your target market.

Intensive distribution is a channel design in which you market your products through as many outlets as possible. Maximizing your exposure in the marketplace is particularly important with convenience products, which are fairly inexpensive and tend to be purchased frequently and quickly. With intensive distribution, customers can find your product in a large number of locations.

Veryfine, which uses intensive distribution to market bottled fruit juices, is reaching customers across the United States through many supermarkets, convenience stores, and vending machines. In the service sector, Travelers, the giant insurance company, expanded its market coverage to reach more buyers of homeowner's and automobile policies. The company arranged for 100,000 agents of Primerica Financial Services to offer Travelers insurance products to customers across the country. Later, Primerica acquired Travelers and took its name for the entire corporation.[32]

Selective distribution is a channel design in which products are marketed through a limited number of outlets. Selective distribution is appropriate when you're restricting your product to a certain geographic area, when you can't afford wider market coverage, or when you want only outlets that fit your product's image. Just as important, with fewer channel partners, you can develop closer relationships with each.

Glidden uses selective distribution to market its paints in a limited number of stores. By being selective, Glidden can concentrate on supporting fewer channel relationships that produce higher sales.[33] In the service sector, movie producers sometimes limit their films' distribution to certain movie houses to assure a quality presentation.

Exclusive distribution is a channel design in which products are marketed through a few carefully selected partners. This is the opposite of intensive distribution. It's appropriate when you want to work only with channel partners that can adequately support or service your product, or when you want to enhance a luxury image.

Department 56, a gift marketer based in Minnesota, uses this channel design. Its limited-edition collectible gifts, such as miniature porcelain buildings, are offered in only 6,000 small U.S. stores. If Department 56's products were more widely available, they would lose the aura of exclusivity that attracts collectors. Small wonder that the company has a waiting list of 3,000 retailers eager to carry its products.[34] In the service sector, Georgette Klinger uses exclusive distribution to limit the number of skin care salons it operates. This exclusivity allows the company strict control over service quality.

Exclusive distribution is one strategy that allows marketers to establish closer ties with their retail outlets and to build better relationships with customers as well. Department 56 makes the Snow Village products that are sold to collectors through carefully selected stores. The stores' personnel can then be trained to discuss the distinctive features of the models so that they can provide more knowledgeable service. Can you think of some disadvantages of exclusive distribution strategies?

exclusive distribution

a channel design in which products are marketed through a few carefully selected partners

Making Channel Decisions

To support decisions about channel partners and market coverage, you'll want to analyze a number of issues that affect channel design and management. Your top priority is understanding marketing channels from your customer's viewpoint. In addition, you'll want to consider the market environment, your organization's objectives and concerns, product issues, legal issues that affect channel relationships, and the costs and profits associated with various channels and relationships.

Customer Considerations

Are you targeting ultimate consumers or organizational customers? Their buying behaviors differ, which means that the channels normally used for one may not be appropriate for the other. Find out how customers prefer to have access to products like yours. Take the marketing exchange as your starting point, and work your way upstream through the value chain, conducting research to answer three questions:

- What functions provided by channel partners do customers in each segment and market value? (For example, do customers need fast delivery—and will they pay for it?)

- How well do available channels and partners meet customer needs in each segment and market? (Can customers get fast delivery from existing channels and partners that offer products like yours?)

- Which new channels or channel partners might do a better job of meeting the needs of specific customer segments and markets? (That is, what channel options will allow you to offer fast delivery to satisfy customers?)[35]

This analysis helps you understand what your customers expect—information that will allow you to avoid certain channels or partners, choosing instead those that better meet your customers' requirements. Consider Brenda French's experience. As the CEO of French Rags, a knitwear marketer, French found that her customers wanted a better selection of sizes, colors, and styles than her channel partners, department stores, offered. So French switched to a direct channel, hiring her best customers as salespeople to hold parties and take orders for custom-made knit clothing. Now her customers can buy exactly what they want—and French's sales have passed the $5 million mark.[36]

Market Environment Considerations

After you've studied your customers' needs and preferences, you'll want to examine the environment in the markets where you plan to offer your products. Analyze the market to see whether customers are geographically close or dispersed, since these patterns affect your choice of channels and partners. Also look at the number of customers in each market and the way products currently reach them. When you want to reach many customers or cover a larger geographic area, you may need longer channels and more partners to efficiently complete all customer exchanges.

Look, too, at what competitors are doing, and consider how your choice of channels and channel partners can give you a competitive advantage. Dial-A-Mattress built a $65 million business using a direct channel design that was, at the time, unique for bedding marketers. Instead of working with department and specialty stores, the company invited customers to call toll-free to buy bedding. Although competitors are now copying this approach, Dial-A-Mattress has stayed a step ahead by adding commercial online services as channel partners.[37]

Internal Considerations

When you make channel decisions, you must take into account your organization's objectives, marketing plans, and resources. If your organization has ambitious goals for entering new markets, adding new products, or increasing profits, it may be advisable to add or change channels or channel partners. Furthermore, if a channel is disrupted, you may need to make changes so you can still achieve your objectives.

That's what happened to Glomar, a small California business that makes professional baseball bats. More than 90 percent of Glomar's bats were marketed directly to major-league baseball players. But after a baseball strike shut down Glomar's most important market, the company shifted channels to achieve its objectives. "When the major-league players went on strike, we turned to where our five-year plan said to go next: retail," says founder Juan Faxas. The company also signed up dealers who outfit amateur baseball teams. As a result of these channel decisions, the company's sales were even higher than originally planned.[38]

Product Considerations

Your product and its positioning have a lot to do with the channels and partners you decide to use. You would work with one type of channel partner to market an expensive, customized, or sophisticated product and use another type to market a less-expensive, standardized, or simpler product. Physical characteristics make a difference, as well. Perishable products such as ice cream call for special handling that isn't necessary for products such as pencils.

Issues for critical thinking

Can a channel partner's positioning affect your product's positioning? Compare the positioning of Costco, a discount warehouse–style retailer, with that of Saks Fifth Avenue, an upscale department store. How would customers perceive a product that was available at Costco? At Saks? Why?

You'll also want to adjust your channel relationships as your product moves through the product life cycle, as shown in Table 14.2. Consider the changes in channel arrangements made by Sharp and other makers of fax machines. When these products were introduced, they were available directly from the manufacturers and, in some cases, through indirect channels such as office equipment dealers. These channel partners added value in the form of training, supplies, and servicing. Then, as more customers became familiar with fax machines, the manufacturers could add channels with lower levels of support, reaching larger numbers of customers through computer stores, electronics stores, department stores, and mail-order companies.[39]

TABLE **14.2**   **Channel Strategies Through the Product Life Cycle**

	Introduction	Growth	Maturity	Decline
Strategic focus	Market creation	Market expansion	Market share	Migration of customers
Value added by channel	Very high	High/medium	Low	Very low
Channel characteristics				
Number	Few; exclusive	Several; selective	Many; intensive	Few; exclusive
Margins	High	High to medium	Low	Very low
Examples	Boutiques Manufacturer's representatives Value-added resellers	Exclusive dealers Direct sales force Franchisees	Discount stores Off-price retailers Commission sales force	Direct mail Mass marketers

Legal Considerations

Every channel decision has to fit into the legal context of relationships in marketing channels. As discussed in Chapter 3, business arrangements that illegally restrain competition are prohibited by a variety of federal laws. These include the Sherman Antitrust Act, the Clayton Act, the Federal Trade Commission Act, and the Robinson–Patman Act. Among the channel relationships that have come under legal scrutiny are exclusive dealing, dual distribution, tying agreements, and resale restrictions.

Antitrust laws forbid marketers from requiring *exclusive dealing*, which means that marketers are not allowed to insist that a channel partner carry its products exclusively or avoid competing products. In addition, antitrust controversies have arisen over dual distribution arrangements in which marketers with company-owned channel outlets undercut prices charged by independent channel partners or drive independents out of business. Also controversial are *tying agreements,* in which a marketer refuses to sell certain products unless the channel partner agrees to also buy other products. Such agreements were once common in franchising. However, a court ruling against franchiser Chicken Delight clarified current judicial thinking; namely, that tying agreements violate the Sherman Antitrust Act when channel partners can buy the same products from other marketers.[40]

Producers sometimes want to control the resale of their products in the marketing channel. *Resale restrictions* are attempts by a marketer to stipulate the customers and the geographic areas that channel partners may target in reselling efforts. Such practices were once considered illegal under the Sherman Act, but the Supreme Court now applies the "rule of reason" doctrine, leaving the door open for legal action if resale restrictions have a "demonstrable economic effect."[41]

Cost and Profit Considerations

All the functions performed by channel partners come at a price. The price that every channel partner charges its customers is added on as the product moves through the value chain. In the end, all the costs are reflected in the price paid by ultimate consumers. As you plan channel relationships, then, you'll want to weigh the cost of having partners perform certain functions, consider the impact on the price customers pay, and be sure that you'll earn the profits you need to make the marketing exchange beneficial for you as well as your customers.

For example, banks are analyzing costs and profits as they take a fresh look at making financial services available through tellers in branches. These days, automated teller machines, telephone banking, and other technology-based channels, such as banking on the Internet, are faster and cheaper ways of giving customers access to banking products. As a result, "This industry is on its way to eliminating the branch as a delivery system," observes Edward E. Crutchfield, Jr., CEO of First Union, a major bank based in North Carolina.[42]

Relationship Marketing with Channel Partners

Just as relationship building is essential to satisfying ultimate consumers, it's essential to satisfying partners in the value chain. This insight is especially important with respect to complex channel arrangements in which partners perform functions for each other. Although channel cooperation is the goal, channel conflict can be a concern in any value chain. In addition, channel leadership and channel power can affect relationships among channel partners.

Channel Cooperation

The role of each channel partner in the value chain is shaped, in part, by interdependencies within the web of channel relationships. Thus even the longest channels and the most geographically dispersed channel relationships can work well when every partner views the next link in the value chain as its customer. By treating downstream partners like customers and building long-term relationships based on trust and mutual satisfaction, marketers can gain the cooperation they need to keep value-chain functions running smoothly.[43]

Look at the cooperation fostered by Spector Photo in Brussels, Belgium. Spector develops film dropped off by consumers at 600 independent photography shops. Its slogan shows it understands the channel partners' needs: "We don't sell you prints. We sell you profit." Spector offers stores a computer system to track consumer purchases. Computer terminals in every store print out a discount coupon after every six purchases to reward consumers for their loyalty. This system helps stores better serve their customers and secures cooperation for Spector.[44]

Because retail partners are closer to customers than marketers that are upstream in the value chain, it pays to cooperate when retailers make suggestions. Computer maker Packard Bell moved quickly when Larry Mondry, head of merchandising for the giant computer retailer CompUSA, suggested product improvements. "Instead of saying, like some companies, 'Thank you for your comments, we'll change some things next year,' they said, 'Give us two weeks,'" notes Mondry. Right on time, Packard Bell sent CompUSA a new shipment of PCs with the changes Mondry had requested.[45] Now that's cooperation.

Working with others in the marketing
channel can take many forms. In this
ad, 3M takes advantage of the popularity
of Hewlett-Packard printers to sell its
transparency film. Can you see why 3M
might want to partner with HP when developing such film? What do you think
is the advantage to HP?

Channel Conflict

Although channel partners depend on each other to
complete the exchange process, conflicts do erupt in the
channel. After all, every organization has its own objectives and operations. Conflicts can arise when the objectives and operations of one partner don't fit with those
of another partner, or when one partner believes that
another is using its power to upset the balance of cooperation.[46] In general, channel partners face two types of
conflict: horizontal and vertical.

Horizontal conflict can occur among partners at the
same level in the channel, such as two drug retailers or
two drug wholesalers. Even though these partners cooperate with upstream marketers to bring products through
the marketing channel, they also compete for customers,
which causes conflict.

The potential for horizontal conflict increases when a
producer sells a product through a variety of partners at
the same level, such as supermarkets, convenience
stores, or retailers of other types. For example, horizontal conflict erupted when the San Marcos Specialty
Shops shopping center opened near a J.C. Penney store
in San Marcos, Texas. Manufacturer-owned stores in the
new shopping center offered some of the same branded
products as Penney's, only at lower prices. This caused
horizontal conflict between Penney's and the manufacturer-owned stores.[47]

Vertical conflict can occur among partners at different levels in the channel,
such as a producer and a wholesaler or a wholesaler and a retailer. Quaker
Oats, which markets Gatorade drinks, found itself embroiled in vertical conflict after acquiring Snapple Beverages. Snapple products were sold through
independent distributors that delivered to delicatessens, while Quaker sold
Gatorade directly to supermarket and convenience stores. The Snapple distributors objected when Quaker tried to take over their larger store accounts,
and Quaker backed off. To strengthen the relationship with distributors,
Snapple set up a distributor advisory council, through which it hoped to improve its understanding of and response to its partners' concerns.[48]

Slotting and Exit Fees

Manufacturers and retailers can come into conflict over **slotting fees**, payments that retailers demand in exchange for placing products on store
shelves. Slotting fees first sprang up in Europe and Canada and have spread
to U.S. drug stores, supermarkets, and computer stores. Stores may ask for
thousands of dollars to place one product in one store, which adds to the already high cost of launching a new product.

Jeff Phillips, vice president of marketing at Seventh Generation in Vermont, had to pay $4 million in slotting fees to get his company's "green"
products onto supermarket shelves across the United States. As if these slotting fees weren't hefty enough, compare them to the size of the company:

slotting fees
payments that some retailers require in exchange for placing products on store
shelves

Many companies complain that they must pay slotting fees to display their products on store shelves. Yet marketers know that such exposure is necessary. For example, Seventh Generation displays its paper towels in Fresh Fields stores. The Fresh Fields approach to retailing promotes a certain "green" image—an image that traditional supermarkets don't offer, which creates value for products the chain sells. Do you agree with the use of slotting fees? Why or why not?

Seventh Generation's annual sales were under $8 million. Phillips knew, however, that if he didn't pay up, he wouldn't be able to reach enough markets and consumers to build sales and profitability.[49]

Many marketers question the ethics of slotting fees, calling them "extortion allowances" that pay stores for merely stocking products. And, since slotting fees are negotiated verbally, you won't know whether stores treat different marketers differently. For their part, retailers point to the need to pay for storing, stocking, and removing the thousands of new products introduced every year. Therefore, they set slotting fees as a way of "renting" valuable shelf space to marketers.[50]

In addition to slotting fees, some retailers have begun levying *exit fees*—payments marketers must make when failed products are pulled off store shelves. And if marketers want to keep their products on store shelves for another year, they may be asked to pay *annual renewal fees*.[51]

Gray Market Conflicts

Another area of conflict between producers and channel partners is over the **gray market**, buying and selling among unauthorized channel partners that bring products from other countries at lower prices than authorized channel partners pay. Unauthorized channel partners are those a marketer didn't intend to use in a particular market. A variety of producers have battled with gray market distributors over this practice. BMW has faced gray market conflicts when marketing its cars, Duracell when marketing its batteries, and Opium, when marketing its top-selling perfume. Although producers oppose the gray market because the prices undercut those in regular channels, their legal remedies are limited.[52]

Channel Leadership and Channel Power

One of the ways to control channel conflict is through channel leadership. A **channel captain** is a manufacturer or channel partner with the power to dominate the chain of channel partners. This power may come from a variety of sources, including sheer size, market dominance, and access to key information.[53] The role of channel captain can be played by a manufacturer, a wholesaler, or a retailer.

gray market

buying and selling among unauthorized channel partners that bring products from other countries at lower prices than authorized channel partners pay

channel captain

a manufacturer or channel partner with the power to dominate the chain of channel partners

For example, channel captain General Electric used its leadership to strengthen channel relationships by changing the way dealers buy and sell GE appliances. Dealers that join the manufacturer's Direct Connect plan are linked to a computer system that lets them check on product availability and place orders 24 hours a day for next-day delivery. Now, rather than keep dozens of refrigerators and stoves on hand—or risk running out of popular models—the dealers can immediately respond to customer inquiries and purchases. GE uses dealer orders to control its manufacturing and delivery systems. From producer to channel partners to customers, everybody benefits.[54]

In recent years, retailers have gained channel power as a result of their relationships with large numbers of customers and their control over customer buying data. Marks & Spencer is a case in point. This $10 billion retailer, the largest in Great Britain, is a channel captain because of its huge customer base and its knowledge of what, where, when, and how consumers buy. The company therefore has the purchasing power to control activities in its marketing channel.[55]

Power in the value chain is moving down to the retail level. The reason is that retailers are closest to customers and have comprehensive databases that contain the names, addresses, and purchasing preferences of millions of people. Using that information as clout, retailers are able to win concessions from wholesalers and manufacturers. This is true all over the world, including in Great Britain where Marks & Spencer is a channel captain. What can smaller retailers do to gain improved leverage with their suppliers?

Using Vertical Marketing Systems

In the past, most marketing channels were fairly loose networks of independent wholesalers, retailers, agents, and brokers working together. However, a more efficient method of managing channel relationships has emerged. A **vertical marketing system (VMS)** is a professionally planned and managed network of channel relationships designed for optimal efficiency and effectiveness. These efficiencies strengthen customer relationships by improving access to needed products while performing all the required channel functions. Also, thanks to better coordination, not only do all participants in a VMS share financial risks, but all can reduce costs through economies of scale and boost productivity by learning from other partners.[56] Figure 14.6 shows the three types of vertical marketing system: administered, corporate, and contractual.

vertical marketing system (VMS)
a professionally planned and managed network of channel relationships designed for optimal efficiency and effectiveness

FIGURE **14.6**   Vertical Marketing Systems

Administered, corporate, and contractual systems are three types of vertical marketing systems in which marketers may participate. Common types of contractual systems include retail cooperatives, wholesaler–sponsored voluntary chains, and franchises. A VMS can strengthen channel relationships and increase efficiency throughout the channel.

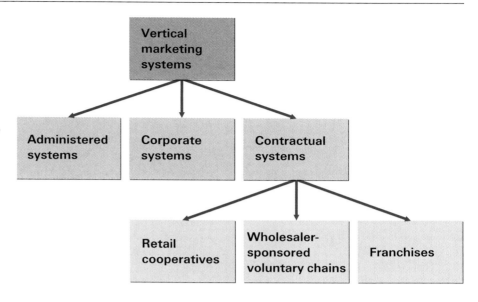

Administered Systems

An *administered system* is a voluntary VMS that achieves a high degree of coordination through the power and influence of the channel captain rather than through formal ownership or contractual arrangements. The system works because all the participants benefit when they cooperate with the channel captain. Wal-Mart in North America and Ikea, the Swedish-based furniture store chain, are retail channel captains that coordinate relationships in their administered systems, determining through their purchasing power what and when goods will be produced and delivered.[57]

Corporate Systems

A *corporate system* is a VMS in which all channel participants are owned and controlled by one company, allowing for closer coordination of activities throughout the channel. One example is manufacturer Levi Strauss, which not only makes jeans but also markets them through its Original Levi's stores. Another example is wholesaler American Hospital Supply, which owns suppliers that make a number of the medical products the company markets to hospitals and other health care providers.[58]

Contractual Systems

A *contractual system* is a VMS controlled and coordinated by formal contracts, not by ownership or channel leadership. Retail cooperatives, wholesaler-sponsored voluntary chains, and franchises are common types.

A *retail cooperative* is a group of independent retailers that voluntarily band together to coordinate their purchases for better buying power. ServiStar, for example, is a retail cooperative of some 4,500 hardware stores that arranges merchandise purchasing and delivery for the entire group. ServiStar coordinates channel activities to ensure that retailers get their products when and where needed to satisfy their customers.

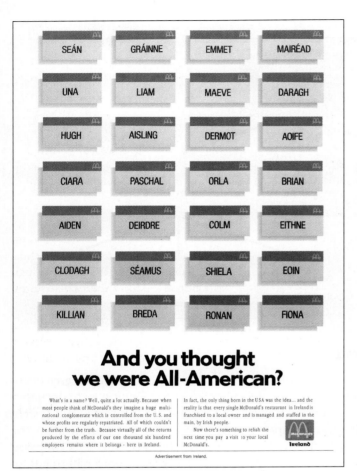

And you thought we were All-American?

What's in a name? Well, quite a lot actually. Because when most people think of McDonald's they imagine a huge multi-national conglomerate which is controlled from the U.S. and whose profits are regularly repatriated. All of which couldn't be further from the truth. Because virtually all of the returns produced by the efforts of our one thousand six hundred employees remains where it belongs - here in Ireland.

In fact, the only thing born in the USA was the idea... and the reality is that every single McDonald's restaurant in Ireland is franchised to a local owner and is managed and staffed in the main, by Irish people.

Now there's something to relish the next time you pay a visit to your local McDonald's.

Advertisement from Ireland.

A *wholesaler-sponsored voluntary chain* is a group of independent retailers whose members agree to concentrate their purchasing at the request of a particular wholesaler. As the channel captain, the wholesaler negotiates product prices and delivery to meet the needs of the retailers downstream in the channel. In the Northeast, Drug Guild is a wholesaler-sponsored voluntary chain that helps independent drug stores get the products and prices they need to compete more effectively with giant drug chains.[59]

A *franchise* is a contractual arrangement in which one company (the franchiser) licenses the right to use its brand name, products, and operational methods to a second company (the franchisee). Many franchisers provide advertising, marketing research, purchasing, and other support services. In exchange, franchisees pay an initial fee and a percentage of their sales of goods or services. Franchising, as you saw in Chapter 4, is growing rapidly all over the world. Franchises account for nearly $800 billion in sales every year, marketing everything from fast food (Taco Bell) and automotive services (Jiffy-Lube) to real-estate brokerage services (Century 21). However, the channel power that franchisers hold over franchisees raises serious ethical issues, as the following section shows.

No franchisor is better known globally than McDonald's. However, the brand name is associated with the United States. This ad stresses the fact that McDonald's franchises in Ireland are owned and staffed by Irish natives. That means that local profits and jobs are created when people eat at the neighborhood McDonald's. Why would this message be important to Irish citizens?

ETHICS & SOCIAL RESPONSIBILITY

Do franchisers abuse channel power?

Franchising allows an entrepreneur to go into business using a franchiser's prepackaged set of products and processes. But even as franchising is booming, the number of lawsuits and complaints to regulatory agencies is growing, reflecting ethical questions about how some franchisers wield channel power.[60]

- *Should franchisers put new outlets near existing franchisees' outlets?* Although in most cases franchisers can legally do this, franchisees protest that adding too many outlets in an area takes customers away from existing outlets. One group of Kentucky Fried Chicken franchisees fought back by getting the Iowa state legislature to pass a bill forbidding franchisers from opening new outlets within 3 miles of existing outlets without payment.

- *Should contracts heavily favor the franchiser?* At one time, the contract offered by Southland Corporation for 7-Eleven convenience stores allowed the company to take 52 percent of a franchisee's gross profits and to shut down a store with only three days' notice if the franchisee performed poorly. Even without such unfavorable clauses, however, many small business owners buying franchises feel they have little leverage to renegotiate contracts with giant franchisers.

- *Should franchisers spend franchisees' money?* Franchisees pay franchisers for advertising services, but they're not always consulted before a campaign breaks. Similarly, franchisers may whip up costly new products without checking with franchisees, who are responsible for selling them to customers.

  As complaints mount, some franchisers are tearing up their old contracts and building new cooperative relationships with franchisees. Also, more franchisees are banding together, with the idea of gaining the power to stand up to franchisers.[61]

  As a franchiser, how would you handle these ethical issues to strengthen relations with franchisees?

Because of contractual arrangements, all channel partners are required to meet specific quality and customer service standards. With consistency thus ensured, customers at the end of the value chain will receive the product they expect in every marketing exchange. The chapter that follows explores two major channel partners in the value chain: wholesalers and retailers.

Before you go on . . .

A. How does intensive distribution compare with selective distribution and exclusive distribution?

B. What legal considerations affect channel decisions?

C. What is channel leadership and why is it important?

D. What are three types of vertical marketing systems?

Summary

1. **Define the marketing channel and explain its position in the value chain.**

   A marketing channel is the network of value-chain partners that participate in bringing a product from producers to ultimate consumers. The activities in the marketing channel occur downstream from the producer's position in the value chain. All value-chain activities are connected through logistics, the management of product and information flows throughout the value chain to increase efficiency and speed.

2. **Show how channel partners add value to satisfy customers along the value chain.**

   Channel partners perform functions of three basic types that add value for customers. Exchange functions relate to matching buyers and sellers. Logistical functions are activities related to transporting, storing, and sorting products. Facilitation functions help complete marketing exchanges.

3. **Contrast direct and indirect channels.**

In direct channels, marketers complete marketing exchanges directly with customers through direct marketing and/or direct selling. In contrast, indirect channels include channel partners such as wholesalers, retailers, agents and brokers, industrial distributors, and manufacturers' representatives that help marketers complete marketing exchanges.

4. **Explain how marketers use multiple channels, strategic channel alliances, and reverse channels.**

Dual distribution is accomplished by using more than one channel to bring a product (or a group of similar products) to several customer segments. In a strategic channel alliance, one marketer uses another marketer's channel to reach the same customers. Reverse channels return products, such as used plastic bottles, from customers to marketers.

5. **Describe how intensive, selective, and exclusive forms of distribution allow for the proper market coverage.**

With intensive distribution, products are marketed through as many outlets as possible. With selective distribution, products are marketed through a limited number of outlets. With exclusive distribution, products are marketed through very few outlets.

6. **Identify the issues that marketers must analyze before making channel decisions.**

The issues are customer considerations, market environment considerations, internal considerations, product considerations, legal considerations, and cost and profit considerations.

7. **Differentiate between horizontal and vertical channel conflict, and show how vertical marketing systems operate.**

Horizontal conflict can occur among partners at the same level in the marketing channel (such as two retailers). Vertical conflict can occur among partners at different levels in the marketing channel (such as between wholesalers and retailers). A vertical marketing system (VMS) is a professionally planned and managed network of channel relationships designed for optimal efficiency and effectiveness. Administered systems, corporate systems, and contractual systems are three types of VMS.

KEY TERMS

channel captain 429
direct channels 415
dual distribution 419
efficient consumer response (ECR) 413
exclusive distribution 423

gray market 429
indirect channels 415
intensive distribution 422
logistics 409
marketing channel 408
reverse channels 421

selective distribution 422
slotting fees 428
strategic channel alliance 420
value-chain management 410
vertical marketing system (VMS) 430

Skill-Building Applications

1. Develop a sales presentation to a business you buy from (such as a hair salon or a bookstore) promising a long-term commitment if you are given a discount on purchases. How well do you think such a reverse marketing relationship-building approach would work?

2. Your video game store is losing out to competitors that get the interesting games first, when the market is hot. What could you do to convince manufacturers to sell to you first?

3. How could the Red Cross use the Internet as a channel to raise funds for helping victims of natural disasters right after such catastrophes occur?

4. What small restaurants in your area could benefit by using a service like Takeout Taxi? Could you profit by starting a service like Takeout Taxi? What channel functions would you perform?

5. In many states, the Department of Motor Vehicles services customers mostly through one channel: retail outlets. What other channels might this department use to better serve customers?

6. Assume that Michelin, based in France, wants to market tires in South Africa. How could Michelin design cross-border channels to reach consumers in South Africa?

Getting Involved in Marketing

1. *On Your Own* Diagram one of the marketing channels that brings a particular product, such as a Sony television set from Japan, to the customer. Identify the partners in that marketing channel and indicate the functions that each performs.

2. *On Your Own* List several issues you think might cause vertical conflicts between manufacturers and their channel partners. How can the manufacturer reduce such conflicts? List several specific ideas for turning conflict into cooperation.

3. *Find Out More* Interview a representative for Mary Kay Cosmetics or another company that uses direct selling in a direct channel. Ask about the exchange, logistical, and facilitation functions that the rep performs. Analyze how the representative's activities add value from the customer's perspective.

4. *In a Partnership* With a classmate, role-play a conversation about slotting fees between a food marketer, who wants to negotiate lower or no slotting fees, and a supermarket executive, who wants

to collect slotting fees. After the role-playing exercise, hold a class discussion to evaluate the arguments of each side.

5. *In a Team* With other students, determine how to research the customer, marketing environment, legal, product, and cost and profit considerations in making channel decisions for a specific good or service. Where would you look for this information? How often would you expect to reevaluate the channel decision for your product? Write a report about your findings.

6. *In a Team* With other students, design a reverse marketing channel to help a customer return all or part of a product (such as a Chrysler Neon car) to the marketer for recycling. Draw a diagram and label each partner in the reverse channel. What value does the customer gain from this exchange? What value does the marketer gain? What value do the channel partners gain?

15

Wholesaling and Retailing

Learning Goals

After you have read and studied this chapter, you should be able to:

1. Differentiate among the three types of wholesaler.

2. Describe how retail image and atmospherics are related to retail positioning.

3. Identify the two main product strategies used by retailers and define scrambled merchandising.

4. Differentiate among discount, off-price, and full-price retail strategies.

5. Analyze why nonstore retailing is becoming more popular.

6. Demonstrate how category management affects relationships among retailers, their value-chain partners, and their customers.

7. Describe the evolution of retailing, based on the wheel of retailing and the retail life cycle theories.

PROFILE

Yaohan puts the world under one roof for shoppers

Kazuo Wada is a world-class marketer who has the knack of offering customers what they want. Wada's Hong Kong–based retail company, Yaohan International, markets everything from cars to cabbage in China, Japan, Europe, and the United States, bringing in $5 billion in annual sales. As chairman, Wada is leading a push for growth by meeting local customers' desires for a wide selection of products in one convenient location.

Long established in Japan, Yaohan has expanded by bringing retailing to other countries on a large scale. Its U.S. retail centers are located in areas with large concentrations of people from Asia. Hungry for a taste of home, customers travel from all over the New York area to shop at New Jersey's Yaohan Plaza. The Yaohan supermarket, specialty stores, and restaurants offer familiar foods, housewares, and videotapes. If it's available back home, it's available at Yaohan.

Wada's latest target market is China, where he plans 1,000 supermarkets and stores. He's launching this growth with a gigantic one-stop shopping center in downtown Shanghai. Known as the Nextage Shanghai Tower, this stylish 21-story retail complex takes up a city block and offers more than a million square feet of selling space for goods and services. The largest retail center in Asia, Nextage can accommodate a million shoppers every weekend.

Wada's customers want an exciting shopping experience, and he gives them a lot of variety in a snazzy atmosphere. Customers can kick the tires in a spotless car showroom, buy merchandise imported from dozens of countries, ice skate, visit restaurants, and even get married, all under one ultramodern roof. With so many choices and such an inviting shopping environment, customers keep coming back, increasing Wada's profits.[1]

Building on the discussion of channels in Chapter 14, this chapter takes a closer look at indirect marketing channels. First, you'll examine the role of wholesaling in the value chain and learn about the various types of wholesaler. Then you'll see how the fast-paced retailing industry creates value for customers and contributes to the economy. A discussion of relationship building in retailing is followed by a look at how retailing is evolving to further satisfy customers.

Wholesaling and Value-Chain Relationships

Are wholesalers an endangered species? **Wholesalers** are channel partners that buy products from producers or agents for resale to retailers or other channel partners. In the past, wholesalers played a key role in moving products through the marketing channel. Today, retailers such as Wal-Mart believe that they can handle those functions more efficiently. Using value-chain management ◄—┘ **(p. 410)**, some marketers are eliminating wholesalers from their value chains. As retailers expand their operations to global markets, the challenge to wholesalers is to provide more efficient services and add even greater value—or lose their position in the value chain.[3] Wholesaling is now performed by some 300,000 U.S. wholesalers with combined sales of $2.5 trillion. And there's room for growth. Many U.S. wholesalers are expanding to reach markets and customers in other countries.

Wholesalers can add value and build relationships by performing several important functions for retailers and value-added resellers, their customers in the value chain. Three such functions are as follows:

- *Create utility*. Wholesalers create time and place utility, making products available for purchase when and where their customers would like to find them. They do this by storing goods at convenient locations until needed. In the next chapter, you'll see how logistics management helps wholesalers orchestrate a seamless flow of goods from producers to consumers. Many wholesalers also create possession utility, allowing their customers to take ownership of products as needed. This way, wholesalers, not their customers, assume the risk that goods will become outdated before they're purchased by ultimate consumers. Finally, wholesalers add information utility ◄—┘ **(p. 10)**, providing details about the products they sell. This added value allows wholesalers' customers to satisfy their consumer or organizational customers.

- *Perform key services*. Wholesalers provide an ever-widening array of services, thus creating service utility. For example, United Stationers, the largest U.S. distributor of office supplies, offers overnight delivery and encourages its customers to place special orders of merchandise not available through ordinary channels. Among other services provided by some wholesalers are suggesting improvements to customers' operations; training customers' employees; and providing computerized systems for ordering, inventory tracking, and other functions.[4]

- *Boost exchange efficiency*. Wholesalers often save retail customers time and money by streamlining the marketing exchanges needed to stock many products from many manufacturers. Manufacturers benefit as well because they don't have to do business directly with many consumers or organizational customers. Working through one or more wholesale channel partners cuts the number of exchanges needed.

Consider the value added by Tech Data, a Florida-based wholesaler of personal computer products to retailers and value-added resellers. Its 45,000 customers find buying from Tech Data extremely efficient because they can order from a single source any of 14,000 products made by 300 manufacturers. Tech Data holds all these products in inventory, so retail customers aren't running the risk of being stuck with obsolete computers. Ordering is

wholesalers
channel partners that buy products from producers or agents for resale to retailers or other channel partners

also convenient. Retail customers simply call in to make a purchase. In addition, they can call Tech Data for technical support, which creates information utility. By performing functions that its retail customers value, Tech Data has grown to $1.5 billion in sales.[5]

Manufacturer-Owned Wholesalers
(not independent, own products they resell)

Sales offices
Sales branches

Merchant Wholesalers
(independent, own products they resell)

Full-function wholesalers
Limited-function wholesalers
    Rack jobbers
    Cash-and-carry wholesalers
    Drop shippers
    Truck jobbers

Agents and Brokers
(independent, don't own products they resell)

Manufacturer's representatives
Selling agents
Brokers

FIGURE **15.1**

Types of Wholesalers
Each of the three broad types of wholesalers functions slightly differently in the value chain. Manufacturer-owned wholesalers are not independent, and they own the products they resell to other channel partners. Merchant wholesalers also own the products they resell, but they're independent. Agents and brokers are independent and don't own the products they resell.

merchant wholesalers
wholesalers that take title to the products they buy for resale to other channel partners

Types of Wholesaler

One way of looking at how wholesalers function in the value chain is to examine the role of the three different types: manufacturer-owned wholesalers, merchant wholesalers, and agents and brokers. As shown in Figure 15.1, you can distinguish among these types by looking at who owns the wholesaler and who owns the products it sells.

Manufacturer-Owned Wholesalers

Many manufacturers prefer to have close control over the flow of their products through the marketing channel, so they set up their own wholesaling operations. This makes sense when no channel partners can adequately handle the manufacturers' products, when manufacturers want to provide special services to larger customers, or when manufacturers serve only a few customers, concentrated in a narrow geographic region.

Sales branches are wholesale outlets, located away from the factory, that stock and sell products to nearby customers. In contrast, *sales offices* carry no inventory but instead serve as a base for sales representatives who call on customers in surrounding areas. Hewlett-Packard, based in California, maintains sales offices in more than 100 countries where it markets its computer products.[6]

Merchant Wholesalers

Merchant wholesalers are wholesalers that take title to the products they buy for resale to other channel partners. This means that they legally own the products until those products have been sold to customers. Unlike manufacturer-owned wholesalers, which are controlled by their parent companies, merchant wholesalers are *independent* businesses that provide such typical channel functions as buying, selling, storing, and transporting large quantities of products. Approximately 60 percent of all sales made in wholesale channels are handled by this type of wholesaler.[7]

Full-function merchant wholesalers handle a wide variety of services for downstream customers. They maintain stocks of goods for fast delivery when needed, help customers finance their purchases, provide information about products and markets, and send representatives to discuss customer product needs. Some full-function merchant wholesalers offer a diverse assortment of unrelated products, some carry a limited line of related products, and some specialize in just a few product lines.

Central Garden & Pet maintains 30 warehouses that stock more than 18,000 gardening, pet, and pool supplies. It delivers products to retailers such as Kmart, Target, Home Depot, and Lowe's, and helps them stock shelves and manage inventory. Central even trains the front-line workers in these retail stores about use of the products so that they can educate their customers. Here, a Central employee checks inventory at a California retailer. What advantages does Central gain from providing these additional services?

For example, Central Garden & Pet in California is a full-function merchant wholesaler with a limited line of garden, pet, and pool products. It buys from manufacturers such as Ortho and Monsanto and resells to retailers such as Home Depot and Target. Its representatives stock store shelves and teach retail employees the benefits and uses of specific products. Such services add value for retail customers and consumers alike.[8]

Merchant wholesalers that operate in organizational markets are known as *industrial distributors*. These wholesalers buy industrial products from manufacturers and resell them to businesses and other organizational customers. One example is Bearings Inc., a large industrial distributor in Cleveland. In addition to industrial bearings, this wholesaler offers motors, belts, and drives. To strengthen relationships with customers, Bearings provides special services that other wholesalers don't offer, such as energy audits of factory motors.[9] The next section shows how an entrepreneur spotted an opportunity that turned into a profitable wholesaling business.

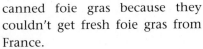

Wholesaling is only the start for D'Artagnan

Ariane Daguin wasn't thinking about starting a business, but she quickly opened the door when opportunity knocked. Daguin was head of marketing for a company that provides pâté for French restaurants when a farmer offered her a new product: fresh foie gras, a rich goose liver produced in upstate New York. She knew this was an important opportunity because many customers had complained of having to use

canned foie gras because they couldn't get fresh foie gras from France.

Daguin's boss wasn't interested in this business. So, armed with $15,000 in start-up funds, Daguin started her own wholesaling business, named D'Artagnan after the character in *The Three Musketeers*. "D'Artagnan is my hero," she explained. "Like him, I wanted to do something reckless and courageous." With partner George Faison, Daguin began wholesaling the farmer's foie gras to upscale

Ariane Daguin and George Faison are partners and entrepreneurs who saw a wholesaling opportunity in the food industry and responded quickly. They now provide foie gras (goose liver) and related game products to restaurants and gourmet food shops. How could the partners determine what additional services would be valued by their customers?

French restaurants around New York. The entrepreneurs took orders on Mondays, traveled to the farm to fill the orders during the week, and delivered the orders to their restaurant customers on Thursdays.

Next, Daguin and Faison began to smoke the remaining goose parts and wholesaled those, too, along with an expanded line of gourmet meats. Soon they expanded to prepared entrées, which they wholesaled to gourmet food shops and other specialty stores. By moving quickly when opportunity knocked, they have built a $14 million wholesaling business.[10]

Do you think Daguin and Faison should move into retailing by opening restaurants or stores? Why or why not?

Limited-function merchant wholesalers perform only some of the functions handled by their full-function counterparts. *Rack jobbers* are limited-function merchant wholesalers that specialize in maintaining the stock of products displayed on store shelves, such as shoe polish and panty hose. In many cases, rack jobbers retain ownership of the products they stock on retailers' shelves, with the result that stores pay only for what shoppers buy. *Cash-and-carry wholesalers* are, as you can guess from the name, limited-function merchant wholesalers that don't offer credit or delivery services. This is a convenient alternative for small retailers such as neighborhood stores that buy in small quantities and don't need delivery.

Another type of limited-function wholesaler is the drop shipper. *Drop shippers* arrange for manufacturers to ship large quantities directly to retail customers that have placed orders. Drop shippers own but don't transport the products they sell. They commonly work in industries where customers buy in large quantity. *Truck jobbers*, on the other hand, regularly visit their customers' locations to sell items from stock maintained in their trucks or vans. A good example is Snap-on Tools. Its personnel drive vans to customers' service stations and sell tools and parts used by auto mechanics.

One way that wholesalers can add value is to make it easy for their customers to purchase their products. For example, Snap-on Tools puts its products on a truck and takes them to locations where mechanics and other potential buyers work. This Snap-on Tools truck carries an elaborate display of products for customers to see and evaluate. In what other ways can wholesalers facilitate the buying process?

Agents and Brokers

Agents and brokers, another category of independent wholesaler, don't assume legal ownership of the products they buy for resale. In some cases they may not even hold or transport the products. Generally, these wholesalers concentrate on bringing marketers together with customers downstream in the value chain, so they offer fewer services than other wholesalers. Among the wholesalers in this category are manufacturer's representatives, selling agents, and brokers.

Manufacturer's representatives, also known as *manufacturer's agents*, are independent salespeople who market to customers in a specific geographic area. Reps market several related but noncompeting product lines, such as a variety of small kitchen appliances, and they're paid a percentage on each sale they make. For example, Buffalo Tank, a steel fabricating company that is part of Bethlehem Steel, uses reps in New England only. Each rep specializes in a particular industry, such as heating and air conditioning or power. This approach has helped Buffalo Tank boost sales considerably in those targeted industries.[11]

manufacturer's representatives

independent salespeople who market to customers in a specific geographic area

Selling agents offer more services than reps, taking on *all* the marketing responsibilities for the manufacturers they represent. They gather marketing information, design promotions, make sales calls, and, in some cases, decide on prices and financing. Makers of industrial equipment and textile goods often reach organizational customers and retailers through selling agents.

Brokers are independent wholesalers who arrange sales between manufacturers and customers. As matchmakers in the marketing channel, brokers offer far fewer services than either reps or selling agents. A broker can work for either the buyer or the seller. The company that hires the broker pays a fee or, sometimes, a percentage of the sale.

Manufacturers interested in getting their products into international marketing channels can work through specialized brokers. *Export brokers* match exporters with customers in other countries. *Export management companies* act as export departments for manufacturers, assuming more channel functions than export brokers. They may conduct market research, arrange financing, handle integrated marketing communication, and plan shipping.[12]

The Changing Role of Wholesaling

The role of wholesaling within the value chain has been changing in recent years. Wal-Mart and other gigantic retailers are increasingly insistent about shortening the marketing channel—and cutting costs—by buying directly from manufacturers. This practice is displacing brokers and some wholesalers that once sold to these retailers.[13] With shorter channels, the functions formerly performed by wholesalers are being handled by manufacturers or retailers.

Against the backdrop of this pressure, more wholesalers are strengthening their channel relationships by adding value in a variety of ways. First, they're taking on functions that were previously handled by their customers. For example, Supervalu, a $16 billion food wholesaler based in Minnesota, doesn't just sell food products to more than 4,000 independent grocery stores in 47 states. It also offers training for store employees, store design services, and other forms of assistance, to help its customers compete more effectively.[14]

Wholesalers are also becoming more flexible about when, where, and how they operate, helping to streamline the movement of products through the entire channel. This cuts costs and improves service for customers. Technology is a key element in this effort. Consider San Francisco-based McKesson, the world's largest drug wholesaler. McKesson uses computer power to respond more quickly and accurately when its drugstore customers place orders for any of the 100,000 products in the wholesaler's 30 warehouses. This system strengthens relationships with upstream partners as well. McKesson's suppliers can quickly find out how any product is selling in a specific region or in certain stores.[15] As a result of such changes, the role of wholesaling in the marketing channel is evolving toward a more value-added approach.

selling agents

agents who gather marketing information, design promotions, make sales calls, sometimes decide on prices and financing, and generally take over the marketing functions for the manufacturers they represent

brokers

independent wholesalers who arrange sales between manufacturers and customers

retailers

channel partners that market goods and services to ultimate consumers

retailing

the set of value-chain activities related to the marketing of goods and services to consumers for personal, family, or household use

Before you go on . . .

A. **What are the similarities and differences among the three types of wholesaler?**

B. **Why is the role of wholesaling in the marketing channel changing?**

Retailers are the organizations at the end of the value chain that provide goods and services to ultimate consumers. The largest shopping mall in the United States is Mall of America in Bloomington, Minnesota, and one advantage of its size is the greater choice it offers consumers. Perhaps the best example of the mall's one-stop shopping approach is the Chapel of Love, which enables couples to get married right in the mall. Many people love to shop in malls, but others dislike the hassle. How can retailers service those who prefer to shop from home?

Retailing in the Value Chain

Unlike wholesalers, which are not well known by most consumers, retailers are highly visible in the value chain. **Retailers** are channel partners that market goods and services to ultimate consumers. The word *retail* is derived from the French verb *retailler*, meaning "to cut up."[16] Retailers buy in bulk and sell in smaller quantities to consumers. Thus **retailing** is the set of value-chain activities related to the marketing of goods and services to consumers for personal, family, or household use. In contrast, wholesalers buy and sell in bulk to retailers and other channel partners.

Because they perform their functions near the end of the value chain, retailers are the customers of upstream channel partners and, at the same time, marketers to downstream customers. This position allows retailers to provide producers and other channel partners with key information about consumer purchases through scanner data and other methods. It also allows retailers to pass along product information from producers to consumers. Finally, it's a prime position for gathering data to respond quickly to competition and the many other changes that are inevitable in the marketing environment.

The Many Faces of Retailing

In colonial America, retailing meant trading posts, general stores, and itinerant peddlers. These days, retailing takes a wider variety of forms. Service retailers include hotels, amusement parks, car washes, movie theaters, and restaurants. Retailers of goods include supermarkets, clothing stores, gas stations, and automobile dealerships. But these are just the beginning, as technology opens the way for many new forms of retailing. The World Wide Web of the Internet, CD-ROM catalogs, and interactive kiosks are just a few of the developments that are changing the face of retailing in the 1990s—and beyond, as you'll see later in this chapter. Table 15.1 shows a half-dozen ways of classifying retailers.

Retailing is such an important value-chain activity that many manufacturers are setting up their own stores. For example, Haggar now operates stores that retail its own men's apparel. This approach builds brand equity **(p. 266)** by creating special showcases for the products. It also allows for improved customer service and timely feedback about products. "We want our people to be good listeners," says Ronald Batts, vice president of Haggar's retail division. "Today, you go into a lot of retailers, and unfortunately, customer service is not priority one. Through good listening, we want to find out what the customers like about us and what they don't like."[17]

T A B L E **15.1** **Types of Retailer**

Classification Method	Types of Retailer
Ownership	• Independent • Chain stores • Members of vertical marketing systems
Product strategy	• General merchandise • Limited-line merchandising
Pricing strategy	• One-price • Full-price • Discount • Off-price
Location strategy	• Freestanding • Urban business district • Shopping center • Strip center
Service strategy	• Full service • Limited service • Self-service
Operations strategy	• Store • Nonstore

How Retailing Satisfies Customers

Retailing satisfies customers by offering time, place, possession, form, information, and service utility ◄——┘ **(p. 10)**. Research indicates that time utility is the U.S. consumer's top priority, which is why Holiday Inn, for example, helps customers book rooms quickly and easily at any hour. In addition to taking room reservations through travel agents, Holiday Inn maintains a toll-free telephone hotline and a World Wide Web site through which customers can reserve rooms day or night.[18]

Customers gain place utility by having convenient access to products where needed. Consider how Friedman's Shoes in Atlanta, which stocks a huge selection of large-size men's shoes, creates place utility for Shaquille O'Neal and other athletes who can't easily find shoes to fit. Retailers also create possession utility by helping customers get and use products. Tom Elo, owner of Snyder Drug of Buffalo, a small Minnesota retailer, competes with Wal-Mart by offering possession utility in the form of free delivery of prescription drugs.[19]

Many retailers also create form utility, by transforming raw materials into finished products. Form utility is the big draw for customers who shop the heat-and-eat food counters at Ukrop's in Richmond, Virginia. Pasta, stir-fry, and premade meals of many other kinds are available at Ukrop's. Says Jacquelyn G. Legg, the store's vice president of creative food merchandising, "We have traditional groceries, and food for the people who want to make believe they are having a home-cooked meal."[20]

Retailers create information utility by providing customers with information about goods and services. For example, MacWarehouse is an East Coast catalog retailer that uses faxes and the Internet to offer customers information about the computer programs and accessories it markets. Customers key in a four-digit product code, and MacWarehouse immediately transmits the requested product details.[21]

Finally, retailers create service utility by responding to customers in a fast and friendly manner and resolving any problems professionally. Retailers such as Home Depot have gained market share and cemented customer relationships with service-oriented strategies. The following case shows how a retailer uses computer power to satisfy its customers.

Applying the Concepts
Peapod puts groceries online

Groceries are just a keystroke away for customers who use Peapod, a small, rapidly growing computer-based shopping service in Chicago and San Francisco. Founded by Thomas and Andrew Parkinson, Peapod allows subscribers to shop for 18,000 grocery items via home computer. The idea is catching on as more customers log on for enhanced time, place, possession, and service utility via computerized shopping.

Here's how Peapod works. Customers call up a series of screens on their home PCs to locate products by category or by brand name, to check prices, and to see coupons and specials. When they find what they want, they press a key to transmit their orders. They also select a specific 90-minute period for delivery and choose a payment method (credit card or other means).

Online shopping for groceries offers consumers several advantages. One advantage is that online shoppers tend to buy only what they need; they are not tempted by displays and in-store promotions. Furthermore, they save the time usually spent driving, parking, and searching for what they want. What are the advantages of actually shopping in the store? What kinds of changes may make online shopping much more attractive to consumers in the future?

Now Peapod's small army of shoppers and delivery personnel takes over. The shoppers handpick the groceries from a Jewel supermarket (for Chicago customers) or a Safeway (for San Francisco customers). Then the delivery people whisk the groceries to the customer. From order to door takes about 4 hours. Subscribers buy the software, then pay a monthly fee to participate, as well as a delivery charge for each order.

The Parkinson brothers know that customers won't order again if service quality doesn't measure up, which is why they want their employees, not store employees, thumping the melons and driving the delivery vans. This approach is helping them forge long-term relationships with customers like Sarah White, who calls the service an "incredible timesaver."[22]

Make marketing decisions

1. What can Peapod do to thwart competitors who want to lure its customers away?

2. Should Peapod stress expert shoppers, fast delivery, or both in its integrated marketing communication? Why?

3. Why would Jewel and Safeway welcome Peapod's shoppers?

4. Would you recommend that Peapod start offering food products under its own brand name? Why or why not?

How Retailing Contributes to the Economy

Retailing not only creates value for individual consumers, it contributes to the overall economy. In the United States alone, 1.5 million retail outlets employ 20 million people, which means that one in five workers are employed in retailing. The combined annual sales of the leading 100 U.S. retailers tops $600 billion, a sizable chunk of the $2.2 trillion in sales the retail industry generates in one year. To put this into perspective, consider that the U.S. gross domestic product is about $6.7 trillion. Table 15.2 shows the

TABLE **15.2**   **Top Global and U.S. Retailers**

Top Global Retailers

Rank	Company	Type of Retailing	Home Country
1	Wal-Mart Stores, Inc.	Discount	United States
2	Metro International AG	Diversified	Germany
3	Kmart Corporation	Discount	United States
4	Sears, Roebuck, Inc.	Department	United States
5	Tenglemann	Supermarket	Germany
6	Rewe Zentrale AG	Supermarket	Germany
7	Ito-Yokado Co., Ltd.	Diversified	Japan
8	Daiei Inc.	Diversified	Japan
9	Kroger Company	Supermarket	United States
10	Carrefour SA	Hypermarket	France

Top U.S. Retailers

Rank	Company	Headquarters	1994 Sales (U.S. $ Millions)
1	Wal-Mart	Bentonville, Ark.	82,494
2	Kmart	Troy, Mich.	34,025
3	Sears, Roebuck	Chicago	29,451
4	Kroger	Cincinnati	22,959
5	Dayton Hudson	Minneapolis	21,311
6	J.C. Penney	Plano, Tex.	20,380
7	American Stores	Salt Lake City	18,355
8	Price/Costco	Issaquah, Wash.	16,161
9	Safeway	Oakland, Calif.	15,627
10	Home Depot	Atlanta	12,477

10 largest retailers in the United States and in the world.[23]

Retailing is also an important contributor to the world economy. The world's 100 largest retailers ring up over $1.13 trillion in sales every year. Because 68 of these 100 retailers operate in more than one country, their marketing activities boost not only local economies but also global trade. This trend toward globalization is expected to continue. "By the year 2000, 90 percent of the 100 largest retailers of the world will be operating as global retailers," predicts Daniel J. Sweeney, vice chairman of retail industry services for Management Horizons, a retail consulting firm.[24]

How Ownership Affects Value-Chain Relationships

Retail ownership has a definite influence on value-chain relationships. The way a retailer buys products for resale to consumers—even the choice of suppliers—depends on whether it's independent, part of a chain, or part of a vertical marketing system.

Independent retailers, owned by individuals or families, form the backbone of U.S. retailing, capturing nearly half of all retail sales. Most independent retailers operate just one or two stores, and they usually buy from wholesalers rather than from manufacturers. However, to compete with the buying clout of larger stores, many are joining *buying groups*, organizations that coordinate or pool the purchasing power of retail members to form larger orders placed directly with major manufacturers.[25]

Chain stores are groups of retail outlets that are owned and operated by a corporate parent, which handles many buying and marketing activities from one central location. Chain stores sell food, apparel, and other types of merchandise. The world's largest chain-store organization is Arkansas-based Wal-Mart, which currently has over $93 billion in sales and more than 2,500 stores. The second largest is Metro International, a German retailer with $48 billion in sales and 2,750 stores across Europe.[26]

As you saw earlier, a growing number of chain stores are buying directly from manufacturers so they can obtain the best prices, delivery, and buying terms. For example, Target stores, Sears, and Wal-Mart all go directly to Koss when they want to carry that company's stereo headphones. Chain stores are Koss's best customers, accounting for more than 75 percent of its sales revenues. Small wonder that Koss works hard to nurture these value-chain relationships.[27]

chain stores

groups of retail outlets that are owned and operated by a corporate parent, which handles many buying and marketing activities from one central location

T A B L E **15.3** Franchisee Checklist

1. What are the required franchiser fees: initial fee, advertising appropriations, and royalties?

2. What degree of technical knowledge is required of the franchisee?

3. What is the required investment in time by the franchisee? Does the franchisee have to be actively involved in the day-to-day operations of the franchise?

4. What is the extent of control of a franchise by a franchiser in terms of materials purchased, sales quotas, space requirements, pricing, the range of goods to be sold, required inventory levels, and so on?

5. Can the franchisee accept the regimentation and rules of the franchiser?

6. Are the costs of required supplies and materials purchased from the franchiser at market value, above market value, or below market value?

7. What degree of name recognition do consumers have of the franchise? Does the franchiser have a meaningful advertising program?

8. What image does the franchise have among consumers and among current franchisees?

9. What are the level and quality of services provided by the franchiser to franchisees: site selection, training, bookkeeping, human relations, equipment maintenance, and troubleshooting?

10. What is the franchiser policy in terminating franchisees? What are the conditions of franchise termination? What is the rate of franchise termination and nonrenewal?

11. What is the franchiser's legal history?

12. What is the length of the franchise agreement?

13. What is the failure rate of existing franchises?

14. What is the franchiser's policy with regard to company-owned and franchisee-owned outlets?

15. What policy does the franchiser have in allowing franchisees to sell their businesses?

16. What is the franchiser's policy with regard to territorial protection for existing franchisees? With regard to new franchisees and new company-owned establishments?

17. What is the earning potential of the franchise during the first year? The first five years?

Retailers that are part of a vertical marketing system ◄———┘ **(p. 430)** typically follow specific guidelines for buying goods and services. For instance, all company-owned OshKosh B'Gosh stores market only clothing by their namesake corporate owner. The Speedo Authentic Fitness Stores, which sell Speedo's sports apparel and accessories, have the same policy.[28]

Similarly, small business owners can get a lot of guidance and marketing support when they buy a *franchise*. JoAnne Shaw, president of the $50 million franchise chain the Coffee Beanery, offers franchisees a full line of specialty coffees as well as equipment and services such as training.[29] However, as you saw in Chapter 14, some franchisees complain about the way franchisers use their channel power. That's why franchisees must review any franchise agreement in advance, as discussed in Table 15.3.

Before you go on . . .

A. How do retailers add value to satisfy customers?

B. In what ways does retail ownership affect value-chain relationships?

retail image

the perceptions of a retailer by its customers and other stakeholders

atmospherics

the physical design of the interior and exterior retailing space coupled with lighting, music, fragrance, and other sensory cues

Retailers are discovering that dramatic atmospherics can generate value. Rainforest Cafe advertises itself as "A wild place to shop and eat." This restaurant/retailer recreates a tropical rain forest with live and animated wildlife and special effects. The first outlet opened in the Mall of America in Minnesota. Others are now opening across the country. Do you think customers are likely to continue a relationship with a restaurant/retailer solely because of dramatic atmospherics?

Building Relationships Through Retail Marketing Strategy

Like every other partner in the value chain, retailers have to maintain close relationships with customers as well as with suppliers and other stakeholders. Put yourself in the position of a retailer. To build relationships, you apply the eight universal processes of marketing, starting with environmental scanning and marketing research (p. 134). Then you develop strategies for targeting and positioning, product, pricing, location, integrated marketing communication, service, operations, and value-chain partnerships.

Targeting and Positioning Strategy

As a retailer, you, like other marketers, must select a target market and position your business to appeal to the customers you're targeting. First you evaluate target markets and segments by considering demographics, lifestyles, and buying behavior, among other factors. For example, Lerner New York, a $1 billion apparel chain owned by the Limited, targets women aged 35 to 55 who have busy lifestyles. Chief executive Pamela S. Goodman points to some 40 million customers in this fast-growing target market—customers who want to buy entire outfits, not just individual pieces of clothing.[30]

Once you have an idea of each segment's wants and needs and potential profitability, you can select the one (or more) you want to serve. Then you can use positioning (p. 224) to encourage the people in your targeted segments to form a particular impression of your stores.

A **retail image** consists of the perceptions of a retailer by its customers and other stakeholders.[31] Products, employees, pricing, location, integrated marketing communication, service, and operations all combine to project a particular retail image. In the United States, Toys "Я" Us, for example, is positioned as a low-price store with a vast selection of toys. In Europe and Asia, however, the retailer stresses selection more than low prices.[32]

Retail image is also supported by atmospherics. The components of **atmospherics** are the physical design of the interior and exterior retailing space coupled with lighting, music, fragrance, and other sensory cues.[33] For example, Pam Del Duca, president of a $10 million gift and clothing retail business, says that "retail is theater." She carefully plans her atmospherics: any customer who enters one of her 16 stores "is bombarded with a bunch of things—the visual displays, the music playing, and the aroma of potpourri. And we use all those ways as opportunities to sell merchandise."[34]

Atmospherics are important in all types of retail establishments. For instance, the Dadeland Marriott in Miami has installed a $12,000 machine that circulates floral and citrus aromas throughout the lobby to enhance the atmospherics, making the hotel more appealing to travelers.[35] On the World Wide Web, snazzy graphics, sound, and motion are the equivalent of atmospherics. Holiday Inn's Web site, for example, includes colorful virtual-reality tours of its hotels as well as an interactive version of the Travel Buff board game.[36]

Product Strategy

In developing product strategy, retailers face a variety of choices, including type of products, product mix width (the number of product lines offered), and product line length (the number of products in each line carried). The product strategy chosen determines whether a retailer is in general merchandise retailing or limited-line retailing.

General Merchandise Retailing

General merchandise retailers carry a wide product mix **(p. 299)**; they are differentiated by the variety of goods and services they offer. *Department stores* such as Nordstrom and Dillard are general merchandise retailers that stock a wide range of products, including some lengthy product lines. Because they offer a number of value-added services (such as credit, delivery, and gift wrapping), their costs are higher than those of retailers of many other types. By comparison, *variety stores* such as McCrory and Woolworth stock a wide variety of relatively inexpensive products but offer far fewer services than department stores.

Hypermarkets are mammoth retail stores that sell food and nonfood products under one roof, at low prices but with few services. Hypermarkets first surfaced in Europe during the 1960s. The largest, French retailer Carrefour, rings up $20 billion a year in Europe, South America, and Asia. The concept has been less successful in the United States, however. Carrefour opened and then closed two U.S. hypermarkets during the early 1990s. Kmart and Wal-Mart tested but didn't retain hypermarket stores. On the other hand, Meijer's, an 86-store hypermarket chain in the Midwest, has successfully used high-quality foods, attractive displays, and low prices to build strong customer relationships.[37]

Kmart and Wal-Mart have been converting their U.S. hypermarket stores to *supercenters*, also known as superstores, huge combination food–nonfood stores with few services or frills but low prices and a varied product selection. Whereas hypermarkets average 230,000 square feet in size, supercenters average under 200,000 square feet, carrying about 100,000 items. Both Kmart and Wal-Mart have changed the product mix in their supercenters to emphasize food products, competing directly with supermarkets.[38]

Warehouse club retailers are general merchandise retailers that offer a narrower product mix and shorter product lines at discount prices in a warehouse setting. Customers pay a membership fee to buy at low "member" prices. The largest retailer of this type is Price/Costco, which operates 221 cavernous stores and rings up $18 billion a year in U.S. sales.[39] Warehouse retailers keep prices low by offering very few services and spending little on atmospherics.

general merchandise retailers

carry a wide product mix; they are differentiated by the variety of goods and services they offer

Single-line retailers have started offering some unusual items. Famous Fido's Doggie Deli in Chicago, Illinois, sells gourmet treats for canines. There are also stores that deal exclusively in sunglasses, ties, baseball caps—even socks. What kind of selection do you think consumers will be able to enjoy as more single-line retailers begin operating on the Internet?

limited-line retailers

offer fewer types of product than are sold by general merchandise retailers, but they stock many more choices in each product line

single-line retailers

offer many choices of only one type of product

scrambled merchandising

a strategy in which a retailer carries product lines that are not related to its main product focus

discount retailers

retailers that market top-quality and lower-quality products in large volumes at low prices but with few services

off-price retailers

retailers that offer specially purchased branded products, with limited services, at prices below those charged by full-price retailers

Limited-Line Retailing

Limited-line retailers offer fewer types of product than are sold by general merchandise retailers, but they stock many more choices in each product line. Supermarkets, for example, use a product strategy of carrying a relatively narrower range of products in considerable depth: they offer mostly food and household products, with a sometimes staggering variety of brands in each type of product. Of course, some supermarkets limit their product mixes more than others. Fresh Fields, for example, is a Maryland-based supermarket chain that sells only natural, healthy, environmentally correct groceries.[40]

Limited-line nonfood retailers are also known as *specialty stores* because they specialize in products of certain types and offer a much more extensive selection in each product line. For instance, Botanix, in Canada, specializes in gardening products. Similarly, Darryl McCray's New York City store, House of Nubian, carries only shirts and other products made or designed by African American companies.[41]

Computer City (computers), Barnes & Noble (books), Autozone (auto parts), and Toys "Я" Us (toys) have taken the product strategy of limited-line retailing a step further. These stores are called *category killers*, retailers that offer an enormous selection—and low prices—in one product category. Some specialty stores offer selection, some offer price; but category killers combine the two for a potent competitive advantage. Consider Computer City, with giant, 23,000-square-foot outlets stocked almost to the ceiling with competitively priced personal computers, printers, and accessories. Alan Bush, president of Computer City, notes, "Our intent is to be the lowest price in the market—period."[42]

An even more narrowly focused product strategy is used by **single-line retailers**, which offer many choices of only one type of product. The names of single-line retailers such as Just Bulbs (lightbulbs), Just Shades (lamp shades), and Just Kidding (children's clothing and toys) let customers know exactly what kind of product awaits them.[43]

Scrambled Merchandising

Groceries in warehouse club stores and drug products in general merchandise retailers illustrate a growing retail trend. **Scrambled merchandising** is a strategy in which a retailer carries product lines that are unrelated to its main product focus. One popular product line popping up in different stores is prescription drugs. To lure more shoppers and earn higher profit margins, Kmart, Target, Safeway, and other retailers have added drugs, even though pharmaceuticals are unrelated to their other product categories. Another popular product line is groceries, which can now be found in drug stores, general merchandise stores, warehouse club stores, and some gas stations.[44]

Retailing of Services

Many retailers concentrate on service products. Service retailers include beauty salons, auto repair shops, print shops, insurance stores, banks, tax preparers, and medical clinics. Such businesses often sell related goods, but their primary purpose is to provide fast, friendly, and quality service. For example, Mail Boxes Etc. franchise stores offer an array of services, including private mailboxes, packing and shipping, e-mail, and photocopying. Audrey Ritt's

New technology continues to change the way retail businesses operate. In this example, an employee uses a hand-held order-entry system to electronically record a sports fan's food order at the Omni Arena in Atlanta, where the Atlanta Hawks play. This technology allows the food marketer to more quickly respond to customer requests and to track inventory at the push of a button. What other types of retail businesses might profit from using such hand-held ordering devices?

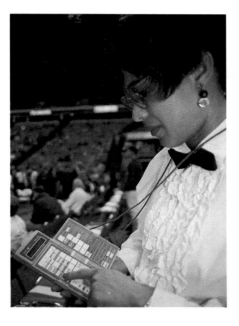

Mail Boxes Etc. on the campus of the University of Michigan is located inside the student union, making its services more convenient for the 15,000 students who pass through daily.[45]

Frontline employees are the key to success for service retailers because they perform the services that form the basis for the value package. Internal marketing ◄——┘ **(p. 9)** is critical in such stores because customers are more likely to come back when they are treated well by friendly service personnel who are properly trained and adequately empowered. Many service retailers harness technology to support their employees. At Tony and Joe's Seafood Place in Washington, D.C., servers send customer orders from the table to the restaurant's kitchen using handheld computers. This system speeds service and prevents servers from accepting orders for items that have sold out.[46]

Pricing Strategy

Pricing can be an effective customer draw—and a powerful competitive tool—for retailers. Some U.S. stores follow a *one-price policy*. At Everything One Dollar stores in the Midwest, every product is of course priced at $1.00. The merchandise can be priced so low because the quality isn't top-notch. In Japan, many independent "100 yen" stores sell housewares at that one low price, made possible by a foreign-exchange situation in which imported goods cost much less than domestic goods.[47]

Discount retailers market top-quality and lower quality products in large volumes at low prices but with few services. As the term suggests, discount retailers sell merchandise at a reduced price, compared with full-price stores. They carry lower product and service costs and lower profit margins. Wal-Mart is the largest discount general merchandise retailer in the world.

Tokyo, Japan, has single-price stores similar to those found in the United States. These "100 yen" shops offer all kinds of items at one low price. Many consumers like knowing that every item will be very inexpensive and that they may find some real bargains. Which product strategies do you think would be most successful with such a pricing strategy?

Off-price retailers offer specially purchased branded products, with limited services, at prices below those charged by full-price retailers. To implement this strategy, off-price retailers buy first-quality goods (or sometimes seconds) from manufacturers before or after the regular selling season. This opportunistic purchasing means that the products in stock may vary from week to week. However, because the stores pay less than the ordinary wholesale price—and because they add only a tiny profit margin—they can offer lower prices than other retailers. Leading off-price retailers include T.J. Maxx and Marshall's (now owned by the same company).

Issues for critical thinking

How does off-price retailing differ from discount retailing? Why would a customer care about the difference? Should retailers clarify the distinction in their integrated marketing communication? Why or why not?

Rather than sell out-of-season or irregular merchandise to off-price or discount stores, some manufacturers prefer to open factory outlets. More factory outlets are opening as manufacturers seek to control the way their products reach customers. There are more than 10,000 factory outlets across the United States, ringing up over $10 billion in annual sales. Factory outlets include Calvin Klein (apparel), Mikasa (china, cutlery), and Seiko (clocks, watches).[48]

In contrast, *full-price* retailers such as Bloomingdale's and Tiffany offer better quality brands without discounts (except during sales). Their prices reflect a profit margin higher than that established by discount and off-price retailers. To attract customers (and to clear out slow-moving goods), these retailers periodically use promotional pricing, placing selected items on sale. However, frequent sales and steep reductions have undermined consumer confidence in the value represented by the regular prices of many full-price retailers.[49]

As you saw in Chapter 13, retailers generally set prices by adding a certain percentage, known as the *markup*, to the product's wholesale cost. When the product doesn't sell as well as expected—or when retailers want to generate excitement—they authorize a *markdown*, reducing the original price by a particular percentage. (For more information on markups and markdowns, see Appendix B at the end of the text.) However, Sears, Wal-Mart, and other retailers minimize markdowns by using an everyday low pricing (EDLP) strategy to reassure customers that their regular prices offer good value.

Location Strategy

One of the most critical factors for retail success is location. But a location that's right today may not be right tomorrow as a result of changes in customer buying habits, population trends, real-estate values, and competition. A.J. Cohen learned about such changes from personal experience. For decades his family had run the Lady Jane women's apparel stores in downtown Savannah, Georgia. Over time, however, customers moved to the suburbs and shopped there too. "Our customers' habits changed because of where they were living," explains Cohen. "Shopping malls were just more convenient for them than coming back into town to shop at my stores." Finally, Cohen closed Lady Jane forever.[50]

Generally, retailers have four location options: a freestanding location, an urban business district, a shopping center, and a strip center. When retailers such as Lowe's home improvement centers or Ford car dealers choose *freestanding locations*, they build on a busy highway or street without adjacent stores. This keeps real-estate and occupancy costs low and lets the retailer

planned shopping center

a group of stores in an architecturally unified site that is designed and marketed together as a shopping destination

control the building's look and the parking. At the same time, freestanding stores can't rely on neighboring stores to attract customers, so they often need ongoing marketing campaigns to draw shoppers.

A second option is to open in an *urban business district*. Macy and Marshall Field's, two of the oldest U.S. department stores, started in such locations. Downtown stores draw shoppers who work or live in the city, as well as tourists. In cities all over the world, such concentrations of stores in one area create a magnet for shoppers.

Many stores choose to locate in a **planned shopping center**, a group of stores in an architecturally unified site that is designed and marketed together as a shopping destination. Such centers usually include one or more *anchor stores*, major department or discount stores that draw shoppers. One variation is the *regional shopping center*, a large shopping center with several anchor stores and 50 or more specialty stores. The largest one in the United States is Mall of America in Bloomington, Minnesota. This colossus, which occupies 4.2 million square feet, boasts four anchors, 400 other retailers, an indoor amusement park, and dozens of restaurants.[51] A smaller variation is the *community shopping center*, which has fewer anchor stores and fewer specialty stores.

Strip centers are groups of stores clustered along a major street or route. Even when the stores are connected, each has its own exterior entrance and facade. Taking strip centers a step further are *power centers*, strips with a number of category-killer retailers or discount stores. Strip and power centers are becoming more popular as shopping habits change. Time-pressured customers can dart into one or two stores and complete their errands faster than would be possible during a visit to an enclosed shopping center. Seven Corners Center in Falls Church, Virginia, which wanted to offer its customers this quick-getaway feature, converted from an indoor shopping center to a strip center. *Niche malls* are now emerging to appeal to selected customer segments such as working women. For example, Shops at Somerset Square in Glastonbury, Connecticut, targets working women.[52]

In addition to Wal-Mart, this power center includes Home Depot, PETsMART, Circuit City, and a Super Crown bookstore. At power centers like this one, consumers enjoy the convenience of being able to drive to a store, run in, and finish their shopping quickly. What are the disadvantages of power centers? What are the advantages of enclosed malls?

In choosing a store location, retailers analyze the demographics and buying behavior of people in the surrounding area; they also examine transportation patterns, investigate the competition, and research local regulations. Geodemographic analysis ◄——┘ **(p. 228)** helps a retailer find an area with a population that reflects the income level and other demographic characteristics that match the targeted customer segment. Many retailers use computer-generated maps to study the demographic characteristics of a specific area. Executives of the Target chain, for example, map the area around each store to determine where population and income trends will support an additional store.[53]

Location is so important that a number of stores of all sizes outsource site selection to experts. Large stores such as Saks Fifth Avenue do this, as do small stores such as Creative Kidstuff in Minneapolis. "The issue of retail site selection is too important and complicated not to use the best help available to find the most suitable site for your business," says Creative Kidstuff's owner, Cynthia Gerdes.[54]

One of the newest locations for retailers is the Internet. It is relatively inexpensive for a small retailer to establish a Web site and reach a global market. Consequently, Internet retailing is expected to grow dramatically in the next few years.

Integrated Marketing Communication Strategy

Whether they want to attract new customers or maintain their relationship with current customers, retailers can choose among an almost endless variety of integrated marketing communication approaches: advertising, personal selling, direct marketing, store displays, special events—the list goes on and on. Here are just a few of the ways that retailers large and small are communicating with their customers:

Tesco, a supermarket chain in Great Britain, practices relationship marketing using a customer database. Its loyalty program features cash discounts and gifts that customers earn by making purchases over time. What integrated marketing communication techniques would you use to promote this program?

- Tesco, a U.K. supermarket chain, uses database marketing to operate a customer loyalty program offering discounts and other benefits for members. When customers show membership cards at the cash register, their purchases are credited toward awards of cash discounts and gifts. Tesco stays in constant touch with its members through newsletters and other promotional materials. More than 5 million members are in Tesco's database, which is used to analyze purchasing patterns and promotional effectiveness.[55]

- The Body Shop, which retails personal care products through 238 stores in the United States, uses special events to draw attention to its products and to social causes. The company recently turned a truck into a portable store. Driving to markets where Body Shop stores are located, the truck stops at colleges, shopping centers, and other sites to demon-

Each new friend is just as important as the first.

Welcome.

Thank you for your order. I remember so vividly a day eleven years ago, I had mailed the first catalog and was literally waiting for the phone to ring—and when the first call came at last, you can imagine my excitement!

Each call today is just as important as that first one, because without you we wouldn't be here.

Please let me take this opportunity to extend a warm 'thank you' for being a part of Hanna, with a savings of 10% on your next order. We're convinced that hannas will give your family lots of softness and wear (if you don't agree, please let me know about it!).

Enjoy the savings, and we'll talk with you soon.

Take **10%** off your next order.
Just mention code 'WB15' when you call, and we'll credit your order!

Good through December 31, 1995. Not valid with any other offer. Hanna Andersson Corporation. Printed on recycled paper.

A good integrated marketing communication strategy will use targeted media to build and enhance customer relationships. This illustration shows how Hanna Andersson, a direct-mail firm, uses relationship marketing to retain customers over time. The firm offers customers a discount of 10 percent on their next order to thank them for their patronage. What other incentives or actions might a catalog marketer provide to retain its customers?

strate products and to give away samples, coupons, and catalogs. This approach has boosted both store and mail-order sales.[56]

- Hanna Andersson, a $52 million children's clothing catalog based in Portland, Oregon, thanks every first-time customer for ordering by sending a 10-percent-off gift certificate good for the next order. It also invites customers to return the company's clothes after children have outgrown them. Customers receive a credit of 20 percent of the average purchase price, which can be used toward any new purchases, and the used clothing goes to children's charities. The socially responsible "Hannadowns" program builds Hanna Andersson's name and, at the same time, strengthens customer relationships.[57]

- K. Barchetti, a two-store fashion clothing retailer in Pittsburgh, Pennsylvania, maintains an extensive database of customer purchases and preferences. Using database marketing, the store periodically mails special offers tailored to each customer's buying behavior. It also mails "Oops!" research forms to find out why customers haven't shopped in a year or more—and to entice them back with a discount. One recent "Oops!" mailing brought in $58,000 in sales.[58]

In the next section, you'll see how a South African retailer strengthens long-term relationships with its customers.

Global Issues

Both education and customers win at The Club

Retailing is never easy, but it's a special challenge in South Africa, where unemployment tops 40 percent. Still, one department store has consistently achieved double-digit growth in sales and profits. How does Edgar's do it? The answer is The Club, a relationship-building program that includes a monthly sweepstakes benefiting members and schools.

More than a million members from all over the country have joined The Club, paying about $20 a year to belong. In exchange, they receive a monthly 80-page magazine with book reviews, beauty tips, and exclusive merchandise offers, as well as discount coupons, surprise gifts, invitations to fashion shows and members-only discount days, and other benefits. Perhaps the biggest draw, however, is the monthly sweepstakes.

Members can win one of 620 cash prizes, including a first prize of 250,000 rands (about $70,000). In addition, the top five winners decide which schools will receive a cash donation from Edgar's. In all, the store donates nearly $1 million to South African schools every year.

Edgar's uses integrated marketing communication to spread the word about the results of this philanthropy. It runs television commercials showing the recipient schools' improved facilities, new computers, and so on. It also hosts Prize Winner Days at local schools and stores to give winners, Club members, and customers a sense of pride in the program. Members feel good about Edgar's and about helping their schools—and they remain loyal.[59]

How can Edgar's find out what additional benefits would bring in more loyal members?

Both large and small store-based retailers are enhancing their IMC strategies by reaching out through the Internet. For example, NationsBank's World Wide Web site provided information about special financial services available during the 1996 Olympic Games in Atlanta. Similarly, Fly & Field, a small store in Glen Ellyn, Illinois, sells fishing rods and reels to customers in Europe, South America, and Asia—via its Web site.[60]

Service Strategy

To satisfy or delight customers, retailers need to offer flexible services that respond to the needs and expectations of each customer segment.[61] Long John Silver's fast-food seafood restaurants, for example, offer drive-through, sit-down, and take-out services. Why so many choices? "We just weren't competing," says a spokesperson."You really have to go where the fish are biting."[62]

The U.S. Postal Service has also developed a retail service strategy. Based on marketing research, the U.S.P.S. has changed thousands of post offices into attractive postal stores staffed by friendly personnel. "The idea is to make the post office a one-stop shopping place," says spokesperson Vic Laudisio. "It's the same one-on-one service that retailers have been doing for years."[63]

Issues for critical thinking

How can you determine what level of service is right for your retail business? What kind of marketing research can you conduct to support decisions about your retail service strategy?

Full-service retailers such as Nordstrom, the Seattle-based department store chain, offer customers many services, including credit, returns, and personal sales attention. Nordstrom is, in fact, a role model for exemplary service: its employees are empowered to do whatever is necessary to satisfy customers.

These days, most department stores are *limited-service retailers*, offering selected services such as merchandise returns and credit. Supermarkets, discount stores, and off-price stores are examples of *self-service retailers*, where customers choose products without sales assistance and bring their selections to a central checkout area. These retailers offer fewer services—but their prices are also lower than those of full- or limited-service retailers.

When it comes to service, customers have a long memory. Their perceptions of service quality change slowly over time, even after improvements have been in place for considerable periods. In one recent U.S. government survey, customer satisfaction with retailers in general and department stores in particular had dropped, indicating that retailing has some negative customer perceptions to overcome.[64] That's why service improvements must be long-term and consistent to start new customer relationships or rebuild current ones.

For example, Mobil Oil is bringing full service back to gasoline retailing, which in recent years had steered toward self-service. The Mobil Friendly Serve program is building repeat business through fast, friendly service and clean, attractive stations.[65] Checking on the quality of retail service can raise ethical issues, as the next section shows.

ETHICS & SOCIAL RESPONSIBILITY

Using mystery shoppers ethically

Mystery shoppers are no mystery to the Au Bon Pain restaurant chain, to Safeway supermarkets, and to many other retailers. These marketers hire people who, by pretending to be ordinary customers, test service quality at retail outlets. Store employees never know when and where mystery shoppers will arrive, which helps management get a realistic picture of what happens in each location. But how can marketers avoid crossing the ethical line from service monitoring to spying? Here are a few tips for using mystery shoppers ethically.

- *Let employees know the criteria by which service is being judged.* Au Bon Pain posts the judging criteria in each store—along with a list of employees who have received perfect scores in six of the service areas examined by mystery shoppers.

- *Reward employees for good service rather than punishing them for poor service.* "Some companies give bonuses or praise when staff members get good write-ups," says an executive at one firm. "And the primary benefit is, when employees know they're being monitored, all customers tend to get treated better."

- *Judge service quality by a series of visits rather than a single visit.* "I'm not worried about whether one shift was good or bad," explains Au Bon Pain's CEO. "That happens to everybody. But I'm certainly interested in whether we have a systematic problem across a specific district or a store, whether it's service speed or product quality."[66]

How would you suggest that marketers explain a mystery shopper program to employees?

Operations Strategy

Your operations strategy, like your service strategy, will be geared to your customers' needs and expectations. The majority of retailers operate stores in fixed locations. Because today's consumers want to be able to buy goods and services in a variety of ways, however, nonstore retailing has become an increasingly important part of operations strategy.

Nonstore retailing now accounts for $60 billion in annual sales—just under 3 percent of all U.S. retail sales—and it's growing rapidly, fueled by technological advances and changes in consumer buying behavior and lifestyles.[67] Among the many nonstore methods of retail operation are catalogs, vending machines, interactive kiosks, television home shopping and interactive television, and computer-based retailing on the Internet.

- *Catalogs*. Mail-order catalogs are hardly new—Sears, Roebuck Inc. and Montgomery Ward were retailing through catalogs more than 100 years ago—but they've become more popular in the past three decades. Marketers mail 13 billion catalogs every year to time-pressured consumers interested in shop-at-home convenience. The latest wrinkle is the CD-ROM catalog, which allows customers whose home computers are equipped with CD-ROM drives to look up product information. For example, Microsoft placed its software products on a CD-ROM catalog sent to 250,000 customers of Egghead Software stores.[68]

Customers can buy a pair of Levi's jeans, using a credit card, at this vending machine in Lyon, France. Vending machines are an increasingly popular and a frequently used means for selling products in many countries. In Japan, for example, consumers can buy a wide array of products—not just food—from vending machines. What do you think accounts for the popularity of vending machines in Japan? Do you envision a similar use developing in the United States? Why?

- *Vending machines*. A $23 billion business in the United States, vending machines sell an ever-increasing variety of products. Although food products top the list, nonfood products are becoming more commonplace in vending machines. The Electronic Merchandising Systems in Cincinnati, a $10 million company, sells Kodak film and cameras from vending machines placed in sports stadiums and other locations in 20 states.[69]

- *Interactive kiosks*. An interactive kiosk is a computerized machine with a touch-sensitive screen that allows consumers to view product photos, ask questions, and buy products by credit card. By one estimate, 500,000 of these devices will soon be in place in shopping centers and other locations around the United States. Interactive kiosks go well beyond traditional vending machines: they can offer detailed information, make sales, and dispense coupons, as well as collect data about customer needs and preferences. Interactive kiosks placed by Campus Interaction at U.S. colleges let students hear samples of music from Warner Music recordings, sign up for a subscription to *huH Music Magazine*, and more.[70]

- *Television home shopping and interactive television*. QVC and Home Shopping Network are two of the main U.S. channels that allow viewers to call a toll-free number to buy goods they've seen on television. But sales through television home shopping are plateauing. Interest is growing in interactive television, in which viewers use a special remote control to request product information and place orders. Canada's UBI, planned as the world's largest interactive television system, serves as a

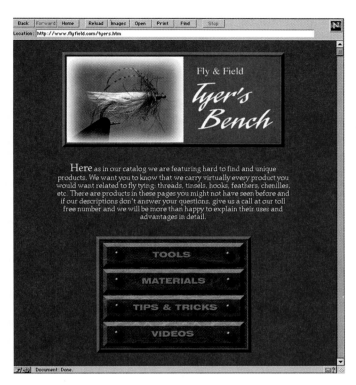

In many areas, consumers can't easily find just the right fly-fishing equipment. Now, these enthusiasts can use their computers to browse the Internet, visit Fly & Field's Web site, and go shopping. What are some of the changes in wholesaling and retailing you anticipate as a result of marketing on the Web?

category management

the practice of managing each product category as a separate business, tailoring the product mix on a store-by-store basis to satisfy customers

nonstore retail outlet for National Bank of Canada, Sears Canada, and other marketers.[71]

- *Computer-based retailing on the Internet.* Commercial online database services such as CompuServe as well as the World Wide Web of the Internet are part of computer-based retailing, in which customers use a personal computer and a modem to browse through product offerings and place orders. Store-based retailers such as Gottschalk's department store have jumped onto the Web, as have retailers without stores. Over 35,000 Web retailers are still experimenting with merchandise, pricing, and atmospherics, even as sales grow.[72]

Value-Chain Partnership Strategies

Like all marketers, retailers need strong relationships with their suppliers and channel partners as well as with their customers. In this way, they can secure a seamless, timely flow of products to satisfy customers at the end of the value chain. Good relationships are equally important for upstream marketers, which depend on the information about consumer needs and buying patterns that retailers can provide. Many retailers offer special membership cards to shoppers who fill out questionnaires about household buying. Supplementing this information with scanner data about actual purchases, the stores can tell manufacturers a great deal about who is buying what—and when.

Managing information flow up and down the value chain is one key to long-term profits. As you saw in Chapter 14, retailers are using techniques such as efficient consumer response (ECR), quick response, and electronic data interchange (EDI) to exchange information and build closer channel relationships.

In addition, many retailers are stressing category management. **Category management** is the practice of managing each product category as a separate business, tailoring the product mix on a store-by-store basis to satisfy customers. The purpose is to stock, price, and promote the products in each category on the basis of the actual buying behavior of each customer segment in each store. As a result, customers get the exact products they want, retailers don't waste shelf space on unneeded products, and manufacturers and channel partners sell more.[73]

To be effective, category management must be a team effort, and it is necessary to speed communication by breaking down the boundaries that separate value-chain partners. Instead of thinking in terms of individual brands, manufacturers take a broader view and help their retail partners expand overall sales and profits in a particular category. Then category management is "a win/win situation," observes Yosi Heber of Dannon Yogurt. When Dannon teamed up with its retail partners to implement category management, the stores got the products they wanted—and Dannon's sales doubled, thanks to the flow of timely sales information.[74]

One of the ways 7-Eleven Japan earns above-average profits is by using technology to carefully monitor the purchasing patterns of its customers; it can then quickly adjust inventory or introduce new products to meet demand. The stores thus build close relationships with both customers and suppliers. 7-Eleven stores in the United States are now trying to modernize to become as successful and profitable as their counterparts in Japan. What changes will you expect to see in your local 7-Eleven as a result?

The 7-Eleven Japan convenience store chain goes a step further, using a computer system that tracks individual purchases, pairing the data with demographic information about its customers. In each store, clerks key in the gender and approximate age of each customer as well as the items purchased. Using store-by-store data, the system generates purchase orders for channel partners and manufacturers. As a result, any product local customers want is always in stock, and products local customers don't want are quickly dropped. This system has helped the retailer forge closer relationships with more than 15 manufacturers, which maintain special factories devoted to 7-Eleven products.[75] That system is now being introduced in U.S. 7-Eleven stores.

Before you go on . . .

A. Why are atmospherics important?

B. What are four options for retail location strategy?

C. What is nonstore retailing and what are some examples?

D. Why is category management important?

Retailing Evolves to Satisfy Customers

Retailing is like every other aspect of marketing in that it never stands still. Newer forms of retailing such as interactive kiosks and computer-based retailing on the World Wide Web have emerged, even as older forms such as trading posts have all but disappeared. Two theories that describe the nature of retail evolution are the wheel of retailing and the retail life cycle.

The Wheel of Retailing

The **wheel of retailing** theory describes retail evolution as a cycle in which newcomers, beginning as low-cost, low–profit margin, low-price retail operations, gradually upgrade their products and services to better serve customers, while raising their prices, which attracts more upscale customers. As shown in Figure 15.2, the cycle continues when new businesses enter at the low end to challenge established retailers—businesses that have traveled up the wheel from their stripped-down beginnings. The wheel is constantly turning, as retailers upgrade to satisfy customers and to compete more effectively with the low-price appeal of retailers just starting out.[76]

Woolworth provides a good example of a spin on the wheel of retailing. During the late nineteenth century, the company rocketed to success with variety stores selling an assortment of products for 5¢ and 10¢. Over time, Woolworth traveled up the wheel, adding services, enlarging and upgrading

wheel of retailing
a theory that describes retail evolution as a cycle of continuing to upgrade to serve more upscale customers

Long-Established Retailers

- Top-quality products, customer services
- Higher prices, costs, profit margins
- Appeal to upscale consumers

Established Competitors

- Upgraded products, customer service
- Moderate prices
- Appeal to both value-conscious and service-conscious consumers

New Entrants

- Low cost, low profit
- Limited offerings and customer services
- Appeal to price-sensitive consumers

FIGURE **15.2**

Wheel of Retailing

According to this theory of retail evolution, new retailers enter the industry at the low-price, low-cost part of the wheel. Then they gradually move up the wheel, adding more services to satisfy customers and upgrading to compete with established retail competitors.

retail life cycle

describes the four-stage cycle of innovation, accelerated development, maturity, and decline that characterizes retail strategies

the product mix, and raising prices. In the 1960s, the company had to compete with discounters entering the low end of the wheel. By the 1980s, the ever-expanding product mix of discount stores such as Wal-Mart overshadowed the mix offered in Woolworth's variety stores. Finally, in the 1990s, Woolworth responded to added competition from lower price challengers such as Dollar General by closing hundreds of its less-profitable variety stores.[77]

Not all retail innovations fit the wheel of retailing model. It doesn't apply to interactive kiosks and computer-based retailing, for example, because these newcomers don't focus on low prices. Still, many businesses do seem to follow the evolutionary cycle suggested by the wheel of retailing. Consider factory outlet stores, which are moving upscale from their bargain-basement origins, offering better atmospherics, more sales help, and more services. Or note that customers at selected Wal-Mart stores can buy gourmet foods at Harry's in a Hurry convenience-style grocery departments or have purchases sent home; the company is also moving up the wheel by testing a fancy foods catalog.[78]

The Retail Life Cycle

Like products, retail strategies pass through a series of predictable stages during their time in the market. The **retail life cycle** theory describes the four-stage cycle of innovation, accelerated development, maturity, and decline that characterizes retail strategies. In the innovation stage, the retailer adopts a new strategy that's distinctly different from those of existing retail marketers. As the innovation draws more customers, the life cycle attains the second stage, where sales and profits grow rapidly. In the third stage, the retail strategy faces many competitors, and sales and profits grow more slowly. In the fourth stage, sales and profits go downhill, as customers migrate to competitors with more innovative retail strategies.[79]

In the context of the retail life cycle, Woolworth's variety store strategy is in the decline stage. The company's original five-and-dime stores were innovative, so they attracted much customer attention. Sales and profits soared as Woolworth expanded to bring its new strategy to more customers. As an increasing number of competitors emerged, however, growth and profits grew more slowly, and the strategy moved into the maturity stage. Now the variety store strategy is barely profitable, and Woolworth is concentrating on specialty stores that are in earlier stages of the retail life cycle. Among these are Foot Locker, Lady Foot Locker, and After Thoughts, specialty store chains that provide extensive product choices but limited services.[80]

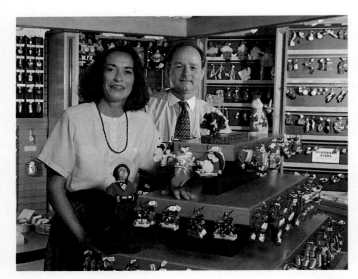

Temporary retailing is gaining popularity in the United States. It involves opening temporary retail venues to bring customers seasonal goods and then closing them when the season passes. Pattie and Robert MacCool's Ornament House sells Christmas decorations in three permanent retail locations and 10 temporary locations, sometimes using kiosks in the middle of malls. What other kinds of seasonal products and services might appeal to consumers in your area?

You can't predict the exact timing of the stages in the retail life cycle, any more than you can predict the timing of the product life cycle. Since, however, the life cycle of many retail strategies is becoming compressed, the time between innovation and decline is shorter than ever before. One of the hottest trends in retailing is *temporary retailing*, a retail strategy that is planned to last for only a brief period.

Small business owners Pattie and Robert MacCool are among the growing number of entrepreneurs active in temporary retailing. Their first temporary store did well during its six months in operation selling Christmas ornaments. Now the MacCools operate up to 10 temporary stores in shopping centers around Baltimore and Washington, D.C. When sales fall off in any temporary store—or when the lease runs out—the MacCools can begin again with an innovative new retail strategy.[81]

An important part of retail strategy is getting the right products to the right people at the right time. This calls for an effective strategy for managing logistics throughout the value chain. That is the subject of the next chapter.

Before you go on . . .

A. How does the wheel of retailing explain retail evolution?

B. What is the retail life cycle theory?

Summary

1. **Differentiate among the three types of wholesaler.**

   Manufacturer-owned wholesalers control the flow of their products through the marketing channel. Merchant wholesalers take title to the products they buy for resale. Agents and brokers don't assume legal ownership of the products they buy for resale.

2. **Describe how retail image and atmospherics are related to retail positioning.**

   Positioning encourages people in the retailer's targeted segments to form a particular impression of its stores. The retail image consists of the perceptions of a retailer held by its customers and other stakeholders. Atmospherics—the physical design of the interior and exterior retailing space, along with lighting, music, fragrance, and other sensory cues—are part of retail image.

3. **Identify the two main product strategies used by retailers and define scrambled merchandising.**

   Retailers can use either general merchandise retailing or limited-line retailing to build customer relationships. General merchandise retailers carry a wide product mix, whereas limited-line retailers carry a narrower range of products in more depth. In scrambled merchandising, a retailer carries product lines that are not related to its main product focus.

4. **Differentiate among discount, off-price, and full-price retail strategies.**

   Discount retailers sell top-quality and lower quality products in large volumes at low prices with few services. Off-price retailers offer specially purchased branded products, with limited services, priced below items sold by full-price retailers. Full-price retailers offer better quality brands without discounts.

5. **Analyze why nonstore retailing is becoming more popular.**

   Consumers want to be able to buy goods and services in a variety of ways, to accommodate changes in buying behavior and lifestyles. These changes, coupled with technological advances, are adding to the popularity of nonstore retailing, such as marketing on the Internet.

6. **Demonstrate how category management affects relationships among retailers, their value-chain partners, and their customers.**

   Category management is the practice of managing each product category as a separate business, tailoring the product mix store by store to satisfy each customer segment. Thus the retailer can satisfy local customers while providing manufacturers and channel partners with timely information about customer needs.

7. **Describe the evolution of retailing, based on the wheel of retailing and the retail life cycle theories.**

   The wheel of retailing describes retail evolution as a cycle in which newcomers begin at the low end and gradually upgrade products and services, raising prices and attracting more upscale customers. The retail life cycle describes retail evolution as a cycle with four stages: innovation, accelerated development, maturity, and decline.

KEY TERMS

atmospherics 448

brokers 442

category management 459

chain stores 446

discount retailers 451

general merchandise retailers 449

limited-line retailers 450

manufacturer's representatives 441

merchant wholesalers 439

off-price retailers 451

planned shopping center 453

retail image 448

retail life cycle 461

retailers 443

retailing 443

scrambled merchandising 450

selling agents 442

single-line retailers 450

wheel of retailing 460

wholesalers 438

Skill-Building Applications

1. What kind of information could you give your local supermarket that would help it better meet your needs? Should all supermarkets request such information from customers?

2. A merchant wholesaler calls on your local stationery store, which is competing with Staples, a category-killer store. How can the merchant wholesaler help the smaller stationery store compete?

3. If France's Carrefour announced plans to reenter the U.S. market, which product strategy would you recommend? Why?

4. One of the fastest growing segments of the U.S. population consists of people over the age of 65.

Pick a local retailer and show how it could develop strategies to cater to that market.

5. Peapod now delivers groceries to people in their homes. What other retailers in your area could benefit from home delivery? How could you provide that service for them at a profit?

6. 7-Eleven stores in the United States are adopting the database marketing approach used by 7-Eleven Japan. What kinds of questions should the U.S. stores ask to elicit information about the exact items desired by customers?

Getting Involved in Marketing

1. *On Your Own* From the wholesaler's viewpoint, what are the advantages and disadvantages of taking title to goods before selling them to customers? What value does taking title provide for the wholesaler's customers? For the wholesaler's suppliers?

2. *On Your Own* Visit three retailers in a shopping center or urban business district. How would you classify each? Identify the target market and positioning for each. Are all the elements of each retailer's marketing strategy consistent with the target market and positioning? What improvements can you suggest?

3. *Find Out More* Find an article (in a newspaper, magazine, or online information service) about a successful wholesaler. Who are the wholesaler's customers? What services does this wholesaler provide? Why would customers value these services? How can this wholesaler add more value to satisfy its customers?

4. *In a Team* Are department stores obsolete? Divide into two-person teams and debate this issue in class. One student will argue the pro side and the

other will argue the con side. Consider the threat posed by printed and CD-ROM catalogs, television home shopping, and computer-based retailing (such as on the Internet). Also look at the impact of specialty stores and discount stores. Which side is more persuasive? Why?

5. *In a Team* With classmates, tune into a television home-shopping channel or access the World Wide Web. What kinds of products are being marketed? Describe the product selection and the price range. Determine how customers pay for and receive their purchases. Choose one of the featured products and report on the pros and cons of buying in this way rather than by visiting a store.

6. *In a Team* With other students, research the beginnings of a particular retailer. You can select a large, well-known retailer or a smaller, local retailer. How did this retailer get started? Over the years, what changes have been made in product, pricing, service, and positioning? Did this retailer's evolution follow the wheel of retailing? Share your findings with the class.

VideoCase   In Store at Von Maur: Service and Atmospherics

Even a department store known for top-notch customer service has to move up a notch when competing with such world-class retailers as Nordstrom, Neiman-Marcus, Marshall Field's, and Saks Fifth Avenue. But Von Maur is more than meeting the challenge. In fact, in Lombard, Illinois, the location of one of its 12 stores, Von Maur is taking service to new heights.

"The level of customer service at this store has to exceed even current Von Maur standards," notes Richard von Maur III, who is general manager and a member of the fourth generation in the family to run this Davenport, Iowa, retail business. "Other stores talk about customer service, but no one delivers like Von Maur."

To enter the Lombard market, Von Maur spent $20 million to completely renovate an abandoned building that formerly housed another (now defunct) department store. The investment shows in ways that are pleasing to customers. Background piano music adds to the classy atmosphere created by the stylish decor. The store boasts an impressive three-story atrium with arched window skylights, in addition to marble floors, Oriental carpets, working fireplaces, and more than 30 comfortable seating areas.

Shoppers can browse more than two dozen departments featuring quality brands of clothing, cosmetics, shoes, and accessories. New products often debut at Von Maur. This is because the store has made a conscious decision to strengthen relationships with suppliers in its value chain. Rather than pressing suppliers for discounts, says Richard von Maur, "we ask them to ship their new merchandise to Von Maur first." As a result, shoppers can buy new items at Von Maur that may not be available in other stores for weeks or even months.

Staying close to the customer helps Von Maur maintain its competitive edge. Store executives spend part of every work day on the selling floor interacting with customers. In this way, they can continually assess customer satisfaction and find new ways of attracting and delighting shoppers.

But the real secret of Von Maur's success is its staff of 250 salespeople, who take on the challenge of delighting every customer every day. They receive good hourly wages and are offered incentives for boosting customer satisfaction and sales. Top salespeople receive a gold card that entitles them to a 33 percent discount on store merchandise. In addition, many employees feel that the job itself is rewarding. The atmosphere is exciting, the cooperation with other employees is great, and the job provides an opportunity to learn and grow.

Thanks to its customer-oriented retail strategy, attentive service, and welcoming atmospherics, Von Maur has boosted chainwide annual sales to over $200 million. For other stores in the Lombard area, Von Maur has become *the* department store to benchmark.[82]

Strategies and applications

1. How does Von Maur's product strategy help the store compete with specialty apparel stores such as The Limited?

2. Where on the Wheel of Retailing would you place Von Maur? Why? What are the implications for the store's competitive strategy?

3. Is Von Maur in direct competition with Wal-Mart, Price Club, and other discount retailers? Explain your answer. What are the implications for Von Maur's pricing strategy?

4. How does Von Maur's service strategy stimulate word-of-mouth communication to attract new customers?

5. What other stores have outstanding atmospherics? What makes their atmospherics so attractive: Physical appearance? Pleasant aromas? Eye-catching displays? Can you suggest enhancements for Von Maur's atmospherics?

6. How can Von Maur and other department stores create long-term relationships with customers, encouraging them to come back time after time? What might they do—inadvertently—to hurt those relationships?

Team project

Rank the elements of retail marketing strategy in order of importance to you as a department store customer. Include strategies for products, location, pricing, communications, service, operations, and value-chain partnerships. Compare your ranking with another student's ranking. Discuss the differences and similarities in your rankings. As a team, what suggestions can you make for how Von Maur might plan its strategy, taking into account differences in individual priorities and preferences?

16

Logistics Management

Learning Goals

After you have read and studied this chapter, you should be able to:

1. Explain the role of logistics in the value chain and identify the six major activities in logistics management.
2. Show how to use logistics to deliver quality customer service and to support relationship building.
3. Identify the role of transportation in logistics management and list the five basic modes of transportation.
4. Distinguish between storage warehouses and distribution centers.
5. Analyze the use of inventory and apply the three methods of streamlining inventory management.
6. Show how order processing and shorter order cycles contribute to customer satisfaction.
7. Demonstrate how marketers use reverse logistics.

PROFILE

Dell Computer hitches a ride with Roadway

Dell Computer knows personal computers inside and out. But that doesn't make the $3.5 billion company an expert in shipping. Dell has to get computer chips, disk drives, and other parts to manufacturing plants to be assembled into PCs. Then it has to deliver the finished products to stores and to customers who receive PCs by mail. Fast-paced growth, however, was straining the company's ability to keep up with the details of moving materials and products through the value chain at the right time and at the right cost.

Dell had kept costs down by carrying about one-third less inventory than competitors. Its system was designed to get parts to the plant exactly when needed. About 200 Dell employees were handling shipping chores, but many more were needed to do the job right. Scott Flaig, senior vice president of worldwide operations, estimated that he would need up to 2,000 more employees to handle Dell's current and future sales. Instead of hiring employees, Flaig decided to outsource all the company's shipping activities to Roadway Logistics Systems, which specializes in managing inbound and outbound transportation for other companies.

"We expect multimillion-dollar savings annually," says Flaig. "This allows us to grow without adding people." Since shipping and other logistical details account for as much as 40 percent of the cost of a Dell computer, the deal with Roadway is an extremely important one. Roadway selects the transportation method and the carrier, tracks the progress of parts and PCs as they move to their destinations, and handles shipping for service and repairs. By hitching a ride with Roadway, Dell is free to concentrate on selling PCs rather than on managing logistics.[1]

In this chapter, you'll learn how logistics management links all channel partners and value-chain activities. First, you'll take an in-depth look at the role of logistics in the value chain. Then you'll see how marketers build customer relationships through logistics management, with quality customer service, timely response, cost efficiencies, and tailored logistics. Finally, you'll explore the six basic activities that make up logistics management.

If a company can master all the logistics and supply-chain efforts, it is a key competitive advantage.

Richard E. Belluzzo
Hewlett-Packard[2]

The Role of Logistics in the Value Chain

Scott Flaig of Dell and his counterparts in organizations the world over take logistics very seriously. They recognize the importance of logistics in linking the various functions in the upstream and downstream sides of the value chain. Without logistics, marketers could not organize the flow of products and information throughout the value chain.[3]

Logistics management is the process of managing the movement of raw materials, parts, work in progress, finished products, and related information through the value chain in an efficient, cost-effective manner to meet customer requirements. Notice that *customer requirements* drive the entire process. Every aspect of logistics management is geared toward completing a marketing exchange that provides the customer with the right product at the right time and the right place, in the right condition, and at the right price.[4] Clearly, understanding what customers expect is a prerequisite to creating a logistics management system.

Logistics management is, for many marketers, the final frontier of competition. A great product, priced right, in the right marketing channels, with top-notch integrated marketing communication, is no longer enough. To profitably build long-term customer relationships—and fend off competitors—wise marketers are devising strategies for more efficiently moving products and information through the value chain.

Consider how Glen Johnson, the owner of Oakley Millwork in Illinois, put customers at the center of his building supply company's logistics management system. Surveying customers, he found that no one wanted to wait for products that had been ordered. That's when Johnson issued a new guarantee: if any item ordered is out of stock and not immediately available from a supplier, the customer gets it free. Johnson also created an internal marketing program **(p. 9)** to communicate the guarantee and its implications to the staff. Then he promised a trip to Hawaii for his 30 employees and their spouses if the company went through an entire year without running out of any ordered items.

Johnson's employees quickly mobilized to stand behind the guarantee, developing a computerized inventory tracking system and better internal procedures to closely match demand to supply. Sure enough, Oakley Millwork notched an entire year without running out of ordered items, which delighted both customers and employees. "I directly attribute a 20 percent increase in our sales to that guarantee the year it came out," notes Johnson.[5]

Glen Johnson and his employees at Oakley Millwork guarantee that any product will be available at the time it is ordered or the customer gets it free. That is a strong guarantee and one that could be quite costly unless everyone in the firm is willing to work together to avoid mistakes. To motivate his employees, Johnson offered them a trip to Hawaii if they were able to live up to his challenge for a full year. How can Johnson communicate the benefits of this guarantee to internal and external customers?

How Logistics Moves Products and Information

As you saw in Chapter 14, the producer or service provider stands at a point between the upstream and downstream sides of the value chain. Logistics management is what ties together upstream and downstream activities. **Inbound logistics** is the inflow of raw materials, equipment, and other goods, services, and information needed to make the product or provide the service from the upstream side until the product is actually produced. This process is also known as *materials management*. The downstream side—after the product has been made—is covered by **outbound logistics**, also known as

F I G U R E **16.1** Logistics Management for Music CDs

Inbound logistics brings the flow of raw materials, packaging, other goods and services, and information from upstream suppliers to the producer who manufactures and assembles the music CDs. Outbound logistics manages the flow of finished products and information to channel partners and customers, to complete marketing exchanges.

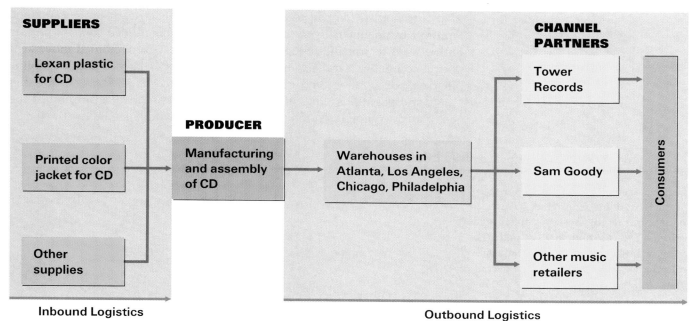

physical distribution, the outflow of finished products and information to the customer to complete a marketing exchange.[6] Figure 16.1 diagrams logistics management in action.

Six major logistical activities occur in the flow of products and information through the value chain: transportation, warehousing, materials handling, inventory management, order processing, and reverse logistics. Managing these activities means cutting across both the boundaries that separate an organization's internal departments and the external boundaries between value-chain partners such as suppliers, wholesalers, and retailers. Seamlessly integrating every activity calls for a high degree of cross-functional coordination, communication, and teamwork.[7]

logistics management

the process of managing the movement of raw materials, parts, work in progress, finished products, and related information through the value chain in an efficient, cost-effective manner to meet customer requirements

Not every marketer places the same emphasis on each of these activities. Many service marketers don't have to worry about transportation, warehousing, materials handling, inventory management, or bringing products back for disposal, repairs, or recycling. The stock brokerage firm Merrill Lynch, for example, doesn't have tangible products to transport or store, so it emphasizes order processing and related logistics functions. Other service marketers such as the Marriott chain of hotels focus on the logistics of processing orders (reservations) and managing inventory (towels and other materials) to refresh hotel rooms.

inbound logistics

the inflow of raw materials, equipment, and other goods, services, and information needed to make the product or provide the service from the upstream side until the product is actually produced

In contrast, Dell Computer is so concerned about getting parts and products to plants and customers that it outsources its transportation activities. Compaq Computer, one of Dell's competitors, takes a different approach, stressing materials handling. Its suppliers share a warehouse near Compaq's Houston factories, so that parts are available when needed on the assembly line.[8]

outbound logistics

the outflow of finished products and information to the customer to complete a marketing exchange

The cost of moving products and information through the value chain is staggering, as you can see in Figure 16.2. In one recent year, U.S. marketers spent $670 billion—nearly 11 percent of the nation's gross domestic product—on logistics activities such as packaging, transportation, and storage. Simply managing logistics more efficiently can therefore net significant savings for marketers and, ultimately, for customers.

For example, Compaq slashed its annual supply costs by more than $600 million by taking delivery of parts exactly when needed and by finding other ways to streamline logistics management. This combined move kept prices competitive and also improved profits. Dixie-Narco, a South Carolina marketer of soda vending machines, was able to cut $800,000 in logistics costs and pass the savings along to customers. The price cut improved the company's competitive stance against European and Japanese rivals.[9]

FIGURE **16.2**   **Where the Logistics Dollar Goes**

Logistics accounts for about 10.5 percent of the gross domestic product. Transportation costs the most, but inventory carrying costs are quite high as well. The latest techniques, such as electronic data interchange (EDI), greatly reduce overall costs. Total costs are now about $670 billion a year.

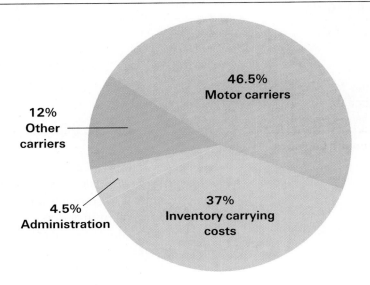

12% Other carriers

46.5% Motor carriers

4.5% Administration

37% Inventory carrying costs

How Logistics Management Adds Value and Builds Relationships

As a marketer, you can apply logistics management to directly create time, place, information, and service utility for customers throughout the value chain. You create time utility by ensuring that the product and information is available to your customers when needed. You create place utility by using logistics to get your products and information to locations that allow customers to conveniently purchase or use them. You provide information utility by applying logistics management to communicate information about product benefits and usage to channel partners and, ultimately, to customers.[10] Finally, you provide service utility by supplying follow-up services such as installation and training.

Indirectly, logistics management supports both form utility and possession utility. By efficiently and effectively managing the movement of raw materials, supplies, and information needed to produce goods and services, you make possible the transformation into a finished product that provides form utility. In addition, the combination of logistics management and channel strategy allows customers to take ownership of your product.[11] By

Sometimes marketing efforts can be so effective that a company generates more demand for goods or services than it can satisfy. This happened to IBM, which historically has been known for great service and responsiveness. IBM was unable to satisfy the initial demand for the Aptiva, putting their customer relationships in jeopardy. However, IBM was able to quickly step up production and overcome the initial problems—something many other companies are unable to do. What steps could IBM have taken to avoid this situation?

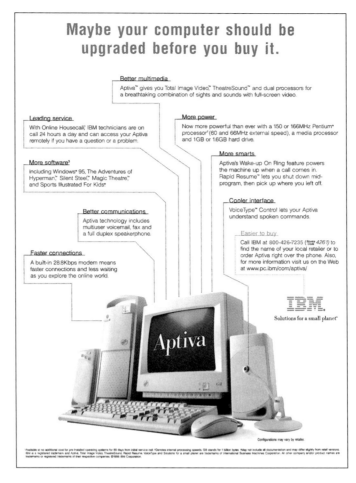

providing all six utilities, you can satisfy your customers' requirements and, at the same time, generate profits.

The reverse is also true: when you don't apply logistics management to create the value your customers require, you may lose their business. Consider what happened when IBM couldn't get its Aptiva personal computer to stores on time or in sufficient quantities. The Aptiva came out of development late, and when it finally reached stores 10 days before Christmas, it nearly missed the holiday selling season. Then dealers couldn't get enough machines to satisfy customer demand. After these logistical problems, IBM had to redouble its efforts to repair relationships with disappointed channel partners and customers.[12]

Marketers are continuously improving their logistics management systems to be able to offer extra value that gives them a competitive edge. By strengthening the linkages between value-chain activities and partners (largely through relationship marketing), many firms are providing more options and more flexibility.[13] This extra value strengthens relationships with customers and encourages long-term loyalty.

For example, Domino's Pizza has added value for customers by using logistics management to streamline its order processing. When someone who has ordered from a particular store calls again to order a home-delivered pizza, Domino's computerized system automatically matches the caller's phone number to a database that includes names, addresses, delivery directions, and past orders. Then Domino's employees can address customers by

Domino's Pizza has received a great deal of free publicity as a result of installing a database that enables employees to answer the phone and immediately access information about the customer placing the call, including previous orders and directions to the customer's location. This makes pizza ordering fast and customer-friendly. It also indicates the direction in which technology is taking logistics management. What other marketers might successfully adapt Domino's system of logistics management?

name, ask whether they want the same order as last time, and avoid asking questions that slow the order process. Once customers have learned how the system works, they can dial in, say they want their regular orders, and hang up—in three seconds.[14]

Ways of Handling the Logistics Function

Some marketers that prefer to handle the entire logistics function themselves are centralizing logistics management at headquarters for better control over quality and costs. Rather than approaching logistics as a series of isolated transactions, these marketers think in terms of relationships up and down the value chain.[15]

For example, John Deere, which markets $7 billion worth of agricultural and construction equipment around the world, manages its own transportation to ensure control over service quality. "We have a long-term relationship with our dealers," explains Ann F. Salabar of Deere's export order department. "It's in our best interest to do the [transport] job." This way, Deere employees can monitor products in transit and, if a tractor's windshield breaks during shipping, a new one can be installed before the equipment reaches the dealer or the customer.[16]

In contrast, other marketers prefer to leave logistics details to specialists. That's why they use outsourcing (p. 40), turning to outside companies that are better equipped to handle one or more logistics activities. For example, Xerox outsources delivery and installation of its giant copying machines to the Ryder System. Ryder truckdrivers haul the quarter-ton machines to Xerox's organizational customers, set up and test the copiers, and clean up after the installation.[17]

Competing Through Logistics Leadership

By integrating the management of all the logistics activities needed to move products and information through the value chain, marketers can lower costs, boost profits, improve quality, and achieve higher levels of customer satisfaction.[18] Information plays a starring role in the integration of activities for logistics leadership. The *virtual value chain* uses information to add value to activities throughout the value chain. The inclusion of "virtual" in this term signifies that the value chain can adapt quickly to any change in the marketing environment. Such quick response depends on gathering, organizing, selecting, analyzing, and distributing information to enhance logistics activities. Information technology is the key to the virtual value chain.[19]

For example, Sweden-based Volvo uses a sophisticated computer system to add value by expediting the flow of information and goods among suppliers, transportation companies, manufacturing plants, and dealerships. The system also allows Volvo dealers to satisfy their customers by tracking down a specific car model no matter where it might be in Volvo's value chain—at another dealership, on a ship, or being built at the factory. Thanks to this capability, Volvo has a competitive edge, one it uses to strengthen relationships with customers as well as with channel partners.[20] The following case describes Wal-Mart's world-class logistics management system.

Applying the Concepts

Benchmarking on Wal-Mart's logistics management

The world's largest retailer has arguably the world's best private logistics management system. Wal-Mart's 20 distribution centers cover more than 18 million square feet in total and hold some 80,000 items. Thus if you want to benchmark against a marketer with world-class logistics management, you might well choose Wal-Mart.

Each distribution center is located within a day's drive of the stores it serves, so that merchandise reaches the stores soon after goods are ordered. The period between ordering merchandise and receiving shipment averages only two days, compared to four to five days for some competitors—and some Wal-Mart stores get delivery in a day. The retailer is linked to its suppliers by electronic data interchange for more timely and accurate communication of merchandise orders and receipts.

Wal-Mart also has one of the nation's largest private truck fleets. The retailer can pinpoint the location of every one of its 2,000 trucks and 11,000 trailers, so it can track the timing of deliveries. But company drivers don't just deliver merchandise: they also gather and report details about the stores they visit, which helps the marketers back at headquarters meet customer needs more effectively.

Through advanced technology and continuous improvement ◄─┘ **(p. 288)**, Wal-Mart has reduced its shipping costs to levels well below those of its competitors. As a result, if Wal-Mart sells the same goods for the same price, it can make up to 2.5 percent more profit. Clearly, Wal-Mart's superior logistics management goes straight to the bottom line—in the form of higher profits.[21]

Make marketing decisions

1. What would Wal-Mart want to investigate when considering whether to outsource some or all of its logistics activities?

2. What kinds of information should Wal-Mart's logistics management system be passing up and down the value chain?

3. How can Wal-Mart research additional improvements to its logistics management system?

4. Do you think Wal-Mart should talk about its superior logistics management in consumer advertising? Why or why not?

How Logistics Supports International Marketing

If moving products and information through a value chain in one country can be complicated and expensive, imagine the complexities of sourcing from and marketing to other countries. As a manufacturer, you can't control many of the environmental elements that affect your ability to obtain supplies or export products to other countries, such as political and legal regulations, economic conditions, competition, geographic location of customers, or infrastructure. You can, however, develop logistics management strategies to overcome the unique challenges and take advantage of the unique opportunities in each country where you do business.[22]

When you think global marketing, think logistics. A key to success in global marketing is getting goods from one country to another in the least expensive way. Starbucks imports coffee beans to Seattle from 20 countries. Each year, the company ships over 1,000 cargo containers by ocean vessel. Therefore, a key task for Starbucks is to look at the total cost of transportion for these raw materials from door to door, one country to another. What factors, other than cost, must Starbucks consider in making a decision regarding mode of transport?

In some countries, marketers have to start from scratch to build logistical links, as Coca-Cola did in Romania in the early 1990s. After Romania's economy emerged from communist control, Coca-Cola built eight bottling plants and put together a fleet of colorful delivery trucks. Coke personnel traveled the country signing up stores, restaurants, and food stands to create distribution channels. Nistor Branescu, a local entrepreneur, was one of the logistical links in this value chain. He trucked Coke to stores outside Bucharest, selling for cash and replenishing stock when needed. Soon he needed two warehouses and six trucks to keep retailers supplied. Thanks to Branescu and thousands of other individuals who perform logistical functions, Coke became the market leader in soft drinks in Romania within four years.[23]

Coca-Cola and other marketers realize that international customers not only expect the same quality service as domestic customers but have serious concerns about buying from distant marketers. Topping the list of concerns are availability of parts and access to technical advice.[24] International marketers can respond to these concerns—as well as to others raised by ultimate consumers—by building logistics management systems around customers' requirements.

Before you go on . . .

A. **What is logistics management and why is it important for marketers?**

B. **How does logistics management add value for customers?**

Building Customer Relationships Through Logistics

Because the purpose of logistics management is to satisfy customer requirements, it's a central ingredient in building and maintaining long-term customer relationships. When you use this marketing tool to deliver quality service, remember that quality is defined by customers, whose criteria include reliability, responsiveness, assurance, empathy, and tangibles; service gaps, as well, are a major consideration ◄─┘ **(p. 323)**. On-time response is therefore a basic logistical component of service quality.

Customers also apply the value equation to weigh the value of the perceived quality and perceived benefits against the price ◄─┘ **(p. 346)**. To give customers more value for their money, it's important to continuously search for cost efficiencies. And, as you'll see later in the chapter, it may make sense to design tailored logistics to meet specific requirements of your key customers.

Delivering Quality Customer Service

Quality customer service is, in effect, the goal of all your logistics activities.[25] To be able to meet such requirements, you begin by researching what customers want and determining how to use logistics to deliver the appropriate level of quality service. Then you can set specific service standards and measure your performance in managing logistics to provide what customers expect.

Customer Service Expectations

Although specific needs vary, customers generally expect logistics to support quality customer service in several areas.

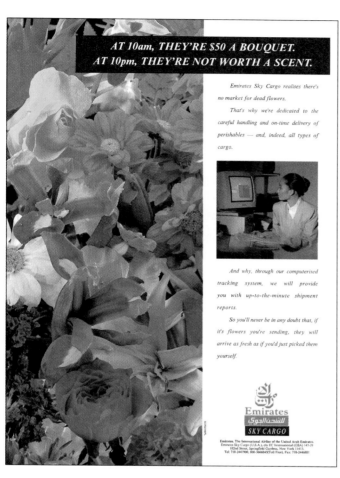

Few products offer a greater shipping challenge to logistics experts than flowers. Because they are so easily damaged, a company that can successfully handle flowers should be able to transport almost anything. That is why Emirates Sky Cargo promotes its ability to ship something as delicate as flowers. What factors would you consider in selecting a shipper if you needed to transport live animals or birds?

- *Accurate and timely communication about products, orders, and deliveries.* Information is the basic building block in the value chain, which is why it's critical to quality customer service. For example, until recently Levi Strauss could not tell retailers the location of jeans on order or give them an exact date of delivery. Considering the roundabout route jeans take from textile mill to sewing plant to stonewashing facility to warehouse, Levi's unresponsiveness wasn't surprising, but it irked retailers who had questions about their orders. Now Levi's uses a computerized logistics management program that tracks the progress of products from fabric suppliers to factories to stores.[26] This system can't help but please Levi customers.

- *Availability of products and information.* It's not enough to know where products *are*; customers also want products and information *available* when and where needed. You risk damaging customer relationships when you can't locate or deliver a product. Business customers, in particular, may be forced to delay making their products if the component you supply isn't available. At the very least, if availability is a problem, you need to let customers know it.

- *Short, reliable order cycles.* It is essential to customers throughout the value chain to know that marketers will deliver orders as agreed. Beyond that, most organizations want to reduce the time between ordering and receiving products so that they can more quickly serve their own customers. Keeping less inventory on hand also slashes costs. For retailers and other channel partners, receiving goods soon after ordering is one of the most important measures of quality customer service.[27]

- *Convenient, cost-effective delivery.* No matter what goods or services you're marketing, your customers will want delivery on their schedules and at a price they can afford. That's why Kansas-based Coleman, which markets coolers, sleeping bags, and lanterns around the world, analyzes every order to find the cheapest and easiest way to provide on-time delivery. Coleman negotiates shipping rates to rein in costs, and it works with channel partners to find the best route for each order.[28]

- *Complete, correct orders.* Many retailers say accuracy is their top priority when placing orders with suppliers. An incomplete or incorrect order sets off a chain reaction: the supplier isn't satisfying its customer, which in turn isn't able to satisfy its customers. Sometimes, if an ordered product isn't available, marketers receive permission to substitute a product in another size or a product that performs as well or better. Substitution is a good solution in such cases, but only if marketers and customers agree on it in advance.[29]

- *Damage-free products.* No customer wants to open a shipment and find smashed, wet, or otherwise damaged goods. Therefore, it's not enough for ordered goods to arrive on time and on budget; they also must be in usable or salable condition. Damage is a particular concern when you are marketing abroad. Often, products have to survive long journeys and differences in temperature and humidity. So to satisfy customers with products that arrive intact, marketers need to pay close attention to packaging, shipping, and handling. At the same time, growing concern about responsible disposal of excess packaging is leading some marketers to reduce the amount of materials used and incorporate recycled and recyclable materials into their products.

- *Appropriate billing and after-sale support.* Customers always expect on-time, accurate billing. In addition, they often need after-sale support for installation, repairs, and so on. If you're not equipped to handle these services, you can establish strategic alliances or use outsourcing to provide them. For example, James and Peter Kovolsky, who own Frustration Solvers in North Carolina, provide after-sale support for Service Merchandise, Sports Authority, and other stores. When a customer needs help assembling a new picnic table or basketball hoop, these stores recommend Frustration Solvers for the job. The Kovolsky brothers have built a $1 million business offering such services.[30]

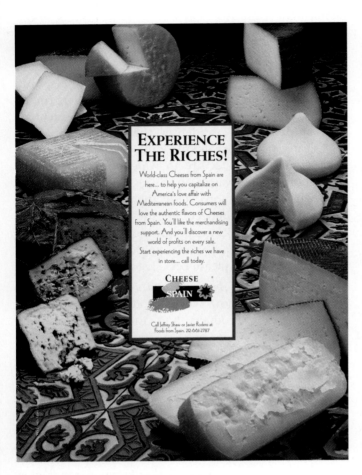

Time has become one of the most important factors in evaluating the logistics function in firms. Not all products need to be delivered quickly. However, when moving perishable or time-sensitive items, quick delivery is critical. Producers of world-class products like these cheeses from Spain can advertise globally knowing that their goods will be delivered quickly and without damage or deterioration. What other international products can you identify that are available for purchase due to an efficient logistics system?

Customer Service Standards

Knowing what your customers expect is the first step toward developing a written set of standards to track your progress in delivering quality customer service. You'll want to analyze every area in which logistics management supports customer service. You'll also want to look at cost considerations as well as how your competitors manage their logistics. Then you can establish specific, measurable goals for using logistics management to profitably satisfy your customers. In particular, pay careful attention to areas in which service gaps can damage a customer's assessment of your service quality.

Issues for critical thinking

What role does internal marketing play in communicating customer service standards to employees throughout the organization? How can you use internal marketing to support your organization's delivery of quality customer service?

Depending on your product and your targeted customer segments, you may decide on a variety of customer service standards, such as number of days or hours between order and delivery, percentage of orders filled completely and accurately, or percentage of deliveries made on time. National Semiconductor, the California maker of computer chips, set a standard of delivering products from factory to customer within four days. Once you have such standards, you can regularly check your performance and pinpoint areas for improvement. As time goes on, you'll want to apply continuous improvement, raising your standards higher and higher to enhance service and strengthen long-term customer relationships. National's next goal was to shave a day off its standard, providing chip delivery within three days.[31]

The Australia–New Zealand Direct Line (ANZDL), a water transportation company, went a step further. As part of a bid to win ISO 9000 quality certification, the company set performance standards in 16 categories. Every month, it measures its performance and tells customers the results. The company also asks customers to rate its performance every year. As a result of this initiative, ANZDL boosted on-time delivery to 85 percent (from under 50 percent) and cut documentation errors from 5 percent to 1 percent. Customers noticed the improvement in quality customer service: ANZDL's market share almost doubled in just two years.[32]

Seamless Customer Service

Although logistics management covers six major activities, savvy marketers know how to satisfy customers by smoothly blending these activities to deliver seamless customer service. After all, customers care about the overall quality of the customer service, not about the activities of individual departments. By promoting teamwork and empowering employees, marketers can move products and information more smoothly through all the logistical activities needed to serve their customers.

Roller-bearing manufacturer Timken is a case in point. The company's plants in Virginia and North Carolina are staffed by teams empowered to make adjustments to serve their customers. The teams have cut the time needed to produce and ship orders from two days to three hours. At the North Carolina plant, teams can also tailor some products to specific customer requirements. This kind of flexibility is unusual in a firm that's called on to fill small orders, but Timken's attention to logistics makes the entire process run smoothly. Now the company delivers quality customer service while running with leaner inventories.[33]

More and more marketers are adding customers to their project teams, which brings the voice of the customer into every aspect of logistics management. This approach gives marketers and customers a better understanding of how to use logistics management to boost customer satisfaction. For example, United Stationers, the largest U.S. wholesaler of office products, formed teams of personnel from operations and sales to work with retailers and other customers on upgrading services. As a result, the company started guaranteeing that orders called in or transmitted electronically by 7 P.M. would be delivered by noon the next day, a quick-response program that customers appreciate.[34]

Providing Timely Response

Notice how often *time* comes up as an element in quality customer service. Speedy-response strategies to differentiate products are designed around the ability to expedite the movement of products and information up and down the value chain. Speed is important in product development (to compress the period between developing and producing products) as well as in the order cycle (to compress the period between customer order and supplier delivery). In the broader context of the overall value chain, timely response includes the ability to react not only to shifts in customer requirements but also to changes in suppliers' needs, to competitive pressures, and to other changes in the marketing environment.[35]

Only UPS guarantees delivery at these three speeds: Fast. Faster. And impossible.

Your customers rarely ask, "How?" They just want to know, "How soon?" Now you can answer with a question of your own, "How soon do you need it?" Because now UPS offers three express delivery options, each one guaranteed. Overnight delivery by 10:30 a.m. If needed earlier there's overnight by 8:30 a.m. (8:00 a.m. in major cities). And for those increasingly frequent emergencies that can't wait until tomorrow, there's even same-day delivery. Only UPS offers all these ways to keep pace with the speed of business. A speed measured less by miles per hour, than by crises per hour.

MOVING at the SPEED of BUSINESS.

In fact, next-day delivery will not meet all customers' needs for timely response. More and more customers want same-day delivery, which has created a logistical opportunity for UPS, FedEx, and other delivery services. "It's no longer an issue of overnight, but rather what time of [the same] day," says Peter Fredo, vice president of advertising for UPS. To handle time-sensitive deliveries, UPS maintains one of the world's largest airplane fleets as well as a huge fleet of trucks. Its ability to track the progress of items from pickup to delivery permits customers to find out where their packages are at any time.[36]

Information technology is critical to timely response. In many industries, electronic data interchange **(p. 210)** is the standard way of exchanging information about products, pricing, orders, and delivery via computer-to-computer links. EDI expedites communication with suppliers and customers and incorporates built-in checks to ensure greater accuracy. PPG Industries, for example, is a Pittsburgh-based manufacturer that routinely exchanges orders and billing data electronically with auto manufacturers and other buyers of its glass and related products. Using the company's EDI system is much faster—and more accurate—than handling such information manually, as paperwork.[37]

As discussed in Chapter 14, a growing number of nonfood retailers are applying information technology to implement quick response, in which products are automatically reordered to replenish store shelves. In grocery retailing, efficient consumer response (ECR) **(p. 413)** improves logistics by electronically sending data about consumer purchases from supermarkets to upstream members of the value chain. Suppliers and channel partners can then plan production and delivery so that supermarkets will have the right goods in the right stores at the right times. [38]

Timely response depends on faster delivery, and many manufacturers depend on UPS for this. While some companies say in their ads, "Allow four to six weeks for delivery," those who use UPS can say, "We'll deliver it tomorrow." Is it a good idea for companies to outsource their logistics needs to rapid delivery companies like UPS? What are the advantages and disadvantages as you see them?

Achieving Cost Efficiencies

Moving products and information through the value chain can be quite costly. One of the goals of logistics management is to achieve cost efficiencies so that customers get more value for their money and, at the same time,

suboptimization

the lowering of logistics costs in one area while increasing them elsewhere, with resulting damage to overall cost-efficiency

total cost concept

looks at each logistics activity as part of an integrated whole and balances changes so that overall costs are lowered

marketers earn higher profits. This win-win approach to logistics can strengthen relationships throughout the value chain.

Bear in mind, however, that logistics activities are closely linked, and beware of **suboptimization**, the lowering of logistics costs in one area while increasing them elsewhere, with resulting damage to overall cost-efficiency. If, for example, you want to minimize the cost of keeping parts in inventory, the trade-off may be to ask suppliers to ship more frequently. In this case, inventory costs may be lower, but shipping costs will be higher.

To avoid the pitfalls of suboptimization, you can use the **total cost concept** to balance the overall costs of logistics management for optimal efficiency.[39] Rather than taking the cost of each logistics activity separately, you analyze the combined cost of all these activities, because they're part of an integrated process. Each activity is connected to the next, so a change in one will effect a change in one or more of the others.

Notice that holding more parts in inventory, for example, is likely to lead to an increase in the cost of warehousing. By the same token, bringing in smaller shipments more frequently—rather than holding parts in inventory—will mean higher transportation costs. With the total cost concept, you look for efficiencies that make sense in terms of the *overall* expense of logistics management, not just the cost of one activity.

For example, California-based Adaptec manufactures computer parts in Singapore and markets them around the world, using the total cost concept to manage its overall logistics management bill. Adaptec spends $6.5 million to make 60,000 air shipments every year, rushing parts from 150 global suppliers to its Singapore plant, then speeding finished goods to industrial customers in Europe, Asia, and the Americas. In return, the company saves $20 million annually by avoiding extensive inventories and huge warehouses. Equally important, Adaptec gets its products to customers faster than ever before, which fosters customer loyalty and creates a powerful competitive advantage.[40]

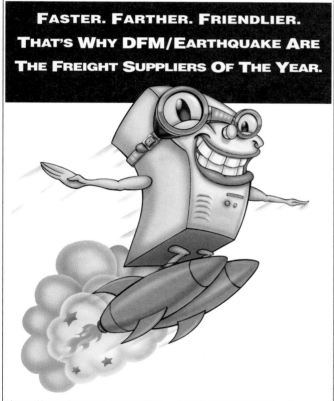

FASTER. FARTHER. FRIENDLIER. THAT'S WHY DFM/EARTHQUAKE ARE THE FREIGHT SUPPLIERS OF THE YEAR.

Adaptec would zoom to the moon to win customers and keep them happy. And we figure that DFM Custom Brokers and Earthquake Distribution Services have the same spirit. It's our business to provide an uninterrupted supply of products that speed the flow of data between PCs, peripherals, and networks. Without DFM/Earthquake speeding materials to and from our manufacturing facilities, Adaptec's record of delivering on time, just in time, every time may not look as good as it does.

Our solutions are incorporated into the products of virtually all major computer and peripheral manufacturers around the world. DFM and Earthquake deliver these solutions. Their teamwork makes much of our success possible. That's why we are pleased that they are Adaptec's Freight Suppliers of the Year.

Fast deliveries help profits soar.

 **adaptec**

One marketer that represents the future is Adaptec, a California-based computer company with manufacturing facilities in Singapore. Adaptec clearly recognizes the importance of logistics and fast delivery, spending millions of dollars delivering goods by air. This is a more expensive way of shipping, but some of the costs are offset through savings that result from being able to maintain smaller inventories. Adaptec is confident that fast, superior customer service builds a bond of trust and loyalty that more than justifies the incremental shipping costs. If you were competing with Adaptec, how would you go about designing a superior logistical system?

Applying Tailored Logistics

Just as you can customize a product to meet an individual customer's needs, you can also customize your logistics for individual customers. When you apply **tailored logistics**, you customize your logistics activities to better satisfy the specific requirements of a particular customer or market segment.[41] In the past, many marketers provided the same logistical services for *every* customer. However, some customers prefer fewer services and lower prices, while others are willing to pay more for more services. With tailored logistics, you design a program and a price to meet the specific needs of selected customers, which strengthens customer relationships and, ultimately, increases your sales and profits.

For example, New Jersey–based Becton Dickinson, which markets medical supplies and equipment internationally, empowers its cross-functional teams **(p. 47)** to offer tailored logistics to key customers and supply-chain partners. Depending on the requirements of the customer, the team will arrange for special services such as continuous replenishment of frequently ordered items or electronic links to track shipments in transit. The company's vice president of corporate logistics notes that tailored logistics helped Becton Dickinson sign Asian customers that "we couldn't even approach before because we couldn't perform to the level of need they had, both in terms of cycle-time reliability and customizing a delivery mechanism."[42]

Tailored logistics isn't just for big companies. Small businesses can also use tailored logistics to strengthen customer relationships, as the next section shows.

SMALL BUSINESS WATCH

Tailored logistics goes to college

How do you serve an organizational customer that demands perfection? That was the challenge facing John Leinweber, the founder of American Office Equipment in La Grange, Illinois. Leinweber had sold more than 300 photocopiers to a university in the Chicago area, which expected perfection in three respects: every new copier was to be up and running immediately after delivery; all copiers were to be operational 100 percent of the time; and the number of copies made by each machine every month was to be provided.

None of these requirements would have imposed unusual demands if Leinweber's business had been located near the campus. However, its closest branch was 35 minutes away. How could Leinweber deliver perfection? The answer: tailored logistics.

After analyzing the university's requirements, Leinweber created a special logistics program to provide everything the customer wanted. He arranged to store spare parts and replacement copiers right on campus, for instant availability when any installed unit went on the blink. He also assigned an on-site crew of technicians to set up new copiers, make repairs, and gather the details about usage that university officials wanted.

tailored logistics

customizing logistics activities to better satisfy the specific requirements of a particular customer or market segment

Thanks to tailored logistics, Leinweber has received glowing customer satisfaction ratings from university personnel. He's also been able to renew his company's contract with the university again and again.[43]

How can marketers decide whether to apply tailored logistics to an individual customer?

Before you go on . . .

A. **How can marketers avoid suboptimization and instead apply the total cost concept?**

B. **What is tailored logistics and what are its benefits?**

Inside Logistics Management

Earlier in the chapter, you learned that logistics management covers six major activities: transportation, warehousing, materials handling, inventory management, order processing, and reverse logistics. Here is a closer look at each one, since no matter what good or service you're marketing, you will perform one or more of these activities. Because all logistics activities are interrelated, the costs and results of one affect the costs and results of others. That means that the ideal overall logistics management strategy balances optimal costs with optimal results.

Transportation

The first major component of logistics management is *transportation*, moving raw materials and parts from point of supply to point of production, then moving finished products to point of sale or point of consumption. You can choose among five basic modes of transportation: rail, truck, air, water, and pipeline. In making your selection, you'll take into account six criteria, shown in Table 16.1:

TABLE **16.1** **Comparing Five Modes of Transportation**

Characteristic	Best ⟵				⟶ Worst
Speed	Air	Pipeline	Truck	Rail	Water
Frequency	Pipeline	Truck	Air	Rail	Water
Dependability	Pipeline	Truck	Rail	Water	Air
Capacity	Water	Rail	Truck	Air	Pipeline
Availability	Truck	Rail	Air	Water	Pipeline
Cost	Pipeline	Water	Rail	Truck	Air

- *Speed.* How quickly can products be transported?
- *Frequency.* How frequently can shipments be scheduled?
- *Dependability.* How reliable is the mode of transportation? Can it deliver products safely and on schedule?
- *Capacity.* How large or how heavy a quantity can be transported?
- *Availability.* What modes of transportation to your destination are available? How can you gain access to the transportation?
- *Cost.* How much will transportation cost?

Over the past two decades, the U.S. transportation industry has changed as government restrictions on competition, pricing, and operations have been relaxed in the course of a move toward deregulation. Now transportation companies are able to tailor their services, schedules, and rates to meet the needs of individual customers. Changes in other countries, including government deregulation, infrastructure development, and increasing competition, are reshaping international transportation choices for marketers as well.

In addition, companies such as FedEx have altered the competitive environment by challenging established providers of transportation in two ways. First, they're offering a variety of speedy, dependable delivery options for marketers of all sizes. Second, they're capable of taking over some or all of a customer's logistics activities through outsourcing. As a result, transportation choices are both more varied and more complex than in the past.

Transportation by Rail

Measured by the ton-mile (the movement of one ton of freight for one mile), rail is the most commonly used mode of transportation for freight shipped within the United States. Figure 16.3 shows the proportion of domestic freight carried by each mode of transportation. Rail is also the number one mode in China, Russia, and many other countries. Rail service can reach nearly every urban area in the world, although it's not always available to smaller communities. Manufacturers rely on rail transportation when moving heavy materials long distances. Ford, for example, transports parts and finished goods by rail between facilities and markets in Canada, the United States, and Mexico.[44]

FIGURE **16.3**   **Freight Transport Within the United States**

Most freight moves by rail within the United States. Shipments by rail, air, and truck transport have been increasing in recent years, while shipments by pipelines and waterways have been decreasing.

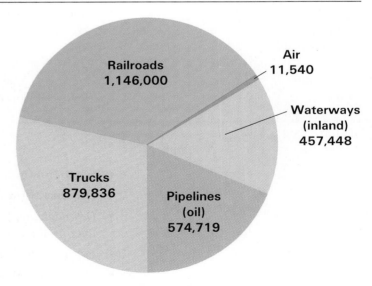

Railroads
1,146,000

Air
11,540

Waterways
(inland)
457,448

Trucks
879,836

Pipelines
(oil)
574,719

Volume of freight (millions of ton-miles)

Modernization of tracks and facilities in many developing countries, including China, has led to more efficient rail shipping, which is particularly important for inexpensive but bulky commodities (such as coal and grain) that are typically transported on trains. To accommodate shippers, railroads now run *unit trains* dedicated to transporting one type of commodity from the source to the market destination. The latest innovation, high-speed rail links between major cities, will soon offer U.S. marketers new options for shipping small packages.[45]

Transportation by Truck

Truck transportation is a good choice for shippers and customers interested in door-to-door pickup and delivery. Often, highways and roads can be laid out where railroad tracks can't, so virtually every market, everywhere, can be reached by truck transportation. Trucks are able to carry a variety of products, whether large and heavy or tiny and fragile. Small wonder that more than 75 percent of all U.S. agricultural products—including meats, dairy products, and baked goods—travel by truck as they move through the value chain from farmer to consumer.[46]

Truckers have the flexibility to adjust their schedules to fit their customers' needs. One example is Roberts Express, based in Akron, which will pick up and deliver at any hour on any day of the year anywhere in the United States. It helped Starr Hydraulics out of a tight spot when the company needed to get a 900-pound pump to a customer over a weekend. A Roberts truck picked up the pump late Friday night in Philadelphia and delivered it to the customer in Toledo, Ohio, early Saturday morning. "It was nothing short of a miracle," marvels Louis Starr, vice president of Starr Hydraulics.[47]

Roberts Express offers extraordinary service—they will pick up and deliver at any time of day or night. One of the primary advantages of transporting goods by truck is the ability to reach almost any market relatively quickly. This is especially true when truck containers are moved by train, plane, and/or ship and then trucked to their ultimate destination. What other advantages in transporting goods do trucks have over railroads? What are some disadvantages?

Transportation by Air

When you need speed—and can afford to pay for it—choose air transportation. As you saw earlier, the high cost of shipping by air may be offset by the benefits of the result—getting products to their destinations faster—leading to savings in inventory and warehousing costs. No longer reserved for shipping perishable, valuable, or emergency products, air transportation is becoming a priority as increasing numbers of marketers race to get their products to customers halfway across the country or halfway around the world.

Air cargo within the United States is dominated by FedEx and UPS, which together log more ton-miles than the next six largest air carriers. Northwest, American, and other passenger airlines have cleared more space in their jets for cargo, and they're developing better technology to track packages in transit. Some carriers differentiate themselves by specializing in certain types of cargo. KLM Royal Dutch Airlines, for example, specializes in transporting horses from country to country. The airline even maintains an animal hotel to accommodate horses between flights.[48]

intermodal transportation

the use of more than one mode of transportation to complete a single movement of products

Transportation by Water

If you're moving heavy, bulky, low-value goods that don't have to be anywhere in a hurry, you can use water transportation. Shipping by barge, freighter, or tanker on rivers, canals, lakes, and oceans is a slow but inexpensive way to transport raw materials, parts, or finished products. However, low speed can be an advantage for marketers that use cargo ships as floating warehouses. Nanco, a Massachusetts importer of toys made in China, times its shipments to arrive at U.S. ports when needed—and when the billing and customs paperwork have arrived.[49]

Many products are *containerized*, or stored for water transportation in containers that are sealed for protection against water and weather damage. The containers are marked with bar codes that can be read by automated equipment at each port. This is just one of the ways of expediting the movement of containerized freight. The Port of Singapore, for example, is developing a fully automated system for controlling its cranes and heavy equipment, and for tracking the containers they load, unload, and put into storage berths. Because many containers get to ports by rail, the Port of Houston and many other ports are upgrading rail facilities to make the transfer more convenient.[50]

Transportation by Pipeline

Natural gas, oil and petroleum products, water, and chemicals are among the limited number of products you can ship through pipelines. Coal—in the form of coal slurry—can also be shipped by pipeline. The process involves grinding the coal into powder, mixing it with water, sending the resultant slurry through the pipeline, and then separating the coal from the water at the destination.

Pipeline speeds are rather slow, and pipelines aren't available everywhere, but this mode of transportation is dependable and costs very little. More than 440,000 miles of pipelines connect cities in the United States, and more pipelines are being constructed around the world to accommodate demand for energy products.[51]

One of the most efficient ways to move the cargo of a truck across water is to simply drive it onto a ferry or boat and float it to its destination. This particular ferry terminal is located in Great Britain, but there are similar terminals around the world. Cooperation among companies providing various modes of distribution is essential, especially when international destinations are involved. What products do you think require cooperation among various international distribution companies to deliver to local retailers?

Intermodal Transportation and Freight Forwarding

Intermodal transportation, the use of more than one mode of transportation to complete a single movement of products, allows you to choose the modes of transportation that offer the best combination of service and cost. Often, intermodal transportation can cut shipping costs while offering a route or schedule that meets your needs. In the common form of intermodal transportation known as *piggyback*, products are packed in special containers so that shipments can be conveniently and safely transferred between trucks, ships, or railroad cars without unpacking. Piggybacking on ships is called *fishybacking*. Because of these advantages, half of all products moving between countries travel in containers.[52]

Containers play a central role in the intermodal transportation system devised by Starbucks Coffee in Seattle. Starbucks imports enough coffee beans, coffeemakers, and other products to fill 1,000 containers every year, using ships and then switching to truck or rail transportation to and from ports. It cut its yearly transportation costs by 10 percent just by choosing the right ports. No wonder Darrow Weiss, Starbucks's transportation manager, calls himself "a port shopper."[53]

Smaller marketers or marketers that don't ship enough products to fill a container, truck, or railcar can still get good rates and service. The answer is to use **freight forwarders**, companies that put many smaller shipments together to create a single, large shipment that can be transported more cost-efficiently to the final destination. Freight forwarders act as wholesalers of transportation services, buying shipping space and reselling it to customers at lower rates than small shippers would otherwise pay. Some freight forwarders are broadening their offerings, moving beyond pickup and delivery to offer warehousing, customs assistance, and other services.[54]

Warehousing

Warehouses are a vital link in the value chain, holding raw materials, parts, or finished products until needed for operations or assembly, until ordered by customers, until seasonal demand increases, competition eases, or some other change occurs in the marketing environment. In some cases, you will save money by buying and transporting goods in quantity, then warehousing them until you can break the larger lots into smaller lots for customers. In other cases, you may need to warehouse smaller lots until you have accumulated enough for a large shipment, which is how some marketers handle international shipments. With warehousing, you can be sure of a constant supply of parts or materials when needed, and you can also accommodate customers that need goods right away.

There are two types of warehouse. **Storage warehouses** are repositories for parts, raw materials, or products that need to be stored for a period of days, weeks, or months before being moved to a factory, a customer's site, or another location. **Distribution centers** are warehouses in which products are briefly stored before being moved to wholesale, retail, or customer locations.

Warehousing operations of both types have been transformed by computerized applications that can quickly and accurately receive products, assign storage space, monitor climate and security, locate products when needed, and organize items for packing and shipping. For example, with the help of sophisticated software, employees at the Hudson's Bay Company distribution centers can log in, price, and sort thousands of items for shipment to 375 stores across Canada—in one day.[55]

Like Hudson's Bay, Wal-Mart and other marketers are looking for ways to minimize the time products spend sitting in distribution centers. One such technique is *cross-docking*, receiving incoming products and immediately transferring them to waiting trucks for delivery. Wal-Mart, for example, coordinates the movements of incoming and outgoing shipments so that goods arrive when needed and cross through the distribution center to go instantly out to the stores.[56] This makes warehousing more efficient and speeds products to customers.

freight forwarders

companies that put many smaller shipments together to create a single, large shipment that can be transported more cost-efficiently to the final destination

storage warehouses

repositories for parts, raw materials, or products that need to be stored for a period of days, weeks, or months before being moved to a factory, a customer's site, or another location

distribution centers

warehouses in which products are briefly stored before being moved to wholesale, retail, or customer locations

Materials Handling

Materials handling is the movement of products, parts, and raw materials within and between warehouses and manufacturing facilities. Moving goods or parts can be costly and time-consuming—and it can lead to damage, theft, spoilage, or waste. Effective materials handling can minimize the number of times items are moved and the distance covered. In addition, good materials-handling practices can help to efficiently maintain a uniform flow of goods and materials throughout the production process.

Nearly every aspect of materials handling has been touched by technology. Automatic guided vehicle systems (AGVS), for example, are electronically controlled vehicles that transport cases, pallets, or products within a facility by following a preset route embedded in the floor. At the Oldsmobile factory in Lansing, Michigan, each AGVS can ferry 185 cars to various points within the plant. These systems also bring chassis to locations where an overhead conveyor system leaves engines for installation. In other plants, computerized robots are used to stack, load, and unload products, cases, and containers. Many materials-handling systems rely on computer-generated labels that code packages for sorting, storage, or shipment, using codes that automated equipment can scan and identify.[57]

Use of the just-in-time approach to inventory control has minimized the amount of inventory carried in many plants. In modern facilities such as this Oldsmobile assembly plant, inventory is handled using the latest in technology, including these electronically controlled vehicles that move goods to the assembly line. Every dollar saved in shipping, storing, and moving goods can go directly to profit. Can you see why understanding logistics is crucial to competing successfully in a technologically driven environment?

Inventory Management

For many marketers, inventory is a major investment—and managing inventory is a delicate balancing act. Traditionally, marketers have used inventory (1) as a buffer against mismatches in supply and demand, (2) as a guard against shortages when supplies can't be delivered, (3) as a means of quickly filling orders, (4) as a means to accommodate extra quantities bought at advantageous prices, and (5) as a way to support efficient production and shipping schedules.

The balancing act starts when you try to determine the right amount of inventory to have on hand. Consider the inventory situation Robbie Guyette faces as a production supervisor at H.P. Hood in Connecticut. Guyette knows that Hood ice creams sell best in the summer, but finding the right inventory level isn't easy. "You don't want too much inventory because then you run out of space to store it," he notes. "You don't want too little, because you can't supply your customers with what they need when they need it. It's a real balancing act." The balance that Hood strikes is to begin building inventory in its warehouses as early as January to meet summer demand.[58]

Storage isn't the only issue. If you hold too much inventory, you tie up your money for longer than necessary, which leaves you with less to invest in other profitable activities. On the other hand, if you have too little inventory, you risk disrupting your customer and channel relationships. To properly weigh these issues, you must understand your inventory costs and determine the level of efficiency and responsiveness that makes sense for optimum customer satisfaction as well as for profitability.

materials handling
the movement of products, parts, and raw materials within and between warehouses and manufacturing facilities

Inventory Costs

Although holding partially or completely finished products in inventory can be costly, many marketers can't easily gauge the true amount because costs are spread over so many departments and facilities. At any given moment, some products may be awaiting final assembly in the factory, moving between the factory and the warehouse or a customer's site, or sitting in storage at the warehouse. Table 16.2 shows four types of inventory cost: capital costs, inventory service costs, storage costs, and risk costs.

TABLE **16.2** Analyzing Inventory Costs

Inventory Cost	Issues to Consider
Capital costs Costs associated with investing in inventory rather than in other areas	What activities are you unable to undertake because your money is invested in inventory? What profits are you foregoing because your money is tied up in inventory?
Inventory service costs Costs associated with holding products in inventory	What taxes and insurance expenses are you paying on products in inventory?
Storage costs Costs associated with storing products held in inventory	What are you paying to store goods in warehouses and distribution centers?
Risk costs Potential losses due to holding goods in inventory	Will products become obsolete while in inventory? How likely is it that products will be damaged, stolen, spoiled, or lost while in inventory?

If you understand your costs, you can see how your inventory level affects profitability. Martha Morgan, president of Metropolitan Apparel Group in Wilmington, Delaware, is a small business owner who has become very aware of capital and risk costs in particular. Instead of buying large quantities of clothing for her upscale women's apparel store, she now buys fewer items more frequently, leaving money available for other purposes—and minimizing profit-squeezing markdowns when styles go out of fashion. "I can see a 5 to 10 percent increase in our gross margins since using this method," Morgan says.[59] Appendix B discusses markdowns and gross margins in more detail.

Lean inventories don't work for every marketer, as the Wisconsin-based catalog retailer Lands' End found several years ago. Cutting inventory levels to reduce costs, the company ran out of some sizes and colors, which delayed shipments and disappointed customers. Now President William T. End is determined to maintain an in-stock inventory position 90 percent of the time during the winter holiday season, even though the extra inventory adds $20 million in costs.[60] Clearly, customer service is a priority at Lands' End.

Just-in-Time and Stockless Inventory Management

just-in-time (JIT) inventory management

an approach in which inventory is kept at a very low level to meet immediate production demands, and additional supplies are delivered as they're needed

In an ideal world, marketers would be able to perfectly match their inventory levels to their customers' purchasing patterns. Because of the difficulty in forecasting how much and when customers are likely to buy, marketers have developed a number of methods for streamlining inventory management. One popular method is **just-in-time (JIT) inventory management**, an approach in which inventory is kept at a very low level to meet immediate production demands, and additional supplies are delivered as they're needed.

With JIT, producers carry little inventory and therefore have lower storage costs. To make this technique work, however, they need strong value-chain relationships with suppliers whose commitment to total quality management ◄──┘ **(p. 48)** ensures prompt and error-free products and deliveries. Since the producer has no extra inventory to fall back on, a late delivery or incomplete shipment will delay production. In turn, the producer must be equally committed to customers who depend on JIT deliveries.[61]

The step beyond JIT is *stockless inventory*, in which suppliers make daily deliveries directly to the locations that require parts or products. Figure 16.4 compares ordinary, JIT, and stockless inventory systems. Baxter International, which supplies medical products to hospitals, offers its customers stockless inventory by making small, daily deliveries to the operating rooms, nursing wards, and other areas where products will be used. Thanks to stockless inventory, St. Luke's Episcopal Hospital in Houston has eliminated storerooms and excess inventory, saving more than $500,000 every year.[62]

FIGURE **16.4**   **Ordinary, JIT, and Stockless Inventory Management**

(1) Hospitals using ordinary inventory management receive periodic shipments of supplies. To avoid running out, they have to maintain a large inventory of supplies. (2) Hospitals using JIT inventory management can allocate less space for inventory, because they receive more frequent deliveries.

(3) With stockless inventory management, hospitals need to keep only minimal inventory on hand. Instead, they receive daily deliveries from suppliers, sometimes even getting supplies delivered directly to specific wards.

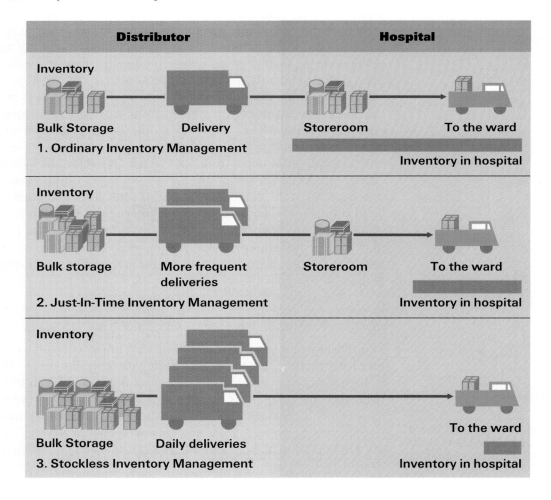

Small businesses are especially concerned about minimizing inventory because of the high cost of holding products or parts in reserve until needed. Here's how one Mexican wholesaler helps its small customers minimize inventory.

GLOBAL ISSUES

Helping farmacias minimize inventory

How can a small store—with little money to invest in inventory—stock all the products customers want? In Mexico, the answer is provided by wholesaler Grupo Casa Autrey. Autrey carries such U.S. products as Lysol cleaners, Mars candies, Kodak film, Duracell batteries, and Gillette razors, plus thousands of other local and imported food, household, and pharmaceutical products. Although it serves some large retailers, including Cifra and Gigante, most of its 20,000 customers are independent drugstores known as *farmacias*. These small businesses can't afford to tie up money in inventory, and that's where Autrey comes in.

If a *farmacia* calls Autrey with an order by noon, it can have the merchandise in hand before the end of day. "When the *farmacia* says come back this afternoon for your medicine, it usually gets it from us," confirms company president Sergio Autrey. Here's how the system works. The store's order goes to the nearest of Autrey's 19 automated warehouses. Robots pick the products off the shelves, then employees pack and send them down chutes to the waiting trucks. The drivers of the delivery trucks also collect the amount due from each *farmacia*.

This pay-as-you-go method allows *farmacias* to minimize the stock they hold in inventory. Although the stores pay a bit more for Autrey's same-day service, they make it up by opening large packages and selling products one by one at a slightly higher price.[63]

What other logistical services do you think *farmacias* might want from a wholesaler like Autrey?

Grupo Casa Autrey, a wholesaler in Mexico, sells a wide variety of products to thousands of independent drugstores across the country. Using advanced technology, the company can fill orders and make same-day delivery to retailers who order before noon. This means that cash-starved stores can buy in small quantities and still satisfy their customers. Do you think trade agreements like NAFTA increase or decrease the need for firms such as Grupo Casa Autrey? Why?

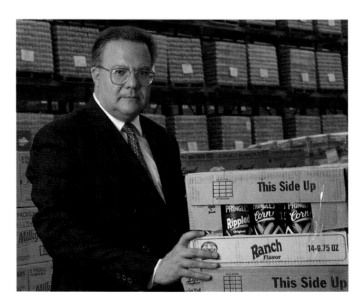

Vendor-Managed Inventory

In recent years, some retailers have turned over responsibility for maintaining inventories of certain store products to their suppliers, a technique known as *vendor-managed inventory*. Here's how it works. The retailer collects information on store-by-store, product-by-product customer purchasing patterns and inventory levels. It makes the data available electronically to suppliers, who need it to reach decisions about timing production and delivery. When inventory has dropped to a predetermined level, suppliers rush replacements to the retailer's distribution center or directly to each store—and let the retailer's computer know that replacements are on the way, so they can be tallied as part of each store's inventory.[64]

With vendor-managed inventory, the store doesn't have to check its stock or place orders. Instead, it relies on its suppliers to analyze consumer purchasing data and keep shelves full. For example, Leviton Manufacturing in Little Neck, New York, makes electrical accessories. It manages inventory of its products for a number of its customers, including Ace Hardware, Home Depot, and Wal-Mart. Tom Parisi, Leviton's business systems specialist, says that he now has to think like a retailer. "We have to change hats, make believe we are Ace Hardware and process data that's not ours," he explains. Once Parisi has developed a sense of how consumers buy from each retail customer, he can adjust his production and deliveries to replenish the inventory as needed.[65]

Order Processing

Order processing may be a basic logistics activity, but it's essential to customer satisfaction. From the way you accept orders to the way you check on available quantities, pricing, payment options, packing, shipping, billing, and returns or damage claims, every step in order processing has the potential to delight—or disappoint—your customer. Often, orders crisscross departmental lines as they move through the processing system, increasing the potential for errors and delays. Experts therefore recommend tracing the route that orders take to uncover hidden problems, smooth the passage between departments, speed fulfillment, improve accuracy, and lower costs.[66]

As Leviton's experience shows, order processing doesn't mean waiting for orders before taking action. To be ready to satisfy your customers, you have to anticipate what they may need so you can plan production (for goods) or staffing (for services) and have channel partners lined up to help. If you have strong ties to customers, as Leviton does, you will have access to information about how each customer's customers buy. This helps you forecast volume and timing of purchases, which is a step in the direction of shortening the order cycle time.

Order cycle time, also known as *lead time*, is the period between the placement of an order and its receipt. For faster, more accurate, less costly order processing, many marketers maintain computer links such as electronic data interchange, so they can send orders to suppliers and receive orders from customers automatically.

Issues for critical thinking

What lengthens the order cycle time for a product? What kinds of product have longer order cycle times? What can you suggest to shorten the gap between order and receipt for long-lead-time products?

order cycle time

the period between the placement of an order and its receipt

reverse logistics

the process of managing the return flow of products from customer to marketer

Reverse Logistics

What do you do when customers have finished with your products or need to return them for repair or replacement? You use **reverse logistics**, the process of managing the return flow of products from customer to marketer. This logistical activity has become more urgent as landfills approach capacity, regulations governing disposal and recycling have become stricter, and consumers speak out about protecting the environment. It's also a concern for marketers of durable goods such as computers or appliances, which are able to be serviced to extend product life.

Marketers can use reverse logistics to retrieve products for servicing, replacement, recycling, or disposal. Here's how three marketers apply reverse logistics in socially responsible ways.

ETHICS & SOCIAL RESPONSIBILITY

The greening of logistics management

Can logistics management help save the environment? Target stores, Nike, and Eastman Kodak think so. These three marketers are incorporating social responsibility into their logistics management plans in a variety of ways.

Target, a midwestern chain, uses plastic wrap to anchor goods on pallets during shipping from distribution centers to stores. Instead of throwing the tie-down material away, however, the retailer collects the used plastic from each store and sends it to a recycler. In turn, the recycler sells the plastic to a company that uses it to make trash bags—which are sold in Target stores.

Nike is saving landfill space by finding new uses for cast-off sneakers. The company has piloted reverse logistics programs in which customers bring used sneakers to Foot Locker and other retailers. The sneakers go back to Nike, where they're ground up and delivered to a company that uses the recycled rubber to make—what else?—running tracks.

Reverse logistics brings used products back to the manufacturer for reuse or recycling. The process is part of "green marketing" and benefits several stakeholders. In this ad, Xerox provides directions for recycling drum cartridges for its copiers. Note that the company pays the postage and offers a $5.00 incentive. What are the potential benefits of this strategy to Xerox?

Kodak has also been putting touches of green in its reverse logistics. Confronted by environmentalists protesting the waste of FunSaver disposable cameras, Kodak decided to recycle the units. Now, when customers return cameras to photofinishers for film processing, the cases are sent back to Kodak for disassembly. Plastic parts are ground up to make new camera parts, but some mechanical parts are reused as many as 10 times.[67]

What other steps do you think Target, Nike, or Kodak might take to use logistics management to preserve the planet?

When you design your reverse logistics system, take into account your customers' behavior patterns as well as your organizational needs and goals. If customers or channel partners can't easily and conveniently return products, you may damage those relationships. Hewlett-Packard and Apple Computer, for example, make it easy to return empty toner cartridges from laser printers. The customer simply puts the empty cartridge into the original carton (or the carton left over from the replacement cartridge), sticks on a label, and gives the carton to UPS, which delivers it to the original manufacturer.

Before you go on . . .

A. How can marketers evaluate their transportation choices?

B. How do storage warehouses differ from distribution centers?

C. What is just-in-time inventory management and why is it important?

D. What is reverse logistics and how is it used?

Summary

1. **Explain the role of logistics in the value chain and identify the six major activities in logistics management.**

   Logistics management is the process of managing the movement of raw materials, parts, work in progress, finished products, and related information through the value chain in an efficient, cost-effective manner to meet customer requirements. The six major activities in logistics management are transportation, warehousing, materials handling, inventory management, order processing, and reverse logistics.

2. **Show how to use logistics to deliver quality customer service and to support relationship building.**

   To deliver quality customer service, first research what customers want and determine how logistics can be used to deliver the appropriate level of quality service. Then strengthen relationships by setting specific service standards and measuring performance in managing logistics to provide what customers expect.

3. **Identify the role of transportation in logistics management and list the five basic modes of transportation.**

   Transportation moves raw materials and parts from point of supply to point of production, and finished products to point of sale or point of consumption. The five basic modes of transportation are rail, truck, air, water, and pipeline.

4. **Distinguish between storage warehouses and distribution centers.**

   Storage warehouses are repositories for parts, raw materials, or products that at some point will be moved to a factory, a customer's site, or another location. In contrast, distribution centers are warehouses in which products are briefly stored before being moved to wholesale, retail, or customer locations.

5. **Analyze the use of inventory and apply the three methods of streamlining inventory management.**

   Inventory is used (1) as a buffer against mismatches in supply and demand, (2) as a guard against supply shortages, (3) as a means of quickly filling customer orders, (4) as a means to accommodate extra quantities bought at advantageous prices, and (5) as a way to support efficient production and shipping schedules. With just-in-time (JIT) inventory management, inventory is kept at low levels to meet immediate production demands, and additional supplies are delivered as needed. With stockless inventory, suppliers deliver daily to the locations requiring parts or products. With vendor-managed inventory, retailers turn over responsibility for maintaining inventories of certain products to their suppliers.

6. **Show how order processing and shorter order cycles contribute to customer satisfaction.**

   Order processing includes accepting orders, checking on available quantities, and arranging pricing, payment options, packing, shipping, billing, and returns or damage claims. Customers appreciate a short order cycle time, the period between placing an order and receiving the products.

7. **Demonstrate how marketers use reverse logistics.**

   Reverse logistics entails the management of the return flow of products from customer to marketer for servicing, replacement, recycling, or disposal.

KEY TERMS

Skill-Building Applications

1. What career prospects do you see in logistics management? What courses would you have to take to prepare yourself?

2. What are the chances that companies like Roadway Logistics Systems might take over additional logistics functions such as order processing and materials handling for manufacturers? What would be the advantages and disadvantages to Roadway? To the manufacturer?

3. Could the U.S. Postal Service benefit by benchmarking on companies that have learned how to deliver goods the same day? What specific logistical activities should the Postal Service study? Why?

4. Imagine you're marketing Hammermill paper for printing and photocopying. How might your emphasis on logistics activities differ according to whether you were dealing with a service customer like Pip Printing or a manufacturer like Chrysler?

5. What issues are likely to influence UPS and other transportation firms as they go global? How will the number and condition of roads and railroad lines in less developed countries affect on-time performance? How might other infrastructure issues affect UPS's ability to serve customers around the world?

6. How would logistics management affect a small business such as a local hardware store? List several logistics management issues that would affect the store's ability to compete with Home Depot.

Getting Involved in Marketing

1. *On Your Own* Diagram the inbound and outbound logistics involved in marketing a perishable product such as ice cream. Indicate the role of logistics in this value chain, and determine which logistics activities should be stressed to deliver the product to the customer in the best condition. Identify aspects of the operation that might be computerized for increased speed and accuracy. Share your findings during a brief presentation to your class.

2. *On Your Own* Identify one marketer that stresses order processing to satisfy its customers and another that stresses transportation to satisfy its customers. Next, suggest at least five specific standards each marketer might set for delivering quality customer service through logistics.

3. *Find Out More* Research how an imported product such as a toy or a toaster enters this country. What logistical activities can you identify in the movement of the product from inbound transportation to customers? If importers wanted to outsource these logistical activities, what are their alternatives? What are the cost implications of changing to an outsourcing approach? Write a brief report summarizing your findings.

4. *In a Partnership* Team up with another student to role-play a conversation between a marketer and a customer about tailored logistics. The student playing the customer should explain his or her special requirements, making up any details about products and delivery needed to make a reasonable case. The student playing the marketer should respond with a proposal to satisfy the customer's requirements in a timely, cost-effective manner. Afterward, analyze the customer's concerns and the marketer's response. What is the best way to profitably sustain a relationship with this customer?

5. *In a Team* With two other students, select a specific country as well as a specific product that U.S. marketers export to that country. What requirements might that country's customers have when purchasing the product? How might marketers apply technology to logistics management to address these requirements? Prepare a brief report or presentation summarizing your group's ideas.

6. *In a Team* With other students, recommend appropriate transportation method(s) for moving each of the following products from supplier to marketer or from marketer to customer. In each case, be prepared to explain your reasoning.

   a. natural gas

   b. photocopying paper

   c. fresh fish

   d. granite chips

   e. sewer pipes

VideoCase Arizona's Logistical Know-How Shakes Up the Beverage World

Logistics is one of the key weapons that Arizona uses to compete with the giants in the cola and tea wars. Despite its name, Arizona beverages come from a company based in Lake Success, Long Island. Battling Coca-Cola, Pepsi, Snapple, and other major competitors, Arizona's founders, John Ferolito and Don Vultaggio rely on a savvy channel strategy to keep sales bubbling.

The beverage market is both huge and extremely competitive. Together, Coke, Pepsi, and Snapple spend some $2 billion on advertising in the United States alone. PepsiCo's Lipton brand and Coca-Cola's Nestea brand hold first and second place, respectively, in the $1 billion U.S. iced tea market. Despite the odds, Arizona has been able to grab a 13 percent share of the national iced tea market by dominating sales in four areas: New York, New Jersey, Florida, and Michigan.

Arizona's value-chain strategy is to rely on wholesalers—mostly distributors of Budweiser and Miller beers—to deliver its products to retail locations such as neighborhood grocery stores, gas stations, and convenience stores. These wholesalers have well-established delivery networks and can service a large number of stores on their routes quite efficiently. Vultaggio and Ferolito were aware of this because they started out as small, independent New York beer distributors, learning the business from the ground up. Their knowledge of logistics served them well as they made plans to build the Arizona brand.

For their part, retailers are happy to carry Arizona drinks because the profit margin is more than 50 percent on each item—and sales are brisk. Although Arizona is a premium-priced product (higher priced than Coca-Cola or Pepsi beverages), it provides more for the money because it comes in a larger bottle and offers more exotic flavors. The packaging acts as in-store advertising, with eye-catching color and graphics. Strengthening the relationship with partners in the marketing channel, Arizona offers point-of-purchase displays to attract customer attention.

Unlike its major competitors, the company doesn't use splashy television, newspaper, and magazine advertising campaigns to build brand recognition. "What good is advertising when studies show that 50 percent of ready-to-drink purchases are not decided until the door of the cold box is opened?" asks Vultaggio. Instead, Arizona ads on billboards and buses capture consumer attention on the way to the store. Then, when consumers reach into the store cooler, the colorful packaging helps Arizona drinks stand out from the competition.

Vultaggio and Ferolito's strategy of getting Arizona products into as many stores and coolers as possible has paid off. The company has grown rapidly, from $10 million in sales to more than $400 million in only three years. The Arizona brand now appears on an expanded line of candies and other products produced under license, which allows the company to use its overall channel strategy to make more sales to the stores it already services. Keep your eye on Arizona—there's no telling where its logistics management will take it next.[68]

Strategies and applications

1. If you were a marketing advisor to Arizona, would you recommend that the founders use television, newspaper, or magazine advertising to support their channel partners? Why or why not?

2. What competitive moves might you expect from Coke and Pepsi to challenge the inroads made by the Arizona brand? How could Arizona meet such challenges?

3. How might Arizona use logistics management to expand beyond the United States into Canada and Mexico? Think about existing marketing channels and the brand's current competitive strengths as you answer.

4. If Arizona were asked for slotting fees by major supermarket chains, what arguments might it offer to prove the brand's value and avoid paying the fees?

5. Ferolito and Vultaggio want to license the Arizona brand to other marketers. What types of products do you think would be most appropriate under the Arizona name? Why?

6. What could Arizona do to establish a longer term relationship with consumers?

Team project

With another student, assume the role of partners in a local convenience store. What specific functions would you expect Arizona's delivery people to perform? How active should they be in helping you manage your Arizona inventory? Would you want them to monitor your sales and automatically place and confirm orders as needed? Would you want them to increase orders when peak selling periods are approaching, or to arrange reverse logistics for bottle and can deposits? How would these activities cement your relationship with Arizona? What concerns would you have about handing over certain functions? Summarize your ideas in a brief written or oral report.

internet

http://www.amazon.com

Marketing on the Net   Turning a New Page in Book Retailing

Competing with book superstores isn't easy. Retailers such as Borders and Barnes and Noble stock over 50,000 books in each store, offer comfortable reading chairs, and—in some locations—even sell coffee and desserts. But entrepreneur Jeffrey Bezos has not only found a way to compete, he seems poised to dramatically change the way books are marketed through the value chain.

Bezos is the founder of Amazon.com, an online bookstore that rings up $5 million per year operating solely on the Web. Unlike conventional bookstores, Amazon.com never closes, and it draws customers from 66 countries. Instead of walking through aisles of bookshelves, customers simply click on their favorite subjects or enter a title or author. In a flash, the screen fills with information about the requested books. At any given time, more than one million books are in the store's catalog, and others can be ordered on request. Bezos minimizes inventory costs by stocking only the fastest-selling books. He buys other books only after receiving orders from customers.

The way Bezos designed his retail operation defies the tradition of the wheel of retailing. Amazon.com is hardly a stripped-down, low-service, low-price store. To the contrary, it offers unique services that aren't easily matched by conventional book retailers. One example is Eyes, an automated system that customers can use to request notification via e-mail when certain books become available. This mass customization allows Amazon.com to respond to individual customers' needs and interests without sacrificing the logistical efficiency it needs to keep costs low.

In addition to satisfying customers, Bezos is mindful of his relations with suppliers. He has set aside special Web pages to show how linking with Amazon.com can help a publisher sell its books. By helping his value-chain partners market more effectively, Bezos is able to start new relationships and strengthen existing relationships with suppliers. This enables the value-chain partners to achieve their ultimate goal of delighting book-lovers, who are their mutual customers.

Fueled in part by the enormous increase in Web commerce, Amazon.com has been growing at an incredibly rapid rate. At the start, Bezos operated out of a 400-square-foot office. After doing business on the Web for six weeks, he was forced to move to a 2,000-square-foot warehouse to keep up with the orders. Six months after opening, he had to move again—to a 17,000-square-foot building.

One of Amazon.com's resources is the giant database it is building on customers and their reading preferences. However, Bezos is careful about the way he uses this database, because he knows customers are concerned about privacy. One false move, and he may get flamed from all directions. "If someone thinks they are being mistreated by us, they won't tell five people—they'll tell 5,000," he says. As a retailer that thrives on positive word of mouth, customer satisfaction is his top priority. Since nearly half of the people who buy from Amazon.com are repeat buyers, it is clear that Bezos is very successful at building customer marketing relationships that last.[1]

Strategies and applications

1. Visit Amazon.com's Web site and look at how its Eyes service operates. How could a conventional book retailer compete with this automated notification service? From the customer's perspective, what value does such a service add? From the retailer's perspective? From the publisher's perspective?

2. Call up a few book listings and look for book reviews by customers as well as comments by authors. Why would other customers want this information?

3. Where in the retail life cycle would you place book retailing? Where would you place Amazon.com? Do you think the retail life cycle of Web-based stores will be about the same as conventional stores? Explain your answers.

4. Compare the Web site of Borders (http://www.borders.com) with that of Amazon.com. What can Borders do to compete more effectively for book buyers who use the Web—without copying the unique features of Amazon.com?

5. Should Amazon.com move to vendor-managed inventory? What are the pros and cons of using this method to maintain stock for a Web-based retailer?

6. Of the six major logistics management activities, to which do you think Amazon.com should pay special attention? Why?

Team project

Work with other students to consider whether Bezos should change its location strategy by opening one or more physical stores. Now that conventional book retailers are on the Web competing with Amazon.com, Bezos might want to compete with them in physical locations. What are the advantages and disadvantages of doing this? Prepare a presentation to your class to summarize your recommendations.

one-to-one IM

http://www.nettuno.it/mall

Marketing on the Net Inviting Global Visitors to a Weekend in Florence

Florence, Italy, is a shopper's paradise famous for leather goods, jewelry, and other hand-made products. Now, instead of packing a suitcase and flying to Florence, shoppers can point their Web browsers to the *Weekend a Firenze* (WAF) site. The largest commercial Web site in Italy, WAF enhances the shopping experience by presenting colorful views of Florence along with artistic photos and detailed descriptions of local merchandise for sale. The result is an atmospheric cyberspace shopping trip that draws customers from all over the world.

Allessandro Naldi, managing director of WAF, notes that the Web site has been carefully designed to nurture relationships with customers. People are invited to return again and again, whether or not they buy anything. In successive visits, people may examine different products, ask for more information, or request products that aren't displayed at the Web site. After they have visited a few times, people feel more comfortable buying because they are confident about the quality of the products and the professionalism of the marketers.

To avoid misunderstandings and minimize post-purchase dissonance, WAF clearly explains its sales policies and return procedures. It also ensures security of payment information—and compliance with Italian laws—by requesting that customers sign and fax in their order forms when buying by credit card.

As part of its relationship-building program, WAF has personalized the shopping experience. First, every purchaser receives an individual thank-you message via e-mail. Then customers are invited to join a frequent-buyer club that rewards customer loyalty. Customers receive points for every purchase. The points can be used toward discounts on future purchases. The club also has other benefits. Members receive advance notification of new offers and special sales. They can also request a personalized search to locate specific products in which they are interested.

Like any good retailer, Naldi is concerned about building traffic. That is why he has arranged to have the site listed with selected Web shopping malls and search engines. "The enormous range of goods today available on the Internet demands the greatest visibility in terms of quantity (occasions to see the address and name of the Web site in different places) and quality (displaying *"Weekend a Firenze"* on the most prestigious malls)," he says. And, in choosing products for display on the Web site, Naldi warns that "the choice of local products must not make one forget that the market is international. For instance, summer in Europe is winter in Australia."

Along with product offers, WAF presents tourist and hotel information to assist people who want to travel to Florence. This reinforces the site's positioning as the premier guide to the Florence experience. Armchair travelers and globe-trotters alike can enjoy the ambiance and convenience of spending a weekend in Florence on the Web.[2]

Strategies and applications

1. Visit the WAF Web site. How would you characterize its product strategy? Offer specific evidence to support your answer.

2. Some of the merchandise offered by WAF is breakable. How can WAF reassure customers that items they order will arrive in good condition? How can WAF use reverse logistics to allow customers to return damaged items?

3. The title, Weekend in Florence, implies that the Web site is more than a store. What else can WAF do to the site to enhance the visit for browsers and shoppers alike?

4. WAF ships its merchandise by air so that customers receive their orders within 48 hours. Why is this transportation method appropriate for WAF? Would transportation by rail or truck be appropriate in some cases? Explain your answers.

5. Imagine you're an artisan marketing hand-crafted leather briefcases through the WAF Web site. Could you use just-in-time inventory management? Why or why not?

6. WAF uses local programmers to prepare the software used in all its operations. Should Naldi publicize this fact on the Web site? Would any stakeholders care? Why?

Team project

With other students, use a Web search engine such as Excite to locate two or three online shopping malls. Compare their offerings, atmospherics, and ordering methods to what WAF offers at its Web site. What can WAF learn from these other shopping malls? What can the other malls learn from WAF? Write a brief team report about your findings, including at least one specific suggestion for improving each Web site your team visited.

internetempowerment

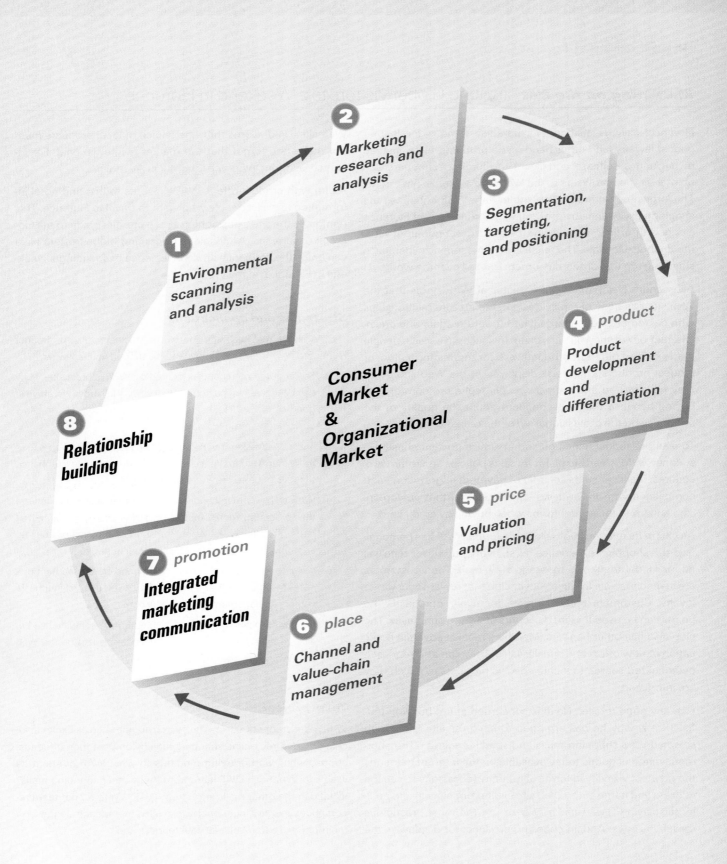

PART 7

Management of Integrated Marketing Communication

Part 7 covers strategy, implementation, and evaluation of integrated marketing communication (IMC) as part of a relationship-building strategy. First, Chapter 17 presents an overview of communication and the IMC mix. The chapter opening profile of Kodak Singapore shows the use of IMC to build relationships with customers and channel partners. Chapter 18 discusses the latest developments in advertising and direct marketing. The profile describes how Pleasant Company uses direct marketing to communicate with families that buy children's dolls. Chapter 19 explores the application of sales promotion and public relations in the IMC mix. The profile details how Microsoft launched Windows 95 using a worldwide sales promotion and PR blitz. Finally, Chapter 20 discusses the role of personal selling and sales management in building customer relationships. Learn in the profile how Capitol Concierge strengthens relationships with customers using database-driven personal selling.

17

Integrated Marketing Communication

Learning Goals

After you have read and studied this chapter, you should be able to:

1. Define integrated marketing communication (IMC) and explain its goal.

2. Show how the two-way dialogue of integrated marketing communication contributes to stakeholder relationships.

3. Identify the techniques marketers can use in the IMC mix and analyze the role of IMC in generating positive word-of-mouth communication.

4. Demonstrate how the five broad IMC objectives add value to marketing relationships.

5. Trace the steps in planning, implementing, and evaluating an IMC program.

6. Describe five ways of setting IMC budgets.

7. Show how an IMC audit is used.

PROFILE

A Kodak Moment for all audiences

Kodak Singapore wanted to make the moment last. Its challenge: to encourage more film purchases. Its response: a yearlong integrated marketing communication program anchored by the theme, "A Kodak Moment." The company's long-term goal was to strengthen relationships with consumers, channel partners, and professional photographers. But it didn't overlook internal marketing as it planned its communications program.

According to Kodak's marketing research, teenagers and parents are the heaviest users of film and cameras. To reach this audience, the company developed eye-catching advertising, public relations, and in-store materials featuring a Kodak Moments photo contest. Kodak gained wider public exposure by providing striking, colorful photographs for the reverse side of fare cards used in the Singapore subway system.

To build excitement among film retailers, the company sent out flyers, posters, and displays featuring the contest. In addition, retailers received copies of testimonials from consumers who were delighted by what they could do with Kodak film. Kodak also used direct mail to stay in touch with photographers in its marketing database.

Tying the campaign together was an internal marketing program keyed to the external marketing program. First, Kodak established an employee version of the Kodak Moments photo contest. Then the company held a series of employee briefings on how to take better photographs. This prepared every employee—not just those in marketing—to represent the company and its products to family, friends, neighbors, retailers, and consumers. By coordinating all its communications with the contest theme, Kodak Singapore focused attention on the brand name and its link with product benefits.[1]

This is the first of four chapters about the relationship-building abilities of integrated marketing communication (IMC), one of the most visible—and creative—of the eight universal marketing processes. In this chapter, you'll explore IMC's role in marketing, learn why two-way communication is the heart of IMC, and examine the techniques used in the IMC mix. Then you'll see how IMC adds value to marketing relationships and the process for planning, implementing, and evaluating IMC programs. With this foundation, you're ready to advance to the following chapters for an in-depth look at individual IMC techniques.

Integrated Marketing Communication and Marketing Relationships

In IMC we move from looking at products and units and share of market and transactions to customers and income flows and relationships over time.

Don E. Schultz
Northwestern University[2]

Having the right product at the right price in the right channels is a prerequisite for marketing success, as the people at Kodak Singapore well know. But the picture isn't complete without a means for building bridges to customers, channel partners, employees, and other stakeholders to strengthen relationships. Kodak reached out to its internal and external stakeholders using a variety of carefully controlled communications, all crafted around the Kodak Moment theme. This approach to relationship building exemplifies integrated marketing communication.

Integrated marketing communication (IMC) is a cross-functional process for establishing and strengthening profitable relationships with customers and other stakeholders; all marketing messages are coordinated to create a unified image for the organization and its products.[3] Such messages include those communicated through personal selling, advertising, public relations, direct mail pieces, store displays, Web sites, and other communication vehicles.

The goal of IMC is to maintain a dialogue with customers and other stakeholders, to enable the marketer to respond quickly to their ever-changing needs and wants. Note that IMC is *cross-functional*; that is, people in every department help create and maintain relationships through their contacts inside and outside the organization. Notice, also, that IMC is aimed at new as well as existing relationships, both of which are important to any marketer.

In addition, IMC is broader than traditional marketing communication because it is designed to reach not just customers and channel partners but also employees and other stakeholders who can influence the organization's success or failure. That's why every contact with stakeholders must be consistent with your marketing objectives and relationship-building strategy.

For example, Converse, the Massachusetts-based marketer of athletic shoes, reaches out to a number of stakeholders. Seeking to increase global sales, the company communicates with customers, wholesalers, retailers, and employees. It's also in touch with officials and players in the National Basketball Association, the National Football League, and selected college football teams. Converse's messages are consistent in their presentation of the brand and of product benefits. This consistency reinforces relationships that directly affect product sales and indirectly influence what people buy after seeing what players wear.[4]

Another key aspect of IMC is the need to coordinate the content and the look (or sound) of *every* marketing message. Few marketing activities are as dynamic and creative as designing and producing marketing communication materials. The choices of communication tools go on and on, from entertaining television commercials and informative CD-ROM catalogs to exciting contests and unusual public relations announcements. At the most basic level, careful coordination of these messages ensures consistency, so stakeholders won't be confused by conflicting or divergent messages. But that's not the only purpose. Coordinating all messages can lead to *synergy*— that is, the overall impact of all the messages together will be greater than the sum of the individual messages.[5]

Think for a moment about how customers might react to a number of different ads from one marketer in one magazine. That's what Abby Kohn-

integrated marketing communication (IMC)

a cross-functional process for establishing and strengthening profitable relationships with customers and other stakeholders; all marketing messages are coordinated to create a unified image for the organization and its products

stamm, IBM's vice president of corporate marketing, thought about as she flipped through an issue of *Client/Server Journal* and found 24 separate IBM ads, each with a distinct look and message, each created by a separate ad agency. Small wonder that Kohnstamm quickly took steps to avoid such duplication by consolidating all IBM advertising under a single ad agency.[6] IBM and other marketers that coordinate all internal and external messages around a common theme or concept are better able to use these communications to support their marketing objectives.[7]

The full power of IMC comes from its ability to sustain a *dialogue* with stakeholders. By exchanging information with stakeholders, you can strengthen each relationship and make the marketing exchange mutually beneficial for you and your stakeholders.[8] This calls for a two-way dialogue rather than the traditional one-way communication that marketers tended to emphasize in the past. This is why many marketers are turning to Web sites and e-mail. These new tools enable marketers to maintain a dialogue with all stakeholders.

One-Way Marketing Communication Versus a Two-Way IMC Dialogue

Integrated marketing communication is a specialized form of communication. In traditional communication models, the *sender* (marketer) is the source of the *message*, which is the information the sender wants to share with one or more *receivers*, the people (customers or prospects) to whom the message is directed. This process is shown in Figure 17.1.

Marketing has taken on an exciting new dimension as a result of the Internet. Marketers can now establish an ongoing dialogue to learn what information individual consumers are seeking and provide it quickly. Magazines such as *Black Enterprise* have opened Web sites, both to be more accessible to consumers and to generate information for use in planning future issues. How could *Black Enterprise* use the information-gathering capability of the Internet to increase the number of advertisers in its magazine?

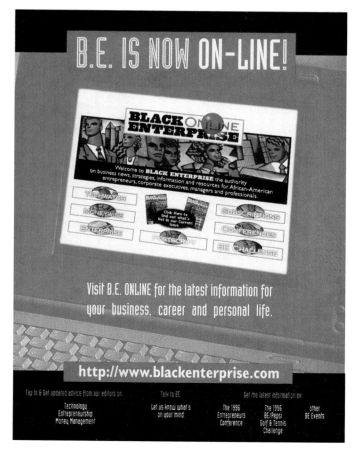

FIGURE   **17.1**   One-Way Versus Two-Way Communication Process

In the traditional one-way communication process, the marketer encodes a message and transmits it via a medium to the receiver. The receiver decodes the message and offers feedback to the sender. In contrast, integrated marketing communication relies on two-way communication. In this process, the marketer and the customer are both senders and receivers, encoding and decoding messages at the same time.

One-Way Communication Process

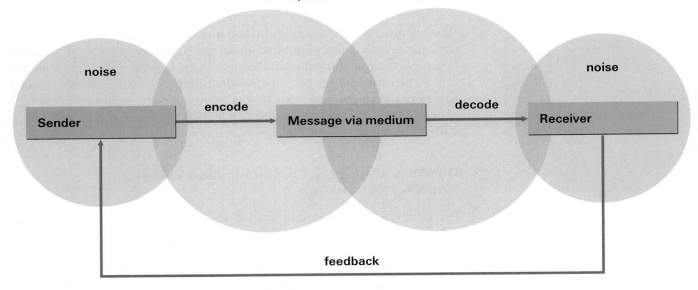

Two-Way Communication Process

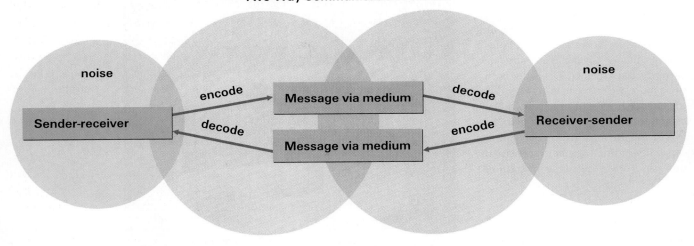

To start the process, the sender *encodes* the message by putting it into words, numbers, symbols, or graphic formats the intended receiver can understand. Then the sender transmits this message by choosing the appropriate *medium:* a television commercial, a posting on the Internet, a newspaper ad, a flyer placed on doorknobs, a billboard, an ad in the Yellow Pages, or any other way of reaching the receiver for whom the message is designed.

The receiver *decodes* the message by interpreting the sender's encoded message to uncover the meaning. Both encoding and decoding are influenced by the sender's and receiver's values, attitudes, and backgrounds, known as their *fields of experience*. Both sender and receiver also can be influenced by *noise*, extraneous factors such as distractions or printing errors that interfere with successful encoding and decoding. Closing the communication loop, the receiver responds to the message by offering *feedback*. Feedback lets the sender know whether the message was received and correctly decoded.

In the context of marketing, this traditional one-way model plus feedback describes *promotion*, marketing communication designed to inform and influence customers and potential customers. Too many marketers have stressed the encoding and sending aspects of communication and have paid less attention to the receiver's willingness and ability to decode the message and offer feedback. But promotion is only a subset of IMC. Instead of simply sending promotional messages to customers, channel partners, and other receivers, then awaiting feedback, an increasing number of marketers are using IMC to forge *two-way* communication links (a dialogue).

In the two-way communication model shown in Figure 17.1, the sender (marketer) is also a receiver, and the receiver (customer) is also a sender. Thus the sender is listening and responding to the receiver's messages, just as the receiver is listening and responding to the sender's messages. Such a dialogue is much more effective in establishing relationships than promotion plus feedback.

As marketers and their customers exchange information and ideas, they learn more about each other and about how to interpret the meaning of the messages they exchange. Marketers can also monitor purchases, returns, marketing research, letters, e-mail messages, telephone calls, and other sources of customer input to keep the dialogue going. Then they can refine their communications, products, prices, and channel strategies accordingly. For their part, customers come to know more about the marketer's offering, and they get better at expressing their needs and wants. In this way, the information shared by marketer and customer makes the marketing exchange more meaningful for each, which strengthens the relationship.[9]

The dialogue of IMC can be extended to every stakeholder group, including past customers, prospects, stockholders, employees, channel partners, suppliers, media representatives, bankers, and regulators. What's more, IMC marketers work hard to maintain the dialogue on a one-to-one level. This means building a database ◄——┘ **(p. 138)** of the needs, preferences, and profiles of the people in each stakeholder group so that communication can be customized for each individual.[10]

For example, American Express's Privileges On Call marketing program invites credit card customers to call for information about special services, such as access to health clubs while traveling. The automated telephone system routes the call to the appropriate recorded message and captures the inquiry for American Express's marketing database. Then, by analyzing each customer's history of inquiries, the company's computer can issue special offers keyed to individual interests. This dialogue has helped American Express do more business with its customers. Customers like it too: 81 percent of those who've used the program rate it good or excellent.[11]

The Role of IMC in Marketing

What makes IMC particularly relevant to marketing in the 1990s is the move from targeting a mass market to targeting specific market segments ◄──┘ **(p. 220)**. In the past, marketers had difficulty identifying individual customers and uncovering individual needs, so they tended to use standardized, one-way marketing communication to reach what they saw as a largely homogeneous market. These promotional messages were aimed at moving customers through the product adoption process ◄──┘ **(p. 305)**, a series of attitudinal and behavioral changes leading to a purchase.

According to this linear process, customers (1) become aware of the product, (2) develop an interest in learning more about the product, (3) evaluate the product's features and benefits, (4) try the product for the first time, and then (5) adopt the product for continued use through repeat purchasing.[12] This linear process is illustrated in Figure 17.2.

F I G U R E **17.2**   **Linear Product Adoption Process**

Lacking the tools to target individual customers, marketers traditionally used standardized, one-way communication to move customers along a linear path from awareness to trial and adoption of a product. Today, sophisticated technology allows marketers to build customer relationships by shaping IMC programs around individual needs, behaviors, and attitudes.

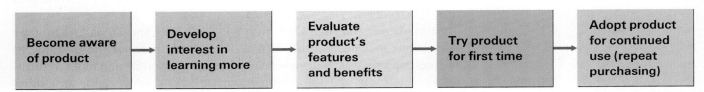

However, some researchers have questioned the linear sequence of steps in traditional models of product adoption. For one thing, these models don't consider that people have differing levels of involvement ◄──┘ **(p. 170)** with the products they purchase. Yet involvement affects the way customers gather information and evaluate products prior to purchase. The models also neglect the full range of customer behaviors that can occur during the buying process. Some customers may continually postpone adoption by reevaluating the product after every purchase. Others may prefer the novelty of constant brand switching. Linear models don't reflect such behaviors. They also don't take into account external factors (such as competitive messages) and internal factors (such as self-concept) that can influence a customer's buying behavior.[13]

Rather than using IMC to move a mass market of customers along a linear progression of steps toward product adoption, marketers can now take a more individualized approach. These days, marketers have the tools to appeal to *individual* needs and purchasing behaviors. Using detailed information such as store scanner data and database information, marketers can move backward from actual purchases to determine where and when individuals buy, what media they use, when and which marketing messages are most relevant, and when individuals are most receptive to these messages.[14] They can also set up interactive Web sites where potential customers can select the kind of information they need and get that information immediately.

Building the IMC program around individual needs and preferences enables customers to choose how, when, and where they want to receive messages from or send messages to the marketer. Customers can reach marketers using telephone, mail, fax machines, online information services, and many other methods. Marketers and customers have never had so many opportunities to share information and build relationships as a result.

In turn, marketers can use criteria such as customer needs or product usage to build one or more market segments made up of individual names. The vast amount of information in the marketing databases (past purchases, addresses, and so on) also offers clues to the profit potential of building a long-term relationship with each individual. Based on this information, marketers can use marketing communication to establish and sustain relationships with the individuals in targeted segments, rather than attempting to simply sell specific products.[15]

To see how IMC contributes to relationship building, consider the experience of Earth's Best, a Colorado-based business that annually sells nearly $20 million worth of all-natural baby foods. Now owned by Heinz, the company prices its products higher than those of rivals Gerber and Beech Nut. It targets two main segments: parents (who buy baby food) and pediatricians (who recommend baby food brands).

Although the company advertises in parenting magazines, it devotes most of its IMC budget to direct-mail programs. Earth's Best sends pediatricians information about the hazards of pesticides in foods, along with a handout that doctors can give to new parents. For parents, there's *Earth's Best Family Times*, a folksy newsletter with nutrition information, child-care advice, discount coupons, and a form asking for the names of others who might like a free subscription. The company prints its toll-free number in the newsletter and on every label. Nearly a million people call yearly for nutrition details and to find out where Earth's Best foods are sold. Customers are fiercely loyal to the company.[16]

Relationship building with customers can take many forms, but few are more powerful than a *useful* newsletter that keeps customers in touch with a company and its products. Shown here are three from Earth's Best baby food. *The Earth's Best Family Times* contains attractive illustrations and provides helpful advice for new parents. As effective as they may be, such newsletters are only one part of a successful, fully integrated marketing communication program. What are some of the other ways Earth's Best should promote its baby food?

The IMC Mix

The marketers at Earth's Best know that IMC blends a variety of communication techniques. The *IMC mix* is the particular combination of communication techniques that a marketer uses to achieve its objectives. The IMC mix you choose to meet your marketing objectives depends on your organization's unique situation, target market, strategy, and budget.

Earth's Best uses three techniques: advertising (magazine ads), direct marketing (newsletter mailings), and sales promotion (coupons). As shown in Table 17.1, other IMC techniques marketers may use are public relations, personal selling, and word of mouth. In addition, marketers can blend support techniques such as publicity, product placement, and event sponsorship into the IMC mix.

T A B L E   **17.1**   Summary of IMC Techniques

Technique	Definition	Application
Marketer Initiated		
Advertising	Paid, nonpersonal communication by an identified marketer to create or continue relationships	Useful for reaching large target audiences cost-effectively to stimulate a dialogue about needs and offerings
Direct marketing	Two-way process of marketing communication through which marketers interact directly with customers to exchange information and sell products	Useful for direct two-way exchange of information so communications and offerings can be tailored to individuals
Sales promotion	Communication of incentives that enhance a product's value for a limited time, encouraging channel members and employees to market it and customers to buy it	Useful for accelerating current purchasing and encouraging repeat purchasing to establish, continue, or renew relationships
Public relations	Process of evaluating stakeholder attitudes, identifying a marketer's products and activities with stakeholders' interests, and using nonpaid communications to build long-term relationships	Useful for communicating messages through a credible medium
Personal selling	Interpersonal communication process in which marketing representatives identify prospective customers, examine their needs, present product information, gain commitment, and follow up to maintain relationships	Useful for building and sustaining long-term relationships based on personal two-way communication; especially important in business-to-business and other organizational marketing efforts
Marketer Influenced		
Word-of-mouth communication	Interpersonal communication in which users and nonusers of products share experiences with products and opinions about them	Useful for stimulating positive attitudes toward a product, leading toward trial and adoption

Advertising

Advertising is any paid, nonpersonal communication initiated by an identified marketer to create or continue exchange relationships with customers and, often, with other stakeholders. Note that advertising is paid for by the marketer, who therefore controls the content, look, and sound of the message. This is in contrast to public relations, which is not paid for by marketers and is not under their control. The marketer also has considerable authority over where, when, and how often advertising messages reach the target market. Again, this degree of control is not possible with public relations.

Advertising is considered to be nonpersonal because the message is not delivered from one person to another or others but is sent through media such as television, radio, newspapers, magazines, direct mail, the Internet, and billboards. It is this characteristic that separates advertising from personal selling and word-of-mouth communication, two IMC techniques in which messages are communicated through personal contact.

Increasingly, marketers are including a variety of response mechanisms (ways for customers to reply, such as tear-off post cards) in their advertisements. This way, customers and other stakeholders can respond more easily to strengthen the relationship. For example, a recent Ford magazine ad invited readers to get information about the Taurus model by calling a toll-free number, mailing in a postcard, or visiting online sites on the World Wide Web. Ford television advertising invites viewers to see the car at nearby Ford dealers. But Ford's IMC mix isn't limited to advertising. Like most marketers, the company also uses other techniques—including sales promotion, public relations, and personal selling—to keep the dialogue going.[17] You'll learn more about advertising in Chapter 18.

Electronic catalogs are one of the fastest-growing areas in marketing. This direct marketing tool gives more power to customers by allowing them to easily and conveniently request additional information and, in many instances, receive an immediate response via their computers. Customers can view pictures of products, read descriptions, check specifications, and even place orders electronically. How important is this development to the idea of relationship marketing?

Direct Marketing

Direct marketing is a two-way process of marketing communication through which marketers interact directly with customers to exchange information and sell products. Like advertising, direct marketing is paid for by the marketer, who controls the message that customers receive. In addition, as you saw in Chapter 14, direct marketers control their marketing channels, bypassing wholesalers, retailers, and other channel partners to communicate directly with customers.

Direct marketing is an extremely powerful way of building and maintaining customer relationships. In part, its power comes from the control the marketer exerts over the exchange of information. But it's also due to the direct marketer's ability to gather a great deal of information about the target market. By analyzing the details stored in customer databases, direct marketers can tailor both their value packages and their communications to individual customers' needs.

For example, AT&T uses direct marketing to contact prospects for its discounted international telephone service. For one promotion, it built a database of Russian and Israeli immigrants who had recently come to the United States. Then the company tailored a letter that presented the offer as an opportunity to call home for less. To enhance the effectiveness of the message, AT&T prepared both Russian- and Hebrew-language versions of the letter. Such customized communications draw three to four times as many responses as nondatabase communications.[18]

Although building a good database is the key to effective direct marketing, marketers face serious ethical questions about invasion of customer privacy and misuse of personal information when using such resources. You'll find out more about these ethical questions when you learn more about direct marketing in Chapter 18.

Sales Promotion

Sales promotion consists of limited-time incentives that encourage value-chain members and/or ultimate consumers to buy now rather than later. The incentive may be a discount coupon, a sample, a special display, a chance to win a prize, or some other deal that has the potential to change the way customers, value-chain partners, and employees perceive the product's value. By enhancing the product's short-term attraction, sales promotion accelerates current purchasing and encourages repeat purchases.

When coordinated with other IMC techniques, sales promotion is a good way to kick off, continue, or renew relationships with various stakeholders. In the past, it took a backseat to advertising in the IMC mix. However, sales promotion has become increasingly important, and marketers like Nestlé spend more on sales promotion today than on advertising. "A number of years ago, Nestlé's marketing budget consisted of roughly 75 percent advertising, 25 percent promotional dollars," observes Timm Crull, CEO of Nestlé USA. "Today, it's just the opposite."[19]

Coca-Cola has been using sales promotion to combat intense competition from archrival PepsiCo. To get thirsty European customers hooked on the taste, Coca-Cola frequently offers free cola samples. German consumers received a full gallon of Coke to sample, in the hope that they would develop a taste for the brand. Supported by a multipronged IMC program, the sampling program helped boost Coke's European sales.[20] See Chapter 19 for a more in-depth discussion of sales promotion.

Public Relations

Public relations (PR) is the process of evaluating stakeholder attitudes, identifying a marketer's products and activities with stakeholders' interests, and using *nonpaid* communications to build long-term relationships with them. Unlike advertising, direct marketing, and sales promotion messages, PR messages are not directly paid for or controlled by the marketer. As a result, stakeholders often see PR messages as less biased and more believable than advertising.

The perceived believability of publicity adds power to the message. Some marketers pay agencies to help place stories with the media; but neither the marketers nor the agencies can dictate where, when, how, or whether the media will present the messages to the public.

Consider how Linda McCartney used public relations to market 400,000 copies of vegetarian cookbooks and 150 million packaged vegetarian meals in the United Kingdom and around the world. When she came to New York to publicize her second cookbook, *Linda's Kitchen*, she talked with news reporters about the book and about doing business as the wife of rock legend Paul McCartney. "In the beginning, the McCartney name was it," she says of her early PR efforts. "But as someone said, in the food business, they'll try

Linda McCartney, wife of Paul McCartney, former member of The Beatles, relies heavily on public relations to promote her crusade for vegetarianism, her two cookbooks, a line of meatless frozen dinners, and a vegetarian dog food. What other promotional tools would you recommend she use in an integrated communication campaign? In what ways could she generate positive word of mouth to help sell her products?

your product once, and if it doesn't taste good, they don't come back."[21] You'll look more closely at public relations in Chapter 19.

Personal Selling

Personal selling is an interpersonal communication process in which the marketer's representatives identify prospective customers, examine their needs, present product information, gain commitment, and follow up to maintain customer exchange relationships. As the term suggests, personal selling relies on personal contact to fuel two-way communication. In contrast, the other IMC techniques are distinctly nonpersonal (except word of mouth). Even when marketers like Linda McCartney meet one-on-one with reporters, their messages are carried to the public by newspapers, magazines, television reports, and radio coverage, rather than by individual contacts.

Personal selling takes place throughout the value chain. It's widely used in business-to-business (organizational) marketing, where suppliers of parts and raw materials, industrial equipment, and business services help organizational customers make purchases that will solve specific problems or satisfy specific needs. It's also used in consumer marketing. Among the marketers that emphasize personal contact are retailers (such as Hecht's department stores), multilevel marketers (such as Mary Kay, which markets personal care products), and service marketers (such as MCI, which markets long-distance telephone services). Both face-to-face and telephone contacts provide excellent opportunities for the kind of two-way communication that sustains long-term exchange relationships. Chapter 20 examines personal selling in more detail.

Support Techniques

Advertising, direct marketing, sales promotion, public relations, and personal selling are the most frequently used marketing communication techniques. However, they aren't the only techniques that fit into the IMC mix. Cause-related marketing, product placement, and event sponsorship are three of many other techniques you can use to support your IMC programs.

With *cause-related marketing*, a marketer contributes to a nonprofit organization every time a customer buys its products. The purpose is to link the products with a specific cause so customers can feel good about buying from a socially responsible marketer. By communicating this connection, the marketer builds a reputation for social responsibility and, in the process, offers support for a cause that customers (and other stakeholders) care about. American Express, Procter & Gamble, and many other corporations use cause-related marketing to link their products to a variety of causes such as the Special Olympics.[22]

Joining products and causes to make sales

Cause-related marketing, pioneered by American Express, has become increasingly popular as marketers search for ways to differentiate their products. In the early 1980s, American Express reaped a public relations bonanza from its support of the Statue of Liberty restoration. However, consumers are apparently less enthusiastic than marketers about linking social responsibility with marketing communications.

According to recent studies, consumers won't buy (or switch to) a product just because of a cause-related marketing effort. In fact, consumers are often cynical about ties between products and social causes. If a product doesn't seem to have a meaningful connection with a particular cause, "Why would a consumer be motivated any more than normal to buy the brand?" asks Professor Stephen Greyser of Harvard Business School.

At the same time, consumers say they want marketers to demonstrate a real commitment to local issues such as education and environmental cleanup. That's the approach taken by Fresh Choice, a family-oriented restaurant chain operating in California, Washington State, and Texas. The chain selects local schools to host preopening fund-raising dinners at new locations. Students sell tickets, earning as much as $3,200 for their schools, and the restaurant makes a good impression on its new community.[23]

How might Fresh Choice communicate its cause-related marketing efforts to families in its target audience?

Citymeals-On-Wheels

We Salute You.

Diamond Crystal® Salt is proud to be an Associate Sponsor of the *1996 American Chefs' Tribute to James Beard*, the founder of the Citymeals-On-Wheels program. Providing more than 1 million meals to over 13,000 elderly home-bound New Yorkers a year, Citymeals-On-Wheels continues to raise money for this great cause, and Diamond Crystal® Salt is proud to be a part of it.

Diamond Crystal® Salt — the Choice of Great Chefs.

FOR FURTHER INFORMATION CIRCLE 16 ON READER SERVICE CARD.

Cause-related marketing can add spark to any product, as illustrated by this ad for Diamond Crystal Salt. Citymeals-On-Wheels provides meals to over 13,000 elderly home-bound New Yorkers each day. Restaurants that participate in this program have every right to be proud of their contribution since it addresses an important organizational goal—to satisfy all stakeholders, including the local community. What benefits should Diamond Crystal Salt expect from sponsoring this ad?

product placement

paying to have products or brands featured in an entertainment production such as a movie, television program, or video game

Marketers who use **product placement** pay to have their products or brands featured in an entertainment production such as a movie, television program, or video game. The payment may be in cash or in supplies of the featured product. One of the most highly publicized uses of this technique was the placement of Reese's Pieces candies in the movie *ET*. When Reese's Pieces sales jumped 66 percent in three months, other marketers began going after product placements. Coca-Cola used product placement in the movie *Falling Down*, in which star Michael Douglas fights for a Diet Coke. United Biscuits used it in the European video game called James Pond, with Penguin brand biscuits popping up during the game.[24]

Although it is popular, product placement is also controversial. Critics question the ethics of product placements, especially in video games that children play over and over. Researchers also question the technique's usefulness. Studies suggest that viewers don't remember many of the products or brands that appear. Even when products are remembered, viewers aren't necessarily more likely to buy because of the placement. For now, some marketers and ad agencies are shunning placements. "We have yet to be con-

event sponsorship

underwriting all or part of a special event such as a sports activity or a concert as a promotional device

vinced of their effectiveness," says an executive at the D'Arcy Masius Benton & Bowles agency in London.[25]

A marketer who uses **event sponsorship** pays to underwrite all or part of a special event such as a sports activity or a concert. This technique helps put the brand in front of customers and other stakeholders, build goodwill through links with well-liked events, and enhance the brand's image. Marketers spend about $5 billion yearly to sponsor sporting events around the world. For example, Nokia, a Finnish telecommunications marketer, sponsors U.S. college football games on prime-time television. Although the company holds 20 percent of the mobile phone market in Europe and 19 percent in North America, it is seeking more brand recognition in its drive to become a truly global brand.[26]

Word-of-Mouth Communication

Word-of-mouth communication ◄──┛ **(p. 175)** is an interpersonal process in which one person, who usually has some experience with an organization or its products, tells someone else about his or her experience and offers an evaluation of it. Marketers seldom can directly control word of mouth, but they can use any or all of the techniques in the IMC mix to help generate such discussions. That's what makes it an important part of any IMC strategy.

Word-of-mouth communication is extremely powerful because the message is perceived as being unbiased. Often such messages are communicated among friends who are eager to share information about products. In such situations, since the source of the message is trusted, the information has much higher credibility than it would have if it came directly from a marketer. Thus negative word of mouth can be quite damaging to a marketer, while positive word of mouth can strongly motivate customers to try or buy products.[27]

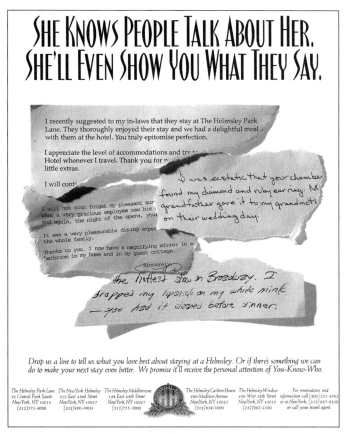

Ever hear of Leona Helmsley? Word of mouth is an important and sometimes underrated promotional tool. Virtually all marketers can benefit from positive endorsements from customers. The Helmsley Hotel chain uses customer endorsements to build an image of extraordinary service. Sampling is a good way to generate word-of-mouth communication; so is advertising to customers, who may then share desirable information about your product or service when speaking with others. What kinds of experiences might prompt a customer to say positive things about a company's service or products?

Issues for critical thinking

Nasty rumors can circulate quickly and hurt a marketer's reputation. What can a marketer do to combat negative—but inaccurate—word-of-mouth communication?

Manny and George Dragone, who refurbish and sell antique cars, generate word of mouth by participating in radio talk shows about antique cars. Car buffs in the audience hear their ideas, share the information with others through word of mouth, and bring them business. Similarly, Wizards of the Coast, which markets the game Magic, generates word of mouth by sponsoring championship tournaments. These competitions get young fans talking about the latest Magic cards and winners' strategies.[28] Here are some ways that marketers can use IMC to encourage positive word-of-mouth communication.

MARKETING IDEAS

Using IMC to generate word of mouth

Word-of-mouth communication is a vital part of building strong marketing relationships. How can marketers generate positive word of mouth for their products? Here are four ideas.

1. *Offer a sample.* Get products to opinion leaders who can talk them up with other people. This is what Approach Software did with its first database software product. The company targeted small business owners, offering a low introductory price and a 90-day money-back guarantee. Within six months, the company had tripled its sales, thanks to word of mouth from the opinion leaders.

2. *Ask for referrals.* When asked, satisfied customers are generally glad to pass the word to their friends and colleagues. Indy Lube, a fast-oil-change chain in Indianapolis, offers customers a $10 gift certificate when they give friends a referral card (that includes $5 off the first oil change).

3. *Go online.* Laurence Ostrow has built ChiPants Concepts, his apparel business, on word of mouth spread through online information services. When a satisfied customer posted a message on an online service, Ostrow was deluged with e-mail inquiries. He quickly set up a World Wide Web site where people can request fabric swatches or order forms and enter their names into the company's database. The site also includes testimonials from satisfied customers.

4. *Advertise to users.* People who buy complex or expensive products often read ads for those products—after a purchase—to reinforce their purchase decision. The additional information in the ads gives customers more to talk about, which encourages word of mouth. The Bose Company sends such ads to its users, who then explain to noncustomers through word of mouth how its Wave acoustic radios actually work.[29]

These are just four of many ways that marketers use IMC to generate word of mouth. What other ideas can you suggest?

Before you go on . . .

A. Why does IMC require a two-way dialogue between marketers and stakeholders?

B. What are the major communication techniques marketers can use in an IMC mix?

C. Why do marketers use IMC to generate positive word-of-mouth communication?

IMC Objectives: Adding Value to Marketing Relationships

To effectively build and strengthen relationships, an integrated marketing communication (IMC) program must add value for both the marketer and the stakeholder. Therefore, before planning such a program, you should decide what is meant to be accomplished—and what value customers, channel partners, or other stakeholders will get from the program. Broad objectives for IMC include building brand equity, providing information, managing demand and building sales, differentiating products, and influencing attitudes and behavior.

You'll notice that these objectives are often interrelated. By building brand equity, for example, you can also build sales, differentiate products, and influence attitudes and behavior. Regardless of the specific IMC objectives you set, your overall aim is to add value to establish or reinforce relationships with customers and other stakeholders.

How do you win consumers over to "100% Colombian Coffee?" One way is to stress the unique flavor through a humorous ad like this one. The ad focuses attention on one coffee bean. But it is not an ordinary bean, it is Colombian, and that's the difference. Building brand equity is a major responsibility of integrated marketing communication. That means, for one thing, having a strong message and repeating it often in different media. How could marketers of Colombian coffee reinforce the flavor message in other media?

Building Brand Equity

When you offer a branded product, often the most important objective of IMC is to build brand equity **(p. 266)**. The stronger the brand equity, the stronger the bond with customers and channel partners. This bond translates into repeat purchases and, ultimately, a more profitable, mutually satisfying relationship with customers and channel partners.

By making brand equity a priority for IMC activities, you're aiming to communicate the unique value your brand provides. You can use IMC to reinforce the connection with customers and make your brand even more desirable. As long as customers perceive that your brand's unique value can't be matched by competitive brands, they are likely to remain loyal to the relationship.[30]

Providing Information

A second objective of IMC, after building brand equity, is to add value to stakeholder relationships by providing information. This gives customers, channel partners, suppliers, employees, community groups, and other stakeholders a better sense of what your organization does, what it stands for, and how its products add value. In fact, delivering information through IMC programs can be a competitive advantage. For example, Fidelity Investments, a marketer of mutual fund investments, is known for its information-packed communications. Michael Hines, senior vice president, says the objective is to "add value to our products by giving more information and assistance to potential customers than any other company does." Along with direct mail and print advertising, Fidelity has aired infomercials about personal financial planning.[31]

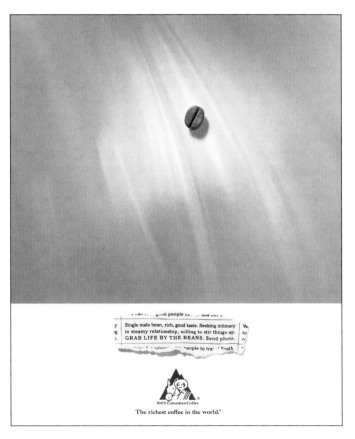

Single male bean, rich, good taste. Seeking intimacy in steamy relationship, willing to stir things up. GRAB LIFE BY THE BEANS. Send photo.

100% Colombian Coffee

The richest coffee in the world.®

Using IMC to disseminate information is crucial when you're launching new products and reaching out to new markets. Just ask Motoh Katsumata, who owns five car dealerships in Japan. When he began to import Ford cars, he started an aggressive IMC campaign of direct mail, newspaper, and radio advertising. His dealers sparked word of mouth by driving Taurus cars and other Ford models. These messages, coordinated with Ford's own multi-million-dollar IMC campaign, focused on the cars' safety features and competitive pricing. Although Katsumata sells only a few hundred Fords every year, he's positioning his dealerships for the future, when imported cars will be more popular.[32]

One of the best ways to provide information today is to establish an effective World Wide Web site. Information may be updated constantly in response to market changes or requests from stakeholders. The information is available at all hours of the day or night.

Managing Demand and Building Sales

A third objective of IMC is to help manage demand and build sales for your products. When supply is short or when you want to spread demand to slower periods, IMC messages can temporarily discourage customer buying or show customers the value of buying at another time. In addition, IMC can help boost both primary and selective demand.

Primary demand is demand for all products in a particular category. For example, Sweden's dairy industry used an IMC campaign to encourage teenagers to drink more milk. Messages on posters, bumper stickers, milk containers, and in other media played up milk's health benefits. This campaign increased overall demand for milk products, which benefited all dairy producers.[33]

After you've established primary demand, you can use IMC programs to increase *selective demand*, demand for your own brand. For example, Valvoline doesn't have to build primary demand for antifreeze products used in car and truck radiators because consumers already recognize a need. Instead, it uses IMC to build selective consumer demand for its Zerex brand of antifreeze, using television commercials, commercials in movie theaters, store displays, and a limited-time rebate offer.[34]

Differentiating Products

A fourth objective for IMC is to differentiate products from those of rivals. This is especially important when you're using IMC messages to build selective demand in a highly competitive market. As you saw in Chapter 8, differentiation sets a product apart from its competitors when the added value in the point of differentiation is meaningful to the target market. Then, to reinforce the differentiation, all your IMC messages must work together to communicate the uniqueness of this added value.[35]

For instance, GE Plastics, a Massachusetts-based division of General Electric, differentiates itself on the basis of its leading-edge technology, broad spectrum of products, and dedication to customer support. The company focuses on these points of differentiation in every message to the business-to-business market. In addition to using traditional advertising and personal selling, GE Plastics reaches its customers through the Internet. "We were the

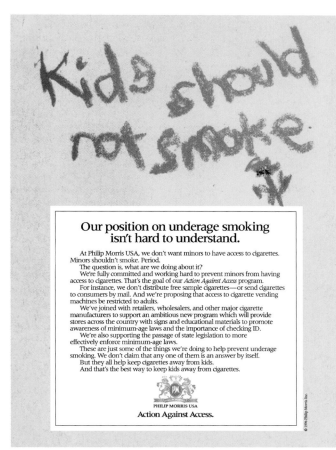

Our position on underage smoking isn't hard to understand.

At Philip Morris USA, we don't want minors to have access to cigarettes. Minors shouldn't smoke. Period.

The question is, what are we doing about it?

We're fully committed and working hard to prevent minors from having access to cigarettes. That's the goal of our *Action Against Access* program.

For instance, we don't distribute free sample cigarettes—or send cigarettes to consumers by mail. And we're proposing that access to cigarette vending machines be restricted to adults.

We've joined with retailers, wholesalers, and other major cigarette manufacturers to support an ambitious new program which will provide stores across the country with signs and educational materials to promote awareness of minimum-age laws and the importance of checking ID.

We're also supporting the passage of state legislation to more effectively enforce minimum-age laws.

These are just some of the things we're doing to help prevent underage smoking. We don't claim that any one of them is an answer by itself. But they all help keep cigarettes away from kids. And that's the best way to keep kids away from cigarettes.

PHILIP MORRIS USA

Action Against Access.

A cigarette company clearly has stakeholders other than customers. Research has shown that the general population in the United States is very much opposed to underage smoking, and tobacco companies are using advertising in an attempt to convey a responsible position on this issue. This ad promotes Philip Morris USA's Action Against Access program, which discourages underage smoking by limiting minors' access to cigarettes. This communicates to their stakeholders that they too are against smoking by minors. Do you believe these types of ads are sincere? What kind of impact do you think ads like this one have on Philip Morris USA's sales, if any?

first large business outside of computer-related companies to seek a serious online presence," notes Rick Pocock, general manager of marketing communications. The Internet presence backs up the company's leading-edge positioning ◄─┘ **(p. 224)** and provides instant support for customers seeking detailed technical information.[36]

Influencing Perceptions, Attitudes, and Behavior

The fifth objective of IMC is to influence stakeholder perceptions, attitudes, and behavior. Some IMC programs are aimed at changing public attitudes toward political or social issues. Others are aimed at influencing employees, stockholders, and other stakeholders. The nonprofit American Cancer Society recently used IMC to influence the attitudes and behavior of sunbathers. Its message: using a suntan lotion with SPF 15 or higher allows safe tanning and helps prevent skin cancer. The campaign featured models from the annual *Sports Illustrated* swimsuit issue. In addition to ads on television and radio, in magazines and newspapers, on billboards, and on posters, the campaign included publicity, sales promotion, and direct marketing. Over a three-year period, these messages convinced millions in the United States to tan safely with SPF 15 lotion.[37]

For IMC programs aimed at customers and prospects, the objective is to build positive attitudes toward the product and spark first-time or repeat purchases. Kool-Aid, for example, recently put together an IMC campaign to support the introduction of its Piña-Pineapple powdered soft drink mix. Targeting Hispanic families, the marketer's campaign used Spanish-language television commercials, coupons, samples, and a sweepstakes. These messages encouraged a positive feeling that translated into product trial and positive word of mouth. Sales of Piña-Pineapple soared, as did sales of other Kool-Aid flavors.[38] The following case shows how A.B. Dick uses IMC in business-to-business marketing.

Applying the Concepts

A.B. Dick's IMC links color and money

How do you capture a printer's attention? In A.B. Dick's case, the answer is to mention color and money in the same message. The Chicago-based company had long been known for duplicating machines, but not full-size printing presses. So when it introduced a two-color printing press, the Century 3000, it was necessary to influence customer perceptions, attitudes, and buying behavior. In marketing the new product, therefore, Dick used the theme "The Color of Money" to convey the product's key benefit: making short-run color printing profitable.

The marketer targeted three customer segments: small printing firms, corporate printing departments, and large commercial printers. Dick's ad agency coordinated a multifaceted IMC program of magazine advertising, direct mail, public relations, newsletters, and personal selling around the theme. Every element in the campaign pointed the audience toward a free, six-minute videotape showing the Century 3000's capabilities and benefits.

The company kicked off the campaign with a news conference in Chicago, demonstrating the new product and screening the video for the media. Its magazine ads in trade publications offered the video, as did its direct mail campaign. Dick's salespeople also brought copies of the video along on sales calls. The company gave away 12,000 videos during the two-year campaign, building its marketing database in the process.

Then Dick continued the dialogue with a free newsletter for prospects, customers, and salespeople. The newsletter told the customers' side of the story, showing how printers used the Century 3000 to boost business. These word-of-mouth success stories are "far more credible than a pitch from us," says Patricia Fortini, Dick's director of marketing communications. "They've helped us expand on different ways to help our customers market color." The Color of Money theme led to sales of 350 presses at $70,000 each.[39]

Make marketing decisions

1. What else can Dick do to keep up two-way communications with customers and prospects?

2. Why would printers see Dick's video as adding value?

3. What new theme would you suggest for an IMC campaign to introduce a new, improved Century 3000?

4. How could Dick have adjusted its campaign to spread demand for the new product over a longer period?

Before you go on . . .

A. How does IMC build brand equity?

B. What value might customers and prospects see in the information conveyed by IMC messages?

IMC Planning, Implementation, and Evaluation

With such a wide array of integrated marketing communication techniques available, putting together the optimal mix is a challenge. The process of planning, implementing, and evaluating an IMC campaign covers six steps: (1) examining the marketing situation and the product life cycle, (2) selecting the target audience and positioning, (3) setting program objectives, (4) establishing a budget, (5) designing and implementing the IMC strategy, and (6) evaluating results, then adjusting communications as needed. As you can see in Figure 17.3, this process is circular rather than linear, and step 6 leads back to step 1 for continuous improvement.

FIGURE **17.3** Planning, Implementing, and Evaluating IMC

The process of planning, implementing, and evaluating IMC is circular. The final step of evaluation and adjustment provides critical information for the initial step of examining the marketing situation.

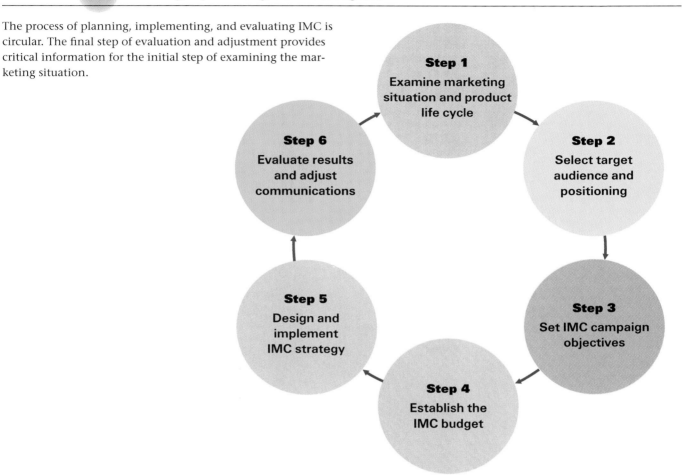

Step 1: Examine Marketing Situation and Product Life Cycle

Planning for an IMC campaign, like marketing planning, starts with a situation analysis. Start by reviewing your marketing plan, your marketing objectives, and your strategies for product development, channel management, and pricing. Then you can use marketing research to investigate the market, the industry, the competition, and the factors in the marketing environment that might affect internal and external communication. Also examine the effectiveness of previous IMC programs and determine how the strategy and tactics affected marketing results.[40]

Next, analyze the product's stage in the product life cycle ⟵⏋
(p. 302). As shown in Figure 17.4, the IMC support a product needs in the introduction stage differs from the support required in the growth, maturity, and decline stages. During the introduction stage, you can use advertising, public relations, and word of mouth to build market awareness of your new product. To stimulate initial purchases, you may want to use sales promotion techniques such as sampling and discount coupons. This is also the time to use personal selling and other techniques to cement relations with channel partners.[41]

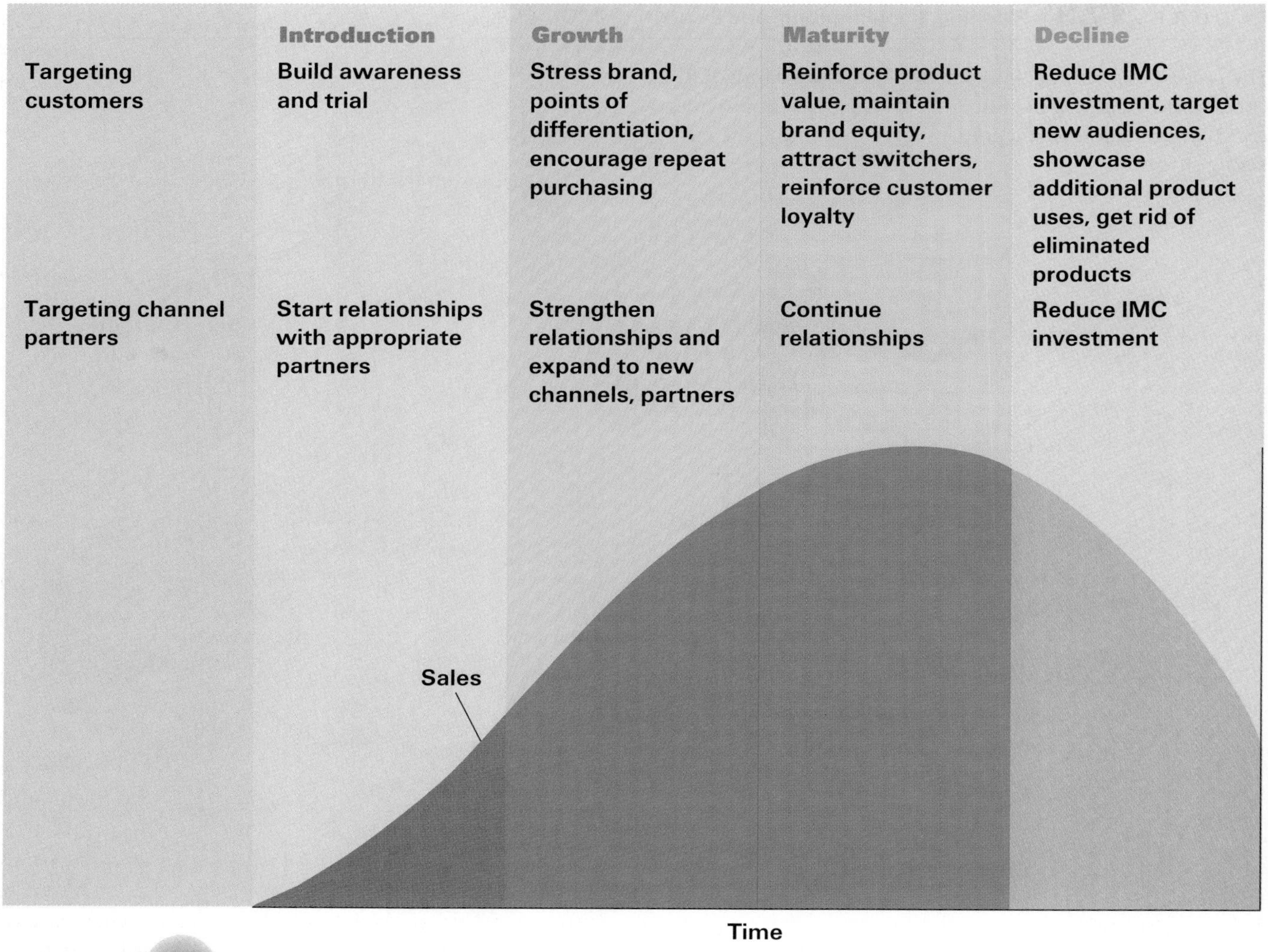

	Introduction	Growth	Maturity	Decline
Targeting customers	Build awareness and trial	Stress brand, points of differentiation, encourage repeat purchasing	Reinforce product value, maintain brand equity, attract switchers, reinforce customer loyalty	Reduce IMC investment, target new audiences, showcase additional product uses, get rid of eliminated products
Targeting channel partners	Start relationships with appropriate partners	Strengthen relationships and expand to new channels, partners	Continue relationships	Reduce IMC investment

Sales

Time

FIGURE **17.4**

IMC and the Product Life Cycle
In each stage of the product life cycle, marketers have a different focus for using IMC to target customers and channel partners.

target audience
the group of people a marketing message is intended to reach

communication objectives
IMC objectives geared toward influencing customer attitudes and behavior at particular points in the buying process

In the growth stage, you can attract more customers and enhance relationships with existing customers using advertising and direct marketing to clarify points of differentiation and boost brand equity. In addition, sales promotion can help increase demand by encouraging repeat purchasing. To support this growth, you will need to strengthen value-chain relationships using IMC techniques such as personal selling, direct marketing, and sales promotion aimed at channel partners and their employees. This is also a great time to set up a Web site to provide information to all stakeholders.

In the maturity stage, you can defend your product against competitive pressures by using advertising and sales promotion both to remind customers of the product's value and to maintain brand equity. Advertising and promotions can encourage switchers to defect from competing products, while direct marketing and other communications can reinforce customer loyalty. At the same time, you'll want to continue personal selling, sales promotion, and other techniques that support channel relationships.

When the product is in the decline stage, you may reduce your investment in advertising, promotion, personal selling, and other IMC techniques. To extend the life of a product in decline, you might try aiming advertising and sales promotion at new audiences or showcasing additional product uses and improvements.[42] If a product is being phased out, sales promotion and direct marketing can help empty the shelves. After a product has been eliminated, direct marketing and other communications can help meet customers' needs for ongoing service support.

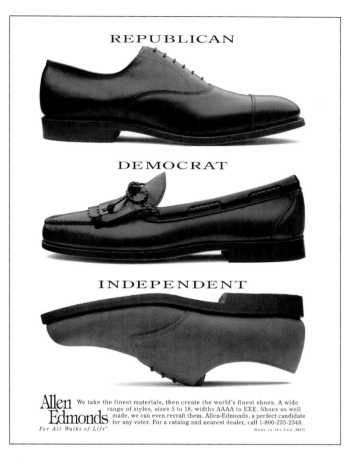

REPUBLICAN

DEMOCRAT

INDEPENDENT

Allen Edmonds We take the finest materials, then create the world's finest shoes. A wide range of styles, sizes 5 to 18, widths AAAA to EEE. Shoes so well made, we can even recraft them. Allen-Edmonds, a perfect candidate for any voter. For a catalog and nearest dealer, call 1-800-235-2348.
For All Walks of Life™

Made in the USA (MET)

Allen-Edmonds makes very high quality shoes. Since many of its products are in the mature stage of the product life cycle, the company's strategy calls for continuous advertising in an attempt to maintain market share. This particular ad pokes fun at image stereotypes to capture attention and promote the idea that the variety of styles offered will appeal to all tastes. By providing a toll-free number, the company ensures that potential customers can easily access information on its products and retailers. What image of the company and its product line does this ad suggest?

Step 2: Select Target Audience and Positioning

The **target audience** is the group of people your marketing message is intended to reach. To be effective, the IMC program should be developed to add value for a particular target audience, such as a specific market segment of customers, prospects, or channel partners. If you're targeting organizational markets, be sure to identify the decision makers and other participants in the buying center ◄——⏋ **(p. 207)**. Using marketing research, determine what your target audiences know (and need to know) about your product—and how you can reach these audiences most effectively. Then you can gear each marketing message and medium to the needs of the intended audience.

Once you've identified specific target audiences, you can use IMC activities to position your products according to each target audience's needs. Repositioning ◄——⏋ **(p. 242)** is a special challenge, especially when it involves changing long-held customer perceptions and attitudes. Just ask Dun & Bradstreet Information Services, which repositioned itself with an expanded product line. "One of the greatest challenges we have is communicating our services," says David S. Murray, vice president of U.S. sales and product marketing. "We do this with our more than 500 salespeople and through trade shows—getting the message out that we are a business information company, not simply a credit information company as we were in the past."[43]

Step 3: Set IMC Campaign Objectives

The next step is to decide exactly what the IMC program should accomplish. As you saw earlier, you can set five broad objectives for an IMC campaign. Now it's time to get more specific by setting measurable objectives that cover an identified target audience for a particular period. Then you'll be able to compare your results with your objectives to determine whether the campaign worked as planned.

IMC campaign objectives come in two types: communication and sales. **Communication objectives** are geared toward influencing customer attitudes and behavior at particular points in the buying process. Before customers buy, they move through a series of steps as they learn about specific products and brands, evaluate the alternatives, and test a product. A communication objective that corresponds to one of these interim steps would measure how customers are progressing toward a purchase.[44]

The ultimate objective of integrated marketing communication is to create a dialogue that leads to a long-term relationship that satisfies both customer and marketer. Nike has successfully established its brand name not only with television ads but through many other forms of IMC. For example, when customers call the number in this ad, they hear two mountain climbers discussing the merits of these shoes. Callers are then encouraged to leave their names and addresses to receive more information. In this way, Nike hopes to establish a dialogue with customers. What potential benefits does Nike hope to receive by reaching out directly to consumers?

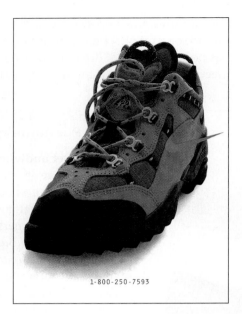

1-800-250-7593

Communication objectives can be expressed in several ways, such as

- the number of product inquiries received,
- the number of test drives taken, and
- the number of samples requested.

Sales objectives are specific, measurable sales and customer relationship goals to be met. Sales objectives can be expressed in a variety of ways, including

- the number of new customer or channel relationships started,
- the number of sales made to new or existing customers,
- the specific dollar amount or number of units to be sold,
- the specific increase in sales expected over an earlier period, and
- the specific market share or increase in share to be attained.

It is important that your IMC objectives make sense in the context of the overall marketing plan and marketing objectives. Be sure also that the results of your IMC program can be measured against the objectives. Finally, look ahead and think about whether the objectives being set for the current campaign will help achieve your organization's mission over the longer term.

Step 4: Establish the IMC Budget

How much should you spend to reach your target audiences and achieve your IMC objectives? This is a key question, because the budget determines how much can be spent to create and produce IMC materials and how much can be spent on media time and space. Some marketers budget a percentage of sales, some match what competitors spend, some budget what they can afford, some set budgets according to their IMC objectives, and some spend based on their expected return on investment.

sales objectives

specific, measurable sales and customer relationship goals to be met by an integrated marketing communication strategy

- *Percent-of-sales.* With a **percent-of-sales budget**, a certain pe annual sales is earmarked for communications. For instance, tual or expected annual sales are $500,000, and you plan ιο spend ɔ percent on IMC programs, your budget will be $25,000. However, be aware that this approach can lead to the mistaken conclusion that the more you expect to sell, the more you should spend on communications. In fact, the idea is for IMC to build sales. Sales aren't intended to build IMC spending.[45] Conversely, think twice before cutting IMC spending when sales are down—because that's the period when IMC can be most valuable.

- *Competitive parity.* When you prepare a **competitive-parity budget**, you plan to spend the same amount for advertising as your competitors spend. This information is available in rivals' annual reports and in trade association figures, among other sources. Finding out what competitors spend can help you avoid over- or underspending. However, be careful not to slavishly copy a rival's budget. IMC objectives generally differ from marketer to marketer, so what any given competitor does may not be right for you.

- *Affordability.* When you can't afford to spend much on IMC, you may use an affordability budget. An **affordability budget** is based on what money is available after all other expenses are met. Of course, when money is tight, reducing IMC spending may hamper your ability to meet communication or sales objectives. In general, affordability budgets are not effective planning tools because they are not related to sales or other meaningful figures.

- *Objective and task.* An **objective-and-task budget** is based on specific tasks that will help reach specific objectives: you set IMC objectives and then determine the IMC techniques that will help you reach each one. The cost of completing all the IMC tasks becomes the IMC budget. This is an effective budgeting method because it links IMC expenditures to specific objectives, permitting you to account for results. If affordability is an issue, you can revise both your objectives and your tasks to more realistic levels.

- *Return-on-investment.* A **return-on-investment budget**, which views IMC spending as an investment in developing additional customer business, is based on achieving a certain payback on the amount invested. For example, if you want a 200 percent payback, you must look for additional revenues of $20,000 from a $10,000 IMC investment.[46] Although this approach helps you look at IMC as an investment that is needed to build relationships, it may not help you to link results directly to IMC activities.

Many technology-based IMC tools are relatively inexpensive and therefore appropriate for marketers of all sizes. For example, Select Comfort Direct, a direct marketer of air-cushioned bedding, sends videocassettes at a cost of only $1.45 per prospect request. The tape includes product information and customer testimonials—and a toll-free number for ordering.[47]

Communicating globally on the Internet through commercial online information services such as America Online needn't be costly either. Small businesses like Mr. Upgrade, a computer parts retailer in Arizona, can spend

percent-of-sales budget

a certain percentage of annual sales is earmarked for integrated marketing communication

competitive-parity budget

spending the same for advertising and other IMC activities as your competitors spend

affordability budget

a budget based on what money is available for IMC after all other expenses are met

objective-and-task budget

a budget based on specific tasks that will help reach specific IMC objectives

return-on-investment budget

budgeting for IMC spending as an investment in developing additional customer business; based on achieving a certain payback on the amount invested

More and more firms are going into cyberspace to sell their products. Once a Web site is established, buyers from all over the world can peruse what you have to sell and place orders directly or through other means. Mr. Upgrade now gets half of its international business through the World Wide Web. Like all other forms of IMC, marketing on the Web requires careful attention to design and copywriting. What types of products do you think will have the greatest appeal to shoppers on the Internet?

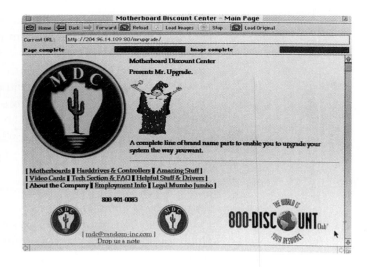

as little as $1,000 to set up a home page and $25 per month to stay on the World Wide Web. "It's actually our cheapest form of advertising," observes Robert Wood, Mr. Upgrade's sales manager. Yet, he notes, "Half our international business comes from the Web."[48]

Step 5: Design and Implement IMC Strategy

Once you've determined how much to spend, you're ready to design and implement the IMC strategy. For marketers that work through channel partners to complete marketing exchanges with customers, IMC can support a pull strategy, a push strategy, or a combination. These strategies are shown in Figure 17.5.

FIGURE **17.5** Pull and Push Strategies

Marketers can use IMC to support both pull and push strategies. In a pull strategy, marketers aim their communications at the customer, who then requests the product from the channel partner. In a push strategy, marketers aim their communications at the channel partner, encouraging cooperation in bringing the product to the customer.

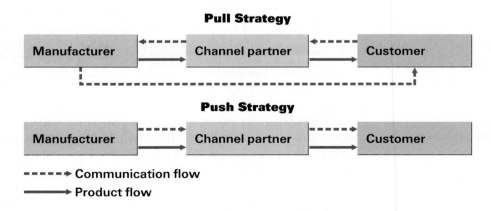

Pull and Push Strategies

A **pull strategy** aims communications at customers, who ask retailers (or other channel partners) for the advertised product, creating demand that pulls your product through the channel. Because a pull strategy encourages customers to seek out your product, it indirectly encourages channel partners to carry and support the item. A growing number of pharmaceutical marketers are using pull strategies for prescription drugs, targeting consumers who then talk to their doctors. Merck, for example, aims advertising for Zocor, a cholesterol-reducing drug, at consumers. One ad includes questions that consumers can ask their doctors about the drug.[49]

A **push strategy** aims communications at channel partners to carry the product through the channel to reach customers. Whereas a pull strategy targets customers, a push strategy targets channel partners, encouraging mutual cooperation to market your product. In turn, channel partners communicate with their customers to sell your product.

For example, when start-up USAfrica Airways began flying between the United States and South Africa, the company used a push strategy to build ticket sales. Its publicity and advertising efforts targeted travel agents who book trips for vacationers and business travelers. Travel agents then began to recommend USAfrica Airways to their clients. As a result of this IMC strategy, the airline was able to fill 83 percent of its seats, exceeding its objectives by one-third.[50]

In many cases, marketers blend push and pull strategies, aiming communications at both customers and channel partners. This is how Procter & Gamble, Kraft, and Campbell's Soup align their IMC strategies. P&G, for example, uses advertising and other IMC techniques to focus consumer attention on its Pampers brand of disposable diapers. At the same time, its promotions support the sales efforts of supermarkets and other channel partners that carry Pampers. Together, the two strategies are helping P&G defend against Huggies and other competing brands.[51]

From Strategy to Execution

The IMC strategy sets the overall direction for the IMC mix. After that, you'll develop individual strategies for each individual IMC technique you plan to use. This means devising a separate strategy for advertising, for Web site development, for sales promotion, and for all other techniques in the mix. In addition, each individual strategy should carry a budget and a set of specific objectives. No matter how many techniques are in your IMC mix, however, all your messages and media should be coordinated for maximum impact.

Timing is critical to IMC success, so before executing the individual strategies, you need to prepare a schedule showing all IMC activities. Use marketing research and environmental analysis to verify that each communication effort is scheduled to reach the target audience at the appropriate time and place and through the appropriate medium. Once the creative development and production of communication materials have been completed, you'll need a plan for evaluating the results. Here's how one small business owner updated his company's IMC strategy.

pull strategy

aims communications at customers, who ask retailers (or other channel partners) for the advertised product, creating demand that pulls the product through the channel

push strategy

aims communications at channel partners to carry the product through the channel to reach customers

Larry's Shoes retraces its IMC steps

Can you imagine Ringo Starr's psychedelic sneakers and 30,000 pairs of men's shoes under one roof? Step into Larry's Shoes, a 10-store shoe chain based in Texas. Marketing research showed store president Elliot Goodwin that Larry's had what customers wanted: huge selection, quality shoes, and value prices. Yet only 16 percent of the people in the target market were customers. So Goodwin revamped his IMC strategy in an effort to communicate more effectively with the other 84 percent, and to stay in touch with the 16 percent who were already customers.

Larry's had long relied on newspaper ads to communicate both brand selection and price. Goodwin dropped some of the print ads and moved into cable television to reach potential customers. The commercials showcased Larry's selection and vast array of sizes and prices, lingering on shots of the stores' interiors and the museum of celebrity footwear. Research soon confirmed that the cable campaign was drawing new shoppers.

Simultaneously, Goodwin strengthened the store's relationship with existing customers using a steady stream of direct mail communications. In addition to twice-yearly catalogs, salespeople sent thank-you cards, birthday cards, notices of sales, and new product announcements. Anchoring the IMC strategy was an internal marketing program (including training and employee newsletters) designed to stress customer satisfaction and product knowledge. After this IMC strategy was executed, Larry's sales jumped nearly $2 million in a year.[52]

Should Larry's Shoes also advertise on the World Wide Web? Why or why not?

Larry's Shoes of Dallas is willing to try almost anything to please and keep its customers—even installing coffee bars in its stores. You can see for yourself how attractive the store is and why customers feel comfortable shopping there—again and again. Larry's Shoes is an excellent example of relationship marketing in action. How does its approach compare with that of local shoe stores in your area?

Step 6: Evaluate Results and Adjust Communications

Executing an IMC strategy without being prepared to evaluate the results is like taking a test without being able to check the answers. Assessing IMC results can be a complex undertaking, though, one of the toughest challenges marketers face.[53] As you saw in Chapter 5, marketing research can help you determine the effectiveness of your IMC programs. If results are not as expected, you'll want to adjust communications. If results are on track or above expectations, you can apply what you learn from these successful strategies to develop future strategies.

On the other hand, you can't necessarily attribute good results to IMC alone. Isolating the effect of communications is quite difficult because so many environmental forces can influence marketing performance. One exception is direct marketing, where you can look at customer responses and trace results to specific communications. Another is couponing, where you can determine the number of coupons redeemed.

Issues for critical thinking

Apart from IMC, what environmental forces might affect sales results? How can marketers use environmental scanning and market analysis to identify and track these forces?

To overcome the measurement difficulty, more marketers are building response mechanisms into their communications. Then they can evaluate results by counting the number of inquiries or sales from a particular communication. For example, SmithKline Beecham posted a message in an Internet newsgroup offering a free sample of its Aquafresh Whitening toothpaste. Thousands of respondents called the marketer's toll-free hotline to request a sample. Not only could SmithKline count the responses, it also could and did gather the names and addresses for its marketing database.[54]

Measuring the results of marketing communications in newer media, such as online services, can be tricky but not impossible. Most marketers want to know more than just the number of daily "hits" (the number of people who access, or visit, a marketer's online site). That's why the World Wide Web site for *Pathfinder*, an online magazine set up by Time Inc., provides its advertisers with demographic data about first-time and repeat visitors to sponsored pages. These data help the marketers who advertise on *Pathfinder* better match their messages to the audience.[55]

Another way to evaluate the full range of IMC communications is to use an **IMC audit**: a comprehensive assessment of all the organization's communications with stakeholders. The purpose is to determine whether the communications (1) are appropriate and meaningful to their target audiences, (2) convey messages that are consistent with the marketer's objectives, and (3) are properly integrated. In an IMC audit, you look at

- whether the product's positioning and benefits are clearly expressed,
- whether the content, look, and sound of each communication fit the positioning and the target audience, and
- whether the unique value of the brand is appropriately communicated in a way that's meaningful for the audience.[56]

This audit helps you pinpoint individual communications that need improvement as well as communications that are effective. Then you can take steps to adjust your communications and better integrate all techniques into a cohesive IMC strategy.

Before you go on . . .

A. What is a target audience?

B. How do communication objectives differ from sales objectives?

C. What methods can marketers use to set IMC budgets?

D. How do pull strategies differ from push strategies?

IMC audit

a comprehensive assessment of all the organization's communications with stakeholders

Summary

1. **Define integrated marketing communication (IMC) and explain its goal.**

   Integrated marketing communication (IMC) is a cross-functional process for establishing and strengthening profitable exchange relationships with customers and other stakeholders by controlling or influencing all marketing messages to create a unified image for the organization and its products. The goal of IMC is to maintain a dialogue with customers and other stakeholders, to be able to respond to their needs and wants.

2. **Show how the two-way dialogue of integrated marketing communication contributes to stakeholder relationships.**

   With a two-way dialogue, both marketers and stakeholders send and receive messages. The information shared through IMC strengthens the relationship by making the marketing exchange more meaningful for each party.

3. **Identify the techniques marketers can use in the IMC mix and analyze the role of IMC in generating positive word-of-mouth communication.**

   The IMC mix can include advertising, direct marketing, sales promotion, public relations, personal selling, word of mouth, and support techniques such as cause-related marketing, product placement, and event sponsorship. Word-of-mouth communication is powerful because the message is perceived as being unbiased. Although marketers can't always control word-of-mouth communication, they can use the IMC mix to generate positive word of mouth for their products.

4. **Demonstrate how the five broad IMC objectives add value to marketing relationships.**

   Broad objectives for IMC include building brand equity, providing information, managing demand, differentiating products, and influencing attitudes and behavior.

5. **Trace the steps in planning, implementing, and evaluating an IMC program.**

   In step 1 you examine the marketing situation and the product life cycle. In step 2 you select the target audience and positioning. In step 3 you set IMC campaign objectives. In step 4 you establish the IMC budget. In step 5 you design and implement the IMC strategy. In step 6, which leads back to step 1, you evaluate results and adjust communications if necessary.

6. **Describe five ways of setting IMC budgets.**

Percent-of-sales budgets set aside a percentage of annual sales for IMC activities. Competitive-parity budgets match what competitors spend. Affordability budgets are based on money remaining after all other expenses are met. Objective-and-task budgets are based on the tasks needed to reach IMC objectives. Return-on-investment budgets calculate the return on investment of IMC activities.

7. **Show how an IMC audit is used.**

An IMC audit is a comprehensive assessment of all the organization's communications with stakeholders. The purpose is to determine whether the communications (1) are appropriate and meaningful to their target audiences, (2) convey messages that are consistent with the marketer's objectives, and (3) are properly integrated.

KEY TERMS

affordability budget **523**
communication objectives **521**
competitive-parity budget **523**
event sponsorship **513**
IMC audit **527**

integrated marketing communication (IMC) **502**
objective-and-task budget **523**
percent-of-sales budget **523**
product placement **512**

pull strategy **525**
push strategy **525**
return-on-investment budget **523**
sales objectives **522**
target audience **521**

Skill-Building Applications

1. One of your most important IMC tasks will be to generate a positive message about yourself as you seek out employers and build your career. How can you apply the concepts from this chapter? How can you use word of mouth to help your cause?

2. Business-to-business marketing relies heavily on personal selling. How might an advertising agency such as Leo Burnett win customers using other IMC techniques besides personal selling?

3. The American Cancer Society holds an annual "Smoke Out" day, encouraging smokers to quit for the day—and for longer, if possible. How can the organization use IMC techniques to get smokers to participate? Suggest several specific ideas.

4. Should Lufthansa, the German airline, vary ad messages for different customer segments? What

segment might respond to a message stressing on-time service? What segment might respond to a message stressing price? Should the airline communicate a consistent message to all segments? Why or why not?

5. What are some of the least expensive IMC techniques the owner of a small business like Sam's Deli could use to attract more customers? Discuss specifically how such a deli could use word of mouth and direct mail to get and keep customers.

6. Should a service marketer like AT&T have a different IMC program for each country it serves? What limitations to the use of various IMC techniques might the company anticipate?

Getting Involved in Marketing

1. *On Your Own* Select three different ads for a particular product, such as 3M Post-It notes or Dodge Grand Caravan minivan. Based on these ads, identify the target audience and the product positioning. How does each ad invite a two-way dialogue with the audience? If one or more ads contain sales promotion elements such as a contest or a discount coupon, how do these elements enhance the product's value for a limited time?

2. *On Your Own* Choose a product that is receiving a great deal of in-store promotion support, such as special displays, on-shelf couponing, or product demonstrations. Is this an example of a push or a pull strategy? Who is the target audience? How are the producer, the customer, and the store benefiting from the in-store communications? Prepare a brief report on your findings.

3. *Find Out More* Find an article in a magazine, newspaper, or an online database service (or interview a local marketer) about using a push or a pull strategy. What does the marketer want to accomplish? How does the strategy selected help the marketer meet its objectives? How does the IMC mix support this strategy? What can you suggest to strengthen this marketer's IMC program? Draft a letter to the marketer explaining your ideas.

4. *In a Team* With two other students, assume the role of executives in an advertising agency that handles all IMC programs for Mars's M&M chocolate candies. If Mars wants to build year-end holiday sales for M&Ms, which IMC techniques would your agency recommend? Prepare a report or a presentation relating your recommendations to Mars's objective.

5. *In a Partnership* With another student, look for possible product placements in a recent movie. How does each placement relate to the product's target market and benefits? How long does each brand or product appear on the screen, and in what context? How effective do you think each placement is? Hold a debate in class, with one student arguing for product placements in the movie, and the other arguing against. Which side is more persuasive? Why?

6. *In a Team* With two or three other students, develop an IMC plan for a specific product, such as Rayban sunglasses or FedEx overnight shipping services. Prepare a situation analysis, looking carefully at product life cycle and competition. Then select a target audience and positioning, establish objectives, set a budget, and suggest an IMC strategy. How will results be measured? Be prepared to defend your plan during a class presentation.

VideoCase Building Relationships at Biltmore Estate

The welcome mat is out at Biltmore Estate, the largest private home in the United States. Biltmore Estate was built in 1895 in Asheville, North Carolina for multimillionaire George Vanderbilt. Now owned by William Amherst Vanderbilt Cecil, George Vanderbilt's grandson, the Estate is open to the public as a tourist attraction. And what an attraction it is, with 250 rooms in Biltmore House, acres of manicured grounds, a winery, and restaurants. Small wonder that nearly one million visitors annually flock to this one-of-a-kind destination.

Biltmore Estate marketers have worked closely with Price/McNabb, their IMC agency, to craft a successful communication strategy for building customer relationships. The focus is on three distinct market segments. Passholders are people who buy one-year admission passes to the Estate. General Visitors are people who pay for one-day admission to the Estate. Prospects are people who have never visited but may be interested in the Estate.

Each year, the marketers establish goals for all three segments, and then design an IMC mix for each segment. They measure results according to the number of contacts made, the number of inquiries, the number and value of sales transactions, and the outcome of surveys about customer satisfaction.

The Estate maintains an ever-growing internal database of customer names and, in addition, taps external databases for prospect names. As a result, its marketers are able to establish and strengthen relationships by sending a steady stream of direct mail to prospects and customers.

To strengthen the relationship with Passholders, Biltmore Estate mails newsletters, invitations to special events, and other communications to this segment. Direct mail is also used to encourage guests who have visited in the past to come back again. These visitors are sent a colorful brochure detailing upcoming events and are provided special offers to encourage visits.

To encourage first-time visits from Prospects and repeat visits from General Visitors, the Estate uses a variety of advertising techniques. Ads in upscale magazines convey the grandeur of Biltmore House as well as the beauty of the gardens and grounds. Readers can call toll-free for more information, and all inquiries are entered into an internal database. In addition, radio advertising is used to promote seasonal events such as the annual "Christmas at Biltmore."

Public relations helps draw visitors from around the country—and around the world. Biltmore Estate marketers work with media contacts in newspapers, magazines, television, and radio to promote special events and keep Biltmore House, gardens, and the winery in the public eye. Coordinated with other IMC activities, public relations helps to reinforce the Estate's overall image and positioning.

This IMC strategy has been quite successful, boosting attendance and increasing sales of Biltmore Estate products. But competition in the travel and tourism industry never ends. That's why Estate marketers aren't about to slow down as they plan, implement, and evaluate IMC activities for relationship marketing.[57]

Strategies and applications

1. What kind of information should Biltmore Estate offer in advertising to Prospects? Why?

2. Can you suggest additional ways of using direct marketing and external databases to reach Prospects and boost attendance?

3. How would you recommend that Biltmore Estate promote its Christmas at Biltmore celebration on a World Wide Web site?

4. In planning an IMC campaign for the Christmas celebration, what would you examine in the marketing situation? Why?

5. What else could Biltmore Estate do with IMC to reinforce its positioning and differentiate itself from competitors?

6. How can Biltmore Estate use IMC to generate positive word of mouth to increase attendance?

Team project

With another student, prepare to stage a public relations interview. One student, playing a Biltmore Estate marketer, should write a one-page press release promoting the special Christmas at Biltmore event (make up any needed details). The other student, playing a television news reporter, should write at least ten questions to ask. Conduct the role play in class, then hold a discussion to critique its results. What could each student do better to communicate with the audience?

18

Advertising and Direct Marketing

Learning Goals

After you have read and studied this chapter, you should be able to:

1. Define advertising and show how the various types support relationship building.
2. Comment on the value of advertising to customers, marketers, and channel partners.
3. Explore the creative role of appeals, copy, and art in the development of an advertisement.
4. Apply advertising research to create, place, and evaluate advertising.
5. Demonstrate the importance of reach and frequency in selecting media.
6. Explain the factors to consider in making media decisions.
7. Show how marketers use direct marketing and database marketing to build customer relationships.

PROFILE

Pleasant Company: Direct marketing gets all dolled up

Addy Walker and Kirsten Larson are two dolls that don't drive pink sports cars or wear spike heels. Instead, they wear period clothing and star in storybook adventures out of America's past. These historically accurate dolls are a world away from the glamor and glitz of high-fashion Barbie—and that's exactly the way Pleasant T. Rowland planned it.

Rowland decided to create dolls that are fun and educational after looking without success for dolls she would like to give to her young nieces. The result was the American Girls Collection, a line of dolls, clothing, and books for girls aged 7 and up. Because of the historical detail and quality, the dolls are priced close to $100, compared with some Barbie dolls that can be bought for $10 or less.

From the start, Rowland planned to bypass stores to market directly to consumers. "Direct mail was the best way to sell a new, relatively complex product line in a softer and gentler voice to girls, mothers, and grandmothers," she says. The books are also sold in bookstores and contain a reply card so customers can get the doll and accessory catalog. Customers can call toll-free with questions and orders. Employees capture customer information in Pleasant Company's database, including names and addresses; children's birth dates, ages, and grade levels; and the source of the inquiries. Knowing these facts, the company can analyze customer purchasing patterns and better target future mailings.

Rowland's direct marketing approach to two-way communication has paid off. Pleasant Company mails some 36 million catalogs a year. The payoff: more than $150 million in purchases by a loyal customer base.[1]

Advertising and direct marketing are key elements of integrated marketing communication, one of the eight universal marketing processes. In this chapter, you'll examine the use of advertising to build and sustain exchange relationships. The chapter opens with an overview of advertising and relationship marketing. Then you'll learn how to develop advertising that works, from planning to implementation to evaluation. Finally, you'll explore the diverse world of direct marketing, including database marketing, direct mail advertising, and direct response advertising to establish and maintain relationships.

Advertising and Relationship Marketing

Advertising can't sell any product; it can only help to sell a product the people want to buy.

Jeremy Tunstall

The words and images of advertising are all around us, in magazines and newspapers, on television and radio, on the Internet and in mailboxes, and on buses and blimps. **Advertising** is any paid form of nonpersonal communication link, initiated by an identified marketer, to establish or continue exchange relationships with customers and, at times, with other stakeholders.

Notice that advertising is communication that has been *paid* for by the marketer, who is *identified* as the source of the information. In contrast to personal selling, which takes place one-on-one, advertising is a *nonpersonal* communication method. As a *communication link*, advertising is part of a two-way dialogue supporting the relationships between marketers and their customers and other stakeholders.

Many companies, nonprofit organizations, and government agencies allocate a large portion of their IMC budgets to advertising. In all, U.S. marketers spend over $162 billion annually on advertising. The top category advertised is automotive products, as shown in Table 18.1. Worldwide, total advertising expenditures top $355 billion per year, an amount that is expected to grow as more marketers seek to reach global markets.[2]

advertising

any paid form of nonpersonal communication link, initiated by an identified marketer, to establish or continue exchange relationships with customers and, at times, with other stakeholders

product advertising

focuses on a good or a service, either for ultimate consumers or for organizational customers

institutional advertising

focuses on the organization, presenting a particular image or concept

pioneering advertising

introduces a new product or brand

reminder advertising

keeps the marketer's or product's name in front of the target market

competitive advertising

stresses the ways in which one product or product category is superior to others, without naming specific competitors

comparative advertising

demonstrates how a product is superior to a particular competing brand

T A B L E **18.1**   Top U.S. Advertising Categories

Rank	Category	1994 Advertising Spending (millions of dollars)
1	Automotive products	$1,241
2	Direct response marketers	1,234
3	Toiletries and cosmetics	877
4	Services	686
5	Apparel, footwear, accessories	567
6	Foods and food products	557
7	Drugs and remedies	501
8	Travel, hotels, resorts	472
9	Computers, office equipment	420
10	Cigarettes and tobacco products	307

Types of Advertising

There are two basic types of advertising: product advertising and institutional advertising. **Product advertising** focuses on a good or a service, either for ultimate consumers or for organizational customers. This type of advertising seeks to encourage product purchases, so the marketer's name is less in the spotlight than the product itself. Much of advertising falls into this category. For example, when Timex advertises its Indiglo wristwatches, the products are prominently featured, the brand name tucked discreetly into a corner. Product advertising works for Timex, which saw its share of the U.S. watch market rise from 25 to 33 percent following a recent Indiglo ad campaign.[3]

Institutional advertising focuses on the organization, presenting a particular image or concept. Unlike product advertising, which aims to stimulate purchases, institutional advertising aims to influence attitudes. Nintendo, for instance, used institutional advertising to recast its brand image among boys ages 8 to 14, the target market for video games, and especially among boys 12 to 14, who serve as opinion leaders in the product category. Nintendo's ad campaign communicated a hip, contemporary image that appealed to the target market—and helped the company overtake Sega as the market leader.[4]

Beyond these two broad categories, individual ads can be categorized as pioneering, reminder, competitive, or advocacy, depending on what the ad is designed to communicate. Here's an overview of these four categories.

- **Pioneering advertising** introduces a new product or brand. Such advertisements usually present a great deal of information to educate customers about the new product or brand and its benefits. Since research shows that customers prefer pioneering brands over later entrants, pioneering advertising is an important tool for building early sales. For example, pioneering ads helped Accent Software International launch a word processing program that accommodates as many as 35 languages in one document. The ads linked product features to benefits. This way, says president Bob Rosenschein, "Our customers typically knew from the outset what [problems] we solved for them."[5]

- **Reminder advertising**, as the name suggests, keeps the marketer's or product's name in front of the target market. Once pioneering advertising has paved the way for new product sales, you need to reinforce customers' purchasing behavior. Reminder advertising reassures customers of the continuing value of your product, to encourage them to keep it on their shopping lists. Eastman Kodak, for example, developed a series of reminder ads after research showed that customers wanted photos of as many as 40 special occasions during the year—but had trouble remembering cameras and film. The Kodak campaign ties reminders to Mother's Day, graduations, and other occasions.[6]

- **Competitive advertising** stresses the ways in which one product or product category is superior to others, without naming specific competitors. Some marketers take competitive advertising a step further. **Comparative advertising** demonstrates how a product is superior to a particular competing brand. Comparative advertising can be effective when a marketer wants to show how a product offers more value than a particular rival. Visa, for example, runs comparative ads saying that more travel and shopping locations accept its credit card than American Express cards. "All of our advertising is comparative," notes Jan Soderstrom, Visa's senior vice president of advertising. "I can't imagine a strategy that would have worked better."[7]

Product advertising for Timex's Indiglo watches focuses attention on reliability as well as the special light features. What group or groups of consumers do you think Timex is targeting with this product advertisement?

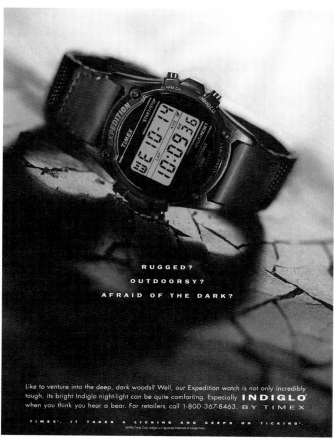

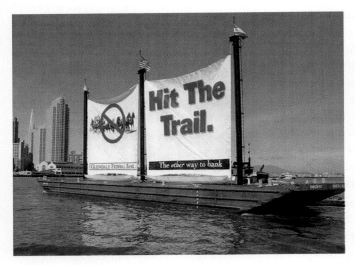

Integrated marketing communication means using a variety of media to communicate a strong and consistent message to the public. As this photo shows, IMC can include the use of unusual media such as these two 40-foot-square billboards mounted on a barge. Because mounting billboards on a barge is out of the ordinary, it gives Glendale Federal Bank, based in San Francisco, even greater visibility in its attempt to compete against its larger rivals. What other unusual or unique media can smaller marketers use to challenge larger, well-financed rivals?

- **Advocacy advertising** communicates a marketer's position on an issue. Both profit-seeking and non-profit marketers use this type of advertising to influence people's attitudes toward social or legislative issues. For example, the Massachusetts Department of Health advocates a nonsmoking, healthy lifestyle. By stressing how smoking leads to wrinkled skin and yellowed teeth, the agency's ads try to turn teenagers against smoking.[8] This advocacy ad by a state department of health is a good example of **public service advertising (PSA)**, ads by government or nonprofit groups that address social issues such as smoking and drunk driving. Television stations and other media often donate time or space to run PSAs as a community service.

The Value of Advertising

Advertising is one of the most visible forms of integrated marketing communication, and its pervasiveness stokes the debate over its value. But precisely because there are so many ads, the effect of any one message is lessened. This leads marketers to present even more ads and try different media in the hope of breaking through the clutter—which only fuels the debate. Advertising has been attacked for being wasteful, manipulative, and so persuasive that it encourages people to buy products they don't need. Consider the reaction to the controversial advocacy ads produced for the "United Colors of Benetton" campaign. One ad called attention to a social problem by picturing a man dying of AIDS. A French court ruled that the ad exploited AIDS sufferers and fined Benetton $28,300. Another ad, which also resulted in a fine, showed a person sporting an "HIV positive" tattoo. Many Benetton retailers protested the United Colors campaign. German retailers even took Benetton to court, claiming that the ads kept customers away. Meanwhile, sales floundered. Benetton then began downplaying the advocacy ads in favor of more restrained product ads spotlighting clothing and prices.[9]

On the other side of the argument, proponents believe that advertising adds real value for customers, channel partners, and marketers. First, effective advertising is geared toward helping customers buy as well as helping marketers sell. This approach, which fits well with the concept of a customer orientation, focuses on long-term exchange relationships rather than isolated marketing transactions. The aim is not to make one sale but to sustain an ongoing dialogue that enhances product value for customers and reinforces commitment and loyalty to the marketer's products.

In the past, many marketers looked inward when making decisions about what, when, and how they wanted to advertise. A relationship-building approach makes marketers look outward. They then use customer and market research to uncover customer needs, determine what media their customers prefer, when ad messages might be most relevant to customers, when customers would be most receptive to advertising, and how customers prefer to respond to ad messages.[10] With this background, they can create ads that give customers information to assist in making decisions about buying and using products. Ads also offer a variety of ways to communicate—from toll-free telephone numbers to World Wide Web or other Internet addresses—to let customers request product specifications and prices or place an order.

advocacy advertising

communicates a marketer's position on a certain issue

public service advertising (PSA)

ads by government or nonprofit groups that address social issues such as smoking and drunk driving

Despite these benefits, advertising is by no means the only or the best way for customers to obtain information about products. As technology speeds the growth of new media, expanded online services, and other sources of information and entertainment, customers are gaining more options to support decisions about buying and using products. They will be able to bypass advertising if it doesn't provide what they need, when they need it, in a form they can use.[11]

Finally, advertising can add value by serving as an efficient and effective method for maintaining communication among customers, channel partners, and marketers. Few marketers have the resources to communicate one-on-one with every customer and prospect in the value chain. So advertising is usually a more productive way of keeping up a dialogue, and its impact can be enhanced by customization and targeting.

Even when advertising is entertaining and informative, it doesn't add value unless it's also effective in building profitable customer exchange relationships. This is an important point, because studies show that popular or memorable ads don't automatically lead to higher sales or profits. For example, in a year when PepsiCo's Shaquille O'Neal television commercial was one of the most popular ads in America, the company's soft drink sales were down 1.6 percent. The ad may have brought in sales that otherwise would not have been made, but other factors—including competition—affected Pepsi's sales results.[12] As you'll see later in the chapter, marketing research can help determine whether ads have been effective and whether other factors have contributed to changes in sales.

Ads don't have to be wildly popular to build sales and profits. Consider the effectiveness of the ads beef producers placed when they wanted to slow a decline in sales. These advertisements clearly created value: for each dollar of advertising, the beef marketers gained $5 in sales.[13] Whether results are measured in dollars and cents, votes cast, or lives saved, ad effectiveness has to be the marketer's bottom line.

Advertising in International Markets

When you use advertising to establish or expand customer relationships in other countries, you'll face a variety of challenges. You'll have to comply with the legal and regulatory requirements imposed by the host government. China and many other nations ban television and radio advertising for certain products, such as cigarettes, and regulate the way other products, including drugs, are advertised. As in the United States, consumer protection rules often restrict the use in advertising of terms such as *free* and *low calorie*. China, Germany, and other countries forbid some forms of comparative advertising.[14]

At times, the host government will want to see all advertising before it runs. This is true in Iran, where strict government controls apply. Under the rules, the appliance marketer Damavand was not allowed to compare the effectiveness of its refrigerators to the cold conditions created by nature.[15]

Although "surfing the Net" is becoming more and more popular with consumers, they are still uncertain about which company offers the best access to the Internet. CompuServe has been providing Internet access for years. However, other companies are challenging CompuServe with attractive value packages; note the number of free items new subscribers are offered in ads. The small print shows that this is an ad for CompuServe in the United Kingdom. What problems do you think CompuServe will face when marketing in countries where English is not the primary language?

Both language and cultural differences affect the way local audiences respond to ad messages. Merely translating an ad word for word isn't enough. Dig deeper to understand the nuances of meaning that a word takes on in another culture. For example, Gillette changed the name and advertising of its Trac II razor after research showed that in some European countries "trac" is associated with fragility. Also be aware of the cultural implications of the colors and symbols in your advertising. When Amoco prepared an institutional ad campaign to raise brand awareness in China, the company emphasized colors with positive connotations. It used red to symbolize life, gold to indicate brilliance, and purple to stand for quality.[16]

Finally, use of media will vary from country to country. Hong Kong, for example, has more than 600 magazines and 40 newspapers to choose from, which complicates media selection but gives you many options. On the other hand, in countries such as Pakistan, where the literacy rate is low, nonprint media may be more appropriate. By carefully researching media availability, usage, and customs in the host country, you can determine which media are most likely to influence your target audience.[17]

Advertising and IMC Strategy

As marketers jockey for customer attention and competitive advantage in the ever-changing global marketplace, advertising plays a key role in shaping customer opinions and behavior. It's vital in the introduction stage of the product life cycle ←┘ **(p. 302)**, when pioneering ads build awareness of a new product and explain its benefits. In the growth stage, competitive ads help combat pressure from rival products. In the maturity stage, reminder ads keep the brand name on the minds of loyal customers. Less advertising is used in the decline stage, where the function of ads may be to help clear out merchandise or reposition the product for a new market.

However, advertising alone often can't do the job. As you saw in Chapter 17, marketers now spend more on sales promotion than on advertising. Public relations and other IMC tools also play an important role in communicating with the target audience. By coordinating advertising with other communication techniques, you can tailor your IMC strategy to the needs and interests of the people in your target market. In addition, the synergy created by a well-coordinated IMC campaign can build brand equity ←┘ **(p. 266)** and reinforce your message, thus enhancing your ability to start or maintain relationships with customers and other stakeholders.[18]

A case in point is the IMC strategy used by Port Aventura, a theme park in Spain, to kick off its first year in business. The multinational strategy included advertising, public relations, and sales promotion activities. Every message was designed to communicate the park's positioning as an exotic adventure destination. Billboards, television and radio commercials, newspaper and magazine ads, plus ads in movie theaters, brought the message to consumers in Spain, while special events spread the word to other European markets.

Port Aventura also advertised in publications targeted toward tour operators and travel agents who influence consumer decisions about vacation destinations. Then the park devised special ticket promotions to be included in hotel and tour packages. Thanks to this carefully orchestrated IMC strategy, Port Aventura drew 2.7 million visitors, 8 percent more than expected, in its inaugural season. Demand was so high that the park planned to open two months earlier in its second year.[19]

advertising agency

an organization that specializes in helping marketers plan and implement advertising campaigns

The Role of Advertising Agencies

An **advertising agency** is an organization that specializes in helping marketers plan and implement advertising campaigns. Some marketers, especially small businesses, create their own advertising concepts and materials. In these businesses, the advertising specialists work in an *in-house agency*, an agency that develops advertising only for its parent company.

Larger marketers often hire independent agencies as marketing partners to handle some or all of the tasks associated with advertising planning and implementation. A *full-service agency* such as Young & Rubicam is able to do everything from researching target audiences and preparing ads to buying media time or space and tracking audience response. The trend in full-service agencies is to provide help in creating a wide range of IMC materials using all available promotional tools, including direct marketing. When Blockbuster Video wanted an agency that could manage every detail of the retail chain's national advertising, it hired Y&R. "It's full service that won the account," said Blockbuster's vice president of marketing, alluding to Young & Rubicam's capabilities.[20]

Some marketers hire *limited-service agencies* to work on a particular aspect of their advertising, such as creating the ads, selecting the media in which ads will run, or preparing ads for a specific medium. Xerox, for example, hired Lowe Direct to create direct mail packages targeting businesses that buy duplicating equipment. The agency's "Docu-Drama" package, sent to top executives at the 1,000 largest U.S. companies, led to $7 million in equipment sales.[21]

Giants such as Xerox, AT&T, and McDonald's often have a number of full- and limited-service agencies handling such diverse tasks as researching and developing ad messages for specific customer segments, creating direct mail materials to attract new customers, and scripting and filming television commercials. Coca-Cola, for example, works with 30 ad agencies around the world to adapt global Coke advertising themes to local tastes and interests.[22]

Before you go on . . .

A. How does product advertising differ from institutional advertising?

B. What are the arguments for and against advertising?

C. What do marketers have to consider when developing advertising for target audiences in other cultures?

D. How do marketers work with advertising agencies?

Developing Advertising That Works

Whether you're a large marketer aiming at a gigantic market with a huge advertising budget or a small business trying to reach local customers on a shoestring, you'll use the same process to plan, implement, and evaluate your advertising communications. This process is shown in Figure 18.1.

FIGURE **18.1** Planning, Implementing, and Evaluating Advertising

The process of planning, implementing, and evaluating advertising is circular, because evaluation helps the marketer improve planning.

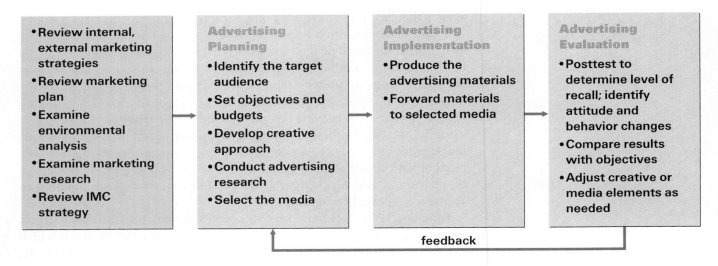

- Review internal, external marketing strategies
- Review marketing plan
- Examine environmental analysis
- Examine marketing research
- Review IMC strategy

Advertising Planning
- Identify the target audience
- Set objectives and budgets
- Develop creative approach
- Conduct advertising research
- Select the media

Advertising Implementation
- Produce the advertising materials
- Forward materials to selected media

Advertising Evaluation
- Posttest to determine level of recall; identify attitude and behavior changes
- Compare results with objectives
- Adjust creative or media elements as needed

feedback

More and more marketers are targeting specific cultures within the United States, including the large and rapidly growing Hispanic and Latino market. This Wrangler ad, produced by Ornelas & Associates of Dallas, is targeted to that market. It celebrates Wranger's long-standing relationship with Hispanic and Latino customers. Why do advertisers need to target their advertising as specifically as possible?

Before you begin, review your internal and external marketing strategies, your overall marketing plan, and your IMC strategy. Also examine the market and customer information collected through environmental analysis and marketing research. This background sets the stage for the advertising process, starting with the identification of the target audience.

Identifying the Target Audience

At the most basic level, your choice is to target either ultimate consumers or organizations. *Consumer advertising*, as the name suggests, is geared toward individuals who purchase products for personal or household use. In contrast, *organizational advertising* is geared toward people in businesses, government agencies, or nonprofit organizations who buy or influence the purchase of products for organizational use.

Beyond this distinction, you'll want to be as specific as possible in defining whom you want to reach, so you can plan for their unique needs. When Pioneer Electronics readied an advertising campaign for its car stereos, for example, the company targeted men aged 18 to 24. When Casio planned ads for an electronic product called My Magic Diary, the company targeted girls aged 6 to 11.[23] Selecting an exact target allowed these marketers to research audience needs and develop relevant advertising messages for the appropriate media.

Setting Advertising Objectives and Budgets

Once you've identified the target audience, you can decide exactly what you want your advertising to accomplish. Your objectives should be specific and measurable and should cover a particular period, so you can determine whether your advertising worked. As discussed in Chapter 17, you may want to set communication objectives or sales objectives or both ◄──┘ **(p. 521)**. The choice depends, in part, on your ability to measure specific results.

For example, when the New York State Department of Economic Development advertised to attract vacationers, it didn't set sales goals because of the difficulty of accurately measuring results. Instead, the agency set a communication objective of receiving 50,000 requests for information during the campaign.[24]

Communication objectives represent milestones on the road to building and maintaining exchange relationships. However, their usefulness is limited because they don't reflect how or indeed whether customers actually buy. "Awareness of a brand, if it doesn't elicit sales, is not a particularly useful advertising benefit," states market researcher Mark Gleason. "The challenge is to get advertising that elicits purchase behavior."[25]

That's where sales objectives come in. Sales objectives lead to ads that attain a specific dollar or unit sales level, a specific increase in sales over an earlier period, or a specific level or increase in market share. For example, Compaq set two sales objectives for a recent Presario advertising campaign: (1) to increase market share of Presario PCs bought for home use by 47 percent and (2) to increase sales of Presario computers by 97 percent.[26]

Of course, you can't always attribute sales results to advertising alone. If you're a direct marketer and have no other marketing channels, you can easily track sales that come as a result of toll-free telephone numbers, coupons, and other response mechanisms you place in your ads. But sales are influenced by so many factors—including competition, economic pressures, and all the elements in marketing strategy—that it's seldom possible to isolate the effects of advertising. Therefore, sales objectives are generally linked to overall marketing plans rather than to specific ads or ad campaigns.

Next, set a budget for your advertising program. This subset of your IMC budget indicates how much you'll allocate to creating ads and buying media time and space. Major marketers often establish multimillion dollar advertising budgets to build brand equity and support relationship-building strategies. Table 18.2 shows the advertising budgets of America's largest advertisers.

T A B L E **18.2** **What the Largest U.S. Advertisers Spend**

Rank	Marketer	1994 Advertising Expenditures (billions of dollars)
1	Procter & Gamble	$2.7
2	Philip Morris	2.4
3	General Motors	1.9
4	Ford Motor	1.2
5	Sears, Roebuck	1.1
6	AT&T	1.1
7	PepsiCo	1.1
8	Chrysler	1.0
9	Walt Disney	0.9
10	Johnson & Johnson	0.9

Not every marketer can afford a lavish advertising campaign. Still, small businesses have advertising options even when money is tight, as the following section shows.

SMALL BUSINESS WATCH

Stretching limited advertising dollars

Even if you don't have the multibillion-dollar advertising budget of Procter & Gamble, you can still build or maintain customer relationships through advertising. Here are a few ideas from small business owners who have found ways to get more bang for their advertising dollars.

Relax. With Amtrak's Air Rail Travel Plan you can take twice the vacation without doubling your time. Travel Amtrak to your destination and fly home on United Airlines. All for one surprisingly low price.* Air Rail gives you a unique opportunity to really see America up close. Because Amtrak lets you make up to three stopovers along the way. And at most destinations, special hotel and tour packages are available. You'll also enjoy United Airlines' Mileage Plus credit, and for a limited time Amtrak is offering an additional 500 miles† credit. For information and reservations call your travel agent or Amtrak Air Rail at 1-800-440-8202.

*Subject to availability, advance purchase required, other restrictions may apply. †Applies to Amtrak portion, regardless of distance traveled. Offer good for travel booked by March 31, 1996 and completed by June 30, 1996. Subject to Mileage Plus rules.

Customers may be surprised to see an ad for two competing modes of transportation making a joint appeal. Together, the two organizations can offer a value package that is unique. You can see how hotels, restaurants, auto rental firms, and theaters might benefit by joining these two companies in providing a complete vacation value package. Are there disadvantages to this form of cooperation?

- *Consider automated telemarketing.* Katherine Moser, who owns a chimney sweep service in Oregon, spent thousands of dollars on flyers, newspaper ads, and Yellow Pages advertising, but "we were still practically starving to death." Then she found success using telemarketing equipment that automatically dials homeowners and plays a taped message offering Moser's services. Starting new relationships this way cost just $1.43 per customer. Many consumers dislike this type of marketing, however.

- *Take advantage of co-op advertising.* Many manufacturers offer *cooperative advertising programs* (co-op for short), in which they'll pay part of the cost when their products are featured in retailers' ads. David Lang takes advantage of this to feature brand-name products in ads for his lawn equipment store in St. Louis. In the past, he spent only $20,000 a year, but "now we can spend $40,000, because we're getting $20,000 back," says Lang.

- *Mail postcards.* For just pennies, Bill Boyd and Bill Lawder maintain relationships with customers of their Java Coffee & Tea Company in Houston. They send attractive, handwritten postcards to customers who haven't bought recently, saying, "We haven't seen you in a while. Let us know if you need anything." Customers respond, saying they appreciate the gentle reminder.[27]

- *Hand-deliver flyers.* You can hire local teenagers to deliver inexpensive photocopied flyers to consumers or businesses in your area. For a small total cost to cover the designing, printing, and distribution of the flyers, you may achieve a big impact.

Can you think of other ways to stretch a limited ad budget? How might cash-strapped marketers advertise on the World Wide Web?

Developing the Creative Approach

When you develop an ad, you start by selecting a basic creative appeal. This appeal drives the two components of every ad: the words that make up the message, known as the *copy*, and the visual elements, known as the *art*.

Effective Advertising Appeals

The way you appeal to people in your target audience shapes their perceptions of your brand and product. Among the advertising appeals you can use are logic, emotion, celebrity, sexual attractiveness, fear, and humor.

Logical appeals depend on rational reasons and hard evidence to prove that a product is a logical choice. Typically, ads based on logical appeals are loaded with product facts and figures for the target audience to analyze and evaluate. Ads for cameras, computers, and banking services frequently feature logical appeals, stressing special value or unique benefits. In contrast, *emotional appeals* focus on feelings about a product or its benefits. Ads that rely on emotional appeals aim for the heart by evoking emotions such as love. Love is the emotional appeal used by many jewelry and perfume marketers.

Celebrity appeal, a popular creative approach, puts well-known personalities in ads to attract attention and boost credibility. Often people in the target market want to emulate celebrities, which adds to the strength of this appeal. Celebrity appeal is used when basketball star Michael Jordan leaps into Nike ads and television star Candice Bergen speaks out from Sprint ads. However, choose your famous spokesperson with care: the appeal can backfire if the celebrity in your ad becomes embroiled in a scandal, as happened with pop star Michael Jackson and skater Tonya Harding.[28]

Ads based on *sex appeal* encourage audience members to believe that the advertised product will increase their attractiveness. This approach is used by cosmetics and apparel marketers, among others. However, some ads relying on sex appeal have raised ethical questions. For example, one recent campaign for Calvin Klein jeans featured young models in provocative positions. As the ads began appearing on billboards and television screens, Calvin Klein was accused of crossing the line into child pornography. The company quickly apologized and withdrew the ads.[29]

Marketers of burglar alarms and weight-loss products often use a *fear appeal*, which plays on audience worries to drive home a point about the advertised product. Ads that use the fear appeal imply that the audience can avoid some problem (such as becoming a crime victim) by buying the marketer's product. Ads for the Club, an antitheft device for cars, use a fear appeal.

Another common creative approach is the *humor appeal*, which aims for the audience's funny bone to make a point about the product. Humor appeals run the gamut from slapstick to bizarre, eliciting smiles, chuckles, or belly laughs. For example, the advertising agency for Bob's Stores used a humor appeal to create a funny television commercial for the northeastern casual clothing chain. The commercial featured a dog enthusiastically chewing up an old sneaker, a cute and funny image that set viewers up for the real message: buy sneakers at Bob's.[30]

Humor is a commonly used tactic in advertising. This is true for all kinds of organizations, as this ad for Chicago's Shedd Aquarium shows. Were you attracted to the ad? Do humorous pictures in such ads increase your motivation to buy or visit? Do you think consumers prefer ads that provide more information? Why?

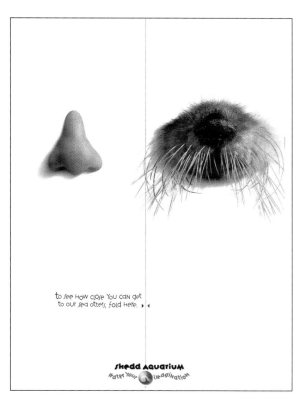

to see how close you can get to our sea otters, fold here.

Shedd Aquarium
Water your imagination

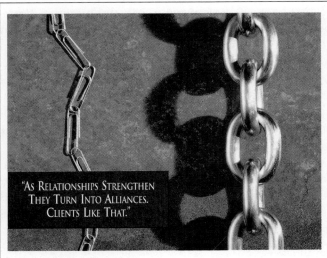

"As Relationships Strengthen They Turn Into Alliances. Clients Like That."

Re-engineering. Restive boards. Ravenous competitors. Revenue-seeking governments. CEOs and CFOs need strong financial allies now more than ever.

Now more than ever, Chemical is committed to building strong and mutually valuable relationships with our clients—operating as banker, advisor, and trading and investment partner.

We forge relationships that last by serving clients better than our competitors, by providing more of the products and services our clients need than our competitors, by solving more problems and finding more opportunities.

Our broad-based approach produces results. For example, we rank first in the world in loan syndications, thanks to

structuring expertise and our strong emphasis on distribution. As a natural extension of these strengths, Chemical Securities Inc. can now underwrite and deal in all types of debt securities in the United States, including corporate bonds.

Chemical also has leadership positions in trading, treasury, corporate finance, operating services and capital markets activities worldwide. And, at a time when others have retreated from international arenas, we have a global network across 35 countries.

Our formidable market presence, growing capital strength and higher credit ratings have demonstrably increased our usefulness to our clients. Put Chemical to the test. We're a financial ally with a multitude of strengths.

 **CHEMICAL**

EXPECT MORE FROM US.℠

© 1993 Chemical Banking Corporation   Chemical Securities Inc.-Member SIPC

Relationship marketing has permeated the marketing process in virtually every industry. This ad for Chemical Bank—which has merged with Chase Manhattan Bank—uses strong visuals and imagery to convey the strength of its relationship building with customers. What IMC techniques might Chase Manhattan Bank use to explain its relationship-building approach to customers who were with Chemical Bank before the merger?

Effective Copy and Art

With the basic appeal in place, you are ready to develop copy and art. The combination of these two components is used to attract audience attention and interest, provide information, and persuade the audience to take a specific action that starts or continues a marketing relationship.

If you're working with an advertising agency, the copywriters and creative directors will prepare the copy and art for your approval. If you're doing your own advertising, you'll write copy for the magazine, newspaper, Web site, or billboard ad or a script for a television or radio commercial. Copy in a print ad includes the *headline*, the line of words in large type that dominates the ad, the *body copy*, the words in the main part of the ad, and the *signature*, which includes the marketer's name and, on occasion, its logo. In addition, the ad may have a *slogan* or a *tag line*, a catchy phrase that relates to the marketing message, such as insurance marketer Allstate's slogan, "You're in good hands" and FedEx's "Our most important package is yours."

The visual aspects of a print or electronic ad are as important as the copy. Art is what gets the ad noticed, preparing viewers to attend to the copy that communicates your marketing message. Color, shape, texture, space, and size are some of the elements of design that contribute to an eye-catching ad. In the electronic media, motion, visual effects, and sound are additional creative elements that can bring an ad message to life. Ads available on CD-ROM, for example, have the benefits of sight, sound, and motion—and they can be quite long, allowing the customer to fully understand the product.

Keep cultural differences and taboos in mind when you're creating ads for other countries and cultures, including groups in the United States. Often it helps to have a member of that group or a specialized agency help prepare the ad to make sure that it is appropriate and effective. Also, certain words or images may be offensive in other cultures, so check local customs before you finalize your ads. As the following section shows, one question multinational marketers face is whether to use the same creative approach in every market.

Announcing the opening of our newest location.

A|X

ARMANI EXCHANGE

http://www.ArmaniExchange.com

More and more companies are jumping on the bandwagon of marketing on the Internet, including companies based in other countries. Companies from other countries are eager to reach the affluent U.S. market. This ad announces the opening of the Armani Exchange World Wide Web "location." Can you see how this same ad and theme could be used in any country? How might the availability of foreign products on the Internet influence domestic competitors?

advertising research

provides information about the target audience that helps marketers make better decisions about advertising messages and media

GLOBAL ISSUES

One ad fits all?

Globalization or localization? That's the debate, as marketers seek out relationships with customers in other markets and cultures. *Globalization* means applying one marketing approach in multiple countries and cultures by appealing to the similarities, rather than the differences, among customers. In contrast, *localization* means adapting to the unique characteristics of each local market. Which works best for advertising?

Those who prefer globalization say they're riding a trend toward homogenization of tastes and preferences that transcends cultural boundaries. Building on these similarities, marketers can save money and present a unified global message by using much the same advertising (translated and otherwise modified) in every market. Fisher-Price, the U.S. toy marketer, does this. "Our Fisher-Price global advertising is effective because no matter what country, we're talking to parents as parents," says an executive at the company's ad agency.

Supporters of localization argue that advertising must be responsive to local needs and cultural nuances. Sensitivity in this regard can help marketers avoid cultural blunders and, at the same time, to compete more effectively with local rivals. Audi, for example, develops different ads for each market, so its U.K. advertising is nothing like its U.S. advertising, because the audiences are quite different. Similarly, Levi Strauss advertising in Europe stresses the same all-American lifestyle as its U.S. advertising, but the creative approach and actual messages are distinctly different.[31]

What kind of product ads do you think are best suited to globalization? To localization? Why?

Conducting Advertising Research

Before producing and placing your ads, you'll need to conduct advertising research to investigate your target audience's responses to the message and the media. **Advertising research** provides information about the target audience that helps marketers make better decisions about advertising messages and media. This type of research focuses on *advertising* issues, as opposed to general marketing research, which provides information to support *all* marketing processes, not just advertising.

Message research helps you understand how your target audience perceives what your ads are communicating and how effective the messages are in influencing attitudes and behavior. Acquiring this information before an ad runs is known as *pretesting*. For example, Honda's ad agency conducted advertising research to develop and pretest a new ad campaign to launch a redesigned Accord car. With input from 44 focus groups, the agency pretested advertising messages under consideration. The process helped the agency settle on the slogan "A Car Ahead" to reinforce Honda's competitive superiority.[32]

Media research helps you understand the makeup and preferences of media audiences, so you can pick the right media (radio, TV, newspapers, or other choices) to reach your target audience. Because today's audiences are exposed to more media than in the past, selecting the right medium or media is a complicated process.

Media research helps by showing how many people with the characteristics of your target audience use a particular medium. For example, *Spin*'s research shows that the music magazine has more than 400,000 readers, the average reader is 24 years old, and subscribers have a median income over $43,500.[33] Knowing this, marketers that want relationships with people who fit that profile will consider advertising in *Spin*.

When you conduct advertising research after your advertisements have run, you're using *posttesting*. As you'll see later in this chapter, posttesting is a good way to find out whether your ads are having the desired effect.

Selecting the Media

Using the advertising research you've gathered, you're ready to select the media and vehicles for your advertising message. **Media** (the plural of *medium*) are the communication channels that carry your messages to the target audience. You'll also identify the individual *media vehicles* (publications, programs, and so on) to be used. In this way, you can communicate with the target audience at the appropriate time and place.

Selecting media and vehicles can be tricky because you have to stretch your budget to cover the number of people you want to reach, as well as the number of times you want to reach them. **Reach** is a measure of how many different people in the target audience are exposed to an ad in a specific media vehicle. The higher the reach, the more people are exposed to the message.

Frequency is a measure of how many times audience members are exposed to a media vehicle during the period an ad runs. The higher the frequency, the more times your audience is exposed to the message. Most people don't absorb or remember the information in your message the first time your ad runs. Depending on your objectives and what you can afford, you'll want to build more frequency into your media plans.

Balancing the cost of reach with the cost of frequency is a challenge, even for marketers with big budgets. Media costs are usually expressed in **cost per thousand (CPM)**, the cost of using a media vehicle to reach 1,000 audience members one time. The higher the CPM, the more you'll pay to reach 1,000 people. Mass media such as television and radio have a lower CPM than more targeted media such as direct mail and specialized magazines.

When planning an advertising schedule, think not only about which media you'll use, but also about when and for how long. In a *continuous advertising schedule*, advertising runs without interruption. This mode is appropriate for products that customers buy throughout the year. A *flighting advertising schedule*, which covers on-and-off advertising with gaps between "flights" of advertising, is appropriate when you want to advertise during peak purchasing periods but not during slower periods. A *pulsing schedule*

media

the communication channels that carry advertising messages to the target audience

reach

a measure of how many different people in the target audience are exposed to an ad in a specific media vehicle

frequency

a measure of how many times audience members are exposed to a media vehicle during the period an ad runs

cost per thousand (CPM)

the cost of using a media vehicle to reach 1,000 audience members one time

FIGURE **18.2**

U.S. Expenditures on Advertising Media, 1984–1994
Of the total amount spent on U.S. advertising, the proportion spent on newspaper advertising declined significantly over the decade from 1984 to 1994. Over the same period, the proportion spent on direct mail increased a great deal. Much of this increase is due to technological advances that allow marketers to better target individuals.

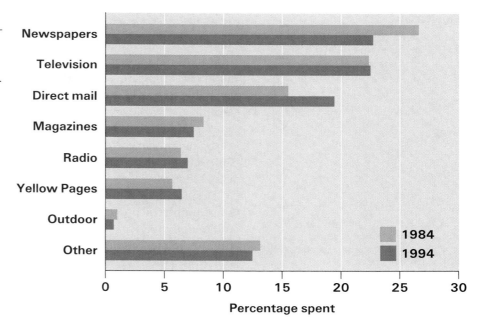

combines continuous advertising with isolated periods of heavier advertising activity. This approach is useful when you're trying to create higher demand, introduce a new product, or respond to competitive pressures.

Of the money spent on media in the United States, about 23 percent goes into newspapers, and a nearly equal amount goes into television advertising. Figure 18.2 compares advertising spending in 1984 and 1994, showing how spending in each medium changed. The third largest media category is direct mail, followed by magazines, radio, Yellow Pages, and outdoor advertising. As you read the following sections, you can refer to Table 18.3 for a summary of each medium's advantages and disadvantages.

TABLE **18.3** Comparing the Major Advertising Media

Medium	Advantages	Disadvantages
Television	Can reach large audiences cost-effectively; many creative possibilities using color, motion, sound, special effects.	Difficult to target narrow audience segments; medium cluttered with commercials; high production costs.
Radio	Low media and production costs; can target geographically; can appeal to imagination.	Lack of visual effects; brevity of message; cannot convey complex messages; product cannot be demonstrated.
Newspapers	Can accept and change ads on short notice; can reach local markets; production costs low; can deliver lengthy, complex message to be saved for future reference.	Color reproduction not as good as magazines; medium cluttered with other ads; less extensive reach.
Magazines	Good color reproduction; can target some specialized audiences; can deliver lengthy, complex message to be saved for future reference.	Difficult to reach broad geographic areas; need long lead time to accept or change ads; medium cluttered with other ads.
Direct mail	Can target precisely and tailor message; can deliver lengthy, complex message to be saved for future reference; can deliver samples; many creative possibilities.	Relatively costly; at times, mailbox clutter is a problem; lower reach potential; perception of junk mail.
Outdoor	Low cost for high reach and frequency; color and creative possibilities; can target geographic areas.	Difficult to target specific segments; can carry only short, simple messages.
Interactive	Audience can get involved in the message; many creative possibilities; can deliver lengthy, complex messages cost-effectively.	Limited media research available; limited, growing audience.

infomercials

longer commercials that market goods and services in a program format

Television

Television is an extremely popular advertising medium among national and international marketers, who rely on its sound, color, and motion to attract audience attention and convey messages in a creative way. Television is available to nearly every U.S. household and to a growing number of homes around the world, which means access to mass audiences. However, television is less efficient for reaching small segments. As Chris Perry, national advertising manager of American Isuzu Motors, says, "If I want to reach 750,000 Isuzu owners and my TV ad reached 10 million viewers, that isn't very efficient."[34]

Despite an overall mass reach, television finds its audience fragmenting as the number of broadcast and cable networks rises. The good news is that cable networks are more efficient than broadcast networks at reaching highly targeted audiences. The bad news is that you may have to advertise on more programs to reach larger audiences, because broadcast network viewership is down and cable viewership per program is still relatively small.[35] In addition, many people switch channels during commercials, or don't watch them at all.

Because television time is so expensive, most marketers use brief commercials (15, 30, or 60 seconds). A 30-second network commercial during the Super Bowl costs more than $1 million, which is a huge amount even for an ad that reaches more than 120 million viewers. Producing commercials can be costly as well.[36]

At the same time, more marketers are running **infomercials**, longer commercials that market goods and services in a program format. Infomercials may run as long as 90 minutes, and they often air late at night or at times when TV costs are lower. This longer commercial format, used by Fidelity Investments, Sega, and other major marketers, is useful for explaining product benefits or demonstrating unique features. Infomercials work: in the United States alone, they bring in $1 billion in product sales each year. However, infomercials that seem to be talk shows, news reports, or entertainment programs raise serious ethical issues. In response, infomercial makers have developed voluntary guidelines for content and for identification of commercials.[37]

Still in its infancy is *interactive television*, in which viewers use a remote control or joystick to interact with televised games, programs, and advertise-

Cher is one of many celebrities who demonstrate their products during infomercials. This is a good way to show customers how a product looks and operates. An increasing number of marketers are going beyond television to offer product demonstrations on CD-ROMs, video, and on World Wide Web sites. What types of goods or services do you think would benefit from being demonstrated during an infomercial?

ments. For example, Ford Canada has run ads on the Videoway interactive television system, which has 300,000 subscribers in Quebec and two other Canadian cities. Subscribers were invited to choose which of four commercials they wanted to view, and they competed for prizes based on their recall of points made in the ads.[38]

Radio

Although radio lacks the visual excitement of television, it can spark the imagination and conjure up memorable images. What's more, radio is much less expensive and more precisely targeted than television. As a result, you can fine-tune your targeting and increase frequency without busting the budget. Since each of the 10,000 U.S. radio stations targets a specific customer segment within a market, you will be able to get a good idea of who will hear your ads. You can use network and syndicated radio to reach larger audiences, relying on local radio stations to reach narrowly defined geographic areas.[39]

The ability to target audiences more precisely and more frequently—at a much lower cost than television—has drawn Sears, AT&T, Marriott, and many other marketers to radio advertising. Sears, for example, uses Spanish-language radio to communicate with its Hispanic/Latino customers. Business-to-business marketers such as Marriott also find radio an effective medium. Targeting business travelers, radio commercials for the Courtyard chain have brought the brand the highest recognition of any Marriott hotel brand.[40]

Newspapers

Newspapers, the number-one U.S. advertising medium, are particularly strong in reaching target audiences in specific markets. Small wonder, then, that retailers are by far the heaviest users of newspaper advertising, followed by car marketers seeking to drive customers into local showrooms. But businesses also find newspapers an effective advertising medium. Blue Cross/Blue Shield of Virginia, for example, advertises in newspapers to explain its alliances with health care providers and insurers and to solicit new health care contracts.[41]

Newspapers offer flexibility. You can place or change an ad on short notice, you can choose a particular section of the paper to reach a particular audience, and you can print in color or black and white. If you prefer, you can get better color reproduction by preprinting a flyer and having it inserted into the newspaper. True Value Hardware, J.C. Penney, and many other retailers do this. Newspapers can deliver samples too, as Chesebrough-Pond knows. The company recently bagged a sample of a new Mentadent toothpaste and a money-saving coupon with the daily newspaper in several U.S. cities.[42]

Magazines

Magazines are a good choice for communicating with narrowly defined target audiences. When beverage marketer Gatorade wanted to reach a target audience of sports-oriented young men, it advertised in *Sports Illustrated*. When computer marketer IBM wanted to reach a top-level audience of busi-

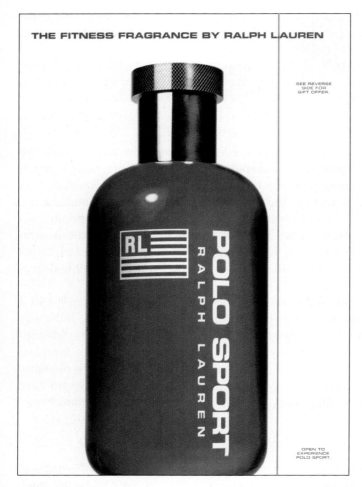

THE FITNESS FRAGRANCE BY RALPH LAUREN

SEE REVERSE
SIDE FOR
GIFT OFFER.

RL

POLO SPORT

RALPH LAUREN

OPEN TO
EXPERIENCE
POLO SPORT.

Magazine ads for fragrances often include a sample to try. Since customers find it difficult to imagine what a product like Polo Sport smells like, Ralph Lauren provides a sample in its magazine ads. What are some other advantages and some disadvantages of this practice?

ness executives, it advertised in *Forbes*.[43] Whether you use geographic segmentation ◄┘ **(p. 226)**, demographic segmentation, or another segmentation method, there's a magazine to fit your customers' profile. In addition, many magazines can print ads in just the issues that reach specific cities or readers with certain characteristics (income, occupation, etc.), which is more efficient than reaching out to all readers.

Thousands of consumer, business, and farm magazines are published in the United States every year. Magazines such as *Mustang Monthly* (a consumer magazine for Mustang car enthusiasts) and *Billboard* (a business magazine for music retailers) are geared toward small, highly specialized audiences, while general-interest magazines such as *Reader's Digest* reach larger and broader populations. Magazines offer better color reproduction than newspapers as well as the flexibility to include minisamples (such as perfume scents). However, some consumers complain about the strong odor given off by such ads.

Direct Mail

Talk about narrow targeting: you can select exactly the individuals or businesses you want to reach when you use direct mail letters, packages, or catalogs. In contrast to the mass media of television and magazines, which blanket large groups with a single message, direct mail offers pinpoint precision for one-to-one marketing communication. Although not all direct marketers do this, you can tailor your message, sending information geared specifically to the needs and behavior of each individual.[44]

What's more, direct mail has staying power: television and radio ads go by in a flash, but direct mail pieces can be any length, to be read and reread by the audience. This means that people have a chance to absorb and analyze a great deal of information about your product and its benefits. To reach your target market, you can buy a mailing list from another marketer or use your own marketing database.

Direct mail can be effective in business-to-business marketing too. Avis, for example, bought a list of business executives for a campaign to encourage corporate car rentals. Tailoring its message to the needs of each company, Avis mailed four packages in succession. Then its employees followed up with phone contact. The campaign generated enough first-year sales to cover its cost a dozen times over.[45]

Outdoor and Transit Media

Advertising isn't confined to media that reach people at home. People see *outdoor* media such as billboards when they're traveling to and from work, school, or other destinations, such as vacation areas. Billboards are large, elevated signs that dot many highways and busy urban streets. Although you can't fit much copy on a billboard, people passing by won't have much time to read it, either. That's why billboards need strong visual elements for greatest impact. Billboards are banned on some roads, so check before planning to use this medium.

Transit ads are a good way to reach commuters and travelers by advertising on or in buses, trains, and transportation terminals. For example, Korean Airlines and the International Bank of Asia are just two marketers that have splashed colorful advertising over the sides of the double-decker streetcars that wind through the streets of Hong Kong. Such ads act like moving billboards, capturing the attention of passengers, pedestrians, and drivers of other vehicles along the route.[46]

Interactive Media

To increase the involvement of your target audience in your message, you can put it into *interactive media* such as the Internet and CD-ROMs, which invite audience participation in programming and advertising. These media are increasingly popular. Millions of people subscribe to commercial online services such as America Online, and millions surf the Internet. Marketers are pouring $6 billion annually into interactive media purchases, a figure expected to reach $14 billion by 1999, when 22 percent of all U.S. households are expected to be hooked to an online service.[47]

Issues for critical thinking

Are interactive media appropriate for every audience or product? What should marketers consider before using interactive media?

Interactive media offer color, motion, sound, and special effects. Some World Wide Web sites are elaborately produced to attract and maintain audience interest. These run the gamut from the promotion by Paramount Pictures of its *Star Trek* movies to the efforts of the U.S. Postal Service to promote mailing services.[48] In addition, interactive media help you reach specialized audiences and allow audience members to work through the message at their own pace. Even if you simply read and respond to online messages, you can gain customers. Russian Information Services, a small business, sold $2,000 worth of travel books over six months by following up messages on CompuServe's Travel and International Trade forums.[49]

Although marketers are excited about interactive media's potential for engaging customers in an ongoing dialogue, troubling ethical issues have arisen, as the next section shows.

ETHICS & SOCIAL RESPONSIBILITY

Ethical issues in cyberspace

As advertising picks up speed on the information superhighway, ethical issues are coming to the forefront. One is the question of personal privacy. How much should marketers be able to find out about visitors to online ads? CompuServe, for example, can track subscribers' visits to online areas and record how long they spend at each site. Internet surfers are sometimes asked to register at Web sites so that sponsors can learn more about them. Matching such data with demographics gives marketers a powerful tool for targeting specific customer segments—down to the individual level. How can the individual's right to privacy be protected in interactive media?

A second ethical issue is access to tobacco and liquor ads on the Internet. Cigarette ads have been illegal on U.S. television and radio since 1970, and liquor marketers (with the exception of beer) have stayed away from television and radio. However, Internet ads are a legal and ethical gray area. The Federal Communications Commission, which regulates radio and television advertising, has no control over Internet advertising.

For now, some marketers are moving ahead. DeKuyper offers a "virtual bar" that can be entered via *Vibe* magazine on the World Wide Web. Although prospective visitors are warned "You must be 21 or older," DeKuyper makes no attempt to block underage visitors.[50]

Do you think liquor and tobacco marketers should be allowed to advertise on the Internet even when minors can visit?

Other Media

Marketers are constantly searching for media that reach people when and where the ad message can make an impact. One of the hottest areas for advertising away from home is at the *point of purchase*, meaning the store or restaurant or other location at which the customer actually buys the product. In the words of Joseph T. Ricci, promotion service manager of Duracell USA, "the retail space is the final frontier of your ad campaign. It is the last opportunity you have, especially with a high-impulse item like batteries."[51] You'll learn more about point of purchase in Chapter 19.

Interest is also growing in *place-based media*, ad locations away from the home that are ideal for reaching certain narrowly defined target audiences. Television commercials beamed to television receivers in health clubs, for example, reach people interested in physical fitness. The idea is to communicate with the target audience when they're likely to be interested in an ad for a product related to their surroundings.[52]

Marketers are constantly looking for ways to reach consumers when they are most receptive to their messages. One good place to reach consumers is when they are waiting for service at locations such as the offices of dentists and physicians and airports. The CNN Airport Network reaches travelers waiting in airports for their flights. What kinds of products and services do you think would benefit most from using this medium?

Making Media Decisions

Deciding which media to use is both an art and a science, which is why many marketers hire experts to tackle the task. Both marketers and advertising agencies generally use specialized software to compare media and to test alternative media schedules. Some programs also take into consideration the effect of competitive advertising and other environmental factors that can influence media decisions.

The wide number of media choices helps marketers reach narrowly defined target audiences. At the same time, reaching larger audiences is difficult because consumers are splitting their attention among so many media and vehicles. Balanced against the need for reach is the need for a frequency that allows your target audience to absorb your message. How can you get both reach and frequency and stay within your budget? Here are several factors to consider when making media decisions.

- _Consider the target audience's use of media._ Through media research, you can determine which media are used and when. In this way, you can eliminate media that the audience doesn't use and identify those in which the audience are interested.

- _Be sure your creative approach and your media are compatible._ An ad filled with detailed or technical copy about product performance will work better in newspapers or magazines. Similarly, an ad that relies on sight and sound to make a point about product performance calls for television or interactive media. Also think about the content and complexity of your message. If one brief exposure isn't enough to communicate your message, think about media such as newspapers, magazines, or direct mail, which allow the audience to reread and save your ad.

- _Analyze the way competitors use media._ If you're on a tight budget, and competitors' spending threatens to drown out your message, you may want to choose a medium where you'll face less competition. You can also differentiate your product by using a medium that rivals don't use.

- _Compare the reach, frequency, and CPM of the media you're considering._ Media costs can take a big bite out of any advertising budget, so be sure you're getting the impact you need at a price you can afford. Instead of spreading your budget among several media, you may want to consolidate to get more frequency in a single medium. Conversely, if one medium isn't giving you the reach you need, you may want to advertise in two or more.

Media selection is important in business-to-business marketing also. Consider how New Jersey–based Astra Jet selected media to reach executives that buy corporate aircraft. The company placed print ads in _Fortune, Business & Commercial Aviation,_ and other magazines that reach its target audience. It also aired television commercials on CNN in Europe during the Paris Air Show, a major industry event that draws executives from around the world. This limited television schedule helped Astra communicate its message when executives were getting ready to buy. Then, using direct mail, Astra was able to provide the target audience with more detailed information than could have been packed into other types of advertising. This integrated campaign helped Astra sell 30 planes (at $14 million each).[53]

Producing Advertising

Once you've chosen the media and vehicles you'll use, you can move ahead to produce the advertising, based on your creative approach and copy. For print advertising, this means combining the copy and the art into a finished page and then into photographic film for distribution to the magazine, newspaper, or direct mail printer that will reproduce the final ad. Many marketers and ad agencies use computerized desktop publishing packages that eliminate the need for typesetting and other interim steps.

For television advertising, production starts with a _storyboard_, a layout of every major scene in the commercial, and a script of the spoken words. Once the script has been approved, the material is filmed and edited; then you can send duplicate videotapes of the finished commercial to the networks and stations that will air the ads. With radio, you either supply each station with a script for local announcers to read or tape the commercial (with voices, music, and any sound effects) and send finished cassettes to stations on the schedule.

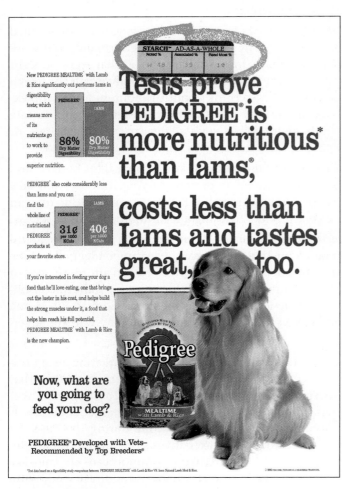

This ad for Pedigree dog food has been annotated with Starch scores. As indicated, only 10 percent of the people exposed to the ad read most of it, but 48 percent noted the ad and 39 percent read part of it. Starch scores emphasize the importance of targeting ads to the right audience using the right media. What could Pedigree do to encourage more people to read more of the ad?

Evaluating Advertising

Now you come to the moment of truth: Is your advertising working? If your advertising is having the effect you want—by bringing you closer to your goals—then it's working. On the other hand, if it's not getting you where you want to go, you'll have to change the creative approach, the copy, the art, the media, the media vehicle, or the media schedule and evaluate the result of the new mix.

As mentioned earlier, you can use posttesting to evaluate an advertisement after it has been run. Many marketers start by determining whether their ads are recalled by people in the target audience. With *readership research*, the researcher presents a printed ad and then asks people whether they noticed it and, if so, what they remember about it. See the photo for a sample of an ad that has been posttested by the Starch Readership Report. In contrast, *unaided recall tests* (which ask questions such as "Did you see any automotive commercials on television yesterday?") reveal what people remember without prompting. Also, marketers can compare the impact of two ads using a *split-run experiment* in which half the media audience sees one ad while the other half sees the second.

However, studies haven't found a strong relationship between recall and purchasing behavior.[54] So some marketers go beyond recall to measure attitude and behavior changes. *Attitude tests* indicate how feelings toward a brand or product have changed over the course of an advertising campaign. *Inquiry tests* measure how many people requested information or product samples offered through an ad. For example, New York State counted 117,000 inquiries to its tourism ads, far exceeding the 50,000 goal.[55]

Of course, the ultimate measure of effectiveness is whether your advertising increased sales, garnered votes, or changed behavior as intended. Depending on your advertising goals, you can measure effectiveness according to sales or market share, or you may use another measure that's appropriate for your organization. When Compaq toted up the sales results for its Presario campaign, it found that its share of the home PC market had increased by 97 percent, compared with the objective of 47 percent—and sales had jumped 164 percent.[56]

You can also evaluate your advertising in terms of the number of new relationships you gain. For example, the Springfield Institution for Savings, a small bank battling giant competitors in Massachusetts, set an advertising

This diagram shows how Communicus, a marketing research supplier, helps marketers evaluate the results of their advertising. By understanding changes in brand attitudes and usage, marketers can then refine their advertising to enhance relationship building with customers in the target market.

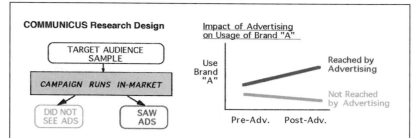

COMMUNICUS Research Design

TARGET AUDIENCE SAMPLE

CAMPAIGN RUNS IN-MARKET

DID NOT SEE ADS   SAW ADS

Impact of Advertising on Usage of Brand "A"

Use Brand "A"

Reached by Advertising

Not Reached by Advertising

Pre-Adv.   Post-Adv.

The Communicus System provides a way for advertisers to evaluate the results of their advertising. Interviews are conducted with consumers before the advertising is run to measure brand attitudes and usage. Then, after the advertising appears in-market, the same consumers are interviewed again. The analysis of the effectiveness of the advertising involves comparing changes in attitudes and buying behavior among those who have seen advertising for the brand with changes in attitudes and behavior among those who have seen none of the advertising for the brand. Many national advertisers in product categories as diverse as automobiles, cereal, computers, fast food and banking services use the Communicus System to understand the value of their advertising in producing sales of their products and services.

goal for establishing new banking relationships with consumers. After running radio, print, and billboard ads, the bank measured results and found that it had started three times as many new relationships as planned.[57] Now that's effective advertising.

Before you go on . . .

A. **Why do marketers identify the target audience before creating and placing an ad?**

B. **How do marketers use advertising research?**

C. **Why do marketers balance frequency and reach?**

D. **What does posttesting measure and why is it important?**

Direct Marketing: Going Direct to Build Relationships

One of the most effective ways to start or maintain an exchange relationship with individuals in your target audience is to use **direct marketing**, a two-way process of marketing communication through which marketers offer and customers buy products without contact with other channel partners. In the United States, direct marketers bring in more than $300 billion in sales every year.[58] Direct marketing covers a number of techniques, including direct mail and direct response advertising, that help marketers communicate directly with target audiences. To use direct marketing, you have to know a good deal about customers and prospects. That's where database marketing comes in.

direct marketing

a two-way process of marketing communication through which marketers offer and customers buy products without contact with other channel partners

Using Database Marketing

Database marketing is the process of collecting information about customers and potential customers, storing the data in computer files, and then analyzing the data to find out how best to start or support profitable long-term exchange relationships. This is critical for any customer-oriented organization. Imagine the possibilities for satisfying your customers and strengthening relationships when your database holds details about individual needs and buying patterns (gleaned from marketing research, sales files, and other sources). You'll be able to match customers with appropriate products and advertising messages, building a target audience one name at a time. Small wonder, then, that Kraft Foods, American Express, and other marketers rely on databases for more effective marketing.[59]

Database marketing allows you to target more precisely and gear advertising messages to individual customer needs and preferences. This personalized approach is an effective way to start new exchange relationships and strengthen existing relationships. Database marketing also helps you reach out to customers who might be interested in your other products, thereby deepening the relationship. The tricky part is making sure that customers recognize the value of being part of your database, so take care to tailor your offers to customer needs. When you are successful in this respect, your response rates can rise by as much as 200 percent—and when you fail, you leave yourself open to competitors that use database marketing more skillfully.[60]

Because database marketing depends on details about individuals, many people are concerned about invasion of privacy. Worries about inappropriate disclosure or misuse of personal details are especially troubling in an age when computers can swap huge quantities of information quickly—and without customer knowledge. Government regulations in the United States and abroad are helping to curb abuses, but marketers are also taking voluntary steps such as notifying customers of information sharing and removing names from lists on request.[61]

One regional unit of IBM has taken an unusual step in building a database of business customers and prospects. IBM asked the 300 executives in the target audience how often they prefer to be contacted, what information they want to see, and how they want that information delivered. Now the executives can receive the information they want by fax, mail, telephone, e-mail, or in a face-to-face meeting. Customers are pleased that their needs and preferences are heeded, and IBM saves money by targeting and timing messages more precisely.[62]

database marketing

the process of collecting information about customers and potential customers, storing the data in computer files, and then analyzing the data to find out how best to start or support profitable long-term exchange relationships

direct mail advertising

uses the medium of mail or private delivery to bring an advertising message to the target audience

Using Direct Mail Advertising

Direct mail advertising uses the medium of mail or private delivery to bring an advertising message to the target audience. (When direct marketers such as L.L. Bean advertise and deliver products to customers by mail, they're involved in *mail order*, a form of direct mail advertising.) Retailers such as Eddie Bauer, nonprofit organizations such as the ASPCA, and political parties—Republicans and Democrats alike—use direct mail advertising.

Direct mail advertising formats include catalogs, letters, packages, or inserts slipped into other mail communications. Catalogs are an increasingly popular communication vehicle. U.S. marketers mail nearly 13 billion catalogs every year, generating over $57 billion in sales. The average U.S. consumer receives more than 12 pieces of direct mail advertising every week—and throws away one-third of these ads without reading them.[63] These unwanted pieces have become known as *junk mail*.

But if the right offer is mailed to the right list, based on a consumer-oriented approach to communication, recipients will read and respond. Just ask small business owner Ruby Montana. She started a catalog, Pinto Ponies, to supplement her store's sales of western-style apparel and novelties. With the catalog, Montana's business was able to grow past $1 million in annual sales.[64]

Using Direct Response Advertising

Direct response advertising uses any medium to elicit an immediate response from the target audience. You can use mail, television, radio, newspapers, magazines, billboards, or online services to carry direct response advertising. Include a communication mechanism such as a coupon to be mailed, a phone number to call, or an online address so your audience can respond.

Because direct response advertising can be targeted to specific individuals in the buying center, about 36 percent of business-to-business marketers use it. But it's also a valuable technique for inviting responses from consumers. For example, World Vision, a nonprofit relief organization that helps 1 million children worldwide, supplements direct mail advertising with direct response brochures inserted into selected newspapers in major cities and direct response television advertising. Consumers can respond by phone or by mail, and they do, charging their donations or sending checks.[65] The following application showcases direct response advertising on the World Wide Web.

Applying the Concepts
Advertising for a song on the Web

Direct response advertising that works 24 hours a day, 365 days a year—that's Windham Hill Records's World Wide Web site. One thousand daily cybervisitors sample songs, order recordings, and get details about the musicians. The company's Web advertising is a good example of two-way marketing communication: while visitors are accessing information about recordings, musicians, and concerts, the marketer is gaining information about the interests and preferences of its target audience.

The Web service provider tells Windham Hill's marketing director, Roy Gattinella, exactly what site visitors do during their visits. "On the Web we know what ads people look at, for how long, and how involved they get," he says. "We can break the data down by sections—each recording artist's page. That tells me who's more popular." This daily feedback helps Windham Hill make marketing decisions about products, concerts, and so on.

direct response advertising
uses any medium to elicit an immediate response from the target audience

Online site management is relatively new for most marketers. By monitoring visits, marketers learn which pages are most interesting to consumers and can then adapt products and messages accordingly. Windham Hill Records, whose America Online site is shown here, has learned that online marketing is both effective and relatively low cost. What are the advantages and disadvantages to online selling and buying?

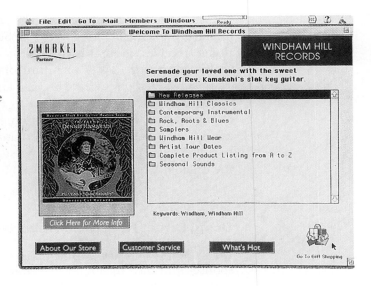

By analyzing Web site traffic, the company was also able to correct an unintentional marketing error. At first musicians' names were listed alphabetically, and those near the beginning of the alphabet received many more visits than the others. Gattinella quickly realized that people weren't taking the time to browse the entire menu of performers. So he changed the listing to showcase musicians Windham Hill wanted to emphasize.

Windham Hill's Web site advertising accounts for less than 5 percent of its marketing budget, yet it's more productive than many alternatives. Compared with print advertising, which includes only "an 800 number and a list of local retailers," Gattinella likes the direct response interaction that the Web allows—for a song.[66]

Make marketing decisions

1. How might Windham Hill use its Web site to pretest advertising messages?

2. How might Windham Hill reach music retailers, its customers in the value chain, through Web site advertising?

3. What other media would you suggest that Windham Hill use to advertise its recordings? Explain your answer.

4. Should Windham Hill use an emotional or a logical appeal? Why?

Before you go on . . .

A. How does direct marketing relate to direct mail advertising and direct response advertising?

B. What is database marketing and how do marketers use it?

Summary

1. **Define advertising and show how the various types support relationship building.**

   Advertising is any paid form of nonpersonal communication link, initiated by an identified marketer, to establish or continue exchange relationships with customers who buy or use goods, ideas, or services. Advertising can be either product or institutional. Within those categories are pioneer, reminder, competitive, and advocacy advertising, all designed to provide the right message about the right product at the right time to build customer relationships.

2. **Comment on the value of advertising to customers, marketers, and channel partners.**

   Critics complain that advertising is wasteful, manipulates attitudes and behavior, and encourages people to buy unnecessarily. On the other hand, customer-oriented advertising is valuable because it helps customers buy, as well as helping marketers sell. Advertising can open a dialogue that enhances product value for customers and builds commitment and loyalty to a marketer's products. Finally, advertising adds value by serving as an efficient and effective method for maintaining communication among customers, channel partners, and other stakeholders.

3. **Explore the creative role of appeals, copy, and art in the development of an advertisement.**

   In creating an ad, the first step is selecting a basic appeal such as logic, emotion, celebrity, sexual attractiveness, fear, or humor. The appeal drives the copy and art that make up the creative portion of an ad.

4. **Apply advertising research to create, place, and evaluate advertising.**

   Advertising research provides information about the target audience that helps marketers make better decisions about advertising messages and media. Message research (used in pretesting and posttesting) shows how the target audience perceives what the ads are communicating and how effective the messages are at influencing attitudes and behavior. Media research helps reveal the makeup and preferences of media audiences, so marketers can select appropriate media for the target audience.

5. **Demonstrate the importance of reach and frequency in selecting media.**

   Reach measures how many different members of the target audience are exposed to an ad in a specific media vehicle; frequency measures how many times audience members are exposed to a media vehicle while the ad runs. Balancing the two is a challenge because both higher reach and higher frequency are desirable but costly.

6. **Explain the factors to consider in making media decisions.**

In selecting media, marketers examine the target audience's use of media, match the ad's creative approach to the media, check competitors' use of media, and compare reach, frequency, and cost per thousand for media being considered.

7. **Show how marketers use direct marketing and database marketing to build customer relationships.**

Direct marketing is a two-way process of marketing communication through which marketers offer and customers buy products without contact with other channel partners. Database marketing is the process of collecting information about customers and prospects, storing the data in computer files, then analyzing the data to find out how to start or maintain profitable long-term marketing relationships. Both forms help marketers reach target audiences with appropriate products and advertising messages geared to their needs and behavior. This is a good example of a customer-driven communication approach.

KEY TERMS

advertising **534**

advertising agency **539**

advertising research **545**

advocacy advertising **536**

comparative advertising **535**

competitive advertising **535**

cost per thousand (CPM) **546**

database marketing **556**

direct mail advertising **556**

direct marketing **555**

direct response advertising **557**

frequency **546**

infomercials **548**

institutional advertising **535**

media **546**

pioneering advertising **535**

product advertising **534**

public service advertising (PSA) **536**

reach **546**

reminder advertising **535**

Skill-Building Applications

1. How could you use the Internet to help find a job when you graduate? What other interactive media might be helpful?

2. Should a company like Goodyear use institutional or product advertising when trying to market tires to auto manufacturers like Chrysler and Ford? Explain your answer.

3. What forms of advertising have charities like the American Heart Association used to reach you? Which have been most effective? Why? What kind of ads would you recommend?

4. Small businesses such as Katherine Moser's chimney sweep service are limited in the amount they

can spend on advertising. In addition to the suggestions in the text, what are some inexpensive yet effective ways such small businesses can use to reach potential customers?

5. How could H&R Block and other income tax preparers more effectively use advertising to win your business?

6. What kind of company is more likely to be able to use global advertising campaigns and what kind is better off customizing ads for each country? Can an argument be made that every company should customize its ads, regardless of the greater expense?

Getting Involved in Marketing

1. ***On Your Own*** Analyze a product ad and an institutional ad. Who do you think is the target market for each? Be as specific as possible. What objectives might the marketers have set for these ads? How does the medium used for each ad reach the target market? Summarize your findings in a presentation to your class.

2. ***On Your Own*** Explore several Web sites on the Internet and evaluate their effectiveness. What makes one site more attractive than others? What kind of information is available on Web sites? Write a two-page paper analyzing the present status of Web site development.

3. ***Find Out More*** Collect consumer and business advertisements that illustrate the various types of advertising appeal. Analyze each to discover how both copy and art support the appeal. Which do you find most effective? Why? Prepare a brief report summarizing the results of your analysis.

4. ***In a Team*** With two classmates, select a societal issue such as recycling or drug abuse. Decide how you would use advertising to change behavior—encouraging recycling, for example, or discouraging drug use. Prepare a presentation in which you identify your target audience, show your objectives, suggest a creative approach and appropriate media, and explain how you would determine advertising effectiveness.

5. ***In a Partnership*** With another student, analyze a comparative ad to determine what it says about the competing product. If your team were making advertising decisions for that competitor, how would you use advertising to respond? Draft a report about your ideas.

6. ***In a Team*** With other classmates, make a list of at least six issues that a marketer should consider when developing direct response advertising. Indicate one or more sources a marketer might consult to get information about each.

19

Sales Promotion and Public Relations

Learning Goals

After you have read and studied this chapter, you should be able to:

1. Differentiate between consumer and trade sales promotion.
2. Show how sales promotion can build consumer, trade, and internal relationships.
3. Analyze the strategic balance between sales promotion and advertising.
4. Identify the eight major consumer sales promotion techniques.
5. Demonstrate the use of the five major trade sales promotion techniques.
6. Distinguish between public relations and publicity used in integrated marketing communication.
7. Show how public relations can be used to reach stakeholder audiences.

PROFILE

Promotions open windows for Microsoft

"Start me up!" was the theme of the most widely trumpeted software promotion in history. On August 24, 1995, Microsoft launched its Windows 95 operating system amid unprecedented marketing hoopla. Microsoft wanted to persuade 85 million computer users around the world to buy its operating software, a special challenge because so many would have to invest in computer and software upgrades to use some Win95 features.

Based on this marketing objective, Microsoft put together a $200 million integrated marketing communication campaign spanning 22 countries, including a prime-time 30-minute infomercial. To complement its splashy advertising, the company whipped up excitement in local markets using sales promotion, publicity, and special events to highlight the new product's value and support local retailers' marketing efforts.

To start, Microsoft gave away thousands of sample computer disks and CD-ROMs to show what Win95 could do. Targeting corporate users, the company also sent out 10 million demonstration disks so businesspeople could test the product. In addition, Microsoft supported its retail partners by providing colorful signs, on-screen demonstrations, and informative brochures. A number of stores mounted promotions of their own, and many opened at midnight on August 23—for 95 minutes—to sell the software.

Win95 dominated the news as the launch date approached, thanks to the company's public relations efforts. In addition to mentioning product details, news reports focused on special events around the world, including launch parties in dozens of cities, prizes in Cracker Jack boxes, and a giant banner unfurled on the CN Tower in Toronto. These carefully coordinated activities made Windows 95 one of the fastest-selling software products in history.[1]

For Microsoft, as for many marketers, sales promotion and public relations are key ingredients in the recipe for success in relationship marketing. This chapter opens with a discussion of how sales promotion adds value that builds relationships with external customers, channel partners, and internal customers. After analyzing the strategic role of sales promotion, you'll look at specific techniques used in consumer and trade sales promotion. Then you'll learn how to use public relations, including publicity and special events, to build relationships with stakeholders.

Sales Promotion and Relationship Marketing

Like Microsoft, all marketers are looking for ways to strengthen exchange relationships with customers and value-chain partners by communicating extra value and providing special incentives for buying. Sales promotion is one marketing tool that can help to achieve this. **Sales promotion** is the communication of any incentive that enhances the basic value of a product for a limited period, to encourage channel members and sales people to market it and customers to buy it.

The incentive (which can be anything from a free sample to a cash reward) changes the way customers, channel partners, and salespeople perceive the product's value ◀━━┛ **(p. 346)**. The addition of the incentive changes the value equation and extends the product's existing benefits without increasing the price, a maneuver that boosts the value—but only temporarily.[3] Much of the power of sales promotion comes from its sense of urgency, which stimulates the target audience to respond quickly.

Sales promotion has become a key element in an integrated marketing communication (IMC) strategy ◀━━┛ **(p. 13)**. This means of accelerating purchasing and encouraging repeat purchasing is a good complement to the long-term relationship-building abilities of advertising, public relations, and personal selling. When sales promotion is carefully blended into the IMC strategy, it contributes to brand equity ◀━━┛ **(p. 266)**, reinforces positioning ◀━━┛ **(p. 266)**, and invites continued buying.[4] As a consequence, marketers overall now spend more of their IMC budgets on sales promotion than on advertising. Table 19.1 shows this clearly.

Consider how Kraft Foods's Post division combined sales promotion with television advertising to successfully introduce a new breakfast cereal. Creative television commercials for Blueberry Morning built awareness and stimulated interest in the product's flavorful, naturally dried blueberries and crunchy flakes. In-store sampling (one sales promotion technique) gave consumers a free taste while they were shopping— and money-saving coupons (another promotion technique) offered the final incentive to buy. Added to the aggressive advertising schedule, these two incentives helped Blueberry Morning zoom to $47 million in sales in just 8 months.[5]

T A B L E **19.1**   Spending on Sales Promotion Versus Advertising

| Year | Percentage of Marketer's IMC Budget Spent on | | |
	Media Advertising	Trade Sales Promotion	Consumer Sales Promotion
1985	35	38	27
1986	34	40	26
1987	33	41	26
1988	32	42	25
1989	31	44	26
1990	28	47	25
1991	25	48	27
1992	25	48	27
1993	24	49	27
1994	24	50	26
1995	25	51	24

Numbers do not always add up to 100 because of rounding.

sales promotion

the communication of any incentive that enhances the basic value of a product for a limited period, to encourage channel members and sales people to market it and customers to buy it

You can use sales promotion to support relationship-building marketing strategies with three distinct audiences: (1) ultimate consumers, (2) organizational customers such as channel partners, who are collectively referred to as the *trade*, and (3) salespeople and other internal customers. You'll learn about sales promotion strategies for reaching each group in the following sections.

How Sales Promotion Builds Consumer Relationships

Consumer sales promotion covers a range of promotional incentives that marketers offer to ultimate consumers to encourage product purchases. Marketers allocate about 25 percent of their IMC budgets to consumer sales promotions, which include coupons, samples, frequency marketing programs, sweepstakes and contests, premiums, price promotions, refunds and rebates, and displays.[6] Consumer sales promotion is a key ingredient when marketers use pull strategies. As you saw in Chapter 17, a pull strategy **(p. 525)** is one in which marketers aim their communications at ultimate consumers, who then ask retailers for the product being promoted. This creates demand that pulls the product through the channel.

Depending on their overall goals, marketers can use consumer sales promotion to accomplish one or more of the following objectives:

Sampling is a very effective sales promotion tool. If you have a product you think is superior, why not let customers see and decide for themselves by providing a free demo or sample? That is exactly how Myst, now the most successful CD-ROM game on the market, got started. Demo games were widely distributed and word of mouth helped spur sales. What are some other products that would benefit from a similar sampling strategy?

consumer sales promotion

a range of short-term promotional incentives that marketers offer to ultimate consumers to encourage product purchases

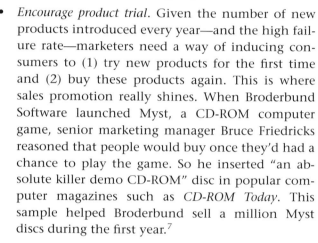

- *Encourage product trial.* Given the number of new products introduced every year—and the high failure rate—marketers need a way of inducing consumers to (1) try new products for the first time and (2) buy these products again. This is where sales promotion really shines. When Broderbund Software launched Myst, a CD-ROM computer game, senior marketing manager Bruce Friedricks reasoned that people would buy once they'd had a chance to play the game. So he inserted "an absolute killer demo CD-ROM" disc in popular computer magazines such as *CD-ROM Today*. This sample helped Broderbund sell a million Myst discs during the first year.[7]

- *Encourage continued buying and usage.* Marketers also have to defend against competitive threats by strengthening customer relationships over the long term. To do this, they can offer incentives such as coupons, special pricing, contests, and rewards that encourage consumers to keep buying and using the promoted products. For example, the Superquinn supermarket chain in Dublin, Ireland, awards points according to how much customers spend. Customers keep buying to earn points that can be exchanged for gifts such as toys, sporting goods, and discount certificates.[8]

- *Encourage purchase and usage of related products.* Marketers often use sales promotion to encourage consumers to try or buy more than one product from the product line. This is the approach chosen by Salon Selectives and other marketers of hair care products when they insert coupons for shampoo, conditioner, and other related products in a single ad.

- *Support IMC strategy to gain faster, more measurable response.* Sales promotion can sharpen the focus on extra value and add a note of immediacy to complement other IMC messages. As a result, consumers may speed up their buying decisions and buy sooner. This is especially important with seasonal products such as Halloween candies.

- *Build a marketing database.* One of the most effective ways of encouraging customers and prospects to provide details for a marketing database is to offer a special gift or other incentive in return for information. T.S. Cyclesports, a small bicycle retailer in Wichita, Kansas, drew a large response when it announced a drawing for high-tech sunglasses and invited customers to fill out free entry forms.[9]

How Sales Promotion Builds Value-Chain Relationships

Trade sales promotion refers to promotional incentives offered by marketers to wholesalers, retailers, and other value-chain partners for supporting certain products. Among the most common types of trade sales promotion are trade allowances, trade shows, deals and incentives, cooperative advertising, and training and marketing support. Trade sales promotions are rarely seen by consumers, but they are an important investment for most marketers, accounting for nearly half of all IMC spending.[10] Trade promotions help build relationships with channel partners, which is vital when using a push strategy. As discussed in Chapter 17, a push strategy is one in which marketers aim their communications at value-chain partners, to induce them to carry the product through the value chain to reach ultimate consumers ◀─┘ **(p. 50)**.

In the value chain, marketers can use trade sales promotion to achieve a variety of objectives:

- *Add value-chain partners.* Given the constant stream of new product introductions, marketers using indirect channels ◀─┘ **(p. 415)** can't simply assume that value-chain partners will carry their products. Trade sales promotion can help persuade wholesalers and retailers to carry a particular product or product line. Castle Springs, a small bottled-water marketer in New Hampshire, offers tours of its mountain spring location as a promotion to encourage wholesalers to carry its water—and no visiting wholesaler has ever refused the product, notes the company's founder.[11]

- *Induce partners to carry more stock.* Marketers can encourage wholesalers and retailers to stock more than the usual quantity by offering discounts or allowances, sales incentives, cooperative advertising, or other incentives. Although this practice can encourage partners to more aggressively market the product, it can also backfire—because value-chain partners that load up with stock are likely to buy less for a while afterward. That's why Procter & Gamble, Quaker Oats, and other marketers have de-emphasized load-up promotions, hoping to smooth out the peaks and valleys of trade purchasing.[12]

- *Enhance value-chain support.* Trade sales promotion is a good way to encourage wholesalers and retailers to give a product special attention. To do this, producers can provide sales literature or displays, show how an upcoming advertising or promotion campaign will generate consumer interest, or offer incentives in exchange for enchanced sales support.

- *Strengthen value-chain relationships.* Producers often provide sales training, brochures, and other types of trade sales promotion to supplement the sales efforts of wholesalers and retailers. These joint promotions help channel partners serve their customers better, and, in turn, allow them to market products more effectively. In addition, with efficient

trade sales promotion

promotional incentives offered by marketers to wholesalers, retailers, and other value-chain partners for supporting certain products

consumer response **(p. 413)**, manufacturers have the ability to check store scanner data and reward grocery retailers for promoting certain products.[13] The result: stronger exchange relationships up and down the value chain.

Bear in mind that aggressive consumer sales promotion can benefit trade relationships as well by attracting consumers who buy value-chain partners' products. For example, when Nestlé held a summerlong in-store sweepstakes promotion, tying its pet foods and food products to Walt Disney's *Pocahontas* movie, retail partners benefited from higher traffic and sales—and made more room on store shelves for the products.[14]

Sales promotion efforts aimed at consumers can also strengthen relationships with value-chain partners. This Nestlé promotion, featuring Disney's movie *The Hunchback of Notre Dame*, encouraged retailers to stock up on the candy bars and display them prominently so consumers could buy them. How could Nestlé use the same theme for a trade sales promotion geared toward convenience stores and other food retailers who sell candy bars?

How Sales Promotion Builds Internal Relationships

Marketers can adapt sales promotion techniques to enhance relationships with internal customers, who often are as important to marketing success as external customers and value-chain partners. For maximum impact, many marketers are looking beyond individual salespeople to also reward cross-functional teams **(p. 47)** for enhancing relationships with others. By applying some of the techniques usually found in consumer and trade sales promotions, marketers can achieve several objectives:

- *Build internal commitment.* Organizations can get employees lined up behind marketing programs and objectives—and everything the organization does to satisfy customers—by offering premiums, prizes, samples, and other incentives. Small businesses such as Big Wheel/Rossi Auto Stores in Minnesota do this, using more modest versions of incentives than larger organizations offer. Big Wheel motivates employees to become committed to store activities and goals by awarding prizes such as tickets to sporting events and concerts.[15]

- *Encourage closer teamwork.* Sales promotion can encourage better teamwork throughout the organization by offering employee incentives. Many short-term incentives such as contests are aimed at teams who serve customers, including salespeople, installation and repair technicians, and others. In addition, some marketers extend contests and other incentives to people throughout the organization who team up to work on new products or help major customers through crisis situations.

- *Shape employee attitudes and behavior.* Marketers can use sales promotion to give employees incentives for delivering superior service, for working toward new organizational goals, and for developing new products—or to otherwise shape attitudes and behavior. For example, Holiday Inn hotels in Tennessee have used a "praising coupon" promotion to reward high-quality service. Guests filled out coupons on which they listed the names of employees who had provided especially good service. The hotel's general manager publicly praised employees for their efforts, which raised morale and reinforced superior customer service.[16]

The Strategic Role of Sales Promotion

The power of sales promotion to build and strengthen relationships with consumers, channel partners, and internal customers has made this marketing tool an increasingly vital part of IMC strategy. Yet in the past, sales promotion played a relatively minor role. What happened to bring about this change? And how does sales promotion fit with IMC strategy today? This section examines those two key questions.

The Strategic Balance Between Sales Promotion and Advertising

Until about 20 years ago, marketers spent more of their IMC budgets on advertising than on sales promotion. Then, in the mid-1970s, the balance began to tilt away from advertising, with more and more dollars flowing toward sales promotion. Looking back at Table 19.1, you can see that trade and consumer sales promotion now accounts for 74 percent of the IMC budget and advertising accounts for only 26 percent, a loss of nine percentage points for advertising in the course of a decade.[17]

Marketers are increasing their investment in sales promotion for several reasons. For one thing, retailers have become more powerful players in the value chain. They have daily contact with customers and can determine, through scanner data gathered at checkout time, exactly which products sell and which don't, information that manufacturers can't easily get on their own. In many industries, value-chain power is consolidated in the hands of a few major retailers. Toys "Я" Us, for example, is responsible for 25 percent of all U.S. toy sales. As a result, manufacturers that want to reach store customers must build and sustain good exchange relationships with their retail partners, which they can do through trade sales promotion.[18]

Also propelling the movement toward sales promotion was a change in consumer behavior away from brand loyalty and toward price sensitivity. In part, this change reflected heightened consumer interest in getting better value, as well as uncertainties related to job security and economic conditions. It was also a reaction to the flood of new products. When consumers detected little differentiation among functionally comparable items, they relied more on price and price promotions as indicators of value. With the onslaught of promotions, consumers grew accustomed to buying on the basis of price alone. Over time, this bargain-hunting pattern hurt brand loyalty and eroded relationships—and profits.[19]

The growth in new products has put pressure on marketers to build customer relationships in a hurry. Marketers feel that they must make back their investments in new product development within a short time, which means bringing customers on board quickly. Many forms of integrated marketing communications take time to show results, but consumer and trade sales promotion can help speed the process—and the results are measurable.

In addition, use of sales promotion has risen because the effectiveness of this tool is measurable. Marketers can count the responses they get from coupons and other sales promotion tools, whereas advertising results aren't so easily measured. Measuring response helps marketers see the relationship-building effect of each communication and teaches them how to improve communication over time.

However, when marketers develop quick-hit sales promotions, launching them without careful coordination with advertising and other IMC techniques, they run the risk of jeopardizing long-term objectives—such as relationship building and profit. One study concluded that a large percentage of promotions actually cut into profits. Brand equity can also be damaged by sales promotions that don't fit well with overall IMC plans.[20] Now some marketers are cutting back on the use of coupons and other price-oriented promotions and beginning to focus more on IMC messages that emphasize value and quality rather than price.

Look at the way BF Goodrich, the tire manufacturer, integrated sales promotion with advertising. Teaming up with Timberland, the footwear company, Goodrich gave away an $80 pair of hiking boots to consumers who purchased its light-truck tires. Advertising the two-month promotion in magazines and newspapers and on radio brought customers to its tire dealers. An in-store display of Timberland boots perched atop a five-foot stack of logs reinforced the outdoor theme of the campaign. As a result, dealers ordered and marketed the tires more aggressively. Goodrich sold over 70,000 tires, lifting market share 30 percent while reinforcing the brand image of quality, value, performance, and durability.[21]

Increasingly, marketers are looking at ways of making advertising and promotional expenditures do double duty, building both consumer and trade relationships at once. Procter & Gamble, for example, is replacing some traditional trade promotions with consumer advertising. By customizing product ads in direct mail, television, and other media to feature specific retailers, P&G can simultaneously support its brands' images and draw customers to key partners such as Target, Kmart, and Wal-Mart.[22]

Sales promotion can be both effective and less expensive when companies work together to design joint promotions. A product can be made much more attractive when a free premium accompanies its purchase. This consumer promotion by BF Goodrich, featuring Timberland boots, is a good example. What other products would you recommend for a joint promotion to boost truck tire sales for BF Goodrich?

Sales Promotion and IMC Strategy

Balancing sales promotion and advertising within the IMC strategy is a complex task. Every marketer must find the best balance for its unique situation by examining such variables as the product, overall marketing objectives, time considerations, target audience, media used, competition, and the internal and external marketing environment.[23] The ideal balance should have the largest promotional effect while still maintaining profits.

Like every IMC technique, sales promotion has a part to play in the overall IMC strategy. Both consumer and trade sales promotion are crucial to launching a new product. In the introduction stage of the product life cycle ◄┘ **(p. 302)**, promotions such as samples encourage consumers to try your product. In that stage, trade sales promotion such as trade shows help open doors to value-chain partners, while contests motivate your salesforce to focus on the new item.

In the growth stage, channel relationships can be reinforced by trade promotions such as training and marketing support, and consumer promotions

coupon

a document that allows customers to buy a product at a specific discount

such as rebates often help expand the customer base. In the maturity stage, consumer promotions such as coupons and frequency marketing programs are useful for fighting competitors, while trade promotions such as cooperative advertising satisfy value-chain partners and support brand loyalty. By the time a product is in decline, it often receives little sales promotion support.

Despite its potential for relationship building, sales promotion can't fix a poor value-chain strategy or an inadequate product. Also, sales promotion is intended to enhance product value for a limited time, not indefinitely. Excessive promotion may harm brand share over time as customers hop from brand to brand, seeking the best price. So for maximum effect, be sure to coordinate your sales promotion objectives with your long-term IMC objectives and overall marketing objectives.[24]

Before you go on . . .

A. What are the major objectives of consumer sales promotion?

B. What are the major objectives of sales promotion in the value chain?

C. How does sales promotion build internal relationships?

Using Consumer Sales Promotion to Add Value

Consumer sales promotion techniques include coupons, samples, frequency marketing programs, sweepstakes and contests, premiums, price promotions, refunds and rebates, and displays. These techniques are shown in Table 19.2. Rarely does any marketer use them all, however. The choice depends on a variety of factors, including product, target audience, and overall IMC strategy.

TABLE **19.2** Using Consumer Sales Promotion

Technique	How Marketers Use Technique
Coupons	Give first-time or loyal customers a document good for a specific discount on a particular product, encouraging trial and repeat purchasing.
Samples	Offer products free or at low price to allow customers to personally experience and evaluate the product and its benefits.
Frequency marketing programs	Reinforce brand loyalty by offering rewards to customers who repeatedly purchase product over time.
Sweepstakes and contests	Invite customers to compete for prizes by using skills (contests) or returning entries for random drawing (sweepstakes), which builds awareness and excitement.
Premiums	Offer a gift free or at a low price to induce customers to buy or try a product.
Price promotions	Offer a short-term price reduction for every purchase during the promotional period to change the value equation and encourage purchasing.
Refunds and rebates	Return some or all of the purchase price if customers buy during a specific period, which enhances the product's value for a limited time.
Displays	Set up displays in retail outlets to promote the purchase of a particular product where and when customers make buying decisions.

Coupons are an effective way to get consumers to buy a particular brand or shop in a certain store. However, overuse can reduce profits. As a consequence, some companies are dropping the use of coupons and going to everyday low pricing (EDLP). How would you resolve the impact on profitability if you were a retailer issuing coupons?

Coupons

A **coupon** is a document that allows customers to buy a product at a specific discount. Nearly all U.S. manufacturers of consumer products, some business-to-business marketers, and many retailers offer coupons. Coupons encourage customers to try new products, to switch from competing products, and to continue buying products from certain stores. Among the most frequent users of coupons are makers of breakfast cereals, medications and health aids, and household cleaning products. Despite the popularity of coupons, some marketers are starting to de-emphasize this marketing tool in favor of a more consistent value position communicated through everyday low pricing (EDLP).[25]

Although 327 billion manufacturer coupons (and 400 million retailer coupons) are issued every year, customers redeem fewer than 8 billion manufacturer coupons. Nonetheless, coupons can build exchange relationships simply by being seen by potential customers. Someone who notices a coupon may buy the product later, with or without a cents-off slip—and many who clip coupons forget to bring them along during shopping trips.[26]

In line with customer-oriented marketing, and to increase redemption rates, marketers are learning to target customers and potential customers better. One way to do this is by sending coupons to past users and those who live near them. Adrian Fredericks of Five Buck Pizza, a small restaurant near Provo, Utah, targets customers for coupon mailings using zip codes, and then measures the results. With new technology, marketers can identify individual users of coupons and tailor couponing programs to reward brand loyalty and build stronger exchange relationships. Both McDonald's and Pizza Hut use computerized targeting and tracking to adapt coupon promotions to customer purchasing patterns by neighborhood.[27]

Marketers get coupons to customers in a variety of ways, as shown in Figure 19.1. Most of the time, coupons are printed in freestanding inserts (FSIs) that are delivered with Sunday and daily newspapers. In addition, issuing coupons inside the store (through shelf dispensers, for example) has become

FIGURE **19.1**

How Marketers Get Coupons to Consumers

By far the most commonly used method for getting coupons to consumers is through free-standing inserts in newspapers. In the coming years, marketers will use more electronic couponing to reach consumers when and where they make buying decisions.

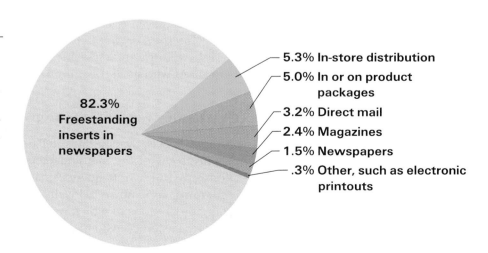

- 82.3% Freestanding inserts in newspapers
- 5.3% In-store distribution
- 5.0% In or on product packages
- 3.2% Direct mail
- 2.4% Magazines
- 1.5% Newspapers
- .3% Other, such as electronic printouts

increasingly popular because it allows marketers to reach consumers when and where they make purchasing decisions. These days, marketers are moving beyond traditional paper couponing to electronic couponing. Computer-generated coupons can be printed at the checkout, issued through interactive kiosks that print coupons on request, or printed at home by PC users who browse the World Wide Web.[28]

Couponing is not as popular around the world as it is in the United States. "It is far less or nonexistent in most other countries, simply because the cultures don't accept couponing, or it is emerging as it is in the U.K. with retailers now being made aware of couponing and how to handle it," says Joseph Potacki, who teaches sales promotion for the Promotional Marketing Association of America. Coca-Cola's marketers in Moscow, for example, can't offer coupons there because they have no way to collect redeemed coupons from retailers, as a prelude to reimbursement. For now, Coke is concentrating on advertising and sweepstakes promotions in Russia.[29]

Samples

A **sample** is a good or service offered free or at a very low price to encourage customers to experience its benefits. People who have sampled a good or service are better able to appreciate its superiority—especially when sensory experiences such as taste or sight are involved. For example, when CPC International promoted the taste and convenience of Thomas' Sandwich Muffins, the marketer persuaded supermarkets to provide sliced meats for lunch-time samples of sandwiches made with the muffins. Sampling helped CPC get across the message that "these muffins are not just for breakfast. They're also for sandwiches and barbecues," noted Bruce Malinowski, a CPC director of consumer marketing.[30]

Sampling is a must in the hotly competitive video game market, where Sega's Saturn game equipment competes with Sony's PlayStation and Nintendo's Game Boy. "Firsthand experience is what sells these games, and there's no better way to get word of mouth out there than to get kids face to face with the game," notes Tim Dunley, Sega Saturn's director of marketing. During the summer that the Saturn was launched, Sega invited thousands of teenagers to play free games on machines installed at Orlando's Universal Studios and Disney World's Epcot Center.[31]

Marketers can offer samples in stores, in or on product packages, at local events, via direct mail, inserted in newspaper or magazines, in shopping centers, and even electronically. Digital Equipment Corporation recently invited Internet browsers to try certain DEC computer products online. Thanks to this virtual test drive, DEC sold $5 million of Alpha computers to customers who liked the online sample.[32]

sample
a good or service offered free or at a very low price to encourage customers to experience its benefits

frequency marketing programs
ongoing promotions in which marketers reinforce brand loyalty by offering rewards to customers who make repeat purchases

Frequency Marketing Programs

Airlines, banks, long-distance telephone marketers, restaurants, and retailers are just some of the many marketers that support long-term exchange relationships through frequency marketing programs. **Frequency marketing programs**, also known as loyalty or relationship marketing programs, are ongoing promotions in which marketers reinforce brand loyalty by offering rewards to customers who make repeat purchases. In contrast to most consumer sales promotions, which last only for a short period, frequency marketing programs go on and on, allowing customers to rack up points toward an array of awards. The more customers buy, the more prizes they can earn.[33]

The real power behind frequency marketing as a relationship-strengthening tool comes not from the prizes but from the explicit recognition of the customer's importance. Frequency marketing programs such as American Airlines' AAdvantage and National Car Rental's Emerald Club let customers know that they're valued through regular newsletters, award statements, and other communications. And every time a customer flashes a frequency marketing membership card, it's a signal to employees to provide extra-special treatment. From the customer's viewpoint, participating in a frequency marketing program heightens the feeling of collaboration in the marketing exchange, which enhances the overall relationship.[34]

Most often, marketers use frequency marketing programs to deepen relationships with current customers and to defend themselves against competitive pressures. They also find frequency marketing a good way to start relationships with new customers. And, as customers buy products over time, marketers can gather vital information about customer preferences, frequency of purchasing, and other details that support better targeting, more effective database marketing ◄——▌ **(p. 138)**, and future product development.[35]

American Express takes frequency marketing a step further, combining it with market segmentation to tailor rewards and offers to more closely fit the needs of cardholders in specific segments. For example, one key target population consists of people who pay the annual card fee but don't use the card very often. To stimulate card usage in this segment, Amex offers two free airline tickets to customers who charge a great deal over a 6-month period. Although this promotion is costly, it helps Amex retain potentially profitable customers who would be even more costly to replace with new customers.[36]

Handling frequency marketing programs can be tricky. The following case contrasts a successful experience in Canada with an unsuccessful experience in the United States.

Citibank is one of the many partners that have connected specific products with the highly successful American Airline AAdvantage frequency marketing program. Citibank's AAdvantage card earns cardholders one mile on American Airlines for every dollar they charge. The idea, of course, is to keep consumers using a single credit card so they can build up air miles and earn free trips. Do you think such incentives are more attractive than a lower interest rate?

Applying the Concepts

Air Miles soars in Canada, crashes in U.S.

The Air Miles frequency marketing program is flying high in Canada—but it crashed in the United States. Both were based on the original Air Miles Reward Program launched in the United Kingdom in 1988, rewarding customers who loyally buy sponsors' products with points that can be redeemed for air travel. Why did the program succeed in Canada and fail south of the border?

One reason for the U.S. failure was the hassle of crediting points to consumer accounts. While some of the 40 marketers could credit points electronically, many manufacturers had to ask consumers to go through the tedious process of cutting out and mailing proofs of purchase to get credit. A second reason was that some products were worth just a few points per purchase, which discouraged customers eager to earn travel rewards quickly. At its peak, U.S. Air Miles signed up 2.2 million consumers—but only half were active. The program disappeared in less than two years.

In contrast, the Canadian program enlisted retail and service marketers (rather than manufacturers) such as Canada Safeway, Bank of Montreal, and Shell Oil. Whereas consumers might buy a particular manufacturer's product sporadically, they bank, shop for groceries, and buy gasoline regularly, so they can earn Air Miles points more quickly as they make basic household purchases. The Canadian program allows participants to earn at least one trip a year, which reinforces the value of remaining loyal. Finally, points are credited electronically: consumers present a card each time they buy from a sponsoring marketer, and points are automatically tallied and credited.

Canadian marketers like the customer-friendly program because it strengthens exchange relationships. "We see Air Miles as a long-term way to reward and retain our loyal customers," comments Shell Oil's Oly Boersma. The proof: Shell's market share rose from 13 percent to 15 percent in two years, despite many station closings. Bottom-line results like these are keeping Air Miles flying high in Canada.[37]

Make marketing decisions

1. How could Air Miles Canada use advertising or other IMC techniques to expand the number of participating consumers?

2. How could Air Miles Canada use advertising or other IMC techniques to expand the number of sponsoring marketers?

3. What are the pros and cons for Air Miles Canada of offering prizes other than air travel?

4. How might Air Miles Canada market itself to employers seeking to strengthen relationships with employees?

Sweepstakes and Contests

Looking to stir up some promotional excitement? Try sweepstakes or contests. A *sweepstakes* is a good way to expand a customer database while attracting new customers and giving loyal customers an extra reward. It requires no special skill or talent; winners are chosen at random from among the entries.

For example, Argencard, which markets MasterCard credit cards in Argentina, recently used a sweepstakes promotion to boost charge sales. Every receipt from an Argencard purchase was entered into a prize drawing. Winners whose receipts were selected were reimbursed for those purchases. Global marketers should note that although sweepstakes promotions are popular in the Americas, they're banned in Scandinavian countries and in some other European nations.[38] Here's how Bristol-Myers mounted a sweepstakes in South Africa.

premium

an item of value offered free or at a low price to customers who buy or try a particular product

Contests seek to attract consumers' attention by engaging them in some challenge to win a prize. In this photography contest sponsored by *Traveler* magazine, the person with the best photo submission wins the first prize—a dream holiday in Nepal. What do you think the magazine is hoping to gain by sponsoring such a contest?

GLOBAL ISSUES

Sweepstakes builds Mum's brand in South Africa

Mum's the word for Bristol-Myers. Mum is the name of the marketer's line of deodorants for men and women—as well as an affectionate colloquialism for "mother." Bristol-Myers played on both meanings when it started a national sweepstakes to boost brand image and increase sales in South Africa. The top prizes were two convertible Porsche Speedster replicas and 20,000 rands (U.S. $60,000). But the real star of the show was Mum.

To kick off the promotion, Bristol-Myers ran a magazine ad and attached a bumper sticker reading "I love Mum." The ad detailed the benefits of Mum deodorants and invited readers to put the bumper stickers on their cars. Here's where the sweepstakes comes in: anyone who saw a bumper sticker on another car could send in the car's license number, which entered both the car's owner and the sharp-eyed reader in the prize drawing.

During the seven weeks of the promotion, about 300,000 South African cars displayed the Mum bumper sticker, serving as mobile billboards circulating around the country. Eager spotters were on the lookout for the Mum stickers, which reinforced the brand name and generated considerable word of mouth. As excitement mounted, sales skyrocketed. But the promotion didn't stop working after the sweepstakes ended. In fact, Mum bumper stickers remained on South African cars long after the drawing, extending the promotion's effect for more than a year.[39]

Should Bristol-Myers make the sweepstakes an annual event? Explain your answer.

A *contest* requires people to use certain skills to win prizes. For example, OshKosh B'Gosh, which makes work clothes, used a "Building America" contest to reinforce its relationship with professional and amateur do-it-yourselfers. The marketer invited customers to mail in photos and descriptions of their best projects, from furniture to houses, and awarded Stanley tools to the winners.[40]

Premiums

A **premium** is an item of value offered free or at a low price to customers who buy a particular product. Promotions featuring premiums such as toys, apparel, or prepaid telephone cards can encourage customers to buy for the first time or reinforce the relationship over time by rewarding multiple purchases. Premiums can be offered by mail, on or inside product packages, or in the store. For example, Cracker Jack puts a premium—usually a small toy—in every package of caramel-covered popcorn, while Hershey asks consumers to mail in candy bar wrappers to receive basketballs and other premiums.[41]

Trading cards are popular premiums for cementing customer relationships. For several years, Sears has produced trading cards depicting its Craftsman Tool line, sold in packs of 12 for 99 cents. The Denny's restaurant chain gives away baseball trading cards during its annual summer promotions. "Each year we give away all the cards, and that's millions of cards," says Debbie Atkins, Denny's public relations manager, describing the premium's success. Trading cards act as tiny billboards, reinforcing the marketer's name and generating goodwill.[42]

Price Promotions

A *price promotion* is a price reduction offered to every purchaser during a limited period. Whereas marketers sometimes require consumers to hand in coupons to get the lower price, price promotions offer a discount to everyone. This discount changes the value equation and therefore encourages customers to try a product when it's first introduced or to buy more of an established product.

Price promotions can be handled in several ways. Some promotions lower prices by a fixed percentage (such as "30 percent off"). Some lower prices by a fixed dollar amount (such as "$10 off"). Others effectively lower the price by providing two or more items for the price of one. Although price promotions can be used to fight back in competitive situations, overuse can severely hurt profitability.

Refunds and Rebates

Refunds take the risk out of trying a new product because under the terms of this type of promotion, the customer may request the return of all or part of the price paid for the item. This is an effective way to encourage first-time purchases. Customers who know they can get their money back often lose some of their doubts about buying a product they've never used before.

Rebates are partial refunds offered by makers of expensive products like cars and appliances. Rebates tip the value equation by reducing the price without lessening benefits, so they're often used to blunt competitive initiatives. For example, Chrysler used rebates to build sales of its minivans in the months before Ford introduced its Windstar minivan.[43]

Refunds and rebates, being limited-time promotions, temporarily enhance the value of a product. Such promotions may persuade customers to switch from competing brands, encourage repeat purchasing, accelerate rate of purchase, and help marketers expand sales in a product category.[44] However, rebates can hurt profits when many consumers wait for a promotion rather than paying the price the marketer counts on in the normal course of business. Therefore, to be effective and profitable, rebates should be used sparingly.

Displays

In-store promotions are becoming increasingly popular among marketers looking for ways of communicating with shoppers who are in the process of deciding what to buy. **Point-of-purchase (POP) displays** are set up in retail outlets to encourage the purchase of a particular product. Responding to the continuing flood of new products competing for customer attention,

point-of-purchase (POP) displays

display material set up in retail outlets to encourage the purchase of a specific product

Point-of-purchase displays are used throughout the world to attract consumers as they shop. This display for Gillette products is in a store in Shanghai, China. With global marketing, producers can offer goods virtually anywhere in the world and set up POP displays to reach shoppers in local stores. What do you think attracts a shopper to a POP display?

marketers see shelf signs, special shelving units, and other POP displays as opportunities to set their products apart from those of rivals. With store or restaurant displays, marketers can grab customer attention, provide product information, and encourage more *impulse purchases*—unplanned, spur-of-the-moment purchases.[45]

Consider how Holland's Van Bloem Gardens uses displays to create a quality image for brand-name flower bulbs sold in U.S. garden centers. Stores usually pile packaged bulbs on a table or dump them into a cardboard carton. Van Bloem has changed that system by standardizing its bulb packages, adding colorful and informative labels, and developing attractive units that allow stores to separate and display bulbs according to type. The displays also come with informative garden-planning brochures to help customers plan where and when to plant the bulbs.[46]

Of course, displays do more than catch the eye of passing shoppers. They also build value-chain relationships by satisfying the merchandising needs of channel partners. Chesebrough-Ponds is one of several manufacturers that design displays specifically for Wal-Mart, for example. Not every display is right for every channel partner at every time, however. Kraft found this out when it offered displays for Kool-Aid powdered drink mix during the winter. Kraft's objective was to expand demand for Kool-Aid beyond the summer season, but many supermarkets refused the displays. "There was a lot of trade resistance," says Matthew Bostwick, Kool-Aid's senior product manager. "People said, 'No way, Kool-Aid is summer.'"[47]

Before you go on . . .

A. Why do marketers give away coupons? Samples?

B. What are frequency marketing programs designed to achieve?

C. How do price promotions, refunds, and rebates change the value equation? How might they affect profits?

D. Why do marketers provide POP displays?

Using Trade Sales Promotion to Add Value

Just as consumer sales promotion adds value to enhance relationships with ultimate consumers, trade sales promotion builds relationships with value-chain partners. Forging closer value-chain relationships is especially important to marketers introducing new products or entering new markets.[48]

Among the most commonly used trade sales promotion techniques are trade allowances, incentives and contests, trade shows, cooperative advertising, and training and marketing support. These techniques are summarized in Table 19.3.

TABLE **19.3** Using Trade Sales Promotion

Technique	How Marketers Use Technique
Trade allowances	Offer cash payments or deductions to reward channel partners for promoting products to customers.
Trade shows	Exhibit products to current and prospective customers and channel partners during industry events.
Incentives and contests	Offer extra rewards when channel partners promote certain products or achieve specific marketing goals.
Cooperative advertising	Share the cost when channel partners feature certain products in their advertisements.
Training and marketing support	Provide training and other marketing support to help channel partners serve customers more knowledgeably.

Trade Allowances

Trade allowances are payments or discounts offered to reward value-chain partners for promoting products to customers through personal selling, advertising, more shelf space, special displays, or other techniques. Many trade allowances take the form of cash payments or deductions. For example, an *off-invoice allowance* lets value-chain partners deduct a certain amount or percentage from invoices on products ordered during the promotion. Sometimes marketers ship extra allotments of products when wholesalers or retailers buy a minimum—for example, "Order 10 cases, get a case free."

At times, some value-chain partners abuse trade allowances by engaging in forward buying and diverting. *Forward buying* is the practice of buying large quantities when products are being promoted with trade allowances and reselling the extras at regular prices after the promotional period has ended. Value-chain partners can fatten their profit margins through forward buying, although costs are incurred because of the need to carry some of the promoted products as inventory until the promotion is over. *Diverting* is the practice of buying large quantities during trade allowance promotions and selling some to another wholesaler or retailer outside the area. Because both forward buying and diverting affect manufacturers' abilities to manage production and value-chain relationships, some manufacturers are cutting back on trade allowances in favor of everyday low pricing.[49]

Incentives and Contests

Another way to boost relationships is by offering value-chain partners extra rewards, through incentives and contests, for promoting certain products or achieving specific marketing goals. *Push money* is the industry term for cash awards to salespeople who sell certain products. As the term suggests, push money is used to support a strategy that gets products through the value chain to customers; specifically, a predetermined reward (such as $5) is paid to salespeople who sell the promoted brand or model.

Issues for critical thinking

Do you think push money is unethical? Might it motivate a salesperson to sell a product that doesn't fit a customer's needs? Should marketers use such promotions? Why or why not?

trade show

an event at which marketers exhibit their products to current and prospective customers and to buyers from various organizations

Trade shows are a critical part of many organizations' sales promotion strategies. These shows give companies exposure to their competitors' goods or services and their promotion strategies, as well as to potential buyers. Trade shows provide marketers with opportunities to display and demonstrate products, answer questions, and gather information about customers for use in a database. How does the image a company projects at a trade show contribute to its success?

Just as marketers use contests to spark excitement among consumers, they can use contests in business-to-business markets to whip up enthusiasm for products among value-chain partners. For example, one 3M contest was geared toward industrial distributors that handle its occupational health and safety products. The contest rewarded distributors' employees with free prizes, including sweatshirts and vacations, for selling 3M products during the promotional period.[50] Such contests can generate much goodwill and strengthen exchange relationships.

The use of incentives and contests can, however, violate the idea of a customer focus. To win prizes, retail or wholesale employees may be overly aggressive in selling products that don't meet customers' needs, and they may downplay other products as they focus on the promoted line. That's why marketers are working more closely with value-chain partners to design and implement appropriate (and ethical) programs.

Trade Shows

A **trade show** is an event at which marketers exhibit their products to current and prospective customers and to buyers from various organizations. Nearly every industry has a trade show at which wholesalers, retailers, and other customers in the value chain can meet manufacturers and examine the latest products. In fact, more than 4,300 trade shows take place every year in the United States and Canada, attracting 1.3 million marketers and 85 million attendees.[51] International trade shows enable marketers from all over the world to get together and exchange product information.

For Ken Schwartz of the Hand Tool Division of Stanley Works in Connecticut, trade shows like the National Hardware Show and the National Home Builders Association Show are wonderful opportunities for supporting relationships with value-chain partners such as home centers and hardware stores. "It's important for us to be there because trade shows are a major communication device," notes Schwartz. Stanley uses both push and pull strategies, coordinating trade sales promotion activities with consumer sales promotion activities for maximum impact.[52]

Exhibiting at a trade show is usually a more cost-effective way to start exchange relationships than making personal sales calls. That's why Vibra Screw, a New Jersey maker of industrial machinery, spends half its IMC budget on one trade show, where its salespeople meet representatives from as many as 350 organizations that are potential customers for the company's products. The company displays working models so visitors to the booth can see how its products operate. It also segments visitors according to size of firm, needs, and position in the organizational buying center, as a means of determining quickly what marketing approach to take. Most important, the company follows up after the show by communicating with every interested visitor within a few days. This creates a solid foundation for an ongoing relationship.[53]

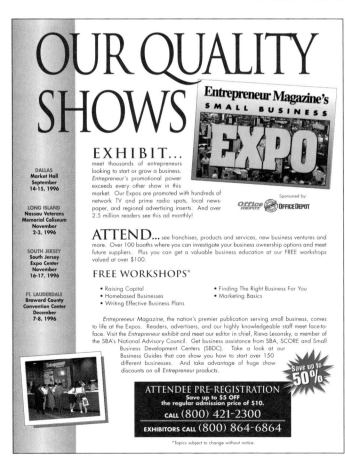

The next section shows how a small business uses trade shows to build strong exchange relationships with its value-chain partners.

SMALL BUSINESS WATCH

Koss meets and greets at the show

For audio and video marketers, the Consumer Electronics Show in January is the trade show of the year, and John Koss, Jr., is always ready. As sales vice president for Koss Corporation in Milwaukee, Koss starts planning his trade show strategy months in advance. His target: buyers from Wal-Mart, Target, Home Depot, and other retail giants that resell Koss's stereo headphones and other audio products to consumers across America. The retailers are out in force at the CES, examining products and talking prices and delivery. "I like to see people we'd otherwise never be exposed to," comments Teri Kohler, a buyer for Target stores.

Knowing the importance of this huge industry event, Koss takes special care with his plans. One recent year, he dubbed the firm's booth "The Quiet Zone," promising a welcome respite from the unrelenting din of the crowd. The availability of Koss noise-cancellation headphones, which visitors could try for themselves, is what earned the booth its name.

Koss provides product and sales training for the representatives who staff his booth. At any given time, at least six are in the booth to talk with retailers. But Koss also makes specific appointments with buyers from key retail partners like Target and Blockbuster Music. He and his reps demonstrate products, explain promotional plans, and—when everything goes just right—take orders for delivery throughout the year.[54]

How might John Koss use direct mail advertising to encourage retail buyers to visit his CES booth?

Koss, like many marketers, exhibits in major trade shows to reach a large number of buyers at one time. In just a few days—in one location—Koss can meet with buyers from a wide variety of stores, both large and small. What kinds of product and value messages do you think Koss can convey to buyers during a trade show?

cooperative (co-op) advertising

an arrangement in which manufacturers share the cost when their products are featured in value-chain partners' advertising

Cooperative Advertising

Cooperative (co-op) advertising, another key tool in trade sales promotion, is an arrangement in which manufacturers share the cost when their products are featured in value-chain partners' advertising. Often, manufacturers agree to share as much as 50 percent or more of an ad's cost. Some peg the exact amount to the volume of purchases by wholesale or retail customers. For example, if a retailer buys $100,000 worth of products, a manufacturer might set aside up to 5 percent of the purchase price, or $5,000, for its share of cooperative advertising. Some manufacturers also provide advertising materials ready to be customized for individual retailers and wholesalers.

Co-op can bolster exchange relationships in two ways. First, it puts dollars in the pocket of wholesalers and retailers that carry the marketer's products, giving them a bottom-line reason to continue the relationship. Second, it encourages a closer link between the marketer's brand and the partner's name, bringing all the power of the brand name to support the wholesaler's or retailer's marketing efforts.

For example, the American Automobile Association (AAA), a Florida-based association of local auto travel clubs, recently started a national television ad campaign. The campaign had co-op advertising support from Walt Disney World, Carnival Cruise Line, and Hertz, among other marketers, and everyone benefited from the relationship. Hertz saw its rental car bookings through AAA travel agencies nearly triple in two years.[55]

Training and Marketing Support

Both wholesalers and retailers can benefit from training and marketing support programs that help them serve their customers better. Many marketers hold in-depth training sessions when they introduce new products and provide ongoing help to channel partners by making available printed materials on product specifications, brushup training on product features and benefits, newsletters with product and sales tips, and other marketing support.

General Motors has committed significant training and marketing support to help dealers market Saturn cars. GM offers weeklong training sessions for employees of Saturn dealerships at the plant in Spring Hill, Tennessee, so dealer personnel can see how quality is built into every car. Employees also receive training in customer pampering and no-haggle selling, two key elements that differentiate Saturn from its competitors. With this training as background, dealers can be more effective in marketing Saturn cars and make the buying experience a pleasure instead of a headache.[56]

Before you go on . . .

A. How can marketers use trade allowances to strengthen channel relationships?

B. What are trade shows and why do marketers use them?

C. What is cooperative advertising and how does it enhance channel relationships?

Public Relations and Relationship Marketing

Public relations (PR) is the process of evaluating stakeholder attitudes, identifying a marketer's products and activities with stakeholders' interests, and using nonpaid two-way communication to reach stakeholder audiences and build long-term relationships. As you can see, public relations is a key IMC tool, and it begins with good marketing research to understand stakeholder attitudes about the marketer, its products, and its policies. PR also causes the marketer to see how its products and procedures fit with the needs and interests of its many stakeholders. Finally, PR opens a dialogue that helps the marketer build stronger, more enduring stakeholder relationships.

Corporate public relations is a broad-based PR effort to build and sustain a general climate of goodwill for the marketer. Although corporate public relations may indirectly boost product marketing efforts, its main thrust is creating a solid foundation for marketing activities through open two-way communication with all the stakeholders of the firm. **Marketing public relations (MPR)**, on the other hand, is more targeted, aimed at customers, channel partners, and other stakeholders that directly influence marketing efforts and results. When part of an IMC program, MPR is an effective and cost-efficient way to support relationship-building strategies and achieve marketing objectives through maintaining an open dialogue.[57]

Be careful not to confuse public relations with publicity. **Publicity** is a subset of public relations that encourages nonpaid media coverage of the marketer and its products. Publicity is one-way communication as opposed to a dialogue. Messages conveyed through publicity are more believable because they're seen as coming from an objective source (the media), compared with sales promotion and advertising messages that are controlled and paid for by marketers.[58]

On the other hand, marketers can't directly influence how, when, where, or even *whether* publicity is communicated. As a result, publicity can be either positive or negative, and it may come about without the marketer's direct involvement or consent. Just ask Intel, which initially ignored postings on the Internet about a flaw in its Pentium computer chip. When the cyberspace discussion had attracted worldwide media attention, Intel said it would provide replacements only when the company deemed them necessary. Facing a rising tide of negative publicity from customers—and critical press coverage—Intel changed its policy and offered free replacements to all Pentium users.[59]

public relations (PR)

the process of evaluating stakeholder attitudes, identifying a marketer's products and activities with stakeholders' interests, and using nonpaid two-way communication to reach stakeholder audiences and build long-term relationships

corporate public relations

a broad-based PR effort to build and sustain a general climate of goodwill for the marketer

marketing public relations (MPR)

communication with customers, channel partners, and other stakeholders that directly influences marketing efforts and results

publicity

a subset of public relations that encourages nonpaid media coverage of the marketer and its products

Issues for critical thinking

Think of a recent negative news report about a product or a marketing organization. What kind of impression did you form from this negative publicity? What can a marketer do to present its side of the story in such a situation?

For a good example of how to fight negative publicity with positive publicity, consider the Florida Division of Tourism's experience. Florida was up against worldwide negative publicity about devastating storms and crimes against tourists, which had kept vacationers away. Knowing that people planning vacations pay attention to reports by travel writers, officials spent

WE CAN FIT ANYONE'S IDEA OF THE PERFECT VACATION.

Florida is full of wonderful, exciting places to visit. By concentrating on the positive, the state hopes to attract more tourists. Ads of this type have been effective in drawing people to the state—not only to visit, but to retire. What message would you suggest that Florida's division of tourism generate to appeal to potential vacationers from other states?

$70,000 to arrange a tour for writers from all over the world. The writers liked what they saw and turned out the equivalent of $23 million in media coverage. Florida also spent $6 million on advertising to get its message across. Soon tourism began to pick up, giving the state a sizable return on its relationship-building investment in publicity and advertising communication.[60]

The "Public" in Public Relations

As Florida's experience shows, PR communication goes beyond customers and prospects. In the broadest sense, the "public" in public relations refers to all stakeholders who have the potential for affecting or being affected by the organization. This includes individuals, groups, government agencies, suppliers, media, stockholders, labor groups, and employees, among other stakeholders.

Note that an important public is inside the firm—employees. Communicating the value of products and practices internally through publicity enables employees to become ambassadors of goodwill, spreading the news to other publics. This word-of-mouth communication can be valuable in building relationships with outside audiences.

Objectives of Public Relations

Marketers can use PR to accomplish a variety of objectives, all of which help establish or enhance relationships with customers and other audiences. These objectives include the following:[61]

- *Raise awareness.* Public relations can help to expose audiences to a marketer and its product, which is particularly important for little-known or new products. For example, few people knew about Breathe Right, made by CNS, a Minnesota medical equipment maker, until San Francisco 49er's star Jerry Rice and other athletes began wearing the adhesive strips on their noses. The plastic strips that look like Band-Aids open nasal passages and help breathing, which allows for better breathing and limits snoring. Publicity about football players using this product helped Breathe Right sales zoom to $3 million within a year.[62]

- *Inform and educate.* Public relations can also provide details about product usage and benefits, which adds value to the product and enhances customer and channel-partner relationships. Butterball Turkey, for example, provides a toll-free hotline for consumers to call with questions about cooking turkeys. Publicizing the hotline makes stores that carry Butterball products look good too.

- *Build trust and understanding.* Central to any marketing relationship is a climate of trust and understanding, an aspect that assumes special priority after negative publicity. Consider the classic case of Tylenol, which suffered a devastating drop in sales when someone put poison into some capsules, causing several deaths. Johnson & Johnson,

Tylenol's maker, acted swiftly and decisively to remove products from store shelves. The pharmaceuticals giant also urged consumers not to use Tylenol capsules, publicized new safety packaging, and offered coupons for free products to replace bottles that consumers had destroyed. Thanks to publicity about these steps, consumers came to trust Tylenol again, and its market share quickly rebounded.[63]

• *Open communication lines*. Through external contacts, PR helps marketers collect and analyze information about the marketing environment. Multinational marketers use PR to clarify local cultural influences, permitting management to maintain an appropriate dialogue with the publics in each host country.[64] With two-way communication, PR builds relationships among customers as well as between customers and marketers. This is the goal of the Harley-Davidson's Harley Owners Group, or HOG, which is made up of 220,000 customers who gather for special events. By sponsoring this group, Harley helps its motorcycle customers connect with each other and express their commitment to the product, which ultimately enhances their relationship with Harley.[65] The company has received much favorable publicity as a result of these efforts.

Public Relations and IMC Strategy

Public relations and publicity play an important role in IMC strategy. Publicity is especially powerful in the introduction stage of the product life cycle, when a marketer wants to build awareness of a new product among prospective purchasers and potential channel partners. As the product moves through the life cycle public relations is a good way to keep up a dialogue, making it possible for the marketer to stay abreast of changes in the marketing environment and to respond to its various publics. Setting up an exciting Web site can generate extra media exposure for a product in any phase of the life cycle.

Publicity is a relatively inexpensive way to reach potential customers. Newspapers, magazines, and the broadcast media are typically eager to report on new and innovative goods and services. However, marketers must still provide reporters with useful information. When they do, as Gary Kvistad did with his perfectly tuned wind chimes, the results can be amazing. How might Kvistad use public relations to keep orders coming in month after month?

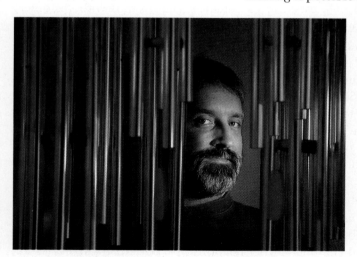

Publicity helped Garry Kvistad establish a new business, Kvistad's Woodstock Percussion, maker of perfectly tuned wind chimes. The entrepreneur enjoyed National Public Radio, so he sent a set of his wind chimes to commentator Susan Stamberg, who invited him to talk about the product on the air. His first radio interview brought in more than 1,000 orders. Following up on this success, Kvistad sent chimes to other radio and television personalities. As a result of interviews on the *Today Show* and other programs, Kvistad has received thousands of calls from consumers and from retailers that want to carry the chimes.[66]

Using Public Relations for Relationship Building

You can choose a variety of publicity techniques to relay your PR message. Three commonly used techniques are news releases, news conferences, and event sponsorship.

News releases are announcements to the media presenting information about the organization, its employees, its products, or its activities. News releases aren't always on paper or audiotape. A *video news release (VNR)*, with videotaped material provided by the marketer, is a good way to get footage on television newscasts. In addition, some marketers send news releases via electronic mail, some use computer-readable CD-ROMs, and some post news on the Internet. The Investment Company Institute, for example, keeps its home page on the World Wide Web supplied with news releases that are useful to radio reporters and others preparing stories about mutual fund investments.[67]

MARKETING IDEAS

Using VNRs to defuse a crisis

For many audiences, seeing is believing. That's why video news releases (VNRs) can be so valuable. In the middle of a crisis, it's important to have a fast, efficient, believable way of getting your points across. Because so many Americans get most of their news from television, VNRs can help marketers communicate using a medium that audiences watch and trust.

For example, after reports of injuries caused by its Colorblaster 3-D spray art toy, Kenner Products cooperated with the U.S. Consumer Safety Product Commission in a voluntary recall. The company produced a VNR to show what might happen if children didn't operate the toy correctly and to explain the company's recall decision. Then it beamed the VNR via satellite to stations around the country, many of which immediately put the tape on the air. This demonstration of Kenner's concern for child safety reassured customers that they could still trust the company, minimizing the damage to customer relationships.

For its part, PepsiCo used a series of VNRs to respond to reports that syringes had been found in Diet Pepsi cans. The first VNR showed Pepsi's high-speed bottling process and demonstrated that tampering was impossible during this phase of production. The second VNR featured Pepsi CEO Craig Weatherup. The third VNR was the clincher: it included footage, shot in a Colorado store, of a customer inserting a syringe into a Diet Pepsi can. Television stations used that VNR to expose the tampering as a hoax—and the crisis was defused.[68]

What kinds of crises do you think VNRs are best suited for? Why?

Event sponsorship is often an effective way for a marketer to get positive public exposure. Tostitos, a Frito-Lay product, is the primary sponsor for the annual Fiesta Bowl football game. Brand familiarity is important to marketers, so many organizations consider having their brand name displayed at various events an important part of a comprehensive IMC. From your perspective, is event sponsorship an effective promotional strategy for a product like tortilla chips? Why?

For especially newsworthy events, many PR people call *news conferences*, meetings of reporters and representatives of the marketing organization during which new products, major organizational changes, and other information can be announced. Unlike news releases, which communicate information from a marketer to the news media, news conferences encourage two-way communication as reporters ask questions and interact with the marketer's managers and representatives.

A third way to communicate with customers, channel partners, and other publics is through *event sponsorship*, a PR technique to build excitement and goodwill by backing a sports, cultural, agricultural, or entertainment event that draws significant public attention. The point is to link the marketer and its products with an event that is anticipated and enjoyed by the public, strengthening stakeholder relationships and, many times, providing extra media coverage to extend the benefits.[69]

For example, Visa, the credit card marketer, is a sponsor of the annual Indianapolis 500 race. "We are looking for additional exposure," explains Sandra Stairs, Visa's corporate relations manager, and "racing has millions of fans around the world." Another Indy 500 sponsor, motor oil marketer Valvoline, pays for the right to supply racers with its products and to sponsor a racing team; in addition, it advertises during the race. This event sponsorship puts Valvoline's brand name in front of 400,000 on-site fans as well as millions of international viewers who see the race on television—no matter which racer wins.[70]

Before you go on . . .

A. Why are public relations and publicity considered to be believable yet uncontrollable communications?

B. How does corporate PR differ from marketing PR?

C. How do marketers use PR techniques to reach various publics?

Summary

1. **Differentiate between consumer and trade sales promotion.**

   Consumer sales promotion provides incentives that encourage ultimate consumers to purchase specific products, whereas trade sales promotion provides incentives to encourage channel partners to support certain products.

2. **Show how sales promotion can build consumer, trade, and internal relationships.**

   Sales promotion is used in consumer markets to encourage product trial, stimulate additional buying and usage, encourage purchase and usage of related products, reinforce marketing communication for faster response, and build a marketing database. Sales promotion is used in the trade to gain channel partners, encourage stronger support, induce partners to carry more stock, and strengthen channel relationships. Sales promotion is used internally to build commitment, encourage closer teamwork, and shape employee attitudes and behavior.

3. **Analyze the strategic balance between sales promotion and advertising.**

   Marketers are emphasizing sales promotion over advertising for several reasons. First, retailers have more power because of their knowledge of customer buying, and consolidation has concentrated this power, making trade sales promotion more important. Second, since today's consumers are increasingly price sensitive, consumer sales promotion can help marketers address heightened interest in better value. Third, marketers under pressure to recover investments in new products are using sales promotion for faster results. And fourth, sales promotion is attractive because its results can be measured more easily than advertising results. Increasingly, however, marketers concerned about the prospect of sales promotions hurting profits are looking for ways to enhance value while maintaining profit margins.

4. **Identify the eight major consumer sales promotion techniques.**

   Eight major consumer sales promotion techniques are coupons (documents for product discounts), samples (products offered free or at a low price to allow customers to experience the benefits), frequency marketing programs (ongoing promotions that reward customers for repeat purchasing), sweepstakes and contests (which invite consumers to win prizes), price promotions (short-term price reductions available to all customers), refunds and rebates (which return some or all of the purchase price), premiums (gifts offered free or at a low price to customers who buy a product), and displays (which encourage purchasing while the customer is in the store).

5. **Demonstrate the use of the five major trade sales promotion techniques.**

   Five major trade sales promotion techniques are trade allowances (payments or deductions to reward channel partners for promoting products), incentives and contests (rewards for channel partners that promote products or achieve marketing goals), trade shows (gatherings at which marketers exhibit products to channel partners and customers), cooperative advertising (in which manufacturers share the cost when their products are featured in channel partners' advertising), and training and marketing support (to help channel partners serve customers).

6. **Distinguish between public relations and publicity used in integrated marketing communication.**

   Public relations (PR) is the process of evaluating stakeholder attitudes, identifying a marketer's products and activities with stakeholders' interests, and using nonpaid two-way communication to reach stakeholder audiences and build long-term relationships. In contrast, publicity is a subset of PR that encourages nonpaid media coverage of the marketer and its products. It is one-way communication, as opposed to PR's dialogue.

7. **Show how public relations can be used to reach stakeholder audiences.**

   Three PR techniques commonly used to reach stakeholder audiences are news releases (announcements to the media about the organization, its products, and other details), news conferences (meetings between reporters and a marketer's representatives to announce new products and other information), and event sponsorship (a way of building excitement and goodwill by backing a sports, cultural, agricultural, or entertainment event that draws significant public attention).

KEY TERMS

consumer sales promotion **565**

cooperative (co-op) advertising **581**

corporate public relations **582**

coupon **571**

frequency marketing programs **572**

marketing public relations (MPR) **582**

point-of-purchase (POP) displays **576**

premium **575**

public relations (PR) **582**

publicity **582**

sales promotion **564**

sample **572**

trade sales promotion **566**

trade show **579**

Skill-Building Applications

1. The value to the marketer of a sales promotion depends greatly on how consumers value it. Bring to class as many sales promotion pieces as you can (coupons, price promotions, and the like) and make a case for or against each of them from the consumer's perspective.

2. List all the publics you can think of that have an influence on the success of the Walt Disney Company. How can Disney use public relations to understand and respond to the needs of its publics?

3. The Million Man March brought nearly a million African American men to Washington, D.C. Publicity created much of the excitement around the event. If you were organizing such an event, how would you use publicity to influence the attitudes of participants? Nonparticipants?

4. Should service marketers such as MCI and Sprint use trade shows to reach businesses in various industries? Are there more effective or less expensive ways for telecommunications firms to reach business customers? Explain your reasoning.

5. How can a local optician use consumer sales promotion to compete against chains such as Lenscrafters? Identify three specific ideas for starting and reinforcing customer relationships in a pressured competitive environment.

6. Exxon suffered a great public relations setback with its handling of the oil spill in Alaska in 1989. What can the company do now to reverse the impact of that negative publicity and to show its concern for protecting the environment?

Getting Involved in Marketing

1. *On Your Own* Find and analyze one example each of consumer and trade sales promotion. Who are the specific target audiences? What does the marketer want to achieve? What is the incentive being offered? Is a time limit mentioned? How does each promotion build or enhance the relationship? Prepare a brief report about your findings.

2. *On Your Own* Imagine that as the marketing manager for Doritos corn chips, you're introducing a new spicy barbecue flavor to extend your product line. Suggest a sales promotion to encourage consumers to try the new product. Next, suggest a trade promotion to encourage grocery stores to stock the product. How might you balance sales promotion and advertising to get the most out of your promotional budget when reaching both audiences?

3. *Find Out More* Visit a trade show or find an article about a large trade show, such as the Consumer Electronics Show. Who are the exhibitors? Who are the customers visiting the show? What are the ob-

jectives of the exhibitors? The customers? How do exhibitors invite visitors to their booths? If you were an exhibitor, what would you do to attract visitors, and how would you continue the relationship with visitors after the show?

4. *In a Team* With two or three classmates, plan a two-month sales promotion to encourage local Pizza Hut customers to order two pizzas, not one, for home delivery. Consider local competition, your target audience, the media you'll use to convey your message, other Pizza Hut marketing efforts, and the potential impact on profitability. Think about the timing of your sales promotion activities, as well. Present your plan to the class and get feedback on its strengths and weaknesses.

5. *In a Partnership* Pair up with a classmate to debate the pros and cons of consumer price promotions, using a specific product category as an example. Research the product, develop a profile of the target audience, and outline likely channel relationships. Hold the debate in front of the class.

Which side was more persuasive? Why?

6. *In a Team* Working with other students, prepare a PR plan for introducing a new product, such as a high-performance car, a walk-in medical care facility, or a shampoo. Identify the publics you want to reach, your specific objectives, and the techniques you'll use to build relationships. How will you measure results? Would you consider using a home page on the World Wide Web? Why or why not?

VideoCase   Mobil Builds Relationships with Many Publics

All kinds of stakeholders care about the environment, and Mobil wants them to know about its actions to prevent pollution. From consumers, employees, and dealers to government regulators, media commentators, and fishing enthusiasts, many publics are on the gasoline marketer's list of stakeholders. These publics have the ability to directly affect the company's success, which is why Mobil uses public relations (among other marketing techniques) to build and strengthen stakeholder relationships.

Mobil has several goals for its PR programs. One goal, in the aftermath of well-publicized oil spills by a number of gasoline marketers, is to increase trust and understanding by focusing attention on the company's efforts to protect the environment.

By using video news releases and other PR tools, Mobil can demonstrate how its employees and dealers are joining with others to prevent air, water, and land pollution. This encourages stakeholders to believe in the company's commitment to environmental protection and see Mobil as a trustworthy gasoline marketer.

A second goal is to inform and educate stakeholders about specific antipollution activities. People may not know the purpose of the vapor recovery systems used at gasoline pumps, for example. By explaining how such systems work and why they are important, Mobil helps consumers understand why its gas dealers use special pumping equipment. When consumers become aware of the steps that the company and its dealers take, they may be more open to starting or continuing relationships with Mobil.

A third goal is to invite participation in Mobil activities. Communication through PR accomplishes more than merely providing information. It also invites stakeholder participation in pollution prevention activities, inviting a two-way dialogue with the marketer and active support of its efforts. For example, once consumers realize that certain Mobil gas stations recycle used motor oil, they will know what to do with the used oil from their oil changes. They will also be encouraged to recycle the empty plastic containers from motor oil at the Mobil gas stations where they were purchased. Thus, consumers will be pleased by Mobil's efforts and encouraged to join in protecting the environment.

Protecting the environment is an important component of Mobil's social responsibility agenda. Because so many stakeholders are deeply concerned about air, water, and land pollution, Mobil not only supports antipollution activities, it also uses PR to communicate this support and encourage participation. In this way, Mobil is able to strengthen its bond with stakeholders and pave the way for long-term success.

Skill-Building Applications

1. Assume you work in Mobil's PR department. How many uses can you find for a videotape demonstrating the company's antipollution efforts? In each case, indicate the public you want to reach and the goal(s) you want to achieve.

2. As a member of Mobil's PR department, would you invite dealer participation in specific PR efforts? Would you invite environmental activists to participate? Explain.

3. If Mobil wanted to use event sponsorship to tout its environmental efforts, which events would you suggest? Why? How would you communicate the event sponsorship to Mobil's publics?

4. Why would individual Mobil dealers want to publicize their local recycling efforts? What can you suggest to publicize a local dealer's program for collecting and recycling used motor oil?

5. What consumer sales promotions might dealers use to encourage customers to buy Mobil oil at a local gas station and return used oil there for recycling after a do-it-yourself oil change? How do you think such an environmental protection promotion would build customer relationships?

6. Should Mobil use cooperative advertising to encourage individual dealers to run ads about specific environmental protection actions benefiting local communities? Is this a good idea? If so, how could Mobil accomplish this?

Team Project

With other students, outline a marketing program to communicate the company's antipollution activities using a combination of PR and sales promotion. Identify the stakeholders who will be the target audience for this program. What goals should be set? How will results be measured? What tracking and follow-up would your team recommend? Prepare a team presentation to explain your ideas to the class.

20

Personal Selling, Sales Management, and Customer Relationships

Learning Goals

After you have read and studied this chapter, you should be able to:

1. Contrast transaction selling with relationship selling, and inside selling with outside selling.
2. Show how customers and marketers benefit from sales teams and sales partnering.
3. Discuss the process of identifying and qualifying prospects before the sales call.
4. Explain why salespeople make presentations during sales calls.
5. Demonstrate how follow-up after the sales call strengthens customer relationships.
6. Analyze the methods of organizing the sales force and determining its size.
7. Explain how to set standards for sales force evaluation.

PROFILE

How Capitol Concierge builds service sales

Mary Naylor's marketing motto is "Consider it done." She's done it all in the course of starting Capitol Concierge, a service business employing 85 concierges in office buildings around Washington, D.C. The service handles everyday chores like booking airline tickets and picking up dry-cleaned clothes for harried office workers. Naylor built a $5 million business on personal selling to two target markets, businesses and individuals.

The entrepreneur's first target was businesses that manage office buildings. Research showed that building managers would pay a monthly fee if they could add to tenant value by offering on-site concierge services. However, when Naylor presented her capabilities during sales calls, she ran into the same objection again and again. Businesses wanted some proof of her expertise. After eight months of sales calls, she signed her first building, and more followed. Then competitive pressures forced her to cut monthly fees, and she began focusing on her second sales target—individuals.

Many individuals were already using their building's concierge for a single service, but Naylor knew she could get additional business by offering personal service geared to solving specific customer problems. "It takes a lot of trust for someone to hand over their to-do list," she observes. So Naylor's concierges began making sales presentations one office at a time, explaining how they could make life easier for executives and office workers.

To better satisfy the needs of individual customers, Naylor created a computerized marketing database of customer wants, purchases, and interests, which she's expanding with the help of customer questionnaires. Now concierges can consult the database and offer customers selected services as they're needed. Thanks to personal selling—backed by top-quality personal service—Mary Naylor's Capitol Concierge is growing rapidly.[1]

Personal selling is a demanding but rewarding way to build long-term exchange relationships. In this last chapter covering integrated marketing communication, you'll take a closer look at how personal selling has moved beyond individual transactions to relationship selling. Then you'll explore techniques for keeping satisfied customers throughout the value chain. Included are concepts such as total quality sales, sales teams, sales partnering, and sales profitability. This chapter ends with a discussion of the role of sales management.

Personal Selling: Seeking Customers and Keeping Customers Satisfied

It takes time, professionalism and a caring attitude to build a trusting relationship with the customer.

Jim Quinn
executive vice president of sales, Tiffany & Co.[2]

One of the most important tools in the integrated marketing communication (IMC) toolbox is personal selling. **Personal selling** is an interpersonal communication process in which a marketer's representatives identify prospects, determine needs, present product information, gain commitment, and follow up after sales to maintain customer relationships.

Unlike advertising, sales promotion, and public relations, which are all *nonpersonal* forms of marketing communication, personal selling is based on *personal* contact with customers and prospects. As the Profile shows, Mary Naylor meets with building managers when she's selling Capitol Concierge's services, and her concierges use in-person or telephone contact to sell specific services to individuals in each building.

Why personal selling? The personal contact provides a good opportunity to analyze customer problems and present product information to help solve those problems. Such contact is important to customer-driven marketing. Although other IMC techniques permit two-way communication, personal selling adds the person-to-person dimension that enhances in-depth understanding and regular exchange of ideas. This is especially critical in many business-to-business marketing situations, where complicated problems, large purchases, and customized, technological solutions are the norm.

Personal selling is a growing field with many career opportunities. Nearly 15 million people in the United States hold sales jobs, and the number is expected to increase 24 percent by the year 2005. This growth is due, in part, to the need to bring a marketing message to a variety of customer segments and geographic markets. It's also due to the increasingly complex nature of customer needs and available products. Making a good match requires more personal sales attention than ever before.[3]

Salespeople play a vital role in customer-oriented marketing organizations. Consider their role at PPG Industries, the Pittsburgh-based marketer of glass products for industrial customers worldwide. PPG's salespeople are trained to explain how new technology and other changes will affect customers' needs and to enlist customer participation in creating products to meet those emerging needs. As one PPG sales manager observes, "The pivotal function of the sales organization is to exercise leadership with, and on behalf of, the customer." This means that salespeople represent customers and their needs to the marketer's organization, mustering internal support to serve and satisfy customers. Salespeople also represent the marketer and its products and problem-solving capabilities to customers.[4]

But salespeople aren't the only individuals responsible for sales; today every employee plays a role. Ball Corporation believes this so strongly that its aluminum container division foots the bill to bring prospects to its plant in Muncie, Indiana. "All of us together can sell better than one of us can sell individually," says Clifton Reichard, Ball's director of business development. Production people, not salespeople, squire prospects around, answering questions and introducing engineers, research scientists, and other employees. Well over half the prospects who visit become customers, says Reichard.[5]

What's more, the role of personal selling within marketing is changing. Not so long ago, marketers saw selling as applying pressure and persuasion to get a customer to buy then and there. Although this *hard sell* approach often alienated customers, some marketers found it an effective (if ethically

personal selling

an interpersonal communication process in which a marketer's representatives identify prospects, determine needs, present product information, gain commitment, and follow up after sales to maintain customer relationships

As this ad indicates, effective relationship marketing and relationship selling demand proper training and active participation by everyone in the organization. With training, sales personnel learn how to improve productivity, increase performance, and ultimately boost profitability. Understanding the lifetime value of a customer helps keep employees focused on delighting customers with outstanding goods and services. Why do you think companies sometimes fail to get all of their employees committed to relationship building with customers?

lifetime customer value

the total amount of money that a customer is likely to spend with a marketer throughout the ongoing exchange relationship

transaction selling

the marketer focuses on making an individual sale to a customer

questionable) way of increasing sales and profits.[6] Now hard sell is largely on the way out. Marketers have come to see personal selling as the process of getting and keeping customers by helping them make purchases that satisfy their needs over the long term.

General Motors' Saturn division knows the difference between selling a car and helping a customer buy. "Sales consultants" at Saturn dealers are trained to listen, answer questions, explain the one-price policy, and encourage comparison shopping. Instead of using traditional car sales techniques, such as haggling and high pressure, the consultants offer a single price and treat customers with respect before, during, and after the sale. Mechanics, office staff, and all other dealer employees are also ready to listen and respond to customer needs. "Our goal," says one Saturn dealer, "is to exceed customer expectations." This approach has had car buyers flocking to Saturn.[7]

From Transaction Selling to Relationship Selling

Why is GM turning away from traditional methods of selling cars? The company has been studying customer loyalty and purchasing patterns, especially the lifetime value of a customer. **Lifetime customer value** is the total amount of money that a customer is likely to spend with a marketer throughout the ongoing exchange relationship. As mentioned in Chapter 1, GM found that the lifetime value of one loyal customer is $400,000, including purchases of cars, service, and auto loan financing.[8] These numbers showed that GM would profit more in the long run by fostering customer goodwill to build loyalty and enduring relationships than by pushing to make an immediate sale. You can read more about lifetime customer value in Appendix B.

GM, like many marketers, is moving away from transaction selling and toward customer-oriented relationship selling. Table 20.1 contrasts the two forms. With **transaction selling**, the marketer focuses on making an individual sale to a customer. In this approach, each transaction is a discrete selling encounter designed to promote the one-time purchase of a specific

TABLE **20.1** Contrasting Transaction Selling with Relationship Selling

In transaction selling, the salesperson . . .	In relationship selling, the salesperson . . .
focuses more on selling than on learning about the customer's needs;	focuses more on learning about the customer's needs than on selling;
does more talking than listening;	does more listening than talking;
works toward adding buyers and sales through persuasion, price, presence, and terms.	works toward long-term customer relationships through credibility, responsiveness, and trust.

product. Once the sale has been completed, the relationship may well end. That's how many marketers, including car dealers, traditionally approached personal selling. Frequently, however, transaction-oriented sellers, pressing to complete sales, alienated customers. That customer, dissatisfied with the buying experience, will likely buy from another marketer the next time around. As one Saturn dealer points out, "You can shear a sheep many times in its life, but you can only skin it once."[9]

These days, salespeople from IBM, Saturn, and many small firms use *consultative selling*, acting as consultants, providing information, and helping solve customer problems. Consultative selling positions the sales force as a source of knowledge and ideas, not just products.[10] By serving as problem solvers, the salespeople move beyond a single sale to forge longer term relationships with their customers.

Consultative selling is part of **relationship selling**, a process whereby salespeople learn about and satisfy customer needs during an ongoing series of transactions that result in long-term exchange relationships. The initial sale is only the start of a continuing dialogue designed to build mutual trust and commitment. Then, each succeeding transaction may build on its predecessors to reinforce the relationship.[11]

Roles in Personal Selling

Sales personnel fill three roles in sales transactions. **Order getters** make both initial sales that start relationships with new customers and additional sales that strengthen relationships with existing customers. They actively investigate the needs of customers and prospects, show how their organization's goods and services can satisfy those needs, and follow up after sales to be sure customers are satisfied. Order getters play a particularly important role in organizational marketing, where multiple contacts may be needed to analyze a customer's complex or technical requirements and then to customize an appropriate value package ◄──┘ **(p. 11)**.

For example, at Tchibo, a German coffee manufacturer, salespeople don't just sell to retailers, their customers in the value chain. They also apply category management ◄──┘ **(p. 459)** to help retailers boost profitability of coffee products on the store shelves. In addition, they look for ways to help stores stock what shoppers want while minimizing inventory investment.[12]

Order takers accept new orders and process repeat orders. Unlike order getters, who seek out new customers and take a problem-solving approach to satisfying their needs, order takers handle routine transactions. They accept orders from new customers, help existing customers reorder products they've purchased before, and work to expand the number or type of products customers buy. For instance, customers who call to order from a Spiegel catalog deal with order takers. These salespeople answer questions about products, accept orders, and make payment and shipping arrangements.

Sales support staff don't get or take orders, but they handle a variety of tasks to supplement the efforts of order getters and order takers. *Missionary salespeople* are support staff that pave the way for sales by providing customers and prospects with details about new and existing products. *Technical specialists*, who lend their expertise to the analysis of customer problems, help customers get the most benefit from products they purchase.

relationship selling

a process whereby salespeople learn about and satisfy customer needs during an ongoing series of transactions that result in long-term exchange relationships

order getters

salespeople who make both initial sales that start relationships with new customers and additional sales that strengthen relationships with existing customers

order takers

salespeople who accept new orders and process repeat orders

sales support staff

people who don't get or take orders but handle a variety of tasks to supplement the efforts of order getters and order takers

Telemarketing is now used as a selling tool on a global basis because it allows marketers to reach consumers and businesses at a relatively low cost. What products are particularly well-suited to this form of personal selling? Why?

Inside and Outside Selling

Selling by order getters, order takers, and sales support staff can take place in the field (outside selling), over the counter (inside selling), or by telephone (telemarketing). **Field sales** are personal sales calls made at the customer's home or business location. Field calls are the most costly way to sell. The cost of one such call on a business averages $252—and it has been increasing as much as 10 percent per year.[13]

Most business-to-business marketers that offer complex, technical, or expensive products use field salespeople to make buying as convenient as possible for their customers. Some consumer products, such as beauty aids, are also marketed through field sales. For customer convenience and, often, for privacy, salespeople go to either homes or offices.

Over-the-counter sales are made in retail or wholesale locations when customers visit the facility. Instead of the salesperson visiting the customer, the customer goes to the wholesale or retail site to look at the products, get more information, and complete the purchase. Sales at Computer City stores involve over-the-counter selling, as does selling at other retail and wholesale locations.

In contrast, **telemarketing** is personal selling in which contact between sales representatives and customers takes place by telephone. For many marketers, and their customers, telemarketing is the most convenient and least expensive method of completing a person-to-person sales transaction. The cost of telemarketing is about 20 percent of the cost of field sales, and thanks to technological advances such as automated dialing equipment, it has been dropping steadily.[14]

Issues for critical thinking

What annoys consumers about telemarketing? What ethical issues are raised by automated dialing equipment that can call consumers over and over? What can marketers do to respond to consumer complaints and add value to telemarketing sales efforts?

field sales

personal sales calls made at the customer's home or business location

over-the-counter sales

personal sales made in retail or wholesale locations when customers visit the facility

telemarketing

personal selling in which contact between sales representatives and customers takes place by telephone

With *outbound telemarketing*, sales personnel dial out to reach prospects and customers. For example, at Massachusetts Envelope, a $25 million company, telemarketing reps call smaller businesses, freeing field sales personnel to concentrate on larger accounts. In one year, the telemarketing effort doubled small-account sales—and its lower cost boosted sales profitability too.[15]

With *inbound telemarketing*, sales personnel are ready to receive calls from customers. This is a popular way to make sales and provide support to customers who respond to catalogs, offerings on the World Wide Web, media advertising, and other marketing communications. For example, Singapore's Creative Technology, which makes Sound Blaster and other computer parts, set up an inbound telemarketing center in Ireland to support its sales efforts in Europe. Telemarketing reps who speak English, French, German, Spanish, and Italian answer questions and arrange after-sale support. Since the opening of this telemarketing center, European revenues have doubled.[16]

Personal Selling in the Value Chain

Personal selling in all its forms has a place in every link of the value chain ◀━━┘ **(p. 50)**. At the upstream end, raw materials suppliers use personal selling to market to manufacturers. In turn, manufacturers use personal selling to market to channel partners, such as wholesalers and retailers, who then sell to organizational customers or ultimate consumers. When selling to channel partners, smart marketers try to help customers satisfy *their* customers as part of a comprehensive customer-driven approach.

Understanding not only the customer's customer but also the customer's situation—the environment, the opportunities, and the challenges—is a powerful competitive advantage for any sales force.[17] For example, salespeople at Nalco, an Illinois-based marketer of water-treatment chemicals, use laptop computers to analyze prospect data and suggest improvements. One rep recommended that a paper mill change the chemicals in its water to boost paper quality and cut costs. That suggestion made Nalco and its products more valuable to the mill—and helped the mill better satisfy its customers as well.

Similarly, James River, which markets Dixie cups and other paper products, helps its retail partners by providing marketing data to boost store sales of all paper products. With the help of salespeople from James River, Lucky Stores was able to grab market share in paper goods from competing stores.[18]

Direct selling is selling directly to customers rather than through channel partners. This direct contact can be face-to-face or by telephone. For example, a Royal Bank of Scotland subsidiary markets automobile insurance in the United Kingdom by telephone. Because it sells to consumers without having to maintain sales offices or pay channel partners, its prices are lower than those of its rivals.[19]

Total Quality Selling for Customer Satisfaction

As you learned in Chapter 2, total quality management means putting quality at the heart of every organizational operation ◀━━┘ **(p. 48)**. In personal selling, total quality means keying sales activities to customer needs and buying behavior, doing whatever is necessary to help customers buy and use products that satisfy their needs. Two-way communication is vital, because dialogue helps marketers shape and refine the sales process to make buying more satisfying. Sales staff who use total quality principles influence and monitor their organizations' internal activities to ensure that sales meet or exceed customer expectations. To make total quality selling effective, marketers have to view their own salespeople as internal customers whose needs must be met so that they can serve external customers.[20]

Lonnie Carver exemplifies total quality sales. As a top salesperson for Entergy Corporation, a New Orleans electric utility, Carver sells heating and cooling equipment and support services to resellers in the Southeast. She'll meet with dealers whenever and wherever they need help. She knows her products, her market, and her customers. She saves customers time by com-

direct selling

selling directly to customers rather than through channel partners

Team selling in certain industries is becoming increasingly popular. Specialized skills and knowledge possessed by team members allow them to better inform and meet the needs of customers. What products or services can you identify that would benefit from team selling? Why?

pleting documents on her computer, submitting them, and following up internally to get things done properly—and on time. For their part, fellow Entergy employees treat Carver like a valued internal customer. When she asked the credit department for fast turnaround on one dealer's application, the response came through in half a day. That's total quality sales at work.[21]

Total quality sales also means putting together the right value package to satisfy customer needs. For a customer who has a complex or technically challenging problem, one product may not be enough. To satisfy such customers, marketers often turn to system sales. **System sales** are sales of a special value package that bundles goods and services to satisfy a specific customer's needs. For example, a computer marketer may sell a value package of hardware, software, training, and service. System sales provide more value because the package components are designed to work together to meet each customer's specific needs.[22] At times, a salesperson will bundle products from other manufacturers to offer customers a total package that best meets their needs.

Sales Teams and Sales Partnering

Just as one product may not be sufficient to satisfy a customer, one salesperson may not have all the expertise required to service a particular customer. And when a marketer is working with an organizational customer's buying center **(p. 207)**, one salesperson may not be able to maintain all the contacts needed to initiate and sustain the relationship. That's why many marketers are reducing reliance on individual salespeople in favor of teams. A **sales team** is a group of employees from various functional areas who work together to ensure that customer needs are satisfied throughout the sales process.[23]

Companies such as DuPont, Digital Equipment, Data General, and Tandem Computers use sales teams to add value for customers and, at the same time, broaden internal support for meeting customer needs. From the customer's perspective, team selling provides access to more specialists who can help solve problems. At Reebok, teams that include support staff help retailers (their customers in the value chain) do a better job of selling the company's athletic shoes. One expert analyzes how each Reebok model is selling in each store. Another works with retailers to come up with strategies for boosting shoe sales.[24]

As effective as they can be in the right situations, sales teams aren't appropriate for every marketer, product, or customer. Individuals may do a better job than teams selling simple, long-established products and products that don't require after-sales service. Also, a team can sometimes delay, not shorten, the sales cycle, causing confused communications as well.

However, when customers buy in teams, when competitors sell in teams, and when the product is highly technical or requires ongoing support, you can use sales teams to give your customers the support they need to benefit from your products. The added value strengthens customer relationships and creates a bond that competitors will have difficulty breaking.[25] Here's how one small business used teams to boost productivity and satisfy customers.

system sales

sales of a special value package that bundles goods and services to satisfy a specific customer's needs

sales team

a group of employees from various functional areas who work together to ensure that customer needs are satisfied throughout the sales process

SMALL BUSINESS WATCH

Teaming up for sales and satisfaction

The telephones were ringing off the hook at Electronic Label Technology, a Tulsa, Oklahoma, marketer of bar code printers. However, the phone lines were jammed not by customers placing orders but by salespeople calling for answers to customers' questions. The calling started CEO Tim Wright thinking about how customer service should begin on the very first sales call. That insight led Wright to the use of cross-functional sales teams.

Now when a salesperson visits with a customer or prospect to demonstrate the product or make a presentation, a technical expert goes along, ready to provide details and answer questions. Once the sale has been made, Wright sends in a new cross-functional team of hardware and software specialists who, with the salesperson, provide after-sale support. The team approach makes customers feel that they have the answers they need to make informed buying decisions—and the support they need to wring the most benefit from their purchase.

Sales teams have been so effective at building sales for Electronic Label Technology that its competitors had to adopt the same approach. "Without the technical people to prove that their systems worked," says Wright, "they couldn't compete with us."[26]

Can you see how Electronic Label Technology's use of sales teams supports an ongoing relationship with its customers?

A growing number of customers are taking a more active role in the sales process. **Sales partnering**, also known as *collaborative selling*, is an approach in which the customer forms an alliance with a supplier to tailor the sales process and meet ongoing customer objectives. The salesperson is treated as an integral part of the buyer's organization. This is customer-driven marketing at its best. The partners work together to investigate problems, identify opportunities, and develop workable solutions. This fosters two-way loyalty and an enduring, mutually profitable relationship.[27]

Xerox and General Electric take sales partnering a step further. They buy from each other, so each enrolls its salespeople in the other's employee training sessions. "To really focus on customer needs, you must understand more about them than how they use your product," explains Waylon Hicks, executive vice president for marketing and customer relations at Xerox. The ongoing partnership allows General Electric (as the customer) to shape the sales process used by Xerox so Xerox is more responsive to GE's ever-changing problems and needs. The same holds true for Xerox as the customer, with GE acting as the supplier.[28]

Personal Selling and Profitability

High sales don't necessarily mean high profits, because all sales are *not* equal. Even when you sell at the same price to two customers, your profit may be significantly higher on one sale than the other because of the costs involved in servicing the customer, such as delivery costs. To balance the investment in a customer relationship against the expected profits, you must look closely at costs and at lifetime customer value.[29]

sales partnering
an approach in which the customer forms an alliance with a supplier to tailor the sales process and meet ongoing customer objectives

TABLE **20.2** How Dun & Bradstreet Segments for Sales

Segment of Market	Number of Prospects	Size of Sale	Sales Approach
High potential	10,000	$10,000+	Personal sales visits
Medium I	40,000	$3,000 to $10,000	Telephone sales
Medium II	200,000	Under $3,000	Direct mail
Small businesses	240,000	Under $3,000	Direct mail

Add up all the costs associated with selling, producing, and delivering the product as well as providing support after the sale, and you'll find some customers more costly to serve than others. As mentioned earlier, field sales are more costly than telemarketing sales. That's why some marketers sell differently to each customer segment. For example, Dun & Bradstreet segments the market for financial services information according to the size of the potential sale, as shown in Table 20.2. To keep costs in line with the size of the sale, D&B uses field sales with businesses that are expected to spend the most on D&B services, while businesses that spend less are covered by telemarketing or direct mail.[30]

Because exchange relationships aren't based on a single sale, it's important to think about the lifetime value of a customer when determining profitability. For example, a loyal customer of Domino's Pizza is worth about $5,000 over a 10-year period. Similarly, a loyal customer of Marriott hotels will spend $125,000 during 10 years. Looking at lifetime customer value has helped Joe Girrard sell more new cars and trucks than any other car salesperson in the world. His success, mentioned in the *Guinness Book of World Records*, is based on seeing every customer "as a long term investment." Girrard doesn't just calculate the profit from the immediate sale—he also counts the profitability of future sales that make up the relationship.[31]

Cross-selling is a way to boost the profitability of a customer over the long term. *Cross-selling* means selling a number of different products to customers who initially buy a single product. Norwest Financial, a bank headquartered in Minneapolis, is a master at cross-selling financial services to its consumer and small business customers. Bank employees are trained to determine whether a customer who opens a checking account also needs a savings account, a mortgage, or a credit card. Cross-selling helps Norwest cover the high fixed costs of maintaining branch banks. It also strengthens customer relationships by giving customers more reasons to remain loyal to the bank.[32]

Before you go on . . .

A. What do marketers and customers gain from relationship selling?

B. Why do marketers use sales teams?

C. How important are sales costs and lifetime customer value when determining the profitability of a customer?

The Sales Process and Relationship Building

As you've seen, personal selling is a key element in forging and sustaining ongoing relationships with channel partners, organizational customers, and ultimate consumers. Although the interaction between the customer and the salesperson or sales team is critical, it's only one aspect of the three-part sales process, shown in Figure 20.1. Before the sales call, the marketing and sales staff does much planning and research. They identify and qualify prospects, gather background research, and plan the approach. During the sales call, the salesperson determines customer needs, presents information, answers questions and objections, and gains customer commitment to close the sale. After the sales call, the sales staff follows up to ensure customer satisfaction and to maintain customer relationships.

F I G U R E   **20.1**   The Sales Process

The sales process involves a series of activities before, during, and after the sale. Note that the process is ongoing, rather than finite, because what salespeople do during and after each sale affects their ability to maintain or renew relationships by making additional sales to these customers.

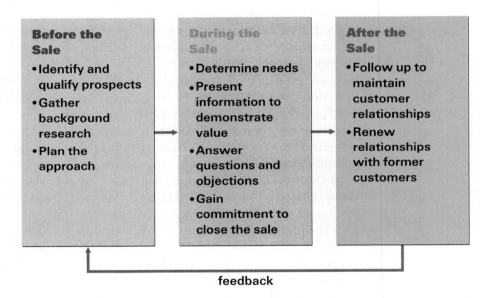

In customer-oriented marketing organizations, planning and follow-up usually take more time than the actual sales call. Using these procedures, the sales and marketing staff can better anticipate customer needs, be prepared to demonstrate how goods and services will benefit the customer, and check on customer satisfaction after the sale.[33] Marketers can also learn how to improve the sales process to strengthen relationships with current customers and renew relationships with former customers.

Before the Sales Call

The most important sales activities take place *before* any interaction with prospects or customers.[34] Marketers determine which consumers or organizations are prospective buyers and investigate in detail what these prospects may need. Upon completion of the planning and research, salespeople are ready to make the sales call.

prospecting

identification of potential customers who may be qualified to purchase the product being sold

qualified prospect

one who not only needs the product but also has the financial ability and the authority to pay for it

Identifying and Qualifying Prospects

The first stage of the sales process is **prospecting**, the identification of potential customers who may be qualified to purchase the product being sold. Marketers can search for prospects in a variety of ways. People who respond to ads, visit a Web site, attend special events, and indicate an interest in other marketing communications can be good prospects. Other ways to prospect include asking customers, suppliers, and channel partners for referrals; searching online databases; and asking community contacts.[35] Some salespeople prospect by *cold calling*—contacting by telephone or in person people who have had no previous contact with the marketer. This practice, however, is both expensive and inefficient.

The names obtained from prospecting are known as *leads*, until the marketer confirms that the individuals or organizations need its goods or services. The next step is to qualify leads, to determine whether any further steps should be taken to make a sale. A **qualified prospect** is one who not only needs the product but also has the financial ability and the authority to pay for it.[36] These three qualifying factors act as a screen, weeding out nonprospects and leaving a smaller group of people who are more likely to become profitable customers.

Salespeople can't call on every prospect at once, so it's important to organize prospects' names to reflect some order of priority. Methods used to prioritize prospects include the size of the potential sale and the expected profitability of the sale. NSS, a small software marketer in New Hampshire that markets to banks, ranks prospects according to the timing of the purchase. An "A" prospect is one that will make a buying decision within a year, a "B" prospect is one that will make a buying decision within two years, and so on. Now NSS's 10 salespeople have an objective, uniform way of deciding which prospects to call on first.[37]

Today, successful selling in other countries means learning not only the language but also the local customs, such as bowing in Japan. The extra work this requires is well worth the effort given the level of worldwide competition. To research prospects in other countries, you can check books or magazines, attend seminars, or go online to use Internet sources. In what other ways can technology be applied to overcoming language and cultural barriers to selling globally?

Gathering Background Research

After leads have been found, it's time to gather the background research needed to plan the sales call. This research is used to profile each prospect. For organizational prospects, that means gathering demographic, geographic, and behavioral information. It also means researching the financial health of the buyer, as well as determining who is in the buying center, the timing of purchases, and buying criteria. In addition, marketers look at the prospect's situation, problems and needs, rivals, and suppliers. For sales to individuals, demographic, geographic, and behavioral information is relevant, as are data on buying influences such as lifestyle. This research goes into the marketing database for use before, during, and after the sales call.

Where will you find this information? Secondary sources **(p. 144)**, such as those described in Chapter 5, can provide a wealth of details. Sales expert Brian Tracy advises asking prospects directly for background materials. In addition, field sales staff usually have firsthand knowledge of markets and prospects. Timely information is especially important when marketing in other countries, where research data may be difficult to obtain.[38]

Part of the salesperson's homework before a call consists of deciding on the specific objective of the visit or telephone call. The objective may be to get the customer to agree to a product demonstration or to negotiate purchasing terms. For example, John Heitzenroder of Occidental Chemical, a chemical and plastics manufacturer in Dallas, often sets fact-finding as the objective for initial sales calls. He probes for the prospect's specific needs, and he may not even discuss individual products during the first meeting. Yet he's already looking beyond the first sales call to the second one, which has another objective. Regardless of the specific objective for a sales call, the ultimate aim is to forge a relationship and pave the way for future contacts.[39]

Planning the Approach

After doing research, you must plan the approach to take during the sales call. This is where you apply your research to make the sales call more effective. Think about whom you should call on first. When selling to organizational customers, consider how to approach a gatekeeper, who controls access to other members of the buying center. Think, too, about what a decider wants to know and what a user wants to know, and determine how influencers might affect purchasing or usage decisions. Factor in the need for more than one sales call, since most business customers don't actually buy until the seventh sales call.[40]

As you plan the approach, work out how to set an appointment for the sales call. Some salespeople send letters or e-mail before calling for an appointment. Others qualify prospects and ask for appointments during the initial call. When making an appointment, explain why the prospect will benefit from a relationship with you. Previewing the value you'll bring to the relationship attracts the prospect's attention and builds interest in the upcoming sales call.

During the Sales Call

Precall planning and research form the foundation for the sales call. After a brief period of introduction, the salesperson or sales team focuses on understanding what prospects need, presenting information that adds value relative to those needs, answering questions and objections, and gaining commitment to close the sale. Good communication skills are a must. Salespeople working with customers in other countries or cultures need to be sensitive to language, cultural, and political differences that can interfere with communication.

Determining Needs

What, exactly, do prospects (and customers) need and want? Background research can uncover some possible needs, but prospects will certainly have more to say. Here's where good listening skills are especially important, along with probing to explore prospects' problems, situations, and expectations. This exploration may take more than one meeting. In fact, a good salesperson is on the lookout for unmet needs and changes in needs throughout the relationship.

New technology is changing the look of many sales presentations. This Crystal Eyes Projection System from Stereographics enables a salesperson to show customers product concepts in three dimensions (3-D). With laptop computers, salespeople can show photos, video, and other kinds of exciting and informative images to potential buyers. What products do you think would benefit most from the use of computer-assisted presentations? Can you think of any that would not?

Selling is truly a problem-solving process. During the first sales call, agents for Northwestern Mutual Life Insurance, based in Wisconsin, determine a consumer's insurance needs by asking questions according to a structured survey. They use a conversational tone, listening carefully as consumers answer. By the end of the survey, the agent and the consumer have laid a solid foundation of trust and rapport on which to build a relationship. In later sales calls, agents can ask about changes in customer needs.[41]

Presenting Information to Demonstrate Value

Once salespeople have come to understand prospects' needs, they show how their goods or services add value. The value may lie in the way a product solves a particular problem, helps prospects achieve their objectives, or provides other benefits. The *presentation* is the point in the sales call at which the salesperson delivers the marketing message, showing how products add value.

One traditional presentation method is the **canned sales presentation**, based on recall of memorized information. This type of presentation can help less experienced salespeople remember what to say, and it's often used in telemarketing, where salespeople have only a few moments to deliver a message. Canned presentations, however, do not prepare salespeople to be responsive to prospects' questions or comments. In contrast, a **need-satisfaction presentation** is tailored to satisfying the needs of the customer or prospect. Properly used, such presentations can position salespeople as a source of knowledge and ideas, which adds value beyond that of the product itself.[42] Some salespeople use canned presentations to start a conversation, but switch to a need-satisfaction mode as the sales process progresses.

Answering Questions and Objections

canned sales presentation

based on recall of memorized information

need-satisfaction presentation

tailored to satisfying the needs of the customer or prospect

More often than not, prospects will have questions and objections during the presentation. Some may want more details about product capabilities or other aspects of the value package. Others may have *objections*, voicing doubt or disagreement about statements made in the presentation.[43] Objections won't necessarily prevent prospects from purchasing. In fact, objections open the door for sales personnel to show competitive superiority, explain benefits, justify price by emphasizing quality and value, and learn more about an individual prospect's buying process. The best salespeople anticipate objections and provide answers—even before prospects raise the issues.[44]

When a prospect raises an objection, savvy salespeople listen carefully and ask questions to determine what is at issue. At that point, the salesperson can decide to:

- *Postpone responding.* This is appropriate when later parts of the presentation will address the prospect's concerns.

- *Transform an objection into an advantage.* If, for instance, a prospect objects that a product is too big, the salesperson can explain that larger equipment is easier to operate.

- *Acknowledge the objection's validity.* But don't stop there. This is an opportunity to discuss a related benefit.

- *Present additional information.* Show a relevant research report or some other data that will allay the prospect's concerns.

- *Tactfully deny the objection.* If the objection is based on a mistaken impression or inaccurate information, now is the time to offer clarification—in a polite and respectful way.

Gaining Commitment to Close the Sale

After all objections and questions have been answered, it's time to gain the prospect's commitment. **Closing** is the part of the sales process in which the salesperson obtains a commitment from the prospect. The entire sales call has been pointed in this direction, as prospect and sales personnel come to agreement about the product's value in satisfying needs. If the objective is to schedule a product demonstration, closing means getting the prospect to commit to a demonstration. If the objective is to negotiate a contract, closing means getting the prospect to sign the contract. Of all the actions that salespeople take, closing is one of the most difficult to master.[45]

To find out whether the prospect is ready to buy, many salespeople start with a *trial close*, a question or statement designed to elicit a reaction that shows the prospect's readiness to commit. A typical trial close might be a question about delivery, color preferences, or another decision that prospects have to make when buying a product. Depending on the answer, the salesperson can move ahead to a firmer close or provide additional information to answer new questions or objections.

Closing is not a mechanical process: salespeople must be sensitive to customer comments and reactions. There are a variety of closing techniques. Using the *direct close*, for example, the salesperson makes a direct request for commitment. With the *assumptive close*, the salesperson progresses on the supposition that the prospect is committed.

In an *alternative-decision close*, the salesperson asks which decision the prospect prefers, gaining commitment to one or the other. This close might take the form of a question such as "Will that be cash or charge?" The alternatives might be delivery dates, payment options, or other choices. With the *standing-room-only close*, the salesperson emphasizes the urgency of making a commitment to take advantage of limited quantities, special pricing, or another temporary condition. Of course, using this close when the limitations don't exist is unethical.

closing
the part of the sales process in which the salesperson obtains a commitment from the prospect

After the Sales Call

Closing may be the climax of the sales call, but it's not the end of the process. Turning a prospect into a long-term customer sets in motion a new series of activities. Now the marketer gears up to satisfy the customer as agreed. The salesperson also has much work ahead, following up to maintain customer relationships and renew relationships with former customers who have taken their business elsewhere.

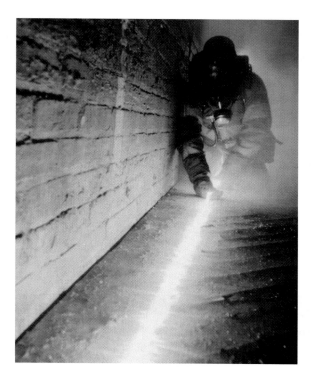

Flexlite is a life-saving product that firefighters can lay down as they enter a burning building and then follow to retrace their steps out of the building in thick smoke. By offering a lengthy product guarantee and replacing any Flexlite strips that didn't work properly, marketer Paul Manley was able to build strong customer relationships and expand his small business. Why is personal selling the best way to get this product into the hands of firefighters across the country? How else might Manley market this product?

Following Up to Maintain Customer Relationships

After the sale, the salesperson (or another member of the sales team) follows up to be sure the customer is satisfied. Checking internally first, the salesperson finds out whether the goods were shipped on time or the service performed as agreed. Checking then with the customer, the salesperson learns whether the product delivery, installation, and performance have met expectations. This is also the time to ask about any problems, arrange for additional services the customer may need, and—equally important—thank the customer.

Thorough, timely follow-up shows customers that the salesperson cares. It also reinforces the trust and commitment the salesperson and the customer bring to the relationship. Finally, it can head off or minimize post-purchase dissonance, the doubt that sometimes grips customers who have just made an investment in goods or services. By following up to ensure customer satisfaction, the salesperson brings each sales transaction to a successful conclusion, improving the odds that the customer will buy again.[46]

Considering the lifetime value of a customer—and the expense of finding and selling to new customers—you can see why salespeople work hard to maintain customer relationships. The more ways you can satisfy your customers, the stronger the relationship. That's why many salespeople look for ways to add value to every sale. They may offer service contracts, consulting services, or additional goods that enhance the benefits from the original purchase. Satisfaction usually leads to repeat purchasing, which in turn builds customer loyalty throughout the relationship.

Follow-up helped Paul R. Manley, the owner of Flexlite in New Jersey, stay on top of problems that threatened his small business. The product, a plastic rope studded with tiny lightbulbs, tended to turn black with use. To reassure customers, Manley offered a five-year product guarantee and followed up relentlessly. "I kept my customers by replacing anything that went wrong, listening to their complaints, admitting my mistakes, and asking for another shot," he says. "Almost everybody gives you another chance." By following up and continually improving his product, Manley kept his customers and added more to exceed $1 million in annual sales.[47]

Issues for critical thinking **Think about a time when you left a relationship with a marketer. Did the marketer try to keep you as a customer? What else could this marketer have done to renew the relationship?**

Renewing Relationships

Once a customer, always a customer? Not necessarily. Customers do leave, because of pricing, product problems, service difficulties, changes in needs, or other reasons. These are expensive losses, for marketers have invested resources to satisfy customers and build long-lasting relationships. Customer defections may also signal a deeper problem that can threaten relationships with other customers. That's why the best marketers don't let customers slip away unnoticed. They have a service recovery plan ◄━━┛ **(p. 327)** to deal with customer problems. They also make a point of finding out why customers leave, so they can take steps to renew the relationships.

For example, Rich Gevertz, the director of sales for the AmeriSuites Hotel in Irving, Texas, moved quickly when he heard that Honda North America, which spends $40,000 a year on employee accommodations, was leaving. He asked his contact at Honda, "What can we do to regain your confidence and win back your business?" The executive listed several areas of dissatisfaction and told Gevertz not to call back until all the problems had been solved. Gevertz's staff quickly got to work on the problems. Two months later, he invited Honda to inspect the improvements. The result: the hotel regained the customer's trust and renewed a profitable relationship.[48] Adding value through personal selling is important all over the world, as the next section shows.

Professional salespeople such as Jean Louis Decaix add special value to the relationship that they build with their customers. Decaix's technical knowledge, reliability, honesty, and problem-solving ability help customers get the best results from the products they purchase. How can marketers apply the concepts of internal marketing to support the efforts of their salespeople?

GLOBAL ISSUES

Adding value helps customers say "oui"

Jean Louis Decaix knows how to help his customers say "oui" in a sales situation. As the top salesperson in France for Advanced Technology Laboratories, he sells $250,000 digital ultrasound imaging machines to hospitals and radiology centers. Each sale can be a year or more in the making, not counting after-sale services. To build and maintain customer relationships before, during, and after the sale, Decaix works hard to add value during every contact.

"Since our sales cycle is very long, I have to build long-term relationships based on trust, respect, and value," explains Decaix. "In the early stages, I offer the value of listening; later, I use the value of references, connections, and testimonials." He also offers a great deal of information about the product and the technology. In this way, he trains prospects to associate added value with the product and the company—and to expect extra value as part of the ongoing relationship.

In addition, notes Decaix, "Good teamwork creates more value for our customer." When he's getting to know a prospect, he works with the people in the organization's buying center to develop internal support for the purchase. After the purchase, he puts together special teams to help customers solve thorny technical problems. The problem-solving value that Decaix adds helps customers better serve *their* customers. Ultimately, that's what encourages customers to say "oui" to Decaix again and again.[49]

How might Decaix use his added-value approach to renew relationships with former customers?

Salespeople need every advantage they can get when making presentations, and technology is increasingly being used to achieve a competitive edge. For example, the Z-Noteflex Multimedia Presenter enables salespeople to show sight and sound presentations anywhere. The display screen is detachable so it can be placed in front of prospects in an office or home, on the factory floor, or at a trade show. What kinds of products could be effectively featured on a laptop-based multimedia presentation during a personal sales call?

Technology in the Sales Process

Thanks to technology, salespeople are able to work more efficiently and effectively before, during, and after the sale. Computers, online services, fax machines, cellular telephones, electronic mail, and many other advances are powerful tools that help sales personnel work smarter and faster to satisfy customers and enhance relationships. In fact, Pfizer's International Pharmaceuticals Group found that applying technology to the sales process cut costs drastically and enabled salespeople to make more calls and book more sales.[50]

Before and after the sale, salespeople can use computers to comb online database services for details about prospects, customers, markets, and competitors. By referring to computerized marketing databases, they can more thoroughly plan upcoming sales calls. Computer software also helps salespeople organize their calling schedules. And with cellular telephones, e-mail, and online services, sales staff can quickly and easily communicate with prospects and customers.[51]

Computers are an integral part of many sales calls. For example, salespeople at Genentech, a biotechnology company, take laptop computers along on sales calls to physicians. Part of the value these salespeople bring to the relationship is access to timely information. They use their computers to find medical articles and technical reports to help keep doctors up to date. In turn, this information helps doctors determine how their patients can benefit from Genentech's growth hormone Protropin. The reps also use their laptops to speed doctors' questions to company specialists via electronic mail for fast response.[52]

A growing number of salespeople use personal computers to make multimedia presentations. These computerized presentations can include CD-ROM product catalogs, video clips or slides of product demonstrations, and taped customer testimonials. In addition, salespeople can use their PCs to connect with company systems and check on available product stock, place orders, schedule delivery, and review previous orders.[53] Some tap into their company's electronic data interchange ◄—— **(p. 210)** systems to transmit orders and requirements instantly. As a result, orders are more accurate—and they're filled and delivered more quickly. After the sale, salespeople can use electronic means to check on orders, track deliveries, check invoicing, and handle other follow-up chores.[54]

Before you go on . . .

A. How do field sales, over-the-counter sales, and telemarketing work?

B. Why and how do marketers qualify prospects?

C. What does it mean to "close a sale"?

D. How do marketers renew relationships with former customers?

Sales Management for Customer Satisfaction

Like every other aspect of IMC, personal selling must be carefully managed and integrated with the organization's overall marketing activities. This is the role of **sales management**, a coordinated set of actions to plan sales efforts, organize the sales staff, and develop an effective, motivated sales force. In today's increasingly global marketing environment, managing a far-flung, multinational sales force can be a real challenge. At the same time, even start-up firms can use sales management to keep sales moving in the right direction.

Sales Planning

All sales activities are driven by the *sales plan*, a document that identifies the target market, lays out sales objectives, and details the actions, budget, and timing needed to reach those objectives. Although it's based on the marketing plan, the sales plan focuses more narrowly on personal selling interactions with prospects and customers. A sales plan starts with a situational analysis of the marketing environment, including competitive pressures. It also includes details about the target market, including the estimated size and composition of market segments where prospecting will take place.

So that the sales force knows exactly what results are expected, every sales plan includes the organization's overall sales objectives for a given period. In turn, each salesperson is responsible for helping to set and achieve individual sales objectives. These objectives can be expressed in terms of customer satisfaction, market share, unit or dollar sales of products, sales to new markets, new customer acquisition, more sales to existing customers, customer loyalty, and profitability. For example, Massachusetts Envelope sets separate sales objectives for field sales and telemarketing sales. During a recent year, field sales aimed for $22.5 million in sales, while telemarketing aimed for $2.5 million.[55]

The sales plan also summarizes the *sales strategy*, the steps the sales force will take to achieve the sales objectives. This strategy describes how salespeople will work within the target market and within each customer segment, including the use of field sales, over-the-counter sales, and telemarketing. It also indicates how salespeople should prioritize and approach customers and prospects as well as how they will be assigned to work with customers and prospects.

sales management

a coordinated set of actions to plan sales efforts, organize the sales staff, and develop an effective, motivated sales force

Sales Force Organization and Size

A marketing sales staff can be organized in a variety of ways. The most common methods of organizing sales personnel, shown in Figure 20.2, are by geography, product, and customer. No one method is best for all marketers, and some marketers use a combination of methods. The choice depends on the number and type of customers and prospects, the way customers prefer to buy, the number and type of products sold, the number and types of markets targeted, the competitive situation, and the size of the sales force.

To organize a sales force by *geography*, the marketer divides its target market into distinct districts or territories, such as sections of a city or country,

FIGURE **20.2** **Three Methods of Sales Force Organization**

Marketers can organize salespeople in three ways: by geography, by product, or by customer. A food marketer, for example, might organize (1) by geography, assigning salespeople to the eastern, central, or western region of a market; (2) by product, assigning salespeople to sell one of three product lines; or (3) by customer, assigning salespeople to work with one of four types of customers.

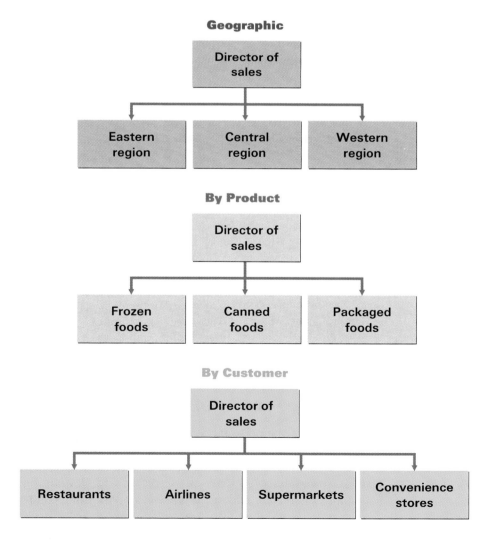

and assigns salespeople to each area. Because sales personnel don't have to travel far, they get to know the local marketing environment, and they're available when customers need them. One limitation of this organizational method is that the local sales staff may not have the specialized knowledge required by some customers.

To organize by *product*, the marketer assigns a separate sales force to each product line. For example, ConAgra, the giant U.S. food marketer, has more than a dozen sales forces, each handling a particular product line.[56] With a limited number of products to sell, salespeople quickly gain in-depth product knowledge to share with prospects and customers. However, customers who buy more than one product wind up seeing more than one rep, which can be confusing and inefficient.

When marketers organize by *customer*, they assign salespeople to customers of specific types or, on occasion, to specific customers. This is how Eastman Kodak's Consumer Imaging division assigns its sales force. Each Kodak salesperson sells film and related products to specific customers in the marketing channel, such as photography stores or drug stores. For even sharper focus on a specific customer's needs, many marketers organize by *major accounts*, assigning salespeople to strengthen relationships with certain customers. Kraft Foods, ConAgra's competitor, uses this organization approach, aligning each of 300 sales and marketing support teams with a single retail chain.[57]

How many salespeople does a marketer need? Too many will drive expenses sky-high, while too few will hold back the selling effort. A common way of determining the number of sales personnel needed is by applying the equalized workload method. The **equalized workload method** is a formula for determining the size of the sales force based on the number of sales calls to be made, the number of customers, and the average number of calls per salesperson. As you can see in Table 20.3, a marketer that segments its customers by size needs 11 salespeople to make 22,000 calls yearly. If any part of the formula changes—for example, if there is an increase in the number of customers—the marketer can recalculate, then adjust the sales force accordingly.

TABLE **20.3**   **Using the Equalized Workload Method**

Customer or Prospect Size	Call Frequency		Number of Accounts		Number of Sales Calls per Year
Large	2 per month	×	200	=	4,800
Medium	1 per month	×	1,000	=	12,000
Small	1 per quarter	×	1,300	=	5,200
			Total sales calls per year:		22,000

Assuming that each salesperson makes 2,000 calls per year, the size of the sales force should be

$$\frac{\text{total sales calls}}{\text{average yearly sales calls per salesperson}} = \text{number of salespeople}$$

$$\frac{22,000}{2,000} = 11$$

Sales Force Development

equalized workload method

a formula for determining the size of the sales force based on the number of sales calls to be made, the number of customers, and the average number of calls per salesperson

Because of the personal nature of selling, who does the selling is a key issue in sales management. Moreover, how salespeople are trained, supervised, and motivated to sell will make all the difference between meeting and missing sales objectives. By selecting and developing a top-quality sales force, marketers can set themselves apart from competitors—and lay the groundwork for relationships that turn prospects into long-time customers.

Recruitment and Selection

What do marketers look for when hiring sales personnel? The specific characteristics favored by individual marketers vary, but one study shows that the best salespeople have the following characteristics:

- *They influence others.* Salespeople should be able to influence the attitudes and actions of prospects, customers, and colleagues.
- *They reach high.* Top sales personnel set ambitious goals and work hard to achieve them.
- *They show initiative.* Selling takes much persistence and creativity. Salespeople have to be enthusiastic self-starters.
- *They communicate effectively.* Strong communication skills are a must, including the ability to listen and ask probing questions.
- *They go to bat for customers.* To be successful, a salesperson must be truly interested in satisfying customers.
- *They have self-confidence.* No matter what the challenge, the sales rep must move ahead with poise and professionalism.[58]

Before hiring sales staff, sales managers should clarify the specific tasks salespeople are expected to handle. Then they can match individual candidates' skills and experiences against the particular job description. Not all marketers use highly analytical recruiting and selection procedures, however. When recruiting sales personnel, the Nordstrom department store chain looks for friendliness above all else. Nordstrom managers use their judgment when hiring, and employees receive little training in customer relations.[59]

Training

New salespeople need training to learn about the marketer's products, sales strategies, customers, and target market. On average, companies invest more than $6,000 over nearly four months to train each new salesperson.[60] Then, in the spirit of continuous improvement, marketers keep up the training schedule. Ongoing training helps experienced salespeople sharpen their selling skills and stay abreast of new products, industry trends, new technology, and changes in customer requirements.

For example, the American Bankers Insurance Group (ABIG) in Miami markets life insurance through banks and retail channel partners. Most of its contracts with channel partners span three years or more, so ABIG salespeople use relationship selling. The company's initial training focuses on building credibility, solving customer problems, and negotiating effectively. Every other week, sales managers reinforce key concepts in full-day training sessions. In addition, the sales force receives a week of training every six months. Such extensive training has helped ABIG grow sales 20 percent per year for the past five years.[61] The following case, which features a very different type of maketer, shows how 3M involves customers in planning for sales training.

Telemarketers need ongoing training in product knowledge and updates on how to handle customer inquiries and orders. Sales training, in general, is a continuous process because new products are constantly being introduced, as are new methods of promotion. How will telemarketers be influenced, if at all, by the Internet?

Applying the Concepts

3M asks customers about sales training

Who knows better than customers whether salespeople need to brush up their skills? 3M, the Minnesota-based global marketer of industrial and consumer products, had long conducted customer surveys to get feedback about products. But it had never asked about its sales personnel, who play a crucial role in assessing customer needs and suggesting solutions. So a few years ago, 3M decided to find out how its salespeople were doing—and give them the tools they need to do better. 3M's sales training process is named ACT, which stands for assessment and analysis, curriculum content, and training transfer.

Here's how ACT works. First, key customers are asked to complete a written questionnaire in which they evaluate 3M sales personnel on selling skills, knowledge of goods and services, teamwork, and commitment to quality. The answers are scored by an outside training company, which lets each salesperson know what customers said and suggests additional training that would address any problems.

Next, each salesperson works with his or her sales manager to develop an individualized training curriculum. Sales personnel can choose among various 3M seminars and workshops, self-paced study courses, or university courses. To help the sales staff transfer this new knowledge to sales situations, 3M managers help reinforce sales skills, coach those who need additional help, and encourage staff members to coach each other.

What makes ACT so powerful is that it's "customer-focused, just-in-time, on-demand sales training," notes Janet Quinto, sales training manager for the company's Dental Products Division. Because ACT is ongoing, it leads to continuous improvement, enhancing customer relationships and helping sales personnel to achieve both personal and professional goals.[62]

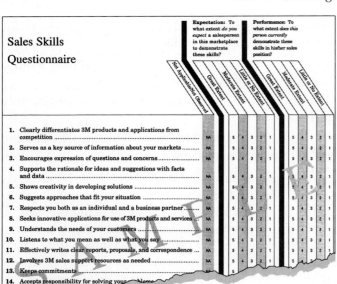

Customers use this form to evaluate the sales effectiveness of 3M salespeople. The sales training at 3M is ongoing, and sales personnel are fully supported by their managers through individualized coaching. What questions would you add to this form to determine whether 3M salespeople are indeed customer-driven and relationship-oriented?

Make marketing decisions

1. How might 3M extend the ACT program to telemarketing reps who serve small business customers?

2. What specific sales skills should 3M ask customers to rate?

3. Should 3M ask former customers to rate sales personnel? Why?

4. Should 3M have all customers rate all sales personnel every year? Explain your answer.

Supervision

The managers who supervise sales personnel play a key role in sales management. They're responsible for deploying the sales force to call on both prospects and customers. In addition, they act as coaches, helping salespeople manage calling schedules, develop customer-specific strategies, and

straight salary compensation

salespeople receive a fixed amount of money weekly, monthly, or yearly

straight commission compensation

salespeople are paid according to results such as sales or profits

combination compensation

salespeople are paid a salary plus commissions, bonuses, or other incentives for performance

progress toward sales objectives. These days, sales managers are emphasizing empowerment, allowing salespeople flexibility in accomplishing their objectives and satisfying customers. "I leave my people alone as much as I can," says Jay Sferra, a sales manager for AT&T. "They know I trust them to do a great job. I'm here to be called on when they need help."[63]

Motivation and Compensation

Day in and day out, as salespeople work to establish and maintain customer relationships, they have to stay motivated. In the course of calling on prospects and customers, they're likely to feel frustration and rejection as well as accomplishment. Although the motivation to perform comes from within, sales managers can help inspire sales staff in a number of ways. First, they can provide salespeople with a clear, specific description of the sales job. Second, they need to effectively supervise sales efforts. Third, they should build on the salesperson's interest in achieving objectives. And fourth, they have to design a reward system that reinforces success.[64]

Many marketers offer noncash rewards such as plaques, gifts, and trips to motivate sales personnel. In terms of cash compensation, salespeople can be rewarded in three ways: straight salary, straight commission, and a combination of salary and commission or another incentive. These three methods are compared in Table 20.4.

With **straight salary compensation**, salespeople receive a fixed amount of money weekly, monthly, or yearly. The amount doesn't vary, no matter how much the salesperson sells. In contrast, with **straight commission compensation**, salespeople are paid according to results such as sales or profits. Thus, salespeople are paid more when they achieve or exceed the expected results.

With **combination compensation**, the marketer pays a salary plus commissions, bonuses, or other incentives for performance. About two-thirds of all U.S. companies use this method to motivate salespeople to develop customer relationships without pressure to make immediate sales. For example, Rega Plaster sells for Marshall Industries, an electronics distributor. When Marshall switched from straight commission to a combination of salary and bonus based on profits, Plaster found new motivation to sell. "Now I can spend time with smaller accounts and nurture them, and I can do it with a clear mind and conscience," she says.[65] Some compensation plans, however, may tempt salespeople to stray into ethically questionable areas, as the next section shows.

T A B L E **20.4** **Comparing Sales Compensation Methods**

	Straight Salary Compensation	Straight Commission Compensation	Combination Compensation
Advantages	Tight control over compensation costs; lowers pressure to make immediate sales; easy to administer	Rewards high achievers; can vary the commission to promote selected products or target other segments	Offers salespeople some security plus incentives for meeting objectives; has flexibility to change emphasis when needed
Disadvantages	Less incentive to achieve or exceed objectives; costs fixed regardless of sales results	Salespeople feel pressure to make sales; sales costs can vary widely	Can be complex, costly to administer; costs are less predictable

ETHICS & SOCIAL RESPONSIBILITY

Ethical issues in personal selling

Unlike many marketing activities, personal selling is a relatively private situation, involving direct, one-to-one contact with customers. Under these circumstances, and knowing that they're being evaluated on sales performance, not on how they get their results, some salespeople may yield to the temptation to cut ethical corners. The pressure to act unethically is even greater when competition is fierce, when a troubled economy is dampening sales opportunities, or when salespeople are eager to reach high objectives or earn commissions. Here are some of the ethical questions raised in connection with personal selling.

1. Should a salesperson withhold information about a product's potential problems, or promise what the company cannot deliver?

2. Should a salesperson sell an inappropriate product or quantity to win a contest, make an objective, or earn a bonus?

3. Should a salesperson disparage a competitor or a competitor's products, spy on competitors, or tamper with rival products?

4. Should a salesperson misrepresent the purpose of a call?

Some of these issues are addressed by laws governing marketing actions. For example, telemarketing salespeople are legally required to say they're selling something; they cannot claim to be conducting a survey. However, some of the issues are less clear-cut. That's why marketers need to set and communicate ethical standards for employees to follow, establish reasonable objectives and compensation rules, and stress fairness and honesty in dealings with customers.[66]

How can a marketer determine whether its salespeople are acting ethically?

Sales Force Evaluation

Salespeople, like other employees, need feedback about their performance so they can track progress toward individual and organizational objectives. Sales force evaluation provides this feedback and turns up performance problems that may impair results. It is important to work with sales personnel to define specific, measurable standards for individual and team results.

Marketers can set both qualitative and quantitative standards for sales performance, linking the measures to sales objectives. *Quantitative standards* are objective standards derived from calculable measures such as number of sales completed, number of products sold, number of customers contacted, and average profit per sale during a particular period. In some cases, each salesperson or team has a **sales quota**, a minimum level of sales or profits to be attained. At IBM, however, the large number of products complicated the quota system. These days, IBM's standards are far simpler: it has one quantitative standard, based on profitability.[67]

Qualitative standards are tied to more subjective measures of sales performance such as customer satisfaction, service quality, or repeat purchases. For example, IBM has a single qualitative standard: customer satisfaction. Setting qualitative standards helps guard against overzealous sales personnel who might otherwise push for sales to make quotas or other standards.

sales quota

a minimum level of sales or profits to be attained

Typically, standards for team performance are a blend of individual and team measures. Consider what Baxter International, the Illinois-based marketer of health care products, does with its teams. The company wants total team cooperation in selling and servicing customers, so it sets customer satisfaction standards and rewards the whole team for meeting customer needs. In addition, it sets standards for tasks such as invoice accuracy and delivery speed, which gives individuals specific results to seek.[68]

It is also important to analyze performance by comparing actual results against standards. After this evaluation, marketers should reward sales accomplishments and pinpoint areas for improvement. Some marketers extend the analysis and evaluation to the sales process itself. "We have always measured sales performance in terms of end results [such as] quota, growth, and new accounts," says one Hewlett-Packard sales manager. "That may not be the best way to measure performance. We also need to look at the steps of the [sales] process and measure those. If we do well at the steps, the end results will absolutely come."[69] In today's market, those end results depend on pleasing customers every time.

Before you go on . . .

A. **Why do marketers set sales objectives?**

B. **In what three ways can a marketer organize its sales force?**

C. **Which compensation methods can marketers use to reward sales personnel?**

D. **What types of standards do marketers set for sales force evaluation?**

Summary

1. **Contrast transaction selling with relationship selling, and inside selling with outside selling.**

   In transaction selling, the marketer focuses on an individual sale to a customer. In relationship selling, the marketer wants to learn about and satisfy a customer's needs during an ongoing series of transactions that form a long-term customer relationship. Personal selling can occur in the field (outside selling), over the counter (inside selling), or by telephone (telemarketing).

2. **Show how customers and marketers benefit from sales teams and sales partnering.**

   A sales team is a cross-functional group of employees who work together to satisfy customer needs throughout the sales process. Teams can add value for customers and broaden support within the marketer's organization for meeting customer needs. Teams help marketers strengthen customer relationships and keep competitors at bay. Sales partnering is an approach in which the customer forms an alliance with a supplier to tailor the sales process and meet ongoing customer objectives.

3. **Discuss the process of identifying and qualifying prospects before the sales call.**

Before the sales call, marketers use prospecting to identify potential customers that may be qualified to purchase the product being sold. Marketers turn leads into qualified prospects by confirming that they need the product, can pay for the product, and have the authority to pay for it.

4. **Explain why salespeople make presentations during sales calls.**

The presentation is the point in the sales call at which salespeople deliver the marketer's message, showing how their goods and services add value for the customer. Canned sales presentations are based on recall of memorized information. In contrast, need-satisfaction presentations are tailored to stress satisfying the needs of the customer or prospect. It is possible to use both a canned presentation and a need-satisfaction presentation at different stages in the selling process.

5. **Demonstrate how follow-up after the sales call strengthens customer relationships.**

When the salesperson checks after the sale to be sure that the customer is satisfied, the follow-up shows that the salesperson cares. This essential step in the sales process reinforces the trust and commitment between the salesperson and the customer; moreover, it can head off or minimize postpurchase dissonance and solve problems that have developed. Finally, follow-up improves the odds that customers will buy again.

6. **Analyze the methods of organizing the sales force and determining its size.**

The most common methods of organizing sales personnel are according to geography, product, and customer. Many marketers use the equalized workload method to determine the size of the sales force. This method relies on a formula based on the number of sales calls to be made, the number of customers, and the average number of calls per salesperson.

7. **Explain how to set standards for sales force evaluation.**

Marketers can set two types of standard for sales performance. Quantitative standards are objective standards derived from calculable measures such as number of sales completed. Qualitative standards are tied to more subjective measures of sales performance such as customer satisfaction or repeat purchases.

KEY TERMS

canned sales presentation 603
closing 604
combination compensation 613
direct selling 596
equalized workload method 610
field sales 595
lifetime customer value 593
need-satisfaction presentation 603
order getters 594

order takers 594
over-the-counter sales 595
personal selling 592
prospecting 601
qualified prospect 601
relationship selling 594
sales management 608
sales partnering 598
sales quota 614

sales support staff 594
sales team 597
straight commission compensation 613
straight salary compensation 613
system sales 597
telemarketing 595
transaction selling 593

Skill-Building Applications

1. How can you use the concepts of relationship selling to get and keep the kinds of jobs you want during your entire career?

2. Imagine that you are an AT&T salesperson trying to sell long-distance telephone service to a major corporation. What information would you need about the corporation and its telephone usage? How could the latest technological tools help you handle prospecting? Closing the sale?

3. Using the concept of lifetime value, explain why Pizza Hut should or should not return the customer's money if a particular pizza is not satisfactory.

4. Imagine a sales team working at Best Buy, an electronics retailer. One member of the team would sell in the store. Another team member would visit customers' homes or offices to set up the equipment and demonstrate proper use. How would such a team benefit customers? The store?

5. Melissa Johns works for a travel agency. What are the advantages and disadvantages of paying her a commission to sell the agency's services to businesses? What are the advantages and disadvantages of paying a salary?

6. Tom Parker has been taught to sell vacuum cleaners door to door using a canned sales presentation. What are the advantages and disadvantages of using this strategy?

Getting Involved in Marketing

1. *On Your Own* Assume you're a sales representative for a specific business product, such as Steelcase office furniture or General Electric turbine engines. How would you identify and qualify prospects in the target market for the product you selected? How could online database services help you?

2. *On Your Own* As in exercise 1, you're a salesperson marketing a business product, and you're planning for a sales call with a prospect who is nearly ready to buy. Identify the kind of information you expect the prospect to provide and predict questions and objections you are likely to face. Then show how you would respond to each item.

3. *Find Out More* Research the training and background needed to become a salesperson for a company in your area. Also find out what this company looks for when recruiting sales personnel and what training and supervision it provides for new hires. How does the company set standards, evaluate, and reward performance?

4. *In a Partnership* With another student, select a product such as a Nikon camera that is sold by manufacturers to retailers for resale to consumers. Work independently to list three needs of retailers that a manufacturer's sales staff should satisfy dur-

ing the sales process. Also list three needs of consumers that retailers' sales personnel should satisfy. Then list suggestions for responding to each need. Exchange lists with the other student and critique the needs and suggestions.

5. *In a Team* With other students, select a specific product, such as a Xerox photocopier or Sprint long-distance telephone service, that is marketed to organizational customers. Working independently, identify the costs the marketer is likely to incur when selling to one customer. Next, outline how this marketer might go about calculating the lifetime value of one organizational customer. Now share your ideas with your classmates and come to agreement about both costs and calculations of lifetime value. Be prepared to present your work to the class.

6. *In a Team* Working with two other students, select and research one marketer each to illustrate making sales in the field, over the counter, and through telemarketing. Suggest how each marketer should set sales objectives and measure sales performance, organize its sales force, and apply technology to the sales process. Prepare a detailed report or presentation of your recommendations.

http://www.relaxtheback.com

Marketing on the Net Relax the Back Goes Global on the Web

Taking care of people's backs is what Relax the Back does best. From ergonomically correct chairs to exercise equipment, Relax the Back markets a range of products to relieve and prevent back pain. But even with more than four dozen franchised stores across North America, the Texas-based company can't easily reach potential customers in other countries. For founder and president Virginia Rogers, the answer was to use the World Wide Web to launch an integrated marketing communication (IMC) effort in cyberspace.

"The Internet introduces people to us," says Rogers. "They get a clearer picture of what Relax the Back is and the variety of products that are available." Franchisee Fred Boyd designed the Relax the Back Web site as an electronic catalog. The site includes pages about products, back pain, and store locations. The site also includes links to related Web sites and more educational information about back pain. Visitors can now follow links to a site about ergonomic resources (at ErgoWeb) and a site about repetitive stress injuries (at the University of Nebraska). In addition, visitors can move at their own pace through pages with information about back problems related to working, driving, playing, and sleeping.

As an integral part of Relax the Back's IMC strategy, the Web site reinforces the company's focus on customer needs. Before they see any products, visitors are invited to click on pages that will help them deal with back pain. Only then are they steered toward pages featuring specific products and store locations.

Then, with award-winning graphics and clear explanations, Relax the Back presents the benefits of its products and tells why customers should buy them. When customers go to the store listing, they can choose to make contact in any of four ways: they can call toll-free, click on a store to see its individual home page, send e-mail to a specific store, or visit a store in person. By offering Web customers so many ways to communicate, Relax the Back invites an ongoing dialogue that supports profitable relationship building with customers near and far.

What makes the Web an especially attractive communication tool for franchise owners (each a small business owner) is the ability to find customers who might not otherwise know about

Relax the Back. Gerry Austin, a Relax the Back franchise owner in Ardmore, Pennsylvania, says, "You can do something relatively simple like this and increase your business by 5 percent in a couple of months." Fred Boyd, the franchisee in Tacoma, Washington, has received e-mail inquiries from Hawaii and Australia. For Boyd, the cost of being on the Web is less than $30 per month—and the customers who buy after visiting the Web site increase profits, too. "I'm getting more bang for my buck," he says.[1]

Strategies and applications

1. Visit the Relax the Back Web site and analyze its home page. How does the page show customers that the company cares about their needs and concerns? Be specific.

2. Examine the part of the Web site where the company explains how its franchising system operates. Why is it a good idea for Relax the Back to use its Web site to attract new franchisees?

3. How does the Relax the Back Web site work toward influencing the perceptions, attitudes, and behavior of visitors? Cite specific areas on the Web site to support your answer.

4. How can Relax the Back franchisees use their other IMC activities to support the Web site and, in turn, use their individual home pages to support other IMC activities?

5. Doctors who treat patients for back pain are in a good position to recommend appropriate products. What IMC activities might Relax the Back use to build relationships with this stakeholder group?

6. Why would visitors to the Web site be interested in reading clippings from newspaper coverage of Relax the Back? How does this help generate positive word of mouth and build brand equity?

Team project

With a partner, think about how Relax the Back can use consumer sales promotion to attract more first-time visitors to its Web site and, at the same time, encourage repeat visits. Develop two consumer sales promotion ideas and indicate the specific communication goals each will help achieve. How could Relax the Back measure the results of each idea?

http://www.ohiobiz.com

Marketing on the Net   How Ohio Is Gathering Speed on the I-Way

The state of Ohio is in the express lane on the information superhighway. Its World Wide Web site has something for almost everyone. One target audience is businesses that will employ local residents and build tax revenues. A second is tourists who are interested in travel information. A third is residents who want to learn more about jobs, colleges, and cultural events. The goal is to communicate the benefits of living, working, visiting, and doing business in the Buckeye State.

Web visitors can get a sense of the state's vitality by jumping to pages describing more than 100 cities and towns, businesses, sports teams, and cultural sites. "This site helps us sell the state in its entirety," notes John Damschroder, special projects director for the Department of Development, which directed the creation of the Web site. "If people are interested in technology, in media, it's there. If they look at the site, I don't have to say a word about the critical mass of businesses in the state. They can go in and look around for themselves."

The Web site draws 17,000 people every week, including visitors from Scandinavia and Asia. "Through this Web site, we are able to link to any Ohio organization that has a Web site and back again, which creates traffic," says Donald Jakeway, the state's development director. The idea of reciprocal links is so important that Ohio won't link with another site unless it links back.

Just as important, the Webmasters don't allow the Ohio site to become stale, which can alienate repeat visitors and dampen budding relationships. "You have to avoid the downside to the interactive world," says Damschroder. "That is the 'been there, done that' situation when a site is rarely updated." The Ohio home page is never the same two days in a row. Featured Ohio sites rotate weekly, and a special section titled "Postcards from Ohio" changes daily, packed with tidbits on a wide range of timely topics. Another feature that supports relationship building is the Graffiti Wall, a section where visitors can send an inquiry or sound off on Ohio topics.

While a growing number of states are setting up World Wide Web sites, not all are as bottom-line oriented as Ohio. California, for example, had to rework its site to include wage and tax information that businesses need when making relocation decisions. The Illinois Web site, on the other hand, is linked to a Web-based

industrial buying guide so that businesses can find customers and suppliers in the state. For its part, Ohio's special pages on state resources and statistics provide very concrete evidence of the state's dedication to helping local businesses succeed. That approach has helped the state create and maintain relationships with its business, resident, and tourist stakeholders.[2]

Strategies and applications

1. Visit the Ohio Web site and click on the section titled "Bottom Line Ohio." Why would a relocating business need the data described in this section?

2. Visit the home page of the Rock and Roll Hall of Fame, which can be accessed through the Ohio site or through its URL (universal resource locator) (http://www.rockhall.com). How does this tourist attraction encourage cyberspace visitors to return frequently? How does it encourage in-person visits?

3. Bearing in mind the three target audiences, how would you evaluate the Web site's slogan, "Ohio: America's Economic Development Leader"? Is this slogan effective? If not, can you suggest an alternative that would appeal to all three audiences?

4. If you were in charge of the Web site, what communication objectives would you set? How would you measure results? How would you research the response of the target audience in order to adjust your Web communications?

5. Many Web sites use contests or other consumer sales promotions to attract visitors. Should Ohio's Web site use a promotion to draw people interested in traveling to the state? What kind of promotion would you suggest? How would results be measured?

6. Businesses that want to reach many buyers at once can exhibit at a trade show. How could Ohio create a virtual trade show for businesses in a particular industry?

Team project

With other students, use a search engine to locate and visit the Web sites of two other states. Explore those sites to see how they appeal to relocating businesses. How does Ohio's Web site differentiate the state from other states that compete to attract businesses? What can your team suggest to enhance Ohio's differentiation?

internetempowerment

Relationship Building with Visitors to Biltmore Estate

A Marketing Plan for the Grandest Home in America

The travel and tourism business is one of the top industries in the United States. Now it's your turn to make marketing decisions and take marketing actions in this dynamic field. This integrative capstone case shows how Biltmore Estate and its communications agency, Price/McNabb, developed, implemented, and evaluated a marketing plan for building exchange relationships with employees and visitors to the largest home in the country. Follow along as they apply all eight universal marketing processes within the framework of a marketing strategy to delight more than 800,000 visitors every year. The processes are shown in Figure CC.1 on the next page. You can also check Table CC.1 below to review the elements of a marketing plan. Then, after you've read the case, you can build your marketing skills and get more involved in marketing by answering questions about how *you* would market Biltmore Estate.

TABLE **CC.1** Inside a Marketing Plan

Element	Purpose
Situation analysis	Investigate the organization's present state and evaluate the external and internal factors that can influence its future prospects.
Target market	Indicate the group of people or organizations whose needs the marketer's products are specifically designed to satisfy.
Marketing goals and objectives	Identify specific long-term and interim results to be achieved.
Marketing strategies	Show how the organization will establish and sustain relationships with internal customers and customers in the target market.
Marketing programs	Detail the actions and steps for implementing marketing strategies to achieve marketing goals and objectives.
Program budgets	Indicate the allocated amount of money and the expected financial return for each marketing program.
Program schedules	Lay out the timing of each marketing program to guide employees in planning and implementation.

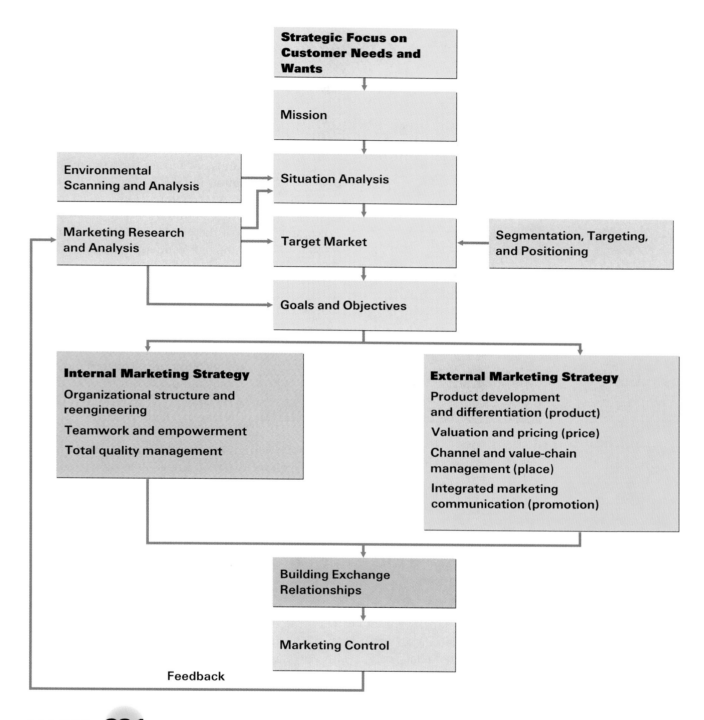

FIGURE **CC.1**

The Framework of Marketing Strategy

Background

Nestled among the majestic peaks of the Blue Ridge Mountains, the 250-room Biltmore House was modeled after the castles in France's Loire Valley. Multimillionaire George Vanderbilt spared no expense in constructing this impressive home, with its 390-foot facade, 32 guest rooms, 43 bathtubs, 65 fireplaces, and 1,354 windows. Completed in 1895, the home was filled with treasures brought back from Vanderbilt's world travels, including paintings by John Singer Sargent and Pierre-Auguste Renoir.

The setting in Asheville, North Carolina, was equally impressive. Designed by the creator of New York's Central Park, the lush grounds and gardens were carefully tended for year-round enjoyment. Then, as now, every season brought a different outdoor spectacle, from thousands of tulips in spring to masses of mums in fall.

After 35 years as an opulent private home, Biltmore Estate was opened to the public. Owner William Amherst Vanderbilt Cecil has continued his family's tradition of gracious hospitality. For an admission charge, guests can tour Biltmore House, stroll the grounds, visit the winery, and dine at several restaurants. Christmas is especially magical at Biltmore. The grounds and rooms are decked in holiday finery. A decorated 35-foot fir dominates the massive Banquet Hall. Crackling fires in nineteenth-century fireplaces, hundreds of candles, and musical performances add to the spirit of the season. At holiday time and throughout the year, impeccable service remains the hallmark of Biltmore Estate.

Research has shown that once people have seen a photograph of Biltmore Estate, they are more likely to want to visit. Therefore, in its promotional efforts, Biltmore Estate needs to expose as many people as possible to its beauty and grandeur. Do you think an infomercial would be successful in promoting the Estate? Would a Web site or a CD-ROM be appropriate for demonstrating a guided tour? Why?

Setting the Stage for a New Marketing Strategy

A strategic focus on the customer has helped Biltmore Estate thrive during 65 years as a tourist attraction. As in George Vanderbilt's day, the comfort and satisfaction of visitors is the driving force behind the organization's internal and external marketing strategies. For years, the Estate had steadily gained relationships with new customers. Interest in the special Christmas tours became so strong that the celebration was extended by several weeks to meet demand.

Then, early in 1994, when its marketers used the universal marketing process of *environmental scanning and analysis* to examine the marketing environment, they found that the increase in new customer relationships had plateaued. Marketers attempting to determine whether this was a problem only for Biltmore Estate found many other tourist attractions in the same position. This lack of growth pointed to some change in the environment that required further investigation—and an action plan for reversing the trend.

To create a foundation for an integrated marketing strategy, the Estate worked with Price/McNabb on a comprehensive situation analysis. In the competitive environment, Disney World and other Florida attractions were considered to be competitors, as was Colonial Williamsburg in Virginia. The marketers noted that many of these tourist attractions were increasing their entertainment value by adding new rides and facilities to enhance the value package and build repeat business. Museums, another type of competitor, were unveiling new interactive and involving exhibits. Another source of competition was the trend toward spending vacation time at home rather than traveling to a destination such as the Estate.

Exploring the economic environment, the marketers found that real disposable income—a necessary prerequisite for spending on tourist attractions—was rising across the country. Income per person in the South was also rising, indicating that customers and prospects in the region were better able to afford the attraction.

As for the social environment, the population from Virginia to Florida was growing at a faster pace than the U.S. average. This trend increased the pool of potential customers for day trips to the Estate. Occupancy at Asheville hotels, motels, and inns was also rising, showing that more tourists were visiting the area. In addition, vacation travel by car was on the rise. Such travel data helped agency marketers determine where to concentrate their IMC efforts.

The marketers used information from the situation analysis to prepare the SWOT analysis shown in Figure CC.2. This matrix presentation helped them understand the strengths, weaknesses, opportunities, and threats likely to influence the Estate's ability to build marketing relationships. The attraction's strengths were important for differentiating it from competitors, and opportunities revealed in the SWOT analysis presented ideas for establishing new relationships and strengthening current relationships. However, the marketing strategy would also have to address the Estate's weaknesses and help the attraction neutralize the threats. After completing this SWOT analysis, the marketers looked more closely at the target market.

F I G U R E **CC.2**

SWOT Analysis for Biltmore Estate

Strengths
- Largest house in America
- Gardens and natural beauty
- Winery
- Art/architecture
- Culture
- History
- Offers a chance to envision/ imagine life at its best

Weaknesses
- Possibly considered high-priced
- Not as interactive/ involving as some competitors
- Fixed location
- Not getting fair share of repeat visitation

Opportunities
- Great potential to increase Passholder retention
- Especially conducive to development of relationships with some guests
- Asheville-area tourism is growing
- Opportunities exist for increased interactivity

Threats
- Competition is more interactive
- Increasing popularity of other Asheville-area attractions
- Lack of understanding among nonvisitors of the depth of the Biltmore experience

Exploring Biltmore Estate's Target Market

The agency investigated the market for pleasure travel through *marketing research and analysis*. Using secondary data sources, it identified two distinct segments: people who wanted a close-to-home, impulse, low-cost holiday, and people who wanted a distant, expensive dream vacation. This information helped the marketers dig deeper to see how the Estate's customers and prospects fit into these segments.

TABLE **CC.2**   Profile of Biltmore Estate Customer Segments

Passholders

Demographics	Yearly value of each passholder: $207.75
	Most are female, married, no children at home
Psychographics	Quality of life and environmental responsibility is important
	Like to identify with some aspect of the Estate (art, gardening, decor, etc.)
Geographics	50% from the Asheville area
Behavior	Visits last 3–4 hours
	Visit more than three times per year
	Walk through gardens more than any other activity
Expectations	In general, spectacular gardens, experience history/culture, new or variety of experience, special opportunities, opportunity to interact and give feedback
	From products: quality; benefits or discounts for loyalty; elegance and sophistication; variety
	From employees: sincere appreciation, rewards for loyalty, mutual relationship

General Visitors

Demographics	Yearly value of each visitor: $39.35
	Most are female, married, no children at home, older than 35, and well educated
Behavior	Visits last 6+ hours
	Unlikely to visit twice in same year
	Slightly more likely to tour House
	62% plan to revisit within 3 years
Expectations	In general, to experience history, to view stunning architecture, to be entertained/amused
	From products: quality, style and elegance, quality dining
	From employees: to be appreciated, to be informed; courtesy and good service

The marketers set up four focus groups to get a better understanding of how customers and noncustomers in the target market view the Estate. As a result of this research, they learned that visitors and nonvisitors alike associated the attraction with flowers, gardens, and landscaping. Visitors also cited the historic and cultural significance of the Estate and its grandeur and beauty.

Using data from the focus groups to shape the questionnaire, the marketers surveyed 400 respondents in each of three segments: Passholders, General Visitors, and Prospects. Passholders were the 22,000 individuals who had bought a one-year pass to the Estate for 1994. General Visitors were the 726,000 individuals who had bought a one-time admission to the Estate that year. Prospects had never visited the Estate but, based on their characteristics, were likely to become either General Visitors or Passholders.

This research helped the Estate apply the universal marketing process of *targeting, segmentation, and positioning,* and the demographic, psychographic, geographic, and behavioral characteristics thus identified were used in segmenting the target market. This information, summarized in Table CC.2, also revealed each segment's expectations of the Estate experience. Knowing these expectations helped the marketers position the Estate as representing "the vision of George Vanderbilt to do everything in the grandest, finest, and most enduring way possible." Then the marketers set marketing objectives and developed both internal and external marketing strategies for relationship building.

Setting Goals and Objectives

Biltmore Estate set long-term goals for profitable growth through the addition of new customer relationships and the strengthening of current customer relationships. Next, it established specific 1995 objectives for attracting more prospects as General Visitors, converting more General Visitors to Passholders, and strengthening relationships with Passholders and all customers. These objectives included:

Passholder	General Visitor	Prospect
Start new relationships:	*Start new relationships*	*Start new relationships*
*Increase number of paid guests brought along	*Increase paid admissions and revenues	*Increase paid admissions and revenues
		*Increase number of first-time visits.
Strengthen relationships:	*Strengthen relationships*:	
*Increase yearly spending per Passholder	*Increase upgrades of visitors to Passholders per visitor	
*Increase Passholder renewals	*Increase spending	

In addition, the Estate set specific objectives for the 1994 Christmas campaign, which would serve as a test for the overall marketing plan. These objectives were (1) to build closer relationships with customers, (2) to increase paid admission by 5 percent, (3) to shift visitation from crowded weekends to less crowded weekdays, and (4) to increase average party size. All these objectives were supported by internal and external marketing strategies keyed to the expectations and characteristics of the targeted segments.

Developing Internal Marketing Strategy

The Estate's internal marketing strategy incorporated training, empowerment, teamwork, and attention to quality. These are the key elements that allowed Biltmore employees to provide the level of professionalism and service expected by customers. In-depth training included background about George Vanderbilt, the Estate's construction, cultural and historical highlights, and Vanderbilt's role in the economic development of Asheville.

According to the strategy, every employee—from the parking lot attendants to the ticket takers to the people who worked in the restaurants, House, Winery, and Garden locations—would operate as a team member to provide a gracious, memorable experience for all visitors. Each room on the Biltmore House tour was attended by a knowledgeable employee who acted as host for that room. The host would answer visitors' questions, provide historical background, discuss the room's art, and help when called on by visitors. Visitors taking a behind-the-scenes guided tour would also be able to ask questions. For visitors who prefer the flexibility of a self-guided tour, Biltmore Estate offered audiotape tours, supplemented by comments from hosts.

As in the days when George Vanderbilt was in residence, quality has been a high priority at the Estate. No detail is too small. To be sure that quality was meeting customer expectations in the period of the 1994 Christmas campaign, the Estate regularly conducted customer-satisfaction research. This feedback, part of the ongoing dialogue between customers and marketers, helped the Estate strengthen exchange relationships for the long term.

Developing External Marketing Strategy

Biltmore Estate's internal marketing strategy laid the groundwork for an external marketing strategy build around the four Ps of the marketing mix.

Product Development and Differentiation

Using *product development and differentiation,* the Estate's marketers designed a value package around Biltmore House's original function as a luxurious showplace for entertaining family and friends. The features of this value package included Biltmore House and its opulent appointments, the ever-changing natural beauty of Biltmore Estate's 8,000 acres, and all that the restaurants, shops, and Winery had to offer. Special events also supported the positioning.

The Winery is one of Biltmore Estate's most popular attractions. By promoting tours of the Winery and describing seasonal events in glowing terms, the Estate's marketing personnel can encourage people to return. How might the Estate promote return visits by travelers from outside the United States?

The service component included the expertise of the tour guides and room hosts, attentive service in the restaurants, and courtesy and appreciation shown by all employees. Service quality was built into every aspect of the value package, from the meticulous care taken of the buildings, grounds, and walkways to the food, music, and personal service.

To celebrate the Estate's first 100 years, the marketing team developed a special yearlong Centennial Celebration for 1995. Capping the Centennial

One of the most popular times to visit Biltmore Estate is during the Christmas season. How could Estate marketers use direct mail materials featuring photos from that season to promote return visits at other times of the year?

was an expanded version of the Estate's traditional Christmas Celebration, including Victorian-style trimmings, live music, candlelight tours, and more than three dozen lavishly decorated Christmas trees.

The marketers encouraged frequent visitation by mounting a series of special events that reflected the image of Biltmore Estate that customers described to the market researchers. Events such as flower festivals, interpretive forestry walks, special dinners, and artisan demonstrations gave Passholders and past visitors a reason to return again and again. Passholders were also encouraged, through newsletter articles, to share the experience by giving twelve-month passes as gifts to family and friends.

Valuation and Pricing

Valuation and pricing was a critical factor in the external marketing strategy. Supply and demand influenced the price, especially during the ever-popular Christmas Celebration. Regular ticket prices were in effect for daytime tours, but the special Candlelight Evening tours—in high demand—were priced higher for General Visitors. Passholders were offered discounted tickets to Candlelight tours as a way of reinforcing the value of this customer relationship.

To alleviate the pressures caused by high demand for weekend visits, the marketers offered incentives to shift visitation to weekdays. They also offered discounts to current customers making a return visit and to a select group of prospects who were likely to visit for the first time. All these pricing decisions were followed by database research to determine the success of various offers.

Channel and Value-Chain Management

In developing its strategy for *channel and value-chain management,* the Estate was careful to select suppliers that would provide high-quality goods and services. This emphasis on quality was important for reinforcing the "grandest/finest" position the attraction was projecting. To boost brand equity, the marketers featured Biltmore Estate's brand on all products sold through its marketing channels.

Biltmore Estate chose both direct and indirect marketing channels to reach customers and prospects. It mailed a catalog to customers and prospects in its marketing database. It also maintained direct contact with visitors through on-site ticketing, shops, and restaurants.

Strengthening relationships with other channel partners, such as hotel personnel who advise guests about tourism and sell Biltmore Estate tickets, was also a priority. The Estate placed displays in selected area hotels with informative brochures about the attraction. This channel strategy helped the Estate combat the threat of losing visitors to competing attractions near Asheville.

Integrated Marketing Communication

The strategy for *integrated marketing communication* was based on the Estate's in-depth customer research. From the focus groups and the surveys, the marketers were able to identify the unique characteristics that set each of the three market segments apart. Rather than use one communication approach for all segments, the marketers focused their IMC tactics on the differences among segments.

For prospects, the objective was to start new exchange relationships by focusing on the benefits of visiting the Estate during any season. For past visitors, the objective was to strengthen relationships by focusing on the added excitement of visiting the Estate during special events. In this way, a visitor who had experienced the Estate before had new reasons to make a return visit.

Past visitors received a direct mail package with a seasonal brochure and an opportunity to enter a drawing for a free weekend at the Estate's private guest cottage. This provided an incentive for visitors to attend the Spring Festival of Flowers. Both prospects and General Visitors were the target audience

Relationship marketing demands contact over time. Biltmore Estate accomplishes this through use of various media, including direct mail, as shown here. The idea is to maintain contact, inform, and build an image that will encourage additional visits. What might Biltmore Estate say or show on its envelopes to encourage recipients to open and read its brochures?

for ads in 16 upscale magazines selected through research, shown in Figure CC.3. Each ad invited response by means of a toll-free telephone number, and since there was a different toll-free number for every magazine, marketers were able to track every response to its ad source. When people called, their names and addresses were added to Biltmore Estate's internal database. The Estate then sent all callers a direct mail package about the benefits of visiting.

FIGURE **CC.3**   Biltmore Estate's Print Recommendation

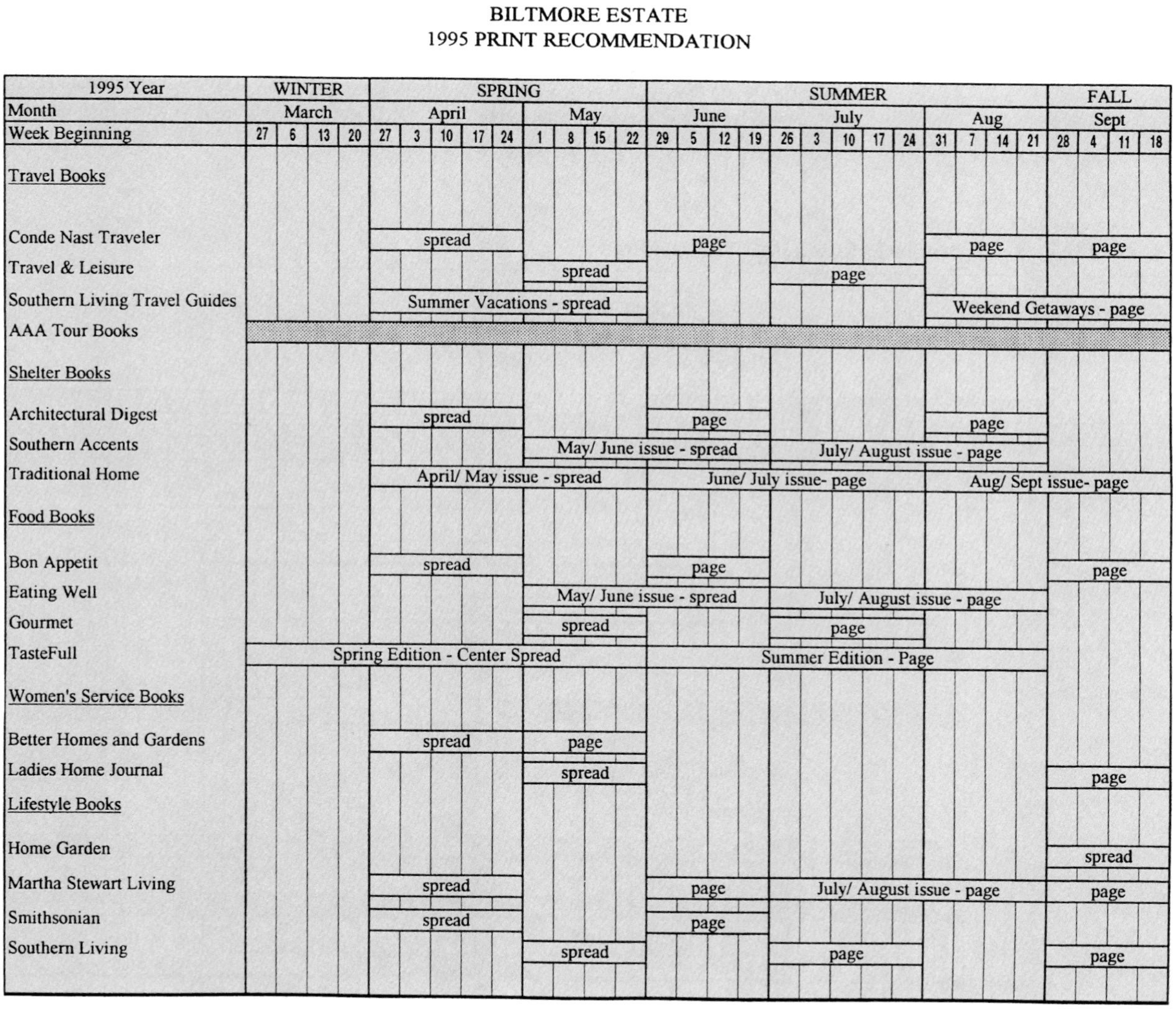

BILTMORE ESTATE
1995 PRINT RECOMMENDATION

Publication	March (Winter)	April	May	June	July	Aug	Sept (Fall)
Travel Books							
Conde Nast Traveler		spread		page		page	page
Travel & Leisure			spread		page		
Southern Living Travel Guides		Summer Vacations - spread				Weekend Getaways - page	
AAA Tour Books	(year-round)						
Shelter Books							
Architectural Digest		spread		page		page	
Southern Accents			May/ June issue - spread		July/ August issue - page		
Traditional Home		April/ May issue - spread		June/ July issue - page		Aug/ Sept issue - page	
Food Books							
Bon Appetit		spread		page			page
Eating Well			May/ June issue - spread		July/ August issue - page		
Gourmet			spread		page		
TasteFull	Spring Edition - Center Spread			Summer Edition - Page			
Women's Service Books							
Better Homes and Gardens		spread	page				
Ladies Home Journal			spread				page
Lifestyle Books							
Home Garden							spread
Martha Stewart Living		spread		page	July/ August issue - page		page
Smithsonian		spread		page			
Southern Living			spread		page		page

Ads in the Automobile Association of America tour guides and on radio stressed the natural beauty and the cultural and historical significance of the Estate. Throughout the year, sponsorship of National Public Radio programming helped keep awareness high among all segments. These communications encouraged prospects to visit for the first time (starting new relationships) and General Visitors to return again (strengthening existing relationships).

New for 1994 was an internal database created from records of visits by Passholders and General Visitors. Using this database, the Estate arranged a series of mailings keyed to the interests and behavior of each segment. To reinforce continued customer loyalty, Passholders received special treatment. Continuing a tactic from earlier years, the Estate mailed its *Ambassador* newsletter to Passholders, providing details about the benefits of visiting through all the seasons. The newsletter also introduced the people who work at the Estate, putting a more human face on the product.

Encouraging visitation during seasonal events, the Estate mailed each Passholder an elegant personal invitation to the Christmas Celebration with a letter and a Centennial trip planner, plus tasteful notices of exclusive offers tied to other activities. By staying in continual contact with this key segment, the Estate marketers strengthened the relationship and solicited feedback as part of an ongoing dialogue geared toward understanding and satisfying customer needs. The IMC schedule for General Visitors and prospects is shown in Figure CC.4.

FIGURE **CC.4** **Biltmore Estate's IMC Tactical Plan**

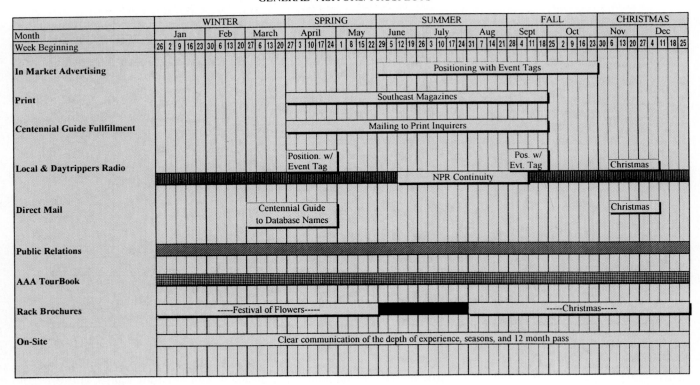

BILTMORE ESTATE
1995 IMC TACTICAL PLAN
GENERAL VISITORS/ PROSPECTS

Public relations plays a key role in the Estate's IMC strategy. Working closely with media contacts across the country, the Estate marketers arranged for photos and articles to appear in time to bring visitors to seasonal or special events. For the 1994 Christmas Celebration, Biltmore experts decorated the New York set of the *Today Show* and hosted a *Today* broadcast from the Banquet Hall in all its holiday splendor. These and other PR activities reinforced the image and positioning of the Estate and spread the word about the experience.

Evaluating the Marketing Plan

To determine the effectiveness of the marketing plan after implementation, the Estate marketers measured customer behavior and attitudes related to *relationship building*, the eighth universal marketing process. These measures included:

- *Contacts.* Number of people reached through IMC activities and media coverage. This was the starting point for making prospects aware of the Estate and reminding General Visitors and Passholders of the benefits of visitation.

- *Inquiries.* Number of telephone calls and requests for information traced to advertising campaign. This showed the effectiveness of IMC in encouraging prospects to consider visits.

- *Transactions.* Number of visitors, amount of admission revenue, purchases of meals and Biltmore products. These data revealed how many customers visited and showed their purchasing patterns.

- *Attitude.* On-site and telephone surveys about customer satisfaction. These gauged satisfaction with the overall experience and with the ticket office, the parking area, the shopping and dining, and the host staff, among other elements.

Every marketer needs to conduct customer satisfaction research to uncover areas for improvement. By asking for customer feedback, the marketer can identify real opportunities for strengthening relationships with customers. This customer satisfaction survey provides a formal mechanism for understanding whether customers enjoyed their visit to Biltmore Estate and for pinpointing what customers would like improved. What questions do you think Biltmore Estate might ask to probe its customers' satisfaction levels?

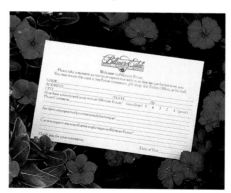

Comparing the measurements to the specific objectives set for the marketing plan, the Estate marketers were able to see what worked and what needed improvement. For both the Christmas 1994 campaign (see Table CC.3) and the 1995 campaign (see Figure CC.5), results were dramatically better than expected. These results—as well as the feedback from customers and prospects—

T A B L E **CC.3**   **Christmas 1994 Results**

Objective	Result
Build relationships with customers and prospects	Attracted new General Visitors and Passholders; received personal notes of appreciation from people who received invitations; 92% of customers satisfied with courtesy and professionalism of host staff
Increase paid admission by 5%	Paid admissions up by 20%
Shift visitation to weekdays	Weekday visitation up 38%
Increase average party size	Average party size increased 12.5%

FIGURE **CC.5**

Actual Revenues vs. Goals for Marketing Plan

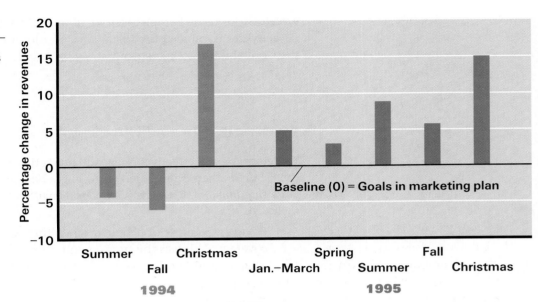

were used by the marketers as they planned the 1996 marketing strategy for building relationships during Biltmore Estate's second century.

The success of Biltmore Estate's strategy demonstrates the power of building relationships one customer at a time. "The goal of relationship marketing is to reach customers on a personal level—to make connections with them as individuals," observes Tom Eppes, president of Price/McNabb. "The proof of the effectiveness of the Estate's Christmas campaign was revealed to us in ways beyond just record sales; many of the people who received the invitational mailer took the time to actually sit down and write a personal response. By gaining an understanding of existing customers to craft messages they could relate to, using that understanding to effectively target prospects, and by crafting a top-quality creative piece, we were able to affect sales as well as customer loyalty."[1]

Skill-Building Applications

1. Develop a marketing plan for Biltmore Estate that would help it establish better relationships with travel agents, holiday planners, and tour organizers, as well as employees and customers.

2. Imagine that Biltmore Estate wants to reach out to a new segment, international travelers visiting the southeastern United States. How should the Estate use marketing research to determine the proper positioning? How can it use IMC to communicate this position?

3. How would you use public relations to make prospects aware of the benefits of visiting the attraction? List at least three PR ideas for reaching prospects in the Southeast.

4. What can Biltmore Estate do to empower its employees to satisfy customers before, during, and after a visit? What decisions do you think employees at this tourist attraction might face in satisfying customers? What information about customers do employees require to be prepared to meet their needs? How can top management reinforce the empowerment message using internal marketing?

5. How often should the Estate evaluate its marketing results? How can its marketers use feedback about marketing effectiveness to improve future strategies and plans?

Getting Involved in Marketing

1. *On Your Own* What mission statement would you write for Biltmore Estate? Why? How would you communicate this mission statement to employees? To customers? To suppliers?

2. *On Your Own* Assume that the Estate wants to forge a strategic alliance with one or more attractions near Asheville as a way of drawing more visitors from other states and countries. How can attractions work together to demonstrate the value of vacationing in the Asheville area? Outline a marketing plan for such a collaborative effort.

3. *Find Out More* Find one or two recent articles about Colonial Williamsburg (Virginia) or Hearst Castle (California) in a newspaper, magazine, or online database service. What features are emphasized? How do these features compare with the Estate's value package? How do these features compare with the expectations of the customer segments researched by Biltmore marketers? How would you suggest that the Estate sharpen its product differentiation to compete with the tourist destination you researched?

4. *In a Team* With two classmates, diagram the value chain you see for the Estate. How do its suppliers and its channel partners fit in this diagram? What

would you suggest the Estate do to strengthen relationships with its suppliers? Prepare a two-minute presentation to your class summarizing your team's ideas.

5. *In a Team* With two other students, assume roles of Price/McNabb staff members helping the Estate explore possible media vehicles for advertising. How would you use audience research to select media? What creative strategy might be effective? Where and when would you place your ads? Draft a brief presentation that you, as agency personnel, can make in front of the Estate marketers.

6. *In a Partnership* Working with another student, design a marketing research questionnaire to use in a telephone survey of recent General Visitors who did not become Passholders. You want to determine why these visitors did not upgrade to a twelve-month pass. What questions will you ask? How will you decide which General Visitors to select for this survey? How will you be able to use the survey results to encourage more General Visitors to become Passholders? Write a three-page report summarizing your ideas, including at least six questions for such a survey.

A Career in Marketing

Why pursue a career in marketing? One good reason is the unusually large variety of job opportunities available. Marketing is a broad field offering many different career paths—from advertising, selling, marketing research, logistics, and telemarketing to multilevel marketing, direct mail marketing, and developing Web sites on the Internet. In addition, continual expansion and ongoing changes in the global marketing environment are opening more opportunities for marketing jobs here and in other countries. And if you enjoy customer contact—with consumers or with businesses—a job in marketing is the place for you.

The most exciting aspect of marketing may be the possibility of creating your own job: you can "find a need and fill it." By filling an unmet need, you can prosper as an entrepreneur/marketer—this may be as simple as giving massages in malls to weary shoppers or as complex as creating new software for helping companies to invest. As long as there are individuals or groups with needs, there will be a need for new marketers.

To prepare you for selecting from the diversity of careers in marketing, this appendix covers three topics. The first topic is the skills necessary for success in the marketing field. In assessing and developing your skills, consider yourself as the product to be marketed. Developing an attractive product is as important to your success as it is for any marketer. The second topic is the job search: from performing a self-analysis through resumé writing and the job interview. The final section looks at potential career paths in marketing and provides brief job descriptions for some entry-level positions.

How to Succeed in Marketing

Each type of marketing job requires a particular set of technical skills, but those outlined here are important in all areas of marketing.

A few years ago, the U.S. Secretary of Labor appointed a commission, the Secretary's Commission on Achieving Necessary Skills (SCANS), to identify the skills that students need to succeed in the marketplace of the 21st century. The commission named five types of skills—the ability to (1) allocate time, money, and resources (*resource skills*); (2) work on teams and serve customers (*interpersonal skills*); (3) acquire and evaluate information and use computers to process information (*information skills*); (4) understand social, organizational, and technological systems and improve on such systems (*systems skills*); and (5) apply technology to specific tasks (*technology skills*). Beyond these basic skills, job-seekers in the marketing field also need motivation skills. The following sections expand on several of these key skills.

Interpersonal/Communication Skills

Being able to interact effectively with people is perhaps the most important marketing skill—not simply interacting with customers but being able to work with peers on a team or knowing how to supervise other employees. Marketers must be able to present their thoughts and ideas clearly, both in oral presentations and in written reports. They also need to listen closely to customers so they can identify wants, needs, and expectations.

Building long-term relationships with customers and other stakeholders is one of the most important aspects of marketing. Therefore, interpersonal skills must be combined with the ability to respond quickly to customers' suggestions, wants, and complaints, especially in service recovery. Learning to say "I apologize for the mistake and will make it right" is often as important to marketing as any other skill. Customers may be more loyal to a firm that has made a mistake and then gone out of its way to correct it than to a firm that hasn't had to prove itself in that way.

Information/Problem-Solving and Technology Skills

A marketer must be able to use technology to find information and apply that information in the decision-making process. Today, this means being familiar with surfing the Internet, using e-mail, and conducting information searches by computer, including database research. Beyond simple information gathering is the pursuit of learning—the successful marketer must acquire both general and job-related knowledge in order to guide future decisions. Finally, the marketer must be a flexible thinker. Two quite similar problems will probably require different solutions, as the different dynamics surrounding each problem affect the solution choices. Marketers must be able to recognize these differences and come up with creative ideas to address the unique factors in each marketing situation.

Motivation Skills

Two types of motivation are required in marketing. From the outset a marketer must be highly self-motivated, taking the initiative in a project and following it through until completion. As the marketer begins to take on a leadership role, often within a cross-functional team, the ability to motivate others becomes essential.

This text was designed to assist you in developing all of these skills. You have improved your interpersonal skills by doing the exercises at the end of each chapter, especially those involving teams. You have learned about the processes of marketing and how to implement and improve those processes. You have learned about marketing technology; now you need practice using computers, e-mail, fax machines, and the like. Your work experience will be a valuable asset. Try to find summer jobs that improve the skills you will need when you graduate. For example, you may want to find an internship with an advertising agency or retailer. Such on-the-job training can help you develop your talents and let you gain experience in a marketing function. The goal of this text is to prepare you for the marketplace of the future—thus its emphasis on relationship marketing, technology, ethics, and global thinking.

How to Find a Job in Marketing

FIGURE **A.1**

Sixteen Traits Recruiters Seek in Job Prospects

The career search in marketing is not unlike searching for jobs in any other field. What is different is the way you must present yourself to prospective employers.

1. **Ability to communicate.** Do you have the ability to organize your thoughts and ideas effectively? Can you express them clearly when speaking or writing? Can you present your ideas to others in a persuasive way?
2. **Intelligence.** Do you have the ability to understand the job assignment? Learn the details of operation? Contribute original ideas to your work?
3. **Self-confidence.** Do you demonstrate a sense of maturity that enables you to deal positively and effectively with situations and people?
4. **Willingness to accept responsibility.** Are you someone who recognizes what needs to be done and is willing to do it?
5. **Initiative.** Do you have the ability to identify the purpose for work and to take action?
6. **Leadership.** Can you guide and direct others to obtain the recognized objectives?
7. **Energy level.** Do you demonstrate a forcefulness and capacity to make things move ahead? Can you maintain your work effort at an above-average rate?
8. **Imagination.** Can you confront and deal with problems that may not have standard solutions?
9. **Flexibility.** Are you capable of changing and being receptive to new situations and ideas?
10. **Interpersonal skills.** Can you bring out the best efforts of individuals so they become effective, enthusiastic members of a team?
11. **Self-knowledge.** Can you realistically assess your own capabilities? See yourself as others see you? Clearly recognize your strengths and weaknesses?
12. **Ability to handle conflict.** Can you successfully contend with stressful situations and antagonism?
13. **Competitiveness.** Do you have the capacity to compete with others and the willingness to be measured by your performance in relation to that of others?
14. **Goal achievement.** Do you have the ability to identify and work toward specific goals? Do such goals challenge your abilities?
15. **Vocational skills.** Do you possess the positive combination of education and skills required for the position you are seeking?
16. **Direction.** Have you defined your basic personal needs? Have you determined what type of position will satisfy your knowledge, skills, and goals?

Know Yourself—The Self-Evaluation

The first step in any job search is to perform an analysis of what you want out of a job. What are your strengths? What are your weaknesses? What new skills do you want to learn? What talents do you have to offer an employer? What are your long-term career objectives? What type of salary do you hope to earn immediately? Ten years from now? How important is this job compared with your nonworking life—your friends, family, leisure time?

By answering such questions you should be able to determine what you are looking for in a job—be it establishing a career or just achieving short-term financial stability. Either way, this self-evaluation will give you an idea of what you want out of a job, what your skills and abilities are, and what you are willing to sacrifice in order to achieve your goals. Figure A.1 summarizes some traits of successful job seekers.

Know Your Customers—Getting to Know the Position

Once you have analyzed your career requirements, you should spend time searching for the type of position that most closely matches your interests, strengths, and traits. This is only the first step in developing a marketing strategy for getting a job. A position that seems ideal at first may seem less so when you analyze other factors, such as company size, geographic location, compensation programs, and other factors, all of which come into play when narrowing the search for a potential employer. Once you have narrowed your choices, you must make a realistic assessment of the current job market. You may decide to work for a while at a company that is not your first choice in order to acquire essential skills and knowledge.

Search industry periodicals, online resources, area newspapers, and college job postings for positions that fit your criteria. Many marketers now have Web sites where you can learn about the company and its products. An increasing number of students are finding jobs by advertising on the Internet. If you are not yet familiar with this technology, get some help. Once you have targeted specific companies, use every possible resource available to get that all-important "foot in the door." Direct contact with a potential employer by letter or telephone is one way to go. If the company has on-campus recruiting, that path may prove more effective.

Knowing someone already established within the firm you are targeting is invaluable. Ask friends, professors, parents, or alumni if they know anyone in the company. The chances of getting an interview and a job offer are greater when you have an insider ushering your resumé through the company's required review process, instead of dealing only with the human resources department.

The Resumé

With or without some sort of direct contact within the organization, you will need to create a resumé that attracts the attention of recruiters, human resources personnel, or a functional decision maker in the company. Entire books have been devoted to formatting and writing a resumé and cover letter. Several themes recur and should be used as guidelines for anyone in the hunt for a job.

First, the resumé should be targeted to a specific position. This doesn't necessarily mean that you need a separate resumé for every job application, but you will want to prepare different resumés for different *types* of jobs.

Second, the resumé should spell out what you can bring to the job. Either create a section that highlights your qualifications or integrate this information in the work experience section. You need to build a strong case for yourself: a seemingly unqualified individual won't get the job. See Figure A.2 for some key "action" words to use in your resumé.

Third, if you include a section on work experience, focus on relevant accomplishments. Don't note that you spent 20 hours a week on filing if it isn't relevant to the

FIGURE **A.2**

Some Action Words to Describe Work Experience in a Resumé

Administered	Handled	Planned
Budgeted	Implemented	Produced
Conducted	Improved	Scheduled
Coordinated	Increased	Served
Designed	Investigated	Sold
Developed	Managed	Supervised
Directed	Operated	Trained
Established	Organized	Wrote

job for which you are applying. Describe how you designed a database, helped solve customer service problems, or carried out any tasks that relate to the job you are seeking.

Fourth, if you lack work experience, focus on other personal accomplishments. Achievements that show leadership skills, self-motivation, persistence in the face of adversity, and the pursuit of knowledge are viewed favorably by recruiters.

A superb resumé can get you an interview even if you have some weaknesses, and a poor resumé can eliminate even an eminently qualified candidate from consideration. There are several pitfalls to avoid. (1) Keep it short. Unless you have years of related work experience, the resumé should be one or two pages only. Nobody wants to read extraneous information; "fluff" only increases the chance that your resumé will not be fully read. (2) Make sure it is grammatically and typographically perfect. The slightest typing error gives the recruiter a negative impression. (3) Be honest about what you have accomplished. Stretching the truth, or lying about what you have done, is unethical and can cost you a job when the truth comes to light.

Using the Internet

Use the Internet to research industries and companies, to identify specific job openings, and to get your resumé to prospective employers. Altavista and other search engines can help you find the latest information on employment trends, recent announcements by companies in your chosen field, and news items about the companies that interest you.

A variety of online services list specific jobs available at companies, universities, and government agencies. One of the largest is JobTrak (http://www.jobtrak.com), which covers job openings across the United States. FedWorld (http://www.fedworld.gov) posts federal government jobs, and other services are coming online all the time.

If you want to make your resumé available to employers on the Internet, you can check with your campus placement office and search the Web for posting services such as Job Tailor Employment Online Service (http://www.jobtailor.com). Some of these services are free and others charge a fee, so check carefully before you sign up.

The Interview

Assuming everything goes well—your resumé and cover letter have made a good impression on the potential employer—you will be faced with the first interview. Interviews have many formats. More often than not (particularly with on-campus interviews), the first interview is a get-to-know-you interview: the recruiter is trying to get to know the person behind the resumé, gauging both your personality and your level of interest in the position. However, interview styles vary, depending on the interviewer.

The following tips are helpful in preparing for your interview:

1. *Know yourself.* Be prepared to discuss your accomplishments and strengths and how they relate to the position you are seeking. Anticipate questions about your qualifications and prepare good answers for them.

FIGURE **A.3**

Some Questions to Ask an Interviewer

- What are the advantages of working for your company?
- Who are your major competitors? How do their products and marketing compare with yours?
- How would you describe your corporate culture?
- What is your highest priority in the next six months? How could someone like me help in meeting that priority?
- How long does the training period last? What is included in the program?
- When would I be expected to start?
- What is the working environment like in my area?
- What is the managerial style in my area?
- How much travel is associated with the position?
- What is your promotion policy?
- How would I be evaluated?
- What is the next step in the selection process?
- When can I expect to hear from you?
- What other information can I give you about my background, experience, or education?

2. *Know the company*. Be prepared to ask insightful questions about the company (see Figure A.3). Be up to date on all current events involving the company and the industry. Identify specific company needs that your skills and background can fill.

3. *Practice*. Nothing beats practice. Role-play with a friend and ask for a critique.

4. *Dress appropriately*. Normal business dress is advisable for a job interview. Even when you're interviewing for a position in which employees normally wear casual clothing on the job, you should look professional and businesslike when meeting the interviewer.

5. *Be prompt*. Arrive 10 to 15 minutes ahead of the scheduled interview time.

Once in the interview, your goal is simple: to sell yourself to the interviewer. From the time you enter the room until the time you leave, your aim is to make a good impression and convince the interviewer that you and you alone are the one for the job. Several things can increase your chances of getting the job.

First of all, relax. You have a presentation to make, and you won't get your points across effectively if you are too tense. Greet the interviewer with a firm handshake, smile during the interview, and maintain eye contact. These all show enthusiasm on your part and give the interviewer a positive impression. Be sure to say what you went in there to say. You achieve this only by preparing and practicing a comprehensive outline of your strengths and then using that outline as you progress. For example, if the interviewer asks you why you want the job, you can use the opportunity to relate your skills and interests to the employer's needs. Don't try to dominate the discussion, but make sure that you cover all the points you want to cover.

Don't be afraid to make a final sales pitch. Restate that you are interested in the position and that you feel you would fit in well with the firm. Make sure to get a contact address/phone number for following up, and ask when you can expect to hear from the company.

Your self-marketing presentation doesn't end when the interview is over. After the interview, send a thank-you note to the interviewer. You can add to this any additional items that you need to reemphasize. Most importantly, learn from each interview. Make notes of what went well and what you can improve. Revamp your presentation if certain elements need to be stressed more or eliminated. Analyzing your performance will help you in other interviews.

Positions Available in the Field of Marketing

Numerous career paths are available within marketing. This section gives a brief outline of the major marketing career paths, the types of skills and knowledge required in each path, and the potential in each field.

Advertising and Sales Promotion

Advertising provides career opportunities for individuals with varied marketing backgrounds. Positions include copywriter, art director, and media planner, among others. Some crucial traits for work in advertising are creativity, communication skills, and artistic ability. Keep in mind that with the downsizing trend of the 1990s, many firms are cutting back or completely outsourcing their advertising function. Therefore, independent advertising agencies and sales promotion firms may offer more job opportunities.

The trend today is toward sales promotion. For those with skills in design, display, contest development, or other creative areas, sales promotion is a good option because it is a faster-growing field. Sales promotion includes building displays at trade fairs, designing couponing programs, developing sampling programs, and generally creating excitement and incentives for "buying now."

Sales and Purchasing

Sales is perhaps the largest employment segment within the field of marketing. Sales positions are found in nearly all types of organizations. Salespeople need to be highly self-motivated and able to handle rejection. They also need strong communication skills and enthusiasm. The growth prospects for sales positions are about average and are generally tied to the economic strength of the specific industry.

Career opportunities in business-to-business sales are growing rapidly. This involves selling products to businesses rather than consumers, but the skills involved—communication and problem-solving—are similar.

The other side of the marketing process is buying. You may find a rewarding career as a buyer for retail stores or as a purchasing agent for a major manufacturing firm. The same negotiating and interpersonal skills necessary for a good salesperson can be used to become a good buyer.

Public Relations

Public relations professionals design and communicate messages targeting the various stakeholders of a firm. The goal is to establish and maintain positive relationships. Public relations workers must have excellent writing and oral communication skills; writing news releases or newsletters and giving speeches are common tasks. Like all marketing jobs, public relations requires an ability to understand the views and values of the target audience. Competition for entry-level public relations positions is steadily increasing.

Retail Management and Customer Service

Many people mistakenly equate retailing with sales. While retail managers often begin on the sales side, there is much more to retail management than selling. Retail managers must wear many hats, overseeing store functions such as security, promotions, and inventory control in addition to sales force management. In the past, salespeople typically worked their way up into retail management positions, but some retailers recruit individuals directly out of college for management training programs. Success in this field depends on strong decision-making skills, strong personnel management abilities, and a strong customer service orientation.

In this new era of relationship marketing, customer service representatives play a key role in selling products, offering service support, and building enduring ties with consumers and business customers. Some customer service reps work exclusively by telephone, helping customers buy products, answering questions, and offering ideas for making products more productive. Some customer service reps meet customers face to face in a retail location; some respond to customer inquiries via e-mail, fax, or letter. These positions require excellent communication skills (listening, writing, and speaking), plus empathy and an ability to respond under pressure.

Marketing Research

Marketing researchers perform a vital function within marketing firms: collecting and analyzing data in order to solve marketing problems. Researchers may start by handling statistical duties, later assuming more of a consultant role, searching for problems and investigating possible solutions. Future growth in marketing research is expected to be strong, offering particular opportunities for those with advanced degrees or significant industry experience. Many marketing research positions require a strong background in math and statistics.

Product Management

The position of product manager requires a broad base of knowledge, including both business and logistics. Product managers are responsible for the marketing of a product or product family. They deal with manufacturing, sales, pricing, advertising, promotion, and all other aspects of effective product marketing. With experience, a product manager can move up to become a category manager and ultimately assume higher-level management responsibilities.

Transportation and Logistics

As marketing becomes increasingly global, tremendous job opportunities are being created in logistics—the movement of goods from one place to another, including order processing, storage, and transportation. Marketers need to get orders to customers when and where the products are needed, so this field is growing in importance. Transportation specialists help marketers analyze and select the right method for moving goods from factories or warehouses to customer locations. Warehouse managers oversee inventory, security, ordering, and shipping functions. Careers in transportation and logistics call for information technology skills as well as interpersonal skills for working collaboratively with suppliers, transportation companies, and customers.

Marketing Careers in Nonprofit Organizations

This text has provided numerous examples of marketers working in non-business organizations. Nonprofit hospitals, charities, government organizations, schools, trade associations, arboretums, and other nonprofit groups need marketers as much as do profit-making firms. You have learned, for example, how some motor vehicle departments have become more customer-oriented and how some cities and counties have improved their services through consumer surveys. Working in a nonprofit organization often has its own rewards because it usually entails work that directly benefits others and society. But the financial rewards can be substantial as well. Don't ignore this important area when considering a marketing career.

Starting Your Own Business

There is nothing quite so rewarding and exciting as running your own business, and no college degree better prepares you for starting your own business than a degree in marketing. You learn how to pick a good site for your business, how to assess the market and competition, and how to serve customers well. You also need to understand business operations, accounting, human resources management, and other functions. You may want to work for another small business for a while to learn business management and marketing skills.

As an entrepreneur, you can use the eight universal marketing processes to successfully build relationships with customers in consumer or organizational markets. Environmental and market analysis can lead you to business opportunities; segmentation, targeting, and positioning can help you determine the appropriate market and approach; product development and differentiation will result in a unique product for your small business to market; valuation and pricing are used to set a price for a mutually beneficial marketing exchange; channel and value-chain management can help you make connections with suppliers, resellers, and customers; integrated marketing communication is the key to maintaining a dialogue with customers; and relationship building will allow you to attract and keep customers over the long run.

Emerging Marketing Fields: Internet Marketing and More

One exciting aspect of a career in marketing is that new jobs are constantly emerging. For example, one of the hottest areas of the late 1990s is the development of Web sites for companies wanting to market on the Internet.

The Internet is creating new opportunities for artists who can design a creative Web site; for copywriters who can draft the content for a compelling Web site; for marketing researchers who can find ways to measure and analyze Web site traffic; for advertising and sales promotion specialists who can devise ways of drawing surfers to Web sites; and for product managers and entrepreneurs who can develop new products geared to the needs and interests of Internet visitors.

More job opportunities are being created by a trend toward nonstore selling through catalogs, vending machines, interactive kiosks, and television home shopping. Catalog marketing is more than 100 years old, but new technologies such as CD-ROM and video catalogs are opening doors for more job seekers. Also, Japan and other countries are far ahead of the United States in selling goods through vending machines. Everything from pasta to popcorn can be sold this way, creating profit opportunities for all types of entrepreneurial businesses. Creative and technical people are in demand for designing and implementing interactive kiosks, another emerging marketing channel. Growth in television home shopping has resulted in more jobs for telemarketers to take inbound customer orders as well as for communication experts who can help marketers do a better job presenting their products to viewers.

Marketing is now entering the era of mass customization. Future marketers must be able to develop a customer database, use that database to learn what customers are buying, and then develop value packages that will retain those customers over time. Database management is becoming a critical part of marketing, as is establishing linkages in the value chain through electronic data interchange. Those who understand the technology and the concepts—and can apply them—will have long and successful careers in marketing.

As this appendix shows, marketing offers a wide range of diverse career opportunities. All kinds of organizations need people with marketing skills. Some jobs will put you in direct contact with external customers while others involve functions that satisfy internal customers. No matter what kind of marketing career you're considering, your success will depend, in part, on your commitment to both internal and external customer satisfaction. As part of a team—working collaboratively with other employees, with suppliers, and with channel partners—you can move beyond customer satisfaction and delight your customers, forging an enduring relationship that competitors can't easily disrupt.

Quantitative Analysis for Marketing Decision Making

As a marketer, you will need to apply a variety of quantitative methods to inform and support the decisions you make. Because quantitative analysis is also important when working with people from other departments on cross-functional teams, handling product development and other key activities, you must be familiar with quantitative terms and concepts used by other areas of the firm, such as accounting and finance. Furthermore, there are certain calculations that you will be using in your everyday management of the business. This appendix highlights some of the terms, concepts, and formulas every marketer should know. Using the example of Bountiful Bakery, a small business, you will learn how quantitative analysis techniques are applied to a real marketing situation.

First, you will see how the bakery analyzes its overall financial performance using an income statement and a balance sheet. By using these financial statements to calculate operating ratios, the owner can identify adjustments that need to be made to improve profitability and to support marketing decisions.

Next, you will explore financial concepts that apply to pricing and product management. The bakery uses markup and markdown techniques to set prices. The formula for markup helps the bakery set initial prices for its products; the formula for markdown helps it set prices for clearing out day-old baked goods or accessories that are not selling well enough to be retained. In addition, the bakery can use break-even analysis to determine whether to go ahead with a new product introduction and to determine the price at which it becomes profitable.

Finally, you will learn how to calculate the lifetime value of a customer—an analysis essential to relationship marketing because it can demonstrate to employees why they should pay attention to maintaining good relationships with customers over an extended period. Even a small business such as Bountiful Bakery can benefit from analyzing the lifetime value of its customers. This helps the bakery to determine who its best customers are and to develop marketing ideas for reinforcing their loyalty, such as offering free delivery.

Income Statement and Balance Sheet

Every business keeps track of its financial health and performance through two important financial statements. The *income statement* (also called the profit and loss or P&L statement) summarizes the business's income, expense, and profit results over a specified period, usually a month or a year. The purpose is to deduct expenses from revenues to arrive at net income or profits. *Net operating revenues* is the term for sales revenues.

The *balance sheet* summarizes the business's assets and liabilities on a specified date. The purpose is to provide a snapshot of what the company owns (assets such as bank deposits and buildings) and what it owes (liabilities such as loans as well as equity invested by owners) on that date. The balance sheet acts like a scale, helping managers to weigh assets owned against liabilities owed and equity invested in the business.

These financial statements are usually produced by the accounting department or bookkeeper, but they are very useful to marketers and managers in other departments. Apart from helping managers prioritize strategic decisions such as increasing sales or reducing expenses, an income statement also enables a business to estimate its tax liability.

Publicly traded U.S. companies are legally required to publish these financial statements as part of their annual reports to stockholders. Generally, however, private businesses do not release income statements or balance sheets to the public, although they do maintain them for tax and internal purposes and for inspection by lenders and owners.

Figure B.1 shows the income statement for Bountiful Bakery; Figure B.2 shows the balance sheet. Notice that these statements cover a defined time frame of one year. Year-to-year changes in these statements are important indicators of trends, such as decreasing profitability or rising debt load.

The income statement shows that in 1996 the bakery had a net income (also known as net profit) of $24,667. The balance sheet shows that in 1996 the bakery had total assets of $134,170. The assets included: current assets of $52,470; property, plant, and equipment of $59,800; investments and other assets of $12,460; and goodwill of $9,440. The company's liabilities included: current liabilities of $43,480, long-term debt of $30,410, and owners' equity of $60,280.

FIGURE **B.1**

Income Statement for Bountiful Bakery

Bountiful Bakery
INCOME STATEMENT
Year ending December 31, 1996

Net Operating Revenues		$180,018
Cost of Goods Sold		69,238
Gross Profit		$110,780
Operating Expenses		
Selling expenses	$21,020	
Administrative expenses	8,750	
General expenses	40,090	
Total operating expenses		69,860
Operating Income		$40,920
Other Income & Expenses		
Interest income	(1,110)	
Interest expense	6,280	
Total other income & expenses		5,170
Income before taxes		$35,750
Less: Corporate taxes		11,083
Net Income		$24,667

FIGURE **B.2**

Balance Sheet for Bountiful Bakery

Bountiful Bakery
BALANCE SHEET
Year ending December 31, 1996

ASSETS

Current Assets
Cash	$11,670	
Accounts receivable	16,950	
Inventories	11,170	
Prepaid expenses	12,680	
Total Current Assets		$52,470

Property, Plant, and Equipment
Vehicles	$15,000	
Machinery and equipment	41,350	
Containers	3,450	
Total Property, Plant, and Equipment Assets		59,800

Investment and Other Assets
Marketable securities, savings account	$12,460	
Goodwill	9,440	
Total Investment and Other Assets		21,900

Total Assets $134,170

LIABILITIES

Current Liabilities
Accounts payable	$43,480	
Total Current Liabilities		$43,480

Long-Term Debt   30,410

Owners' Equity   60,280

Total Liabilities $134,170

Operating Ratios

Using figures from the income statement and balance sheet, managers can compute *operating ratios* that serve as diagnostic measures of the business's overall health.

Gross profit ratio (also known as the gross margin ratio) is calculated by dividing the gross profit by the net operating revenues:

$$\text{Gross profit ratio} = \frac{\text{gross profit}}{\text{net operating revenues}}$$

Applying this to Bountiful Bakery:

$$\text{Gross profit ratio} = \frac{\$110,780}{\$180,018} = 0.615 = 61.5\%$$

Operating margin ratio is computed by dividing operating income by net operating revenues:

$$\text{Operating margin ratio} = \frac{\text{operating income}}{\text{net operating revenues}}$$

Applying this to the bakery:

$$\text{Operating margin ratio} = \frac{\$40,920}{\$180,018} = 0.227 = 22.7\%$$

The higher the bakery's gross margin and operating margin ratios, the more profitable it is. Increasing or decreasing margins over time indicate that performance is improving or declining, respectively. Similarly, comparing these ratios with the profit and operating margins of competitors (when available) helps managers pinpoint areas for improvement.

Gross margin may be increased by reducing the cost of goods sold, and operating margin can be increased by reducing selling, administrative, and general expenses. Both the gross margin and operating margin ratios can be increased by increasing net operating revenues through higher sales volume or price increases that enhance sales revenues.

Inventory turnover ratio, also called the stock turnover ratio, is calculated by dividing the cost of goods sold by the average inventory figure over the period being analyzed. The purpose is to see how quickly products are selling. In this example, Bountiful Bakery's average inventory level for non-baked goods over the year 1996 is $10,820. Thus,

$$\text{Inventory turnover ratio} = \frac{\text{cost of goods sold}}{\text{value of average inventory}}$$

$$= \frac{\$69,238}{\$10,820} = 6.4 \text{ times}$$

This indicates that the bakery sells and replaces its accessory inventory more than six times during the year. Again, comparisons over time and with competitor turnover ratios will help determine whether the bakery's performance needs improvement.

Return-on-investment ratios indicate the overall performance of a business. Three such ratios are return on assets (ROA), return on investment (ROI), and return on equity (ROE).

Return on assets is computed by dividing net income by total assets. For Bountiful Bakery,

$$\text{ROA} = \frac{\text{net income}}{\text{total assets}}$$

$$\text{ROA} = \frac{\$24,667}{\$134,170} = 0.184 = 18.4\%$$

Return on investment is computed by dividing net income by total investment. The figure for total investment is obtained by subtracting total current assets from total assets. For the bakery, the total investment is $134,170 − $52,470 = $81,700. Thus,

$$\text{ROI} = \frac{\text{net income}}{\text{total investment}}$$

$$= \frac{\$24,667}{\$81,700} = 0.302 = 30.2\%$$

Return on equity is a measure of owner (or shareholder) value, which is computed by dividing net income by owners' equity. For Bountiful Bakery,

$$\text{ROE} = \frac{\text{net income}}{\text{owners' equity}}$$

$$= \frac{\$24,667}{\$60,280} = 0.409 = 40.9\%$$

All three return-on-investment ratios should be compared with rates of return available to the business from other investment opportunities and with standard results for similar businesses. In this way, management can determine whether the business is doing as well as it should. Bountiful Bakery's ratios indicate that it is delivering outstanding value to its owner and producing a good return on its assets and investment.

Markup and Markdown Pricing

Marketers use a variety of quantitative analyses to determine selling prices and pricing profit margins. In particular, retailers and other resellers rely on markup and markdown pricing techniques that make it easier to calculate the selling price of the products they offer.

Markups

As you saw in Chapter 13, retailers often add a specific percentage of dollar amount to a product's cost to come up with the selling price. This is known as *markup pricing*, with the markup representing the margin per unit.

Markup pricing can be calculated on the basis of either the cost or the selling price of the product. The *percentage markup on cost* is the ratio of the dollar amount of markup on one unit to the dollar amount of each unit's cost:

$$\text{Markup on cost (\%)} = \frac{\text{dollar markup on one unit}}{\text{dollar cost per unit}}$$

In contrast, the *percentage markup on selling price* is the ratio of the dollar amount of markup on each unit to the selling price of one unit:

$$\text{Markup on selling price (\%)} = \frac{\text{dollar markup on one unit}}{\text{dollar selling price per unit}}$$

As you can see, each formula gives a different markup percentage.

How would Bountiful Bakery use these markup formulas? If the bakery is selling a package of party favors that costs $2.00 and the owner marks up each package by $1.00 to a selling price of $3.00, then:

$$\text{Markup on cost (\%)} = \frac{\$1.00}{\$2.00} = 50\%$$

On the other hand, if the bakery uses markup on selling price:

$$\text{Markup on selling price (\%)} = \frac{\$1.00}{\$3.00} = 33.3\%$$

If you know one type of markup percentage you can calculate the other. Knowing the markup on cost, you can find the markup on selling price:

$$\text{Markup on selling price (\%)} = \frac{\text{markup on cost (\%)}}{100\% + \text{markup on cost (\%)}}$$

In the case of Bountiful Bakery, the markup on selling price can be determined using the markup on cost of 50%:

$$\text{Markup on selling price (\%)} = \frac{50\%}{100\% + 50\%} = \frac{50}{150} = 33.3\%$$

Similarly, you can find the markup on cost when you know the markup on selling price:

$$\text{Markup on cost (\%)} = \frac{\text{markup on selling price (\%)}}{100\% - \text{markup on selling price (\%)}}$$

For Bountiful Bakery:

$$\text{Markup on cost (\%)} = \frac{33.3\%}{100\% - 33.3\%} = \frac{33.3}{66.7} = 50\%$$

You can easily calculate the selling price per unit if you know the unit cost and either the markup percentage on cost or the markup percentage on selling price. The selling price is calculated from the cost and the markup on cost as follows:

$$\text{Selling price (\$)} = \text{unit cost (\$)} \times [100\% + \text{markup on cost (\%)}]$$

Thus Bountiful Bakery's selling price for the party favors would be

$$\text{Selling price (\$)} = \$2.00 \times (100\% + 50\%) = \$2.00 \times 150\% = \$3.00$$

What if the bakery commonly uses the markup on selling price? In this case, the owner would use a different formula to find the selling price:

$$\text{Selling price (\$)} = \frac{\text{Unit cost}}{[100\% - \text{markup on selling price (\%)}]}$$

The selling price for the party favors would be

$$\text{Selling price (\$)} = \frac{\$2.00}{100\% - 33.3\%} = \frac{\$2.00}{66.7\%} = \$3.00$$

Markdowns

At times, Bountiful Bakery (like most resellers) will want to lower the price of selected items to sell them off. This is the way retailers encourage shoppers to buy products that are being eliminated because they are obsolete, are not as fresh as current items, or are not selling well enough to be retained in the product mix.

A *markdown* is a reduction in the selling price per unit. The percentage of markdown is computed by dividing the dollar amount of the reduction by the dollar amount of the original selling price:

$$\text{Markdown (\%)} = \frac{\text{reduction in selling price (\$)}}{\text{original selling price (\$)}}$$

Imagine that Bountiful Bakery wants to take a markdown on a cake carrier that didn't sell as well as expected. The owner decides to advertise the percentage markdown so that bargain hunters will buy quickly. The original selling price of $10.00 is being reduced by $3.00 to a new selling price of $7.00. The owner calculates the percentage markdown in this way:

$$\text{Markdown (\%)} = \frac{\$3.00}{\$10.00} = 30\%$$

If the owner wants to use a markdown percentage to determine the selling price, the new price is calculated as follows:

New selling price = original selling price × [100% − markdown (%)]

For the cake carrier being marked down by 30%:

New selling price = $10.00 × (100% − 30%) =$10.00 × 70% = $7.00

Break-Even Analysis

All marketers need to analyze the profit potential of a new product before introducing it. One tool you can use is *break-even analysis*, which helps you analyze revenues and costs to find the profit at various levels of quantity sold. As you saw in Chapter 13, the purpose of break-even analysis is to determine how many units of a product must be sold to recover variable and fixed costs. In this way, a marketer can figure out whether it is worthwhile to invest in a new product.

The *break-even point (BEP)* is the point at which revenues equal costs and beyond which you begin to make a profit. The formula for finding the break-even point is

$$\text{BEP (in units)} = \frac{\text{fixed costs}}{\text{price per unit} - \text{variable cost per unit}}$$

The two key principles in a break-even analysis are (a) identifying the time frame for the analysis, and (b) identifying the relevant fixed and variable costs. Typically, break-even analysis is done for a one-year time frame. Knowing the time covered by the analysis helps you identify the costs that should be included in the calculation. However, the analysis can be extended to cover several years into the future. For a major new product launch that entails thousands or even millions of dollars in advertising and sales promotion, a marketer may not break even in the first year and will require a multiyear break-even analysis to compute the break-even point for each year.

The *payback period* is the time it takes the marketer to break even on a project. Many companies have guidelines for funding projects based on the payback period. For instance, if the payback period for a new product launch exceeds three years, management may not fund it.

In a break-even analysis, cost components have to be carefully classified as variable or fixed. *Variable costs* vary directly with the number of units produced and sold. These costs include direct labor, direct material, sales commissions, and similar costs. *Fixed costs* do not vary with the number of units produced or sold, at least in the short term. These include salaries, rent, utilities, manufacturing and administrative overhead, advertising, market research, and similar costs.

Finally, in order to compute the break-even point using the formula given above, you must use the correct selling price per unit. For a retailer, this selling price is the price a shopper pays for the product in the store. For a manufacturer who sells through wholesalers or retailers, the selling price is the price that it charges channel partners, not the retail price paid by ultimate consumers or business customers at the end of the channel.

To see how break-even analysis works, consider the decision to be made by the owner of Bountiful Bakery. She is considering launching a new dessert pastry and has gathered some data for her break-even analysis:

1. Retail selling price	$4 per unit
2. Raw material	$1 per unit
3. Direct labor	$1 per unit
4. Rent and administrative overhead	$24,000
5. Advertising and promotion in year 1	$8,000
6. Advertising and promotion in year 2	$6,000
7. Sales forecast	14,000 units/year 1
	18,000 units/year 2

The owner wants to (a) compute the break-even point (in units) for this new product in years 1 and 2 and (b) determine the payback period on the new product launch. If the owner's guideline is that the payback period for new products should not exceed two years, should she launch the new dessert product?

First, identify fixed and variable costs. In year 1, the fixed costs are the sum of items 4 and 5 above, which total $32,000. In year 2, the fixed costs are the sum of items 4 and 6, totaling $30,000—lower than in year 1 because the advertising cost declines. The variable costs are the sum of items 2 and 3, for a total variable cost of $2 per pastry. The costs in each year can be summarized as follows:

	Year 1	*Year 2*
Fixed costs	$32,000	$30,000
Variable cost per dessert	$2	$2
Selling price per dessert	$4	$4
Sales forecast	14,000	18,000

With these details arranged, the owner can calulate the break-even point for each year:

$$\text{Year 1 BEP} = \frac{\$32,000}{\$4 - \$2} = 16,000 \text{ desserts}$$

$$\text{Year 2 BEP} = \frac{\$30,000}{\$4 - \$2} = 15,000 \text{ desserts}$$

According to the owner's sales forecast, the bakery will not break even on this product in the first year: it needs to sell 16,000 desserts to break even and the forecast is for 14,000. However, the bakery will break even in year 2, when forecasted sales of 18,000 desserts will exceed the break-even point of 15,000 desserts for that year. The payback period for the new dessert is therefore two years, which meets the owner's guidelines. Using this analysis, the bakery owner feels confident in launching the new product.

Lifetime Value of a Customer

A key quantitative concept in relationship marketing is the *lifetime value of a customer,* the revenue potential of a customer over time across all the goods and services offered by the marketer. This calculation recognizes the value of building a long-lasting relationship with a customer rather than thinking about each transaction in isolation. When you add up all the goods and services a customer may buy during a relationship that stretches over months or years, you can see why it is extremely important to stress customer satisfaction in every interaction.

This quantitative tool is useful for reinforcing a relationship orientation, prioritizing customer targets, and setting product, pricing, and service policies. For instance, after conducting such an analysis, Bountiful Bakery might decide to adopt a policy of offering free delivery to customers who buy more than $200 worth of baked goods each month.

Every marketer can apply the lifetime value concept. Consider the lifetime value of a car buyer to a car dealer. The dealer may sell a $15,000 car to a customer this year. Then, over the life of the car, the dealer can also earn revenues from maintenance services and parts replacement as well as interest from financing the purchase. A detailed computation of the revenues that the dealer can make on this one sale is shown in Figure B.3.

FIGURE **B.3**

Lifetime Customer Value

	Potential Revenue from a Typical Automobile Customer												
Year	1	2	3	4	5	6	7	8	9	10	11	12	13
Selling price	15000												
Oil change	60	60	60	60	60	60	60	60	60	60	60	60	15
Minor service	100	100		100	100	100	100		100	100	100	100	
Major service		300	300	300	300		300	300	300	300		300	
Timing belt								200					
Tire replacement					200								
Battery replacement					50								
Other parts				200					200			200	
Interest	1500.00	1384.60	1269.20	1153.80	1038.40	923.00	807.60	692.20	576.80	461.40	346.00	230.60	115.20
Total revenue	16660	1844.6	1629.2	1813.8	1748.4	1083	1467.6	1252.2	1036.8	921.4	506	890.6	130.2
Discount factor		1.05	1.10	1.16	1.22	1.28	1.34	1.41	1.48	1.55	1.63	1.71	1.80
Discounted revenue	16660	1756.76	1477.73	1566.83	1438.41	848.56	1095.15	889.92	701.75	593.94	310.64	520.72	72.50
Net Present Value	27932.90												

Notes:
1. The life of the car is assumed to be 150,000 miles.
2. The average usage is assumed to be 12,000 miles per year.
3. Oil changes are recommended every 3000 miles.
4. Minor service recommended every 7500 miles, major service every 15,000 miles.
5. Simple interest is computed on a declining balance basis at 10% per year.
6. Discounted revenue is based on a 5% discount rate.
7. Net present value is the sum of the discounted revenue across all 13 years.

The total yearly revenue expected from the sale varies from $16,660 in year 1 to $130 in year 13. A technique called *discounted cash flow* or *net present value analysis* is used to arrive at the discounted revenue each year. This is necessary because of the time value of money: $130 in year 13 is worth a lot less than $130 this year. The discounted revenue of $72.50 in year 13 means that if this amount were invested today at an interest rate of 5%, it would be worth $130 in year 13. Aggregating the discounted revenues across the 13 years yields a net present value of about $28,000, almost double the selling price of the car.

Remember: this is the potential revenue from the sale of a single car. Consider the additional revenue potential of a 22-year-old car buyer. She might buy a new car three or more times over the years, and she might trade in lower-priced cars for more expensive ones as her income climbs. Some car companies estimate the lifetime value of such a customer to be close to $300,000. Every automobile dealer should look at each car buyer as being worth $300,000 rather than just the price of the car being sold. With this long-term view, the dealer's employees would be more motivated to provide better service and take more care to keep customers happy.

You can see how a bakery would also benefit from such an analysis. Employees who have been taught the lifetime value of customers would be inclined to treat each customer better. It is one thing to calculate the profit from selling a customer two donuts and a cup of coffee. It is quite another to calculate how much profit the customer will generate by coming into the bakery five days a week, for the next 15 years.

The Model of a Modern Marketing Plan

Successful Companies Are Rewriting Their Strategies to Reflect Customer Input and Internal Coordination*

In a world where competitors can observe and rapidly imitate each other's advancements in product development, pricing, packaging, and distribution, communication is more important than ever as a way of differentiating your business from those of your competitors.

The most successful companies are the ones that understand that, and are revamping their marketing plans to emphasize two points:

1. Marketing is a dialogue between customer and supplier.

2. Companies have to prove they're listening to their customers by acting on their input.

What Is a Marketing Plan?

At its most basic level, a marketing plan defines a business's niche, summarizes its objectives, and presents its strategies for attaining and monitoring those goals. It's a road map for getting from point A to point B.

But road maps need constant updating to reflect the addition of new routes. Likewise, in a decade in which technology, international relations, and the competitive landscape are constantly changing, the concept of a static marketing plan has to be reassessed.

Two of the hottest buzz words for the 1990s are "interactive" and "integrated." A successful marketing plan has to be both.

"Interactive" means your marketing plan should be a conversation between your business and your customers. It's your chance to tell customers about your business and to listen and act on their responses.

---

*By Shelly Reese. Reprinted with permission from *Marketing Tools*, January/February, 1996.

"Integrated" means the message in your marketing is consistently reinforced by every department within your company. Marketing is as much a function of the finance and manufacturing divisions as it is the advertising and public relations departments.

Integrated also means each time a company reaches out to its customers through an advertisement, direct mailing, or promotion, it is sending the same message and encouraging customers to learn more about the product.

Why Is It Important?

The interaction between a company and its customers is a relationship. Relationships can't be reproduced. They can, however, be replaced. That's where a good marketing plan comes into play.

Think of your business as a suitor, your customers as the object of your affection, and your competitors as rivals. A marketing plan is your strategy for wooing customers. It's based on listening and reacting to what they say.

Because a customer's priorities are constantly changing, a marketing plan should change with them. For years, conventional wisdom was 'prepare a five year marketing plan and review it every year.' But change happens a lot faster than it did 20 or even 10 years ago.

For that reason, Bob Dawson of The Business Group, a consulting firm in Freemont, California, recommends that his clients prepare a three year plan and review it every quarter. Frequent reviews enable companies to identify potential problems and opportunities before their competition, he explains.

"Preventative maintenance for your company is as important as putting oil in your car," Dawson says. "You don't wait a whole year to do it. You can't change history but you can anticipate what's going to happen."

FIGURE **C.1**

Three Components of a Marketing Plan

Essential Components

Most marketing plans consist of three sections. The first section should identify the organization's goals. The second section should establish a method for attaining them. The third section focuses on creating a system for implementing the strategy. [See Figure C.1.]

Although some plans identify as many as six or eight goals, many experts suggest a company whittle its list to one or two key objectives and focus on them.

"One of the toughest things is sticking to one message," observes Mark Bilfield, account director for integrated marketing of Nissan and Infinity cars at TBWA Chiat/Day in Los Angeles, which handles national advertising, direct marketing, public relations, and promotions for the automaker. Bilfield argues that a focused, consistent message is easier to communicate to the market place and to different disciplines within the corporation than a broad, encompassing one. Therefore, he advises, "unless there is something drastically wrong with the idea, stick with it."

Section I: Goals

The goals component of your plan is the most fundamental. Consider it a kind of thinking out loud: Why are you writing this plan? What do you want to accomplish? What do you want to achieve in the next quarter? The next year? The next three years?

Like taping your New Year's resolution to the refrigerator, the goals section is a constant reminder of what you want to achieve. The key difference between a New Year's resolution and your marketing goals, however, is you can't achieve the latter alone.

To achieve your marketing goals you've got to convince your customers to behave in a certain way. If you're a soft drink manufacturer you may want them to try your company's latest wild berry flavor. If you're a new bank in town, you need to familiarize people with your name and convince them to give your institution a try. Or perhaps you're a family-owned retailer who needs to remind customers of the importance of reliability and a proven track record in the face of new competition.

The goals in each of these cases differ with the audiences. The soft drink manufacturer is asking an existing customer to try something new; the bank is trying to attract new customers; the retailer wants to retain existing customers.

Each company wants to influence its customers' behavior. The company that is most likely to succeed is the one that understands its customers the best.

There's no substitute for knowledge. You need to understand the demographic and psychographic makeup of the customers you are trying to reach, as well as the best methods for getting their attention.

Do your research. Learn as much as possible about your audience. Trade associations, trade journals and government statistics and surveys are excellent resources, but chances are you have a lot of data within your own business that you haven't tapped. Look at what you know about your customer already and find ways to bolster that information. Companies should constantly be asking clients what they want and how they would use a new product.

"If you're not asking people that use your end product, then everything you're doing is an assumption," argues Dawson.

In addition, firms should ask customers how they perceive the products and services they receive. Too often, companies have an image of themselves that they broadcast but fail to live up to. That frustrates consumers and makes them feel deceived.

Companies that claim to offer superior service often appear to renege on their promises because their definition of 'service' doesn't mesh with their customers' [definition], says Bilfield.

"Airlines and banks are prime offenders," says Bilfield. "They tout service, and when the customers go into the airport or the bank, they have to wait in long lines."

The problem often lies in the company's assumptions about what customers really want. While an airline may feel it is living up to its claim of superior service because it distributes warm towels and mints after a meal, a business traveler will probably place a higher value on its competitor's on-time record and policy for returning lost luggage.

Section II: The Strategy

Unfortunately, after taking the time and conducting the research to determine who their audience is and what their message should be, companies often fail by zooming ahead with a plan. An attitude of, "OK, we know who we're after and we know what we want to say, so let's go!" seems to take over.

More often than not, that gung-ho way of thinking leads to disaster because companies have skipped a critical step: they haven't established and communicated an internal strategy for attaining their goals. They want to take their message to the public without pausing to get feedback from inside the company.

For a marketing plan to work, everyone within the company must understand the company's message and work cooperatively to establish a method for taking that message to the public.

For example, if you decide the goal of your plan is to promote the superior service your company offers, you'd better make sure all aspects of your business are on board. Your manufacturing process should meet the highest standards. Your financial department should develop credit and leasing programs that make it easier for customers to use your product. Finally, your customer relations personnel should be trained to respond to problems quickly and efficiently, and to use the contact as an opportunity to find out more about what customers want.

"I'm always amazed when I go into the shipping department of some company and say, 'What is your mission? What's the message you want to give to your end user?' and they say, 'I don't know. I just know I've got to get these shipments out on time," says Dawson.

Because the success of integrated marketing depends on a consistent, cohesive message, employees throughout the company need to understand the firm's marketing goals and their role in helping to fulfill them.

"It's very important to bring employees in on the process," says James Lowry, chairman of the marketing department at Ball State University. "Employees today are better than any we've had before. They want to know what's going on in the organization. They don't want to be left out."

Employees are ambassadors for your company. Every time they interact with a customer or vendor, they're marketing your company. The more knowledgeable and helpful they are, the better they reflect on your firm.

At Nordstrom, a Seattle-based retailer, sales associates are empowered to use their best judgment in all situations to make a customer happy.

"We think our sales associates are the best marketing department," said spokeswoman Amy Jones. "We think word of mouth is the best advertising you can have." As a result, although Nordstrom has stores in only 15 states, it has forged a national reputation.

If companies regard marketing as the exclusive province of the marketing department, they're destined to fail.

"Accounting and sales and other departments have to work together hand in hand," says Dawson. "If they don't, you're going to have a problem in the end."

For example, in devising an integrated marketing campaign for the Nissan 200SX, Chiat/Day marketers worked in strategic business units that included a variety of disciplines such as engineers, representatives from the parts and service department, and creative people. By taking a broad view of the business and building inter-related activities to support its goals, Chiat/Day was able to create a seamless campaign for the 200SX that weaves advertising, in-store displays, and direct marketing together seamlessly.

'When everybody understands what the mission is, it's easier," asserts Bilfield. "It's easier to go upstream in the same direction than to go in different directions."

After bringing the different disciplines within your company on board, you're ready to design the external marketing program needed to support your goals. Again, the principal of integrated marketing comes into play: The message should be focused and consistent, and each step of the process should bring the consumer one step closer to buying your product.

In the case of Chiat/Day's campaign for the Nissan 200SX, the company used the same theme, graphics, type faces, and message to broadcast a consistent statement.

Introduced about the same time as the latest Batman movie, the campaign incorporates music and graphics from the television series. Magazine ads include an 800 number potential customers can call if they want to receive an information kit. Kits are personalized and include the name of a local Nissan dealer, a certificate for a test drive, and a voucher entitling test drivers to a free gift.

By linking each step of the process, Chiat/Day can chart the number of calls, test drives, and sales a particular ad elicits. Like a good one-two punch, the direct marketing picks up where the national advertising leaves off, leveraging the broad exposure and targeting it at the most likely buyers.

While the elaborate 200SX campaign may seem foolproof, a failure to integrate the process at any step along the way could result in a lost sale.

For example, if a potential client were to test drive the car and encounter a dealer who knew nothing about the free gift accompanying the test drive, the customer would feel justifiably annoyed. Conversely, a well-informed sales associate who can explain the gift will be mailed to the test driver in a few weeks will engender a positive response.

Section III: Execution

The final component of an integrated marketing plan is the implementation phase. This is where the budget comes in.

How much you'll need to spend depends on your goals. If a company wants to expand its market share or promote its products in a new region, it will probably have to spend more than it would to maintain its position in an existing market.

Again, you'll need to create a system for keeping your employees informed. You might consider adding an element to your company newsletter that features people from different departments talking about the marketing problems they encounter and how they overcome them. Or you might schedule a regular meeting for department heads to discuss marketing ideas so they can report back to their employees with news from around the company.

Finally, you'll need to devise a system for monitoring your marketing program. A database, similar to the one created from calls to the 200SX's 800 number, can be an invaluable tool for determining if your message is being well received.

It's important to establish time frames for achieving your goals early in the process. If you want to increase your market share, for instance, you should determine the rate at which you intend to add new customers. Failing to achieve that rate could signal a flaw in your plan or its execution, or an unrealistic goal.

"Remember, integrated marketing is a long-range way of thinking," warns Dawson. "Results are not going to be immediate."

Like any investment, marketing requires patience, perseverance, and commitment if it is to bear fruit. While not all companies are forward thinking enough to understand the manifold gains of integrated marketing, the ones that don't embrace it will ultimately pay a tremendous price.

GETTING STARTED

A nine-step plan that will make the difference between writing a useful plan and a document that gathers dust on a shelf**

In his 1986 book, *The Goal*, Eliyahu M. Goldratt writes that most of us forget the one true goal of our business. It's not to deliver products on time. It isn't even to manufacture the best widget in the world. The goal is to make money.

In the past, making money depended on selling a product or service. Today, that's changed as customers are, at times, willing to pay for what we stand for: better service, better support, more innovation, more partnership in developing new products.

This section . . . assumes that you believe a plan is needed, and that this plan should weave together your desires with those of your customers. [The editors of *Marketing Tools* magazine have] reviewed a number of marketing plans and come up with a nine-step model. [See Figure C.2.] It is perhaps more than what your organization needs today, but none of the steps are unimportant.

Our model combines some of the basics of a conventional plan with some new threads that we believe will push your plan over the edge, from being satisfactory to being necessary. These include:

- Using and improving the former domain of public relations, image, as a marketing tool.

- Integrating all the business functions that touch your customers into a single, customer-focused strategic marketing plan.

FIGURE **C.2**

The Nine-Step Marketing Plan

1 Describe the Business

2 Market Analysis

3 Marketing Strategy

4 Marketing & Sales Organization

5 Revenue/Expenses

9 Measure/Renew

8 Sell the Plans

7 Executive Summary

6 Management Issues

** By Carole R. Hedden and the *Marketing Tools* editorial staff. Reprinted with permission from *Marketing Tools*, January/February, 1996.

- Borrowing from Total Quality theories to establish performance measures beyond the financial report to help you note customer trends.
- Making sure that the people needed to deliver your marketing objectives are part of your plan.
- "Selling" your plan to the people whose support is essential to its success.

. . . First, let's look at the model itself. Remember that one of the primary criticisms of any plan is that it becomes a binder on a shelf, never to be seen again until budget time next year. Planning should be an iterative process, feeding off itself and used to guide and measure.

Whether you're asked to create a marketing plan or write the marketing section of the strategic plan for your business, your document is going to include what the business is trying to achieve, a careful analysis of your market, the products and services you offer to that market, and how you will market and sell products or services to your customer.

1. Describe the Business

You are probably in one of two situations: either you need to write a description of your business or you can rely on an existing document found in your annual report, the strategic plan, or a capabilities brochure. The description should include, at minimum:

- Your company's purpose [mission];
- Who you deliver products or services to [target market]; and
- What you deliver to those customers [products].

Too often, such descriptions omit a discussion about what you want your business to stand for—your image. This is increasingly important as customers report they are looking for more than the product or service; they're in search of a partner. The only way to address image is to know who you want to be, who your customers think you are, and how you can bridge the gap between the two.

Part of defining your image is knowing where you are strong and where you are weak. For instance, if your current yield rate is 99.997 percent and customers rate you as the preferred supplier, then you might identify operations as a key to your company's image. Most companies tend to be their own worst critics, so start by listing all your strengths. Then identify weaknesses or the threats you face, either due to your own limitations or from the increased competency of a competitor.

The description also includes what your business delivers to its owners, be they shareholders, private owners, or employees. Usually this is stated in financial terms: revenue, return on investment or equity, economic value added, cash generated, operating margin or earnings per share. The other measures your organization uses to monitor its performance may be of interest to outsiders, but save them for the measurement section of your plan.

The result of all this describing and listing is that you should have a fairly good idea of where you are and where you want to be, which naturally leads to objectives for the coming 6, 12, or 18 months, if not longer.

2. Analyze the Market

. . . [L]ook at this as a section jointly owned by [almost] everyone working with you. In a smaller company, the lead managers may own various pieces of this section. In a larger organization, you many need to pull in the ideas and data available from other departments, such as logistics, competitor intelligence, research and development, and the function responsible for quality control or quality assurance. All have two things in common: delivering value to customers, and beating the competition.

Together, you can thoroughly cover the following areas:

- **Your target markets.** What markets do you currently compete in? What do you know about them in terms of potential, dollars available, and your share of the market? Something frequently prepared for products is a life cycle chart; you might want to do the same for your market. Is it embryonic, developing, mature or in decline? Are there new markets to exploit?

- **Customer knowledge.** Your colleagues in Quality, Distribution, Engineering, or other organizations can be helpful in finding what you need.

  The customer's objectives. What threats does your customer face? What goals does the customer have? Work with your customer to define these so you can become a partner instead of a variable component.

  How is the customer addressing her or his markets? Do you know as much about your customer's position as you know about your own? If not, find out.

  How big is each customer, really? You may find you're spending more time on a less important customer than on the customers who can break you. Is your customer growing or in decline? What plans does the customer have to expand or acquire growth? What innovations are in development?

  What does your customer value? Price, product quality, service, innovation, delivery? The better you know what's driving your customer's purchasing decision, the better you'll be able to respond.

- **Clearly identify the alternatives your customer has.** As one customer told employees at a major supplier, "While you've been figuring out how to get by, we've been figuring out how to get by without you." Is backward integration—a situation in which the customer develops the capability inhouse—possible? Is there an abundance of other suppliers? What is your business doing to avoid having your customers looking for alternatives?

- **Know your competition.** Your competitors are the obvious alternative for your customer, and thus represent your biggest threat. You can find what you need to know about your competitors through newspaper reports, public records, at trade shows, and from your customers: the size of expansions, the strengths that competitor has, its latest innovations. Do you know how your competition approaches your customers?

- **Describe the environment.** What changes have occurred in the last 18 months? In the past year? What could change in the near future and over a longer period of time? This should include any kinds of laws or regulations that might affect you, the entry or deletion of competitors, and shifts in technology. Also, keep in mind that internal change does affect your customers. For instance, is a key leader in your business planning to retire? If so, decision-making, operations or management style may change—and your customer may have obvious concerns. You can add some depth to this section, too, by portraying several different scenarios:

- What happens if we do nothing beyond last year?
- What happens if we capitalize on our strengths?
- What might happen if our image slips?
- What happens if we do less this year than last?

3. The Marketing Strategy

The marketing strategy consists of what you offer customers and the price you charge. Start by providing a complete description of each product or service and what it provides to your customers. Life cycle, again, is an important part of this. Is your technology or product developing, mature or in decline? Depending on how your company is organized, a variety of people are responsible for this information, right down to whoever is figuring out how to package the product and how it will be delivered. Find out who needs to be included and make sure their knowledge is used.

The marketing strategy is driven by everything you've done up to this point. Strategies define the approaches you will use to market the company. For instance, if you are competing on the basis of service and support rather than price, your strategy may consist of emphasizing relationships. You will then develop tactics that support that strategy: market the company vs. the product; increase sales per client; assure customer responsiveness. Now, what action or programs will you use to make sure that happens?

Note: strategy leads. No program, regardless of how good it is, should make the cut if it doesn't link to your business strategies and your customer.

The messages you must craft to support the strategies often are overlooked. Messages are the consistent themes you want your customer to know, to remember, to feel when he or she hears, reads, or views anything about your company or products. The method by which you deliver your messages comes under the heading of actions or programs.

Finally, you need to determine how you'll measure your own success, beyond meeting the sales forecast. How will you know if your image takes a beating? How will you know whether the customer is satisfied, or has just given up complaining? If you don't know, you'll be caught reacting to events, instead of planning for them.

Remember, your customer's measure of your success may be quite different from what you may think. Your proposed measures must be defined by what your customer values, and they have to be quantifiable. You may be surprised at how willing the customer is to cooperate with you in completing surveys, participating in third-party interviews, or taking part in a full-scale analysis of your company as a supplier. Use caution in assuming that winning awards means you have a measurable indicator. Your measures should be stated in terms of strategies, not plaques or trophies.

4. The Marketing and Sales Organizations

The most frequently overlooked element in business is something we usually relegate to the Personnel or Human Resources Office—people. They're what makes everything possible. Include them. Begin with a chart that shows the organization for both Marketing and Sales. You may wish to indicate any interdependent relationships that exist (for instance, with Quality).

Note which of the roles are critical, particularly in terms of customer contact. Just as important, include positions, capabilities, and numbers of people needed in the future. How will you gain these skills without impacting your cost per sale? Again, it's time to be creative and provide options.

5. Revenue and Expense

In this section, you're going to project the revenue your plan will produce. This is usually calculated by evaluating the value of your market(s) and determining the dollar value of your share of that market. You need to factor in any changes you believe will occur, and you'll need to identify the sources of revenue, by product or service. Use text to tell the story; use graphs to show the story.

After you've noted where the money is coming from, explain what money you need to deliver the projected return. This will include staff wages and benefits for your organization, as well as the cost for specific programs you plan to implement.

During this era of budget cuts, do yourself a favor by prioritizing these programs. For instance, if one of your key strategies is to expand to a new market via new technologies, products, or services, you will need to allocate appropriate dollars. What is the payback on the investment in marketing, and when will revenues fully pay back the investment? Also, provide an explanation of programs that will be deleted should a cut in funding be required. Again, combine text and spreadsheets to tell and to show.

6. Management Issues

This section represents your chance to let management know what keeps you awake at night. What might or could go wrong? What are the problems your company faces in customer relations? Are there technology needs that are going unattended? Again, this can be a collaborative effort that identifies your concerns. In addition, you may want to identify long-term issues, as well as those that are of immediate significance.

To keep this section as objective as possible, list the concerns and the business strategy or strategies they affect. What are the short-term and long-term risks? For instance, it is here that you might want to go into further detail about a customer's actions that look like the beginnings of backward integration.

7. Executive Summary

Since most senior leaders want a quick-look reference, it's best to include a one-page Executive Summary that covers these points:

- Your organization's objectives
- Budget requirements
- Revenue projections
- Critical management issues

When you're publishing the final plan document, you'll want the executive summary to be Page One.

8. Sell the Plan

This is one of the steps that often is overlooked. Selling your plan is as important as writing it. Otherwise, no one owns it, except you. The idea is to turn it into a rallying point that helps your company move forward. And to do that, you need to turn as many people as possible into ambassadors for your marketing efforts.

First, set up a time to present the plan to everyone who helped you with information and data. Make sure that they feel some sense of ownership, but that they also see how their piece ties into the whole. This is one of those instances where you need to say your plan, show your plan, discuss your plan. Only after all three steps are completed will they *hear* the plan.

After you've shared the information across the organization, reserve some time on the executive calendar. Have a couple of leaders review the plan first, giving you feedback on the parts where they have particular expertise. Then, present the plan at a staff meeting.

Is It Working?

You may think your job is finished. It's not. You need to convey the key parts of this plan to coworkers throughout the business. They need to know what the business is trying to achieve. Their livelihood, not just that of the owners, is at stake. From their phone-answering technique to the way they process an order, every step has meaning to the customer.

9. Measure/Renew

Once you've presented your plan and people understand it, you have to continuously work the plan and share information about it. The best way to help people see trends and respond appropriately is to have meaningful measures. In the language of Total Quality, these are the Key Result Indicators—the things that have importance to your customers and that are signals to your performance.

For instance, measure your ability to deliver on a customer request; the amount of time it takes to respond to a customer inquiry; your productivity per employee; cash flow; cycle time; yield rates. The idea is to identify a way to measure those things that are critical to you and to your customer.

Review those measurements. Share the information with the entire business and begin the process all over again. Seek new ideas and input to improve your performance. Go after more data and facts. And then renew your plan and share it with everyone—all over again.

It's an extensive process, but it's one that spreads the word—and spreads the ownership. It's the step that ensures that your plan will be constantly in use, and constantly at work for your business.

Glossary

A

accessory equipment (p. 256) relatively small and inexpensive products required by an organization, shorter-lived than components

advertising (p. 534) any paid form of non-personal communication link, initiated by an identified marketer, to establish or continue exchange relationships with customers and, at times, with other stakeholders

advertising agency (p. 539) an organization that specializes in helping marketers plan and implement advertising campaigns

advertising research (p. 545) research that provides information about the target audience to help marketers make better decisions about advertising messages and media

advocacy advertising (p. 536) advertising that communicates a marketer's position on a certain issue

affordability budget (p. 523) a budget based on what money is available for integrated marketing communication after all other expenses are met

atmospherics (p. 448) the physical design of the interior and exterior retailing space coupled with lighting, music, fragrance, and other sensory cues

attitudes (p. 181) enduring positive or negative responses to people, products, or information

B

barter (p. 346) the exchange of goods, services, and ideas without the use of money (or money substitutes)

behavioral segmentation (p. 230) a way of grouping people within a market on the basis of behaviors such as product usage, benefits sought, or brand loyalty

benchmarking (p. 15) rating practices, processes, and products against the world's best to see how the organization can

match or improve on them for a competitive advantage

benefits (p. 252) the satisfaction or need-fulfillment gains that customers receive from products

bid (p. 203) a formal indication of the price to be charged, the goods and services to be provided, and other details about how the marketer will meet the buyer's requirements

brand (p. 261) a name, phrase, design, symbol, or a combination that identifies a product and differentiates it from rival products

brand equity (p. 266) the long-term value of a marketer's brand in the marketplace

brand extension (p. 264) applying an existing brand to a new product in another category

brand loyalty (p. 184) a favorable attitude toward a brand that prompts consistent purchasing over time

breakeven analysis (p. 378) a tool for analyzing revenues and costs to find the profit at various levels of quantity sold

breakeven point (BEP) (p. 378) the point at which revenues equal costs and beyond which the marketer begins to make a profit

brokers (p. 442) independent wholesalers who arrange sales between manufacturers and customers

bundle pricing (p. 383) setting one price for a package (bundle) of two or more products

business cycle (p. 84) the pattern of economic activity created by successive stages of prosperity, recession, and recovery

business services (p. 256) specialized, intangible products that keep operations running smoothly

business strength–market attractiveness matrix (p. 40) a tool that compares strategic alternatives according to business strength and market attractiveness

buying center (p. 207) the group of people within an organization who participate in the buying process

C

canned sales presentation (p. 603) a sales presentation based on recall of memorized information

cannibalization (p. 292) the potentially undesirable result of a new product cutting into sales of the marketer's existing product line

category management (p. 459) the practice of managing each product category as a separate business, tailoring the product mix on a store-by-store basis to satisfy customers

causal research (p. 144) research designed to help identify cause-and-effect relationships among certain elements in marketing problems

cause-related marketing (p. 95) a marketing program that links donations to non-profit organizations to sales of a particular product

census (p. 147) a study incorporating every person, place, or thing in the defined population

chain stores (p. 446) groups of retail outlets that are owned and operated by a corporate parent, which handles many buying and marketing activities from one central location

channel captain (p. 429) a manufacturer or channel partner with the power to dominate the chain of channel partners

closing (p. 604) the part of the sales process in which the salesperson obtains a commitment from the prospect

code of ethics (p. 92) a written guide to help employees understand what is considered ethical and what is unethical

cohort subculture (p. 177) people of similar ages who have undergone similar experiences

combination compensation (p. 613) salespeople are paid a salary plus commissions, bonuses, or other incentives for performance

commercialization (p. 295) putting a new product into full-scale production and introducing it with full marketing support into the market

communication objectives (p. 521) integrated marketing communication (IMC) objectives geared toward influencing customer attitudes and behavior at particular points in the buying process

comparative advertising (p. 535) advertising that demonstrates how a product is superior to a particular competing brand

competition (p. 86) every alternative that a customer might consider in place of a particular product

competitive advertising (p. 535) stresses the ways in which one product or product category is superior to others, without naming specific competitors

competitive environment (p. 86) includes all organizations offering product alternatives to a specific target market

competitive-parity budget (p. 523) spending the same for advertising and other integrated marketing communication activities as competitors spend

components (p. 255) parts supplied by other marketers that are incorporated into finished products

concentrated marketing (p. 238) a marketing strategy in which one marketing program is directed toward a single market segment

concept testing (p. 291) marketing research to determine what potential customers think of an idea for a new product

consideration set (p. 169) options a consumer considers before deciding on a purchase

consumer behavior (p. 164) all the consumer decisions and activities connected with choosing, buying, using, and disposing of goods and services

consumer sales promotion (p. 565) a range of short-term promotional incentives that marketers offer to ultimate consumers to encourage product purchases

consumerism (p. 80) a movement to promote the rights and powers of buyers in relation to marketers

continuous improvement (p. 288) a total quality management process that leads to constant, incremental improvements in products (as well as in all organizational processes)

convenience products (p. 254) fairly inexpensive goods and services that consumers buy frequently, quickly, and with a minimum amount of effort

cooperative (co-op) advertising (p. 581) an arrangement in which manufacturers share the cost when their products are featured in value-chain partners' advertising

core competencies (p. 39) an organization's competitively superior knowledge and use of particular technologies, processes, and specialists' skills

corporate public relations (p. 582) a broad-based public relations effort to build and sustain a general climate of goodwill for the marketer

cost per thousand (CPM) (p. 546) the cost of using a media vehicle to reach 1,000 audience members one time

cost-plus pricing (p. 386) a pricing method in which a marketer adds a certain amount or percentage to cost to arrive at the product's selling price

countertrade (p. 110) marketing exchanges in which customers pay for their purchases with local products instead of money

coupon (p. 571) a document that allows customers to buy a product at a specific discount

credence qualities (p. 322) qualities of a product that customers can't easily evaluate even after purchase and consumption

cross-cultural marketing (p. 122) marketing to people who belong to various cultures

cross-functional teams (p. 47) groups of employees from various functions or departments who work together to satisfy customers

culture (p. 77) the set of values and beliefs shared by a group of people and passed down from one generation to the next

customary pricing (p. 388) pricing a product according to a traditional or standardized price

customer (p. 7) an individual or organization that buys or exchanges something of value for a marketer's products

customer service (p. 271) assistance that marketers provide to customers when they buy or use a product

customized marketing (p. 238) marketing programs that are tailored for each market or to individual consumers or organizations in the market

customized marketing strategy (p. 118) an approach to international marketing in which the marketing mix is tailored to each local market

D

database (p. 138) a computerized file of data that can be searched for particular details

database marketing (p. 556) the process of collecting information about customers and potential customers, storing the data in computer files, and then analyzing the data to find out how best to start or support profitable long-term exchange relationships

deceptive pricing (p. 365) pricing that misleads and deceives customers by hiding the true or final price for a product

demand curve (p. 357) a graphic illustration of the way customer demand responds to a series of possible prices

demand-backward pricing (p. 384) a pricing method in which the price that will create a desired level of demand is determined first; the product is then developed and marketed to fit that price

demarketing (p. 85) a type of marketing that discourages demand for goods and services in short supply

demographic segmentation (p. 226) a way of creating smaller groups within a larger market using variables, such as age and income, that describe the population

demography (p. 76) the study and measurement of a population as described by such factors as age, gender, birthrate, education, family size, income, nationality, race, and occupation

derived demand (p. 199) demand for organizational products linked to (or derived from) the demand for consumer products

descriptive research (p. 143) research that gives a rather precise picture of the nature of a marketing problem and the frequency with which it occurs

differentiated marketing (p. 237) a strategy in which separate and distinct marketing strategies are devised for each of the market segments to be reached

direct channels (p. 415) marketing channels in which the marketer completes the marketing exchange directly with the customer

direct investment (p. 115) in international marketing, owning manufacturing or marketing facilities in another country

direct mail advertising (p. 556) use of the medium of mail or private delivery to bring an advertising message to the target audience

direct marketing (p. 555) a two-way process of marketing communication through which marketers offer and customers buy products without contact with other channel partners

direct response advertising (p. 557) the use of any advertising medium to elicit an immediate response from the target audience

direct selling (p. 596) selling directly to customers rather than through channel partners

discount retailers (p. 451) retailers that market good quality and lower quality products in large volumes at low prices but with few services

distribution centers (p. 485) warehouses in which products are briefly stored before being moved to wholesale, retail, or customer locations

domestic marketing (p. 102) marketing exchanges with customers in the marketer's home country

dual distribution (p. 419) the use of more than one channel to bring the same product (or similar products under different brand names) to several customer segments

dumping (p. 368) the practice of pricing products in host countries below cost or for less than their price in the marketer's home country

E

economic environment (p. 84) the set of economic factors that influence customer buying and organizational marketing efforts

efficient consumer response (ECR) (p. 413) in the grocery industry, an electronic system that creates an efficient, continual flow of products through the value chain in response to store-by-store data on consumer purchases

electronic data interchange (EDI) (p. 211) the computer-to-computer exchange of information between marketer and customer in organizational markets

embargo (p. 109) a ban on importing or exporting certain products

empowerment (p. 17) allowing employees at all levels of the organization to use their power and discretion to make decisions and take steps to satisfy customers

equalized workload method (p. 610) a formula for determining the size of the sales force based on the number of sales calls to be made, the number of customers, and the average number of calls per salesperson

ethnocentrism (p. 112) the assumption that a specific culture is superior to others

event sponsorship (p. 513) underwriting all or part of a special event such as a sports activity or a concert as a promotional device

everyday low pricing (EDLP) (p. 389) setting prices that are consistently low

exchange rate (p. 109) the value of one currency relative to the currencies of other countries

exclusive distribution (p. 423) a channel design in which products are marketed through a few carefully selected partners

experience curve pricing (p. 386) setting a low price to maximize sales while keeping total costs down; made possible as a marketer gains technical proficiency in making the product

experience qualities (p. 322) qualities of a product such as taste that customers can evaluate only after purchase or consumption

experiment (p. 153) a scientific way of comparing and measuring data under controlled conditions—that is, one or more elements are changed while others remain the same

exploratory research (p. 143) a type of preliminary research designed to disclose more fully the nature of the problem and of the present situation, and to point the way toward further research

export (p. 103) marketing products to customers in other countries

extended problem solving (p. 172) an approach to decision making in which the consumer consciously searches for information, carefully evaluates the alternatives, and analyzes the result

external environment (p. 70) the set of factors outside the marketer's value chain that can influence marketing success

F

features (p. 252) characteristics or attributes of products

field sales (p. 595) personal sales calls made at the customer's home or business location

fixed costs (p. 375) all the expenses that remain the same no matter how many goods or services are sold

focus group interview (p. 150) meeting of a market researcher with a small group of people to discuss a particular product or topic

four Ps (p. 20) the elements of the marketing mix: product, price, place, and promotion

franchising (p. 114) a form of licensing in which a company pays a fee for the right to use another company's brand name, products, and operational methods in a particular area

freight forwarders (p. 485) companies that put many smaller shipments together to create a single, large shipment that can be transported more cost-efficiently to the final destination

frequency (p. 546) in advertising, a measure of how many times audience members are exposed to a media vehicle during the period an ad runs

frequency marketing programs (p. 572) ongoing promotions in which marketers reinforce brand loyalty by offering rewards to customers who make repeat purchases

G

general merchandise retailers (p. 449) stores that carry a wide product mix; they are differentiated by the variety of goods and services they offer

generic brand (p. 263) identifies a product by the category alone

geocentrism (p. 112) the assumption that successful international marketing requires respecting both home- and host-country cultures

geodemographic segmentation (p. 228) combines geographic and demographic data to define market segments

geographic information system (GIS) (p. 228) a computerized method of merging and analyzing details about an area and displaying the results in map form

geographic segmentation (p. 227) a way of grouping people within a market using geographic variables such as countries or regions

global corporation (p. 103) an organization that has markets worldwide

global marketing strategy (p. 117) standardization of product, pricing, channel management, and communication activities, wherever possible, for use in all countries

goals (p. 44) specific long-term results a marketer wants to achieve

goods (p. 252) tangible products which can physically be touched

goods–services continuum (p. 313) a tool for classifying products according to their tangibility

government market (p. 198) federal, state, local, and foreign government agencies that buy goods and services

gray market (p. 429) buying and selling among unauthorized channel partners that bring products from other countries at lower prices than authorized channel partners pay

green marketing (p. 94) marketing products that are safe or beneficial to the environment

growth-share matrix (p. 40) an analytical tool for comparing the market growth and market share of various divisions or products

H

home country (p. 107) the nation where an organization has its headquarters

host country (p. 107) any nation where a marketer sells or sets up operations

hypothesis (p. 142) in marketing research, tentative explanation of the relationship between marketing elements

I

IMC audit (p. 527) a comprehensive assessment of all the organization's communications with stakeholders

import (p. 103) bringing products from other countries into the marketer's home country

inbound logistics (p. 468) the inflow of raw materials, equipment, and other

goods, services, and information needed to make the product or provide the service from the upstream side until the product is actually produced

inconsistency (p. 316) in services marketing, variability that occurs because delivery is highly dependent on the people providing the service or operating the equipment that provides the service

indirect channels (p. 415) marketing channels that include one or more channel partners that help the marketer complete exchanges with customers

industrial market (p. 197) businesses that buy goods and services to use directly or indirectly in producing other goods and services

industry–competition model (p. 42) provides a structure for analyzing the effect of competition on profitability within an industry

infomercials (p. 548) longer television commercials that market goods and services in a program format

inseparability (p. 317) in services marketing, service production can't be separated from service consumption

installations (p. 256) large, expensive, long-lasting capital purchases such as buildings

institutional advertising (p. 535) advertising that focuses on the organization, generating a particular image or concept

institutional market (p. 199) hospitals, charities, civic groups, religious institutions, schools, prisons, museums, libraries and other profit-making and not-for-profit organizations

intangibility (p. 315) in services marketing, the quality of services that cannot be physically examined before purchase

integrated marketing (p. 13) the unification and coordination of the marketer's internal activities with its partners' activities to complete marketing exchanges that delight customers

integrated marketing communication (IMC) (p. 502) a cross-functional process for establishing and strengthening profitable relationships with customers and other stakeholders by coordinating all marketing messages to create a unified image for the organization and its products

intensive distribution (p. 422) a channel design in which products are marketed through as many outlets as possible

intermodal transportation (p. 484) the use of more than one mode of transportation to complete a single movement of products

internal environment (p. 70) the set of factors inside the marketer's value chain that can influence marketing success

internal marketing (p. 9) the process of satisfying internal customers (employees) as a prerequisite to satisfying external customers

internal products (p. 257) reports and advice delivered to internal customers (employees) in organizations

international marketing (p. 102) exchange relationships between marketers and customers located in two or more countries

inventory restrictions (p. 317) in services marketing, services can't be stored in inventory

involvement (p. 170) the level of importance or interest that a consumer attaches to a certain product or purchase situation

ISO 14000 (p. 95) a collection of the best practices for managing an organization's environmental impacts

J

joint venture (p. 114) a partnership in which two or more companies share the work, costs, and rewards of a major project

just-in-time (JIT) inventory management (p. 487) an approach in which inventory is kept at a very low level to meet immediate production demands, and additional supplies are delivered as they're needed

L

learning (p. 183) the process of applying experience or knowledge to consumer behavior

licensing (p. 114) an agreement in which one company pays for the right to make or sell another company's product

lifestyle (p. 186) an individual pattern of living as exhibited in a person's activities, interests, and opinions

lifetime customer value (p. 593) the total amount of money that a customer is likely to spend with one marketer throughout the ongoing exchange relationship

limited problem solving (p. 172) buying process in which a consumer chooses among a number of unfamiliar alternatives in a familiar purchase situation

limited-line retailers (p. 450) retailers who offer fewer types of product than are sold by general merchandise retailers, but stock many more choices in each product line

line extensions (p. 283) products bearing the marketer's brand that are added to the marketer's existing line of products in a particular category

list price (p. 393) the official price a marketer quotes for a product

logistics (p. 409) the management of product and information flows throughout the value chain to increase efficiency and speed

logistics management (p. 468) the process of managing the movement of raw materials, parts, work in progress, finished products, and related information through the value chain in an efficient, cost-effective manner to meet customer requirements

loss-leader pricing (p. 388) pricing selected products well below what competitors ordinarily charge, to attract customers

M

make-or-buy decision (p. 202) organizational decision to solve a problem by producing what is needed or by buying (or leasing) from an outside supplier

mall intercepts (p. 151) individual interviews conducted by market researchers in shopping centers

manufacturer brand (p. 262) a national brand frequently advertised throughout the country

manufacturer's representatives (p. 441) independent salespeople who market to customers in a specific geographic area

marginal analysis (p. 377) a tool for understanding the financial implications of producing one more unit and determining the point of maximum profitability

marginal cost (p. 376) change in total expense of producing one more unit

marginal revenue (p. 377) the change in sales revenue generated by selling one more unit

market (p. 135) the group of customers or prospects who need or want a product and have both the resources and the willingness to exchange something of value to get it

market modification (p. 304) looking for new users of a product or increased use among present users

market price (p. 393) the price that customers actually pay for a product

market segmentation (p. 220) the process of grouping people or organizations within a market according to similar needs, characteristics, or behaviors

market share (p. 40) measures the marketer's portion of total units sold or dollar sales made of a given product, relative to competitors

marketing (p. 4) the process of establishing and maintaining mutually beneficial exchange relationships with customers and other stakeholders

marketing audit (p. 57) a comprehensive review of an organization's marketing strategies, tactics, and performance

marketing channel (p. 408) the network of partners in the value chain that cooperate to bring products from producers to ultimate consumers

marketing concept (p. 15) the idea that organizations can satisfy their own long-term objectives, such as profitability, by coordinating and focusing all their activities on identifying and satisfying customer needs and wants

marketing control (p. 56) the four-step process of setting standards for performance, measuring progress toward marketing goals, comparing results with the standards, and making changes or reinforcing good results to stay on track

marketing decision support system (MDSS) (p. 140) a computerized system that links internal databases and allows marketers to analyze data for marketing decisions

marketing environment (p. 69) all the internal and external factors that directly or indirectly influence a marketer's success

marketing ethics (p. 88) the moral standards and values that are applied to marketing issues

marketing information system (MIS) (p. 138) a structured system for managing the ongoing collection, analysis, storage, and reporting of marketing data

marketing management (p. 19) the system-wide process of planning and implementing marketing programs, measuring results, and making adjustments to ensure the establishment and maintenance of mutually beneficial exchange relationships with customers and other stakeholders

marketing mix (p. 20) the combination of product, price, distribution, and marketing communication that most effectively satisfies customer needs

marketing myopia (p. 35) the tendency to view the organization as a means of producing goods or services rather than as a means for creating and satisfying customers

marketing plan (p. 54) a detailed document that describes (1) the target market, (2) the goals, objectives, and strategies for reaching that market, (3) the marketing tactics, budget, and timing needed to reach those goals, and (4) the expected return to the organization

marketing public relations (MPR) (p. 582) public relations communication with customers, channel partners, and other stakeholders that directly influences marketing efforts and results

marketing research (p. 134) the function that links the consumer, customer, and public to the marketer through the gathering of marketing information

markup pricing (p. 385) pricing technique in which resellers in the marketing channel set prices by adding a standard, predetermined percentage to the cost of each product

mass customization (p. 274) offering individually tailored, quality goods and services to a large number of customers at a relatively low cost

mass marketing (p. 220) the process of using one standardized strategy to market standardized, mass-produced products to everyone in the market

materials handling (p. 486) the movement of products, parts, and raw materials within and between warehouses and manufacturing facilities

media (p. 546) the communication channels that carry advertising messages to the target audience

merchant wholesalers (p. 439) wholesalers that take title to the products they buy for resale to other channel partners

mission (p. 38) the fundamental purpose of the organization, which forms the foundation of all organizational activities

mission statement (p. 38) a declaration of an organization's purpose and direction

modified rebuy (p. 206) a purchase situation in which an organizational buyer who has made a particular kind of purchase before now faces some changed circumstances such as additional alternatives

motives (p. 180) the internal factors that propel individuals to take actions that satisfy their needs

multinational corporation (MNC) (p. 103) company with operations and activities in more than one country

N

need-satisfaction presentation (p. 603) sales presentation tailored to satisfying the needs of the customer or prospect

new product development process (p. 289) the sequence of activities a marketer uses to transform product ideas into marketable goods and services

new-task buy (p. 206) situation in which the organizational buyer has no experience making a particular type of purchase

niche market (p. 220) a very small market segment

nonprice competition (p. 356) the practice of differentiating a product on the basis of elements other than price

nonprobability sample (p. 147) a sample in which the chance that any one member of the population will be selected can't be accurately calculated

nonprofit marketing (p. 318) seeks to achieve a goal other than generating profits

nonprospects (p. 220) people or organizations that are not potential customers

O

objective-and-task budget (p. 523) a budget based on specific tasks that will help reach specific integrated marketing communication (IMC) objectives

objectives (p. 44) specific, measurable interim targets that must be met to reach the organization's goals

observation (p. 149) in marketing research, watching and recording the actions of the people, objects, or events being studied

odd–even pricing (p. 383) setting prices to end in a certain digit rather than being rounded to whole dollars

off-price retailers (p. 451) retailers that offer specially purchased branded products, with limited services, at prices below those charged by full-price retailers

opinion leaders (p. 174) people who can influence the attitudes or behaviors of others

order cycle time (p. 490) the period between the placement of an order and its receipt

order getters (p. 594) salespeople who make both initial sales that start relationships with new customers and additional sales that strengthen relationships with existing customers

order takers (p. 594) salespeople who accept new orders and process repeat orders

organizational culture (p. 48) the pattern of shared values and beliefs that influences employee attitudes and behavior

organizational marketing (p. 192) the process of marketing to customers in the organizational market; also known as business-to-business marketing

outbound logistics (p. 469) the outflow of finished products and information to the customer to complete a marketing exchange

outsourcing (p. 40) hiring other companies to perform certain functions that the selected firms can handle more efficiently or more effectively

over-the-counter sales (p. 595) personal sales made in retail or wholesale locations when customers visit the facility

P

penetration pricing (p. 381) a pricing strategy in which a new product is given a low initial price to attract many customers quickly while discouraging competitors

perceived benefits (p. 346) anything and everything customers believe they receive from the overall value package

perceived price (p. 346) whatever customers believe they have to give up in exchange for the benefits received

perceived risk (p. 168) the chance that the wrong choice of product might result in negative consequences

percent-of-sales budget (p. 523) budgeting a certain percentage of annual sales for integrated marketing communication (IMC)

perception (p. 180) the process of determining meaning by selecting, organizing, and interpreting stimuli in the environment

perceptual map (p. 240) a graph of how customers perceive the competing products in a category along two or more important dimensions

personal selling (p. 592) an interpersonal communication process in which a marketer's representatives identify prospects, determine needs, present product information, gain commitment, and follow up after sales to maintain customer relationships

personality (p. 185) the unique set of behavior patterns an individual exhibits in response to recurring situations

philanthropy (p. 95) the direct donation of money, goods, and services to nonprofit organizations of all sorts

pioneering advertising (p. 535) advertising that introduces a new product or brand

planned shopping center (p. 453) a group of stores in an architecturally unified site that is designed and marketed together as a shopping destination

point-of-purchase (POP) displays (p. 576) displays set up in retail outlets to encourage the purchase of a particular product

political environment (p. 79) governmental rules, policies, and legal rulings that influence marketing

population (p. 147) the total group that might be included in a particular research study

positioning (p. 224) the use of marketing to encourage people in the target market to form a particular mental image of a product relative to competing products

postpurchase dissonance (p. 170) feelings of anxiety or doubt about the wisdom of a purchase decision that has been made

predatory pricing (p. 365) the illegal practice of setting unreasonably low prices to force competitors out of business

premium (p. 575) an item of value offered free or at a low price to customers who buy or try a particular product

prestige pricing (p. 382) setting a higher price than competitors to attract customers who are willing to pay more for a product that is higher in quality or status

price (p. 346) the amount of money or some other valuable that the marketer asks in exchange for a product

price competition (p. 355) the practice of differentiating a product from competitive products primarily on the basis of price

price discrimination (p. 365) the practice of unfairly pricing the same quality, grade, and quantity of goods differently for different customers

price elasticity of demand (p. 359) a measure of the degree to which customers are sensitive to changes in product pricing

price fixing (p. 364) an illegal conspiracy among competitors to set prices for particular products

price leader (p. 362) the first company to announce price changes that competitors quickly imitate

price lining (p. 383) setting a separate, specific price for each product in a line

price war (p. 362) a situation in which competitors continually undercut each other's prices in an effort to be perceived as offering the lowest price

primary data (p. 146) facts, figures, or details gathered for a specific marketing research study

private brand (p. 262) a brand that is owned by a wholesaler or retailer

probability sample (p. 147) a sample in which every person, place, or thing in the population has a known chance of being selected for the research

product (p. 5) a good, service, or idea that the customer acquires to satisfy a need or want through the exchange of money or something else of value

product adoption process (p. 305) the series of attitudinal and behavioral changes leading up to product purchase and adoption; also known as response model

product advertising (p. 534) advertising that focuses on a good or a service, either for ultimate consumers or for organizational customers

product differentiation (p. 224) creating a value package that is better than the competition in a way that is meaningful to the target market

product diffusion process (p. 305) the process by which new products are adopted by various groups in the market

product life cycle (p. 302) the four-stage cycle of introduction, growth, maturity, and decline that characterizes a product's movement through the marketplace

product line (p. 299) a group of closely related products offered by one marketer

product management (p. 306) form of organization that groups employees according to the products they work on

product managers (p. 306) employees who are responsible for planning and implementing marketing decisions for specific products or brands

product mix (p. 299) the assortment of product lines and individual products offered by one marketer

product modification (p. 304) changing product quality, features, or style to attract new users or more usage from present customers

product placement (p. 512) paying to have products or brands featured in an entertainment production such as a movie, television program, or video game

promotional pricing (p. 388) temporarily setting and communicating lower prices on selected products

prospecting (p. 601) identification of potential customers who may be qualified to purchase the product being sold

prospects (p. 220) people or organizations that are potential customers

prototype (p. 293) a sample of the actual product made to test production methods as well as product performance

psychographic segmentation (p. 229) grouping people or organizations in a market according to similarities in lifestyles, interests, activities, and opinions

public relations (PR) (p. 582) the process of evaluating stakeholder attitudes, identifying a marketer's products and activities with stakeholders' interests, and using nonpaid two-way communication to reach stakeholder audiences and build long-term relationships

public service advertising (PSA) (p. 536) ads by government or nonprofit groups that address social issues such as smoking and drunk driving

publicity (p. 582) a subset of public relations that encourages nonpaid media coverage of the marketer and its products

pull strategy (p. 525) aims communications at customers, who ask retailers (or

other channel partners) for the advertised product, creating demand that pulls the product through the channel

push strategy (p. 525) aims communications at channel partners to carry the product through the channel to reach customers

Q

qualified prospect (p. 601) a prospect who not only needs the product but also has the financial ability and the authority to pay for it

quality (p. 259) the degree to which the product meets customer needs, wants, and expectations

quality function deployment (QFD) (p. 297) a cross-functional effort to identify customer requirements and translate them into specifications to be used in defining, designing, producing, and marketing a quality product

quotas (p. 109) government-set limits on the number of products in certain categories that can be imported or exported

R

raw materials (p. 256) basic, natural materials and agricultural goods that become part of manufactured products

reach (p. 546) in advertising, a measure of how many different people in the target audience are exposed to an ad in a specific media vehicle

reciprocity (p. 210) the practice of buying from suppliers that are also customers

reengineering (p. 46) the fundamental rethinking and radical redesign of organizational processes to achieve dramatic improvements

reference groups (p. 175) in consumer behavior, groups that influence the behavior of members, people wanting to be members, and people who do not want to be members

relationship marketing (p. 6) the process of establishing and maintaining mutually beneficial long-term relationships among organizations and their customers, employees, and other stakeholders

relationship selling (p. 594) a process whereby salespeople learn about and satisfy customer needs during an ongoing series of transactions that result in long-term exchange relationships

reminder advertising (p. 535) advertising that keeps the marketer's or product's name in front of the target market

repositioning (p. 241) the use of marketing to change a product's relative position in the minds of the target market

request for proposal (RFP) (p. 203) asking marketers to compete for an order by showing how they will meet the product specifications, the delivery dates, and other requirements

reseller market (p. 198) wholesalers and retailers that buy products for resale to others; also called commercial market

respondents (p. 149) in market research, the people being studied in a survey

retail image (p. 448) the perceptions of a retailer held by its customers and other stakeholders

retail life cycle (p. 461) the four-stage cycle of innovation, accelerated development, maturity, and decline that characterizes retail strategies

retailers (p. 443) channel partners that market goods and services to ultimate consumers

retailing (p. 443) the set of value-chain activities related to the marketing of goods and services to consumers for personal, family, or household use

return-on-investment budget (p. 523) budgeting for integrated marketing communication spending as an investment in developing additional customer business; based on achieving a certain payback on the amount invested

reverse channels (p. 421) channels that bring products from customers to marketers

reverse logistics (p. 491) the process of managing the return flow of products from customers to marketers

reverse marketing (p. 210) the use of marketing by customers to build stronger relationships with suppliers

routine problem solving (p. 172) in the buying decision, the consumer makes a quick choice, taking little time to consider the alternatives or the outcome of the decision

S

sales management (p. 608) a coordinated set of actions to plan sales efforts, organize the sales staff, and develop an effective, motivated sales force

sales objectives (p. 522) specific, measurable sales and customer relationship goals to be met by an integrated marketing communication strategy

sales partnering (p. 598) an approach in which the customer forms an alliance with a supplier to tailor the sales process and meet ongoing customer objectives

sales promotion (p. 564) the communication of any incentive that enhances the basic value of a product for a limited time, to encourage channel members and sales people to market it and customers to buy it

sales quota (p. 614) a minimum level of sales or profits to be attained by sales people

sales support staff (p. 594) employees who don't get or take orders, but handle a variety of tasks to supplement the efforts of order getters and order takers

sales team (p. 597) a group of employees from various functional areas who work together to ensure that customer needs are satisfied throughout the sales process

sample 1. (p. 147) in marketing research, a segment of the total population selected to represent the whole; **2. (p. 572)** a good or service offered free or at a very low price to encourage customers to experience its benefits

sampling error (p. 147) a measure of the difference between the results obtained from studying a sample and the results that would have been obtained from studying the entire population

scrambled merchandising (p. 450) a strategy in which a retailer carries product lines that are not related to its main product focus

search qualities (p. 322) qualities of a product such as color and fit that customers can examine before they purchase

secondary data (p. 144) in marketing research, facts and figures that have already been collected for another purpose

selective distribution (p. 422) a channel design in which products are marketed through a limited number of outlets

self-concept (p. 185) the way a person feels and thinks about himself or herself

selling agents (p. 442) agents who gather marketing information, design promotions, make sales calls, sometimes decide on prices and financing, and generally take over the marketing functions for the manufacturers they represent

service encounter (p. 324) point of interaction between a customer and a service provider

service gap (p. 323) discrepancy between the service provider's performance and the customer's expectations

service recovery plan (p. 327) a set of actions designed as a response to service problems

service strategy (p. 326) a broad plan for delivering quality service

services (p. 253) products that are intangible and offer financial, health, cosmetic, or other benefits that satisfy customer needs

shopping products (p. 254) goods and services that are relatively costly and bought infrequently, and for which consumers usually take time and effort to compare alternatives

simulated test marketing (STM) (p. 294) a form of computer modeling that predicts a new product's future based on consumer behavior in a laboratory setting, on details of the competitive environment, and on the planned marketing activities

single-line retailers (p. 450) retailers that offer many choices of only one type of product

situational influences (p. 178) elements of time and place that can affect consumer behavior

skimming pricing (p. 381) a pricing strategy in which a new product is initially priced high to attract customers who are willing to pay for unique benefits and high quality

slotting fees (p. 428) payments that some retailers require in exchange for placing products on store shelves

social audit (p. 96) evaluates an organization's progress toward implementing programs that are socially responsible and responsive

social class (p. 176) groupings of people who share similar lifestyles, values, interests, behaviors, and status

social environment (p. 75) the set of characteristics, cultural elements, and attitudes that affect customers' perceptions of and reactions to marketers

social responsibility (p. 92) the belief that organizations should look beyond their own interests and profits to make a real contribution to society

specialty products (p. 254) goods and services that consumers value and see as unique, so that they are willing to expend considerable time and effort when purchasing them

stakeholders (p. 8) individuals and organizations, including employees, suppliers, stockholders, and the community, that influence or are influenced by what the organization does

standard industrial classification (SIC) codes (p. 232) U.S. government system for categorizing organizations according to the products they sell

storage warehouses (p. 485) repositories for parts, raw materials, or products that need to be stored for a period of days, weeks, or months before being moved to a factory, a customer's site, or another location

straight commission compensation (p. 613) method of paying salespeople according to results such as sales or profits

straight rebuy (p. 206) a situation in which the organizational buyer makes a routine repeat purchase

straight salary compensation (p. 613) compensation method in which salespeople receive a fixed amount of money weekly, monthly, or yearly

strategic alliances (p. 39) long-term relationships with other organizations in which the partners pool their resources to develop or share competencies

strategic channel alliance (p. 420) an agreement in which a marketer uses another marketer's channel to reach customers

strategy (p. 34) a broad plan used to guide the decisions and actions of everyone in the organization

suboptimization (p. 479) the lowering of logistics costs in one area while increasing them elsewhere, with resulting damage to overall cost-efficiency

supplies (p. 256) items that are used up in the course of business but don't become part of the finished product

survey (p. 149) collecting data by asking the target population a series of questions

SWOT analysis (p. 38) an assessment of the organization's strengths (S) and weaknesses (W) as well as its opportunities (O) and threats (T)

system sales (p. 597) sales of a special value package that bundles goods and services to satisfy a specific customer's needs

T

tailored logistics (p. 480) customizing logistics activities to better satisfy the specific requirements of a particular customer or market segment

target audience (p. 520) the group of people a marketing message is intended to reach

target market (p. 220) the group of people or organizations whose needs a product is specifically designed to satisfy

target marketing (p. 220) the process of selecting customer groups within a larger market and developing products and marketing programs geared to their specific wants and needs

target-profit pricing (p. 387) establishing the dollar amount of profit to be achieved through pricing

target-return pricing (p. 387) setting prices to reach a specific measure of profit, such as return on sales, return on investment, or return on assets

tariffs (p. 109) taxes levied on specific products coming into a country

technological environment (p. 83) innovations and new ideas from scientific or engineering research that help marketers satisfy customers in a new or better way

telemarketing (p. 595) personal selling in which contact between sales representatives and customers takes place by telephone

test marketing (p. 153) research to measure reaction to a new product offered in a specific geographic area

total cost (p. 376) total amount spent to produce every unit of a product

total cost concept (p. 479) looks at each logistics activity as part of an integrated whole and balances changes so that overall costs are lowered

total quality management (TQM) (p. 48) puts quality at the heart of every organizational operation to satisfy the needs of both internal and external customers

trade protectionism (p. 108) the use of government regulations to set limits on the marketing of goods and services by foreign producers

trade sales promotion (p. 566) promotional incentives offered by marketers to wholesalers, retailers, and other value-chain partners for supporting certain products

trade show (p. 579) an event at which marketers exhibit their products to current and prospective customers and to buyers from various organizations

transaction selling (p. 593) an approach to selling in which the marketer focuses on making an individual sale to a customer

transactional marketing (p. 6) an approach to marketing in which marketers focus on individual, isolated exchanges that satisfy a customer's needs at a particular time and place

U

undifferentiated marketing (p. 236) a single marketing strategy to reach the entire market

unsought products (p. 255) goods and services that consumers are unaware of, haven't necessarily thought of buying, or find that they need to solve an unexpected problem

utility (p. 10) the value a product provides for the customer

V

value (p. 346) the ratio of a product's perceived benefits to its perceived price

value analysis (p. 202) examination of the balance between a product's cost and its design, quality, and performance

value chain (p. 50) the sequence of linked activities that must be performed by suppliers, channel partners, and the marketer to create and deliver a value package that satisfies customers

value-chain management (p. 410) the coordination of all the functions and partner relationships in the value chain

value marketing (p. 347) the process of designing, developing, and marketing products to give customers extra benefits and higher quality at fair prices

value package (p. 11) the combination of tangible and intangible elements that potential customers evaluate when deciding whether to buy a particular product

value pricing (p. 348) the process of holding prices steady or cutting them while improving product benefits

variable costs (p. 375) expenses that change according to the level of production and sales

vendor analysis (p. 205) rating each supplier's performance on factors such as price and service

vertical marketing system (VMS) (p. 430) a professionally planned and managed network of channel relationships designed for optimal efficiency and effectiveness

W

wheel of retailing (p. 460) a theory that describes retail evolution as a cycle of continuing to upgrade to serve more upscale customers

wholesalers (p. 438) channel partners that buy products from producers or agents for resale to retailers or other channel partners

word-of-mouth communication (p. 175) the informal transmission of information from person to person

Notes

PREFACE

1. Christian Gronroos, "Relationship Marketing: Strategic and Tactical Implications," *Management Decisions*, 34, no. 3 (1996): 5–14.

2. A. H. Walle, "Will Marketing Be Nibbled to Death?" *Marketing News*, 26 February 1996, 4.

3. Stephen R. Covey, "300 Degree Quality," *Quality Digest*, April 1996, 27.

CHAPTER 1

1. Don Taylor and Jeanne Smalling Archer, *Up Against the Wal-Marts* (New York: AMACOM, 1994); Mark Lewyn, "MCI: A Smaller Family and Fewer Friends," *Business Week*, 6 February 1995, 147–148; Mark Lewyn, "MCI Attacking on All Fronts," *Business Week*, 13 June 1994, 76–79; Terry Lefton, "Telecommunications: 800 Ways to Call Long-Distance," *Superbrands*, 18 October 1993, 106–107; Stan Rapp and Thomas L. Collins, *Beyond MaxiMarketing* (New York: McGraw-Hill, 1994), 233–240; Don Peppers and Martha Rogers, *The One-to-One Future* (New York: Currency Doubleday, 1993), 125–126.

2. "Committee Reports," American Marketing Association, October 1948, 202–217; Frederick E. Webster, Jr., "The Changing Role of Marketing in the Corporation," *Journal of Marketing*, October 1992, 1–17.

3. Adapted from Robert M. Morgan and Shelby D. Hunt, "The Commitment–Trust Theory of Relationship Marketing," *Journal of Marketing*, July 1994, 20–38; Regis McKenna, *Relationship Marketing* (Reading, Mass.: Addison-Wesley, 1991).

4. Rapp and Collins, *Beyond MaxiMarketing*, 261–272.

5. Laura M. Litvan, "Increasing Revenue with Repeat Sales," *Nation's Business*, January 1996, 36–38; Thomas Woods and Judith Remondi, "Relationships Vital for High-Tech Marketers," *Marketing News*, 20 May 1996, 8–9.

6. Gianni Lorenzoni and Charles Baden-Fuller, "Creating a Strategic Web of Partners," *California Management Review*, Spring 1995, 146–163; Roberta Maynard, "Striking the Right Match," *Nation's Business*, May 1996, 18–28.

7. David Osborne and Ted Gaebler, *Reinventing Government* (Reading, Mass.: Addison-Wesley, 1992).

8. W. Benoy Joseph, "Internal Marketing Builds Service Quality," *Journal of Health Care Marketing*, Spring 1996, 54–59; Sybil F. Stershic, "Internal Marketing," in *Marketing Encyclopedia*, edited by Jeffrey Heilbrunn (Chicago: NTC Business Books, 1995), 101–106.

9. Stan Rapp and Thomas L. Collins, *The New MaxiMarketing* (New York: McGraw-Hill, 1996), 249–287; B. G. Yovovich, "Swamped Customers Erect Voicemail Walls," *Business Marketing*, February 1996, 26.

10. Jagdish N. Sheth and Rajendra S. Sisodia, "Feeling the Heat," *Marketing Management*, Fall 1995, 8–23; Ken Blanchard, "Raving Fans: African Style," *Quality Digest*, May 1996, 19.

11. Theodore Levitt, "Marketing Success Through Differentiation—of Anything," in *Levitt on Marketing* (Boston: Harvard Business School Press, 1991), 65–73; Ian C. MacMillan and Rita Gunther McGrath, "Discover Your Products' Hidden Potential," *Harvard Business Review*, May–June 1996, 58–73.

12. Kathleen Kerwin, "Forget Woodstock—These Folks Are Headin' to Spring Hill," *Business Week*, 27 June 1994, 36; Chad Rubel, "Partnerships Steer Saturn to New Marketing Mix," *Marketing News*, 29 January 1996, 5.

13. Eugene W. Anderson, Claes Fornell, and Donald R. Lehmann, "Customer Satisfaction, Market Share, and Profitability: Findings from Sweden," *Journal of Marketing*, July 1994, 53–66; "Saturn Learns a Lesson," *Marketing News*, 26 February 1996, 1.

14. Jayashree Mahajan, Asoo J. Vakharia, Pallab Paul, and Richard B. Chase, "An Exploratory Investigation of the Interdependence Between Marketing and Operations Functions in Service Firms," *International Journal of Research in Marketing*, 11 (1994): 1–15; McKenna, *Relationship Marketing*, 5.

15. Adapted from Bill Fromm and Len Schlesinger, *The Real Heroes of Business* (New York: Currency Doubleday, 1993), 23–43, 241–254.

16. Dean Tjosvold, Lindsay Meredith, and R. Michael Wellwood, "Implementing Relationship Marketing," *Journal of Business and Industrial Marketing*, 8, no. 4 (1993): 5–17; Janet Smith, "Integrated Marketing," *Marketing Tools*, November–December 1995, 63–67.

17. For an elaborate discussion of the evolution of the marketing concept, see R. A. Fullerton, "How Modern Is Modern Marketing? Marketing's Evolution and the Myth of the Production Era," *Journal of Marketing*, January 1988, 108–125.

18. Frederick E. Webster, Jr., *Market-Driven Management* (New York: John Wiley, 1994), 5–6; Susan Caminiti, "Troutt Fishing in America," *Fortune*, 26 May 1996, 24.

19. Theodore Levitt, *The Marketing Imagination* (new expanded edition) (New York: Free Press, 1983), 141–172.

20. Webster, *Market-Driven Management*, 7–8.

21. John Ridding and Andrew Gowers, "Michelin Men Make Their Mark," *Financial Times*, 5 October 1995, 13.

22. Robin T. Peterson, "Small Business Adoption of the Marketing Concept vs. Other Business Strategies," *Journal of Small Business Management*, January 1989, 38–46; Philip Kotler and Sidney J. Levy, "Broadening the Concept of Marketing," *Journal of Marketing*, January 1969, 10–15; Joanne Scheff and Philip Kotler, "How the Arts Can Prosper Through Strategic Collaborations," *Harvard Business Review*, January–February 1996, 52–62.

23. Joanne Lawson, personal communication, January 1994.

24. Theodore Levitt, "After the Sale Is Over. . . ," in *Levitt on Marketing* (Boston: Harvard Business School Press, 1991), 55–61; Jakki J. Mohr and Robert E. Spekman, "Perfecting Partnerships," *Marketing Management*, Winter/Spring 1996, 35–43.

25. Amal Kumar Naj, "Shifting Gears" and

"Your Enemy's Mind," *Wall Street Journal*, 7 May 1993, A1, A6; "Benchmarking: Past, Present, and Future," *The Quality Observer*, March 1996, 45.

26. General Electric Company, 1993 Annual Report, 2–3.

27. Adapted from Ron Zemke and Dick Schaaf, *The Service Edge* (New York: Penguin Books USA, 1990); Hoover's Handbook Database, accessed 8 November 1995.

28. Daniel J. Sweeney, "Marketing: Management Technology or Social Process?" *Journal of Marketing*, October 1972, 3–10; "Responsible Care," advertisement by the Chemical Manufacturers Association in *Forbes*, 24 April 1995, 187ff.

29. "Ben and Jerry's: Corporate Ogre," *Fortune*, 10 July 1995, 30; "Ben & Jerry Tell on Themselves," *Business Week*, 26 June 1995, 8.

30. Neil H. Borden, "The Concept of the Marketing Mix," in *Marketing Classics*, 7th ed., edited by Ben M. Enis and Keith K. Cox (Boston: Allyn & Bacon, 1991), 361–369; Philip Kotler and Gary Armstrong, *Marketing: An Introduction*, 4th ed. (Upper Saddle River, NJ: Prentice-Hall, 1997), 49.

31. Mark Hendricks, "Mass Appeal," *Entrepreneur*, August 1996, 68–72; R. Lee Sullivan, "Custom-Made," *Forbes*, 6 November, 1995, 124–125.

32. Lefton, "Telecommunications: 800 Ways to Call Long-Distance," 106–107.

33. Marian B. Wood and Evelyn Ehrlich, "Segmentation: Five Steps to More Effective Business-to-Business Marketing," *Sales & Marketing Management*, April 1991, 59–62; Wendell R. Smith, "Product Differentiation and Market Segmentation as Alternative Marketing Strategies," *Marketing Management*, Winter 1995, 63–65.

34. Kevin J. Clancy and Robert S. Shulman, *Marketing Myths That Are Killing Business* (New York: McGraw-Hill, 1994), 87.

35. Joshua Hyatt, "Guaranteed Growth," *Inc.*, September 1995, 68–70, 72, 75–76, 78.

36. David Woodruff, "Can a Tune-Up Make Chevy a Contender?" *Business Week*, 25 July 1994, 70–71.

37. Adapted from Cory Johnson, "Instant Exports," *Success*, December 1993, 20.

38. Tom Duncan, "The Concept and Process of Integrated Marketing Communication," *Integrated Marketing Communications Research Journal*, Spring 1995, 3–10.

39. Thomas Petzinger, Jr., "Two Executives Cook Up Way to Make Pillsbury Listen," *Wall Street Journal*, 27 September 1996, B1.

40. Peppers and Rogers, *The One-to-One Future*, 37; Stan Rapp and Thomas L. Collins, *The New MaxiMarketing* (New York: McGraw-Hill, 1996), 250–251.

41. Peppers and Rogers, *The One-to-One Future*, 49–50.

42. Adapted from Donna Fenn, "Leader of the Pack," *Inc*, February 1996, 31–38.

CHAPTER **2**

1. Laxmi Nakarmi, "Look Out, World—Samsung Is Coming," *Business Week*, 10 July 1995, 52–53; Louis Kraar, "Korea Goes for Quality," *Fortune*, 18 April 1994, 153–154, 156–159; Julia Flynn, "Korea's Big Leap into Europe," *Business Week*, 18 March 1996, 52.

2. Quoted in William A. Band, *Creating Value for Customers* (New York: John Wiley, 1991), 49.

3. Thomas F. Wallace, *Customer-Driven Strategy: Winning Through Operational Excellence* (Essex Junction, VT.: Oliver Wight Omneo, 1992), 8; Tom Stein, "Outselling the Giants," *Success*, May 1996, 38–41.

4. Joe Panepinto, "Special Delivery," *Computerworld*, 7 March 1994, 79–81; Leslie Brokaw, "Twenty-Eight Steps to a Strategic Alliance," *Inc.*, April 1993, 96–100, 102, 104; Stephanie Strom, "Capital Cities Buys Stake in Mail-Order Flower Company," *New York Times*, 26 September 1994, D3.

5. Theodore Levitt, *The Marketing Imagination* (new, expanded edition) (New York: Free Press, 1986), 141–172.

6. Martin Christopher, Adrian Payne, and David Ballantyne, *Relationship Marketing* (Oxford, U.K.: Butterworth-Heinemann, 1991), 21–22; Vincent P. Barabba, "Meeting of the Minds," *Marketing Tools*, March–April 1996, 49–56.

7. Kevin J. Clancy and Robert S. Shulman, *Marketing Myths That Are Killing Business* (New York: McGraw-Hill, 1994), 104–105; "What's a Loyal Customer Worth?" *Fortune*, 11 December 1995, 182.

8. Clancy and Shulman, *Marketing Myths*, 106; Jill Griffin, *Customer Loyalty: How to Earn It, How to Keep It* (New York: Lexington Press, 1995), 42–43.

9. Gary Hamel and C. K. Prahalad, *Competing for the Future* (Boston: Harvard Business

School Press, 1994), 16–17; Howard Davies, Thomas K.P. Leung, Sherriff T.K. Luk, and Yiu-hing Wong, "The Benefits of 'Guanxi,' the Values of Relationships in Developing the Chinese Market," *Industrial Marketing Management* 24, (1995), 207–214.

10. Hamel and Prahalad, *Competing for the Future*, 16–17, 111–114.

11. "Corporate Community Service: Seeking America's Leaders," special advertising section in *Fortune*, 29 November 1994; Larry Witham, "Morality and the Marketplace," *Washington Times*, 21 December 1992, D1, D2; Robert Kuttner, "Rewarding Corporations That Really Invest in America," *Business Week*, 26 February 1996, 22.

12. Hamel and Prahalad, *Competing for the Future*, 73; Robert S. Kaplan and David P. Norton, "Using the Balanced Scorecard as a Strategic Management System," *Harvard Business Review*, January–February 1996, 75–85.

13. Bill Lombardo, "Another Company's Mission Statement," *Nation's Business*, April 1994, 4–5.

14. Ronald Grover, "Can This Man Lift Motown's Blues?" *Business Week*, 6 November 1995, 164, 168.

15. Adapted from Sharon Nelton, "Beating Back the Competition," *Nation's Business*, September 1994, 18–22, 24–25.

16. Frederick E. Webster, Jr., *Market-Driven Management* (New York: John Wiley, 1994), 85; C. K. Prahalad and Gary Hamel, "The Core Competence of the Corporation," *Harvard Business Review*, May–June 1990, 79–91; Hugh Carnegy, "Ericsson Battles to Stay in the Number One Slot," *Financial Times*, 6 September 1995, 13.

17. Shawn Tully, "The Modular Corporation," *Fortune*, 8 February 1993, 106–108, 112, 114–115; "Core Competencies," *Success*, December 1994, 18.

18. Julie Cohen Mason, "Strategic Alliances: Partnering for Success," *Management Review*, May 1993, 10–11, 13–15; Yoichi Clark Shimatsu, "Ford's New Engine, Mazda's New Driver," *World Business*, July–August 1996, 9.

19. Brenton R. Schlender, "How Toshiba Makes Alliances Work," *Fortune*, 4 October 1993, 116–118, 120.

20. Steven L. Goldman, Roger N. Nagel, and Kenneth Preiss, *Agile Competitors and Virtual Organizations* (New York: Van Nostrand Reinhold, 1995), 166; Bill Thomas,

"Entrepreneur's Notebook: Developing Passion for a Product," *Nation's Business*, December 1993, 9.

21. David J. Collis and Cynthia A. Montgomery, "Competing on Resources: Strategy in the 1990s," *Harvard Business Review*, July–August 1995, 118–128; Henry Mintzberg, *The Rise and Fall of Strategic Planning* (New York: Free Press, 1994), 356; Webster, *Market-Driven Management*, 47–49.

22. Michael E. Porter, *Competitive Advantage: Creating and Sustaining Superior Performance* (New York: Free Press, 1985), 4–6; J. Scott Armstrong and Fred Collopy, "Competitor Orientation and Effects of Objectives and Information on Managerial Decisions and Profitability," *Journal of Marketing Research*, May 1996, 188–199.

23. Christopher, Payne, and Ballantyne, *Relationship Marketing*, 43–45.

24. Karen Benezra, "Brand Builders: Pop Goes the Orville," *Brandweek*, 4 September 1995, 20–21.

25. John C. Narver and Stanley F. Slater, "The Effect of a Market Orientation on Business Profitability," *Journal of Marketing*, October 1990, 20–35; Murray Raphel and Neil Raphel, "Action Plan for Efficiently Building Customer Loyalty," *Bottom Line/Business*, 1 February 1996, 1–2.

26. Kathleen S. Kelly, "The Fund-Raising Behavior of U.S. Charitable Organizations," *Journal of Public Relations Research* 7(2), 1995, 111–137.

27. David E. Bowen, "Market-Focused HRM in Service Organizations: Satisfying Internal and External Customers," *Journal of Market-Focused Management* 1, (1996), 31–47.

28. Steve Gelsi, "Michelle Lange, Chevrolet," *Brandweek*, 13 November 1995, 29.

29. Ronni T. Marshak, "Business Process Reengineering," *Fortune*, 5 February 1996, advertisement.

30. Michael Hammer and James Champy, "The Promise of Reengineering," *Fortune*, 3 May 1993, 94–97.

31. Jerry Bowles, "The Enterprise Rewards," *Fortune*, 19 February 1996, 8–18.

32. Band, *Creating Value for Customers*, 55; Rohit Deshpande and Frederick E. Webster, Jr., "Organizational Culture and Marketing: Defining the Research Agenda," *Journal of Marketing* 53 (January 1989): 3–15; Pete Engardio, "Live-Wire Management at John

son Electric," *Business Week*, 27 November 1995, 80.

33. Webster, *Market-Driven Management*, 51–53; Christopher, Payne, and Ballantyne, *Relationship Marketing*, 63.

34. Jack Neff and Pat Sloan, "Proctor and Gamble Out to Simplify Its Product Lines," *Advertising Age*, 30 September 1996, 21.

35. "NHL Reaches Out in New Ways," in "The NHL," special advertising section in *Advertising Age*, 26 June 1995, NHL-10.

36. Peter Coy, "Supply-Chain Secrets," *Business Week*, 13 May 1996, 77. Webster, *Market-Driven Management*, 68–69.

37. Alex Taylor III, "The Auto Industry Meets the New Economy," *Fortune*, 5 September 1994, 52–54, 56, 58, 60; Peter Burrows, "Giant Killers on the Loose," *Business Week/The Information Revolution 1994*, 108–110; Warren Brown and Frank Swoboda, "Ford's Brave New World," *Washington Post*, 16 October 1994, H1, H4.

38. Barbara A. Gutek, *The Dynamics of Service* (San Francisco: Jossey-Bass, 1995).

39. Thomas O. Jones and W. Earl Sasser, Jr., "Why Satisfied Customers Defect," *Harvard Business Review*, November–December 1995, 88–99; "Training: Sales and the Seven Habits," *Inc.*, December 1995, 117.

40. John Goodman, "Customer Loyalty: Hard to Earn, Easy to Lose," *Boardroom Reports*, 15 June 1993, 7–8; Anne Murphy, "Entrepreneur of the Year," *Inc.*, December 1995, 38–40, 43–44, 46, 48, 51.

41. Thomas Petzinger, Jr., "Audio Legacy Shows Value of Feedback in Speaker Sales," *Wall Street Journal*, 2 August 1996, B1.

42. Stan Rapp and Thomas L. Collins, *Beyond MaxiMarketing* (New York: McGraw-Hill, 1994), 52–54; "Hotel Chain in India Sells 'First Class' Rooms to Business Travelers," *MaxiMarketing Insights*, November 1995, 12.

43. Shelly Reese, "The Very Model of a Modern Marketing Plan," *Marketing Tools*, January–February 1996, 56–65.

44. Jay Finegan, "Everything According to Plan," *Inc.*, March 1995, 78–80, 82, 84–85.

45. Pam Weisz, "Andrea Jung, Avon," *Brandweek*, 13 November 1995, 22.

46. Andrea Dunham and Barry Marcus with Mark Stevens and Patrick Barwise, *Unique Value: The Secret of All Great Business Strategies* (New York: Macmillan, 1993), 76–83.

47. Hamel and Prahalad, *Competing for the Future*, 243–245.

48. Band, *Creating Value for Customers*, 249.

49. Kevin J. Clancy and Robert S. Shulman, *The Marketing Revolution* (New York: HarperBusiness, 1991), 257–258.

50. Steve Gelsi, "George Burnett, AT&T," *Brandweek*, 13 November 1995, 24; Mark Lewyn, "MCI: A Smaller Family and Fewer Friends," *Business Week*, 6 February 1995, 147–148; Kate Fitzgerald, "Hellbent for the Digital Highway," *Advertising Age*, 28 September 1994, 10; Terry Lefton, "Truth Hurts AT&T's Rivals," *Superbrands 1995*, 17 October 1994, 128, 130–132.

51. Daniel Lyons, "How Home Depot Built Its Own Support Network," *INFOWORLD*, 7 August 1995, 48; Don Taylor and Jeanne Smalling Archer, *Up Against the Wal-Marts* (New York: Amacom, 1994); Greg Johnson, "Making Hardware Easy," *Los Angeles Times*, 15 October 1995, D1.

MARKETING ON THE NET FOR PART 1

1. Adapted from Jim Carlton, "Think Big: The Net Gives Small Business a Reach They Once Only Dreamed Of," *Wall Street Journal*, 17 June 1996, R27.

2. Adapted from Kim Cleland, "How Sprint Does Business on the Web," *Advertising Age's Internet Marketing*, May 1996, M4.

CHAPTER 3

1. Greg Burns, "'French Fries with That Quart of Oil?'" *Business Week*, 27 November 1995, 86–87; Eleena de Lisser, "Fast-Food Drive-Throughs Lose Speed," *Wall Street Journal*, 27 October 1994, B1, B7; Karen Benezra, "Fast Food: The Battle of the Bundles," *Superbrands 1995*, 17 October 1994, 89-99; Jeanne Whalen, "Shops Shift as Fast-Food Struggles for Answers," *Advertising Age*, 28 September 1994, 32; Ellen Neuborne, "Busy People Want Meals on Demand," *USA Today*, 4 October 1994, B1, B2; McDonald's 1993 Annual Report; Margaret Mannix, "A Big Whopper Stopper?" *U.S. News & World Report*, 6 May 1996, 60–61.

2. Steven L. Goldman, Roger N. Nagel, and Kenneth Preiss, *Agile Competitors and Virtual Organizations* (New York: Von Nostrand Reinhold, 1995), 3.

3. Rudolph A. Pyatt, Jr., "In Making Plans for Theme Park, Disney Let Arrogance Be Its Guide," *Washington Business*, 3 October 1994, 3, 43.

4. Stan Rapp and Thomas L. Collins, *The New MaxiMarketing* (New York: McGraw-Hill, 1996), 2–4; Stan Rapp and Thomas L. Collins, "A Generation Leads Technology Battle," *Business Marketing*, February 1996, 8.

5. PepsiCo, 1993 Annual Report, 2–3, 49.

6. Nancy A. Nichols, "From Complacency to Competitiveness: An Interview with Vitro's Ernesto Martens," *Harvard Business Review*, September–October 1993, 163–171.

7. Richard Brandt, "Bill Gates's Vision," *Business Week*, 27 June 1994, 56–62; Richard Brandt, "Top 10 Business Marketers," *Business Marketing*, February 1996, 3, 18, 30.

8. Adapted from Larry Armstrong, "From Riot to Ruin, A Surprising Harvest," *Business Week*, 9 May 1994, 38.

9. Robert H. Waterman, Jr., *What America Does Right* (New York: W. W. Norton, 1994), 90–91.

10. Christopher Caggiano, "What Do Workers Want?" *Inc.*, November 1992, 101–102; Keith Ferrazzi, "Minimize the Pain of Reengineering," *Wall Street Journal*, 13 November 1995, A14.

11. Fara Warner, "Circle Line: Nissan, GM Shy," *Brandweek*, 11 October 1993, 4.

12. Michele Galen, "White, Male, and Worried," *Business Week*, 31 January 1994, 50–55.

13. Kenneth Labich, "Making Diversity Pay," *Fortune*, 9 September 1996, 177–180.

14. Leon E. Wynter, "New Ideas Can Also Be Found Down the Hall," *Wall Street Journal*, 30 March 1993, B1.

15. Lilli Gordon, "New Deal for Shareholders," *Wall Street Journal*, 4 February 1993, A18; Lynn Asinof, "Something for Nothing," *Wall Street Journal*, 8 December 1995, R11.

16. Rosabeth Moss Kanter, "Collaborative Advantage: The Art of Alliances," *Harvard Business Review*, July–August 1994, 96–108; Christopher Palmieri, "A Process That Never Ends," *Forbes*, 21 December 1992, 52.

17. Russell Mitchell, "Managing by Values," *Business Week*, 1 August 1994, 46–52; Alice Z. Cuneo, "Nimble VF Strips Levi of Jeans Market Lead," *Advertising Age*, 28 September 1994, 30; Elaine Underwood, "Apparel: Casual Conquers the Market," *Superbrands 1995*, 17 October 1994, 56–57.

18. Bruce G. Posner, "The Best Small-Business Banks in America," *Inc.*, July 1992, 86–89, 92–93.

19. Shannon Dortch, "A Slow Fade for the Echo Boom," *American Demographics*, July 1994, 15–16; Peter Francese, "America at Mid-Decade," *American Demographics*, February 1995, 12–31.

20. Robert J. Samuelson, "Generational Economics: The Gap Is Real," *Washington Post*, 14 April 1994, A31; U.S. Bureau of the Census, *Statistical Abstract of the United States 1993* (Washington, D.C.: U.S. Government Printing Office, 1993), 15, 17.

21. Jay Finegan, "A Bootstrapper's Primer," *Inc.*, August 1995, 49–51.

22. Francese, "America at Mid-Decade," 28; Brad Edmondson, "The Big Picture," *American Demographics Desk Reference Series, No. 1*, 2–3; Kathy Bodovitz, "Black America," *American Demographics Desk Reference Series No. 1*, 6–7; Kathy Bodovitz, "Hispanic America," *American Demographics Desk Reference Series, No. 1*, 8–9; Kathy Bodovitz and Brad Edmondson, "Asian America," *American Demographics Desk Reference Series, No. 1*, 10–11.

23. Gail Baker Woods, *Advertising and Marketing to the New Majority* (Belmont, Calif.: Wadsworth, 1995), 6.

24. Joel Millman, "Zen and the Art of Fresh Produce," *Forbes*, 15 February 1993, 220.

25. Don E. Schultz, Stanley I. Tannenbaum, and Robert F. Lauterborn, *The New Marketing Paradigm: Integrated Marketing Communications* (Lincolnwood, Ill.: NTC Business Books, 1993).

26. Stephanie N. Mehta, "Number of Women-Owned Businesses Surged 43% in 5 Years Through 1992," *Wall Street Journal*, 29 January 1996, B2.

27. Robert F. Hartley, *Marketing Mistakes*, 6th ed. (New York: John Wiley, 1995), 13–25; Sue Shellenbarger, "Work & Family," *Wall Street Journal*, 14 February 1996, B1.

28. "Government's Role in Business," *CNN's Money Week/Management*, 24 October 1993, 2; Kenneth J. Meier, *Regulation: Politics, Bureaucracy, and Economics* (New York: St. Martin's Press, 1985), 235.

29. Amy Cortese, "Next Stop, Chicago," *Business Week*, 1 August 1994, 24–26.

30. Meier, *Regulation*, 254.

31. James R. Healey, "Rules Re-Define Origin," *USA Today*, 29 June 1994, 2B.

32. Julia Miller, "Ad Propping Today: Shoot Fast, 'Cut Back on Trickery,'" *Advertising Age*, 17 October 1994, 29; Catherine Arnst and Michael Mandel, "Telecom's New Age," *Business Week*, 8 April 1996, 63–66.

33. Andrea Gerlin, "A Matter of Degree: How a Jury Decided That a Coffee Spill Is Worth $2.9 Million," *Wall Street Journal*, 1 September 1994, A1, A4.

34. Theodore B. Olson, "The Dangerous National Sport of Punitive Damages," *Wall Street Journal*, 5 October 1994, A17.

35. Thomas Hine, "The Front Line of Marketing," *Brandweek*, 16 October 1995, 24–25, 28, 30, 34, 36; Pat Sloan, "Private Labels Win in Court," *Advertising Age*, 10 October 1994, 2.

36. Archie B. Carroll, *Business & Society: Ethics and Stakeholder Management*, 2nd ed. (Cincinnati: Southwestern Publishing, 1993), 284.

37. Carroll, *Business & Society*, 227, 234–235.

38. Peter Burrows, "Giant Killers on the Loose," *Business Week Information Revolution 1994*, 18 May 1994, 108, 110.

39. David B. Montgomery and Charles B. Weinberg, "Toward Strategic Intelligence Systems," in *Marketing Classics*, 7th ed., edited by Ben M. Enis and Keith K. Cox (Boston: Allyn & Bacon, 1991), 341–358; Gail Edmondson, "In the Cold and the Dark, High-Tech Heat," *Business Week*, 25 September 1995, 120, 122.

40. "Mom and Pop Go High Tech," *Business Week*, 21 November 1994, 82–86, 90; Christopher Power, "How to Get Closer to Your Customers," *Business Week Enterprise 1993*, 42, 44–45.

41. Stephanie Anderson Forest, "Dillard's Has a Dilly of a Headache," *Business Week*, 3 October 1994, 85–86.

42. Warren Strobel, "Isolated No Longer: Hanoi Races for Riches," *Washington Times*, 9 May 1994, A1, A7; Pete Engardio, "Rising from the Ashes," *Business Week*, 23 May 1994, 44–46, 48.

43. Adapted from Daniel Burrus, *Technotrends* (New York: HarperBusiness, 1993), 173.

44. Michael E. Porter, *Competitive Advantage* (New York: Free Press, 1985), 6; Jeanne Wahlen, "Nabisco Brand Is the Cookie

Scent," *Advertising Age*, 27 September 1995, 18.

45. Maria Mallory, "Checkmate Electronics: Beating Bad-Check Artists Right at the Cash Register," *Business Week*, 23 May 1994, 95–96.

46. Carroll, *Business & Society*, 122–124.

47. "Right-Action Ethic Really Works," in "Problem-Solving Partnerships," a special advertising section of *Business Ethics* magazine, July–August 1994, 29.

48. Fara Warner, "Find a Niche. . . Then Defend It," *Superbrands 1995*, 17 October 1994, 133–134.

49. Ralph M. Gaedeke, Craig A. Kelley, and Dennis H. Tootelian, "Practitioners' Perceptions of Ethical Standards in Marketing," *Journal of Professional Services Marketing*, 8, no. 2 (1993): 11–26; N. Craig Smith, "Marketing Strategies for the Ethics Era," *Sloan Management Review*, Summer 1995, 85–97; David M. Messick and Max H. Bazerman, "Ethical Leadership and the Psychology of Decision Making," *Sloan Management Review*, Winter 1996, 9–22.

50. Michael Elliott, "Corruption," *Newsweek*, 14 November 1994, 40–42; Dana Milbank and Marcus W. Brachli, "Greasing Wheels: How U.S. Concerns Compete in Countries Where Bribes Flourish," *Wall Street Journal*, 29 September 1995, A1, A16; Sharon Nelton, "Promoting a World Ethical Standard," *Nation's Business*, April 1996, 12.

51. Russell Mitchell, "Managing by Values," *Business Week*, 1 August 1994, 46–52.

52. Robert McGarvey, "Do the Right Thing," *Entrepreneur*, October 1992, 138–143; Michael Lane, "Improving American Business Ethics in Three Steps," *CPA Journal*, 1 February 1991; Susan Sonnesyn, "A Question of Ethics," *Training and Development Journal* 45, 1 March 1991, 29–37; Dawn Blalock, "For Many Executives, Ethics Appear to Be a Write-Off," *Wall Street Journal*, 26 March 1996, C1, C15.

53. Kenneth Blanchard and Norman Vincent Peale, *The Power of Ethical Management* (New York: William Morrow, 1988); Diane Cole, "Companies Crack Down on Dishonesty," *Managing Your Career*, a *Wall Street Journal* publication, Spring 1991, 8–10; Smith, "Marketing Strategies for the Ethics Era," 85–97.

54. Shelby D. Hunt and John J. Burnett, "The Macromarketing/Micromarketing Dichotomy: A Taxonomical Model," *Journal of Marketing*, Summer 1982, 11–26.

55. "Allstate Chairman Stresses Community Service," in "Corporate Community Service: Seeking America's Leaders," advertising supplement to *Fortune*, 28 November 1994, 122.

56. "Corporate Community Service: Seeking America's Leaders," advertising supplement to *Fortune*, 28 November 1994; Paul N. Bloom, Pattie Yu Hussein, and Lisa R. Szykman, "Benefiting Society and the Bottom Line," *Marketing Management*, Winter 1995, 8–18.

57. Janean Huber, "Social Graces," *Entrepreneur*, December 1994, 121–127.

58. Faye Rice, "Who Scores Best on the Environment?" *Fortune*, 26 July 1993, 114–116, 118–120, 122; Jessica Mathews, "Business Goes Green," *Washington Post*, 12 February 1996, A19.

59. Elaine Underwood, "Green Jeans and Pop Bottles," *Brandweek*, 10 October 1994, 8; "Sprouting Sales with 'Green' Products," *Nation's Business*, May 1996, 11; Gregory J. Hale and Caroline G. Hemenway, "ISO 14001 Likely to Join Regulatory Framework," *Quality Digest*, February 1996, 29–34.

60. Joan C. Szabo, "Business Initiatives for Better Schools," *Nation's Business*, September 1992, 44, 46, 48; "A Team Approach Is Used for Oracle's Community Service Program," in "Corporate Community Service: Seeking America's Leaders," advertising supplement to *Fortune*, 28 November 1994, 124; Carroll, *Business & Society*, 374; Jacquelyn Ottman, "Mandate for the '90s: Green Corporate Image," *Marketing News*, 11 September 1995, 8.

61. Carroll, *Business & Society*, 380; McDonald's, 1993 Annual Report, 13; Avon, 1993 Annual Report, 14.

62. Edmund M. Burke, letter to the editor, *Harvard Business Review*, July–August 1994, 142; Thomas Petzinger, Jr., "This Auditing Team Wants You to Create a Moral Organization," *Wall Street Journal*, 19 January 1996, B1.

63. "Be Socially Responsible," advertisement in *Utne Reader*, November–December 1994, 31; Robert McGarvey, "Natural Wonder," *Entrepreneur*, September 1995, 160–164.

CHAPTER 4

1. Jeffery D. Zbar, "Blockbuster's Fast-Forward," *Advertising Age*, 18 September 1995, I-32; Edward R. Silverman, "Global Go-Getters," *International Business*, October 1992, 20–21; Blockbuster Entertainment, 1993 Annual Report; "Block-buster to Expand in Asia," *Financial Times*, 5 October 1995, 18.

2. Robert L. Rose, "Success Abroad," *Wall Street Journal*, 29 March 1991, A1, A5.

3. Toni Mack and Andrew Tanzer, "The Jewel in the Crown," *Forbes*, 26 September 1994, 76, 78; Shelley Neumeier, "An American Way to Invest in a European Recovery," *Fortune*, 19 September 1994, 33–34; Karl Schoenberger, "Motorola Bets Big on China," *Fortune*, 17 May 1996, 116–124.

4. John Scholes, "A Global Paradigm," *International Business*, November 1995, 60–62; William Knoke, "Bold New World," *Success*, April 1996, 68.

5. Noel M. Tichy and Stratford Sherman, *Control Your Destiny or Someone Else Will* (New York: Doubleday, 1993), 242.

6. Tom Keane, "Aspire Makes Impressive Debut with Much to Offer for 8K Plus," *Washington Times*, 18 March 1994, E1, E10.

7. Walter B. Wriston, "Big Brother, We Are Watching You," *Forbes*, 4 January 1993, 57; Rosabeth Moss Kanter, *World Class* (New York: Simon & Schuster, 1995).

8. Michael E. Porter, "The Competitive Advantage of Nations," *Harvard Business Review*, March–April 1990, 73–93; Shelby D. Hunt and Robert M. Morgan, "The Comparative Advantage Theory of Competition," *Journal of Marketing*, April 1995, 1–15.

9. Michael R. Czinkota, Pietra Rivoli, and Ilkka A. Ronkainen, *International Business*, 2nd ed. (Fort Worth, Tex.: Dryden Press, 1992), 24–25.

10. Neil Gross, "In the Digital Derby, There's No Inside Lane," *Business Week 21st Century Capitalism*, 1994 bonus issue, 146–150, 152, 154.

11. Rob Norton, "Strategies for the New Export Boom," *Fortune*, 22 August 1994, 124–127, 129–130, 132.

12. Charles Batchelor, "Letting the Train Take the Strain," *Financial Times*, 16 October 1995, 8.

13. Ken Labich, "NBA's David Stern: Still a Gamer," *Fortune*, 30 October 1995, 28; Hillary Rosner, "Dream Team's Sisters," *Brandweek*, 6 November 1995, 24, 26; Carl Desens, "The NBA's Fast Break Overseas," *Business Week*, 5 December 1994, 94; David

Halberstam, "David Did It," *World Business*, January/February 1996, 34–39.

14. David E. Moore, "Davos '94: A Reporter's Notebook," *International Business*, March 1994, 12; David Halberstam, "David Did It," *World Business*, January–February 1996, 34–39.

15. Czinkota, Rivoli, and Ronkainen, *International Business*, 181–182.

16. Douglas Harbrecht, William C. Symonds, Elisabeth Malkin, and Geri Smith, "What Has NAFTA Wrought? Plenty of Trade," *Business Week*, 21 November 1994, 48–49; Daniel B. Moskowitz, "Opening the Services Door," *International Business*, March 1996, 70–72.

17. Edward Russell-Walling, "Europe's Time of Trial," *International Business*, April 1994, 66, 68, 70–72, 74, 76; Martin Sieff, "With AFTA Here, Is TRAFTA on Way?" *Washington Times*, 16 April 1995, A1, A13; Martin Sieff, "Robust EU Confronts Crippling Growing Pains," *Washington Times*, 11 August 1996, A10.

18. Dana Milbank, "Can Europe Deliver?" *Wall Street Journal World Business Report*, 30 September 1994, R15, R23.

19. Robert West, "The Big New Import/Export Opportunities," *Boardroom Reports*, 15 February 1995, 11–12; Sherman E. Katz, "The Quiet Ways the WTO Is Working Well," *Washington Times*, 12 April 1996, A19.

20. Yuri Kageyama, "Saturn Tries to Sell Japanese on New Service," *Washington Times*, 9 July 1996, B10.

21. Douglas Harbrecht, "'Delay Would Mean the Death of GATT,'" *Business Week*, 5 December 1994, 34–36.

22. Amy Borrus, Bill Javetski, John Perry, and Brian Bremmer, "Change of Heart," *Business Week*, 20 May 1996, 48–49.

23. Czinkota, Rivoli, and Ronkainen, *International Business*, 180.

24. "Making Shoes in Brazil: Not Just a Load of Cobblers," *The Economist*, 24 June 1995, 61–62.

25. Andrew Joncus, "German Faucet Maker Hoping to Tap Fresh Markets, Particularly in the U.S.," *Wall Street Journal*, 17 July 1995, A5C.

26. Zhao Xiniuo, "Barter Tourism: A New Phenomenon Along the China–Russia Border," *Journal of Travel Research*, 32, no. 3 (Winter 1994): 65–67.

27. Susan Douglas and Bernard Dubois, "Looking at the Cultural Environment for International Marketing Opportunities," in *Marketing Classics*, 7th ed., edited by Ben M. Enis and Keith K. Cox (Boston: Allyn & Bacon, 1991), 542–549; Margo Lipschitz, "Using Culture to Promote Fruit," *Ad Age International*, May 1996, 14.

28. Janet L. Willen, "Marketers to the World," *Nation's Business*, February 1994, 11; 205–206; Czinkota, Rivoli, and Ronkainen, *International Business*, 205–206.

29. Brian Toyne and Peter G.P. Walters, *Global Marketing Management* (Boston: Allyn & Bacon, 1993), 250.

30. Rahul Jacob, "Where's the Beef?" *Fortune*, 24 January 1994, 16; Cheryl Nakata and K. Sivakumar, "National Culture and New Product Development: An Integrative Review," *Journal of Marketing*, January 1996, 61–72.

31. "Chinese Cheetos," *New York Times Magazine*, 27 November 1994, 31.

32. Daniel B. Moskowitz, "Taking Aim at Bribes Overseas," *International Business*, February 1994, 110.

33. Peter Fuhrman with Michael Schuman, "'Now We Are Our Own Masters,'" *Forbes*, 23 May 1994, 128ff.

34. Roger E. Axtell, *The Do's and Taboos of International Trade: A Small Business Primer* (New York: John Wiley, 1989), 57–59.

35. Tony Munroe, "Kitsch Sells Via Kokomo," *Washington Times*, 31 October 1994, A19.

36. Nanette Byrnes, "Stars of Stage, Screen, and Toys 'R' Us," *Business Week*, 5 December 1994, 46.

37. "No Kidding," *St. Louis Post-Dispatch*, 30 August 1991, 1F.

38. Mark Nicholson, "Honda and Siel to Build India Car Plant," *Financial Times*, 6 September 1995, 5; P. Theron Johnson, "Delivering to the Global Village," *MAST*, July 1991, 20–26.

39. Amy Barrett, "It's a Small (Business) World," *Business Week*, 17 April 1995, 96–101.

40. Peggy Salz-Trautman, "Tectonic Stirrings in European Insurance," *International Business*, June 1995, 56, 58–59.

41. "Thailand: An Asian Powerhouse," *International Business*, February 1994, 62.

42. Jeffrey J. Ake, "Easier Done than Said," *Inc.*, February 1993, 96–99; Mary Beth Sammons, "Preparing for the Plunge," *Chicago Tribune*, 27 October 1993, sec. 7, 5.

43. Lourdes Lee Valeriano, "How Small Firms Can Get Free Help from Big Ones," *Wall Street Journal*, 30 July 1991, B2; William Holstein and Kevin Kelley, "Little Companies, Big Exports," *Business Week*, 13 April 1992, 70–72.

44. Daniel B. Moskowitz, "More than a Band-Aid," *International Business*, December 1992, 110; Susan Hayes, "Source 1993," *Success*, July–August 1993, 37–40; "International Chamber of Commerce," *International Business*, June 1995, 28.

45. Donna G. Albrecht, "Small-Business Help from the Government," *Entrepreneur*, May 1992, 208–211.

46. David A. Ericson, "Standardized Approach Works Well in Establishing Global Presence," *Marketing News*, 7 October 1996, 9.

47. "Sergio Zyman," *Brandweek*, 14 November 1994, 34–36, 38, 40–42; Robert T. Moran, Philip R. Harris, and William G. Stripp, *Developing the Global Organization* (Houston, Tex.: Gulf Publishing, 1993), 184–187; Betsy Morris, "The Brand's the Thing," *Fortune*, 4 March 1996, 72–86.

48. Brenton R. Schlender, "Matsushita Shows How to Go Global," *Fortune*, 11 July 1994, 159–160, 162, 164, 166.

49. S. Tamer Cavusgil and Shaoming Zou, "Marketing Strategy–Performance Relationship: An Investigation of the Empirical Link in Export Market Ventures," *Journal of Marketing*, 58 (January 1994): 1–21.

50. Roderick Oram, "The Slippery Business of Soap," *Financial Times*, 17 November 1995, 13.

51. David Woodruff, "Mercedes' Maverick in Alabama," *Business Week*, 11 September 1995, 64–65.

52. Melanie Wells and Bradley Johnson, "Going Global Via E-mail, Online," *Advertising Age*, 12 September 1994, S-6.

53. Paul B. Carroll, "'Nafta Superhighway' Sought for Trade," *Wall Street Journal*, 19 September 1995, A19.

54. Eric Hollreiser, "Mercedes Veers from Value Line," *Brandweek*, 10 October 1994, 6.

55. Bill Saporito, "Behind the Tumult at P&G," *Fortune*, 7 March 1994, 74–76, 80–82.

56. Allyson L. Stewart, "International Business," *Boardroom Reports*, July 15, 1994,

7–8; Robert F. Hartley, *Marketing Mistakes*, 6th ed. (New York: John Wiley, 1995), 113–127, 146–160; Moran, Harris, and Stripp, *Developing the Global Organization*, 196–197; Andrew Jack, "Euro Disney Makes Communication Its Theme," *Financial Times*, 16 November 1995, 20.

57. Rick Yan, "To Reach China's Customers, Adapt to *Guo Qing*," *Harvard Business Review*, September–October 1994, 66–68, 70–74.

58. T. N. Somasundaram and C. David Light, "Rethinking a Global Media Strategy," *Journal of International Consumer Marketing* 7, no. 1 (1994): 23–38; Yan, "To Reach China's Customers," 66–68, 70–74; Louis Kraar, "TV Is Exploding All Over Asia," *Fortune*, 24 January 1994, 98–101.

59. Jane Z. Sojkia and Patriya S. Tansuhaj, "Cross-Cultural Consumer Research: A Twenty-Year Review," *Advances in Consumer Research*, 22 (1995), 461–474; Kathy Bodovitz, "Black America," *American Demographics Desk Reference Series*, No. 1, 6–7; Kathy Bodovitz, "Hispanic America," *American Demographics Desk Reference Series, No. 1*, 8–9; Kathy Bodovitz and Brad Edmondson, "Asian America," *American Demographics Desk Reference Series, No. 1*, 10–11; Gail Baker Woods, *Advertising and Marketing to the New Majority* (Belmont, Calif.: Wadsworth, 1995), 38–50.

60. Woods, *Advertising and Marketing to the New Majority*, 8–33; Michael R. Solomon, *Consumer Behavior* (Boston: Allyn & Bacon, 1992), 417–418.

61. Woods, *Advertising and Marketing to the New Majority*, 44.

62. Bodovitz and Edmondson, "Asian America," 10–11.

63. Sandra Sugawara, "A Blooming Business in Any Language," *Washington Post*, 4 May 1994, D1, D3; Gary Levin, "Marketers Learning New Languages for Ads," *Advertising Age*, 10 May 1993, 33

64. Allan Wagner, "Asian Grocers Succeed with Anglo Shoppers," *American Demographics*, December 1994, 19.

65. Adapted from "Ad Agency Speaking to the Hispanic Market," *Chicago Tribune*, 8 January 1995, 7.

MARKETING ON THE NET FOR PART 2

1. Sarah Shafer, "Will Your Web Page Fly in Japan?" *Inc. Technology*, 18 June 1996, 20;

Isa Gucciardi, "Language Helps Expand Markets on the Internet," *DM News*, 17 June 1996, 4; Michael J. Mandel, "A World Wide Web for Tout Le Monde," *Business Week*, 1 April 1996, 36.

2. Adapted from Jacquelyn Ottman, "Stalking the Green Consumer on the Internet," *Marketing News*, 26 February 1996, 7.

CHAPTER 5

1. Stan Rapp and Thomas L. Collins, "Nestlé Banks on Databases," *Advertising Age*, 25 October 1993, 16, S-7, S-10; Stan Rapp and Thomas L. Collins, *Beyond Maxi-Marketing* (New York: McGraw-Hill, 1994), 135–142; Stan Rapp and Tom Collins, *The Great Marketing Turnaround* (Englewood Cliffs, N.J.: Prentice-Hall, 1990), 125–126, 202–203, 305.

2. "AMA Board Approves New Marketing Definition," *Marketing News*, 1 March 1985, 1, 14.

3. Frederick E. Webster, Jr., *Market-Driven Management* (New York: John Wiley, 1994), 263; Bradley Johnson, "Behind All the Hype Lies a Hidden, Crucial Asset," *Advertising Age*, 2 October 1995, 30–32.

4. Ray Verdon, "Innovation May Be Wonderful, But Naught Without User Demand," *Brandweek*, 12 December 1994, 17; Betsy Spethmann, "SnackWell's Rolls Challenge to Jell-O," *Brandweek*, 27 November 1995, 3.

5. David Osborne and Ted Gaebler, *Reinventing Government* (New York: Plume, 1993), 174–175; Chad Rubel, "Some Colleges Guarantee Their Students Will Succeed at Work," *Marketing News*, 9 October 1995, 1–2.

6. "Customizing for the New Consumer," *Fortune*, 27 December 1993, 45; Garth R. Hallberg, "Intelligent Use of Databases Can Nurture Brand Loyalty," *Advertising Age International*, June 1996, I-16.

7. Christina Del Valle, "They Know Where You Live—And How You Buy," *Business Week*, 7 February 1994, 89; "PRIZM: Lifestyle Segmentation," a brochure from Claritas Inc., 1995.

8. Jennifer Derryberry, "Calling All Young, Hip Scientists," *Business Marketing*, July 1995, 2.

9. Jeanne Whalen, "Category Insight Bonds Marketers to Retailers," *Advertising Age*, 16 October 1995, 24.

10. Edward Parker, "The Spy Fighters," *Success*, April 1994, 33–39.

11. "Creative Strategies: Radio Shack's New Tune," *Direct*, November 1994, 50; Mark Halper, "Welcome to 21st-Century Data," *Forbes ASAP*, 8 April 1996, 49–56.

12. Rapp and Collins, *Beyond MaxiMarketing*, 186–192.

13. Laura Loro, "Downside for Public Is Privacy Issue," *Advertising Age*, 2 October 1995, 32; Judith Waldrop, "The Business of Privacy," *American Demographics*, October 1994, 46–51, 54–55; ". . . And Way Out on the Leading Edge," *Fortune*, Autumn–Winter 1993, 41; Mark Lewyn, "You Can Run, but It's Tough to Hide from Marketers," *Business Week*, 5 September 1994, 60–61.

14. Kevin J. Clancy, Robert S. Shulman, and Marianne Wolf, *Simulated Test Marketing* (New York: Lexington Books, 1994), 243; Raymond R. Burke, "Virtual Shopping: Breakthrough in Marketing Research," *Harvard Business Review*, March–April 1996, 120–131.

15. William R. Dillon, Thomas J. Madden, and Neil H. Firtle, *Marketing Research in a Marketing Environment*, 3rd ed. (Burr Ridge, Ill.: Irwin, 1990), 656–663.

16. Don Peppers and Martha Rogers, *The One-to-One Future* (New York: Currency Doubleday, 1993), 82–84.

17. Sam Walton with John Huey, *Sam Walton: Made in America* (New York: Doubleday, 1992).

18. Thomas C. Kinnear and James R. Taylor, *Marketing Research*, 4th ed. (New York: McGraw-Hill, 1991), 48; Susan M. Detwiler, "Secondhand Prose," *Marketing Tools*, January–February 1995, 12–16.

19. Information on MicroScan has been adapted from Patricia Sellers, "Keeping the Buyers You Already Have," *Fortune*, Autumn–Winter 1993, 56–58.

20. Rita Koselka, "The New Mantra: MUT," *Forbes*, 11 March 1996, 114–118.

21. Osborne and Gaebler, *Reinventing Government*, 177; Nevin J. Rodes, "Marketing a Community Symphony Orchestra," *Marketing News*, 29 January 1996, 2.

22. Aimée Stern, "Do You Know What They Want?" *International Business*, March 1993, 102–103.

23. "42,496 Secrets Are Bared," *Fortune*, 24 January 1994, 13.

24. David Parmerlee, "Information, Please," *Marketing Tools*, November–December 1994, 15–17; Jack Edmonston, "Syndicated Research Attack 'Uninformed'," *Business Marketing*, February 1996, 28.

25. Michael R. Czinkota, "Take a Shortcut to Low-Cost Global Research," *Marketing News*, 13 March 1995, 3.

26. Stern, "Do You Know What They Want?" 102–103.

27. Sellers, "Keeping the Buyers You Already Have," 56–58.

28. Earl Naumann, *Creating Customer Value: The Path to Sustainable Competitive Advantage* (Cincinnati: Thomson Executive Press, 1995), 145–146.

29. Gary G. Brush, *How to Choose the Proper Sample Size*, vol. 12 (Milwaukee: American Society for Quality Control, 1988), 27; Vicki Douglas, "Questionnaire Too Long? Try Variable Clustering," *Marketing News*, 27 February 1995, 38.

30. Regis McKenna, "Real-Time Marketing," *Harvard Business Review*, July–August 1995, 87–95.

31. Betsy Wade, "Smoke-Free Flights Increase," *New York Times*, 1 January 1995, sec. 5, 4.

32. Kinnear and Taylor, *Marketing Research*, 400.

33. Esther D'Amico and L. Maxine Sanford, "Pint-Size Purchasers," *Home Office Computing*, October 1994, 98–99.

34. Alice Z. Cuneo, "Prying the Truth Out of Consumers," *Advertising Age*, 12 September 1994, S–4; Stuart Elliott, "The Latest in Market Research: Videogenic Self-Analyzing Shoppers," *New York Times*, 23 August 1993, D1.

35. Terence P. Pare, "How to Find Out What They Want," *Fortune*, Autumn–Winter 1993, 39–41; Susan Carroll, "Questionnaire Design Affects Response Rate," *The Honomichl 50*, a supplement to *Marketing News*, June 1994, H25–H26; James P. Dickson and Douglas L. MacLachlan, "Fax Surveys: Return Patterns and Comparison with Mail Surveys," *Journal of Marketing Research*, February 1996, 108–113.

36. "The NPD Group," in *The Honomichl 50*, a supplement to *Marketing News*, 6 June 1994, H8.

37. "Focus Groups: Face to Face with Customers," *Outlook*, 6 March 1995, 7; Thomas

L. Greenbaum, "Focus Groups by Video Next Trend of the '90s," *Marketing News*, 29 July 1996, 4.

38. William Weylock, "Focus: Hocus Pocus?" *Marketing Tools*, July–August 1994, 12, 14, 16; Leah Rickard, "Focus Groups Go to Collage," *Advertising Age*, 14 November 1994, 39.

39. Debra Goldman, "Cyber-Chat 101," *Brandweek*, February 1995, IQ6; Tibbett Speer, "Nickelodeon Puts Kids Online," *American Demographics*, January 1994, 16–17; Cyndee Miller, "Focus Groups Go Where None Has Been Before," *Marketing News*, 4 July 1994, 2, 14; "Get Fast, Cheap Research Online," *Success*, April 1996, 6.

40. Paula Kephart, "Think Globally," *Marketing Tools*, November–December 1994, 74–76; Stern, "Do You Know What They Want?" 102–103; Kenneth Wylie, "International Researcher Growth Surges Nearly 20%," *Advertising Age*, 20 May 1996, 44–45.

41. Kevin J. Clancy and Robert S. Shulman, *Marketing Myths That Are Killing Business* (New York: McGraw-Hill, 1994), 256.

42. Clancy, Shulman, and Wolf, *Simulated Test Marketing*, 44–47, 49–78.

43. Clancy and Shulman, *Marketing Myths*, 255–259.

44. Bart Ziegler, "Old Market Research Tricks No Match for New Technology," *Wall Street Journal*, 1 November 1994, B1, B9; Tim Triplett, "Survey System Has Human Touch Without the Human," *Marketing News*, 24 October 1994, 16; Howard Schlossberg, "Shoppers Virtually Stroll Through Store Aisles to Examine Packages," *Marketing News*, 7 June 1993, 2; "Spiegel Keeps in Touch," *Stores*, October 1993, 78.

45. Susan Spiggle, "Analysis and Interpretation of Qualitative Data in Consumer Research," *Journal of Consumer Research* 21 (December 1994): 491–503; Arthur Middelton Hughes, "Boosting Response with RFM," *Marketing Tools*, May 1996, 4–10.

46. Lester E. Coleman and Donald G. Reynolds, "Benchmarking Customer Satisfaction," *Personal Selling Power*, November–December 1994, 52–55.

47. Rita Koselka, "The New Mantra: MUT," *Forbes*, 11 March 1996, 114–118.

48. Coleman and Reynolds, "Benchmarking Customer Satisfaction," 52–55.

49. Margaret R. Roller, "Virtual Research Exists, But How Real Is It?" *Marketing News*, 15 January 1996, 13–15.

50. Larry B. Christensen, *Experimental Methodology*, 4th ed. (Boston: Allyn & Bacon, 1988), 350–356; William G. Zikmund, *Exploring Marketing Research*, 4th ed. (Chicago: Dryden, 1991), 295–296.

51. Adapted from Jay Finegan, "In the Customer's Shoes," *Inc.*, May 1995, 45–53.

CHAPTER 6

1. "Saturn Starts 2nd Generation of Models, Opens Internet Site," *Washington Times*, 19 July 1996, E13; Raymond Serafin, "Saturn Bounces Back with Its Basic Appeal," *Advertising Age*, 30 January 1995, 4; John Bissell, "Saturn 'Homecoming': Publicity Stunt, or Triumph of Relationship Marketing?" *Brandweek*, 8 August 1994, 18; Warren Brown, "What If You Had a Party and 28,000 Saturn Owners Showed Up?" *Washington Post*, 26 June 1994, A20; Kathleen Kerwin, "Forget Woodstock—These Folks Are Headin' to Spring Hill," *Business Week*, 27 June 1994, 36.

2. Don Peppers and Martha Rogers, *The One-to-One Future* (New York: Currency Doubleday, 1993), 140.

3. William D. Wells, "Discovery-Oriented Consumer Research," *Journal of Consumer Research* 19 (March 1993): 489–504; Morris B. Holbrook, "What Is Consumer Research?" *Journal of Consumer Research* 14 (June 1987): 128–132.

4. Gerald Karush, "The CIF and the Market Planning Process," *Bank Marketing*, May 1990, 32–36; Ken Blanchard, "Raving Fans: African Style," *Quality Digest*, May 1996, 19.

5. Matthew Grimm, "Pizza Hut's Perkins Has No Time to Stop," *Brandweek*, 11 January 1993, 20–21; Chad Rubel, "Pizza Hut Explores Customer Satisfaction," *Marketing News*, 25 March 1996, 15.

6. "Building 'Share-of-Customer' Becomes a Priority at U.S. Shoe's Women's Specialty Retailing Group," *Colloquy*, 4, no. 21 (1993): 8–9, 11.

7. Jerry Adler, "Have We Become a Nation of Slobs?" *Newsweek*, 20 February 1995, 56–62.

8. Peter F. Drucker, *Managing the Nonprofit Organization: Principles and Practices* (New York: HarperCollins, 1990); David Osborne and Ted Gaebler, *Reinventing Government* (New York: Plume, 1993); Debra Hale, "Seriously Casual," *Washington Times*, 9 December 1995, C4.

9. Michael R. Solomon, *Consumer Behavior: Buying, Having, and Being,* 2nd ed. (Boston: Allyn & Bacon, 1994), 220.

10. William P. Putsis, Jr., and Narasimhan Srinivasan, "Buying or Just Browsing? The Duration of Purchase Deliberation," *Journal of Marketing Research,* 31 (August 1994): 393–402.

11. Adapted from Solomon, *Consumer Behavior,* 228.

12. Niraj Dawar and Philip Parker, "Marketing Universals: Consumers' Use of Brand Name, Price, Physical Appearance, and Retailer Reputation as Signals of Product Quality," *Journal of Marketing,* 58 (April 1994): 81–95.

13. Solomon, *Consumer Behavior,* 340–341; Dale D. Buss, "The Little Guys Strike Back," *Nation's Business,* July 1996, 18–34.

14. Daniel Pearl, "More Firms Pledge Guaranteed Service," *Wall Street Journal,* 17 July 1991, B1, B4.

15. Osborne and Gaebler, *Reinventing Government,* 174–177; Chad Rubel, "Some Colleges Guarantee Their Students Will Succeed at Work," *Marketing News,* 9 October 1995, 1–2.

16. Henry Assael, *Consumer Behavior and Marketing Action,* 4th ed. (Boston: PWS-Kent, 1992), 32–33.

17. Adapted from Stuart Elliott, "The Latest in Market Research: Videogenic Self-Analyzing Shoppers," *New York Times,* 23 August 1993, D1.

18. Judith Lynne Zaichkowsky, "Consumer Behavior: Yesterday, Today, and Tomorrow," *Business Horizons,* May–June 1991, 51–58; Edward M. Tauber, "Why Do People Shop?" *Marketing Management,* Fall 1995, 58–60.

19. Patrick E. Murphy and William A. Staples, "A Modernized Family Life Cycle," in *Marketing Classics,* 7th ed., edited by Ben M. Enis and Keith K. Cox (Boston: Allyn & Bacon, 1991), 156–173; Sue Shellenbarger, "Two-Income Couples Are Making Changes at Work and at Home," *Wall Street Journal,* 14 February 1996, B1.

20. Zaichkowsky, "Consumer Behavior," 51–58.

21. U.S. Bureau of the Census, *Statistical Abstract of the United States 1995* (Washington, D.C.: U.S. Government Printing Office, 1995), 57.

22. Nancy Coltun Webster, "Marketing to Kids: The New Whiz Kids," *Advertising Age,* 13 February 1995, S-1; Sharon E. Beatty and Salil Talpade, "Adolescent Influence in Family Decision Making: A Replication with Extension," *Journal of Consumer Research* 21 (Summer 1994): 332–341.

23. Julie Liesse, "Ralston Thinks Younger for Chex," *Advertising Age,* 9 January 1995, 12.

24. Eric Hollreiser, "Reebok, L'eggs Roll with USA Gymnastics," *Brandweek,* 16 January 1995, 5.

25. Regis McKenna, *Relationship Marketing: Successful Strategies for the Age of the Customer* (Reading, Mass.: Addison-Wesley, 1991), 90.

26. Terry L. Childers and Akshay R. Rao, "The Influence of Familial and Peer-Based Reference Groups on Consumer Decisions," *Journal of Consumer Research* 19, no. 2 (September 1992): 198–211.

27. Elaine Underwood, "Penney Books Heart-Throbs for Teen Fashion Dream Event," *Brandweek,* 30 January 1995, 8.

28. Kenneth Labich, "Class in America," *Fortune,* 7 February 1994, 114–116, 120, 122, 124, 126; Richard P. Coleman, "The Continuing Significance of Social Class in Marketing," *Journal of Consumer Research,* December 1983, 265–280; Lynn Martin, "The Middle Class Is Not Disappearing," *Washington Post,* 31 December 1991, A17.

29. Labich, "Class in America," 114–116, 120, 122, 124, 126; Lisa Gubernick and Marla Matzer, "Babies as Dolls," *Forbes,* 27 February 1995, 78–82.

30. John Thornhill, "To Russia with Baked Beans," *Financial Times,* 7 October 1995, 8.

31. Gail Baker Woods, *Advertising and Marketing to the New Majority* (Belmont, Calif.: Wadsworth, 1995), 70–74.

32. Cynthia Webster, "Effects of Hispanic Ethnic Identification on Marital Roles in the Purchase Decision Process," *Journal of Consumer Research,* 21 (September 1994): 319–331.

33. Solomon, *Consumer Behavior,* 500.

34. Solomon, *Consumer Behavior,* 501–502; William Dunn, "Sinatra Has the Last Dance," *American Demographics,* July 1994, 39.

35. Marcia Mogelonsky, "The Blueberries of Wrath," *American Demographics,* February 1995, 17–18.

36. Vicki Clift, "Who's Influencing Your Customer's Decisions?" *Marketing News,* 27 February 1995, 33.

37. Laurie Freeman, "No Tricking the Media Savvy," *Advertising Age,* 6 February 1995, 30.

38. John A. Howard and Jagdish N. Sheth, "A Theory of Buyer Behavior," in *Marketing Classics,* 7th ed., edited by Ben M. Enis and Keith K. Cox (Boston: Allyn & Bacon, 1991), 87–105; Sam Bradley, "We Want Our Food . . . Now!" *Brandweek,* 30 January 1995, 17.

39. Elaine Underwood, "Levi Woos Firms: Get into Our Pants," *Brandweek,* 30 January 1995, 19.

40. Todd Pruzan and Ivy Silverman, "Multinationals Pouring Earthquake Aid into Japan," *Advertising Age,* 30 January 1995, 34.

41. Del I. Hawkins, Roger J. Best, and Kenneth A. Coney, *Consumer Behavior: Implications for Marketing Strategy,* 6th ed. (Burr Ridge, Ill.: Irwin, 1995), 254–255.

42. Catherine Arnst, "Phone Frenzy," *Business Week,* 20 February 1995, 92–97.

43. Betsy Spethmann, "Pork Gets New Look," *Brandweek,* 23 January 1995, 10.

44. Kathleen Deveny, "Marketers Exploit People's Fears of Everything," *Wall Street Journal,* 15 November 1993, B1, B3; Judy Quinn, "Promotions Provide Emotional Rescue," *Incentive,* May 1996, 8.

45. Eric Hollreiser, "Maintaining Momentum," *Brandweek,* 2 January 1995, 20–23, 26.

46. Hawkins, Best, and Coney, *Consumer Behavior,* 364; Leaf's Jolly Rancher coupon, 12 February 1995; Trichy Krishnan, "FSIs Bad Rap Unwarranted," *Marketing Management,* Winter–Spring 1996, 5.

47. Laura M. Litvan, "Going 'Green' in the '90s," *Nation's Business,* February 1995, 30–32; "Consumers' True Colors," *Nation's Business,* February 1995, 31; Jessica Mathews, "Business Goes Green," *Washington Post,* 12 February 1996, A19.

48. Gary Levin, "'Price' Rises as Factor for Consumers," *Advertising Age,* 8 November 1993, 37; Betsy Morris, "The Brand's the Thing," *Fortune,* 4 March 1996, 72–86.

49. Greg Erickson, "Seeing Double," *Brandweek,* 17 October 1994, 30–32, 34–35; John A. Quelch and David Harding, "Brands Versus Private Labels: Fighting to

Win," *Harvard Business Review*, January–February 1996, 174.

50. Betsy Spethmann, "Partners Shoot for the Stars in Alliances with $54M Milky Way," *Brandweek*, 2 January 1995, 8.

51. Assael, *Consumer Behavior and Marketing Action*, 87; Tamasin Doe, "Designers Who Want to Keep Jeans on the March," *Financial Times*, 21 October 1995, VI.

52. Cyndee Miller, "Rewards for the Best Customers: Loyalty Programs Increase as Marketers Try to Build Relationships," *Marketing News*, 5 July 1993, 1, 6; Murray Raphel and Neil Raphel, "Action Plan for Efficiently Building Customer Loyalty," *Bottom Line Business*, 1 February 1996, 1–2.

53. Rajiv Grover and V. Srinivasan, "Evaluating the Multiple Effects of Retail Promotions on Brand Loyal and Brand Switching Segments," *Journal of Marketing Research* 29, no. 1 (February 1992): 76–89; Levin, "'Price' Rises as Factor for Consumers," 37; Laura Bird, "Back to Full Price," *Wall Street Journal*, 29 May 1996, A1, A10.

54. Adapted from Frances Huffman, "Marketing Smarts: Meal Ticket," *Entrepreneur*, October, 156, 158–159.

55. Assael, *Consumer Behavior and Marketing Action*, 293.

56. Meera P. Venkatraman, "The Impact of Innovativeness and Innovation Type on Adoption," *Journal of Retailing* 67, no. 1 (Spring 1991): 51–67.

57. Cyndee Miller, "Men Drop Their Dull Drawers for Something More Colorful," *Marketing News*, 24 October 1994, 1–2.

58. Leah Haran, "Chevy Tastes Persist on Cadillac-Like Income," *Advertising Age*, 18 September 1995, 3.

59. Adapted from "Fly & Field—a Website Worth Studying," *MaxiMarketing Insights*, March 1996, 11.

CHAPTER **7**

1. George R. Walther, *Upside-Down Marketing* (New York: McGraw-Hill, 1994), 128–132; Aberdeen Group, "Profile: Brock Control Systems," *Inc.*, February 1995, 1–8.

2. Michael P. Collins, *The Manufacturer's Guide to Business Marketing* (Burr Ridge, Ill.: Irwin, 1995), 36.

3. Frank G. Bingham, Jr., and Barney T. Raffield III, *Business-to-Business Marketing Management* (Homewood, Ill.: Irwin, 1990),

5; "The Business-to-Business Census," *Advertising Age*, June 1996, S1–S22.

4. Jan Jaben, "A One-Stop Shop," *Business Marketing*, November 1992, 86–87; Bradley Johnson, "Dell Tests TV as Phone Order Generator," *Business Marketing*, March 1996, 2–4.

5. Robert M. Morgan and Shelby D. Hunt, "The Commitment–Trust Theory of Relationship Marketing," *Journal of Marketing*, July 1994, 20–38; Collins, *The Manufacturer's Guide to Business Marketing*, 9–10; Donald V. Fites, "Make Your Dealers Your Partners," *Harvard Business Review*, March–April 1996, 84–95.

6. David Smith and Mary Bard, "Everything You Always Wanted to Know About Industrial Buying Behavior, but Were Afraid to Ask—In Case It Made the Research Too Expensive," *Journal of the Market Research Society*, July 1989, 307–330; Frederick E. Webster, Jr., and Yoram Wind, "A General Model for Understanding Organizational Buying Behavior," *Marketing Management*, Winter–Spring 1996, 52–57.

7. Webster and Wind, "A General Model for Understanding Organizational Buying Behavior," 52–57.

8. Raymond Bolger, "For Environmental Entrepreneurs, Saving the Earth Is Selling Point," *Business Record*, 14 October 1994, 13–14.

9. Michael D. Hutt and Thomas W. Speth, *Business Marketing Management*, 4th ed. (Fort Worth, Tex.: Dryden Press, 1992), 58; Peggy Saltz-Trautman, "Creating an Industry," *International Business*, February 1996, 51–54.

10. Jan Larson, "The Bicycle Market," *American Demographics*, March 1995, 42–43, 46–48, 50.

11. B. Joseph Pine II, Don Peppers, and Martha Rogers, "Do You Want to Keep Your Customers Forever?" *Harvard Business Review*, March–April 1995, 103–114.

12. Geoffrey L. Gordon, Roger J. Calantone, and C. Anthony di Benedetto, "Business-to-Business Service Marketing: How Does It Differ from Business-to-Business Product Marketing?" *Journal of Business & Industrial Marketing*, 8, no. 1 (1993): 45–57; Sharon Nelton, "Rising Hurdles for Vendors," *Nation's Business*, June 1996, 46–48.

13. James R. Norman, "'So We're Faust,'" *Forbes*, 7 November 1994, 139–140.

14. Suneel Ratan, "Uncle Sam's Paper Wars," *Fortune*, 24 January 1994, 16.

15. Earl Naumann, *Creating Customer Value* (Cincinnati: Thomson Executive Press, 1995), 185–187.

16. James Worsham, "The Flip Side of Downsizing," *Nation's Business*, October 1996, 18–25.

17. Mark Amtower, "Marketing to Government: There's Room for Players of All Types and Sizes," special advertising supplement to *Business Marketing*, July 1994, G-1; U.S. Bureau of the Census, *Statistical Abstract of the United States 1993* (Washington, D.C.: U.S. Government Printing Office, 1993), 291.

18. Philip Lader, "Smooth Selling," *Entrepreneur*, February 1995, 156; Laura M. Litvan, "Selling to Uncle Sam: New, Easier Rules," *Nation's Business*, March 1995, 46–48.

19. Hutt and Speth, *Business Marketing Management*, 6–7.

20. Tom Stundza, "Metal Cans: Lusting for Market Share," *Purchasing*, 22 February 1990, 61–64; Bradley Johnson, "Microsoft Reboots Marketing," *Advertising Age*, 4 March 1996, 1, 36.

21. Gregory Matusky, "Power Partnerships," *Success*, October 1993, 60, 62–63, 66–67.

22. William H. Davidow and Michael S. Malone, *The Virtual Corporation* (New York: HarperBusiness, 1992), 146.

23. Matusky, "Power Partnerships," 60, 62–63, 66–67.

24. Barbara Kline and Janet Wagner, "Information Sources and Retail Buyer Decision-Making: The Effect of Product-Specific Buying Experience," *Journal of Retailing* 70, no. 1 (1994): 75–88.

25. Raydel Tullous and J. Michael Munson, "Organizational Purchasing Analysis for Sales Management," *Journal of Personal Selling & Sales Management* 12, no. 2 (Spring 1992): 15–26; Jan B. Heide and Allen M. Weiss, "Vendor Consideration and Switching Behavior for Buyers in High-Technology Markets," *Journal of Marketing*, July 1995, 30–43.

26. Matusky, "Power Partnerships," 60, 62–63, 66–67.

27. Andrea Gerlin, "Deals on the Side: How a Penney Buyer Made Up to $1.5 Million on Vendors' Kickbacks," *Wall Street*

Journal, 7 February 1995, A1, A16; Gene R. Laczniak and Patrick E. Murphy, *Ethical Marketing Decisions* (Boston: Allyn & Bacon, 1993), 134–137, 194–197; Harriet McCullough, "Heed the Ethical Boundaries of Marketing to Government," special advertising supplement to *Business Marketing*, July 1994, G-2.

28. Tullous and Munson, "Organizational Purchasing Analysis for Sales Management," 15–26.

29. Bingham and Raffield, *Business-to-Business Marketing Management*, 50–54.

30. Adapted from Mary Robbins, "Frequency Marketing 'Down Under,'" *Colloquy* 4, no. 1: 14–15.

31. Elizabeth J. Wilson, Gary L. Lilien, and David T. Wilson, "Developing and Testing a Contingency Paradigm of Group Choice in Organizational Buying," *Journal of Marketing Research*, November 1991, 452–466.

32. Allyson L. Stewart, "The Challenges of Business-to-Business Marketing in Europe," *Marketing News*, 6 December 1993, 11.

33. "Team Buy Breaks Communication Wall," *Purchasing World*, September 1990, 34, 36–37.

34. Kate Bertrand, "Vertical Teams Require a New Show Strategy," *Business Marketing*, March 1995, 19, 21.

35. James C. Anderson, Håkan Håkansson, and Jan Johanson, "Dyadic Business Relationships Within a Business Network Context," *Journal of Marketing*, October 1994, 1–15; Francis J. Gouillart and Frederick D. Sturdivant, "Spend a Day in the Life of Your Customers," *Harvard Business Review*, January–February 1994, 116–125.

36. Bingham and Raffield, *Business-to-Business Marketing Management*, 11.

37. Michiel R. Leenders and David L. Blenkhorn, *Reverse Marketing: The New Buyer–Seller Relationships* (New York: Free Press, 1988) 2–3; Raymond Serafin, "Changing Relationships," *Business Marketing*, February 1996, 3–5.

38. Leslie Brokaw, "Case In Point," *Inc.*, December 1995, 88–90, 92.

39. John Rossant, "The Man Who's Driving Fiat Like a Ferrari," *Business Week*, 23 January 1995, 82–83; Alex Taylor III, "Fiat Scores Some Points with Punto," *Fortune*, 7 August 1995, 40.

40. Stephen H. Wildstrom, "In Search of the Paperless Contract," *Business Week*, 29 August 1994, 14; "EDI in Action," special advertising section, *Business Week*, 30 March 1992, 85ff.; Arthur Middleton Hughes, "How Panduit Did It," *Marketing Tools*, March–April 1996, 4–7.

41. Andrew Fisher, "Banks' Big Adventure," *Financial Times*, 11 August 1995, 12.

42. Len Egol, "Marching Orders," *Direct*, July 1994, 53–56.

43. Adapted from Egol, "Marching Orders," 53–56.

44. Rahul Jacob, "Corporate Reputations," *Fortune*, 6 March 1995, 54–57, 60, 64.

45. "United They Sell," *Success Selling*, May 1993, 24.

46. Joel Kotkin and David Friedman, "Why Every Business Will Be Like Show Business," *Inc.*, March 1995, 64–66, 69–70, 72, 74, 76–77.

47. Gregory L. Miles, "Tailoring a Global Product," *International Business*, March 1995, 50–52; Joseph Nocera, "Cooking with Cisco," *Fortune*, 25 December 1995, 114–118, 119–120, 122.

48. Leslie Bayor, "Wal-Mart Exec Notes Need for Efficiency," *Advertising Age*, 8 March 1993, 32; Matthew Shifrin, "The Big Squeeze," *Forbes*, 11 March 1996, 45–46.

49. Otis Port, "Quality," *Business Week*, 30 November 1992, 66–72.

50. Port, "Quality," 66–72.

51. Adapted from UPP Business Systems, "Our Business Is Knowing Yours" (Oakbrook Terrace, Ill.: UPP Business Systems, no date).

CHAPTER 8

1. Sharen Kindel, "Eye-Opening Management: Luxottica Group S.p.A.," *Hemispheres*, August 1995, 31–32, 34; Steven L. Wright, "Luxottica Edges Fiat as Italian Bellwether Firm," *Cincinnati Business Record*, 10 July 1995, 1; Ben Edwards, "The Company with No Banks," *Euromoney*, July 1995, 110–111; Bill Saporito, "Luxottica Group: Cutting Out the Middleman," *Fortune*, 6 April 1992, 96; Richard C. Morais, "Luxottica's Golden Spectacles," *Forbes*, 20 May 1996, 98–100.

2. Don E. Schultz, Stanley I. Tannenbaum, and Robert F. Lauterborn, *Integrated Marketing Communications* (Lincolnwood, Ill.: NTC Publishing, 1993), 5; William G. Nickels, James M. McHugh, and Susan M. McHugh, *Understanding Business*, 4th ed. (Burr Ridge, Ill.: Richard D. Irwin, 1996), 411–412.

3. Mark Hendricks, "Mass Appeal," *Entrepreneur*, August 1996, 68–72.

4. Steven L. Goldman, Roger N. Nagel, and Kenneth Preiss, *Agile Competitors and Virtual Organizations* (New York: Van Nostrand Reinhold, 1995), 11–12.

5. Goldman, Nagel, and Preiss, *Agile Competitors and Virtual Organizations*, 11–12.

6. Peter Burrows, "The Computer Is in the Mail (Really)," *Business Week*, 29 January 1995, 76–77; Michael S. Dell, "Service Sells," *Executive Excellence*, August 1993, 6–8; Barry L. Bayus and Ray Mehta, "A Segmentation Model for the Targeted Marketing of Consumer Durables," *Journal of Marketing Research*, November 1995, 463–469.

7. Janet Falon and Mary Ellen Egan, "Not Business as Usual," *Business Ethics*, September–October 1994, 14.

8. Jay Conrad Levinson, "Think Small," *Entrepreneur*, May 1996, 86.

9. Roberta Maynard, "Rich Niches," *Nation's Business*, November 1993, 39, 42.

10. Michael Dempsey, "Rewards for Passengers," *Financial Times*, 4 October 1995, 9.

11. Art Weinstein, *Market Segmentation* (Chicago: Probus Publishing, 1987), 41–43.

12. Jeffrey D. Zbar, "Niche Audiences Are Growing," *Advertising Age International*, July 1996, i18–i21.

13. Kevin J. Clancy and Robert S. Shulman, *Marketing Myths That Are Killing Business* (New York: McGraw-Hill, 1994), 121–122; David E. Schnedler, "Use Strategic Market Models to Predict Customer Behavior," *Sloan Management Review*, Spring 1996, 85–96.

14. Webster, *Market-Driven Management*, 104; Wendell R. Smith, "Product Differentiation and Market Segmentation as Alternative Marketing Strategies," *Marketing Management*, Winter 1995, 63–65.

15. Theodore Levitt, *The Marketing Imagination* (new expanded edition) (New York: Free Press, 1986), 133; Sanjit Sengupta and Louis P. Bucklin, "To Ally or Not to Ally?" *Marketing Management*, Fall 1995, 25–33.

16. Brent Johnson, "A Framework and Procedure for Assessing Market Segment Change and Stability: An Application in a High-Technology Business Market," draft thesis, Smeal College of Business, Pennsylvania State University, October 1994, 1–12; Julia Koranteng, "Tracking What's Trendy, Hot Before It's Old News," *Ad Age International*, May 1996, 130.

17. Don Taylor and Jeanne Smalling Archer, *Up Against the Wal-Marts* (New York: AMACOM, 1994), 228–229; Vincent Alonzo, "The Bigger They Are . . .," *Incentive*, June 1995, 57–60.

18. Kevin J. Clancy and Robert S. Shulman, *The Marketing Revolution* (New York: HarperBusiness, 1991), 70; Jack Bickert, "Focus on the Household," *Marketing Tools*, November–December 1995, 82–86.

19. Cyndee Miller, "Cosmetics Firms Finally Discover the Ethnic Market," *Marketing News*, 30 August 1993, 2; Berna Miller, "A Beginner's Guide to Demographics," *Marketing Tools*, October 1995, 55–64.

20. "Rodeway Seniors Get Choice Room," *Lodging Hospitality*, November 1993, 11; "Video Genie Sells Game to Youngsters," *Direct*, January 1995, 52; "Targeting Generation X," *Success*, April 1996, 24.

21. Dan Gutman, "Technology Clinic: Find Your Customers," *Success*, October 1994, 58.

22. Brian Toyne and Peter G. P. Walters, *Global Marketing Management: A Strategic Perspective*, 2nd ed. (Boston: Allyn & Bacon, 1993), 334–359.

23. Steven A. Holmes, "Shoppers! Deciding? Just Ask Your Child," *New York Times*, 8 January 1995, sec. 4, 4; E. Scott Reckard, "Taco Bell Makes a Run for Families with Low-Fat Items, Children's Meals," *Washington Times*, 22 June 1995, B1, B10.

24. Sudhir H. Kale and D. Sudharshan, "A Strategic Approach to International Segmentation," in *The International Marketing Digest*, edited by Malcolm H. B. McDonald and S. Tamer Cavusgil (Oxford, U.K.: Heinemann Professional Publishing, 1990), 103–135; Joan Delaney, "Vive La Difference," *International Business*, May 1996, 42–43.

25. Pat Sloan, "U.S. Business Is Key to Colgate's Future," *Advertising Age*, 19 December 1994, 4.

26. Glenn Gaslin, "Take the Local," *Chicago Tribune*, 7 July 1994, sec. 7, 8.

27. U.S. Bureau of the Census, *Statistical Abstract of the United States 1993* (Washington, D.C.: U.S. Government Printing Office, 1993), 916–917; Thomas G. Exter,

"Taming the Tiger for 2000," *Marketing Tools*, June 1996, 10–13.

28. Clancy and Shulman, *The Marketing Revolution*, 268–269; Berna Miller, "Where in the World Is Hallcrest Dr.?" *Marketing Tools*, January–February 1996, 18–22.

29. *PRIZM Lifestyle Segmentation*, Claritas brochure, 1995.

30. Peter Francese, *Marketing Tools*, July–August 1994, 42–50; Sarah Lubman, "A 'Student of Value' Means a Student Who Can Pay the Rising Cost of College," *Wall Street Journal*, 5 January 1994, B1, B7.

31. Ann S. Badillo and Elizabeth A. Kunze, "Don't Know Much About Geography?" *Marketing Tools*, November–December 1994, 54–61.

32. Melita Marie Garza, "Credit-Card Trade Attempts to Cash In on Ethnic Loyalty," *Chicago Tribune*, 28 February, 1994, sec. 4, 1, 2.

33. Gayle Sato Stodder, "The Greeting of America," *Entrepreneur*, September 1994, 210, 212–214.

34. Judith Waldrop, "Markets with Attitudes," *American Demographics*, July 1994, 22–32; Arnold Mitchell, "The VALS Typology," in *Marketing Classics*, 7th ed., edited by Ben M. Enis and Keith K. Cox (Boston: Allyn & Bacon, 1991), 192–207; Weinstein, *Market Segmentation*, 114–117.

35. Michael R. Solomon, *Consumer Behavior: Buying, Having, and Being*, 2nd ed. (Boston: Allyn & Bacon, 1992), 506.

36. Webster, *Market-Driven Management*, 101; Clancy and Shulman, *Marketing Myths*, 112–114; Weinstein, *Market Segmentation*, 116–117.

37. William G. Nickels, James M. McHugh, and Susan M. McHugh, *Understanding Business*, 4th ed. (Burr Ridge, Ill.: Irwin, 1996), 425.

38. Rahul Jacob, "The Big Rise," *Fortune*, 30 May 1994, 74–76, 78, 82, 86, 90.

39. Laura Loro, "Single-Use Cameras Snap the Photo Industry Awake," *Advertising Age*, 28 September 1994, 28.

40. Chip Walker, "Meet the New Vegetarian," *American Demographics*, January 1995, 9–11; William McCall, "Veggieburger Creator Aims for McDonald's," *Marketing News*, 24 October 1994, 8; James R. Norman, "With or Without Ketchup," *Forbes*, 14 March 1994, 107; Yumiko Ono, "Catering

to Part-Time Vegetarians' Tastes," *Wall Street Journal*, 24 August 1994, B1–B2.

41. Don Peppers and Martha Rogers, *The One-to-One Future* (New York: Currency Doubleday, 1993), 108–109; Anthony Faiola and Albert B. Chrenshaw, "Marketing by the Mile," *Washington Post,* 21 April 1996, H1, H5.

42. Len Egol, "Sherwin-Williams Paints a Database," *Direct*, June 1994, 11; "The Business-to-Business Census," *Business Marketing*, June 1996, 518–522.

43. Weinstein, *Marketing Segmentation*, 152.

44. Jeffrey M. O'Brien, "Ameritech Seeks B-to-B Efficiencies," *Direct*, September 1994, 14.

45. Marian B. Wood and Evelyn Ehrlich, "Segmentation: Five Steps to More Effective Business-to-Business Marketing," *Sales & Marketing Management*, April 1991, 59–63.

46. "Trade Finance: You Need a Business Ambassador," *Global Trade*, July 1990, 20; Len Egol, "Chemical's Loyalty Power," *Direct*, November 1994, 65; Michelle Singletary, "Checking an Image, Coining a Phrase," *Washington Business*, 25 March 1996, 9.

47. Barbara Benson, "Physician-Friendly HMO Targets City," *Crain's New York Business*, 2 January 1995, 2.

48. Shannon Oberndorf, "Creative Breakthrough: Celebrating the Past," *Direct*, December 1994, 51; Jon Bigness, "Impersonal Touch: More Hotels Automate Front Desk," *Wall Street Journal,* 18 June 1996, B1, B6.

49. Clancy and Shulman, *Marketing Myths*, 116–117; Wood and Ehrlich, "Segmentation," 59–63.

50. Michael Schrage, "Manager's Journal: Fire Your Customers!" *Wall Street Journal*, 16 March 1992, A14; Jill Griffin, *Customer Loyalty: How to Earn it, How to Keep It* (New York: Lexington Books, 1995).

51. Robert F. Hartley, *Marketing Mistakes*, 6th ed. (New York: John Wiley, 1995), 233–247.

52. Kate Bohner Lewis, "Thou Better Not Steal," *Forbes*, 7 November 1994, 216–217.

53. Hartley, *Marketing Mistakes*, 129–145; Robert Frank, "Root Beer, Bit Player, May Yet Be a Star," *Wall Street Journal*, 20 November 1995, B1, B8.

54. "Niche Marketing in Honduras," *Bank Marketing*, March 1993, 22, 24–25.

55. John S. DeMott, "New Mission," *Nation's Business*, November 1994, 20–27.

56. Roberta Maynard, "Branching Out," *Nation's Business*, November 1994, 53.

57. Gerry Khermouch, "New Age Beverages Target Young Consumer," *Superbrands 1995*, 17 October 1994, 72–73; Mark Gleason, "Iced Tea Marketers Declare War," *Advertising Age*, 17 June 1996, 4.

58. Michael S. Malone, "Chips Triumphant," *Forbes ASAP*, 26 February 1996, 53–78.

59. Peppers and Rogers, *The One-to-One Future*, 134–135.

60. Wendy Marx, "The New Segment of One," *Direct*, September 1994, 45–48; "Tailoring Products for a Niche of One," *Nation's Business*, November 1993, 42.

61. Jack Trout and Al Ries, "Positioning Cuts Through Chaos in Marketplace," in *Marketing Classics*, 7th ed., edited by Ben M. Enis and Keith K. Cox (Boston: Allyn & Bacon, 1991), 216–233; Geoffrey A. Moore, *Crossing the Chasm* (New York: HarperBusiness, 1991), 156; Martin R. Lautman, "The ABCs of Positioning," *Marketing Research*, Winter 1993, 12–18; Jeff Jensen, "Chief Auto Steers for Quality Positioning," *Advertising Age*, 1 April 1996, 8.

62. Taylor and Archer, *Up Against the Wal-Marts*, 101–102; Johnson A. Edosomwan, "Empowering the Organizational Reengineering Team," *Quality Observer*, March 1996, 5.

63. Bill Fromm and Len Schlesinger, *The Real Heroes of Business* (New York: Currency Doubleday, 1993), 139–164.

64. Adapted from Laura Mazur and Annik Hogg, *The Marketing Challenge* (Wokingham, U.K.: Addison-Wesley, 1993), 151–152.

65. Regis McKenna, *Relationship Marketing: Successful Strategies for the Age of the Customer* (Reading, Mass.: Addison-Wesley, 1991), 80–81; Jack Trout, "Repositioning: When to Do It, How to Do It," *Bottom Line/Business*, 1 December 1995, 3.

66. Adapted from Maria Elena Toraño, "Entrepreneur's Notebook: New Opportunities, New Directions," *Nation's Business*, November 1994, 6.

67. Terry Lefton, "Truth Hurts AT&T's Rivals," *Superbrands 1995*, 17 October 1994, 128, 130–132.

68. Valerie Reitman, "Buoyant Sales of Lever 2000 Soap Bring Sinking Sensation to Procter & Gamble," *Wall Street Journal*, 19 March 1992, B1.

69. "I'm Glad We Did This Ad," advertisement by Magazine Publishers Association in *Advertising Age*, 16 January 1995, 15.

70. Charles Siler, "Body Shop Marches to Its Own Drummer," *Advertising Age*, 10 October 1994, 4.

71. Jack Russell, "At Last, a Product That Makes Japan's Subways Safe for Men," *Advertising Age*, 16 January 1995, I-24.

72. Jeffrey A. Tannenbaum, "Video Distributor Thrives at Last in Offering 'Culture'," *Wall Street Journal*, 4 May 1994, B2.

73. Melinda Newman, "Consumer Music Mags Win Clout," *Billboard*, 23 December 1995, 1; Ann Marie Kerwin, "Alternative Options," *Inside Media*, January 18–31, 1995, 33; "Readers' Key Facts," *Option* media kit, no date.

MARKETING ON THE NET FOR PART **3**

1. "Secure Transaction Ability Boosts Spiegel's Web Sales," *Interactive Marketing News*, 24 May 1996, 1, 7; Bruce Judson, *Netmarketing* (New York: Wolff New Media, 1996), 27, 65.

2. Adapted from Larry Jaffee, "Ad Banners, Links and Tracking Build List Company's Web Services," *DM News* 27 May 1996, 19, 21.

CHAPTER **9**

1. Adapted from Bob Weinstein, "Drinking Buddies," *Business Start-Ups*, February 1995, 52–57.

2. Phone interview, February 1996.

3. Roy A. Bauer, Emilio Collar, and Victor Tang, *The Silverlake Project* (New York: Oxford University Press, 1992), 167–173.

4. Philip Kotler and Gary Armstrong, *Marketing: An Introduction*, 4th ed. (Upper Saddle River, NJ: Prentice-Hall, 1997), 242.

5. Alex Taylor III, "Why an Industry That Was Up a Tree Is on a Big Roll," *Fortune*, 17 April 1995, 134–136, 140, 142.

6. Michael Treacy and Fred Wiersema, "How Market Leaders Keep Their Edge," *Fortune*, 6 February 1995, 88–90, 94, 96, 98.

7. Jeffrey M. Ferguson, Lexis F. Higgins, and Gary R. Phillips, *Industrial Marketing Management*, August 1993, 187–193; John Ratcliffe-Smith and Roger Brooks, "Service from Within," *TQM Magazine*, October 1993, 41–43; Marc H. Meyer and Michael H. Zack, "The Design and Development of Information Products," *Sloan Mangement Review*, Spring 1996, 43–59.

8. Alan W. H. Grant and Leonard A. Schlesinger, "Realize Your Customers' Full Profit Potential," *Harvard Business Review*, September–October 1995, 59–72.

9. Pam Weisz, "StainMaster Gets $10M+ Boost," *Brandweek*, 20 March 1995, 16; Kevin J. Clancy and Robert S. Shulman, *The Marketing Revolution* (New York: HarperBusiness, 1991), 229.

10. Clancy and Shulman, *The Marketing Revolution*, 142.

11. This discussion is based on Theodore Levitt, *The Marketing Imagination* (new expanded ed.) (New York: Free Press, 1986), 74–85.

12. Jacqueline Mitchell, "Automobiles: Without 2 Air Bags, Sales May Deflate," *Wall Street Journal*, 12 October 1993, B1.

13. Eugene W. Anderson, Claes Fornell, and Donald R. Lehmann, *Economic Consequences of Providing Quality and Customer Satisfaction* (Cambridge, Mass.: Marketing Science Institute, 1993), 7; John A. Byrne, "Never Mind the Buzzwords. Roll Up Your Sleeves," *Business Week*, 22 January 1996, 84–85; Louis Kraar, "Korea Goes for Quality," *Fortune*, 18 April 1994, 153–154, 156–159.

14. David Drobis, "Premium Brands," *Boardroom Reports*, 15 September 1993, 9; T. L. Stanley, "1995 EquiTrend Survey: How They Rate," *Brandweek*, 3 April 1995, 45–48; Betsy Morris, "The Brand's the Thing," *Fortune*, 4 March 1996, 72–86.

15. Earl Naumann, *Creating Customer Value* (Cincinnati: Thomson Executive Press, 1995), 44–49; Michael D. Hutt and Thomas W. Speh, *Business Marketing Management*, 5th ed. (Fort Worth, Tex.: Dryden Press, 1995), 289–293; Roberta Maynard, "A Company Is Turned Around Through Japanese Principles," *Nation's Business*, February 1996, 9.

16. David Greising, "Quality: How to Make It Pay," *Business Week*, 8 August 1994, 54–59.

17. Karl T. Ulrich and Steven D. Eppinger, *Product Design and Development* (New York: McGraw-Hill, 1995), 155–174.

18. Ulrich and Eppinger, *Product Design and Development*, 167–168; "John Doerr," *Adweek*, 8 July 1996, IQ 16–21.

19. Tom Peters, *Liberation Management* (New York: Knopf, 1992), 293–295.

20. David Field, "Delta, American Team with Giants in Credit Cards, Raising Flyer Miles," *Washington Times*, 7 February 1996, B6, B10.

21. Marcia Mogelonsky, "When Stores Become Brands," *American Demographics*, February 1995, 32–36, 38; Marcia Mogelonsky, "What's the Difference?" *American Demographics*, February 1995, 37; John A. Quelch and David Harding, "Brands Versus Private Labels: Fighting to Win," *Harvard Business Review*, January–February 1996, 174.

22. Andrew A. Caffey, "Mark Your Words," *Entrepreneur*, September 1992, 128, 130–131.

23. James Rosini, "Playing the Brand Name Game: Preventative Medicine Required," *Brandweek*, 3 April 1995, 18; "Business Bulletin," *Wall Street Journal*, 16 January 1992, A1.

24. David E. Sanger, "What's What in the Trade Pact," *New York Times*, 27 November 1994, 34; Gene R. Laczniak and Patrick E. Murphy, *Ethical Marketing Decisions: The Higher Road* (Boston: Allyn & Bacon, 1993), 89–91; Brian Toyne and Peter G. P. Walters, *Global Marketing Management*, 2nd ed. (Boston: Allyn & Bacon, 1993), 460–465.

25. "'AAI' Picks Next Major Marketers," *Advertising Age*, 18 September 1995, I-33, I-43.

26. Zachary Schiller, Greg Burns, and Karen Lowry Miller, "Make It Simple," *Business Week*, 9 September 1996, 96–104.

27. "Mr. Clean," *Forbes*, 26 February 1996, 116.

28. Schiller, Burns, and Miller, "Make It Simple," 96–104.

29. Toyne and Walters, *Global Marketing Management*, 445.

30. Time Warner, 1993 Annual Report, 10; Kate Fitzgerald, "License to Sell," *Advertising Age*, 12 February 1996, S1–S10.

31. Henry Assael, *Consumer Behavior and Marketing Action*, 4th ed. (Boston: PWS-Kent Publishing, 1992), 87; Pat Sloan, "Brands Are Back," *Advertising Age*, 8 May 1995, 1, 40–41; Sanjay Sood, "Brand Equity and the Marketing Mix: Creating Customer Value," *Marketing Science Institute Conference Summary*, no. 95-111, September 1995, 1–34.

32. Frederick E. Webster, Jr., *Market-Driven Management* (New York: John Wiley, 1994), 108–109; Chip Walker, "How Strong Is Your Brand?" *Marketing Tools*, January–February 1995, 46–53; Betsy Morris, "The Brand's the Thing," *Fortune*, 4 March 1996, 72–86.

33. Martin B. Rosen, "Changing a Brand? TLC Pays Dividends," *Advertising Age*, 1 January 1996, 10; Mark Bergen, Shantanu Dutta, and Steven M. Shugan, "Branded Variants: A Retail Perspective," *Journal of Marketing Research*, February 1996, 9–19; David A. Aacker, "The Value of Brand Equity," *Journal of Business Strategy*, July–August 1992, 27–32.

34. Jim Carlton, "Marketing Plays a Bigger Role in Distinguishing PCs," *Wall Street Journal*, 16 October 1995, B4.

35. Katrina Carl, "Good Package Design Helps Increase Consumer Loyalty," *Marketing News*, 19 June 1995, 4.

36. Michael Prone, "Package Design Has Stronger ROI Potential Than Many Believe," *Marketing News*, 11 October 1993, 13.

37. Sterling Anthony, "Warning: Marketers Must Do Better with Product Warnings," *Marketing News*, 19 June 1995, 4, 11.

38. Betsy Spethmann and Sam Bradley, "Kleenex Wiping Up Kids Market," *Brandweek*, 17 October 1994, 26; Peter Coy, "A Package for Every Person," *Business Week*, 6 February 1995, 44; Raju Narisetti, "Plotting to Get Tissues into Living Rooms," *Wall Street Journal*, 3 May 1996, B1, B12.

39. Eliot Schreiber, "Retail Trends Shorten Life of Package Design," *Marketing News*, 5 December 1994, 7; "Campbell Soup's New Labels Stir Mightily Against Tradition," *Chicago Tribune*, 21 April 1994, N1.

40. John Morris, "Packaging Smarter," *International Business*, November 1992, 23–24.

41. Eben Shapiro, "Portions and Packages Grow Bigger and BIGGER," *Wall Street Journal*, 12 October 1993, B1, B6.

42. Pam Weisz, "Repackaging," *Brandweek*, 27 February 1995, 25–27.

43. Alison L. Sprout, "Technology to Watch: New Packaging That's Thriftier! Niftier! And Cooks Your Food!" *Fortune*, 5 September 1994, 109.

44. Adapted from Eve Nagler, "A Macaroni Company with Homespun Appeal," *New York Times*, 12 December 1993, 22–23.

45. Frances Cairncross, "How Europe's Companies Reposition to Recycle," *Harvard Business Review*, March–April 1992, 34–36, 38, 40–42, 44–45; "'Green' Product Design," *Business Week*, 10 June 1996, 109.

46. Catherine Marenghi, "Less Is More: Stopping Packaging Waste at the Source," *Management Review*, June 1992, 18–23; Jacquelyn Ottman, "A Little Creativity Could Lead to a Big Advantage," *Marketing News*, 27 March 1995, 11.

47. Monica Kass, "Packaging's Three-Part Challenge," *Restaurants & Institutions*, 1 March 1993, 112–118.

48. "Toy and Game Safety," *Consumer Reports*, December 1994, 765.

49. John M. Ivancevich, Peter Lorenzi, and Steven J. Skinner, with Philip B. Crosby, *Management: Quality and Competitiveness* (Burr Ridge, Ill.: Irwin, 1994), 118; Laczniak and Murphy, *Ethical Marketing Decisions*, 215–216.

50. Marianne Kyriakos, "The Tangle over Product Liability Law Reform," *Washington Business*, 6 April 1992, 8; John R. Hayes, "The Bundler," *Forbes*, 22 April 1996, 82–88.

51. Stephen H. Wildstrom, "Bundles of Trouble," *Business Week*, 11 March 1996, 16; Hayes, "The Bundler," 82–88.

52. David Osborne and Ted Gaebler, *Reinventing Government* (New York: Plume, 1992), 180; Carolyn Magnuson, "Grads for Hire, Warranty Included," *Nation's Business*, June 1996, 83.

53. Michael E. Porter, *Competitive Advantage* (New York: Free Press, 1985), 154.

54. William Boulding, Eunkyu Lee, and Richard Staelin, "Mastering the Mix: Do Advertising, Promotion, and Sales Force Activities Lead to Differentiation?" *Journal of Marketing Research*, May 1994, 159–172; Mark Gleason, "Sprite," *Advertising Age*, 24 June 1996, S-28.

55. Raymond Serafin, "The Marketing 100: Marty Levine, Dodge Ram," *Advertising Age*, 4 July 1994, S-27.

56. Kraar, "Korea Goes for Quality," 153–154, 156–159.

57. Ivancevich, Lorenzi, Skinner, and Crosby, *Management: Quality and Competitiveness*, 11; Martha E. Mangelsdorf, "Insider: Why 99.9% Just Won't Do," *Inc.*, April 1989, 26; Harley-Davidson, 1993 Annual Report, 11.

58. "Competitive Edge: Fast Product Development," *Inc.*, October 1992, 92; Gerard J. Tellis and Peter N. Golder, "First to Market, First to Fail? Real Causes of Enduring Market Leadership," *Sloan Management Review,* Winter 1996, 65–75.

59. B. Joseph Pine II, Bart Victor, and Andrew C. Boynton, "Making Mass Customization Work," *Harvard Business Review,* September–October 1993, 108–119; Michael S. Malone, "Chips Triumphant," *Forbes ASAP,* 26 February 1996, 53–78.

60. Don Peppers and Martha Rogers, "The End of Mass Marketing," *Marketing Tools,* March–April 1995, 42–52; Louise Lee, "Garment Scanner Could Be a Perfect Fit," *Wall Street Journal,* 20 September 1994, B1, B8.

61. George R. Walther, *Upside-Down Marketing* (New York: McGraw-Hill, 1994), 157–158; "Coach and Toyota Link Brands," *Incentive,* June 1996, 14.

62. Cathryn Conroy, "Marketing by Modem," *CompuServe Magazine,* April 1995, 30–32.

63. Stan Davis and Jim Botkin, "The Coming of Knowledge-Based Businesses," *Harvard Business Review,* September–October 1994, 165–170.

64. Kevin Kelly, "It Really Can Pay to Clean Up Your Act," *Business Week,* 7 November 1994, 141; Jessica Matthews, "Business Goes Green," *Washington Post,* 12 February 1996, A19.

CHAPTER 10

1. Joseph Weber, "A Better Grip on Hawking Tools," *Business Week,* 5 June 1995, 99; Susan Caminiti, "Product Innovation: A Star Is Born," *Fortune,* Autumn–Winter 1993, 44–47; Black & Decker, 1994 Annual Report.

2. Willard I. Zangwill, "Lightning Strategies for Innovation," *Success,* September 1993, 42–43.

3. Rahul Jacob, "Corporate Reputations," *Fortune,* 6 March 1995, 54–57, 60, 64; "New-Product Development Secrets," *Boardroom Reports,* 1 December 1994, 5–6; Anirudh Dhebar, "Speeding High-Tech Producer, Meet the Balking Customer," *Sloan Management Review,* Winter 1996, 37–49.

4. Justin Martin, "Ignore Your Customer," *Fortune,* 1 May 1995, 121–122, 124, 126.

5. Peter F. Drucker, *Innovation and Entrepreneurship: Practice and Principles* (New York: Harper & Row, 1985), 220–223; "Mr. Clean," *Forbes,* 26 February 1996, 116.

6. Patty LaNoue Stearns, "Butter Makes a Comeback: New in '94," *News-Times* (Danbury, Conn.), 19 April 1995, C-4.

7. David Olson, "Challenges in 'Creating Customers' via Really New Products," in Marketing Science Institute, *And Now for Something Completely Different: "Really" New Products* (Cambridge, Mass.: Marketing Science Institute, 1994), 32–36; Martin, "Ignore Your Customer," 121–122, 124, 126.

8. Robert G. Cooper, "New Products: The Factors That Drive Success," *International Marketing Review* 11, no. 1 (1994): 60–76; Fahri Karakaya and Bulent Kobu,"New Product Development Process: An Investigation of Success and Failure in High-Technology and Non-High-Technology Firms," *Journal of Business Venturing* 9 (1994): 49–66; Lori Calabro, "Manufacturing: Secrets of Success," *CFO,* September 1993, 18; Martin, "Ignore Your Customer," 121–122, 124, 126; Glen L. Urban and John R. Hauser, *Design and Marketing of New Products,* 2nd ed. (Englewood Cliffs, N.J.: Prentice Hall, 1993), 28–30; Zangwill, "Lightning Strategies for Innovation," 42–43; Abdul Ali, Robert Krapfel, Jr., and Douglas LaBahn, "Product Innovativeness and Entry Strategy: Impact on Cycle Time and Break-Even Time," *Journal of Product Innovation Management* 11 (1995): 54–69.

9. Scott McCartney, "PC Servers Making Inroads as Their Power Accelerates," *Wall Street Journal,* 17 January 1995, B3; Martin, "Ignore Your Customer," 121–122, 124, 126; Compaq, 1994 Annual Report, 9.

10. Betsy Spethmann, "New Product Development 1995: Big Talk, Little Dollars," *Brandweek,* 23 January 1995, 20–23, 25–26, 29; "It's New, but Is It Improved?" *Marketing Tools,* November–December 1994, 20; Kevin J. Clancy and Robert S. Shulman, *Marketing Myths That Are Killing Business* (New York: McGraw-Hill, 1994), 81–88; Cyndee Miller, "Little Relief Seen for New Product Failure Rate," *Marketing News,* 21 June 1993, 1, 10.

11. Kevin J. Clancy, Robert S. Shulman, and Marianne Wolf, *Simulated Test Marketing* (New York: Lexington Books, 1994), 3–6.

12. Dan Dimancescu, *Seamless Enterprise: Making Cross Functional Management Work* (New York: HarperBusiness, 1992), 41; Hugh Carnegy, "Time to Chart a Different Course," *Financial Times,* 7 August 1995, 19.

13. Barry L. Bayus, "Tradeoffs in New Product Development: Really New or Just Improved," in Marketing Science Institute, *And Now for Something Completely Different: "Really" New Products* (Cambridge, Mass.: Marketing Science Institute, 1994), 42–45; Dhebar, "Speeding High-Tech Producer, Meet the Balking Consumer," 37–49.

14. Neal Templin and Jeff Cole, "Working Together: Manufacturers Use Suppliers to Help Them Develop New Products," *Wall Street Journal,* 19 December 1994, A1, A8; Edwin E. Bobrow, "Participative Process Can Shape New Product Development," *Marketing News,* 22 April 1996, 9–11.

15. H. Kent Bowen, Kim B. Clark, Charles A. Holloway, and Steven C. Wheelwright, "Make Projects the School for Leaders," *Harvard Business Review,* September–October 1994, 131–140; Hewlett-Packard, 1993 Annual Report, 8.

16. John M. Ivancevich, Peter Lorenzi, and Steven J. Skinner, with Philip B. Crosby, *Management: Quality and Competitiveness* (Burr Ridge, Ill.: Irwin, 1994), 152–153; Jeffrey D. Swaddling and Mark W. Zobel, "Beating the Odds," *Marketing Management,* Winter–Spring 1996, 21–33.

17. John Ridding, "Renault Steers Around Potholes," *Financial Times,* 7 August 1995, 10.

18. Booz, Allen, and Hamilton, "New Product Management for the 1980s," in *Marketing Classics,* 7th ed., edited by Ben M. Enis and Keith K. Cox (Boston: Allyn & Bacon, 1991), 378–391; Paul S. Adler, Avi Mendelbaum, Vien Nguyen, and Elizabeth Schwerer, "Getting the Most Out of Your Product Development Process," *Harvard Business Review,* March–April 1996, 134–152.

19. Wendy Zellner, "Go-Go Goliaths," *Business Week,* 13 February 1995, 64–70; Laurie Flynn, "Intel Looks Beyond the Pentium," *New York Times,* 26 February 1995, sec. 3, 23.

20. Marshall Sella, "Will a Flying Doll . . . Fly?" *New York Times Magazine,* 25 December 1994, 20–25, 40, 43–45.

21. "New-Product Development Secrets," *Boardroom Reports,* 1 December 1994, 5–6.

22. Marshall Loeb, "How's Business? How to Grow a New Product Every Day," *Fortune*, 14 November 1994, 269–270.

23. Adapted from Vern Terpstra, "On Marketing Appropriate Products in Developing Countries," *International Marketing Digest* (Oxford, U.K.: Heinemann Professional Publishing, July 1990), 177ff.

24. Albert L. Page and Harold F. Rosenbaum, "Developing an Effective Testing Program for Consumer Durables," *Journal of Product Innovation*, 9, no. 4 (December 1992): 267–277; Gerald J. Tellis and Peter N. Golden, "First to Market, First to Fail? Real Causes of Enduring Market Leadership," *Sloan Management Review*, Winter 1996, 65–75.

25. Martin, "Ignore Your Customer," 121–122, 124, 126.

26. Sella, "Will a Flying Doll . . . Fly?" 20–25, 40, 43–45.

27. Robert F. Hartley, *Marketing Mistakes*, 6th ed. (New York: John Wiley, 1995), 67; Joan E. Rigdon, "Cruel World: Cannibalism Is a Virtue in Computer Business, Tandem's CEO Learns," *Wall Street Journal*, 24 August 1994, A1, A5.

28. Sella, "Will a Flying Doll . . . Fly?" 20–25, 40, 43–45.

29. Tom Peters, "Proper Way to Develop Products: Just Do It," *Washington Times*, 24 June 1994, B9; Philip A. Himmelfarb, "Being First to Market Isn't Enough," *Quality Digest*, February 1996, 39–41.

30. Sella, "Will a Flying Doll . . . Fly?" 20–25, 40, 43–45.

31. Gene Bylinsky, "The Digital Factory," *Fortune*, 14 November 1994, 92–94, 96, 100, 104, 106, 110.

32. Gene Bylinksy, "Manufacturing for Reuse," *Fortune*, 6 February 1995, 102–104, 108, 110, 112; Frances Cairncross, "How Europe's Companies Reposition to Recycle," *Harvard Business Review*, March–April 1992, 34–36, 38, 40–42, 44–45.

33. Faye Rice, "Secrets of Product Testing," *Fortune*, 28 November 1994, 166–171, 172.

34. James Daly, "For Beta or For Worse," *Forbes ASAP*, 5 December 1994, 36–38, 40.

35. Michael Treacy and Fred Wiersema, "How Market Leaders Keep Their Edge," *Fortune*, 6 February 1995, 88–90, 94, 96, 98.

36. Sella, "Will a Flying Doll . . . Fly?" 20–25, 40, 43–45.

37. Clancy, Shulman, and Wolf, *Simulated Test Marketing*, 44–47, 49–78.

38. John Labate, "Companies to Watch: Norton McNaughton," *Fortune*, 20 February 1995, 118.

39. Karl T. Ulrich and Steven D. Eppinger, *Product Design and Development* (New York: McGraw-Hill, 1995), 6; Marco Iansiti, "Shooting the Rapids: Managing Product Development in Turbulent Times," *California Management Review*, Fall 1995, 37–57.

40. Sella, "Will a Flying Doll . . . Fly?" 20–25, 40, 43–45; Rachel Beck, "What's the Hot Toy This Year? It's Anyone's Guess," *News Times* Business Extra, 23 November 1995, B-8.

41. Sanjit Sengupta and Louis P. Bucklin, "To Ally or Not to Ally?," *Marketing Management*, Fall 1995, 25–33; "A New Approach," *Forbes ASAP*, 8 April 1996, 45–47.

42. Jay Mathews, "Utensile Strength," *Washington Post*, 2 April 1995, H1, H4; Alan Farnham, "America's Most Admired Company," *Fortune*, 7 February 1994, 50–52, 54; Loeb, "How's Business?" 269–270.

43. A. Ansari and Batoul Modarress, "Quality Function Deployment: The Role of Suppliers," *International Journal of Purchasing and Materials Management*, Fall 1994, 28–35.

44. Discussion of House of Quality based on Glen L. Urban and John R. Hauser, *Design and Marketing of New Products*, 2nd ed. (Englewood Cliffs, N.J.: Prentice Hall, 1993), 341–347.

45. Pam Weisz, "Hershey Hits Aisle to the Final Four," *Brandweek*, 20 February 1995, 8.

46. Jennifer Comiteau and Karen Benezra, "Blimpie Founder Takes Spotlight to Declare Sub-War on Subway," *Brandweek*, 20 March 1995, 9.

47. Michael McCarthy and Terry Lefton, "Card Game," *Brandweek*, 31 October 1994, 1, 6.

48. Pam Weisz, "Slim-Fast Targets Snackwell's," *Brandweek*, 14 November 1994, 4.

49. Eastman Kodak, 1993 Annual Report; Mark Maremont, "Will a New Film Click?" *Business Week*, 5 February 1996, 46.

50. Adapted from Les Burch, "Moving Away from 'Me Too,'" *Nation's Business*, August 1994, 6.

51. Bill Saporito, "The Eclipse of Mars," *Fortune*, 28 November 1994, 82–84, 86, 90, 92; Julie Liesse, "Brand Extensions Take Center Stage," *Advertising Age*, 8 March 1993, 12.

52. John A. Quelch and David Kenny, "Extend Profits, Not Product Lines," *Harvard Business Review*, September–October 1994, 153–160; "The Logic of Product-Line Extensions," *Harvard Business Review*, November–December 1994, 53–55, 58–60, 62.

53. Lorraine Sunde and Roderick J. Brodie, "Consumer Evaluations of Brand Extensions: Further Empirical Results," *International Journal of Research in Marketing* 10, no. 1 (March 1993): 47–53; David A. Aaker and Kevin Lane Keller, "Consumer Evaluations of Brand Extensions," *Journal of Marketing* 54, no. 1 (January 1990): 27–41; "The Logic of Product-Line Extensions," 53–55, 58–60, 62; Kevin J. Clancy and Robert S. Shulman, *The Marketing Revolution* (New York: HarperBusiness, 1991), 121.

54. Emily DeNitto, "Today's Special on the Marketing Menu: Jelly: Smucker Looks Beyond, to Frozen Pies," *Advertising Age*, 7 March 1994, 3; Betsy Spethmann, "Food: Returning to Core Business," *Superbrands 1995*, 17 October 1994, 102.

55. Andrew Wallenstein, "Coca-Cola's Sweet Return to Glory Days," *Advertising Age*, 17 April 1995, 4.

56. Dow, 1993 Annual Report, 4.

57. Pam Weisz, "Cosmetics/Fragrances: Mass Brands Continue to Rise," *Superbrands 1995*, 17 October 1994, 79.

58. Information in the following section based on Theodore Levitt, *The Marketing Imagination* (new expanded edition) (New York: Free Press, 1986), 174–178; John E. Smallwood, "The Product Life Cycle: A Key to Strategic Marketing Planning," in *Marketing Classics*, 7th ed., edited by Ben M. Enis and Keith K. Cox (Boston: Allyn & Bacon, 1991), 370–377; Neelam Kinra, "Offensive and Defensive Combat Strategies and Strategems: Their Relation to the Product Life Cycle," *Marketing and Research Today* 21, no. 3 (September 1993): 185–192.

59. Glenn Rifkin, "Product Development: The Myth of Short Life Cycles," *Harvard Business Review*, July–August 1994, 11.

60. Don E. Schultz, "Integration Helps You Plan Communications from Outside-In," *Marketing News*, 15 March 1993, 12.

61. "Death of the Brand Manager," *The Economist*, 9 April 1994, 67–68; Jack Ryder,

"Category Management: A Matter of Less of the Same," *Brandweek*, 8 August 1994, 16.

62. Stephen Drucker, "Who is the Best Restaurateur in America?" *The New York Times Magazine*, 10 March 1996, 45–47, 104; Judann Pollack, "Ronald's Road Show Pumps Up Arch Deluxe," *Advertising Age*, 6 May 1996, 4; Judann Pollack, "McDonald's to Aim Its Arch at Grown-Ups," *Advertising Age*, 8 April 1996, 3, 37.

CHAPTER 11

1. Adapted from Suzanne Oliver, "Money-Raising in the Men's Room," *Forbes*, 13 February 1995, 72, 74.

2. Ronald Henkoff, "Service Is Everybody's Business," *Fortune*, 27 June 1994, 48–52, 56, 60.

3. U.S. Bureau of the Census, *Statistical Abstract of the United States 1995* (Washington, D.C.: U.S. Government Printing Office, 1995), 793, 794; Ripley Hotch, "In Touch Through Technology," *Nation's Business*, January 1994, 33–35.

4. Debra Phillips, "The New Service Boom," *Entrepreneur*, August 1994, 134, 136, 138, 140; Stratford Sherman, "You Can Have It All," *Fortune*, 4 March 1996, 193.

5. Larry Holyoke, "Can AT&T Get Through to Japan?" *Business Week*, 15 May 1995, 112–113.

6. Leo Ryan, "Canada Courts New Markets for Its Services and Expertise," *Journal of Commerce*, 15 September 1995, 1A; Henkoff, "Service Is Everybody's Business," 48–52, 56, 60; Myron Magnet, "Good News for the Service Economy," *Fortune*, 3 May 1993, 46–52; Rita Koselka, "BlockBusted?" *Forbes*, 26 February 1996, 42–47.

7. David Mercer, *Marketing* (Oxford, U.K.: Blackwell Publishers, 1992), 341; Emil E. Becker, "Service Quality Requires Strategy and Tactics," *Marketing News*, 29 January 1996, 4.

8. Brian Dumaine, "Volume Down at Bloomberg," *Fortune*, 6 March 1995, 33–34.

9. Thomas A. Stewart, "A New 500," *Fortune*, 15 May 1995, 166–167, 170, 174, 178; Maggie Jackson, "Service Industries Crack the Vaunted 500," *Washington Times*, 26 April 1995, B7, B9.

10. Stewart, "A New 500," 166–167, 170, 174, 178.

11. Ronald Henkoff, "Inside Andersen's Army of Advice," *Fortune*, 4 October 1993, 78–80, 82, 84, 86.

12. Adapted from Stan Rapp and Thomas L. Collins, *Beyond MaxiMarketing* (New York: McGraw-Hill, 1994), 203–219.

13. Ron Zemke and Dick Schaaf, *The Service Edge* (New York: Plume, 1990), 15; Lisa Miller and Gabriella Stern, "Crazy Drivers," *Wall Street Journal*, 15 January 1996, A1, A6.

14. Andrew E. Serwer, "McDonald's Conquers the World," *Fortune*, 17 October 1994, 103–104, 106, 108, 112, 114, 116; Judann Pollack and Mark Gleason, "Wendy's, McD's to Add Menu Sizzle," *Advertising Age*, 12 February 1996, 12.

15. Judy Temes, "A Hard Hat Worn with Style," *Crain's New York Business*, 13 March 1995, 14.

16. Ron Zemke, "The Emerging Art of Service Management," *Training*, January 1992, 37–42; Christopher Lovelock and George S. Yip, "Developing Global Strategies for Service Businesses," *California Management Review*, Winter 1996, 64–86.

17. B.G. Yovovich, "Business Info's New Power Tools," *Advertising Age*, 20 February 1995, 13; Terry Lefton, "Credit Cards: Co-Branding Proves Its Point," *Superbrands 1995*, 17 October 1995, 82, 84; Janet N. Hunter and David B. Zenoff, "The Marketing of a New Bank Image," in *Customer-Focused Marketing of Financial Services*, edited by David B. Zenoff (New York: Harper & Row, 1989), 33–56.

18. Jerry Buckley, "Why the Prognosis for Reform Is Poor," *U.S. News & World Report*, 23 November 1992, 30, 33, 36–39.

19. "Review & Outlook: Public Service," *Wall Street Journal*, 18 March 1994, A10.

20. Adapted from Steven J. Simurda, "Doing Good," *Entrepreneur*, October 1994, 133–137.

21. Dave Savona, "Out-Sourcing Profits," *International Business*, April 1995, 66.

22. Wade Leftwich, "Counting Eyeballs," *Marketing Tools*, January–February 1996, 53; Conner Middelmann, "German Giant Stakes Its Claim," *Financial Times*, 6 November 1995, 7, 8.

23. Lisa Belkin, "In Lessons on Empathy, Doctors Become Patients," *New York Times*, 4 June 1992, A1, A15.

24. Leonard L. Berry, "Services Marketing Is Different," in *Marketing Classics*, 7th ed., edited by Ben M. Enis and Keith K. Cox (Boston: Allyn & Bacon, 1991), 392–400; Stratford Sherman, "You Can Have It All," *Fortune*, 4 March 1996, 193–194.

25. Mark Peyrot, Philip D. Cooper, and Donald Schnapf, "Customer Satisfaction and Perceived Quality of Outpatient Health Services," *Journal of Health Care Marketing*, Winter 1993, 24–33.

26. Robin Kamen, "Restaurateur Meyer New Arbiter of Taste," *Crain's New York Business*, 13 February 1995, 2.

27. Zemke and Schaaf, *The Service Edge*, 512–515.

28. Valarie A. Zeithaml, "How Consumer Evaluation Processes Differ Between Goods and Services," in *Services Marketing*, edited by Christopher H. Lovelock (Englewood Cliffs, N.J.: Prentice Hall, 1984), 191–199; Praveen K. Kopalle and Donald R. Lehmann, "The Effects of Advertised and Observed Quality on Expectations About New Product Quality," *Journal of Marketing Research*, August 1995, 280–290.

29. Amy Ostrom and Dawn Iacobucci, "Consumer Trade-Offs and the Evaluation of Services," *Journal of Marketing*, January 1995, 17–28; Glenn B. Voss and A. Parasuraman, "Prepurchase Preference and Post-consumption Satisfaction in a Service Exchange," Marketing Science Institute Working Paper, no. 95-113, October 1995, 1–60.

30. Based on information from the SERVQUAL model developed by A. Parasuraman, Valarie A. Zeithaml, and Leonard L. Berry, cited in Frederick E. Webster, Jr., *Market-Driven Management* (New York: Wiley, 1994), 77–78, and Martin Christopher, Adrian Payne, and David Ballantyne, *Relationship Marketing* (Oxford, U.K.: Butterworth Heinemann, 1991), 70–71.

31. Tom Peters, *Liberation Management* (New York: Knopf, 1992), 715–716; Christopher, Payne, and Ballantyne, *Relationship Marketing*, 71.

32. Kenneth Labich, "Is Herb Kelleher America's Best CEO?" *Fortune*, 2 May 1994, 45–47, 50, 52; Richard S. Teitelbaum, "Southwest Airlines: Where Service Flies Right," *Fortune*, 24 August 1992, 115–116.

33. Zemke and Schaaf, *The Service Edge*, 8; Nilly Landau, "Are You Being Served?" *International Business*, March 1995, 38, 39–40; "Privileged Information," *Boardroom Re-*

ports, 15 December 1992, 2; Howard Scott, "Winning Back a Lost Account," *Nation's Business*, July 1989, 31R.

34. "Numbers for the '90s," *Advertising Age*, 2 January 1995, 3.

35. Karl Albrecht and Lawrence J. Bradford, *The Service Advantage* (Homewood, Ill.: Dow Jones–Irwin, 1990), 30–31.

36. Albrecht and Bradford, *The Service Advantage*, 33–34.

37. Richard A. Melcher, "Why Hyatt Is Toning Down the Glitz," *Business Week*, 27 February 1995, 92, 94.

38. Mary Jo Bitner, Bernard H. Booms, and Louis A. Mohr, "Critical Service Encounters: The Employee's Viewpoint," *Journal of Marketing*, 58 (October 1994): 95–106; Chad Rubel, "Buying a Car: What a Pain," *Marketing News*, 25 March 1996, 4.

39. Leonard L. Berry, *On Great Service* (New York: Free Press, 1995), 64–65, 137–139.

40. Zemke and Schaaf, *The Service Edge*, 7.

41. Berry, *On Great Service*, 100.

42. Zemke and Schaaf, *The Service Edge*, 21–22; Dwayne Gremler and Mary Jo Bitner, "Classifying Service Encounter Satisfaction Across Industries," in *Marketing Theory and Application*, edited by Chris Allen et al. (Chicago: AMA Winter Educator Conference Proceedings, 1992), 111–118.

43. Berry, *On Great Service*, 95; Robert Johnson, "Service Failure and Recovery: Impact, Attributes and Process," in *Advances in Services Marketing and Management*, edited by Teresa A. Swartz, David E. Bowen, and Stephen W. Brown (Greenwich, Conn.: JAI Press Inc., 1995), 211–228.

44. Berry, *On Great Service*, 106.

45. Berry, *On Great Service*, 179; Gary L. Clark, Peter F. Kaminski, and David R. Rink, "Consumer Complaints: Advice on How Companies Should Respond Based on an Empirical Study," *Journal of Services Marketing*, Winter 1992, 41–50.

46. Leonard A. Schlesinger and James L. Heskett, "Customer Satisfaction Is Rooted in Employee Satisfaction," *Harvard Business Review*, November–December 1991, 148–149; Susan Chandler, "Lands' End Looks for Terra Firma," *Business Week*, 8 July 1996, 128–131.

47. Kathleen Murray, "Make Nice, and Make It Snappy: Companies Try Courtesy Training," *New York Times*, 2 April 1995, sec. 3, 13; Joan C. Szabo, "Brushing Up on Customer TLC," *Nation's Business*, May 1995, 42, 44; Berry, *On Great Service*, 197–198.

48. Berry, *On Great Service*, 232–234.

49. Karl Albrecht, *At America's Service* (Homewood, Ill.: Dow Jones–Irwin, 1988), 131–132.

50. Brian Dumaine, "The Trouble with Teams," *Fortune*, 5 September 1994, 86–88, 90, 92.

51. Zemke and Schaaf, *The Service Edge*, 70–74.

52. Zemke and Schaaf, *The Service Edge*, 14–15; Voss and Parasuraman, "Prepurchase Preference and Postconsumption Satisfaction in a Service Exchange," 1–60.

53. Zemke and Schaaf, *The Service Edge*, 266–269.

54. Paul N. Bloom, "Effective Marketing for Professional Services," *Harvard Business Review*, September–October 1984, 102–110.

55. "10 Ways to Generate Customer Feedback," *Nation's Business*, April 1993, 63; William J. Glynn, "Service Quality: It's the Why That Counts," *Marketing News*, 29 January 1996, 4.

56. George R. Walther, *Upside-Down Marketing* (New York: McGraw-Hill, 1994), 86; David Osborne and Ted Gaebler, *Reinventing Government* (New York: Plume, 1993), 177; Emil E. Becker, "Service Quality Requires Strategy *and* Tactics," *Marketing News*, 29 January 1996, 4.

57. Joe Whalen, "Qualitative Research Adds the 'Why?' to Measurement," *Marketing News*, 9 May 1994, 8.

58. Albecht and Bradford, *The Service Advantage*, 5–6; Michael Brogan, "Death of a Shoe Salesman," *Business Week*, 20 February 1995, 16E4–16E8.

59. Albrecht, *At America's Service*, 42; Patricia Davis, "If You Can't Reach the Front Desk Clerk, He May Be Outside Tending the Flowers," *Wall Street Journal*, 24 January 1996, B1.

60. Zemke and Schaaf, *The Service Edge*, 426–429.

61. Chip R. Bell, *Customers as Partners* (San Francisco: Berrett-Koehler, 1994), 84–91.

62. Hal F. Rosenbluth and Diane McFerrin Peters, *The Customer Comes Second* (New York: William Morrow, 1992).

63. Ron Zemke and Dick Schaaf, *The Service Edge* (New York: Plume, 1990), 544–547; Osborne and Gaebler, *Reinventing Government*, 177.

64. "Profiting a Nonprofit," *Nation's Business*, February 1995, 51.

65. Peter F. Drucker, "What Business Can Learn from Nonprofits," *Harvard Business Review*, July–August 1989, 88–93.

66. "Let's Play Patient," *Consumer Reports*, February 1995, 83; Belkin, "In Lessons on Empathy, Doctors Become Patients," A1, B5.

67. "Patient-Centered Care: Feeling Comfortable in a Hospital," *Consumer Reports*, February 1995, 84–85.

68. John Elson, "Campus of the Future," *Time*, 13 April 1992, 54–58.

69. Kenneth Eskey, "Government to Put Customer First," *Washington Times*, 20 September 1994, A6.

70. Eskey, "Government to Put Customer First," A6.

71. Pam Black, "Finally, Human Rights for Motorists," *Business Week*, 1 May 1995, 45.

72. Osborne and Gaebler, *Reinventing Government*, 142–145.

73. Marc Gunther, "Travel Planning in Cyberspace," *Fortune*, 9 September 1996, 187–188.

74. *Advertising Age's Netmarketing*, a special supplement to *Business Marketing*, September 1996, M-1–M14.

75. Peter Kaminsky, "Why Ask for the Moon When He Already Has Three Stars?" *New York*, 18 July 1994, 18–25; "Local Restaurants Provide Charity During Blizzard," *Town & Village*, 11 January 1996, 3; Union Square Cafe newsletters, 1995–1996.

MARKETING ON THE NET FOR PART **4**

1. Adapted from Susan Greco, "Website of the Week: Joe Boxer," *Inc. Online*, 10 June 1996, 1–2.

2. Doug Abrahms, "Little Bank, Big World," *The Washington Times*, 7 June 1996, B7; "Business in Brief," *Investor's Business Daily*, 23 May 1996, online access; Ted Bunker, "As Electronic Banking Looms, Kentucky Firm Forges Ahead," *Investor's Business Daily*, 15 May 1995, online access; Toddi Gutner, "Surfing the Net for Better Returns," *Business Week*, 18 March 1996,

116; "The Future of Money," *Business Week*, 12 June 1995, cover story, via online access.

CHAPTER **12**

1. Adapted from Don Taylor and Jeanne Smalling Archer, *Up Against the Wal-Marts* (New York: AMACOM, 1994), 222–224.

2. Ingrid Abramovitch, "Mongoose," *Success*, April 1995, 38–42.

3. Marsha Bertrand, "Let's Make a Deal," *Nation's Business*, February 1995, 27–29.

4. Neil Gross and Peter Coy, "The Technology Paradox," *Business Week*, 6 March 1995, 76–81, 84.

5. Linda Gorchels, "Prices Should Wed Intuition, Technique, Customer Value," *Business Marketing*, May 1995, 9; Gabriella Stern, "The Frills Are Gone in GM's Showrooms, but Profits Are Back," *Wall Street Journal*, 15 January 1996, A1, A7.

6. Holly Heline, "Brand Loyalty Isn't Dead—But You're Not Off the Hook," *Brandweek*, 7 June 1993, 14–15; Bob Taska and Peter Caldwell, "You Will Be Satisfied," *Success*, May 1996, 59–66.

7. Riccardo A. Davis, "'Value' and 'Quality' Show Popularity in New Trademarks," *Advertising Age*, 1 March 1993, 41; Bradley Johnson, "Hyundai Parks Low-Price Pitch; Emphasizes Value," *Advertising Age*, 26 February 1996, 16.

8. Frederick E. Webster, Jr., *Market-Driven Management* (New York: Wiley, 1994), 55–56.

9. Kent B. Monroe, *Pricing: Making Profitable Decisions*, 2nd ed. (New York: McGraw-Hill, 1990), 15–16, 55; Peter F. Drucker, "The Five Deadly Business Sins," *Wall Street Journal*, 21 October 1993, A18.

10. O. P. Malik, "The Great Indian Brand Bazaar," *Brandweek*, 5 June 1995, 31–32; Karen Benezra, "Fast Food: The Battle of the Bundles," *Superbrands*, 17 October 1994, 98–99.

11. Kathleen Kerwin, "Value Will Keep Detroit Moving," *Business Week*, 10 January 1994, 71; B. Joseph Pine II, Bart Victor, and Andrew C. Boynton, "Making Mass Customization Work," *Harvard Business Review*, September–October 1993, 108–119; Martha Brannigan and Eleena De Lisser, "Delta Air May Try New 'Lite' Service," *Wall Street Journal*, 9 February 1996, B8.

12. Seth Mydans, "High Ceilings and High Tech on the Triple 7," *New York Times*, 4 June 1995, sec. 5, 14.

13. Robert J. Dolan, "How Do You Know When the Price Is Right?" *Harvard Business Review*, September–October 1995, 174–176, 178, 180–183.

14. Robin Kamen, "New York Hotels Seize the Per Diem," *Crain's New York Business*, 23 January 1995, 3, 48.

15. Rubbermaid, *Philosophy, Management Principles, Vision & Mission, Objectives* (Wooster, Ohio: Rubbermaid, 1994), 5.

16. Jim Carlton, "Apple's Choice: Preserve Profits or Cut Prices," *Wall Street Journal*, 22 February 1995, B1, B6; Peter Burrows, "Apple: Another Bout of Bad Tidings," *Business Week*, 8 January 1996, 33.

17. Gross and Coy, "The Technology Paradox," 76–81, 84.

18. Catherine Arnst, "Say Goodbye to the Bare-Bones Phone," *Business Week*, 29 May 1995, ENT18.

19. Webster, *Market-Driven Management*, 51–58.

20. Tom Ehrenfeld, "The New and Improved American Small Business," *Inc.*, January 1995, 34–36, 38, 40, 42, 44–45.

21. T. L. Stanley, "Mitsubishi Raises Halo with Spyder," *Brandweek*, 27 February 1995, 33.

22. Jonathan Berry and Zachary Schiller, "Attack of the Fighting Brands," *Business Week*, 2 May 1994, 125.

23. David Osborne and Ted Gaebler, *Reinventing Government* (New York: Plume, 1993), 90–92.

24. Ylonda Gault, "Whitney Lures New Crowd by Breaking Down Walls," *Crain's New York Business*, 24 April 1995, 20.

25. Working Assets ad in *Utne Reader*, November–December 1994.

26. Brian Blomquist, "Dulles Greenway May Cut Toll to Gain Drivers," *Metropolitan Times*, 5 February 1996, C7.

27. Alfred R. Oxenfeldt, "A Decision-Making Structure for Price Decisions," in *Marketing Classics*, 7th ed., edited by Ben M. Enis and Keith K. Cox (Boston: Allyn & Bacon, 1991), 428–436.

28. Monroe, *Pricing*, 295–299.

29. Monroe, *Pricing*, 303–312.

30. Earl Naumann, *Creating Customer Value* (Cincinnati: Thomson Executive Press, 1995), 118–119.

31. Webster, *Market-Driven Management*, 182–183.

32. Michael L. Rozansky, "Soaring Cost of Paper Pinches Publications," *The News-Times* (Danbury, Conn.), 8 March 1995, D-8; Mark Langlois, "Local Publishers Tighten Their Belts," *The News-Times* (Danbury, Conn.), 8 March 1995, D-8.

33. Mark Lewyn, "MCI: A Smaller Family and Fewer Friends," *Business Week*, 6 February 1995, 147–148; Eric Mitchell, "More Profitable Pricing Strategies," *Boardroom Reports*, 15 July 1994, 1–2.

34. Gayle Sato Stodder, "Paying the Price," *Entrepreneur*, October 1994, 54; Peter R. Dickson and Joel E. Urbany, "Retailer Reactions to Competitive Price Changes," *Journal of Retailing* 70, no. 1 (1994): 1–21; Jim Juback, "It's Not Gonna Be Easy," *Worth*, March 1996, 51–52.

35. Robert A. Garda and Michael V. Marn, "Price Wars," *The McKinsey Quarterly*, no. 3 (1993): 87–100; Francis J. Mulhern and Daniel T. Padgett, "The Relationship Between Retail Price Promotions and Regular Price Purchases," *Journal of Marketing*, October 1995, 83–90; Laura Bird, "Back to Full Price?" *Wall Street Journal*, 29 May 1996, A1, A10.

36. Based on information from Taylor and Archer, *Up Against the Wal-Marts*.

37. Stephen H. Haeckel, "Engineering Customer Experience," Conference Summary Report, no. 96–100, March 1996, 9.

38. David Greising, "Watch Out for Flying Packages," *Business Week*, 14 November 1994, 40.

39. Bill Saporito, "Behind the Tumult at P&G," *Fortune*, 7 March 1994, 74–76, 80–82.

40. Laurel Wentz, "Cachet and Carry," *Advertising Age International*, 12 February 1996, I-15, I-16, I-18.

41. Alex Taylor III, "Why an Industry That Was Up a Tree Is on a Big Roll," *Fortune*, 17 April 1995, 134–136, 140, 142; Judith Messina, "Boxed In by Hikes," *Crain's New York Business*, 5 June 1995, 1, 21; Rozansky, "Soaring Cost of Paper Pinches Publications," D-8.

42. "Scalpers Lick Chops Over Harley Hogs," *Chicago Tribune*, 20 November 1994, sec. 7, 8; Richard Melcher, "Tune-Up Time for Harley," *Business Week*, 8 April 1996, 90–94.

43. Steve Malanga, "NY Inflation Debate: Alan, Meet Suellen," *Crain's New York Business*, 13 February 1995, 3, 26.

44. Kevin J. Clancy and Robert S. Shulman, *The Marketing Revolution* (New York: McGraw-Hill, 1991), 148–149; Venkatesh Shankar and Lakshman Krishnamurti, "Relating Price Sensitivity to Retailer Promotional Variables and Pricing Policy," *Journal of Retailing*, forthcoming.

45. Russell Mitchell and Richard A. Melcher, "'Thanks for Your Deposit. That'll Be $3,'" *Business Week*, 15 May 1995, 46; Maria Mooshil, "Bank's $3 Teller Fee Has PR Pros Wondering," *Advertising Age*, 15 May 1995, 12.

46. John Huey, "Eisner Explains Everything," *Fortune*, 17 April 1995, 44–48, 52, 56, 58–60, 64, 68; Robert F. Hartley, *Marketing Mistakes*, 6th ed. (New York: Wiley, 1995), 113–128.

47. Monroe, *Pricing*, 390–391; Garda and Marn, "Price Wars," 87–100.

48. Andrew E. Serwer, "How to Escape a Price War," *Fortune*, 13 June 1994, 82–85, 88, 90; Martha Brannigan and Eleena De Jesser, "Delta Air May Try New 'Lite' Service," *Wall Street Journal*, 9 February 1996, B8.

49. Lori Ioannou, "How to Win Price Fights," *International Business*, May 1994, 24, 26.

50. Edith Terry, "Japan: Where the Prices Are Insane!" *Fortune*, 31 October 1994, 21; James Sterngold, "Is Japan's Sam Walton Up to the Job?" *New York Times*, 4 December 1994, sec. 3, 1, 4.

51. Ionannou, "How to Win Price Fights," 24, 26.

52. Gerry Khermouch and Karen Benezra, "Resource Ripples: From Coke to P&G," *Brandweek*, 9 January 1995, 3.

53. "Catalogers Resort to Bartering," *Catalog Age*, February 1994, 38.

54. Kenneth J. Meier, *Regulation: Politics, Bureaucracy, and Economics* (New York: St. Martin's Press, 1985), 244–246; Monroe, *Pricing* 389–390; Steven C. Bahls and Jane Easter Bahls, "The Price Is Wrong," *Entrepreneur*, May 1996, 74–75.

55. Monroe, *Pricing*, 404–405; Terry, "Japan: Where the Prices Are Insane," 21.

56. "Wal-Mart's Price War: David Versus Goliath," *U.S. News & World Report*, 25 October 1993, 14; Thomas J. Winninger, *Price Wars* (Rocklin Calif.: Prima Publishing, 1996), 12–13.

57. Monroe, *Pricing*, 393–394.

58. Monroe, *Pricing*, 399–403.

59. Gene R. Laczniak and Patrick E. Murphy, *Ethical Marketing Decisions: The Higher Road* (Boston: Allyn & Bacon, 1993), 130.

60. Christine Gorman, "Border Bargains," *Time*, 19 February 1996, 54.

61. Laczniak and Murphy, *Ethical Marketing Decisions*, 131–132.

62. Adam Bryant, "This Absolutely Free Article Will Explain Everything About the World of Advertising!" *New York Times*, 29 January 1995, sec. 4, 5; Laczniak and Murphy, *Ethical Marketing Decisions*, 133–134.

63. Laczniak and Murphy, *Ethical Marketing Decisions*, 132–133.

64. Nilly Ostro-Landau, "Currencies, Prices and Profits," *International Business*, July 1995, 16, 18–19.

65. Joel R. Evans and Barry Berman, *Marketing*, 7th ed. (Upper Saddle River, NJ: Prentice-Hall, 1997), 170.

66. John Delmar, "Foreign Law Report: The Price Is Wrong," *International Business*, March 1994, 132; Monroe, *Pricing*, 405–406; Gorman, "Border Bargains," 54.

67. Jay Finegan, "Unconventional Wisdom," *Inc.*, December 1994, 44–59; Hoover's MasterList Database and Hoover's Company Profile Database, accessed online 12 September 1996.

CHAPTER 13

1. Howard Banks, "When the Going Gets Tough . . ." *Forbes*, 2 January 1995, 16; Kenneth Labich, "Is Herb Kelleher America's Best CEO?" *Fortune*, 2 May 1994, 44–47, 50, 52; Howard Banks, "A Sixties Industry in a Nineties Economy," *Forbes*, 9 May 1994, 107–112; Martha Brannigan and Eleena De Lisser, "Delta Air May Try New 'Lite' Service," *Wall Street Journal*, 9 February 1996, B8.

2. Linda Gorchels, "Prices Should Wed Intuition, Technique, Customer Value," *Business Marketing*, May 1995, 9.

3. Kevin J. Clancy and Robert S. Shulman, *The Marketing Revolution* (New York: HarperBusiness, 1993), 144–148.

4. Helen L. Richardson, "Pricing: Carriers Calculate Their Risks," *T&D*, March 1994, 29–30, 32.

5. Kevin Clancy, "Pricing Strategies . . . For These Very Tricky Times," *Boardroom Reports*, 15 January 1994, 1, 6; Gene Koprowski, "Testing, Testing, $1, $2, $3 . . ." *Marketing Tools*, September 1995, 59.

6. Susan Greco, "Smart Use of 'Special Offers'," *Inc.*, February 1993, 23.

7. Kevin J. Clancy, Robert S. Shulman, and Marianne Wolf, *Simulated Test Marketing* (New York: Lexington Books, 1994), 174–177.

8. Kevin J. Clancy and Robert S. Shulman, *Marketing Myths That Are Killing Business* (New York: McGraw-Hill, 1994), 203; Clancy, Shulman, and Wolf, *Simulated Test Marketing*, 170–173.

9. Dhruv Grewal, Kent B. Monroe, and R. Krishman, "The Effects of Price-Comparison Advertising on Buyer's Perceptions of Acquisition Value and Transaction Value," Working Paper Report, no. 96–103, May 1996, 1–34.

10. Neil Gross and Peter Coy, "The Technology Paradox," *Business Week*, 6 March 1995, 76–81, 84.

11. Richardson, "Pricing," 29–30, 32.

12. Brian Coleman, "Daimler Aerospace Comes Down to Earth," *Wall Street Journal*, 21 July 1995, A6.

13. Robin Cooper and W. Bruce Chew, "Control Tomorrow's Costs Through Today's Designs," *Harvard Business Review*, January–February 1996, 88–97.

14. Richard Rosen, "If Neil Simon Likes the Nabe, It Must Be Off Broadway," *New York Times*, 26 March 1995, sec. 4, 7, 18.

15. Adapted from Kevin D. Thompson, "Planning for Profit," *Black Enterprise*, April 1993, 93–94, 96, 98.

16. David Kirkpatrick, "IBM Moves to Fix Its Microsoft Problem," *Fortune*, 10 July 1995, 102–111; Paul C. Judge, "Lotus Is Learning to Live with the Net," *Business Week*, 29 January 1996, 70–71.

17. Theodore Levitt, *The Marketing Imagination* (new expanded ed.) (New York: Free Press, 1986), 182.

18. Gross and Coy, "The Technology Paradox," 76–81, 84.

19. William Echikson, "Luxury Steals Back," *Fortune*, 16 January 1995, 112–114, 116, 118–119; Bill Richards, "Kemper's

Shows Even Root Beer Has a Premium Niche," *Wall Street Journal*, 19 May 1993, B2; Laurel Wentz, "Cachet and Carry," *Ad Age International*, 12 February 1996, 115–116.

20. Monroe, *Pricing*, 312.

21. Pam Weisz, "Stores Need More Cavities on Shelves for New Toothpastes," *Brandweek*, 2 January 1995, 12.

22. Gerald E. Smith and Thomas T. Nagle, "Frames of Reference and Buyers' Perception of Price and Value," *California Management Review* 38, no. 1 (Fall 1995): 98–116.

23. Edith Hill Updike, "Japan Is Dialing 1 800 BuyAmerica," *Business Week*, 12 June 1995, 61, 64.

24. Milind M. Lele, *Creating Strategic Leverage* (New York: Wiley, 1992), 272, 282; John R. Hayes, "The Bundler," *Forbes*, 22 April 1996, 82–88.

25. Betsy Spethmann, "Campbell Bundles Up for Kit War," *Brandweek*, 27 February 1995, 4.

26. Gerald J. Tellis, "Beyond the Many Faces of Price: An Integration of Pricing Strategies," in *Marketing Classics*, 7th ed., edited by Ben M. Enis and Keith K. Cox (Boston: Allyn & Bacon, 1991), 437–459; Lele, *Creating Strategic Leverage*, 272, 282.

27. "Gen X Makes Neon Product of the Year," *Advertising Age*, 19 December 1994, 17; Christopher Farrell and Zachary Schiller, "Stuck! How Companies Cope When They Can't Raise Prices," *Business Week*, 15 November 1993, 146–148, 150, 154–155.

28. Peter F. Drucker, "The Five Deadly Sins," *Wall Street Journal*, 21 October 1993, A18; Clancy and Shulman, *The Marketing Revolution*, 151–152.

29. "Pricing: Your Fees Are Obsolete. Now What?" *Inc.*, June 1995, 87.

30. G. Dean Kortge, Patrick A. Okonkwo, James R. Burley, and Jeffrey D. Kortge, "Linking Experience, Product Life Cycle, and Learning Curves," *Industrial Marketing Management* 23 (1994): 221–228.

31. Brent Schlender, "Why Andy Grove Can't Stop," *Fortune*, 10 July 1995, 88–92, 94, 98; Gerald J. Tellis, "Beyond the Many Faces of Price: An Integration of Pricing Strategies," in *Marketing Classics*, 7th ed., edited by Ben M. Enis and Keith K. Cox (Boston: Allyn & Bacon, 1991), 437–459; Frederick E. Webster, Jr., *Market-Driven*

Management (New York: John Wiley, 1994), 46–47.

32. Black & Decker, 1994 Annual Report, 5.

33. David Mercer, *Marketing* (Oxford, U.K.: Blackwell Publishers, 1992), 425–426; "Procter & Gamble Will Reduce Marketing Expenses, Cut Prices," *Washington Times*, 19 February 1996, B20.

34. Monroe, *Pricing*, 47–48.

35. Adapted from Robert F. Hartley, *Marketing Mistakes*, 6th ed. (New York: John Wiley, 1995), 100–112.

36. Holman W. Jenkins, Jr., "Brand Managers Get Old Time Religion," *Wall Street Journal*, 23 April 1996, A23. Holman W. Jenkins, Jr., "Brand Managers Get Old-Time Religion," *Wall Street Journal*, 25 April 1996, A23.

37. Jennifer Lawrence, "7-Eleven Opens Up to Low Pricing," *Advertising Age*, 10 January 1994, 27; Fara Warner, "The New Formula," *Superbrands 1994*, 18 October 1993, 16–18, 20, 22; Robert Wals, "EDLP Not Good for All," *Advertising Age International*, April 1996, I-6.

38. Susan Reda, "Is EDLP Coming Up S.H.O.R.T.?" *Stores*, October 1994, 23–24, 26; Stephanie Anderson Forest, "Dillard's Has a Dilly of a Headache," *Business Week*, 3 October 1994, 85–86; "Everyday Low Profits," *Harvard Business Review*, March–April 1994, 13; Richard Gibson, "Broad Grocery Price Cuts May Not Pay," *Wall Street Journal*, 7 May 1993, B1, B8.

39. Jeannie Mandelker, "Pricing with Precision," *Profit*, September–October 1994, 18–20, 22.

40. Gabriella Stern and Rebecca Blumenstein, "GM Expected to Expand 'No Haggle' Pricing Plan," *Wall Street Journal*, 24 April 1996, A3.

41. Brian Toyne and Peter G. P. Walters, *Global Marketing Management*, 2nd ed. (Boston: Allyn & Bacon, 1993), 484–485.

42. Monroe, *Pricing*, 445–448.

43. Toyne and Walters, *Global Marketing Management*, 495–497; Monroe, *Pricing*, 450–451.

44. Toyne and Walters, *Global Marketing Management*, 495–496.

45. Toyne and Walters, *Global Marketing Management*, 532–535; Michael R. Czinkota, Pietra Rivoli, and Ilkka Ronkainen, *International Business*, 2nd ed.

(Fort Worth, Tex.: Dryden Press, 1992), 426–427.

46. J. L. Hazelton, "Post Cereal to Cut Prices 20 Percent, Issue New Coupon," *Washington Post*, 16 April 1996, D3.

47. Mercer, *Marketing*, 436.

48. Tom Ehrenfeld, "The New and Improved American Small Business," *Inc.*, January 1995, 34–36, 38, 40, 42, 44–45.

49. David Woodruff, "How Many Rebates Can Fit in a Minivan?" *Business Week*, 13 February 1995, 72, 74.

MARKETING ON THE NET FOR PART 5

1. Jack Edmonston, "Cost-per-Contact Fees Will Win on the Web," *Business Marketing*, June 1996, 14; Jeffery D. Zbar, "How to Buy Ad Banners: A Step-by-Step Guide," *Advertising Age's Internet Marketing*, May 1996, M1, M6; "New Pricing Models Emerge from Better Web Measurement," *Interactive Marketing News*, 10 May 1996, 1, 8.

2. Adapted from Bruce Judson, *Netmarketing* (New York: Wolff New Media, 1996), 292.

CHAPTER 14

1. Adapted from Bev Farrar, "Dressings for Success," *Nation's Business*, July 1995, 13–14.

2. Jennifer Patterson, "Adding Value by Managing Supply Chain Activities," *Marketing News*, 17 July 1995, 6.

3. Gregory L. Miles, "Breaking Down Turf Barriers," *International Business*, June 1995, 25.

4. Patterson, "Adding Value by Managing Supply Chain Activities," 6; Robert C. Borsch, "Supply Chain Management," *Boardroom Reports*, 15 July 1994, 9–10.

5. David J. Bowersox and M. Bixby Cooper, *Strategic Marketing Channel Management* (New York: McGraw-Hill, 1992), 17.

6. Bert Rosenbloom, *Marketing Channels*, 5th ed. (Fort Worth, Tex.: Dryden Press, 1995), 51–53.

7. Robert Benjamin and Rolf Wigand, "Electronic Markets and Virtual Value Chains on the Information Superhighway," *Sloan Management Review*, Winter 1995, 62–71.

8. Bob Jones, "Know Your Place," *Entrepreneur*, June 1994, 52, 54–55; "Leave the

Driving to Us," *Restaurant Business*, 10 October 1992, 80, 84.

9. Myron Magnet, "The New Golden Rule of Business," *Fortune*, 21 February 1994, 60–64; James A. Narus and James C. Anderson, "Rethinking Distribution: Adaptive Channels," *Harvard Business Review*, July–August 1996, 112–120.

10. Douglas M. Lambert and James R. Stock, *Strategic Logistics Management*, 3rd ed. (Homewood, Ill.: Irwin, 1993), 29.

11. Donald G. Howard, "The Role of Export Management Companies in Global Marketing," *Journal of Global Marketing* 8, no. 1 (1994): 95–110; Lee Smith, "Does the World's Biggest Company Have a Future?" *Fortune*, 7 August 1995, 124–126; Jeffrey H. Dyer, "How Chrysler Created an American Keiretsu," *Harvard Business Review*, July–August 1996, 42–56.

12. John Kavanagh, "Focus Is on Supply Chain Information," *Financial Times*, 4 October 1995, 17.

13. Mark Maremont, "Next, A Flap over Film?" *Business Week*, 10 July 1995, 34; "Snapping Back," *Business Week*, 24 June 1996, 48.

14. Laurie Freeman, "CRP Sticks as Product Movement Mantra," *Advertising Age*, 8 May 1995, S-1, S-6, S-9; Kurt Salmon Associates, "Efficient Consumer Response" (Washington, D.C.: Food Marketing Institute, 1993), 1–2, 7; Judann Pollack, "The Food Chain," *Advertising Age*, 6 May 1996, 28, 30.

15. Lisa R. Williams, "Understanding Distribution Channels: An Interorganizational Study of EDI Adoption," *Journal of Business Logistics* 15, no. 2 (1994): 173–203; Daniel J. Biby, "Electronic Data Interchange," *Mast*, March–April 1993, 16–21; Peter Bradley, "Power Leasing," *Success*, April 1996, 63–66.

16. Joseph Weber, "Just Get It to the Stores on Time," *Business Week*, 6 March 1995, 66–67.

17. Michael Selz, "Firms Innovate to Get It for You Wholesale," *Wall Street Journal*, 23 July 1993, B1, B2.

18. "Communication: Finding Ways to Talk with Customers," *Nation's Business*, March 1995, 12.

19. John Tagliabue, "Spain's Olive Growers Seek Their Day in the Sun," *New York Times*, 27 November 1994, sec. 3, 7.

20. Anne Murphy, "The Missing Link," *Inc.*, June 1995, 58–60, 62–66; Dori Jones Yang, "The Pied Piper of Kids' Software," *Business Week*, 7 August 1995, 70–71.

21. Alpine Lace Brands, Form 10–K, 31 December 1993, 5.

22. Julia Flynn, "An Ever–Quicker Trip from R&D to Customer," *Business Week 21st Century Capitalism*, 18 November 1994, 88.

23. Black & Decker, Form 10K, 31 December 1994, 10.

24. Greg Burns, "Can It Play Out of Peoria?" *Business Week*, 7 August 1995, 58–59.

25. Robert Muraskin, "Workers of Hungary Unite—In Amway," *Washington Post*, 6 August 1994, D1, D8; Veronica Byrd, "The Avon Lady of the Amazon," *Business Week*, 24 October 1994, 93, 95–96.

26. Byrd, "The Avon Lady of the Amazon," 93, 95–96; Avon, 1993 Annual Report, 1, 4, 8, 11; Laurel Wentz, "Global Village," Advertising Age International supplement to *Advertising Age,* 15 January 1996, I-3.

27. Rosenbloom, *Marketing Channels*, 113.

28. Kathy Rebello, "Cidco: Picking Up on Caller ID," *Business Week*, 22 May 1995, 78.

29. Andrew Wallenstein, "Coke–Blockbuster Link," *Advertising Age*, 10 July 1995, 8; Pat Sloan, "Sheila Hewitt: CK One," *Advertising Age*, 26 June 1995, S-18.

30. Gary Levin, "Green Marketing Gets Cautious," *Advertising Age*, 5 July 1993, 4.

31. David Shenk, "Buy a Hat, Save the Earth," *Hemispheres*, May 1993, 25–26, 28.

32. Gerry Khermouch, "Veryfine Battles Nestlé for Kids," *Brandweek*, 17 April 1995, 8; Tim Smart, "How Travelers Got Moving Again," *Business Week*, 4 December 1995, 96.

33. George S. Day, *Market-Driven Strategy* (New York: Free Press, 1990), 225.

34. Judann Pollack, "Susan Engel: Department 56," *Advertising Age*, 26 June 1995, S-14; "These Low-Risk Growth Stocks Could Average 28% Gains in the Next 12 Months," *Money*, December 1995, 170.

35. Alexandra J. Campbell, "The Effect of Fast Market Responsiveness on Supply Partnerships," *Marketing Science Institute Working Paper*, no. 95-112, October 1995, 1–36.

36. Hal Plotkin, "Riches from Rags," *Inc. Technology*, Summer 1995, 62–64, 67.

37. Kim Cleland, "Leave Off the Last 'S' for Surfing," *Advertising Age*, 6 February 1995, 14.

38. Susan Biddle Jaffe, "Still a Player During a Strike," *Nation's Business*, February 1995, 6.

39. Bowersox and Cooper, *Strategic Marketing Channel Management*, 242–243.

40. Rosenbloom, *Marketing Channels*, 111–116.

41. Rosenbloom, *Marketing Channels*, 119–121.

42. Kelley Holland, "Why Banks Keep Bulking Up," *Business Week*, 31 July 1995, 66–67.

43. Jan B. Heide, "Interorganizational Governance in Marketing Channels," *Journal of Marketing*, January 1994, 71–85; Walfried Lassar and Walter Zinn, "Informal Channel Relationships in Logistics," *Journal of Business Logistics* 16, no. 1 (1995): 81–105.

44. Murray Raphel, *Customerization* (Atlantic City, N.J.: Raphel Publishing, 1993), 17.

45. Alison L. Sprout, "Packard Bell," *Fortune*, 12 June 1995, 82–84, 88.

46. Brett A. Boyle and F. Robert Dwyer, "Power, Bureaucracy, Influence, and Performance: Their Relationships in Industrial Distribution Channels," *Journal of Business Research*, 32 (1995): 189–200; James C. Anderson and James A. Narus, "A Model of Distributor Firm and Manufacturer Firm Working Partnerships," *Journal of Marketing* 54 (January 1990): 42–58; Keith J. Kelly, "Publishers Wary of Wholesaler Consolidation," *Advertising Age*, 26 February 1996, 3, 43.

47. Rosenbloom, *Marketing Channels*, 132–133.

48. Ylonda Gault, "Acquisition Aftertaste Sours Snapple," *Crain's New York Business*, 24 July 1995, 1, 24; Andrew Wallenstein, "Summer Slugfest for Snapple and Fruitopia," *Advertising Age*, 12 June 1995, 6.

49. "A National Brand—At What Price?" *Inc.*, February 1995, 108.

50. Gene R. Laczniak and Patrick E. Murphy, *Ethical Marketing Decisions* (Boston: Allyn & Bacon, 1993), 117–118.

51. Laczniak and Murphy, *Ethical Marketing Decisions*, 117–118; Don Peppers and Martha Rogers, *The One-to-One Future* (New York: Doubleday, 1993), 269.

52. Rosenbloom, *Marketing Channels*, 395–396.

53. Laczniak and Murphy, *Ethical Marketing Decisions*, 111.

54. Michael Treacy and Fred Wiersema, "Customer Intimacy and Other Value Disciplines," *Harvard Business Review*, January–February 1993, 84–93.

55. Carla Rappaport, "Retailers Go Global," *Fortune*, 20 February 1995, 102–104, 106, 108.

56. Bowersox and Cooper, *Strategic Marketing Channel Management*, 308–313; Rosenbloom, *Marketing Channels*, 485.

57. Peter F. Drucker, "The Economy's Power Shift," *Wall Street Journal*, 24 September 1992, A16; Day, *Market-Driven Strategy*, 231–233.

58. Alice Z. Cuneo, "Levi Strauss Sizes the Retail Scene," *Advertising Age*, 23 January 1995, 4; Rosenbloom, *Marketing Channels*, 502.

59. Rosenbloom, *Marketing Channels*, 491–492.

60. Adapted from Andrew E. Serwer, "Trouble in Franchise Nation," *Fortune*, 6 March 1995, 115–116, 118, 122, 124, 127, 129.

61. Serwer, "Trouble in Franchise Nation," 115–116, 118, 122, 124, 127, 129; Rosenbloom, *Marketing Channels*, 155–157; Laczniak and Murphy, *Ethical Marketing Decisions*, 118–121.

CHAPTER 15

1. Carla Rappaport, "Retailers Go Global," *Fortune*, 20 February 1995, 102–104, 106, 108; Peter Kaminsky, "Japan on the Hudson," *New York*, 24 July 1995, 48.

2. Quoted in Jon Taylor and Jeanne Smalling Archer, *Up Against the Wal-Marts* (New York: AMACOM, 1994), 215.

3. Richard A. Melcher, "Cut Out the Middleman? Never," *Business Week*, 10 January 1994, 96; Keith Kelly, "Publishers Wary of Wholesaler Consolidation," *Advertising Age*, 26 February 1996, 3, 43.

4. Melcher, "Cut Out the Middleman?" 96.

5. Matt Walsh, "Automation Begins at Home," *Forbes*, 25 April 1994, 158, 160.

6. Hewlett-Packard, 1993 Annual Report, 48.

7. Donald J. Bowersox and M. Bixby Cooper, *Strategic Marketing Channel Management* (New York: McGraw-Hill, 1992), 40–41.

8. "Companies to Watch: Central Garden & Pet," *Fortune*, 7 February 1994, 137.

9. Melcher, "Cut Out the Middleman?" 96.

10. Adapted from Richard Phalon, "Diversifying into Pâté de Foie Gras," *Forbes*, 21 November 1994, 176, 178.

11. Michael P. Collins, *The Manufacturer's Guide to Business Marketing* (Burr Ridge, Ill.: Irwin, 1995), 134–135.

12. Brian Toyne and Peter G. P. Walters, *Global Marketing Management*, 2nd ed. (Boston: Allyn & Bacon, 1993), 626–627.

13. Judann Pollack, "The Food Chain," *Advertising Age*, 6 May 1996, 28–30.

14. Matthew Schifrin, "Middleman's Dilemma," *Forbes*, 23 May 1994, 67, 69; Melcher, "Cut Out the Middleman?" 96.

15. Joseph V. Barks, "Squeezing Out the Middleman," *Distribution*, January 1994, 30–34; John W. Verity, "A Trillion-Byte Weapon," *Business Week*, 31 July 1995, 80–81.

16. Barry Berman and Joel R. Evans, *Retail Management*, 6th ed. (Englewood Cliffs, N.J.: Prentice Hall, 1995), 9.

17. Elaine Underwood, "Store Brands," *Brandweek*, 9 January 1995, 22–27.

18. Joe Peritz, "Retailers Who Keep Score Know What Their Shoppers Value," *Marketing News*, 24 May 1993, 9; Debra Aho Williamson, "'Net Helps Find Room at the Inn," *Advertising Age*, 19 June 1995, 18.

19. "How to Reach the Major Leagues of Shoe Shopping," *Fortune*, 7 August 1995, 36; Erika Kotite, "Store Wars," *Entrepreneur*, July 1992, 158–163.

20. Bill Saporito, "What's for Dinner?" *Fortune*, 15 May 1995, 50–52, 56, 60, 64.

21. Stan Rapp and Thomas L. Collins, *The New MaxiMarketing* (New York: McGraw-Hill, 1996), 9.

22. Ronald Henkoff, "Why Every Red-Blooded Consumer Owns a Truck," *Fortune*, 29 May 1995, 86–90, 94, 96, 100; Susan Reda, "Interactive Shopping," *Stores*, March 1995, 20–22, 24; David J. Wallace, "Logging On for a Loaf of Bread," *Advertising Age*, 10 October 1994, 20.

23. U.S. Bureau of the Census, *Statistical Abstract of the United States 1995* (Washington, D.C.: U.S. Government Printing Office, 1995), 451, 777, 780; David P. Schulz, "Top 100 Retailers," *Stores*, July 1995, 16–22, 24–27, 32–33; Berman and Evans, *Retail Management*, 5–7; Management Horizons, "The Top 100 Retailers Worldwide: Third Annual Survey," *Retail World* (Columbus, Ohio: Management Horizons, n.d.), 1.

24. Management Horizons, "The Top 100 Retailers Worldwide," 1–3; "Ou Est Le Kmart?" *American Demographics*, September 1994, 17, 20.

25. Taylor and Archer, *Up Against the Wal-Marts*, 190–191.

26. Management Horizons, "The Top 100 Retailers Worldwide," 5.

27. Susan Greco, "Selling the Superstores," *Inc.*, July 1995, 54–56, 58–61.

28. Mary Kuntz, "These Ads Have Windows and Walls," *Business Week*, 27 February 1995, 74.

29. Heather Page, "Something's Brewing," *Entrepreneur*, March 1995, 198.

30. Ylonda Gault, "Lerner NY Looking for Un-Limited Recovery," *Crain's New York Business*, 7 August 1995, 3, 37.

31. Berman and Evans, *Retail Management*, 42.

32. Kate Fitzgerald, "Competitors Swarm Powerful Toys 'R' Us," *Advertising Age*, 27 February 1995, 4; Rappaport, "Retailers Go Global," 102–104, 106, 108.

33. Julie Baker, Michael Levy, and Dhruv Grewal, "An Experimental Approach to Making Retail Store Environmental Decisions," *Journal of Retailing*, 68, no. 4 (Winter 1992): 445–460; James C. McElroy, Paula C. Morrow, and Sevo Eroglu, "The Atmospherics of Personal Selling," *Journal of Personal Selling and Sales Management* 10, no. 4 (Fall 1990): 31–41; "Scents and Profitability," *Wall Street Journal*, 22 February 1996, A1.

34. Meg Whittemore, "Survival Tactics for Retailers," *Nation's Business*, June 1993, 20–22, 24, 26–27; "Scents and Profitability," A1.

35. Mitchell Pacelle, "Many People Refuse to Check In if a Hotel Has Odors in the Lobby," *Wall Street Journal*, 28 July 1992, B1.

36. Williamson, "Net Helps Find Room at the Inn," 18.

37. Zina Moukheiber, "Squeezing the Tomatoes," *Forbes*, 13 February 1995, 55; Emily DeNitto, "Hypermarkets Seem to Be Big Flop in U.S.," *Advertising Age*, 4 October 1993, 20.

38. Leah Rickard, "Supercenters Entice Shoppers," *Advertising Age*, 20 March 1995, 1, 10; Moukheiber, "Squeezing the Tomatoes," 55; DeNitto, "Hypermarkets Seem to Be Big Flop in U.S.," 20.

39. Schulz, "Top 100 Retailers," 16–22, 24–27, 32–33.

40. Betsy Pisik, "Selling Bio-Friendly Products Is Good for Fresh Fields' Health," *Washington Times*, 1 March 1994, B7, B9; Fresh Fields is now owned by Whole Foods Market, see Candy Sagon, "Store Wars," *Washington Post*, 31 January 1996, E1, E10.

41. Ylonda Gault, "Pride Powers Retailers," *Crain's New York Business*, 31 July 1995, 3, 20.

42. John Schmeltzer, "Signing On in Chicago," *Chicago Tribune*, 7 December 1994, sec. 3, 1; Howard Rudnitsky, "Category Killer?" *Forbes*, 11 March 1996, 52–54.

43. Suzanne Slesin, "Why Shops' Names Say 'Just': Because," *New York Times*, 16 January 1992, C10.

44. Kate Fitzgerald, "Retailers Prescribe Pharmacies," *Advertising Age*, 15 March 1993, 3, 51; Steven Pratt, "Big Merchandisers Eat More of Food Dollar," *Chicago Tribune*, 10 March 1994, sec. 7, 4, zone C.

45. Carol Steinberg, "Break All the Rules," *Success*, October 1995, 83–85.

46. Martha M. Hamilton, "Computers on the Menu," *Washington Post Washington Business*, 18 December 1995, 5.

47. Christina Duff, "Single-Price Stores' Formula for Success: Cheap Merchandise and a Lot of Clutter," *Wall Street Journal*, 30 June 1992, B1, B2; Edith Terry, "Japan: Where the Prices Are Insane," *Fortune*, 31 October 1994, 21.

48. Margaret Webb Pressler, "The Not-So-Far-Out Outlets," *Washington Post Washington Business*, 6 March 1995, 1, 12–13.

49. Walter K. Levy, "Beware, the Pricing Genie Is Out of the Bottle," *Arthur Andersen Retailing Issues Letter*, November 1994, 1–3.

50. Kate Fitzgerald, "All Roads Lead to . . ." *Advertising Age*, 1 February 1993, S-1; Whittemore, "Survival Tactics for Retailers," 20–22, 24, 26–27; Dale D. Buss, "The Little Guys Strike Back," *Nation's Business*, July 1996, 18–24.

51. Tony Kennedy and Randy Furst, "Mammoth Mall Shows Promise with Surprisingly Solid First Year," *Washington Times*, 14 August 1993, C5, C12; Chad Rubel, "Three Malls Turn to Tourists—and Thrive," *Marketing News*, 6 May 1996, 5.

52. Susan Reda, "Do Power Centers Make Sense?" *Stores*, May 1995, 20–22, 26; Margaret Webb Pressler, "And the Mall Comes

Tumbling Down," *Washington Post*, 9 November 1994, B1, B3; Kelly Shermach, "Niche Malls," *Marketing News*, 26 February 1996, 1–2.

53. Berman and Evans, *Retail Management*, 267–268.

54. "At Deadline: Saks Taps C&W," *Crain's New York Business*, 3 July 1995, 55; Richard J. Maturi, "Site-Seers," *Entrepreneur*, January 1994, 282.

55. Richard Brookes, "Retailing Fresh Produce: Recent Lessons from the United Kingdom," *Stores*, July 1995, RR1–RR4.

56. Pam Weisz, "Body Shop, in Lieu of Ads, Hits the Road," *Brandweek*, 24 April 1995, 42.

57. Murray Raphel and Neil Raphel, *Up the Loyalty Ladder* (New York: HarperBusiness, 1995), 83–88.

58. Ingrid Abramovitch, "Operation: Oops!" *Success*, June 1994, 34–35.

59. Adapted from "In South Africa, Edgar's Department Stores Buck Recession with 'Relationships Retailing' Innovations," *MaxiMarketing Insights*, 11 September 1995, 1, 12.

60. "Ringing Up the Web," *Advertising Age,* 8 January 1996, 22; Rob Jackson, "Angling DMer Casts a Long Line," *Direct*, January 1996, 62–63.

61. Ruth N. Bolton and James H. Drew, "A Multistage Model of Customers' Assessments of Service Quality and Value," *Journal of Consumer Research*, March 1991, 375–384; Emil E. Becker, "Service Quality Requires Strategy *and* Tactics," *Marketing News*, 29 January 1996, 4, 5.

62. Carl Quintanilla, "Come and Get It! Drive-Throughs Upgrade Services," *Wall Street Journal*, 5 May 1994, B1, B7.

63. "Post Office Tries Retail Image to Keep Its Customers Happy," *The News-Times* (Danbury, Conn.), 21 February 1995, C-8.

64. Ruth N. Bolton and James H. Drew, "A Longitudinal Analysis of the Impact of Service Changes on Customer Attitudes," *Journal of Marketing*, January 1991, 1–9; "Service Survey," *USA Today*, 23 February 1995, 1B.

65. Jeffery D. Zbar, "Mobil Returns Service to Service Stations," *Advertising Age*, 31 July 1995, 23.

66. Ellen Ryan, "Mystery Shopper," *Washington Post*, 23 January 1995, B5; Leslie Brokaw, "The Mystery-Shopper Question-

naire," *Inc.*, June 1991, 94–95, 97; Paula Kephart, "The Spy in Aisle 3," *Marketing Tools*, May 1996, 16–19.

67. Stratford Sherman, "Will the Information Superhighway Be the Death of Retailing?" *Fortune*, 18 April 1994, 98–101, 105–106, 110; Michael H. Martin, "What's Online?" *Fortune*, 5 February 1996, 127.

68. Personal communication, Direct Marketing Association April 1995; Charles Waltner, "Interactive Catalogs a Tough Sell," *Advertising Age*, 6 March 1995, 19; Janean Chun, "Going the Distance," *Entrepreneur*, February 1996, 114–120.

69. Timothy L. O'Brien, "Vending Scams Are on the Rise, Officials Warn," *Wall Street Journal*, 1 July 1994, B1, B2; Leah Singer, "Push-Button Profits," *Success*, October 1993, 18; Mary Jordan, "On a Vendor Bender," *Washington Post*, 20 March 1996, A21, A24.

70. Jeffrey A. Trachtenberg, "Interactive Kiosks May Be High-Tech, But They Underwhelm U.S. Consumers," *Wall Street Journal*, 14 March 1994, B1, B8; Roberta Maynard, "New Directions in Marketing," *Nation's Business*, July 1995, 25–26; Cyndee Miller, "Kiosk Targets Those Techno-Savvy Students," *Marketing News*, 23 October 1995, 2.

71. Mark Robichaux, "TV Shopping Losing Its Shine for Retailers," *Wall Street Journal*, 22 November 1994, B1, B4; Debra Aho Williamson, "Want Two-Way TV? Head North," *Advertising Age,* 13 February 1995, 17, 20.

72. Joan E. Rigdon, "Blame Retailers for Web's Slow Start as a Mall," *Wall Street Journal*, 16 August 1995, B1, B5; Kim M. Boyne, "Is Your Site a Success?" *Marketing Tools*, March–April 1996, 68–72.

73. Frank Maritato, "Have Baseline, Will Analyze," *Marketing News*, 23 September 1996, 24–25.

74. "Category Management: Management for the '90s," *Marketing News*, 14 September 1992, 12–13; Hume and Bayor, "Category Management Concept Gains Momentum," 26.

75. Karen Lowry Miller, "Listening to Shoppers' Voices," *Business Week Reinventing America 1992*, 69; Southland Corporation, 1995 Annual Report.

76. Berman and Evans, *Retail Management*, 135–136; "I Can Get It for You Retail," *Business Week*, 18 September 1995, 84–85;

Louise Lee, "Upward Mobility," *Wall Street Journal*, 7 February 1996, A1, A8.

77. Leah Rickard, "Woolworth Walking Down a New Path," *Advertising Age*, 15 May 1995, 4.

78. Christina Duff, "Brighter Lights, Fewer Bargains: Outlets Go Upscale," *Wall Street Journal*, 11 April 1994, B1; Kathleen Barnes, "Wal-Mart Goes Gourmet with Harry's," *Advertising Age*, 13 March 1995, 10; Laura Loro, "Home-Shopping Tests Spread," *Advertising Age*, 21 November 1994, 22; Ellen Neuborne, "Wal-Mart Division Tests Catalog Business," *USA Today*, 7 December 1994, 2B; Lee, "Upward Mobility," A1, A8.

79. Berman and Evans, *Retail Management*, 137–141.

80. Rickard, "Woolworth Walking Down a New Path," 4.

81. Randy Myers, "Temporary Tenants," *Nation's Business*, August 1995, 39–40.

82. Adapted from Mary Peterson Kauffold, "Taking Care of Business: Von Maur, the Chicago Retail Community's New Kid on the Block, Is in Love with Its Customers," *Chicago Tribune*, 5 March 1995, 6.

CHAPTER **16**

1. Scott McCartney, "Dell Computer to Outsource All Shipping," *Wall Street Journal*, 15 February 1995, B6; Peter Burrows, "The Computer Is in the Mail (Really)," *Business Week*, 23 January 1995, 76–77.

2. Ira Sager, "The Man Who's Rebooting IBM's PC Business," *Business Week*, 24 July 1995, 68–70, 72.

3. John Conley, "The Shakeout in Global Logistics," *International Business*, December 1995–January 1996, 50–57.

4. Douglas M. Lambert and James R. Stock, *Strategic Logistics Management*, 3rd ed. (Homewood, Ill.: Irwin, 1993), 4–11; Lisa H. Harrington, "Logistics for Profit," advertisement in *Fortune*, 1 April 1996, 137–145.

5. Mark Henricks, "Satisfaction Guaranteed," *Entrepreneur*, March 1993, 48, 50–51.

6. Douglas M. Lambert and Robert L. Cook, "Integrating Marketing and Logistics for Increased Profit," *Business*, July–September 1990, 22–29; James A. Narus and James C. Anderson, "Rethinking Distribution: Adaptive Channels," *Harvard Business Review*, July–August 1996, 112–120.

7. Marita van Oldenborgh, "Power Logistics," *International Business*, October 1994, 32–34; "Partnerships Are Essential for Seamless Transporation," advertisement in *International Business*, April 1995.

8. Lambert and Stock, *Strategic Logistics Management*, 4; Ronald Henkoff, "Delivering the Goods," *Fortune*, 28 November 1994, 64–66, 70, 74, 76, 78; Dan McGraw, "Compaq's Flexible Factories Go with the Flow," *U.S. News & World Report*, 8 July 1996, 46.

9. Henkoff, "Delivering the Goods," 64–66, 70, 74, 76, 78; Gregory L. Miles, "Exporters' New Bully Stick," *International Business*, December 1993, 46, 48–49.

10. Lambert and Stock, *Strategic Logistics Management*, 8–9.

11. Lambert and Stock, *Strategic Logistics Management*, 9; Holly M. Werner, "Enesco Corporation," *Incentive*, December 1995, 30–31.

12. Sager, "The Man Who's Rebooting IBM's PC Business," 68–70, 72.

13. Richard Normann and Rafael Ramirez, "From Value Chain to Value Constellation: Designing Interactive Strategy," *Harvard Business Review*, July–August 1993, 65–77; Craig H. Wood, Allen Kaufman, and Michael Merenda, "How Hadco Became a Problem-Solving Supplier," *Sloan Management Review*, Winter 1996, 77–88.

14. Brian S. Akre, "Pizzerias and FedEx Find New Uses for Caller I.D.," *The News-Times* (Danbury, Conn.), 5 February 1995, D1, D2.

15. Tom Richman, "Logistics Management: How 20 Best-Practice Companies Do It," *Harvard Business Review*, September–October 1995, 11–12.

16. Miles, "Exporters' New Bully Stick," 46, 48–49.

17. Laurie M. Grossman, "Truck Cabs Turn into Mobile Offices as Drivers Take On White-Collar Tasks," *Wall Street Journal*, 3 August 1993, B1, B5.

18. Craig M. Gustin, Patricia J. Daugherty, and Theodore P. Stank, "The Effects of Information Availability on Logistics Integration," *Journal of Business Logistics* 16, no. 1 (1995): 1–21.

19. Jeffrey F. Rayport and John J. Sviokla, "Exploiting the Virtual Value Chain," *Harvard Business Review*, November–December 1995, 75–85.

20. Robert G. House, "The Logistical Advantage," *North American International Business*, January 1991, 56.

21. Sam Walton with John Huey, *Sam Walton: Made in America* (New York: Doubleday, 1992); Patricia Sellers, "Can Wal-Mart Get Back the Magic?" *Fortune*, 29 April 1996, 130–136.

22. John Conley, "The Shakeout in Global Logistics", 50–57.

23. Nathaniel C. Nash, "Coke's Great Romanian Adventure," *New York Times*, 26 February 1995, sec. 3, 1, 10.

24. Martin Christopher, Richard Lancioni, and John Gattorna, "Managing International Customer Service," *International Marketing Digest* (Oxford, U.K.: Heinemann Professional Publishing, 1990), 151–157.

25. Daniel I. Innis and Bernard J. La Londe, "Customer Service: The Key to Customer Satisfaction, Customer Loyalty, and Market Share," *Journal of Business Logistics*, 15, no. 1 (1994): 1–27.

26. George Harrar, "Levi's: Cool Brand, Lousy Distribution, IT to the Rescue," *Forbes ASAP*, 5 December 1994, 140, 142.

27. Mary Collins Holcomb, "Customer Service Measurement: A Methodology for Increasing Customer Value Through Utilization of the Taguchi Strategy," *Journal of Business Logistics* 15, no. 1 (1994): 29–51; David Field, "UPS, Federal Express Fight to Set Same-Day Standard for Deliveries," *Washington Times*, 13 July 1995, B6, B7.

28. "The Convert," *International Business*, March 1993, 64.

29. Lisa M. Ellram, Bernard L. LaLonde, and Mary Margaret Weber, "Retail Logistics," *International Journal of Physical Distribution and Materials Management*, 19, no. 12 (1989): 29–39; Lambert and Stock, *Strategic Logistics Management*, 117–118.

30. Patrick M. Byrne and William J. Markham, "How the Flow of Materials Can Lead to Customer Satisfaction: A Study Points the Way," *National Productivity Review*, Spring 1992, 169–180; Dorothy Elizabeth Brooks, "Putting It All Together," *Nation's Business*, September 1995, 16.

31. Henkoff, "Delivering the Goods," 64–66, 70, 74, 76, 78.

32. Gregory L. Miles, "Cheaper Sailing," *International Business*, February 1995, 29–30, 32.

33. Louis S. Richman, "Managing Through a Downturn," *Fortune*, 7 August 1995, 59–60, 64.

34. Michael D. Hutt and Thomas W. Speh, *Business Marketing Management*, 5th ed. (Fort Worth, Tex.: Dryden Press, 1995), 413.

35. Donald J. Bowersox and Patricia J. Daugherty, "Logistics Paradigms: The Impact of Information Technology," *Journal of Business Logistics* 16, no. 1 (1995): 65–79; Michael A. McGinnis and Jonathan W. Kohn, "A Factor Analytic Study of Logistics Strategy," *Journal of Business Logistics* 11, no. 2 (1990): 41–63.

36. Lisa Coleman, "Overnight Isn't Fast Enough," *Brandweek*, 31 July 1995, 26–27.

37. James Johnston, "EDI Implementation at PPG Industries," *Journal of Systems Management* 43, no. 2 (February 1992): 32–34.

38. Barry Berman and Joel R. Evans, *Retail Management*, 6th ed. (Englewood Cliffs, N.J.: Prentice-Hall, 1995), 404–405; Judann Pollack, "The Food Chain," *Advertising Age*, 6 May 1996, 28–30.

39. Lambeth and Stock, *Strategic Logistics Management*, 45.

40. "Air and Adaptec's Competitive Strategy," *International Business*, September 1993, 44.

41. Adapted from Joseph B. Fuller, James O'Conor, and Richard Rawlinson, "Tailored Logistics: The Next Advantage," *Harvard Business Review*, May–June 1993, 87–98.

42. van Oldenborgh, "Power Logistics," 32, 34; Gregory L. Miles, "Breaking Down Turf Barriers," *International Business*, June 1995, 25–26.

43. Mark Henricks, "Special Delivery," *Entrepreneur*, November 1993, 43–45.

44. Lambert and Stock, *Strategic Logistics Management*, 169; Gregory L. Miles, "Railroads Redux?" *International Business*, May 1995, 24–27; Gregory Spears, "Planes and Trains Look Great—at Last," *Kiplinger's Personal Finance Magazine*, March 1996, 87–90.

45. Gregory Spears, "Planes and Trains Look Great at Last," *Kiplinger's Personal Finance Magazine*, March 1996, 87–90.

46. Lambert and Stock, *Strategic Logistics Management*, 166–169; John Conley, "Keep on Truckin'," *International Business*, February 1996, 26–30.

47. Julie Candler, "Getting It There in a Hurry," *Nation's Business*, September 1993, 60–61.

48. Carl Quintanilla, "Passenger Carriers Are Rushing to Ride Air-Cargo Boom," *Wall Street Journal*, 2 June 1995, B3; Richard C. Morais, "They Ship Horses, Don't They?" *Forbes*, 7 November 1994, 45–46; John Conley, "Frequent Fliers," *International Business*, April 1996, 22–28.

49. John Morris, "High Seas Warehouses," *International Business*, June 1993, 34.

50. Mark Magnier, "Singapore Battles for Technological Edge," *Journal of Commerce*, 11 July 1994, 3B; "Growth Prospects for North American Ports," *International Business*, March 1994, 141–147; John Davies, "Skipping the Waves," *International Business*, May 1996, 26–28.

51. Lambert and Stock, *Strategic Logistics Management*, 174.

52. Gregory L. Miles, "Intermodal's Next Conquest," *International Business*, April 1995, 24–26; Julie Candler, "Road and Rail Connections," *Nation's Business*, July 1994, 73–74; John Conley, "Coming of Age," *International Business*, March 1996, 36–42.

53. "A Port-Shopper's Secret," *International Business*, March 1994, p. 76.

54. Jon Jacobs, "Fast Forwarding," *International Business*, February 1993, 29–30, 32.

55. James R. Stock, "Managing Computer, Communication and Information Technology Strategically: Opportunities and Challenges for Warehousing," *Logistics and Transportation Review* 26, no. 2, 133–148; "The Wireless Warehouse," Symbol Spectrum One advertisement in *Forbes*, 16 August 1993, 58.

56. Tompkins Associates, *Crossdocking in the '90s* (Raleigh, N.C.: Tompkins Associates, n.d.), 1–2; Thomas J. Andel, "The Pluses and Minuses of 'Value-Added,'" *Transportation & Distribution*, September 1991, 55–62; Dennis Templar, "A Warehous Without Inventory," *APICS*, July 1995, 64.

57. Lambert and Stock, *Strategic Logistics Management*, 288–298.

58. Robert A. Hamilton, "Sweet, Cold Frenzy in the Hood," *New York Times*, 23 July 1995, sec. 13, 1, 4.

59. Meg Whittemore, "When Not to Go with Your Gut," *Nation's Business*, December 1993, 41–42.

60. Tim W. Ferguson, "Shrink Inventory? Lands' End Likes It Loose," *Wall Street Journal*, 18 January 1994, A17.

61. John M. Ivancevich, Peter Lorenzi, and Steven J. Skinner, with Philip B. Crosby, *Management: Quality and Competitiveness* (Homewood, Ill.: Irwin, 1994), 478; Marita von Oldenborgh, "Getting Up to Speed," *International Business*, July 1995, 25–29.

62. Hutt and Speh, *Business Marketing Management*, 428.

63. Adapted from Joel Millman, "Pipeliners," *Forbes*, 12 September 1994, 218, 220.

64. Mitch Betts, "Manage My Inventory Or Else!" *Computerworld*, 31 January 1994, 93–95; Jonathan Friedland, "VW Puts Suppliers on Production Line," *Wall Street Journal*, 15 February 1996, A11.

65. Betts, "Manage My Inventory Or Else!" 93–95.

66. Benson P. Shapiro, V. Kasturi Rangan, and John J. Sviokla, "Staple Yourself to an Order," *Harvard Business Review*, July–August 1992, 113–122.

67. Peter Sibbald, "Manufacturing for Reuse," *Fortune*, 6 February 1995, 102–104, 108, 110, 112; Justin Martin, "Old Soles Live," *Fortune*, 6 September 1993, 14; E. J. Muller, "The Greening of Logistics," *Distribution*, January 1991, 26ff.

68. Glenn Collins, "A Feisty Brand's Newest Frontier: Premium Colas," *New York Times*, 28 October 1995, 19; Mark Gleason, "Beverages," *Advertising Age*, 16 October 1995, S22; "Ferolito, Vultaggio & Sons," Hoover's Company Profile Database, accessed online, 1996.

MARKETING ON THE NET FOR PART 6

1. David Gates, "Cyberspace Superstore," *Business Week*, 10 June 1996, 86; G. Bruce Knecht, "Reading the Market: How Wall Street Whiz Found a Niche Selling Books on the Internet," *Wall Street Journal*, 16 May 1996, A1, A8; "John Doerr," *Adweek*, 8 July 1996, IQ 16–21.

2. Adapted from "'A Weekend in Florence' Shows How a Specialty Merchant in Any Country Can Go Global," *MaxiMarketing Insights*, June 1996, 10–11.

CHAPTER 17

1. Don E. Schultz, "IMC Is a Great Idea, but Does It Have 'Legs'?" *Marketing News*, 8

May 1995, 12; Claudia Montague, "This Is Not a Fad," *Marketing Tools*, November–December 1995, 68–70.

2. Don E. Schultz, "Integration Helps You Plan Communications from Outside-In," *Marketing News*, 15 March 1993, 12.

3. Adapted from Tom Duncan, "The Concept and Process of Integrated Marketing Communication," *Integrated Marketing Communications Research Journal*, Spring 1995, 3–10.

4. Dave Savona, "Footloose in Foreign Markets," *International Business*, August 1995, 39–40, 42, 44–45.

5. Thomas R. Duncan and Stephen E. Everett, "Client Perceptions of Integrated Marketing Communications," *Journal of Advertising Research*, May–June 1993, 30–39; Don E. Schultz, "IMC Has Become a Global Concept," *Marketing News*, 26 February 1996, 6.

6. Bradley Johnson, "Global Thinking Paces Computer Biz," *Advertising Age*, 8 March 1995, 10.

7. Don E. Schultz, "IMC Is All Right in Seattle," *Marketing News*, 23 October 1995, 43; Don E. Schultz, Stanley I. Tannenbaum, and Robert F. Lauterborn, *The New Marketing Paradigm: Integrated Marketing Communications* (Lincolnwood, Ill.: NTC Publishing, 1994), 58.

8. Schultz, Tannenbaum, and Lauterborn, *The New Marketing Paradigm*, 59; Tom Duncan, "Integrated Marketing? It's Synergy," *Advertising Age*, 8 March 1993, 22; Janet Smith, "Integrated Marketing," *Marketing Tools*, November–December 1995, 63–67.

9. Schultz, Tannenbaum, and Lauterborn, *The New Marketing Paradigm*, 59; Don E. Schultz, "Be Careful Picking Data Base for IMC Efforts," *Marketing News*, 11 March 1996, 14–15.

10. Audrey Ward, "Interactive Marketing: An Integrated Approach," *Integrated Marketing Communications Research Journal*, Spring 1995, 44–49; Ernan Roman, "The Under Achieving Database," *Marketing Tools*, June 1996, 48–55.

11. Ward, "Interactive Marketing," 44–49.

12. Schultz, "Integration Helps You Plan Communications from Outside-In," 12.

13. Schultz, "Integration Helps You Plan Communications from Outside-In," 12; "Distributors vs. Marketers: An IMC Approach," *Focused Communications News* (From Price/McNabb, 1996).

14. Don E. Schultz, "The Many Views of Integrated Marketing Communications," in *Marketing Encyclopedia*, edited by Jeffrey Heilbrunn (Lincolnwood, Ill.: NTC Publishing, 1995), 190–194.

15. Don E. Schultz, "We Simply Can't Afford to Go Back to Mass Marketing," *Marketing News*, 15 February 1993, 20; Stanley Marcus and Carole Sweet, "Narrowcasting vs. Broadcasting," *Bottom Line/Business*, 15 February 1996, 9–10.

16. Leah Rickard, "Mike Mondello: Earth's Best," *Advertising Age*, 26 June 1995, S-27; "Baby-Feeder Becomes Giant-Killer," *Maxi-Marketing Insights*, 11 September 1995, 6–8.

17. Dottie Enrico, "Ford Cranks Up $120 Million Taurus Promotion," *USA Today*, 28 July, 1995, 1B; Taurus ad in *Newsweek*, 9 October 1995, 15; Robert L. Dilenschneider, "Marketing Communications in the Post-Advertising Era," *Public Relations Review* 17, no. 3 (Fall 1991): 227–236.

18. Jonathan Berry, "Database Marketing," *Business Week*, 5 September 1994, 56–62.

19. Timm Crull, "Nestlé to Agencies: 'Shake Mindset,'" *Advertising Age*, 3 May 1993, 26; Dagmar Mussey and Laurel Wentz, "Integration Emphasis in Germany," *Ad Age International*, May 1996, I-28.

20. Maria Mallory, "Behemoth on a Tear," *Business Week*, 3 October 1994, 54–55.

21. Maggie Jackson, "Singer Grows Veggie Empire," *The News-Times* (Danbury, Conn.), 30 October 1995, C-8.

22. Kristen Traeger, "Mission Marketing," *Integrated Marketing Communications Research Journal*, Spring 1995, 35–38; Genice Jacobs, Mary Ann Stutts, and Larry T. Patterson, "The Effects of Cause-Related Marketing Appeals on Consumer Purchase and Donation Behavior," *Journal of Promotion Management* 2, no. 3/4 (1994): 105–119; V. Kasturi Rangan, Sohel Karim, and Sheryl K. Sandberg, "Doing Better at Doing Good," *Harvard Business Review*, May–June 1996, 42–54.

23. "Cause-Related Marketing: What Works," *Inc.*, August 1994, 102; Yumiko Ono, "Advertisers Try 'Doing Good' to Help Make Sales Do Better," *Wall Street Journal*, 2 September 1994, B8; "Numbers for the '90's," *Advertising Age*, 23 October 1995, 3; Joanne Sheff and Philip Kotler, "How the Arts Can Prosper Through Strategic Collaborations," *Harvard Business Review*, January–February 1996, 52–62.

24. Damon Darlin, "Junior Mints, I'm Gonna Make You a Star," *Forbes*, 6 November 1995, 90, 92–94; Beng Soo Ong and David Meri, "Should Product Placement in Movies Be Banned?" *Journal of Promotion Management* 2, no. 3/4 (1994): 159–174; Kyle Pope, "Product Placements Creep into Video Games," *Wall Street Journal*, 5 December 1994, B1, B9.

25. Pope, "Product Placements Creep into Video Games," B1, B9; Ong and Meri, "Should Product Placement in Movies Be Banned?" 159–174; Fara Warner, "Why It's Getting Harder to Tell the Shows from the Ads," *Wall Street Journal*, 15 June 1995, B1, B11; David Leonhardt, Peter Burrows, and Bill Vlasic, "Cue the Soda Can," *Business Week*, 24 June 1996, 64–66.

26. Richard L. Irwin, Makis K. Assimakopoulos, and William A. Sutton, "A Model for Screening Sport Sponsorship Opportunities," *Journal of Promotion Management*, 2, no. 3/4 (1994): 53–69; "'AAI' Picks Next Major Marketers," *Advertising Age*, 18 September 1995, I-33, I-43; Tim Kelly, "Money Is Not Enough. Become Part of the Event." *Brandweek*, 23 October 1995, 17.

27. Regis McKenna, *Relationship Marketing* (Reading, Mass.: Addison–Wesley, 1991), 89–92.

28. Wirt M. Cook, "Growing a Business," *Entrepreneur*, July 1992, 50–53; Seanna Browder, "Zero to $50 Million: Now That's Magic," *Business Week*, 2 October 1995, ENT10, ENT12.

29. Jill Griffin, *Customer Loyalty* (New York: Lexington Books, 1995), 159–180; Julie Tilsner, "Using Chi—and the Net—to Rebuild," *Business Week*, 2 October 1995, ENT13.

30. David A. Aaker, "The Value of Brand Equity," *Journal of Business Strategy*, July–August 1992, 27–32; Chip Walker, "How Strong Is Your Brand?" *Marketing Tools*, January–February 1995, 46–53; Larry Light, "Brand Loyalty Marketing Key to Enduring Growth," *Advertising Age*, 3 October 1994, 20; Bradley Johnson, "Compaq's Brand Ads Go Global," *Advertising Age*, 24 June 1996, 1, 48.

31. Kathy Haley, "Expect Wider Brand-Name Use of Half–Hours," infomercials advertising supplement to *Advertising Age*, 6 March 1995, A2.

32. Edith Updike, "Roadblocks, Roadblocks Everywhere," *Business Week*, 19 June 1995, 58.

33. Faye Rice, "A Cure for What Ails Advertising?" *Fortune*, 16 December 1991, 119–120, 122; Mark Gleason, "Men Are Newest Target for 'Milk Mustache' Ads," *Advertising Age*, 1 July 1996, 10.

34. Steve Gelsi, "Zerex Joins Valvoline Youth Push," *Brandweek*, 11 September 1995, 6.

35. William Boulding, Eunkyu Lee, and Richard Staelin, "Mastering the Mix: Do Advertising, Promotion, and Sales Force Activities Lead to Differentiation?" *Journal of Marketing Research*, May 1994, 159–172; Kim Cleland, "Skytel," *Advertising Age*, 24 June 1996, S-16.

36. Len Egol, "Home Sweet Home Page," *Direct*, July 1995, 49–50, 52–53.

37. Schultz, Tannenbaum, and Lauterborn, *Integrated Marketing Communications*, 180–196.

38. "Non–English Language: Kook-Aid," insert in *Brandweek*, 12 June 1995, EFFIES 25.

39. Adapted from Nancy Arnott, "Money," *Sales & Marketing Management*, February 1995, 64–67, 69.

40. NKH&W Integrated Marketing Communications, *A Guide to Creating Integrated Marketing Communications Plans* (Kansas City, Mo.: NKH&W, 1995), 1–4.

41. Glen L. Urban and John R. Hauser, *Design and Marketing of New Products*, 2nd ed. (Englewood Cliffs, N.J.: Prentice Hall, 1993), 565–569.

42. NKH&W, *A Guide to Creating Integrated Marketing Communications Plans*, 15.

43. James G. Kimball, "DBIS Revamps Sales," *Business Marketing*, December 1994, 3, 32.

44. Adapted from Schultz, Tannenbaum, and Lauterborn, *The New Marketing Paradigm*, 114–134.

45. Kevin J. Clancy and Robert S. Shulman, *Marketing Myths That Are Killing Business* (New York: McGraw-Hill, 1993), 142.

46. Don E. Schultz, "How to Generate an Unlimited ICM Budget," *Marketing News*, 5 June 1995, 7.

47. Jamie Goldman, "Mattress Seller Wakes Up Market with Video Tool," *Advertising Age*, 22 May 1995, S-2.

48. Tony Seideman, "Making Net Export Profits," *International Business*, August 1995, 47–51.

49. Kathleen Day, "The Doctor Is Out; the Consumer Is In," *Washington Post*, 22 November 1995, E1, E3; Zocor ad in *Newsweek*, January 1996.

50. "Transportation: USAfrica Airways," insert in *Brandweek*, 12 June 1995, EFFIES 29.

51. Bert Rosenbloom, *Marketing Channels*, 5th ed. (Fort Worth, Tex.: Dryden, 1995), 404–406; Jack Neff, "Diaper Battle Puts EDLP on Injured List," *Advertising Age*, 14 August 1995, 3, 33.

52. Adapted from Jay Finegan, "In the Customer's Shoes," *Inc.*, May 1995, 44–46, 48, 51–53.

53. Janet Smith, "Integrated Marketing," *Marketing Tools*, November–December 1995, 63–67.

54. "Road Kill," *Advertising Age*, 10 April 1995, 20.

55. Scott Donaton, "Pathfinder Blazes a Trail to Ads," *Advertising Age*, 10 April 1995, 19.

56. Lexis F. Higgins, Toni Hilton, Kathryn Babcock, and Monte Smith, "Style and Tone in Marketing Communications," *Journal of Promotion Management* 2, no. 3/4 (1994): 37–51; Tom Duncan, "Is Your Marketing Communications Integrated?" *Advertising Age*, 24 January 1994, 26; Don E. Schultz, "Maybe We Should Be 'Customerizing,'" *Marketing News*, 17 June 1996, 4, 15.

57. Based on materials provided by Biltmore Estate and Price/McNabb. Published sources include Hugh Meenan, "Media Strategy: You're Invited . . ." *Inside Media*, 12 July 1995, 38; and Suzanne MacNeille, "Cheer Around the Country," *New York Times*, 3 December 1995, sec. 5, 1, 3, 18.

CHAPTER **18**

1. Brian Dumaine, "Pleasant Co.: How to Compete with a Champ," *Fortune*, 106; "Rejecting Barbie, Doll Maker Gains," *New York Times*, 1 September 1993, D1, D4; Mollie Neal, "Cataloger Gets Pleasant Results," *Direct Marketing*, May 1992, 33–36.

2. Robert J. Coen, "Insider's Report" (New York: McCann-Erickson, June 1995), 2.

3. "Apparel and Accessories: Timex Indiglo," insert in *Brandweek*, 12 June 1995, EFFIES 6.

4. "Corporate Reputation/Image/Identity: Nintendo," insert in *Brandweek*, 12 June 1995, EFFIES 18.

5. Frank R. Kardes and Gurumurthy Kalyanaram, "Order-of-Entry Effects on Consumer Memory and Judgment: An Information Integration Perspective," *Journal of Marketing Research*, August 1992, 343–357; Margo Lipschitz Sugarman, "Accent Software: Bob Rosenschein," *Advertising Age International*, 20 November 1995, I-12.

6. "Coalition for Reinforcement," letter to the editor by Roy J. Bostock and Harry Davis, *Advertising Age*, 17 May 1993, 24; Gerry Khermouch, "Kodak to Promote Occasion-ally," *Brandweek*, 27 February 1995, 14.

7. Judann Pollack, "Global 100 Overcomes Obstacles," *Business Marketing*, June 1995, 6; Gene Koprowski, "Theories of Negativity," *Brandweek*, 20 February 1995, 20–22.

8. "Government/Institutional: Mass. Tobacco Control," insert in *Brandweek*, 12 June 1995, EFFIES 21.

9. Dagmar Mussey, "Benetton, German Retailers Squabble," *Advertising Age*, 6 February 1995, 1, 46; Bruce Horovitz, "Benetton Takes Conventional Turn," *USA Today*, 13 March 1995, 1B.

10. Don E. Schultz, "Integration Helps You Plan Communications from Outside-In," *Marketing News*, 15 March 1993, 12; Stan Rapp and Thomas Collins, "The New Maxi Marketing," *Success*, April 1996, 39–46.

11. Kelly Shermach, "'New World Order' Will Change Life for Marketers," *Marketing News*, 21 November 1994, 9; Jim Carlton, "Think Big," *Wall Street Journal*, 17 June 1996, R27.

12. Chad Rubel, "Dr. Pepper–7 Up Join Pepsi, Coke in Soda Wars," *Marketing News*, 10 April 1995, 8.

13. Pamela Sebastian, "Business Bulletin," *Wall Street Journal*, 18 May 1995, A1.

14. Dexter Roberts, "Winding Up for the Big Pitch," *Business Week*, 23 October 1995, 52.

15. Peter Waldman, "Please Don't Show Your Lingerie in Iran, Even if It's for Sale," *Wall Street Journal*, 21 June 1995, A1, A14; Brian Toyne and Peter G. P. Walters, *Global Marketing Management*, 2nd ed. (Boston: Allyn & Bacon, 1993), 556.

16. Toyne and Walters, *Global Marketing Management*, 542–543.

17. Geoffrey Lee Martin, "West Unraveling Mysteries of Culture," *Advertising Age International*, 16 October 1995, I-15, I-16; Joan

Delaney, "Vive La Difference," *International Business*, May 1996, 42–43.

18. Robert L. Dilenschneider, "Marketing Communications in the Post-Advertising Era," *Public Relations Review* 17, no. 3 (Fall 1991): 227–236; Janet Smith, "Integrated Marketing," *Marketing Tools*, November–December 1995, 63–70.

19. Deborah Klosky, "Port Aventura: Lluis Rullán," *Advertising Age*, 20 November 1995, I-12.

20. "Late News: Blockbuster Video Picks Y&R for $140 Mil Account," *Advertising Age*, 15 January 1996, 1.

21. Diane Cyr, "X Man," *Direct*, December 1995, 1, 51–53.

22. Joshua Levine, "Makeovers on Madison Avenue," *Forbes*, 27 March 1995, 110–111.

23. "Consumer Electronics: Pioneer Electronics," insert in *Brandweek*, 12 June 1995, EFFIES 18; "Leisure Products: Casio," insert in *Brandweek*, 12 June 1995, EFFIES 23.

24. "Travel/Tourism/Destination: NY State Dept. of Econ. Dev.," insert in *Brandweek*, 12 June 1995, EFFIES 29.

25. Tim Triplett, "Researchers Probe Ad Effectiveness Globally," *Marketing News*, 29 August 1994, 6, 7; Thomas Robinson, "The Age of Accountability," *Marketing Tools*, June 1996, 4–8.

26. "Computer Hardware: Compaq," insert in *Brandweek*, 12 June 1995, EFFIES 14.

27. Denise Osburn and Dawn Kopecki, "A Way to Stretch Ad Dollars," *Nation's Business*, May 1994, 68; John Morris, "The New Basics of Advertising," *Office Advisor*, Spring 1993, 1, 6; Don Taylor and Jeanne Smalling Archer, *Up Against the Wal-Marts* (New York: AMACOM, 1994), 64–78.

28. Cyndee Miller, "Celebrities Hot Despite Scandals," *Marketing News*, 28 March 1994, 1, 2, 5.

29. Jennifer DeCourse, "Klein's Apology Wearing Thin," *Advertising Age*, 4 September 1995, 35; Bob Garfield, "Forum: Publicity Monster Turns on Klein," *Advertising Age*, 4 September 1995, 18; "Editorial: Calvin Crosses the Line," *Advertising Age*, 4 September 1995, 16.

30. Anthony Vagnoni, "Dweck Humors Clients with Unique Attitude," *Advertising Age*, 17 July 1995, 30–31.

31. James Caporimo, "Worldwide Advertising Has Benefits, but One Size Doesn't Always Fit All," *Brandweek*, 17 July 1995, 16;

Jacques R. Chevron, "Global Branding: Married to the World," *Advertising Age*, 15 May 1995, 23–24; Bradley Johnson, "For Computer Giants, It Really Is a Small World," *Advertising Age*, 14 November 1994, S–2; Theodore Levitt, *The Marketing Imagination* (new, expanded ed.) (New York: Free Press, 1986), 30–49; "Ad Age Best: Apparel," *Advertising Age*, 9 May 1994, 36; "Ad Age Best: Magazine," *Advertising Age*, 9 May 1994, 42.

32. George Belch and Michal Belch, *Introduction to Advertising and Promotion* (Burr Ridge, Ill.: Irwin, 1994), 276.

33. Jacqueline Gaulin, "Music Magazine Notes Rise in Pitches as Ads," *Washington Times*, 3 March 1995, B7, B12.

34. Raymond Serafin and Cleveland Horton, "Still No Substitute for Traditional Ads," *Advertising Age*, 28 March 1994, S24.

35. "From Gutenberg to Katzenberg," *Fortune*, 4 September 1995, 84–85; Junu Bryan Kim, "Living on the Edge," *Advertising Age*, 12 June 1995, S-2.

36. Stuart Elliott, "Super Bowl Campaigns Break Long Lasting Streak," *New York Times*, 31 January 1995, D1, D21; Sally Goll Beatty, "Super Bowl Ad Play: 'Hut, Hut, Value,'" *Wall Street Journal*, 16 January 1996, B6.

37. Jacqueline M. Graves, "The Fortune 500 Opt for Infomercials," *Fortune*, 6 March 1995, 20; Gene R. Laczniak and Patrick E. Murphy, *Ethical Marketing Decisions: The Higher Road* (Boston: Allyn & Bacon, 1993), 168–169; Peter Bieler and Suzanne Costas, "How to Create a $100 Million Craze," *Success*, July/August 1996, 59–66.

38. Gene Koprowski, "Plus la Même Chose," *Marketing Tools*, September–October 1994, 6, 8–10.

39. "Radio Formats," advertising supplement to *Brandweek*, 4 September 1995, 9, 13, 34, 38.

40. "Radio Formats," 9, 13, 34, 38.

41. "Total Measured U.S. Ad Spending by Category and Media," *Advertising Age*, 2 January 1995, 17; "Newspaper," *Advertising Age*, 9 May 1994, 42.

42. Stan Rapp and Thomas L. Collins, *The New MaxiMarketing* (New York: McGraw-Hill, 1996), 193–194.

43. Keith J. Kelly, "Magazine of the Year," *Advertising Age*, 6 March 1995, S1, S5; Alan Mirabella, "Forbes Finds 4,000 Reasons to Cheer," *Advertising Age*, 6 March 1995, S8.

44. Kevin J. Clancy and Robert S. Shulman, *The Marketing Revolution* (New York: HarperBusiness, 1991), 278–279; Edward L. Nash, *Database Marketing: The Ultimate Marketing Tool* (New York: McGraw-Hill, 1993), 4–8; Stanley Marcus and Carole Sweet, "Marketing 1996," *Bottom Line/Business*, 15 February 1996, 9–10.

45. Nash, *Database Marketing*, 210–211.

46. Robert Goldsborough, "Hong Kong Trams Keep Ads Rolling," *Advertising Age*, 8 May 1995, 36.

47. Debra Aho Williamson, "Digital Media Future Looks Rosy," *Advertising Age*, 7 August 1995, 13; Kim Cleland, "Infomercials Plugging into the Internet," *Advertising Age*, 3 June 1996, 18.

48. "Ad Age Names Awards Finalists," *Advertising Age*, 27 February 1995, 12–14; Kate Bertrand, "IBM Joins Crowded Online Sphere," *Business Marketing*, March 1996, 2, 4.

49. Phaedra Hise, "The Flameproof On-Line Marketing Pitch," *Inc.*, March 1995, 87–89.

50. Fara Warner, "Cheers! It's Happy Hour in Cyberspace," *Wall Street Journal*, 15 March 1995, B1, B5; Debra Aho Williamson, "Web Searching for a Yardstick," *Advertising Age*, 9 October 1995, 21–22; Charles Waltner, "Tracking Traffic Beyond the 'Net,'" *Advertising Age*, 9 October 1995, 22.

51. Lisa Z. Eccles, "P-O-P Scores with Marketers," advertising supplement to *Advertising Age*, 26 September 1994, P1, P2, P4.

52. Mary Kuntz and Joseph Weber, "The New Hucksterism," *Business Week*, 1 July 1996, 76–84.

53. Char Kosek, "Astra Sales Merge Emotion with Logic," *Business Marketing*, December 1995, 3, 5.

54. Leonard M. Lodish, Magid Abraham, Stuart Kalmenson, Jeanne Livelsberger, Beth Lubetkin, Bruce Richardson, and Mary Ellen Stevens, "How T.V. Advertising Works: A Meta–Analysis of 389 Real World Split Cable T.V. Advertising Experiments," *Journal of Marketing Research*, May 1995, 125–139; David M. Bender, Peter H. Farquhar, and Sanford C. Schulert, "Growing from the Top," *Marketing Management*, Winter–Spring 1996, 10–19.

55. "Travel/Tourism/Destination: NY State," insert in *Brandweek*, 12 June 1995, EFFIES 29.

56. "Computer Hardware: Compaq," insert in *Brandweek*, 12 June 1995, EFFIES 14.

57. "Financial Services/Not Cards, Reg. & Loc.: SIS," insert in *Brandweek*, 12 June 1995, EFFIES 21.

58. Lynn Jones, "This Is Getting Complicated," *Direct*, January 1996, 53–54.

59. Jonathan Berry, "Database Marketing," *Business Week*, 5 September 1994, 56–62; Garth R. Hallberg, "Intelligent Use of Databases Can Nurture Brand Loyalty," *Advertising Age International*, June 1996, I-16.

60. Don E. Schultz, "Some Comments on the Absolute Value of the Database," *Journal of Direct Marketing* 8, no. 4 (Autumn 1994): 4–5; Richard P. Derks, "Business Trends: The Competitive Advantages of Database Marketing," *Information Strategy*, Spring 1994, 5–11; Don E. Schultz, "Be Careful Picking Data Base for IMC Efforts," *Marketing News*, 11 March 1996, 14–15.

61. Richard J. Leighton and Alfred S. Regnery, *U.S. Direct Marketing Law* (Washington, D.C.: Libey Publishing, 1993), 85–87, 243–250; Nash, *Database Marketing*, 228–230.

62. Len Egol, "Advise and Consent," *Direct*, April 1995, 55–56, 60, 62–63; Laura Loro, "IBM Mends Marketing Using Database," *Business Marketing*, February 1996, 29.

63. Sam Bradley, "By the Numbers . . ." *Brandweek*, 9 October 1995, 38; George E. Bardenheier, Jr., "More to Database Brand Building Than Filling Up a Lot of Mail Boxes," *Brandweek*, 2 May 1994, 20–21.

64. Kevin McLaughlin, "Crazy Catalogs," *Entrepreneur*, February 1992, 75–81.

65. Jonah Gitlitz, "Direct Marketing Boosts B-to-B Selling," advertising supplement to *Advertising Age's Business Marketing*, August 1995, B2, B4; Lynn Jones, "World Vision Grows Weary of Mail," *Direct*, March 1995, 21.

66. Adapted from Phaedra Hise, "Hits That Rate Attention," *Inc.*, September 1995, 115.

CHAPTER **19**

1. Adapted from Bradley Johnson, "Windows 95 Opens with Omnimedia Blast," *Advertising Age,* 28 August 1995, 1, 32; "For Microsoft, Nothing Succeeds Like Excess," *Wall Street Journal*, 25 August 1995, B1, B3; Kathy Rebello, "Feel the Buzz," *Business Week*, 28 August 1995, 31.

2. Stan Rapp and Thomas L. Collins, *The New MaxiMarketing* (New York: McGraw-Hill, 1996), 170.

3. Terence A. Shimp, *Promotion Management and Marketing Communications*, 3rd ed. (Fort Worth, Tex.: Dryden Press, 1993), 442; Daniel McQuillen, "A Case for Incentives," *Incentive*, February 1996, 16–17.

4. Betsy Spethmann, "Money and Power," *Brandweek*, 15 March 1993, 21; Donnelley Marketing, *The 17th Annual Survey of Promotional Practices* (Oakbrook Terrace, Ill.: Donnelley Marketing, 1995), 29–31.

5. Julie Ralston, "Bob Lowe: Blueberry Morning," *Advertising Age*, 26 June 1995, S8.

6. Donnelley Marketing, *17th Annual Survey*, 30.

7. Richard K. Skews, "Bruce Friedricks: Myst," *Advertising Age*, 26 June 1995, S12.

8. "Irish Supermarket Chain Turns Its Club Members into Quality Control Inspectors," *MaxiMarketing Insights*, October 1995, 1–4.

9. Don Taylor and Jeanne Smalling Archer, *Up Against the Wal-Marts* (New York: AMACOM, 1994), 70.

10. Donnelley Marketing, *17th Annual Survey*, 30.

11. Gerry Khermouch, "Brand Builders: Sticht's Moat Operandi," *Brandweek*, 11 September 1995, 22, 24.

12. Andrew Leckey, "Some Firms Clip Coupons Out of Their Sales Strategy," *Washington Times*, 11 April 1996, B8.

13. Jeanne Whalen, "ECR Opens Promo Pandora's Box," *Advertising Age*, 21 March 1994, S10, S13; Judann Pollack, "The Food Chain," *Advertising Age*, 6 May 1996, 28, 30.

14. T.L. Stanley, "Poca-Coca-Motion," *Brandweek*, 13 March 1995, 1, 6.

15. William G. Nickels, James M. McHugh, and Susan M. McHugh, *Understanding Business*, 4th ed. (Chicago: Irwin, 1996), 323.

16. William A. Band, *Creating Value for Customers* (New York: John Wiley, 1991), 202.

17. Donnelley Marketing, *17th Annual Survey*, 29.

18. Carla Rappaport, "Retailers Go Global," *Fortune*, 20 February 1995, 102–104, 106, 108; Peter F. Drucker, "The Economy's Power Shift," *Wall Street Journal*, 24 September 1992, A16; George S. Day, *Market-Driven Strategy* (New York: Free Press, 1990), 235–237.

19. Shimp, *Promotion Management and Marketing Communications*, 445–446; Laura Bird, "Avoiding a 'Sale du Jour,'" *Wall Street Journal*, 29 May 1996, A1, A10.

20. Laura Mazur and Annik Hogg, *The Marketing Challenge* (Wokingham, U.K.: Addison-Wesley, 1993), 187.

21. T. L. Stanley, "BF Goodrich," *Brandweek*, 20 March 1995, 24, 26.

22. Betsy Spethmann, "Trade Promotion Redefined," *Brandweek*, 13 March 1995, 25–26, 28, 30, 32; Jack Neff, "P & G Extends Co-Branded Coupons," *Advertising Age*, 3 June 1996, 9.

23. Dae Ryun Chang, Minhi Hahn, and Ik-Tae Kim, "SPAD: A Contingency Framework for Integrating Sales Promotion and Advertising," *Journal of Promotion Management* 2, no. 2 (1994): 45–57; Cyndee Miller, "Consumer Marketers Spend Most of Their Money on Communications," *Marketing News*, 11 March 1996, 1, 5.

24. Rapp and Collins, *The New MaxiMarketing*, 170–171; Don E. Schultz, Stanley I. Tannenbaum, and Robert F. Lauterborn, *The New Marketing Paradigm: Integrated Marketing Communications* (Lincolnwood, Ill.: NTC Publishing, 1993), 58; John L. Stanton, "How Top Execs Kill Brands," *Marketing News*, 25 September 1995, 4.

25. Darlene Superville, "Coupons: The Declining Road to Redemption," *Washington Times*, 12 March 1995, A12; Jane Perrin, "Secrets of Much More Effective Couponing," *Boardroom Reports*, 15 January 1994, 5–7; "Targeted Couponing Slows Redemption Slide," *Marketing News*, 12 February 1996, 11.

26. Janine S. Pouliot, "Coupons as Compasses," *Nation's Business*, October 1995, 37R.

27. Betsy Spethmann, "Breakthrough Program Tracks Coupon Users," *Brandweek*, 26 September 1994, 1, 6; Pouliot, "Coupons as Compasses," 37R.

28. Lisa Krakowka, "Savings in Cyberspace," *Marketing Tools*, October 1995, 31–33; Adrienne Ward Fawcett, "Trading Scissors for Modems," *Advertising Age*, 5 June 1995, 14, 19; Kate Fitzgerald, "Paper Coupons Losing Lure in High-Tech Store," *Advertising Age,* 21 March 1994, S14.

29. Leslie Ryan, "Sales Promotion: Made in America," *Brandweek*, 31 July 1995, 28.

30. Gabriella Stern, "With Sampling, There Is Too a Free Lunch," *Wall Street Journal*, 11 March 1994, B1, B6.

31. Kate Fitzgerald, "Just Playing Along," *Advertising Age*, 17 July 1995, 24.

32. Donnelley Marketing, *17th Annual Survey*, 41; Rick Tetzelli, "The Internet and Your Business," *Fortune*, 7 March 1994, 86–88, 92, 94, 96.

33. Patricia J. Daugherty, "Frequency Marketing Programs: A Clarification with Strategic Implications," *Journal of Promotion Management* 2, no. 1 (1993), 5–26; Louise O'Brien and Charles Jones, "Do Rewards Really Create Loyalty?" *Harvard Business Review*, May–June 1995, 75–82.

34. Don Peppers and Martha Rogers, *The One-to-One Future* (New York: Currency Doubleday, 1993), 59; Jodi M. Wallace, "The 'Buys' That Bind," *DM News*, 27 May 1996, 40.

35. Richard G. Barlow, "Frequency Marketing," in advertising supplement to *Advertising Age*, 21 August 1995, P13; Eleena De Lisser, "Marketing: Fast-Food Chains Reward Loyalty," *Wall Street Journal*, 7 June 1993, B1; Stephanie Seacord, "Who's Been Sleeping in Our Beds?" *Marketing Tools*, March–April 1996, 58–65.

36. Louise O'Brien and Charles Jones, "Do Rewards Really Create Loyalty?" *Harvard Business Review*, May–June 1995, 75–82.

37. "Air Miles Conquers Canada with 'Coalition Database Marketing,'" *MaxiMarketing Insights*, November 1995, 1–4; "Why Air Miles Failed in the U.S. and Worked So Well in Canada," *MaxiMarketing Insights*, November 1995, 4; O'Brien and Jones, 75–82.

38. Jo Bedingfield, "Credit Cards Scurry in Latin America," *Advertising Age*, 18 September 1995, I16; Charles Roda, "Sweepstakes Degenerating into Database Collections," *Advertising Age*, 19 September 1994, 23; Mazur and Hogg, *The Marketing Challenge*, 188.

39. Adapted from "The Secret of Stretching Your Advertising and Sales Promotion Expenditures," *MaxiMarketing Insights*, November 1995, 7.

40. "Consumer Incentive Strategy Guide: Promotion Close–Up," advertising supplement to *Incentive*, May 1995, 59.

41. "Cracker Jack Gets More Mature Twist," *Advertising Age*, 14 November 1994, 14; Christy Fisher, "Candy Bars Pack on the Promotions," *Advertising Age*, 19 September 1994, 29.

42. Jan Koch, "Driving Relationships," *Advertising Age*, 6 March 1995, 1, 8.

43. Raymond Serafin, "Steve Lyons: Ford Windstar," *Advertising Age*, 26 June 1995, S27.

44. Abdul Ali, Marvin A. Jolson, and Rene Y. Darmon, "A Model for Optimizing the Refund Value in Rebate Promotions," *Journal of Business Research* 29 (1994): 239–245.

45. Kathleen Deveny, "Displays Pay Off for Grocery Marketers," *Wall Street Journal*, 15 October 1992, B1, B6.

46. Betsy Spethmann, "Brand Builders: Branding of the Bulb," *Brandweek*, 21 August 1995, 28.

47. Leah Rickland, "Wal-Mart Shares POP Pointers," *Advertising Age*, 7 November 1994, 64; Eben Shapiro, "Food Firms Seek a Plan for All Seasons," *Wall Street Journal*, 29 July 1993, B1, B12.

48. Kusum L. Ailawadi, Paul W. Farris, and Mark E. Parry, "Share and Growth Are Not Good Predictors of the Advertising and Promotion/Sales Ratio," *Journal of Marketing*, 58 (January 1994), 86–97; Roberta Maynard, "Striking the Right Match," *Nation's Business*, May 1996, 18–28.

49. Bert Rosenbloom, *Marketing Channels*, 5th ed. (Fort Worth, Tex.: Dryden Press, 1995), 418.

50. Rosenbloom, *Marketing Channels*, 418.

51. William Dunn, "On with the Show!" *Marketing Tools*, July–August 1995, 46–49, 52–55; Kevin Kearney, "Technology Revolutionizes Trade Show Data Collection," *Business Marketing*, April 1996, B5.

52. Edmund O. Lawler, "Trade Shows Drive 'Push–Pull' Marketing," advertising supplement to *Advertising Age*, November 1994, A3–A4.

53. Michael D. Hutt and Thomas W. Speh, *Business Marketing Management*, 5th ed. (Fort Worth, Tex.: Dryden Press, 1995), 493; Dunn, "On with the Show," 46–49, 52–55.

54. Adapted from Susan Greco, "Selling the Superstores," *Inc.*, July 1995, 54–56, 58–61.

55. Elaine Underwood, "AAA Sets $14M Co–Op Debut," *Brandweek*, 22 August 1994, 8.

56. Mark Maynard, "Saturn Uses Some Customer Suggestions," *Washington Times*, 7 June 1996, E11.

57. Thomas L. Harris, "How MPR Adds Value to Integrated Marketing Communications," *Public Relations Quarterly* 38, no. 2 (Summer 1993): 13–18; Anne B. Fisher, "Corporate Reputations," *Fortune*, 6 March 1996, 90–98.

58. Prema Nakra, "The Changing Role of Public Relations in Marketing Communications," *Public Relations Quarterly* 36, no. 1 (Spring 1991): 42–45; Gene Koprowski, "Smart Companies Use Public Relations Tactics to Get Good Ink," *Marketing Tools*, October 1995, 46–53.

59. Wendy Marx, "PR Joins the Interactive Parade," *Advertising Age*, 17 April 1995, 15; Carole Hedden, "Build a Better Image," *Marketing Tools*, May 1996, 69–72.

60. Jeffery D. Zbar, "Florida Banks on Increased Media, PR to Boost Tourism," *Advertising Age*, 18 September 1995, 43.

61. Harris, "How MPR Adds Value to Integrated Marketing Communications," 13–18; Nakra, "The Changing Role of Public Relations in Marketing Communications," 42–45.

62. Ann Marsh, "Nose Jobs," *Forbes*, 13 March 1995, 140.

63. Shimp, *Promotion Management and Marketing Communications*, 592–593.

64. James E. Grunig, Larissa A. Grunig, K. Sriramesh, Yi-hui Huang, and Anastasia Lyra, "Models of Public Relations in an International Setting," *Journal of Public Relations Research* 7, no. 3 (1995): 163–186; Martha M. Lauzen, "Toward a Model of Environmental Scanning," *Journal of Public Relations Research* 7, no. 3 (1995): 187–203.

65. Laura Loro, "Everyone's Talkin' in the 'Multilogue,'" *Advertising Age*, 4 September 1994, 28; Richard A. Melcher, "Tune-Up Time for Harley," *Business Week*, 8 April 1996, 90–94.

66. Minda Zetlin, "A Ringing Success," *Nation's Business*, February 1996, 12, 14.

67. Larry Weber, "Why Getting Wired Makes Sense," *Public Relations Tactics*, June 1995, 11; Adam Shell, "Ways to Attract Visitors to Your Web Site," *Public Relations Tactics*, June 1995, 14.

68. Adapted from Nick Peters, "Using Video to Snuff Out a Crisis," *Public Relations Tactics*, 2 May 1995, 14–15.

69. Sydney Roslow, J. A. F. Nicholls, and Henry A. Laskey, "Hallmark Events and Measures of Reach and Audience Characteristics," *Journal of Advertising Research*, July–August 1992, 53–59.

70. Alan Saloman, "Charged Up for Indy," *Advertising Age*, 5 June 1995, 35.

C H A P T E R   **20**

1. Adapted from Susan Greco, "The Road to One-to-One Marketing," *Inc.*, October 1995, 56–58, 60, 63, 65–66.

2. Gerhard Gschwandtner, "A Jewel of a Company," *Personal Selling Power*, March 1995, 14–19, 22–24.

3. U.S. Bureau of the Census, *Statistical Abstract of the United States 1995* (Washington, D.C.: U.S. Government Printing Office, 1995), 412; Roger Brooksbank, "The New Model of Personal Selling: Micromarketing," *Journal of Personal Selling & Sales Management*, Spring 1995, 61–66.

4. Thomas R. Wotruba, "The Evolution of Personal Selling," *Journal of Personal Selling & Sales Management*, Summer 1991, 1–12; Alan Test, "Hire a Sales Rep, Not a Product Person," *Marketing News*, 12 February 1996, 4.

5. Bill Wagner, "Not Business as Usual," *Business Ethics*, July–August 1994, 12.

6. Wujin Chu, Eitan Gerstner, and James D. Hess, "Costs and Benefits of Hard Sell," *Journal of Marketing Research* 32 (February 1995): 97–102.

7. Raymond Serafin, "Saturn Bounces Back with Its Basic Appeal," *Advertising Age*, 30 January 1995, 4; Jaclyn Fierman, "The Death and Rebirth of the Salesman," *Fortune*, 25 July 1994, 80–82, 86, 88–89, 91; Yuri Kageyama, "Saturn Tries to Sell Japanese on New Service Style," *Washington Times*, 9 July 1996, B10.

8. Don Peppers and Martha Rogers, *The One-to-One Future* (New York: Currency Doubleday, 1993), 37.

9. Benson P. Shapiro, "Close Encounters of the Four Kinds: Managing Customers in a Rapidly Changing Environment," in *Seeking Customers*, edited by Benson P. Shapiro and John J. Sviokla (Boston: Harvard Business School Press, 1993), 127–155; Paul

Gray, "Nice Guys Finish First?" *Time*, 25 July 1994, 48–49.

10. Irving Goldmacher and Charles Diekmann, "Value–Balanced Selling for the '90s," *Marketing News*, 29 August 1994, 4; Nancy Arnott, "A Woman's World," *Sales & Marketing Management*, March 1995, 54–59.

11. Theodore Levitt, "After the Sale Is Over," in *Seeking Customers*, edited by Benson P. Shapiro and John J. Sviokla (Boston: Harvard Business School Press, 1993), 39–52.

12. Francis J. Gouillart and James N. Kelly, *Transforming the Organization* (New York: McGraw-Hill, 1995), 247–249.

13. Kevin J. Clancy and Robert S. Shulman, *Marketing Myths That Are Killing Business* (New York: McGraw-Hill, 1994), 216.

14. N. Andrew Cohen, "How to Sell Much More," *Boardroom Reports*, 1 July 1994, 5–6; Jack Freker, "Secrets of Successful Telephone Selling," *Boardroom Reports*, 1 November 1995, 5–6.

15. Howard Scott, "How to Handle Smaller Accounts," *Nation's Business*, September 1994, 48R; Thomas A. McCafferty, *In-House Telemarketing* (Chicago: Probus Publishing Co., 1994).

16. Nilly Landau, "A Call Center to Call Your Own," *International Business/IT Special Report* 7, no. 9, September 1994, 22, 24–26.

17. Daniel C. Smith and Jan P. Owens, "Knowledge of Customers' Customers as a Basis of Sales Force Differentiation," *Journal of Personal Selling & Sales Management*, Summer 1995, 1–15; Michael Warshaw, "The Golden Key to Selling," *Success Selling*, May 1996, 44–46.

18. John T. Hiatt, "Empowering the Global Sales Force," *International Business/IT Special Report* 7, no. 9, September 1994, 16, 18, 20; Fierman, "The Death and Rebirth of the Salesman," 80–82, 86, 88–89, 91.

19. Charles Fleming, "European Insurers Are Calling Up Customers as Direct Selling Captures Changing Market," *Wall Street Journal*, 4 April 1994, B4D.

20. Cas Welch and Pete Geissler, *Bringing Total Quality to Sales* (Milwaukee, Wis.: ASQC Press, 1992), 14; Steve Ditlea, "Managing Sales with Software," *Nation's Business*, March 1996, 29–31.

21. Arnott, "Woman's World," 54–59.

22. Shapiro, "Close Encounters of the Four Kinds," 127–155.

23. Mark A. Moon and Gary M. Armstrong, "Selling Teams; A Conceptual Framework and Research Agenda," *Journal of Personal Selling & Sales Management*, Winter 1994, 17–30.

24. Jay M. Orlin, "Selling in Teams," *Training & Development*, December 1993, 26–32; "Team Selling Catches On," *Wall Street Journal*, 29 March 1994, A1; Jack Falvey and Robert Lavery, "Team Selling: Strengths/Weaknesses," *Boardroom Reports*, 1 March 1994, 9–10.

25. Jack Falvey, "Selling Is Not a Team Sport," *Wall Street Journal*, 24 April 1995, A12; Falvey and Lavery, "Team Selling," 9–10; Cathy Hyatt Hills, "Everybody Sells," *Small Business Reports*, October 1992, 31–40.

26. Adapted from Hills, "Everybody Sells," 31–40.

27. Tony Alessandra, "Collaborative Selling: The Future of the Sales Process," in *Marketing Encyclopedia*, edited by Jeffrey Heilbrunn (Lincolnwood, Ill.: NTC Publishing, 1995), 144–150.

28. Jill Griffin, *Customer Loyalty: How to Earn It, How to Keep It* (New York: Lexington Books, 1995), 153.

29. Benson P. Shapiro and John J. Sviokla, eds., *Keeping Customers* (Boston: Harvard Business School Press, 1993), xiii.

30. Benson P. Shapiro, V. Kasturi Rangan, Rowland T. Moriarty, and Elliot B. Ross, "Manage Customers for Profits (Not Just Sales)," in *Seeking Customers*, edited by Benson P. Shapiro and John J. Sviokla (Boston: Harvard Business School Press, 1993), 277–291; Len Egol, "Marching Orders," *Direct*, July 1994, 53–56.

31. Griffin, *Customer Loyalty*, 42–43, 149.

32. Jonathan D. Glater, "The Big Bank That Thinks Small," *Washington Post*, 8 January 1995, H1, H7.

33. Brooksbank, "The New Model of Personal Selling," 61–66; Thomas Petzinger, Jr., "Hal Becker Preaches the Virtue of Sales to Fellow Climbers," *Wall Street Journal*, 8 March 1996, B1.

34. "Must-Have Selling Skills," *Inc.*, December 1992, 27; Thomas Siefel and Michael Malone, "Virtual Selling," *Success*, June 1996, 59–66.

35. Stephan Bowman, "New Lead Generation Tools Reshape Insurance Industry," *DM News*, 3 June 1996, 19; Thomas Woods and Judith Remondi, "Lead Management

Tools Critical to Measuring Marketing Success," *Business Marketing*, June 1996, 9.

36. Ray A. DeCormier and David Jobber, "The Counselor Selling Method: Concepts and Constructs," *Journal of Personal Selling & Sales Management*, Fall 1993, 39–59; Tweed Robinson and Mark L. Boos, "Get 'Em While They're Hot," *Marketing Tools*, June 1996, 64–68.

37. "Sales Automation: Tracking Sales Leads On-Line," *Inc.*, January 1993, 31.

38. Robert McGarvey, "Listen Up!" *Entrepreneur*, August 1995, 104–108, 110; Lawrence B. Chonko, John F. Tanner, Jr., and Ellen Reid Smith, "Selling and Sales Management in Action: The Sales Force's Role in International Marketing Research and Marketing Information Systems," *Journal of Personal Selling & Sales Management*, Winter 1991, 69–78.

39. John C. Hafer, *The Professional Selling Process* (St. Paul, Minn.: West Publishing, 1993), 249–250.

40. Griffin, *Customer Loyalty*, 38.

41. Kevin J. Corcoran, Laura K. Petersen, Daniel B. Baitch, and Mark F. Barrett, *High Performance Sales Organizations* (Chicago: Irwin, 1995), 19, 89.

42. Irving Goldmacher and Charles Diekmann, "Value-Balanced Selling for the '90s," *Marketing News*, 29 August 1994, 4; Arnott, "Woman's World," 54–59.

43. Maurice G. Clabaugh, Jr., and Jessie L. Forbes, *Professional Selling: A Relationship Approach* (St. Paul, Minn.: West Publishing, 1992), 292.

44. Jay Conrad Levinson, "Basic Sales Success Secret," *Boardroom Reports*, 15 June 1992, 5–6.

45. David J. Lill, "Closing Time," *Personal Selling Power*, September 1995, 56; John Cleese, "Lessons from Legends," *Success Selling*, May 1994, 8; Danielle Kennedy, "Close the Sale," *Entrepreneur*, March 1996, 102–103.

46. Griffin, *Customer Loyalty*, 116.

47. Ingrid Abramovitch, "Inside Track: See the Light," *Selling Success*, May 1994, 25.

48. Griffin, *Customer Loyalty*, 200–201.

49. Adapted from Gerhard Gschwandtner, "Portrait of a World Class Sales Professional," *Personal Selling Power*, July–August 1992, 54–62, 64.

50. Nilly Landau, "Holistic Salespeople," *International Business*, April 1995, 50–52.

51. Josh McHugh, "Holy Cow, No One's Done This!" *Forbes*, 3 June 1996, 122–128; Kristin Dunlap Godsey, "Sell Yourself," *Success*, May 1996, 51.

52. Regis McKenna, *Relationship Marketing* (Reading, Mass.: Addison-Wesley, 1991), 17–18.

53. Mark Kasperowicz, "Customer Focus Reaps Strategic Advantage," *Business Marketing*, April 1995, 21–22.

54. Ned C. Hill and Michael J. Swenson, "The Impact of Electronic Data Interchange on the Sales Function," *Journal of Personal Selling & Sales Management*, Summer 1994, 79–87; Owen Edwards, "Bow Tech," *Forbes ASAP*, 3 June 1996, 54–58.

55. Scott, "How to Handle Smaller Accounts," 48R.

56. Greg Burns, "Will So Many Ingredients Work Together?" *Business Week*, 27 March 1995, 188, 191.

57. Michael Wilke, "Kodak Customizes Sales Force for Retailers," *Advertising Age*, 20 January 1995, 8; Julie Liesse, "Kraft Retires General in Reorganization," *Advertising Age*, 9 January 1995, 4.

58. Niklas von Daehne, "Hiring Top Performers," *Success Selling*, May 1994, 34–35.

59. Tibbett L. Speer, "How to Be a Friend to Your Customers," *American Demographics*, March 1995, 14–15.

60. "Hands On: Sales & Marketing," *Inc.*, April 1995, 107; "The Cost of Training New Salespeople," *Inc.*, April 1993, 28.

61. Andy Cohen, "Training for Success," *Sales & Marketing Management*, March 1995, 27.

62. Adapted from William Keenan, Jr., "Getting Customers into the A.C.T.," *Sales & Marketing Management*, February 1995, 58–63.

63. Jenny C. McCune, "The Sales Arsenal," *Selling Success*, May 1994, 11; Ray Cusato,

"Empowering Salespeople to Boost Sales," *Small Business Reports*, March 1991, 26–31.

64. Stephen X. Doyle and Benson P. Shapiro, "What Counts Most in Motivating Your Sales Force?" in *Seeking Customers*, edited by Benson P. Shapiro and John J. Sviokla (Boston: Harvard Business School Press, 1993), 237–253; "Sales Incentive Programs," *Bottom Line/Business*, 1 March 1996, 11.

65. "How Do You Pay Your Sales Force?" *Inc.*, February 1993, 26; Fierman, "The Death and Rebirth of the Salesman," 80–82, 86, 88–89, 91.

66. Gene R. Laczniak and Patrick E. Murphy, *Ethical Marketing Decisions: The Higher Road* (Boston: Allyn & Bacon, 1993), 185–204; Hafer, *The Professional Selling Process*, 429–488; Petzinger, "Hal Becker Preaches the Virtue of Sales to Fellow Climbers," B1.

67. Ira Sager, "IBM Leans on Its Sales Force," *Business Week*, 7 February 1994, 110.

68. Gilbert Fuchsberg, "Selling Isn't Everything," *Wall Street Journal*, 13 April 1994, R8.

69. Corcoran, Petersen, Baitch, and Barrett, *High Performance Sales Organizations*, 30.

MARKETING ON THE NET FOR PART 7

1. Adapted from Carol Steinberg, "Selling in Cyberspace," *Selling Success*, May 1996, 77–78, 80–83.

2. "Business Bulletin," *Wall Street Journal*, 30 May 1996, A1; "Your Link to All Things Ohio!" advertisement for ohiobiz.com, *Forbes ASAP*, 3 June 1996, 60–61.

INTEGRATIVE CAPSTONE CASE: BILTMORE ESTATE

1. This case is based on materials provided by Biltmore Estate and its communications agency, Price/McNabb. Published sources include Hugh Meenan, "Media Strategy: You're Invited . . ." *Inside Media*, 12 July 1995, 38; and Suzanne MacNeille, "Cheer Around the Country," *New York Times*, 3 December 1995, sec. 5, 1, 13, 18.

Illustration Credits

AUTHOR PHOTOS
Bill Nickels by Silvia Dinale; Marian Wood by Treë.

CONTENTS

p. viii John Thoeming; **p. x** John Thoeming; **p. xii** Paul Stuart; **p. xv** Kaku Kurita/Gamma-Liaison Network; **p. xvii** Sprint; p. **xix** Associated Air Freight, Inc.; **p. xxi** Jim Leynse/SABA.

CHAPTER **1**

p. 3 Price McNabb/Biltmore Estate; **p. 5** *(left & right)* Treë, 1996; **Table 1.1** Based on Martin Christopher, Adrian Payne, and David Ballantyne, *Relationship Marketing* (Oxford, U.K.: Butterworth-Heinemann, 1991), 9; William A. Band, *Creating Value for Customers* (New York: John Wiley, 1991), 120; **p. 7** Acclivus Corporation; **p. 10** Courtesy of the Store 24 companies; **p. 12** *(top)* David R. Frazier/Photo Researchers, Inc.; **p. 12** *(left)* Joseph Nettis/Stock, Boston; **p. 12** *(right)* Eldred Wheeler Co., Hingham, MA.; **p. 14** Intel Corporation; **p. 16** Courtesy of L.L. Bean, Inc.; **p. 19** Marc PoKempner; **p. 20** John Thoeming; **p. 23** Chrysler Corporation; **p. 26** Eric Millette.

CHAPTER **2**

p. 33 P. Robert/Sygma; **p. 34** Calyx & Corolla, 1-800-800-7788; **Figure 2.1** Adapted from Martin Christopher, Adrian Payne, and David Ballantyne, *Relationship Marketing* (Oxford, U.K.: Butterworth-Heinemann, 1991), 35; **p. 38** Taken from Unipart Group of Companies mission statement from Francis J. Gouillart and James N. Kelly, *Transforming the Organization* (New York: McGraw-Hill, 1995), 59-60. Reproduced with permission of McGraw-Hill Companies; **p. 40** Sal DiMarco/Black Star; **Figures 2.2, 2.3, and 2.4** Based on Michael E. Porter, *Competitive Strategy: Techniques for Analyzing Industries and Competitors* (New York: Free Press, 1980), 362-363; **p. 43** John Thoeming; **Table 2.2** Based on information from Maurice G. Clabaugh, Jr., and Jessie L. Forbes, *Professional Selling: A Relationship Approach* (St. Paul, Minn.: West Publishing, 1992), 459; Michael D. Hutt and Thomas W. Speh, *Business Marketing Management*, 5th ed. (Fort Worth: Dryden Press, 1995), 202–209; **Figure 2.5** Adapted from William G. Nickels, James M. McHugh, and Susan M. McHugh, *Understanding Business, 4th ed.* (Chicago: Irwin, 1996), 261-262; **p. 48** Greg Girard/Contact Press Images; **p. 50** John Thoeming; **Figure 2.6** Based on Michael E. Porter, *Competitive Strategy: Techniques for Analyzing Industries and Competitors* (New York: Free Press, 1980), 362–363.

CHAPTER **3**

p. 67 Courtesy of McDonald's Corporation; **p. 69** Joseph Nettis/Photo Researchers, Inc.; **p. 72** Lester Sloan/Gamma-Liaison Network; **Fig**-

ure 3.2 based on "White, Male, and Worried," *Business Week*, 31 January 1994, 52–53; **p. 76** Graco Children's Products, Inc.; **Figure 3.3** *American Demographics* Magazine, ©1995, Reprinted with permission; **Table 3.2** "Minority Markets," *American Demographics*, February 1995, 26. *American Demographics* Magazine, ©1995, Reprinted with permission; **p. 82** ©1996 by Consumers Union of U.S., Inc., Yonkers, N.Y. 10703-1057. Reprinted with permission of Consumer Reports, 1996. To subscribe call 1-800-234-1645; **p. 85** John Thoeming; **p. 88** Reprinted with permission of the American Marketing Association; **p. 89** CEEM, Inc.; **pp. 90–91** © *Business Ethics* magazine. Reprinted with permission. Copies are available from *Business Ethics* magazine, (612) 962–4700; **p. 92** Levi Strauss & Company; **p. 94** Lee Apparel Company.

CHAPTER **4**

p. 101 Courtesy of Blockbuster Entertainment, Inc.; **Table 4.1** Based on "The 100 Largest U.S. Multinationals," *Forbes*, 15 July 1995, 274–276; **p. 104** Juha Sarkkinen; **p. 106** National Basketball Association; **p. 107** Lennox McLendon/AP Wide World; **Figure 4.1** TIOS, Trade Inflo; **p. 111** J. P. Laffont/Sygma; **p. 114** George Olson; **p. 115** Steve Fischer Photography; **p. 120** John Thoeming; **p. 122** Sears, Roebuck & Co.

CHAPTER **5**

p. 133 Nestlé; **p. 136** Claritas; **p. 140** John Thoeming; **p. 143** Village of Hinsdale; **p. 145** Information Resources, Inc.; **p. 151** Bob Daemmrich/Stock, Boston; **p. 152** Maritz Marketing Research, Inc.; **p. 153** Lawrence Migdale/Stock, Boston; **p. 156** MRI; **p. 157** Spencer Grant/Photo Researchers, Inc.

CHAPTER **6**

p. 163 David Graham; **p. 169** Photo Courtesy of Rollerblade, Inc.; **p. 170** Promus Hotel Corporation; **p. 173** Larry Dale Gordon/The Image Bank; **p. 175** Waterman; **p. 176** Glenn Turner; **p. 177** Ornelas & Associates; **p. 179** John Thoeming; **Table 6.1** Based on Michael R. Solomon, *Consumer Behavior*, 2nd ed. (Boston: Allyn Bacon, 1994), 93; **p. 182** Prodigy; **p. 184** National Fluid Milk Processor Promotion Board; **p. 185** Morris Garages.

CHAPTER **7**

p. 191 John Thoeming; **p. 193** Peter Menzel/Stock, Boston; **p. 196** Bob Daemmrich/The Image Works; **p. 199** B & J Supply; **p. 200** AST Research, Inc.; **p. 202** Savin Corporation; **p. 204** American Business Information; **p. 207** Courtesy of 3M; **p. 208** Courtesy of W.W. Grainger, Inc.; **p. 209** American Express Travel Related Services

Company, Inc.; **p. 211** Dun & Bradstreet; **p. 213** Cinnabar California, Inc.; **p. 214** Delta Air Lines.

CHAPTER **8**

p. 219 Courtesy of the Luxottica Group; **p. 222** William Filmyer; **p. 223** Douglas Burrows/Gamma-Liaison Network; **p. 225** Map produced by ESRI, Redlands, California using ESRI's ArcView GIS software; **p. 226** Pavion, Ltd.; **Tables 8.1 and 8.2** Based on Andrea Dunham and Barry Marcus with Mark Stevens and Patrick Barwise, *Unique Value: The Secret of All Great Business Strategies* (New York: Macmillan, 1993), 166–167; Kevin J. Clancy and Robert S. Shulman, *The Marketing Revolution* (New York: HarperBusiness, 1991), 74–75; **p. 229** First Consumers National Bank; **p. 230** Kraipit Phanvut/SIPA; **p. 234** Executive Woman; **p. 238** ©1996 Nation's Business/T. Michael Keza; **Figure 8.6** Adapted from Steven A. Sinclair and Edward C. Stalling, "Perceptual Mapping: A Tool for Industrial Marketing: A Case Study," *The Journal of Business and Industrial Marketing*, 5(1), (Winter-Spring 1990): 55-66; **p. 242** Stephan Savola/AP Wide World.

CHAPTER **9**

p. 251 Nantucket Allserve, Inc.; **p. 253** Maytag Company; **Tables 9.1 and 9.2** Based on information from J. Paul Peter and James H. Donnelly, Jr., *Marketing Management*, 3rd ed. (Burr Ridge, Ill.: Irwin, 1992), 111; Philip Kotler, *Marketing Management*, 8th ed. (Englewood Cliffs, N.J. : Prentice-Hall, 1994), 436–437; **p. 255** Rolls-Royce Motor Cars, Inc.; **p. 257** Cable and Wireless, Inc.; **Figure 9.1** Reprinted by permission of Harvard Business Review. An exhibit from "Marketing Success Through Differentiation—of Anything," by Theodore Levitt, January-February 1980. In *The Marketing Imagination* by Theodore Levitt. New York: The Free Press, 1986. Copyright © 1979 by the President and Fellows of Harvard College, all rights reserved; **Table 9.3** John M. Ivancevich, Peter Lorenzi, and Steven J. Skinner with Philip B. Crosby, *Management: Quality and Competitiveness* (Burr Ridge, Ill.: Irwin, 1994), 12; **p. 260** Richard E. Brown; **p. 261** Microsoft; **p. 263** John Thoeming; **Figure 9.3** *American Demographics* Magazine, ©1995, Reprinted with permission; **p. 264** Ed Bailey/AP Wide World; **p. 265** John Thoeming; **p. 266** John Thoeming; **p. 268** Photo Courtesy of Arizona Beverages; **p. 270** Bud Lee; **p. 272** Cross; **p. 275** entertainment MCI; **p. 276** Courtesy of 3M.

CHAPTER **10**

p. 281 Individual, Inc.; **p. 283** Courtesy of McDonald's Corporation; **p. 284** GE Information Services; **p. 285** Michael J. Okoniewski/Gamma-Liaison Network; **p. 288** Hewlett Packard; **p. 290**

Bob Daemmrich/The Image Works; **p. 597** John Thoeming; **Table 20.2** Len Egol, "Marching Orders," *Direct*, July 1994, 53-56 © Cowles Business Media; **p. 601** Larry Dale Gordon/The Image Bank; **p. 603** Stereographics; **p. 605** Flexlite, Inc.; **p. 606** Albert Berenguier; **p. 607** Zenith Data Systems Corporation; **Table 20.3** Based on Maurice G. Clabaugh, Jr., and Jessie L. Forbes, *Professional Selling: A Relationship Approach* (St. Paul, Minn: West Publishing, 1992), 465; **p. 611** Charlie Westerman/Gamma-Liaison Network; **p. 612** Created & Copyrighted 3M, 1995.

INTEGRATIVE CAPSTONE CASE

p. 622 Biltmore Estate/James Valentine; **p. 626** Biltmore Estate/James Valentine; **p. 627** Biltmore Estate/James Valentine; **p. 628** John Thoeming; **p. 631** John Thoeming.

Name, Product, and Company Index

Subject Index

Learn these concepts to become a world-class marketer

Relationship marketing pp. 6-11, 16-17, 27, 53-54, 74-75, 134-137,164-166, 184-185, 191-193, 206-207, 209-211, 222, 252, 266, 393, 427-432, 470-472, 474-480, 515-517, 538, 555-558, 564-566, 582-585, 592-594

Database marketing pp. 138-139, 164-165, 210-212, 281, 505, 556

Lifetime value of the customer pp. 27, 593-594, 598-599

Integrated marketing and cross-functional teams pp. 11-13, 18, 208-209, 288, 296-297, 567, 597-598

Internal marketing pp. 9, 46-48, 70, 72-73, 257, 327-328, 501, 567, 596-597

Benchmarking pp. 15-16, 115-116, 214, 259, 273, 331-332, 473

Total quality management pp. 48-49, 69, 259-260, 273-274, 288, 297-298, 410, 596-597

After-sale service and service recovery pp. 23, 169-170, 195, 271-272, 322-329, 600, 605-606

Mass customization pp. 118, 238-239, 274-275, 313

Value-chain management pp. 24-25, 50-52, 209-214, 286, 363, 408-427, 438-439, 459-460, 468-470, 566-567

Integrated marketing communication pp. 26-27, 454-455, 501-527, 536, 538, 565, 569-570, 584, 592

Ethics and social responsibility pp. 18-19, 36, 69-70, 72, 75, 88-96, 123, 139, 157-158, 182-183, 205, 269-271, 276, 293, 353, 366-367, 432-433, 457, 491-492, 512-513, 551-552, 589, 614